PLATO'S PHILOSOPHERS

Plato's Philosophers

THE COHERENCE OF THE DIALOGUES

Catherine H. Zuckert

THE UNIVERSITY OF CHICAGO PRESS

CHICAGO AND LONDON

Catherine H. Zuckert is the Nancy Reeves Dreux Professor of Political Science at the University of Notre Dame. She is the author of *Postmodern Platos* and a coauthor of *The Truth about Leo Strauss*, both published by the University of Chicago Press.

The University of Chicago Press, Chicago 60637
The University of Chicago Press, Ltd., London
© 2009 by The University of Chicago
All rights reserved. Published 2009
Printed in the United States of America

18 17 16 15 14 13 12 11 10 09   1 2 3 4 5

ISBN-13: 978-0-226-99335-5   (cloth)

ISBN-10: 0-226-99335-3   (cloth)

Library of Congress Cataloging-in-Publication Data
Zuckert, Catherine H., 1942–
Plato's philosophers : the coherence of the dialogues / Catherine H. Zuckert.
p. cm.
Includes bibliographical references and index.
ISBN-13: 978-0-226-99335-5 (cloth : alk. paper)
ISBN-10: 0-226-99335-3 (cloth : alk. paper) 1. Plato. Dialogues. 1. Title.
B395.Z77 2009
184—dc22
2008043514

♾ The paper used in this publication meets the minimum
requirements of the American National Standard for Information
Sciences—Permanence of Paper for Printed
Library Materials, ANSI Z39.48-1992.

Contents

PART III
The Trial and Death of Socrates

Acknowledgments

"No one takes twelve years to write a book anymore," a colleague commented at a recent political science convention. I did, and I would like to thank the institutions and individuals who made this lengthy study possible.

Carleton College, Fordham University, and the University of Notre Dame provided me with both the financial support and teaching opportunities necessary to pursue the project. Fellowships from the National Endowment for the Humanities and the Earhart Foundation gave me uninterrupted time to read and write. As a visiting scholar at the Liberty Fund in Indianapolis, I also had time to work on this book.

Earlier versions of some of the arguments to be found in chapters 1, 2, 3, and 9 were published in the *Journal of Politics* 66 (May 2004): 374–95; *Review of Metaphysics* 51 (June 1998): 840–71, and 54 (September 2001): 65–97; *History of Political Thought* 25 (Summer 2004): 189–219; and the *Journal of the International Plato Society* (Winter 2005). The overlapping sections are published here with permission.

I particularly thank the colleagues who read and commented on parts of the manuscript: Mary Nichols, Michael Davis, Mary Sirridge, Laurence Lampert, Gretchen Reydams-Schils, Vittorio Hösle, and Ken Sayre. I also recognize some of the many students who have contributed to my understanding of the dialogues by reading and discussing them with me: Lisa Vetter, Andrew Hertzoff, Xavier Marquez, Jill Budny, Catherine Borck, Kevin Cherry, Jeffrey Church, Alex Duff, Elizabeth L'Arrivée, and Rebecca McCumbers.

I also thank John Tryneski and Rodney Powell for shepherding the manuscript through the publication process and the anonymous readers for the University of Chicago Press for their suggestions and corrections.

Most of all, however, I express my gratitude to my husband, Michael Zuckert. He not merely read, reread, and commented on the many drafts of each and every chapter. His enthusiasm for the project buoyed my spirits when I became discouraged by its size and complexity. I could not have written this book without his love and support.

INTRODUCTION

Platonic Dramatology

Alfred North Whitehead's quip that all subsequent philosophy is merely a footnote to Plato has often been repeated, but those who repeat it do not seem to have thought much about the difference between the source and the scholarship on it. Whereas all subsequent philosophers have written treatises (even if they have also produced some more literary works), Plato wrote only dialogues.[1] And in these dialogues he not merely presented various philosophers in conversation with non-philosophers, but he gave the philosophers and their interlocutors specific individual identities, backgrounds, and views. Plato's depiction of philosophy is, in other words, neither impersonal nor abstract. The conversations are shown to have occurred at different times and places, and mostly but not always in Athens. The philosophical figure who guides the conversation in most of the dialogues is Socrates, but he is not Plato's only philosopher. Plato also presents conversations in which an "Athenian Stranger," Parmenides, Timaeus, or the Eleatic Stranger takes the lead. Socrates is said to be present at some of these conversations but not all. Sometimes Socrates and another philosopher question the same interlocutors; more often, however, Plato shows them talking to different individuals. Some of these individuals are known historical figures; others are not. As depicted in the Platonic dialogues, then, philosophy is not an activity undertaken by a solitary individual in his or her study, attempting to replicate or ascend to Aristotle's first principle of thought, thinking itself. Philosophy is an activity

---

1. The authenticity of his letters has often been questioned, and letters are not, in any case, treatises.

undertaken by a variety of different embodied human beings, coming from different cities and schools, having different views and concerns, talking in different ways to nonphilosophers.[2] In this book I investigate the significance of these differences: first, for Plato's own understanding of the nature of philosophy, and second, for ours.

Previous scholars have, of course, noticed that Plato presents more than one philosopher and that there are differences not only among his philosophers but also in his depictions of Socrates. Nineteenth-century commentators may have followed the lead of Friedrich Schleiermacher in trying to understand the dialogues in terms of Plato's "development," because they were convinced that the only way the work of any author could or should be understood was to trace the changes in his thought over time.[3] But many twentieth-century students of Plato adopted the essentially speculative "chronology of composition" rather than the "unitarian" reading championed by Paul Shorey and Hans von Arnim, at least in part because the "chronology" provided an explanation for the differences in the philosophical "spokesmen" whereas the unitarian reading did not.[4]

2. Among other things, I am arguing that not merely Socrates, but Platonic philosophy more generally, is not "impersonal," that is, not concerned with the individuality of others; pace Martha Nussbaum, *The Fragility of Goodness* (Cambridge: Cambridge University Press, 1986), 165–99; and Gregory Vlastos, "The Individual as an Object of Love in Plato," in *Platonic Studies* (Princeton: Princeton University Press, 1973), 3–34.

3. C. C. W. Taylor traces the "assumption that the works of Plato (and indeed of any other writer) are to be approached in this most general historical sense" to the "development of serious critical study in Germany at the beginning of the nineteenth century, . . . ultimately to the predominant intellectual and cultural climate of that particular country and epoch, Romanticism, and specifically to the philosophy of Hegel"; Taylor, "The Origins of Our Present Paradigms," in *New Perspectives on Plato, Modern and Ancient*, ed. Julia Annas and Christopher Rowe (Cambridge: Harvard University Press, 2002), 74. Jacob Howland, "Re-Reading Plato: The Problem of Platonic Chronology," *Phoenix* 45 (1991): 189–214, quotes A. E. Taylor's statement about the necessity of knowing the order in which an author wrote his works, from Taylor, *Plato: The Man and His Work* (Cleveland: World Publishing, 1956), 16. This conviction is reflected in the "classic" studies of Plato's thought as a whole by George Grote, *Plato, and the Other Companions of Sokrates*, 3 vols. (London: J. Murray, 1865); W. K. C. Guthrie, *A History of Greek Philosophy*, vols. 4–5 (Cambridge: Cambridge University Press, 1976–78); and Paul Friedländer, *Plato*, trans. Hans Meyerhoff, 2nd ed., 3 vols. (Princeton: Princeton University Press, 1969); as well as more recent studies such as that of George Klosko, *The Development of Plato's Political Theory* (New York: Methuen, 1986). Kenneth Sayre endorses the chronological understanding of the development of Plato's thought and treats the "late dialogues" as statements of arguments or doctrines much like treatises, but in *Plato's Literary Garden* (Notre Dame, IN: University of Notre Dame Press, 1995) he emphasizes the pedagogical function of the "middle" dialogues.

4. Paul Shorey, *The Unity of Plato's Thought* (Chicago: University of Chicago Press, 1903); and Hans von Arnim, *Platos Jugenddialoge und die Entstehungszeit des Phaidros* (Leipzig: G. B. Teubner, 1914; repr., Amsterdam: A. M. Hakkert, 1967). As von Arnim notes (iii), Schleiermacher began the attempt to understand Plato in terms of the development of his thought. Friedrich Daniel Ernst Schleiermacher, *Über die Philosophie Platons*, including *Geschichte der Philosophie: Vorlesungen über*

These scholars agreed that there are "early" dialogues, like the *Apology* and *Crito*, in which Plato depicts the historical Socrates refuting his interlocutors; "middle" dialogues, like the *Republic* and *Phaedo*, in which Plato attributes his own arguments to Socrates; and "late" dialogues, like the *Sophist* and *Laws*, in which Plato generally presents his more mature philosophical understanding in the mouth of a non-Socratic spokesman.[5] Building on the pioneering studies by Lewis Cambpell and Wilhelm Dittenberger, scholars undertook "stylometric" computer studies to show regularities and changes in word use to support this "dating."[6]

Recently, however, serious questions have been raised about the evidence for, and the validity of the assumptions underlying, the "chronology of composition" and the "stylometric" studies used to confirm the "theory."[7] "In no ancient source is there ever any suggestion that Plato changed

---

Sokrates und Platon (1819–23) and *Die Einleitungen zur Übersetzung des Platon* (1804–28) (Hamburg: Felix Meiner, 1996). According to Holger Thesleff, *Studies in Platonic Chronology* (Helsinki: Societas Scientiarum Fennica, 1982), 1, Wilhelm Gottlieb Tennemann first suggested the study of the dating of the composition of the various dialogues, in *System der Platonischen Philosophie* (Leipzig: Barth, 1792), in contrast to studies of the development of Plato's thought, such as that later undertaken by Schleiermacher. Thesleff recognizes that the two concerns have often been mixed and were finally merged in many Anglo-American commentaries. E. N. Tigerstedt, *Interpreting Plato* (Stockholm: Almqvist & Wiksell, 1977), 13–51, breaks down the various attempts to interpret Plato even further by individual author—in terms of the development of his thought, the order of the presentation of his thought, the chronology of composition, and his biography (about which, Tigerstedt assures us, after reviewing the scarce ancient sources or gossip and citing one of the most famous "biographical" studies by Ulrich von Wilamowitz in support, that we know very little).

5. The exception is, of course, the *Philebus*, which most commentators regard as "late," even though Socrates is the major philosophical spokesman. For a recent claim regarding the "remarkable . . . degree of consensus that has emerged" concerning Platonic chronology, see David Sedley, *Plato's "Cratylus"* (Cambridge: Cambridge University Press, 2003), 6. Debra Nails, *Agora, Academy, and the Conduct of Philosophy* (Dordrecht: Kluwer Academic Publishers, 1995), 55–68, observes, on the contrary, that "there is unanimity about almost nothing across the various methods of ordering the dialogues" (55). Nevertheless, Charles H. Kahn, "On Platonic Chronology," in Annas and Rowe, *New Perspectives on Plato*, 93–127, defends the general chronological schema.

6. According to Nails (*Agora*, 101–14), Gerard R. Ledger, *Re-Counting Plato* (Oxford: Oxford University Press, 1989), is the best of the stylometric studies. The varying results of the stylometric analyses are summarized in Leonard Brandwood, *The Chronology of Plato's Dialogues* (Cambridge: Cambridge University Press, 1990); and Thesleff, *Studies*, 65–95. From the nineteenth century onward, stylometric research has shown that the *Critias, Laws, Philebus, Statesman, Sophist,* and *Timaeus* are characterized by certain linguistic mannerisms absent in other dialogues. Because this group includes the *Laws*, it is often said to be "late," although Thesleff, in *Studies*, points out that the linguistic affinity among these dialogues does not, in fact, prove anything about their date or Plato's "development," even though many scholars seem to think it does.

7. Howland, in "Re-Reading Plato," was the first to bring out and criticize the assumptions underlying the "chronology of composition," especially concerning the "development" of Plato's thought. Howland's critique was soon followed by that of Kenneth Dorter, *Form and Good in Plato's Eleatic Dialogues* (Berkeley: University of California Press, 1994), 1–17; Nails, *Agora*; Charles H. Kahn, *Plato and the Socratic Dialogue: The Philosophical Use of a Literary Form* (Cambridge: Cambridge University Press, 1996); and the exchange Kahn had with Charles Griswold in *Ancient Philosophy*

his views in a radical way," Kenneth Dorter reminds us. "Aristotle, for example, always write[s] as though Plato consistently defended the theory of forms throughout his life. . . . Neither does Diogenes Laertius, that repository of anecdotes of every stripe, provide the slightest hint of such an occurrence." In the *Politics* (2.6.1264b26–27), Aristotle says that the *Laws* was written later than the *Republic*, and Diogenes Laertius (3.3) reports that "some say that Philip of Opus transcribed the *Laws*, which were in wax."[8] But Aristotle's remark does not give us any guidance about the order of the rest of the dialogues, and an inference from a centuries-old rumor that Plato must have left the text of the *Laws* unfinished does not provide a firm basis for determining the order or dates at which the dialogues were written.[9] Reviewing the scant historical evidence for the "chronology of composition" in his introduction to *Plato: The Complete Works*, John M. Cooper "urge[s] readers not to undertake the study of Plato's works holding in mind the customary chronological groups of 'early,' 'middle,' and 'late' dialogues . . . and to concentrate on the literary and philosophical content."[10] The fact is, we do not know when or in what order Plato wrote the individual dialogues. If we want to discover how Plato saw the world or

---

19 (1999): 361–97, 20 (2000): 189–93, 195–97, revisited in "Platonic Chronology," in Annas and Rowe, *New Perspectives on Plato*, 93–144.

8. Dorter, *Form and Good*, 3. As G. E. L. Owen observed, "There is no external or internal evidence which proves that the *Laws* or even some section of it was later than every other work. . . . Diogenes' remark that it was left on the wax does not certify even that it occupied Plato to his death"; Owen, "The Place of the *Timaeus* in Plato's Dialogues," *Classical Quarterly*, n.s., 3 (1953): 79n4, 93n3. Dionysius of Halicarnassus' report in *On Literary Composition*, ed. W. Rhys Roberts (London: Macmillan, 1910), that "Plato did not leave off combing and curling and in every manner replaiting his dialogues, even at eighty years of age" (25), should also make commentators hesitant to date the dialogues in terms of their composition. Dionysius also relates a story told about the finding of a tablet which showed that Plato had set down the first sentence of the *Republic* in many different ways. This story lends support to Thesleff's contention that the dialogues cannot be dated by stylistic or stylometric evidence, because they were constantly being rewritten. Marks of their early composition were thus cancelled out by traces of later revisions (Thesleff, *Studies*, 71).

9. Dorter observes with regard to the stylometric studies attempting to determine the date or order in which the dialogues were composed: "The search was on for measures of stylistic affinity. Candidates that were found included reply formulas (the responses of the interlocutors—useless, however, in the case of a narrative like the *Timaeus*), clausula rhythms (the ends of periods or colons), avoidance of hiatus (following a word ending in a vowel with one beginning in a vowel), and use of *hapax legomena* (unique appearances of words) or unusual words. But each of these encounters difficulties in measurement. In measuring reply formulas do we take into account the personality of the interlocutor and the nature of the questions being asked? And do we count slight variations as being the same; or formulas imbedded within longer sentences in the same way as isolated formulas? . . . we must also decide whether to take into account the nature and subject matter of the dialogues. Should we expect to find the same stylistic features in a narrative myth (*Timaeus*), an exercise in abstract dialectic (*Parmenides*) . . . , or a set of speeches (*Symposium*), as in dialogues like the *Republic*, *Theaetetus*, or *Laws*?" (Dorter, *Form and Good*, 5–6).

10. John M. Cooper, ed., *Plato: The Complete Works* (Indianapolis: Hackett, 1997), xiv.

what he thought, we need to find another way of showing how more than a few dialogues are related to one another by theme or shared characters. We need, in other words, to formulate another account of the character, the organization, and content of Plato's corpus.

I. Taking Account of the Literary Form and Context of the Dialogue

Plato did not write treatises, although commentators following Aristotle have tended to present him and his thought as if he had.[11] Because Plato himself does not speak in the dialogues, we discover what Plato thinks—or at least what he wants to show his readers—in his selection of the characters, the setting, and the topic to be discussed by these individuals at that time and place, as well as the outcome or effects of the conversation. Socrates is usually but not always the philosopher guiding the conversation. Because Socrates is not the only philosopher Plato depicts—indeed, in some dialogues (like the *Timaeus* and *Sophist*), Socrates mostly sits and listens to another, possibly superior philosopher present his arguments—we cannot assume that Socrates speaks for Plato. Because Socrates is by far the most common philosophic voice, however, we cannot take one of the others— the Athenian stranger, Parmenides, Timaeus, or the Eleatic stranger—as Plato's spokesman either. These philosophers do not merely articulate different understandings of the best way to argue as well as of the character of philosophy, politics, the cosmos, and being; they also engage different interlocutors.[12] In addition to the complex interplay of characters, moreover, the dialogues also have settings—indications of specific times and places— and depict a variety of actions or outcomes.[13] To be sure, Plato does not

11. Cf. Andrea Nightingale, "Writing/Reading a Sacred Text: A Literary Interpretation of Plato's *Laws*," *Classical Philology* 88, no. 4 (October 1993): 282; and Rudolph H. Weingartner, *The Unity of the Platonic Dialogue* (Indianapolis: Bobbs-Merrill, 1973), 1–4. On the problems involved in taking Aristotle as a guide to reading Plato, see Harold Cherniss, *Aristotle's Criticism of Plato and the Academy*, vol. 1 (Baltimore: Johns Hopkins University Press, 1944); John R. Wallach, *The Platonic Political Art* (University Park: Pennsylvania State University Press, 2001), 26–29; Rosyln Weiss, *The Socratic Paradox and Its Enemies* (Chicago: University of Chicago Press, 2006), 10n29.

12. On the different kinds of dialogue represented by Plato's different philosophical interlocutors, see Michael Frede, "Plato's Arguments and the Dialogue Form," in *Methods of Interpreting Plato*, ed. James C. Klagge and Nicholas D. Smith (Oxford: Clarendon Press, 1992), 202–19; Diskin Clay, *Platonic Questions: Dialogues with the Silent Philosopher* (University Park: Pennsylvania State University Press, 2000), 256–58, 268.

13. In *Platonic Questions*, Clay reminds his readers that "Plato was hardly the first to write a Socratic dialogue, [but] he was, so far as we can now determine, the first to invest his dialogues in

dramatize any murders or celebrate any marriages; the dialogues are neither tragedies nor comedies. But in some of the conversations (like the *Statesman* and the *Philebus*), the interlocutors are convinced; in others, like the *Protagoras*, they admit that they have been defeated in argument but remain unpersuaded; and in some, like the *Meno*, they get angry when they are refuted. In all cases, readers are encouraged to understand the status and character of the arguments not simply in themselves or in the abstract, but as presented by this particular philosopher with his distinctive background and approach to a specific person or persons at the time and place indicated, with a discernible (sometimes lack of) effect.

Since Plato does not speak himself, it is necessary to look at the arguments in context. Each dialogue is a specific conversation. In the following account of Plato's thought, I have therefore proceeded dialogue by dialogue. Since Plato presents a variety of philosophers speaking to different interlocutors, in different circumstances, with different results, I begin the discussion of each dialogue by reminding readers of the situation, that is, what we know about the characters and the setting.[14] To show how the characteristics and interests of the interlocutors affect the arguments that the philosopher speaking puts forth, I have also taken up the arguments in the order in which they occur and looked at each step at the results, which are not always logical.[15] At times we are told about the emotional reaction the philosopher or his interlocutor has. Sometimes characters leave; sometimes others take their place. Why? And why at this particular juncture? It is, of course, possible to abstract out arguments from the dialogues; it is

recognizable historical settings. . . . [Moreover,] Plato is concerned not only with the words spoken and arguments made but the record of significant action. These actions tend to be lost sight of in philosophical readings of the Platonic dialogues" (10).

14. Ruby Blondell, *The Play of Character in Plato's Dialogues* (Cambridge: Cambridge University Press, 2002), represents a big step toward the kind of reading of the dialogues I am advocating. James Arieti, *Interpreting Plato: The Dialogues as Drama* (Savage, MD: Rowman and Littlefield, 1991), also emphasizes the dramatic character of the dialogues, but he does not bring out any connections among them.

15. It seems obvious, if not axiomatic, to say that even the arguments, narrowly construed, are presented in stages, that is, that they develop and are developed in the course of a dialogue. But David Roochnik, *Beautiful City: The Dialectical Character of Plato's "Republic"* (Ithaca: Cornell University Press, 2003), 15–23, shows that many commentators have isolated Socrates' presentation of the three-part soul in the *Republic* from its context, even though they have found it necessary to refer to later parts of the dialogue in explicating it, and have presented it as "Plato's" argument. Grace Hadley Billings, *The Art of Transition in Plato* (Menasha, WI: George Banta, 1920), observes: "One of Plato's favorite methods of developing a theme [is that a] partial or superficial view of the subject is first presented, only to be superseded or supplemented by further discussion" (21).

also possible to read arguments taken from several dialogues thematically. But by taking the arguments out of context, a commentator loses most, if not all, of what Plato is showing his readers. And Plato only shows; he does not state or say anything in his own name.[16]

The price of presenting the arguments in context is that the presentation tends to look like a summary. The following accounts of the individual dialogues are not mere summaries, however; they represent attempts to bring out what is shown: who is persuaded or not, by what arguments, with what results. Plato's understanding is to be found in what he shows, first in individual dialogues, taken as a whole, and then in his corpus, read as a whole. It is not to be found in individual arguments Plato puts in the mouths of specific characters conversing under particular conditions.

The results of one conversation are, moreover, often indicated only in a later conversation. It is not sufficient to read single dialogues in complete isolation from the others. We do not learn from Plato's *Parmenides*, for example, what young Socrates' reaction to the elderly Eleatic's demonstration of argumentative gymnastics was. Only by reading the dialogues shown to take place afterward do we see that Socrates never followed Parmenides' advice. In other words, the context of the conversation(s) depicted in each individual dialogue is determined not only by the immediate setting but also by the order or sequence of the dialogues Plato indicates by means of their dramatic dates.

Commentators as early as Thrasyllus observed that some of the conversations are explicitly linked to each other.[17] If we go beyond the traditional tetralogies (for example, *Euthyphro*, *Apology*, *Crito*, and *Phaedo*) and look at the dramatic dates (the indications Plato gives of the time at which readers are to imagine the dialogue having taken place, not the much later and more speculative time of composition), however, we see that the dialogues represent incidents in one overarching narrative. They depict the problems that gave rise to Socratic philosophy, its development or maturation, and its limitations.

---

16. Cf. Leo Strauss, *The City and Man* (Chicago: Rand McNally, 1964), 59–60.

17. Diogenes Laertius, *Lives of Eminent Philosophers*, trans. R. D. Hicks (Cambridge: Harvard University Press, 1925), 3.61–62, reports that Aristophanes the grammarian divided some but that he could not arrange all of the dialogues into trilogies. Bernard Suzanne, http://plato-dialogues.org/tetralog.htm, has tried to revive and update the Thrasyllan approach to the organization of the dialogues in tetralogies, although the sets of four that Suzanne identifies differ from those posited by Thrasyllus and have not been adopted or endorsed by anyone else.

II. The Overarching Narrative Indicated
by the Dramatic Dates

Each of Plato's other philosophers takes charge of the conversation in one or two dialogues: the Athenian Stranger in the *Laws* and *Epinomis*, Parmenides and Timaeus in the dialogues that bear their names, and the Eleatic Stranger in the *Sophist* and *Statesman*. The problem with determining whether Plato's characterization of the philosophers is consistent or differentiated, for example, whether the various philosophers articulate fundamentally the same Platonic understanding of things (the unitarian thesis) or whether they represent fundamentally different positions (which may or may not correspond to stages in Plato's own development), arises first and foremost with regard to Socrates. Present in thirty-three of the thirty-five dialogues, Socrates certainly appears to be Plato's most important philosopher. As readers we learn more about his education, background, appearance, family, city, and associates than we do about any of the other philosophers. It is not so clear, however, whether Plato always attributes the same arguments and views to the character named Socrates. The advocates of the chronology of composition argue that he does not.[18]

Plato gives us our first view of the young Socrates in the *Parmenides*, a dialogue in which the conversation is directed by the older Eleatic philosopher. And if we list the dialogues in the order of their dramatic dates, we see not only that the dialogues featuring Socrates can be so ordered, but also that the non-Socratic dialogues can be incorporated into the narrative that emerges on the basis of the dramatic dating.

That order can be summarized as follows:

460–450 BCE *Laws* (followed by the *Epinomis*)

455–450 (Socrates' turn from the study of nature or the beings to the examination of the *logoi*, related in the *Phaedo*)

450 *Parmenides*

450–433 (Socrates' turn from the *logoi* to the *doxai*, related in the *Symposium* and *Apology*)

433–432 *Protagoras*

432 *Alcibiades I* and *II*

---

18. Two of the best-known versions of the developmental thesis, particularly with regard to Socrates, are found in Terence Irwin, *Plato's Ethics* (New York: Oxford University Press, 1995); and Gregory Vlastos, *Socrates, Ironist and Moral Philosopher* (Ithaca: Cornell University Press, 1991).

429	*Charmides* (after the battle of Potidaea)
423	*Laches*
421–420	*Hippias Major* and *Minor*

416	*Symposium*
415	*Phaedrus*
413	*Ion* (treated thematically in note to the *Republic*)
411	*Clitophon* (introducing the *Republic*)
411	*Republic*
n.d.	*Philebus* (thematically related to the *Republic*)
409–408	*Timaeus-Critias*

409	*Theages*
407	*Euthydemus*
406	*Lysis*
405	*Gorgias*
402–401	*Meno*

| 399 | *Theaetetus, Euthyphro, Cratylus, Sophist, Statesman, Apology, Crito,* and *Phaedo* |
| 387–386 | *Menexenus* |

In this list I use horizontal lines to group the dialogues into periods or stages of Socrates' development as a philosopher. I have organized the subsequent account of the dialogues on this basis.

In attempting to establish the dramatic dates of the dialogues, I have relied on the philological, philosophical, and archeological work of many scholars.[19] These dates are admittedly subjects of ongoing controversy. At the beginning of each chapter in which I treat a set of dialogues, I have therefore noted some of the relevant disagreements. Plato often gives slight indications of the time at which a conversation occurred—by means of an ambiguous reference, as to a battle at Megara in the *Republic* (there are several such battles) or to the presence of a person whose identity and life span are known independently of the dialogues. In two important cases, the *Republic* and the *Phaedrus*, scholars have shown, partly on the basis of internal evidence and partly on the basis of inscriptions, that the conversations depicted could not have taken place among those persons indicated

19. Debra Nails, *The People of Plato: A Prosopography of Plato and Other Socratics* (Indianapolis: Hackett, 2002), is invaluable to scholars pursuing questions about the dramatic dates of the dialogues. I have not agreed with her in every case, for example, concerning the specific dates of the *Euthydemus* and *Lysis*, but I have found her analyses of other scholars as well as her own arguments about the dates and the personae of the dialogues extremely helpful.

at the time and place indicated.[20] Likewise, scholars have long known that there are anachronistic references to events that occurred after the conversation is supposed to have taken place, for example, in the *Protagoras* (327d) and the *Symposium* (193a), two other dialogues whose authenticity has rarely been questioned.[21] Both the impossibility of the actual occurrence of some of the conversations and the occasional anachronistic references serve, or should serve, to remind readers that the dialogues are Platonic literary inventions, not historical reports.[22] I have taken Plato's indications of the times at which the conversations took place merely as hints of the order in which he wanted his readers to imagine the conversations taking place.[23] The coherence of the narrative that emerges when one strings the

20. Kenneth Dover, *Lysias and the Corpus Lysiacum* (Berkeley: University of California Press, 1968); Nussbaum, *Fragility*, 212–13nn24–25; Nails, *People*, 314, 324–26.

21. In the heyday of such debates, Eduard Zeller went so far as to question the authenticity of the *Laws*, upon which most of the stylometric analyses of the chronology of composition rest, but he later withdrew his doubts. Recognizing that the "authenticity," that is, Platonic authorship, of many of the dialogues was brought into question in the nineteenth century, and in some cases, such as those of the *Alcibiades* and the *Theages*, continues to this day, I am struck by the fact that most of those judgments involve a decision by a commentator concerning what sort of writing or argument is truly Platonic, based on a reading of part of the corpus, which is then applied to the rest. Do we know the character and extent of Plato's literary and philosophical abilities? Are our presumptions about what Plato thought or could have written to be preferred to an examination of the works long attributed to Plato himself? In line with an increasing tendency in current scholarship, I have accepted the traditional list of thirty-five authentic dialogues to be found in Diogenes Laertius, acknowledging that Diogenes is not an altogether reliable source but believing that he is closer to Plato and his students than the authors of more recent constructions and speculations. For excellent if critical accounts of the various debates about the authenticity of the dialogues, see Tigerstedt, *Interpreting Plato*, 13–22; and Thesleff, *Studies*, 86–94. See Thomas L. Pangle, "Editor's Introduction," in *The Roots of Political Philosophy* (Ithaca: Cornell University Press, 1987), 3–17, for a more thorough account of the reasons to accept the ancient lists of authentic dialogues, not as perfect but as the best we have.

22. Walter Nicgorski, "Cicero's Socrates," in *Law and Philosophy*, vol. 1, ed. John A. Murley, Robert L. Stone, and William T. Braithwaite (Athens: Ohio University Press, 1992), reminds us that Cicero recognized that "Plato's Socrates is, in a sense, made or created by Plato" (216) in *De finibus* 2.2 and *De oratore* 3.67. One of the clearest instances of such a recognition on Cicero's part occurs, ironically, when he describes the last speech in Plato's *Apology of Socrates* as "that which Plato made him employ" (*Tusculanae disputationes* 1.97; Nicgorski, "Socrates," 228). But contemporary commentators have not always adhered to this earlier insight. Kahn, in *Plato and the Socratic Dialogue*, argues that the *Apology of Socrates* alone is historical. Donald Morrison, "On the Alleged Historical Reliability of Plato's *Apology*," *Archiv f. Gesch. d. Philosophie* 82 (2000): 235–65, gives a detailed critique of Kahn's argument. For a more general discussion of the reasons the *Apology of Socrates* should be read as a literary work by Plato, with a historical basis rather than a historical report, see R. B. Rutherford, *The Art of Plato* (Cambridge: Harvard University Press, 1995), 29–34. David Wolfsdorf, "Interpreting Plato's Early Dialogues," *Oxford Studies in Ancient Philosophy* 27 (Winter 2004): 20, also observes that "the particular configuration of the historical elements is not historically accurate. Among other things, the ubiquity of anachronism . . . [suggests that] the dialogues are not intended to represent conversations that actually occurred."

23. I make no claim about the order and time in which the dialogues were written or conceived. Plato may have composed some of the dialogues depicting Socrates late in life, like the

dialogues together in the order indicated corroborates the character and significance of the dramatic dates. Because in some dialogues the date is sketchily presented, and there are in a few cases contradictory indications, I do not think the dramatic dates can do anything more than indicate the order and connections among the dialogues.

Read in the order indicated by their dramatic dates, the dialogues tell a story. The evidence for the dating of the dialogues as well as for the readings that are summarized here is more fully presented in the relevant chapters of this book.

The story begins not with the *Parmenides*, the earliest appearance of Socrates, but with the *Laws*, usually taken to be the last dialogue Plato wrote. As noted earlier in the introduction, the evidence for the dating of the composition of the *Laws* is slight and highly questionable. But whenever Plato wrote it, in this dialogue Plato asks his readers to imagine a conversation that took place after the Persian Wars, to which there are many references, but before the Peloponnesian War, to which there is no reference at all. Occurring before the Peloponnesian War, the dialogue also occurs before Socrates became a public figure in Athens. Indeed, the *Laws* shows us why Socratic philosophy emerged and was taken up with such passionate interest.[24] In the conversation he has with two elderly Dorian statesmen, an anonymous Athenian stranger draws extensively upon pre-Socratic Greek poetry, pre-Socratic Greek political experience or "history," and pre-Socratic philosophy in proposing a new and better regime. But at the end of his legislative proposals (*Laws* 965c–66a), the Athenian tells his interlocutors that the city he has described in speech will not come into being unless they and the people who will help them found the new colony in Crete join together in an investigation of the unity of the virtues as well as of the noble and the good. Such an investigation is necessary if the city is to

---

Apology, before he wrote dialogues depicting a younger Socrates, like the *Parmenides*; he may have "filled in" lacunae in the story. We don't know. All we have are the finished products, and there is some dispute about which dialogues he actually wrote. Since I take each of the dialogues to depict a separate conversation, I do not think the overall narrative would be seriously harmed if some of the more questionably authentic dialogues were ignored. In this respect I follow both the reasoning and the practice of Rutherford (*Art*, 3). I have treated the *Alcibiades II* and *Ion* only in the notes as thematically related, respectively, to the *Alcibiades I* and the discussion of Homeric poetry in the *Republic*. For the dramatic dating of the *Ion*, see John D. Moore, "The Dating of Plato's *Ion*," *Greek, Roman, and Byzantine Studies* 15 (Winter 1974): 425–39.

24. An abbreviated version of the argument put forward in fuller form in chapter 1 can be found in Catherine H. Zuckert, "Plato's *Laws*: Postlude or Prelude to Socratic Political Philosophy?" *Journal of Politics* 66 (May 2004): 374–95.

achieve its stated goal (770c–d). To make every member of the community as virtuous as possible, the leaders need to know what human virtue or excellence (aretē), traditionally defined in ancient Greece as the kalokagathia (nobility and goodness), really and truly is. In other words, to establish the best possible form of common human life and thus solve the political problem, it is necessary to raise the questions characteristic of Socratic philosophy. But, as the Athenian also has to explain to his philosophically untutored interlocutors, raising such questions will be politically problematic, if not pernicious, because the questioning of accepted opinions encourages the tendency of young men to become impious and rebellious and thus threatens the stability of the laws as well as the future of the regime.

As everyone knows from reading the Apology, Socrates' questions concerning the noble and good finally provoked his fellow citizens to accuse and convict him of impiety, although it took them more than forty years (and possibly defeat in war) to act against him. But, as Plato indicates in the Parmenides (dramatically dated 450, shortly after the Laws), there were perhaps even more serious philosophical problems with Socrates' search for knowledge of the "ideas" of the virtues, the noble, and the good. In this dialogue a youthful (nineteen- or twenty-year-old) Socrates is not able to tell the elderly Eleatic philosopher why he thinks there are ideas of relations and the virtues, but not of natural species or more lowly phenomena like hair and mud. Nor is Socrates able to explain how sensible things participate in purely intelligible beings or how purely intelligible beings can be known by non–purely intelligible humans.

In the two dialogues he suggests occurred earliest, Plato thus shows that it would not be possible to establish the best possible form of political order without engaging in something like Socratic philosophy. But that philosophy involved two different kinds of problems—philosophical as well as political—from its very inception. Plato does not devote a single dialogue to depicting Socrates' own philosophical education and development. There is, indeed, a gap of seventeen years between the first glimpse we get of the young Socrates in the Parmenides and his emergence "on stage" in Athens, so to speak, in the Protagoras. What we do see, negatively, is that Socrates never followed Parmenides' advice to engage in the sort of argumentative gymnastics that the Eleatic models in the last two-thirds of the Parmenides. Plato does have Socrates give three retrospective accounts of his own education and development in three dialogues that are shown to have occurred much later. On the last day of his life, Socrates famously explains how he turned away from the investigations of nature we now call pre-Socratic philosophy and formulated the argument concerning the ideas we see him present in the *Parmenides*. In the *Symposium* Socrates tells his friends how he learned from "Diotima" to move beyond thinking in terms of opposites, the "is" and "is not" characteristic of Parmenides and his student Zeno, to investigating opinions, especially about the noble and good.[25] In his *Apology* Socrates attributes that turn in his thought to the oracle at Delphi in explaining how and why his philosophy has aroused the enmity of some of his fellow citizens. In both the *Symposium* and the *Apology*, the divine instruction or inspiration, we might say, that led Socrates to turn to examining opinions, especially about the noble and good, rather than merely criticizing previous philosophical arguments (*logoi*), appears to have occurred after 450 but before 433.[26]

In the dialogues that follow the initial presentation of the problems to which he was responding, Plato presents four stages or periods of Socrates' philosophizing. In the first stage, the two sets of conversations that Plato indicates took place at the very beginning and then at the end of the first part of the Peloponnesian War—the *Protagoras*, *Alcibiades*, and *Charmides*, followed a decade later by the *Laches*, *Hippias Major*, and *Hippias Minor*—we see Socrates repeatedly demonstrate the inadequacy of the understandings of virtue, the noble, and the good held by his contemporaries. In the face of the proven inadequacy of their current understanding, Socrates urges his interlocutors to join him in further philosophical investigations of the good and the noble, but his invitations do not bear fruit. His two most notorious sometime associates, Alcibiades and Critias, do not stay with Socrates long enough to acquire nontraditional or noncontradictory conceptions of a human life that is truly *kalos k'agathos* (noble and good).[27] The two generals or statesmen to whom Socrates speaks in the *Laches* are too busy with public affairs to engage in any further conversations, and the sophists (Protagoras and Hippias), who claim to be able to teach politically ambitious young Athenians how to succeed, do not seek to be corrected (and embarrassed) by Socrates again.

25. I have been asked several times why I do not include "Diotima" (and Aspasia in the *Menexenus*) among the Platonic philosophers (whom I do not think should, strictly speaking, be called spokesmen, because no one in the dialogues speaks for Plato simply or directly). Although Socrates tells his interlocutors what he learned from Diotima and Aspasia, and explicitly calls them his teachers, Socrates reports what they told him. Plato does not show either of the women speaking directly to other interlocutors. Nor does either of these women present as comprehensive a view as Plato's philosophers.

26. See Catherine H. Zuckert, "The Socratic Turn," *History of Political Thought* 25 (Summer 2004): 189–219; and chapter 3 in the present volume.

27. Cf. Xenophon *Memorabilia* 1.2.24.

In the second stage, constituted by a group of dialogues that Plato indicates occurred during the second part of the Peloponnesian War between 416 and 411, Socrates no longer remains content merely to show the
inadequacy of the opinions held by his interlocutors. He begins to put forth a
kind of positive teaching of his own, albeit in the form of images and myths.
He also asserts that he possesses a certain limited kind of knowledge of *ta
erōtika*. In the *Symposium* (unquestionably dated in 416), Socrates meets again
with many of the Athenians present at his initial encounter with Protagoras.
But instead of questioning the opinions of the sophists, with whom these
Athenians had associated, in the *Symposium*, *Phaedrus*, and *Republic* Socrates
engages in a contest with the poets, the origin of the traditional notions of
kalos k'agathos to which the sophists adhered. Rather than demonstrate the
internal incoherence of the traditional notions as he had in previous conversations, in these dialogues (completed, I argue, by the argument concerning the human good in the *Philebus*, which has no definite dramatic date)
Socrates puts forth a vision of another, better understanding of a noble and
good human life, the life of those who join together in seeking knowledge of
what is truly noble and good. As we see in later dialogues, Socrates succeeds
in attracting a certain number of regular associates, even though he does
not persuade everyone to whom he speaks of the pressing need for, and the
unparalleled enjoyment to be gained by, such philosophical investigations.

Socrates does not succeed, however, in putting forth a comprehensive
view of the intelligibility of the whole. That is the reason he always describes himself literally as a philosopher, a seeker of wisdom, rather than a
knower or wise man. The *Timaeus* clearly follows the conversation related
in the *Republic*, although not necessarily immediately; in the *Timaeus* Plato
reminds his readers that Socrates never presents a cosmology, that is, an
account of nature as a whole, by having Socrates sit silently listening to an
explicitly mythical account of the intelligible construction of the cosmos
given by another philosopher-statesman.[28] Indeed, in the person and speech
of Timaeus Plato presents a model or paradigm of philosophy that is notice-

28. The closest Socrates comes is a mere assertion that the cosmos must be the work of intelligence, to which he gets Protarchus to agree without giving any supporting arguments in *Philebus*
28c–30e. Francis MacDonald Cornford, *Plato's Cosmology: The "Timaeus" of Plato* (London: Routledge and Kegan, 1937), 75–79, points out that Socrates' description of the orbits of the spheres
in the myth of Er at the conclusion of the *Republic* does not correspond (and makes no claim to
correspond) to empirical observations of the orbits of the heavenly bodies the way Timaeus' account does. Aristotle's observation (*Metaphysics* 987b1–8) that Socrates busied himself about ethical matters and neglected the world of nature as whole, although he sought the universal in these
ethical matters, thus describes the character presented in Plato's dialogues.

ably different from that represented by Socrates. Socrates seeks knowledge by examining the opinions of others, particularly about the true objects of their endeavors, the noble and the good. According to Timaeus, philosophers not only acquire knowledge of the intelligible order of the cosmos, but also duplicate that order within their own souls by observing and then contemplating the intelligible order of the movements of the heavenly bodies. They and only they are truly happy. To acquire the skills and self-control needed to learn about the orderly movements of the heavens, however, such philosophers need to be raised under a certain regime. To show how the regime described in the first four books of the *Republic* could actually come into being, Timaeus is asked to explain how the cosmos came into being up to the point where there are human beings capable of becoming citizens of that regime. Although Timaeus' account of the construction of the cosmos by the demiurge is a philosophical tour de force, incorporating the best of ancient Greek natural science (and has, therefore, often been taken as "Plato's cosmology"), he does not perform the job assigned. Toward the end of the dialogue, Timaeus suggests that women arise from cowardly males. There are not and never have been any potential female guardians in Timaeus' cosmos, but in the city Socrates initially describes, as in the *Republic*, there are to be both male and female guardians. In the conversation that follows, Critias thus has to present another, more traditionally mythological account of the origin of ancient Athens and Atlantis to replace Timaeus' defective beginning. Although Timaeus' account of the generation of the various kinds is laughable, it nevertheless points to a fundamental difference between his philosophy and that of Socrates. Socrates never presents an explanation of the order or generation of the cosmos, but he can account for human eros in a way Timaeus does not. Indeed, Socrates presents philosophy as a fundamentally erotic activity.[29]

Because he and his readers are human beings animated by a variety of desires, Plato turns his readers' attention back from Timaean contemplation

29. Pace Jill Gordon, "Eros in Plato's *Timaeus*," *Epoche* 9, no. 2 (Spring 2005): 255–77, both A. E. Taylor, *A Commentary on Plato's "Timaeus"* (Oxford: Clarendon Press, 1928), 260, 263–64, 493; and Cornford, *Plato's Cosmology*, 281n3, 145n1, correctly observe that eros becomes a part of the human soul only after it is attached to a mortal body and confused. When Timaeus states that lovers of *nous* and *epistēmē (ton de nou kai epistēmēs erastēn)* regard the intelligible principles as first causes (46d–e), he is referring to the same and the other, which the god forced together in the world soul and embedded in the orbits of the heavenly bodies. Qua intelligible, these principles may be beautiful and good, but they are not the beautiful or the good in themselves, that is, the objects of philosophical eros as Socrates describes it. The intelligible principles embedded in the orbits are copies of the purely intelligible beings made by the Demiourgos.

to the Socratic search for wisdom, especially concerning the best life for human beings, in the third stage of his depiction of the philosophical life and career of Socrates, in a series of dialogues said to occur in the last decade of the fifth century. These dialogues have often been grouped with the dialogues depicting Socrates' primarily critical encounters with the sophists and infamous young Athenians during the first part of the Peloponnesian War as "early" and "elenctic." In fact, however, there are two important differences between the two sets of dialogues. In the *Theages*, *Euthydemus*, *Lysis*, *Gorgias*, and *Meno*, Socrates has acquired the reputation and following that he is shown merely to be seeking in the earlier set of dialogues. As a result, Plato is able to show us the effect Socrates has on some of his regular associates as well as the kinds of people he does not attract or retain as regular companions. Having shown that Socrates does not claim to be able to give a coherent account of the whole and that he encourages his companions to join with him in a search for knowledge, Plato depicts the personal more than the philosophical results as well as some of the characteristic misunderstandings of that search. He does not have Socrates present a grand doctrine.

In the fourth stage or period, constituted by the eight dialogues with dramatic dates that explicitly connect them to Socrates' trial and death, Plato presents a defense of his teacher. In the first three of these dialogues, he presents the grounds and consequently a defense of Socrates' claim that he is wise only so far as he knows that he does not know. In the *Theaetetus* he has Socrates show the brilliant young mathematician why the art in which he takes so much pride cannot be considered knowledge, properly speaking. In the *Euthyphro* Plato dramatizes the dangers of relying on divine inspiration, especially the sort of inspiration that gave rise to the stories told by the ancient Greek poets. And in the *Cratylus* he has Socrates demonstrate the inadequacy of names or words as a source of knowledge of the beings.

If human beings cannot acquire knowledge by means of number or divine inspiration or words, however, how can we come to understand anything about ourselves and our world? Does it make sense to continue seeking knowledge we can never attain? Socrates' famous disclaimer concerning his own knowledge, combined with his persistent questioning and refuting of others, made him appear to be merely a destructive critic of traditional morality, an eristic "sophist." That criticism is leveled in its most fundamental form by an anonymous Eleatic Stranger. In a set of conversations said to take place the day after the *Theaetetus*, *Euthyphro*, and *Cratylus*, the stranger first accuses Socrates, in effect, of being a sophist. By refuting the opinions of others in private conversations, Socrates appears to know all the things about which he questions his interlocutors, even though he himself knows "ironically" that he does not. (In other words, Socrates fits the last and apparently best definition of a sophist.) In the *Statesman* the stranger then suggests that the questioning of traditional opinions about the just and the noble in which Socrates engages undermines the rule of law, and with it the best possible form of government.

Plato presents Socrates' response to these charges in his *Apology, Crito,* and *Phaedo.* In the *Apology* Socrates argues that his questioning of the opinions of his contemporaries with regard to the just, noble, and good constitutes the greatest possible service not only to Athens but also to the god of Delphi. In the *Crito* Socrates then demonstrates that he and his philosophy do not undermine the rule of law both in argument and in deed. And in the *Phaedo* Socrates finally presents his close associates in private with both arguments and an example he hopes will enable them to persist in their philosophical investigations after his death. The fact that many of the individuals present went on to write "Socratic" dialogues and to establish various philosophical schools suggests that Socrates succeeded in leaving a philosophical legacy. In the *Menexenus* Plato dramatizes the political legacy Socrates left to his own city, anachronistically and thus from the grave, so to speak, by having the philosopher present a speech he attributes to Aspasia in which he shows the Athenians how to understand their city's history and thus their own political lives more moderately and justly.

Reading the dialogues as discrete incidents in an ongoing story allows us to preserve the integrity of the individual works of art. By stringing them out in the order of their dramatic dates, we not only get a "through-line" that helps us see the shape of Plato's corpus as a whole; we also follow Plato's own indications about the relations of the conversations to one another. In contrast to the chronology of composition, we are not led to present inferences based on interpretations of the content of the dialogues as if they were based on externally determined historical "facts" about the time at which the dialogues were written—facts, to repeat, that we do not know.[30]

---

30. As Eduard Munk, *Die Natürliche Ordnung der Platonischen Schriften* (Berlin: Dümmler, 1857), vii, pointed out long ago, attempts to date the dialogues on the basis of style or word use involve inferences from highly questionable assumptions. Plato was a consummate artist who was able to use many styles in depicting exchanges between different individual characters. Even if, as the stylometric studies show, there are six dialogues in which Plato uses similar phrases and constructions, Thesleff observes, the evidence that these dialogues were written "late" is slight. Nor does it follow that Plato intended these conversations to be read as "late" productions (Thesleff, *Stud-*

The order in which we read the dialogues affects the way we understand them, both singly and in relation to one another.[31] To mention some particularly egregious examples: on the basis of a supposed chronology of composition, the *Apology of Socrates* is usually considered to be an early work, whereas the *Parmenides* is thought to be a middle or even late production. According to the indications of the dramatic dates, however, the *Parmenides* depicts one of Socrates' first public appearances, whereas the *Apology* occurs at the end of his life. In the *Parmenides* we look forward to Socrates' future development; in the *Apology* he tries to explain to his fellow citizens what he has already done. According to the same chronology of composition, the *Crito* is early, the *Phaedo* a dialogue from Plato's middle period, and the *Sophist* and *Statesman* late. But if we follow the dramatic dating, we see that the *Sophist* and *Statesman* are explicitly shown to occur the day after Socrates is indicted. Following the conversations in which an Eleatic "stranger" implicitly accuses Socrates of being a sophist and of having brought the charges on himself, the *Apology*, *Crito*, and *Phaedo* all appear to be responses to his more philosophical accusations as well as to the legal indictment.

Reading the dialogues in the order indicated by their dramatic dates thus yields two immediate benefits. First, it enables us to take account of the

---

ies, 69–71). The order Munk proposed resembles the order I have presented on the basis of the dramatic dates inasmuch as he also relies on the dramatic dates and suggests that the dialogues represent three periods in the development of Socrates' philosophy: (1) Socrates' dedication to philosophy and his battle against sophistry: *Parmenides*, 446; *Protagoras*, 434; *Charmides*, 432; *Laches*, 421; *Gorgias*, 420; *Ion*, 420; *Hippias Major*, 420; *Cratylus*, 420; *Euthydemus*, 420; and *Symposium*, 417; (2) Socrates' true wisdom: *Phaedo*, 410; *Philebus*, 410; and *Republic*, *Timaeus*, *Critias*, 410; and (3) Socrates proves the truth of his teaching through a critique of opposed insights and his martyrdom: *Meno*, 405; *Theaetetus*, *Sophist*, *Statesman*, *Euthyphro*, *Apology*, *Crito*, and *Phaedo*, 399. Some of these dates have been challenged (as I show in notes to the chapters that follow). Munk is forced, moreover, to set aside some dialogues as not belonging to the cycle (and thus possibly representing early works by Plato): *Alcibiades I*, *Lysis*, *Hippias Minor*, as well as later works like the *Laws* and *Menexenus*. That is, Munk has to recur to the chronology of composition he himself criticized in accounting for some Platonic writings, and he entirely omits others—including the *Phaedrus*—as well as possibly inauthentic dialogues such as the *Theages* and *Alcibiades II*. He does not see the way in which the Eleatic Stranger challenges Socrates in the *Sophist* and *Statesman*; he regards these dialogues, on the contrary, as showing the way in which Plato combined Eleatic philosophy with Socratic morality.

31. Charles Griswold, "E Pluribus Unum? On the Platonic 'Corpus,'" *Ancient Philosophy* 19 (1999): 386–93, takes a step in this direction, but he gives only general principles supporting the dramatic chronology he sketches in note 29, and barely indicates (387–95) some of the interpretive results such a reading of the dialogues might bring. Joseph Cropsey, *Plato's World* (Chicago: University of Chicago Press, 1995); and Jacob Howland, *The Paradox of Political Philosophy: Socrates' Philosophical Trial* (Lanham, MD: Rowman and Littlefield, 1998), both emphasize the sequence of dialogues explicitly connected by their dramatic dating to Socrates' death.

differences in Plato's presentation of Socrates that led most commentators to adopt the developmental thesis rather than maintain a unitarian reading of Socrates, much less of Plato, without claiming historical knowledge that we in fact lack about the times at which Plato wrote individual dialogues. Second, and more important, the dramatic chronology enables us to see the way in which Plato used his other philosophical spokesmen, first to set up the problems, philosophical and political, that were bequeathed to Plato and his teacher by the pre-Socratics and then to indicate the limitations of the "solutions" Socrates proposed, both cosmological and logical. Socrates is clearly the central figure in the Platonic corpus, but Plato's understanding is more comprehensive than his chief protagonist's. That is not to say that Plato simply agrees with Timaeus or the Eleatic Stranger, however. On the contrary, he uses Socrates to critique them. Plato's own understanding is to be found, I argue, in the way he juxtaposes the different philosophical positions, dramatizing the limitations of the arguments that Socrates articulates but showing in the end that there is no better alternative.

III. Atypical Kinds of Dialogues

A. The Narrated Dialogues: Socrates' Interior

Most of the dialogues are presented as prose dramas, but some—nine, to be precise—are narrated.[32] And like the narrative that emerges on the basis of the dramatic dates, the narrated dialogues highlight the role and figure of Socrates. Four of these dialogues—*Lovers, Lysis, Charmides,* and *Republic*—are entirely narrated by Socrates. Two—*Protagoras* and *Euthydemus*—are narrated by Socrates, following an introductory dramatic exchange. The three dialogues that are not narrated by Socrates—*Parmenides, Symposium,* and *Phaedo*—all contain accounts or reports of incidents in the education of Socrates, discoveries or lessons that, I argue in chapter 3, contributed to making Socrates the distinctive kind of philosopher he became.[33]

---

32. The dialogue the slave boy reads in the *Theaetetus* was originally narrated to Euclides by Socrates, but Euclides tells Terpsion that he removed all the signs of its narration, for example, "he said," and thus transformed it, in effect, into a dramatic dialogue. As a result, we readers do not know whether Socrates made any comments on the conversation as he related it to Euclides. Scholars disagree about the historical status of narrated dialogues. Whereas Thesleff argues (*Studies,* 56–62) that narrated dialogues probably preceded the dramatic, Rutherford observes (*Art,* 45) that Xenophon never makes Socrates the narrator and suggests that Plato was first to do so.

33. Cf. Leo Strauss, *On Plato's "Symposium,"* ed. and with a foreword by Seth Benardete (Chicago: University of Chicago Press, 2001), 186.

The four dialogues entirely narrated by Socrates are conversations he himself chooses to relate, in all cases to an anonymous audience of an indeterminate number. By relating these conversations, Socrates appears to be trying to affect, if not to control, what people in general know and thus think about his interrogations of others.[34] He often seems to be trying to correct some widespread misapprehensions and misunderstandings of his philosophical activity. The fact that he chooses to relate these conversations makes them stand in contrast to the explanation of his philosophical activity that he was required, if not forced by law, to give in the *Apology.*

In all four of the dialogues narrated entirely by Socrates, we hear about conversations he had with noble young Athenians. Rather than corrupting the young with whom he associated, in all four cases Socrates shows that he was trying to help them become better by encouraging them to seek the most important kind of knowledge. In two of these dialogues, the *Charmides* and *Lovers*, Plato shows that Socrates himself went to a gymnasium in search of young people with whom to conduct his philosophical investigations. In two others we see that Socrates was either invited or forced to take part in the conversation that ensues by the desires of his young associates. The primary reason Socrates engaged in conversations with others, it becomes clear, was his concern for the young. He was not trying to learn something himself so much as to attract them to a life of philosophy.

As narrator, Socrates is able to explain how he happened to talk to these specific individuals and comment on how they or others reacted to the exchange. In the *Lovers* he does not tell us why he went to the school of Dionysius, but once there, he uses the opportunity to challenge other misconceptions of philosophy and to encourage all of his auditors to seek the most useful form of knowledge, how to be just and moderate. In the *Charmides* Socrates explains that, arriving home with the army from Potidaea, he went to the wrestling school of Taureas, anxious to resume his usual conversations and to discover whether any of the youths had proved themselves to be particularly noble or handsome and wise in his absence. As in the *Lovers* and the *Lysis*, so in the *Charmides*, it becomes clear that the other men and boys do not gather in the gymnasia primarily to philosophize.

---

34. To be sure, on the basis of Plato's comments in the *Seventh Letter*, we might read all the dialogues as, at bottom, constituting a defense of Socrates. This seems, nevertheless, to be emphatically the case in the dialogues Socrates himself narrates (and not so obviously the case in dialogues like the *Philebus* or *Statesman*).

Socrates is forced, therefore, to take account of their concerns—whether about the course of the war or attracting lovers—in order to induce them to take part in the philosophical conversations he himself prizes. This need to speak, at least initially, to the political concerns or personal desires that move his young associates was one of the reasons Socrates' compatriots did not understand the true character of his own philosophy or its potential benefits for the city. As in the *Lovers*, so in the *Charmides*, Socrates admits that he is excited by the presence of handsome youths, but he also shows that he conquered his bodily desires by conversing rather than seeking to lie with them. (If we did not have Socrates' testimony about his own feelings, we might, on the basis of what Alcibiades says in the *Symposium*, think that Socrates was simply indifferent to bodily beauty or frigid.) In the *Charmides* we also see Socrates try to convince two future tyrants of Athens, both relatives of Plato, to become moderate. He and we both know that he did not succeed; Charmides and Critias found Socrates' conversations amusing and wanted to compel him to stay and talk more, but they were not persuaded to become more moderate. As narrator, Socrates is nevertheless able to show that he understands the difficulty human beings experience in exercising self-restraint, and that he was trying to make these young aristocratic Athenians more moderate and more pious.

Socrates famously begins the *Republic* by explaining that he went down to the Piraeus with Plato's brother Glaucon to see the first celebration of a new foreign goddess, and that he stayed to talk about justice as a result of a combination of Polemarchus' threat to restrain him by force and his own desire to accommodate Glaucon. When Polemarchus' father Cephalus leaves, readers are reminded that Socratic conversations were more attractive to the young than the old, and that Socrates preferred to talk to the former. It is impossible for human beings to become better, more just, or more moderate without questioning, challenging, and finally replacing old opinions and conventions. But, Plato shows in the *Republic* (as in all his other dialogues), Socrates challenged accepted opinions, particularly about the noble and the good; he challenged these opinions in private, however, by talking to individuals, not in public, by speaking in the assembly or disobeying the law.[35] In the *Republic* Socrates describes a new and more

35. In his *Apology* 29d, Plato's Socrates states that he will disobey "the men of Athens," if they forbid him to philosophize in the future. Until the Athenians convicted Socrates of the capital crimes of impiety and corrupting the young, the law of Athens did not forbid philosophy. If, as "the laws" in the *Crito* claim afterward, it was the particular members of the Athenian jury who

beautiful "city in speech" in an all-night secret meeting, but he concludes that the purpose of that city is to serve as an internal paradigm for the individual to use in ordering his soul. As in the *Charmides*, so in the *Republic*, Socrates begins by taking account of the political ambitions and interests of his interlocutors. He gradually attempts to show them, however, that they will be able to realize their desire to live the best possible form of human existence only by philosophizing in a Socratic manner. It is not clear at the end of the dialogue that he succeeded. Plato's brothers did not become tyrants like Critias and Charmides, but they did not become philosophers either.

At the beginning of the *Lysis*, readers are also reminded of the unconventional, possibly illegal and impious character of Socratic philosophy when Socrates explains that he accompanied a group of young men at their behest to a gymnasium where some handsome young boys were celebrating a festival. It is not clear that older men like Socrates were allowed to attend such celebrations; at the end of the dialogue, the slave tutors of the two boys to whom Socrates has been talking take them home forcibly. The young men want Socrates to demonstrate his erotic knowledge by showing one of them how to attract a beloved boy. As in the *Lovers*, so in the *Lysis*, Socrates shows that a lover attracts his beloved by providing him with useful knowledge more than by preening himself or the beloved. As in the *Lovers*, so in the *Lysis*, Socrates does not claim to have shown what the *philon* is, or even what the search for knowledge of it, philosophy, would entail. He does say, however paradoxically at the end of the dialogue, that he and the two young boys have become friends. Socrates claims, in other words, to have established a kind of community with the boys, dedicated to their mutual improvement, even if and when he has not succeeded in explicitly answering the question they are debating to his or their satisfaction. As in the *Republic*, so at the end of the *Lysis*, it is not clear whether the boys will remain Socrates' friends. In fact, we learn from the *Phaedo* that Menexenus became a regular companion of Socrates but Lysis did not. Menexenus did not become a philosopher, however; as we learn

---

treated Socrates unjustly and not the laws per se, they presumably did not forbid such philosophizing after the trial either. There was, of course, a complex relation between the law and opinion in ancient Greece, where *nomos* referred to customs and thus to unwritten as well as to written laws. Then as now, however, there was also a difference, often brought out in the Platonic dialogues, between what individuals wanted for themselves and what they were willing to say in public was right or just. After Socrates' trial and death, Plato left Athens but later returned. Aristotle also came to fear prosecution and fled.

from the dialogue that bears his name, he had political ambitions which Socrates tried to help him realize in a way that would benefit all Athenians. From the narrated dialogues, we learn that Socrates did not always have the effect he sought. He was not able to convince most of his young interlocutors to pursue a life of philosophy. He was not even able to persuade some of them to act more justly in conventional, political terms. His comments as narrator nevertheless show us what he intended as well as his own recognition of the limited kinds of effects he could have on his interlocutors in a single conversation.

In the two dialogues narrated by Socrates after a dramatic prologue, the *Protagoras* and *Euthydemus*, we see him interrogating the sophists. Those who accused Socrates of corrupting the young thought that he was a sophist. Socrates' interrogations of the sophists not only highlight the differences between him and the sophists, but also indicate the reasons his compatriots confused him with them. Because they claimed to teach virtue, the sophists charged fees for their lessons. As Socrates emphasizes in his *Apology*, he did not claim to teach virtue, nor did he charge a fee. In his conversations with the sophists, Socrates nevertheless shows that he knows how to argue better than the sophists do by proving that they do not know what virtue is. In other words, he shows that the sophists do not really know what they are talking about and that they do not, therefore, justly charge fees for their lessons. At the same time, Socrates (or Plato) indicates that he was familiar with the sophists personally as well as with their doctrines, and that Socrates' familiarity with the sophists contributed to his compatriots' belief that he was one of them. Before taking a young Athenian to meet the famous sophist, in the *Protagoras* Socrates warns Hippocrates, who had awakened him to ask for an introduction to the sophist, to be careful about the lessons he acquires. But we also observe that Socrates relates an account of his victory over Protagoras to an anonymous Athenian audience immediately thereafter and thus contributes to the formation of his own reputation as a kind of "super-sophist." In the *Euthydemus*, Socrates' old friend Crito asks Socrates to relate the conversation he had with a pair of sophists the day before.[36] Although Socrates makes

---

36. The fact that the two narrated dialogues that are related to named individuals (as opposed to an anonymous audience), the *Euthydemus* and the *Phaedo*, are related in the first case to one of Socrates' closest friends present at his death, and in the other, by another of Socrates' friends present at his death, to a friendly figure who asked specifically what Socrates said and did (*Phaedo* 57a–58e), suggests that these two dialogues are particularly concerned with what Socrates wanted his friends to know about his activity.

the sophists look ridiculous, at the end of the conversation he neverthe-less urges Crito to bring his sons and come along with him to take lessons from the brothers. In these dialogues Plato shows not only that Socrates was not a sophist but also that the sophists were not his primary targets or enemies, as some commentators have claimed.[37] The sophists may not have possessed the knowledge they promised to purvey, but they at least recognized the importance of speech or argument in learning to be virtu-ous. Without the insight provided by Socrates' comments about his own intentions and efforts, it was difficult to distinguish him from them.

Whereas the dialogues narrated by Socrates emphasize the effects he had, or at least wanted to have, on young Athenians, the dialogues nar-rated by others contain sections explaining how and why Socrates came to engage in the kinds of inquiries he did for his own sake, to discover the truth, and not simply for the sake of the effect his investigations might have on his interlocutors or audience. On the last day of his life, in the *Phaedo*, we hear Socrates retrospectively relate the reasons he gave up the investigations of natural phenomena in which he had engaged as a youth and turned to an examination of the arguments (*logoi*) of others. In the *Parmenides* we then see Socrates use the argument about the ideas he de-veloped as a hypothesis in the *Phaedo* to critique Zeno. However, Socrates was unable to respond to the questions Parmenides raised about his argu-ment concerning the ideas. We do not learn how Socrates responded to Parmenides' demonstration of philosophical gymnastics at the time. Only later, in the *Symposium*, does Socrates tell a story about the way "Diotima" taught him to examine opinion, as that which is between knowledge and ignorance, being and not-being, and so enabled him to escape the *aporia* that results from Eleatic arguments in terms of mutually exclusive "is" and "is not."

If Plato had not written these narrated dialogues, his readers would have only the external view of Socrates provided by the dramatic dialogues. Judging only on the basis of appearances in the absence of Socrates' own account of his endeavor, readers, like Socrates' compatriots, might have found it difficult to distinguish his attempts to attract young companions from those of the foreign sophists or older male lovers. We might have observed that Socrates did not charge a fee to listen to him converse, nor

---

37. See, e.g., Hans-Georg Gadamer, *The Idea of the Good in Platonic-Aristotelian Philosophy*, trans. P. Christopher Smith (New Haven: Yale University Press, 1986), 61, 99; and Weiss, *Socratic Paradox*. I fill in the reasons for my own controversial claims about Socrates' relation to the soph-ists in the chapters on these dialogues.

did he seem to seek physical pleasure from his intercourse with young men. But why, then, was he so anxious to talk to them and to persuade them, as opposed to more mature thinkers and philosophers, to join him in his examinations of opinion? In other words, why did Socrates become the distinctive kind of philosopher he was? In the dramatic dialogues we see how he interrogated others about their views of the noble and good. We learn about the steps or stages in Socrates' own education that led him to undertake these investigations, however, only through the retrospective indirect discourse that a narration makes possible.

B. The Undated Dialogues: A General External View of Socrates

An attentive reader will have noticed that the narrative I've just sketched does not include three of the four dialogues that have no dramatic date: *Hipparchus, Minos, Lovers,* and *Philebus.* Socrates is the major spokesman in all, so they clearly take place during his lifetime—even more precisely, during the period in which he was known to be examining the opinions of his contemporaries about the just, the noble, and the good. His interlocutors in all appear to be young, if nameless, Athenians.[38] The absence of specific personalities and times is one of the main reasons many commentators think the *Hipparchus, Minos,* and *Lovers* are spurious, composed by an imitator, not by Plato himself. It would be easiest for a commentator attempting to show the coherence of the Platonic corpus in terms of the dramatic characteristics of the dialogues, including particularly the dramatic dating, to dismiss the three brief undated dialogues as inauthentic and to relate the *Philebus* thematically to the *Republic,* as in the list above. However, because the grounds for declaring these as well as other dialogues inauthentic are problematic and therefore a source of contention, it appears better (and safer) to show how these and other possibly, but not certainly, spurious dialogues can be included in a coherent account of the corpus.[39]

Like the dialogues with more specific dramatic dates, these dialogues point to the centrality of Socrates to the Platonic corpus. Even if they are not genuine, these dialogues reflect what are, and what Plato's contemporary

38. Leo Strauss, "On the Minos," in *Liberalism Ancient and Modern* (New York: Basic Books, 1968), observes: "As for the character of the companion, we suspect that he was no longer quite young" (74).

39. Cf. Strauss, *Symposium,* 11: "Today, some of the dialogues which have come down to us as Platonic dialogues are regarded as spurious. I believe it is wise to suspend our judgment on this subject and simply to accept all dialogues which have come down to us as Platonic."

admirers saw to be, central themes in his presentation of Socrates: the desire on the part of all human beings to acquire and possess the good, the questioning of the justice of established laws and customs, and the true character and utility of philosophy. The failure to name the individual interlocutors or to indicate the specific time at which these conversations occurred may, as some commentators have argued, reflect a lack of artistry on the part of the author. It may, however, serve to indicate the general pervasiveness of these themes or questions in Socratic philosophizing. Few scholars have expressed doubts about the authenticity of the *Philebus*, although it has no specific time or setting beyond Athens, and Socrates' interlocutors have only generic names meaning "lover of or beloved by the young" and "first principle or ruler." This dialogue also begins, rather inartistically, in the midst of a conversation already under way and ends before it is completed.

The *Hipparchus* and the *Minos* are the only two dialogues that begin abruptly, without any dramatic introduction, with one of the "what is . . . ?" questions for which Socrates was famous. These are also the only two dialogues that bear the names of ancient tyrants. The reason appears initially and externally to be that no other characters in these dialogues are named except Socrates.[40] Upon examination, however, there also appears to be a thematic connection between the naming of the tyrants and the questions posed in these dialogues. In the *Hipparchus* Socrates tries to persuade a young moralist that "lovers of gain" may not be the "shameless rascals" he takes them to be, if gain is a good, and all human beings seek the good. And in the *Minos* Socrates tells a slightly less young and thumotic Athenian that law cannot be defined merely in terms of what the Athenians say is law. Other cities also have laws, different laws, and all these cities claim that their laws are just. "Laws" so understood look like a variety of attempts to discover what is truly just and should be judged accordingly. Both these dialogues thus dramatize the way in which Socrates challenges the basis and content of traditional morality. And we see that the specific questions Socrates raises about the content and basis of the traditional morality that declares gain seeking to be base, if not bad, and the law to be just, also lead him to question the grounds on which the self-seeking, lawless rule

---

40. As Strauss explains: "Since no one else appears to be present at the conversation, the work could not carry as its title, as most Platonic dialogues do, the name of a participant in a Socratic conversation or of a listener to it" ("Minos," 65).

of tyrants had been castigated.[41] In the *Hipparchus* Socrates claims that the Athenian tyrant was in fact a wise and good man who tried to educate his subjects, although Socrates then points out that Hipparchus wanted to educate his subjects so that they would admire his wisdom more than that of the god at Delphi. And in the *Minos* Socrates suggests the Athenian belief, propagated by the tragedians, that the founding legislator of Crete was a tyrant may not be true.[42] No reader exposed solely to these two dialogues would be surprised to learn that Socrates had aroused the ire of some of his fellow citizens and that he was accused and convicted of illegally corrupting the young. In other words, even if these dialogues are not authentic, they present a popular view of Socrates that is consistent with Plato's other works.

In the *Lovers* Socrates tells an anonymous audience that he went to the school of Dionysius, where he saw two young boys disputing.[43] Because Plato had a teacher named Dionysius (Diogenes Laertius 3.5), one translator has wondered whether Plato did not represent himself as one of the handsome youths from families of good repute, who quit their own debate to listen to Socrates' interrogations of others.[44] Because Socrates asks what it is to philosophize, the dialogue seems to raise the central question of the entire Platonic corpus. Its authenticity has been questioned, however, even in ancient times.

Unable to hear what the boys were saying, but inferring from their gestures that they must be talking about the theories of Anaxagoras or

41. Christopher Bruell, *On the Socratic Education* (Lanham, MD: Rowman and Littlefield, 1999), observes that, according to Socrates in the *Republic* (344a), "a tyrant is believed to be one who defers neither to law nor to any other consideration in his grasping for more" (3).

42. Socrates cites the authority of Homer, a poet whose authority was more widely respected in ancient Greece generally, in opposition to the tragedians. The fact that the story about Zeus educating his son Minos in the cave comes from a tale Odysseus fabricates to test, if not simply to deceive, his wife should make us wonder how seriously Socrates himself takes the story about the divine origins of the laws of Crete. Some think Zeus and Minos had something more like a "drinking party" than an intellectual "symposium" in the cave, Socrates admits, but he suggests that if that were the case, Minos would not have forbidden drinking by law among the Cretans. No wise ruler would treat the ruled in a way so obviously different from himself. The question the dialogue leaves open, however, is whether Minos was a wise legislator.

43. See Michael Davis, "Philosophy and the Perfect Tense: On the Beginning of Plato's *Lovers*," *Graduate Faculty Philosophy Journal* 10, no. 2 (1980): 75–97, for a close reading of the beginning of the dialogue.

44. James Leake, trans., "*Lovers*," in Pangle, *Roots*, 80n1. In the quotations from the dialogue that follow, I have departed somewhat from Leake's translation on the basis of my own reading of the Greek. For the Greek I have referred, unless otherwise noted, to *Platonis Opera*, vol. 1 (Oxford: Oxford University Press, 1995) and vols. 2–5 (Oxford: Clarendon Press, 1901–7).

Oinopides, Socrates opens the conversation by asking another observer what the boys are talking about, "no doubt something great and noble" (*Lovers* 132b). On the contrary, the observer responds, "they are philosophizing, babbling about the heavenly bodies, and other such nonsense" (132b). When Socrates asks in surprise whether it is shameful to philosophize, we are reminded of the difference between Socrates and his cosmological predecessors. Socrates investigates human opinions, especially about what is noble and good; he does not contemplate or record the movements of the heavenly bodies, although he is familiar with the arguments of those who do.

A second observer breaks in and urges Socrates not to question the first about the nobility of philosophy. Having "passed his whole life putting others in a headlock, stuffing himself, and sleeping" (132c), the first observer knows nothing about philosophy. The second reveals himself to be a rival of the first when, denigrating the gymnast as the gymnast had denigrated philosophy, he declares that he would not regard himself as a human being if he considered it shameful to philosophize.

Socrates observes that the two rivals represent the two traditional poles or components of ancient Greek education, gymnastics and music. And, as represented by these two lovers, he shows that neither of these poles, in itself or in conjunction with the other, constitutes an adequate understanding of either love or education. As in the *Lysis*, so in the *Lovers*, Socrates demonstrates both in the action and the argument of the dialogue that an older man can persuade handsome youths to associate with him more effectively by promising to teach them something of use to them than by trying to make himself attractive through gymnastic exercise or learning a great many things with which to ornament his own speeches and make himself look wise.

By questioning the observer who believes that it is noble to philosophize, Socrates quickly shows that this young man understands philosophy to consist of the acquisition of much learning that gives a man a reputation for wisdom. This youth is a lover of honor who wants to be admired for his learning more than a seeker of wisdom per se. Socrates exposes the vapidity of this understanding of "general" or "liberal" education by observing that it is impossible for any human being to learn everything, certainly not to learn everything well. He reasons as follows: since we cannot learn everything, we should learn what is noblest and best. The best, which is to say, the most useful kind of knowledge human beings can acquire, is how to make ourselves better. From observing what goes on in cities, we see that making people better involves knowing how to correct or punish them. That art or science of punishment is called justice. We recognize, moreover, that in order to know how to make human beings better, we need to know what a human being is. Such knowledge, in the case of a single human being, is called self-knowledge; following the adages of the god at Delphi (in contrast to the inscriptions of the tyrant Hipparchus), we identify such self-knowledge with moderation. Justice and moderation are thus fundamentally the same. This knowledge constitutes what we call the political art, and this art belongs to anyone who rules others justly and moderately, whether we call him a king, a tyrant, a statesman, a household manager, or a slave master.

As does the *Hipparchus* and the *Minos*, so the *Lovers* culminates in an erasure of the distinction between tyrannical and other forms of rule. It is not the law, the limits placed on the power of the ruler, or the participation or the consent of the governed that determines whether rule is good or not. The only factor that determines whether rule is good or bad, noble or base, just or unjust, is the knowledge of the ruler. Socrates does not claim to possess this knowledge. Nor does he seek or claim to rule. All he claims to know is that knowledge of the noble and good is the most important kind of knowledge for human beings to acquire, and we should therefore seek above all to acquire it.

The only dialogue in which Plato shows Socrates expressly inquiring about a definition of the human good is the *Philebus*, the fourth dialogue that lacks a specific date. Here there is no explicit reference to politics. In fact, Socrates suggests both in his arguments and in his action that the human good is to be found in the private intellectual life of an individual, either thinking by himself or in conversation with others. Although the dialogue is not set at any particular place or time in Athens, and Plato seems to have named Socrates' two interlocutors on the basis of their function in the conversation, no one has questioned the authenticity of the *Philebus*— probably because the subject discussed is so central to Socratic philosophy, if not to the Platonic corpus as a whole.[45] It is treated more fully in the analysis of Plato's presentation of Socrates that follows.

45. On the basis of Aristotle's statements and Plato's own report of a lecture he gave concerning "the good," members of the so-called Tübingen school have argued that the dialogues are merely protreptic and that Plato presented an "esoteric" or secret teaching to members of his Academy. See, e.g., Thomas A. Szlezak, *Reading Plato*, trans. Graham Zanker (New York: Routledge, 1999), 116–19; Hans Joachim Krämer, *Plato and the Foundations of Metaphysics*, trans. John R. Catan (Albany: SUNY Press, 1990), 93–114. Kenneth Sayre, *Plato's Late Ontology: A Riddle Resolved* (Princeton: Princeton University Press, 1983), 168–74, has pointed out that there is, in fact, more

IV. Plato's Other Philosophers

Socrates is obviously the most important character in the Platonic dialogues, but he is not the only character, or even the only philosopher. Indeed, many commentators have claimed to find stages in the development of Plato's thought represented first by a historical Socrates, then a spokesman named Socrates who puts forth Plato's own "theory of the ideas" (as announced by Aristotle),[46] and finally a series of other spokesmen who articulate Plato's later thought. Such a reading, however, flies in the face of some of the dramatic details Plato himself put into the dialogues. By having Socrates not only be present but also engage in introductory exchanges with the other philosophers before they take charge of the conversation, Plato seems to go out of his way to show that his philosophers do not represent interchangeable names for the figure serving as his "spokesman." Two of the five dialogues in which other philosophers take charge of the argument are shown to have occurred, moreover, at the very beginning, if not before the inception, of Socrates' public career. In terms of the dramatic dating, these dialogues are not "late."

Even when presented merely as anonymous "strangers," Plato's philosophers represent distinct individuals who exemplify and articulate different understandings of philosophy—the manner in which philosophical

---

continuity than some of the esotericists are willing to admit between the dialogues, especially the arguments Socrates presents concerning the character of the human good in the *Philebus* and the "puzzling" characteristics of the lecture Plato gave on the good. Szlezak admits some overlap but argues that the critique of writing in the *Phaedrus* as well as some gaps in the arguments in dialogues like the *Republic* point toward the oral teaching. In chapter 5 I argue that Szlezak, among others, has drawn too sharp a distinction between oral and written discourse in reading Socrates' critique of the latter in the *Phaedrus*. Like Tigerstedt (*Interpreting Plato*, 63–82), I find it difficult to accept an account of Plato's teaching based not on his own writings, at least primarily, but on statements by Aristotle and secondhand reports. For a brief summary of critiques of the Tübingen school, see Rutherford, *Art*, 37–38.

46. Although Aristotle attributes a theory of the ideas to Plato, in the dialogues Plato has three different philosophers present three different arguments about the ideas (which are in themselves, to be sure, in all cases purely intelligible and unchanging). As in the *Parmenides*, *Republic*, and *Phaedo*, Socrates talks about ideas of the good, the noble, the virtues, and quantitative relations. According to Timaeus, the demiurge or god constructs the cosmos by copying the eternal ideas, including the ideas of the same and the other that he forces together in constructing the soul of the cosmos. Although the god and the cosmos he fabricates are said to be good, he does not refer to an idea of the good. Like Timaeus (and unlike Socrates) the Eleatic Stranger includes the same and the other among the five greatest ideas (which include being, rest, and motion but not the good or the noble). In the myth the Eleatic tells about the effects of the changes in the direction of the movement of the cosmos, the god does not construct a soul of the cosmos or the particular kinds of beings present in it as imitations of the ideas.

investigations can and should be conducted as well as the results that can be gained through such inquiries.[47] Plato uses the contrast between Socrates and the other philosophers to dramatize both the advantages and the limitations of Socratic philosophy. The irreconcilable differences between and among these philosophers point to the irresolvable problems that led Plato to conclude that the most human beings could ever do or achieve would be to seek wisdom, like Socrates. They would never be able simply to possess wisdom or to become wise. The following introductory sketch is merely that; I present the arguments for these suggestions much more fully in the chapters that follow.

A. The Athenian Stranger

Because Socrates is not said to be present when the Athenian Stranger proposes a set of laws to his old Dorian interlocutors in the *Laws*, many commentators have taken the Athenian to represent Plato himself. If we pay attention to the indications Plato gives about when the conversation took place, however, we see that it occurred before Socrates became an active participant in Athenian public life. It is not likely, moreover, that Plato himself would have ignored the Peloponnesian War entirely in putting forward his own understanding of Greek political history. Convinced that the *Laws* is Plato's last work—whether by the rumor that it was left in wax and copied, if not composed, by Philip of Opus; by Aristotle's statement that the *Laws* was written after the *Republic*; or simply by the observation that all the interlocutors are elderly—most commentators have not noticed that all the poetry, history, and philosophy to which the Athenian refers are pre-Socratic. The anonymous "stranger" in the *Laws* is emphatically Athenian; as Glenn Morrow has shown, many of the institutions and laws he recommends have precedents in pre-Periclean Athens. Unlike Socrates, who stayed in Athens except for his military service, but like all the other philosophers Plato depicts, the Athenian "stranger" has traveled to another city, perhaps to learn, but demonstrably to share his wisdom—

---

47. George Kimball Plochmann, "Socrates, the Stranger from Elea, and Some Others," *Classical Philology* 49, no. 4 (October 1954): 223–31. Other scholars who have emphasized the differences among Platonic philosophers include Clay, *Platonic Questions*; Gerald Mara, "Constitutions, Virtues, and Philosophy in Plato's *Statesman* and *Republic*," *Polity* 13 (Spring 1981): 355–82; and Michael Kochin, "Plato's Eleatic and Athenian Sciences of Politics," *Review of Politics* 61 (Winter 1999): 1–28.

philosophical and political. The dialogue itself points to a reason for the Athenian to remain anonymous (rather than merely hiding the presumed identity of the criminal Socrates, who is fleeing prosecution). If he succeeds in convincing the old Dorians that the laws he proposes are better than those they now have in Crete, the Athenian will have replaced Zeus as the purported source of the laws. The anonymous Athenian stranger represents the "intelligence" or "mind," which he argues is the only true source of law and is itself divine. This mind may in principle belong to all human beings, but, the stranger shows, people develop the requisite kind of intelligence only in communities like Athens, where they can learn and compare the different ways human beings have ordered their communities. At the very end of the *Laws* the Athenian provides for such learning in the city he proposes in the Nocturnal Council. The Athenian's account of the need for such a council and the questions its members will discuss convince his Dorian interlocutors that they will not be able to establish the city he has recommended if they do not compel the Athenian to stay and help them. The Athenian has promised Clinias the "credit" or glory for founding the new colony, however; he himself will remain the invisible brains behind the operation.

Socrates would not have been able to persuade the old Dorians to accept his recommendations, because, we know from the *Apology*, Socrates would not have accepted the constraint initially put on the discussion by the Dorian "law of all laws," which commands everyone to praise the law and forbids anyone to question its justice unless they are old and there are no young people present. Nor would Socrates have been allowed to practice philosophy in his accustomed manner in the city the stranger proposes, as we see in the laws the Athenian proposes concerning piety and the punishments for impiety, as well as in the prohibition of "busybodies" who voice their thoughts about the laws, education, or upbringing outside the council.

Some readers have suggested that the differences between the Athenian Stranger and Socrates can be explained by the differences in their interlocutors and circumstances. These differences are integrally related, however, to differences in the content and form of the two philosophers' arguments. The Athenian never directly and explicitly confronts his interlocutors with the contradictions inherent in their opinions and so never "corrects" them the way Socrates does Polus and Callicles in the *Gorgias*. On the contrary, the Athenian characterizes the first third of their conversation as one of the "preludes" he himself has been the first to suggest are necessary to persuade people to obey the laws. The Athenian never raises the "what is . . . ?"

(law, in this case) question that is typical of Socrates. The Athenian does not, because he does not see or describe a world organized into a variety of unchanging kinds of beings or ideas. He points rather to "the god, just as the ancient saying has it, holding the beginning and the end and the middle of all the beings, [who] completes his straight course by revolving, according to nature. Following him always is Justice, avenger of those who forsake the divine law" (*Laws* 716a). To support the necessary beliefs in the existence of gods, and in the propositions that these gods care about human beings and that they cannot be bribed, he emphasizes the priority of motion or "soul" to body and the intelligibility of the orbits of the heavenly bodies. The gods that are in or behind these motions can look down and survey human affairs, but they cannot be reached or affected by human pleas or gifts. They have agreed, he concludes, "that heaven is full of many good things, and also of the opposite, and that [because] there are more of the latter, there is an immortal battle going on" (906a). Understanding the cosmos in terms of such unending strife is characteristic of Socrates' predecessors, but not of Socrates himself. At the very end of the dialogue, the Athenian suggests that the "guardians of the laws" must seek knowledge of the unity of the virtues as well as of the noble and good. Without knowledge of the goal, these "guardians" will not be able to direct or preserve the city and its laws. The Athenian does not explain, however, whether or how such knowledge is compatible with the cosmology he also insists the guardians must learn, if they and their citizens are to remain pious.

In sum, in the *Laws* Plato shows that the Athenian Stranger is able to have a much greater and more direct effect on politics than Socrates, without encountering the same danger of prosecution and death, precisely because the Athenian does not act or think like Socrates in some decisive respects. On the other hand, Plato also indicates, the Athenian will not succeed in establishing and maintaining the laws he recommends without introducing something like Socratic philosophy into his city. Because it seems impossible to incorporate that kind of philosophy and to preserve the kind of piety the Athenian argues is necessary in the citizen body, it appears at the end of the dialogue that he has not been able to solve the political problem or the philosophical quandaries associated with it.

B. Parmenides

Several commentators have seen that the arguments the elderly Eleatic philosopher of that name presents in Plato's *Parmenides* bear a family resemblance to, but are not identical with, those found in the historical philosopher's poem. A few have observed that the argument about the ideas young Socrates uses to critique Zeno's defense of Parmenides (by showing the paradoxes that result from a denial of the unity and homogeneity of being) constitutes a kind of modified Eleaticism. Like Parmenides, Socrates argues that what truly is, is always and unchanging, and that only what truly is, because it does not change, can be known. For that reason, perhaps, Parmenides concludes his critique of Socrates by conceding that something like Socrates' argument about the ideas is necessary if philosophy is to be possible. If there is nothing purely intelligible, hence unchanging and eternal, there is nothing we can seek to know. Everything we declare to be true will change.

Unlike Parmenides, Socrates maintains that there are essentially and hence always different kinds of being. He "solves" some of Zeno's paradoxes this way, but he does not and cannot resolve all the problems associated with an assertion of purely intelligible forms of being. As Plato's Parmenides points out in his famous critique of Socrates' argument concerning the ideas, Socrates cannot say exactly what there are ideas of. (The lists of "things in themselves" of which we can have knowledge that Socrates gives as examples change from dialogue to dialogue. Sometimes, as in the *Phaedo*, the list includes equality; at other times, as in the *Phaedrus*, it includes knowledge; only in the *Republic* is the Idea of the Good said to be the source of all other ideas or kinds of being and thus "beyond" them.)[48] Nor, Plato's Parmenides famously points out, can Socrates explain how sensible things participate in purely intelligible ideas. As some astute critics have observed, Plato's Parmenides spatializes being in a way that neither his nor Socrates' argument would, strictly speaking, allow.[49] Nevertheless, as Plato shows in the *Phaedo*, on the very last day of his life Socrates admits that he still cannot explain exactly how sensible things participate in the purely intelligible ideas. He insists only that we have to refer to such ideas to determine what things are. It is not clear, moreover, that Socrates is ever able to explain how sensible human beings can acquire knowledge of the purely intelligible.

48. Stanley Rosen, *The Question of Being* (New Haven: Yale University Press, 1993), points out: "Although these Ideas are 'frequently mentioned' in the dialogues, there is no uniform account of their nature" (47).

49. R. E. Allen, *Plato's "Parmenides"* (New Haven: Yale University Press, 1997), 131–45; Mitchell H. Miller, Jr., *Plato's "Parmenides": The Conversion of the Soul* (Princeton: Princeton University Press, 1986), 50–51.

Because Parmenides presents his demonstration purportedly to show Socrates how he can improve as a philosopher, most commentators have sought to show how the arguments Parmenides gives first to prove that one is and then to show the consequences of the proposition that one is not represent an improvement of "Plato's" argument about the ideas.[50] Few commentators have observed the parallel between the organization of Parmenides' demonstration and the historical philosopher's poem. If one takes seriously the parallel and the references implicit in both the name and the similarity in the arguments presented, however, one sees that the demonstration constitutes a critique of the historical Parmenides' argument. His argument, as presented in the poem as well as in the dialogue, cannot generate a conclusion about the intelligible character or organization of being, because that intelligibility is not and cannot be revealed on the basis simply of the opposition between "is" and "is not." As G. W. F. Hegel later saw, and both Socrates and the Eleatic Stranger maintain, being is intelligible if and only if it is essentially differentiated. The question then becomes how and into what kinds. As Plato humorously shows in the *Euthydemus*, sorting things according to whether they are or are not but without any consideration of what they are or are not leads to a series of ridiculous *aporiai*. Because Parmenides' demonstration leads to just such an *aporia*, some commentators have concluded that the dialogue is a joke.

In the dialogues that follow the *Parmenides* in terms of the dramatic date, we see that Socrates' differentiated understanding (or hypothesis about the character) of being leads him to argue in a different way from Parmenides, Zeno, and their sophistical followers. Instead of asking whether something is or is not, Socrates asks what it is. For Socrates the character of his interlocutor is important, moreover, in a way it is not for the Eleatics. In selecting an interlocutor, Parmenides explicitly seeks someone tractable. Aristotle raises few objections and so performs his role to the satisfaction of the elderly Eleatic. Since Aristotle later became one of the Thirty, Plato's readers might be led to contrast Parmenides' utter lack of concern about the character and opinions of his interlocutor or the effect his interrogation might have on either with Socrates' attempt to convince Charmides and Critias to become more moderate. In the narrative introduction to the *Parmenides*, Plato shows his readers that Parmenides'

---

50. Nails, *Agora*, 98. Cf. Mary Louis Gill, introduction to *Plato: "Parmenides"* (Indianapolis: Hackett, 1996), 1–12; Miller, *Plato's "Parmenides,"* 43–189; Kenneth M. Sayre, *Parmenides' Lesson* (Notre Dame, IN: University of Notre Dame Press, 1996), 57–299; Weingartner, *Unity*, 141–201.

austere form of argumentation did not have the attraction that Socrates' refutations of others had for young listeners. Both in the *Parmenides* and other dialogues, Plato shows that young men like his brothers Glaucon and Adimantus and his half brother Antiphon, who initially were attracted by the "antilogistical" refutations of the claims of others, gradually became convinced that no one knew anything and so dropped philosophy as a useless endeavor. Precisely because he concentrated on seeking knowledge particularly of the noble and good, instead of arguing simply about what is and is not, Socrates continued to attract young aristocratic associates in a way the Eleatic and his followers did not.

C. Timaeus

Timaeus is a singular character in the Platonic dialogues who gives a singular speech. Unlike Parmenides and Socrates, there is no evidence outside the dialogues that Timaeus ever existed. Yet, unlike the Athenian and Eleatic "strangers," Timaeus is given a name. No other philosopher in the dialogues gives such a long, uninterrupted speech without any interlocutor. No one presents such a detailed account of the intelligible organization of the cosmos or suggests that the four elements have geometrical shapes that explain their distinctive properties and interpenetration in the shifting contents of *chōra*. No other Platonic philosopher explains how the human body is constructed or how our senses work.

At first glance, Timaeus' account of the construction of the cosmos appears to be truly comprehensive, incorporating the insights of virtually all previous philosophers. Like Parmenides (and Socrates), Timaeus begins by distinguishing the being(s) that are always and purely intelligible from those that come to be and are only imitations of the former. Because the cosmos is visible, Timaeus reasons, it cannot be eternal. But because the cosmos is beautiful, he infers that it must have an intelligible order and a good origin or maker. Like Socrates in the *Symposium*, Timaeus thus traces the beautiful to the good and suggests that the origin—at least of all sensible beings—is good. Adapting Parmenides' argument about being, Timaeus emphasizes the unity and completeness of the cosmos; he too gives it a spherical shape. In the construction of the cosmic soul, which not only holds it together but also makes the motions of the heavenly bodies intelligible, Timaeus brings together being, sameness, and difference, three of the greatest *eidē*, according to the Eleatic Stranger. Like the

Athenian Stranger, Timaeus insists not only that the movements of the heavenly bodies are intelligible but also that the discovery and observation of the orbits of the heavenly bodies have beneficent effects on human beings. And in showing that lower forms of bodily existence also have an intelligible structure and organization, Timaeus incorporates not only Pythagorean geometry but also Empedoclean medicine.

Timaeus does not present his lengthy speech merely to display his erudition, however. He gives it as part of the just compensation that he, his host Critias, and Critias' other guest, Hermocrates of Syracuse, offer to pay Socrates in exchange for the presentation of the "city in speech" described in the *Republic* that he had given them the day before. Charged specifically with showing how the people who would populate Socrates' city come into being, so that Critias can then describe that city at war in the guise of ancient Athens, Timaeus gives a speech that is supposed to provide the cosmological basis for the political analysis Socrates gives in the *Republic* and so, in effect, to complete Socratic philosophy.

Including "ideas" of the four elements or places where they are typically found, however, Timaeus' understanding of the intelligible organizing principles of the cosmos proves upon examination to differ from the understandings of the "ideas" put forward by Socrates and the Eleatic. His description of the basis and character of the intelligible movements of the heavens also differs from that given by the Athenian Stranger. But the most significant differences and defects in Timaeus' account arise in his description of the constitution of human beings.

Human beings are able to understand the intelligible movements of the cosmos, Timaeus suggests, because the divine part of our souls is made of the same "stuff" as the soul of the cosmos. But even though the divine part is encased in the head and separated as much as possible from the rest of the body, the intelligible order in human beings is completely disrupted when the divine part of the soul is joined to a mortal soul and body. Philosophy is the happiest and best way of life for human beings, Timaeus argues, because contemplation of the intelligible order of the movements of the heavenly bodies enables human beings to recapture and reconstitute a similar kind of order in their souls. Only those who have become orderly themselves can introduce or impose order on the lives of others, moreover. Timaeus' account of the construction of the cosmos—and the living beings within it—thus points to the need for a philosopher-statesman of the kind he himself is said to be. The kind of philosophy Timaeus both practices and advocates does not involve the questioning of opinion in which Socrates engages, or even the copying of the ideas of the virtues onto the souls of citizens that Socrates attributes to philosopher-kings in the *Republic*. Timaeus does not mention any such ideas; the "things" he calls "ideas" are the intelligible divisions that enable us to distinguish different kinds of beings. His ideas are closer to those of the Eleatic Stranger, although Timaeus says that the demiurge has to force being, sameness, and difference together in constituting the soul of the cosmos, whereas the Eleatic argues that these great ideas coexist.

The three parts of the human soul Timaeus describes resemble the three parts of the soul Socrates analyzes in the *Republic*. Timaeus does not say anything about the need to enlist *thymos* in controlling the desires, however. Indeed, Timaeus says little about *thymos* or the virtue of courage most clearly associated with it—even though he is supposed to be describing people who become warriors. Timaeus' failure to describe the coming into being of people who could become citizens of Socrates' city is most manifest, however, when he explains that there were not any women at first and hence no need for sexual organs. The first men were constituted by the gods. Generation is not natural, according to Timaeus, although degeneration seems to be. Only after the souls of cowardly men are reincarnated as women do humans have to be equipped for sexual procreation. If there are no courageous women by nature, however, Socrates' city cannot have both female and male guardians.

Timaeus' "likely" story about the divine construction (or making) of the cosmos shows what has to be the case for human beings to acquire even the limited knowledge of the world we now possess. He does not and cannot give a plausible explanation of how the world or anything else was, is, or will be generated. In order to be good, Timaeus argues, the cosmos has to be complete; to be complete, it has to contain all other possible forms of incomplete life. Precisely because they are incomplete, these defective and needy beings have desires; they do not contain the means of supporting their own continued existence or motion within themselves. Unlike Socrates, Timaeus never characterizes sexual generation as the manifestation of an implicit or instinctive desire for immortality.

Nor does he talk about the higher forms of that desire, which lead poets and legislators to create new forms of human life, much less a desire on the part of philosophical educators "to beget in the beautiful." For Timaeus, human eros is merely the sign of our incompleteness; it becomes part of the human soul only after it is joined to a mortal (as opposed to a starry, cosmic) body. Eros heightens the confusion and disorder caused by the bodily desires; it does not direct human effort and striving toward the noble and good. Timaeus does not, therefore, like Socrates, urge his listeners to seek self-knowledge by examining their opinions to see what they truly desire. He urges them rather to look outside themselves to the heavens to find an order they can not only comprehend but also incorporate. Later readers have tended not to notice the differences between Socratic striving and Timaean contemplation, because Plato's student Aristotle sought to combine them. Plato dramatized the differences between the two kinds of philosophy by attributing them to two different individuals.

D. The Eleatic Stranger

The day after he has been indicted for a capital crime, Socrates is introduced to an anonymous visitor from Elea. In the two conversations that follow, the stranger implicitly accuses Socrates, first, of being a sophist and, second, of having brought the accusation on himself.[51] The stranger is too polite to name Socrates, however, and few readers have paid much attention to the implicit charges.[52] They have been more impressed by the critique the Eleatic gives of all previous philosophy, Parmenidean as well as materialist.

---

51. The Eleatic's final definition of the sophist as someone who knows how to make others think that he is all wise, even if he knows that he is not, by refuting his interlocutors in private conversations looks much more like Socrates than it does like Protagoras, Hippias, Prodicus, Euthydemus, and Dionysodorus, all of whom sought students by claiming to teach them how to be virtuous, especially how to become a persuasive public speaker and so acquire influence in public assemblies. Along the way to this final definition the Eleatic argues that sophists cannot be adequately distinguished simply by their seeking young students, charging fees, or knowing how to compose and deliver speeches. Since most people are not able to recognize a truly knowledgeable statesman, the Eleatic observes, they will not trust anyone who seeks to exercise political power unchecked by law. Not able to distinguish someone who steps outside the letter of the law on the basis of knowledge, or who questions the law for the sake of learning how to rule better from someone who merely seeks to escape legal restraints on his own desires, they will accuse the former of seeking tyrannical power and corrupting the young.

52. There are, of course, exceptions. Mitchell H. Miller, Jr., *The Philosopher in Plato's "Statesman"* (The Hague: Martinus Nijhoff Publishers, 1980), 2–3, characterizes the *Sophist* and *Statesman* as Socrates' "philosophical trial." Stanley Rosen, *Plato's "Statesman": The Web of Politics* (New Haven: Yale University Press, 1995), 6–7, and Howland, *Paradox*, vii, 3–8, also see the Eleatic accusing Socrates of political and philosophical failings. Christopher Rowe, "Killing Socrates," *Journal of Hellenic Studies* 121 (2001): 63–76, attempts to forestall such a reading. All these commentators nevertheless conclude that the Eleatic's position is compatible with Socratic philosophy.

Even more explicitly than Socrates, the anonymous stranger is a follower of Parmenides. He is introduced as a member of the Eleatic school,
but he finds it necessary to break with his philosophical "father" in order to
explain how it is possible for something like a sophist to exist. Like Socrates,
the Eleatic suggests that being must be differentiated in order to be intelligible. Also like Socrates, the Eleatic calls the intelligible divisions or kinds
"ideas." Unlike Socrates, however, the Eleatic does not speak of ideas of
the good, the noble, or the just. He refers rather to the five greatest ideas:
being, rest, motion, sameness, and difference. He criticizes "friends of the
forms (or ideas)," such as Socrates, for insisting on a complete disjunction between being and sensible becoming. Because they maintain such a
complete disjunction, the Eleatic points out, "friends of the forms" cannot
explain cognition or *logos*, because both thought and speech or argument
involve motion. Indeed, the Eleatic announces, the purpose of his own
account of the ideas is to explain how *logos* is possible. One of the reasons
he initially breaks with his teacher Parmenides is that it is impossible to
account for the difference between the name and the thing to which it refers, if being is one.[53] By showing that being itself is divided into different
kinds, some of which can coexist, like being and rest or being and motion,
but others of which cannot, like rest and motion, the Eleatic suggests that
being itself is organized in the same way that languages are. Just as some
letters (vowels and consonants) can be combined but others (consonants
only) cannot in making words, so some words (nouns and verbs) can be
combined but others cannot in making sentences. It is necessary to learn
which can and cannot be combined in order to determine which are true,
that is, possible, combinations of words, and which are not, that is, false.

At first glance it might appear that, like Timaeus, the Eleatic represents
both an extension and an improvement of Socratic philosophy. Understanding being to be differentiated, like Socrates, the Eleatic asks what
something (in this case, a sophist, statesman, or philosopher) is. Also like
Socrates, the Eleatic understands philosophy to consist in the dialectical sorting of things, according to the traits they share or do not. Unlike
Socrates, however, the Eleatic states that he sorts things solely according to
their similarities or differences; unlike "the most well-born form of sophist," he does not sort or define things according to whether they are noble

---

53. In the lectures he gave at the University of Marburg in 1924–25, Martin Heidegger, *Plato's
"Sophist,"* trans. Richard Rojcewicz and André Schuwer (Bloomington: Indiana University Press,
1997), emphasizes the importance of Plato's discovery of the significance of this difference.

or not. Although both Socrates and the Eleatic divide things "diairetically" into two as well as by their joints, the Eleatic begins and continues to divide things down the middle, according to whether they are the same or different, departing from this process only when necessary (as in the case of politics), whereas Socrates asks whether and to what extent something shares in one of the eternal ideas, like beauty or nobility, or not. Although both philosophers use the same words in asking what something is, they prove upon examination not to be asking the same question in fact (and so illustrate the difference between word and deed [or fact] as well as the confusion that difference causes). When Socrates asks what something is, he is seeking to find out what it is in itself. When the Eleatic asks what something is, he is trying to determine in what respect or respects it is the same as itself and different from others. Things do not exist and cannot be known "in themselves," according to the Eleatic. They are known only in comparison to others, as same or different.

Important differences between the Eleatic and Socrates also emerge in the discussion of statesmanship. According to Socrates, just rulers need to be philosophers. At the beginning of the *Sophist*, the Eleatic declares that the sophist, statesman, and philosopher are three different types, although he admits that it is difficult to distinguish them. Like Socrates, the Eleatic characterizes those who pretend to be wise, whether about everything or only about ruling, as sophists. Unlike Socrates, however, the Eleatic never suggests that someone who possesses political science or the royal art needs to know philosophy. According to the Eleatic, a statesman knows how to direct and use the arts that have practical effects. More precisely, he needs to know how to mix courage and moderation in his citizens. Unlike those who consider courage and moderation to be virtues, and so like Socrates would encourage people, both individually and in groups, to acquire as much of each as possible, the Eleatic maintains that courage and moderation are opposed traits that need to be balanced, if a city is to survive. A city composed entirely of moderate people who mind their own business will become too gentle to defend itself against aggressors, whereas courageous peoples tend to risk wars with others until they are defeated and destroyed. A statesman knows how to join people with the two opposed natural inclinations with bonds both human (mating) and divine (inculcated opinions). He supervises "lawful educators and nurses" (*Statesman* 308e) in making citizens "better from worse" (293d–e) and distributes tasks and offices justly "as far as possible" (297b) in order to keep the city safe. According to the myth the Eleatic relates in the middle of the dialogue, human beings had to develop the political art (like all other arts) to protect themselves from wild beasts (who might include other human beings) after the gods ceased to care and provide all the necessities for them. Political associations and knowledge are, in other words, primarily defensive. Nature, as the Eleatic depicts it in his myth of the reversed cosmos, is not kind. It was not constructed as an image of the eternal ideas by a good god, as Timaeus suggests, nor does it have its source and ruling principle in the idea of the good, as Socrates says in the *Republic*.

The Eleatic demonstrates more concern about the character of his young interlocutors than does either Parmenides or Timaeus. He indicates that he himself possesses at least some of the knowledge he attributes to the statesman by attempting literally to en-courage the modest, if not moderate Theaetetus and to moderate the "manly" young Socrates. The Eleatic does not try to impart this knowledge to the young Athenians, however, or inspire them to seek it on their own. He is, indeed, generally unconcerned with human desires or motivation. To the extent that he is trying to teach his young interlocutors anything, it is dialectics or philosophy. At one point he says they have not posed the problem of the statesman "for it own sake, but for the sake of becoming more skilled in dialectics" (285d). The demonstration he gives the young mathematicians of the particular way in which he sorts things may be related to, but it is also obviously different from, the demonstration Parmenides gave young Socrates of the kinds of arguments he should practice in order to become more proficient at philosophy.

The differences among the Platonic philosophers in comprehensive view, interlocutors, and approach are summarized in table 1.

This brief sketch of the varied characteristics and doctrines of the Platonic philosophers suggests that, in the Platonic dialogues, the Athenian Stranger and Parmenides present the problems, both political and philosophical, that confronted later thinkers, and that Socrates, Timaeus, and the Eleatic Stranger all represent related but differing attempts to solve these problems. There are common elements. All five of the Platonic philosophers recognize that neither being nor the cosmos is homogeneous; all five draw a distinction between the purely intelligible aspects and the sensible, changing manifestations of the intelligible elements. This distinction is central to what is often called Platonism. There are, nevertheless, important differences among Plato's philosophers with regard to the character and "location" of the intelligible aspects of being. According to the Athenian Stranger, there is an immortal war going on between the orderly and disorderly souls; Parmenides, on the other hand, presents the propositions that one is and that one is not as mutually exclusive. According to Parmenides, there cannot be a battle. The Athenian is centrally concerned about the direction, regulation, and ordering of human life; Plato's Parmenides appears to be almost completely indifferent to human needs, sensations, and desires. Like the Athenian, Socrates, Timaeus, and the Eleatic all explicitly attempt to show human beings how we can best order our lives. The principles and goals of the orders they propose differ significantly, however. Socrates insistently urges his interlocutors to seek what is truly noble and good by examining opinions, their own, first and foremost. Timaeus urges his listeners to observe the order of the heavens so that they can reconstitute such an order within themselves. Because no human being is apt to be able to acquire the knowledge of how to use and coordinate all the kinds of arts needed to weave together moderate and courageous people in order to preserve them by preserving the city, the Eleatic argues, people have to rely on a kind of approximate, practical knowledge, based on trial and error, that gradually becomes embodied in laws. He does not urge people to observe the order in the heavens, because he thinks that order has been, and may well again be, reversed. Nor does he argue that a statesman or his people must seek knowledge, first and foremost, of what is truly noble and good. On the contrary, he observes, in a world in which human beings find themselves naturally unprotected against the ravages of climate and wild beasts, they have to concentrate on organizing themselves politically to defend themselves if they are to survive. Goodness and justice, though desirable, must be subordinated to the requirements of safety.

All three of Plato's "second-generation" philosophers' recommendations concerning the way human beings should organize and conduct themselves in order to live the best possible lives are supported by three different views of the partially intelligible organization of the world in which we find ourselves. Because Timaeus and the Eleatic (as well as the Athenian) Stranger include motion in the intelligible aspects of being, they are able to present better, certainly fuller, cosmological explanations of the context and grounds of their recommendations for the best form of human life than is Socrates. This is one of the reasons many later commentators have identified Plato more with the views articulated by these non-Socratic philosophers; they seem to give better, more comprehensive views of the whole. But if Plato thought the views presented by Timaeus or the Eleatic were truer than the arguments presented by Socrates, why did Plato

Table 1. Differences among Platonic Philosophers

| | PHILOSOPHERS | | |
	Athenian Stranger	*Parmenides*	*Socrates*
Comprehensive view	Motion (soul) prior to body; good soul/gods eternally battle disorderly/bad soul/gods.	One is (or is not).	Separate ideas are always and intelligible. Sensible things participate in the eternal ideas. The idea of good is also the knowledge humans want most.
Argumentative and investigative procedure	Persuasive preludes; nonconfrontational	Investigates the logical consequences of the proposition that One is; then, that One is not.	Confrontational refutations or "corrections"
	Does not ask What is *x*?		Asks What is *x*? (which follows from a doctrine of separate ideas); investigates opinions (a mix of intelligible and sensible).
	Seeks ways of enlisting human emotions in educating and controlling them.	Little concern about human motives or emotions	Erotic
	Mixes *logos / mythos*	Quotes only one line of poetry.	Relates myths and gives arguments.
	Proposes legislation, a "city in speech," to elderly Dorians able to establish it.	No politics or legislation.	Claims to practice the "true political art" but does not legislate; proposes a "city in speech" to Plato's brothers to show them how to live as individuals.
	Travels.	Travels.	Does not leave Athens except for military duty.
Interlocutors	Elderly Dorian legislators	Socrates; tractable youths. Aristotle becomes one of the Thirty.	Young politically ambitious; foreign teachers. Crito is an exception, but he is concerned about the education of his sons.
	Does not criticize laws in front of the young.	No concern about the effects of his arguments on his interlocutors.	Interested most in his fellow Athenians.
Problems	The incompatibility of the Socratic ideas needed to define the goal of the polity (virtue) with the doctrine of the intelligible motions of the cosmos and strife between good and bad souls needed to support piety. The secrecy and mixed composition of the Nocturnal Council—in sum, the conflicting requirements of politics and philosophy.	Cannot explain how "intelligible" and "sensible" are related or how human beings can acquire knowledge of the purely intelligible. In other words, he lacks self-knowledge.	His doctrine of the "imitation" or "participation" of sensible beings in purely intelligible beings does not explain motion or the relations human beings have to the world around them. Antagonizes fathers. Uncertainty of knowledge gained.

Timaeus	Eleatic Stranger
Cosmos is constructed by a good god, looking to eternal ideas. World soul is a forced mix of sameness, difference, and being. Its body is composed of four geometrically defined elements in space/time (*chōra*).	"Greatest" *eidē* of being, motion, rest, same, difference; some coexist, some are mutually exclusive. Things/ideas are known only in relation to each other, not in themselves. The motion of the cosmos changes direction.
Gives an extended speech, combining *mythos* and *logos*.	Prefers *diairesis*, dividing down the middle into same and other, but defines arts by separating off different kinds, if necessary, as in politics.
Asks What must be the case for humans to be able to understand the organization of the cosmos? He bases his account on observation and mathematics, not an examination of opinions.	
Nonerotic	Nonerotic
Is a poet, according to Socrates.	Does not mention poetry.
Is a statesman.	Defines the statesman but does not engage in politics, at home or abroad.
Travels.	Travels.
None. Audience of other antidemocratic politicians	Young mathematicians and gymnasts, not politically ambitious
Can't give a plausible account of generation or eros. Does not show how a just city could come into being, as promised.	No account of human motivations, even to seek knowledge. No account of the attraction of the *kalon*, of poetry, or of sex.

continue to make Socrates the most prominent philosopher? Plato is known to have reworked the dialogues until his death. He could have changed the name, if not the entire character of his leading philosophical speaker, if he wanted. The prominence of Socrates in the dialogues, which I stressed earlier in this introduction, suggests that Plato thought that Socrates' position or practice was most important. The question to which the remainder of this study is dedicated to answering is, why.

Although Socrates did not and apparently was not able to give a plausible account of the intelligible organization of the sensible world, to say nothing of a coherent account of the intelligibility of the whole, Plato seems to have thought that Socrates represented the necessary and hence best place from which human beings should begin their inquiries. He emphatically and explicitly began with the question that is, in Aristotelian terms, first for us, although not necessarily first per se—namely, how should we live? In presenting Socrates as his leading but by no means only philosophical "spokesman," in contrast to other philosophers who give better accounts of the world or the intelligibility of the whole but not of distinctively human concerns, Plato shows that he understood full well the problem that has bedeviled human thought since the nineteenth century: The mathematical, sometimes materialistic concepts that enable us to understand and manipulate the nonhuman world do not explain human actions—unconscious or conscious and intentional—very well. But Aristotle's extension to the cosmos, even simply to biological organisms, of the purposive, teleological accounts that fit human affairs better than the more reductive, quantitative alternatives has not withstood the onslaught of modern physics. Plato does not present the problem merely as a matter of different forms of knowledge or ways of understanding things, however. Unlike modern philosophers, he does not contrast the humanities and their fundamentally hermeneutical approaches or interpretations of things with the quantitative or process studies characteristic of the natural and social sciences. Plato suggests that there is no one, fully comprehensive way of understanding the whole, because the whole is made up of essentially different kinds of beings. The real problem is identifying what these essentially different kinds of being are and how they are interrelated. Because of the inherent limitations of our mortal minds, human beings may never be able to comprehend the whole. In the meantime, we still have to live as well as we can. To do so, we need to know our peculiar situation and powers, limited as they are. That means we need to seek self-knowledge, first and foremost. By making Socrates the most prominent philosopher in his dialogues, Plato privileges the study of the human things. He and his work thus challenge the modern tendency to privilege science, particularly modern natural science, by making it paradigmatic of science or knowledge per se. By emphasizing the limits of human reason, Plato also preserves an awareness of the superhuman or divine, even while criticizing some of the more irrational beliefs human beings have about it. By studying the depiction of the world and the peculiar place human beings have in it in Plato's dialogues, we can therefore acquire a better understanding of our own situation and problems as well.

V. The Organization of This Book

The account of the dialogues in subsequent chapters follows the order indicated by the dramatic dates. Attempting to preserve the integrity of each conversation depicted, I have sought not only to show how the dialogues read in this order constitute a coherent narrative but also how reading them in this order affects the way we read and understand each of the individual dialogues. Although I have studied and presented the dialogues individually, none of the studies presented here can possibly be as thorough or as definitive as a monograph dedicated to a single dialogue. I am presenting a new framework in which to view the corpus as a whole, and that attempt alone has resulted in a very long book. There is much more detailed work to be done.

Read in the order indicated by their dramatic dates, I argue, the dialogues can be divided into three basic groups or parts. Part I of this study concerns the problems posed by previous philosophy and Socrates' initial response. In three of his autobiographical statements we learn how Socrates formulated his response to the problems posed by the Athenian Stranger in the *Laws* and the elderly Eleatic in the *Parmenides*. But we also see that Socrates failed to attract followers or future philosophers merely by refuting his contemporaries' opinions about the noble and good. In part II, I thus argue, Plato presents two different paradigms of philosophy, represented by Socrates and Timaeus, as potential answers to the political and philosophical problems dramatized in the earlier dialogues. Although Timaeus articulates a more comprehensive account of the whole than Socrates ever does, we see that he is not able to give a plausible account of human life. In the dialogues that follow the *Timaeus* in terms of their dramatic dating, Plato suggests that, despite its philosophical and political limitations, Socratic dialogic practice is more effective than Timaean contemplation. In part III, I then argue that in the eight dialogues explicitly leading up to his trial and death, Plato presents a defense of Socrates—philosophical as well as political. In the conclusion I seek to explain why, in light of the criticism represented by the other four philosophers, Plato made Socrates his chief philosophical protagonist.

PART I

The Political and Philosophical Problems

1

Using Pre-Socratic Philosophy to Support Political Reform

THE ATHENIAN STRANGER

The *Laws* and the *Epinomis* are the only Platonic dialogues in which Socrates does not appear. They are usually thought to be the last dialogues Plato wrote.[1] All three of the interlocutors are elderly, and there is an ancient report that *Laws* was left unedited in a wax impression only.[2] In the course of the conversation, both the Athenian and his Dorian associates emphasize the advantages of recording such conversations in writing. Since the most obvious difference between Plato and his teacher Socrates is that Plato wrote and Socrates did not, some critics have concluded that the anonymous Athenian Stranger who seems to replace Socrates as Plato's spokesman in these dialogues is Plato himself.[3] In the

---

1. See, e.g., Eduard Zeller, *Die Philosophie der Griechen in ihrer geschichtlichen Entwicklung*, 5th ed. (Leipzig: O. R. Reisland, 1922), 2:436, 976, 978–82; Ulrich von Wilamowitz-Möllendorff, *Platon* (Berlin: Weidman, 1920), 1:647; Friedländer, *Plato*, 3:387; Harold Cherniss, *The Riddle of the Early Academy* (Berkeley: University of California Press, 1945), 4; Eric Voegelin, *Plato* (Baton Rouge: Louisiana State University Press, 1981), 215–68; Gregory Vlastos, *Socratic Studies* (Cambridge: Cambridge University Press, 1994), 135; Christopher Bobonich, *Plato's Utopia Recast: His Later Ethics and Politics* (Oxford: Clarendon Press, 2002). As noted in the introduction to this book, most stylometric studies of the dialogues assume that the *Laws* was written last and compare other dialogues with it.

2. Diogenes Laertius 3.37 reports that Philip of Opus transcribed the *Laws* from wax tablets. Some later commentators have thus supposed that Plato was working on the dialogue until his death in 347, or even that Philip composed the *Laws* and the *Epinomis* on the basis of Plato's notes. Glenn Morrow, *Plato's Cretan City* (Princeton: Princeton University Press, 1960), 515–18, provides a sober account of the reasons most scholars now take the *Laws* to be genuinely Platonic. For a review of the debates concerning the *Epinomis*, see Edouard Des Places, *Études platoniciennes* (Leiden: E. J. Brill, 1981), 105–19, 172–79.

3. Cicero (*De Legibus* 1.4.15) appears to have been the first classical author to identify the Athenian Stranger with Plato. Hans-Georg Gadamer, "Plato and the Poets," in *Dialogue and Dialectic*, trans. R. Christopher Smith (New Haven: Yale University Press, 1980), concludes that it is "the

guise of an anonymous Athenian, he both responds to and corrects proposals he himself put forth in Socrates' mouth in the *Republic*.[4] Others
have argued that the *Laws* constitutes a kind of thought experiment. What
if Socrates had, contrary to the reports in the other dialogues, left Athens?[5] What if he had had an opportunity to hold such a conversation as an
anonymous Athenian Stranger with practicing statesmen from the reputedly best-governed regimes in ancient Greece?[6] In the *Laws* we see what
Socrates would then have said. These commentators tend to deny that the
understanding of politics to be found in the *Laws* differs fundamentally

Athenian in whom more than anyone Plato has most obviously hidden himself" (71). The Athenian not only makes the written text of their conversation, that is, Plato's dialogue itself, the basic
text for the education of citizens but also calls it the noblest drama. Klosko also thinks the Athenian Stranger is "probably a stand-in for Plato himself" (*Development*, 198). Jacques Derrida emphasizes the importance of writing in distinguishing Plato from Socrates: Derrida, *Otobiographies:
L'enseignement de Nietzsche et la politique du nom proper* (Paris: Galilée, 1984); Derrida, *The Ear of the
Other*, ed. Christie V. McDonald (New York: Schocken Books, 1985), 7; and Derrida, *The Postcard*,
trans. Alan Bass (Chicago: University of Chicago Press, 1987), 20.

4. See, e.g., Trevor J. Saunders, "Plato's Later Political Thought," in *Cambridge Companion
to Plato*, ed. Richard Kraut (Cambridge: Cambridge University Press, 1992), 469; R. F. Stalley, *An
Introduction to Plato's "Laws"* (Oxford: Basil Blackwell, 1983); Morrow, *Cretan City*; Grote, *Plato*,
3:301–2, 350. The first three see the main difference between the *Republic* and the *Laws* to be in the
generality of the former and the specific character of the proposals in the latter. Grote argues
that Plato had become more intolerant; he emphasizes the differences between the openness of
Socratic questioning and the imposed theological beliefs in the *Laws*. Diskin Clay agrees that the
Laws is probably Plato's last work, but he refuses to identify Plato with the Athenian Stranger.
"In the Laws we seem to hear his unfamiliar voice projected through the mask of the Athenian
Stranger. But this voice is distorted by a mask that . . . is the mask of a character and not an indi-
vidual" (*Platonic Questions*, 268).

5. Cf. Leo Strauss, *The Argument and the Action of Plato's "Laws"* (Chicago: University of Chicago Press, 1975), 1–2. If Socrates had been younger, Strauss points out, he might not have been
limited to the escape options he sketches in the *Crito* (53b–d); he could have traveled to a well-
governed regime far away (like Crete) and continued to hold conversation with others as an
anonymous Athenian stranger. However, in the *Menexenus* (where he has Socrates refer to an
event that occurs after Socrates' death) Plato shows that he was not constrained by historical fact
or probability. Strauss thus concludes that there must be a reason other than the setting in Crete
for the absence of Socrates in the *Laws*. Strauss points out in "How Farabi Read Plato's *Laws*," in
What Is Political Philosophy? and Other Studies (Glencoe, IL: Free Press, 1959), 153–54, that Socrates
did not make laws. According to both the *Apology* (31c–32a) and the *Republic* (496c–e), Socrates intentionally never spoke to the Assembly. In the *Laws* the Athenian Stranger proposes a set of laws
to be used, if they see fit, by officials charged with establishing a new colony on Crete.

6. In the *Politics* 1265a10, Aristotle calls Plato's spokesman in the *Laws* "Socrates." Zdravko
Planinc, *Plato's Political Philosophy: Prudence in the "Republic" and the "Laws"* (Columbia: University of Missouri Press, 1991), argues that the "human being [both of these dialogues] describe is
Socrates, who Aristotle says is present in both dialogues" (26). Thomas L. Pangle, in the "Interpretive Essay" he appends to his translation *Plato's "Laws"* (New York: Basic Books, 1980), observes
that "in the *Laws*, Plato presents a nameless old Athenian philosopher who acts and talks in a
manner reminiscent of Socrates. . . . In the *Laws* we learn what Socrates would have said and done
if his quest for self-knowledge, and his friendships, had ever allowed him the leisure to engage in
giving advice to political reformers—and if he had ever found himself in the appropriate circum-
stance" (378–79).

from that to be found in the *Republic*—that is, to deny that Plato changed his understanding of politics late in life. Differences in the specific proposals for political reform in the two dialogues reflect differences in setting and interlocutors.

Both these interpretations of the significance of the absence of Socrates from the *Laws* and the *Epinomis* fall afoul of one fact: not once is the Peloponnesian War or any of the persons and events associated with it mentioned in either dialogue.[7] Is it likely that Plato would have given his own, final political understanding or practical proposals for constitutional reform without even mentioning the war in which his own city had been defeated and subjected to a series of unstable regimes? In his *Seventh Letter* (324b–26b), Plato says that his own understanding of the relation of politics and philosophy was fundamentally affected by the postwar events leading up to Socrates' trial and death. In book 3 of the *Laws* the Athenian Stranger gives an account of the corruption of Athenian politics, but he does not mention the war, the plague, or any of the leaders—for example, Pericles, Cleon, or Alcibiades—from the period following the Persian Wars. Can an anonymous Athenian—whether Socrates or Plato—be imagined trying to convince two experienced Dorian politicians to introduce a series of institutions drawn from prewar Athens after her defeat by Sparta without giving an account or explanation of that defeat?[8] The absence not merely of any mention of the war but of the war itself might well be taken, however, to be a necessary precondition of a peaceful

7. I am indebted to Michael Zuckert for this crucial observation.

8. Arguing that the dramatic date of the *Laws* should be imagined to be 408/407, Slobodan Dusanic, "The Laws and the Foreign Policy of Eubulus' Athens," in *Plato's "Laws" and Its Historical Significance*, ed. Francisco L. Lisi (Sankt Augustin: Academia Verlag, 2001), observes that in 408/407 a Spartan named Megillus came to Athens as the youngest member of a three-man diplomatic mission and that 408/407 was "perhaps the critical moment in the history of the Peloponnesian War" (232). But if a Spartan peace mission toward the end of the Peloponnesian War were the background, if not occasion for the conversation, one would think that the war would at least have been mentioned. Pointing out that the name is unusual, Dusanic argues that Clinias is also associated with Athenian politics at that time because he bears the same name as Alicibiades' father. A connection with Alcibiades would not have furthered a potential alliance at that time, however, because Alcibiades had already become a problem for the Spartans. The connection between Clinias the Cretan and Alcibiades is, as I argue later, more likely to be a connection in character; both are shown to have tyrannical desires. Dusanic's suggestion that all three interlocutors in the *Laws* are official representatives of their respective regimes is belied by the anonymity of the Athenian. It does not seem likely, moreover, that Dorians would ask or accept advice in formulating laws for a new colony from an official representative of Athens, a regime with which they both claim to have family connections but that they initially despise. In general, Dusanic looks for details to support reading the *Laws* as promoting a foreign policy Plato was advocating in fourth-century Athens, and not in terms of the dialogue's own drama or setting.

conversation between an Athenian and two Dorians about the best possible set of laws or regime. The fact that there is no reference to any specific event in Greek political history after Salamis and Plataea (the battles at which the Athenians and Spartans won the Persian War in 479) suggests that the dramatic date of the *Laws* is some time during the following two—or perhaps three—decades, that is, at a period when Athens and Sparta were still allies. At that time Socrates had not yet emerged as a public figure.[9]

The suspicion created by that probable dramatic date that the Athenian Stranger is a pre-Socratic figure grows when we look at some of his central teachings. Like Socrates in the *Republic*, but even more like the Pythagoreans, the Athenian emphasizes the utility of the study of number (*Laws* 747b).[10] Again like Socrates in the *Republic*, but also like the Pythagoreans, the Athenian suggests it would be best if all citizens held all property in common and if males and females were to receive the same education.[11] Unlike Socrates or Pythagoras (or Plato's Timaeus, for that matter), the Athenian does not put forth a teaching concerning the immortality of indi-

9. The earliest point at which we see Socrates in the Platonic dialogues is as a youth of approximately twenty years of age in conversation with Parmenides (in the dialogue, if not in fact) in 450. Cf. Allen, *Plato's "Parmenides,"* 72. Plato shows Socrates beginning to make a reputation for himself as a "clever speaker," if not a philosopher in the *Protagoras*, in a conversation that occurs shortly before the outbreak of the Peloponnesian War.

10. Since Pythagoras left no writings, there is considerable uncertainty about what he taught. Scholars disagree, moreover, about whether Pythagoras or his followers engaged in the mathematical studies associated with his name before the late fifth century. Cf. Walter Burkert, *Weisheit und Wissenschaft: Studien zu Pythagoras, Philolaus, und Platon* (Nuremberg: Hans Tarl, 1962), 202; W. K. C. Guthrie, *A History of Greek Philosophy* (Cambridge: Cambridge University Press, 1962), 1:181; John Burnet, *Early Greek Philosophy* (London: Adam and Charles Black, 1892), 83–109, 301–21; Wilbur Richard Knorr, *The Evolution of the Euclidean Elements* (Dordrecht: D. Reidel, 1975), 21–28. However, many commentators believe that Pythagoras' followers were engaged in the study of mathematics by the 460s. Cf. Charles H. Kahn, *Pythagoras and the Pythagoreans: A Brief History* (Indianapolis: Hackett Publishing, 2001), 5–18. Ancient sources credit Pythagoras and his followers with the discovery of incommensurability: Pappus, *Commentary on Book X of Euclid's "Elements,"* ed. Gustav Junge and William Thomson (Cambridge: Harvard University Press, 1930), 63–64; Proclus, *A Commentary on the First Book of Euclid's "Elements,"* trans. Glenn Morrow (Princeton: Princeton University Press, 1970), 65; and Iamblichus, *Life of Pythagoras,* trans. Thomas Taylor (London: John M. Watkins, 1965), 95, 126–27. Burkert and Knorr suggest that it was probably not discovered until 430. These modern scholars base their claims about what the Pythagoreans did not know primarily on Plato and Aristotle. An earlier dramatic date for the *Laws* would lend credence to the ancient view that the Pythagoreans discovered incommensurability but kept it secret until approximately 450 when they were expelled from Italy.

11. Pythagoras asked his followers to hold their property in common and gave lectures to women as well as to men; he also educated children separately from their parents. Cf. G. S. Kirk, J. E. Raven, and M. Schofield, *The Presocratic Philosophers,* 2nd ed. (Cambridge: Cambridge University Press, 1983), 226–27 (Dicaearchus frag. 33 [Porphyry *Vita Pythagorae* 18]; Timaeus frag. 13a).

vidual souls or reincarnation.[12] When the Athenian suggests that some of the citizens of his "city in speech" should study not only numbers but also commensurable and incommensurable lines, figures, and solids, he adds that he himself has learned about the latter only recently (819d–20b). If so, the Athenian indicates once again that he probably belongs to the generation after Pythagoras (ca. 560–500) and before Socrates (469–399).[13]

When the Athenian offers an argument to prove that the gods exist (something no other Platonic philosophical spokesman even attempts), he seems to be addressing and refuting pre-Socratic philosophers like Archelaus (who was reputedly a student of Anaxagoras and a teacher of Socrates) as well as Anaxagoras himself.[14] Even though the Athenian recognizes three possibilities with regard to motion and change—that everything moves and changes, that some things move and change others, and that some things never change or move—he never explicitly posits the existence of anything eternal and unchanging except motion or the soul and the battle between good and bad. In other words, unlike Anaxagoras, to

12. At the very end of the *Laws* the Athenian does say that "it is a noble saying that the bodies of the corpses are images of the dead, while the being that is really each of us—named 'the immortal soul'—goes off to other gods to give an account, as the ancestral law says. To the good man this is heartening, but to the bad man very frightening" (959b). He does not, however, affirm or argue for the truth of this saying himself.

13. Socrates does not present the incommensurability of the hypotenuse of a square with its one-unit sides as a new discovery in the famous exhibition with the slave boy in the *Meno* (82a–84a).

14. In *Tusculanae disputationes* 5.10 Cicero reports that "Socrates sat under Archelaus, a disciple of Anaxagoras." As in the case of many pre-Socratic philosophers, the events and dates of Anaxagoras' life are somewhat uncertain. Apollodorus says in his *Chronicles* that the philosopher was born in the seventieth Olympiad (500–497) and died in the first year of the eighty-eighth (428/427). Anaxagoras is credited with having brought Pythagorean teachings to Athens in approximately 480. There is much debate about the time at which he was accused of impiety and whether he was actually tried. According to Plutarch, Anaxagoras was the victim of a decree against atheists introduced by Diopeithes around 433. In his *Succession of Philosophers* Sotion says that Anaxagoras was prosecuted by Cleon for impiety because he maintained that the sun was a red-hot mass of metal, and that after Pericles, his pupil, had made a speech in his defense, the philosopher was fined five talents and exiled. According to A. E. Taylor, "On the Date of the Trial of Anaxagoras," *Classical Quarterly* 11 (1917): 81–87, Satyrus was right in placing Anaxagoras' prosecution at the beginning and not at the close of Pericles' political career, that is, around 450. According to Satyrus, the charge against Anaxagoras was brought by Thucydides in his political campaign against Pericles, and the charge was for Medism as well as for impiety. The philosopher was condemned to death in his own absence and finally withdrew to Lampsacus, where he died. By all accounts, the persecution of Anaxagoras for impiety to which the Athenian refers at the very end of the dialogue would have occurred before the outbreak of the Peloponnesian War. Kirk, Raven, and Schofield conclude that "there is a fair amount of evidence which cumulatively supports the conclusion that Anaxagoras' immediate impact as a philosopher was made mostly in Athens before 450" (*Presocratic Philosophers*, 353–54).

say nothing of Socrates and the Eleatic Stranger, the Athenian shows no sign of having been influenced by or of incorporating (if only a part) of Parmenides' famous argument concerning the complete and unchanging but therefore intelligible character of Being in itself and as a whole. He sounds more like Heraclitus when he concludes (*Laws* 906a–b) that human beings are caught in an immortal cosmic battle between good and bad, orderly and disorderly motions.[15] The Athenian does not appear to represent any one particular school or teaching of pre-Socratic philosophy; indeed, his own argument concerning the priority of soul to body constitutes an important modification of previous arguments, that is, an innovation. Nevertheless, his arguments concerning the priority of soul and the importance of the orderly motions of the heavens are based on, and formulated primarily in reaction to, the doctrines of the pre-Socratic cosmologists. When the Athenian suggests at the very end of the dialogue that the members of the Nocturnal Council will need to investigate the unity and diversity of the virtues as well as the ideas of the good and the noble—questions pressed particularly by Socrates—Plato thus leads his readers to ask whether the pre-Socratic philosophy on which the Athenian has relied up to this point is adequate to support his political project.

Not merely are the probable dramatic date of the conversation and hence the philosophical doctrines to which the Athenian refers primarily pre-Socratic; so is the most notable and likely precedent for his political project. Reputedly having fled from the tyranny of Polycrates on Samos in 530, Pythagoras so impressed the governing council of elders in Croton with his wisdom and virtue that they asked him to educate their young men, schoolchildren in the absence of their parents, and even their women.[16] Under his guidance, the morale and discipline of the citizens of Croton improved so greatly that they not merely recovered from their defeat by Locri but became the dominant city in southern Italy.[17] The Athenian appears to want to do something similar in Crete. Like Pythagoras,

15. Cf. Charles H. Kahn, "A New Look at Heraclitus," *American Philosophical Quarterly* 1, no. 3 (July 1964): 198n.: "Book X of the Laws . . . is essentially concerned with the reinterpretation of Nature in terms of Reason—a reinterpretation different in kind, but not in tendency, from that of Heraclitus himself."

16. Plato, *Laws*, Loeb ed., trans. R. G. Bury (Cambridge: Harvard University Press, 1926), 2n313, relying on Diogenes Laertius 2.16 on Archelaus, 967b–c, with regard to Anaxagoras.

17. By way of contrast, Socrates himself never founded a school. In Plato's *Apology of Socrates*, Socrates claims he let anyone who wished listen to him conversing. Plato himself did found the "academy." He established his "school" on his own land, however, and not with political support or control from the Areopagus (the old Athenian council of elders, which had been deprived of most of its power by Pericles).

the Athenian appears to be fleeing incipient tyranny resulting from the destruction of law and order in Athens after the Persian Wars (cf. *Laws* 701b–c) and seeking to establish a more virtuous regime with the support of the elders in a faraway city.[18] At the end of the dialogue (968e–69a) he explicitly recognizes that they will be undertaking a risky enterprise and offers to share the risk by giving them his opinions about education and upbringing. Knowledge of the fate of the Pythagoreans in southern Italy would have made some of the danger or risk clear. In the first half of the fifth century, democratic forces in the Greek cities in southern Italy organized in opposition to the Pythagorean influence on the aristocratic governments. By 450 all but two of the Pythagoreans in Croton had been killed (when their meetinghouse was burned down), and these two fled; the leading Pythagoreans in other southern Italian cities were also expelled. In this context, it is not surprising to see the Athenian reveal the end or purpose (*telos*) of his "city in speech" to the elder Dorians with whom he is conversing only after a long and complex discussion.[19] At the same time he refers obliquely to the persecution of Anaxagoras for impiety in Athens. If these philosophers had drawn the correct conclusions from their observations, he argues, they would not have been prosecuted. Like the Athenian himself, they would have shown instead how philosophy could be used to establish and support a more virtuous political order.

The question raised by both the argument and the action of the *Laws* is whether the Athenian could have succeeded. If the dialogue is supposed to have taken place before the Peloponnesian War, the Athenian cannot be either Socrates (who was too young to take part in a conversation of old men) or Plato (who was yet to be born). What the dialogue presents (whenever it was written) is a hypothetical history, a "could have been." If we are convinced by the end of the conversation that his project was feasible, we must conclude that in the *Laws* Plato shows how a philosopher could have influenced the laws of a city in a way Socrates insisted he could not (*Apology* 31c–32a; *Republic* 496c–e). In that case, it also indicates something about what should be tried in the future. If, however, we find that the Athenian's project could not work, we will have discovered some of the reasons not only why Plato thought there would be no real political

18. Planinc (*Prudence*, 221–33) emphasizes the Pythagorean elements in the Athenian's regime.

19. As Strauss points out (*Argument and Action*, 9), the Athenian says that death is the end of the political regime, in book 1 (*Laws* 632c). The Athenian corrects this statement only in book 12 (960b).

reform until philosophers became kings, but also why that combination might be impossible to achieve.

I. Differences between the Athenian Stranger and Socrates

A brief comparison of the *Minos*, traditionally taken to serve as a preface or introduction to the *Laws*, and the beginning of the *Laws* itself brings out striking differences between Socrates and the Athenian Stranger in the content and manner as well as the circumstances of their respective inquiries.[20] In the first sentence of the *Minos*, Socrates characteristically but bluntly asks: "What is the law for us?" Not only is the "what is . . . ?" question characteristic of Socrates, but so also is the character of his interlocutor. He is an Athenian. In the Platonic dialogues, we are reminded, Socrates never left Athens except to do his military duty.

In the *Minos* Socrates' anonymous Athenian interlocutor initially gives a characteristically Athenian definition of law: it is what the council and assembly (*boulē*) agree is law. Socrates objects to this conventional, but democratic definition by observing that virtually all nations and people agree that laws are supposed to be just. In the same way that doctors need to know what a healthy constitution is, so, Socrates maintains, those properly called lawmakers need to know what is just—indeed, what is good and bad for the soul. In response to his interlocutor's objection that laws differ from place to place and time to time, Socrates states that the law "wishes" or aims (*bouletai*) at what truly is.[21] As in the *Republic* (and many other dialogues), Socrates' definition of law suggests that to be a true legislator one must know what truly is. To become a legislator, a person must, therefore, seek knowledge—above all, of what is just or, more generally, what is good for the human soul. In other words, according to Socrates,

20. Clay observes, "The character of the discussion [in the *Laws*] is very much unlike the discussions of Plato's earlier dialogues and what we think of as the Socratic method" (*Platonic Questions*, 268).

21. Seth Benardete, *Plato's "Laws": The Discovery of Being* (Chicago: University of Chicago Press, 2000), makes this Socratic statement fundamental in his interpretation. The problem is not only that the statement proceeds from Socrates in a different dialogue and not the Athenian Stranger. The problem is also that the distinction between nature (*physis*) and convention (*nomos*) from which Socratic political philosophy is often said to arise does not emerge in the *Minos*, where the word *physis* does not occur even once. If, as Socrates states in the *Minos*, the law aims at what truly is, most laws in most places are failures, that is, they are not truly laws. We see here, as in the *Republic*, the potentially revolutionary character of Socratic philosophizing.

to become a legislator, properly speaking, one must first have been a philosopher.[22]

In the first sentence of the *Laws*, the Athenian Stranger asks Clinias whether a god or a human being was the cause (*aitia*) of the laws of Crete.[23] He never asks "what is law?" Nor does he ever explicitly say that a legislator must first have been a philosopher. He does suggest, both in practice and precept, that a legislator must learn about the laws of other regimes, ideally by traveling around, observing, and interviewing the inhabitants. He himself seems to have come to Crete to investigate the source and character of their laws; in contrast to Socrates, the Athenian has clearly not stayed in Athens to conduct his investigations. At the end of the *Laws* (951a–c) he suggests that elderly emissaries from Magnesia should travel abroad to learn how other regimes are ruled. Both the questions the Athenian Stranger asks and the way he seeks to answer them thus differ from those characteristic of Socrates.[24]

So does the presupposition with which the Athenian begins. Whereas the *Minos* begins with the democratic premise that laws are the results of human agreements, the *Laws* begins with the premise that the old is the good.[25] One reason critics have viewed the *Minos* as an introduction to the *Laws* is that the *Minos* begins with the democratic notion that laws are conventions but ends with the traditional conviction that the old is the good. At the conclusion of the *Minos*, Socrates reminds his interlocutor that the laws of Crete are some of the oldest. Laws that have lasted a long

22. Bruell (*Socratic Education*, 7–15) argues that the *Minos* represents the true beginning of a Socratic education.

23. Because *aitia* was used with reference to court cases, the sentence could be translated: who is responsible for your laws? It could, in other words, be read as an accusation or charge.

24. Malcolm Schofield, *Plato* (New York: Oxford University Press, 2006), observes: "The Athenian Visitor is not an anonymized Socrates, but a successor to wise lawgivers like Solon (at Athens) and Lycurgus (at Sparta). The very designation 'Athenian Visitor' is doubtless meant to bring Solon to mind. Herodotus has Solon greeted on his arrival in Sardis by the Lydian king Croesus with the following words (1.30): 'Athenian visitor, a great deal of talk has reached us about you, on account of your wisdom and your traveling. You have traversed much of the earth in your philosophical efforts to contemplate things.' Just so the *Laws*' Athenian has a wide experience of a range of different social and political institutions (1.639D), unlike his Spartan and Cretan interlocutors. He comes to Crete not just to give of his wisdom, but to learn: this time like Lycurgus, of whom Herodotus reports that he borrowed the Spartan social and political system from Crete, according to the Spartans' own version of the matter (1.65)" (75–76).

25. A critic might object that the difference in presuppositions merely reflects a difference in interlocutors. But, as I argue later, the difference in interlocutors (old in the case of the Athenian and generally young for Socrates) is a reflection of their habits—Socrates always stayed in Athens (cf. *Crito* 52b) except to do his military duty—and characteristic manner of proceeding. Socrates did not and claimed that he could not (*Apology* 37d–e) accept the "Dorian law of laws," which forbade anyone from criticizing the laws in the presence of young people.

time without being changed have presumably proved in practice to be good. There is, moreover, a story that the original legislator, Minos, received instruction in a cave from his father Zeus. Although that story was transmitted to later generations by Homer in a highly dubious form (as a lie Odysseus tells when he returns to Ithaca disguised as a Cretan foreigner and beggar), Socrates appears to take it at face value.[26] Minos' laws were good because they were based on divine wisdom. The Athenians regard Minos as a tyrant, Socrates explains, because he is depicted as such in the tragedies. They show Minos to be a tyrant because he not only defeated the Athenians with his navy but also demanded a sacrifice of seven young women and seven young men every year thereafter.[27] Athenians have thus been misled by their poets into looking at Minos in terms of the pain he caused them rather than the excellence or defects of the laws he gave his own people. The *Laws* begins with an inquiry into the excellence of the Cretan legislator. It might thus appear to be intended as a "Socratic" correction of the democratic Athenian dislike of Minos.[28]

As we see from the very beginning of the *Minos*, Socrates regularly questions both the wisdom and the justice of the laws of his own regime. The Athenian, on the contrary, recommends many of the institutions of pre-Periclean Athens to his Dorian interlocutors.[29] Despite his military service or defense of Athens in deed, Socrates rarely appears in the Platonic dialogues as an explicit advocate or defender of Athenian laws and institutions in speech. The stance the Athenian Stranger and Socrates take toward their native city also appears to be different.

So are the mode and conditions under which they conduct their respective inquiries. Having asked about the source of Crete's laws, the Athenian suggests that the three old men occupy themselves by discussing laws and regimes as they walk the long path from Cnossus to the cave of Zeus, taking periodic rests from the heat of the sun under the shade of the cypress trees. At the beginning of the *Phaedrus* Socrates observes that in leading him outside the city into the countryside (where they also seek shade un-

---

26. *Minos* 319b–c; *Odyssey* 19.179.

27. At beginning of the *Phaedo* (58b–c) we learn that Socrates' death was delayed a fortnight because the law forbade public executions during the time the Athenians sent a ship to Delos each year to commemorate the saving of the fourteen young men and women who had been sent to Crete.

28. According to Morrow (*Cretan City*, 35–39), it was taken to be such by later commentators.

29. Morrow, in *Cretan City*, extensively documents the extent to which the laws the Athenian recommends for the new colony to be founded in Crete are taken from pre-Periclean Athenian practice.

der a plane [*platonos*] tree) by means of his love of speeches, Phaedrus has induced him to depart from his ordinary habits. Rather than roam about the countryside, Socrates usually remains in the city. The trees have nothing to teach him, he explains; his fellow citizens do. Remaining in Athens, Socrates can and does converse with foreign teachers as well as with his fellow citizens. Both the philosopher and his interlocutors enjoy the protection of democratic Athenian law, which allows an extensive freedom of speech (*parrhēsia*). On the island of Crete, the Athenian Stranger later points out, no one is allowed to question the justice or beneficence of the laws in public. A few elderly men conversing in private may, however, do so—so long as no one young is present. Not only their habits and physical circumstances but also the political or legal conditions under which Socrates and the Athenian converse differ significantly.

So do their interlocutors. As depicted in the *Symposium* and *Phaedrus*, Socrates is explicitly an erotic. In the *Laws* the Athenian just as explicitly criticizes the homosexual and other extramarital relations Socrates appears to tolerate, if not condone. Socrates' "erotic" desire for knowledge leads him to converse with others, especially young men. In Crete the Athenian also appears to seek knowledge by conversing with others, but the people with whom he seeks to converse are not only foreigners but also experienced elder statesmen. They seek knowledge of the best way of life both for an individual and for a regime primarily by comparing the institutions and practices of their respective regimes.

In most evident contrast to Socrates, the Athenian's investigations would not appear to make him subject to the accusation traditionally leveled at philosophers—that as students of things in the heavens and under the earth, they are atheists. On the contrary, in book 10 of the *Laws* the Athenian presents a speech explicitly designed to convince youths corrupted by such philosophers that the gods exist. He would apparently not have to worry about being hauled into court and charged, like Socrates, with the capital crimes of not believing in the gods of the city and corrupting the young. Because there are no young people present, they will not be apt to anger their elders by imitating the philosopher's interrogations. Nor will these elders be able to repeat the standard charges against philosophy; they do not know them. The philosophical doctrines that they and future citizens are to learn in the regime the Athenian proposes are explicitly designed to foster piety.

The Athenian purchases his immunity from political persecution, however, at a price. Although he asserts the Socratic dictum that no one willingly commits an injustice, because no one willingly harms himself (860c–d), the Athenian never encourages either his current elderly interlocutors or their projected younger colleagues of the future to seek self-knowledge as the only and necessary means of discovering what is good for the human soul. The self-reflective, critical character of Socratic philosophizing appears, therefore, to be almost entirely absent from the *Laws*.[30] Because the Athenian never embarrasses his elderly interlocutors by confronting them directly with their ignorance or contradictory opinions as individuals rather than as representatives of their respective regimes, he never subjects them to the shame Aristotle suggests (*Nicomachean Ethics* 1128b15–16) is appropriate only for the young. As a result, the Athenian's elderly interlocutors never learn how very much they do not know. Readers are led to wonder whether the old Dorians will continue to be willing to inquire into the goodness and effectiveness of the laws they propose in the presence of younger people, when it becomes clear, in response to questions younger people raise, that the elders do not understand and therefore cannot give the reasons for the institutions they have established.

II. The Athenian's Political Project in the *Laws*

The problems with the Athenian's characteristic mode of proceeding and the laws he proposes gradually become evident in the course of the dialogue. Although many commentators have found the *Laws* to be a sprawling, repetitive discussion full of historical detail, the dialogue is clearly organized into three parts.[31] In the first part (books 1–4) the Athenian demonstrates the way in which he is able to show the elderly Dorians that he has a superior knowledge of politics and so persuade them to listen to his legislative proposals (books 1–3). He concludes this part of the conversation in book 4 by announcing the two basic principles or requirements of law: (1) that it originate in intelligence (*nous*) and (2) that lawgivers direct the actions of others by means of persuasion (the preludes) rather than

---

30. Nightingale asks, "[is] the discussion designed to reduce the interlocutors to perplexity and expose the inconsistencies in their souls in the 'Socratic' manner? Certainly it does not have this effect on Megillus," she observes. And "Clinias cannot participate in a truly 'philosophical' discussion because he is uneducated." She concludes, "The argumentation in the *Laws* is . . . wholly unsocratic" ("Literary Interpretation," 294–95).

31. See, e.g., Morrow, *Cretan City*; George Klosko, "The Nocturnal Council in Plato's *Laws*," *Political Studies* 36 (1988): 74–88; Bobonich, *Utopia*, 114; Stalley, *Introduction*, 171; Wilamowitz-Möllendorff, *Platon*, 1:655.

simply with force. In the second part of the dialogue (books 5–8) the Athenian then proposes a set of specific laws, drawing on his knowledge of
Athenian as well as Dorian institutions and practices. As he makes his recommendations, readers see that his elderly Dorian interlocutors will not
be able to establish or maintain the arrangements the Athenian proposes,
because they lack the requisite scientific, poetic, historical, and mathematical education. Readers also learn that all legislators face a constant and
fundamentally insoluble problem in trying to impose a lasting, if not unchanging, order on ever new generations. In the last four books (9–12) the
Athenian thus shows his interlocutors (and Plato's readers) the necessity
of establishing four other kinds of institutional responses to the ineradicable resistance to the regulation of their passions by law, which all human
beings experience, especially when they are young: punishments, a public
teaching about the gods' support for the laws, regulations concerning the
inheritance and exchange of property, and a school for future legislators.
In recounting and explicating the reasons for the Athenian's proposals, I
intend to show how orderly his presentation of the problems confronting
a legislator is.[32]

32. Because the *Laws* contains a long, complex, and detailed discussion, readers may find it
useful to refer to the following more detailed outline of its contents, as analyzed in this chapter:

    I. Differences between the Athenian Stranger and Socrates
    II. The Athenian's political project in the *Laws*
        A. How the Athenian persuades the elderly Dorian legislators to listen
            1. Playing Crete off against Sparta
            2. Replacing Crete and Sparta with Athens as the model
            3. The defect of both the Dorian militarists and the democratic Athenians
            4. Drawing lessons from ancient Greek legends and political experience
        B. The Athenian's "city in speech"
            1. Necessary conditions
                a. The location, population, knowledge, and power needed to
                   found a new regime
                b. The role of the god—or the true source of law
                c. The Athenian's innovation: Preludes
                d. The limits of preludes (or persuasion)
                e. Inculcating moderation by restricting differences in wealth
            2. The regime: Further problems confronting the legislator
                a. Transitional officeholders
                b. Imperfect justice in the allocation of offices or honors
                c. The need to adapt "unchanging" laws to changing
                   circumstances
                d. Problems posed by generation
                    1) Regulating private relations between the sexes: How to use and maintain
                     shame
                  2) Supervising the behavior of women and children
                  3) Replacing laws with songs or "play"

Although Plato shows that the Athenian's proposals represent improvement on past Greek political practice, readers see in the end that his legislative proposals do not solve the political problem as he first described it. If the legislator's goal is, first and foremost, to make every citizen as virtuous as possible, legislators have to know what virtue is. At the end of the *Laws* the Athenian thus tells his old Dorian interlocutors that members of the Nocturnal Council will have to take up the characteristically Socratic questions about the unity of the virtues, the good, and the noble. As most readers know from Plato's "later" depiction of the trial and death of Socrates, such investigations are not compatible with the regulations, particularly the enforcement of a public teaching about piety, that the Athenian has recommended.

A. How the Athenian Persuades the Elderly Dorian Legislators to Listen

In the course of the first three books of the dialogue, Plato shows the Athenian acquiring students of a kind Socrates never attracted by persuading two Dorian elders that he may be able to propose a set of laws superior to those of their own cities. Since Crete and Sparta were reputed to be among the best-governed cities in Greece, the Athenian's initial achievement is remarkable.

1. PLAYING CRETE OFF AGAINST SPARTA

One reason the Athenian is able to persuade the old Dorians to listen to his suggested improvements on their laws is that he tailors his questions to their particular characters and habits of mind and then, at crucial junctures, plays one off against the other. He is able to verify presuppositions he has about them with a few questions, because, as he later intimates (*Laws* 641e), all three of the participants in this discussion are typical of their respective regimes.

From the time of Homer, Cretans had been (in)famous as liars. By asking Clinias whether the source of Crete's laws is human or divine, the Athenian quickly learns that the wily old Cretan is apt to say what he thinks is publicly acceptable or "most just" (understanding the "just" as the "legal" or conventional). As the Athenian's follow-up questions reveal, however, Clinias' own opinions are somewhat different. Queried about the reasons for Crete's distinctive institutions—its military training, common meals and gymnastic exercises—Clinias praises "the lawgiver" for arranging everything with an eye to winning victories in war, through which the victors acquire the goods of the vanquished. Whereas his first answer was pious, his second—an explanation of the basis of the law—is functional; at bottom it feeds human greed.

One reason the Athenian persuades Clinias to listen is that he never directly embarrasses or threatens to anger or silence the old Cretan by confronting him with the contradictions in his opinions, as Socrates would. Rather than point out the tension between Clinias' functional account of the laws and his "most just" account of their origin, the Athenian merely indicates the problem with maintaining that victory in war is the supreme and all-encompassing end of politics by asking whether it might not be possible for a numerous body of lesser men in a city to overpower their few betters. Expressing surprise, Clinias admits that it would. The Athenian then asks whether it would be better for the best men to rule themselves and kill the evil ones, for the best to force lesser people to serve and obey them, or for a wise judge to reconcile the two warring factions? Even though he had just stated that everyone is always at war—with everyone else and even himself—Clinias chooses the third option. Contrary to his own first statement, he thinks that achieving peace at home is more important than winning victories abroad.

Clinias objects that the laws of Crete were nevertheless designed to enable them to win wars. But the Athenian deflects the discussion from a direct criticism of either Clinias or the Cretan lawgiver by asking his interlocutor to consider the contrasting views of two poets. Whereas Tyrtaeus, an Athenian who had become a citizen of Sparta, praised courage in war as the greatest virtue, Theognis of Sicilian Megara suggested that a courageous but untrustworthy soldier would not make a good fellow citizen or comrade-in-arms. Courage is only one of several virtues, the Athenian points out (630a); it is better to have justice (*dikaiosynē*), moderation (*sōphrosynē*), and practical wisdom (*phronēsis*) as well.

Clinias objects again to his demeaning of "our lawgiver," and the Athenian again deflects the criticism by suggesting that it is not the legislator of Crete but their statement or understanding of his intention that is at fault. The aim of any "divine" legislator must be to enable his people to attain happiness by acquiring not only the four human goods—health, beauty, strength, and wealth—but also, and more important, the four divine goods—prudence (*phronēsis*), intelligent moderation (*meta nou sōphrōn psychēs hexis*), the justice that arises from moderation mixed with courage, and courage itself (*Laws* 631b–d).[33] To do so effectively, a legislator must supervise their associations and passions from birth to death.

Recognizing Clinias' increasing resistance to engaging in an exchange that appears critical of the Cretan legislator, the Athenian turns to the less clever, but more forthright, courageous, and generous Spartan.[34] Rather than continue to skewer Clinias with his interrogation, as Megillus desires (633a), the Athenian asks the Spartan to explain how his regime inculcates courage. Megillus responds that it does so by requiring the young to learn

33. As Pangle points out in a note to his translation of the *Laws* (515), the translation of this crucial passage is vexed because there is a lacuna in the manuscripts that have only the adjective "divine" (*theias*) and do not add a substantive noun. In quoting the *Laws* in this chapter, I have generally used the Pangle translation, although I have occasionally, as here (by using "legislator" instead of "man" to maintain the ambiguity concerning whether the legislator is human or divine), departed from it slightly on the basis of my own understanding of the text.

34. Megillus demonstrates both his honesty and his generosity a bit later in the conversation when he recalls how he had defended Athens from his angry compatriots. Like many others, he believes that the "Athenians who are good . . . are good by nature, not compulsion" (*Laws* 642c–d). The Spartan is more direct, honest, and generous than his Cretan companion because he feels himself and his regime to be stronger. He has the simplicity often associated with a certain kind of nobility. Feeling himself able to defend his opinions, he says what he thinks. There are at least two other occasions later in the dialogue when the Athenian confronts and provokes the honest Spartan in a way he never does the crafty Cretan in order to move the conversation onto another, higher plane. The first occurs in book 4 when the Athenian insists on the novelty of his teaching about preludes (721e–22b); the second occurs in book 7 when Megillus' objection to the Athenian's demeaning of the race (804b) leads him to propose a more intellectual education for the rulers.

to hunt, to serve in the secret service, and to endure pain—as well as through the common meals and gymnastic training Sparta has in common with Crete. But the Athenian inquires: Can people not be overcome by pleasures as well as by pains? How do Spartan laws teach them to master or control their pleasures? Megillus is at a loss.

The Athenian uses the opportunity created by Megillus' (expected) incapacity to show Clinias that he will not risk contravening Cretan laws and customs by persisting in their inquiry. Instead of immediately and directly pointing out the obvious defect of both Dorian regimes—that they inculcate courage, but not moderation—the Athenian wins the hearts of his two interlocutors by praising one of their laws.[35] That law commands everyone in the regime repeatedly to chant in unison how good and just the laws are. Only the elderly, meeting in private with no young people present, are allowed to inquire into the soundness of their own legislation and the possible advantages of the institutions of others. It is not clear that any Dorian has heard of such a law before this; Clinias praises the Athenian for "divining" the intention of their legislator. It has now been established, however, that their inquiry is legally sanctioned. Clinias does not need to be quite as guarded as he has been thus far.

The Athenian then uses the freedom offered by the privacy of their exchange to challenge, if not to provoke, the forthright Megillus. In this way he moves their inquiry concerning laws and regimes to a new, second stage in which the Athenian symposium replaces Dorian military training as the model or locus of a good education.

2. Replacing Crete and Sparta with Athens as the Model

Having used the time or opportunity given him by the Athenian's excursus on the law to reflect, Megillus asserts (Laws 636a) that the Spartans inculcate moderation or mastery of pleasure the same way they teach their citizens to overcome their fears—through gymnastic training and sparse (Spartan) common meals. These famed institutions may be said to promote virtue,

---

35. We see here the grounds for the distinction Farabi drew in his *Philosophy of Plato* between the confrontational "way of Socrates," which required an open break with accepted opinions, and the "way of Plato," which demands judicious conformity with accepted opinions. In his *Summary of Plato's "Laws,"* Farabi does not name or distinguish among the speeches of the interlocutors. He writes simply of what Plato said, intended, or wrote. *Alfarabi's "Philosophy of Plato and Aristotle,"* trans. Muhsin Mahdi (Glencoe, IL: Free Press, 1962), 62–67; Strauss, "How Farabi Read Plato's *Laws,"* 153.

the Athenian responds, but in fact they encourage licentious, unnatural sexual relations between men. Stung by the criticism of his beloved city, Megillus retorts, at least we are not as shameless as the Athenians, who appear drunk in public. The Athenian then uses the opportunity created not only by the freedom of a private conversation and the attack he himself has provoked but also by the respect he knows his interlocutors have for the expression of patriotic feelings to defend a distinctive institution of his own city. At the same time he instructs Megillus about the proprieties of conversational inquiry: Athenians might respond to his attack by pointing to the notoriously loose behavior of Spartan women, but such exchanges of insults serve no useful purpose. They should inquire, instead, into the best way of dealing with drink. Peoples vary. Whereas the Spartans entirely forbid the consumption of alcohol, Persians and others imbibe wine undiluted with water. Which way is best?

Megillus retorts that Spartans defeat any and all of these peoples on the battlefield. But the Athenian points out that the Dorians confuse might with right. Victory on the battlefield often reflects the size of the nation more than the excellence of its regime. Leaving aside victory for the moment—along with the disparagement of others and praise of one's own—they should inquire whether the institution in question is noble. To do that, they have to examine it rightly ordered and conducted, which means with an appropriate ruler (*archōn*).

Clinias easily concedes that any organized activity requires a ruler with the necessary skill and virtue, but he asks: what possible use or benefit can drinking parties (*symposia*) have? Rather than respond immediately with the parallel he subsequently draws between the way social drinking gives people practice in controlling their pleasure and the way Spartan institutions teach their citizens to overcome fear by forcing them to confront pain, the Athenian simply states: the benefit in question is education. Well-educated men not only become good, but they also conquer others in battle, whereas conquerors often give way to hubris. Dorian institutions tend to make the inculcation of virtue merely a means of conquest and acquisition; a better set of institutions would make self-mastery, or more, the acquisition of virtue as a whole, the goal.

Clinias immediately perceives that what is at stake is not mere drink or intoxication but fostering the freedom and friendship that makes convivial association possible. What he does not understand, although he and Megillus are about to experience an example, is that such convivial association proceeds primarily through exchanges of words or speeches (*logoi*), as opposed to contests of arms or exchanges of goods. Lacking such experience, he asks the Athenian to show how drinking parties contribute to the education of citizens.

The Athenian immediately demonstrates his own superior experience and expertise in leading such a conversational exchange by insisting on the need to begin with a definition of education: what it is and what powers it has. He defines education as a kind of playful practice, undertaken from childhood onward, in the pursuits that enable a person to become a perfect citizen, to rule and to be ruled justly. This playful practice is implicitly contrasted to the serious preparations for war emphasized by the Dorians. Rather than operate primarily through restraint and pain like Dorian regulations, this education (*paideia*) aims at attaching the pleasures and desires of the child (*pais*) to appropriate objects by means of play (*paizonta*). Such practice is necessary, because human beings, as if puppets, are pulled in opposite directions by their pleasures and pains. These attractions and aversions need to be directed and regulated by reason (*logismos*) in individuals and by law in cities. Because reason itself exercises little push or pull, it has to be strengthened through association with the other sources of motion.

The Athenian indicates the way, if not the reasons why the education he is about to describe is superior to Dorian laws, when he observes (645b) that the image of human beings as puppets enables us to understand somewhat better what is meant by achieving a victory over oneself. Clinias' original statement was cast in terms of conflict and forceful repression; the Athenian's image points to the desirability of harmony and the need for leadership—pulling or attracting, rather than merely subduing or repressing. Symposia provide opportunities for developing this form of leadership not only by giving the participants practice in controlling their pleasure but also, and more importantly, by providing the ruler with an opportunity to learn the true character of their souls and desires by watching what they do when uninhibited.

Symposia have a third function, moreover, which is to preserve in adults the effects of the education they received as children. As the image of people as puppets suggests, human beings are not internally ruled or directed by nature. Like other animals, human beings utter inarticulate sounds and are in constant motion from birth. Unlike other animals, humans have the capacity to learn to order their motions and give their utterances regular

meaning by learning to dance and sing in harmony with others.[36] All songs
and dances do not have the same effects, however; some tend to make
people too soft, others too frenzied. If legislators want to train and educate virtuous citizens, they will have to regulate the content of the songs
and the kinds of dances performed in their city.

3. THE DEFECT OF BOTH THE DORIAN MILITARISTS AND THE DEMOCRATIC ATHENIANS

Responding to Clinias' objection that Crete and Sparta are the only cities
that even try to regulate musical productions, and that they have been unable to protect their citizens from the corruption of taste, the Athenian
admits he is talking about what should happen more than what does. He
is, indeed, gradually moving the conversation and thus his initial education
of the two old Dorians beyond the praise of Athens to a third and even
higher stage. In Athens people recognize the importance of music more
than they do in Crete or Sparta, he points out, but in Athens the many
judge musical performances according to their pleasure; they do not accept the judgment of those wiser and better.

Clinias easily and enthusiastically agrees that it would be a great improvement if all peoples followed the example of the Dorian cities. The
Dorian cities are, however, no longer the prime examples of good legislation.[37] Nor is Athens.[38] On the contrary, the Athenian shows, both the mili-
taristic oligarchs and the demos share the same mistaken understanding of
the human good. Legislators should compel poets to teach "that the good
man, being moderate and just, is happy and blessed, whether he be great

36. Elizabeth Belfiore ignores the significance of this crucial introduction to the discussion of
choral education in her analysis, "Wine and Catharsis of the Emotions in Plato's *Laws*," *Classical
Quarterly* 36, no. 2 (1986): 421–37.

37. Although Greek education was traditionally understood to be a combination of gymnastics and music, this exchange serves to remind readers (as well as, perhaps, the two old Dorians
themselves) that neither Clinias nor Megillus had mentioned the regulation of music or poetry
as one of the ways in which their regimes fostered virtue. They had referred only to the regulation of bodily functions and activities—eating and gymnastics. As the Dorians see it, defense and
acquisition are important, serious activities—matters of life and death; poetry, like speech making in general, is a frivolous enterprise for those at leisure. Although they grant the traditional
attribution of the theater, poetry, and song to the gods—Dionysus, Apollo, and the Muses—the
old Dorians do not understand the implication of the divine origins—that these activities are as
important, as beneficial, as good for human beings as the "laws" they attribute to Zeus (who has
traditionally been understood to be the source and enforcer of justice).

38. Unlike the Dorians, the Athenians prize music. They, however, leave judgment of its excellence to the uninformed.

and strong or small and weak, whether he be rich or not" and that "the things said to be good by the many are not correctly so described, . . . that the best thing is health, and second is beauty, and third is wealth . . . ; and then, by becoming a tyrant, to do whatever one desires; and finally . . . to become immortal" (Laws 660e). Clinias, however, demurs. He agrees that the just life is noble and that the unjust acquisition of what the Athenian had previously called "the human goods" is base (662a), but he does not believe that the unjust acquisition of wealth and power is bad. Like the many, Clinias himself believes, at bottom, that pleasure is the good and it is best to be a tyrant.[39]

Having brought out the tyrannical root of both Doric and Athenian opinions and practices, the Athenian explicitly dissents. If he were a legislator, he would try to compel the poets and all the other citizens to chant regularly in unison, not, as in the Dorian regimes, that the laws are good and just but rather that the just life is the best and most pleasant.[40] Indicating his own view of the true source of Dorian laws, he says he would not attribute the desire to acquire goods and power unjustly to the gods; he would attribute such statements to human ancestors and lawgivers.[41]

Clinias concedes that a lawgiver might find it useful to propagate such a view among the populace, even if it were a lie (pseudos). So the Athenian drops the question of the truth of the teaching and asks instead how it can be spread.[42] Returning to choral training, he suggests that citizens should be divided into groups according to age. Children should be required merely to chant the identity of the good and the just; those from eighteen to thirty years of age will be taught to attribute the truth of this claim to Apollo. It is only the third chorus, composed of those from thirty to sixty years of age and their elders, no longer able to sing, whose characters are to be tested by drink and so revealed. They will have to learn what the

---

39. It is probably not an accident that Plato gave the old Cretan the same name as Alcibiades' father (and son). In this case the son inherited and acted out his father's desire. Barry Strauss first pointed out the connection of the names to me.

40. "There are many other things contrary to what is now said, as it seems, by Cretans and Lacedaemonians—and, of course by the rest of mankind—I should persuade my citizens to proclaim" (Laws 662b).

41. Like Aristophanes in the Clouds and Adimantus in the Republic, the Athenian would also remind fathers that they urge their sons to be just; in declaring the unjust life to be happiest, they are inconsistent. Fame (the human form of immortality) is pleasant, and fame goes to the just.

42. He later returns in his monologue on the soul in book 5 to insist on the importance of truthfulness for the attainment of human happiness (Laws 730c) and that the most pleasant life is, on balance, the most moderate (732e–34e).

content of the songs and the forms of the dances must be in order to inculcate virtue in the people—and how constantly to vary them to maintain
the pleasure people take in singing and so the effect of the songs.

The primary and most important purpose of symposia thus turns out
to be the education of these elders, an education that would enable them
to know the nature of things so that they can judge what is a correct imitation and recognize how the true and the beneficial can be presented pleasantly (667b–69b). The elders must become expert, in other words, not only
about the nature of the world and of human beings but also in the arts of
persuasion.[43] Only those who possess such knowledge will be able to judge
what songs should be allowed. Only those who possess such knowledge
can make and administer just laws.

The Athenian has provided an example in action of what such an education of elders would look like in his exploration of the proper use and
benefit of symposia with the old Dorians. By leading Clinias to examine
the nature and use of music, he has led Clinias not merely to reveal but
to recognize the fundamental defect in his own character: he wishes, at
bottom, to be a tyrant. At the same time the Athenian has pointed out the
most glaring defect of the laws and institutions that shaped the character
of the old Cretan. When Clinias remarks that Dorians know of no songs
for a chorus of godlike elders to chant (and so obtain the desired knowledge), the Athenian responds:

> Of course not. For you have really never attained to the noblest song. Your
> regime is that of an armed camp and not of men settled in cities. You keep
> your young in a flock, like a bunch of colts grazing in a herd. None of you
> takes his own youngster apart. . . . None of you gives him a private groom
> and educates him by currying and soothing him. . . . If you did, he would
> become not only a good soldier but someone capable of managing a city
> and towns. . . . He would always and everywhere honor the possession of
> courage as the fourth, not the first, part of virtue, for private individuals and
> the whole city. (666e–67a)

43. He also indicates (*Laws* 674a–c) that wine drinking per se plays a very small part in the
education and hence life of the "musical" regime he has described. There will be no drinking, in
fact, except for bodily training or health during the day. No city official, no soldier, no servant, or
potential parent at night shall drink. There are other occasions when men of right reason and law
would not drink. In sum, there would be less drinking in the Athenian's regime than there was in
either Crete or Sparta. He reminds his Dorian interlocutors of the effects of wine in order to show
them what rulers really need to know. Cf. Strauss, *Argument and Action*, 37.

In his description of the requirements of a true education, the Athenian thus points to something like Socrates' questioning of individuals in private about their views of the good and the noble. The Athenian cannot develop this thought with his Dorian interlocutors, because, as he says, they lack the requisite knowledge of *mousikē*, much less of philosophy. The education he can provide the Dorian elders is limited by their (lack of) experience and training as youths.

4. Drawing Lessons from Ancient Greek Legends and Political Experience

Having inquired into the correct content, use, and form of an education in music, the Athenian suggests that they look at "gymnastics."[44] Clinias exults, because he thinks that the Dorians are experts in such. In the survey of Greek political experience that follows, however, the Athenian shows that the defects of Dorian education have produced great defects in Dorian practice as well. He thus sets the stage for introducing a new and better understanding of political practice.

The Athenian agrees with Clinias that human beings become hostile after they have organized themselves into cities. But, he suggests, they do not view each other antagonistically before they are organized into discrete political units. He posits something like a modern "state of nature" to counter Clinias' initial claim that war is necessary and natural.

We have to seek the origin (*archē*) of political regimes in a time human beings no longer remember. As we know from our own experience, many different regimes have come into being and passed away. This stream of becoming does not flow without interruption, however. There are ancient stories of great disasters—floods, for example—as a result of which most human beings, their settlements, the arts, and thus the means of recording what they had learned were destroyed. Those who survived would probably be solitary herdsmen living on mountain tops. The question thus becomes how such people could and would have developed cities, laws, virtues, and vices. From the source of Cretan law, the Athenian thus broadens the scope of their inquiry into the source of laws and regimes per se.

Lacking arts (*Laws* 679d), human beings were innocent and peaceable at first. Having everything they needed to survive and rarely encountering

---

44. As traditionally conceived in Greece, education consisted of instruction in music and gymnastics. Cf. Gadamer, "Plato and the Poets," 53–54.

others, they had no incentive to fight.[45] Without any reason or experience to make them fear others, they took pleasure in meeting their kind. Characterized by a kind of natural or naive courage associated with lack of fear as well as the moderation and justice that results from absence of need or greed (but lacking intellectual development and hence wisdom), these people did not need laws. They nevertheless lived under a certain kind of regime (*politeia*): the rule of the household by the father, usually called "dynasty" (*dynasteia*), that Homer describes among the Cyclopes. They did not have deliberative assemblies or clan rules but lived separately in caves and ruled their own children and wives.

Like other inhabitants of Crete, Clinias admits, he is not familiar with the works of foreign poets like Homer. Nor does he notice the fundamental antagonism between the sketch of human prehistory the Athenian has just given and his own initial claim that human beings are always and everywhere at war. The Spartans are familiar with Homer, Megillus observes (680c–d), but he points out that the poet depicts a different, Ionic rather than Laconic, way of life. Apparently without conscious irony, Megillus alerts Plato's readers to the questionable use the Athenian has made of the poet by commenting that Homer appears to be a good witness to the Athenian's argument because Homer attributes the ancient ways of the Cyclopes to their "savage" or uncivilized condition.[46] In the *Odyssey* Homer depicts the Cyclops as a cannibal who refuses to honor Zeus or his guest laws. Homer's view of "uncivilized" nature is closer to Clinias' initial warlike view than to the originally pacific condition described by the Athenian.[47]

Neither Clinias nor Megillus understands the issue raised by the Athenian's account of the origin of political association, because neither old Dorian has had enough training in philosophy to distinguish between nature and convention. They simply see that different peoples have different ways and believe that those ways that prove to be most powerful are best.[48] The reader of the dialogue is invited, however, to view the Athenian's

45. Cf. Montesquieu *Spirit of the Laws* 1:2–3.

46. E. B. England, *The "Laws" of Plato* (Manchester: Manchester University Press, 1921), *ad* 1.316, prefers "wild" in this context.

47. In *Theaetetus* 152e, Socrates points out that all poets and philosophers before Parmenides, Homer chief among them, taught that everything was fundamentally in flux. Later in the dialogue (*Laws* 782a–d) the Athenian suggests that this view leads to the conclusion that human nature itself is extremely malleable, not that it is essentially warlike.

48. Cf. Leo Strauss, *Natural Right and History* (Chicago: University of Chicago Press, 1953), 81–94.

account of Greek political experience with some skepticism. Surely the Athenian knows that he has distorted the view Homer presents of the Cyclops. He appears to be taking advantage of Clinias' lack of learning and Megillus' simplicity in an attempt to change their opinions.[49] His contention that human beings originally lived in peace stands in tension with, if not complete opposition to, his earlier observation that, like other animals, young human beings are constantly in motion and that this motion becomes orderly only through poetry or art.

Moving from his sketchy depiction of the natural condition to answer his initial query, the Athenian identifies the emergence of political life proper with the explicit formulation of laws that occurred when various clans gathered together behind walls they built to defend themselves from wild beasts.[50] Once the various clans came together, they perceived the need to deliberate about which of their different customs the community as a whole should adopt. The people chosen to decide became the first lawgivers and constituted a kind of aristocracy.

Having used poetry and prehistorical myths, again indirectly, to challenge Clinias' contention that human beings are hostile by nature, the Athenian admits that cities became characterized by enmity, both internally and with regard to others, when, forgetting the original disaster, peoples moved down from the mountains onto the plains. Human beings did not simply forget, however. The Athenian suggests that they lost their fear of natural forces by developing arts like shipbuilding and navigation to manage if not entirely to overcome them, when he mentions, apparently only in passing, that a military expedition probably came against Troy by sea (as Homer had shown) because everyone was then making use of the sea without fear.

49. One of the more notable differences between the Athenian's mode of proceeding in the *Laws* and Socrates' in the *Republic* is that the Athenian always cites or quotes both Homer and Hesiod positively, whereas in the *Republic* Socrates is critical of the poets. One reason the Athenian can be as positive about the teachings of the epic poets as he is seems to be that he can reshape the content of their poems to suit his own purposes. Because his young Athenian interlocutors are more familiar with the works of the poets, Socrates does not have the same opportunity to "rewrite."

50. The Athenian maintains the ambiguity introduced by his misuse of Homer by failing to say how "wild beasts" differ from human beings without cities. Cf. *Statesman* 274c, where the Eleatic Stranger also associates the emergence of political associations with the development of the arts necessary to preserve the human race. In the *Republic* Socrates, by way of contrast, has "the true city" emerge out of a division of labor among artisans, that is, those who possess arts already. In the "myth" Protagoras tells in the dialogue that bears his name, knowledge of how to associate politically comes after the development of other arts.

Human beings living under different conditions have changed over time, the Athenian shows here (and reiterates later). They have learned how to organize themselves into cities and to protect themselves in other ways from hostile natural forces, but the changes, even the increase in knowledge, have not all been simply good.[51] Just as human beings learned to overcome the dangers posed by natural forces by learning how to use or manipulate them, he now suggests, they can learn how to overcome the danger posed by the enmity of other human beings. The learning or lesson to be derived from past political experience is not, however, what his Dorian interlocutors first think.[52]

The Athenian points out that after the attack on Troy, the stories (*mythologia*) of the poets come together with the history of Sparta.[53] When the Achaean forces returned home, they were confronted with rebellions against their rule. Putting the youthful rebels down, the victors changed their name to Dorian in honor of Dorieus, who gathered the exiles together. Having thus arrived at the fourth stage in the development of political regimes, when order is reinstituted and restored on the basis of experience with war, he notes, they have come back to the point at which they diverged from their initial inquiry into the laws of the Dorian regimes by taking up questions about music and drink. To determine what is noble and good and so worthy of preserving in these regimes, they will have to begin again, as it were, at the beginning. They will, however, now be examining the laws of the Dorian regimes in a very different light. The standard of excellence will no longer be military victory. As the Athenian insisted it should be from the very beginning

51. Cf. Andrea Nightingale, "Historiography and Cosmology in Plato's *Laws*," *Ancient Philosophy* 19, no. 2 (Fall 1999): 304, 306–7, 311.

52. It is a mistake, I think, to write about the discussion of past political experience in the *Laws* as "history," although several commentators have done so: e.g., R. G. Bury, "Plato and History," *Classical Quarterly* 45 (1951): 86–93; J. H. Callahan, "Dialectic, Myth and History in the Philosophy of Plato," in "Interpretations of Plato," ed. Helen North, special issue, *Mnemosyne* (1977): S64–S85; Konrad Gaiser, *Platon und die Geschichte* (Stuttgart: Fromman, 1961); and P. Vidal-Naquet, "Platon: L'histoire et les historiens," in *Histoire et structure*, ed. J. Brunschwig, C. Imbert, and A. Roger, 147–60 (Paris: Vrin, 1985). For the ancient Greeks, *historia* meant "inquiry"; what we call "history" was merely a record of what had happened. It did not have any necessary direction or causal principle(s).

53. The account the Athenian gives does not entirely coincide with those found in other sources. The Athenian himself later refers to stories that suggest the conquerors of Troy and those who reinstituted order in the cities of the Peloponnesus were two different peoples when he reminds Megillus at 685d that the sons of Heracles were considered to be better rulers than the descendants of Pelops. Cf. Pangle, *Laws*, 522.

of the conversation, the standard will be the inculcation of virtue as a whole.[54]

The Athenian uses the history of Sparta to prove his point. The initial arrangements instituted by the Dorians—an alliance of three monarchies based on popular consent for their mutual defense against both domestic and foreign threats—were faulty. The alliance itself and two of the three monarchies quickly collapsed because their rulers suffered from the same lack of learning (*amathia*) Clinias confessed to earlier: the Dorian kings did not truly believe that the things they publicly proclaimed to be noble and just were truly good. They sought, therefore, unjustly to aggrandize themselves at the expense of their allies. To Megillus' amazement, the Athenian shows that the excellence of the Spartan regime does not lie in its armies. The alliance of the three Dorian kings enabled them to amass an armed force of unprecedented size and power capable of defending Greece as a whole, but the alliance and its army quickly disintegrated because the kings could not trust each other.[55] The Dorian kings revealed their lack of political experience and wisdom in thinking an oath would suffice to restrain the unlawful desires of uneducated rulers.[56]

A legislator would have needed great foresight to have known what would have been required to forestall the dissolution of the confederacy, the Athenian admits, but the three of them can learn from past experience. Of the three monarchies, Sparta alone survived because a "god" blessed her king with two sons; as a result, the power of the monarchy was divided and checked from the outset. Some time later a human being perceived that there was still too much power concentrated in the monarchy and sought to check it further by establishing a council of elders with power equal to that of the two kings. Even that did not suffice to quell the insolence

54. Megillus, who enters the conversation when it concerns his city in particular, avers that he would be willing to engage in an even longer walk and talk if the arguments were of the kind he has thus far heard. Just as in his earlier praise of the natural virtue that individual Athenians manifest (*Laws* 642c–d), so Megillus here shows that his understanding is not simply bound or limited by the laws of Sparta.

55. As the Athenian indicated in his first response to Clinias, the poet Theognis was right to maintain that civic friendship is the precondition for, and therefore more important than, the ability to fight wars with others.

56. The Athenian makes the same point about the inefficacy of relying merely on human oaths, in book 12 (*Laws* 948b–e) when he contrasts human rulers and judges with legendary divine judges like Minos and Rhadamanthus, who could rely solely on oaths. Late in the dialogue he thus indicates much more clearly than he had at the beginning that the storied origins are unsuitable, if not flawed, and cannot serve as models for lawgivers now.

of rule, so a third "savior" was needed to establish the ephorate as yet another check. The excellence of the Spartan regime does not lie in its military might, as Megillus first bragged, but in the laws, which have gradually evolved to limit the power of any part or individual. Correcting the traditional account that traced Spartan laws to Lycurgus and Apollo, the Athenian shows that these institutions were not the products of any single intelligence, divine or human. They were the results of a combination of good luck with trial and error.

Contemporary admirers of constitutional government might expect the Athenian to make the Spartan mixed regime exemplary or at least to declare it an example of the best set of laws generally possible. Instead, he blames the lack of learning of the "so-called statesmen and lawgivers of old" (693a). If their greed had not broken up the original Dorian confederacy, the Persians would never have dared invade Greece, and Athens would not have been left alone to defend her. When Clinias asks what a lawgiver should do to foster prudence, freedom, and friendship among his fellow citizens, the Athenian does not urge him to consider adopting or adapting Spartan institutions. On the contrary, he says, they should examine models of the two extreme forms or "mothers" of rule—monarchy and democracy—which are to be found in every regime (as they were in the original three Dorian monarchies, based as they were on consent).

What they learn from this examination of the two extremes is that neither works well unless it is checked by the other, informally, if not formally. Both in Persia and in Athens, the paradigms of monarchy and democracy, the destabilizing tendencies of the extreme were initially counteracted by external factors or conditions. As a result of the habits Cyrus and his men developed living as shepherds in rough country, in Persia the soldiers initially felt free and friendly. Those who were prudent were allowed to give the king advice. Raised in luxury by women at court, Cyrus's sons were not able to maintain the same kind of equality and friendliness with their men; lacking the habitual self-restraint imposed by harsh circumstances, they not only killed but were also killed.[57] Having seized rule from the

---

57. "By going too far in depriving the populace of freedom, and by bringing in more despotism than is appropriate, they destroyed the friendship and community within the city. Once this is corrupted, the policy of the rulers is no longer made for the sake of the ruled and the populace, but instead for the sake of their own rule. . . . When they come to need the assistance of their populaces to fight in their defense, they discover that there no longer exists a community with a spirit eager to run risks and fight. They have myriads of subjects, but all of them are useless in war; so they have to hire helpers as if they lacked human subjects" (Laws 697c–e).

usurpers, Darius was not the son of a king and had not, therefore, been corrupted by the luxury of the court; his son Xerxes, however, was. There has not been a "great king" since except in name, because the Persians have not been able to provide anyone with the education necessary to preserve freedom, friendship, and intelligence.[58]

Turning from the problems of monarchy (one-man rule) to rule by the many, the Athenian observes that at the time of the Persian invasion there was a regime in Athens based on a division into four classes. The people were held in check by awe (*aidōs*) of the law and fear (*phobos*) of the invading force. After their victory over the Persians at Salamis, however, the Athenians lost their fear and were corrupted by the poets.[59] Before the war, musical forms had been divided according to type (as the Athenian had earlier [669c] argued that the Muses would divide them) and judged by the educated. But after the war, poets mixed up all the different types (as Nietzsche argues they were in Greek tragedy) and appealed to the people as a whole to judge the excellence of the product according to the pleasure it afforded them.[60] Once the people became accustomed to judging excellence in one area, they became increasingly unwilling to recognize and obey authority in any other. They began to contemn the laws, their parents and elders, and finally even the gods. In the end the Athenians displayed "what is called the ancient Titanic nature" (701c), that is, complete lack of order and continual conflict.[61]

When the Athenian "pulls himself up short" and asks rhetorically what the point of all this is, the reader has no doubt. If cities are to have well-made laws, their lawgivers must know more about the political experiments and experiences of both Greek and non-Greek peoples than the

58. In denying that there has been a Great King since, except in name, the Athenian seems to be referring to the weak rule of Artaxerxes. If so, this comment serves to support a dramatic date between 460 and 450.

59. We see how the terms of the discussion have gradually changed at 699d when Megillus praises the Athenian for recognizing the greatness of his city's achievement at Salamis and the Athenian responds, first, that it is appropriate to do so with a citizen of Sparta with whom Athens was allied in this great endeavor, but then reminds both his interlocutors that he is not speaking for the sake of the "myths" but to show how the Persians led their people into slavery, whereas his city has led them in the opposite direction, into complete freedom. Not patriotic pride but political understanding has explicitly become the goal, and the acquisition of political understanding requires criticism of both Doric and Attic regimes.

60. Cf. Friedrich Nietzsche, *Die Geburt der Tragödie*, in *Sämtliche Werke*, vol. 1, ed. Giorgio Colli and Mazzino Montinari (Berlin: De Gruyter, 1980), secs. 7–9, pp. 52–71; trans. Walter Kaufman, *Birth of Tragedy*, in *Basic Writings* (New York: Modern Library, 1968), 56–72.

61. Like Socrates *Republic* 568c, the Athenian suggests that tragedy corrupted Athens by appealing to the people and so fostering democratic if not tyrannical politics.

closed Dorian regimes allow. That is the reason the old Dorians need instruction by an Athenian stranger. What those experiences show is that lawgivers must provide their citizens with a better or more complete education in virtue than the military training the Dorians now stress. People will not live in freedom and friendship or develop their prudence unless they learn to associate voluntarily, on the basis of their own desire or pleasure rather than external force. Instead of seeking to master others, they must first and foremost learn to control themselves.

Even though the Athenian does not state his lesson in so many words, Clinias seems to understand. When the Athenian asks how they can test what he has said, the Cretan elder says he has an idea. He and nine other Cnossians have been charged with establishing a new colony on Crete, which will have the same laws as the mother city—or better, if they can find them. "Let's construct a city in speech, just as if we were founding it from the very beginning. That way there will be an examination of the subject of our inquiry, while at the same time I may perhaps make use of this construction." When the Athenian quips, "At least you're not declaring war, Clinias" (702d), we see how far he has brought the old Dorians. Rather than competition and conflict, they are now looking to cooperation and conversation to help them establish a better form of polity.

B. The Athenian's "City in Speech"

In describing his "city in speech," the Athenian shows the old Dorians that even a much-improved kind of "herd" education will not suffice to make citizens truly virtuous.[62] He thus prepares his interlocutors gradually—very gradually—for the much more radical reform he suggests at the end of the dialogue.[63] In showing why such a radical reform is needed, the Athenian also brings out the problems that face any legislator.[64]

62. In order to maintain that in the *Laws* Plato shows that nonphilosophers can become truly virtuous, Bobonich has to conflate true opinion with knowledge, as he does when he writes, "virtue as a whole consists in knowledge of (or true opinion about) what is good" (*Utopia*, 288). Neither Plato nor his Athenian Stranger equates opinion with knowledge.

63. Trevor J. Saunders, "Plato on Women in the *Laws*," in *The Greek World*, ed. A. Powell (London: Routledge and Kegan Paul, 1995), points out that the Athenian's "city in speech" does not constitute an exact "blueprint"; on the contrary, it "incorporates all sorts of tensions within itself" (603).

64. Herwig Görgemanns, *Beiträge zur interpretation von Platons Nomoi* (Munich: Beck, 1960), 25, 72–110, also argues that the dialogue is addressed primarily to people interested in politics. Albert Keith Whitaker, *A Journey into Platonic Politics* (Lanham, MD: University Press of America, 2004), seeks to extend that political education to readers today.

1. NECESSARY CONDITIONS

a. The Location, Population, Knowledge, and Power Needed to Found a New Regime

Before outlining the regime he proposes for the new colony on Crete, the Athenian asks about the conditions in which it will be established. Socrates never does any such thing in the *Republic*. This is one reason why some commentators view the *Laws* as Plato's practical political proposals; they are located more specifically in space and time. The Athenian's subsequent discussion of the particular physical location, resources, and population of the colony nevertheless points to the constraints under which any legislator must work. As in the case of the origins of political associations and laws, he broadens the scope of the discussion without stating explicitly what he is doing.

A city will not last if it is not founded in a region that can provide its citizens with food and other necessities; the location must also enable citizens to defend it against external attack. Inquiring whether the new colony will be located on the seacoast, the Athenian observes that people who engage in commerce with other nations or build navies will not retain their virtue. The former cannot maintain the purity of their morals in trading with others; the latter do not train their citizens to stand and fight rather than flee.[65]

The composition of the population poses an even greater, less soluble problem than the location. If the people of the new colony are drawn from the same or similar regimes, they will come together in friendship, but they will not be prepared to accept new or different laws. If they are drawn from a variety of regimes, they will be more apt to accept new laws, but they will find it difficult to trust one another. The populace of this particular colony will probably be drawn from Dorian cities on the mainland as well as on Crete. Will these Dorians be willing to accept strange laws suggested by an Athenian? Probably not. Plato indicates at the very

---

65. Readers of the dialogue cannot help but notice a contradiction between the isolated conditions necessary for a city to retain its virtue and the conditions necessary for obtaining the knowledge of practical politics the Athenian has gained—as a result, at least in part, of the commercial activity of his own regime. This contradiction between the conditions necessary to acquire the knowledge required to found the regime and the conditions necessary to maintain the virtue it is designed to foster is one of the central problems the Athenian attempts to overcome with his final reform—the introduction of a "nocturnal council," composed of elders and promising younger citizens, which both receives foreign visitors and sends representatives abroad, to be questioned later in private.

beginning that this "city in speech" is not more apt to be adopted in practice than Socrates' "city" in the *Republic*.

The difficulties of legislating for a new city are so great, indeed, that the Athenian says he is tempted to conclude that "no human being ever legislates anything, but that chance and accidents . . . legislate everything for us" (*Laws* 709a).[66] Meditating on the pilot's art (and so reminding us once again that his knowledge is the product in a sense of Athens' seafaring commerce), however, he concludes that "it seems equally true to say . . . that in all things god—and together with god, chance and opportunity—pilots all human things. One must, indeed, concede that these are accompanied by yet a third gentler thing . . . art [*technē*]" (709a–b).

The third necessary condition for the successful founding of a city thus becomes the presence of a man who knows what and how to legislate. (As we have seen, he cannot be a product of the regime itself.) Like a pilot, such a man knows how to save the ship of state from foundering among forces neither he nor any other human being can create or control. Like the pilot who can guide or direct a ship by looking at the heavens, the man who knows how to legislate understands both the goal and the markers that enable him to move others in the desired direction. He may not be able to produce or possess the means of achieving the goal or even merely of moving in the right direction, but he does know how to identify and use natural forces that might oppose him, like winds or emotions, to balance or counteract others, like waves or selfish desires.

To put his knowledge into effect, a legislator needs tyrannical power. The best situation, the Athenian thus states, would be one in which an older legislator, with the requisite knowledge, had the confidence and cooperation of a young tyrant (with a good memory, quick intelligence, courage, nobility, and the sort of moderation sometimes found in young children or animals), who could immediately put the old legislator's suggestions into effect. A tyrant can quickly establish laws and customs with little difficulty by his mere example; the tyrant only needs to possess, not necessarily to use, complete power over others.

Unfortunately, the Athenian concludes, conditions in the new colony to be established on Crete are far from the best. If not a tyrant, a legislator would wish to have the cooperation of a king or, lacking that, a people

---

66. Both in Persia and Athens, he shows, when the pure or extreme regimes functioned well, it was a result of external conditions beyond the control of the government. Even the benefits of the mixed Spartan constitution were products only in part of human intention and design.

ready and willing to adopt and carry out his dictates. An oligarchy of the kind that is to establish the laws of the colony on Crete is the most difficult to direct, because it has the largest number of rulers who, believing that they are better and hence wiser than others, are difficult to persuade to follow the advice of another.[67] The Athenian seems to be predicting that there will be a gap between the suggestions he makes to Clinias and the laws actually proposed for the government of the colony by the ten Cnossians. Clinias himself may or may not accept all that the Athenian proposes (858b–c); his colleagues will be even less apt simply to do so.

b. The Role of the God—or the True Source of Law

People are less apt to bridle at commands issued from a superior divine power than they are at orders emanating from another human. So, we were reminded at the beginning of the dialogue, the founders of both Crete and Sparta attributed their laws to gods. The Athenian has already shown that neither Clinias nor Megillus has the requisite experience or intelligence to become a lawgiver; their regimes have not educated them properly. Instead of emphasizing their defects and his own superiority and so arousing their envy or ire, the Athenian thus posits a divine source of his suggestions—in the way, perhaps, that Minos and Lycurgus had before him.[68]

The Athenian asks his interlocutors to invoke a god and then say what kind of regime they would like to establish. Because they still take their own cities as exemplary, Clinias and Megillus declare they are not able to say. Since they are "mixed regimes," Crete and Sparta cannot be accurately described in terms of a pure regime, such as an aristocracy, oligarchy, or democracy. These so-called regimes are not really regimes at all, the Athenian contends; they merely represent the domination of one part of the city by another for its own advantage.[69] The regime that truly deserves to

67. The Athenian appears to break here with his Pythagorean precedent. Perhaps he saw that the elders of Croton were willing to follow the advice of the sage only because they had recently been severely defeated in a war with a nearby city. The Athenian could hardly state such a wish for the new colonists of Cnossus.

68. Such a notion of the "legislator" is also to be found in Niccolò Machiavelli, *Discourses on Livy* 1:10, and in Jean-Jacques Rousseau, *Social Contract* 2:7.

69. Here, as in the title of the *Republic* (*Politeia*), Plato does not use the term for "order" the way Aristotle does. In both the *Laws* and the *Republic*, Plato suggests that a political "order" properly speaking serves the good of all; it does not favor the ruling part as the "regimes" (*politeiai*) in Aristotle's *Politics* do. In book 3 (*Laws* 690a–c) the Athenian Stranger lists seven incommensurable titles or claims to rule—of parents, the well born, elders, masters over slaves, strong over the weak, the wise, and the fortunate. The problem is that the other claims, especially of strength,

be called such would be named after the god who despotically rules all those who have minds. The Athenian does not answer Clinias, however, when the old Cretan asks what the name of that god is. Instead he suggests they "should imitate the way of life that is said to have existed under Cronus . . . by obeying whatever within us partakes of immortality, giving the name 'law' to the arrangements ordained by intelligence [*nous*]" (713e–14a).[70] Identifying *nomos* basically with the dictates of *nous*, the Athenian equates the "god" who is the origin (*archē*) of the laws with "intelligence" or "mind."[71]

c. The Athenian's Innovation: Preludes

Having explained the necessary conditions for successful legislation, the Athenian suggests that everything they now say should be imagined as said in the presence of the future citizens of the colony. Such a literary move or device is required by the logic of the legislative project. If Clinias is to communicate their proposals to his colleagues, these three old men can no longer be imagined to be having a private conversation. Legislation has to take place in public.

The deliberations that lead up to specific proposals must enable not only the legislators but also their people to see the reasons for the regulations and so become more willing to obey them.[72] Laws made for a free people cannot be issued merely as commands backed up by the threat of punishment; they require persuasive preludes to obtain the voluntary compliance and cooperation of the ruled.

Making the function of their conversation thus far explicit, the Athenian informs his interlocutors that it has constituted just such a prelude. He himself has become the model of a legislator. The contrast with Socrates, who never went into the assembly to propose policies or laws, could not be more evident.

---

are difficult to combine with the claims of wisdom. Whereas the Theban poet Pindar thought that strength was most natural because it was the most universal, the Athenian suggests that the rule of the wise over the ignorant is the greatest of the claims and that the rule of law over willing subjects is most natural (for human beings?). The problem of creating a regime or *politeia* is somehow combining or coordinating these incommensurable claims.

70. Cf. England, *Laws* ad 1.714a1.

71. Morrow, *Cretan City*, 478, also emphasizes the identification between *nomos* and *nous* in the *Laws*.

72. For this reason he later suggests (*Laws* 811c–e) that a written record of their conversation become the basic educational text in the regime.

Nowhere does the Athenian differ more from Socrates, indeed, than in his emphasis on the need for "preludes," which are not arguments, proofs, or dialectical examinations of one's own opinions but persuasive speeches, often quite lengthy. In the terms of Aristotelian rhetoric, such speeches would be called deliberative. But the word "rhetoric" (*rhētorikē*) does not appear in Plato's *Laws*.[73] Unlike the poets who preceded them (cf. *Protagoras* 316d–17b), teachers of rhetoric and sophistry claimed that their knowledge was autonomous; unlike the poets, these masters of argumentation did not trace the source of their wisdom to the gods. In the *Laws* the Athenian identifies the kind of persuasive speech that should be employed in legislation with poetry, not only because he explicitly and repeatedly acknowledges the need to strengthen reason with appeals to the desire for pleasure or the aversion to pain, but also because poetry, unlike rhetoric or sophistry, does not claim to be autonomous. In contrast to Socrates in the *Republic*, in the *Laws* the Athenian does not therefore expel the poets from his city in speech.[74] On the contrary, he explicitly incorporates a certain amount of poetry subject to the control of the legislators. But he does not allow autonomous poetry, which appeals to the pleasure of the greatest number, any more than he allows forensic rhetoric into his "city in speech."

The Athenian provides an example of the kind of speech he has in mind in the prelude he addresses to the future colonists. The god he invokes in this prelude is both like and unlike Zeus and Apollo, the fabled founders of the Dorian regimes. Unlike these Olympian gods, the Athenian's deity has no name or individual personality. "The god [who] just as the ancient saying has it, holding the beginning and the end and the middle of all there is, completes his straight course by revolving, according to nature" (*Laws* 715e–16a), would appear to be like the sun or the heavens in general, moving in predictable regular motion and controlling thereby what comes into being and passes away on earth.[75] Like Zeus, the Athenian's god not only

73. The Athenian will later (*Laws* 937e) ban those who claim to possess an art that enables them to escape from punishments, whether just or unjust, without naming the so-called art.

74. Görgemanns (*Beiträge*, 56–69) does not distinguish adequately between rhetoric and poetry in emphasizing the Athenian's use and advocacy of both.

75. The Athenian blurs the difference between what he is proposing and what has been traditionally received if, as the scholiast suggests, the ancient saying to which he refers is the Orphic: "Zeus is the original cause, Zeus is the middle, from Zeus all things are created." Cf. *Laws*, Loeb ed., 293n; Pangle, *Laws*, 525; England, *Laws ad* 1.716a. One is reminded of the Heraclitean fragment, "That which alone is wise is one; it is willing and unwilling to be called by the name of Zeus";

holds all the beings together; he is also always followed by justice, even if he himself does not "personally" see that justice is done with his thunderbolts. Retribution follows almost automatically on those who forsake the divine law.[76] Swelled with hubris on account of their riches, honors, or physical beauty, they deny the need to follow the leadership of a superior intelligence and associate with others like them. As a result, like the kings of the original Dorian confederacy, they bring ruin on themselves, their families, and cities.

In the *Laws* we thus see an anonymous legislator appeal to an anonymous god. The threat to the preservation of a just and law-abiding regime appears to be the desire on the part of its leaders to attain recognition and power for themselves as individuals. The Athenian sets a contrary example. In the end (969a) he promises all the glory of founding the new community to Clinias—as a reward, it seems, for his following the prescriptions of the Athenian or *nous*.[77]

The Athenian's anonymous god is also selfless. *Nous* would certainly not be overcome by erotic passion or fight with his elders for power like the Olympian deities depicted by Homer. As the god who rules those who have minds, he loves those who are like him, the sensible and moderate (*sōphrōnes*).[78] Only such people can safely pray to the gods. As the Athenian

Kathleen Freeman, trans., *Ancilla to the Pre-Socratic Philosophers: A Complete Translation of the Fragments in Diels, "Fragmente der Vorsokratiker"* (Cambridge: Harvard University Press, 1948), 27.

76. The Athenian's statement is reminiscent of the Anaximander fragment: "And the source of coming-to-be for existing things is that into which destruction, too, happens, according to necessity; for they pay penalty and retribution to each other for their injustice according to the assessment of Time" (Kirk, Raven, and Schofield, *Presocratic Philosophers*, 118). The notion here (*Laws* 716a–b)—as opposed to what might appear to be the surface meaning of the Athenian's attempt in book 10 to show that the gods "care" about human affairs, especially the punishment of injustice—is not that personified gods take direct action to punish transgressors but rather that in the same way that things come into being and pass away as a result of natural causes, so unjust people suffer from their own actions. The Athenian is putting forth a very rational religion.

77. Nightingale points out that "the Athenian links his own legislative principles to those of Minos and Lycurgus at the same time as he disclaims his own expertise in lawgiving. . . . The Athenian . . . must speak for the ideal lawgiver (who is, after all, only a fictional presence), but he tries to avoid identifying himself with this figure" ("Literary Interpretation," 245).

78. In contrast to Socrates in the *Republic*, the Athenian does not make the way in which he is editing, censoring, and selecting from the old tales explicit, although he later explicitly urges the legislators and guardians of the laws in his regime to do so (*Laws* 802a–b). No doubt, Clinias' ignorance of the works of Homer and Hesiod makes it easier for the Athenian to revise the traditional stories without commenting on the fact that he is doing so. The Athenian does point out the difference between his teaching and that of the sophist Protagoras—without naming the latter (presumably for the sake of Plato's readers, since Clinias and Megillus cannot be imagined to be familiar with the teachings of the sophists). Playing upon the famous sayings inscribed at Delphi, Protagoras had declared that "man is the measure"; each of us knows and can only know or recognize (*gignōskō*) what he or she perceives. Consequently, Protagoras declared that he did

pointed out earlier in his analysis of the defects of the Dorian confederacy, ignorant people often pray to the gods for what they believe is good only to find that it is not, really, when their prayers are granted. *Sōphrosynē* is, moreover, the virtue Clinias has shown that he lacks. Although the initial invocation of the god is purportedly addressed to the populace of the new colony, the Athenian continues to have his old Dorian interlocutors in mind as well.

Even if the law is understood to be the dictate of intelligence for the good of everyone concerned, persuasion, if not compulsion, is necessary to get compliance. Human beings do not spontaneously move or act in an orderly or intelligible manner. They have to be taught, and reason is weak. It has to be strengthened by appeals to the desire for pleasure or the aversion to pain.

To fabricate such appeals, the Athenian suggests that legislators learn from the poets how to tailor their speeches to their audience, even though he previously had argued that legislators had to supervise the poets. As a sort of practice, he asks his interlocutors to imagine that they are addressing the legislator rather than the people. Using a poetic metaphor, he suggests that legislators who wish to see their people become free, friendly, and intelligent should not treat them the way a slave doctor treats his slave patients, by giving orders based on the experience or knowledge of others and threatening them with punishment or pain if they do not comply. Someone who wishes to make laws for a free people should proceed, instead, like a free doctor who cares for the maladies of a free people:

> by investigating their illnesses from the beginning and according to nature, communing with the patient himself and his friends, both learning himself from the invalids and teaching, as much as he can, the one who is sick. He doesn't give orders until he has in some sense persuaded; when he has on each occasion tamed the sick person with persuasion, he attempts to succeed in leading him back to health. (720d)

As the Athenian later remarks (857d), by using arguments much the way a philosopher would, the "free doctor" may appear to be teaching his

---

not and could not know whether the gods exist; that which is said to be immortal is beyond the purview of any mortal. The Athenian argues, on the contrary, that we should obey the immortal we perceive in our own minds, not that the human being as a whole or the mortal per se but that the trace of the divine we perceive partly within us, in our minds, should become the rule or "measure" for the rest.

patient to become a doctor more than curing him.[79] The doctor is not simply the equivalent of a philosopher or teacher, however. He teaches "as much as he can." His patient is sick; he may not listen to reason. In the image of the threefold legislative process the Athenian describes as "free," both the doctor (or legislator) and his patients (or people) learn to understand their own condition better by conversing with one another; among other things, the legislator (or doctor) learns how to persuade his patients (or people) to do what he recommends; only then does he formulate a set of orders, backed up by a threat of punishment. The threat nevertheless remains. If education were sufficient, no command or force would be necessary. Philosophers both teach and learn from their students as individuals in private conversation; legislators may give reasons for their commands in public, but their commands are enforced.[80]

Although the Laconic way is to favor brevity of speech, Megillus affirms that he thinks the dual mode of legislation is better. Once again he demonstrates his willingness not only to recognize the excellence of others but also to learn from them. We are surprised, therefore, to see the Athenian cut him off abruptly, if not rudely, by stating that it is stupid to argue about whether writings should be long or short.[81] Earlier (641e–42a) the Athenian had contrasted the Athenian tendency to speak at length with Spartan terseness and Cretan wiles. He is curt now because he does not want his interlocutors to mistake his central teaching about the character of legislation for a mere reflection of the differences in their respective regimes.

Although earlier the Athenian had been self-effacing, he now emphasizes the novelty of his own approach. Like songs (also *nomoi*), he points out, all speeches or arguments have introductions, "yet with regard to things that are really 'laws' [*nomoi*], . . . no one has ever either uttered a prelude or become a composer . . . as if it were a thing that did not exist in

79. This instance is one of only two occurrences of any form of the word *philosophia* in the *Laws*.

80. The Athenian does not even consider, much less rebut, the claims later made by "sophists" and "rhetoricians" that they could teach their pupils how to persuade persons to adopt whatever measures they wanted as laws, that is, that one who knows the "art" can rule completely on the basis of persuasion and hence, apparently, without any need for force. His interlocutors do not know anything about the claims made by these followers of the pre-Socratic philosophers. Because their regimes are not democratic, popular audiences do not determine what is law. Nor does the Athenian think such claims are sound. Because "human nature is not capable of regulating human things, when it possesses autocratic authority over everything, without becoming swollen with insolence and injustice" (*Laws* 713c), enforced limits will always be needed.

81. Socrates, on the other hand, often insists on brief exchanges, as we shall see in the *Protagoras* (334c–35c).

nature. But the way we've been spending our time has shown us, it seems to me, that such a thing really does exist" (722e).

If all previous legislators have proceeded like slave doctors who give orders without making the reasons for their orders clear, no previous legislation (including that of the Dorian cities) has been suitable for ruling a free people. If laws suitable for a free people are to come into existence, legislators must learn how and why they should use preludes. Because there is a reason for every law that deserves to be called such, the Athenian tells the old Dorians, every law has a prelude. "Yet, if we should ordain that every law, great or small, is to have a prelude, we would not be speaking correctly" (723c). It is not necessary to give a prelude, for example, when the reason for the command is obvious. Sometimes the people to whom the law is directed will not understand the reasons for it. The Athenian's observation that all laws do not need preludes suggests that his own explanations for the laws he will propose will not be complete. In the first and last reference to their own progress in space and time toward the "cave of Zeus" (the traditional locus of the source of divine wisdom and education of the founding legislator), the Athenian observes (722d) that it is now high noon; they have been talking since dawn. From this point on, he and his wisdom or the god (*nous*) in full sunlight will replace Zeus and the twilight of his cave as the source of the laws of the future colony.

d. The Limits of Preludes (or Persuasion)

Impatient with all the talk of gods and ancestors, Clinias breaks in and urges the Athenian to get on with it. But instead of gratifying his interlocutor's desire to move quickly to the pronouncement of the laws themselves, the Athenian gives two long monologues. Demonstrating the ways he argues a legislator must teach or persuade citizens to obey the law through his own deeds—or example—as well as speeches, the Athenian thus gives Clinias a practical lesson in self-restraint, the virtue Clinias has shown he most needs to learn if he is to give his colony better laws.[82]

---

82. The Athenian had given two versions of the law concerning marriage (*Laws* 721b–e) as an example of the difference between a simple command and a law with a prelude—the simple command that a man marry between the ages of thirty and thirty-five or pay a fine and suffer dishonor, and the dual version, in which the command is preceded by a reminder of the desire for immortality inherent in human nature that can be satisfied by leaving children behind as well as by fame. In his impatience, Clinias is perhaps demonstrating some of the homosexual proclivity for which the Athenian had criticized Cretan laws. Plato never lets his readers forget that the Athenian's immediate audience is composed of two old Dorians and that the laws of their regions do not explicitly promote moderation. These future legislators would also confront an audience

In his first long speech, the Athenian urges both his Dorian interlocutors and their future colonists to embrace moderation not merely as the best and truest way to honor their own souls, but also as the most effective way of achieving happiness. In the second he sketches a way of distributing property among citizens in a roughly equal fashion and maintaining that distribution over time in order to prevent conflict between rich and poor. As the order of the speeches suggests, the Athenian does not believe that sermons of the first variety have much effect on the opinions and desires, to say nothing of the behavior, of most people. Although preludes are necessary, the Athenian recognizes that persuasive speech alone will not suffice to institute good laws.

The way in which most people are not, but should be, self-restrained is in the acquisition of property.[83] Hence the Athenian begins, "Of all the things that belong to one, the most divine—after the gods—is the soul, that which is most one's own."[84] Echoing Clinias' initial emphasis on the importance of self-mastery, the Athenian observes, "Everyone's possessions fall into two classes. The superior and better sort are masterful, while the inferior are slavish. . . . So I speak correctly when I urge people to honor their souls second after the gods, who are masters, and those who follow after the gods" (726a). Although the Athenian does not say so explicitly, his statement suggests that neither the old Dorians nor their colonists should honor their ancestors, because their ancestors sought empire without limit. They are among those who do not assign honor correctly, because they believe that they honor themselves or their souls when they indulge their desires rather than when they seek to improve themselves.[85]

After the gods and the soul, the Athenian states, we should honor the body. And in describing the "honorable body," the Athenian makes the

---

composed, in the first place, of other Dorian elders and, later, of Dorian elders combined with younger people educated by their laws. The model of the teacher of legislators he presents is that of a superior leading inferiors. It contrasts greatly with the freedom and equality Socrates says must characterize a philosophical community of fellow inquirers.

83. Cf. Aristotle *Politics* 1257b40.

84. He emphasizes the connection to property by using the word *oikeiotaton*. As Strauss points out (*Argument and Action*, 66), the Athenian skips over parents or ancestors in saying that one's soul should be honored after the gods. His *sub silentio* replacing or writing-over of tradition continues.

85. The Athenian lists seven kinds of such false honors: the boy who brags about his ability to learn and is willing to try anything; the human being who refuses to take responsibility for his own actions and blames others; those who delight in pleasures contrary to the law; those who cannot endure hardships that are praised; those who believe that survival is the greatest good; those who honor beauty more than virtue; and those who seek ignoble gain.

character and theme of his entire long monologue clear. Contrary to what he said about the "human goods" of health, beauty, strength, and wealth at the beginning of the dialogue, he argues that the body we should honor is a middling, not a particularly healthy, beautiful, or strong one, so that possession of a praiseworthy body will not give its owner's soul occasion to become boastful or rash. He applies the same reasoning to the possession of money. Encapsulating the lesson he will state forthrightly at the end of his sermon (731e)—that excessive self-love is the source of all ignorance and injustice—he suggests that no one should seek too much of anything for him or herself.[86]

In delivering his lecture, the Athenian recognizes the limited effectiveness of all such attempts at moral suasion. Understanding that most people find deeds more persuasive than words (cf. *Apology* 32a), he observes: "What really makes a difference in education—not only of the young but of ourselves—is not so much the precepts one gives others as the way one exemplifies the precepts one would give to another, in one's conduct throughout life" (*Laws* 729b–c). Even though the Athenian had urged the colonists to honor their ancestors and bear their parents' anger, he now advises elders not to admonish their children (much less threaten them with loss of their patrimony) but "to be ashamed before the young" and to take care that they never do or say anything shameful when a young person is present (an adaptation of the Dorian law that forbids questioning of the law in the presence of the young).

The tyrant is not the only one who guides others primarily by example. The Athenian is teaching Clinias how to become a teacher of legislators (his nine colleagues), if not a legislator himself, primarily through his own example, in deed as well as in speech. Clinias will be able to persuade his fellow citizens to be moderate and just only if he himself becomes so. It is not possible to lie, even if the lie is salutary (as suggested earlier [663d]). On the contrary:

> Truth is the leader of all good things for gods, and of all things for human
> beings. Whoever is to become blessed and happy should partake of it from
> the very beginning, so that he may live as a truthful man for as long a time
> as possible. Such a man is trustworthy. The untrustworthy man is one who
> finds the voluntary lie congenial; . . . [and] every man who is untrustworthy

---

86. Readers should not forget that this fault was displayed not only by the three Dorian kings but also by Clinias.

is also ignorant and friendless. As time goes on such a man is discovered, and in the hard time of old age, near the end of life, he makes himself completely deserted, so that whether his comrades and children are living or not he lives almost as if he were an orphan. (730c)[87]

e. Inculcating Moderation by Restricting Differences in Wealth

Explicitly bringing his prelude to an end (*Laws* 734e), the Athenian appears ready to turn to the laws or the regime. Instead he turns back to the preconditions—the population and the land. As in the case of any herd, he observes, so in the case of any people, it is necessary for the legislator to purge at the outset those who cannot be reared to be healthy both in body and soul.[88] "If the same man were a tyrant as well as a lawgiver he could employ the purges that are harsh and best," that is, exile and death (735d). Since such a combination of knowledge and power is not available to them, they will have to use one of the gentler methods. Under the euphemistic name of "colonization," they will expel the have-nots ready to attack the haves.[89] The Cnossian founders of the colony are oligarchs; the reason they are establishing a new colony, we infer, is to avoid domestic unrest.

What initially appeared to be a problem of different natures and nurture in the human material with which the legislator had to deal now appears to be a problem of the extent and distribution of wealth as well as of the class conflict to which it gives rise. The legislator must attend not only to the composition of the people, in terms of their origins, and the implications of the location of the city for its economic support and defense. He also has to arrange things so his people do not come into economic or class conflict with one another; and to do that, he has to determine the number

87. The first claim about truth is said to have been borrowed from the Pythagoreans (England, *Laws ad* 1.730c1). Unlike the Pythagoreans, however, the Athenian characteristically argues on the basis of results in this life. One reason is the character of his interlocutor. Although he is old, Clinias does not appear to be as concerned with the afterlife as Socrates' elderly interlocutor, Cephalus, is in the *Republic*. Clinias is still concerned with making his mark here.

88. The Eleatic Stranger makes the same observation in the *Statesman* 308e–9a. Presuming knowledge on the part of the ruler, the Eleatic recommends the harsh but best form of purge, death.

89. The fact that Cnossus is sending out a colony suggests that its lawgivers were not able to solve or manage the problems of economic supply and distribution. If the future citizens of the colony were scheming against the oligarchy in charge of the mother city because they were unable to feed themselves, they are not apt to have a musical education, much less training in truth telling and justice. They are not apt to be well disposed, therefore, to obeying the laws of Cnossus transplanted to another location.

of citizens and the extent of the land needed to support and defend them as well as its distribution among them.[90]

The Athenian avoids the need to address the specific composition of the population of the colony by observing (736b) that they are founding it now only in speech, not in fact. He thus states a series of general considerations and recommendations without reference either to the particular people—their origin or character—or to the land. As in the prelude concerning the honoring of the soul, so he now gives another long monologue concerning the principles of an economic arrangement that would make a virtuous, law-abiding citizenry possible. (People who are starving are not apt to have time or opportunity to be virtuous, but as the Athenian points out, riches do not make people virtuous either. People gain more using a combination of just and unjust means than using only the just.) He has to give this argument on his own, because his Dorian interlocutors lack knowledge of the necessary economic arrangements as much as of the soul. By stating the necessary arrangements in general, he also avoids the need to criticize existing institutions, especially the distribution of economic goods, in Crete or Cnossus in particular.

His suggestion that there be 5,040 divisions of people and land or households seems at first to be a matter primarily of administrative convenience. He "chooses the number that has the most numerous and consecutive divisions within itself," including all integers between 1 and 10 as well as 12. "These divisions are useful in war and peace—in all contracts and associations, in revenue-gathering and disbursements" (738a). The actual division of the land into districts must not be determined simply abstractly or according to number, however. A lawgiver should not change any of the ancient shrines, sayings, or rites, but he should make sure that every group has a god or hero and establish sanctuaries in choice spots where the people will get together in celebrations at regular intervals. The purpose of such institutions is less to instill piety than to enable the people to get to know each other. "There is no greater good for a city than that its inhabitants be well known to one another; for where men's characters are obscured from one another . . . , no one ever obtains . . . the honor he deserves" (738e). The purpose of the division of the land into districts is not division

90. Because the Athenian explicitly contemplates birth control, I do not understand why Aristotle Politics 1265a38 claims that in the Laws, "Socrates" does not take account of the need to regulate population as well as the distribution of property; he does (Laws 737d, 740d–e).

for its own sake or even distribution; it is to produce certain effects on the attitudes and opinions of the citizens.

The Athenian insists that the city they are constructing is second best. In the most virtuous regime, everyone would share everything in common (as in the *Republic*), but "such a city is inhabited presumably by gods or children of gods" (*Laws* 739c–e).[91] One might be tempted to dismiss the city in which friends hold everything in common as inappropriate because impossible for humans, but, the Athenian urges, it should be the model. They will approximate this model as closely as they can by dividing up the land into equal portions of a never-changing number, to be used by the present occupant who can choose his own heir, although the land continues to belong to the city.

In contrast to the practice of most cities now, the Athenian emphasizes, they are not trying to make the city or its citizens as rich as possible; that would encourage citizens to be unjust, to gain at the expense of others. He proposes a series of measures designed to preserve the original distribution, but, he admits, it is impossible to maintain complete equality.[92] Different colonists will bring different goods with them; some will use their resources better than others. The best a lawgiver can do is to limit the inequality. No one should be allowed to amass more than four times the basic allotment; if someone does, the surplus should go to the city. As in ancient Athens (698b), there will be four classes. For the sake of administrative efficiency and defense, the city should be located as close to the center of the territory as possible, and the land should be divided into

91. This is one of the two basic reasons later readers have concluded that the *Laws* follows the *Republic*. Cf. England, *Laws* 1.4. It is important to remember, therefore, that Pythagoras had also asked the members of his community (sect or school) to share their property. In the *Republic* Socrates suggests that all three of his most radical suggestions—that women receive the same education and hold the same offices as men, that all things be held in common, and that philosophers become kings—will arouse "waves" of laughter, but that the third will arouse most. Glaucon adds (474a) that the third, the proposal that seems to be the only one unique to Socrates, will also arouse hostility.

92. To keep the number and extent of the landholding households the same, children who do not inherit are to be married off or adopted by other families. If too many are born, means of preventing or aborting births can be used. The city could also send out a colony. To keep the divisions of the land the same, occupants will not be allowed to buy or sell them. Commercial enterprise or moneymaking is generally to be discouraged. As in Sparta, residents will need a medium of exchange, but it should be a kind that can only be used locally. The city will have gold to use in foreign affairs, but any citizen found hoarding it in private will be punished. To maintain as much economic equality as possible and so to prevent disputes and lawsuits from arising, no one will be allowed to give a dowry or to loan funds at interest (*Laws* 740b–42c).

twelve parts, radiating from the center. Each part should be equal to the others in productivity but not necessarily, therefore, in size. The people should also be divided into twelve parts. The land should then be divided into 5,040 allotments and each of these allotments cut in two, so that every household can have one place near the center of the city and one at the periphery. All will feel equally involved in the defense and maintenance of all.

Reminding Plato's readers, if not his interlocutors, of the general rather than specific character of his recommendations, the Athenian emphasizes that these things may never come to pass. They may not be possible under the circumstances; the citizens may not accept the restrictions he has recommended on money or childbirth. He has been talking "as if he were telling dreams or molding a city and citizens from wax" (746a–b).

By having the Athenian reiterate the utility of mathematics not merely for administering the city but for the education of citizens—"both the variations that exist within numbers themselves and also those that exist in plane and solid figures, in sounds, and in motions" (747a)—Plato reminds his readers that the old Dorians do not possess the education the Athenian has indicated would be required for citizens of his regimes, much less its lawgivers. The old Dorians lack the requisite knowledge of mathematics, he intimates (747c), because their regimes suspect that the study of calculation leads to illiberality and the love of money. They must take measures to prevent such a distortion and misuse of mathematical studies in the city they are founding. The Athenian underlines the inadequacy of his interlocutors' education and knowledge when, addressing them by name, he reminds them that "some places differ from one another in their tendency to breed better and worse human beings, and such factors shouldn't be defied when one makes laws. All sorts of winds and different exposures to the sun can presumably make places unfavorable or favorable, as can the local waters, and the type of plants" (747d). To found and maintain the regime he has recommended, lawmakers would have to study not only mathematics but also natural science. Relatively early in this dialogue, readers are thus shown that this "city in speech" is no more apt to come into being through the action immediately contemplated by those who listen to the suggested innovations than the "city in speech" sketched in the *Republic*. Its founders do not have the requisite knowledge. In the next section the Athenian tells his interlocutors that their laws will thus need to be modified by those who come later.

2. THE REGIME: FURTHER PROBLEMS CONFRONTING THE LEGISLATOR

a. Transitional Officeholders

The Athenian emphasizes the difficulty of founding again when he turns to the regime itself—the offices and the laws that the various officers will administer. The colonists will not be apt to know each other and thus will be unable to select those who will guide them wisely. Those who are selected will not have been raised under the laws, and so will be ill prepared to apply and preserve them.

The first "solution" the Athenian proposes seems obviously impractical: he and his elderly interlocutors must somehow manage to stay alive (and in control) until the first generation of youths has been educated under their laws and thus has been prepared to maintain them.[93] Admitting the impossibility of that conceit (which in harshness falls short of Socrates' proposal to expel all people more than ten years of age from his city but has the same rationale and function), the Athenian next proposes that half of the first "guardians," including Clinias, be sent from the mother city Cnossus and given to the new colony. Clinias asks why he should be given and not Megillus or the Athenian himself, and the Athenian suggests that the founding of this new colony is not terribly important to anyone outside of Crete.[94] What is important is the model of founding and the laws formulated, as well as the reasons for them. Having set out the way the colonists ought to select their most outstanding citizens to "guard" or maintain the laws, the Athenian makes a concession to Clinias' unwillingness to move by allowing the Cnossian founders to return to their own city after they help the colonists select their first guardians.[95] Readers see an example of the problem the Athenian is describing. He has not yet succeeded in transferring the allegiance of his interlocutors from their native cities to the colony they are founding. He has to make the project

93. Impossible or not, the Athenian's final suggestion that they attempt to institute the Nocturnal Council in order to establish and then to preserve the laws of the city amounts to a return to this first suggestion.

94. "Athens thinks big—as does Sparta. And both are far away, while for you it is convenient" (*Laws* 753a).

95. Morrow (*Cretan City*, 204–5) takes the fact that the Athenian suggests two different ways of selecting the first guardians as an indication that the text was not finished. He thinks that Plato had not decided which to keep and which to excise. Morrow does not see the reason for the two suggestions, because he does not see the problem of succession to which the Athenian was responding.

more attractive to them, if he and they are truly to found a new kind of regime.

b. Imperfect Justice in the Allocation of Offices or Honors

Once again the Athenian thus emphasizes the difficulties they will encounter (and so the potential glory of overcoming them). Not only are the foundations of the regime or its first governors almost necessarily defective, because they lack knowledge of, and education by, the laws, but the justice of every appointment thereafter will necessarily also fall short of political justice, strictly understood. The ancient saying that equality breeds friendship is true, but it is important to understand what kind of equality is meant. It is not the equality used in measuring the length and weight of things but what Aristotle later calls proportional equality: "greater honors [should] always [go] to those who are greater in virtue" (757c). Nonetheless, the Athenian acknowledges, political communities have to blur the distinction between giving each his or her due and treating all citizens as equals if they are to avoid civil war. Equal or stable distribution of property will not suffice, because some citizens desire honor as well.[96] In the city they are founding, pure recognition of merit will thus have to be qualified by having the highest officials elected by their inferiors in virtue— and, in some cases, by lot.[97] For some offices, considerations of merit are

96. Cf. Aristotle *Politics* 1267a2. Once more the Pythagorean precedent may be instructive. In Croton the democratic opposition was organized by a man named Cylon who had reputedly been denied admission to the sage's school.

97. The electorate differs from office to office. In the case of the highest officials, called guardians of the laws, people who have borne heavy arms first nominate (and then challenge) 300 candidates. These are reduced to 100 and then to 37 by another series of challenges and elections. Military officers are then nominated by the guardians but can be challenged by anyone who has taken part in war or is ready to do so; these past or potential soldiers then select from the nominees by voting. Members of the council are nominated and elected according to their economic class; those who are wealthiest are penalized for not voting, whereas the poorest are excused from some elections. Priests and priestesses are selected either by heredity or lot, because both processes are believed to be controlled by the gods. Since everything and everyone must be watched or guarded to the greatest extent possible, there must be public supervision and hence supervisors of all areas—city, country, and market. City supervisors, country supervisors, and market supervisors are selected from the wealthiest classes by a combination of election and lot. Everyone is required to vote, and all citizens are allowed to attend the assembly (which would hear reports from the part of the council receiving foreign emissaries), but only members of the two wealthiest classes are penalized for not attending. Officials in charge of musical and gymnastic contests are selected by a combination of election and lot. At one end of the spectrum, the most important official of all, the supervisor of education, is elected by the other magistrates for a five-year term. At the other end, as many citizens as possible are to be made jurors, because those who do not share in the right of judging do not consider themselves to share in the city (*Laws* 768b).

further reduced or qualified by the requirement that candidates come from specified economic classes, especially the two wealthiest.[98]

c. The Need to Adapt "Unchanging" Laws to Changing Circumstances

Because they are elderly, the Athenian reminds his interlocutors (770b–c), they will need to make the guardians of the laws (*nomophylakes*) they have selected to carry out their provisions into legislators (*nomothetai*) as well. Application or enforcement of established laws in changing circumstances is apt gradually to change them. To prevent corruption of the laws through gradual, unnoticed deviations, the guardians must understand the end or purpose. Every effort ought to be directed toward enabling every member of the community—male or female, young or old—to acquire the virtue of soul that befits a human being (and so to become a good man [*anēr agathos*]) by any possible means. Nothing is to be given precedence over this end—not even the preservation of the city itself (770d).

Clearly the means of educating people to become virtuous, that is, the city and its laws, cannot be rationally substituted or preferred to the end. Yet the difficulty remains. Those with the power or authority to establish the city (Clinias and his colleagues, for example) have not received such an education to virtue. If political associations are ever to achieve their goals, some one will not merely have to persuade human beings with less than full virtue or knowledge to institute laws different from those under which they have lived. Lacking the necessary education, these founders will indubitably make mistakes or miss things. Their works will have to be corrected by those who follow them, but those followers will have also grown up under partly defective laws. It appears to be impossible ever to establish a perfect set of laws, much less to maintain them over time in practice. The need to educate potential legislators and the necessarily defective character of their education persist.[99]

---

98. When the Athenian states, "This selection procedure would strike a mean between a monarchic and a democratic regime, which is the mean the regime should always aim for" (*Laws* 756e), we see that the "monarchic" principle he saw represented in Persia was not so much the rule of one as the rule of those who acquire power as a result of their own virtue, and not because they are children of the previous emperor. As Aristotle observes in *Politics* 1266a5, there is no "monarchical" principle or rule of one in the city the Athenian sketches—unless one attributes that "role" or function to the god or *nous*. As Aristotle argues at the end of book 3 of the *Politics*, the rule of law is incompatible with, and inferior to, the rule of a completely virtuous and wise human being. In contrast to the Spartan kings, no offices in the Athenian's city in speech are reserved or restricted to a specific group of citizens by heredity or birth.

99. When the Athenian turns back to what he now calls "the beginning of their laws" with the sacred, the division of the land into 5,040 segments, he thus points out the slightly defective

d. Problems Posed by Generation

The problem confronting legislators, in a word, is generation. That problem takes several different forms.

First and most obviously, the fact that there are generations means not only that the composition or people of the city is continually changing. Knowledge distilled from past experience has to be communicated to present and future generations in a way that enables them to pursue virtue under changing circumstances. A literal or mechanical application of the laws will not suffice; some members of the next generation must learn to be prudent.

Second, future generations have to be conceived. But conception requires the conjunction of male and female, and so maintaining a difference between the sexes that an education in virtue appears designed to overcome by making members of both sexes as alike as possible. There appears, indeed, to be a tension between the end of the city, making everyone—both male and female—as virtuous as possible, and one of the basic requirements of preserving the city—reproduction. This tension is reflected in a series of vacillations in the Athenian's later specifications of the educational regime. At times he insists that males and females be treated exactly the same way; at other times he suggests that females should perform only the gymnastic exercises to which they are inclined (cf. *Laws* 794d, 795d, 796c, 802a, 804d–5c). Women are excluded from military service and other public offices during their childbearing years. They do not participate in public life in the same way or to the same extent as men.[100]

The requirements of procreation pose another sort of difficulty for the legislator. Among human beings, the sexual urge is not simply instinctive or automatic. Coitus does not occur on command. Human desire must be aroused, then directed and controlled. As the law requiring men to marry by age thirty-five indicates, all are not so inclined. Nor are all humans sexually attracted to each other, equally and indifferently. Marriages in this city are arranged by families or households, but the Athenian suggests that allowances should be made for individual inclinations. At the monthly celebrations that enable citizens to get to know each other, youths are to dance

---

character of the number or division; it can be evenly divided by all numbers between 1 and 12, except 11 (*Laws* 771b–c). There is no perfectly rational order or arrangement of the land and people in a city. Cf. Benardete, *Laws*, 176–82.

100. Cf. Michael S. Kochin, *Gender and Rhetoric in Plato's Political Thought* (Cambridge: Cambridge University Press, 2002), 88–90, 94–96.

as scantily clad as possible within the bounds of modesty, so that they and their families can select mates more knowledgeably. Both individuals and families should be admonished not to marry on the basis of wealth. Citizens should be encouraged to mate with those of opposite dispositions (as in the *Statesman*, the courageous and hasty with the moderate and slow) in order to give the city's people an evenly balanced temperament. In contrast to the explicit teachings of both Socrates in the *Republic* and the Eleatic Stranger in the *Statesman*, however, the Athenian recognizes that such policies cannot be legislated. People would not merely find it ridiculous to prohibit the children of the rich from marrying the rich; they would get angry at the attempt to force them to mate with their opposites—in character even more than in wealth.[101]

(I) REGULATING PRIVATE RELATIONS BETWEEN THE SEXES: HOW TO USE AND MAINTAIN SHAME. Once married couples form separate units with their own houses and servants, the problem of public regulation of private behavior becomes even more severe, because most people will resist invasions of their privacy (*Laws* 799e). Nevertheless, the Athenian states, "whoever leaves private things unregulated by law and believes the people will be willing to live with the common and public things regulated by the laws is incorrect" (780a). The problem the Athenian has already noted in the case of the selection of mates is that private desires and acts cannot be subjected entirely to command or compulsion.

In Sparta, public regulation of men's behavior did not prevent women from becoming licentious in private. In Crete, separation of the sexes fostered pederasty. The Athenian's educational proposals are designed primarily to counteract, if not entirely to overcome, the most notable vices of the cities from which his interlocutors come. He seeks cautiously and gradually to loosen the old Dorians' attachment to the laws of their own cities by leading them to contemplate even better arrangements. He does

---

101. Generation also appears to be the source of corruption and decay of the best regime in the *Republic* (546a–47d). Socrates traces the corruption, however, to the guardians' "forgetting" or inability to calculate the "nuptial number." The existence of such a number assumes that the elements to be combined can be reduced somehow to commensurable units. The Athenian does not suggest that there is a numerical solution to the problem of generation. He treats it more in terms of the pre-Socratic concern with the attraction of like to like, along with the mutual repulsion of opposites, which are apt to produce an imbalance by concentrating everything of one kind in one place, in the absence of art. The art with which the Athenian tries to remedy the imbalance that would occur in the population if like were able to follow its natural inclination to marry and mate with like, moreover, is the art of persuasion, and the Athenian explicitly recognizes that the power of the art of persuasion or poetry in this area is limited.

not initially associate resistance to public regulation with male sexual desire so much as with female weakness. Turning from the critique of Sparta implicit in the admonitions and regulations designed to prevent the concentration of wealth in a few families through marriage, a critique that becomes explicit in his discussion of the treatment of slaves, the Athenian pacifies Megillus by praising his city's policy of not relying on fortifications but rather on the training of men to defend it.[102] The common meals that contribute to this training were probably discovered by accident, but they were preserved when people saw how much they contributed to the common defense. Although no one has yet proposed it, the Athenian suggests that common meals should be extended to women as well. A city that does not train half its citizens to contribute to its defense is weakened by half.

To show that such regulation might be possible, the Athenian asks Clinias and Megillus to consider how much human life has changed and varied over time: in some places human beings have eaten others, like animals; in other places, they have abstained from meat entirely. Although he does not say so explicitly, the same range of behavior might be found in human sexual relations, varying from complete abstinence to omnivoracity (including bestiality as well as homosexuality). The only things that remain constant in human life are the three basic desires for food, drink, and sex and the three checks on those desires—fear, law, and true reasoning (*logos*).

The problem that becomes evident in the educational practices the Athenian advocates is that the gymnastic training intended to make citizens virtuous by overcoming their native or primal fear (790e–91a) necessarily weakens one of the three basic checks on human desire—shame. At

---

102. The critique of Sparta with regard to slavery occurs when Megillus briefly reenters the conversation at 776b and is addressed explicitly, along with Clinias, by the Athenian at 778d and 780e. The Athenian explains that there is a controversy concerning the proper way to manage slaves. Because human beings resist enslavement, some argue that masters should treat them harshly. In light of the revolts of the Helots in Sparta and the fact that slaves are members of the household who have, upon occasion, proved themselves more reliable than other members of the family, however, others urge kindness. Rather than endorse either the harsh or the kind extreme, the Athenian characteristically advocates moderation—for the sake of the masters more than the slaves themselves. Citizens should not learn to be arrogant in their treatment of their inferiors. But he insists that they should not destroy the order of the household or discipline by treating their servants as equals or joking with them. Although he advocates moderation, the Athenian does not propose any explicit legal restriction on the force a master may use in disciplining his own slaves. Having criticized Spartan slavery, the Athenian nevertheless praises the absence of walls in Sparta (778b). He also notes his own inability to follow an entirely rational order in presenting the stages or steps whereby a city is established. There cannot be households without houses, but he has treated the parts of the household and their relations with one another before he has dealt with the buildings. A reader might ask whether there can or should be houses before there are people.

the beginning of their conversation, the Athenian admitted that reason is weak, so laws become effective only by combining reason with pleasure or pain. Since food, drink, and sex are all sources of pleasure, the strengthening of true reasoning in the form of law or public opinion had to come from pain—the pain of public disapprobation or actual, physical penalties designed to make that disapproval effective. But, as the Athenian pointed out early in their conversation (646e–47b), shame (*aidōs*) is a kind of fear. To the extent to which citizens become courageous and hence able not only to endure physical pain but also to overcome their fear of public disapprobation, they are apt to become shameless or immodest.[103]

The Athenian attempts to prevent training in courage from producing shameless behavior in two ways. First, although he prescribes the same exercises for both men and women (at times), he separates the sexes from age six onward. Further measures are necessary, however. Separation of the sexes may seriously hamper, if it does not altogether prevent, shameless heterosexual behavior, but members of the two sexes must eventually be publicly exposed to the sight of others in order to choose mates. Members of the two sexes cannot therefore remain entirely segregated from each other. As we are reminded in the discussion of erotic relations that follows the description of the education, moreover, separation of the sexes does not prevent and may even encourage homosexual attraction or desire.[104] To prevent citizens from behaving shamelessly when he makes their life as public or common as possible, the Athenian attempts to transform the shame human beings feel in the sight of others into shame or an admission of their inferiority in the sight of god.

(2) SUPERVISING THE BEHAVIOR OF WOMEN AND CHILDREN. Virtuous acts are not truly virtuous if they are coerced (cf. *Laws* 730b, 822d–23a), which is the reason education for virtue cannot be a matter of law (*nomos*), strictly speaking. Like the attempts to persuade but not force people to marry those of opposing dispositions and fortunes, the recommendations the

103. Fear of shame may lead males particularly to act courageously, but courage may make members of either sex indifferent to shame.

104. Whereas Megillus explicitly objects to the Athenian's denigration of his city when the Athenian points out that none of the attempts to give women a different regime than men—in Thrace by making them shepherds or farmworkers, that is, the equivalent of slaves, in Athens by making them stewards of the household, or in Sparta by giving them the same education but not the same public, military responsibilities as adults—has worked (805d–6c), Clinias refuses to state his own opinion when Megillus and the Athenian agree that homosexual relations must be banned (842a).

Athenian makes concerning the conception, nurturing, and education of children take the form of admonitions or adages, exhortations, and threats of dishonor by exclusion from ceremonies rather than trials for illegal acts followed by punishments.

Women and children are to be watched by public officials, not only during common meals but also in their homes. Female officials appointed by the guardians of the laws will visit the homes of young married couples "and by exhortations and threats prevent them from doing anything wrong or foolish" (*Laws* 784c). If the female officials don't succeed, they will report to the guardians of the laws, and if the guardians don't succeed in persuading the young couples to do their duty, their failure to reform these individuals will be made public. Neither publicity nor command suffices to regulate the nurture of infants once born, however. Nurses would not merely laugh but refuse to obey laws ordering them to soothe the fears of the newborn by singing lullabies and rocking or walking them. Lawgivers should nevertheless attempt to persuade masters and free citizens to adopt and enforce such policies on their own.

Public supervision and instruction of children are to begin explicitly at age three. The female inspectors are to appoint others to collect and supervise the games of those children aged three to six years old at district temples. From the ages of six to sixteen or twenty, young women are to be gathered together to learn the same sorts of military exercises—horseback riding, archery, javelin throwing, sling, and use of heavy arms—that boys do. Youths of both sexes are to learn to dance, fully armed, arrayed with weapons, and accompanied by horses, in the processions in honor of the gods. Once the appropriate exercises and songs have been determined by the lawgiver or appropriately educated elders, they should be sanctified and never changed.

(3) REPLACING LAWS WITH SONGS OR "PLAY." "Our songs [*nomoi*] have become laws [*nomoi*]," the Athenian announces (*Laws* 799e), which is as much as to say that our laws have become songs.[105] Rather than slavishly ordering the lives of citizens with commands backed up by the threat of the use of force (like Dorian regimes in the past), legislators for the new colony will train citizens to take pleasure in performing their civic duties. "Playing at

---

105. As Pangle notes, "The Greek word for law, *nomos*, was also the word for a form of poetry, a song sung by a chorus or by soloists to the accompaniment of the kithara. (Cf. 700b)" (*Laws*, 526).

certain games—sacrificing, singing, and dancing—they will make the gods propitious; as a result, the city will be able to defend itself and be victorious over its enemies in battle" (803e).

Citizens of the new city may believe that they are victorious because their prayers have been answered, but the Athenian has clearly shown that they will be able to defend themselves because they are constantly practicing the requisite skills. There is a reason for the practices he recommends that goes beyond worship or even a successful defense of the city, however. Citizens acquire moderation or self-restraint as a result not only of the restrictions put upon their imagination and desires, but also of the inculcation of the notion that their fate, both as individuals and as a community, depends not on their own resources or intelligence but on the favor of the gods.

If human beings were as malleable as the Athenian suggested in his account of the variations in food (782a–83a) and training in ambidexterity (794d–95d), such a regime could be established. But the Athenian gives us several reasons to doubt it. First, it is more difficult to prevent any change from occurring in the songs, games, or practices than the Athenian admits here. In his first discussion of music (796e), he had also praised the Egyptian practice of sanctifying songs in order to prevent change (656d–57a), but in that earlier discussion he observed that the "singing . . . must in one way or another be continually changing, presenting variety in every way, so that the singers will take unsatiated pleasure in their hymns" (665c). In making their songs into laws, the Athenian does not allow for the need to vary them in order to prevent citizens from becoming satiated or bored. Perhaps he counts on the games being ever new for new generations. In describing the early games of children, he admits that there is a natural tendency to invent or change, an observation suggesting that the supervision of the nurses might be more repressive than it first seems. The Athenian also raises questions about the extent of human malleability when he insists (802e) on the importance of distinguishing between the gentle, moderate songs fitting for females and the splendid, brave tunes fitting for males. Just as it is necessary to preserve two different sexes to propagate future generations, so the city needs citizens who have two opposed dispositions. The city will not survive if all citizens become the same.[106]

---

106. Aristotle takes his primary criticism of Plato in *Politics* 1260b36–61a32, it seems, from Plato himself. Cf. Michael S. Kochin, "The Unity of Virtue and the Limitations of Magnesia," *History of Political Thought* 19, no. 2 (1998): 125–41.

If citizens could be trained or conditioned to become as fearless and self-less as the Athenian's image of the city at play suggests, moreover, neither courage nor moderation would be a virtue.[107]

e. Intellectual Instruction

In book 3 the Athenian argued that political associations must seek, above all, to develop the intelligence of their citizens, but he has not thus far included such an understanding in the education of the citizens of this regime. He has treated them as puppets of the gods. He explicitly acknowledges the need for instruction in writing, music, and mathematics only after Megillus vociferously protests the Athenian's suggestion that human beings confuse what is truly serious with what is not by treating war (or other issues of life and death) as serious rather than the god, which, being eternal, is the only truly serious thing (803c–e), as demeaning of the race.[108]

(1) WHY TEACHERS MUST BE "STRANGERS." Instruction in letters and numbers introduces a "foreign" element into a Dorian regime. From the very beginning of the dialogue, the Athenian's emphasis on the importance of educating intelligent citizens has been contrasted with the Dorian emphasis on the importance of winning wars. We have already seen some of the reasons the founder of the regime would need to have a broader education and experience than was possible in existing Dorian cities. It is not clear, however, why the Athenian says that instructors after the founding should continue to be foreigners. According to the admonition the Athenian gave the elders about providing good examples for the young, it seems that teachers should also exemplify the excellence to be fostered by the education they claim to provide. The Athenian insists, however, that citizens are to devote every waking moment to acquiring virtue. All necessary but not inherently choiceworthy functions in this regime must therefore be

---

107. The Athenian states (*Laws* 800b–802a) that the songs should never include dirges or lamentations, which suggest that death is bad or that good people can suffer evil; either or both might arouse fear or the suspicion that the gods are not kind. All songs must, rather, take the form of prayers. Poets must be supervised to make sure that their songs are prayers, that they are prayers for what is truly good, and that they honor the gods, demigods, and dead heroes. As in the tragedies, no one can be considered truly good or happy (and worthy of honor in song) until his or her life has come to an end. Again, he worries that they will be thought ridiculous in their attempt to specify the content of (frivolous or unserious) songs.

108. The Athenian here displays the same tendency to denigrate the merely "ephemeral" in seeking knowledge of, if not union with, the eternally unchanging that Aristophanes ridicules in the "pre-Socratic" sophist "Socrates" in the *Clouds*.

performed by slaves or foreigners. So long as there is nothing like a philo-sophical community of friends, instruction is for the sake of students, not the teachers. The latter must therefore be justly compensated for their ser-vice with pay.[109] But the fact that the teachers remain foreigners indicates that the necessary intellectual development has not yet been fully inte-grated into the regime.[110]

(2) LITERACY AND THE INTRODUCTION OF THE *LAWS* AS A TEXT. To be-come truly virtuous, citizens require instruction in reading and writing, music, and mathematics. But the question immediately arises with regard to writing: what text or texts should citizens be allowed to read? Nothing could serve better as a paradigm of the kind of writing that should be allowed, the Athenian suggests, than a record of their conversation. By re-quiring instructors to know the text themselves (by testing them on it) and to teach it, knowledge of the fundamental principles of the regime will be incorporated into their city in speech.

The difficulties inherent in this proposal begin to become evident if we ask who is to recall this conversation, much less to record it in writing. Only if Megillus and Clinias succeed in compelling the Athenian to stay, as Megillus suggests at the end of the dialogue (*Laws* 969c), could he relate this long conversation to someone else (as Socrates does at the end of the *Protagoras*) or review the written record and check for errors (as Socrates is said to have done in the *Theaetetus*). Neither of the old Dorians will be able to remember all the arguments with sufficient precision or in sufficient detail. Nor would most citizens who had studied reading for a mere three years between ages ten and thirteen be able to read and comprehend the founding document.

"It is dangerous to imbue children with much learning" (811b). This is presumably a second reason to have foreigners as instructors; as resi-dent aliens they will have to leave after twenty years (that is, within one generation). Nothing between complete conditioning or supervision and complete understanding is to be allowed in this city. Anything in between

109. We can and should note the contrast with Socrates, who in his *Apology* says emphatically that he never taught anyone anything and hence did not take pay.

110. Without some explicitly intellectual development, the Athenian admits (*Laws* 807a–b), the feasting, singing, and dancing citizens of his regime, whose necessities are provided for by foreigners and slaves, might be compared to animals being fattened like cows for sacrifice.

might lead a citizen to question the laws without understanding the reasons for them. In this city it begins to appear that there will be a small group of guardians who understand the reasons for the laws and another, much larger group of citizens who basically do as they are told.

(3) MUSIC: THE *LAWS* AS THE BEST AND NOBLEST TRAGEDY. Like literacy, the Athenian suggests, the musical training all citizens receive should be restricted. By learning how to play simple melodies between ages thirteen and sixteen, they will not become skilled performers so much as good judges of the performances of others. In music as in literary productions, the Athenian distinguishes the recipients from the originators.

The distinction between audience and performance leads him to reconsider a part of the citizens' gymnastic training in dance as well. There are different kinds of dance: noble, shameful, and ecstatic. The Athenian excludes the latter, disorderly and frenzied movements, because they are entirely apolitical. Somewhat surprisingly in light of the previous emphasis on restricting poets, the Athenian argues that the citizens should watch shameful, comic choral performances. "For someone who is going to become prudent can't learn the serious things without learning the laughable, or, for that matter, anything without its opposite" (816d–e). They are to learn only as spectators, however. Citizens should not imitate and thus risk acquiring base habits; comedies may be performed only by slaves or foreigners. It is not clear whether "serious" plays will be allowed.

The Athenian responds most explicitly to Megillus' objection to his demeaning of the human race when he tells serious poets, whom he describes as "divine men" and "best of strangers" and addresses as "friends," that he and his Dorian colleagues are also poets who "have to the best of our ability created a tragedy that is the noblest and best." Their city in speech is a poetic work inasmuch as it is an imitation intended to persuade its audience that it represents "the noblest and best way of life" (817b). That life does not belong to an individual, as in most of the tragedies that have come down to us, so much as to a community. Earlier the Athenian had described life in this city as play—sacrificing, singing, and dancing in honor of the god—in choruses. Now he describes his work as serious poetry or tragedy, perhaps because it incorporates an understanding of the incompletely rational character of political, if not human life. In contrast to the tragedies written by other poets, the Athenian's play does not depict the desirability of achieving unlimited power or wealth—tyranny—nor does it make the pleasure of the majority the standard of excellence (cf. *Laws* 658d). Insofar as the other tragic poets say something different, he concludes, their works will not be admitted.

(4) MATHEMATICS: EXPLICITLY DIVIDING THE FEW FROM THE MANY. The difference between what a few and most citizens will learn becomes explicit in the case of mathematics. All citizens need to know enough about numbers and calculation, geometry, and astronomy to tell time, keep track of the calendar, and undertake military operations. Only a few need to study lines, figures, and volumes to determine which are commensurable and which not.[111] Not everything can be measured, at least not according to a common standard of measurement.[112] But the few who become learned about the orbits of the "gods," the sun and moon, have to learn, contrary to current Greek opinion, that their courses are regular (and hence mathematically calculable).[113] In striking contrast to Socrates in the *Republic*, however, the Athenian does not proceed to argue that these few must ascend from what are there five and here three kinds of mathematical studies to engage in dialectics.[114] The word does not even occur in the *Laws*.

---

111. Planinc (*Prudence*, 161) ignores this distinction in arguing that the city depicted in the *Laws* is intended by Plato to be simply the best. Much of Bobonich's argument that Plato, in his *Laws*, concedes that nonphilosophers can become virtuous also depends on Bobonich's assertion (*Utopia* 107–9, 200, 392, 572n57) that all citizens will receive "sophisticated" instruction in mathematics and astronomy, even though Bobonich admits that the Athenian says (*Laws* 818a) only a few will be required to study these subjects precisely—as if there could be "sophisticated" instruction in mathematics that was not precise.

112. In other words, the Athenian Stranger is not as close to the Pythagoreans as Timaeus is, at least according to Taylor, in *Commentary on Plato's "Timaeus."* He wants the educated few to know that the world is not simply and completely organized by number. In the *Meno* Socrates gives a slave boy (!) a similar lesson. Socrates does not restrict the audience for his teaching the way the Athenian does.

113. As Morrow points out (*Cretan City*, 482), the mathematics required to show that the orbits are regular are complex. Erich Frank, *Plato und die Sogenannten Pythagoreer* (Halle: Niemeyer, 1923), 15, argues that the necessary proofs were not developed until Plato's time. As we have seen, claims about the entirely nonmathematical character of pre-Platonic Pythagoreans have been strenuously challenged by other scholars. The Athenian's call for a proof of the mathematical regularity of the motions of the heavenly bodies may be the first, but it will by no means be the only historical improbability, if not sheer impossibility readers encounter in Plato's corpus. He gives his readers many reminders that the dialogues are products of the imagination and not historical reports of actual events.

114. The types of mathematical study are grouped in the *Laws* according to their use or practically relevant lesson; in the *Republic* they are grouped more precisely according to the character of the object of study. Both Laszlo Versenyi, "The Cretan Plato," *Review of Metaphysics* 15, no. 1 (September 1961): 74; and Gerhard Müller, *Studien zu den Platonischen Nomoi* (Munich: C. H.

f. The Limits of Education through Play

Postponing until the very end of their conversation his discussion of the education of those few who will preserve the laws, the Athenian turns to a summary description of the festivals the city will organize. And in his description of these festivals, the fundamental tensions or problems within the educational regime he has described come explicitly to the fore.

(I) OVERCOMING THE FEAR OF DEATH WITH WAR GAMES. The first concerns fear of death. In the scheduling and dedication of the festivals, the Athenian urges, the gods of the underworld should be kept separate from the heavenly and their celebrations relegated to the twelfth, Pluto's month. Such a separation, with its implicit contrast of light and dark, is not intended to suggest that death is bad. "Warlike human beings should not abhor such a god; they should rather honor him as being always the best for the human race, because, I would seriously affirm, for soul and body, community is not superior to dissolution" (*Laws* 828d).[115] Nevertheless, in describing the war games in which citizens should engage during the festivals, at least monthly, the Athenian insists that the contestants should be heavily armed with lethal weapons, so that "the play they engage in with one another will not be altogether lacking in fear, and through the fear it will in a certain way make apparent who has a stout soul and who does not" (830e). Courage in the face of death is not much of a virtue if death is not fearful.

No one has ever suggested that a city continually stage armed battles of citizens to keep them prepared to defend the city from foreign aggression, the Athenian acknowledges. Other cities have not adopted such a practice for two reasons: (1) in most polities citizens are too busy trying to enrich themselves to devote full time to military preparedness for the common defense; and (2) in all other regimes, the (self-interested) ruling party fears rebellion on the part of the ruled too much to arm and train them to fight in opposition to other citizens. By instituting strict limits on the acquisition of wealth and providing for the necessities of all citizens, their regime

---

Beck Verlag, 1951), 22–28, also emphasize the absence of dialectics in the *Laws* in contrasting the education the Athenian suggests with that which Socrates proposes in the *Republic*.

115. As readers of the Platonic dialogues know, Socrates makes a similar affirmation on the last day of his life; in the *Republic* he also argues against the rationality of a fear of death.

will escape the major source of faction in the conflict between the rich and poor. Their regime will be able, therefore, to inculcate courage in an unprecedented fashion by sponsoring armed battles between groups of citizens.

(2) THE DIFFICULTY OF REGULATING HUMAN EROS BY LAW. The erotic desires of human beings are not so easily or effectively restrained as their economic desires. Limits on the acquisition of wealth and public supervision, along with the requirement of continuous gymnastic training and the honors given to those who win athletic contests, will not suffice to prevent homosexuality or adultery, even though a law that prohibited them would be according to nature (*Laws* 836c, 839a–b). By nature, sexual intercourse results in procreation, but human sexual desire is not regulated by nature. Human beings do not regard the behavior of lesser animals as exemplary; even though there is no lawgiver or community that considers homosexual or adulterous love manly and so tries to encourage it, such intercourse regularly occurs. The Athenian first claims to have an art (*technē*) that would persuade human beings to refrain from extramarital intercourse as they now do from incest—by declaring it abhorrent not merely in the sight of other people but to the gods. Nevertheless, he finally admits, rigorous gymnastic training (which leads some athletes to abstain from sexual relations), an appeal to people's pride (by observing that they ought to be able to order their own lives as well as birds), and the declaration that such behavior is impious may not suffice to control the erotic impulses of a passionate youth. If their citizens "become corrupted by the other Greeks and most of the barbarians" (840e), the guardians of the laws will have to lay down a second law: sexual desire should never be indulged without shame. In support of such a law, guardians could appeal to citizens' reverence for the gods, love of honor, and desire not merely for the body but for nobility of soul in the beloved. Such an appeal might be considered a prayer more than a command. The only regulation the guardians could enforce is

> either that no one is to dare to touch any well-born and free person except the woman who is his wife, and no one is to sow unhallowed, bastard sperm in concubines or go against nature and sow sterile seed in males; or we should abolish erotic activity between males altogether, and in the case of women, if anyone should have sexual intercourse with someone other than those who enter his house with . . . the sacred marriage ceremony . . . and

fails to escape notice, . . . he should be barred from all honors in the city on the grounds that he is really a stranger. (841d–e)[116]

In both versions of the law, bodily intercourse between males is forbidden. In the first, male friendships for the sake of improving the souls of the friends would be tolerated; there is to be no bodily intercourse allowed outside marriage. In the second, homosexual relations are banned and any known heterosexual adultery punished, although it is implicitly recognized that some will secretly occur. Human sexual desire cannot be entirely repressed or controlled, ironically, because it is not simply instinctive or bodily.

Would the Athenian's proposals prevent the problematic sexual behavior characteristic of Crete and Sparta from arising in his city? As in Sparta, women are given almost the same education as men, but they do not serve in the army or hold public office for most of their adult lives. What is to prevent them from becoming licentious in the privacy they will enjoy between common meals when the men are off exercising, fighting, or supervising? Public regulation not only of the accumulation of wealth but also of food and drink limits private license, and the requirement of common meals for women adds opportunities for more public supervision. From age three onward, males would live in public from dawn to dusk. But if all fighting is defensive, they should return to their homes at night unless they are on field duty, where they are to be supervised by an officer elected by the tribe. Citizens are supposed to sleep as little as possible in order to supervise their servants (as well as, perhaps, their wives and children). There are also the female inspectors. Nevertheless, the Athenian admits, it is impossible to prevent extramarital sexual relations completely—whether between the officer and the youths he chooses in the field or between master and female slaves in the household.[117] By requiring not only that citizens be born of citizen parents but also that they themselves generate others, the Athenian seeks to avoid one of the major effects of Spartan vice, the depletion of the citizen population over time, if not the vice itself.[118]

116. The Athenian uses a word literally for "force," *biasaimetha*, because there is no persuasion in the case of this law.

117. In an earlier discussion of the common meals for women, the Athenian concluded that "the things they are seeking would probably not be realized with adequate precision so long as women and children and homes are private. . . . But if the second-best arrangements would come into being, . . . things would achieve due measure" (*Laws* 807b).

118. The Athenian makes this requirement explicit at 930a–d. Cf. Aristotle *Politics* 1270a34. In the *Symposium* and *Phaedrus*, Socrates "cures" the Cretan (but by no means solely Cretan) vice by urging his interlocutors to sublimate and thus elevate their bodily pederastic desires into philosophical friendships. The Athenian's dual formulation of the law concerning eros does not

g. The Limitations of the Regime

(1) IMPERFECT JUSTICE: A PEOPLE DIVIDED ACCORDING TO OCCUPATION
AND BIRTH RATHER THAN NATURE OR TALENT. Having shown that human desire can be shaped but not entirely controlled by educational training, habituation, and persuasion, the Athenian turns back to the economic
regulations that constitute the effective basis of the regime. After his discussion of the need for, but limitations of, legal regulation of human eros,
we are not surprised to see him reassert the sanctity of boundaries and the
need to punish those who violate them. If human desire recognizes no
limits, restrictions have to be enforced. Boundaries have to be drawn not
only between plots of land but also between the different kinds or classes
of people in the city.

Because citizens are supposed to devote themselves wholly to the pursuit of virtue, they cannot practice any other art. Nor should they allow
their domestic servants or slaves to work as craftsmen, that is, to practice
two arts or activities. Because productive or instrumental arts are not practiced for their own sake but only for what can be gained by them, such arts
should be performed only by resident aliens. These artisans and merchants
should live in separate areas and leave after twenty years, so that their practices and opinions will not corrupt the behavior and attitudes of citizens.

Each person should practice one art, the Athenian explains, because human nature hardly allows anyone to do more than one thing precisely. He
thus enunciates the principle on which Socrates builds his city in speech in
the *Republic*, but he applies that principle quite differently. In the Athenian's
regime, tasks are not allocated on the basis of natural aptitude, as in the
Republic. Tasks are allocated on the basis of birth (citizen, slave, or foreign),
that is, on an accidentally (we do not choose our parents) and conventionally defined basis. The division of labor is not put forward or defended as a
matter of justice; it is merely a means of preserving the relation between
the end or purpose of the city, the attainment of virtue, and provision of
the necessary means, goods, and services. But insofar as the division of
tasks and the status that accompanies it are not based on natural aptitude
or achievement and are not just, the institutional means the Athenian uses

---

foreclose fostering male friendships for the sake of the improvement of the soul, but his interlocutors' ignorance of philosophy makes it difficult, if not impossible, for him to suggest such an option explicitly. Readers have to decide, when they reach the end of the dialogue, whether Clinias'
desires could be satisfied by the institution of the Nocturnal Council. Megillus explicitly accepts
the Athenian's two-pronged law regulating erotic relations, but Clinias just as explicitly abstains.

to supply the goods necessary to enable some people to become virtuous undermine the end of the organization and operation of the city—to make all citizens as virtuous, and therefore as just, as possible.

(2) THE NEED FOR PUNISHMENTS. From the very beginning of the dialogue, the Athenian has insisted that human beings cannot be ruled by reason alone. The attraction of pleasure and aversion to pain we share with other animals is too strong. To bring order to human life, laws must therefore combine the directives of reason with appeals to pleasure in persuasive preludes and back up its commands with threats of painful punishment. Precisely because they represent such a combination of reason with appeals to the passions, the Athenian, in sketching his city in speech, has been forced to admit that laws alone never make human beings completely prudent, intelligent, or virtuous.

C. Remedying for the Defects of Law Per Se: The Problem of *Thymos*

In the last four books of the dialogue, the Athenian shows that the laws—or the legislators who formulate and the guardians who apply them—must try to compensate for the difference between law and reason in four different ways. First, in determining penalties for lawbreakers, the law must try to make lawbreakers just by persuading them not to repeat the infraction or—if they prove intractable—try to purify the community of those who would contaminate it by exiling or killing them and dissuade others from following the criminals' example. Punishments must also be designed to quell the anger of the citizens who have been harmed and so restore friendship between them and the accused, if the community is to be preserved. Second, legislators must compensate for the difference between knowledge or intelligence and the wisdom of the elders supposedly incorporated in the laws by showing how worship of the gods is based on an observable natural order. If no explanation of the foundation of the laws in a rational order is provided, young people will rebel at the command to honor and obey their elders simply because they are older, and the elders will get angry at the rebellious youths. Such intergenerational division also threatens the preservation of community. Third, because they are unable to train or mold human beings entirely, the laws must forbid citizens from engaging in commercial activities that threaten to arouse their cupidity or from engaging in speeches or actions—disowning children or ridiculing their peers, for example—that, again, arouse the anger of others. Finally, because the laws themselves do not clearly or completely communicate the reasons for them, those who are to apply and maintain the laws must receive an extralegal education. The question arises whether it is possible to give younger men such an education without arousing the anger of their elders.

I. WHY PUNISHMENTS ARE NECESSARY

As this provisional sketch of the contents of the last third of the dialogue indicates, the psychology on which the Athenian has based his suggestions thus far is incomplete. Using his image of the puppet as a model, he has treated human beings as if they could be controlled by pulling the strings of pleasure or pain.[119] He has not taken sufficient account of the anger (*thymos*) citizens feel toward lawbreakers. He has assumed this anger would simply make them eager to help magistrates bring criminals to justice (*Laws* 730d, 731b–d). He has admitted that attempts to regulate marriage and child rearing with laws would arouse both the scorn and anger of citizens (773c, 790a) and has tried to avoid it by making regulation of family life customary rather than matters of law with penalties attached. Now he admits, if only indirectly, that the anger citizens feel at those they believe have wronged them threatens to destroy the community as much, if not more, than the excessive love of self that leads human beings to try to take more than their fair share of common goods. Laws must therefore be formulated and enforced with an eye to assuaging this anger as much as preventing the injustice that arouses it.[120]

The Athenian admits that the need for a penal code is in some ways shameful, but he observes, "we aren't in the same position as the ancient lawgivers who gave their laws to heroes or the children of gods. . . . We're human and legislating for the seed of humans" (853c). From the begin-

---

119. Arthur J. Jacobson, "The Game of the *Laws*," *Political Theory* 27, no. 6 (December 1999): 769–88, emphasizes the calculations of pleasure and pain in the *Laws* by recasting and analyzing them in terms of contemporary game theory. For a parallel critique of the psychological assumptions of game theory, see Catherine H. Zuckert, "On the Rationality of Rational Choice," *Political Psychology* 16, no. 1 (1995): 179–98.

120. Even though he quotes the relevant passage from book 9, Bobonich, in *Utopia*, does not notice the change in the psychological basis of the laws. He maintains that the tripartite understanding of the soul in the *Republic* has been dropped in the *Laws*. Like desire and reason, *thymos* is present in the *Laws*. It has a somewhat different status, however, than it does on the surface of the argument in the *Republic*. There Socrates argues that *thymos* serves to help reason check the desires. In the *Laws* the Athenian admits that *thymos* itself can cause disruptions; he therefore seeks means of assuaging it.

ning of the dialogue he has insisted that human beings are not amenable to the rule of reason simply; some can only be controlled with force or, ultimately, killed. Now he explicitly states, "The laws . . . come into being partly for the sake of the worthy human beings, to teach them how they might mingle and dwell in friendship, and partly for the sake of those who have shunned education, having a tough nature and in no way softened so as to avoid everything bad" (880d–e). Even those who are educated to become rulers or guardians of the laws must be restrained by the threat of exposure and punishment, because "there is no human being whose nature develops so as to know what is most beneficial in a political regime and to be able and willing always to do what is best" (874e–75a). The attachment human beings have to themselves and their private interests is simply too strong. If there were such a human, he or she would not be subject to law, "for no law or order is stronger than knowledge, nor is it right for intelligence to be subordinate or slave to anyone" (875c–d). The reason we must choose what comes second—order and law, which see and look to most things, but are incapable of seeing everything—is that there is no completely intelligent or knowing person to take charge. The problem with which the Athenian is centrally concerned in the last third of the dialogue thus becomes how can the law not only educate but also restrain those who make and enforce it?

a. Replacing Revenge with Reparation and Reconciliation

Because they are unable to predict all exigencies or foresee the effects of all the measures they put in place, the guardians of the laws should experiment with the operation and application of the laws for ten years, and then set them in stone, so to speak, by sanctifying them. Because neither they, the founders, nor those who will apply, preserve, and modify their work possess complete knowledge, the regime as a whole looks to the god (or *nous*, here as the distillation of practical experience) as its first principle—its origin, justification, and goal. A resident who steals from the temple demonstrates his failure to learn this most fundamental lesson or principle. His crime is thus treated as the first and most serious crime against the city, worse even than sowing the seeds of sedition.

In this as in all lesser crimes, the prosecution and punishments are intended to be educative. In contrast to the trial of Socrates by the city of Athens, the Athenian recommends that citizens accused of these crimes be tried not by a popular assembly but by a more knowledgeable and experienced "supreme court" composed of guardians of the laws along with justices selected from the other, lower courts. Both the arguments and the verdicts of the judges are to be rendered in public over three days; there will be no immediate, possibly emotion-based verdict. Deliberative reason is to rule. If the person convicted is a slave or foreigner, he will be whipped and his face disfigured before he is killed and his body is thrown naked beyond the borders; if a citizen, he will not be disfigured but merely killed and disposed of in the same way, without fame, to serve as a negative example for others. Such punishments benefit the city in two ways, the Athenian explains; they both deter others from like behavior and rid the city of bad people. Plato's readers should nevertheless observe the tension between the formative and punitive laws of the regime. The education the Athenian prescribed was intended to overcome the fear of death and so make citizens courageous, but we see that the penal law depends on the persistence of such fear in the hearts of all.

From temple robbery the Athenian turns to treat all theft in a summary fashion. If convicted, thieves should pay their victims twice the value of what they have stolen. The haste and simplicity with which he initially treats crime and its punishment reflect his belief that all crime is involuntary, a result of mistaken judgment; most such errors have their origins in the self-love that leads most people to prefer their own pleasures and thus to seek the means of satisfying them (money) at the expense of the common good. Clinias points out that nearly all lawmakers differentiate crimes and punishments in terms of both the importance of the objects and the character of the criminal. But the Athenian reminds him "that law giving has never been done correctly" (*Laws* 857c). The model has been the slave doctor who gives commands with threats of penalties for noncompliance rather than trying to educate his patients to follow his advice voluntarily. Those who would lay down laws must themselves be educated. Admitting, in effect, the flawed character of his own efforts up to this point, he tells his interlocutors, "we're becoming lawgivers but we aren't yet lawgivers" (859c). As a result of their misconception of lawgiving as command rather than as education, virtually all past legislators—poets such as Tyrtaeus and Homer as well as statesmen such as Lycurgus and Solon—have erroneously distinguished between voluntary and involuntary crimes. Like Socrates, the Athenian insists that no one harms himself willingly and to be unjust is to harm oneself. The virtually automatic penalty that follows from injustice (716b, 728b) is to be deprived of the company of good people and forced to associate with other bad characters. That virtually automatic or divine penalty is reflected, if not duplicated, in the penalties of exile or death that the Athenian proposes.[121]

Rather than attempt to distinguish voluntary from involuntary crimes, lawmakers should distinguish injury (*blabē*) from injustice (*adikia*), that is, the harm suffered from the character of the harm doer. In cases of injury, the city should attempt to compensate the victim in such a way as to restore friendship between the victim and the perpetrator. In cases of injustice, the city should attempt first to cure the evildoers, or, if they prove incurable, cast them out. Even in the case of injustice, the purpose of the punishment is not simply to "rehabilitate" the criminal; it is to restore good relations or friendship among the citizens.[122] The Athenian defines injustice as "the tyranny in the soul of spiritedness, fear, pleasure, pain, envy and desires . . . and justice as the opinion about what is best, even if it is mistaken" (864a), although, he notes, many take the latter to be an instance of involuntary injustice. Because human laws are never the product purely of knowledge but always involve opinion and so the possibility, if not probability, of mistakes in application, if not articulation, the Athenian recognizes that law could never be considered just, if justice were to require knowledge of what is right with no mistakes.

In the discussion of violent crimes, we see that the problem a legislator faces in devising a criminal code is not merely how to treat or cure the criminal. The law also has to recognize that a wrong was done, in order to satisfy the possible anger of the victims and their families. For this reason even injuries cannot merely be compensated for by a return in kind; the victims must be given more. Murder poses a particular difficulty. Taking someone's life might look like an especially heinous form of theft, but how could that theft be compensated for not merely once but twice? In the case of slaves it might be possible to reimburse the owner double the market value of his lost property. That would not be possible, however, in the case of a citizen and his family (although some contemporary public choice theorists believe a price can be set for anything). Rather than treat the death of a fellow citizen as an injury requiring compensation, the Athenian

---

121. Imprisonment also represents a way in which problematic individuals are removed from the society of good citizens. If, as Stalley states (*Introduction*, 138), Plato was the first to suggest such a penalty (which Greek polities did not use as a penalty per se, although they did imprison people awaiting trial), he is extending the general principle.

122. Most commentators on this section have not recognized the second function of punishment. See, e.g.,. Trevor Saunders, "Penology and Eschatology in Plato's *Timaeus* and *Laws*," *Classical Quarterly* 23 (1973): 232–44; and Stalley, *Introduction*, 137–65, although Stalley emphasizes in opposition to Saunders that the penalties do not aim simply or purely at curing the criminal.

distinguishes causes of death in terms of degrees of injustice. The punishments vary accordingly, although the Athenian does not always spell out the reasons. Those who kill in performing their public duty—participating in war games, for example—are to suffer no penalty but simply to undergo a ritual purification. (The dead have been sacrificed for the sake of the community, not the self-interested desires of the perpetrator.) Doctors whose patients die despite efforts to cure them will be declared to be unpolluted by law (presumably so that the doctors will remain able and willing to attempt to heal others). Citizens who kill other free persons accidentally must stay away from the places frequented by their unintended victims for a year (lest they arouse the memories and anger of those who loved the deceased). Those who kill in anger must suffer the dishonor of exile, but they are allowed to return in two years if they killed in immediate rage, three years if the murder was premeditated. Although the injustice is not, strictly speaking, involuntary, the Athenian recognizes that people are in effect seized by rage. The penalty constitutes a cooling-down period not only for the perpetrator but also for the friends and family of his victim. The desired goal is a reconciliation. The extent to which the Athenian subordinates means to ends is reflected in the relative leniency with which he treats violent capital crimes. Nevertheless, that leniency has limits. If the perpetrator repeats his crime, he is to be banished permanently.[123] The Athenian also recognizes that when murders occur within families, reconciliation is unlikely. Those who kill children, siblings, or spouses must not only suffer banishment but must also separate from their family when they return. Those who kill parents, even in self-defense, must be killed themselves. Second to the gods and the demigods, one's ancestors are sacred.[124] Indeed, we increasingly see, to the extent to which the laws are not and cannot be based on reason or knowledge alone, age with its presumed superior experience becomes the substitute.

123. The repeat offender is banished rather than killed, we suspect, so that there will be no excuse to begin a cycle of murders in revenge.

124. In reading this section, we see the Athenian responding to many of the problems dramatized in tragedies—Agamemnon's killing of his daughter, Clytemnestra's killing of Agamemnon, Orestes' killing of Clytemnestra, Oedipus' angry murder of his own father, Medea of Jason's and her own children, and Polyneices and Eteocles' battle for Thebes. The Athenian does not name or quote any of these plays, in part because the extant works postdate the dramatic date of the *Laws*. The stories were known, however, and his presentation of the penal code is rather explicitly a critique of the understanding of justice as retribution (as criticized by Aeschylus in his *Oresteia*). The Athenian's indications—and they are sketchy—of how such problems might be solved through law could be another reason he claims the *Laws* to be "the best and noblest tragedy."

Those who kill others to satisfy their own desires or from envy are treated more severely than those who kill in fits of rage, because desires and envy tend to be both more calculating and longer lasting. Such crimes appear to be voluntary; they are, according to the Athenian, more unjust and, like fear, have more common motives, which need to be more forcefully counteracted. Murders committed from desire or envy should be tried in the same manner as temple robbing; they should be tried by the same court and have the same punishments. Crimes for the sake of gain represent the same inversion of the fundamental principles of the regime, putting self-love and pleasure above virtue and the god(s). The penalty is death or perpetual exile, because there is not the same hope of the heat of anger cooling with the passage of time, or of reconciliation in the long term between the criminal and those he has harmed.

The penalty for murder of a family member in cold blood is even more severe. Someone convicted of killing a family member is not only to be put to death; he or she is also to be deprived of his or her individual identity, traceable to the family. Upon execution, the naked body is to be taken to a specified crossroads outside the city, where each of the magistrates is to throw a stone at the head (and so obliterate the face, the most identifying feature) and the body then carried to the borders of the country, where it is to be cast out, unburied. Someone who refuses to recognize the bonds of family has no place in this city. A suicide, not having harmed another, will be buried, but in a place without company or identification. Beasts and even lifeless things that accidentally cause the death of a citizen shall also (if comically) be prosecuted and, if convicted, killed and cast out—presumably to satisfy the potential anger of the bereaved family. (Human beings have been known, irrationally but angrily, to kick the stools over which they have tripped.) Because the family with its affective and economic bonds is the fundamental unit of the regime, those who kill intruders to preserve their property, wives, or children from attack are to be as blameless as the soldiers who defend the city from surprise attacks from abroad.

b. Enforcing Respect for Elders

The Athenian had admitted in passing that the citizens of his regime would probably never be perfectly nurtured and educated, so long as there were private households (*Laws* 807b). Nevertheless, in his description of the penal code he now indicates that where there are private households, their integrity must be preserved above all, because they are the source not only of individual existence but also of the preservation of the regime. Even though he had argued earlier (729b–c) that elders should and would educate the young more effectively by example than by precept, his criminal code makes it clear that youths have no right to resist unreasonable demands or even bodily harm at the hands of their parents.

As he turns from violent acts that cause death to wounds, the Athenian reminds his interlocutors that the need for laws arises from the limits of human intelligence and our inability to free ourselves entirely from self-love. Because the types of injuries or wounds people can inflict on each other are so numerous and varied, it is impossible for legislators to specify all the appropriate responses or remedies. The Athenian thus limits himself to enunciating two or three basic principles. First, if such disputes must be settled in court, the constitution and character of the court proceedings must reflect the regime. In good regimes composed of well-educated citizens, the proceedings and judgments should be as public as possible. If citizens and the judges they select are not well educated, however, such publicity will produce even more unjust results. Second, although wounds can be treated as injuries to a certain extent, and individuals, families, and city compensated for the loss, in the case of families, wounds should be treated as capital crimes and punished with death or exile. As the need for the guardians of the laws to reorganize or choose a successor family to manage each of the 5,040 plots when a head of household dies without leaving an heir indicates, he who strikes out at the family strikes out at the basis of the regime.

In the *Republic* Socrates attempts to make the city or its guardians into one big family (if not individual) by instituting a community of women and children; in the *Laws* the Athenian attempts to make the city into one big family with regard to punishment. Having admitted the impossibility of human beings sharing all property as well as the impossibility of entirely controlling erotic attraction and sexual relations, the Athenian falls back on a generalized rule of the elders and a generalized enforcement of such. He concludes his discussion of punishment by stating:

> Every man, child, and woman ought always to think about such things in the following way: The elder is to no small degree more venerable than the younger, in the eyes of gods and of human beings who are going to be saved and become happy. It is therefore shameful, and hateful to the gods, to see in the city an assault by a younger man on an elder. And it's reasonable

for every young man who is beaten by an old man to endure his rage. . . .
Whoever exceeds us by twenty years in age, male or female, should be considered as a father or a mother. (879c)

Everyone thus has a responsibility not merely to respect but to defend any
member of an older generation as if that person were a parent.

If someone should dare to strike his father or mother . . . , while not af-
flicted with madness, then one who happens along should help. . . . If a
stranger who's a resident alien helps, he is to be invited to take a front seat
at the contests, while if he hasn't helped, he is to be exiled perpetually. . . .
A slave who has helped is to become a free man, while if he hasn't helped,
he is to be beaten a hundred strokes. . . . If someone should be convicted in
a judicial trial for assault on his parents, he must . . . be perpetually exiled
from the city . . . and must avoid all sacred places. (881b–d)

Membership or participation in this city depends ultimately on respect
shown for elders. No one is to associate in any way with a person who
does not display such respect.

2. Mandating a Public Teaching about the Gods

Insofar as the operative principle of the regime becomes a requirement
that younger people respect and obey their elders—without question or
objection—the most direct and immediate threat to civic order becomes
the insolence youths sometimes display toward the gods and the law as
well as their parents. Since no one who believes in the gods as the laws
require has ever performed an impious deed, the Athenian suggests, they
will need to persuade young people to believe (a) that the gods exist, (b)
that they care about human affairs, and (c) that they cannot be bribed.

a. Why a Philosophical Defense of the Belief in the Gods Is Needed

Clinias cannot imagine why anyone would deny that the gods exist. "First,
there is the beautiful order of the earth, sun, stars, and seasons, marking
years and months. And then all barbarians as well as Greeks think that
there are gods" (Laws 886a). Clinias does not seem to remember that he
himself thought the story of the divine origin of Crete's laws was "most
just" but not necessarily true. Nor does he appear to recall that he had
thought (821c) some of the heavenly bodies wandered. The Athenian has
persuaded him that the laws of the regime they propose to found can
be traced to the god, nous, and that those who know can prove that the

heavenly bodies move in regular courses. The Athenian told Clinias, in fact, that it was blasphemous to deny it. Clinias does not, therefore, refer to Zeus or any other Olympian deity in objecting to the young atheists. He has learned a great deal already from his conversation with the Athenian. Nevertheless, the Athenian now informs him, his learning is not sufficient to enable him to understand the fundamental difficulty.

There are writings banned by their virtuous cities which describe the coming into being of the heavens and other things, including the gods. Although he would not praise the effects these stories have on the respect shown to parents, the Athenian does not propose banning tales about battles between fathers and sons or their incestuous mating with mothers and sisters, as Socrates does in the *Republic*. On the contrary, in line with the general respect that is to be shown to elders, the Athenian suggests that what pertains to the ancient should be left alone and spoken of in whatever way is pleasing to the gods. In legislating for the new colony, he and his interlocutors should be concerned with a new kind of teaching, a form of ignorance that seems to be the greatest wisdom and has very bad effects. The older writings show the gods acting in questionable ways, but they do not persuade young people that the sun and moon are stones, incapable of thought about human concerns. The older writings might thus lead their readers to wonder whether the gods are just, but they do not lead their readers to believe that the gods do not exist. To persuade a young atheist that he is in error, the Athenian and his interlocutors have to refute new arguments. Rather than attribute the same "flux" understanding of the cosmos to both the poets and most other philosophers the way Socrates does in the *Theaetetus*, the Athenian clearly distinguishes them.

Inasmuch as he and his companions are concerned primarily with preventing insolent or impious behavior on the part of the young, one might have thought that (like Socrates in the *Republic* and the Dorian cities) the Athenian would have been more concerned about the propagation of stories depicting gods engaging in precisely the kinds of insolent acts that threaten both political and familial order—and so setting bad examples—than with cosmological doctrines. The Athenian's focus on the latter reflects his conviction, announced from the very beginning of the dialogue, that legislation should foster the intelligence of citizens—first and foremost. Although legislators have to persuade their fellow citizens to obey laws by appealing to their passions as well as to their reason, the laws will fail to achieve their ultimate goal if they keep citizens perpetually in the dark by telling them "noble lies." Unlike Clinias, the Athenian knows that the "myths" legislators of old used to legitimatize their regimes had been subjected to debunking skeptical critiques that deprive all laws and regimes of any basis but force.[125] Clinias had doubts about the truth of the story concerning the origins of his own city's laws, even though he was not willing to state them as such or in public. By asking his interlocutors how they can argue against the atheists without anger (*mē thymō[i]*), the Athenian points to the political, as opposed to the purely intellectual, problem (887d). Elder statesmen like his interlocutors are apt to become enraged not only at the youths, who dare to question the veracity of stories they have heard since they were young from their parents, but also at those who teach them the grounds for doubt.[126]

As in his initial questions about the source of Crete's laws, the Athenian seeks to avoid arousing the anger of his Dorian interlocutors by using indirect discourse. He urges them to speak mildly to the young atheist they imagine. He will assure the youth that he is not the first to deny that the gods exist; he will, however, also tell the young man that no one has maintained this opinion throughout his life, although some have continued to assert that the gods do not care about human affairs or that they can be bribed. Together they will ask the youth to investigate the question further and to do nothing impious until he has made further inquiries.

Because the Athenian is familiar with the arguments of the atheists, he volunteers both to state and to refute them. He thus relieves Clinias of the burden of showing that he could not.[127] The atheists claim that all things that come to be do so by nature, chance, or art. The elements out of which everything that comes into being is composed—fire, water, earth, and air—exist entirely by nature and chance and not at all by art. The bodies that first come into being from these—earth, sun, moon, and stars—are wholly inanimate (*apsycha*) and exist as a result of the chance interplay of the elements in motion. The movement of these heavenly bodies is responsible for the coming to be and decaying of mortal things

125. See, e.g., the Sidonian story concerning the founding of Thebes to which the Athenian referred earlier (*Laws* 663e).

126. Cf. the excellent discussion of this problem by Thomas Pangle, "The Political Psychology of Religion in Plato's *Laws*," *American Political Science Review* 70, no. 4 (December 1976): 1059–77.

127. Although Clinias appeals here to the regular order of the movement of the heavens, earlier in the conversation (822a–b) he had voiced the erroneous opinion, common among the Greeks, that sun, moon, and stars wander. His claim that all Greeks and barbarians believe in gods is disproved by the existence of atheists; the fact that all peoples may publicly claim to believe in gods does not, moreover, prove that they believe in the same gods (they don't) or that these gods exist. Clinias would have been easily embarrassed had his "proof" been subject to question.

on earth. Art is one of those mortal things. Most arts produce imaginary playthings, but when they are based on knowledge of natural processes, as in medicine or agriculture, arts can have real, if derivative effects. The arts of politics and legislation have a few such real effects (for example, when they serve to preserve peoples from external attacks). The gods exist by law or convention and not by nature. Like the laws and the various conceptions of justice they express, the gods differ from place to place and continually change, because human beings disagree about them. On the basis of such an understanding, both private individuals and poets teach young people that what is most just is determined by those who have the most force. The best life in truth is to be a master of others rather than a slave to others under law.

The challenge the Athenian has laid down for himself is similar to that Glaucon and Adimantus pose to Socrates in the *Republic*: he has to prove that the just life is superior to the unjust. But the Athenian's response to the challenge is very different from Socrates'. Instead of investigating what is just—or any eternal, unchanging intelligible being such as the ideas—the Athenian presents a series of arguments to show (*a*) that soul is prior to body, (*b*) that as images of the motion of soul with *nous*, the sun, moon, and stars should be called gods (which evidently exist), (*c*) that the gods care about human beings, and (*d*) that they cannot be bribed.

Such a response is fully in line with the suggested dramatic date of the dialogue—between the years 460 and 450. The position to which the Athenian is responding appears to be a summary of the doctrines of Archelaus, a pupil of Anaxagoras and teacher of Socrates.[128] Like Anaxagoras, the Athenian seems to make *nous* into the ruling principle. But unlike Anaxagoras, the Athenian does not try to show in response to Parmenides that the elements of everything have always existed; they simply mix and remix continuously. Although the Athenian initially posits three possibilities—that everything moves, that some things move and others stay the same, and that nothing moves (*kineitai*; 893b–c)—he does not mention any examples or give a general account of things that do not move or change. He avoids the objection Socrates makes to Anaxagoras in the *Phaedo* (97b–98c)—that he does not show how *nous* intends and effects the good—by attributing human psychic characteristics to soul or self-motion per se and then uniting soul, or a certain kind of soul, with *nous*. One cannot conceive of *nous* outside of soul, he observes; the price of the union, however, is that *nous*

---

128. *Laws*, Loeb ed., 2.313; Cicero *Tusculanae disputationes* 5.10.

can no longer be said to rule or control the entire cosmos, which becomes the site of an ongoing battle between order and disorder, good and bad.

If all the bodies we perceive result from the interaction of the four basic elements in motion, the Athenian argues, the existence of inanimate bodies presupposes motion, and motion must find its origin or source in self-motion. What we call self-motion or soul must therefore be prior to body. Attributing human psychic characteristics such as mood, character, wishes, calculations, true opinions, cares, and memories (which all living or ensouled [*empsycha*] beings do not share) to self-motion (*psyche*) per se, the Athenian suggests that soul must be the cause of good and bad, noble and base, just and unjust. And if it is, there must be at least two different kinds of soul that control the movements of things in the heavens—that which is conjoined with *nous* and so produces beneficial happy effects, and that which is not and so is disorderly and wreaks havoc.

The motion of *nous* itself is not visible; indeed, human beings cannot look directly at *nous* with their minds any more than they can look directly at the sun with their eyes and not be blinded. Like Socrates in the *Phaedo*, the Athenian thus seeks an image of the motions (or effects) of intellect and finds it in the regular revolutions of bodies in the heavens. He and his interlocutors need not decide whether soul exists in the sun as in our bodies, whether soul moves the sun externally by acquiring another body, or whether soul is without body in some mysterious way. (In the latter two cases, the Athenian could agree with Anaxagoras [cf. *Apology* 26d] that the sun and moon are stones and still maintain that in their revolutions they are the images of the god—*nous*—that moves them by means of soul.) "This soul . . . should be held to be a god by everyone . . . ; and since soul or souls are evidently the causes of the stars, moon, years, months, and seasons—and souls good with every virtue—we will declare that they are gods." Emphasizing the pre-Socratic character of the argument he has presented, the Athenian asks: "Is there anyone who accepts this argument and does not agree [with Thales] that all things are full of gods?" (899a–b).

It is not difficult to see that some if not all the heavenly bodies move in calculable and hence intelligible ways and to infer that both the motion and its intelligibility must have a divine cause (because they are not subject to human manipulation and regularity could not be sustained over long periods of time merely by chance). It is more difficult to see how or why the sources of such motion must have intentions or virtues (like courage [900e]). The intelligible is not necessarily intelligent, although the existence of intelligible motions seems to point to some intelligent cause.

This may be the reason the Athenian says that no one continues to deny the existence of the gods for his entire life, although some people continue to deny that these gods care about humans or assert that they can be moved by sacrifices and prayers.

Insofar as the gods direct the motions of the heavenly bodies, they could be understood to order or even determine (through the weather) what comes into being, moves, and decays on earth. From their heights they might even be said to oversee everything on earth—down to the smallest detail. But can the Athenian show that the cosmic gods or the souls that move them actually care (*epimeleia*) about human beings? The Athenian does not even try to prove that the gods he has shown to exist reward the just and punish the unjust in the afterlife, if not in this. For this purpose he adds some "myths" (903b) to "charm the doubters." According to these myths, the gods care for the whole (and hence may not appear to care for each and every individual part); to preserve the order of the whole they arrange for the evil to sink to lower regions such as Hades and for the virtuous to rise to higher places.

Gods of the heavenly kind the Athenian has described clearly could not be bribed or appeased with prayers and sacrifices. They are not all powerful, moreover; they do not control everything that happens. They direct the orderly motions of the heavenly bodies; the Athenian reminds his interlocutors, however, that they have agreed that all motion is not orderly. Indeed, "we assert there is an immortal battle going on between the good and bad" (906a).

The notion that everything in the cosmos exists in opposition or strife characteristic of pre-Socratic philosophy is compatible with Clinias' initial belief that human beings are always at war. The suspicion arises, therefore, that the Athenian's argument to show that the gods exist is ad hominem. His arguments concerning the gods do not refer to the Olympians or to the punishments inflicted on souls in Hades; his main interlocutor has admitted that he does not know the poetry of Homer or his successors. The Athenian observes that "their speeches have been given rather vehemently on account of a fondness for victory over bad human beings," and so in line with Clinias' initial desires, if not, strictly speaking, with a search for truth. Not having thought it difficult to prove that the gods exist, Clinias is easily persuaded that the arguments the Athenian has given will not discredit the legislator, even if they do not persuade the atheists (907c–d).

The picture of the cosmos as a huge battleground between the forces of good and evil does not provide a firm foundation for political order, however.[129] The Athenian explicitly concedes that there are powerful natural forces or "disorderly motions" that constantly threaten to undermine the laws and regime they have established. We have seen the many ways in which this is true of generation. The cosmic battle between the forces of order and disorder or good and evil does, however, provide justification for the thorough surveillance the Athenian has argued will be necessary if their laws are to be maintained. Because neither the cosmos nor the human soul is or ever will be ordered as a whole, neither constitutes a model to be copied by the city and its lawgivers.[130] They must therefore use pleasure and pain (or persuasion and compulsion or preludes and laws) in addition to reason to produce even an approximation of order, and that approximation is always in danger of being upset or disturbed by the results of generation.

Because the laws are always in danger of being undermined by the changes associated with generation, the Athenian has stated (in line with Dorian law), they cannot be openly questioned or changed. He has admitted,

129. Perhaps because it does not provide a firm foundation for political order, the picture of the cosmos the Athenian presents proves on examination to be fundamentally incompatible with the teachings of two other Platonic philosophical spokesmen with which his argument is often compared. Cf. Benardete, Laws, 293–306; Nightingale, "Historiography," 299–326; E. Dönt, "Bemerkungen zu Phaidros 249 und Nomoi 897," Hermes 96 (1968): 369–71; J. B. Skemp, The Theory of Motion in Plato's Later Dialogues (Cambridge: Cambridge University Press, 1942). In the Phaedrus (245c–46a), Socrates also identifies the soul with self-motion. Because that which moves itself cannot be thought to be moved by something else, he argues that soul must be understood to be eternal. He does not, like the pre-Socratic thinkers to whom the Athenian refers (895a), conceive of soul emerging from the opposition of things standing still. Like the Athenian, Socrates recognizes that there are different types of souls. He too contrasts the orderly (divine) with the disorderly (human and lower animals). Socrates does not, however, envision a battle between the orderly and the disorderly. The orderly movements of the disembodied divine souls are determined by their particular functions in caring for the cosmos and by their need to feed or sustain themselves by contemplating the eternal and unchanging. Fighting is characteristic only of the disorderly human souls, who damage each other in their attempt to ascend to a view of the things that are always what they are in themselves. The fall of the injured human souls to earth, where they acquire bodies, is joined, moreover, as it is in the Timaeus, with a notion of reincarnation. Whereas those souls who seek knowledge and live justly are rewarded by losing their bodies, those who do not are born again in the bodies of lesser animals. As in the myth of Er at the end of the Republic, so in the Phaedrus, rewards and punishments in the afterlife are meted out on an individual basis, according to the virtues and vices of the person in question. As in the Timaeus, so in the Phaedrus, disorderly motion is encompassed within a broader, intelligible order. According to the Athenian, the revolution of the heavenly bodies is a product of soul or souls and an image of the movement of nous, but this soul or souls are not, as in the Timaeus, intentionally constructed by the god as copies of the eternal ideas. Nor does the Athenian, like Socrates in the Republic, describe the education he prescribes as making copies of the eternal ideas of the virtues in the souls of humans.

130. Grote (Plato, 3.305) thus contrasts the reasons the study of astronomy is advocated in the Timaeus (47b–c)—to bring the revolutions of the human soul into an order that parallels the orderly motions of the cosmos—with the Laws, where the study of astronomy is used to support the official theology and not to bring order to individual souls.

however, that the guardians must adapt or change the laws, and that the guardians will need to make their changes look "ancient." Their changes cannot therefore be presented to the public as "improvements."[131] On the contrary, the laws are to be sanctified after ten years of experimentation (772b–c) and so, presumably, to remain unchanged; the prescribed practices, dances, songs, and gymnastic contests that constitute the greater part of citizen education are also described as worship of the god (803e). Those who would throw doubt on the existence of the god or gods (even as untraditionally defined as soul[s] or *nous*) would therefore raise questions about the very foundation and goal of the entire regime.

The Athenian's proposals represent the best form of political order that can be erected on the basis of pre-Socratic philosophy. By dramatizing the difficulties of instituting and maintaining this order, Plato indicates some the reasons for the emergence of Socratic philosophy.

b. The Law concerning Piety

The primary purpose of the prelude and law concerning impiety is to prevent anyone from voicing doubts about the existence of the gods in public and so challenging the wisdom of the elders. The young atheist to whom the Athenian and his interlocutors are purportedly speaking is asked to make further inquiries before he expresses or acts on his doubts. As we learn from the law itself, no one will be allowed to make such inquiries freely or in public. The types of atheism to be outlawed and punished are divided into the original three kinds—denying that the gods exist, denying that they care about humans, and asserting that they can be bribed; the atheists are also divided according to whether their intentions are just or unjust, that is, whether they express their views frankly out of love of truth or whether they seek to take advantage of others by playing on their credulity (or incredulity). If convicted, those who seek to profit by persuading others to engage in practices, concerning the divine, that have not been publicly sanctioned should be thrown into a prison in the middle of

131. In arguing that the laws are changeable, neither Saunders ("Women," 603) nor David Cohen, "Law, Autonomy, and Political Community in Plato's *Laws*," *Classical Philology* 88 (1993): 314, observes the difference between publicly maintaining the principle that the laws do not change (arbitrarily) and recognizing, privately in the case of the *Laws*, that changes in fact do and should occur when the laws, even though they are not officially changed, are applied over time in specific circumstances. Both Americans and British familiar with case law should, however, be familiar with the phenomenon.

the country, where they cannot be visited by any freeman. Fed by slaves so long as they live, the unjust atheists, when they die, will have their corpses cast beyond the borders unburied (presumably so as not merely to be dishonored but forgotten). Those with just dispositions who simply don't believe that the gods exist or care—and declare such beliefs in public—are to be incarcerated in the "moderation tank" (sōphronistērion) located near the places where the Nocturnal Council meets.[132] For five years they will talk only to members of the council; if, after five years, they seem to be "moderate," that is, if they have learned to keep their doubts to themselves, they will be allowed to live with the moderate. If they have not learned and are convicted of saying impious things, again at trial, they will be put to death.

Because the Athenian later states that members of the Nocturnal Council will have to investigate the questions Socrates raised about the unity of the virtues as well as the noble and the good, commentators have asked whether Socrates would have been prosecuted for impiety under this law (as he had been prosecuted in fact in Athens).[133] Socrates never denied or doubted the existence of the gods per se; he merely criticized the stories told about the Olympian "gods of the city," including the suggestion that they could, in effect, be bribed. However, his willingness to converse with sophists like Protagoras, who stated that they did not know whether the gods exist, or youths like Alcibiades and Critias, who openly expressed their doubts, would probably have made him liable to prosecution under the Athenian's law. As the Athenian makes clear in book 12 when he outlaws "busybodies," Socrates would not have been allowed to converse in his usual manner in the Athenian's city.

132. As Strauss observes (Argument and Action, 155), the name of the sōphronistērion reminds of phrontistērion, the name Aristophanes gave Socrates' school in the Clouds. Like Socrates' school, we might recall, the Pythagoreans in Croton were destroyed when forces organized by a disgruntled, rejected student burned down the house in which they met.

133. Strauss (Argument and Action, 156) points out that "it is not clear whether a man who believes in the kosmic gods, . . . without believing in the Olympian gods, is guilty of impiety; he will be guilty of impiety if the mythoi supporting the second dogma are assigned the same status as the logoi. Furthermore, the disjunction made by the law is not complete: what happens to the atheist who is a just man and does not ridicule others because they sacrifice and pray and who to this extent is a dissembler? Is it literally true of him that he deserves not one death or two, i.e., no death at all, nor imprisonment? . . . One could say that he will become guilty if he frankly expresses his unbelief—but what if he expressed it only to sensible friends? Can one imagine Socrates denouncing him to the authorities?" Socrates did not always talk to "sensible" men, however. In the Meno (90a–95a) Plato shows that Socrates angered one of his future accusers, Anytus, by denying that Athenian "gentlemen" were able to teach their sons how to become virtuous.

3. The Need to Regulate All Forms of Exchange

As the Athenian's discussion of the law concerning impiety makes clear, both the deeds and the speech of citizens must be constantly policed if the regime is to endure. The need for such rigorous supervision does not arise simply from the ineradicable tendency of human beings to favor their own pleasures over the needs of others. Challenges to the law, especially unjust attempts to profit at the expense of others, provoke the fellow citizens of the injured, especially members of their immediate family, to retaliate in anger—and hence cause further injustice.

Having discussed the penal laws concerning violent crimes and impiety, the Athenian thus returns to the law concerning the unjust appropriation of the goods of others. Once again he asserts that no one should take the property of another without permission. No one is to seek or appropriate buried treasure (which was presumably left for another). No one is to take up property left unattended. No one is covertly to steal the property of another. The temptation to seek gain at the expense of others, by deceit or sharp trading, is so great that even though commerce is in the common interest, no citizen will be allowed to engage in it. All commercial activities will be relegated to slaves or resident aliens. The strict division of labor that had previously been justified as necessary to enable citizens to spend their entire lives acquiring virtue is now presented as a means of preventing them from giving way to temptation. What had first been described positively as an aspect of formative education becomes a negative restraint.

The aim of the restraint is to maintain friendship among the citizens. Exchanges of goods, especially bequests, within families are particularly apt to become sources of conflict. The power of fathers, who tend to become irascible with age, to bestow their property to those who will come after them must therefore be strictly regulated by law.[134] Because marriages between heirs may be contrary to their inclinations and so cause rebellion against the laws, the lawgivers must ask forgiveness for the hardships they may occasion and make provision to forgive those who find it impossible to comply by establishing a means of arbitration in such cases. Provision must be made for those left without families; the guardians of the laws

---

134. All property within the city, especially the 5,040 allotments, belongs to the city itself and not to the individuals who are allowed to use it.

must care for orphans as if they were their own children. Procedures must be established to enable fathers to disown sons and daughters with cause (and then to find a place within the city or in a colony for the dispossessed); children must also be able to have their parents declared incompetent, if that proves to be the case. There should also be a way in which couples who prove incompatible can divorce.

Because speeches can also provoke anger and retaliation, words as well as deeds must be subject to regulation and prosecution. Rather than risk the vengeance of the gods for the curses of parents, children who neglect to honor their elders shall be liable for punishment. Also liable are those who utter venomous words (as well as those who deliver venomous potions) in the forms of incantations or spells. (They would appear, indeed, to be guilty of the most serious form of impiety.) No one is allowed to curse or to ridicule another citizen. Those who have been given license to engage in comic speech must aim their ridicule only at other slaves or foreigners—and make clear that it is in jest. No one who is mad is to be allowed to rave in public; nor is anyone to be allowed to beg. Those who conspire (agree in word) to commit a crime will be subject to prosecution. All citizens (including women aged forty and above) shall be required to serve as witnesses in trials, if they have relevant information. Those who claim to teach an art of speaking that enables people to escape prosecution shall not be allowed to practice or promote it.

The public services that citizens render others must also be regulated; these too constitute a kind of exchange, although no one is to expect a reward for merely obeying the law (955c). No one is to be allowed to falsify a public message, to steal from the public, or to refuse to fight, if asked, in defense of the city, although people who lay down their arms and flee as a result of misfortune rather than cowardice are not to be prosecuted.

In light of the Athenian's emphasis on the need for constant supervision and surveillance, we are not surprised to learn that the highest, most honorable offices in his city in speech are those of the auditors, that is, the officials who make sure that other public officials have performed their duty—for no personal gain.[135] The auditors' examinations and prosecutions

135. Some of these officials were, the Athenian reminds his interlocutors, selected at least in part by lot. All offices in the regime are not filled simply, solely, or completely justly on the basis of merit. After the initial twelve auditors are selected, he suggests, the three best citizens over the age of fifty should be elected every year at the same time as the select judges (Laws 767c) to serve until they are seventy-five years old.

of other officials for malfeasance can be challenged in court, and if the auditors are found to be in error, they will be deprived of their office and honors.[136]

The Athenian recognizes that such legal checks will not suffice to make or keep the guardians of the guardians either prudent or virtuous. Filling in details of the judicial process that he had left incomplete in his initial description of the offices of the regime, he observes (948c) that, in contrast to the times of Rhadamanthus (or the purported founding of the laws of Crete with which they began), legislators now cannot simply rely on the oaths people swear. Despite the law he set down forbidding public expressions of impiety, some people will not believe in the gods or that the gods care—and others will believe that the gods can be bribed.[137] They cannot allow the opposing parties in a court case to swear that they are going to tell the truth, because half of them will be proved to have sworn falsely. Although he has just reiterated the law against theft and declared that any citizen convicted of stealing public goods should be killed because that citizen clearly did not absorb the education he or she was given and so

136. Selected by their fellow citizens as the best among them, the Athenian suggests, these guardians of the guardians should be named priests of Apollo and the Sun and live on the temple precincts; they should also represent the city at ceremonial functions and games, at home and abroad, and be given special burials when they die. As in the burials that all citizens who have performed their duties and obeyed the laws will receive, no public singing of dirges or other expressions of grief will be allowed. (The Athenian recognizes that private expressions of grief cannot be prevented.) Nor will the original distribution of property be disturbed by expenditures on lavish funerals; the amount of money any citizen can spend on the burial of another will be limited according to their economic class. (At the beginning of his description of his city in speech [719c–e] the Athenian had suggested that poets would criticize legislators for failing to make such distinctions or varied provisions. Here he shows that his city can and does.) The economic base of his city will also be maintained intact by laws forbidding burials on arable land.

137. In filling out his description of the courts, he also shows how members of the Nocturnal Council could introduce improvements on the laws they learn from foreigners without admitting that they are making changes. The guardians of the laws are supposed to examine the laws adopted by decent men in other cities and then to select, test, and correct them on the basis of experience for ten years before they set them down as final, the Athenian "repeats." (Having argued that the city should both send and receive a certain number and kind of foreign visitors, despite his earlier warnings against the contamination of morals that results from foreign trade, he makes the foreign sources of the innovations explicit as he had not in his previous statements about such ten-year experiments. Cf. Laws 772a–d, 846c.) At that point guardians are to set the laws down in writing. The judges who apply them are then to interpret and so modify the "ancient" law explicitly in light of the writings of the lawgiver, that is, the basic text of the Laws itself. As in the provisions encouraging the Nocturnal Council to send and receive foreign visitors in order to learn how different cities order their affairs and other related matters, the Athenian explicitly incorporates the wisdom conveyed through their conversation into the law at the end. Nevertheless, he is about to show, this single conversation is not enough to establish a new form of regime.

must be regarded as incurable (941c–42a), the Athenian also suggests (954a) that citizens who receive permission to search the premises of others for stolen goods be required to strip when they conduct the search. Even in his city, thievery will continue to be common enough for people to suspect their neighbors of using the cover of law to steal. Likewise, although he mandated a law that forbade people not merely from stealing but from picking up property left unattended, he proposes (954d–e) that they legislate limits on the amount of time owners have to bring suit against people they claim appropriated their property when they were not using it. In sum, the Athenian admits that even the best laws cannot make the people who live under them virtuous. If the city is to achieve its end or purpose, he thus concludes (965a), it will be necessary to introduce a new, more precise (*akribesteran*) form of education. But to do that, they will have to begin their discussion of education and the laws over from the beginning (968c–69a), with a somewhat broader audience and more participants.

4. THE END OF THE REGIME—AND THE NEW BEGINNING

The "Nocturnal" Council the Athenian finally urges his Dorian interlocutors to establish is needed to save (*charin sōtērias*) the regime in two different ways. First, the council—consisting of the ten oldest guardians of the laws, the auditors, observers they send abroad, and young people between thirty and forty years of age selected by the elders—is designed to solve the problem of succession by creating a pool of younger people who will come to understand the basis or reasons for the laws and so in the future be able to apply and preserve them.[138] Second, if these guardians of the laws are to do whatever may enable a member of the community to possess the virtue of soul that befits a human being, as the Athenian and his interlocutors agreed earlier (770c–d), the guardians must discover what

---

138. When the Athenian suggests that members of the Nocturnal Council (*nykterinos sullogos*) will meet with the just people convicted of atheism in the "moderation tank" (*Laws* 909a), he does not specify the composition of the council. (I put "Nocturnal" in quotation marks because the council is to meet from dawn to daybreak and not at night [951d].) The first time the Athenian mentions the council in book 12 as the body that will both send and receive official (noncommercial) foreign visitors (951d–e), it includes the auditors, ten oldest guardians of the laws, the current supervisor of education and his or her predecessor, and the younger people they select. When he reintroduces the council at 961a–b, he drops the supervisors of education and adds the observers sent abroad, because, as he subsequently explains (968c), the members of this council will have to determine the contents of their own education before they set about establishing the laws. It is not clear, therefore, whether the office of supervisor of education will exist.

virtue truly is—and discovering it, try to achieve it, first and foremost, in themselves.[139]

Although the Athenian had begun the description of his city in speech by arguing that the laws of a city that traded with others would necessarily become corrupted as a result, at the end he admits that legislators or guardians of the laws will not be able to formulate or preserve their own institutions on the basis of knowledge unless they become familiar with the ways of others, both good and bad. To acquire such knowledge, the city should both send and receive foreign visitors. To prevent such exchanges from corrupting their own customs and laws, they should carefully restrict the kinds of visits and visitors they allow as well as the places to which they can go and the people to whom they can speak. No citizen less than forty years of age will be allowed to travel on public business (military expeditions excepted); no one will be allowed to travel on private business. Foreign traders will be confined to the marketplace. Public visitors will be received and housed by public officials. To acquire the knowledge of the laws of others, which they need in order to preserve their own, the council should allow only the most incorruptible citizens to travel—those who are no less than fifty years of age—and they may not remain away beyond the age of sixty. These travelers should seek especially those "divine human beings—not many—whose intercourse is altogether worthwhile, and who do not by nature grow any more frequently in cities with good laws than in cities without" (*Laws* 951b). These official travelers should be required to report to the council immediately on their return about what they have learned. If they come back unchanged or improved, they should be praised. If they return corrupted by their experience, they are to be allowed to live as private individuals so long as they do not associate or converse with anyone else, young or old, making a claim to be wise. If, however, they are convicted in court "for being a busybody concerning the

---

139. It is not entirely clear whether members of the Nocturnal Council would include both men and women. As Kochin (*Gender*, 94–96), argues, the prohibition of women serving in public office from age twenty to forty suggests not; so does the fact that the supervisor of education must be a father. If each elder in the Nocturnal Council is to choose one male (*ton neon*, 961b), it also looks as if women would never be included in the younger generation being schooled for future leadership. Selection as one of the younger members is not by public election, however; nor is membership in the council a prerequisite for election as a "guardian." It could not be, so long as the selection of younger members remained secret. Selection was kept secret so that young people who were nominated and then rejected would not know. The Athenian probably knew that the attack on the Pythagoreans was said to have been led by a youth who had been rejected.

education and the laws" (952d), they are to die. In other words, Socrates would not be allowed to live in this city. By urging them to receive foreign observers who wish to learn about their laws like the observers the council sends abroad as friends and to give them complete freedom to go where they want and talk to whom they wish, however, the Athenian brings his own inquiries and knowledge into the city.

Knowledge of the ways of others will not benefit the guardians of the laws if they do not understand the purpose for which such knowledge is to be employed. The most important thing for a legislator to know, the Athenian suggested at the beginning of his description of his city in speech (709b–c), is the goal of the laws. Rulers of other cities have not achieved their goal, he now explains, because they have pursued many different ends or visions. Chasing in various, if not simply contradictory, directions, they have worked at cross-purposes and necessarily fallen short of the goal. Coming to the end of his description of his city in speech, the Athenian asks Clinias and Megillus: what does a legislator seek the way a pilot seeks to bring his ship safely to harbor, a doctor seeks the health of his patients, or a general seeks victory? Remembering the Athenian's initial criticism of the Dorians for fostering only one part of virtue, courage, as well as the Athenian's emphasis on fostering intelligence, first and foremost, Clinias responds: virtue, which we said had four parts, with mind leading the way.

If the end of the city is virtue, the Athenian suggests, members of the council who are to safeguard the regime must be able to determine in what respects or why virtue has many forms and in what way it is one. The Athenian thus sounds very Socratic. He even proposes to show Clinias and Megillus how such investigations would be conducted through question and answer. He thus tests his interlocutors' ability to learn and hence to become members of the council he urges them to organize. To show how the virtues of courage and prudence differ, the Athenian points out that courage, which some beasts and children have by nature, can be had without reason (*logos*), but that no one can acquire prudence (*phronēsis*) or intelligence (*nous*) without reason. Since he has already brought out the intellectual limitations of his interlocutors, we are not surprised to learn that neither can say how the virtues are one. Readers of other Platonic dialogues know that Socrates would not have accepted the Athenian's definition of courage (which he rejects in the *Laches* 196c–99e). Unschooled by the sophists, Clinias is not able like Nicias to respond that true courage consists in knowledge of what is truly fearful. The Athenian does not tell his interlocutors, as Socrates tells Glaucon and Adimantus (*Republic* 518d–e), that all the virtues can be subsumed in *phronēsis*. In the face of his interlocutors' admitted incapacity to answer the question concerning the unity of the virtues, the Athenian drops the Socratic method (*methodos*; 965a) almost as quickly as he introduced it. He does not, however, drop his insistence on the need for such investigations of the unity and diversity not only of virtue but also of the good and the noble.[140]

For their present purposes, the Athenian tells Clinias, it suffices for them to agree that it will be necessary for guardians of the law to know the truth about virtue, goodness, and nobility, to be able to articulate the reasons for that truth in speech, and to act on the basis of it. Like a legislator, the Athenian accepts the sufficiency of agreement on a true opinion rather than insist like Socrates on the importance of acquiring knowledge of the truth itself. Adding (966b) that knowledge of these truths will enable the guardians to judge (*krinontas*) what comes into being well (literally, "nobly") and what not according to nature (*ta te kalōs gignomena kai ta mē kata phusin*), the Athenian moves the discussion even further in a non-Socratic direction. It is not altogether clear what it means to judge those things that come into being nobly or well by nature. It could mean according to the natural order, that is, to be born, mature, and die in an appropriate time rather than wither prematurely on the vine; it could refer to deciding what is a noble, if not good, or bad form of existence. What is clearer is that Socrates seeks truth in and about things that never change, whereas the Athenian is most concerned with judging what comes into being. If he himself is not a legislator, he is a teacher of legislators, and legislators for human beings are concerned primarily with "things" that come to be. At most, the knowledge he states the members of the Nocturnal Council must acquire of the differences and unity of the virtues as well as the ideas of the noble and good would give them the standards by which they would become able to judge things that come to be. The knowledge they are to acquire of virtue, the noble, and the good thus appears to be a means of making such judgments, that is, instrumental. Among those

140. The central problem is essentially the same in all three cases. Virtue, good, and nobility are all qualities most ancient Greeks would agree belong to a completely developed, excellent, and happy human being. The phrase they used to describe an admirable man was *kalos k'agathos*. Although these qualities are obviously interrelated, good (especially when associated with pleasure), nobility (associated particularly with courage) and virtue (including justice and wisdom) are, nevertheless, just as obviously different.

things (unstated, but which apparently come to be), the Athenian continues, are the gods.[141]

Instead of a teaching about the *eidē* or *ideai* of the virtues, the noble, or the good, the Athenian thus reverts to the cosmological teaching about the gods he has already presented as the fundamental teaching of the regime (or now, of the school for legislators and guardians) he proposes to found.[142] Admitting that human knowledge of the divine is limited, he insists nevertheless on the centrality of two elements of his doctrine. The first is the priority of soul to body—or of motion to becoming. The second is the significance of the discovery of the orderly motions of the heavenly bodies. He concludes by insisting that the political persecution of philosophers who engaged in such studies in the past and promulgated similar doctrines was their own fault. If the thinkers (like Anaxagoras) who taught that the orderly movement of the stars exhibited the power of *nous* had drawn the correct inferences (like the Athenian)—that this order not only provides evidence of the role of intelligence in the construction of the whole but also points to an intention to effect the good—they would not have been accused of atheism. It was their own erroneous conclusion, that things come into being as a result of chance and necessity rather than intelligence, and their contention that the sun, moon, and stars are lifeless stones rather than embodiments or signs of the movement of soul, that led the many to conclude that astronomical studies were destructive of piety and wonder or awe (*aidōs*).

In advocating the need for foreign exchanges as well as in his cosmological teaching, the Athenian shows how philosophical investigations of certain kinds could be incorporated into a political order without having the disintegrating or corrupting effect that open questioning of the adequacy of the existing laws necessarily would. A city that established a council of the kind he recommends to educate its future rulers would certainly increase their intelligence without encouraging the development of

141. Cf. Strauss, *Argument and Action*, 183–84.
142. The authenticity of the *Epinomis* has been questioned. This dialogue purports to be a continuation of the conversation related in the *Laws* in which the same interlocutors specify what the wisdom (*sophia*) that members of the Nocturnal Council should acquire is. And in the *Epinomis* we see that an investigation of the unity and diversity of the four traditional virtues is not central to the council's deliberations. (If not Plato, his editor or imitator drew such a conclusion.) In the *Epinomis* (989b) the Athenian states that piety (*eusebeia*) is and will be the supreme virtue, encompassing wisdom, courage, moderation, and justice. There is little dialogue, much less dialectical exchange of questions and answers, among the interlocutors in the *Epinomis*. To acquire the necessary piety that results from the two major principles of his cosmology, he emphasizes, members of the Nocturnal Council will have to study number, geometry, and astronomy.

greed and naked ambition that resulted from both Spartan conquests and Athenian commerce.[143] The Athenian succeeds, moreover, in persuading two old Dorians who have not themselves had the advantage of such an education that it would be desirable for their successors. The elders seem to recognize that the successful founding of a new and desirable kind of polity depends crucially upon his wisdom. When the Athenian finally asks Clinias point blank whether they should establish such a council, the Cretan asks him how they could not. Even though the Athenian volunteers to share the risk with them and suggests that he might even be able to find others who could help, when they begin their discussions of education and lawmaking all over again from the beginning with the individuals they think most qualified to participate in them, Megillus tells Clinias that they must abandon all hope of founding their city unless they persuade the Athenian to stay and help. Clinias agrees.

III. Conclusion: On the Compatibility of Philosophy and Political Order

If the realization of the Athenian's city in speech depends on the creation of the Nocturnal Council, some modern critics have contended, the argument of the *Laws* is incoherent. In place of the rule of unchanging law, the Athenian has finally, as Aristotle suggests (*Politics* 1265a), brought back the rule of philosophers he advocated in the *Republic*.[144] This criticism seems misdirected, however, in two fundamental respects. First, it is by no means clear that all or even most members of the Nocturnal Council would qualify as philosophers.[145] They are supposed to seek knowledge about the laws and related matters, which might even include the order of the cosmos;

---

143. Thucydides provides an incomparable account of both in his history of the Peloponnesian War. See *The Landmark Thucydides*, ed. Robert B. Strassler, trans. Richard Crawley (New York: Free Press, 1996).

144. See, e.g., Eduard Zeller, *Plato and the Older Academy*, trans. F. Alleyn and A. Goodwin (London: Longmans, Green, 1888), 539–40; Ernest Barker, *Greek Political Theory: Plato and His Predecessors* (London: Methuen, 1918), 406; George H. Sabine, *A History of Political Theory*, rev. ed. (New York: Henry Holt, 1950), 85; P. A. Brunt, "The Model City in Plato's *Laws*," in *Studies in Greek History and Thought* (Oxford: Clarendon Press, 1993), 250–51; and Klosko, "Nocturnal Council," 74–88, on the "incoherence" of the argument. Cf. the critique of this position by W. Bradley Lewis, "The Nocturnal Council and Platonic Political Philosophy," *History of Political Thought* 19, no. 1 (1998): 1–20. Paul Shorey, *What Plato Said* (Chicago: University of Chicago Press, 1933), 405; and Guthrie, *History*, 5:373–74, argue that at the end the *Laws* becomes the same as the *Republic*.

145. Cf. Bobonich, *Utopia*, 393–94.

their investigations are nevertheless targeted at a practical and partial subject. Most of the members of the Nocturnal Council serve, moreover, ex officio—as a result of their election to high office by their fellows, not primarily or directly by virtue of their education, love of truth, or intellectual potential. Second, it is clear that neither the council nor any of its members has tyrannical, that is, unlimited, power. The council comes into being to preserve the laws by studying the grounds for them and ways they might be improved. As Aristotle observes (*Politics* 1266c5), there is no monarchical, much less tyrannical, element in the regime proposed in the *Laws*. Several individuals are to be elected for limited terms to all the highest offices. These officials are required not merely to announce but to justify their decisions in public. In both these ways the Athenian has put a number of legal restraints on the power of any single individual as well as a good deal of deliberation and public accountability into his regime.

The reason no single human being can be trusted to rule others, and why the rule of law thus becomes necessary, is that few human beings have the requisite knowledge, and none can be expected, always and in every case, to subordinate his or her own private interest to the common good. By giving the highest offices to a number of different individuals at once, limiting their terms, holding elections, having the performance of public officials audited by others afterward, and subjecting them to the penal code as well as the complex system of educational customs and practices, the Athenian has prescribed a great many legal means of restraining the selfish desires and fears to which human beings are prone. Nevertheless, as the Athenian has insisted from the beginning of the dialogue, such restraints do not and will not suffice to produce virtuous or happy people. To rule themselves—both as individuals and as a community—and so attain and retain their freedom and friendship, people have to develop their intelligence.

Contemporary liberals might object that citizens of his regime are hardly free; they are constantly supervised, and they are explicitly discouraged from doing anything independently—in action or thought.[146] The Athenian insists, however, that human beings who act or react on the basis of their momentary and fleeting inclinations are not free. They cannot rule or direct themselves. Because they have no steady direction themselves,

---

146. See especially *Laws* 942c, where the Athenian urges that "one should teach one's soul by habits not to know, and not to know how to carry out, any action at all apart from the others; as much as possible everyone should in every respect live always in a group, together, and in common." The reason he gives is that this will facilitate victory in war.

they cannot be trusted or relied on by others. They cannot or will not, therefore, long be regarded as friends. People must be trained to control their passions, if not to follow the dictates of reason, and as anyone who has dealt with infants knows, this training involves some habituation or conditioning. Human beings do not learn to rule themselves or to reason without the assistance and cooperation of others. The goal of the laws is to make every citizen as virtuous as possible; laws that mandate training are necessary because human beings are not born with the capacity to rule themselves.

Because human beings are mortal, no single individual or city can acquire the knowledge required to formulate and maintain effective laws. Both in practice and precept, the Athenian has shown, people need to learn from the experience of others—what works, what doesn't, and why. They must also preserve in writing their reflections on and conclusions drawn from these experiences, so that later generations can learn from them. In striking contrast to Socrates, who famously did not write, the Athenian thus proposes that a written transcript of his conversation with the two old Dorians become the basic text or, we might say, constitution of the regime. All citizens will learn to read it; foreigners will have to master the basic text before they are allowed to teach; and judges will have to refer to it in applying the laws. Judges will, indeed, introduce necessary or desirable modifications of the law in light of experience—whether of their own people or of others—by means of their interpretations and applications of the basic text.

Like Socrates, however, the Athenian recognizes that no writing or law is simply self-explanatory. That is why he has, in effect, written into the regime itself the need for active and ongoing discussion of the laws—written and unwritten—in comparison with those of others. The elders of his city are not allowed to believe, as Clinias and Megillus do at the beginning of their conversation, that the laws of their city are superior to others because its army wins wars. Citizens of this regime are to be trained to be both moderate and courageous. Their military training is designed to enable them to defend themselves from the incursions of others and to aid their allies.[147] Citizens of this regime are emphatically not supposed to enrich themselves with the goods of those they vanquish.

147. Because the city the new colony is most apt to come in contact, and thus potential conflict, with is Cnossus, it is important to show that its relations with its neighbors on the island of Crete will be friendly, not hostile. Otherwise the mother city might try to maintain control and

The Nocturnal Council is designed to respond to virtually all the difficulties the Athenian himself pointed out in founding and maintaining the rule of law. It combines the need for foreign knowledge with safety from corruption of its own laws and customs by unregulated exchange. All the citizens will be not merely Greeks but Dorians, drawn, however, from different cities, who will therefore probably be relatively friendly but also somewhat open to change. (If they are composed primarily of potentially rebellious have-nots, they are apt to be satisfied initially with the distribution of the land into 5,040 equal parts.) Since the general regulations of education the Athenian prescribes do not differ much from those already in place in both Crete and Sparta—his major and most explicit innovation is the extension of common meals to women—their citizenry are not apt to rebel. The Athenian himself will presumably provide the requisite knowledge of legislation, especially of its goal. Clinias and Megillus are to provide the combination of persuasion and force necessary to convince the nine other Cnossian elders to adopt the Athenian's suggestions. Although it may initially appear to be unlikely, it is not impossible to imagine the other nine accepting the Athenian's proposals on trust, the way Clinias says that he has—after they have heard him discourse and they themselves are invited to serve as elder members of the council with the power to modify the laws on the basis of experience—especially with a representative of Sparta standing there ready to help.

The Nocturnal Council is explicitly designed to respond to the difficulty of succession. The primary purpose of having the elders select younger citizens to join their discussions is to prepare the latter to preserve the regime and its laws by teaching them about its end and rationale. (This education will not suffice to make them rulers, however; they have to be elected. Before, during, and after their education, the Athenian urges, these promising citizens should be carefully watched.) It is not as clear how the council responds to the other two difficulties associated with generation—the conflict between the need to make all citizens as virtuous as possible, and thus the same, and the need to recognize and take account of the differences between the sexes, not merely with regard to the act of procreation but also with regard to the effects of the biological differences on temperament and public functions, or the regulation of erotic inclinations. Because women are excluded from office from age twenty until

---

deny the new colony its freedom—or friendship. Since the colony is not going to have a navy, its military forces are not apt to go farther abroad.

forty, they may appear to be effectively excluded from the council, whose younger members are to be between thirty and forty years old. Since the younger members are not elected by the public, however—their selection and meetings are indeed to be kept secret—females could be nominated. Women could be elected as elders, although some of the offices appear to require active military service.[148] But would they be elected? Would the citizens of this city escape the preference for men and male attributes that characterized Crete and Sparta? The answer to that question depends on what the members of the council learn about virtue, both its different forms and its unity. As the Athenian admits at one point, moderation is a feminine virtue whereas courage is (literally) manly. Would the citizens of this city learn to prize both equally? That is one of the major goals of the education the Athenian mandates. The existence of the Nocturnal Council would also require the legislators to adopt the second of the Athenian's suggested laws with regard to eros, the law that allows nonsexual male friendships.

Questions about the practicability (as well as desirability) of the council thus center on the character of the discussions or studies its members could and would undertake. The first question they are to address, according to the Athenian, is the question of the unity and diversity of virtue. Clinias and Megillus demonstrated their incapacity to engage in such an inquiry, so the Athenian temporarily put it aside. Would Clinias and Megillus and their Cnossian associates allow the Athenian to raise the question with younger people in the presence of their elders behind closed doors? Would they not be embarrassed by their own demonstrated lack of knowledge of the most important things? Would they not refuse, if not initially, after some experience to select or keep younger people who asked such embarrassing questions? Would they not get angry at the stranger who prompted their young people to ask?

The Athenian's teaching about the gods, which he reintroduces at the end of the dialogue as an essential part, even core of the discussions and studies to be undertaken by the council, was introduced to assuage the anger of the elders. Their anger was aroused by younger people who questioned their practices and opinions, as well as by the teachers who pro-

148. The Athenian explicitly says (*Laws* 953e) that the foreign visitors and divine human beings can be male or female. He also states (770c–d) that the laws should do everything possible to enable all members of the community, male and female, young and old, to possess virtue of soul, and that securing the virtue of citizens is more important even than the preservation (and so presumably the military defense) of the city itself.

voked the youths to ask. Indeed, the penal code as a whole was formulated explicitly with an eye to soothing the anger citizens feel toward those who disobey the law, especially those who fail to respect family ties or, more generally, their elders. The Athenian reformulated and responded to the arguments of the cosmologists particularly in order to provide support for the law on the basis of reason, not mere command or, worse, force. He insisted that it was the cosmologists' own fault that they had been persecuted as atheists. The discoveries they had made about the orderly movements of the heavenly bodies could be used to provide a true rather than a merely mythical or simply false foundation for the laws of the regime. Rather than opposition or hostility between philosophy and political authority, the Athenian suggested, both could benefit from an alliance—an alliance that took the form of the cooperation between the Athenian and his Dorian colleagues in the *Laws* in educating a new generation or two of legislators in the Nocturnal Council.

If, as the Athenian tells his colleagues in the *Epinomis* (989b), piety were not merely the first but the unifying core of the virtues, such an alliance would be possible.[149] Unfortunately, the Athenian's account of the studies that members of the Nocturnal Council need to undertake reminds us that he did not list piety among the "divine" or the "human" goods he initially said a legislator should seek by regulating all his citizens' associations for their entire lives. Nor was piety among the four cardinal virtues for which, Clinias and the Athenian agree at the end of the *Laws*, members of the Nocturnal Council must seek to identify the differences as well as the unity. Piety—or, to be precise, the law against impiety—was introduced for the sake of preventing the outrages of the young, that is, as a means of supporting the law in general and respect for elders in particular. It would not, therefore, qualify as the end or purpose.[150] In the Athenian's city, philosophy becomes the source of a kind of natural theology that begins to look very much like what modern thinkers call "ideology," that is, the use of philosophically derived concepts and arguments to support a specific political order.

149. Even if the *Epinomis*, in which the Athenian explicitly discusses the kind of wisdom members of the Nocturnal Council would have to acquire with Clinias and Megillus, is the product of a later editor, its contents indicate that the editor and reader close to Plato concluded that the *Laws* pointed in the direction of piety or respect for elders as the central principle of the regime to be supported by studies of number, geometry, and astronomy.

150. Megillus, we recall, objected to the Athenian's depiction of the city as engaged in continuous worship of the god(s), because it demeaned the human race, that is, because it did not recognize the importance or potential excellence of human existence.

Even if the conclusions the Athenian draws from the orderly motions of the heavenly bodies are true and thus would emerge strengthened from any discussion of the findings of the cosmologists by members of the Nocturnal Council, the mathematical and astronomical studies pursued by most pre-Socratic philosophers did not include investigations of the unity and diversity of the virtues, the noble or the good. They did not because the pre-Socratic philosophers' reflections on the sensible things they observed led them to conclude that everything is in motion, and if everything is in motion, there are no eternal types or an all-encompassing unity. Even if their findings were reformulated, as the Athenian suggests, to show that motion is prior to body and that there is an intelligible order to the motions of the heavens as well as, therefore, to what comes into being and goes away on earth, these findings could not answer the first but most basic question that arises out of the attempt to institute political order: what is the best, the most excellent, noblest form of human existence?

The problem with the course of studies the Athenian recommends for the Nocturnal Council is thus not merely that investigation of the true meaning of virtue would almost surely reveal the ignorance of the elders and so embarrass and anger them. The Athenian has treated Clinias very gently and diplomatically; he might extend that treatment by questioning the younger rather than the senior members of the council. The ignorance of the founding elders is not his or their fault or responsibility. It might be unlikely—he has explicitly said that they will be undertaking a risky enterprise—but the ignorance of the elders might be cured or abolished within a generation or two, *if* the elders were persuaded, as Clinias apparently has been, that they could acquire great glory as founders of a new and better regime by trusting in him and his recommendations, *and* the Athenian and his foreign assistants had an opportunity to educate not merely one but maybe even two decades of the younger members of the Nocturnal Council in mathematics, astronomy, and philosophy.[151]

The problem that makes the education the Athenian seeks to provide members of the Nocturnal Council impossible to achieve is that the two kinds of studies or investigations he says are necessary presuppose two incompatible views of the universe. The studies of nature (especially the movements of the heavens) he recommends point to the conclusion that everything is in motion—some of that motion is orderly, some not—which

---

151. The Athenian said that he was younger than his colleagues. If he is approximately fifty years old, he would have approximately two decades in which to work.

is why there is an immortal war. The other study of the end or purpose of the polity—understood not to be the mere preservation of the community or race but the achievement of excellence—points not only to the existence of enduring standards but also to the possibility of achieving completeness by ordering the disparate parts within a whole. The fundamental problem is not, therefore, so much political as it is philosophical.[152] It is not simply or primarily that the older and more powerful members of a community will not allow their opinions to be challenged; the problem is not simply or primarily that communities cannot be based on or guided by the unadulterated truth. The problem is that the "truths" the philosophers would teach are not coherent.

As readers of the Platonic dialogues know, Socrates, unlike his predecessors, raised the question of the unity and diversity of the virtues, the noble, and the good. As he himself indicates at the beginning of the *Timaeus*, however, he did not have or articulate a cosmology (although he recommended studying all forms of mathematics, including astronomy). As Plato indicates in his depiction of the young Socrates' first encounter with Parmenides (to which we are about to turn), moreover, it is not clear whether Socrates himself ever succeeded in showing how the enduring parts or types were related to each other or to the whole.

In the combination of studies the Athenian recommends for future legislators at the conclusion of the *Laws*, Plato introduces his readers to a problem that has become all too familiar to us in the twenty-first century: the presuppositions of the study of the human good appear to contradict the presuppositions of the observed, intelligible characteristics of the universe. Familiarity should not blind us, however, to the severity of the dilemma. If no connection can be found between the most pressing concerns of human existence and the order of the whole, we humans would appear to be set adrift in a fundamentally indifferent, if not hostile environment.[153] The Athenian offered a proof that certain kinds of non-Olympian gods exist, but he did not give very convincing or valid arguments to show that they cared much about human existence—individual or as a whole.

The conclusion of the *Laws* thus points to the "beginning" or central concern of Platonic political philosophy. The question concerning virtue, the noble, and the good arises directly out of political life. To answer it

---

152. Müller (*Studien*, 13–32) also emphasizes the tension between the teaching or arguments about the virtues and their ideas, on the one hand, and the astronomically based theology, on the other.

153. Joseph Cropsey, *Plato's World* (Chicago: University of Chicago Press, 1995), makes this the central problem in his analysis.

and thereby achieve knowledge of their own purpose or goal, lawgivers need to become philosophers (or at least to study philosophy). It is not clear, however, that philosophers can answer the question. The problem is not simply that a good or effective legal order cannot tolerate the complete and unregulated questioning of its assumptions and goals, in which Socrates engaged in private conversations in Athens. As Athens showed, it can. Inquiry can be free. And, as the Athenian shows, a logical defense of the existing order can be formulated. The problem Plato dramatizes in the differences between the Athenian Stranger and Socrates is, first, whether we can discover an all-encompassing, intelligible order, and second, if such an order can be found, whether it supports or fosters human happiness. To discover that, we obviously have to know what happiness is.

2

Plato's *Parmenides*

PARMENIDES' CRITIQUE OF SOCRATES AND PLATO'S CRITIQUE OF PARMENIDES

Plato takes up the philosophical problems to which he points, but only points, at the end of the *Laws*, in the dialogue that follows the *Laws* most closely in terms of its dramatic date—the *Parmenides*.[1] Rather than solve the problems with which the *Laws* concluded, however, Plato relates a conversation in the *Parmenides* that complicates the problems further. At the end of the *Laws* the Athenian suggests that future rulers will need to investigate the unity and diversity of human virtue(s) as well as the *ideai* of the good and the noble. They will also need to learn the arguments establishing the priority of soul to body and the existence of the gods on the basis of the orderly movements of the heavenly bodies. The problem with which the *Laws* leaves its readers is that the presuppositions of the investigations of virtue and the ideas are not compatible with a cosmos in

---

1. Whereas the conversation related in the *Laws* appears to have occurred sometime in the decades following the defeat of the Persians by the Athenians and Spartans in 479 (before the explicit end of their alliance and the outbreak of the Peloponnesian War), the conversation between the elderly Eleatic and the young Socrates seems to have taken place in 450. Cf. Allen, *Plato's "Parmenides,"* 72. This estimate of the dramatic dating is based on the ages attributed to Parmenides, Zeno, and Socrates in the dialogue at 127b–d. They differ from Diogenes Laertius' estimate (9.23) of Parmenides' *akmē* or *floruit*, when he was forty years of age, as the sixty-ninth Olympiad (504–501), which was, in turn, based on the chronologist Apollodorus (9.29), who also makes Zeno forty years younger. However, as Burnet, in *Early Greek Philosophy*, has shown, Diogenes' account is problematic. Like the Olympic games, the Great Panathenaea was celebrated at four-year intervals. Since Socrates is said to have been very young at the time, and he died in 399, the most likely festival during which Parmenides, explicitly said to be sixty-five years of age, might have visited Athens and talked to him was that in 450. On the same grounds, Munk (*Natürliche Ordnung*, 59–60) dates the conversation in 446 or 442. As both Allen and Munk point out, there is no evidence outside of Plato's dialogues that the meeting took place. If it did (as Plato has his readers imagine that it did, in any case), the conversation related in the *Parmenides* took place almost twenty years before that recounted in the *Protagoras* (which has a dramatic date of 433–432).

which everything is in motion (and nothing but the fact of motion itself stays the same). In the dialogue that follows the *Laws*, Plato shows that the philosophical foundations of good politics are even more problematic by having Parmenides give a critique of Socrates' argument concerning the ideas, including the just, the good, and the noble (*Parmenides* 130b), which Socrates cannot answer.

The conversation depicted in the *Parmenides* between the elderly Eleatic and Socrates is usually thought to have occurred in 450. The *Parmenides* thus gives Plato's readers their first view of the young Socrates, when he was eighteen or nineteen years old. This fact alone has produced a certain amount of scholarly controversy. Relying on Plato's student Aristotle's characterization of Socrates as concerned solely with moral questions (*Metaphysics* 987b) and of Plato himself as the author of the "theory of the ideas" (*Metaphysics* 987a–b, 1078b–79a, 1086a–b), twentieth-century commentators like Gregory Vlastos and Terence Irwin have attempted to distinguish the "historical" Socrates depicted in the "early" elenctic dialogues from the "Socrates" of the *Republic* and other "middle" or "middle-late" dialogues such as the *Parmenides*.[2] Plato himself does not draw any such distinction. On the contrary, he not only shows Socrates presenting an argument about the ideas in his very first appearance as a philosopher in the dialogues, but in the *Phaedo* Plato also shows Socrates continuing to put forward his thesis concerning the ideas until the day he dies.[3] As a youth Socrates admitted that he could not respond to Parmenides' questions or objections, and it is difficult, if not impossible, to find a place in later dialogues (that is, Socratic conversations that are shown to have taken place after this early encounter with Parmenides) where he did. Why did Socrates continue to put forth a teaching he himself knew to be flawed? In the *Phaedo* he claims somewhat modestly that he has not been able to find a better argument. Did Plato want his readers to see that whatever advantages it might have as a way of life, as a search for knowledge Socratic philosophy was a failure? If so, why did Plato make Socrates the leading figure in most of his dialogues?[4]

2. Vlastos, *Socrates: Ironist and Moral Philosopher*; Irwin, *Plato's Ethics*.

3. Cf. Munk, *Natürliche Ordnung*, 70. As I show in more detail in later chapters, moreover, the version of the teaching concerning the ideas that Socrates presents is distinctive. His understanding of the ideas is not the same as that put forth by either Timaeus or the Eleatic Stranger.

4. Mary Louise Gill raises similar questions at the beginning of her introduction to *Plato's "Parmenides,"* 1–2. But Gill treats Parmenides' demonstration as a sustained reflection on "Plato's theory of the ideas" and not as one of the first dialogues in a dramatically indicated sequence.

A preliminary look at the argument—or, to be more precise, the aporetic stand-off—that Plato presents in the *Parmenides* in conjunction with
the *Laws* suggests that in the conversations he presents as occurring earliest, Plato is more interested in laying out a complicated problem than in
solving it. In the *Laws* he shows that even a refined version of the Ionian
understanding of the cosmos in terms of continuous motion cannot support the investigation, much less the realization, of human excellence. In
the *Parmenides* he then dramatizes the *aporia* that resulted from Eleatic
attempts to account for everything in terms of unchanging intelligible
principles—whether one or many. Insofar as it recognizes the existence of
essentially different kinds of things, Plato suggests, the Socratic teaching
about the ideas represents an improvement on Eleatic doctrine—an improvement that nevertheless presupposes Eleatic doctrine. As Parmenides'
critique of Socrates' teaching shows, however, his argument about the ideas
does not solve the problem that surfaces at the end of the *Laws*; it does not
and apparently cannot explain how the unchanging principles of order,
necessary for intelligibility per se, much less for a definition of human
excellence, can be combined with motion, sensible existence, or becoming—even though every human being "knows" from his or her own experience that somehow, in some way, they are. As we see later in the *Republic*,
Socrates' argument about the ideas, especially about the idea of the good,
could provide a basis for a teaching about the gods and so replace the Athenian's arguments about the priority of motion and the orderly movements
of the heavens. Even in the *Laws* a Socratic-like argument about the ideas
is said to be necessary to solve the political problem. The problem with
either of these "solutions" to the political problem, Plato shows his readers in the *Parmenides*, is that Socrates' argument about the ideas is itself
philosophically problematic.

I. The Occasion for the Recounting of the Early Exchange between Socrates and Parmenides

In the *Laws* Plato shows an anonymous Athenian putting forth a modified
version of Anaxagoras' claim that mind (*nous*) is the ruling principle (*archē*) of
everything and Heraclitus' contention that everything is in motion, in order to show how philosophy could be used to support political order rather
than to undermine it. He suggests that this cosmological doctrine can be
combined—somehow—with Socratic investigations of virtue and the ideas

of the good and the noble in the course of study he recommends for the Nocturnal Council. At the beginning of the *Parmenides*, Plato then reminds his readers that Anaxagoras and Socrates represent alternative responses not only to the political persecution of philosophers on the grounds of their impiety but also to the questions Parmenides and his student Zeno had raised about the existence and intelligibility of a plurality of things.

The *Parmenides* is narrated by a man named Cephalus who had traveled to Athens with a group of his fellow citizens from Clazomenae explicitly to hear a narration of an earlier conversation between Socrates and Parmenides. Cephalus does not indicate the time at which he and his companions travel to Athens. He merely reports that they went to the agora to look for Plato's brothers Adimantus and Glaucon to find out the name of their half brother, who had reputedly memorized an account of the conversation between Socrates and Parmenides. If Glaucon died along with Critias in the battle for the Piraeus, as Mark D. Munn speculates, the men from Clazomenae must have arrived in Athens before Socrates' trial, conviction, and execution.[5] If so, we are led to wonder why they didn't try to find Socrates to get an account of the conversation directly from him. Perhaps the men from Clazomenae had heard that Socrates had been criticized by Parmenides. They may not have trusted Socrates to give an honest account of the conversation. According to Cephalus, they wanted to hear an account of a conversation Socrates, Zeno, and Parmenides once had simply because they are great lovers of philosophy.

Cephalus does not explicitly mention their most famous compatriot, Anaxagoras, but it seems likely that men from Clazomenae would have wanted to find out whether Socrates had been able to respond to the challenge the old Eleatic had posed to all earlier, particularly Ionian philosophy better than their countryman had. Like Anaxagoras, the visitors from Clazomenae may have heard, Socrates accepted Parmenides' argument that being must be eternal and unchanging if it is to be intelligible, but denied that it must also, therefore, be one and undifferentiated. Like Anaxagoras, Socrates responded to Zeno's defense of Parmenides by arguing that those who maintained that being had a variety or plurality of forms did not contradict themselves by contending that being was thus both like and unlike

5. Mark D. Munn, *The School of History: Athens in the Age of Socrates* (Berkeley: University of California Press, 2000), 239. The fact that Adimantus is mentioned as having been present at Socrates' trial (*Apology* 34a), but Glaucon is not, supports the supposition that Glaucon was not living in 399 and that the men from Clazomenae must have come to Athens to hear about the conversation between Socrates and Parmenides while Socrates was still alive.

itself, if the various kinds or forms of being were themselves eternal. But where Anaxagoras had argued that there were many distinct kinds of being, which he called "seeds," themselves unchanging and too small to be perceived, that continually mixed and remixed in various combinations to form the "things" we perceive with our senses, Socrates contended that the different kinds of being were nonsensible, intelligible ideas in which sensible things participated. The men from Clazomenae probably wanted to know whether Socrates had been able to maintain his position successfully in the face of an Eleatic countercritique. Did Socrates' separation of the intelligible ideas from their sensible manifestations constitute a better response to the difficulties Parmenides' argument raised about the existence and intelligibility of the sensible world than Anaxagoras' teaching about the seeds? Or had Parmenides' criticisms demolished Socrates' thesis? In that case, their countryman's doctrine would remain the major alternative to, and correction of, the arguments of the Eleatics. Clazomenae might even replace Athens as the true home of philosophical inquiry. In that case, they would not have to travel abroad in order to fulfill their desire for wisdom.

Unfortunately for the citizens of Clazomenae, the outcome of the conversation they heard narrated is indecisive.[6] Socrates criticizes Parmenides' student Zeno, whereupon Zeno's teacher critiques Socrates. Socrates asks Parmenides how he can improve his arguments. Parmenides shows Socrates by first defending and then refuting his own thesis that one is. Ending in apparent *aporia*, the dialogue seems to pose a problem or problems more than it provides answers to the questions raised.[7]

II. The Dramatic Prologue: Dramatizing the Difficulties Mortals Encounter in Acquiring and Preserving Knowledge

On their arrival in Athens, Cephalus tells his auditors, he and his companions went straight to the agora in search of Plato's brothers Adimantus

---

6. To learn why Socrates did not follow Anaxagoras' lead, we have to turn to the *Phaedo*. If the men from Clazomenae came to Athens before 399 (see note 5), they could not have heard about the critique Socrates made of their compatriot's arguments.

7. Allen, in *Plato's "Parmenides,"* also emphasizes the aporetic character of the dialogue. W. G. Runciman, "Plato's *Parmenides*" (1959), in *Studies in Plato's Metaphysics*, ed. R. E. Allen (New York: Humanities Press, 1965), concludes: "The moral of the exercise is that . . . [Parmenides'] method has been shown to lead as legitimately to one set of contradictory conclusions as to the other" (181).

and Glaucon to find out the name of their half brother, who had reputedly memorized the conversation. Adimantus not merely identified Antiphon; he offered to take Cephalus and his associates to Antiphon's home in Melite.[8] As they walked, Adimantus explained that in his youth Antiphon had cared a great deal about philosophy, but as an adult he has, like his grandfather of the same name, concerned himself mostly with horses. By pointing out Antiphon's failure to retain his interest in philosophy as an adult, in contrast to the great efforts Cephalus and his colleagues have made to find him, at the very beginning of the dialogue Plato provokes his readers to ask why some human beings continue to pursue knowledge in the face of the enormous difficulties of obtaining, retaining, and communicating it, whereas others do not.

On seeing Cephalus, Antiphon recognizes him from an earlier visit. Although he does not initially want to recount the conversation he had memorized because it would require so much effort (*poly ergon*; 127a), he finally agrees to do so. One reason human beings try to help others learn, Plato indicates, is friendship; one way we learn is through repetition. Over time, however, errors creep in.

In the dramatic prologue to the retelling of the conversation, Plato thus emphasizes both its remoteness in time and the difficulty of relating the arguments (which become extremely abstract). The account we read is fourth-hand. A student of Zeno's at the time, Pythodorus, had recounted the original exchange many times to Antiphon (a child of Plato's mother by a second husband and so younger than Plato, Adimantus, and Glaucon). Antiphon told Cephalus and his companions. And Cephalus relates it to us (his anonymous listeners and Plato's readers).

Both the lapse of time and the number of retellings raise questions about the reliability of the account. Plato's Socrates attests to the fact of the conversation in two later (in terms of their dramatic setting) dialogues: in the *Theaetetus* (183e), when he recalls his youthful meeting with Parmenides, whom he found, in Homer's words, to be "venerable" and yet "terrible"; and in the *Sophist* (217c), when, conversing with a member of the

---

8. As Mitchell Miller, Jr., points out (*Plato's "Parmenides,"* 16), Adimantus' taking Cephalus by the hand (126a) to greet and guide him literally echoes the beginning of Parmenides' poem in which the goddess takes him by the hand to show him the way. As we shall see, this is but one of the ways in which Plato's dialogue parallels the structure of Parmenides' poem. Like the goddess, Adimantus leads Cephalus to the place where he can learn but does not communicate any knowledge directly to him.

Eleatic school, Socrates remembers the beauty of Parmenides' arguments. However, in contrast to the *Theaetetus*, in which someone present at the conversation also relates it later to a third party, Socrates is not said to have reviewed the contents of the narrative or attested to its accuracy.[9] Nor does Socrates say that he learned anything from Parmenides—in even greater contrast to the *Symposium*, where someone present at the conversation tells a third party, who in turn tells others what Socrates said Diotima taught him about eros.[10] Is Plato suggesting that Socrates failed to learn what Parmenides tried to teach him? Or, by showing that Socrates failed to adopt it, is Plato suggesting that Parmenides' method of arguing is defective because it cannot produce an internally consistent, comprehensive view?

The need for repeated retellings dramatizes the problem Parmenides himself announces later in his critique of Socrates—namely, how transitory beings can have access to the eternal truth. The "action" with which Plato introduces the conversation thus reflects what proves to be the central difficulty for both the Eleatics and Socrates, that is, how transitory things can be understood in terms of unchanging eternal ideas.[11]

The dramatic context points, moreover, to a further, related problem: if human beings succeed in acquiring knowledge, how can they preserve and perpetuate it by passing it on to others?[12] Most philosophers tried to communicate their thought to later generations in writing, but Socrates later became famous as the philosopher who did not write.[13] Nevertheless,

9. *Theaetetus* 142d–43a; *Symposium* 173b. As Harrison J. Pemberton, *Plato's "Parmenides": The Critical Moment for Socrates* (Darby, PA: Norwood Editions, 1984), points out, in the *Symposium* we hear (or read) thirdhand Apollodorus' retelling of the discourses he heard about Eros. Moreover, as Stanley Rosen, *Plato's "Symposium"* (New Haven: Yale University Press, 1968), 9, points out, Apollodorus' recollection and account are explicitly said at 178a to be incomplete. Cf. also *Proclus' Commentary on Plato's "Parmenides,"* trans. Glen R. Morrow and John M. Dillon (Princeton: Princeton University Press, 1987), 1.2.618–25.

10. It does not appear to be quite right to claim, as both Pemberton (*Critical Moment*) and Miller (*Plato's "Parmenides"*) do, that Parmenides educated Socrates.

11. The geographical location of the conversation points to the same problem. As *Proclus' Commentary on Plato's "Parmenides"* 1.4.629 observed, the *Parmenides* explicitly represents Athens and its young philosopher Socrates in the midst, if not literally the middle, of the philosophical dispute between the Italians, who emphasized the intelligible ideas, and the Ionians, who studied the sensible realm of becoming or nature.

12. Cf. Jacques Derrida, *Edmund Husserl's "Origins of Geometry,"* trans. John Leavey, Jr. (Stony Brook, NY: Nicolas Hays, Ltd., 1978), 25–107.

13. Martin Heidegger, *What Is Called Thinking?* trans. Fred Wieck and J. Glenn Gray (New York: Harper and Row, 1968), 26, thus calls Socrates the "purest" but not one of the greatest philosophers. Jacques Derrida, *Of Grammatology*, trans. Gayatri Spivak (Baltimore: Johns Hopkins University Press, 1976), 6, also emphasizes Socrates' refusal to write.

both in the *Parmenides* and in the *Phaedrus* (where Socrates gives his famous critique of writing), Plato shows that the written word has considerable power—even over Socrates. In the only two dialogues (again, the *Parmenides* and the *Phaedrus*) in which Plato depicts Socrates voluntarily leaving the city (in contrast to his military service at Potidaea and Delium), Plato shows that Socrates was drawn out of Athens by a desire to hear what another had written.[14] In the *Parmenides*, it is Zeno's treatise.

As in the *Phaedrus*, so in the *Parmenides*, the reading is not merely followed but is supplanted by what is clearly a superior live exchange. The function of writing, Plato suggests, is not so much the direct communication of the thoughts of one into the mind of another, a substitute as it were for memorization, but the eliciting of questions that provoke further thought on the part of listeners or readers. (In both the *Parmenides* and the *Phaedrus* Socrates subjects the written argument to a devastating critique.) The function of writing thus appears, in Socratic terms, to be erotic. Like eros, writing is not simply a medium of communication between two persons; it can take a human being beyond his or her own immediate experience into something that transcends it by arousing questions or objections on the part of readers. Both Socrates and Plato recognize that the search for wisdom cannot be perpetuated simply by recording the conclusions or arguments; its continuation depends on awakening an interest in continued inquiry on the part of other people.

By introducing a man named Cephalus (even though he is not the same as the metic—long dead—in whose home in the Piraeus the *Republic* takes place) as well as Glaucon and Adimantus, Socrates' primary interlocutors in that later, much longer conversation, Plato reminds readers of the *Parmenides* that Socrates had succeeded in arousing and sustaining such an erotic interest among his Athenian compatriots, whereas the Eleatic visitors had not.[15] The Athenians who studied with Zeno—Antiphon and Pythodorus—had given up philosophy. As Plato shows in the *Euthydemus*,

---

14. At the beginning of the *Lysis* (203a), Socrates is shown to be walking right outside the walls of Athens but is drawn in by some youths he knows.

15. Robert S. Brumbaugh, *Plato on the One: The Hypotheses in the "Parmenides"* (New Haven: Yale University Press, 1961), 29, also notes the failure of the young students of Zeno to pursue philosophy. Miller (*Plato's "Parmenides,"* 18–25) emphasizes the connections established by the interlocutors between the *Parmenides* and the *Republic* as part of his argument that the teaching of the *Parmenides* constitutes a more consistent and philosophical presentation of the doctrines, delivered in a lower, less accurate, because political, form and context in the *Republic*. For reasons that become clear in the analysis that follows, I do not agree.

the refutative method represented by Zeno and later recommended by Parmenides first attracts young people, but it later frustrates and finally alienates them when they grow older. This is perhaps one of the reasons Socrates did not take Parmenides' advice and practice such philosophical "gymnastics." As Socrates observes in the *Philebus*, young people enjoy seeing others, especially their elders, refuted. Over time, however, people not merely become frustrated by arguments that first affirm and then negate a given proposition; they begin to distrust the speaker, because it is not possible to determine what he or she actually thinks.[16]

Because the Athenian followers of Zeno subsequently lost all interest in such arguments, the conversation related in the *Parmenides* is revived only at the behest of the men from Clazomenae.[17] Neither Socrates nor any of the other Athenians displays an enduring interest in pursuing the questions raised. In contrast to his exchange with Protagoras, for example, Socrates is never shown relating the exchange he had with Parmenides and his student Zeno to anyone else. The reason is not hard to find. In the *Protagoras* Socrates clearly bests the then much more famous sophist in argument; Protagoras himself admits as much (361d–e). By immediately retelling the conversation to a broader audience, Socrates contributes to building his own reputation. In the *Parmenides*, the older philosopher criticizes the younger man's teaching about the ideas in ways he cannot answer. The young Socrates may not have been as anxious to let others know about his seeming defeat. But Socrates at least retained his interest in philosophy. The other Athenians present at his conversation with the Eleatics subsequently lost their desire for knowledge and turned their attention instead to more practical, political affairs. Antiphon devoted himself to horses, a mark of Athenian nobility. Pythodorus became a general in the Peloponnesian War, and the young Aristotle, whom Parmenides interrogates in the "demonstration" at the end of the dialogue, is explicitly said to have become one of the Thirty. As we know from the *Republic*, Glaucon and Adimantus once pressed Socrates to discuss justice—in some detail

16. Ordinary Athenians like Crito conclude that eristic argumentation constitutes a futile exercise that may even be detrimental to the formation of a good character (*Euthydemus* 506d–e).

17. Kenneth Sayre (*Parmenides' Lesson*, 58) dismisses the association other commentators have drawn between Cephalus and Anaxagoras on the grounds that Anaxagoras left Clazomenae at too young an age to have established a philosophical school or tradition. Cephalus and his associates could, however, have heard about Anaxagoras' doctrines as a result of the books he wrote, the way Socrates did (*Phaedo* 97b–c). Cities often take more pride in their famous residents after they leave (or die) than while they are present.

and at considerable length—and Socrates related that conversation to others. Neither Socrates nor Plato's brothers exhibit the same interest in the conversation Antiphon committed to memory; they certainly make no claim to know or to be able to summarize it.

Both the content of his investigations and the manner in which Socrates conducted them had more popular and lasting appeal than Eleatic philosophy. Socrates had already begun to ask questions of particular concern to human beings by the time he met Parmenides; the old Eleatic comments that he heard Socrates attempting to define the noble, just, and good in a conversation with Aristotle the day before (135c–d). But, Plato shows in the *Parmenides*, Socrates had not yet learned how investigations of human opinions could provide him with a possible response to the objections Parmenides raised to his argument about the ideas. Socrates learned that later from Diotima, as we shall see in chapter 3.

III. In Defense of Plurality:
Socrates' Critique of Zeno

Pythodorus told Antiphon that Socrates had come to his house with some other Athenians to listen to Zeno read his treatise.[18] When Zeno finished, Socrates asked him to reread the first thesis and then inquired: "Is what you mean, Zeno, that if there are many, they must be both like and unlike, which is impossible; for the unlike cannot be like or the like unlike?" (*Parmenides* 127e ; my translation). Receiving an affirmative answer, Socrates then rather impertinently asked Zeno whether his many arguments and treatises were all the same. Socrates implied that Zeno's practice of giving multiple arguments to prove, negatively, the truth of Parmenides' teaching contradicted his teacher's fundamental insight, that being and thinking are the same, as well as the conclusion that Parmenides deduced from it, that being is one.

Turning to the older Eleatic, the young philosopher wondered whether Parmenides' student had tried to be close to him not only in love (*philia*) but also in doctrine (and perhaps eminence) by arguing for the same con-

---

18. The fact the conversation takes place outside the city indicates its apolitical character. The only other dialogue in which Socrates is shown going outside the city is the *Phaedrus*, in which he claims to have been drawn by his love of *logoi*. The subject there is also apolitical—eros.

clusion, that everything is one, but pretending to say something new, that it is not many. In other words, Socrates again suggested, Zeno was contradicting his own explicit argument in deed, as it were, by presenting the same as other. Neither the master nor the student, Socrates intimated, could account for their personal relations or the combination of similarity and difference in their respective doctrines. The two Eleatics had neither observed nor reflected on the implications of the disjunction between their deeds and their words (or arguments).[19] They had not sought self-knowledge or taken account of the distinctively human things. They had not, because they denied that there are fundamentally different forms or kinds of being.

Zeno responded to the surface thrust of Socrates' accusation by denying any intention to deceive others about the novelty of his doctrine. He wrote his treatise to defend his teacher from critics who ridiculed Parmenides by drawing out the preposterous consequences of his denial of plurality. He was young and eristic at the time of composition. Indeed, Zeno said, he was not sure he would have published the treatise; it was stolen from him. Nevertheless, readers cannot fail to observe, Zeno was reading it to a new and foreign audience; he had not disowned it.[20]

Perhaps as a result of Zeno's courtesy, Socrates turned away from personal innuendo and attacked Zeno's argument directly. If there is an idea of likeness itself and another idea of its opposite, unlikeness, and we call things that participate in the first "like" and those that participate in its opposite "unlike," Socrates asked, what is so paradoxical about something participating in opposite qualities, so long as the opposites, the ideas, remain pure? In contrast to the Eleatics, Socrates then explicitly applied his argument to himself by observing that if Zeno were to say that Socrates is a composite of many parts and yet to assert that Socrates is still one, he would say nothing surprising. Zeno's argument would truly arouse wonder (which traditionally became the source of philosophy, according to

19. As Sayre (*Parmenides' Lesson*, 66) notes. Although primarily in criticism, Socrates, on the other hand, uses himself as an example par excellence of a "one" who is, at the same time, many, that is, has many different characteristics. Even at this early stage of his career, we see, in contrast to previous philosophers, that Socrates insists his argument must account for his own situation and activity. In the *Phaedo* (98c–99b), Socrates makes a similar criticism of those (including Anaxagoras) who seek to explain things solely on the basis of their material composition.

20. Once again, we observe, Zeno's deeds contradict his speech. He could not have read the same arguments from a book that was stolen unless he had a copy, that is, a copy of the same *logoi* that was nevertheless different from the original.

Plato and Aristotle) only if Zeno showed that the ideas themselves were somehow mixed.[21]

What Socrates' questions show is that Zeno's argument that one cannot maintain that more than one "thing" is without contradicting himself, because the many must be said to be both like and unlike, itself depends on his positing of opposites, that is, two things—like and unlike. Zeno's negative conclusion that there cannot be more than one, because more than one would have to be both like and unlike, and like and unlike are mutually exclusive, contradicts his positive premise that the mutually exclusive like and unlike are not and can never be one. It is not clear, however, that Parmenides' own negative proposition—that it is impossible to think or to say the "is not"—involves him in a similar contradiction. There might be a difference between the positions of the student and his teacher, as Socrates indicates when he observes that in his poem Parmenides had argued "nobly and well," whereas in his treatise Zeno presented "many, weighty proofs" (*Parmenides* 128b). Perhaps that is the reason Parmenides enters the discussion.

IV. Parmenides' Critique of Socrates

Pythodorus told Antiphon that he thought Socrates would make Parmenides and Zeno angry but that the two Eleatics merely smiled at one another. Since Parmenides said he had heard Socrates arguing with Aristotle the day before, Plato leads his readers to suspect that the older philosopher was familiar with the young Athenian's teaching about the ideas and had a critique ready to deliver.

Praising Socrates' talent for argument, Parmenides first asked the young man whether he himself discovered the distinction between intelligible ideas and the things that participate in them or whether he had learned it from someone else. As Socrates had insinuated about Zeno, so, Parmenides suggested, Socrates might be using the argument of another to further his own reputation. But when Socrates stated that the argument was his, Parmenides quickly stepped back from such innuendoes and inquired, what sorts of things did Socrates think there are ideas of: the opposites of which Zeno had been speaking, likeness and unlikeness, for example? the just,

21. Cf. *Theaetetus* 155d; Aristotle *Metaphysics* A.2 2982b12; Martin Heidegger, *What Is Philosophy?* trans. William Kluback and Jean T. Wilde (New Haven: Yale University Press, 1956), 79–81.

the noble, and the good? Socrates readily agreed that there are ideas of the general standards we use to differentiate kinds or states of being—for example, like and unlike, many and one, rest and motion—and of the just, the good, and the noble.[22] These qualities are clearly not sensible in themselves (although it is by no means clear that we can perceive them directly in themselves without any experience of the sensible things that participate in them). However, when Parmenides asked whether Socrates also thought there is an idea of the human being (a natural species of which there are clearly sensible examples) or of the basic elements of nature such as fire and water (which are also sensible things), the young man admitted he had been unable to make up his mind. And when the Eleatic inquired about base, dishonorable things like hair, mud, and dirt, Socrates said it would be exceedingly strange if there were ideas of such things, which seem to be exactly as they appear to us. Nevertheless, the young man admitted, he sometimes suspected that what is true of some things is true of all. Fearing he would fall into an abyss of nonsense, Socrates had avoided the question about the character of the whole and the relation of its different parts to concentrate on those things of which he was sure there are purely intelligible ideas. One of the major implications, if not conclusions, of the dialogue is that he cannot continue to do so.

As Parmenides' subsequent questions made clear, Socrates was not able to explain the relation between the different kinds of being, intelligible and sensible, he had identified. Socrates admitted he was not able to give an account of the whole. But, Parmenides warned, if Socrates did not pursue the question of the relation between the parts and the whole, which he now avoided (because it led to the paradoxes characteristic of Eleatic philosophy), Socrates would never acquire the knowledge or wisdom that as a philosopher he claimed to seek. Philosophy had not yet taken hold of him as much as Parmenides believed it would when Socrates was older. Wisdom comes—or can only come—with age, Parmenides suggested. Young people are too concerned about looking good in the eyes of others. So, Parmenides thought, Socrates paid too much attention to human opinion, which values the high and rare more than the common or base. As Socrates will learn from Diotima, however, the Eleatics were not able to show

22. The former type of idea is often called "mathematical," but as Allen points out (*Plato's "Parmenides,"* 106), the notions Zeno employs are not, strictly speaking, simply mathematical in the narrow sense (that is, involving number, calculation, and/or geometry), especially if we include generation and destruction along with being and not-being, which are added to the list at 136b.

how sensible things are related to the purely intelligible precisely because they refused to recognize opinion as the in-between.[23]

Moving from a general to a more specific critique of the young philosopher's argument concerning the ideas, Parmenides observed that in his critique of Zeno Socrates had not only distinguished the ideas from their manifestations in sensible objects; he had also claimed that the latter "participated" in the ideas. How? Parmenides asked. First, he queried somewhat rhetorically, does an object partake in the whole of an idea or only a part? If in the whole, he then observed, the idea would have to be both in itself and in the other, and it is impossible for one thing to be in two places at once. As several commentators have noted, Parmenides thus treated the ideas as if they had spatial existence or locus.[24] Socrates did not insist, as he should have, upon his own major insight into the difference between the physical and the intelligible; he was young and inexperienced. Instead, Socrates suggested, an idea may be like the day, in many places (or participants) at once. Changing the metaphor to a sail (and thus from a temporal to a spatial concept once more), Parmenides pointed out that only a part of the overarching "cover" would be over any particular part. So it appears, Socrates hesitantly responded; as Parmenides observed, Socrates did not want to agree that ideas can be divided.[25]

Parmenides pressed the question further by asking: if things do not participate in the ideas either as a whole or in part, how do they partake of them? Socrates probably thinks each idea is one for something like the following reason: "When there are a number of things that seem to you to be great, you may think, as you look at them, that there is one and the same idea in them, and hence you think the great is one" (*Parmenides* 132a). True, Socrates agreed. Parmenides then gave his famous regress argument: for every set of things that share a given characteristic, there will be a broader description or idea of the characteristic that encompasses both the things

23. Cf. *Sophist* 227b; *Statesman* 262a–63a. I discuss the significance of this difference between these two heirs of Parmenides in much more detail in chapters 9 and 10. In the *Phaedo* Socrates explains that his distinctive way of philosophizing consists in an examination of the speeches or arguments, *logoi*, of other human beings. In the *Symposium* he adds a concern with opinions, *doxai*, as that which is in between the Parmenidean opposites, being and not being and/or truth and falsity.

24. Cf. Allen, *Plato's "Parmenides,"* 110–21; Miller, *Plato's "Parmenides,"* 50–51.

25. If ideas can be divided, Parmenides observes, taking away a part of the great will make the great smaller (that is, participate in the small); likewise, if a part of the smaller is divided from the small, the remaining small is still apt to be larger than the part. Parmenides has thus shown how the ideas might be mixed with each other—what Socrates said earlier would be truly wonder provoking.

and the idea in which the things participate.[26] As several commentators have noted, Parmenides' argument depends on an identification of the idea of, say, largeness, with a large thing. If the purely intelligible idea were distinguished from its sensible manifestations, as Socrates argued it should be, the regress would not occur.[27]

Socrates suggested that the ideas might only be in our souls; they are not the same as or in the things that we name after them. Parmenides then inquired whether Socrates thinks that each of the ideas is one. Isn't each an idea of something and of something that exists? If all things that are participate in the ideas and the ideas are thoughts (*noēmata*), Parmenides pointed out, Socrates would be saying that everything that is, which is to say, everything that participates in the ideas, thinks (*noei*). That ridiculous conclusion, ironically, would have brought Socrates very close to Parmenides' own famous saying that to think (*noein*) and to be (*einai*) are the same. For, if Socrates denied that being and thinking are the same, he would have the ideas (being thoughts) thought by something that does not have being or exist.

Quickly retreating from his proto-idealist position, Socrates more characteristically suggested that the ideas are paradigms or models of which the particular things are likenesses. If the ideas are like their copies, Parmenides responded, they confront another infinite regress in which ideas and their likenesses will be like in some broader, third, fourth, fifth, or infinitely large, respect. Once again Socrates temporized with a qualified answer, "So it seems" (132a). He should have objected that the relation between idea and likeness is not reciprocal, because ideas are not in the same way as spatiotemporal things are.

Even if Socrates had shown that Parmenides' refutations were ill founded, the fundamental problem remains: How are the purely intelligible ideas and their sensible counterparts related? How can human beings who exist in time and space have access to the eternal and unchanging? How can like and unlike be combined without self-contradiction? As Parmenides suggests, this is the greatest perplexity (*aporia*).

26. Cf. Gregory Vlastos, "The Third Man Argument in the *Parmenides*," *Philosophical Review* 63, no. 3 (July 1954): 319–49; W. Sellars, "Vlastos and 'The Third Man,'" *Philosophical Review* 64, no. 3 (July 1955): 405–37; P. T. Geach, "The Third Man Again," *Philosophical Review* 65, no. 1 (January 1956): 72–82; and Colin Strang, "Plato and the Third Man," *Proceedings of the Aristotelian Society*, supp. 37 (1963): 147–64.
27. See, e.g., Francis M. Cornford, *Plato and Parmenides* (London: Routledge and Kegan Paul, 1939), 94; Miller, *Plato's "Parmenides,"* 54; Allen, *Plato's "Parmenides,"* 144–45.

If the ideas do really exist separate from the things participating in them, Parmenides pointed out, mortal creatures cannot possibly know them. Once again spatializing the intelligible, he argued that, being in themselves, the ideas cannot be in us or our souls. Existing separately in themselves, these ideas can exist only in relation to other ideas, not for us; as sensible creatures we can obtain knowledge only about the sensible world with which we have contact. Making the unhappy consequences of this limitation on human knowledge explicit, Parmenides concluded: we cannot know the good or the noble or the just itself (134b–c). Only a god can know the atemporal ideas, and having no contact with the sensible world, such a god can have no knowledge of or control over us. If the intelligible ideas exist independent of the sensible world, as Socrates suggested, we live in a godless universe.

Parmenides' questions about the extent or kinds of ideas, the way in which things participate in them, and the possibility of human beings coming to know them all point to the absence of any connection between the intelligible and the sensible. This was the problem the historical Parmenides had dramatized in his poem. Having questioned the validity of Socrates' argument, Plato's Parmenides thus emphasizes the importance of the question. If, because of the difficulties involved, people deny that there are ideas of things that always exist, they will lose the dianoetic ability to separate things into classes, and the possibility of conversing will be completely destroyed (because no term will have any set or lasting meaning). What is at stake is the ground or possibility of philosophy itself.

V. Parmenides' Demonstration

A. The Dramatic Prologue: The Unerotic Eleatic

Apparently recognizing that the questions he raised about Socrates' argument concerning the ideas were not as unanswerable as many readers have thought, Parmenides said his objections might not be insurmountable. If Socrates were going to overcome them, however, he needed more training in argumentation. Having listened to Socrates' conversing with Aristotle the day before, Parmenides admired the young philosopher's passion for argument as well as his insistence on approaching questions in terms of intelligible ideas rather than visible things—an insistence that made him closer to the Eleatics than to the Ionian natural philosophers. Socrates had not yet learned to examine all aspects of a proposition, however. Unlike

Zeno, Socrates only considered what followed if a particular hypothesis was true; he did not ask what followed if it was not true or what the consequences of its being true or not were for other things. In refuting Zeno, Socrates had pointed out that there was not necessarily a contradiction in maintaining that something was both like and unlike, if there were eternal ideas of both the like and unlike in which a thing could "participate." Socrates had not shown, as Parmenides had just claimed would be necessary for the possibility and perpetuation of philosophy, that nothing would be recognizable as something, if there were no such purely intelligible forms of being, because nothing could be distinguished from anything else.

Socrates asked Parmenides to help him learn how to examine a hypothesis by giving a demonstration. At first the old philosopher demurred; it would require a great effort, especially for a man of his age. So Socrates turned to Zeno, who seconded his request. Socrates might not have understood what a great effort he was asking of Parmenides, Zeno observed. If there had been many people present it would not have been appropriate to ask Parmenides to demonstrate, because the many do not know that it is impossible to attain truth without going through everything in detail. But since they were few and Zeno had not heard Parmenides for a long time, he joined Socrates in his petition, as did all the others.

Reluctantly acquiescing, Parmenides said that he felt "like the old race-horse in Ibycus, who trembles at the start of a chariot-race, knowing from long experience what is in store for him" (137a). The poet had compared himself to the horse when he was forced as an old man to enter the lists of love. So the old philosopher is afraid, when he remembers the sea of arguments he has to go through. In the only quotation of poetry in the entire dialogue, Plato's Parmenides thus reminds readers how lacking in eros he and his philosophy are. Socrates is an erotic, he explains in later dialogues, because he knows that he lacks knowledge—and hence seeks it. Parmenides is not an erotic, because he claims to have discovered the truth about being as a whole and thus to be wise. When Parmenides was younger and more actively in love with Zeno, he had perhaps been more eager to display his skill in logical "gymnastics."[28] Older and perhaps wiser,

28. The only other mention or quotation of Ibycus in the Platonic corpus is *Phaedrus* 242c8, when Socrates quotes the poet at the moment he decides that he must give a second speech, recanting his first praise of the nonlover, as having achieved the praise of men at the expense of honoring the god Eros.

he seems to fear that he might fail to demonstrate his superiority or to attract students. In the dramatic prologue, Plato has shown that Parmenides
had reason to be apprehensive.

As Cornford observes, the contrast between the one poetic image and
the rest of the conversation highlights its plain, prosaic character.[29] Other
commentators have argued that the concentration of arguments to the
exclusion of image testifies to the purely philosophical character of the
dialogue—indeed, that it provides an example of the dianoetic investigations of the pure ideas Socrates associates with the topmost part of the
divided line in the famous image (n.b.) in book 6 of the *Republic*.[30] Socrates'
differentiated ideas are not the same, however, as the one(s) or the many
(ones) or the other (than one[s]) in Parmenides' presentation. Rather than
complete the education that a more mature Socrates sketches in the *Republic*, the demonstration in Plato's *Parmenides* reflects, and reflects on, the
defective character of the Eleatic philosopher's work—both poetic and
philosophical. It shows that Parmenides was not able to solve the problem
he pointed out and then left to Socrates.

B. Plato's *Parmenides'* Critique of the
Historical Parmenides' Poem

Like Parmenides' poem, the dialogue Plato named after him has a dramatic introduction followed by a two-part argument presenting the logical
consequences, first, of the proposition "one is" (the way of truth, as the
historical Parmenides calls it) and, then, of the proposition "one is not" (or
the erroneous "two-headed 'way of opinion,'" which combines the "is"
and the "is not"). In the prologue to the dialogue, Plato indicates that Parmenides was not able to account for his own practice—both poetic and
philosophical—on the basis of his own argument. In the two-part logical
demonstration that follows, Plato then proves, in action as it were, that the
argument or doctrine itself—that being is one—is untenable. In the dialogue he names after the Eleatic philosopher, Plato thus shows that "Parmenides" contradicted himself—first in deed (*ergon*) and then in speech
(*logos*).

As the subject of their "laborious play," Parmenides puts forward his
own thesis—one is. He does so perhaps in response to Socrates' criticism

---

29. Cornford, *Plato and Parmenides*, 64; *Proclus' Commentary on "Parmenides"* 1.6.645–46.
30. See, e.g., Miller, *Plato's "Parmenides,"* 29–32.

earlier—namely, that Zeno and Parmenides cannot account for their own activity. The demonstration seems to constitute a reflection on Parmenides' own doctrine. Instead of the "noble" arguments Parmenides presented in his poem to show that being is one, however, Plato's character of the same name gives a Zeno-like reductio ad absurdum to support what appears to be the same conclusion, one is.[31] But both parts of the argument put forth by Plato's Parmenides lead to the opposite conclusion, that nothing is. In his first argument Parmenides proves that if one is, there cannot be anything beyond the one, not even being itself; in his last argument he proves that if the one is not, nothing is.[32] If anything is, readers are left to conclude with Socrates, there must be a plurality. For being to be intelligible, it must be more than one.

Observing that both the form and the substance of the argument Parmenides gives in the dialogue differ from that which the historical Parmenides presents in his poem, some commentators have insisted that Plato's Parmenides speaks for Plato; he does not represent his historical namesake.[33] But in the dramatic prologue, both Plato's Parmenides and the chief student of the historical Parmenides, Zeno, agree that they argue for the same conclusion (or "hypothesis"), if in different forms; also, Plato's Parmenides explicitly urges Socrates to practice Zeno's method. Plato's Parmenides does not suggest that he has any reservations about Zeno's reductio

31. The "one" that "is," according to the historical Parmenides, is also intelligible. (To be and to think are the same.) But the "one" is not an "idea," and Plato's Parmenides does not describe it as such. On the contrary, when he uses the word *eidos* or *idea* in his demonstration, which is rare, he uses them to refer to concepts like greatness and smallness (opposites; 149e7, 9), others as a kind (158c6), and a whole of parts (157d8) that involve plurality. If *to hen* were an idea, as Socrates says when queried by Parmenides, it would be an idea in distinction from or contrast to other ideas (like the many, *polla*); it would not be all encompassing. Commentators who want to read the *Parmenides* in terms of Plato's development of his "theory of the ideas" should pay more attention to the fact that Socrates introduces the "theory" in his exchange with Zeno at the beginning of this very dialogue to remedy the difficulties or "paradoxes" the Eleatics incurred by denying plurality.

32. The demonstration is broken up into two halves of four parts each: (*a*) if the one is, (1) Parmenides shows it has no possible characteristic, including being (hypothesis I, 137d–42a); (2) it has all possible characteristics (hypothesis II, 142b–55e), in transition in successive times (hypothesis IIa, 156e–57b); (3) others both participate in it and as a result have all the possible characteristics (hypothesis III, 157b–59b); and (4) the others do not participate in it and as a result have no characteristics at all (hypothesis IV, 159b–60d); or (*b*) if the one is not, (1) it still is in a sense a referent of speech and knowledge and is different from others in various characteristics (hypothesis V, 160b–63b); (2) it does not participate in being and thus has no characteristics (hypothesis VI, 163b–64b); (3) the others will not truly have but will seem to have characteristics (hypothesis VII, 164b–65e); and (4) that other to one is not either (hypothesis VIII, 165c–66b).

33. See, e.g., Allen, *Plato's "Parmenides"*; Cornford, *Plato and Parmenides*; Miller, *Plato's "Parmenides."*

ad absurdum. On the contrary, he proposes to demonstrate the two-sided method—as Zeno's teacher.[34] And the historical Parmenides was Zeno's teacher.

In recounting Parmenides' demonstration, Plato presents a two-pronged or two-layered critique of the Eleatic philosopher. First, there is the obvious joke in the action: Parmenides' demonstration constitutes a refutation of his own position. His argument culminates in a thoroughly contradictory statement that is absolutely, ridiculously inconclusive: "Whether the one is or is not, the one and the others in relation to themselves and to each other all in every way are and are not and appear and do not appear" (*Parmenides* 166c). From the time of the early Academy, skeptical readers have concluded that Parmenides' demonstration constitutes a playful exercise in logic at best; at worst it illustrates the sophistic consequences of Eleatic argumentation.[35] Parmenides had reason to be apprehensive. In deed or fact (*ergon*), he himself demonstrates the extent to which his own doctrine fails to take account of (or is inconsistent with) his own activity. As a member of Parmenides' school points out in his critique of the "friends of the ideas" in the *Sophist* (248a–49b), there cannot be *logos* (speech) or knowledge without motion, yet Parmenides argues that being cannot move or be moved. Parmenides cannot, therefore, account for the production and/or coming into being of his own poem. In his *Parmenides*, Plato dramatizes this difficulty with comic effect.

If readers follow through the stages of Parmenides' argument, they see the serious or substantive basis of the joke.[36] In critiquing Socrates' argument about the ideas, Parmenides emphasizes Socrates' inability to give an account of the relation between the intelligible and the sensible. But in

34. Although Socrates distinguishes Parmenides' "beautiful" (perhaps because he explicitly presented them in inspired, poetic form) arguments from Zeno's proofs, there is a certain continuity or family relation between Parmenides' deduction of the characteristics of being from the impossibility of positing the "is not," that is, a negative, and Zeno's proving of assertions by showing that their opposites or negatives involve one in a contradiction and are hence impossible to maintain.

35. *Proclus' Commentary on "Parmenides"* 1.5.630–33.

36. As both Sayre (*Plato's Late Ontology and Parmenides' Lesson*) and Miller (*Plato's "Parmenides"*) show in considerable detail and with great rigor, Parmenides' demonstration does not consist in a static vacillation between the affirmation and negation of a series of propositions. Each new hypothesis or stage constitutes a modification of the previous thesis in light of the objections or difficulties that have been pointed out. There is an extremely logical development, therefore, from beginning to end. Nevertheless, the survey of all the possible alternatives culminates in the simultaneous and hence ridiculous affirmation and negation of everything that has been said.

his demonstration, the elder Eleatic proves even less able to give such an account on the basis of his own hypothesis.

Parmenides' mode of arguing certainly differs from that which Socrates later adopted. Looking around for an interlocutor, the elderly Eleatic chooses the youngest man present, because, he says, a youth is not apt to give his questioner much trouble; a young man is more apt to say what he thinks, simply and directly, than one more experienced in debate. Still dreading the effort of making the demonstration (just as Antiphon dreaded the effort of restating it), the old man also observes (137b) that the youth's answers will give him a chance to rest. In marked contrast to Socrates' later practice, Parmenides displays no interest in examining his interlocutor's opinions. Like the Eleatic Stranger in the *Sophist*, Parmenides treats the responses of his interlocutor merely as a means of presenting his own argument more easily.[37] Plato's readers are reminded, however, of the effects the changing body and human mortality have on intellectual activity—effects the historical Parmenides' argument seems to deny.

According to his poem, the goddess who took Parmenides by the hand led him to see that it was impossible to think or to say the "is not." From that impossibility the philosopher deduces the characteristics of the "is" or being: that it is "ungenerated and imperishable; whole, unique, immovable, and complete; nor was once, nor will be, since [it] is, now, all together, one, continuous." For, he reasons, "whence could it grow? Not from what-is-not . . . ; for [the what-is-not] is not to be said or thought. . . . And what need could have impelled it to grow . . . , if it began from nothing? Thus it must either completely be or not at all."[38] According to the historical Parmenides, there is no such thing as "becoming." Human beings have erred in thinking that there is.

Examining the hypothesis that "one is," Plato's Parmenides suggests that if one is, it cannot be many. One cannot, therefore, have parts; and lacking parts, it cannot be a whole. Plato's Parmenides might thus initially appear to agree with the author of the poem. However, the proposition that one has no parts proves to have problematic consequences. If one has

---

37. In the *Sophist* (217–18a), the Eleatic Stranger also begins by emphasizing the magnitude of his intellectual task (*ergon*). He could respond to Socrates' question about the philosopher, sophist, and statesman—do the Eleatics hold them to be one, two, or three like their names?—with a long speech. But, as Socrates reports Parmenides once did when Socrates was young, the Stranger observes, it is easier to proceed through questions if the interlocutor submits to guidance easily and painlessly.

38. Parmenides of Elea, *Fragments*, ed. and trans. by David Gallop (Toronto: University of Toronto Press, 1984), 64–65.

no parts, Plato's Parmenides continues, it can have no beginning, middle, or end, for those would be parts. Because beginning and end are limits, lacking both, one has no limits. Having no limits, it has no shape—neither round, with extremes everywhere equally distant from the center, nor straight, with its middle on the shortest line between the two extremes.[39] In sum, Plato's Parmenides argues, as in mathematics, that the purely intelligible unit has no dimensions. Like his Italian Pythagorean teachers, who thought they could generate figures from numbers, the historical Parmenides does not seem to have distinguished the purely intelligible from the physical with sufficient rigor—even though that very distinction is central to his own argument.[40] Plato thus indicates, through his presentation of the argument by "Parmenides," that the historical Parmenides committed the same error that made it difficult for Socrates to defend his notion of participation.

In his poem the historical Parmenides had reasoned that what is

> is not divisible, since [it] all alike *is*; neither somewhat more here, which would keep it from holding together, nor somewhat less, but all full of what is. . . . Since, then, there is a furthest limit, [it] is complete, from every direction like the bulk of a well-rounded sphere, everywhere from the center equally matched; for [it] must not be any larger or any smaller here or there; for neither is there what is not, which could stop it from reaching [its] like; nor is there a way in which what is could be more here and less there, since all inviolably *is*.[41]

According to the historical Parmenides, being is continuous and homogeneous. Because it must necessarily include everything that is, Plato suggests, Parmenides erroneously concluded that being must have a shape and limit (or definition).

In his poem the historical Parmenides also argued that because it neither came into being nor perished, what-is did not change or move. Having no parts, Plato's Parmenides points out, "one" has no place; it cannot be anywhere, either in anything or in itself. "If it were in something else, it would be encircled by that in which it would be and would be touched in

---

39. The definition of "straight" is important. Otherwise, we might wonder why there could not be "one" infinitely straight line.

40. Cf. Jacob Klein, "The Concept of Number in Greek Mathematics and Philosophy," in *Jacob Klein: Lectures and Essays*, ed. Robert B. Williamson and Elliot Zuckerman, 43–52 (Annapolis: St. John's College Press, 1985).

41. Parmenides, *Fragments*, 68–69, 72–73.

many places by many parts of it" (138a). To be in itself would presuppose a division of itself; to be in something else would require the existence of something other than one, that is, of many.

Not having any place, Plato's Parmenides continues, one can neither move nor be at rest. As the historical Parmenides pointed out in his poem, one indivisible being could not move into something else, because that would presuppose a place of not-being. Nor, Plato's Parmenides points out, could uniform, homogeneous being revolve around its center; where there are no dimensions or distinctions, there can be no center.[42]

Because it does not come into being or perish, the historical Parmenides argued, what is cannot move, because there is nothing outside or beyond being into which it could go, nor change, because that too would entail an assertion of the is-not. "Remaining the same and in the same," he concluded, "[what is] lies by itself and remains thus firmly in place."[43]

If one cannot be in itself or in anything else, Plato's Parmenides objects, one can never be the same. As in the case of motion, Aristotle expresses some doubt, so Parmenides explains: if one were the same as another, it would be that other and hence not one. If the one is the same as itself, it is not one; it has, in effect, been [internally] divided. For the same reason, if being is one, it cannot be like or unlike anything else, because there cannot be anything else. Nor can one be equal or unequal to itself or to anything else; like sameness and likeness, equality entails a distinction between two things which are compared. The historical Parmenides had concluded in his poem that "all is . . . equal to itself," however, because "there is no way in which what is could be more here and less there."[44]

If one cannot be same, other, like, unlike, equal or unequal to itself or to anything else, Plato's Parmenides argues, one cannot be measured; there is nothing beyond it in terms of which it can be defined or judged. Since one does not come into existence, perish, or change, as the historical Parmenides emphasized, one cannot become younger or older—than itself or others; one does not exist in time. One has no past, present, or future.

Parmenides then asks Aristotle, "Can it partake of being in any other way than in the past, present, or future?" Aristotle responds, "Apparently

<hr/>

42. The Eleatic Stranger makes a similar criticism of Parmenides' contention that being is spherical in *Sophist* 244e.

43. Parmenides, *Fragments*, 68–69.

44. Ibid., 72–73. A reader might object that Plato's Parmenides is faulting the author of the poem for his use of images to explain his argument more than the argument itself. However, Parmenides' argument does not allow him to use images or likenesses (like sphere).

not."[45] Parmenides concludes, "Then the one has no share in being at all. It has no being even so as to be one" (141e).[46] In the first part of his demonstration of the refutative method of argumentation, Plato's Parmenides apparently disproves his own hypothesis.[47]

C. Reconsidering the Thesis That One Is

In the first part of his argument, Plato's Parmenides shows that the denial that being can be differentiated or divided, because such a division entails a negation of being, itself involves a negation of being—if, we should add, being is equated with spatiotemporal existence. In the reconsideration of the hypothesis that follows, Plato's Parmenides then in effect makes the same correction of the original thesis by substituting difference for negation, which his "parricide" student, the Eleatic Stranger, will make in a later conversation with Socrates. But that correction also leads to a thoroughly contradictory picture of being as a whole, in which what are often and logically thought to be mutually exclusive opposites—one and many, same and different, infinity and finitude, rest and motion—are said to coincide.[48]

Confronted with the paradoxical, if not simply contradictory, conclusion of their first examination of Parmenides' hypothesis—that if one is, one is not—Aristotle eagerly agrees to reexamine it. The contradictory results of their first investigation resulted from their initial agreement that one has no parts. Now Parmenides suggests that the statement "one is" does not mean "one is one." On the contrary, it means that one partakes of

45. Aristotle seems to be more convinced that being cannot become than that being is only in time. When Parmenides asks the youth whether "was," "has become," and "was becoming" all indicate participation in the past, as "will become" or "will have become" indicate the future, and "is" and "becoming" refer to the present, he answers, "Certainly." And when Parmenides asks him if one does not participate in any such form of becoming, one does not participate in time, he responds, "Very true." Even though, when Parmenides asks him whether one can partake of being in any other way than past, present, or future, Aristotle answers, "It cannot," he expresses some reservations about the conclusion: "Then one has no share in being at all" (Parmenides 151e–52e). Perhaps as a result of his previous conversations with Socrates, Aristotle accepts the distinction between being and becoming much more readily than the understanding of being that Heidegger attributes to the Greeks, namely, that "to be" means to be present.

46. Heidegger would be delighted with this conclusion that being is only in time. The Neoplatonists used this argument of Parmenides to indicate the "one" that is, in the words of the Republic 509b, "beyond being," is the ineffable, that which has no characteristics, including being. As such, it becomes a major source of "negative theology."

47. Cf. Cornford, Plato and Parmenides, 203.

48. Cf. Brumbaugh, One, 11.

being and being partakes of one. Because there are two distinct aspects, the one that is has parts. Since each of these parts has its own integrity, each of the parts is also one. Not merely is the one that is, a whole; it is many.

From the conjunction of one and many in the one that is, Parmenides then deduces the existence of number. Because each unit can be said both to be and to be one, Parmenides continues, each can be said to be two. Because each of the two parts is different not only from the other but also from the whole, that whole "one" can also be said to be three. Because the one that is thus is also many, these even and odd numbers can be multiplied without end. If number has being and numbers are infinite, being must also be infinite, distributed through everything, from the greatest to the smallest. However, Plato's Parmenides points out, if each part of being has its own unity and is part of a whole, both the parts and the whole must be said to have a limit. Being is thus both unlimited and limited in number.

Explicitly reversing his first argument, Plato's Parmenides continues, if being is a whole, it also has a beginning, middle, and end, and thus a shape. It is also both in itself (the whole) and in the other (parts).[49] Being in itself is also at rest, but being in the other, which is never the same, cannot be at rest and is therefore in motion. It is both the same as itself and different. As one, it is both like and unlike itself and others. As Plato's Parmenides goes on to show at considerable length, if the one is also both equal and unequal to itself and to the others, greater and less than itself and the others, younger and older than itself and the others, depending on whether it is seen to be in the whole or its parts, the combination of opposite qualities produces not merely paradoxical but confusing, if not simply contradictory, results. Parmenides concludes that because one has been shown to have being as well as the other qualities they have discussed, there can be knowledge, opinion, and perception of it (as there was not in the first case); it can be named (identified) and talked or reasoned about in *logos*. The reader has to ask what kind of knowledge, opinion, or perception that would be if opposite qualities were simultaneously asserted.

---

49. Only on the basis of differentiation, which becomes possible by conceiving of the one as a whole composed of parts with their own unity, Plato's Parmenides shows, can one say, as Parmenides did in his poem, that what is "is all continuous; for what is is in contact with what is [and never with what is not]" and that "equal to itself from every direction, [it] lies uniformly within limits" and thus has a spherical shape (*Fragments*, 68–69, 72–73).

On the surface Plato's Parmenides' second argument attributes all the qualities to one, understood to be a whole composed of parts, which were denied to one in the first argument on the grounds that as one it had no parts.[50] On the surface the two arguments seem to contradict, if not to negate, each other.

D. Encompassing Opposition by Means of Sequencing in Time

Parmenides thus suggests that they discuss the matter yet another time. "If one is as we have described it, both one and many and neither one nor many, and participates in time," he asks, "must it not sometimes participate in being and sometimes not?" (*Parmenides* 155e). The assertion of existence of opposites would not constitute a contradiction or cancel each other out if the opposites were not said to be simultaneously present but occurred in temporal sequence. This is as much as to say that if one is a whole composed of parts, one must be generated and perish, that is, if one is, one must become. Being and becoming are one.

What Plato's Parmenides has shown in his first two arguments is, in effect, that the purportedly purely intelligible "ideas" of number, size, and condition cannot be known or perceived if being is not spatially and temporally differentiated. The author of the poem did not see this, because he fused or confused space and time. Because what is did not come into being or perish, he argued, it was continuous; remaining always the same, it was equal to itself in all directions. In drawing out the consequences of his initial insight, that what "is not" cannot be said or thought, the author of the poem separated intelligible being from sensible becoming too radically, ironically enough, because he did not distinguish or differentiate the intelligible from the sensible with sufficient rigor. He described purely noetic being in terms of spatial extension and temporal sequence without recognizing that he did (or that he had to, because there is no other way to describe being). What Plato's Parmenides shows is that what "is," conceived as the historical Parmenides conceived it, cannot be thought or said any more than the "is not."

Perhaps the problem lies not so much in Parmenides' poem, however, as in the minds of his later readers. We should note that in his repeated

---

50. Alexander D. Mourelatos, *The Route of Parmenides* (New Haven: Yale University Press, 1970), 186–87, points out that none of the important deductions in the original poem depends on "The All" (*to pan*)—in contrast to the argument presented by Plato's Parmenides.

reexaminations of what the proposition "one is" might entail, Plato's Parmenides traces a line of thought that resembles relatively recent interpretations of the poem by Karl Reinhardt and Martin Heidegger, who argue that at bottom the doctrines of Parmenides and Heraclitus are the same. Although Parmenides' initial description of the way of being and truth seems to proscribe all differentiation, motion, and becoming on the grounds that they presuppose an assertion of the existence of what is not, in the second part of the poem, of which only scattered sentences remain, Parmenides promises he will give an account of the "two-headed" way of mortals and their opinions. In the fragments that have survived, he writes of seeming opposites such as day and night, male and female. What Parmenides may have argued more clearly in the full version, Reinhardt suggests, is that sensible oppositions like light and dark or hot and cold do not really involve the negation (or "not-being") of the alternative state—that is the common misunderstanding. On the contrary, we understand each of the poles of the opposition only in terms of the other.[51] Things cannot simultaneously be hot and cold; they may be lukewarm, that is, neither simply hot nor cold. They can, perhaps even must, change from hot to cold and back. However, the intelligible structure of opposition in terms of which we perceive (and can only perceive) them to be hot or cold, light or dark, does not alter. For reasons like these, Heidegger concludes, Parmenides said essentially the same thing as Heraclitus.[52]

As Plato's Parmenides shows, at least two problems remain. First, he asks Aristotle that if being or one of its parts has different properties at different times, how do we explain the transition from rest to motion? At any given moment, one must either be at rest or in motion—one or many, like or unlike, small or large. If the change from one condition to another does not occur in a moment of time, it must occur "instantaneously," between moments, as it were. But how are we to understand such "instants"? They would appear to constitute the intellectual divisions we make in the otherwise seamless temporal continuum that allow us to record and measure its passage with numbers, which, like the divisions, are not themselves in time

51. Cf. Karl Reinhardt, *Parmenides und die Geschichte der griechischen Philosophie* (Frankfurt-am-Main: Vittorio Klostermann, 1959); selections translated by Matthew R. Cosgrove in Alexander D. Mourelatos, ed., *The Pre-Socratics* (Princeton: Princeton University Press, 1974), 293–311. Mitchell H. Miller, Jr., gives a similar reading of the poem in "Parmenides and the Disclosure of Being," *Apeiron* 13, no. 1 (1978): 12–35.

52. Cf. "*Moira (Parmenides 8.34–41)*," in Martin Heidegger, *Early Greek Thinking*, trans. David Farrell Krell and Frank A. Capuzzi (New York: Harper and Row, 1975), 93.

or space, although they are sequential. As Socrates at one point ventured to suggest about his ideas, these instants would then exist only for us, in our minds and not in the things intellected (cf. Aristotle *Physics* 4.223a–b). The fact that we can perceive motion only in contrast to something at rest may show that rest and motion (as well as other sensible opposites) are and are perceived by us only in conjunction with each other. However, this fact of the coexistence of opposites as alternating states or conditions in time that Parmenides may have described in the second half of his poem does not explain the relation between the intelligible, what would appear to be always the same without spatial or temporal delimitation, and the sensible or changing, which we perceive as such only by means of nonsensible, nonchanging divisions or definitions. In other words, Parmenides' own hypothesis and method of argumentation do not solve the problems he identified in Socrates' theory of ideas.

E. The Consequences for "Others" if One Is

Parmenides makes the problem of the relation between intelligible and sensible or "participation" clearer when he turns, as he promised, to consider the consequences for "others" if one is. Since they are "other" to one, the others cannot be either a unit or a whole. If what is includes both one and what is other to one, however, the others would be parts. Insofar as they are parts, they participate in the one, but what participates in one is not one itself. Because these parts are not one, they must constitute a multitude that, not being a whole, has no limit. Since they are not one, even the smallest amount subtracted from the others will still constitute a multitude. As parts, the others are limited by the whole and in relation to one another. The union of the others with one thus gives them limits that do not belong to their own nature. The other than one is, then, both limited and unlimited; in being both limited and unlimited, the other than one is both like and unlike itself and others.

In his summary restatement of what happens to the others if one is, Parmenides goes even further. One has to be separate from the others and the others from one, because there is nothing besides one and those other than one in which both could be included. Returning to his first argument, Parmenides observes that if what is truly one can have no parts, the others cannot partake of one in any way. They cannot be parts of the whole nor even many, for if they were many, each would be one. Nor can the others be like or unlike the one or participate in likeness and unlikeness, because that which cannot participate in one cannot participate in two things either. For similar reasons, the others cannot be the same or different, in motion or at rest, becoming or perishing, greater or less or equal. "Therefore," Parmenides once again concludes with a perfectly contradictory statement, "if one is, the one is all things and nothing at all in relation both to itself and to all others" (*Parmenides* 160b).

F. If One Is Not

1. HOW AND WHY THINGS IN SPEECH BOTH ARE AND ARE NOT

Faced with his second contradictory outcome, Plato's Parmenides turns to consider the alternative—one is not. However, he immediately observes, speaking about what is not involves some knowledge of what is spoken about and the characteristics in which it participates that differentiate it from other things—in this case, the one that is. Contrary to what the historical Parmenides explicitly argued in his poem (although not to what he seems to have done in practice in describing the "way of opinion"), Plato's Parmenides reminds his interlocutor both in speech and in deed that it is possible to speak about what is not. As the content of speech, what is not both in a sense is and is not. Since speaking the truth is saying what is, such speech is not true, but it is nevertheless speech (*legein*). This speech about what both in a sense is, yet is not, forms a bond between what is and what is not.

The combination of the is and is not in speech follows from the understanding of the one that is as a whole composed of parts with opposite qualities that coexist in temporal sequence, that is, of the conjunction of being with becoming in Parmenides' second examination of the consequences of his hypothesis that one is. In both cases the opposites, is/is not, like/unlike, same/different, rest/motion, are not mutually exclusive. Plato's Parmenides' second analysis of the consequences of the proposition "one is" makes it possible to name or identify certain aspects or parts of the one inasmuch as each part has a certain integrity or unity. These parts exist, however, only in relation to each other and the whole.

At this point it might look as if speech were a perfect or simple reflection of what is—in time.[53] However, as Plato's Parmenides has already

---

53. According to Heidegger, this was the implication of Parmenides' poem, which Plato and Aristotle corrected by recognizing the possibility of false speech. Heidegger, *Platon "Sophistes,"* in *Gesamtausgabe,* vol. 19 (Frankfurt-am-Main: Vittorio Klostermann, 1992).

observed, speech of what-is-not is not true speech. He goes on to point out that what must be said to change (*metabolein*), because it combines the "is" and "is not" and so has motion (*kinēsis*), cannot move, because it is nothing really and thus has no place in which to revolve or from which to move into another (*Parmenides* 162b–e). Affirming the being of the not-being thus also leads to contradiction.

2. The Not-Being of What Is Not

Plato's Parmenides thus goes back to the beginning once more to ask about the consequences of the proposition "one is not." If what is not cannot be in any sense, "what is not cannot be and cannot in any other way partake of being" (*Parmenides* 163d–e). Nor can the one that is not become, because coming into being and perishing consist in acquiring, receiving, and losing being, in which the one that is not does not participate. Nor can the one that is not change or move or rest. If the one that is not were to participate in any aspect of being, to be like or unlike, same or different, it would be.

3. The Consequences for the Other if One Is Not

Plato's Parmenides turns, finally, to considering the consequences for that other than one, if the one is not. Since one is not, the others cannot be other to one; they must be other to each other. Because one is not, the others must also have a certain multitude or mass. Since, as Parmenides argued before, the others do not participate in unity, they do not really constitute a many; the smallest part can always be divided. Although the others would appear to have size and number—at a distance, as it were—having no unity, the other has no determinate limits. Once again, we are reminded of the possible existence of a continuity (such as time and/or space, perhaps), which, having no definition, is not truly intelligible in itself and thus cannot properly be said, according to the understanding common to Socrates and Parmenides, to be. For, Parmenides concludes, if one is not, the others cannot be or be opined to be one or many. Nor can they be like or unlike, same or different, in contact or separate, or anything else. So we can say, in sum, "if the one is not, nothing is" (*Parmenides* 166c).

G. The Results of the Demonstration

What Plato's Parmenides has demonstrated, we see at the end, is that contrary to the claims the historical Parmenides made in his poem, it is not possible to deduce the characteristics of being, to explain the world we experience, or to determine what is knowable and what is not by means of the exclusive oppositions that he and his student Zeno employed. In light of the Eleatic philosopher's urging of Socrates to practice this mode of thought, the conclusion of the demonstration, "that whether the one is or is not, the one and the others in relation to themselves and to each other all in every way are and are not and appear and do not appear" (*Parmenides* 166c), has to be ironic. If being has an intelligible character or structure, making that character or structure evident requires ideas beyond the oppositions Parmenides and the other Italians drew between being and not being or being and becoming, one and many, whole and parts, same and different, like and unlike, equal and unequal, greater and smaller, rest and motion. All these involve or can be defined in terms of quantity.[54] As Plato's Parmenides reminds us, such terms refer, implicitly if not explicitly, to spatiotemporal existence. Parmenides' demonstration reveals the difficulties involved in separating the intelligible from the sensible even more dramatically than his critique of Socrates' teaching about the ideas.

VI. The Inconclusive Conclusion of the Dialogue

Plato's Parmenides is not able to maintain his thesis in the face of the objections he himself raises any more than the historical Parmenides and his student Zeno were able to maintain his thesis in the face of their critics, which include Plato's Socrates as well as Plato's student Aristotle. Nevertheless, Parmenides' criticisms of Socrates' thesis stand.

In the first place, Parmenides points out, Socrates is not able to say exactly what there are ideas of or why. Nor does this problem appear to be solved in the dialogues that follow. Neither Socrates nor any other Platonic philosopher presents a definitive list—or definition—of the ideas. The "idea of the bed," which Socrates says is made by the god in book 10 of the *Republic*, seems to be quite different in kind from the ideas of the virtues he mentions earlier (but also compares to bodily habits) in the same dialogue. In the *Phaedo* (75d), he includes the equal (*ison*), greater (*meizon*), and lesser (*elatton*), along with the just (*dikaion*), good (*agathon*), beautiful

---

54. The Eleatic Stranger's "correction" of his teacher in the *Sophist* will not, therefore, remove the *aporia* with which Plato's *Parmenides* concludes.

or noble (*kalon*), and holy (*hosion*). But none of the measures of quantity seems to be the same—or the same kind of principle—as being (*on*), rest (*stasis*), motion (*kinēsis*), same (*t'auton*), and different (*thateron*)—the *eidē* listed by the Eleatic Stranger in the *Sophist*, even though Socrates agrees that there are ideas of likeness (*homoiotēs*), the one and the many (*hen kai polla*), along with the just and the good, in his first statement of his argument concerning the ideas in the *Parmenides*. Not being sensible, in all cases, lists, or definitions, the ideas do not change or move; they are not (or should not be) divisible; they do not occupy space or have duration in time. Asserting that the ideas are not sensible does not tell us, however, what kinds and which distinctions truly are. All we seem to learn is that if the world is to be intelligible to us, it must be divided and organized according to some unchanging distinctions among, or kinds of, things. That is presumably why Parmenides told Socrates, in concluding his criticism of the young man's argument about the ideas, that something like the ideas is necessary for philosophy to exist.

Second, Parmenides shows, neither he nor Socrates is able to explain how sensible things "participate" or share in the purely intelligible ideas. How do the unchanging ideas shape or define changeable things? In the *Republic* Socrates describes the relation in terms of similarity or geometrical proportion. The divided line is an image, however, or a metaphor—not really an explanation. In the *Republic* the idea of the good seems, moreover, to be different from the other ideas; it is said to be "beyond being" and the source of the other ideas, if not of everything else. Elsewhere the idea of the good appears to be parallel to and of the same kind as the other ideas. Can ideas participate or share in other ideas? Socrates seems to say no; the Eleatic Stranger says, in some cases, yes.

The most important thing we learn from Plato's *Parmenides* is, however, the outcome of the long "demonstration." What Parmenides' proof and disproof of his own thesis that one is show is that it is not possible to give an account of the whole on the basis of one intelligible unit. Neither the Ionians nor the Italians, whether Pythagorean or Eleatic, could provide an adequate explanation, because they tried to reduce everything to one fundamentally undifferentiated underlying substance, motion, unit, or being. Nor, Plato's Parmenides shows, can being be defined simply through negation, as the historical Parmenides seems to have thought. By opposing being to everything it is not, one gets either no attributes or all attributes. In neither case has one discovered what is distinctive about being in itself.

To explain the whole—and so, presumably, being as a whole—one has to explain the interrelation of things essentially different in kind. Whether Socrates, Timaeus, or the Eleatic Stranger succeeded remains to be seen. As Plato indicates first in the *Laws* and then demonstrates dramatically in the *Parmenides*, this was the task facing the philosophers of the future.

3

Becoming Socrates

Seventeen years elapse between Plato's first presentation of Socrates in conversation with Parmenides in 450 and his next public encounter in 433 with another more famous foreigner, Protagoras. In asking the sophist whether virtue is teachable, Socrates raises the question the Athenian Stranger said future rulers needed to address concerning the unity and diversity of the virtues. Plato does not tell his readers what Socrates did or thought in the meantime. Plato does not, in other words, tell his readers directly how Socrates became the peculiar kind of philosopher they see in action in subsequent dialogues. But in three later dialogues Plato does present three retrospective statements by Socrates describing parts of his development. Plato leaves it to his readers to put these parts together.

On the last day of his life, Socrates tells his friends in the *Phaedo* (96a–100a) how he came to formulate his argument concerning the ideas as well as why he began to investigate the arguments of others rather than the beings or being itself. Only in the *Phaedo* do readers learn why Socrates did not follow the path indicated by Anaxagoras. Only on the last day of his life does Socrates explain how he came to the position he announced in his first appearance in the *Parmenides* in opposition to all earlier Greek philosophy. Readers should notice, however, that Plato depicts Socrates as the author of a certain argument about the ideas both in the first and in the last views he gives of his teacher—the bookends of his depiction of Socrates, so to speak.

In the *Symposium* (201b–2a), Socrates tells a group of his fellow citizens at a private dinner party in 416 what he had learned about eros that showed him how to address the difficulties Parmenides pointed out in his teaching about the ideas. As a result of what an otherwise unknown priestess taught him some time between 450 and 433, Socrates began investigating the opinions people have, especially about the noble and the good, because these opinions lie between the eternal intelligibles and the changing sensibles.[1] From Socrates' speech in the *Symposium*, readers thus learn what happened to him between the conversations related in the *Parmenides* and the *Protagoras*.

In the *Apology*, his one public explanation of how he became the distinctive kind of philosopher he is, Socrates highlights the ironic results. Although he ceased investigating natural phenomena before he was twenty years of age (when readers see him first putting forth his thesis about the ideas in the *Parmenides*), Socrates' fellow citizens continued to confuse him with earlier natural philosophers. On trial for his life, Socrates tried to explain the difference between himself and his predecessors by describing the peculiar turn his own investigations took as a result of his instruction by the priestess as a response to the oracle at Delphi, who commanded everyone to "know thyself," but the Athenian jurors thought he was being ironic, if not impious. They did not and could not understand his philosophical activity solely on the basis of his speeches or arguments. He had to resort to deeds to show them that his form of philosophy was not antagonistic to political order in the way that Anaxagoras' atheistic philosophy was.

Putting his retrospective statements together, we see that Socrates became the distinctive kind of philosopher Plato portrays in his dialogues in two stages. Socrates initially developed his argument about the ideas in response to defects he found in previous theories. He then turned to investigate human opinions, especially about the good, the noble, and the just, in response to the critique Parmenides made of Socrates' argument about the ideas in their first and only encounter. Contrary to the inference many scholars have drawn from Aristotle's statement in the *Metaphysics* (1078b9–16), the Socrates whom Plato depicts was not interested solely in moral questions.[2] He sought knowledge of that which is, in itself, always unchanging and purely intelligible. Nor did Socrates turn to his characteristic investigations of human opinions merely as a matter of necessity or

1. On the dramatic date of the *Symposium*, see Gary Alan Scott and William A. Welton, "Eros as Messenger in Diotima's Teaching," in *Who Speaks for Plato?* ed. Gerald A. Press (Lanham, MD: Rowman and Littlefield, 2000), 152.

2. Aristotle says that Socrates did not investigate natural phenomena but emphasizes that Socrates sought the definitions of ethical things in themselves. He did not, in other words, limit himself to questions of human practice.

incapacity, as Xenophon suggests (*Memorabilia* 1.1.11). According to Plato, Socrates turned to the investigation of human opinions in order to solve a philosophical problem. He wanted to show how sensible things participate in, or can be shaped by, purely intelligible forms of being. The only way he thought he could do that was to lead other, younger human beings to adopt a life of philosophy. It was, however, precisely the effect he had on the young that eventually got him into trouble with the city.

Previous commentators have not brought these three statements together to reconstruct the story of Socrates' development as a philosopher as a result of two widely held principles or theories of interpretation.[3] Adherents of the chronology of composition have regarded the *Apology* as an early work and the *Phaedo* as a middle dialogue in which Plato announced his own theory of the ideas, which he then critiques or develops in the *Parmenides*. Their commitment to the chronology of composition prevented these commentators from putting together the incidents and arguments in the order Plato indicates they were put forward by Socrates. Commentators who insist that each dialogue be read in its own terms have also failed to see the philosophical development indicated by the dramatic dates of the incidents, because of their commitment to reading each dialogue as a discrete unit.

I. Socrates' Critique of Previous Inquiries into Nature

Only on the last day of his life (after he has been officially condemned to death) does Plato's Socrates admit that in his youth he had investigated natural phenomena.[4] As he points out in the *Apology*, people think

---

3. Seth Benardete is a notable exception. In *On Plato's "Symposium"* (Munich: Carl Friedrich von Siemens Stiftung, 1993), he states: "Socrates' instruction in erotic things by Diotima . . . constitutes the last of three stages in Socrates' philosophic education. The first stage Socrates gives in the *Phaedo*. There he tells his disciples about his conversion from thinking of cause in an Ionian manner to his discovery of the ideas and his turn to speeches; the second phase is in the first half of the *Parmenides*, where Parmenides . . . [argues] that even if the [ideas] exist they cannot be known by us, for there must be a complete separation between divine and human knowledge. It seems to be Diotima, with her notion of the inbetween or the demonic, who offered Socrates a way out of the impasse" (69–71). Benardete does not work out the steps in the argument or education any more fully, however, or see how the story of the oracle in the *Apology* represents a public explanation of Socrates' private instruction and its effects.

4. In other words, Plato's Socrates seems to acknowledge what he is at pains to deny in the *Apology*—namely, that there is a basis for Aristophanes' depiction of a philosopher named Socrates as a student of nature in his *Clouds*.

philosophers who engage in such investigations are atheists. He himself had been indicted and convicted, at least in part, because his compatriots did not know and could not tell the difference between him and previous natural philosophers.

Speaking to his close friends in private, Socrates says that he had been tremendously eager to discover the causes of things' coming into being, existing for a time, and then passing away. He had asked whether heat and cold produce life by some kind of fermentation? Is it blood or air or fire by which we think? Or does the brain produce our sensations of hearing, sight, and smell? Do memory and opinion arise from these? Socrates' studies of earlier natural philosophy were apparently quite extensive, including the theories of Archelaus (concerning life's origin in decay), Empedocles (blood), Anaximenes (breath or air), Heraclitus (fire), and Alcmaeon (the function of the brain).[5]

Socrates explains that he turned away from such investigations because they did not result in additions to his knowledge so much as subtractions. Before engaging in his study of natural philosophy, Socrates thought he knew that human beings grew through eating and drinking, that a tall man could be taller than a short man by a "head," that ten was greater than eight by two, and that a two-cubit rule exceeded a one-cubit rule by half. But as a result of his studies, he no longer believed he knew the causes of any of the aforementioned phenomena.[6]

The problem with Socrates' investigations of natural causation was not simply that these investigations led him to "forget" his former opinions: these investigations did not and seemingly could not result in adequate explanations of the reasons why each thing comes into being, exists for a

5. David Bostock, *Plato's "Phaedo"* (Oxford: Clarendon Press, 1986), 136. Yet even at this early stage we see evidence of the mature Socrates' distinctive concern with self-knowledge. Michael Davis, "Socrates' Pre-Socratism: Some Remarks on the Structure of Plato's *Phaedo*," *Review of Metaphysics* 33 (March 1980): 560, points out that, in contrast to his Milesian predecessors, Thales, Anaximander, and Anaximenes, Socrates does not ask what is the basic material of all things. Socrates asks about life, thought, sensation, memory, and opinion—the functions usually located in the human psyche (and the subject of the conversation in the *Phaedo* as a whole). As we see in the *Parmenides*, Socrates had a sense of the importance of acquiring self-knowledge early on. He did not make that sense explicit or incorporate it into his specific mode of inquiry, however, until he discovered the significance of human eros.

6. According to the account he gives at his trial, Socrates should thus have become wiser. He had learned that he did not actually know what he thought he did. Such learning would appear to be the prerequisite for philosophy, understood to be the *search* for wisdom. A man does not inquire further about things he thinks he already knows. Cf. Hans-Georg Gadamer, *Plato's Dialectical Ethics: Phenomenological Interpretations Relating to the "Philebus,"* trans. Robert M. Wallace (New Haven: Yale University Press, 1991), 17–65.

while, and then perishes. Human growth is not and cannot be explained merely as a result of addition. The same result does not always follow from the same cause. (For example, old people eat but do not grow.) For food or drink to produce growth, what is not living must be transformed into what is living. The difficulty arises in explaining that transformation. Moreover, it is not simply a matter of the difference between quality and quantity—or life and death. Even in the apparently simpler case of numbers, the problem exists, if in reverse. Two separate units that can become two—something that neither one is by itself—by addition. But the opposite procedure, division, can also produce two units out of one. To explain how a thing comes to be (something different from what it is), it does not suffice merely to specify the component materials or the process of combination and/or separation. It is necessary to specify what makes any particular thing what it is.[7]

Socrates thought at first that he had found the solution to his problem in the Anaxagorean thesis that mind (nous) is the cause of all. But Socrates was soon disappointed to learn that Anaxagoras did not explain why it was best for each thing to be as it was—for the earth to be flat or at the center of the cosmos, for example. In explaining the reasons things are as they are, Anaxagoras did not refer to mind, but, like the other investigators of nature, mentioned things such as air, ether, and water as causes. But, Socrates observes, he and his friends are not having this conversation simply because they have voices, there is air around for them to breathe, or they can hear the sounds others make. He and his friends could not form or understand the sounds if they did not have minds; nor would they stay and listen if they did not, like Socrates, think it was good for them to do so. As both the Athenians' decision to condemn and kill him and his own decision to remain and accept the punishment rather than try to escape show, human actions cannot be explained simply in terms of material or even efficient causation. The material—Socrates' own bones and sinews, for example—constitutes a necessary condition for human action (and life), but it does not determine its shape or length entirely.[8] The fact that human

7. Pace Rosen (*Question of Being*, 62–63), the problem is not simply that these previous accounts did not allow Socrates or anyone else to preserve our everyday knowledge. The problems with them are more specific than that.

8. The distinction Socrates draws here (*Phaedo* 99b) between the cause (*aitia*, a word originally referring to responsibility or guilt for a crime) of a being and a necessary condition (*ekeino aneu hou*, that without which [the cause could not be a cause]) means that he would not accept Heidegger's account of Aristotle's four causes as the necessary conditions for the production of a thing; Martin Heidegger, *Question concerning Technology*, trans. William Lovitt (New York:

action has an intentional aspect does not, however, prove that this is true of everything or of the whole.

Socrates saw that previous philosophers' accounts of things in terms of their components failed to explain human actions, because such accounts left no room for choice or purpose. Yet, he found, none of his predecessors had been able to give an account of the whole in terms of intelligent causation. Nor was he able to do so himself.[9]

Socrates decided, therefore, to take another tack.[10] He called his new mode of inquiry a "second sailing" (an idiomatic phrase for "second best"), because it is indirect, hence takes longer, and thus presumably requires more effort than immediate perception or intellection.[11] Like people who risk blindness by looking directly at the sun during an eclipse rather than at its reflected image in the water, Socrates concluded, he had risked blinding his soul by trying to cognize the beings directly. Rather than attempt to deduce the material (or even immaterial) cause hidden by the different sensible forms and qualities of the beings, he proposed to examine the *logoi*, the accounts given of them. He admitted that *logoi* were only reflections or images of the beings; but, he insisted, speeches are no more images of the beings than are "facts" (*erga*—the "deeds," acts, or effects we perceive with our senses, but only with the assistance of our intelligence).[12] Insofar as he

---

Harper, 1977), 3–35. As several commentators have observed, Socrates' notion of cause is different from Aristotle's, whether Aristotle's is understood in a Heideggerian or a more traditional fashion.

9. When Timaeus (29d) ventures to give an account of the intentional construction of the cosmos, he explicitly calls it *ton eikota mython* (a likely story) and not a *logos*.

10. Pace R. Robinson, *Plato's Earlier Dialectic* (Ithaca: Cornell University Press, 1941), 143–44; and Norman Gulley, *Plato's Theory of Knowledge* (London: Methuen, 1962), 40–41, Socrates' judgment about what is the "strongest" argument follows directly and logically from his previous investigations.

11. Hayden Ausland, "La 'seconde navigation' dans la philosophie politique de Platon," *Revue Française d'Histoire des Idées Politiques* 16 (2002): 275, explains that the understanding of "second sailing" as rowing when the winds are unfavorable is traceable to a later paroemiographic tradition involving much guesswork. As I shall argue, the alternative version, in which the phrase refers to making a second, more secure attempt at some previously failed journey, fits Socrates' description of his new tack better.

12. In an extremely sophisticated, careful reading of this passage, Rosen (*Question of Being*, 67) translates *Phaedo* 99e6–100a2 to say that Socrates does not think "he who investigates beings in *logois* is looking in icons any more than is he who investigates beings in *ergois*." In contrast to most commentators who think of "deeds" or "facts" as sensible and observable, like the things that imitate or embody the concepts on the third section of the divided line in the *Republic*, Rosen denies that human acts are images any more than speeches, words, or propositions are images, even though he admits that in the *Phaedrus* Socrates suggests that the human capacity to speak, that is, to use words to describe and communicate, presupposes some vision, if unclear, partially impeded, and distorted of the things in themselves (which he identifies with the ideas). Rosen does not distinguish between Socrates and the Eleatic Stranger's arguments concerning the ideas.

had previously studied the "theories" of Empedocles, Anaximenes, Heraclitus, and others concerning the fundamental character of being or the beings, Socrates had been studying *logoi* without recognizing that was what he was doing. Rather than a "second best," Socrates' "second sailing" thus constituted an improved understanding of the character of his own activity. The reasons (or "causes," *aitiai*) things are as they are cannot be directly perceived either by our senses or by our intellect. We have to infer them from the speeches we use to describe the things we encounter and then attempt to explain why they are as they are.[13]

Nor does he distinguish between the examination of the *logoi* Socrates explains in the *Phaedo* and the interrogation of other human beings concerning their opinions about the noble and good that Socrates says he later learned from Diotima. Instead, Rosen argues that "Plato's doctrine of the ideas" can bridge the gap between human, intentional actions and the mathematically describable interactions of nonhuman things only if the ideas are understood to be ratios of various characteristics unified by and in the idea of a being. In an impressive attempt to comprehend as well as to account for the similarities and differences in the Heideggerian, Aristotelian, and Platonic accounts of the ideas as basically looks, Rosen has, I believe, lost sight of the truth of the more generally accepted reading and translation, according to which the *logoi* are no more images than the *erga*, that is, that both are images and distortions of the truly intelligible forms of being to which both the *logoi* and the *erga* nevertheless give us some access, if in distorted form. If Socrates remains true to the understanding of the ideas he first presents in the *Parmenides* (but retains in the *Philebus*), the ideas are unities—in themselves, never changing, therefore always and purely intelligible rather than sensible—which thus have no parts to be in ratio with others. Sensible things participate in the ideas, but the ideas do not participate in sensible things or each other. As Rosen states, Socrates is not, therefore, able to give an account of the whole.

13. Because it proceeds in terms of the sun and its reflection in the water, Socrates' account of his turn to the *logoi* has reminded most readers of the three famous images Socrates uses in books 6 and 7 of the *Republic* to describe the character and kinds of knowledge to Glaucon. As in the *Republic*, so in giving the reasons for his "second sailing," Socrates draws an analogy between the sun, as the source of the light that makes both vision and growth possible, and being, as the source of both intelligible existence and intellection. John Sallis argues that in the *Phaedo*, *logos* is the equivalent of light, whereas Seth Benardete suggests that the "medium" is opinion. John Sallis, *Being and Logos* (Atlantic Highlands, NJ: Humanities Press International, 1986), 38–43; Seth Benardete, *Socrates' Second Sailing* (Chicago: University of Chicago Press, 1989), 157–77. Kenneth Dorter, *Plato's "Phaedo": An Interpretation* (Toronto: University of Toronto Press, 1982), 116, argues that the stages of Socrates' education correspond to the levels of knowledge and intelligibility on the "divided line." In identifying the reflections on the bottom part of the line with the images the cave dwellers see, Dorter ignores the distinction between natural and human things that Socrates brings out in his "autobiography" in the *Phaedo*. In general, those who read Socrates' account of his own education in the *Phaedo* in terms of the *Republic* tend to overlook the centrality of his insistence on an irreducible plurality of causes or ideas. In the *Republic* the "idea of the good" is said to be "beyond being." Presented explicitly in an "image" to a young man who is said not to be able to understand or follow, the "idea of the good" is not clearly knowable. It seems to be identical with the cause of everything Socrates hoped to learn from Anaxagoras, but did not and could not discover for himself. If someone were to come to know it as the cause of all being and knowledge, Socrates' hypothesis in the *Phaedo* would be disproved. Paul Stern, *Socratic Rationalism and Political Philosophy: An Interpretation of Plato's "Phaedo"* (Albany: SUNY Press, 1993), argues that Socrates gives up the search for the [idea of the] good and raises questions about his commitment to his own "theory of ideas" on the last day of his life. Because this account is supposed to be

Not having been able to discover a single cause of everything from his previous studies, Socrates began by positing a variety of intelligible elements. He then attempted to discover what those intelligible elements were and how they made or defined the things that come into being, pass away, or persist in being. He put forth (*hypothemenos*) the *logos* that seemed strongest to him and judged the truth or falsity of other claims by determining whether they agreed or not with his *logos*.

The *logos* that seemed, and still seems, strongest to Socrates in the *Phaedo* is what has become known as the theory of the ideas. It contains at least three distinct propositions: (1) The reasons or causes things are as they are, are irreducibly different from one another and hence plural. In opposition to Parmenides, Anaxagoras, and the Milesian philosophers, Socrates maintains that there is no one cause or undifferentiated being (whether purely intelligible or material). (2) Because the different kinds of being are irreducibly different, these differences or kinds are essential. That is, the good, noble, and the like exist as such and not merely as perceived properties of or in other things. And (3), various things are and are called good, noble, great, and so forth because the idea is present in them. Nevertheless, from his first appearance as a philosopher in his conversation with Parmenides until the day of his death, Plato's Socrates admits that he does not know how to explain this participation.

Socrates thinks that his hypothesis concerning the ideas is better than the cosmological theories of his predecessors because it does not lead its adherents into the same kinds of quandaries, for example, the contradiction involved in accounts of the "generation" of "two" by both addition and division, that is, opposite procedures. It does not, because Socrates' *logos* distinguishes twoness or, more generally, the different kinds or intelligible aspects of things in terms of which we recognize, categorize, and define them, from each other as well as from the things themselves. On the basis of his argument about the ideas, Socrates can thus separate out the purely intelligible unit being counted as well as the number of such, from the thing counted, for example, a head, and the extent of the measure, for example, a cubit.[14] All these different kinds of being were mixed up in the

---

autobiographical, I think we are reading about Socrates' intellectual development *before* he puts forward his famous images in the *Republic*, where he posits the good as the goal of learning, not as something known. Since his argument here culminates in his urging Cebes to accept the *logos* concerning the ideas, it is hard to say Socrates gave it or them up.

14. Jacob Klein, in "Concept of Number," argues that this was one of the crucial advances "Plato" made on the Pythagorean understanding.

things Socrates originally thought he knew. Because they tried to reduce all things to their component parts, the cosmological theories did not sort out the different aspects or kinds of parts from one another clearly enough. As a result, they mixed up or confused causes and effects. Their theories or arguments thus became liable to the sort of antilogistics practiced by Zeno, who paradoxically argued that the existence of the sensible world, characterized by a plurality of things in motion, coming to be and perishing, is logically impossible, because things cannot simultaneously both be and not be.[15] In the *Parmenides* Plato shows that as a youth Socrates used his teaching concerning the ideas to critique Zeno. If there is a plurality of different ideas in which things participate, one could say that something is both like and unlike something else without contradicting oneself.

Socrates thinks his admittedly incomplete, if not fatally flawed theory is better than the existing alternatives—both the cosmological theories, which fail to distinguish and hence confuse different kinds of causes, and the Eleatic critique, which denies the existence of the beings altogether. As we see in the *Phaedo*, the alternatives both result in an unintelligible cosmos—a muddle or confusion of things, on the one hand, and a blank slate, on the other. Neither major alternative includes or gives an account of its own source (*archē*) in the thought of a human being.[16] Socrates' hypothesis at least specifies the condition that made such thought possible.[17] If there is an order intelligible to human beings, that order must, like the human knower, combine the intelligible with the sensible. If the sensible and the intelligible remain completely separate, Parmenides reminded the young Socrates, only pure intelligence, a god, could perceive the intelligible.

Although Plato gives his readers their first view of Socrates in the *Parmenides*, Socrates had already formulated his hypothesis about the ideas in response to the confusions and perplexities he experienced as a result of his study of the works of previous philosophers. (Otherwise Parmenides would not have been able to criticize it.) Socrates' admission on the last

15. In the *Phaedrus* Socrates describes "the Eleatic Palamedes" (Zeno) explicitly as an *antilogistikos* (261d).

16. Socrates states this critique of the cosmological teaching concerning the unending "becoming" of things more explicitly in the *Theaetetus* (162c–83d). The Eleatic Stranger makes this critique of the "friends of the forms" (including Socrates) in *Sophist* 248a–49d. In the *Parmenides*, however, Socrates suggests that the Eleatics lack self-knowledge.

17. As Parmenides observed to the young Socrates, something like his *logos* concerning the ideas is necessary for there to be philosophy. Here in the *Phaedo* 102a, Socrates tells Cebes that he will stick to the hypothesis, which prevents him from mixing the causes up, if he is a philosopher.

day of his life that he cannot explain how particular sensible manifestations of the ideas participate in them indicates he never entirely overcame
the difficulties in his *logos* Parmenides had pointed out. Socrates does not
put his *logos* forward as simply true or proven; he puts it forward merely as
the best he knows.

The difficulties with Socrates' *logos* are not restricted to Parmenides'
objections. In the *Phaedo* Socrates says that he formulated his hypothesis
concerning the ideas to avoid the perplexities he encountered as a result of
his inquiries into nature. Unlike his initial inquiries, Socrates' *logos* does not
try to explain why things come to be or perish. On the contrary, Socrates'
hypothesis explicitly abjures any consideration of the *archē* or its consequences. Participation in the ideas explains only why things are what they
are.[18] It does not explain how any particular thing or set of things comes
to be. As Socrates' conversation with Timaeus should remind Plato's readers, Socrates himself never develops a cosmology. His argument about the
ideas is explicitly presented not merely as a provisional but as an incomplete account of the character of the whole.

Socrates learned from his study of previous philosophy, above all, what
the problem is—namely, how to account for the mixture of intelligible and
sensible in the cosmos—and where to look for an answer in the accounts
human beings give of their experience of things, including, preeminently,
themselves. From the *Phaedo* readers learn how Socrates' turn to the human things, that is, speeches or *logoi*, and thus his search, first and foremost,
for self-knowledge, arose out of his critical studies of previous thinkers. In
the *Symposium* Plato indicates more clearly what Socrates hoped to find by
means of such investigations, why he had to extend his investigations from
the arguments of philosophers about the character of being or the beings
to the opinions human beings have about the beautiful and the good, and
how limited the results of his investigations necessarily were.

II. *Symposium*: Socrates' Discovery of the Significance of Human Eros

In the *Symposium* Socrates relates what he learned about eros from a Man-
tinean priestess named Diotima. These lessons apparently made Socrates

18. Cf. Ronna Burger, *The "Phaedo": A Platonic Labyrinth* (New Haven: Yale University Press,
1984), 135–59.

the distinctive kind of philosopher he is. Both in this conversation and in a later encounter with Phaedrus (the young man who proposes that they speak in praise of love, at the banquet held at the home of the tragic poet Agathon in honor of his first victory in 416), Socrates says that he possesses a certain kind of knowledge, knowledge of erotic matters (*ta erōtika*) (*Symposium* 177e; *Phaedrus* 257a). In the *Apology* Socrates suggests that the oracle at Delphi said he was wisest because, in recognizing that he did not know the most important things, Socrates possessed a certain kind of "human" wisdom. If we put these statements together, we see that Socrates claimed to know what human beings most urgently want to know but do not. He thus knew at what and how human efforts should, first and foremost, be directed: at seeking to discover what is truly noble and good in itself.

The name Diotima is a combination of the words for "god" or "Zeus" (*Dio*) and "honor" (*timē*). Its meaning is thus somewhat ambiguous inasmuch as it could be "in honor of Zeus" or "honored by the god."[19] The name thus seems to reflect the two-way path of the communication between human beings and their divinities.[20] Partly because of the symbolic or functional character of her name, most commentators agree that Diotima is a fictional character. There is no historical evidence outside the dialogue that such an individual actually existed.[21] It is nevertheless important that Socrates attributes the only knowledge he claims to possess to

19. Cf. Nussbaum, *Fragility*, 177; Robert Lloyd Mitchell, *The Hymn to Eros: A Study of Plato's "Symposium"* (Lanham, MD: University Press of America, 1993), 116.

20. As W. R. M. Lamb, the editor of the Loeb edition of the *Symposium* (Cambridge: Harvard University Press, 1925), 173n; Allan Bloom, *Love and Friendship* (New York: Simon and Schuster, 1993), 501; and Strauss, *Symposium*, 184, point out, the grammatical form of the Greek word used to describe her as a citizen of Mantineia (*Mantinikē*) is reminiscent of the word for the science of divining (*mantikē*).

21. Taylor (*Plato*, 224) dissents from this judgment because he does not think Plato introduces fictional characters (or deeds) into his dialogues. Hayden Ausland, "Who Speaks for Whom in the *Timaeus-Critias?*" in Press, *Who Speaks for Plato*, 186n, observes that "Diotima's fictionality is a modern development. Ancient writers speak of her as real." Andrea Nye, "Irigaray and Diotima at Plato's *Symposium,*" *Hypatia: A Journal of Feminist Philosophy* 3, no. 3 (Winter 1989): 46–61, sees the characterization of Diotima as fictional to be a sign of male critics' unwillingness to countenance the idea that Socrates might learn from a woman or that a woman could be a public benefactor to Athens. One could (and I shall) argue, on the contrary, that the fact Socrates and/or Plato constructed *a female* instructor emphasizes rather than denies the importance of the female in the development and constitution of Socratic philosophy. (Socrates often takes on female roles and characteristics, as in his famous characterization of himself as an intellectual midwife in the *Theaetetus* 149a–51d.) The likelihood that Diotima is a fictional creation suggests that Socrates' account of his erotic education cannot be taken literally. He dissimulates insofar as he attributes what were probably his own discoveries—both substantive, about the significance of human eros, and "methodological," about the importance of recognizing and communicating with another—to the instruction he received from another.

instruction he received from another. He does not claim to have acquired his knowledge solely on the basis of his own efforts or ability. He had to be taught by someone who was evidently different—not merely a foreigner, a citizen of a different city, but a woman, a human being of a different sex or generative function, with a special relation to the superhuman.[22] As a man, Socrates is only a part of the whole. To comprehend the whole, he must supplement his own experience and consequent opinions with those of another, one who is not the same as he and yet who shares enough with him that they and their knowledge can somehow be combined. Instruction by means of conversation is the means.[23] Diotima's explication of the meaning of eros appears, indeed, to constitute a poetic account of what philosophers such as Socrates are doing when they seek students to teach.[24]

As an indication of her wisdom, Socrates reports (*Symposium* 201d) that Diotima enabled the Athenians to postpone the plague ten years by offering sacrifices.[25] She could not avert it altogether; her power and knowledge were both limited. Socrates' report of Diotima's involvement in Athenian life does, however, show that she was active in 440, ten years before the plague in 430, and ten years after 450, when Socrates purportedly talked to Parmenides.[26]

Before he encountered Diotima, Socrates, like Agathon, believed that Eros was not only beautiful (or noble) but also a great god.[27] He held a traditional Greek belief that was first enunciated poetically and then carried

22. On the significance of the fact that Diotima is a woman, see Luce Irigaray, "Sorcerer Love: A Reading of Plato's *Symposium*, Diotima's Speech," trans. Eleanor H. Kykendall, *Hypatia* 3, no. 3 (Winter 1989): 32–44; Nye, "Irigaray and Diotima"; Arlene Saxonhouse, "The Philosopher and the Female in the Political Thought of Plato," *Political Theory* 4, no. 2 (May 1976): 195–212. As they observe, the female is and is not present in the conversation. Socrates relates what Diotima told him, but Diotima herself is not present among the solely male participants. As priestess and purveyor of wisdom, Diotima is not performing the female role in physical procreation. Instead she generalizes "pregnancy," making it into a state, both physical and mental, shared by men and women. Arlene Saxonhouse, *Fear of Diversity* (Chicago: University of Chicago Press, 1992), 165–75, emphasizes the way in which Socrates combines the male and the female.

23. Søren Kierkegaard, *Philosophical Fragments*, trans. Howard Hong and Edna Hong (Princeton: Princeton University Press, 1985), emphasizes this aspect of Socrates' teaching in contrast to the overflowing of divine love in Christ, which a human being cannot possibly reciprocate.

24. Strauss (*Symposium*, 248) argues that the presentation of philosophy in the *Symposium* is poetic.

25. One might ask whether that delay were truly beneficial. If she had not postponed the plague, Benardete points out (*Plato's "Symposium,"* 73), it would have taken many fewer lives. Ten years earlier the Athenians had not yet crowded into the city from the countryside on account of the war.

26. Cf. Strauss, *Symposium*, 185.

27. In the context of a discussion of love or eros, it seems more appropriate to translate *kalos* as "beautiful" than as "noble."

over in modified form into pre-Socratic philosophy. As Phaedrus reports in the first speech in the *Symposium* (178b), in the *Theogony* Hesiod wrote that "after Chaos came into being, next broad-bosomed Earth, the solid and eternal home of all, and Eros, the most beautiful of the immortal gods" (116f).[28] And Parmenides later said of Genesis that she "conceived Eros before all other gods."[29]

Diotima contested both these poetic and philosophical characterizations of Eros. Contrary to Hesiod's claim that Eros is the most beautiful god, Diotima pointed out that, if Eros is the love, desire, want, or lack of the beautiful, Eros itself cannot be beautiful; so if the gods are happy and beautiful, Eros is not a god. To show Socrates the true character of erotic desire, Diotima also had to rid him of the tendency to think in terms of mutually exclusive opposites, the way Parmenides and his followers did. She thus reminded Socrates that what is not beautiful is not necessarily ugly and that those who lack knowledge are not necessarily ignorant. There is something halfway between knowledge and ignorance. A person who has right opinion has somehow hit upon the truth and so cannot be called simply ignorant; however, because the person who holds it cannot explain why his or her view is true, right opinion cannot be considered knowledge.[30] Diotima persuaded Socrates to change his understanding of eros by asking him to examine his own opinions, the way Socrates later

28. Hesiod, *Theogony*, trans. Norman O. Brown (Indianapolis: Bobbs-Merrill, 1953), 56. Phaedrus omits the lines about softness and overpowering, because in his speech he later argues that love makes lovers brave. In the speech, which immediately precedes Socrates', however, Agathon restores the original poetic characterization of eros as both soft and powerful.

29. Because the argument in the longest-surviving fragments of Parmenides' poem concerning the "way of truth," which forbids us to think or say the impossible "is not," suggests that it is an error to conceive of a mixture of being (is) and nonbeing (is not) in becoming, this quotation is thought to be a fragment of his mostly lost description of the erroneous "way of opinion" on which most human beings lose their way, which the goddess promises to show him after the "way of truth." Cf. Freeman, *Ancilla*, 41–46; Jonathan Barnes, "Parmenides," in *Early Greek Philosophy* (Harmondsworth, UK: Penguin Books, 1987), 136–37; and Kirk, Raven, and Schofield, *Presocratic Philosophers*, 254–62. Mourelatos observes that "the proem in Parmenides shows greater resemblance . . . to Hesiod's 'Hymn to the Muses,' at the beginning of the *Theogony*, than it does to any other single text from the epic. Moreover, there is an unmistakable resemblance between Parmenides' '*Doxa*'—which evidently combined a presentation of the world sanctioned by mortal belief with sections on cosmogony, theogony, and lists of allegories—and Hesiod's great poem" (*Route of Parmenides*, 33).

30. The fact that Diotima makes that which is between knowledge and ignorance "opining correctly without being able to give an account [*to ortha doxazein kai aneu tou echein logon dounai*]" (*Symposium* 202a) suggests that the examining of opinions in which she instructs Socrates by example is not quite the same as the examination of the *logoi* he says that he undertook in the *Phaedo* as a "second sailing," that is, that the education Socrates receives from Diotima constitutes a second stage.

asks his interlocutors to examine theirs. She thus provided him not only with the content of his knowledge (ta erōtika) but also, by means of example, with the method of acquiring it.[31] And, we see, her education of Socrates proceeded in stages.

Socrates initially agreed with "everyone" that Eros is a great god. Diotima first reminded him that all opinions are not equally valid; there is a difference between those who know and those who do not. The mere agreement of a large number of other human beings is not a sufficient test of truth. The traditional, popularly held belief that Eros is the most beautiful of the gods and the philosophical clarification of the definition of eros as the principle of generation derived from the traditional view are not, in fact, the same. Diotima showed Socrates not only that these two opinions of his were contradictory but also that neither was tenable.

Socrates did not simply or immediately accept Diotima's instruction. He asked questions: if eros is not a god, what is he? And tellingly, what power does he have? Diotima responded that eros is neither a mortal nor an immortal, but a daimōn, with the power to communicate between human beings and gods, who do not themselves commingle with men. Socrates then inquired, who were its father and mother?[32] Traditionally, daimones were supposed to be products of the intercourse between gods and humans. According to Diotima, however, gods do not commingle with humans, and eros does not possess the power of generation so much as communication. It does not produce the unending and essentially undifferentiated stream of becoming that the pre-Socratic poets and philosophers had described. Instead, it brings essentially different kinds of beings into association with one another "so that the whole itself has been bound together by it" (Symposium 203a).[33] As a mediator between other forms of existence, eros presupposes their existence; it cannot come first. It is not the source of generation or becoming. It made sense, therefore, for Socrates to ask how and from what or whom eros came to be.

31. Her instruction of Socrates can thus be considered to be an example, in deed, of what she will call "begetting in the beautiful."

32. Note that Diotima's description of the relation between gods and humans fits Socrates' notion of the divine "ideas" but not the Olympian deities, as traditionally described.

33. Eros thus performs the mediating role between sensibles and intelligibles, which the young Socrates could not discover or describe to Parmenides. Diotima's description of the daimonion in its entirety between god and mortal (Symposium 202c) should lead readers to suspect that what Socrates later called his daimonion (e.g., in the Alcibiades I, Phaedrus, Republic, Theages, Euthydemus, and Apology) is closely related to his knowledge of ta erōtika.

Socrates' question about the genesis of eros provoked a long response from Diotima. We would call her reply a story, although neither Socrates nor Plato explicitly calls it "myth" (*mythos*).[34] Lurking outside the door of Zeus's garden, where the gods were celebrating Aphrodite's birth, Diotima told Socrates, Poverty (*Penia*) saw that Resource (*Poros*) had become drunk with nectar, laid down next to him, and became pregnant. Their offspring Eros inherited traits from both parents. Like his mother, he is poor. Neither tender nor beautiful, as most people think, Eros is hard and parched, shoeless and homeless; he sleeps on the barren ground without covers and rests in doorways. Like his father, however, Eros is resourceful. In seeking the good and beautiful, he is a clever hunter, able to devise many prudent strategies; he is not merely a philosopher, but a terrible sorcerer, bewitcher, and sophist. Turning from the personification to the phenomenon, she concluded that as a mixture, neither mortal nor immortal, eros is neither totally ignorant nor completely wise. As the link between the purely intelligible and the sensible, which is not purely intelligible itself, eros is not and could not be always the same or constant. Relating what she had just said to common experience, Diotima reminded Socrates that eros ebbs and flows.

Since Marsilio Ficino (if not on their own), readers have seen that Diotima's description dramatized the similarity between eros and Socrates.[35] Socrates did not perceive the likeness, however. He asked who such lovers of wisdom were, if they were neither ignorant nor wise. Diotima had not yet succeeded in leading Socrates to see that knowledge of eros has to be derived from self-knowledge.

It would be clear to a child, she somewhat condescendingly observed, that as seekers of wisdom, philosophers are neither wise nor ignorant but something in between. Nevertheless, she explained the character and source of Socrates' previous error (and consequent lack of self-knowledge): he had confused that which is truly lovable and beautiful, the beloved or that which is sought, with love or the seeking itself.

Expressing some skepticism, Socrates once again responded with a question: if eros is not a god or beautiful, what use is it to human beings?

34. Cf. Strauss, *Symposium*, 191.

35. Cf. Marsilio Ficino, *Commentary on Plato's "Symposium on Love,"* trans. Sears Jayne (Dallas: Spring Publications, 1985), speech 7, chap. 2, 155–58. Jacques Derrida emphasizes the same connection: Derrida, "La pharmacie de Platon," in *La dissemination* (Paris: Seuil, 1972), 117; trans. by Barbara Johnson as "Plato's Pharmacy," in *Dissemination* (Chicago: University of Chicago Press, 1981), 134.

Having shown Socrates that he did not really believe what he first thought or said he did, Diotima increased his perplexity by answering his query with a series of her own. She first asked, what do lovers of the beautiful seek? Then, when Socrates answered, to possess it, she pressed him further by asking, what then do they have? Admitting his own inability to say, Socrates became fully aware of his need to learn from Diotima (a need he reiterates several times in the report of their further conversations).

Readers of Plato should be struck by the similarity between Diotima's way of leading the young Socrates step by step to see the truth by asking him a series of questions about his own opinions and the way in which he later interrogates his interlocutors. To arouse a desire for knowledge on the part of another, it does not suffice to show him that he has contradictory opinions; the teacher has to show the student that he really doesn't know, that is, that none of his former, contradictory opinions are tenable or correct in their current form.

Having shown Socrates that he does not really believe that eros (as love of the beautiful) is either beautiful or divine, Diotima next led him to see that eros does not really or ultimately consist of love of the beautiful. People desire beautiful things because they believe beautiful things are good, and they want to acquire good things in order to be happy. What we call love is only a part, a particular type, of a more general desire. What human beings really want is happiness. Since it would make us unhappy to lose what happiness we have, we wish to retain the good things we acquire and the happiness we attain by their means forever. Because human beings are mortal, however, the only way we can even approximately fulfill our deepest desire is by reproducing the best parts or aspects of ourselves in members of the next generation. All human beings—not solely the females—thus feel the desire to beget progeny, of the soul as well as of the body.[36] That desire is aroused by a perception of beauty, that is, a feeling of attraction that pulls us outside or beyond ourselves, whether it be in the form of the promise of sexual gratification, fame, or intelligible order.

To show Socrates that this desire to give birth is not a desire merely to reproduce oneself or one's own species, she reminded him on another occasion of the willingness not merely of parents but of lovers of honor

---

36. In mortal, sensible beings, Diotima explains, the contents, both sensible matter and the contents of our minds, are continually decaying and thus have to be constantly replenished, but the form stays the same. This is the way "a mortal thing participates in immortality" (*thnēton athanasias metechei*; *Symposium* 208b).

to die for the sake of their progeny—intellectual even more than physical. Rather than try to replicate themselves or their fellows, poets like Homer and Hesiod, and legislators like Lycurgus and Solon, conceived of a better, more noble way of life, which they tried to bring into being in the souls of their people—or at least its most promising youths—by educating them. Once the seed, the idea or conception of a prudent or virtuous life, was implanted in them, these people too would try to implant and see it develop in subsequent generations.

Erotic desire, as Diotima described it, is thus more radically productive, imaginative, and intellectual than usually thought. It consists in a striving not merely to perpetuate but rather to bring into being new and better forms of human existence by changing the opinions people have about what is both desirable and possible. Because it requires an act of the imagination and hence of the mind in order to arouse it, this desire is not the universal force of becoming or even simply "animal" generation that previous poets and philosophers had taken it to be; it is distinctively human. Because it requires intentional human action for its realization, it is the source of poetry (*poiēsis*) in its broad sense of making or doing as well as in its more restricted sense of literary verse.

Because the youthful Socrates held opinions about eros like those voiced by Hesiod and Parmenides, Diotima believed he would be able to recognize the phenomenon of eros and its effects not only in procreation but also in poetry and legislation. She thought he would understand the superiority of the "immortal" fame he might achieve as an individual to the mere perpetuation of the species through instinctive procreation. She was not so sure he would be able to follow her when she described the third, highest, and most complete manifestation of eros—the ability to beget true virtue in human beings as a result of one's having seen beauty (or nobility) in itself.[37] He had not yet practiced philosophy as she understood it.

Before his "instruction by Diotima" (or, to speak nonmetaphorically, his discovery of the nature and significance of human eros), Socrates seems to have investigated the *logoi*, the accounts other human beings gave of things in general, and of the excellence of human life or the virtues in

---

37. As Benardete (*Plato's "Symposium,"* 81–89) indicates, the achievement of fame perpetuates a memory of the individual and his acts or products, whereas the contemplation of the eternal seems to involve an obliteration of everything individual. Nothing is produced or left. For this reason, Hannah Arendt argues in *The Human Condition* (Chicago: University of Chicago Press, 1958), philosophy constitutes the end of the political search for individual distinction.

particular, but he did not seek young associates. He did not try to "beget in the beautiful" by implanting a notion of virtue in noble youth and seeing whether it would grow. He did not claim to know what virtue is in itself or the particular forms of virtue like justice are. He simply had a hypothesis, that things became just or equal or noble by participating in the just, the equal, or the noble in itself.

To prove that his hypothesis is true, Socrates not only needed to show what there are ideas of; he also needed to show how changeable mortals could know such eternally unchanging, purely intelligible forms of being.[38] But it is not clear from his account of his "second sailing" in the *Phaedo* how Socrates would acquire such knowledge from an examination of the *logoi*. At most, he could test the arguments of others to see whether they were consistent in themselves or consistent with his best hypothesis and gradually refine his hypothesis by showing that some qualities such as largeness were parts of or participants in more general ideas such as size or extension. He could purify the qualities, ideas, or unchanging forms of being from all accidental or other admixtures, but he could not show how and why the person seeking the knowledge could obtain it. This was one of the two major ways in which Socrates had found all previous philosophy to be defective. Not only had the pre-Socratics mixed up different aspects of existence such as number and extent; they had also failed to provide

---

38. Did they include natural species, the paradigms of artifacts like couches, the virtues, and/or intelligible qualities of physical things like equality, number, extension, and duration? Aristotle suggests the first, but it is not clear that this claim is supported by the dialogues. In the *Parmenides* (130c) Socrates expresses uncertainty about whether there are ideas of natural species or elements. In the *Republic* he first speaks (507b) of the noble itself and the good itself for which we set down one idea as that which really is, but then he draws an analogy between the sun, which produces the light necessary both for sight and growth, and a supreme "idea of the good," which as the cause of both knowledge and truth is "beyond being" (508e–9b). Later in describing the "idea" of a couch of which artisans make specific examples and artists paint imitations he says, "we would say, I suppose, a god produced it" (597b). These three conceptions or use of "idea" appear to be very different from one another. In the *Phaedrus* (246a) Socrates speaks of the idea of the soul itself (which he does not in the *Phaedo*, where he also argues for the immortality of soul). In the *Phaedrus* (246e) Socrates also speaks of the soul's contemplation of the beautiful itself, the wise itself, and the good itself as well as (at 247d) justice itself, moderation itself, and science itself, but he does not call these colorless, shapeless, purely intelligible beings *eidē*. In the *Phaedo* he first speaks of equality, the greater and the lesser in themselves, as well as the just, the good, and the noble (75c, 76e, 78d) as changeless beings our souls encountered before they were (re)born into bodies. But later (in explaining the character of his "second sailing"), he speaks of the *eidos* of cause (*aition*) as well as beauty, good, greatness, smallness, and twoness or duality itself. In the *Philebus* (25a–e) he seems to suggest that there are *ideai* of numbers. In other words, although Plato's Socrates consistently maintains that there is a plurality of eternally unchanging, hence perfectly intelligible beings which he sometimes calls *eidē* or *ideai*, he does not present a definite list or complete definition of such.

an explanation of the reasons why the obviously mortal, changeable philosophers themselves seek, or how they could obtain, knowledge of an unchanging and hence intelligible order of reality. That was the problem Parmenides pointed out in Socrates' notion of the ideas; how could changing mortals have access to unchanging things? What Socrates needed was to find a bridge, some other means of connection or communication between the sensible and the intelligible. That was precisely what he claimed to have learned about eros from Diotima.

As we have seen, Socrates learned about eros in stages. First he had to free himself from the traditional misunderstanding of eros as beautiful. Then he had to come to understand that in pursuing the beautiful, he and other human beings are in fact seeking to obtain the good—forever. In the famous "ladder of love," Diotima showed Socrates how he needed to advance from love of the body of a particular youth to all beautiful bodies (a class), from bodies then to souls, from souls to the institutions and laws that form beautiful psyches, and from institutions to beautiful or noble sciences so that he might free himself from undue attachment to any one particular instance of beauty and produce many noble arguments and philosophical conversations until he achieved knowledge of the beautiful in itself. At this stage (or during these stages) of his education, Socrates could employ his hypothesis concerning the ideas; he could examine the opinions of others and see whether they agree with his notion of the beautiful in itself while he purified his own understanding of all accidental accompaniments.

Socrates could not be sure that his final vision was not merely that—a vision, dream, or intimation as opposed to knowledge—unless he could lead others to see it as well, that is, to accept his understanding. But as Diotima pointed out earlier, the agreement of others would not suffice to prove anything true. Their understanding of the beautiful (or just or good) could remain just that—an agreement or convention. To show how an eternal idea could not merely exist in or be intertwined with a sensible body, but the way in which such an idea could give shape and definition to the sensible, Socrates had to persuade others not merely to join him in a search for knowledge of the *kalon* (beautiful or noble) but finally to embody that understanding in their own lives and so achieve the good—at least for us—by becoming truly virtuous themselves.[39] As a result of his

---

39. This is why we see Socrates tell Glaucon in the *Republic*, for example, that the true lover of beauty will seek not merely to see as many particular examples of it as possible (like a sight-seer) but to find the beautiful in itself. Socrates is trying to lead his more philosophically inclined

encounter with Diotima, in his subsequent conversations Socrates concentrated on the question of what makes a man *kalos k'agathos* rather than on more traditional philosophical questions about the relation between the odd and the even or the "is" and "is not." He did so because he observed that human beings have a natural desire to live both nobly and well, but that this aspiration can be fulfilled only through intentional action, in association with others, through the acquisition of arts or knowledge.[40]

Human beings naturally seek what is good, but Socrates came to see that they do not naturally or immediately understand the character of their own desire. In the *Symposium* Plato shows his readers how Socrates came to understand the character of his own desire for wisdom (literally, philo-sophia) only as a result of having his opinions subjected to dialectical examination by another. Through that examination he learned not only that his previous opinions were inconsistent but also that they did not correspond to his own experience. He could not simply leave things at the level of his own experience, however; that experience could be peculiar to him. He had to see whether his ideas, his beliefs and desires, his deeds and the results of those deeds, could and would be replicated by other human beings. He had to try to "sow the seeds," to "plant" his conception of the best life, the philosophic life, in the souls of others and see whether it would grow. To prepare the soil, so to speak, like Diotima, he first had to show his interlocutors, those who were still young and unformed enough to be fundamentally influenced or molded, the inadequacies of their current opinions. But, he recognized, such a negative showing of inconsistencies or errors was only a preliminary step; it did not suffice to persuade or to teach. Insofar as the knowledge claimed was knowledge of human excellence or virtue, the knowledge claimed was of something more than

---

young associates to see that there are "things in themselves or 'ideas.'" Yet Plato also shows that Socrates not merely sought the company of particular youths but also adapted his arguments to them, that is, that he was concerned with and about particular individuals. All human beings live as individuals, that is, as combinations of soul, including the intellect, and body. To show how purely intelligible ideas could not merely be combined with but shape sensible bodies, Socrates needed not merely to persuade his associates to mimic the external peculiarities of his own bodily existence, for example, not usually wearing shoes or questioning the opinions of others (like Aristodemus and Apollodorus), or even merely to adopt his characteristic opinions about the true meaning of the noble and good. He and his associates would demonstrate, in fact, the way in which purely intelligible ideas shape bodily existence by displaying what they argued were truly virtues in action.

40. We thus see why Socrates concentrated on "the human things," even though he argued that human life is—or at least can be decisively shaped by—ideas of the beautiful and good that are not simply or solely human (and thus essentially transitory).

propositions, opinions (*doxai*), or explanations (*logoi*) of the basis of those opinions. Knowledge of the best form of human life had to be demonstrated in deed or in fact (*ergon*). That is the reason Plato presents Socrates not merely as the enunciator of a certain argument about the ideas but emphatically as representing a certain, philosophical way of life.

As Plato indicates in the order in which he presents the speeches in the *Symposium*, Socrates' account of what he learned—internally, so to speak—from Diotima needs to be supplemented by what others can see—externally, so to speak—in Socrates' deeds. That is the role assigned particularly to Alcibiades, who bursts into the dinner party, drunk. In his exposé of the "truth" about Socrates, Alcibiades reminds the assembled guests that the philosopher pretends to be a great lover of young men; but, he assures them, Socrates' interest in young men is not sexual. No young man in Athens was more physically attractive than Alcibiades, but when Alcibiades tried to seduce Socrates, he failed miserably. Socrates was simply not interested.

Alcibiades arrived at the banquet after Socrates gave his speech. If Alcibiades had been present earlier, he would have heard Socrates say that the lover of the beautiful needs to ascend the "ladder of love" from an attraction to a particular young man, through a perception of the beautiful shared by all young men, to that to be found, even more generally, in practices, institutions, laws, and sciences, until he would finally be able to perceive the beautiful in itself. As Alcibiades testifies, Socrates had made at least part of that ascent. Socrates is not interested in getting sexual gratification from physically attractive young men. He reprimanded Alcibiades, indeed, for trying to cheat him by offering him a less valuable, because commoner and fleeting, good—physical pleasure—in exchange for the rarer, more lasting "gold" of wisdom. Wisdom cannot be communicated from body to body, Socrates reminded Alcibiades. At most, one can arouse the desire to acquire wisdom by giving another an inkling of its beauty.

Socrates' erotic desire *is*, as he himself states, a desire to "beget," that is, to bring into being and thus to perpetuate a truly virtuous form of human life in the most promising, beautiful or noble (*kaloi*) members of the new generation. To plant the seed of this conception he obviously needs to be able not only to identify promising youths with the potential to realize his vision, but also to communicate to them the desire to realize it.[41] According

41. Nussbaum's suggestion (*Fragility*, 165–99) that Alcibiades' exposé constitutes a corrective and critique of Diotima's more traditionally "Platonic" doctrine concerning the superiority of

to Alcibiades, Socrates is an expert or accomplished communicator; his speeches have an unparalleled attractive force. Like Diotima's Eros, Socrates has the powers of a "druggist" or sorcerer. But, Alcibiades also shows, again in deed or fact, there is a twofold problem.

First, although Socrates might attract talented students like Alcibiades, these students do not necessarily continue to listen to him. Like Alcibiades, they might stop their ears and run away. Like the young Socrates, they might confuse the object of love, the beautiful, with love, the desire to obtain it. Like Alcibiades, they might therefore seek to become beautiful, that is, desirable, in the eyes of others and so admired and loved in themselves. Rather than seek knowledge of the beautiful itself, they would, like the poets and legislators of old, seek glory or popular acclaim. Only a person who had ascended to a view of the beautiful or noble in itself, Diotima claimed, can inculcate true virtue in another; other conceptions of virtue like those of the poets and founding legislators are mere likenesses of the truth, examples of what in later dialogues Socrates calls political virtue, that is, virtue based on opinion rather than on knowledge. The vision he and other philosophers acquire of the beautiful in itself is admittedly transitory. As Diotima reminded Socrates, human beings cannot retain anything intellectual any more than they can retain any particular part of their body; we constantly need to replace and replenish what we have acquired in the past. Having a vision of the truly beautiful is necessary, according to Diotima, for *begetting* in the beautiful. The beautiful, the good, and the noble are "begotten," in fact or effect, in the human beings who become philosophers, because, as Socrates explains more fully in the *Republic*, a person who loves the truth (having seen that it is beautiful) acquires all the virtues as a result of his overwhelming love for and hence pursuit of the truth.

People who have seen and therefore desire the beautiful in itself will embody it in their actions. But herein lies a second difficulty; like all the virtues and other intelligible forms of being, true nobility or beauty in itself is not visible. It is impossible for an observer to determine whether another person is truly virtuous, whether he or she is performing what seem to be virtuous deeds on the basis of knowledge, for the sake of virtue itself,

---

the general, abstract ideas to the particular, concrete manifestations seems, therefore, misplaced. Neither Socrates nor anyone else can climb the "ladder of love" Diotima describes without distinguishing more and less promising students, that is, particular individuals, in whom to sow their seeds (an image Socrates uses at the conclusion of the *Phaedrus* as well to describe the possible benefits of writing).

or for some other reason. Socrates is *not* beautiful to look at, Alcibiades emphasizes; like the figures of the ugly satyrs, however, Socrates contains things of incredible beauty within. Socrates manifests some of this beauty in his speeches. The problem with speeches (which both Socrates and the Eleatic Stranger investigate at length) is that they can be artful or just plain false. When Socrates stands still and silent, it is impossible for an external observer to know whether, much less what, he is thinking. Is he contemplating the beautiful itself? No one can know. Socrates might manifest some of his virtue in his external behavior—in the courage he displayed in battle, in his physical endurance, in his relative immunity to the pleasures and pains that plague most human beings, as well as in his extraordinary powers of speech. But, as Aristophanes demonstrates in his *Clouds*, it is possible to see or interpret those manifestations as examples of Socrates' extreme hubris, a pride that involves a denial or ignorance of his limitations as a mortal human being, that is, his lack of self-knowledge and/or eros.[42]

In sum, what Socrates' account of what he learned about eros from Diotima and Alcibiades' description of Socrates' actions in the *Symposium* indicate is that if human eros or desire(s) for a good that transcends the limitations of our corporeal existence is the means whereby sensible and intelligible forms of existence come together, it is not possible to know anything about the connection—and, hence, about the character of the whole—for certain. Although all human beings display an inarticulate desire not merely to live forever but to possess the good eternally, most of them do not recognize the character or goal of the desire on whose basis they act. They do not see the way in which their lives are directed and formed by something that is not, properly speaking, sensible, but that is usually not purely or completely intelligible to them. Because we are mortal, changeable beings, we can never attain knowledge, strictly speaking; we can only have true or false opinions for which we can give more or less adequate explanations (*logoi*). Because the eros of human beings may not be aroused sufficiently or by its true objects, the link may not even or always exist. It does not exist necessarily; it is not a matter of logic, much less of efficient cause and effect.

42. Alcibiades' description of Socrates' striding bravely, looking proudly to his right and left, in the retreat from Delium sounds very much like Aristophanes' description of the proud strutting of the sophist. Cf. *Symposium* 221b with *Clouds* 362.

From these two speeches in the *Symposium* we thus learn what it means when Socrates said that all he knows are the erotic things, why that declaration is basically the equivalent of his saying, as he will in the *Apology of Socrates*, that his wisdom consists in his knowing that he does not know, and why Socrates often states, as in the *Phaedrus*, that he seeks self-knowledge first and foremost. In the *Apology* Socrates explains how the critical investigations of the opinions of his contemporaries concerning the good and the noble, which he undertook at the instigation of the oracle (which seems to coincide with his supposed instruction by Diotima), aroused the envy and anger of his fellow citizens. They did not understand the difference between Socrates and the philosophers who preceded him, and as a result of this misunderstanding, they unjustly condemned him.

III. *Apology of Socrates*: The Externally Observable Effects of Socratic Philosophy

Addressed to a gathering of poets and their admirers at a private dinner party, the somewhat metaphorical account Socrates gives of his own development as a philosopher in the *Symposium* might be called the "inside" story. As Alcibiades suggests, it reveals Socrates' inner beauty as well as the power of his speeches. As Alcibiades emphasizes, Socrates was not beautiful to look at—on the "outside," so to speak. When Socrates was required to give an account of himself and his philosophical activity, not behind doors to a small group of Athenian intellectuals in private but outside in public to the demos as a whole, Plato shows in the *Apology*, Socrates was not able to convince his fellow citizens that his inquiries benefited rather than harmed them. He was not able, in other words, to make his inner beauty and goodness manifest. By writing the *Apology* and showing how Socrates' speeches were reflected in his actions, Plato does.[43]

Socrates begins his defense by emphasizing how difficult it will be for him to make himself understood in a public speech. His accusers have

43. As Eva Brann, "The Offense of Socrates: A Re-Reading of Plato's *Apology*," *Interpretation* 7 (May 1978), 2; and Bruell, *Socratic Education*, 136, point out, the *Apology* is the only dialogue in which Plato is explicitly said to be present. As its author, he purports merely to record what he heard Socrates say. Although he indicates the way in which Socrates aroused the anger of his immediate audience, Plato also has Socrates predict the outcome of his trial and death. The Athenians will be blamed and Socrates will be valorized for heroically accepting his death, even though at seventy years of age he would have died soon in any case.

claimed that he is a terribly clever speaker (*deinos rhētōr*), but, Socrates responds, he has no experience in a courtroom.[44] Rather than employ rhetorical stratagems to enlist the sympathy of his judges, he will say nothing but the truth. Nevertheless, he predicts, his judges will convict him on the basis of prejudices they acquired when they were young. These prejudices seem to have arisen from a confusion between Socrates and his predecessors, that is, a failure or inability to distinguish his characteristic activities from those of natural philosophers, sophists, and teachers of rhetoric.

With the exception of the comic poet Aristophanes, Socrates explains, his "old accusers" are nameless. They charge him with being "a wise man, a thinker on the things aloft, who has investigated all things under the earth, who makes the weaker speech the stronger . . . and teaches others the same things" (*Apology* 18b–c, 19b).[45] In his *Clouds* Aristophanes showed Socrates hanging in a basket, claiming to tread on air, and saying many other ridiculous things. But, Socrates assures the jury, he has no knowledge of this kind, although he does not contemn it. He asks them to recall if they had ever heard him conversing about such things. He points out the most obvious, visible ways in which he differs from the foreign sophists and teachers of rhetoric who come to Athens and ask fees for the instruction they give in natural philosophy, mathematics, and public speaking—that he has not left Athens or asked money from those who listen to him conversing with others. Socrates visibly does not act the way previous philosophers or sophists had, yet his fellow citizens are not able, apparently, to see the difference.[46] Why not? Part of the difficulty seems to involve a lag in perception of change over time. As we learn from the *Phaedo*, there *was* a time when Socrates was concerned with natural history; there was even some reason to confuse him, as he subsequently accuses Meletus of doing, with Anaxagoras. Neither his "old" nor his present or "new" accusers in court—Anytus the politician, Meletus the poet, and Lycon the rhetorician—note or understand the significance of the turn in Socrates' thought

44. In an earlier conversation with Callicles (related in *Gorgias* 521d–22a), Socrates predicted what would happen if he were dragged into court: his position would resemble that of a doctor, accused by a pastry chef of prescribing ill-tasting medicines, before a jury of sweet-loving children.

45. The charge can be taken to point to Socrates' hubris. Thomas G. West and Grace Starry West, *Four Texts on Socrates* (Ithaca: Cornell University Press, 1984), 65–66, note that *sophos* can mean "wise guy" as well as "wise man."

46. Hannah Arendt, "Philosophy and Politics," *Social Research* 57, no. 1 (Spring 1990): 73–103, also argues that Socrates was convicted because the Athenians did not see or understand the difference between his investigations and those of previous philosophers.

that distinguishes him from both his philosophical predecessors and other contemporary intellectuals. Thought is not visible. But, readers may ask, had Socrates' practice not changed as a result of his change in thought?

Socrates reminds his auditors of the change in the nature of his inquiries. As in the *Symposium*, so in his *Apology*, Socrates traces his development to an indirect communication (mediated by another mortal) from the god or gods. Here, however, the decisive lesson is attributed to the publicly recognized oracle at Delphi rather than to an otherwise unknown *Mantinikē*; the pronouncement of the Pythia is both initially solicited and subsequently communicated to Socrates by an Athenian partisan of democracy also known (and shown in Aristophanes' *Clouds*) to have been a student of Socrates, Chaerephon.[47] Socrates' account of the crucial turn in his thought in his *Apology* thus seems tailored to fit his audience on this occasion, the Athenian demos.[48] It is a description of his activity particularly intended for an audience whose members have had little, if any, direct experience with Socrates himself or philosophy more generally.[49]

As in the *Symposium*, so in his *Apology*, Socrates admits that he greeted the divine pronouncement with skepticism. He wondered how the oracle could say that no one was wiser than he, who knew only that he did not know. He appears to have responded to the oracular pronouncement, moreover, by trying to prove that it was wrong. He went to those who were reputed to be wise to demonstrate by interrogating them that they did know more than he. Unfortunately, he discovered, they did not. Embarrassed by their inability to respond, Socrates observes, the people he questioned came to hate him. That is the reason he now finds himself in

47. When or even whether Chaerephon went to Delphi is unclear. H. W. Parke and D. E. W. Wormell, *The Delphic Oracle* (New York: Oxford University Press, 1956), 1:401–2, argue that Chaerephon would not have gone during the war, so the trip had to have taken place before 431 or during the 422–419 truce, and that it probably occurred earlier. Socrates had established a reputation for himself, it seems, simply by the questions he raised about the theories put forward by previous thinkers—cosmological as well as Parmenidean. As we learn from the *Parmenides*, Socrates' exchange with the Eleatics was memorized and retold by others.

48. Socrates himself suggests as much when addressing the jury after they vote to convict him. He observes: "if I say that [being silent and ceasing to philosophize] is to disobey the god . . . , you will not be persuaded by me, on the ground that I am being ironic. And . . . , if I say that this even happens to be a very great good for a human being—to make speeches every day about virtue and the other things about which you hear me conversing and examining both myself and others—and that the unexamined life is not worth living for a human being, you will be persuaded by me still less" (*Apology* 37e–38a).

49. For that reason, the *Apology of Socrates* continues to be one of the first works assigned in introductory philosophy or political theory courses. It is a first presentation of Socratic philosophy for the audience or readers, not necessarily the first presentation of the subject by the author as many defenders of its "historicity" have maintained.

court on trial for his life. His three accusers represent the three groups he questioned. Nevertheless, he concludes (*Apology* 28a), it is not these accusers or groups that will convict him; it is the envy and slander of the many. What do they envy Socrates for, readers should ask, and how exactly do they slander him?

The reason most of his old accusers are nameless and ignorantly accused him of engaging in the kinds of philosophical investigations he pursued only as a relative youth, Socrates explains, is that they have had no direct contact with him. They are relying on hearsay—once, twice, or even further removed. Although he never claimed to be able to teach anyone anything, Socrates admits, he had attracted a following. Young men, especially the sons of wealthy men who have the most leisure, enjoy hearing their elders examined (and shown up). They not only follow Socrates around; they also try to imitate him. (Readers thus learn something about the nature of the "attraction" Socrates exercises upon the young; we also see how the "seeds" once planted begin to grow. By mimicking Socrates, the youths were trying to become philosophers [if not "wise guys," *sophoi*] in deed.) Embarrassed by their inability to answer the questions put to them by these young men, their elders became angry. Rather than blame themselves for their ignorance, they condemned Socrates for prompting the young to ask such unanswerable questions. Having little, if any, direct exposure to Socrates, they could not say specifically, when asked, what Socrates taught the offending youths. So the angry elders taxed Socrates with the things often said against other philosophers—that they investigate things in the heavens and under the earth, that they do not believe in gods, and that they make the weaker argument the stronger.

The central charge—that like other natural philosophers Socrates does not believe in the gods—points to the source of the difficulty Socrates predicted he would have defending himself. Insofar as he is being accused of not believing in the gods of the city, he is being charged, basically, with a crime of thought—and it is impossible to determine for certain what another man thinks. All we have to go on are his visible deeds and audible speeches. But, as everyone also knows, both speeches and deeds can be deceptive. The problem concerning the way in which the sensible aspects of the world participate in the intelligible that prompted Socrates to undertake his distinctive investigations of human *logoi* thus arises, ironically, in its most dramatic form with regard to Socrates' own actions and thoughts in court.

Nevertheless, Plato indicates, it is not what Socrates believes or does not believe that really concerns his fellow citizens so much as his ability to attract a following among the young. In other words, the Athenians care more about Socrates' effect on the next generation than they do about his piety or lack thereof.[50] As Diotima pointed out in the *Symposium*, all human beings seek immortality by perpetuating themselves or their way of life in future generations. Insofar as the philosophical way of life Socrates seeks to perpetuate casts doubt on the validity of the practices and opinions of the Athenians, there is ground for real, abiding hostility. In the *Apology* Socrates thus has to try to convince the jurors not only that he is a different kind of philosopher from his predecessors, but also and more importantly that his particular kind of philosophy does not threaten to destroy the respect and affection parents want from their children.[51]

Socrates attempts to show his fellow citizens how he differs from previous philosophers not only in speech but also in deed. First, he emphasizes in his account of the oracle that he investigates human opinions, not things in the heavens or under the earth. Second, he argues in response to his new accusers that instead of corrupting the young, he tries to correct them and those who have involuntarily harmed them. He is not the sophist depicted in the *Clouds* who teaches his students not to believe in the existence of the Olympian gods and instructs them in an art of speaking that makes them immune from legal prosecution.

Socrates has a difficult time persuading an audience unaccustomed to distinguishing among different kinds of intellectual activities. When he introduces the story of the oracle by admitting that he does have a certain kind of human wisdom, he has to ask the audience not to make disturbances. The jury appears to be reacting angrily to what they take to be boasting; in other words, Socrates appears to be acting like the strutting

50. Thomas G. West, *Plato's "Apology of Socrates": An Interpretation, with a New Translation* (Ithaca: Cornell University Press, 1979), 73–76, 79, 104, 107, 118, emphasizes the arrogance that aroused the anger of the jury (Socrates does not call them judges, as was conventional), but he attributes Socrates' conviction to his failure to understand the need political associations have for salutary beliefs; he does not see the way in which Socrates' influence with the younger generation aroused the envy of his fellow citizens. In other words, West takes the piety charge more seriously than the corruption charge (which he sees to be deduced from the former). Support for my contention that the Athenians were more concerned about Socrates' influence on their children than about his beliefs per se can be found in the *Euthyphro* (3c–d).

51. In the *Clouds* Aristophanes showed that Strepsiades finally tried to destroy Socrates not merely for denying the existence of the gods but even more for alienating the affections of his son Pheidippides.

wise guy Aristophanes mocks in the *Clouds*. Socrates might have claimed, more modestly, only to know that he did not know the most important things, but his attempt to disprove the oracle has struck many readers since as being impious.[52] How dare a mere human being challenge the word of a god? Not all the people who claim to be inspired or to speak for the gods can be trusted, Socrates reminds his audience. The poets say many beautiful things (which they attribute to the Muses), but the poets could not explain their own words when he asked what they meant. Assuming that the god would not lie, but not understanding how the oracle could possibly be true, Socrates made further inquiries. These inquiries differed from those undertaken by previous philosophers not only because they concerned human beings and their opinions rather than natural phenomena, but also and more importantly because Socrates' inquiries established the truth of the oracle whereas the materialistic cosmologies of his predecessors cast doubt on the very existence of the gods.

In cross-examining his new accuser, Socrates nevertheless looks very much like a clever speaker who defeats his opponent by bringing out the contradictions in his argument rather than enunciating a doctrine or defense of his own. The philosopher makes mincemeat of the poet by showing that Meletus has made two ridiculous charges: (1) that acting entirely by himself, Socrates could have corrupted the young people of Athens in the face of the efforts of all other citizens to improve them, and (2) that Socrates believes in the children of gods (*daimones*) but not in the gods themselves. When Socrates suggests that Meletus must be jesting, he once again has to ask the audience not to make disturbances.

Socrates' response to Meletus' jest is, nevertheless, serious. As he argues in other dialogues, so he urges his fellow citizens here: no one who understands what he is doing would intentionally seek to make the people with whom he associates vicious. No one would therefore willingly corrupt the young people of his city by making them unjust. If Socrates has corrupted the young, he has done so unintentionally. The proper response or remedy is not to drag him into court and to threaten him with punishment. Instead, the poet should take Socrates aside and show him in private where he has erred.

52. Cf. John Burnet, *Plato's "Euthyphro," "Apology of Socrates," and "Crito"* (Oxford: Oxford University Press, 1924), 21b8n; and Alexander Nehamas, "Socratic Intellectualism," in *Proceedings of the Boston Area Colloquium in Ancient Philosophy*, ed. J. Cleary (Lanham, MD: Rowman and Littlefield, 1986), 2:306.

That is, Socrates explains, exactly how he has treated his fellow citizens. Reflecting on Socrates' argument with Meletus, the judges should have seen that (1) if the young people of Athens had been corrupted, and (2) it was impossible for Socrates acting alone to have had such an effect in opposition to the efforts of all others, then (3) someone else—all the other Athenians with whom the young regularly associated—must have corrupted them, and (4) these Athenians had not corrupted their own youths willingly or intentionally. That is why Socrates has tried to correct them, going to each individually or in private. As we see in the *Apology*, a large group of people cannot learn or be persuaded of the bad effects of their own actions and opinions all at once in one sitting or hearing (cf. *Gorgias* 455a).

Responding to an anonymous interlocutor who asks whether Socrates is not ashamed of having done something so suspicious that it resulted in his being hauled into court, the philosopher presents his interrogations of his fellow citizens as a service to the city as well as to the god. In effect, he transforms his speeches into deeds. Just as he risked his life defending Athens in the army, so Socrates claims that he risked his life, provoking the envy and anger that would result in his conviction, by showing his fellow citizens that they do not know what is truly noble and good. Rather than seeking the good of the body—the safety, wealth, and glory the Athenians sought, for example, in the Peloponnesian War, a war that resulted in the overthrow of the democracy and the rise of the Thirty—Socrates has irritated his compatriots by asking them why they do not strive instead for the goods of the soul, truth, and prudence. By going to each individually, Socrates has tried to show them that they were not achieving what they really wanted but that they were unintentionally corrupting both themselves and their fellows.

As evidence of his acting for the good of the community and not in his own self-interest, Socrates points out that he has been living visibly in ten thousand-fold poverty. What Socrates' poverty shows is that, consistent with his own teaching, he has been seeking the goods of the soul and not of the body. He does not seek his own interest, however, at the expense of his fellows. On the contrary, he is attempting to show that both he and his fellow citizens benefit from his questioning. Unlike riches or fame, truth and prudence can be shared, and not merely without cost to oneself but for the good of all. Having acted for the common good, Socrates claims to be just.

Recognizing that his judges still suspect him of being a clever speaker, Socrates explicitly turns at the end of his speech to what they honor, deeds, rather than arguments. He thus defends himself and his philosophical activity to the Athenian demos in terms of his externally visible and verifiable actions as opposed to his potentially falsifying, self-justifying speeches. The one time he held public office, Socrates reminds the jury, he alone opposed the Athenians when, acting against their own laws, they brought to trial as a group the generals who had won the battle at Arginusae, because the generals had not collected the corpses and given them proper burial. In trying the generals together, the Athenians acted against their own laws on the basis of two interrelated fears—fear of death and fear of the gods. Having learned from his interrogations that no one knows whether death is good or bad—or what the gods desire—Socrates had no such fear. As his action upon this occasion demonstrates, his philosophy makes it possible for him to do what he thinks right; his actions thus conform to his speeches. Likewise, after the Thirty overthrew the democracy, and along with it the rule of law, Socrates reminds the judges, he refused to obey the tyrants' command to summon Leon of Salamis to his death—at the risk of being condemned to death himself. In concluding his defense, he informs the jurors that he will not try to save his life by pleading for mercy, nor will he bring his wife and children to do so on his behalf, although such pleas were common in Athens. To do so would be to divert the judges from their legal duty to determine what is just, not to do what pleases them.

In contrasting his own actions with theirs, at the end of his defense Socrates thus makes explicit the accusation that was implicit in his exchange with Meletus: it is not the philosopher Socrates but the Athenians themselves who have corrupted the young by providing them with examples of unjust behavior. Whereas the Athenians tried to evade their own laws, Socrates accepts both the trial and punishment they are imposing on him in the name of justice. Socrates' deeds coincide with his speeches; the Athenians say one thing in public—what they declare to be good, noble, and just in law—and do something else when they can.

It might seem strange, Socrates concedes, that he tries to serve the public interest at his own expense only by acting in private and that he does not "dare to go up before the multitude to counsel the city." But, he asserts,

> if I had attempted to be politically active, I would have perished long ago, and would have benefited neither you nor myself. . . . For there is no human being who will preserve his life if he genuinely opposes either you or any other multitude and prevents many unjust and unlawful things from happening in the city. Rather, if someone who really fights for the just is going

to preserve himself even for a short time, it is necessary for him to lead a private rather than a public life. (*Apology* 31d–e)[53]

Now that he is seventy years old and about to die in any case, as Socrates reminds the jurors after they have sentenced him to death, he is ready in his one and only public speech to stand up for what is just and, as a result, to lose his life. He is now trying to convince the Athenians as a whole through his actions of what he had tried to persuade them of earlier in speech and in private. No one would willingly corrupt and thus harm the people with whom he lives. In other words, no one would willingly be unjust.

Why did Socrates agree to go on trial in the first place and then accept his punishment, rather than flee as Crito urged (*Crito* 45e)? Anyone who compares Plato's *Apology of Socrates* with Xenophon's account of *Socrates' Defense to the Jury* knows that there are different explanations of his motives.[54] Xenophon's Socrates tells Hermogenes that he "talked big" in order to provoke the jurors into condemning him and so suffer an easy death. Plato's Socrates arouses the ire and envy of his fellow citizens by contrasting his just speech and action with their shamelessness. Plato's Socrates explicitly recounts his actions, however, in order to persuade his audience of the truth of his speeches. He attempts to show them in deed, as it were, that the pursuit of truth results in virtuous—courageous, just, wise, and pious—deeds. He acts to show them the way in which even a partial perception of purely intelligible ideas like the good, the noble, and the just can shape sensible human life. He might not have been able to show how the good determines everything that happens in nature as well as in human affairs or to find anyone to teach him (cf. *Phaedo* 97b–99c), but he could demonstrate in person the impossibility of explaining why he remained in prison merely by giving an account of his bones and sinews and not taking account of the reasons the Athenians thought it best to condemn him and he thought it best to accept the punishment. The proof of Socrates' strongest *logos* is, finally, in his life and death. The knowledge it generates

---

53. Even though commentators like Vlastos and Kahn claim that the *Apology* is the speech of the "historical" Socrates, Plato's philosopher of the same name says the same thing about his relation to political life, in the *Republic* 496a–e, a dialogue in which these commentators argue that "Socrates" is putting forth Plato's opinions. With regard to his political activity, we see, on the contrary, that Plato's characterization of Socrates is the same in both dialogues.

54. Cf. Thomas C. Brickhouse and Nicholas D. Smith, *Socrates on Trial* (Princeton: Princeton University Press, 1989), 60–61, for a summary of the alternatives.

is far from certain or indisputable. The conjunction of the speeches with the deeds or facts is, however, difficult simply to dismiss.

IV. Conclusion

In his three retrospective statements concerning his own development as a philosopher, Socrates explains how he came to differ from his predecessors both in theory and in practice. Although Socrates took his fundamental insight concerning the difference between the intelligible and the sensible from the Eleatics and so confronted the same problem concerning their relation that Parmenides had, Socratic philosophy has a different content and way of seeking it. As a result of a "divinely inspired" insight, Socrates came to see that the place where sensible and intelligible are joined is human *logos*. He thus turned to his famous examination of the opinions of others, first philosophical, but later poetic and political, particularly concerning the good, the noble, and the just.

To show how purely intelligible ideas can shape sensible existence, Socrates discovered, he had to demonstrate the process in deed or fact by persuading younger people to adopt his own philosophical way of life—as a way of life and not merely as a mode of seeking knowledge. That is the reason he incurred the anger of the fathers. His was a risky enterprise in more than one respect. First and most obviously, Socrates lost his life attempting to prove that philosophy does not undermine law and morality. As he himself emphasized, however, he was seventy years old and would soon have died in any case. The second risk was inherent in, rather than external to, his philosophy. Because there was no guarantee that he would persuade others—or that they, in turn, would persuade members of the next generation—the knowledge Socrates thought he might attain was necessarily uncertain. He could not say, moreover, whether the conjunction of sensible and intelligible that he strove to establish in human life could be extended to the whole.

Going beyond the question of the way in which sensible things participate in or are shaped by the intelligible, Socrates' turn to the human thus poses another set of problems that not merely he but all readers of Plato need to confront. First, so long as Socrates remains completely in the realm of the human, does his knowledge not necessarily remain partial—and hence, really, no knowledge at all? Socrates suggests as much when he emphasizes that he is a philosopher, a lover or seeker of wisdom, and not a *sophos* or wise man.

Second, if Socrates were to extend what he learned about the combination of the intelligible and the sensible in human life to the cosmos as a whole, would he not be in danger of losing his own sense of what is distinctively human by anthropomorphizing the nonhuman? By looking at the nonhuman in terms of intention—or the good as final cause—does he not risk losing the distinction between the human and nonhuman and so knowledge of both? In the *Phaedo* Socrates concludes that neither he nor anyone else had been able to show how the good is the origin, cause, or principle of everything (even though, in an earlier conversation recorded in the *Republic*, he had suggested that it was). He falls back on the safest argument he knows, that concerning the ideas. He suggests that he (or others after him) can determine what the basic kinds of being are by gradually sifting out the general from the particular. He himself never carries out that process, nor does he ever give exactly the same, much less a definitive, list of the ideas. Plato's Socrates never shows, therefore, how the whole is organized or structured. As he indicates in the *Theaetetus*, he cannot explain how human knowledge is possible.

To show how purely intelligible ideas or principles can shape sensible existence, Socrates learned, he had to demonstrate the connection in deed or fact by convincing others to adopt a philosophical way of life. The knowledge he sought could not be gained simply through contemplation or even investigation and discovery. But if a philosopher has to reshape his material, so to speak, two further questions arise.

First, can Socrates limit the effect to the relatively few individuals who might choose to follow him and devote themselves to philosophy? Does he not need to influence the opinions of the nonphilosophers as well, to persuade them to tolerate, if not positively to support, philosophy rather than attempting to destroy it? And if he does need to change the opinions of the nonphilosophers, does he not have to engage in a kind of political action, even though he claims in his *Apology* that he did not engage in politics?

Second, if understanding the conjunction or relation of the intelligible with the sensible in human life requires Socrates to have an intentional effect on the way of life of other human beings, does the same principle or requirement not apply to the whole? In other words, if Socrates seeks knowledge, which to be knowledge properly speaking has to be knowledge of the whole and not merely of the human part, does Socrates not have to try to remake the whole cosmos in order to make it intelligible? Does he or Plato thus initiate, knowingly or unintentionally, the attempt to make everything rational, as Friedrich Nietzsche and Martin Heidegger claim?

Plato shows that he recognizes the limitations, if not defects, of Socratic philosophy by contrasting his teacher not only with the Athenian Stranger and Parmenides but also with Timaeus and the Eleatic Stranger. Why, then, does Plato clearly make Socrates the most prominent representative of philosophy in his dialogues? To answer that question we have to examine, in light of the critical contrasts, the conversations in which Plato shows Socrates engaging.

4

Socrates Interrogates His Contemporaries about the Noble and Good

In the dialogues set in the two decades following Socrates' discovery of the importance of examining human opinion, Plato shows the philosopher interrogating his contemporaries—politically ambitious Athenians and the foreign sophists who claimed to be able to teach them—about their understanding of the noble and good. Socrates' investigations of the opinions of his contemporaries reveal that there was an unresolved tension, if not outright contradiction, in the understanding of human excellence expressed by the common Greek phrase used to describe a gentleman, *kalos k'agathos* (literally, "noble and good").

Following Homer's depiction of Achilles, the ancient Greeks associated nobility (*to kalon*) primarily with the virtue of courage, as exemplified by the willingness of young men to risk their lives in battle for the sake of their beloved. Most identified the good, however, with the pleasant.[1] As Socrates demonstrates in his exchange with Protagoras, in the first conversation Plato shows the philosopher having after his instruction by Diotima, courage may reduce the pain of our existence by alleviating various kinds of fear, but it is difficult if not impossible to maintain that the prospect of death is positively pleasant. But, Plato shows in the dialogues following Socrates' initial encounter with the famous sophist, the incoherence of the understanding of human excellence held by Socrates' contemporaries went even further and deeper. In the *Alcibiades I*, Socrates shows, the young man who reveled in the admiration of others and was willing to risk his life in order to obtain not merely extraordinary wealth but the power and prestige of

---

1. Cf. *Republic* 505b.

the greatest emperor, did not know how to realize his own ambitions. Not recognizing the importance of justice, he did not appreciate the need to serve others in order to attain and maintain their gratitude and admiration. Lacking piety, Socrates shows in both the *Alcibiades I* and *II*, this ambitious young Athenian also failed to recognize his own limitations as a mortal.[2] Nor, Socrates demonstrates in the *Charmides*, did his own aristocratic relatives, Critias and Charmides, see the need for self-restraint. It is no wonder they later became members of the Thirty, who seized power after Athens was defeated by Sparta, but they were hated and quickly deprived of their lives along with their rule by their fellow Athenians.[3] In the *Laches* Socrates' interrogations reveal the inability of leading Athenian generals during the Peloponnesian War to say what courage is. Nor, Socrates demonstrates in

2. The *Alcibiades I* was included among the thirty-five dialogues and thirteen epistles comprising the nine tetralogies of the Thrasyllus canon of the Platonic corpus; earlier scholars (like Diogenes) expressed doubts about the authenticity of other dialogues attributed to Plato. Gary Alan Scott, *Plato's Socrates as Educator* (Albany: SUNY Press, 2000), notes that the tendency to discount the *Alcibiades I* as spurious began with Schleiermacher and his student Ast. Their conclusions have been supported by some stylometric considerations, but as noted in the introduction to this volume, the reliability of such studies has been subjected to ever-escalating critiques. Thomas Pangle, in his introduction to *Roots of Political Philosophy*, quotes Theodor Gomperz's warning: "Three of [Plato's] latest works (*Timaeus, Critias*, and *Laws*) contain nearly 1500 words which are absent from his other works. . . . What, then, is proved if in a particular dialogue we detect a small number of words or phrases not met with elsewhere in Plato. . . ? (*Griechische Denker* [Berlin: Walter de Gruyter, 1925], 2, 220)." Scott concludes, "With few exceptions, modern scholars are much less familiar with the language and its conventions than were the early commentators. . . . That this dialogue was considered for 900 years to be not only genuinely Platonic but the crown jewel of the Platonic corpus by ancient and medieval commentators . . . , places the burden of proof on those who wish to undermine its status as a Platonic text" (*Socrates as Educator*, 206). Nicholas Denyer also defends the authenticity of the dialogue in *Plato: Alcibiades I* (Cambridge: Cambridge University Press, 2001), 11–26. Although she does not defend the authenticity of the dialogue per se, Jill Gordon, "Eros and Philosophical Seduction in *Alcibiades I*," *Ancient Philosophy* 23 (2003): 11–29, shows that Schleiermacher's reasons for questioning it are not well founded. Since the authenticity of the second *Alcibiades* is more widely questioned, even though Jacob Howland has defended it in "Socrates and Alcibiades: Eros, Piety, and Politics," *Interpretation* 18, no. 1 (Fall 1990): 63–90, I have relegated consideration of its contents to two endnotes. The picture it gives of Alcibiades and of Socrates' estimate of him, as well as the theme, is consistent with what we see in *Alcibiades I*.

3. W. Thomas Schmid, *Plato's "Charmides" and the Socratic Ideal of Rationality* (Albany: SUNY Press, 1998), 2–39, shows that Charmides and Critias both articulate traditional notions of aristocratic virtue and exemplify the way in which these notions degenerated into sources of tyranny. As a beautiful beloved, Charmides repeats the traditional notion that young men should be modest, characterized by shame or *aidōs*, and defer to the opinions of their elders (voiced, for example, by the "just speech" in Aristophanes *Clouds* 960–99). Critias was known to have written poetry in praise of the Spartan regime, especially the moderation it inculcated. Yet as the interaction between Charmides and Critias in the *Charmides* indicates, the adulation of their elderly lovers, who desired physical pleasure in return, accustomed young men to commanding rather than seeking the consent of others; their elderly lovers, like Critias, not only wanted but also became accustomed to unquestioning compliance.

his examinations of both Protagoras and Hippias, were the sophists able to improve on the incoherence, if not outright misunderstanding, of human excellence held by these politically ambitious Athenians. On the contrary, Socrates forces both Protagoras and Hippias to admit, the "good counsel" the sophists purveyed consists, at bottom, in calculations of the ways in which human beings can maximize their pleasure and minimize the pain of their existence in the long run. Yet, Socrates also compels both sophists to concede, such calculations, characteristic more of the wily Odysseus than of the noble Achilles, do not constitute a simply or entirely appealing vision of human excellence.

By repeatedly showing his contemporaries that they do not know what is truly noble and good, Socrates was trying to persuade them to join him in a philosophical investigation of what the best form of human existence really is. But, Plato shows, by repeatedly demonstrating his ability to refute the views of his contemporaries, Socrates merely convinced them that he was a "super-sophist."[4] In the dialogues set later, during the second part of the Peloponnesian War, we see (chap. 5) that Socrates thus took a different tack.

I. Socrates Bests the Famous Sophist: *Protagoras*

In the *Apology* Socrates reported that he had examined those who claimed to be wise and showed that they were not. Because Protagoras distinguished himself from his predecessors by openly declaring that he was wise, especially about political matters, Plato shows Socrates questioning him first.

At the beginning of the *Protagoras*, Plato indicates that Socrates did not yet have much of a reputation or following. The anonymous Athenian whom Socrates meets as he leaves Callias' house assumes that the philosopher has been pursuing Alcibiades.[5] Socrates admits that he has just been

---

4. That is the way Aristophanes depicted the philosopher in his *Clouds*, first produced in 423.

5. The dating of the conversations recounted in both the *Protagoras* and the *Alcibiades I* is approximate. At the beginning of both dialogues we are reminded that Socrates has been pursuing Alcibiades for a long time and that the youth has now come into late adolescence. If Alcibiades is nineteen years of age, the year is 433. See Nails, *People*, 310–11. The *Charmides* in which Socrates converses primarily with Critias explicitly takes place immediately after Socrates' return to Athens from the battle of Potidaea in 429. Some commentators, e.g., Proclus, *Alcibiades I*, trans. William O'Neill (The Hague: Martinus Nijhoff, 1965), 3–5; *Alfarabi's "Philosophy,"* trans. Mahdi, 53–54; Steven Forde, "On the *Alcibiades*," in Pangle, *Roots*, 222; Mark Blitz, "Plato's *Alcibiades I*," *Interpretation* 22, no. 3 (Spring 1995): 339; and Paul Friedländer, "*Alcibiades Major*," in his *Plato*, 2:231–43, have taken

with the youth but says that he almost forgot about Alcibiades because Protagoras' wisdom was so much more beautiful.[6] In 433 the reasons for and character of Socrates' pursuit of young men were clearly not widely appreciated or known in Athens. He appeared simply to be another frustrated lover.

Explaining how he came to confront Protagoras, Socrates reports that a young friend of his named Hippocrates had awakened him early that morning with an urgent request for an introduction. Hippocrates has just heard that the sophist is in town. Believing that Protagoras is the wisest of all, and that if he were willing, he could teach others to be equally wise for a fee, Hippocrates wants to meet him. Hippocrates obviously knows Socrates well enough to burst into his bedroom before it is light, but the young man shows no sign of thinking that associating with Socrates will make him wise. By the end of the dialogue, however, we realize that Plato has shown us how Socrates used the opportunity to make a reputation for himself. Although Socrates claims twice during the course of the conversation that he must leave to keep another appointment, at the end we see that he actually had time to sit down immediately and give a blow-by-blow account of his victory over the famous foreigner to a group of his fellow citizens.[7]

---

the *Alcibiades I* to be the first conversation in which Socrates displays his characteristic approach to philosophy—seeking self-knowledge by conversing with young men. I believe that the conversation related in the *Protagoras* precedes the one we hear in the *Alcibiades*, because in the *Protagoras* Socrates first demonstrates the refutative ability that led politically ambitious young men like Alcibiades and Critias (both of whom are present in the *Protagoras*) to want to associate with him. At the end of the *Alcibiades I* (135d), the young man tells Socrates that they are about to switch roles. Whereas Socrates had previously pursued Alcibiades as a lover, the youth will now follow Socrates. That reversal of roles has not yet occurred when the conversation in the *Protagoras* takes place. In the *Protagoras* Socrates does not say that Alcibiades has become a student, much less a follower or lover. Nor does the philosopher ever speak directly to the young man. Alcibiades arrives at the home of Callias not in the company of Socrates but with Critias (316a). During the conversation Alcibiades intervenes not so much to support Socrates as to keep the conversation or contest going. Laurence Lampert, "Socrates' Defense of Polytropic Odysseus: Lying and Wrong-doing in Plato's *Lesser Hippias*," *Review of Politics* 64, no. 2 (Spring 2002), also suggests that "*Alcibiades* I and II [were] both probably set shortly after the *Protagoras* in the year Alcibiades turned eighteen and was therefore permitted to begin a political career by addressing the assembly" (234n7).

6. Patrick Coby, *Socrates and the Sophistic Enlightenment: A Commentary on Plato's "Protagoras"* (Lewisburg, PA: Bucknell University Press, 1987), 20, observes that Socrates' comment about the beauty of the sophist's wisdom echoes Diotima's teaching in the *Symposium* about the superiority of the beauty of the soul to the beauty of the body, even if only ironically.

7. By reading the end of the dialogue in light of the beginning, we see, moreover, that Socrates is not altogether truthful. Cf. Cropsey, *Plato's World*, 3, 15. Gregory Vlastos, "The Unity of the Virtues in the *Protagoras*," in *Platonic Studies*, 223n5, can maintain that Socrates was entirely truthful only by ignoring the action of the dialogue.

More familiar with the sophists than his young companion is, Socrates, in the conversation he initiates with the young man to pass the time while they wait for an appropriate hour to call on Protagoras, attempts to prepare Hippocrates to take a critical stance toward the sophist. Rather than parade his own knowledge, Socrates presents himself as a young "comrade" (even though he is in his midthirties) who will join Hippocrates in consulting their elders about whether it will be safe for him to consume the "soul-food" the sophist sells. By suggesting the good of one's soul as the standard by which the merit of the sophist's teaching should be measured, Socrates knows he is setting a standard that the sophist will not be able to meet.[8] Having thus prepared Hippocrates, Socrates accompanies the young man to the home of Callias, where the philosopher knows that not only Protagoras but also Hippias of Elis and Prodicus of Ceos are staying. Presented in terms that remind a reader of Odysseus' fabled trip to Hades, the gathering of the sophists and their Athenian students provides Socrates with an apt occasion to exhibit his own argumentative ability in contrast, if not in direct competition, with theirs.

Sophists had a bad reputation. In consulting with Socrates about the advisability of his associating with the famous foreigner, Hippocrates states emphatically that he does not want to become a sophist. He merely wants to learn the useful lessons or skills he believes Protagoras can teach. He regards the "wisdom" the sophist claims to possess and purvey as merely instrumental.

Protagoras explains the reasons he and his ilk are in bad repute: "When one goes as a foreigner into great cities and tries to persuade the best of their young men to drop their other associations, both old and young, to join one's own, with the promise of improving them by associating with oneself, . . . great jealousies are apt to ensue along with enmities and intrigues" (*Protagoras* 316c–d). His predecessors had sought to avoid arousing the envy of others by disguising the true character of their teaching. Some, like Homer, Hesiod, and Simonides, pretended merely to be poets. Protagoras, however, openly proclaims that he teaches an art—the political art. He thinks it is useless to try to conceal a political teaching, because those who take a leading role in the affairs of the city will perceive the reason for the disguise, and the many simply follow their leaders.

In their subsequent exchange, Socrates indicates how imprudent it is to express such contempt for the people in a democracy. In other words,

8. Cf. Weiss, *Socratic Paradox*, 30.

he shows that Protagoras does not possess the practical wisdom he claims to purvey. Protagoras boasts that he makes those who associate with him better every day. More specifically, he claims to teach young men not only how to order their own households but also how to become most powerful in their cities, both in speech and deed.[9] By questioning Protagoras, Socrates shows that the sophist does not understand democratic politics and is not, therefore, able to teach a young Athenian how to succeed in public life. In the second half of the dialogue Socrates then forces Protagoras to admit that rather than show young men how to become *kalos k'agathos*, like the other sophists he merely teaches people how to calculate pleasure and pain more accurately.[10] Socrates begins questioning Protagoras' practical wisdom by declaring that like the rest of the Greeks, he (in contrast to the sophist) thinks that the Athenians are wise. They consult with experts to get technical advice on specific projects, but they let everyone participate in debates about what the city should do, because they do not think anyone has expert knowledge of political matters. Nor do they think that political prudence can be taught. They see that outstanding politicians like Pericles (whose sons could be seen in Protagoras' retinue) have not been able to teach their own sons the practical wisdom in which they themselves excel. Socrates thus reminds Protagoras that his claim to teach a political art contradicts the assumptions of democratic political practice.

Protagoras responds to Socrates' challenge by telling a story (*mythos*) in which he traces the necessity of political organization to the defects of human nature. When human beings emerged from the earth, they found themselves, with a bit of experience and thus hindsight (the literal meaning of the name Epimetheus), in contrast to other animals, virtually unequipped for survival. By means of foresight (the literal meaning of Prometheus), they learned to make what they needed; that is, they developed arts, which included the making of altars (or fabrication of beliefs about gods) and language (*phōnē* or "sound," and *onomata*, "words"). Lacking knowledge of how to cooperate for a common end, however, they

9. Obviously wanting to add another wealthy young man to his retinue, Protagoras also seeks to discredit his competitors by adding that, unlike his peers (for example, Hippias), he does not force his students to learn arts such as calculation, geometry, and astronomy, in which they are not truly interested. Because he caters to their real desires, Protagoras brags, he is able to let his students judge the value of his instruction. If they do not want to pay his fee, he tells them to go to a shrine and to pay what they swear his lessons were worth.

10. Cf. Weiss, *Socratic Paradox*, 28–29.

fell to fighting among themselves whenever they tried to unite to protect themselves from predatory beasts. To ensure the survival of the species, Zeus sent Hermes to provide all human beings with knowledge of *aidōs* and *dikē*, "reverence" and "right," the qualities necessary to make community possible. In attributing the development or inculcation of both shame and justice to political necessity, Plato shows, the sophist did not display much of either. At most he slightly veiled his impiety by presenting his understanding of the origins of politics in the form of a myth.

The sophist switches from storytelling to argument (*logos*) when he begins explicitly justifying his own teaching—which is the purpose of his speech. The reason Athenians do not believe that anyone is a teacher of virtue, he explains, is not that people have no knowledge to impart or lessons to give. On the contrary, virtually everyone is involved in teaching children virtue from the time of their birth. Parents employ nurses, schoolmasters, and teachers of music to inculcate desired modes of behavior. As adults, young people are forced to learn the laws, which threaten them with exile or death if they do not obey. But as the sons of excellent flutists often lack the natural talent of their fathers, so do the sons of statesmen. All citizens of organized communities are visibly more orderly than uncivilized barbarians, but there are still individual differences among the civilized, traceable not only to nature but also to instruction, which make some better able to learn and others (like Protagoras) best able to teach political virtue or wisdom. In sum, Protagoras claims to do what families and laws attempt, but better. That is the reason, he explained earlier, sophists aroused the envy of others and so acquired their bad name.

"Bewitched" by Protagoras' performance, Socrates says that he is almost persuaded that there is a kind of care that can make people good. He has a slight reservation, however; that reservation initially seems to concern the form more than the content of the sophist's speech. Like writings (and hence laws), Socrates suggests, lengthy perorations relieve the speaker of the need to answer questions. Such speeches may constitute effective defenses of questionable, if not criminal, causes.[11] They may thus be politically useful on certain occasions. But long speeches are not good means of teaching, because they do not provoke questions or responses from the interlocutor. They do not, therefore, really get their listeners to

---

11. Protagoras was in danger of undermining the basic *nomoi* of Athenian democracy. As J. B. Bury reports in *A History of Greece* (New York: Modern Library, 1913), 371 (and Plato's readers would know), the sophist was charged with impiety and eventually had to flee Athens in 415.

think and thus to learn.[12] Having questioned the "well advisedness" of Protagoras' claim to teach a "political art" in a democratic context, Socrates thus raises questions about the effectiveness of the sophist's form of presentation as well.

Socrates' reservation about the form of Protagoras' speech quickly becomes a serious question about its content. Recalling that Protagoras claimed he can answer questions briefly just as well as he can deliver long epideictic speeches, Socrates reminds the sophist of what he has said about justice and shame. Then Socrates asks: is virtue one thing of which justice, moderation, and holiness are parts, or are these all different names for the same thing? In his story Protagoras had suggested that there was a fundamental difference between intelligence and art, on the one hand, and justice and reverence, on the other. The sophist explains that virtues are like the parts of the face, each of which has a different function, rather than like parts, that is, different quantities, of gold. Courage is different from justice, and justice is different from wisdom, which is the greatest of the virtues. But Socrates asks, don't the holy (*hosiotēs*) and the just (*dikaion*) have something in common? In his myth the sophist had suggested that these two virtues have a common source and function that are different from foresight, prudence, or art. Socrates is surprised, therefore, by Protagoras' insistence that these two virtues have no more in common than any other two things chosen at random, because almost anything can be said to be like something else in some respect.

Instead of pressing the question of the similarities and differences and so directly revealing the contradiction between Protagoras' two claims, Socrates asks the sophist about opposites. As the contraries of foolishness (*aphrosynē*), must not *sōphrosynē* (moderation) and *sophia* (wisdom) be the same, if everything has one and only one opposite? Rather than objecting to the questionable proposition that everything has one and only one opposite, Protagoras admits that he would be ashamed to say, as "many" do, that *sōphrosynē* (good sense) and justice are not the same (even though he had implied as much in his myth).[13]

---

12. In his examination of Protagoras, we thus see the effects of what Socrates says he learned from Diotima about the need for dialogic conversation (*Symposium* 201d–12c).

13. Stanley Rosen, "*Sōphrosynē* and *Selbstbewusstsein*," *Review of Metaphysics* 26, no. 4 (1973), urges that "we should bear in mind the connection between *sōphrosynē* and *phronēsis* or shrewdness, practical intelligence" (620). The popular opinion Protagoras claims not to share is articulated by Glaucon at the beginning of the *Republic* in terms of the myth of Gyges: anyone clever enough to evade the laws of man and god without suffering the consequences would do so.

By asking the sophist about the unity and differences among the virtues, Socrates brings out the tension Protagoras sought to conceal in his myth between the virtues or attitudes (justice and holiness sent by Zeus) that need to be inculcated in the citizen body as a whole in order to maintain political order and the wisdom or art of the few who teach those who want to rule. Attempting to avoid answering any further questions that might lead him to contradict his initial position (and so embarrass himself in front of potential students and competitors for them), Protagoras delivers another long speech. His contention that different things are beneficial to different kinds of animals or plants reflects his more general theoretical position concerning the relative nature of all things, which Socrates examines in a conversation with the young geometer Theaetetus more than thirty years later. Socrates' failure on this occasion to probe the grounds of Protagoras' position, when he has an opportunity to question the sophist directly, indicates he is not as interested in examining Protagoras' argument as he is in discouraging his young companion (as well as, perhaps, the other Athenian youths gathered in Callias' home) from studying with the sophist.

Claiming that he cannot remember what is said in such long speeches, Socrates says he cannot continue unless Protagoras gives shorter answers. Making the agonistic character of their exchange explicit, the sophist retorts: "I have undertaken in my time many contests of speech, and if I were to do what you demand, and argue just the way my opponent demanded, I should not be held superior to anyone nor would Protagoras have made a name among the Greeks." Socrates concludes that the sophist "had not been quite satisfied with himself in making his former answers and that he would no longer willingly converse as respondent" (*Protagoras* 335a–b). By threatening to leave, Socrates enlists the desires of the assembled group to hear the debate continue to pressure Protagoras into answering.[14] In the exchange that follows, Socrates shows that he understands democratic politics better and hence is more prudent than the sophists or their Athenian students. Like Polemarchus at the beginning of the *Republic*, Callias tries to detain Socrates not merely by pleading with him but by using force, grabbing his cloak. Socrates protests that he cannot compete on Protagoras' terms and so implicitly accuses both the sophist and his host of treating him unjustly.

---

14. Cf. Robert Bartlett, "Political Philosophy and Sophistry: An Introduction to Plato's *Protagoras*," *American Political Science Review* 47, no. 4 (October 2003): 613.

Objecting to changes in the rules that prevent the best competitor from claiming victory, Alcibiades steps in and demands that the sophist either concede Socrates' superiority in this sort of exchange (as Socrates had apparently conceded the sophist's superiority in lengthy oration) or that he persist.[15] The young Athenian obviously does not believe Socrates' "jest" about his inability to remember; Alcibiades sees, moreover, that it is not Socrates' insistence on short answers but Protagoras' unwillingness to concede defeat that has brought the conversation to a standstill. Aware of Protagoras' concern about his standing in the eyes of others, Alcibiades suggests that they put the matter to a vote. He thus imposes a democratic process. Displaying the desire for distinction that will lead him in later life to join other oligarchs in overthrowing the democracy, Critias claims that he, Prodicus, and Hippias remain above the fray and can serve, therefore, as impartial judges. Prodicus adds that they have a right to decide, on the basis of their wisdom, not merely their superiority in number or the physical force associated with it. Underlining the difference between mere convention and the claim of the wise to rule by nature, Hippias suggests that they elect a supervisor.

In marked contrast to these various attempts to justify the rule of some by others, Socrates proposes that he and Protagoras ask and answer (or rule and be ruled) in turn. Not only does Socrates recognize the need for voluntary cooperation; he also sees the problems—the divisions and stalemates that result from a demand that one party be recognized as better than the others—especially with respect to knowledge.[16] This is the practical wisdom Protagoras has failed to absorb from his predecessors; he thought he could and should be publicly and openly recognized as wisest. This is also the practical wisdom Socrates himself displays by insisting on his own ignorance.

Reluctantly acceding to the will of the assembled group, Protagoras agrees to question Socrates. In explicating a poem by Simonides, the sophist attempts to demonstrate his superiority to his predecessors by showing

---

15. In the *Alcibiades I* (110b) Socrates observes that as a child Alcibiades reacted angrily to the injustice of changes in the rules of games that would deprive him of the victory he thought he deserved.

16. When Socrates himself later proposes the rule of philosopher-kings in the *Republic*, he explicitly says that he knows he will be viciously attacked for doing so. Socrates' emphasis in this dialogue on the undemocratic character of Protagoras' teaching raises questions about the claim that the sophists were friendlier to liberty and democracy than the Socratic philosophers were. See, e.g., Eric Havelock, *The Liberal Temper in Greek Politics* (New Haven: Yale University Press, 1957).

that one of the "wise" contradicted himself: Simonides said that it is hard for human beings to be good; then he denied it. Protagoras' explication of Simonides' poem also serves to remind his auditors (and Plato's readers) that Protagoras had initially claimed not only to make those who associated with him better, but also that his lessons were not hard or unpleasant like those of the other sophists. He did not force his students to learn geometry and astronomy and other difficult subjects in which they were not truly interested. In other words, unlike the sage Pittacus, unjustly criticized by Simonides (but justly superseded by himself), Protagoras claimed that it need not be hard for human beings to be—or at least to become—good.

In responding to Protagoras Socrates first asks Prodicus to come to the aid of his fellow citizen by employing his art of drawing fine distinctions between words. Having thus reminded Protagoras both that compatriots may form a common front against foreign critics and that he is competing for students with the other sophists present, Socrates admits that his appeal to Prodicus was not entirely serious. Nor, we cannot help but conclude, is Socrates' contention that the Dorian peoples of Crete and Sparta practice philosophy in secret in order to keep the advantages of wisdom to themselves. There is, however, a serious point to Socrates' fanciful suggestion. If wisdom is truly a means of acquiring and maintaining political power, as Protagoras claims, those who possess such wisdom will keep it to themselves and not openly try to sell it to any willing customer. In other words, Protagoras' practice contradicts his teaching.

Socrates' reconstruction of Simonides' intended meaning also constitutes a critique of Protagoras' claim to make his students better painlessly. Characteristically distinguishing "being" from "becoming," Socrates contends that Simonides is correct not only in observing that it is difficult for human beings to become good, but also in disputing Pittacus' saying that it is hard to be good. The poet sees that it is impossible for mortals, subject to change and accident, to remain good even if they attain such a condition. However, by once again questioning the value of mere verbal distinctions and so distancing himself from Prodicus, Socrates also distances himself from the poet by reminding his auditors that, on the basis of his own experience, Simonides knew it was sometimes necessary to praise bad men such as tyrants. In the end Socrates' interpretation of Simonides' poem appears to be designed to discredit such rhetorical exchanges. Protagoras began by claiming that knowledge of poetry was a mark of a well-educated man, but Socrates concludes by suggesting that only those who are not able to speak for themselves turn to interpreting the words of others.

Just as Socrates used his question about the unity of the virtues in the first half of the dialogue to expose the tension concerning the teaching of political virtue hidden in Protagoras' myth, so in the second half of the dialogue he returns to the question of the unity of the virtues to expose Protagoras' covert understanding of good as pleasure. He shows that the man who publicly declares that he is wise is not so open in public about the actual character and content of his wisdom.

Having learned from their previous exchange, Protagoras now admits that wisdom, temperance, justice, and holiness can be said to be similar to each other. Courage, however, is different. The principle of division is fairly evident. Wisdom, temperance, justice, and holiness can all be considered to be means of attaining one's own good. Courage involves the risk of self-sacrifice. That is why courage is thought to be especially noble (*kalon*) but not necessarily good (*agathon*) for the person involved, although it is good, that is, useful, for others. Implicit in Protagoras' division is the understanding that virtue consists ultimately in the ability to calculate one's own pleasure correctly, an understanding that Socrates explicitly extracts from the sophist later.

Socrates responds immediately to Protagoras' contention by arguing that courage requires knowledge or wisdom. Those who understand the character of the dangers they confront are thought to be more courageous than mere fools. Protagoras counters by objecting to Socrates' tendency to reduce everything—including power and hence even bodily strength—to knowledge. But Socrates reminds the sophist that he claimed that knowledge is power too.

Socrates brings out the agreement between himself and the sophist in order to draw out the difference. He asks Protagoras to join him (in a cooperative rather than competitive manner) in an imaginary conversation in which they show the many that they are wrong to believe that someone who knows an act is wrong or base can nevertheless be persuaded to do it through passion, the desire for pleasure, or to avoid pain. If those who believe that knowledge is weak also believe that pleasure is good, they speak absurdly when they say that people do things they believe are bad or base because they are overcome by pleasure (that is, the good). Such people say some pleasures are "bad" because these "pleasures," for example, overeating, produce more pain than pleasure in the long run. It is not so much pleasure or passion overcoming knowledge that causes people to do things they think are bad as it is a failure to calculate the pleasure and pain involved correctly.[17] To overcome their ignorance, Socrates concludes, such people should send their sons to study with the sophists. Addressed individually by name, all three of the sophists agree (358a) that Socrates has spoken truly.

In giving what might look like a sales pitch for sophistry, Socrates reveals the incoherence of Protagoras' position.[18] Although Protagoras insists that virtue is the best and highest human achievement, and that wisdom is the greatest of the virtues, like the other sophists he makes "virtue" or the "curing of ignorance" into merely an instrumental means of maximizing pleasure.[19] Contrary to Protagoras' initial pronouncement and like the many, the sophists agree that pleasure is the good (as well as, Socrates also gets them explicitly to agree, the *kalon*, the beautiful or noble). In declaring that he is a sophist who teaches his students how to choose well or be "well advised," Socrates now forces Protagoras to admit, contrary to his original vaunt, that he too teaches a form of *metrētikē*. His instruction is not fundamentally different (or more pleasurable) than that of his colleagues. Returning to the question of the unity of the virtues and the status of courage, Socrates finally gets Protagoras to agree that if going to war is *kalon*, *kalon* is good, and the good is the pleasant, then courageously facing death is also more pleasant than cowardly flight.[20] Cowardice consists in ignorance of what is truly dreadful.

17. Like Aristotle (*Nicomachean Ethics* 7.2), some commentators might object that such people lack moderation or self-restraint. Like some contemporary psychologists, however, Socrates suggests that these people have discounted the value of future pain too rapidly.

18. Socrates himself does not understand virtue to consist in this art of measurement, because he never grants the first premise, that pleasure is the good. Cf. Kahn, *Plato and the Socratic Dialogue*, 240; J. Peter Euben, *Corrupting Youth: Political Education, Democratic Culture, and Political Theory* (Princeton: Princeton University Press, 1997), 254–60. Socrates is not the calculating hedonist that Friedrich Nietzsche (*Jenseits von Gut und Böse* in *Sämtliche Werke*, vol. 5, aphorisms 190, 111; trans. Walter Kaufman, *Beyond Good and Evil*, in *Basic Writings*, 293), Nussbaum (*Fragility*, 88–121), and Cropsey (*Plato's World*, 23–24) take him to be in the *Protagoras*. (Nussbaum does observe that "Superficially, this agreement about the science follows an agreement that pleasure is the end. But the adoption of this single end is notoriously hasty and unargued" [109].) In the *Republic* 505b and *Gorgias* 495a–97a, Socrates explicitly denies the identification of good with pleasure; the closest Socrates comes to embracing pleasure as a necessary part of the human good (along with knowledge) is in the *Philebus*.

19. Cf. Hans-Georg Gadamer, *The Idea of the Good in Platonic-Aristotelian Philosophy*, trans. Christopher Smith (New Haven: Yale University Press, 1986), 47–48.

20. As Weiss (*Socratic Paradox*, 66), argues, this is a reductio ad absurdum. As Alexander Sesonske, "Hedonism in the *Protagoras*," *Journal of the History of Philosophy* 1 (1963): 73–79; J. Tennku, *The Evaluation of Pleasure in Plato's Ethics* (Helsinki: Societas Philosophica, 1956); and Terence Irwin, *Plato's Moral Theory* (Oxford: Clarendon Press, 1977), 112, all point out, people do not generally think that courageous acts are pleasant or admire courageous people for doing what is pleasant.

In the second half of the dialogue Socrates thus punishes Protagoras (1) for claiming to be superior to his predecessors insofar as he openly admits that he is wise, by showing that the sophist also conceals the true character of his own teaching; (2) for contemning the opinions of the many, by showing that the sophist shares one of the most common—the belief that pleasure is the supreme good; and (3) for claiming to be able to teach virtue, by showing that the sophist is not able to say what virtue is. Emphasizing the critical thrust and intention of the argument, Socrates points out at the end that his own position is no more coherent than that of the sophist. Protagoras maintains that virtue is teachable but argues that it is not knowledge (which would seem to be eminently teachable), whereas Socrates maintains the opposite. Explicitly disowning the arguments that have been attributed to him ever since, Socrates suggests that they ought to begin the inquiry anew.[21]

Protagoras demurs. Trying to appear magnanimous in the face of defeat, he says that he is not envious; he has told others before that he would not be surprised if Socrates became reputed for his wisdom. For now, however, the sophist has had enough.

Socrates claims that he has stayed so long only to oblige Callias. "We left," he concludes. That is to say, Hippocrates went with him.[22] Socrates had achieved the most immediate goal of his visit; he had discredited the sophist sufficiently in the eyes of his young friend to preserve his soul from possible corruption.[23] Socrates then relates the story of his victory to the first Athenian he meets.

21. One of the advantages of reading the dialogues in terms of their dramatic dates and noticing the primarily critical thrust of Socrates' initial encounter with the famous sophist is that it removes the inconsistency several commentators have noticed between Socrates' apparent endorsement of a calculus of pleasure or his "instrumental" view of virtue in the *Protagoras* and his insistence later in the *Republic* and *Philebus* on the difference between the good and the pleasant as well as on the need to seek virtue for its own sake. In the *Protagoras*, we recognize, Socrates is bringing out the difficulties in the arguments of the sophists, which he shows can be reduced to such a calculating, instrumental view. When he returns to the question of whether virtue is teachable in the *Meno*, Socrates takes up the question again in a significantly different historical, political, and philosophical context. It should not be surprising that he also employs different arguments and concepts (such as recollection) at a later date.

22. Nussbaum ignores the first-person *plural* form of the final verb (362a), *apē(i)men*, when she claims that we don't know whether Hippocrates chose to leave with Socrates or to stay with Protagoras (*Fragility*, 120).

23. The traditional subtitle of the dialogue "On Sophists: An Arraignment" is thought not to be Plato's but a later addition by the commentator Thrasyllus. It nevertheless suggests that ancient readers thought the dominant purpose of the conversation was for Socrates to rescue Hippocrates from the pernicious influence of the sophists. Cf. Coby, *Protagoras*, 188.

II. Socrates Urges His Associates to Seek Self-Knowledge

Socrates' demonstration of his ability to best Protagoras in speech seems to have impressed two of the ambitious young Athenians present—Alcibiades and Critias. In the dialogues that immediately follow the *Protagoras* in terms of their dramatic dating, Plato shows that both these young men subsequently became associates of the philosopher. As Plato's readers would know from later history, however, Socrates was not able to divert them from their tyrannous ambitions. They did not understand what he meant by the search for self-knowledge or why it would require them to become moderate and just.[24]

A. Socrates' "Seduction" of Alcibiades

Whereas Protagoras approached potential students as an expert who could impart his wisdom for a fee, Socrates approached potential young companions as a suppliant or lover, concerned about their welfare as much as his own. The superiority of Socrates' approach is indicated by the fact that, although the most talented young Athenian of his generation went along with others to listen to the sophists (as shown in the *Protagoras*), Alcibiades did not become publicly identified as an associate of anyone but Socrates.

In the *Alcibiades I* Plato shows how Socrates used his knowledge of *ta erōtika* to "seduce" Alcibiades.[25] He thus gives his readers a more objective account of the encounter Alcibiades presents in a self-serving way in the *Symposium*. Like the anonymous Athenian to whom Socrates speaks in the *Protagoras*, Alcibiades thought Socrates was attracted by his beautiful body, even though in their first conversation Socrates told the young man that he cared about his soul. Socrates persuaded Alcibiades to associate with him in order to learn how to take care of himself. Because he remained attached to the goods of the body, however, Alcibiades was not able to understand the nature of Socrates' love or the search for self-knowledge in which he urged the young man to engage.

---

24. In his *Memorabilia* 1.2.12–48, Xenophon defends Socrates from the charge that his influence on Critias and Alcibiades showed that the philosopher corrupted the young by pointing out that Critias and Alcibiades were moderate and just while they were with Socrates, but that they became unjust—Critias even threatened Socrates—when they ceased to associate with him.

25. Cf. Scott, *Socrates as Educator*, 100–114; Gordon, "Eros and Philosophical Seduction."

From the opening of the *Protagoras*, readers know that Socrates had been pursuing Alcibiades for some time. Nevertheless, at the beginning of the *Alcibiades I*, the philosopher points out, he is talking to the young man for the first time. His *daimonion*, which had prevented him from approaching Alcibiades before, now allows him to speak to the youth for two reasons: (1) the young man is no longer distracted by the flatteries and importunities of his other lovers, and (2) Socrates has had an opportunity to observe why they failed and to devise a more successful strategy.[26] Thinking he does not need anything from anyone else, Alcibiades had repelled the suits of his previous admirers. But seeing that Alcibiades is extremely ambitious, Socrates recognizes that the youth is not as satisfied with himself or his current condition as he thinks. He wants more—wealth, honor, and power. Understanding what the young man desires, Socrates knows how to appeal to him. (Socrates' claim to know *ta erōtika*, we should recall from the *Symposium*, amounts to a claim to understand the character of human desire, that is, what human beings really want [but do not have].)

Socrates' unusual behavior in following him around silently had aroused Alcibiades' curiosity. The youth tells Socrates that he was about to go and ask what the older man wanted, when Socrates approached him. When Socrates tells Alcibiades what he wants, the young man is astonished to learn that Socrates knows better what Alcibiades hopes to achieve than the young man himself. Alcibiades wants to go before the Athenian assembly and prove to them that he deserves more honor than Pericles—more honor, indeed, than anyone who has ever existed in Greece or elsewhere. As a result, Alcibiades expects to acquire very great power, not only in Athens but also in Europe and even Asia. His only competitors will be Cyrus and Xerxes.

Without explicitly admitting that Socrates is correct, Alcibiades inquires how the philosopher can help him. Socrates shows him in deed, as it were, by asking Alcibiades questions that gradually convince the young man he is not equipped to achieve his dreams. Like Protagoras, Socrates appears to promise to help Alcibiades learn how best to order his own affairs and to become most powerful in the city. In other words, Socrates looks like a sophist. However, the means Socrates proposes are altogether different from those the sophist promotes. If the young man had followed the line

---

26. This is the first (dramatically) but by no means the only time Socrates shows that the "divine voice" that holds him back has and can give reasons. Socrates does not always choose to tell his particular interlocutor(s) what these reasons are.

of study Socrates indicates, he would no longer have sought to rule. He would have engaged in philosophical conversations with his friends instead. Socrates succeeds in persuading Alcibiades he can help him realize his ambitions, but he does not convince Alcibiades to give up those ambitions and seek wisdom instead of fame, wealth, and power.[27]

In responding to Socrates' questions, Alcibiades readily admits that he has no craft or skill on the basis of which he can offer expert advice to his fellow citizens. As an aspiring statesman, he plans to concern himself only with the greatest political questions, especially whether to make war or peace. Socrates asks if he would advocate an unjust war, and Alcibiades observes that no one would; to do so would not merely be unlawful but ignoble (and Alcibiades wants above all to appear noble in the eyes of as many people as possible). How did he learn what is just, Socrates asks: did he receive instruction or did he discover it for himself? Echoing Protagoras, Alcibiades claims that he learned about justice the way people learn to speak Greek, from those around him.[28] If people generally know what is just, Socrates retorts, they would not disagree so much about it. He then gets Alcibiades to demonstrate that he does not, in fact, know what is just by making him contradict himself. Socrates leads Alcibiades to state his belief that the just (serving the common interest) is different from the expedient (acting in one's own self-interest), just as the noble (for example, risking one's life to save a friend) is different from the good (for example, surviving a battle), and then he gets Alcibiades to agree that the just, expedient, noble, and good are the same.

Alcibiades admits that he is confused. With a bit of guidance from Socrates, he also agrees that by "wandering about" and saying contradictory things he is manifesting the worst kind of ignorance, thinking that he knows what he does not.[29] Since they are alone, Socrates thinks it safe to say that

27. In *Memorabilia* 1.2.47, Xenophon suggests that both Alcibiades and Critias hoped to learn how to speak or argue from Socrates and so to succeed in politics. They were interested only in acquiring knowledge that was politically useful; they resented his bringing out their errors by questioning them.

28. Alcibiades' use here (111a) of an argument Protagoras employed in the earlier conversation (at 327e) suggests that the young man may be repeating what he heard and that the conversation related in the *Protagoras* thus precedes that to be found in the *Alcibiades I*.

29. In his *Apology*, Socrates claimed that the Delphic oracle proclaimed that no one was wiser than Socrates because he knew that he was not wise. Unlike the politicians, poets, and artisans he interrogated, Socrates knew he did not know the most important things. Socrates is not simply and entirely ignorant; what others think they know, and what Socrates knows that he does not know, is what is good. As he tells Alcibiades in their next conversation, ignorance may at times benefit human beings. Orestes would have been better off if he had not recognized his mother.

Alcibiades is in a miserable condition. (By saying so in public, Socrates would have embarrassed and so alienated the young man.) But, Socrates adds, Alcibiades' condition is not singular. Not only Socrates but most other Athenians also live in the same miserable condition. Alcibiades' guardian Pericles might be an exception, because Pericles associated with wise men like Pythoclides and Anaxagoras. By asking Alcibiades whether anyone had ever become wiser by associating with Pericles the way Pythodorus and Callias (son of Calliades, not the host in the *Protagoras*) became wiser as a result of their association with Zeno, Socrates gets Alcibiades to agree that neither his family nor the greatest statesman of his city could provide him with the requisite education.[30]

If no one else goes into politics with knowledge, the lazy young man concludes, he does not need it either. The praise of his physical beauty by his former lovers, his family heritage, his wealth and connections with Pericles, along with his own sense of his native intelligence have convinced Alcibiades that he is clearly superior to others by nature and does not require further nurture. To overcome the young man's idle complacency, Socrates, in the central section of the dialogue, reminds Alcibiades of the resources and education of his foreign competitors—the kings of Sparta and Persia. The philosopher's description of the care devoted to the nurture and education of these future kings as well as their enormous wealth persuades the young man that he needs more than his natural endowments and Athenian connections to surpass them.

Alcibiades asks Socrates to tell him what to do.[31] Socrates assures the young man that his own condition is no better, except in one respect: he has a better guardian than Pericles—his god. Alcibiades accuses him of jesting, and Socrates concedes that the youth might be right. There is, nevertheless, a serious point in what appears to be a frivolous exchange. As Plato shows at the center of the dialogue, Alcibiades is not willing to

---

To know whether it would be better to know or not in any specific case, one would have to know what is good.

30. According to Plutarch, *Lives of Noble Grecians and Romans*, ed. Arthur Hugh Clough (New York: Modern Library, 1932), I, 232, Pericles also associated with Protagoras. Once again, we should observe, the argument in the *Alcibiades I* follows lines set out, this time by Socrates, in the *Protagoras* 319b–20c. As Socrates stated there, this criticism of Athenian statesmen for not being able to pass on their own prudence to others through blood or precept was common. Although Plato showed that Socrates later angered both Anytus (*Meno* 93e–95a) and Callicles (*Gorgias* 503c, 515c–21c) by repeating it, this criticism did not originate with Socrates. The criticism constitutes a kind of defense of elective rather than hereditary selection of leaders.

31. Cf. Mark J. Lutz, *Socrates' Education to Virtue: Learning the Love of the Noble* (Albany: SUNY Press, 1998), 118–19.

countenance the limits of human power or any dependence on the divine. He thus shows that he lacks self-knowledge. Insofar as his talents are due either to nature or to his family connections, they are not products of his own efforts but the results of chance—or divine providence. If Alcibiades had an accurate view of his own condition, he would have been grateful rather than proud.

Having convinced Alcibiades that he needs further education, Socrates, in the third part of their conversation, again tries to persuade the young man that he needs to learn what is just. He begins by asking Alcibiades what he thinks he needs to know in order to govern his fellow citizens. Echoing Protagoras again, Alcibiades says that he needs "to be well advised" (or "to have good counsel," *euboulia*) about the management and preservation of the city. Socrates then asks what preserves the city, and Alcibiades responds, "friendship" (*philia*), which he defines as the like-mindedness or concord that characterizes members of a single family. "Don't husband and wife have different arts?" Socrates inquires. "Doesn't justice consist in each doing his own job?" Rather than pursue the question of what kinds of knowledge are necessary and for whom, Alcibiades simply concludes, again, that he is confused.

Unable to get the ambitious young man to think seriously about the requirements of justice, Socrates appeals to his self-interest. He gets Alcibiades to agree, first, that there is a difference between oneself and what belongs to oneself; and second, that to use one's belongings well, it is necessary to know what will benefit oneself. "What is this 'self'?" Socrates then asks. Just as artisans use tools to produce goods, so human beings use their bodies. If bodies are the equivalent of tools, they must be used or ruled by something else, and that "something" is the soul.[32] To seek knowledge of oneself one must, therefore, seek knowledge of the soul.

Socrates concedes the inadequacy of his argument by observing that "if the demonstration has not been precise, it is at least enough for now; we will know precisely when we discover what we just passed over . . . the self itself. As it is, we have considered, instead of the self, what each is" (*Alcibiades I* 130d). But, he assures Alcibiades, it suffices for the present to observe that in addressing each other in speech, they are addressing each other's soul. "It is with the soul . . . that we are bid to become acquainted by the

---

32. Socrates prevents Alcibiades from simply identifying the self with a combination or union of body and soul by leading him to agree that "what rules body is man," and that "if one is not a co-ruler, there isn't any way both together can rule" (*Alcibiades I* 130b).

one who enjoins us to know ourselves" (130e). The "one who enjoins" is, of course, the oracle at Delphi (or the author of the inscriptions above the entrance), who commands those entering not only to know themselves but also to have nothing in excess. If, as Socrates has argued, self-knowledge requires understanding the soul, and knowledge of the soul is knowledge of what one is, that is, one's being, then self-knowledge entails an understanding of the definition or limits of human being (as opposed, for example, to divinity or bestiality).[33] Knowledge of one's limits also presumably makes one moderate.

But if moderation requires knowing the soul, Socrates points out, no one who tends to the goods of the body—no doctor, no artisan, no wealth seeker—can be moderate. Although Socrates does not say so explicitly, Alcibiades' desire for political preeminence, fame, and fortune is a desire for the goods of the body.[34] Attempting to persuade the young man to shift his focus, Socrates reminds him of the relevance of the distinction between soul and body to his own recent experience. Those who claimed they loved him because they were attracted to his physical beauty, deserted him when he came of age. Socrates alone has been his true and constant lover, because he cares for Alcibiades' soul. So long as Alcibiades is not corrupted by the Athenian people, the philosopher promises, he will not desert him.

Socrates is not optimistic about his future relations with Alcibiades, however. On the contrary, in this, the very first conversation he has with the young man, Socrates explicitly states his fear that "having become a lover of the people" (dēmos) (132a), Alcibiades will be corrupted. According to Alcibiades' own statement in the *Symposium*, that was exactly what happened. Although Socrates understood what Alcibiades wanted, Alcibiades admitted in the *Symposium*, the young man did not understand the character of Socrates' love for him. He did not understand the character of Socrates' love because he did not really understand Socrates' identification of the self with the soul.

In their first conversation Socrates urges Alcibiades to "learn what needs to be learned" in order to acquire an antidote against his love of the demos

33. Cf. Aristotle *Politics* 1253a27–28. The traditional subtitle of the *Alcibiades I* is "On the Nature of Man." Socrates begins and ends the conversation by emphasizing the way in which his *daimonion* or god limits, guards, and so guides him.

34. In his *Apology* (29d–e) Socrates tells the jury that he has and would continue to address his fellow citizens as follows: "Best of men, you are an Athenian, from the city that is greatest and best reputed for wisdom and strength: are you not ashamed that you care for having as much money as possible, and reputation, and honor, but that you neither care for nor give thought to prudence, and truth, and how your soul will be the best possible?"

before he enters politics so he will suffer nothing terrible as a result. The young man acknowledges that Socrates speaks well, but he reiterates his desire for Socrates to tell him what to do in order to take care of himself. Alcibiades continues to regard the knowledge he seeks as a means of achieving his desires and not as the end or the good in itself. Considering himself an individual who is not merely distinct from, but in competition with others, he retains his desire to be recognized as the most preeminent and powerful man in the world. He does not see how the satisfaction of this desire makes him dependent on the opinions of others. He certainly does not imagine that taking care of oneself involves taking care of others as well.[35]

Socrates emphasizes the need for Alcibiades to work with others in order to achieve what he most wants. You first need to learn about your own soul, Socrates reiterates, and you can do that only by conversing with others. Just as people come to see their own eyes reflected in the eyes of others, so one's soul comes to know itself by looking into the soul of another. This is especially true of the place in which the virtue of the soul—wisdom—comes to exist. As Socrates shows more fully in his exchange with Critias in the *Charmides*, it is not possible to acquire self-knowledge merely through introspection.[36] If Alcibiades had truly been persuaded by Socrates, he would have jettisoned his political ambitions and joined the philosopher in an investigation of what is truly good and noble.[37] In their first meeting Alcibiades is willing to follow Socrates this far.

However, when the philosopher goes on to argue that, since the part of the soul concerned with thinking and knowing is most divine, and that one who comes to know all that is divine—god and thought (*theon te kai phronēsin*)—will come to know himself, Alcibiades merely responds: "So it

---

35. Plato shows that Socrates knows this in his second conversation with the young man when the philosopher supposes and Alcibiades concedes that he would be delighted if the god were to offer him rule over all of Europe and to promise "that all men will perceive that Alcibiades, son of Clinias, is tyrant" (*Alcibiades II* 141b).

36. Both Julia Annas, "Self-Knowledge in Early Plato," in *Platonic Investigations*, ed. Dominic J. O'Meara (Washington, DC: Catholic University of America Press, 1985), 121ff.; and Hugh H. Benson, "A Note on Socrates' Self-Knowledge in the *Charmides*," *Ancient Philosophy* 23 (2003): 31n2, also point out that the ancient understanding of self-knowledge was not introspective. Annas characterizes it as knowledge about one's social role and the duties appropriate to one's station. Granting that an average fifth-century Athenian would have understood the self-knowledge associated with *sōphrosynē* to be knowledge of oneself in relation to others, Benson argues that Socratic self-knowledge does not consist merely in his recognition of his own ignorance but also in his recognition that he is less wise than the gods.

37. Scott (*Socrates as Educator*, 99–100) also argues that "taking care of oneself" amounts to an exhortation to submit to repeated Socratic cross-examinations.

appears."[38] He refuses to acknowledge that what he wants is, in effect, to be a god—to be admired by all as the most powerful and noble of all. As a mortal, Socrates tries to tell him, Alcibiades can approach the divine only by developing the highest part of his soul.

Because Alcibiades is unwilling to admit or countenance a higher form of existence than his own, Socrates has to retreat to an appeal to the young man's more concrete economic and political interests. Alcibiades has agreed that it is necessary to know oneself and one's own things before attempting to take charge of the city. He has also agreed that only a person who possesses such knowledge will be moderate. And he has emphatically consented to Socrates' contention that a man cannot impart knowledge or virtue to others that he does not possess himself. When Socrates goes on to argue that human beings who lack either self-knowledge or virtue would be better off as slaves than as tyrants, however, the young man is once again willing to concede only that "it appears so" (*phainetai*). Alcibiades is convinced that ruling is the best thing a human being can do.

Alcibiades concludes their first conversation by vowing that from this day forward he will pursue Socrates as Socrates had formerly pursued him. The philosopher's conquest (or conversion of the young man to a life philosophy) appears to be complete. In leaving, Alcibiades promises that from this moment he will also begin to care about justice. Socrates says that he hopes so. He recognizes the limits of the "education" he has achieved. Although Alcibiades promises Socrates that from that day forward he will care about justice, it is clear from the conversation that he does not understand why he should. For Alcibiades to learn to care about justice, he

---

38. *Alcibiades I* 133c. As with the "jest" concerning his superior guardian, Alcibiades tends to be particularly skeptical whenever Socrates appeals to his "god." If Socrates had convinced Alcibiades to pursue self-knowledge as the philosopher understands it, the young man would also, it appears, have become pious. That Socrates knows Alcibiades has not become pious becomes evident at the beginning of the *Alcibiades II*, when Socrates expresses surprise at discovering that Alcibiades is on his way to worship. The philosopher then warns the young man not to pray for what he now thinks is good (as we have seen above, world tyranny), because the gods may grant it and it turn out to be harmful. The example Socrates suggests of a man whose prayer for something he thought was good that turned out to be bad is also revealing. Oedipus is famous for having sought self-knowledge. He knew that he was ignorant, but like Alcibiades, Oedipus did not understand the character of his own ignorance. As Socrates tells the young man in the case of Orestes, sometimes it may be good not to know. Oedipus thought that he would learn who he was if he could determine who his parents were. Although he answered the Sphinx's riddle about the animal that walked on four legs in the morning, two at midday, and three in the evening with "man" and so would seem to have perceived the importance of our living in time, Oedipus the tyrant did not recognize the limitations of human existence or the soul. These limitations are not visible. As Tiresias tells Oedipus, he is blind about his own condition so long as he can see.

would have to recognize his own dependency on others and thus his limitations. He would consequently become more pious as well. (As Socrates indicated in the *Protagoras*, there is a connection between justice and piety.) Although Plato (or his imitator) shows, in the *Alcibiades II*, that the young man began to go through the motions by praying to the gods at public shrines, Alcibiades never learned the reasons why human beings do not entirely control their own fates. That is to say, he never attained self-knowledge.

B. Socrates' Attempt to Moderate the Future Tyrants

Instead of teaching his students "to be well advised" like the sophists, Socrates urged his young associates to seek self-knowledge and so to become more moderate and just. But in the *Charmides* Plato shows that Critias did not understand what that search actually involved any better than Alcibiades had.

Like the *Protagoras*, the *Charmides* is a narrated dialogue.[39] By having Socrates tell his anonymous auditor(s) that he had just returned to Athens with the army from Potidaea (a battle that dragged on from 432 to 429, at the beginning of the Peloponnesian War), Plato reminds his readers of one of the most evident differences between Socrates and the sophists (as well as most pre-Socratic philosophers). Whereas they traveled from city to city in search of students who would pay them to talk about virtue, Socrates left Athens only to perform his civic duty.[40] The philosopher thus expressed his loyalty and love for his fellow citizens in deed as well as in word.[41] The fact that Socrates evidently cared about the fate of Athens and

39. Since the four dialogues completely narrated by Socrates (*Charmides, Rivals, Lysis,* and *Republic*) all show him talking to young men who either describe themselves or are described by others as lovers, we might expect him to display his knowledge of *ta erōtika* most emphatically in them.

40. Plato shows Socrates venturing outside the city walls for the sake of hearing specific speeches read in both the *Parmenides* and the *Phaedrus*, but in neither case does the philosopher leave Attica.

41. Socrates' participation in this battle also had an effect on his relations with Alcibiades. From the account a drunken Alcibiades later gives of his relations with Socrates in the *Symposium* (215a–20e), we know that the young man was extremely impressed by the courage and endurance Socrates displayed at Potidaea. Not only had Alcibiades seen Socrates walk barefoot on ice; the young man reports that soldiers watched the philosopher stand still for a whole day and night, presumably contemplating some problem. Socrates did not appear to care any more about public recognition and honor than he did about pain. Although he saved Alcibiades' life, Socrates urged the generals to give the young man the prize for valor, even though Alcibiades thought Socrates should have accepted it himself. Socrates knew that Alcibiades tended to understand his own

its people did not mean, however, that he was able to benefit them the way he desired.

At the wrestling school to which he went to resume his conversations as soon as he could, Socrates greeted and was greeted by everyone present. While the philosopher himself was away from the city, Plato indicates, Socrates' reputation had spread. As we know from the *Apology*, however, that reputation was not altogether beneficial.[42] One of the reasons Socrates was convicted of corrupting the young was that some of the youths who associated with him later became tyrants. In the *Charmides* Plato defends his teacher from this accusation by showing that Socrates tried to encourage Charmides and Critias to become more moderate.[43]

As Socrates proclaimed in the *Protagoras*, so Plato indicates in the *Charmides*, virtue is not something that can be taught by precept; it has to be practiced.[44] In the dramatic prologue Plato thus has Socrates himself exhibit the moderation he told Alcibiades would result from the search for self-knowledge. By rushing to the school upon returning to Athens, Socrates displayed an intense desire to resume his search for wisdom as soon as possible. He recognized, however, that the young Athenians he met at the school wanted to know about the outcome of the battle first. He had to satisfy their desire before he could find out about the state of philosophy and whether in his absence any young man has distinguished himself for either wisdom or nobility. From the very beginning of the *Charmides*, we thus see Socrates exercise a certain kind of self-restraint.[45]

---

value (and so virtue) as it was reflected in the eyes of others; Socrates was trying to show Alcibiades the difference between truth (or what Alcibiades himself thought) and the opinions of others—in deed, as well as in speech.

42. All three of the young Athenians with whom Socrates talks in this dialogue later became (in)famous students or associates of his. In Aristophanes' *Clouds* (423), Chaerephon is lampooned as Socrates' leading pale and emaciated student, and in his *Apology* (20e–21a) Socrates reports that Chaerephon went to the oracle at Delphi to ask if there were anyone wiser than Socrates. Chaerephon's question shows that he shared the understanding of human excellence as superiority recognized by others characteristic of his fellow Athenians. Although he was obviously a loyal and enthusiastic follower of Socrates, Chaerephon remained politically active. In 404 he lost his life defending Athenian democracy from the oligarchs, including Charmides and Critias, who overthrew the democracy and established the rule of the Thirty. In his *Apology* (32c–d), Socrates reports, the Thirty also ordered his death. Cf. Xenophon *Memorabilia* 1.2.31.

43. Cf. Paul Stern, "Tyranny and Self-Knowledge: Critias and Socrates in Plato's *Charmides*," *American Political Science Review* 93, no. 2 (June 1999): 399–412.

44. Cf. Aristotle *Nicomachean Ethics* 1095a1–10; Drew Hyland, *The Virtue of Philosophy* (Athens: Ohio State University Press, 1981), 147.

45. As Schmid (*Charmides*, 4) points out, Socrates could have responded to Chaerephon's question by bragging about the bravery he displayed in the battle, for which, Alcibiades says in

Both the fact and the grounds of Socrates' self-control become evident in the action that follows the initial greetings and exchange. In response to Socrates' query, Critias says that Charmides is a young man who has distinguished himself for beauty. Socrates confesses that he is no judge, because all young people look beautiful to him. If Charmides is willing to strip, Chaerephon suggests, they will see that his form is even more beautiful than his face. Socrates counters with the more radical suggestion that they strip him of his body entirely in order to examine his soul, where the true beauty of a person is to be found. Critias' suggestion that Socrates pose as a physician in order to justify their examination of the young man shows at the outset that he does not understand the significance of the distinction Socrates drew between soul and body. Plato illustrates the need for the soul to rule the body, however, by having Socrates report that in the jostling that occurred as Charmides entered with a group of admirers, the philosopher looked inside the youth's cloak and felt himself overcome with desire.[46] He nevertheless regained possession of himself sufficiently to answer Charmides when he asked whether Socrates truly had a cure for headaches. Despite his insistence on the locus of beauty (or nobility) in the soul, Plato shows (contrary to Alcibiades' self-serving claims in the *Symposium* 219b–d), Socrates was by no means indifferent to its physical manifestations. But knowing what he truly desired (knowledge rather than sensual pleasure), Socrates was able to subdue his immediate physical impulses. Socratic philosophy did not entail complete forgetfulness or abstention from bodily sensation. On the contrary, in the *Charmides* Plato shows that Socrates tried to convince Critias that the search for knowledge, even of the self, requires us to reflect on what we have experienced in the external world as well as how we have experienced it.

In Socrates' first exchange with Charmides, it becomes clear that the young man does not understand the need to rule the body with the soul. Told that Socrates has a cure for headaches, from which he suffers (and which malady suggests that the young man has an immoderate taste for wine), Charmides proposes to write it down. "Don't you need my consent?" Socrates asks. Accustomed to having his admirers do his bidding,

---

the *Symposium* (220d–e), Socrates deserved the highest honor, although Socrates refused it. Socrates did not vaunt his own courage any more than he did his wisdom—until he was required by law to give an account of his deeds as well as his speeches in defending himself in court.

46. Cf. Seth Benardete, "On Interpreting Plato's *Charmides*," *Graduate Faculty Philosophy Journal* 11, no. 2 (1986): 10.

Charmides does not understand the need for persuasion or consent. The seeds of his future tyranny are visible in his youthful behavior.[47]

For the cure to work, Socrates explains, the application of the leaf has to be accompanied by speeches designed to inculcate moderation. The Thracian physicians who taught Socrates the cure criticized Greek doctors for attempting to treat a part (the body) rather than the whole (the soul and body).[48] To heal the body, it is necessary to have the soul in order. Socrates thus proposes to examine Charmides to see whether he is moderate. If he is, he will not need the treatment through speeches in addition to the leaf. Although Critias assures Socrates that the young man already excels in the virtue his "charm" or speeches are supposed to induce, Socrates quickly demonstrates that Charmides neither knows nor possesses moderation.

Asked whether he is moderate, the young man shows why Critias thinks he is by modestly replying that he cannot with propriety answer the question: if he denies that he has the virtue, he contradicts his elder; but if he claims to possess it, he proves himself a braggart. Socrates insists, however, that if Charmides is moderate, he must have some sense of what moderation is. Looking within himself (and so apparently engaging in a kind of self-reflection often associated with the search for self-knowledge), the young man says he believes it consists in a kind of quietness. Socrates objects that moderation is a virtue. It should, therefore, constitute a positive claim to excellence, not merely the absence of a fault. People associate quickness of wit and strength with virtue as much, if not more than gentleness. (In order to discover what is within oneself, Plato's readers see, one has to know beforehand or from "outside" what one is looking for.) Responding to Socrates' objection, Charmides identifies moderation with a traditional virtue by suggesting that it consists in shame (*aidōs*) of a kind he has displayed. But Socrates questions the validity of this definition by citing a traditional authority. In the *Odyssey* (17.347) Homer's hero, disguised as a beggar, observes that "shame is not good for a needy man" (*Charmides* 161a). Unwilling if not unable to resist the authority of his elders, Charmides gives up. (Like Alcibiades, this handsome young man also

47. Laughing and addressing Socrates by name, Charmides also shows that he sees through the ruse. He testifies to Socrates' growing reputation not only by recognizing him on sight but also by explaining that the boys have been talking about him. Charmides is not quite the innocent Critias thinks he is.

48. Cf. Christopher Bruell, "Socratic Politics and Self-Knowledge: An Interpretation of Plato's *Charmides,*" *Interpretation* 6, no. 3 (1977): 148.

shows himself to be intellectually lazy.) By asking Socrates what he thinks of an opinion he has heard, the youth slyly passes the argument on to his guardian.

Socrates guesses that Charmides heard from Critias that moderation consists in minding one's own business, but the older man denies it until Socrates seems to refute the suggestion by getting Charmides to agree that a polity requiring everyone to do everything for himself is not well organized.[49] If Charmides were quick witted, he might have responded to Socrates by arguing that one does not truly control oneself if one depends on others. If moderation means self-control, it entails taking care of oneself—or minding one's own business.[50] Charmides depends on his guardian, however, for intellectual guidance and support. By explicitly as well as implicitly deferring to Critias, Charmides shows that he neither values nor possesses intellectual independence or self-control.[51]

Nor does his guardian. Vexed by Charmides' failure to defend the definition attributed to him, Critias displays the desire for distinction and command that prevents him from being moderate by taking over as interlocutor.[52] Responding to Socrates' suggestion (contrary to the apparent teaching of the *Republic*) that artisans mind not only their own business but also that of others by performing useful services for them (and so are just as well as moderate), Critias points out that there is a difference between making (*poiein*) and doing (*prattein*). When he defined moderation as minding one's own business, he was not talking about vulgar artisans; like Hesiod, he was describing those who perform honorable and beneficial deeds.

---

49. In the *Republic* 369b–71e, Socrates argues that human beings form political communities because individuals cannot provide everything they need for themselves; it is better to do what one is fitted to do by nature and exchange products and services with others. In the *Hippias Minor* (368b–c) the sophist brags that he can do or make everything for himself. He would presumably constitute a (humorous, because he brags so much) example of the virtue of moderation as defined here. Cf. Hyland, *Virtue*, 72–73.

50. In Thomas G. West's introduction to Plato, *Charmides*, trans. T. G. W. West and Grace Starry West (Indianapolis: Hackett, 1986), he points out that "no one in the *Charmides* poses the most obvious definition of moderation/sound-mindedness: self-control" (7). By translating *sōphrosynē* as "sound-mindedness," the Wests, like Rosen ("*Sōphrosynē* and *Selbstbewusstsein*," 620), emphasize the "phron" root common to *sōphrosynē*, *phronēsis* (intelligence or practical wisdom), *phronimos* (prudent), and *euphrōn* (intelligent).

51. He does, however, somewhat resentfully enjoy the prospect of Critias' discomfiture when his covert authority is disclosed.

52. "Critias had clearly desired to compete and win honor before Charmides and the others present for some time," Socrates reports; "now he could no longer restrain himself" (*Charmides* 162c).

By noting that such verbal distinctions were characteristic of Prodicus, Socrates reminds his auditors (and Plato's readers) that he was not the only intellectual who influenced ambitious young Athenians. As we know from the *Protagoras*, Critias had also associated with, and apparently absorbed the teachings of, the sophists. As we shall see in the *Hippias Minor*, the sophist from Elis claims to embody the understanding of nobility as self-sufficiency that Critias praises here. Self-sufficiency might look like self-control and hence constitute a kind of moderation. Socrates shows that it does not.

Socrates characteristically dismisses Critias' appeals to the poets as well as the verbal distinctions (both characteristic of the sophists) by ignoring them; he simply observes that he would rather have Critias as an interlocutor than Charmides. (Critias was clearly the source of Charmides' opinions.) Socrates then asks Critias: do you think moderation is the doing or making of *good* things?

Critias is not willing to follow Socrates in an examination of what is good, however. Exhibiting his desire to lead, Critias attempts to take charge of the discussion by asking Socrates whether moderation does not seem a good thing to him. But Socrates insists on Critias' responding to the following objection to his earlier statement: people can do or make things beneficial to themselves or others without knowing that they will benefit, but no one can be moderate or virtuous without knowing that he is. Doing beneficial deeds does not suffice, therefore, as a definition of moderation (and Charmides cannot be moderate if he does not know that he is).

Critias had expected Socrates to agree with (and hence praise) his first "anonymous" definition, because Critias had heard something like this from Socrates. The philosopher's objection reminds Critias of another Socratic teaching, however: moderation comes from self-knowledge. Rather than admit he has made an error or misstatement, Critias withdraws his first suggestion—claiming erroneously that their exchange has been inconclusive—and replaces it with a novel reinterpretation of the famous adages inscribed over the entrance to the temple of Apollo at Delphi. Characteristically asserting his own superiority, Critias claims that people in the past misunderstood the inscription over the entrance as a command rather than as the god's salutation to those who entered. As a result, they later added the second inscription: nothing in excess. Critias' reinterpretation of the Delphic sayings indicates that he was no more willing than Alcibiades had been to admit his own inferiority as a human being, compared to the god. Nor does Critias recognize a need for self-restraint.[53] On the contrary, his reinterpretation of the order to recall one's limitations as a mortal in the face of the immortal as the god's greeting to his visitors enables Critias to dismiss the god's second admonition to be moderate as spurious.[54]

Responding to Critias' second definition, Socrates asks: is moderation a kind of knowledge (*epistēmē*)? If so, of what? And with what effect? Emphasizing the reflexive meaning of *autos* (self), Critias explains that the distinctive characteristic of self-knowledge or *sōphrosynē* is that it has no particular external object, subject matter, effect, or product (*ergon*). Purely reflexive, self-knowledge is knowledge of knowledge. It is entirely and completely self-contained.

Having heard Socrates not only assert the fundamental importance of seeking self-knowledge but also equate that knowledge with moderation, Critias accuses Socrates of merely trying to refute him in order to demonstrate his own superiority when the philosopher again raises objections.[55] Socrates protests that rather than trying to refute Critias (or demonstrate superiority), he is attempting to examine an opinion he shares with Critias to make sure that he does not think he knows something that he does not.

As with Alcibiades, so with Critias, Socrates emphasizes the need to seek self-knowledge in conversation with another. As Socrates understands it, self-knowledge is *not* a product of introspection. As knowledge of what makes a human being human, self-knowledge is not at all self-contained or independent. It requires knowledge not only of other human beings but also of the nonhuman things to determine the difference between them and thus what is distinctively human. As knowledge of one's limits, self-knowledge as Socrates understands it entails recognition of one's lack of self-sufficiency and the consequent need to join with others. Self-knowledge

53. Benardete points out that "the Delphic inscription, 'Know thyself' (*gnōthi seauton*), is not in intention a command; it is a concealed assertion: 'You are not a god.' Critias moves to *sōphrosynē* as science of science by denying that 'Know thyself' assigns the addressee to the class of man in opposition to the class of gods " ("Interpreting Plato's *Charmides*," 25).

54. Tyrants seem to have seen the Delphic sayings as sources of popular resistance to their rule. In the *Hipparchus* 228e–29a, Socrates reports that the tyrant tried to dissuade his people from admiring the Delphic inscriptions by putting up figures of Hermes and inscribing them with verses of his own. Critias seems to be doing something similar by reinterpreting the existing inscriptions.

55. In his exchange with Protagoras, Socrates argued that *sōphrosynē* and *sophia* were the same because they were both opposites of *aphrosynē*. He also argued that courage consisted in an *epistēmē* of the dreadful.

as Socrates understands it consists in knowledge of one's ignorance rather than, as Critias claims, knowledge of knowledge.[56]

Socrates responds to Critias' definition of self-knowledge by questioning first the possibility and then the utility of seeking knowledge of knowledge, simply and solely in itself. Emphasizing the difference between any particular science and its subject matter (for example, calculation and numbers or weighing and weights), Socrates points out that, having no particular subject, knowledge of knowledge would be perfectly empty. We might know that we know or don't, but we still would not know anything in particular. An even more fundamental objection to this definition of self-knowledge is that no sense or mental operation refers solely to itself. Does vision see itself? Hearing hear hearing? Desire desire desiring (and not some pleasure)? Love love loving (and not some beauty)? The concepts we use to measure and order things we perceive in the world vis-à-vis each other (not, necessarily, as in our senses and passions in relation to us)— greater, smaller, half and double—also make no sense referred reflexively to themselves. (Can "greater" be greater than greater? Double doubled is quadruple, not double.) Like our senses and passions, our minds direct us outward, to the world of things, not back on ourselves. We become aware of the fact that we have senses, passions, and thought only in reaction to the experience of something outside or beyond us.

Having raised the question, Socrates modestly declares himself incapable of determining whether there can be a purely self-reflexive form of knowledge.[57] He does not entirely deny the possibility of such (or find his own arguments conclusive). He does dramatically contrast his own willingness to admit his limitations with Critias' unwillingness to admit error or ignorance (and so to achieve the first step toward self-knowledge as Socrates understands it).

56. Cf. J. Vernant, *L'individu, la mort, l'amour, soi-même et l'autre en Grèce ancienne* (Paris: Gallimard, 1989), 224–25.

57. Socrates has distressed some modern commentators by appearing to dismiss "epistemology" out of hand. Since Socrates raises the question, What is knowledge? in a later conversation with Theaetetus, it does not seem safe to conclude that he thought it was a useless query—even though he and the young geometer do not prove able to formulate a satisfactory answer. What Socrates objects to here is the entirely self-reflexive, completely self-contained character of Critias' formulation, which prevents knowledge from having any subject matter. Even if we were somewhat illegitimately to translate Critias' claim into modern language and concepts that do not appear in the Greek original, self-consciousness is not the same as consciousness—or perhaps, even, consciousness of consciousness. As in Descartes' *Meditations*, the question still arises about what we mean by the self.

Perceiving that Critias' desire for distinction prevents him from conceding that his definition is faulty (*Charmides* 169c–d), Socrates tells his
auditor(s) that he shifted the discussion from the question of the possibility of attaining knowledge of knowledge to a consideration of its possible
benefit.[58] Again in evident contrast to Critias, Socrates declared that he
was at a loss. He did not see how knowledge of knowledge could give us
knowledge of self. Mimicking, if not mocking, Socrates' argument about
the ideas, Critias suggested that as a swift runner has swiftness, so a knower
has knowledge. Knowing knowledge would be knowing oneself.

Socrates pointed out that there are different kinds of knowledge. Knowledge of knowledge would not give us knowledge of medicine or justice.
At most, by enabling us to determine what is and what is not truly knowledge, knowledge of knowledge would allow us to live free of error. But, he
reflected, living free from error would not necessarily make us live happily.
To be happy, he and Critias agreed, human beings do not need a generalized knowledge of knowledge; we require a specific kind of knowledge,
knowledge of what is truly good. At the end of the exchange Socrates thus
returned to the question Critias refused to take up at the beginning, because he thought the answer was obvious and that Socrates was, therefore,
merely toying with him.

The exchange might appear to be purely abortive, but it is not. The objections Socrates raises to Critias' appropriation and reinterpretation of his
own doctrines bring out both some of the inherent limitations of human
knowledge and the reasons for Socrates' peculiar way of seeking it. They
also point to a fundamental opposition between the traditional ancient
Greek understanding of human excellence as the achievement of political
preeminence and Socratic philosophy.

By contrasting this discussion of self-knowledge and moderation with
Socrates' previous discussion with Alcibiades, readers also see one reason
the philosopher said in the *Apology* that education has to be individual and
private rather than public.[59] People are reluctant to admit their shortcomings in public, but they will not learn to do better unless they admit their
shortcomings. In the *Alcibiades I* Socrates explicitly stated that he could say

---

58. The advantage of a dialogue narrated by Socrates is that he can make explicit his own
intentions as well as his observations concerning the reactions of others to what he says.

59. *Apology* 26a. The Athenian Stranger makes a similar critique of education in Sparta and
Crete (*Laws* 666e).

the youth was in a miserable condition (and persuade him to change it) because they were alone. In the *Charmides* Socrates sees that Critias is unwilling to admit error or ignorance because he is speaking in front of a group of his peers, including his young ward, whom Critias wants to impress.

At the end of the argument Socrates points out that they have not learned anything about moderation, because they too readily agreed that there might be a knowledge of knowledge and that living free from error would constitute a great benefit (the two concessions Socrates told his anonymous auditors he made to keep Critias in the conversation by enabling him to save face). To seek knowledge, like Socrates and unlike Critias, people first have to admit that they lack it. Those, like Critias, who seek knowledge in order to appear, if not to become, truly cleverer than others will inevitably fail to acquire what they think they are seeking. Only those who recognize their own inadequacy will look to others for confirmation, contradiction, or assistance. Aware of their own incompleteness and insufficiency, people who genuinely seek knowledge will never become tyrants. If Charmides and Critias had really listened to Socrates or followed his advice and example, their future careers would have been entirely different. Rather than corrupting these young men and encouraging them in their tyrannical ambitions, Plato shows, Socrates tried to counteract them. Unwilling openly to admit their own failings and consequent need to cooperate with others in attaining their goals, Charmides and Critias saw no need to persuade others to join or assist them. At the end of the dialogue we hear them conspiring to force Socrates to continue entertaining them with his speeches. They had not learned the need Socrates pointed out to Charmides at the beginning of their conversation to obtain the consent of other(s).

In the *Alcibiades I* Socrates urges the young man to seek self-knowledge in an attempt to make him more just. In the *Charmides* Socrates reminds his interlocutors that human beings are no more self-sufficient cognitively than we are physically. It is impossible to achieve any kind of knowledge solely on the basis of introspection. We become aware of our own senses, passions, and thoughts only after they are aroused by external objects. We cannot have knowledge (in general or in itself) because there are different kinds of things, and knowledge would not be knowledge if it did not take account of the differences.[60]

60. Neither Socrates nor Plato could have known that two thousand years later, Descartes would attempt to found certain knowledge on the undeniable self-reflexivity of the *cogito*. From

In the *Alcibiades I* and the *Charmides*, Socrates shows that acquiring knowledge is necessarily an interactive process. Human beings have to look outside themselves to the world, in association with others, to discover by means of contrast both what and who they are. Human beings cannot achieve knowledge or improve their own condition, therefore, until they make the sense of incompleteness implicit in their desires explicit. Human beings not only have to recognize their limitations; like Alcibiades, they have to acknowledge that they want to be something better than they now are. As we see in the *Charmides*, preeminently in Critias, the desire for distinction that fuels political ambition makes any such admission effectively impossible. To persuade his contemporaries to seek knowledge and thus to improve their condition, Socrates had to convince them that political preeminence is not the highest good. He had to convince them, in effect, that the traditional understanding of virtue, originating in Homer and reaffirmed in fifth century Athens by Pericles, is wrong.

III. The Generals' Failure to Define Courage

Plato does not show Socrates engaging in any more philosophical conversations during most of the first part of the Peloponnesian War. Such conversations would have appeared frivolous, if not worse, while the city was under attack. Instead, we are told in the *Laches*, Socrates risked his life as a soldier in the Athenian army at Delium. If Socrates had not proved

---

the *Charmides*, we surmise, however, that Socrates would not have been surprised by some of the problematic results. At the beginning of his *Meditations*, Descartes explains that he is seeking a new foundation and means of acquiring knowledge because there are too many opinions for any one man to examine them all during his lifetime. If human beings are to acquire knowledge—as opposed to "considered" opinions—they have to devise another way. In the *Charmides* Socrates admits that he knows only that he does not know; he does not, and he doubts that anyone can, know that he knows. At the end of his life, he explicitly states in the *Crito* (46b–d) and *Phaedo* (100a) that he has only considered opinions, arguments, or hypotheses. He is not at all certain that they are true; all his conclusions are, rather, explicitly open to reexamination—always. His arguments are simply the best, the most consistent, both logically and with the external evidence that he has found. In the *Republic* (475d–80a, 509d–11e) Socrates argues that there is an unbridgeable gap between the requirements and operations of intelligibility and the world as we experience it. The latter changes; the former cannot. In trying to isolate the intelligible and build solely upon it, Socrates would observe, Descartes necessarily separated the mind or consciousness from the world. Such a separation is artificial and ultimately misleading. No wonder post-Cartesian modern philosophy was plagued by the separation of the "real" from the "ideal." Descartes had severed the link between sensible and intelligible in human opinion and perception from the beginning. He tried to reunite them by introducing a superhuman force (God), but to prove the existence of the supra-rational on the basis of reason is impossible. Most commentators have thus found Descartes' proof of the existence of God inadequate.

himself to be a good citizen in this traditional sense, some of the elders (like Laches) would not have been willing to listen to what Socrates had to say about the education of the young.

After a decade of war and a series of defeats, however, some Athenians were beginning to question the adequacy of the education they had received.[61] Attributing their own failure to win renown to their famous fathers' neglect of their education, the sons of Aristides and Thucydides (Pericles' aristocratic political rivals) invited the two generals then leading Athens to join them in considering how they could do better for their own sons.[62] Laches and Nicias, the two generals who subsequently negotiated the peace with Sparta, agreed to take part in the deliberations.

Laches expresses surprise that Lysimachus has not asked Socrates to join them. By having the elder do so, Plato makes it look as if these conservative representatives of old Athens might have cooperated with Socrates in reforming the education of Athenian youths. (Unlike Meletus, the elders do really care.) In the conversation that ensues, however, Plato reminds his readers that men in office are even less likely than ambitious youths such as Alcibiades and Critias to admit their ignorance and join Socrates in a search for wisdom. Socrates might postpone, but he could not avoid a confrontation with traditional authorities.

By showing that Socrates was no longer known only to the young men and foreign teachers who frequented the gymnasia but was now recognized by the leading conservative politicians in Athens (Nicias and Laches), if for different reasons, Plato indicates that the philosopher's reputation had grown in the ten years between this conversation and that depicted in the *Charmides*.[63] Nicias, for example, knows of Socrates. Although Socrates

---

61. Walter T. Schmid, *On Manly Courage: A Study of Plato's "Laches"* (Carbondale: Southern Illinois University Press, 1992), 183n1, points out that the conversation obviously takes place after Delium in 424. It probably occurs before the Athenian defeat at Amphipolis in 423 (at which Socrates [according to the *Apology* 28e] but not Laches was also present) and the first production of Aristophanes' satirical critique of Socrates in the *Clouds*, since there is no mention of either. If so, Nicias would be the current head of the Athenian government; as such he negotiated a temporary truce with Sparta. He and Laches were able to negotiate the peace treaty in 421 only after the capture of the Spartans at Pylos. According to Thucydides (5.16), one reason Nicias could negotiate the peace was that Cleon and Brasidas, the two leaders who most wanted the war to continue, both died at Amphipolis.

62. Pericles was the leader who led Athens into the Peloponnesian War. The sons of his political enemies might well have seen the faltering war effort as an opportunity for their families to rise to prominence again.

63. By failing to depict a Socratic conversation occurring during the ten years of war following the battle at Potidaea, Plato suggests, for reasons indicated by his characterization of Laches, that Athenians generally would not have looked favorably on leisurely philosophical exchanges

had refused to take Nicias' son as a student, and Nicias had taken lessons from Damon, in the course of the conversation the general shows that he is familiar with both the form and content of Socrates' arguments. In contrast to Nicias, Laches regards all mere talkers or sophists with contempt. He respects Socrates for the courage he displayed on the battlefield in the retreat from Delium.[64] Laches later states his willingness, therefore, to be questioned and even refuted by his fellow soldier as part of their common endeavor. Readers learn that young Aristides and Thucydides had also vociferously praised Socrates, but Lysimachus had not paid much attention to their youthful chatter.[65] The Athenian elder invites Socrates to join their deliberations about the education of their sons, not because of his reputation as a teacher but on traditional grounds of personal loyalty and kinship—because Laches vouches for Socrates' character and because, Laches reminds him, Socrates is a fellow demesman whose father Sophroniscus had been a friend of Aristides. In the *Laches* Plato thus shows that Socrates' military service and family ties to the city made the conservative elders more willing to listen to him than to the foreign sophists and to trust their children to his care. Nevertheless, Socrates' evident ties to the city were not sufficient to make Athenian leaders hearken to, or benefit from, his arguments. Like Critias and Charmides, Plato indicates, Laches and Nicias would have been better off had they followed Socrates' example and advice. They did not because they feared the opprobrium of the demos. Like Alcibiades, they cared too much about public opinion.

In the *Protagoras* Socrates observed that the Athenians did not think it was possible to teach political virtue because they saw that great statesmen like Pericles were not able to pass their own excellence on to their sons. In criticizing Aristides and Thucydides for allowing them to waste away their youth in idle pleasures while their fathers attended to public affairs, Lysimachus and Melesias suggest one reason why. Statesmen like Pericles were too busy serving the city to tend to their private affairs, including the education of their sons. Such a sacrifice of one's private interest for the good of the community might have appeared to be virtuous. As

---

among young men who might be serving their city on the battlefield. The spread of Socrates' reputation suggests that he was, nevertheless, active at home as well as abroad.

64. The military service that earned Socrates the respect of Laches may, however, be a product of Plato's art. Leo Strauss points out in *Xenophon's Socratic Discourse* (Ithaca: Cornell University Press, 1970), 89, and *Xenophon's Socrates* (Ithaca: Cornell University Press, 1972), 126, that Xenophon never mentions any military service on the part of Socrates, and Xenophon, not Plato, was the historian.

65. As was customary, the sons were named after their grandfathers.

Lysimachus and Melesias point out, however, such "self-sacrifice" is short-sighted; like all other cities, Athens needs to train excellent leaders for the future. The new educational community they propose to establish seems to constitute an appropriate remedy for past negligence.

By interrogating first Laches and then Nicias, however, Socrates shows that the reason Athenian statesmen were unable to inculcate virtue in their sons was not simply that they did not pay sufficient attention to their sons' education. On examination, neither Athenian leader proves able to give a coherent definition of virtue, even the part—courage—that he can claim to manifest as a general. Like the self-proclaimed sophist Protagoras, the fathers are not able to teach their sons virtue because they do not know, and thus cannot explain or show, what true human excellence is.

Lysimachus begins the deliberations by asking his companions to determine whether they encourage their sons to take lessons in defensive fighting of the kind currently being displayed in the marketplace. Appealing initially to traditional standards, Socrates suggests that Lysimachus should consult with the generals first, because they are older and hence presumably wiser. In responding to the question, each general takes his characteristic stance. On the basis of prospective calculations about what might prove useful in the future, Nicias says yes, whereas on the basis of past experience, Laches says no.[66] Because the elders disagree, Lysimachus asks Socrates to decide the issue with his vote.

Objecting that such decisions should be made by an expert who knows, not merely by the greatest number of votes, Socrates opposes Athenian tradition and democratic politics more directly and emphatically than Protagoras did. Temporarily taking the lead in the conversation, Socrates changes both its subject and form. First, he suggests that they need to find an expert teacher. To find such an expert, however, they have to determine the goal or purpose of their study. It is not merely a question of the utility of learning to fight in armor, as Nicias suggests. They asked about this particular activity in order to learn how best to care for the souls of young men. Socrates does not claim to know, nor does he have the resources to

66. Nicias argues that such lessons will prevent young men from spending their leisure time in less healthy occupations, make them better able to defend themselves in battle, and give them a taste for more noble studies, particularly generalship. Laches responds that if such lessons were truly useful for winning battles, the Spartans would have taken them up, because they do everything they know to win victories. None of the teachers of defensive fighting has become highly esteemed in war; the particular man now giving a demonstration, Stesilaus, made a fool of himself when he tried to employ an unusual weapon at sea.

hire one of the sophists who claim to be able to make their students *kalos k'agathos*. But Nicias and Laches do. Socrates thus urges Lysimachus to question them to find out whether they know of such an expert or, if they have discovered how to rear the young, to point out an example of their work.

Nicias warns those who do not know Socrates that anyone who "keeps him company in discussion, even if he has earlier begun a discussion about something else, will not be allowed to stop until he has given an account of himself, the way he now lives, and the way he has lived his past life" (*Laches* 187e–88a). Nicias knows of whom he speaks. By interrogating the generals, Socrates not only brings out the defects in the understanding of courage each has and the contradictory character of the virtue they jointly represent. He also indicates the common flaw that leads both of them later to defeat and death.

Although Laches has not experienced a Socratic examination, he assures the company that he is willing to learn from a teacher who is younger and not yet a man of reputation, so long as that teacher has proved his merit in action. Socrates has. The general thus commands the philosopher to teach and to refute him in order to learn whatever he may know. Like Nicias, Laches understands himself to be undergoing a test of which he, unlike Nicias, has no previous experience. Laches acts out his own understanding of courage by resolutely facing the unknown.

Lysimachus declares his own inability to conduct the inquiry, because of his failing memory and hearing, so Socrates takes over. He first gets his associates to agree that they are seeking to discover what human virtue is. Because that is a large question, he suggests, they should begin by examining a part. The part at which fighting in armor seems to aim is courage. He thus asks Laches to tell him what courage is. The general says that courage consists in a man's willingness to remain in the ranks and defend himself rather than flee. Apologizing for not having asked the question properly, Socrates says that he wants to know what is courageous under all circumstances—not only in war but also in sickness and poverty and even in politics. Laches generalizes, saying that courage is a kind of steadfastness, and Socrates asks him, does this steadfastness not need to be accompanied by prudence. Laches agrees, until Socrates inquires whether a man who calculates that his force can win a battle is braver than the man who holds his ground despite the odds. Laches sees the contradiction; he has already agreed that a courageous man cannot be a fool. Nevertheless, he cannot agree that courage is more a matter of calculation than of fortitude.

Nicias, when asked the same question, repeats something he has heard Socrates say before—namely, that courage is a certain sort of wisdom. Apparently unaware of the Socratic source, Laches accuses Nicias of giving a ridiculous answer. Socrates responds simply by urging the general to teach rather than merely revile his colleague. Turning to Nicias, Socrates inquires, what sort of wisdom? Nicias responds: knowledge of the things that inspire dread or daring. Unlike farmers, craftsmen, and doctors who know things necessary to preserve life, courageous men know whether and when it is better to live or die. Alluding to his colleague's reputation, Laches accuses Nicias of claiming that seers are courageous. Nicias counters by observing that seers know only the signs of what will happen, not whether it is for the best.[67] Such knowledge, Laches retorts, could belong only to a god.

If human beings were able to predict and control what happens, Laches intuits, they would not need to be courageous. Courage is a human virtue—difficult to acquire and maintain—precisely because human beings are mortal and our knowledge is consequently limited. Laches withdraws from the conversation in disgust, and Socrates begins questioning Nicias on behalf of both of them. Much to Laches' pleasure, Socrates asks Nicias if he denies that animals such as lions have courage. Nicias explains that such animals are bold but not courageous because they have no knowledge of what they do or risk. Observing that Nicias has been taught by Damon, who associated a great deal with Prodicus, Socrates appears to sympathize with Laches' accusation that Nicias is acting like a sophist by "splitting hairs" or distinguishing terms. (Protagoras had drawn the same distinction between courage and boldness in responding to Socrates' suggestion that courage consists in knowledge of what is truly dreadful [Protagoras 350c–e].) Socrates reminds Laches, however, that leaders also need to be prudent. Laches consistently underestimates the need for wisdom.

67. Relying on the criticism of Nicias in Sicily for giving too much credence to signs in both Thucydides 7.50 and Plutarch, "Life of Nicias," 23, Darrell Dobbs, "For Lack of Wisdom: Courage and Inquiry in Plato's Laches," Journal of Politics 48 (1986): 825–40, suggests that Nicias tries to deflect Socrates' questions in order to avoid disclosing himself under examination and that he erroneously understands courage in terms of knowledge as technē, that is, as a kind of know-how that produces secure results. The courage of both Laches and Nicias proves to be defective, Dobbs concludes, because the greatest test of courage is one's ability to deal with the unknown. I argue, on the contrary, that Plato indicates that the defective character of their understanding of courage is associated with their inability to stand up courageously in opposition to public opinion. Human beings know they are going to die, even if we don't know what, if anything, happens thereafter.

Socrates presses Nicias not on the question of whether courage requires a kind of knowledge but on what kind it is. Would not one who knows things that inspire the terror and confidence in the future also know the same things in the present and in the past? If so, the knowledge Nicias is attributing to the courageous man would constitute knowledge of what is good and bad in human life. It would encompass all the virtues, of which courage was initially agreed to be only a part. Nicias somewhat reluctantly agrees that it looks as if they have not discovered what courage is.[68]

Socrates might appear to contradict himself by finding the argument he gave Protagoras, to show that courage is a kind of wisdom, inadequate when Nicias repeats it. But at the end of the *Protagoras* Socrates explicitly admitted that the position he had argued there was not tenable. In the contrast and interplay between the two generals we see the reason why. Like the sophists, Nicias reduces courage (and all other virtues) to a kind of calculation, but Laches deprives it of all intellectual content. Plato thus allows his readers to see that courage requires a combination of foresight and daring that is difficult, if not impossible, to achieve. People who refuse to recognize the fact of their own mortality are fools, Laches recognizes; those who tremble at every threat are, however, cowards. As Nicias points out, people need to know what is truly terrible and what is or should be braved; but, as Laches objects, it is not clear that human beings have the requisite knowledge. In the *Laches*, in contrast to the *Apology of Socrates*, there is no discussion of whether death is truly to be feared.

Laches forestalls any further inquiry by gloating about the sophistically "educated" Nicias having proved no more able than he to provide an adequate definition of courage. Laches is more concerned about not appearing to be inferior to his opponent than with gaining knowledge, Nicias charges. Since the problem with his definition appears, ironically, to be that he had not distinguished clearly enough between the knowledge required for courage and other sorts, he thinks Damon will be able to help him. Nicias faults Laches for ridiculing the teacher of music and other sophists

68. Charles L. Griswold, Jr., "Philosophy, Education, and Courage in Plato's *Laches*," *Interpretation* 14, nos. 2–3 (May and September 1986), points out: "The last definition is not modified or refuted on its own grounds at all. Rather, it is shown to contradict a separately agreed-to premise—that courage is a 'part' of virtue" (188). Cf. also Hermann Bonitz, "Zur Erklärung Platonischer Dialoge," *Hermes* 5 (1871): 413–42; Michael O'Brien, "The Unity of the *Laches*," in *Essays in Ancient Greek Philosophy*, ed. John Anton and George Kustas (Albany: SUNY Press, 1971), 1:303–25; Gerasimos Santas, "Socrates at Work on Virtue and Knowledge in Plato's *Laches*," in *The Philosophy of Socrates*, ed. Gregory Vlastos (Garden City, NJ: Doubleday, 1971), 177–208; and Daniel Devereux, "Courage and Wisdom in Plato's *Laches*," *Journal of the History of Philosophy* 15 (1977): 129–41.

without having any knowledge of them. Once Nicias has "securely estab-lished these things for [him]self," he promises (or threatens), he will teach Laches, who is "in very great need of learning" (*Laches* 200c). Possibly aping Protagoras, Nicias promises he will do so without envy; repeating some-thing else he may have first heard from Socrates, Nicias observes that, un-like political preeminence or reputation, wisdom can be shared.

If Laches is ignorantly prejudiced against intellectuals, as Nicias charges, how does Socrates escape his contempt? The first reason, we are explicitly told at the beginning of the dialogue, is that Socrates had established his credentials on the battlefield. The second reason, we see at the end, is that Laches believes Socrates has helped him neutralize, if not defeat, his so-phistical competitor. Laches is unable to refute Nicias, but his fellow sol-dier Socrates can.

Had Socrates sought to develop a definition of courage as a kind of wis-dom in cooperation with Nicias, rather than explicitly joining with Laches in a critical examination of Nicias, Laches would have felt shamed—and would probably have become angry as a result. Laches admits feeling some irritation at his own perplexity; he might have blamed Socrates, had the philosopher not appeared to be an ally.[69] As Nicias points out, Laches is not interested in acquiring knowledge—of virtue or anything else. He cares only about defeating his opponent—or not being shown up himself. Like Critias, Nicias seeks knowledge and parrots Socrates, because he wants control. Unlike the philosopher, the "pious" general is not willing to admit that he knows only that he does not know.

Laches rushes to remove the threat of further questions and possible embarrassment by advising Lysimachus and Melesias to bid both generals "farewell, as regards the education of young men, and not to let this Soc-rates go" (200c). The generals will return to the business of "real men"—politics and war. Claiming some of the knowledge possessed by a man of courage, as Nicias has defined it, Socrates responds to Lysimachus' plea that he join them in seeking to make the young as good as possible: "*it would be a terrible thing* to be unwilling to join in someone's zeal to become as good

---

69. When Socrates shows him that his understanding of courage is contradictory, Laches confesses that "a certain love of victory . . . has taken hold of [him], and [he is] truly irritated that [he is] unable to say what [he] perceive[s] in his mind to be courage" (*Laches* 194a–b). He does not become angry, however, because he thinks he and his "ally" have won. Mark Blitz, "An Introduc-tion to the Reading of Plato's *Laches*," *Interpretation* 5, no. 2 (Winter 1975), points out that "there is no mention in the *Laches* of *thymos*" (207). It is a curious omission, because *thymos* often appears to be the psychic root of courage. If so, courage is not simply rational, which is why courage is hard to combine with wisdom.

as possible" (200e, emphasis added). Socrates does not join as a teacher, however. Since none of them has proved able to say what virtue is, he insists, they should all seek a teacher in common, "most of all for ourselves, for we are in need, and then for the lads too" (201a).

The apparently amicable conclusion covers up a deep division. By leaving the education of their friends' sons in Socrates' hands, the generals repeat the error of their predecessors by sacrificing their private concerns in order to pay attention to public affairs. Rather than attend to questions of war and peace, Socrates urges, the first and foremost concern of their little community should be to discover what virtue is.

Neither general follows Socrates' admonition, Plato shows, because neither believes he actually lacks knowledge of courage. Both Laches and Nicias conclude merely that they lack the ability to say what they know from experience in their hearts. Nicias proposes to take more lessons from sophists to enable him to speak more correctly. Laches has contempt for mere speech or speakers; so long as he can demonstrate his courage in deed, he does not think it matters what he can or cannot say.

As Plato's readers would know, the subsequent fates of the two generals resulted, in part, from the defective understandings of courage they express in this dialogue. Laches lost his life in the battle of Mantineia in 418 because he imprudently gave in to the pleas of his troops to attack rather than wait for reinforcements that would have given him overwhelming superiority. He was ashamed of appearing unwilling to take a risk before his men. Five years later in Sicily, Nicias lost an entire army after he delayed their retreat on account of bad portents. His men were frightened by the portents; he was afraid of returning in defeat to Athens.[70]

Had the generals hearkened to Socrates' philosophical reflections, Plato suggests, they might have had greater careers and better practical results. Socrates prescribes the cure for the generals' defect when he urges Lysimachus and Melesias not to listen to the opinion of the greatest number but only to the expert who knows. The views of the ignorant should not inspire dread or daring. As Socrates states both in the *Apology* and the *Crito*, the many may be able to kill a man, but human beings have to die in any case. Politically ambitious men like Nicias and Laches pay more attention to the opinions of the demos than to anything else, however, not so much

---

70. Nicias has often been blamed for his excessive piety (or superstition). Since, as Plato tells us, the general had studied with the sophists, one might wonder whether he believed in the gods so much as he believed in the political utility of seeming to believe.

because they fear death as because public acclaim is the source of political honor, especially in a democracy like Athens, and these generals wish to avoid dishonor more than they fear death.[71] Quoting the same passage from the *Odyssey* that he used in the *Charmides* to dispute the youth's identification of moderation with modesty (*aidōs*), Socrates suggests that a truly courageous man would not be afraid of looking ridiculous or acting shamelessly in case of need.[72] The philosopher thus urges his elderly companions not to worry about those who would laugh at them at their age for seeking teachers.

As the quotation from the *Odyssey* ought to remind us, the critique the philosopher gives of the generals' understanding of courage does not apply merely to Nicias and Laches or to democratic Athens. It extends to the entire ancient Greek tradition, to the understanding of human excellence the citizens of all the *poleis* had acquired from Homer. Like Laches and Nicias, Homer's two heroes Achilles and Odysseus represent the two seemingly incompatible aspects or requirements of true courage, fortitude and cunning. As Plato reminds his readers in the *Hippias Minor*, Achilles was generally regarded as the greater precisely because he showed himself courageously willing to face almost certain death on the battlefield. His reward for accepting an early death was undying fame (which in the *Odyssey* 11.486–92 he complains was not worth the sacrifice). The widespread acceptance of this understanding of human excellence was responsible for the divisive, competitive character of ancient Greek politics, both within and among the *poleis*. It underlay the admiration for Sparta, which both Nicias and Laches share. It also prompted the desire of young ambitious men such as Alcibiades to pursue a war in which they could demonstrate that they are more daring and clever, hence better, than their elders, both on the battlefield and in the assembly.

As Plato shows most dramatically in the *Laches*, Socrates attempted to replace the old, competitive *agōn* for political preeminence with a new cooperative search for wisdom as the basis and goal of human community. He did not succeed in persuading his contemporaries, partly because they did not yet see the disastrous effects of their inherited opinions, partly because he could not press his criticism without arousing hostility, especially

71. In the *Laws* (646e–47b), the Athenian Stranger points out that political courage actually constitutes another kind of fear or shame (*aidōs*), the fear of looking like a coward in front of one's peers.

72. "It is not good for shame to be present in a needy man" (*Odyssey* 17.347; *Charmides* 161a).

of anti-intellectual traditionalists like Laches, but mostly because his contemporaries preferred almost anything—death or even dishonor—to looking ridiculous.[73]

In the *Apology* Socrates reminds the jury that he had been made a laughing stock by the comic poet Aristophanes. But, Plato repeatedly reminds his readers, Socrates survived the satirical attack and lived on happily for many years. Ridicule is hardly the worst thing a human being can experience, yet human beings go to great lengths to avoid it. In the *Laches* Socrates goes so far as to suggest that true courage consists in a willingness to challenge common opinion, even if that makes the speaker look ridiculous, when and if common opinion is wrong. To be sure, the demos can kill you. People do and must sometimes risk their lives, however, if they are not to become base and cowardly. In the *Protagoras* Socrates suggested that the sophist lacked prudence when he vaunted his own wisdom and so implicitly criticized democratic norms and practices. Socrates explicitly criticized the same norms and practices, however. Protagoras erred not in challenging popular opinion but in not perceiving the danger that his claim to be wiser than anyone else would arouse the envy and ire of others. In contrast to Protagoras, Socrates emphasized his own ignorance. Knowing himself to be superior, if only in recognizing that he did not know the most important things, Socrates was willing to let people ridicule and revile him—so long as they allowed him to continue philosophizing. Unlike Protagoras, Socrates recognized the danger. As he explains in both the *Apology* and the *Republic*, his *daimonion* kept him from speaking in the public assembly on behalf of justice, because he knew that he would die if he did. Socrates was courageous because he knew what to fear and what not to fear, and thus when and when not to risk his life.

IV. The Sophist's Inability to Say What Is Noble

Although sophists claimed to teach their students how to become *kalos k'agathos*, as Socrates shows in his two conversations with Hippias, the sophist did not understand what was truly noble any better than did the Athenian politicians. He failed to understand what was truly noble for the same reason. He paid too much attention to public opinion. Far from

---

73. As we learn from the *Theaetetus* 150e–51a, the young men who did become associates of Socrates, like young Aristides, did not always have suitable natures for philosophy.

preaching a revolutionary lesson that undermined traditional morality, Hippias reaffirmed conventional norms in an attempt to please his audience. The reaffirmation of these traditional norms contradicted his own practice, however, and thus made him look ridiculous.

A. Hippias' Conventional Understanding of Nobility

If Socrates' conversations with Hippias are supposed to have occurred in 421/420, they occur shortly after the first performance of Aristophanes' satirical attack on the philosopher.[74] In the *Clouds* Socrates looks and acts very much like Hippias—the sophist Plato subjects to ridicule in these dialogues. In the *Hippias Major* Socrates' most famous student seems to have presented a comic response to Aristophanes' comic critique of the philosopher.

There are, to be sure, significant differences between Aristophanes' philosopher and Plato's sophist. Although Aristophanes' Socrates teaches his students how "to make the weaker argument the stronger" (*Clouds* 112–15, 881–1154) and so to defeat any opponent in court, he does not appear to be interested in politics.[75] Hippias is. Prodded a bit by Plato's Socrates, Hippias claims that he far surpasses the sages of old because he is able to combine public service (his diplomatic missions) with private profit by demonstrating his skill as a rhetorician to young men willing to pay for it in the cities to

74. The dramatic date of the conversations with Hippias cannot be determined with precision. They clearly occurred after Gorgias' visit to Athens in 427, which Socrates mentions at 282b. At the beginning of the dialogue, Hippias explains that he has not been seen much in Athens because he has been sent on so many diplomatic missions to other cities by his native Elis. Since Elis was allied with Sparta both before and after the peace of Nicias, it seems likely that Hippias' visit occurred in the interim. Hippias may have come as an ambassador from Elis to negotiate a treaty with Athens and Argos. Disappointed with the Spartans' failure to support Elis' claims against Lepreum, a city south of Elis on the Peloponnesus that used the war as an excuse to stop paying the tribute it owed to Elis, Thucydides reports (5.31), the Eleans temporarily allied with Argos and Athens. If Hippias came to Athens as part of the diplomatic mission that negotiated the treaty, he came in 421–420. If so, there is reason to suspect that Hippias may not have wanted to be altogether frank in his exchange with Socrates. Hippias had encountered Socrates before in the conversation recorded in the *Protagoras*. Even though there is no audience here to impress, Hippias may have recalled that Socrates was a clever interlocutor and thought that as a diplomat he should be guarded in what he said to any Athenian.

75. Aristophanes' Socrates does not concern himself with politics because he thinks that he is immune from prosecution. He does not recognize the danger of, and hence the need for protection from, direct and violent action on the basis of irrational (*alogos*) passion, which the comic poet dramatizes at the end of the *Clouds* when Strepsiades tries to burn down Socrates' school with teacher and pupils still inside.

which he travels.[76] In contrast to Aristophanes' Socrates, however, Hippias does not openly proclaim a new, impious teaching or explicitly claim to be superior to the mere mortals who surround him. On the contrary, anxious not to arouse the envy of his contemporaries or the wrath of the dead, Hippias says that he, unlike Protagoras, praises the wisdom of those who have gone before. Concerned about his safety as well as his income, Hippias does not directly challenge the *nomoi* of the cities to which he travels, particularly the laws of the city to which he goes most frequently—Sparta. At first glance, Plato's sophist thus appears to be much more prudent than Aristophanes' philosopher or Protagoras.

Socrates asks Hippias if they pay him in Sparta, and the sophist says, of course not; in Sparta it is against the law to hire foreign teachers. As "one who knows," Hippias agrees with Socrates that the purpose of law is to improve the character of citizens; that the law forbidding Spartans from hiring foreign teachers like Hippias to educate their sons is, therefore, not really a law; and that the Spartans are not truly law-abiding. But, the sophist also points out, people do not usually see things this way. Hippias may agree with Socrates' argument in private, because it appears to be to his advantage, but Hippias does not publicly challenge the wisdom or authority of the law. Nor does he seek to convey or to share the wisdom in which he himself takes such great pride with young Spartans. He does not try to teach them astronomy, geometry, calculation, speech, and harmony. On the contrary, he learns stories about past heroes and the ancient foundings of cities that he relates to please his auditors.

The sophist's relation to the Spartans, Socrates observes, is like that of the old woman who tells children stories to amuse them.[77] Hippias is satisfied, nevertheless, with the Spartans' praise and applause. He does not care as much about his own comfort, safety, and income as he does about popular esteem. What the sophist wishes, above all, is to be admired. This is the

76. Socrates erroneously claims that sages like Bias stayed entirely out of politics. Herodotus 1.27 says that Bias (or Pittacus) persuaded Croesus not to attack the Ionians of the Islands. In fact, most of the sages (who include the Athenian legislator Solon) *were* actively involved in directing the affairs of their cities. They tended to see a tension, if not outright opposition, however, between their private interest and public service. As Plato reminds his readers in the last sentence of the dialogue, Pittacus (whose statement was critiqued by Simonides in the poem interpreted by both Protagoras and Socrates) resigned from office rather than fall prey to the temptation to become a tyrant. Anaxagoras lost his fortune. Like the philosophers who ascend from the cave to the light in Plato's *Republic*, others regarded public service as a burdensome distraction from their studies.

77. As Socrates will observe in *Republic* 376e–77b, however, such stories constitute the earliest and some of the most influential forms of education.

reason for Hippias' noble (or fine) attire (which Socrates explicitly contrasts with his own poor clothes and unshod feet); it is the reason Hippias
thinks it of utmost importance to be able to deliver well-crafted speeches;
it is the reason he seeks money. He does not try to form or reform his
listeners so much as to arouse their wonder and admiration by his own
performance.[78] He is particularly gratified by the praise of the Spartans,
because they are reputed to be the most virtuous Greeks, but his desire
for acclaim is not limited to his fellow citizens or the virtuous. The sophist
wants to be admired everywhere, by everyone. This is the same desire, we
have seen, that led young men such as Alcibiades and Critias not merely to
associate with the sophists and Socrates but to seek political preeminence.
Unlike their students, however, Plato shows that the sophists understood
that the greatest thing for which one could be reputed is wisdom. That
is one of the reasons Socrates seeks to converse with them, to find out
whether they really have the wisdom they claim to possess.

Seeking to extend his reputation, Hippias proposes, at the request of a
certain Eudicus, to deliver the same address in Athens that he had given in
Sparta, concerning the advice Nestor gave to Achilles' son Neoptolemos
about the pursuits—customary and noble—that would make him well reputed. Socrates promises to attend the sophist's performance, if god is
willing. Unlike Nicias, Socrates does not believe that any human can know
the future. From the *Protagoras*, we know, however, that Socrates does not
like to listen to long speeches. And on the basis of what Hippias has already said about his own "noble" activities, Socrates appears to have some
doubts about the adequacy of the sophist's understanding of the noble.
Having observed Hippias' unwillingness to disagree explicitly with his audience, Socrates does not think he would respond well to direct questioning of his views. Instead of interrogating the sophist, Socrates thus asks
Hippias to assist him in formulating a response to a "hubristic" fellow who
asked Socrates, when he was describing various activities as base or noble,
if he could say what the noble is.

Socrates divides himself, as it were, into an anonymous "vulgar" fellow, who persistently asks the "Socratic" "what is . . . ?" question, and the
respondent, who looks to Hippias for assistance in formulating answers,
in order to bring out the division between what Hippias says to please his

78. What made Hippias' ability to combine public service with private profiteering "noble,"
the sophist explains (*Hippias Major* 282e), is the way in which his ability to bring back money to
present to his father aroused the wonder of his fellow citizens.

audiences—the lines he feeds Socrates in his first three attempts to define *to kalon*—and what the sophist himself thinks—summarized by Socrates in the three definitions he subsequently suggests. One could view this odd procedure as an example of the search for self-knowledge Socrates urged Alcibiades to undertake by looking at the reflection of his own soul in the eyes or knowledge of another. The procedure is also rhetorically effective. By asking for Hippias' assistance in responding to his anonymous interlocutor, Socrates takes responsibility for the views expressed and deflects the criticism or humiliation that might follow from the critique. Only after Hippias has shown himself incapable of learning in this gentle manner in private, in their first conversation, does Socrates publicly ridicule the sophist for claiming to be entirely self-sufficient in their second exchange.

The contrast Socrates draws between his own ignorance and Hippias' wisdom might seem exaggerated to the point of sarcasm, but it points to the fundamental difference between the philosopher and the sophist. Admitting his own ignorance, the philosopher seeks but does not claim to possess either nobility or wisdom.[79] "Hippias, the noble and wise" (*Hippias Major* 281a), claims that he possesses both; he does not, therefore, look beyond himself in yearning for something higher, better, or finer.[80] If Hippias' claims were true, he would be a god. But as his concern for his safety indicates, he is not.[81] It is the gap between the sophist's pretensions and his cautious speech that makes him look so ridiculous.

Readers get a sense of the customary noble pursuits Hippias would say that Nestor recommends to young men like Neoptolemos from the sophist's three attempts to say what is noble (or beautiful)—a noble virgin (whom a young man should take as a wife), gold (which he should amass not merely to support but to adorn himself and his family), and finally, a beautiful burial by one's own offspring (after having become rich, healthy, and honorable enough to reach old age and have provided a noble funeral

79. From Diotima, Socrates says that he learned that human eros is the desire to beget in the beautiful and that this desire can be satisfied, ultimately, only by ascending the "ladder of love" from an attraction to one individual to the contemplation of the beautiful in itself. Diotima expresses some doubt about whether Socrates will be able to follow her description of the last stages; he has certainly not had the vision. Socrates consistently claims to seek knowledge of the beautiful in itself, not to have such knowledge.

80. Seth Benardete, introduction to *The Being of the Beautiful* (Chicago: University of Chicago Press, 1984), xx, points out that the word *erōs* does not appear in this dialogue.

81. It is no accident that, as Benardete points out (ibid., xxi–xxxiii), all three of Socrates' refutations of Hippias' attempted definitions of the beautiful involve references to gods (to which Hippias' definitions do not apply, although the gods might well be taken to embody projections of characteristics human beings find admirable, desirable, and hence "beautiful").

for one's parents). The definitions correspond, loosely, to three stages in a man's adult life.

Socrates objects to Hippias' first definition by pointing out that saying a noble virgin is noble is not to say what the noble is. As many later commentators have observed, the sophist fails to distinguish particular from universal.[82] Hippias denies that there is a difference. No one would disagree that a noble virgin is noble, he tells Socrates, and no one can refute a man who says what everyone else says and thinks. Hippias' express concern about not being refuted may indicate that the sophist remembers how Socrates treated Protagoras and that he wants to avoid a repetition in his own case.[83] At the end of the dialogue, however, readers learn that there is a deeper basis for the sophist's apparently—but only apparently—inept response. If everything is a naturally continuous body (or bodies), as Hippias asserts, then distinctions between noble and base are simply conventional.[84] In questions of nobility, agreement is the test of truth as well as the basis of social standing. Hippias has already pointed out that anyone who disagrees with everyone else looks ridiculous.

Socrates' alter ego asks whether a noble mare, a noble lyre, and a noble pot are not also noble. Hippias objects to the bad taste of the man for introducing such worthless things in a dignified conversation. At most the sophist will admit that a pot can be nobly (or well, in that *kalōs* is usually translated as an adverb) made; properly speaking, he insists, such a lowly thing cannot be said to be noble. "Don't you know the saying of Heraclitus that 'the most noble of monkeys is base compared with the race of man'?" Socrates asks. If this is true, the noblest pots must be base compared with the race of maidens, and the noblest virgin must be base compared to a

82. See, e.g., Dorothy Tarrant, *The "Hippias Major" Attributed to Plato; With Introductory Essays and Commentary* (Cambridge: Cambridge University Press, 1928; repr., New York: Arno Press, 1973); Alexander Nehamas, "Confusing Universals and Particulars in Plato's Early Dialogues," *Review of Metaphysics* 29 (1975): 288–306. Paul Woodruff, *Plato: "Hippias Major,"* trans. with commentary and essay (Indianapolis: Hackett, 1982), 127–31, argues that Hippias' art consists in large part in agreeing with his audience and ridiculing those who do not. None of these critics seem to have seen the connection between the conventional definition of "truth" Hippias offers here and the fundamentally materialistic understanding of the universe he betrays at the end of the dialogue, when he criticizes Socrates for failing to observe "the naturally large and continuous bodies of being" (*Hippias Major* 301b). Cf. David Sweet, "Introduction to the *Greater Hippias*," in Pangle, *Roots*, 345.

83. Woodruff, *Hippias*, 107, 109, 127.

84. In the *Protagoras* 337c–d, Hippias is the one who clearly distinguishes nature and convention. Woodruff (*Hippias*, 131–32) suggests that Plato singles out Hippias for the most devastating critique (by means of ridicule) because Hippias most thoroughly represents the sophistic position and its corrupting effects.

god. But if nobility is relative, so that things are more or less noble in comparison with each other, there must be something they have more or less of. Our interrogator would scoff at your answering of the question "What is noble?" with something that is no more noble than base.

What is it, Socrates asks Hippias, whose addition makes things noble or adorns them? Hippias suggests that it is gold. In that case, Socrates observes, Phidias erred, when sculpting a statue of the virgin goddess, by making the eyes of Athena out of ivory. Since Phidias was a great sculptor and his statue thought to be beautiful, it would appear to be not gold, but what is fitting (*prepon*), that makes something noble (or beautiful). And if that is the case, a figwood soup ladle is nobler than an implement of gold, which looks finer but gets too hot to use. Hippias again objects to the anonymous critic's introduction of such an inappropriate example and says he would not associate with such a vulgar fellow.[85] Socrates placates the sophist by agreeing (some readers might think sarcastically) that such an association would not be fitting for such a nobly clothed and shod man, who is so famous for his wisdom.

Hippias offers a third definition. What "will never appear base anywhere to anybody" is "to be rich and healthy, and honored by the Greeks, to reach old age, and, after providing a noble funeral for his parents, to be nobly and splendidly buried by his own offspring" (*Hippias Major* 291d–e). Socrates praises Hippias for having spoken in a "wonderful, grandiose way that is worthy of him" by giving what looks at first as if it is going to be a universal definition. Their anonymous interrogator, however, would laugh at the inept conclusion.[86] Pointing to the obvious contradiction between what is honored by the Greeks and what "will never appear base anywhere to anybody," Socrates asks Hippias whether his definition of the noble holds for all time as well as all places and all people. If so, it was not noble for Achilles to die young, before his immortal mother, the goddess Thetis,

---

85. The conversation proceeds, we see, only by means of the rhetorical device whereby Socrates introduces a fictional "anonymous" character to ask him the sorts of questions he himself usually addresses to his interlocutors. Since Socrates consistently claims to be asking these questions for the sake of acquiring knowledge himself, as much as if not more than for the sake of his interlocutors, the device does not constitute the break with the other dialogues that the "athetizers" (the critics who deny the authenticity of the dialogue on the grounds primarily of the comedy and the use of this device) claim.

86. Once again Plato reminds his readers of Aristophanes' comic critique of the philosopher, when Socrates suggests that, if his interrogator happens to have a stick, he will beat him—justly—for continuing to give such inept answers. Having studied under Socrates, Pheidippides (in the *Clouds* 1297–1345) convinces his father Strepsiades that, for the same reasons parents have a right to discipline their children, it is just for sons to beat their parents if the sons are wiser.

nor for Heracles to continue living without having buried his father Zeus.[87] When Hippias retorts that he was talking about human beings and not gods, Socrates observes that this definition of the noble does not seem to apply to heroes either. It has the same defect as the previous two inasmuch as it applies to some things but not to others. The reason Hippias' definitions all have this defect, we shall see, is that, according to Hippias (like Protagoras), everything is relative.

Having shown that the conventional understandings of nobility that Hippias first puts forward are not tenable, Socrates turns to the understanding of nobility he thinks Hippias actually holds and proves that it is no more valid. He begins by suggesting, in the name of his alter ego, that they consider what has proved to be the core of all three of Hippias' previous attempts at defining the noble—the fitting.[88] By objecting to the indecorous speech of their interrogator, Hippias demonstrated an attachment to this understanding in deed as well as in speech.[89]

Prepon refers to the clearly visible as well as to the fitting. The problem (implicit in the example of the soup ladle), Socrates points out, is that there is a difference between the apparent and the real. If what is truly noble evidently appeared to be so to everyone, there would be no disagreement about what it is. But, in fact, nothing is more debated both among private individuals and peoples in cities. That is the reason the definition of the noble often appears to be solely a matter of appearance—or, more fundamentally, convention—for example, to the sophist. If what is noble or fitting is merely a matter of convention, however, it cannot be really or truly noble. It is only apparently so.

Admitting that he is puzzled by the failure of "fitting" as a definition of the noble, Hippias assures Socrates that nevertheless he will easily be able to find an answer if he goes off and thinks about it by himself. (Hippias still believes in his own self-sufficiency.) But, after warning Hippias not to

---

87. Socrates may thus have indirectly reminded Hippias that, according to the stories recorded by Homer and Hesiod, younger generations of gods sometimes displaced their elders, as Cronus displaced Uranus and Zeus displaced his father, but that the changes in the generations were marked by violence, not honorable burial.

88. The connection is clearer in Greek. The verb *prepō* from which *prepon* is obviously derived, first means "to be clearly seen, conspicuous, or shine forth"; its second meaning is "to resemble," and its third meaning is "to become, suit, or fit" (*Greek-English Lexicon* [LSJ], s.v. *prepō*). Hippias himself aspires to shine conspicuously and yet do what is suitable or fitting.

89. Anyone tempted to think that the core of Hippias' understanding is merely a reflection of a superficial fop should recall Aristotle's description of virtuous activity in the *Nicomachean Ethics* 1104b20–25, 1106b15–25, as the right deed done in the right way at the right time by the right person, that is, the fitting.

boast, Socrates recants, assures Hippias that he believes him, and begs the sophist to stay to seek the noble with him.

Turning to what he suspects is the core of Hippias' understanding, Socrates suggests that what really makes things noble is their utility. He makes this suggestion in his own name, rather than eliciting it from Hippias or attributing it to their anonymous interlocutor, to see whether the sophist will agree with it. He does. Hippias emphatically agrees that what gives us power (*dynamis*) is noble, especially in politics. Even more than the "fitting," Plato thus indicates, Socrates' second suggestion expresses Hippias' own views (as opposed to those the sophist first suggested, because he thought others would agree). It appears for a moment that Hippias and Socrates will agree with each other, when Socrates surmises that, if power is noble, wisdom must be the noblest of all. Socrates immediately steps back from the identification of the powerful with the noble, however, on the grounds that men with power do not always know how to use it, in which case power is not beneficial. Hippias counters by suggesting that what is noble is what is powerful and useful for the good.

Readers might expect the discussion to turn to the question of what is good. But Socrates responds to Hippias' suggestion by emphasizing the subordination of the noble to the good: "If the noble is the cause of good, the good would come into being through the noble; and this is why we are eager for wisdom and all the other noble things, because their offspring, the good, is worthy of eagerness" (297b). In other words, if Hippias and his wisdom are noble, they are means of producing or attaining the good, but not good in themselves. Discomfited by Socrates' suggestion he and his art are merely instrumental, Hippias again assures the philosopher that he will think of a response if he withdraws to consider the matter by himself.

Insisting again on his ignorance in contrast to Hippias' purported perfection and self-sufficiency, Socrates says he cannot wait. He puts forward a third suggestion: the noble is that which is pleasing through hearing and sight. Hippias has not said what the good is for which he thinks the noble is powerful or useful. In the *Protagoras*, however, Hippias joined the other sophists in affirming that the good is the pleasant. Socrates' third suggestion is designed not only to bring out Hippias' own understanding of the good and the noble, but also to show the problems with it.

Hippias immediately agrees with Socrates' observation that a definition of the noble (or beautiful) in terms of pleasant sights and sounds does not apply very well to customs and laws. (We modern readers are also reminded of the tension we tend to see between the noble and the beautiful.)

But the sophist suggests that their anonymous interrogator may not notice. From beginning to end, readers see, the sophist remains more interested in maintaining appearances and besting his opponent than in the truth.[90] Socrates says that he cannot deceive himself; he thus finally admits that he is the anonymous interrogator. But, Socrates characteristically insists, once again in explicit contrast to the sophist, he cannot acquire wisdom on his own; he needs someone to converse with. And in laying out the problem with his third suggested definition, Socrates indicates the reasons why.

Since all pleasures are not noble, there must be something other than pleasure that distinguishes the noble. That other characteristic cannot be either visibility or audibility, because the pleasures coming from sight or hearing do not have the same source. "Can two things share a characteristic that neither possesses as an individual?" Socrates asks Hippias. The sophist, who prides himself on his mathematical knowledge, replies they cannot. Socrates points out, however, that taken separately, every one is odd, but two together constitute an even number. The whole is more than the sum of its parts; it has characteristics the parts do not share, and vice versa. The case of the noble is even more complicated. According to Socrates' third definition, nobility appears to be something that distinguishes visible and audible pleasures from others, which both visible and audible pleasures thus share, but which visible and audible sources of pleasure each can have separately, not necessarily in combination with each other.

In contrast to the pleasures of taste and touch, the pleasures we experience through sight and hearing not only involve a certain distance between the source of the effect and the one affected; pleasures of sight and sound also involve the perception of a certain pleasing order or harmony of disparate parts. This appears to be why Socrates suggests, both in the *Symposium* and the *Phaedrus*, that philosophy originates in the desire for the noble or beautiful, a desire that provokes some people to ask, first, what is truly noble, and then, what nobility itself is. The complex structure of the noble (reflected in the difficulty translators have of rendering the word *kalos* by a single adjective—beautiful, noble, fair, fine, admirable—applicable to statues, music, laws, and practices as well as to people), whose perception requires a combination of sensation and intellection, points to, if it does not exactly mirror, the complex structure of the whole.

90. Cf. Ivor Ludlam, *"Hippias Major": An Interpretation* (Stuttgart: Franz Steiner, 1991), 69, 78.

The sophist is not willing to join Socrates in a further investigation of this structure or order, however. Although he had admitted to some perplexity in the course of their conversation, at the end Hippias shows he has not been moved.[91] He reiterates the conviction with which he began: the best thing in human life is "to be able to compose a speech nobly and well in a law court or council chamber or any other ruling group to which the speech is addressed and to go away having persuaded them and taking off not the least, but the largest of prizes, the salvation of oneself and one's money and friends" (304a–b). Socrates thus concludes by contrasting his own sense of perplexity (*aporia*) with the sophist's complacent conventionality. When Socrates honestly confesses his perplexity, he is berated by people like Hippias who say that his questions are foolish; when he is convinced by them that he should learn public speaking, however, he is berated by the anonymous interlocutor at home. Nevertheless, Socrates believes that he has benefited from the two-sided critique. He has come to understand the meaning of the proverbial saying, "The noble things are difficult" (304e). The sophists tried to make them look easy.

Although the differences between the sophist and the philosopher appear to concern the way human beings should live, Plato reminds his readers in the *Hippias Major*, these differences have deep foundations. If all things are continuous bodies, as Hippias asserts, all differences of kind and value are established by convention. According to his autobiographical statement in the *Phaedo*, Socrates turned away from the study of pre-Socratic cosmology, which was characterized by the attempt to reduce things to their elements or homogeneous common denominators, precisely because such accounts could not explain human life and action. Insofar as Hippias does not merely articulate a version of the theory but embodies a way of life based on such a homogeneous cosmology, he represents an important test of the rationale for Socratic inquiry.

In the *Hippias Major* Plato shows that the problem with such pre-Socratic science is not merely, as Aristophanes suggests in the *Clouds*, that it leads its practitioners to believe rhetorical skill will render them immune from political prosecution and that it is safe, therefore, to proceed with their studies openly rather than to hide or disguise their wisdom. Hippias is emphatically

---

91. At 300d Socrates wonders, therefore, whether Hippias has not been playing with him—indeed, deceiving him—in an attempt to be pleasing. He obviously has not taken the argument seriously.

concerned about his safety and, consequently, emphasizes the importance of participating in politics. The sophist's problem is that he imagines himself to be all knowing and hence self-sufficient; he does not understand the limits of his knowledge or powers, because he does not recognize the way differences of opinion, particularly about what is important in human life, raise questions about the underlying unity or intelligibility of the whole.[92] He does not, therefore, seek to test his own opinions or to learn from others in philosophical conversations.

Unlike Socrates, Plato shows, Hippias is not erotic himself, nor has he learned the significance of human eros. By depicting Socrates as a sophist as well as a cosmological philosopher like Hippias, Plato suggests, Aristophanes not merely revealed his failure to understand the difference between Socrates and his predecessors. The comic poet demonstrated the inadequacy of his own understanding of human eros.

B. The Homeric Origins of the Incoherence of the Greek Understanding of the Noble and Good

In the *Hippias Minor* Plato shows even more clearly how false, how lacking in integrity and coherence, the sophist's stance was. Precisely because he adapted his speeches to the views of his audience, the sophist contradicted his own words in practice. At the same time, Socrates (or Plato) shows that the incoherence in his contemporaries' understanding of the *kalos k'agathos* could and should be traced back to Homer.

After Hippias delivered the speech he had invited Socrates to hear in their previous conversation, the sophist's Athenian host asked Socrates why he had nothing to say about it either in praise or refutation.[93] Rather than answer Eudicus' question directly, Socrates asked the sophist whether he shared the opinion of his Athenian host's father that Achilles was a better man than Odysseus. Caught by the need to make good his repeated claim at Olympia to be able to answer any question and his desire not to offend his Athenian host any more than the Spartans by contradicting their

92. Like the Socrates Aristophanes portrays, but unlike Plato's philosopher, Hippias is shown to be an emphatically unerotic man. Cf. Leo Strauss, *Socrates and Aristophanes* (New York: Basic Books, 1966), 1–53.

93. By raising as alternatives the two goals of the sophist's speech, Eudicus' question shows how much he has come under the influence of the sophist. Eudicus' observation that he and Socrates are the only auditors left who claim to pursue philosophy shows his inability to distinguish sophistry from philosophy and the reason why Socrates needs to distinguish himself from Hippias.

beliefs and practices, Hippias was pressed by Socrates into defending the proposition that Achilles was better because he was more honest than the "versatile" Odysseus.[94]

As we know from their previous conversation in private, Hippias praised the wisdom of his predecessors to avoid the envy of his contemporaries, even though he thought his own art was far superior to those of old. Like Odysseus, the sophist lied to protect himself. But, Socrates now reminds Hippias in public, his boasting at Olympia before all the Greeks that he had never met anyone wiser than he destroys the effectiveness of his prudential speech.[95]

Socrates shows that the sophist contradicts himself not only in speech but also in deed, when, following Homer, he maintains that simplicity or truthfulness is the most noble human trait. First Socrates gets Hippias to agree that the liar is capable, prudent, and wise (as the sophist claimed he was). Then Socrates gets the sophist to admit that someone (like Hippias) who knows the arts of calculation, geometry, and astronomy would be able to deceive someone else about those subjects better than a person who has no knowledge of them.[96] Socrates reminds Hippias of how many different kinds of knowledge he claims to possess—not only mathematical but also practical; he recalls that the sophist once appeared at Olympia dressed exclusively in things that he had made, bragging not only about his knowledge of poetry—rhyme, harmony, and diction—but also (and most relevantly in the context) about an artful device he had for remembering. Finally Socrates challenges the sophist to refute the logical conclusion that only a man who knows the truth can say what is false.[97]

---

94. Hippias first tries to avoid the question by responding that Homer shows Achilles to be the best, Nestor the wisest, and Odysseus the most versatile. Leaving the question of the character of Nestor's wisdom apparently in abeyance—Hippias was speaking through the mouth of Nestor in his speech—Socrates first questions the sophist about Homer's portrayal of the two protagonists of his two poems, especially in book 9 of the *Iliad*. Then, because Homer is no longer present to answer questions, Socrates asks Hippias about his own views, so pointing out the indirect, if not deceptive way Hippias usually puts them forward (in the mouth and presumably on the authority of another).

95. We should also note the contrast between Hippias' public boasting at a shrine that no one was wiser than he and Socrates' own more modest reaction to the Delphic oracle's pronouncement that no one was wiser than he.

96. Cf. *Plato: "Ion," "Hippias Minor," "Laches," "Protagoras,"* trans. with comment by R. E. Allen (New Haven: Yale University Press, 1996), 27.

97. Mary Whitlock Blundell, "Character and Meaning in Plato's *Lesser Hippias,*" *Oxford Studies in Ancient Philosophy* supp. (Oxford: Clarendon Press, 1992), 149–51, also argues that this "strategically located speech" trivializes Hippias' mastery of so many arts while pointing to the absence of dialectics and argumentative subtlety.

Accusing Socrates of breaking the question up into small details rather than contending with the whole, Hippias offers to demonstrate in an ample speech with many proofs that Homer shows that Achilles is better than Odysseus and not a liar. Socrates can counter with questions, if he wishes, and the audience will know who speaks better. Characteristically trying to replace competition with cooperation, Socrates admits forthrightly that Hippias is wiser; that is the reason Socrates thinks he can benefit from asking the sophist questions. Nevertheless, the philosopher punishes the sophist for not submitting to the discipline of the argument by reciting passages from the *Iliad* that follow the one Hippias quotes about Achilles' hatred for him "who hides one thing in his mind but says something else," in which Achilles clearly contradicts his initial promise to depart the next day. Did "the son of Thetis, who was educated by the most wise Chiron" forget what he himself had said so quickly (*Hippias Minor* 371d)? Had the inventor of the "artful device for remembering" (368d) forgotten what Achilles said?

If Achilles says different things to different people, Hippias responds, it is not a matter of artful contrivance (as Socrates had suggested) but an expression of his guilelessness (*euētheia*).[98] When Socrates concludes that, in that case, Odysseus is the better man because he decides deliberately whether to speak the truth or not, the sophist reminds the philosopher that the laws treat those who do injustice knowingly more harshly than those who do wrong involuntarily.

Just as Hippias tries to have the audience determine who is the better speaker (even though he claims to possess the art, whereas his opponent admits his ignorance), so the sophist appeals to the law to determine what is just, good, and noble. He bases his argument on convention, even though in the *Protagoras* he had stated that by nature the wise should rule. Although Socrates frequently maintains that no one does something bad or wrong voluntarily (and so has puzzled many commentators by arguing the contrary here), the philosopher observes that their conversation has made him think that "those who harm human beings, who do injustice, lie, deceive, and go wrong voluntarily rather than involuntarily are better than those who do so involuntarily" (372d). They are better because they are able to choose to be good or bad; they can choose because they possess

---

98. Following James Leake's translation, *"Lesser Hippias,"* in Pangle, *Roots*, 292n13.

the relevant knowledge or skill.[99] Those without it do not have the capacity to choose.

The philosopher admits that he vacillates, but he claims that this vacillation is a sign of his ignorance. It would be terrible if "wise" men like Hippias also vacillated, because in that case there would be no hope of remedy. The difference between opinion and knowledge, Socrates explains in the *Meno*, is that, having no firm foundation, opinion is easily changed, whereas knowledge is not. As we have seen, Hippias does vacillate—with a vengeance. His vacillation shows that he does not have the wisdom on which he prides himself. Claiming to be wiser than any other human being, he repeatedly bows to the superior wisdom not merely of his predecessors in speech but of his audience in fact. He bows not merely out of respect for their physical power (or concern for his own physical safety) but more fundamentally because his sense of his own superiority depends on their recognition and applause. Although he claims to know what is natural and that it is the same everywhere, he never challenges the justice or wisdom of the laws of the particular cities to which he travels.[100] In this dialogue Socrates claims to have vacillated in his opinion as to whether it is best to do injustice voluntarily or involuntarily. He never vacillated, however, in his desire to find out what is really just or his conviction that it is better to know and act on the basis of that knowledge than to follow the opinion of anyone else.

---

99. Following Aristotle *Metaphysics* 1035a8 and Grote, *Plato*, 1.399, John R. Pottenger argues that Socrates here fuses and so confuses the ethical with an evaluative measure of excellence. Pottenger, "The Sage and the Sophist," *Interpretation* 23, no. 1 (February 1995): 55. The problem with such a distinction—and a reason that the word "ethical" is not found in Plato as it is in Aristotle—is that one who does not know (or lacks the skill) does not have the ability to choose, and the "ethical" good resides in making the good choice. As we see in the case of Hippias, who intends to deceive when he praises the ancients, the liar who does not know the truth may inadvertently state it. Likewise, a man who believes that he is telling the truth, like Hippias when he brags that he has never met anyone wiser than he, may state something false, again without knowing it. When Socrates praises Hippias' superior wisdom he appears to be the man who deceives knowingly—and to be superior to the "truthful" Hippias. (Cf. Friedländer, *Plato*, 2:139.) Whether Socrates is also unjust or bad in taking Hippias at his word is another question. At the end of the dialogue Socrates returns to something like his usual contention that no one willingly does wrong, when he raises the question of whether there is actually a man who knows and would choose to do wrong. As Leake points out in his introduction to the *Lesser Hippias* (303–5), at times it may be better for others as well as oneself not to tell the truth. Lying is probably a requirement of politics; it may even play a role in attracting young people to philosophy. As Socrates insists at the end of his first private conversation with Hippias, however, a seeker of truth must never lie to himself.

100. As Leake points out in a footnote to his translation of the *Lesser Hippias* 376c (299), the Greek word rendered by "vacillate," *planein*, "to lead astray," means "to wander" in the passive.

V. What We Learn from Socrates' First Conversations

In the *Apology* Socrates tells the jury that, in response to the oracle, he had gone first to question the politicians about what they claimed to know. In his first conversations, Plato shows, the philosopher quickly discovered that both Athenian politicians and their would-be teachers considered political preeminence to be the greatest human achievement possible. But neither the sophists nor their students could give a coherent account of what knowledge or other virtues make a man worthy of great honor or why political preeminence constitutes the acme of human nobility and goodness.

Although the sophist Protagoras claimed to teach others how to manage their affairs better in public as well as private, he demonstrated his own lack of practical, political wisdom in openly challenging democratic practices and prejudices of his audience. As Plato reminds his readers in the *Hippias Major*, democracies were the only regimes that allowed sophists to come and teach their young people. More tightly regulated regimes like Sparta did not. Yet, Plato also shows, when Hippias tried to be more prudent than Protagoras by saying only what his audience wanted to hear and not explicitly asserting or sharing his own superior wisdom, he also contradicted his own words in practice. By seeking to entertain and impress his audience with his own learning rather than to instruct them, he appeared to be something of a buffoon.

The sophists at least understood that some kind of knowledge was necessary, if only instrumentally, for human beings to acquire the highest honors. When Socrates asked Alcibiades what he could offer his fellow citizens to convince them to put the direction of their affairs into his hands, the ambitious young man readily admitted that he did not have any particular expertise. Neither he nor Plato's own relatives, Charmides and Critias, understood why they had to concern themselves about meeting the needs of others in order to acquire the honor, wealth, and power they desired. In other words, they did not see why they needed to be just or moderate. Thinking only about their own interests, they did not recognize that the satisfaction of their own desires depended on the opinions and cooperation of others. These self-satisfied young men believed it would suffice to display their own superior beauty, wealth, cunning, or force. They failed to see the way in which they depended on others not merely for reputation or honor but, even more fundamentally, for self-preservation and the knowledge needed to secure it. They did not recognize their own limitations as human beings, ironically, because they were not able or willing to countenance a higher, better form of existence. Lacking self-knowledge, they did not know what is truly noble and good. Nor could they learn from the sophists, who claimed to be wise (and, in the case of Hippias, noble), but presented their wisdom only as means of acquiring political power, honor, and wealth.

Socrates showed that the sophists could not even give an adequate account of the means. The way most, if not all, individuals in antiquity acquired the offices and honors to which ambitious young Athenians such as Alcibiades and Critias aspired was by serving successfully as a general. To lead an army successfully, one had to be not only courageous but also savvy. But in his conversation with Protagoras, Socrates showed that the sophist could not explain how or why courage was a virtue like wisdom, justice, moderation, or piety; he could not explain how the "noble" (courage) and the "good" (the other virtues) were or could be combined. Nor, Socrates then demonstrated in the *Laches*, could men who had already attained the office of general in Athens. Neither Laches nor Nicias could give a coherent account of the way in which a courageous man necessarily combines fortitude in the face of death with prudence. Neither understood or embodied this human virtue, Plato indicates, because neither had self-knowledge. Neither general had recognized, much less thought out, the implications of the fact that he feared and thus tried to avoid public dishonor more than death. Neither acting politician understood what is truly noble and good any better than the sophists or their ambitious young students.

In depicting these early conversations, Plato not only shows how Socrates proved that his contemporaries had an inadequate understanding of the noble and good, and therefore needed to seek a better one. Plato also defends Socrates from his first accuser.

In the *Clouds* Aristophanes suggested that Socrates was politically imprudent and overly proud of his wisdom. In the *Protagoras* Plato shows, however, that Socrates understood democratic politics and the danger of boasting about one's wisdom much better than his famous predecessor. In the *Clouds* Aristophanes indicated that Socrates was not guarded enough about the investigations of things under the earth and in the heavens in which he and his students engaged. He openly announced his disbelief in the gods of the city. But in the *Alcibiades I*, Plato shows that Socrates repeatedly aroused the young man's skepticism by referring to his god. That god might not have been one of the Olympian deities traditionally

worshipped by the Athenians, but the oracle at Delphi was a publicly recognized authority. Instead of bragging about his own wisdom, much less
claiming to be the equal of a god, as Aristophanes' Socrates does in his
basket or Critias in his reinterpretation of the Delphic inscriptions, Plato
shows that Socrates insisted on the need to seek knowledge, first and foremost, of oneself. And that knowledge consisted, first and foremost, in the
recognition that a human being would never be or become a god.

Because he taught both natural science and the art of speaking, Aristophanes (in the *Clouds* 359–60) called Socrates a sophist and associated
him with Prodicus. In the *Protagoras* (341c–d) Plato shows that Socrates first
appealed to Prodicus and the careful distinctions he drew among words,
but that Socrates then denigrated such verbal distinctions and displays of
learning. Plato's accounts of Socrates' early conversations support the philosopher's claim in the *Apology* that he respects those who had cosmological knowledge and wishes that he himself possessed the sort of wisdom
that would enable him to make others virtuous, but that he does not share
in such wisdom. Not claiming to teach anyone anything, Socrates did not,
in contrast to the sophists, ask for money from those who listened to him
converse.

In the *Clouds* Aristophanes also suggested that Socrates was indifferent to, if not unaware of, the danger that he would arouse the envy and
anger of others, not merely by bragging about his own wisdom but by
undermining the affectionate respect sons had for their fathers. But in the
Laches Plato shows that Socrates, instead of taking young men away from
their progenitors, tried to get the elders to discuss what sort of education
they should not merely offer the young but seek for themselves. It was the
elders who refused, because they were either too old or too busy.

Finally, in the *Clouds* Aristophanes suggested that Socrates did not understand the passions that led to violent conflict among men in the absence
of law. Because Socrates was so ascetic, he did not feel and so did not recognize the force of human desire. In the *Charmides*, however, Plato shows
dramatically that Socrates was by no means immune to sexual attraction.
In the *Symposium* Plato reports Socrates' claim that *ta erōtika* are the only
things he knows. In the *Alcibiades I* Plato illustrates the way Socrates could
use his knowledge of human desire not merely to intuit what human beings really want, but also to outline a way they might achieve satisfaction.
We should not be surprised, therefore, to see that Socrates' account of
what he learned about the benefits of eros from Diotima in the *Sympo-*

sium is delivered in response, at least in part, to a speech attributed to Aristophanes.

In the *Laches* and the *Hippias Minor*, Plato suggests that the inadequate understandings of the noble and the good held by Socrates' contemporaries could be traced back to the poets, particularly to Homer. In the next set of dialogues Plato thus shows Socrates formulating a new understanding of the noble and good explicitly in criticism of and in contrast to the poets. Just as Socrates used the argument about the ideas he formulated in response to the difficulties he found in earlier cosmological theories to criticize the Eleatics, so we shall see he uses his contention that there are a variety of purely intelligible, eternal beings (that he sometimes, although not always calls ideas), especially of the noble and the good, to show, contrary to the poets, that there is both a natural (in the constitution of human beings) and an ontological (in the character of being or beings as a whole) basis for a truly satisfying form of human existence.

That way of life is Socratic philosophy. But, as Socrates repeatedly emphasizes, his form of philosophy cannot be practiced alone. What human beings most want to know is what is good for us. In order to know what is good for us, he tells Alcibiades, we have to know who or what we are. We can learn something about our bodies by looking at our own reflections and comparing ourselves to others. We are composites of soul and body, however, and we cannot see our souls. To discover the character of the force or forces that animate us, we have to look at what moves others. Since neither the desires nor the fears that move human beings are visible directly, we have to look at their expressions in words and deeds.

The things most people want are usually called the "noble" or "beautiful" and "good." The problem with knowing what is truly noble and good, Socrates shows in these early conversations, is not simply that people disagree (although they do). Nor is the problem simply that what initially appears to be noble or good proves, upon examination or in practice, not really to be so. The problem that emerges first and most clearly in these conversations with regard to the virtue of courage is that what appears to be noble, in the case of an individual who risks and loses his life in defending those he loves, for example, is not good for the individual. To put the point more generally and abstractly, as in the case of the two odd units that added together make an even two, the characteristics of the particular are not the same as the characteristics of the whole or combination of particulars. The "nobility" of a warrior who risks his life to defend his community may be good in the sense of useful for the community, but the useful appears to be a matter of calculation and thus not noble—or even good—in itself. Is the noble, then, merely a particular characteristic of an individual (or thing) that is useful for others, as Socrates suggested in the only definition he offered in his own name in the *Hippias Major*? If so, the noble is merely instrumental, consisting in characteristics admired by others, because and insofar as these characteristics are useful to others, as the sophists tended to suggest. In that case, the conventional description of an excellent human being as "noble and good" does not make sense, because the noble is subordinate to rather than coordinate with the good, and so essentially redundant. (The noble is noble because it is good for . . .) As Plato reminds his readers in the *Hippias Minor*, nobility, as represented by Achilles, does not appear to be even instrumentally good for an individual. In the *Iliad* Achilles' reward for sacrificing his life in order to revenge the death of his beloved friend Patroclus is immortal fame. But in the *Odyssey* Homer portrays Achilles in Hades reiterating what he told Agamemnon's ambassadors in the *Iliad*: no fame or power or wealth can benefit a dead man. He would rather be a living slave than a dead king. In the *Odyssey* Homer also shows that his other hero has to learn that wealth, knowledge of the world, or even an unending life of pleasure with the beautiful nymph Calypso is not worth the loss of all mortal companions. Friendship or mutual understanding is good. A shared understanding of our condition is possible only among mortals; precisely because human beings are mortal, however, our friendships also must come to an end. And that end, death (or existence as a mere, empty shade who cannot communicate with anyone else), is bad. What people often say is noble is not merely not good. Risking one's life, except to preserve one's friends and family, is irrational. By presenting two heroes who embodied the two different aspects or characteristics thought to be desirable in political leaders, Homer suggested that traditional ideas about what is noble and good in human life were literally incoherent. As Protagoras was forced to admit, the courageous and the wise are not the same, nor can they simply or always be combined.

In seeking to determine whether there is something truly noble or good in itself and not just relative to other things, Plato shows, Socrates was seeking knowledge of something like the ideas about which Parmenides had raised questions, even though he did not explicitly mention the ideas. Parmenides had asked, for example, what there were ideas of. Socrates told Parmenides that he thought there were ideas not only of the one and the many or likeness, but also of "the just, the noble, the good, and all such" (*Parmenides* 130b). To show that there is an idea of the noble, which is essentially different from the good, but that a single character can participate in the noble, the good, and the just, Socrates first had to prove that the understanding of the noble and the good that his contemporaries had inherited from Homer was not correct. Socrates then had to present a new understanding of the noble, the good, and the just. Plato shows him doing just that in the next set of dialogues.

PART II

Two
Paradigms of
Philosophy

5

Socrates' Positive Teaching

In the *Apology* Socrates says that, in response to the oracle's paradoxical pronouncement that there was no one wiser than he, he went first to question the politicians because they claimed to know what is good. But in the first conversations Plato shows Socrates having after his "divine instruction" (by Diotima or the oracle), the philosopher found that neither his politically ambitious compatriots, nor the foreign sophists who claimed to be able to teach them, had a coherent understanding of the noble or good. They had acquired the incoherent opinions they had about human excellence from the poets, especially Homer, who claimed in the *Odyssey* (8.61–64) to teach "the good and bad of human life." As Socrates reports in the *Apology*, so Plato shows in a second set of dialogues that take place during the second part of the Peloponnesian War, Socrates thus went to question the poets after he had interrogated the politicians.

In his first conversations with his contemporaries, Socrates contented himself with showing that their opinions about the noble and good were incoherent and urging them to join him in further investigations to discover what is truly noble and good. None of his interlocutors accepted his invitation, however. Like many later commentators on these "elenctic" dialogues, his interlocutors had to admit that Socrates had refuted them, but they were not persuaded to engage in many further conversations with him. Alcibiades and Critias associated with him for a while, but they eventually left the philosopher to pursue their tyrannical political ambitions. In dialogues set later, during the second part of the Peloponnesian War, Plato shows, Socrates thus took another tack. In the *Symposium* he not only explicitly engaged in a contest with the poets to see who had the best understanding

of human passion or eros. In explicating his own, rather different understanding of the character of the strongest, most fundamental human desire and its object, Socrates also linked his analysis of human eros to his
early argument about the ideas. Rather than merely refuting the opinions
of his contemporaries, in the *Symposium*, *Phaedrus*, *Republic*, and *Philebus* he
provided them with an alternative, more positive teaching about the best
form of human existence.

I. Socrates' Knowledge of the Erotic Things

A. The Philosopher in Contest with the Poets: *Symposium*

Plato indicates that he is depicting a new stage in the emergence of Socratic philosophy by drawing a series of parallels between Socrates' initial confrontation with the sophists in the *Protagoras* and his first contest
with the poets in the *Symposium*. First, all the speakers at Agathon's dinner
party were present at Socrates' initial confrontation with Protagoras except Aristophanes.[1] Second, both dialogues occur a year before the onset
of war—the war between the Peloponnesians and Athens, in the first case,
and the Athenian invasion of Sicily in the second. Third, both dialogues
are narrated; indeed, both have a two-part dramatic introduction preceding the account of the major speeches or contest. Fourth, in both dialogues Socrates takes a young companion with him to hear the speeches
of famous men of words.[2]

In light of these similarities, the differences also stand out. Aristophanes
is the only speaker in the *Symposium* not present in the *Protagoras*, and his
speech proves to be literally central. Since Protagoras does not take part
in the *Symposium*, the comic poet appears to take the sophist's place as
Socrates' chief antagonist. In his *Clouds* Aristophanes had depicted Socrates
not merely as a sophist who overestimated the power of his own argumentative or rhetorical ability to protect him from prosecution in court, but

---

1. In the *Protagoras* 315c–16a, Socrates reports that Phaedrus and Eryximachus were among
those listening to Hippias, whereas Pausanias and Agathon were in the circle around Prodicus.
Alcibiades was also there, as well as, of course, Socrates. Cf. Rosen, *Plato's "Symposium,"* 24–25;
Strauss, *Symposium*, 25.

2. The fact that Hippocrates' father's name is Apollodorus constitutes another link between
the *Protagoras* and the *Symposium*, even though it is unlikely that the two men named Apollodorus
are the same, since the narrator of the *Symposium* becomes an associate of Socrates more than
twenty years after the conversation related in the *Protagoras* takes place.

also as an ascetic who lacked all understanding of human eros.[3] Plato defended his teacher from the charge that he was a sophist who lacked political prudence in the dialogues set at the beginning and end of the first part of the Peloponnesian War. He has Socrates respond to the more serious accusation, that he does not understand eros and its implications for the organization of human life, in the dialogues set during the second part of the war, beginning with the *Symposium*.

Both the change in dramatis personae and the change in setting signal a shift in direction and tone. In the first part of the war, the Spartans had arguably been the aggressors, whereas Athenians merely defended their lands and allies; in Sicily the Athenians were clearly the aggressors. It is not simply the morality of the foreign teachers and their effects on the young that are now in question; it is the morality of Athens and her native philosopher. In the *Protagoras* Socrates tried to protect Hippocrates from the invidious influence of the sophist; in the *Symposium* Agathon threatens to take Socrates to court on account of the philosopher's hubris, and Alcibiades later indicts him before a jury of his lovers.

The differences in the character of the narrative and narrator(s) indicate a change not only in the circumstances but also in the content of the two dialogues. In the *Protagoras* the sophist bragged that, unlike his predecessors, particularly the poets, he openly declared that he was wise. Mimicking the directness of Protagoras' claims to excellence, Socrates immediately related the story of his victory over the sophist to the first group of Athenians he met. In the *Symposium* a recent associate of Socrates named Apollodorus retells the account of the speeches delivered at the party in honor of Agathon's first victory, which Apollodorus had heard from another associate of Socrates named Aristodemus many years after the fact.[4] Like poets, the narrators of the *Symposium* retell a preexisting

3. On Aristophanes' critique of Socrates, see Strauss, *Socrates and Aristophanes*; the gloss on same in Catherine Zuckert, *Postmodern Platos* (Chicago: University of Chicago Press, 1996), 133–37; and Mary P. Nichols, *Socrates and the Political Community: An Ancient Debate* (Albany: SUNY Press, 1987), 8–28.

4. The date at which the events at Agathon's house are retold has been the subject of some debate. Arguing that the retelling cannot have taken place after Socrates' death in 399 because Apollodorus speaks of his discipleship in the present tense (172e) and also that it must have occurred a number of years after Agathon's departure from Athens in 408 or 407, R. G. Bury, *The "Symposium" of Plato* (Cambridge: Cambridge University Press, 1966), lxvi, suggests a date of 400. Nussbaum objects (*Fragility*, 169–70). Alcibiades was recalled to Athens in 407 by the restored democracy but then lost prestige and retired to the Chersonese. In 405 his advice concerning the battle of Aegospotami was disregarded, and he departed for Asia Minor, where he was assassinated in 404 in a small village in Phrygia. Aristophanes' *Frogs* testifies to the importance of the

story of events in the distant past. They relate the deeds and speeches of others rather than their own, and they have to rely, therefore, on their memory (the mother of the Muses traditionally invoked by epic poets).[5]

The characteristics of the two narrators of the *Symposium* also reraise the question about Socrates' influence on those who associated with him, but again, in somewhat different form. Alcibiades and Critias seemed to accept some of Socrates' teachings but did not act according to them; Aristodemus and Apollodorus imitate the philosopher. Like Socrates, Aristodemus is said to be a short man (and hence, according to ancient Greek notions, ugly) who goes around barefoot. He demonstrates his willingness to break the conventions of polite society when he agrees to accompany Socrates, uninvited, to Agathon's party. Apollodorus is extreme in speech. According to Glaucon, Apollodorus constantly rages against himself and everyone else—except Socrates.[6] He too appears to imitate the philosopher insofar as he insists that no one else is wise or virtuous—except Socrates, who admits that he is not.[7] Neither Apollodorus nor Aristodemus becomes a tyrant, but both are manifestly immoderate. Socrates does not appear to have been a better teacher by means of example than he was by precept. He enters a competition with the poets to be the educator of Athenian youths with even greater handicaps—his own bad looks and apparently insidious influence on his associates—than he had entered into his first competition with the famous sophist as a relatively unknown young Athenian.

In the *Protagoras* Socrates engaged in a contest of words at the behest of his young companion Hippocrates, but in the *Symposium* he goes to Agathon's house on his own. Having bathed and put on shoes, Socrates appears to be uncharacteristically concerned about his external appearance. It is not clear, however, that his presence at Agathon's celebration is

---

question of what to do about Alcibiades, in Athens in 405. Nussbaum thus suggests that Athenian aristocrats such as Glaucon would have been particularly interested in hearing an account of the earlier conversation in 405 or 404, before Alcibiades' death. Rosen (*Plato's "Symposium,"* 7) thinks that Glaucon's error in thinking the dinner party had occurred recently points to a dramatic date of 401–400 for Apollodorus' recounting of the story he heard from Aristodemus.

5. Cf. Helen Bacon, "Socrates Crowned," *Virginia Quarterly Review* 35 (1959): 418–20, on the poetic character of the distanced narrative—that is, one removed from the events both in person and in time.

6. The fact that Apollodorus relates the story of the banquet to a man named Glaucon, who could but is not explicitly said to be Plato's brother, links the *Symposium* to the *Republic*. Rosen (*Plato's "Symposium,"* 11–15) points out other similarities in the dramatic introductions of the two dialogues.

7. Plato reminds his readers of the difference in character between Socrates and his associate, however, in the *Phaedo* 117d by showing that Apollodorus cannot restrain his tears at the philosopher's death.

completely voluntary. Disliking crowds, the philosopher explains to Aristodemus, he had refused to go the first night. He has dressed up in order to be a match for his handsome (*kalos*) host. Expecting a contest, Socrates invites Aristodemus to accompany him for support. Observing that "If two go together . . . , there's one [to espy] before another," Socrates suggests that he is expecting serious, if not altogether open, conflict with the poet.[8] Pausing in a doorway apparently immersed in thought (perhaps about the impending confrontation and his strategy therein), Socrates lets the hapless Aristodemus arrive first as a kind of defensive foil.[9] Graciously inviting Aristodemus to join them, Agathon sends a servant to fetch Socrates, but the philosopher refuses to budge. Agathon orders the servant to go again, but Aristodemus refuses to allow him. To this extent Aristodemus protects his mentor and his thought from interruption and forced subordination.

Socrates arrives on his own halfway through the meal, and Agathon asks the philosopher to sit next to him so that he can absorb the wisdom Socrates acquired on the porch. Socrates points to the substantive difference between himself and the poet by wishing that wisdom were the sort of thing that could be acquired through contact, that is, that it would flow the way water does from a full into an empty cup. If it were, he could gain from Agathon. But, according to Socrates, in contrast to almost all previous poets and philosophers, wisdom neither flows nor is it sensible.[10] Socrates suggests, moreover, that the wisdom each of them possesses is of a different sort. What wisdom Socrates has is poor (*phaulos*) and dubious, whereas Agathon's is brilliant and expansive. Only yesterday, the tragedian had astonished a crowd of 30,000. But, Socrates reminds his audience, philosophy appeals to very few. Recognizing the insult implicit in Socrates' emphasis on his popularity, Agathon responds, "Don't be hubristic," and threatens to take Socrates to court later, with Dionysus serving as judge. The poet and the philosopher will compete in the tragedian's home with

8. The saying is taken from *Iliad* 10.224, the spying trip Odysseus and Diomedes take into the Trojan camp, where they secretly kill several soldiers.

9. The two depictions of Socrates standing immersed in thought occur (and only occur) in the *Symposium*: here at the beginning (173d–e) and then in Alcibiades' report of Socrates' behavior at Potidaea (220c–d).

10. In the *Theaetetus* (152d–e), Socrates explicitly states that all earlier poets and philosophers except Parmenides taught that everything is fundamentally in flux. Like Parmenides, Socrates consistently argues that only the eternal and unchanging is truly intelligible; but unlike Parmenides, Socrates consistently suggests that there are a number of such intelligible beings or ideas. We are able to distinguish "sensible" things from one another because and to the extent to which they "participate" in the intelligible forms of being and do not constantly flow or merge into one another.

the god of the theater presiding.[11] Socrates had reason to worry about going into Agathon's court.[12]

1. The Students of the Sophists

It is not Agathon but the physician Eryximachus who sets the terms of the contest that follows. Instead of drink, the doctor suggests, they should compete with speeches in praise of the heretofore neglected god Eros. They dismiss the flute girl, but not, as Socrates urged in his critique of Protagoras (*Protagoras* 347b–48a), simply in order to converse among themselves. Agathon, his lover Pausanias, and Aristophanes feel the effects of their overindulgence the night before, whereas the doctor and his beloved Phaedrus can never imbibe much. Socrates alone appears to be immune to the intoxicating effects of alcohol.[13]

The doctor and his beloved Phaedrus show themselves to be no more independent in making speeches than in their bodily desires. Like sophists with whom they studied, they begin by quoting poets. Giving his beloved credit as his inspiration or muse, Eryximachus observes, "The beginning of my speech is taken from Euripides' *Melanippe*: 'Not mine the tale'—but Phaedrus's here" (*Symposium* 177a). Phaedrus had complained that neither poets nor sophists had praised Love as they had heroes like Heracles, or even useful but lowly substances like salt. He also begins his speech by quoting from Hesiod's *Theogony*.

a. Phaedrus

The references to poetry are not the only way in which the speeches of Phaedrus, Pausanias, and Eryximachus reflect their earlier studies with the sophists. Following the precepts of their teachers concerning the need

---

11. In the *Clouds* Aristophanes depicted a sophist who could talk his way out of any court case. Would Plato's Socrates be able to outtalk not merely sophists and rhetoricians but the popular masters of verse whom, Aristophanes later suggested, the god of theater loved so much that he was willing to brave the terrors of Hades to revive one? The question Aristophanes' Dionysus uses in the *Frogs* (1421ff.) to adjudicate the contest between Aeschylus and Euripides is that of how to deal with Alcibiades, which was a, if not the, question for Athens at the time at which Apollodorus probably recounted the story of the drinking party.

12. He had not apparently known what to do with Alcibiades earlier when the young man was one of his associates. Did the philosopher claim to possess knowledge that he did not share because he did not really have it? Alcibiades quotes Aristophanes' description of Socrates "strutting like a proud marsh-goose, with ever a side-long glance" (*Clouds* 362) in his accusation at 221b.

13. Eryximachus suggests that Socrates' ability to imbibe or not results from an exceptional constitution. Alcibiades will make a similar observation about Socrates' exceptional endurance. From the *Charmides* Plato's readers know, however, that Socrates is not indifferent to physical pleasures and pains so much as he is able to control his own reaction to them.

to calculate one's pleasures and pains accurately, all three speakers show themselves to be fundamentally self-seeking. As a result, their arguments prove to be fundamentally contradictory. It is not possible to understand eros simply as the principle of generation and to use that principle to justify pederasty.[14]

Like his mentor Hippias, Phaedrus uses old stories to promote his own interests. He wants to see love praised because it brings him benefits as a beloved. He begins by eulogizing Eros as one of the oldest and hence most venerable of the gods. Quoting Hesiod, Acusilaus, and Parmenides, Phaedrus seems to recognize that the principle of generation could not itself be generated. He does not praise Eros merely as a source of renewed life; according to Phaedrus, love is the cause of the greatest goods. At first Phaedrus makes it look as if the greatest good in human life is virtue, by arguing that nothing—family, office, or wealth—is more conducive to the attainment of nobility than love. Love makes a man more reluctant than anything else to appear cowardly or shameful in the eyes of his beloved. An army of lovers will, therefore, be the most courageous of all. The attainment of virtue—or at least seeming virtue—on the part of lovers turns out, however, to be for the sake of the beloved. Only lovers will sacrifice themselves for those they love. To a self-interested fellow like Phaedrus, eros represents an unintelligible, seemingly superhuman or divine force that takes human beings outside and beyond themselves. Like Alcestis, he observes, lovers are praised by human beings and gods alike; in contrast to Orpheus, the gods even bring such lovers back to life to enjoy the company of the one for whom they had been willing to give up everything.[15] Having no need to prove his worth or love, Phaedrus nevertheless concludes, a beloved who gives his life for the sake of his lover is even more extraordinary. Like Achilles, he will be rewarded with eternal life in the Isles of the Blessed. Filled with the "god," lovers are more divine than their beloved, but a beloved (like Phaedrus himself) remains superior to his lover and thus even to the god Phaedrus wanted to have praised!

14. As Hesiod shows in his *Theogony*, unregulated generation produces monsters and a great deal of conflict.

15. Phaedrus shows how little he believes there is a natural order of generation that ought to be respected when he contrasts Alcestis' willingness to die for her husband with his parents' refusal to do so. According to the understanding Phaedrus took over from Hesiod, the older generation did not peacefully or necessarily make way for the new. In the *Theogony*, the new forms of life Uranus generated inside Earth could emerge only after Cronus cut off his father's genitals. Even then, there was no order until Zeus forced Cronus to disgorge all his own progeny, put down the rebellious by force, and allocated specific tasks or functions to the other Olympians.

b. Pausanias

There were apparently several other speeches and speakers after Phaedrus (detailing the benefits to be gained from love, we imagine), but Aristodemus did not remember them with any clarity (perhaps because they did not add anything essentially new). The next speech he was able to relate was by Agathon's old lover, Pausanias.

Like his mentor Prodicus, Pausanias began by drawing a distinction. It is impossible, or at least incorrect, to praise love simply, because there are two kinds: the love associated with the Aphrodite born of no mother, but generated by Uranus and thus called heavenly, and that associated with the goddess born of Zeus and Dione, which we call popular because it characterizes all people (*pandēmos*). Like all other practices, Pausanias emphasized, love is neither noble nor base in itself. Its nobility or vulgarity depends on the way it is done, and the way it is done is a matter of convention. Like Hippias, Pausanias thought that the noble does not exist by nature; it is defined by convention.

Some conventions are nevertheless better than others. The argument Pausanias made for the superiority of a certain version of Athenian law reveals not only the self-interested basis of his own position but also the essentially contradictory character of the claims both he and Phaedrus made on behalf of pederasty. In uncivilized nations, Pausanias observed, all forms of sexual intercourse are encouraged, because these peoples do not have sufficient skill in speech to require lovers to persuade others to gratify them. In Ionia and other nations under despotic power, all homosexual relations are forbidden, including philosophy and sports, because these peoples believe that, like Harmodius and Aristogeiton, such relations will prove dangerous to tyrants.[16] Athens represents the right balance or mixture. Here it is customarily said to be better to love openly than in secret. Lovers are allowed to do and say all sorts of things otherwise thought to be shameful. (So much for Phaedrus' argument concerning the ennobling effects of love on lovers' public behavior.) The fact that fathers instruct the slaves who tutor their sons to prevent any conversations between them and potential lovers makes it appear that Athenians do not regard such affairs as desirable or legitimate. But recognizing that nothing is noble or

---

16. In fact, Thucydides shows (6.54–60), Harmodius and Aristogeiton botched the planned tyrannicide. As a result of the exposure of their conspiracy, the government of Hippias became much harsher.

base in itself, Pausanias argued, Athenians regard quick capitulation as disgraceful, especially if favors are bestowed for the sake of money or other gain. "It is our settled tradition," however, "that when a man freely devotes his service to another in the belief that his friend will make him better in wisdom . . . or any of the other parts of virtue, this willing bondage is not base" (*Symposium* 184c). According to Pausanias, a "base" or "common" lover is one who desires only the pleasure he can obtain from the boy's body; his love thus fades and dies as the boy matures.[17] A "noble" lover takes account of the soul and tries to improve his beloved.

If a noble lover truly wishes what is good for his beloved, we readers recognize, he would, like Socrates with Alcibiades, not merely remain true after others have fled; he would also refrain from bodily intercourse in order to concentrate on benefiting his beloved by improving his soul. The distinction Pausanias draws between the noble love of the soul, which desires the betterment of the beloved, and the base desire for physical gratification undermines the legitimacy of his own desire for the latter, which he tries to justify with the former.[18]

c. Eryximachus

Aristophanes was supposed to speak after Pausanias, but the comedian was prevented from speaking by hiccups, a reflection of both his own physical immoderation and the effect his art has on others (in the form of laughter).[19] After prescribing a cure, Eryximachus thus took the comic poet's place. The trading of places suggests that, in some respect at least,

---

17. Pausanias appears to follow his teacher Prodicus, as well as his own self-interest, in emphasizing the virtue of the enduring. In the story of the education of Heracles in virtue and vice, attributed to Prodicus by Xenophon (*Memorabilia* 2.1.21–32), vice promises the hero immediate and effortless pleasure, whereas virtue emphasizes the need for hard work and pain to achieve lasting (but therefore real) goods. Like his fellow sophists, Prodicus appears to be drawing out the rationalized meaning of an old story—in this case the necessity of the labors of Heracles and his ultimate reward of living with the gods on Olympus (rather than as a shade in Hades). As a loyal lover for more than fifteen years, Pausanias wants to remind Agathon of the virtues of enduring affection. Unfortunately for Pausanias, Agathon perceives all too clearly that Socrates would be better able to improve his soul by increasing his wisdom if the poet could manage to attract the philosopher as a lover. Socrates later accuses Alcibiades of jealousy. Because he alone of the speakers is not explicitly mentioned at the end as either having left earlier or remaining (and the drunken revelers are said to have entered through a door that had just been opened for someone who was going out), it looks as if Pausanias may have left the banquet alone after the bantering competition between Alcibiades and Agathon for Socrates.

18. Cf. Strauss, *Symposium*, 57–72.

19. Cf. Socrates' critique of the raucous laughter that comedies produce, in the *Republic* 388e–89a.

their speeches are interchangeable. Both seem to be based, if loosely, on the writings of Empedocles.[20]

Like Empedocles, Eryximachus addresses a man named Pausanias in attempting to teach him the truth about nature as a whole. Eryximachus also follows Empedocles (as well as Pausanias here) in maintaining that there is not one erotic principle, as Parmenides suggested in the fragment Phaedrus quoted, but two. In contrast to Pausanias, however, Eryximachus claims to have learned from his medical art that the two loves—like for like and unlike for unlike—are cosmic principles, operating in all bodies; they are not merely different kinds of attraction to the beautiful in the souls of human beings. Observing that healthy and sick people desire different things, Eryximachus concludes that Pausanias was correct in maintaining that it is noble to gratify good (or "healthy") men, but base to please the base. The doctor suggests, however, that his medical art consists not merely in the ability to distinguish the noble love from the base, but in knowing how to arouse the former and to subdue the latter. In other words, the doctor claims that it is possible not merely to know, but to manage and control the cosmic drive with his art (*technē*).

Eryximachus' speech becomes incoherent, however, when he argues that the doctor "must be able to make friends and happy lovers of the keenest opponents in the body" (186d). The need for art suggests that nature or bodies are characterized more by strife than by love or the attraction of like for like.[21] But in criticizing Heraclitus' famous saying, "The One at variance with itself is drawn together, like harmony of bow or lyre," Eryximachus denies that there can be a harmony (*harmonia*, which he identifies with "agreement," *homologia*) of dissonant things.[22] The reason for Eryximachus' somewhat confused presentation of the power of

---

20. Cf. Kirk, Raven, and Schofield, *Presocratic Philosophers*, 283–321. Although he does not mention the philosopher by name, Eryximachus appears to rely on the argument Empedocles made in opposition to Parmenides, that there is not one but two distinct warring cosmic principles or tendencies at work. Like is attracted to like, whereas unlikes or contraries are opposed. Although he concentrates on human nature rather than the cosmos as a whole, Aristophanes at *Symposium* 304 also appears to follow Empedocles' suggestion that "with rolling gait and countless hands . . . many creatures were born with faces and breasts on both sides . . . compounded partly of male, partly of the nature of female" (*Fragments* 378–79).

21. Strife was, indeed, one of Empedocles' two principles; the attraction of like for like through love or friendship was another.

22. The doctor would reduce chords to a monotone. Despite his studies with Hippias, Eryximachus does not appear to understand the mathematical character or basis of harmony. As Rosen observes (*Plato's "Symposium,"* 117), the speakers in the *Symposium* all ignore mathematics, Socrates' usual example of simply intelligible beings and concepts. Taken in and by itself, the *Symposium* does not, therefore, provide a complete picture of Socratic philosophy.

art to bring order to nature comes to the fore when he turns from medicine and music to his third example, agriculture. There the sign of healthy relations or loves is productivity—or generation—as opposed to disease and decay. As a model for the regulation of human loves, agricultural art points to the desirability of mating males with females for the sake of reproduction. In contrast to Pausanias, Eryximachus thus explicitly includes heterosexual relations within the purview of his art. But if art is necessary to bring order to erotic relations and productivity is the measure of success, it is not clear why the gratification of the orderly love should ever be homosexual. Eryximachus' speech does not serve, as intended, to justify much less elevate his own erotic knowledge and practice.

2. THE POETS

a. Aristophanes

Aristophanes spoke next, and the humorous story he tells constitutes a correction of the accounts of eros presented by the students of the sophists in three fundamental respects. First, if everything is constantly becoming and hence in flux, the comic poet sees, human nature must also change. Second, in presenting an account of the development of a distinctively human form of existence, he shows that eros is not a fundamentally generative, universal, or cosmic force. Third, he suggests, contrary to the sophists, that human beings are moved not by a desire to maximize their pleasures so much as to minimize their pains. Since pain ends only with death, the only way to keep human beings alive or preserve the race is to delude them. The most important thing to learn is not, therefore, how to calculate our pleasures and pains correctly (from the sophists) but how to create and use artistic illusions to relieve human suffering, if only temporarily (like the poets).

Aristophanes began by describing our original nature. Like the cosmic gods by whom they were originally generated, human beings were round with two faces and sets of limbs. There were, moreover, three sexes— males generated by the sun, females generated by the earth, and hermaphrodites generated by the moon. These spherical beings were so strong and had such grand thoughts that they tried, like the giants, to overcome the gods themselves (that is, their forebears).[23] In other words, these spherical

---

23. In this respect, Aristophanes' account of the development of the human race parallels Hesiod's account in the *Theogony* of the generation or development of the Olympian gods. Rather

beings did not try merely to reproduce themselves; they strove to overcome their own origins.

Indicating the existence of different kinds of forces in the cosmos, Aristophanes reported that the Olympian (rather than the cosmic) gods deliberated on how to put down the rebellion without destroying their source of honors and sacrifices. (As in the *Birds* 1230–65, 1513–50, Plato's Aristophanes thus suggested that the Olympian gods exist only so long as they are worshiped by human beings. Unlike the cosmic gods, the Olympians exist by convention rather than by nature. Cf. *Peace* 400–415.) According to the comic poet, these gods are nevertheless responsible for human life as we now experience it. They might ultimately be human inventions (things newly "generated" by us), but belief in such gods is a necessary condition for maintaining human life. To quell the rebellious tendencies of human beings, Aristophanes said, Zeus ordered Apollo to slice the spherical beings in half and so weaken them, and then to turn their faces toward the side bearing the scars to remind them of the gods' threat to divide them again if they refuse to recognize the limits of their strength. This division gave rise to the longing to be reunited with one's other half and so to become whole that Aristophanes identifies with eros.

According to the comic poet, eros is not primarily a generative force; nor does it inhere in all bodies. (The cosmic gods were originally responsible for the generation of human beings, perhaps in the way they may still be said to be responsible for agricultural production, but these gods are not erotic.) The first result of erotic longing is not generation or even self-preservation, but self-destruction.[24] Longing to be reunited with their other half, the new human beings spent all their time seeking their former partners. When they found their other half, they embraced and clung to each other. Failing to eat or do anything else, the couples gradually expired.[25]

To preserve their own source of honor (and existence), the Olympian gods had to effect another change in human nature. By moving the genital organs to the front, the Olympians enabled human beings to find temporary solace in sexual intercourse and, in the case of the former her-

---

than a smooth process of replication, the emergence of a new kind of being requires the suppression, if not destruction, of the old, that is, its own origins.

24. Cf. Strauss, *Symposium*, 140: "We can also say that eros, as understood by Aristophanes, is, in modern language, extinction of the self."

25. This is the reason Sigmund Freud explicitly refers to Aristophanes' speech in Plato's *Symposium* in pointing out the connection between love and death. Freud, *Beyond the Pleasure Principle*, trans. James Strachey (New York: Bantam, 1959), 100–102.

maphrodites, to procreate and so to preserve the race. The preservation of the race was furthered by the fact that the males, being more manly or courageous, became active in politics. As part of their organizational and defensive function, they came to understand the need for heterosexual generation, but they took wives as a matter of law rather than desire.[26]

Aristophanes concluded by emphasizing the importance of human beings' remembering the gods' threat to weaken them further (through the dissolution of their political organizations), if they do not piously recognize the superiority of the gods. Such an admission of their own limitations is necessary because human beings retain their original desire. The sense of one's essential incompleteness, which gives rise, first, to the erotic yearning to be reunited with another, is, as the description of their original nature indicates, at bottom a desire to be subject to no constraint or superior power.[27] It consists, fundamentally, in the desire to end all desires, to have no further sense of wanting or lacking, to be complete or full. So understood, eros is a fundamentally tyrannical desire, which, as Socrates will also argue in the *Republic* (573b–75a, 587b), must be kept in check, if not completely subdued, to preserve political order and thereby human life. (Socrates will also present politics as fundamentally defensive. If

---

26. Aristophanes' silence with regard to the female halves indicates not only the separation of the erotic from the generative but also his recognition that lesbian sexual relations, if not all sexual relations between members of the same sex, were suppressed by law for the sake of maintaining procreative relations between members of the two (naturally separate) and hence arguably opposed sexes, contrary to the natural desires of both. Cf. Saxonhouse, *Fear*, 170.

27. As Paul Ludwig, *Eros and Polis* (Cambridge: Cambridge University Press, 2002), observes, "The word eros does not occur in the myth until after the surgery" (92). Most commentators (e.g., Bloom, *Love*, 483) thus distinguish eros from the desire for domination. Like Strauss (*Symposium*, 122–40), Ludwig nevertheless connects the eros that leads human beings to seek their other half for what proves to be only temporary solace with the impulse that led to the original rebellion. The Olympian gods who weaken human beings are conventional (belonging only to the Greeks), as opposed to the "cosmic" or natural gods also worshipped by the barbarians. Weakening human beings is basically civilizing them. Laws against incest are necessary to establish order in families and, by extension, in cities. But the eros that Aristophanes says leads the originally androgynous to become adulterers, the originally female to become lesbians, and the originally male to become homosexuals, who marry and procreate only because forced to do so by law, would also lead them to rebel against the gods, if they could be reunited. Pointing out that the extra skin Apollo has to gather together can only have come from the other half, which must then have perished, Strauss concludes: "Eros is infinitely more than the desire of lust, it is the desire for oneness, wholeness, and integrity in the literal sense, everlasting integrity, a desire which cannot be fulfilled" (140). The best human beings can do under present circumstances, according to Aristophanes, is to find a partner to their tastes. Although Aristophanes says that such pairs do not know what they want, they would jump at the chance, if offered by Hephaestus, to be indissolubly united not only in this life but also in Hades, neither Ludwig nor Strauss observes the way in which this desire to become whole or "one" (ultimately with the universe) can only be realized, and then only unconsciously, in death.

every human being wants, at bottom, to remove all constraints on his or her desires, then conflict, failure, and universal unhappiness will inevitably result.) Such an understanding of eros rests, however, on an understanding of pleasure as the end of pain. The problematic character of such an understanding of eros is shown, in Aristophanes' speech, by the fact that it leads to an understanding of eros as a yearning for death. It consists, ultimately, in a desire to be like the cosmic gods—to be in motion but without perception (aisthēsis).

Like Protagoras, Aristophanes told a story in which he suggested that human survival depends on political organization (dikē), which, in turn, requires not merely belief in but fear (aidōs) of the gods. But where the sophist intimated that the wise, understanding the requirements of political order, could use or manipulate the nomoi (beliefs, customs, and laws) of their compatriots to serve their own interests, the comic poet saw that the desire for pleasure, insofar as it consists fundamentally in a desire to end all pain, is impossible for any living being to satisfy. People who come to understand the truth of human existence will conclude, like the chorus in Oedipus at Colonus (1223–25), that the best thing is not to be born, and second is to die as quickly as possible.

Political organization will not suffice, Aristophanes saw, to preserve the race. People will continue to live only if they receive some respite from their suffering.[28] Aristophanes attributed such a respite to the god Love (Eros). On reflection, however, we realize that by arousing laughter, his art provides such a respite better than anything else. Although as a comic poet Aristophanes claims that he serves both Dionysus and Aphrodite, Plato indicates the comic poet's immunity, if not superiority, to the latter by having him alone appear in the Symposium as neither lover nor beloved. That Aristophanes does not have a partner suggests independence, if not self-sufficiency, but it also points to the unattractive aspect of his art. Comedy is usually thought to be base.[29] Insofar as it is disproportionate, the ridiculous is also ugly.[30] Although Aristophanes has a deeper and truer understanding of human desire than the sophists do, Plato shows, in the

---

28. This is the understanding of the origins and function of tragic art—the desire to overcome the limitations associated with individuality or finitude—that Nietzsche presents as "Dionysian" in his account of The Birth of Tragedy.

29. In the Laws 816d–e, for example, the Athenian suggested that comic performances should be allowed as means of teaching citizens the difference between noble and base, but that such performances should be executed only by slaves or foreigners. Citizens should never be allowed to do, even only in imitation, what is base.

30. Aristotle Poetics 1449a33–34.

speeches by Agathon and Socrates that follow, that the comic poet's under-standing of the nature of human desire as a desire, fundamentally, to end pain is defective precisely because it does not take account of the pleasure human beings experience in contemplating the beautiful.[31]

b. Agathon

Just as Aristophanes' speech represents an improvement on that of Eryxi-machus, by revealing the essentially unsatisfiable character of human physical desire and so the impossibility of removing the roots of natural disorder, so Agathon's speech represents an improvement on that of the comic poet insofar as the tragedian not merely brings out the essentially transitory character of all human pleasure but makes the centrality of the phenomenon of beauty manifest. Agathon claims he will not, in contrast to the previous speakers, simply praise eros for its effects, that is, the ben-efits it bestowed on human beings. He will begin by describing what sort of thing it is—the happiest of the gods, because most beautiful and best—and then talk about its effects. Eros is beautiful, Agathon argues, first be-cause he is young. In emphasizing the association between eros and youth as well as its antipathy to anything old and rough, Agathon suggests even more clearly than Aristophanes had that the good and noble things in hu-man life are ephemeral. Because eros is associated with youth, Agathon distinguishes it from the necessity associated with the ancient principle of generation described by Hesiod and Parmenides. Precisely because erotic desire is not necessary but gentle and free, is based on consent rather than force, and fluidly assumes many forms, it exists in the souls and character of men and gods. In arguing that love is the source not merely of beauty but of all forms of human excellence, Agathon suggests that everything noble and good in human life is a product of art (and does not, therefore, exist by nature). By nature, as Aristophanes suggested, human beings use force to get what they want; their desires are unsatisfiable and hence im-moderate. There is, as a result, conflict wherever one party is not able to frighten the other into a temporary peace, and the cosmos lacks rational order. Eros is divine because it produces the opposite, antinatural results. Because love is gentle, based like democratic law on consent rather than force, eros neither does nor suffers injustice. Because it is stronger than all other desires, eros controls them and so produces moderation. Since

---

31. Socrates explicitly examines the claim that pleasure consists merely in the absence of pain and finds it wanting in the *Philebus* 43d–52b.

love (Aphrodite) possesses even the god of war (Ares), eros overcomes fear and so produces courage. Most important of all, eros is the source of wisdom or knowledge because it inspires poetry of all kinds.[32] Eros not merely leads human beings and gods to express their feelings in verse; it is responsible for all procreation and artistic production. It is the force (or god) responsible not only for the generation of all living creatures but also for the invention of all the forms of art that contribute to the amelioration of the human condition—crafts, medicine, and government. Eros is a blessing precisely because it is not, like conflict and death, a result of physical necessity. However, since love is attached only to the young and beautiful and so flees the old and ugly, it and its products are essentially transitory.

As Apollodorus suggested by reporting that "there was tumultuous applause from all present at hearing the youth speak in terms so appropriate to himself and to the god" (*Symposium* 197e–98a), Agathon made himself and his art the embodiment of eros more explicitly than Aristophanes had. As a poet, Agathon did not claim merely to produce the beautiful illusions that entice other human beings to continue living; he also claimed to possess and convey the truth about the good and noble things in human life—that they are essentially fleeting and hence illusory. His art is greater than the medicine of Eryximachus or the comedy of Aristophanes not merely because tragedy has beneficial effects; tragedy is beautiful and yet reveals the not-so-beautiful truth about nature or the whole (and therein the need for and supremacy of art).

3. SOCRATES' RESPONSE

Socrates responded to Agathon's speech, first, by protesting its lack of truth. He said that he had foolishly agreed to participate in the contest in the belief that what is said in praise of love has to be true. The truth underlying Agathon's flowery speech is ugly. By interrogating Agathon, Socrates showed that as desire for the beautiful and good, eros is wanting in both. Praising Agathon for having begun by asking what eros is, Socrates related what he learned about eros from Diotima. As we saw in

---

32. The argument Agathon presents here concerning eros as the source of the virtues resembles that Socrates gives in the *Republic* 485b–87a when he describes the nature of philosophers—people whose love of truth is so strong that it overcomes all other desires and fears. The difference between Agathon and Socrates is that the tragic poet describes eros as love of beauty, whereas Socrates connects it with truth.

chapter 3, the first thing he learned was that eros is not a god.[33] Eros is the *daimōn* that communicates and thus is in between mortals and immortals. It consists fundamentally in a desire to beget in the beautiful. This begetting is part of an attempt to possess the good—forever—by giving birth to something better and longer-lived than oneself. Like Agathon, Diotima told Socrates that the power of eros is first to be seen in the generation of animals but that its purest manifestations are psychological and intellectual. Intellectual progeny are longer lasting than the results of physical procreation. Human beings can satisfy their desire to possess what is good forever, however, only by achieving knowledge of the beautiful in itself. Even then, they must continually struggle to regain the knowledge they are in the process of losing as they gain it.

To acquire such knowledge, Socrates suggested, it is necessary to move through a process of generalization from the love of one body to the love of the beautiful in itself. Love of a specific boy leads the lover to give birth to beautiful speeches (*logous kalous*). Having developed his reason in composing such speeches, the lover observes how the beauty of the body of his beloved resembles that of all others. Having abstracted out the general characteristic that makes bodies beautiful with his reason, the lover comes to appreciate the superiority of that which enables him to perceive such general qualities, the soul. He begins not only to love the beauty of soul in any given individual without regard to the body, but also to nurture and care for that soul, begetting virtues in that soul by conversing with it. Having become actively concerned about the education of another, the lover will observe the beauty of laws and customs and then the beauty of all branches of knowledge.[34] Freeing him from his initial attachment to a particular body or practice, this knowledge enables him to produce beautiful speeches and acquire the philosophical intelligence (*dianoia*) that allows him finally to contemplate the beautiful in itself, which never fades or changes.[35] In contrast to both the comic and the tragic poets, Socrates thus claimed that human beings can satisfy their strongest desire and so achieve happiness, if only with effort. We can be happy because our deepest desire is not, as Aristophanes claimed, to encompass the whole or, as

---

33. The following account of Diotima's instruction of Socrates should be supplemented by the more detailed discussion in chapter 3.

34. Socrates thus solves the problem Hippias pointed out by relating noble laws and practices to the pleasures human beings take in beautiful or noble sights and sounds (or speeches).

35. In her brief restatement of the steps (*Symposium* 211c–d), Diotima omits any mention of the soul, speeches, or philosophy.

Agathon suggested, for fleeting manifestations of beauty.[36] It is to possess some share of what is good forever.[37]

4. ALCIBIADES' ACCUSATION AND THE JUDGMENT

Aristophanes wanted to respond to Socrates' contention that human beings desire not to become whole but only to possess what is good (and so, it seems, less than the whole). He was prevented from doing so by the entrance of Alcibiades and a group of drunken revelers. In both praising and criticizing Socrates, Alcibiades in a sense took Aristophanes' place.

Looking very much like the god of drink as well as drama, Alcibiades had come to crown Agathon with ribbons to celebrate his victory. But when Alcibiades discovers Socrates there, he takes back some of the ribbons and crowns the philosopher, observing that "he is victorious over all human beings in speech—not just once, like you, but always" (*Symposium* 213e). Earlier Agathon had suggested that Dionysus would judge the contest between Agathon and Socrates; appearing in the guise of the god, Alcibiades declares the philosopher the winner.

Alcibiades' inability to praise anyone else in the presence of Socrates, not even the god Eros himself, should alert Plato's readers to the fact that, just as Agathon claimed to embody eros in himself and his art, so Socrates has made himself and his philosophy an image of eros. Which is it? Does human eros consist fundamentally of a desire to lose one's sense of one's own limitations in the intoxication of temporary union with the visibly beautiful? Or is it the desire to acquire, if only temporarily and with effort, an intelligible perception of the beautiful in itself and not merely in relation to us?

Although he claimed simply to tell the truth, Alcibiades' "praise" soon became an accusation. Socrates claimed to be a lover of young men, the frustrated youth charged, but the philosopher always succeeded in making the young men he attracted love him. Like Aristophanes in the *Clouds*, Alcibiades accused Socrates of hubris. Socrates was not willing to trade his

36. Mary P. Nichols, "Socrates' Contest with the Poets in Plato's *Symposium*," *Political Theory* 32, no. 2 (April 2004): 186–206, argues more unequivocally than I do that in the *Symposium* Socrates presents a superior understanding not only of human eros but also of poetry and politics.

37. At the end of the *Symposium* (223d), Aristodemus reports that Socrates was trying to get Aristophanes and Agathon to agree that the same man would know how to be both a comedian and a tragedian. However different the form, Socrates suggests, the two kinds of poetry contain fundamentally the same understanding. Because human desire is ultimately unsatisfiable, human beings need to get relief from the pain of their condition. The knowledge of how to make them forget momentarily and the reason why that is necessary belong to both forms of dramatic art.

wisdom for the sexual favors of the most attractive youth in Athens. The philosopher was not willing to admit the excellence or value of the goods of others in exchange for his own. In not recognizing any need for, much less dependence on, others, he was unloving, if not unjust. (Alcibiades was honest enough also to report Socrates' response, which was that Alcibiades was trying to cheat him by exchanging a transitory good like the pleasure that comes from physical beauty for the more enduring "gold" of wisdom.) Like Aristophanes, Alcibiades emphasized Socrates' extraordinary asceticism—his immunity to the effects of alcohol as well as temperature, his ability to stand transfixed in thought for twenty-four hours or more, his freedom from fear. In describing Socrates' behavior at Delium, Alcibiades even quoted Aristophanes' description of proud Socrates' gait, "strutting like a proud marsh-goose, with ever a side-long glance" (*Clouds* 362).

In contrast to Aristophanes (and his later accusers), however, Alcibiades did not charge Socrates with the crime of introducing new gods or complete atheism.[38] Nor did he accuse Socrates of corrupting the young by making them his lovers. On the contrary, Alcibiades testified to Socrates' extreme temperance as well as his courage and wisdom.[39] By emphasizing Socrates' courage in battle, Alcibiades also reminded his auditors that the philosopher performed his civic duty. Indeed, Alcibiades' account of the way Socrates saved his life but refused to accept the city's reward for courage contradicts the youth's earlier charge that the philosopher was both uncharitable and unjust. According to his young lover, the philosopher exemplified all four of the cardinal virtues. If Eros is the source or cause of all human virtue, as Agathon claimed, the externally ugly but internally noble character of Socrates (and not the apparently beautiful but ultimately ugly truth of Agathon's tragic art) is the embodiment or image of Eros.

5. THE QUESTION CONCERNING SOCRATES

The entrance of a crowd of drunken revelers cut off further conversation. But Socrates demonstrated the truth of Alcibiades' (and Aristophanes') claims about his indifference to physical pains and pleasures as well as his consequent powers of endurance by alone remaining awake at the end of the evening. The question that remained unanswered, as a result (dramatically) of Alcibiades' drunken entrance, is whether Socrates represents a

38. As we have seen, Socrates rebuked Alcibiades for his impiety in earlier conversations.
39. Strauss (*Symposium*, 274) emphasizes Alcibiades' failure to mention justice.

desirable or at least enviable form of human existence, because of his in-human, if not superhuman indifference to physical pleasures and pains (in-cluding recognition or honor from others, which takes sensible forms)—in a word, his asceticism—or whether his philosophy constitutes something positively attractive in itself. To put the question differently, does Socratic philosophy merely free human beings from false hopes and endeavors or does it enable them to acquire or do something truly good and satisfy-ing? Is complete freedom or self-sufficiency the highest human good, as Aristophanes suggested, or can human beings satisfy their deepest desires, as Socrates cum Diotima claimed, only by contemplating the beautiful in itself? Socrates admitted that no human insight or grasp of the truth lasts; we have to regain insights continually. How can we know a transitory in-sight is not an illusion? How can one person's vision, insight, or recollec-tion be communicated to others and so preserved? Plato shows Socrates addressing these questions in the *Phaedrus*.

B. Socrates Speaks as a Poet: *Phaedrus*

Socrates' second conversation with Phaedrus about eros appears to be more complete than the speeches given in praise of the god in the *Sympo-sium*. As Socrates observed after Agathon had spoken, a truthful speech in praise of love would say what is good and remain silent about the nega-tive aspects. The negative aspects of eros that Socrates had slighted in the *Symposium* but explicitly takes up in the *Phaedrus* include its apparent lack of reason, its tendency to dissemble and deceive, and its connection with mortality and death.

In the first speech given in praise of eros in the *Symposium*, Phaedrus quoted Hesiod's characterization of Eros as the most beautiful of the im-mortal gods, but omitted the poet's description of the god's power "in every man to soften the sinews and overpower the prudent purpose of the mind" (*Theogony* 120–23). So described, the power of the god hardly seems beneficent, and in his poem Hesiod depicted eros as the source of a good deal of human suffering.[40] In the *Symposium* Phaedrus tried to avoid the is-sue by repressing the commonly recognized opposition between love and reason. In the *Phaedrus* the young man's admiration for Lysias' argument

40. Hesiod (*Theogony* 560–700) gives a rather negative view of the effect of women on the lives of men.

in favor of the superior rationality of the nonlover leads Socrates to confront the apparently irrational character of love more directly.[41]

As a passionate desire to obtain what one wants, love is also associated more frequently with deceit than with truth.[42] With the introductory exchange in the *Phaedrus*, Plato reminds his readers of the connection often drawn between loving and lying in the *Phaedrus* with the introductory exchange.

I. PHAEDRUS AS A FALSE IMAGE OF EROS

When Socrates accosts Phaedrus, asking him from whence he comes and where he is going, Phaedrus responds that he is coming from Lysias, son of Cephalus, and now going on a walk in the country for his health.[43] As a

---

41. Stanley Rosen, *The Quarrel between Philosophy and Poetry* (New York: Routledge, 1988), 78–101, brings out the importance of the emphasis on reason in opposition to eros in the first two speeches in the *Phaedrus*.

42. In the *Philebus* Protarchus observes that "in sexual pleasures . . . even the swearing of false oaths has obtained forgiveness from the gods, as if the pleasures were like children and possessed not even of the smallest bit of mind" (65c).

43. Because Lysias is explicitly said to be in Athens at the beginning of the *Phaedrus*, *Clitophon*, and *Republic*, there has been considerable controversy about the dramatic dates of all three dialogues. The controversies result from uncertainties about the exact dates at which Pericles persuaded Lysias' father Cephalus to move to Attica from Syracuse, his family's return to Sicily to settle at Thurii, and the return of the sons from Thurii to Attica. According to Dionysios of Halicarnassus (1.8.2–17), Cephalus was a Syracusan by birth, Lysias was born after Cephalus moved to Attica, Lysias and his two brothers went to Thurii when it was founded by the Athenians, Lysias was fifteen years old at the time, and he and the others were forced to flee after the defeat of the Athenians in Sicily. If so, Lysias was born in 458 and was forty-seven years of age in 412–411. But K. J. Dover, *Lysias and the Corpus Lysiacum* (Berkeley: University of California Press, 1968), argues that "if . . . Lysias left Athens in 443 and did not return until 412/411, Plato's *Phaedrus* has no possible dramatic date, for Phaidros went into exile in 415 [at the same time as Alcibiades in connection with the defacement of the Hermae] and did not return until 404, by which time Sophokles and Euripides [mentioned as living at *Phaedrus* 268c] were dead" (31). Dover admits that "if Plato was capable of anachronisms as audacious as *Menexenus*, it is hard to assert that he cannot have created an impossible situation for *Phaedrus*" (37). Dover prefers to rely on evidence of opposition to Athens in Thurii before the Athenian defeat in Sicily in order to date Lysias' departure from Sicily earlier and thus the *Phaedrus* in 418–416. Martha Nussbaum, "'This Story Isn't True': Poetry, Goodness, and Understanding in Plato's *Phaedrus*," in *Plato on Beauty, Wisdom, and the Arts*, ed. J. M. E. Moravcsik and Philip Tenko (Totowa: Rowman and Littlefield, 1982), 96–97, concludes more simply that the *Phaedrus* is fictional. Because of the references to Lysias being in Athens, Nussbaum points out (*Fragility*, 213), the problems reconciling the dramatis personae with the apparent date and/or historical circumstances extend to the *Clitophon* and *Republic* as well. Clitophon was active in Athenian politics from 411 to 405 (cf. Aristophanes *Frogs* 967–70; Aristotle *Athenian Constitution* 28–29; Xenophon *Hellenica* 1.7, 2.3, 24–56). The dramatic as well as thematic connections between the *Clitophon* and the *Republic* constitute one reason for accepting A. Boeckh's suggestion about the dramatic date of the *Republic* as approximately 411 (*Kleine Schriften* 4:437–48). Taylor argues (*Plato*, 262–63) that the conversation depicted in the *Republic* took place earlier, between 422 and 421, for four reasons: (1) In book 8, Socrates pictures democracy in full bloom, not defeat. (Taylor assumes that Socrates' description of democracy corresponds to conditions in Athens. But the

figure in motion between two poles, Phaedrus appears to be an image of the *daimōn* who moves in between; he seems, moreover, able to exercise the same kind of power by luring Socrates out of his accustomed habitat in the city into the countryside by appealing to the philosopher's love of speeches. Having appeared in the *Symposium* to be himself an image of Eros, Socrates points out the similarity between himself and his interlocutor in the *Phaedrus* when he comments, "if I don't know Phaedrus, I have forgotten myself" (228a). As with Alcibiades, so with Phaedrus, Socrates claims to see the reflection of his soul in another. Nevertheless, in his love of speeches Phaedrus proves to be an external and hence somewhat distorted reflection of the philosopher.[44]

To know Phaedrus as well as himself, Socrates has to recognize the difference between them as well as the similarity. Phaedrus loves to listen to speeches, especially speeches designed to please him; he also wants to shine in the eyes of others by delivering such cleverly constructed speeches himself. Like Agathon, Phaedrus wishes to be admired not merely for his

---

easygoing democrats Socrates describes would not have made it impossible for him to take part in public life, as he asserts at 496d–e.) (2) At 368a, Plato's older brothers Adimantus and Glaucon are said to have distinguished themselves at the battle of Megara, which Taylor thinks must have been the battle that Thucydides mentions (4.72) as occurring in 424 (although Dover points out that there were several battles at Megara). But it is not clear that Adimantus and Glaucon would have been old enough to participate in the conversation in the way they do in 422. (3) Thrasymachus is said to be at the height of his fame, and we know Thrasymachus had already become a public figure in 425 when he is made the butt of a joke in Aristophanes' *Acharnians*. See Paul Ludwig, "Portrait of the Artist in Politics: Justice and Self-Interest in Aristophanes' *Acharnians*," *American Political Science Review* 101, no. 3 (2007): 483–84. (The rhetorician was still living and famous later, however. Socrates also praises him in the *Phaedrus* 266c, 267c–d.) (4) Most importantly, Taylor points out, Cephalus was dead by 411. In the *Republic* he is said to be an old man but shown to be living. On the other hand, if Lysias left Athens in 443 and returned only in 412–411, he could not have been present at the conversation as he is said to have been at 328b. As in the *Phaedrus*, so in the *Republic*, it seems that the participants said to have taken part in the conversation could not really have been present at the indicated time and place. The *Oxford Classical Dictionary* reports that inscriptions indicate the dramatic date of the *Republic* was 411. I conclude that the references to Lysias at the beginning of all three dialogues indicate they are linked in dramatic date (hence 411 rather than 422 or 418) as well as theme. Plato used the contrafactual conjunctions of characters with settings in these three dialogues to remind his readers of their fictional character. (We see the same kind of problem in the indications of the dramatic dating of the *Ion*, which is thematically linked to book 10 of the *Republic*, and refers at the end [541d] both to Panosthenes, who led an Athenian expedition against Andros in 406–405 [cf. Xenophon *Hellenica* 1.5.18] and Heracleides of Clazomenae, who raised the fee paid to citizens attending the assembly, probably in about 393, six years after Socrates' death.) Such indications of the explicitly imaginary character of the conversations related appear to be particularly appropriate in dialogues that present the competition between Socrates and the poets to become the educators of Athenian youths both by appealing to their imaginations and enlisting their tendency to imitate.

44. Cf. G. R. F. Ferrari, *Listening to the Cicadas: A Study of Plato's "Phaedrus"* (Cambridge: Cambridge University Press, 1987), 6–7, 26–27.

physical beauty but for his wisdom. Phaedrus is not interested in truth, however, so much as in a form of intellectual pleasure that involves no physical pain. His fundamental concerns are closer to those of the poet than to those of the philosopher. Familiar with Phaedrus' character and habits, Socrates quickly uncovers Phaedrus' intended deceit. Spying the book hidden under his friend's cloak, Socrates insists on hearing the words of the original author, not the product of Phaedrus' fallacious memory. Socrates will not accept an inaccurate approximation or imitation if he can have access to the original.[45]

Yet in the *Phaedrus*, Plato hardly ever shows Socrates speaking or arguing in his own name. Something about love seems to require indirect speech. In the *Symposium* Plato depicts Socrates first questioning Agathon and then relating the story of his own instruction by Diotima. In the *Phaedrus* he shows Socrates first delivering the speech of a lover concealed as a nonlover (the polar opposite of Alcibiades' description of Socrates' own deceptive appearance) with his head covered (and so hidden). Then, after his *daimonion* refuses to let him go without disowning the first, shameful speech, Socrates uncovers his head. He nevertheless attributes his second speech to a poet named Stesichorus, son of Euphemus.[46] In both these speeches Socrates explicitly, if uncharacteristically, acts like a poet (1) by appealing to the Muses for inspiration (237a); (2) by relating speeches he claims to have heard from others, thus speaking only through the mouths of his characters and hence in a contradictory fashion;[47] (3) by speaking in dithyrambs (238d) and epic meter (241e); and (4) by presenting his main teaching about the inner condition or soul of human beings as an image or myth. Even in the second, apparently more argumentative and

---

45. Phaedrus had asked Lysias to read his speech not merely once but to repeat it, Socrates speculates; after that, Phaedrus asked to borrow the book so he could memorize the speech. Becoming tired, he then decided to walk out in the countryside not merely to preserve his health but to practice saying the speech out loud. Meeting a lover of speeches, Phaedrus feigned shyness although he yearned to speak.

46. This is the second explicit mention of Socrates' *daimonion*. It seems to be particularly active or relevant to Socrates' pursuit of young men. At the beginning of the *Alcibiades I* (103a–b) Socrates explained that his *daimonion* prevented him from speaking to Alcibiades until all Alcibiades' other lovers departed, that is, until the young man was ready to listen. Here it prevents him from leaving before he says what Phaedrus is now, but only now, prepared to hear.

47. Socrates thus acts in a way he himself criticizes in the *Republic* 393d–98a, where he suggests that all such indirect forms of narration should be banned. The man who is able to imitate many other kinds of human beings has a great talent, but he sets a bad example. The Athenian Stranger indicates the advantage of the poets' characteristic way of speaking through the mouths of different characters, which Socrates adopts in the *Phaedrus*, when the Athenian urges legislators to learn from poets how to speak to and for many different kinds of human beings (*Laws* 719c–e).

dialectical part of the conversation, Socrates has personifications of the "art of persuasion" and its critics give the arguments for and against it rather than presenting them himself. He also relates fanciful accounts of the origin and function of the cicadas as well as of the invention and effects of the art of writing, which he claims to have heard from others. In the guise of a poet Socrates appears to represent the model for Plato, who depicts the erotic character of philosophy only indirectly in writing dialogues among others rather than treatises.

In the *Phaedrus* Socrates not only distances himself from his own speeches by attributing them to others; when Phaedrus leads him into the countryside to hear Lysias' speech, Socrates is also physically distanced from his usual habitat. The only other dialogue in which Plato shows Socrates venturing outside the city to hear an argument is the *Parmenides*, in which Socrates is also drawn by his desire to hear a written treatise (in that case by Zeno) read.[48] Is Plato suggesting that writing constitutes a means of overcoming the limitations imposed on human love of learning by space and time? That an author's thoughts can be preserved in writing after the author dies?[49] As Socrates indicates in his final discussion of writing, the communication of thought by means of writing is, at best, indirect. Written signs serve only as marks or memorials that may reawaken thoughts in the minds of readers.

In the *Phaedrus* Plato reminds his readers of the connection between love and death (as he had not in the *Symposium*) by means of the setting.[50] As they walk along barefoot in the river (into which Heraclitus said one could never step twice), looking for a suitable place on the bank to rest and read, Phaedrus spots a plane tree.[51] A longtime associate of the doctor Eryximachus, Phaedrus thinks only of the desirability of avoiding the

48. At the beginning of the *Lysis*, Socrates says that he was walking outside the gates of the city, but he is enticed back into the city to converse with some young boys. Likewise, we are told that Socrates has been absent from Athens on military duty in the *Charmides*, *Laches*, and *Symposium*, but we do not actually see or hear him discoursing in the field.

49. Both Ronna Burger, *Plato's "Phaedrus": A Defense of a Philosophic Art of Writing* (University: University of Alabama Press, 1980); and C. J. Rowe, "The Argument and Structure of Plato's *Phaedrus*," *Proceedings of the Cambridge Philological Society* 32 (1986): 106–25, argue that the dialogue constitutes, at bottom, a defense of Platonic writings.

50. The connection was suggested by Aristophanes at one point in his speech, but it was purportedly cured or overcome by eros.

51. When Phaedrus remarks that it is fortunate that he is barefoot, as Socrates always is (229a), we are reminded that in at least one respect, Socrates is behaving in a more characteristic fashion in this conversation that he did in the *Symposium*, where he dressed up, including shoes, to confront the poet. Kenneth Dorter, "Imagery and Philosophy in Plato's *Phaedrus*," *Journal of the History of Philosophy* 9 (1971): 281–82, 286, explicates the symbolism of both the plane (*platonos*) tree,

heat and glare of the sun. Readers of the *Republic* might identify the sun as the source of generation and thus of the degeneration that inevitably follows, however, and see the friends attempting to avoid the latter.[52] Readers in Greek might also associate the protection from the sun offered by the *platonos* tree with Plato, who preserved Socrates' name and speeches from oblivion by writing them down.[53] But when Phaedrus asks Socrates whether they are not at the place on the river Ilissus where Boreas is said to have carried off Oreithuia, readers cannot avoid noting the association drawn between love and death.[54] The intrinsic connection between human eros and our foreknowledge of our own demise is *the* negative aspect that Socrates cum Diotima repressed when she talked only of the desire to possess what is good forever and not of the impossibility of any mortal entirely satisfying that desire.[55] Therein lies the source of the apparent irrationality of love.

According to the traditional story, the daughter of Athenian King Erechtheus was abducted by Boreas when she was playing with a nymph named Pharmaceia (drugs), then presumably raped and killed.[56] Phaedrus asks Socrates whether he thinks she was merely blown off the cliff by the wind (Boreas), as the "wise" would say. If he were a materialist like Phaedrus or his friend Eryximachus, who believes that everything can be reduced to and accounted for by natural forces, Socrates responds, he would spend a great deal of time in the country observing nature. But, the philosopher tells Phaedrus, he remains in the city because trees cannot teach him anything; only human beings can. Human beings learn only mediately through *logos*

---

sacred to Dionysus, and the agnus tree, mentioned at 230b, sacred to Hera. (Agnos was associated with *hagnos*, the word for "chastity.")

52. Readers of the *Laws* might think of the cypress trees lining the road to the cave of Zeus on Mount Ida, providing shade but associated with death.

53. See, e.g., Joseph Cropsey, "Plato's *Phaedrus* and Plato's Socrates," in *Political Philosophy and the Issues of Politics* (Chicago: University of Chicago Press, 1977), 238–39.

54. Cropsey (ibid.) also suggests that the love of examining speeches (*logoi*), which leads Socrates out into the countryside, may be said to have caused his death at the hands of the city by means of poison (*pharmakon*). Derrida ("Plato's Pharmacy," 74–180) makes his now famous argument that the "charm" exercised by the written speech Phaedrus carries under his cloak constitutes (and is described by Plato as) a *pharmakon* or drug that can intoxicate, heal, or poison. The positive and negative functions or characterizations are, moreover, inseparable. More generally, the need to write down arguments in sensible material undercuts Plato's intended or surface argument to the effect that philosophy aims at knowledge of eternal, unchanging, immaterial ideas. As I argue at the end of this book, that conclusion does not follow—in or concerning Plato.

55. Charles L. Griswold, *Self-Knowledge in Plato's "Phaedrus"* (New Haven: Yale University Press, 1986), 19, observes: "*anamnesis*, dialectic, and writing—all ways of transcending one's finitude—are treated briefly or not at all in the *Symposium* but in considerable detail in the *Phaedrus*."

56. Cf. Derrida, "Plato's Pharmacy," 75–80; Griswold, *Self-Knowledge*, 37.

from other beings who possess it. As we know from the *Phaedo*, Socrates had once been a student of natural history. Those studies had not been able to show him what was good, especially for human beings, and thus why he and others did what they did. He began studying the *logoi* to find out. As a result, Plato shows here that, although Socrates did not usually take walks in the country, he could identify the place to which Phaedrus referred more accurately than the young man himself, because Socrates knew what human beings said about it and its use—what it was good for. Because of the old story, there was a shrine to mark the site; it also happened to be a place people could cross the river into an old Athenian deme.

Since we mortals have only a limited amount of time, Socrates reminds his interlocutor, we have to seek knowledge of what is first and most important for us. That, he told Alcibiades in their first conversation, is the good. To find out what is good for us, we first must learn about our own souls by looking at their reflection in the souls of others, and then investigate the nature of the combination of that soul with body in a self (*autos*). As the Delphic oracle urged, Socrates thus seeks self-knowledge (and is to that extent pious). He does not attempt to reinterpret all the old stories in terms of natural or physical phenomena, because, as we know from previous dialogues, he does not think that physical phenomena exhaust everything there is. Nor does he attempt to explicate the monstrous mixtures of species in mythical creatures like the Centaurs, Chimeras, Gorgons, and Pegasus; he does not have time. Human beings constitute a mixture of the divine and bestial, and there are many human beings to examine in his search for self-knowledge. He does not know whether he is a many-headed monster like Typho or a simpler, gentler creature. In his great speech about the human soul later in this dialogue, Socrates suggests that he cannot know; both alternatives represent human possibilities.[57] The

---

57. In his second speech in praise of love Socrates suggests that the human soul is a complex mixture of divine intelligence (one head) with two animal drives. In the *Republic*, Socrates also suggests that there are three parts of the soul, although the three parts differ somewhat from the three parts in the palinode. Whereas in the palinode Socrates identifies the driver with *nous* or *dianoia* and the two horses with *aidōs* (shame or fear) and physical desires, in the *Republic* he argues first, in book 4, that calculation (*logismos*) should direct desire with the help of *thymos* (associated more with anger than with fear, the passion anger overcomes), and then, in book 9, that there is a small man in the soul who may or may not be able to use a lion to control a many-headed hydra. Where intelligence rules, there is only one head; the soul is never simple, however, although when it is well ordered it appears to be gentle (and not moving in many contradictory directions). The uncertainty about the character of the human soul persists because there is no necessity that any, much less all, will be well ordered. It seems clear that Socrates would not accept the physicalist interpretation of soul as smoke (a literal meaning of *typhos*). Cf. Seth Benardete, *The Rhetoric of Mo-*

outcome in any particular case depends, in part, on the person's relations with others—whether he is able to find a philosophical lover and thereby become orderly and just. In this very conversation, we see Socrates try to seduce Phaedrus into forming such a philosophical relationship, but fail. In this dialogue Socrates thus demonstrates not only the knowledge he claims to possess of what human beings truly want and how to arouse desire (*ta erōtika*) but also the limited power of such knowledge.

2. LYSIAS' SPEECH—THE PRAISE OF THE NONLOVER

Having found a suitable spot, Socrates asks Phaedrus to read Lysias' speech (*logos*) so they can examine it. Socrates appears to be much more interested in the effect the speech has on Phaedrus than in its content. Even though in the *Symposium* Phaedrus had stated his desire to have Eros praised—because the god brings such great goods to the beloved—Socrates observes that Phaedrus becomes enraptured as he reads the speech in which a non-lover contends that a youth should gratify him rather than a lover.

Because he is not overcome by passion, the nonlover argues, he will not later repent the attention he has lavished on his beloved or the neglect of his own interest.[58] He will not brag about his conquest or fail to observe other public proprieties. Because he is not jealous, he will not strive to keep the youth isolated from others and dependent on him. Although Lysias argues a position contrary to that Phaedrus seems to take in the *Symposium*, the decisive consideration remains the good of the beloved. The rhetorician simply claims to have calculated the benefits more accurately.

Rather than directly object to the calculating view of love that Phaedrus holds (which does not account for his own rapture), Socrates faults first the form and then the content of Lysias' speech. Claiming to have paid attention only to the rhetoric, Socrates complains that Lysias repeats himself. Lysias omits nothing that could be said on the subject, Phaedrus retorts. Socrates disagrees. Even he can give a better speech, based on something

---

rality and Philosophy: Plato's "Gorgias" and "Phaedrus" (Chicago: University of Chicago Press, 1991), 114. The fact that, according to Hesiod (*Theogony*, 820ff.), Typho was the last monstrous progeny of Zeus who threatened to overcome and destroy his progenitor, reminds us not only that eros, whether for generation or pleasure, can produce disorder, as Eryximachus emphasized in the *Symposium*, but also that the precondition for the emergence of new generations is the death of the old. Like Aristophanes, Hesiod seemed to think that the destructive power of generative eros could be regulated only by politics (in this case of Zeus) with the help of poetry (the Muses who counsel the kings). In the palinode, Socrates will present an entirely different understanding of eros and the order to which it can give rise.

58. As Benardete points out (*Rhetoric*, 176), eros is implicitly defined in Lysias' speech as the desire for sexual gratification. Once the "lover" has what he wants, he will regret the cost.

he heard from someone else long ago—he can't remember from whom or when—because he himself is too ignorant. With this apology Socrates shows himself to be the polar opposite of Phaedrus, who would have memorized and delivered Lysias' speech as his own, if Socrates had not uncovered his ruse. In a sense Phaedrus had made that speech his own insofar as it expressed his understanding. By giving a better speech, Socrates corrects Phaedrus without criticizing him directly. Socrates shows in action, as it were, why poets are such effective teachers. They instruct without directly confronting, refuting, and so shaming the audience.

Phaedrus demonstrates his own failure to understand the persuasive advantages of indirect speech when he commands Socrates to give a better speech, less repetitive and more original, without inquiring about the author. Rather than try to induce the philosopher to reveal his true desires by showing that he understands them and so acting toward Socrates as Socrates has acted toward him, Phaedrus simply orders the philosopher to do what he wants and threatens to punish Socrates if he does not.[59]

Although Socrates and Phaedrus are both said to be "lovers of *logoi*," Plato shows, their loves or desires are quite different. As in the *Symposium*, so in the *Phaedrus*, Socrates' interlocutor indicates that he wants to be entertained and flattered by contests in speech, for which he is the judge.[60] Socrates seeks self-knowledge by looking at the reflection of himself in the soul of another (which, we have already seen, involves a perception of the differences as well as the similarities).

3. THE SPEECH OF THE CONCEALED LOVER

Although Socrates claims that he makes himself ridiculous by entering a speech contest with a professional rhetorician without training or preparation, Phaedrus looks equally, if not more foolish when he first impiously swears by the "god" of the plane tree under which they are sitting, and then threatens never to read or relate another speech to the philosopher if he fails to speak now (as if Socrates could not find another source of

59. Phaedrus speaks in legal terms: first, when he promises to erect golden statues of them both at Delphi if the philosopher does give a better speech than the rhetorician (and thus perhaps changes the conventions concerning eros), he promises to do what the Athenian archons did when they broke the law; second, he acts as judge when he concedes the reasonableness of Socrates' objection that neither he nor anyone else could give an entirely novel speech on the topic; and third, he steps into the role of enforcer when he reminds Socrates that they are alone in a solitary place and that he is younger, that is, he has superior force.

60. Phaedrus acts, in this respect, very much like the Athenian public in judging the plays at the festivals of Dionysus.

speeches in Athens!). Neither "lover" seems to take the exchange very seriously; both are playing roles.[61]

Pretending to yield in the face such a "serious" threat, Socrates agrees to deliver another speech—but only with his head covered. He thus indicates both that the position articulated, even in its improved, revised form, is shameful, and that it is not his own.

Socrates calls the first speech he delivers a *mythos*, although he later refers to it as a *logos* (*Phaedrus* 242d) when he attributes it to Phaedrus. The reason he first describes the improved statement of Lysias' argument as a story seems to be that he introduces it with a narrative. It is also presented indirectly, through the mouth of another, purportedly by a lover who conceals the fact that he is a lover in order to best a multitude of others competing for the favors of a very beautiful boy. The speech represents a *mythos* for Socrates because, although it contains a salutary lesson, it does not convey what he thinks; it constitutes a *logos* for Phaedrus because it gives the best argument for his position. The narrative frame in which Socrates places the second speech is, nevertheless, crucial, because it remedies a major flaw in Lysias' position. If the "nonlover" were truly a nonlover, he would have no interest in obtaining the favors of his young addressee. The calculation Phaedrus so admires takes no account of the nonlover's motive, that is, his reason for promising to benefit the beloved. Nor, we shall see, does it take account of the goal of their exchange, acquiring what is truly good or beneficial.

Like Socrates in the *Symposium*, the concealed lover first explains that one ought to begin a speech by defining its subject matter—in this case, love, what it is and what power it has.[62] Implicitly criticizing the definition Socrates had offered in the previous dialogue, the concealed lover observes that desire to possess the beautiful will not suffice, because nonlovers manifest such a desire as well as lovers.[63] As the first three speakers in the *Symposium* maintained, love of the beautiful can be understood simply as particular kind of a more general desire for pleasure. The concealed lover

61. There is perhaps a serious point underlying the foolery here. If, as Socrates suggests in his second speech, the structure of human souls is the same as that of the gods, a human soul in which the desires simply and completely followed the commands of reason would be divine. Did Plato, whose name is the same as the tree, have such a soul? Like many equivalent jokes in Aristophanes' comedies, the brief exchange raises the question, What is a god?

62. Cf. Stanley Rosen, "Socrates as Concealed Lover," in *Quarrel*, 91–101.

63. In the *Symposium* Diotima's initial suggestion that eros consists in love of the beautiful thus represented a gesture on Socrates' part toward Agathon. She corrected her statement later to make eros a desire to possess forever what is good.

proceeds, therefore, to define eros in terms of two antagonistic directing ideas (*ideai*) within each of us—an opinion about what is best, which
moderates our behavior when it is in control, and the irrational desire for
pleasure that leads to excess (*hybris*) when it becomes paramount. When
the desire for pleasure in the beautiful overcomes our opinion about what
is right, it is called "eros."

Enthralled by the latter, the concealed lover argues, a lover would not
seek what he believed was good for his beloved. Attempting to make the
object of his love weak and dependent, the lover would seek to prevent the
boy from developing his mind, for example, by philosophizing. He would
also strive to make the boy physically weak and poor, bereft of family and
friends. Older and uglier, the lover would have to force his company on
the lad, who would find it increasingly repugnant. When he recovered
his senses, the lover would, moreover, regret and renege on the promises
he made when infatuated. In sum, the concealed lover suggests (as had
Aristophanes in the *Symposium*) that, like the desire of Boreas, love is essentially destructive—not merely of the health and virtue of both lover
and beloved, but of the desire itself. It seeks satisfaction and, finding it,
self-destructs.

Phaedrus objects that Socrates does not present the advantages of the
nonlover in contrast to the defects of the infatuated, and Socrates responds
that the two could simply be reversed. If we were to list those advantages—
cultivation of the boy's mind, body, wealth, and associates—we might get
a picture of a nonlover who looks a great deal like Socrates.[64] He is the
true lover—who wants what is good for his beloved. That is how Socrates
presents himself to Alcibiades in their first conversation (in contrast to
the way Alcibiades presents Socrates in the *Symposium*). In the *Alcibiades I*,
the philosopher points out, he remains true after Alcibiades' other lovers
fled, because he does not "love" the young man's body. Love—whether of
the beautiful or the good—has not been properly defined in either of the
speeches "inspired" by Phaedrus, because it has been understood, implicitly, as the desire for physical pleasure. No account has been taken of the
individual person or soul.

4. Socrates' Praise of Love

Socrates thus recants. Although he had been ready to leave, his *daimonion*
prevents him from going away before he retracts his terrible, impious

64. Rosen, "Socrates as Concealed Lover."

speech.[65] He asks Phaedrus whether he does not believe that Eros is son of Aphrodite and a god (in contrast to the *daimōn*, son of Poverty and Plenty, who Diotima described in the *Symposium*). Responding that people say as much, Phaedrus indicates that he does not share this conventional belief. Socrates nevertheless sets out to purify himself of the error he has made in *mythologia* and perhaps even to make Phaedrus less impious.

Although Socrates takes the cover off his head, he still does not speak in his own name.[66] Asking where the boy he was addressing is, Socrates seems to identify himself with the concealed lover. When Phaedrus responds, "Here he is, close at hand, whenever you want him," he seems likewise to identify himself with the boy.[67] Both participants in the conversation thus continue to play roles.[68] Socrates attributes his former speech to Phaedrus, presumably because Phaedrus provoked him to give it (and the argument was based on the consideration Phaedrus finds decisive, what is beneficial to the beloved). Socrates attributes the speech he is about to give to Stesichorus, because that poet avoided the blindness of Homer by retracting what he had said about Helen's going to Troy. Socrates does not want to lose his knowledge of *ta erōtika* by depicting eros as an irrational cause of harm in the way Homer lost his sight of beauty by making it the cause of treachery, war, and death.[69]

---

65. Socrates' *daimonion* prevented him from approaching Alcibiades until all his other lovers had fallen away. In this case it prevents him from leaving, perhaps because Socrates perceives a readiness on Phaedrus' part to listen to a new and different understanding of eros as that which leads us to reason—or to discover the first principles of *logos*—rather than as what opposes calculation. Socrates' *daimonion* thus appears to give him (or represent) the ability to determine when the circumstances are apt for communicating a certain kind of truth to a specific person, the ability Socrates later complains that writings lack.

66. Socrates seems, instead, to "cover" himself with the conventional or accepted opinion about the "god." As he makes clear in the sequel, he wants to defend himself against the possibility of losing his knowledge of *ta erōtika*.

67. Walter Hamilton, in the introduction to his translation of the *Phaedrus* (London: Penguin, 1973), 12, points out on the basis of Phaedrus' presence in the *Protagoras* that he must have been almost forty years old, hardly, literally, a "boy."

68. Alexander Nehamas misses the role-playing when he observes that "at 236b, Socrates refers to Lysias as Phaedrus' *paidika*, that is, as the boy with whom Phaedrus, in the position of an older man, is in love. The point may be a joke, but it strongly suggests that Phaedrus cannot be younger than Lysias. Similarly, at 257b, Socrates says that Phaedrus is Lysias' *erastēs*, thus reinforcing the same point. . . . though Socrates does occasionally address Phaedrus as *pai* (roughly, 'child') and *neania* (roughly, 'youth,' 'young man'), this is not telling. Such terms of intimacy were as common then as they are now." Nehamas, introduction to Plato *"Phaedrus,"* trans. Alexander Nehamas and Paul Woodruff (Indianapolis: Hackett, 1995), xiv. As I shall argue, in his speech Socrates makes the character of the lover and beloved finally the same; the roles are thus, if completely developed, interchangeable. Griswold (*Self-Knowledge*, 67) notices the role-playing but not how long it lasts.

69. At *Phaedrus* 243c Socrates observes that his former speech was not only impious but also shameless. A wellborn man who loved another would never admit that love freely given and received is a cause of enmity.

The part of his previous speech Socrates explicitly retracts is the definition of eros at the beginning. If "being out of one's mind" were always
bad, that definition would have been correct. In fact, however, there are
four kinds of madness that are beneficial to human beings (and thus,
Socrates piously suggests, sent by the gods): (1) the frenzy of the seers and
prophets, who provide us with knowledge of the future; (2) the madness
that temporarily relieves people from extreme suffering they cannot otherwise bear; (3) the inspiration of poets by the Muses, who produce beautiful
works; and (4) the frenzy of the love that benefits lover and beloved alike
and so constitutes our greatest happiness.[70] Whereas the first two speeches
presented eros in terms of an exchange of goods, Socrates now insists that
the good involved is mutual—shared rather than traded.

According to Socrates, to see why love is a divine blessing (rather than
a curse as Hesiod and Homer present it), it would be necessary to learn
the truth about the nature of the soul—human and divine, both its acts or
effects (*erga*) and the way it is acted on (*pathē*). In itself, he argues, soul is
immortal (deathless) because it is self-moving. As such, soul has no external beginning or end; it is self-perpetuating, not generated. This capacity
to move itself is often said to distinguish soul from body.[71] It is, however,
easier to demonstrate why that which is essentially self-moving must be
immortal than to say what it is in itself or its *idea*.[72] To give the long and

70. Although "being out of one's mind" appears to be "madness," the beneficial forms constitute four different kinds of self-forgetting (as opposed to the self-centered calculations Phaedrus
tends to identify with rationality). Benardete notes: "'To be within oneself' is a Greek expression
meaning to be sane (250a7), just as 'to be outside oneself' is to be crazy or to be in a state of motion" (*Rhetoric*, 35). Insofar as life involves motion, being alive or ensouled therefore necessarily appears to involve a certain degree of "craziness." As we have seen in the *Charmides*, Socrates thinks
that looking beyond oneself is necessary for the acquisition of knowledge, even self-knowledge.
As Heidegger has made clear much more recently in his famous analysis of human existence as
"being-in-the-world," we could not have intelligence or understanding of the world if we or our
minds did not extend beyond our individual bodies or "outside ourselves."

71. In book 10 of the *Laws*, the Athenian Stranger also emphasizes the connection between
motion—both cosmic and vital—and the soul. His teaching about the soul (also contained in book
5) and Socrates' are not the same, however. In book 10 the Athenian argues that soul is the cause of
either good or bad. In the *Phaedrus*, Socrates identifies soul with the divine and observably beautiful cosmic "gods" and noetically perceptible pure intelligibles. Both these statements about the
soul differ from that in the *Timaeus* 29e–46c, where soul is connected to reason (*nous*) and comes
into being to give order to the disorderly motion of body when the *dēmiourgos* makes the cosmos
into a living creature that copies the eternal forms. In that dialogue, or according to Timaeus, soul
is neither eternal nor essentially moving. Not surprisingly, we shall see, Timaeus' account of the
construction of the human soul is also different.

72. As in his earlier speech, Socrates uses the word *idea*. The word here seems merely to
mean, as originally, "look." Since the likeness of the soul, both divine and human, Socrates subsequently describes is a composite, and soul itself is said to take different forms, *idea* here does

intricate argument (*logos*) needed to say what soul is would require more time than any mortal has. At most, we can say what it is like (*eoiken*).

Once again Socrates emphasizes the limitations our mortality places on our ability to obtain knowledge. The difficulty we have obtaining knowledge does not result solely from limited time, however; it is also a result of the complexity of what we seek to know. As Socrates' image indicates, saying what soul is would require not only determining the characteristic all souls have in common (self-motion) but also discovering the reasons why souls take different forms and their various relations to each other as well as to soulless bodies and the unchanging, unmoving bodiless intelligibles. This task is more than a mortal can do. Socrates, therefore, can merely present an image—and that image itself is complex.

As a whole (*pan*), Socrates says, soul is responsible for both the motion and the order of everything in the cosmos. Soul cares for all that is soulless by assuming different forms and traversing the heavens. Soul imparts motion to that which has no motion in itself, and by giving that motion direction, soul also defines and orders it.

By likening the soul—both human and divine—to a winged composite of a driver and two horses, Socrates suggests that all souls that take a particular form have a complex structure.[73] Such internal complexity seems to be a necessary condition for self-motion. For soul to move itself, one part or aspect of soul would have to be sufficiently separate or distinct from the others to move them, even if the aspects or parts (like the driver qua driver) do not exist or function on their own, separate from the others.[74] Soul not only moves itself and soulless things, moreover; as Socrates indicates, it can also be moved or affected by the motions of other souls.

---

not seem to refer to the same kind of being as the equal itself—or the beautiful, just, good, and holy—which Socrates says we can recollect in the *Phaedo* 75c–76a and which Socrates calls *eidē* in the *Republic* 511a–c. These *eidē* are like the eternal intelligible forms of being visible only to *nous*, which souls that rise to the edge of the cosmos contemplate. Not only is soul essentially moving, whereas the purely intelligible beings are unchanging and hence static, but the different kinds of soul that make its form so difficult to describe are also not results of the dilution of the pure form in different kinds of things that merely share in it (like different degrees of justice). On the contrary, Socrates will suggest, it is the defective structure of the human soul itself that results in its combination with body.

73. David A. White, *Rhetoric and Reality in Plato's "Phaedrus"* (Albany: SUNY, 1993), 99, argues that because Socrates does not mention a chariot or car but only a "charioteer" and horses, *heniochou* should be translated "driver."

74. In the *Phaedo* (78c) Socrates argues that no composite can be immortal because the parts will inevitably separate. This is true of soul and body, Socrates argues here, but not of soul itself. The different "parts" or aspects of particular kinds of soul can be distinguished from each other and have different functions but are not and cannot be truly or entirely separable.

When perfect and fully winged, he continues, soul soars to occupy and govern the cosmos (which we see to be in motion, rotating) as a whole. When it loses its wings, however, soul sinks until it settles on some earthly body. Uniting with that body, soul makes the amalgam appear to be self-moving. We call such a compound of soul and body a living being and mortal (in contrast to the immortal soul itself), because the compound eventually dissolves. Appearing to criticize the poets, Socrates observes in passing, it makes no sense to posit the existence of immortal gods with both souls and bodies.

Divine souls remain free of bodies because in them, both horses (or drives) are good and therefore obey the driver (later identified with mind [nous] or thought [dianoia]). Their teams cooperate not only in carrying Zeus and his army of gods and daimones throughout the heavens, so they can perform their specific functions in caring for the soulless, but also in lifting the divine souls to the edge of the cosmos, where the mind nourishes itself and its wings by contemplating the purely intelligible beings.[75] Where there is no opposition or strife, there can be motion, but there is no dissolution or decay.

In human souls, however, one of the horses (or drives) is unruly. As a result, the driver has difficulty maintaining order and directing the motion of the soul. The conflict within each human soul that prevents it from rising directly to the edge of the cosmos and acquiring a steady, unimpeded view of the pure intelligibles also produces an external conflict among the souls as they strive, in a confused manner, to move upward. Jostling and bumping against each other in a competitive struggle to feed on the "sight" of the pure intelligibles, human souls not only fail to achieve a steady or complete view; they also bruise and finally break their wings, fall, and so acquire bodily forms. Just as divine souls are distinguished from human souls by having a complete view of the unchanging, purely intelligible beings such as justice, moderation, and knowledge of what is that is regularly refreshed and renewed, so human souls are distinguished from animals by having had some experience of the purely intelligible. Without the ability to group things we sense on the basis of our recollection of the purely intelligible beings, Socrates observes, humans would not be able

75. Neither mind (nous) nor cognition of the eternal intelligibles constitutes a definition of divinity per se, however. As Benardete (Rhetoric, 139) points out, Hestia remains as traditionally "at home" in the center. She does not need to renew her vision of the intelligibles and feed her wings, because she does not move. She does play an essential role in keeping the motion of the cosmos regular, however, by remaining at the center.

to speak.[76] Human souls are also differentiated from one another by the extent of the contact each has had with the purely intelligible.[77] Human souls are further shaped and distinguished from one another by their experiences when embodied. Those who live more justly have better choices with regard to their future lives than those who become accustomed to disorder; the latter may even acquire bestial forms.

The purpose of this imaginative description of the soul—both what it does and how it itself is affected—Socrates reminds Phaedrus, is to show, first, what the fourth form of madness or eros is, and second, why it is a divine blessing. From Socrates' description of soul we see that eros is a distinctively human characteristic; it presupposes some acquaintance with the purely intelligible (which distinguishes human beings from animals), but lack of real knowledge (which characterizes the divine). As Socrates proceeds to describe it, eros proves to be not merely distinctively human; it proves to be distinctively philosophical, not generative or poetic.

When human souls become embodied, Socrates explains, they lose most, if not all, of their memories of the intelligible beings they previously contemplated. Only philosophers—those who have the most extensive contact with the pure intelligibles and have lived justly—are reminded of what they previously contemplated when they confront the beautiful, the only kind of purely intelligible being that can be directly perceived in sensible things.[78] Other people laugh at them for having their "heads in the clouds" when they lose themselves in an attempt to remember what they have forgotten. Contrary to what he first suggested in the *Symposium* in his examination of Agathon, but as he later says Diotima had taught

76. As Jean-Jacques Rousseau argues in his *Discourse on the Origins of Inequality*, part I, the development of language and that of general ideas appear to presuppose one another.

77. Those with most become philosophers, lovers of nobility, some kind of follower of the Muses, or knowledgeable lover; those with somewhat less contact or knowledge, lawful kings or warriors and rulers; those with less than these become statesmen, household managers, or financiers; those with even less become, fourth, gymnastic trainers of the body or those able to give cures; fifth, prophets or conduct rites; sixth, poets or some other kind of imitator; seventh, craftsmen or farmers; eighth, sophists or demagogues; ninth, tyrants (*Phaedrus* 248d–e). Socrates groups philosophers with followers of the Muses, according to his own currently inspired speech, and separates the latter from the poets, whom he demotes to mere imitators.

78. Because Socrates is explicitly presenting only an image of the soul, there does not seem to be sufficient basis for extracting a doctrine of recollection. In his image Socrates appears to be attributing the capacity to cognize the purely intelligible beings to all human souls qua human; this capacity is the source of their ability to speak. It defines the *zō(i)on echon logon*. But knowledge or even awareness of such intelligible beings is not present or innate in the soul per se. Such knowledge has to be brought back into the mind or remembered. Philosophical friendship is presented here as the means of doing so.

him, Socrates insists that eros does not consist in the love of the beautiful. It consists in a desire to recapture the knowledge of the pure intelligibles aroused by the vision of the beautiful in those souls who have the capacity to recognize it for what it is. According to Socrates, eros is thus essentially philosophical.

Socrates admits that most people do not understand the character of their own deepest and strongest desire. Because their bodies prevent human souls from rising to or recalling their previous contemplation of the purely intelligible beings, human beings do not understand the longing that beautiful visions arouse in them. Those whose souls had least contact with the purely intelligible identify the beautiful with the pleasing and rush to have physical intercourse. That is the reason most people associate eros with sexual generation. The few philosophers who perceive the image of the eternal beings in a beautiful face hold back, however, in reverence (aidōs). They regard their beloved as an image of a god.

Socrates proceeds to explicate the physical manifestations of erotic arousal in terms of his image of the winged soul: the pleasurable sensation of heat flowing through the blood vessels, as the sprouting of wings begins; and the painful feeling of constriction when the beloved departs, as the passages through which the wings are growing contract and the feeling ebbs. There is, Socrates concedes, a kind of madness accompanying such intense passion that leads the lover to forget all else—parents, friends, possessions, laws, and propriety—in a desire simply to be near the beloved. That is the reason Lysias urged young men not to gratify lovers, who regret their shameful behavior when they recover their senses. But Socrates argues that this mania constitutes an inchoate desire to rise above and beyond oneself, to become better than one now is, to become more like the god the lover sees imaged in the face of the beloved. Recognized for what it is and mutually felt, this desire forms the basis of a lasting philosophical friendship.

In this imagistic or metaphorical description of eros, Socrates acknowledges the particularistic or differentiated and discriminating character of human love by observing that individuals are attracted to those who resemble the god they followed before they dropped to earth.[79] There are at least twelve such types or proclivities, which are related to, but not the

79. Able to bear the most intense forms of eros, former followers of Zeus seek out those who are philosophers or leaders by nature and try to make them as much like the king of the gods as possible. Those who were followers of Ares tend to be more warlike and jealous; followers of Hera look for kingly natures; those of Apollo for those like that god—and so forth.

same as, the nine degrees of previous contact with, and hence potential for, recalling and recollecting the purely intelligible.[80] Human beings not only differ in the objects and character of their love, Socrates recognizes; they also have varying degrees of success with more or less happy results.

To explain these differences and to show that philosophy constitutes the greatest and most beneficent form of human love, Socrates returns to the image of the soul he initially drew as a composite of driver and two horses. The horses correspond to the two leading *ideai* he identified in his first speech. The white horse that loves honor with moderation and reverence and is guided solely by *logos* resembles the striving for the best on the basis of opinion that Socrates previously described (*Phaedrus* 237d–38a) as moderation. Like the irrational (*alogos*) desire for excessive pleasure he (or the lover disguised as a nonlover) called eros, the dark horse lacks visible order or proportion and is so hubristic that it can hardly be held in check by force.[81] In his second speech, however, Socrates adds the driver with *nous*, which directs the motion of the soul and determines the outcome of the internal struggle. If the rational faculties in conjunction with the "white horse" are able to check the rush of desire associated with the "dark" one by inculcating a fear of pain, he explains, the love remains noble (love of the beautiful rather than of bodily pleasure).[82] It has the potential, moreover, of becoming reciprocal.

Attracted by his lover's willingness to serve him as if he were a god, the beloved begins associating with the lover, despite previous warnings from tutors and friends. Finding his association with this lover more rewarding than any other, he too begins to want to be with his lover more than anything else without initially understanding why. "He sees himself in his lover as in a mirror" (255d), but does not know it. Desiring to be loved as he loves, each strives to become as good as he can in order to be worthy of

---

80. Benardete, *Rhetoric*, 142–49.

81. Like Socrates, the dark horse is said to have a snub nose and to be short and ugly. It corresponds to the way the philosopher appears as a lover to external observers who have no experience of the beauty of his speeches—irrational, hubristic, and out of proportion.

82. R. Hackforth, *Plato's "Phaedrus"* (Cambridge: Cambridge University Press, 1952), states that it is "obvious that the charioteer with his two horses symbolizes the tripartite soul familiar to us from *Republic* IV" (72), even though he, like Benardete (*Rhetoric*, 149–51) and White (*Rhetoric and Reality*, 89–93), sees that there are important differences. The most important of these differences in my mind is that in the *Phaedrus* the white horse controls the dark desires with pain and a kind of fear (*aidōs*) rather than with *thymos*, as in the *Republic*, which, associated with anger, works to overcome fear.

his lover.[83] If the lovers restrain their desires to touch and be touched and let their thought (*dianoia*) rule, they establish a philosophical friendship that lasts a lifetime. Having established a godlike order in their souls that enables their wings to grow, such philosophical lovers are able to regain their disembodied condition in 3,000 years rather than the usual 10,000.

Socrates concludes his speech in praise of love by contrasting the rewards of such a philosophical friendship with the narrow calculations of the nonlover. Blaming the necessity of his speaking as a poet on Phaedrus, Socrates asks love to accept his recantation and allow him to retain his knowledge of *ta erōtika*. All the harsh things said about eros, particularly its irrationality, should be attributed to the "father" of that speech, Lysias. Love should make Lysias stop making such arguments and, like his brother Polemarchus, turn to philosophy. Then Lysias' lover Phaedrus would also stop vacillating between rhetoric and philosophy.

Although Socrates blames the poetic form of his speech on Phaedrus, we are reminded by his image of the soul that the need to represent purely intellectual things in bodily shapes is not peculiar to Socrates' interlocutor. Embodied minds of mortals do not have direct access to the purely intelligible beings. We have to "recollect" them from our sensible experiences. That is one of the reasons Socrates has to use an image; he cannot say what the soul itself is but only what it is like. That is the reason, more generally, that Socrates has to use indirect speech in praising eros in both the *Symposium* and the *Phaedrus*: the objects of our eros are only mediately, not immediately, evident to us.

In the *Phaedrus* Plato thus shows Socrates explicitly speaking as a poet to communicate a truth he claims is not available to poets. At the center of his second speech (247c) Socrates states that no poet ever has or will compose a hymn worthy of the purely intelligible beings. No poet has told or ever will tell the truth, therefore, about eros or human existence.[84] Not only does the desire to recollect these intelligibles distinguish human beings from both gods and animals. It also culminates in a form of friendship that makes human beings happy until they die (and possibly thereafter).

Speaking as a poet in the *Phaedrus*, Socrates makes the substantive difference between his understanding of eros and that of the poets clearer

---

83. Alcibiades fled Socrates' company, we recall, because he felt ashamed when he was with the philosopher. One learns about one's own soul, Socrates told Alcibiades in their first conversation, by looking at its reflection in the soul of another.

84. Socrates may thus indicate the reason he distinguished lovers of the Muses (daughters of memory) from the poets, who merely imitate sensible beings.

than it had been in the *Symposium*. Like the poets, Socrates denies that human eros is merely an animal desire for pleasure or reproduction; like the poets, Socrates understands human eros to be a yearning for something more, beyond our usual experience, more beautiful, better, and longer lasting. Admitting that love is initially experienced as a combination of pleasure and pain, Socrates denies that the pleasure is necessarily transitory and that love functions as a kind of temporary relief.

Like Aristophanes, Socrates associates eros with several different kinds of motion—vertical, cyclical, and horizontal (in the attraction of like to like). In Socrates' speech, however, all three motions have fundamentally different sources, ends, and significance. Whereas the circular men described by the comic poet assaulted heaven in an attempt to displace the gods, Socrates suggests that human souls merely strive to share the gods' contemplative wisdom. Our souls are attracted not by power but by beauty. We have no hope of possessing or controlling the intelligible beings, which exist independent of gods as well as men. Our souls wish to "see," not to be seen like the cosmic gods (and perhaps even worshiped). In Socrates' tale (in contrast to the poems of Homer and Hesiod) there is no envy or competition among the gods. The revolutions of the heavens are beautiful because of the intelligible order we perceive in them. Unlike the divine beings, human souls do come into competition, but the conflict is a result of their own defective order, not of divine enmity or conflict at the core of the whole. Since the resulting damage is a product of their own internal lack of order, human beings have to provide the remedy. In Socrates' story neither the gods nor the purely intelligible beings they contemplate depend on human recognition or worship for their existence, so they demonstrate little concern about what happens to their human followers (although soul in general is said to take care of the soulless).

Like Aristophanes, Socrates observes that human beings in love do not understand what has come over them or what they really want, and that they are attracted to people who are like them. Because love appears to be inarticulate, if not simply unintelligible, and a form of physical attraction, Aristophanes treats it as a bodily desire. Socrates insists that eros constitutes a movement of the soul. In striking contrast to Aristophanes, moreover, the remedy Socrates prescribes for the confusion and pain involved is wholly private. Rather than institute laws that regulate sexual relations and so secure the preservation of the species, Socrates urges human beings to suppress their bodily desires in order to attain greater and more lasting psychic intimacy. Because our bodies are separate, all community is fundamentally a matter of soul or mind. And if our association and communication with others are more a matter of soul than body, he suggests, there are many more than three kinds of unions or attractions. People choose to associate with others on the basis not only (or even primarily) of sex, but also of intellectual potential, knowledge, taste, talent, and experience. The variety of possible combinations is vast.

Like Agathon, Socrates emphasizes the role of beauty in arousing erotic desire. As in the *Symposium*, he insists that the sight of beauty arouses eros, not that eros itself is beautiful or even simply the desire for the possession of such. Beauty plays a crucial role in human life, because it is the only inherently intelligible quality that manifests itself directly or recognizably in sensible shapes.[85] What we really want, but do not initially know and thus cannot initially say that we want, is to recollect the purely intelligible principles that give order to the whole by directing and so regulating the motion of the soul.

Because, in his second speech, Socrates presents eros completely as a property of the human soul, he does not link it, as he had in the *Symposium*, with generation or the institution of political order, the two bodily manifestations of the desire to attain what is good—forever—that the poets emphasized. Instead, Socrates argues much more fully and directly than he had in his previous conversation with Phaedrus that human eros finds its proper expression and fulfillment only in philosophical friendship. In his account of what he learned from Diotima in the *Symposium*, Socrates suggested that procreation and poetry or legislation were two less pure forms of eros; in the *Phaedrus* he draws a clear distinction. Eros is not a desire to perpetuate one's own existence; eros is a desire to rise above and beyond one's current existence, to make one's own, and the lives of others, better.

The imagistic, poetic form of Socrates' second speech in the *Phaedrus* nevertheless produces a somewhat distorted picture of philosophy as an erotic activity. Both at the beginning and the end of his speech in praise of love, Socrates explicitly says that he is giving it in order to preserve his knowledge of *ta erōtika*. In the image of the soul he gives, he presents a great deal of what he knows about eros, but, in contrast to the *Symposium* where he related the lessons he learned from the priestess through

---

85. Unlike beauty, Socrates states, the bodily images of justice and moderation are not recognizable as what they are. The reason seems to be that these virtues often, if not always, appear to be forcibly (hence unwillingly and unpleasantly) imposed restraints on our desires, not intelligible forms of order that we seek and choose.

a process of dialectical interrogation of his own opinions, in the *Phaedrus*
Socrates gives little if any indication of how he acquired the insights he
conveys. He does not even speak in his own name. He claims to be speaking "ecstatically," in a state outside or beyond his usual earthly existence.

From Socrates' imagistic description of eros as the desire to recollect
knowledge of the eternal intelligibles aroused by the sight of beauty in the
face of a youth, we might infer that the source of his knowledge of eros
was the search for self-knowledge, which he told Phaedrus at the beginning of the dialogue left him no time to investigate the natural basis of old
stories. In earlier dialogues we have seen that Socrates seeks knowledge
of himself, as he told Alcibiades, by seeking to find the reflection of his
own soul in the soul of another. He had come to understand the character
of his own desire for knowledge by arousing and then observing it and
its effects on the souls of others. The souls that were particularly apt for
philosophy, as he described them here, were followers of Zeus and hence
usually desirous of rule. As Socrates suggests in his praise of love in the
Phaedrus, the philosopher attempts to arouse the desire to discover what
is truly good in a youth by becoming his lover. Treating his beloved as an
image of the god, he seeks to persuade him of the need to seek knowledge
of what is truly good.

Socrates states the purpose of the poetic speech he gives in praise of
love at its conclusion: he wishes to convince Phaedrus to turn away from
his fascination with rhetoric and to pursue philosophy instead. Socrates
tries to persuade Phaedrus by giving him what we know from the *Symposium* that Phaedrus desires: speeches in praise of love that show how
love benefits the beloved. If, like the beloved in Socrates' second speech,
Phaedrus were to see his own love of speeches mirrored in Socrates, he
would come to understand that his love of speeches is not merely or truly
a desire for the pleasure of listening or impressing an audience. That is the
desire both the sophists and the poets aroused and fed. The desire Socrates
seeks to arouse by means of his speech is a desire to become better than
one now is. To satisfy that desire, one must seek knowledge.

By presenting a beautiful picture of philosophy as love, Socrates wins
Phaedrus' admiration—at least for the moment. In the second half of the
dialogue, Plato shows that Socrates does not succeed in awakening a sufficiently strong desire to find out what is truly good to prompt his companion to undertake the painful effort involved in seeking knowledge or
to endure the humiliation, if not ridicule, that necessarily accompanies
an admission of one's own ignorance. By producing a beautiful image in

words, Socrates has like a poet allowed his auditor to listen passively, rather than forcing him to take an active part in the dialogue or argument. Poetic speech is not, therefore, the usual way in which Socrates seeks to engage his associates in a philosophical discussion. Because the beautiful poetic image he has drawn could at most arouse Phaedrus' desire for more arguments but could not engage the young man in making those arguments himself, or even in submitting his own views to criticism and possible refutation, in the second half of the *Phaedrus* Socrates returns to his more characteristic dialectical mode of interrogating the opinions of others. Nevertheless, his presentation of the benefits of philosophy continues to be indirect.

5. COMMUNICATING AND PRESERVING WISDOM THROUGH SPEECH AND WRITING

With his second speech, Socrates clearly wins the contest with Lysias.[86] Before Socrates began, Phaedrus promised that he would compel Lysias to formulate a new speech in response (*Phaedrus* 243e–44a); at the conclusion of Socrates' second speech, however, Phaedrus expresses doubt about Lysias' willingness or ability to do so (257c). Failing to understand the source of Socrates' demonstrated superiority as a speaker (or the content of his second speech, his knowledge of *ta erōtika*), Phaedrus attributes the outcome of the contest not so much to the merit of Socrates' talk as to the restrictions imposed on Lysias. Lysias might not want to continue the competition with Socrates—not simply because of the rhetorician's inability to do better but also because he had already been criticized by a politician for being a speechwriter. Phaedrus thus defends his friend by suggesting that the inferiority of Lysias' production lies not so much in its organization or content as in its form and circumstances. Unable to speak for himself in public before an audience (because as a resident alien Lysias was not allowed to address the Athenian assembly), the speechwriter risked being called a sophist because he prepared written speeches for others to read aloud.[87]

---

86. V. Tejera, *Plato's Dialogues One by One: A Structural Interpretation* (New York: Irvington Publishers, 1984), 51, describes the action of the first half of the dialogue as Socrates' "converting" Phaedrus from Lysias to himself. I am arguing that Socrates wins the contest concerning who can give the best speech about the benefits of love, but we see in the end that he does not convert Phaedrus.

87. The politician's criticism seems to foreshadow the critique of writing Socrates will deliver at the end of the dialogue. The writer of speeches is contemptible, the politician suggests, on two grounds. First, the writer does not present his own views directly or defend them. He does not, as Phaedrus later puts it, speak in a manly fashion (*andrikōs*; *Phaedrus* 265a). Second, the writer

Socrates won the contest with the rhetorician concerning who could give the best speech about eros, a private matter to be discussed in private, but Phaedrus still believes that public speaking is more important and respectable. In the second half of the dialogue Socrates thus tries to convince Phaedrus that he will never become a good rhetorician if he does not become a philosopher. So long as philosophy is presented as a means of achieving another end, we know from earlier dialogues, Socrates cannot present his own philosophy as what it really is. Attempting to appeal to Phaedrus' desires, he has to distort the picture or presentation of the nature of his own endeavors. The picture Socrates draws of philosophy in the first half of the *Phaedrus* presents no more a complete or accurate depiction of the nature of Socratic philosophy than does the *Symposium*. In the second half of the *Phaedrus*, Socrates attempts to correct the young man's possible misapprehension. Beginning again by appealing to Phaedrus' sympathies and prejudices, Socrates defends Lysias from the criticism of the politicians by pointing out that legislation is nothing but writing. As in the *Symposium*, Socrates identifies poets and statesmen. When the proposals of public speakers are adopted by assemblies and written into law, he reminds Phaedrus, the poet (*ho poiētēs*) leaves the theater (*theatron*) in delight. The greatest politicians—Lycurgus, Solon, and Darius, for example—were legislators. The crucial difference is not between speaking in person or writing for others, Socrates concludes; the question is whether the speaking or writing is noble (beautiful) or base (ugly).[88] The measure of the nobility or baseness of a speech (*logos*) is not its composition or attractiveness, moreover; the excellence of a speech depends on whether it is based on truth and has beneficent effects on others.

Phaedrus enthusiastically agrees to investigate the question of what makes beautiful or ugly (noble or base) writing in public or private, in verse or prose, by questioning Lysias. "What else should one live for," he observes, "but such intellectual pleasures, that unlike physical sensations,

---

deceives the audience—perhaps even the speaker himself—by making the speaker appear to know more and to be able to reason better than he actually can, unless he is subject to questioning about what he has said, in which case his own (in)capacities and knowledge (or ignorance) will be revealed. Afraid of being accused of being sophists, Phaedrus concludes, the most outstanding politicians refuse to write anything down. They do not want to appear to claim knowledge that they do not test directly in public life.

88. Commentators on Socrates' concluding critique of writing often forget the equation of writing and speech with which he begins this part of the dialogue. See, e.g., Jasper Neel, *Plato, Derrida, and Writing* (Carbondale: Southern Illinois University Press, 1988). Gerald Mara, *Socrates' Discursive Democracy: Logos and Ergon in Political Philosophy* (Albany: SUNY Press, 1997), 18, is a notable exception.

can be enjoyed without previous pain?" (*Phaedrus* 258e). But Socrates gently rebukes Phaedrus for his persistent attempt simply to maximize his own pleasure and minimize his own pain by relating a fanciful story about the fate of human beings so excited by the birth of the Muses that they sang and sang without pausing to eat or drink until they (like Aristophanes' first lovers) perished. Reborn as cicadas, they sing without eating or drinking until they die. Those now humming around them will laugh at his and Phaedrus' indolence of thought (*dianoia*), the philosopher supposes, if they see the friends lulled to sleep in the heat. If the cicadas hear human beings conversing, however, they report back to the eldest Muses (Kalliope and Ourania, the "beautiful" and "heavenly") that these men have honored them by spending their life philosophizing.[89]

With this story Socrates seeks to correct the impression Phaedrus may have received from his speeches both in the *Symposium* and the *Phaedrus* that philosophy consists simply in pleasurable contemplation of the overwhelming beauty of the intelligible beings. As a search for knowledge, philosophy is characterized by painful striving to recapture a momentary glimpse of the purely intelligible in an effort that must continually be repeated. Philosophy does not consist merely in passive reception, watching, or "theory." Philosophers have to work to regain and retain their fundamental insights because they have embodied souls. Because human souls are embodied, they also have to attend to the requirements of self-preservation. To imagine that they are simply free from their bodies is a dangerous, indeed, deadly, mystical illusion—not the truth Socrates sought to convey in the image of the soul as a driver of two horses, which emphasized the constant struggle required to establish and maintain order in human life.

Phaedrus objects to Socrates' claim that the first requirement of good speaking and writing is that the speaker know the truth of the matter; Phaedrus has heard that an orator need not know what is really just, only what would seem just to the multitude who decide cases. Phaedrus prefers rhetoric to philosophy not simply because rhetorical speeches appear to be cleverer and more persuasive, but also because rhetoric seems to enable

---

89. Socrates does not call this account a *mythos* (cf. White, *Rhetoric and Reality*, 183), even though it would seem to be an imaginative tale—a narrative that is not literally true. It might seem stranger for Socrates to suppose that human beings existed before the Muses were born. Such a supposition would correspond to what we know of human history, that is, that human beings precede the development of poetry. It would also be consistent with Socrates' palinode in which human souls are immortal, but the Muses are, as traditionally, said to be born from memory.

people to get what they want with less effort. As Socrates suggested indirectly with his story of the cicadas, Phaedrus is lazy. He is not a passionate man so much as an avid consumer of easy entertainment. As a result, he does not learn. Although Lysias and Socrates have both provided him with examples of private speech or rhetoric, Phaedrus does not change his opinions in light of his own experience. He continues to regard rhetoric primarily in terms of public speaking.

Rather than confront Phaedrus directly, Socrates again seeks to correct him indirectly with an example. A public speaker who does not know the truth (for example, the difference between an ass and a horse), but nevertheless convinces others to follow him, causes them harm (for example, defeat in war). An orator needs to know what is good or bad, Socrates concludes, if he is to benefit his listeners. A legislator or rhetorician will not continue to persuade his audience long, if his advice is shown to be bad or fallacious in practice. Knowing how to give a persuasive speech is no substitute for knowing the things (*pragmata*) the speech is about.

"The art of speaking" (*technē tōn logōn*) might respond to his argument, Socrates suspects, by admitting that she would urge a person to learn what is good first, but she would nevertheless insist that such a person would not be able to persuade others to do it without knowing her. The question becomes whether it is possible to have knowledge (an "art") of persuasion separate from and independent of philosophy. Rather than refuting Phaedrus directly, and so perhaps offending or alienating him, Socrates sets up an indirect dialogue by calling forth critics of the so-called art of persuasion to convince Phaedrus that he "will never be able to speak sufficiently about anything if he does not philosophize" (*Phaedrus* 261a). The critics begin by asking Phaedrus whether rhetoric is not the art of leading souls (*psychagōgia*) through speeches, not only in public assemblies but also in private. Phaedrus does not agree; he still thinks rhetoric consists primarily in public speaking. So Socrates asks Phaedrus what public speakers do; don't they argue opposed sides of issues? Doesn't the purported art of rhetoric consist in making the same things appear at some times just and at other times unjust to the same people? If so, the "Eleatic Palamedes" (Zeno) practices such an art of antilogistics in his treatise when he shows that the same things are both like and unlike. Rhetoric is not limited to public speeches, and if the point of rhetoric is to lead people to mistake things for their opposites (for example, the unjust for the just), the person able to point out resemblances between things will have most success. People are more apt to be persuaded that something is the contrary of what it might seem if they are led gradually by a series of comparisons than if the speaker jumps immediately from one pole to its opposite. To know what something is like, however, one needs to know the truth about the thing. Unable to contradict Socrates, but not entirely convinced, Phaedrus replies merely, "so it seems" (262c).

To illustrate his contention, Socrates suggests that they look first at the failings of Lysias' speech and then at his two as examples "of the way in which one who knows the truth may playfully lead his auditors" (262d). He insists that their having such examples ready at hand should be attributed not to him but to the divinities inhabiting this place (who, he claimed earlier, had inspired him), or perhaps to the prophets of the Muses humming about them. He emphatically denies that he himself has any part in an art of speaking. He uses and examines speeches (*logoi*) in seeking truth; he does not try merely to persuade others to adopt his opinions, that is, to legislate. He restricts himself to private conversations and does not address the public (cf. *Apology* 31c–e). Socrates thus points out that there are important differences between philosophy, on the one hand, and rhetoric, legislation and poetry, on the other. These differences are differences in intention and substantive understanding—not in the kind of knowledge required to produce beautiful speeches with beneficial effects. Socrates denies that he or anyone else possesses the art (*technē*) of speaking, because he denies that there can be technical knowledge of the means of persuading people without knowledge of the soul. And, as he suggested at the beginning of the palinode, it would take more time than any mortal has to acquire such knowledge.

As earlier, Socrates begins his critique of Lysias by faulting him for not defining the subject matter of his speech at the beginning. People agree about the meaning of some words, but they disagree about the meaning of others—like "love"—and the latter are the cases in which rhetoricians have most potential power to persuade other people to adopt their opinion. A rhetorician must learn first to distinguish these two kinds (*eidē*) of words (or things to which they refer) and then be able to determine to which his topic belongs. Lysias does not; from the outset he explicitly assumes that everyone shares his understanding of love. As Socrates has demonstrated, they do not. Lysias also fails to divide love, as Socrates had, into its different kinds (*eidē*). Lysias' list of the costs and benefits of love do not appear to have any necessary order, yet, Socrates observes (and, we shall see, the professional rhetoricians agree), like a living being, every speech should have a head, trunk with limbs, and feet (or, as Aristotle put it, a beginning, middle, and end).

Phaedrus balks at Socrates' ridicule of Lysias, so the philosopher turns to his own productions, which he characterizes again primarily as play.[90] By chance (he says modestly), there are two aspects (*eidoin*) of that talk worth learning: (1) how to collect many disparate particulars into one *idea*, and (2) how to divide things according to their *eidē*. But Socrates goes on to declare that he is such a lover of these *diaireseis* and *syntheseis* that "he follows any man he sees able to do them as if that man were a god" (266b). When Socrates engages someone in conversation, we infer, from his earlier statement about souls following their particular gods, that he is seeking first to discover and then to develop that person's dialectical potential or powers. Such is the philosophical intercourse in which, Socrates suggests, true love and lasting human happiness consist.

Phaedrus and Socrates agree that people like Thrasymachus who claim to possess and teach the art of rhetoric do not engage or instruct others in dialectics. Socrates thus inquires whether there is anything beautiful not included in dialectics that could be called art and attributed to rhetoric. Phaedrus assures him that there is—in the many treatises written on rhetoric. By briefly summarizing the teachings of the authors of several such books—Theodorus, Evenus, Gorgias, Tisias, Prodicus, Hippias, Polus, Licymnius, Protagoras, and Thrasymachus—Socrates not only demonstrates his own familiarity with them but also shows that these rhetoricians would agree with his second criticism of Lysias, the criticism at which Phaedrus took umbrage. Comparing their "art" first to medicine (as practiced by Hippocrates) and then to the writing of tragedies (as practiced by Sophocles and Euripides), Socrates suggests that those who know how to compose speeches that arouse different kinds of passions possess only the necessary tools, not the art itself, that is, knowledge of how and when to use those tools to produce good and beautiful results.

Phaedrus is willing to concede that the professional teachers of rhetoric are inferior to the father of the art of medicine and the greatest tragedians. When he asks Socrates to give him an example of an equally outstanding public speaker, Socrates names Pericles, who, as a follower of Anaxagoras, supports the philosopher's contention that if rhetoric is an art, like all great branches of knowledge it would have to include reflections

---

90. This is also, we should note, the way he will characterize writing at the end of the dialogue.

on nature as a whole. Socrates then returns to Hippocrates and the example of medicine to remind the longtime companion of Eryximachus of the need to learn the nature of the subject matter of the particular science. Just as a physician needs to know about the body as a whole in order to restore a diseased person to health, so a rhetorician needs to know about the soul. To make good his claim to possess an art, a rhetorician would need to know (a) whether the soul is simple or complex, (b) how it acts and is acted upon, (c) by what, and (d) if there are many different forms, what these are. That is, the possessor of an art of rhetoric would have to demonstrate precisely the knowledge Socrates said would require a longer discourse (logos) than any mortal has time to give. To possess an art of rhetoric, a man would not merely have to say what the nature (physis) of the soul is; he would also have to be able to classify all the different kinds (genē) of speeches and souls, showing the effect each produced on the other and why. He would need to be able not merely to list the kinds of souls and speeches in theory but to recognize the different types of soul in sensible form and be able, in practice, to produce the kind of speech that would persuade this type.

Phaedrus agrees that a man claiming to possess an art of rhetoric should know all this—and that such knowledge would be extremely difficult to attain. Remembering that Phaedrus is attracted to the easy way, Socrates asks him to investigate the apparently more modest and easier claim that the art of speech need only deal with probabilities or likelihoods, not with truth per se. To illustrate the reasons why likelihoods would not suffice, Socrates introduces an example from Tisias. The rhetorician had argued that neither a large coward from whom a small, weak man stole a cloak nor the thief would tell the truth in court. The thief would point out how unlikely it was that a weakling like himself would overcome a big strong man. Wishing to conceal his own cowardice, the strong man would also deny that he had been outsmarted or physically overcome. Because we have no direct access to or knowledge of the thoughts, desires, or motives of others, it might seem that we have no choice but to judge what people say on the basis of external appearances. But, Socrates suggests, such deceptions may be uncovered through cross-examination. Not saying how or why, he simply reminds Phaedrus that they had agreed that those who know the truth are best able to identify and formulate likenesses. Because such knowledge is acquired, to the extent humanly possible, only with a great effort, a wise man (sophos) would seek it not in order merely to please a human audience but to gain favor with the gods.

Reflecting on the example he took from Tisias, we are nevertheless able to draw out the grounds for Socrates' pious conclusion. The coward's attempted deception is likely to be uncovered through cross-examination, because bald-faced lying requires a certain amount of boldness, precisely the characteristic the coward lacks. It *is* necessary to have the knowledge of different types of souls and the speeches that suit them in practice to argue effectively; familiarity with mere external appearances or probabilities will not suffice. Neither the world nor human experience of it is quite so unformed and hence malleable as the poets and rhetoricians suggest. The speeches of those who base their likenesses on the truth stand up better to examination than falsehoods, precisely because the former point to what is really the case, whereas the latter can be shown merely to be illusions. As Socrates observed earlier, rhetoricians have power in the cases where human beings do not agree. Precisely because human opinion is variable, the ability to persuade a group of people to adopt a certain view on one or more specific occasions does not achieve anything lasting or truly valuable. Attaining knowledge of what is truly the case, of what the gods see, does.

By concluding that what Socrates has said is extremely beautiful (or noble), if it could only be achieved, Phaedrus reminds us of the fundamental difficulty. The knowledge of the soul involved in a true art of speaking would require a discourse (*logos*) of such length that no mortal can give it. But could not a series of human beings formulate such an argument, art (*technē*) or science (*epistēmē*), over time? This is the implicit but unstated reason that Socrates suggests, having completed their discussion of the art of speaking, they should turn to writing. Writing seems to represent a means whereby human beings can amass and preserve knowledge beyond the limitations imposed by their own mortality.

Socrates argues, however, that people cannot preserve or communicate knowledge in writing any more than they can in speech. Our bodily nature makes it impossible for us to cognize purely intelligible beings immediately or to communicate that knowledge directly to others. We human beings become familiar with ourselves and our surroundings first through our senses. As Socrates has repeatedly demonstrated in speaking to Phaedrus, it is necessary to proceed indirectly. Like the image of the beautiful in the face of a beloved, all writings or speeches can do is to arouse a desire on the part of the recipient to recollect a view of the purely intelligible beings for him- or herself. Socrates describes both his own speeches and all writings as forms of "play" because they cannot preserve or communicate truth per se. They are means of leading of the soul to look in the right direction, of helping it remember and pointing the way.

When Socrates relates "something that he has heard from their predecessors without knowing himself whether it is true" (274c) about the reaction one god, King Thamus of Egypt (otherwise called Ammon), had to the invention of writing by another, Theuth, Phaedrus skeptically comments how easy it is for Socrates to make up tales.[91] Reminding Phaedrus that it is the content, not the source, that matters, Socrates nevertheless tries to overcome his interlocutor's skepticism by not merely repeating, but explaining the critique in his own name. Rather than improve human knowledge and memory, the invention of writing leads people to rely on external marks instead of exercising their own minds and memories. As a result, they learn less while ignorantly believing that they know more. Writings have the further defects of not being able to answer questions and saying the same things to everyone, without regard to context, character, or condition. Writings are not, in other words, good means of teaching. Rather than imparting knowledge, they serve merely as reminders that help people to recollect what they already knew.

Socrates contrasts the art of writing with a related activity (its "brother"), which he calls "writing on the soul." Unlike visible marks or pictures, a person who understands an argument (rather than merely memorizing and repeating it word for word, as Phaedrus had tried to do with Lysias' speech) can defend it by answering questions. Someone who understands what it means to learn also knows (like Socrates by means of his *daimonion*) when, where, and to whom to speak (or remain silent). As Phaedrus points out (276a), the written word is an image (*eidōlon*) of the speech of a living knower. Socrates insists that the image is merely that, an incitement to further action on the part of the reader or listener, not a communication of truth. Knowledge consists in active understanding, not passive possession. As Socrates observed in the *Symposium*, we are constantly forgetting and losing; thus not merely as a species or generations, but even as individuals, human beings must constantly strive to remember and recollect.

In response to Socrates' characterization of writing as play, Phaedrus once again expresses his enthusiasm for such intellectual forms of entertainment. Socrates has not succeeded in transforming his companion's de-

91. Socrates does not explicitly call the account he gives of King Thamus' reaction to Theuth a *mythos*.

sire for easy pleasure into a willingness to work hard in order to discover the truth.

Recapitulating the argument in response to Phaedrus' request for assistance in recollecting it (and so reminding us of both the need for, and function of, writing), Socrates suggests that those who understand the need to learn the truth about things, to define them by dividing them into eidē, and to do the same for the soul and speeches addressed to it should be called philosophers, since only the gods are wise. Mortals do not have time to learn the whole in all its complexity. They can, however, come to understand the difference between the truly intelligible and the merely artificial or man-made. Those who know nothing better than written compositions should be called rhetoricians, poets, or legislators. They mistake sensible reminders for the truly eternal.

Socrates brings the conversation to a close by observing that they have amused themselves talking about speeches long enough. He dispatches Phaedrus to tell Lysias that they have been to a spring sacred to the nymphs, where they were charged to deliver a message to the rhetorician along with other composers of speeches, Homer and the poets, as well as Solon and other lawgivers: they deserve honor if they know the truth and can answer questions about what they have written, but not for their writings per se.[92] Knowing Phaedrus as well as he does, Socrates has reason to suspect that his young friend will try to repeat the speeches he has heard without attributing them to their actual author.

Observing that the heat has died down, the materialist seeker of comfort says he would like to leave. Underlining the difference between himself and his impious companion, Socrates offers a parting prayer to Pan to let him be beautiful inside and to consider the wise man rich. When Phaedrus asks to share in the prayer on the ground that "friends have everything in common," Socrates simply repeats, "Let's go" (279c).[93] He recognizes that he and Phaedrus do not share or have the most important thing in common, a desire for wisdom or truth. They are not truly lovers or friends; in this conversation they had simply playacted.

92. This is *the* move, from the "play" (or indeterminate meaning) of writing to moral and political seriousness, for which Derrida chiefly criticizes Plato ("Plato's Pharmacy," 156–71).

93. Cf. Griswold, *Self-Knowledge*, 130: "In the pretense that Socrates and Phaedrus are equal and, by the end of the dialogue, interchangeable (having 'everything in common' like true friends, as Phaedrus—not Socrates—will say) lies the comedy of the *Phaedrus*. Socrates and Phaedrus belong to different types; or at least, Phaedrus is a laughable imitation of the Zeus-like."

In the second half of the *Phaedrus* Plato has shown his readers how Socrates, who spoke as a poet, could nevertheless be distinguished not only from the poets but also from the rhetoricians and legislators with whom he was often confused. Like the sophists, rhetoricians, politicians, poets, and philosophers claimed to educate the young. But where the rhetoricians, politicians, and poets identified such education with the production of speeches—whether spoken or written—Socrates understood that the effect of such speeches or the education occurred and could only occur in the embodied soul of a living human. The real work of speeches is, and can only be, achieved indirectly, by arousing that person's desire to seek knowledge of the good, often by showing the inadequacy and inferiority of other possible objects of desire and the ignorance as well as the unhappiness of those who continue to pursue them.

Socrates calls his knowledge erotic, because the only thing he claims to know is what human beings really want. Perceiving the differences among them, he also recognizes that there is no single way all can approach, much less achieve, the partial knowledge of what is truly *kalos k'agathos* of which mortals are capable. He does not claim the ability to lead anyone, much less everyone, to see the advantages of a life of philosophy. Although Plato shows that Socrates wins virtually every contest in speech that he enters, Socrates never claims to possess an art (*technē*) of speaking.[94]

II. The Difference between Visible Image and Inner Core: *Clitophon*

Having listened to Socratic conversations like those related in the *Phaedrus* and the *Protagoras*, Plato shows in the *Clitophon*, one young Athenian politician concluded, that Socrates was merely an inferior kind of rhetorician. On meeting Clitophon, Socrates informs the young man, he has heard that, in a conversation with Lysias, Clitophon criticized youths who wasted their time with Socrates and praised those who associated with Thrasymachus.[95] Confronted with the report, Clitophon takes the oppor-

---

94. Socrates' youthful exchange with the elder Parmenides and his final defense of himself before the Athenian jury might be regarded as exceptions. It is not clear, however, that either represents a contest.

95. The fact that the conversation Socrates heard about was with Lysias (*Clitophon* 406) links this dialogue to the *Phaedrus* and *Republic*.

tunity to defend himself. Rather than simply faulting those who associated with Socrates, he had praised as well as criticized them.

In stating what he praised and blamed, Clitophon demonstrates both familiarity with and a fundamental misunderstanding of Socratic teachings. In listening to Socrates, the young man asserts, he often thought the philosopher sounded like a god on the tragic stage, rebuking fathers who attended more to making money than to educating their sons.[96] Like Phaedrus, we see, Clitophon was impressed by Socrates' poetry. Attracted by the nobility of Socrates' teaching, Clitophon agreed with the philosopher that instruction in music and gymnastics does not constitute a sufficient education. Lack of musical training does not produce divisions within families and wars among cities; to live in peace and harmony people need to learn to be just and moderate. Even though injustice is base and hateful to the gods, the uneducated claim that people are voluntarily unjust. Like Socrates, Clitophon believes that no one is willingly unjust or mastered by pleasure.

Like him, Clitophon believes, people want to be virtuous; they simply do not know how. He has been persuaded by speeches of the kind Socrates first gave Alcibiades, for example, that those who train their bodies but not their souls are neglecting the part that should rule. Such people should not seek wealth or power, because those who do not know how to use a possession are more apt to be harmed than benefited by it. Clitophon even accepts the conclusion (at which Alcibiades balked) that anyone who lacks such knowledge is better off a slave than a master. From his self-description, it becomes clear that the politically ambitious young man seeks knowledge because he wants to be a master rather than a slave.

Convinced by Socrates that virtue can be taught (although Socrates did not, in fact, argue this in his earlier dialogues) and that it is necessary above all to care for oneself, Clitophon reports that he sought to learn what virtue is and how it could be acquired. Anxious not to risk the possibility of

96. Clifford Orwin, "On the *Cleitophon*," in Pangle, *Roots*, 118–21, observes that Clitophon's defense of himself echoes the *Apology of Socrates* in the description of the philosopher's exhortation of his fellow citizens to virtue. Unlike the *Apology*, the *Clitophon* makes explicit the gap between exhortation and actual teaching or conversion. Arguing in part on the basis of Clitophon's later defense of the proposition that justice is what the makers of the law believe is to their advantage in the *Republic* (340a–b), Orwin concludes that Clitophon speaks, in effect, in defense of the city against Socrates' accusation in the *Apology*. David Roochnik, "The Riddle of the *Cleitophon*," *Ancient Philosophy* 4, no. 2 (Fall 1984): 132–45, contests Orwin's characterization of Clitophon's speech as a defense in court because there is no crime involved.

being refuted or shown not to have understood the philosopher's arguments fully like Critias or Nicias, the young man did not initially seek to converse with Socrates himself. Rather than attempt to free himself of false opinions or to acquire self-knowledge by learning what he did not know by undergoing a dialectical examination, Clitophon imitated Socrates — or, more precisely, the externally visible form of Socratic speech—by going to some of the philosopher's associates and asking them, as he had heard Socrates ask others, by analogy: if they were seeking to care for their bodies, what arts would they need to learn and employ? On receiving the answer—gymnastics and medicine—Clitophon inquired further: and if they were seeking to care for their souls? When the person reputed to be the best of Socrates' associates answered with the word "justice," Clitophon rebuked him, as the young politician had heard Socrates rebuke others, for responding simply with a word. In order to show that justice is truly an art (*technē*) or form of knowledge, the young man insisted that it would be necessary to show, as in the case of medicine or shipbuilding, that those who claim to possess the art can pass their knowledge on to others and give an account of its effects. The art of justice would presumably produce just human beings, but what sorts of works (*erga*) would these just people produce? Socrates' associates responded variously, with "right," "useful," or even "profitable." But Clitophon objected that the same could be said of medicine, and asked, what is the distinctive work of justice? Like Alcibiades, one of Socrates' best associates suggested friendship in polities. So Clitophon asked him what characterizes friendship? The associate responded: agreement in knowledge (as opposed to mere opinion). According to Clitophon, those listening became angry at the circular character of the argument. Doctors, too, could be characterized by their agreement in knowledge.

Having received no satisfactory answer from Socrates' associates (and perhaps content with his demonstration of his mastery of the techniques of elenctic argumentation), Clitophon finally asked the philosopher himself. Socrates first told him that justice consisted in doing good to friends and bad to enemies, but as the argument progressed, it turned out that it was never good to harm anyone.[97] Disgusted by what appeared to be circular argumentation with no satisfactory outcome, Clitophon concluded

---

97. As we shall see, in the first book of the *Republic* Socrates responds to Polemarchus' contention that justice consists in benefitting friends and harming enemies by arguing that it is never just to harm anyone—and Clitophon's teacher Thrasymachus objects.

that, although no one was better at exhorting others to become virtuous, Socrates could not tell him what virtue is, either because the philosopher did not know or because he was not willing to disclose what he knew. Anxious to learn, Clitophon went to Thrasymachus or anyone else who claimed to possess an art and the ability to teach it to others.[98]

Believing that he had learned how to conduct an inquiry by watching Socrates question others, Clitophon never asked himself what he really wanted or why. Although he claimed that he wanted to know what virtue is, in practice he showed what he thought it was—the ability to best others, first in argument and then in fact. Clitophon parroted many of Socrates' teachings, but we observe, he never mentioned the need to seek self-knowledge, moderation, or self-restraint. He was content with the superficial appearance of things, what people say as opposed to what they think.[99] Without understanding why someone might not want to be virtuous, he did not see the problem involved in becoming virtuous. What is good for one person may not be good for others. Caring for one's self may not serve the common good.

From the report of this brief exchange we see that Socrates could not convince young associates to join him in a life of philosophy merely by painting a beautiful picture in words of the potential benefits or by providing an example of argumentative techniques they could learn through imitation. Those who were impressed by Socrates' poetic speeches and tried to copy his characteristic mode of proceeding quickly became disillusioned. Like most human beings, they believed they knew what is good. They did not comprehend the question that animated Socrates' inquiries or share in the passionate desire to find an answer. To arouse a desire on the part of his young auditors to discover what is truly good for us, Socrates not only had to show them that the opinions about virtue, the noble, and the good they had taken over from their friends, families, and fellow citizens were contradictory and hence self-defeating. He also had to give them grounds to believe in the possibility of finding an answer they could incorporate in their own everyday existence.

---

98. Clitophon nevertheless appears to follow Socrates' suggestions, even in his choice of alternative teachers. In the *Phaedrus* (267c–d) Socrates says that Thrasymachus is the best of those who claim to teach the art of persuasion.

99. It is no accident, therefore, that in the *Republic* (340a–b) Clitophon defends the proposition that rulers do what they believe is advantageous to them; they do not need to know what is truly advantageous.

III. The Contest with the Poets Renewed: *Republic*

Some commentators have taken the *Clitophon* to be a discarded draft of an introduction to the *Republic*, because in the *Republic* Socrates appears to answer both of Clitophon's questions by determining what justice is and how it is to be attained.[100] Examining the dialogue in more detail, however, we see that Socrates casts doubt on the adequacy of the definition of justice to which he and his interlocutors come as well as on the possibility of attaining it.[101] What then does Socrates achieve in his longest conversation? Is Socratic philosophy anything more than the moral suasion Clitophon takes it to be?

In the *Symposium* and *Phaedrus* Plato showed that Socrates could persuade young men such as Alcibiades and Phaedrus that philosophy constitutes the most desirable form of human existence but that he could not keep them persuaded over time. One reason Socrates failed to convert his associates to philosophy was that it appeared to be merely a private endeavor, with little, if any, broader popular effect. In the *Republic* Socrates does not succeed in making Plato's brothers into philosophers any more than he had succeeded with Alcibiades, Critias, and Phaedrus, but he does convince Glaucon and Adimantus that philosophers would be better than either poets or rhetoricians as legislators, because philosophers alone can bring a just regime into existence.[102] In order to preserve the perpetuation

100. Clitophon is also said to be present (*Republic* 328b). Indeed, he speaks briefly in defense of Thrasymachus (340a–c). In the *Republic* Clitophon only addresses an associate of Socrates, Lysias' brother Polemarchus, not the philosopher himself.

101. Both Michael Davis ("On the *Cleitophon*," manuscript) and Bruell (*Socratic Education*, 192–99) question the assumption that the conversation related in the *Clitophon* necessarily precedes that narrated in the *Republic*. They do not, however, argue that the *Clitophon* necessarily follows the *Republic* or question the dramatic connections and hence close conjunction of the two conversations in setting or time. Since Clitophon picks up the contrast between what Socrates does and what rhetoricians and legislators claim to be able to do, with which the *Phaedrus* ends and the *Republic* begins, I think the short dialogue is best read between the two longer works.

102. According to the *Seventh Letter* 324b–26b, this was the lesson Plato took from historical events after the conversation depicted in his dialogue. Glaucon and Adimantus appear to be ideal interlocutors for a conversation about politics insofar as they represent the two basic political virtues—courage (Glaucon) and moderation (Adimantus). Both the Eleatic Stranger in the *Statesman* and the Athenian Stranger in the *Laws* explicitly argue that citizens of any political association must have these two virtues if the polity is to survive. Allan Bloom, "Interpretive Essay," in The "*Republic*" of Plato (New York: Basic Books, 1968), 338; and Leon Craig, The War-Lover: A Study of Plato's "*Republic*" (Toronto: University of Toronto Press, 1994), 3ff., argue that Plato's brothers are lovers of honor (timocrats). In contrast to Craig, I argue that Plato shows that young men with such characters do not represent potential philosophers. As Miller (*Plato's "Parmenides*," 15–21) points out, the utter disinterest Glaucon and Adimantus show in the conversation related in the *Parmenides* indicates as much. I agree, therefore, with the observation in Stanley Rosen, *Plato's*

of philosophy as a form of human existence after the immediate intoxication produced by Socratic speeches faded, Socrates had to change the opinions nonphilosophers held about the utility of philosophy. If Socrates convinced people in general that educating philosophers was in the public interest, families would no longer do everything in their power to dissuade their most talented children from seeking wisdom and urge them to pursue fame and fortune instead (*Republic* 491b–95a). The emergence of philosophers would no longer remain an unlikely product of the chance coincidence of extraordinary talent with exceptional circumstances. In the best case, studies preparatory to philosophy, if not philosophy itself, would become a part of accepted public practice.

Socrates clearly could not convince those unable or unwilling to engage in philosophical investigations of the utility of philosophy merely by philosophizing. As we see in the *Republic*, he had to employ both rhetorical arguments and poetic devices. At the same time, he had to persuade his interlocutors that both the rhetoricians and the poets were wrong to claim that it is either unnecessary or impossible to achieve knowledge of what is truly good for human beings.

In book 1 of the *Republic* Plato thus shows Socrates defeat Thrasymachus, the rhetorician to whom Clitophon went instead of Socrates, in an argumentative contest. Although Thrasymachus appears to be an iconoclastic defender of injustice who argues that justice is nothing but the advantage of the stronger imposed on the weaker in the form of law, the rhetorician agrees with Socrates' fundamental contention that rulers need to know what is good—first and foremost for themselves. In the *Phaedrus* we saw that Socrates and the rhetoricians might disagree about the kind of knowledge that is necessary and how much effort it takes to acquire it, but they agree about the desirability of obtaining knowledge—at least of their art. Socrates and the poets do not.

"*Republic*" (New Haven: Yale University Press, 2005), that "the *Republic* (and not only the *Republic*) is an advertisement for philosophy, in terms that are intelligible to the companions of Socrates, and in particular to Glaucon and Adeimantus. That is to say that within the dialogue, Socrates addresses primarily guardians, not philosopher-kings" (8). G. R. F. Ferrari, *City and Soul in Plato's "Republic"* (Chicago: University of Chicago Press, 2005), 11–15, argues that Plato's brothers are aristocratic "quietists," too gentlemanly to engage in the vulgar politics of a democracy or the tyrannical designs of their relatives, even though they are willing to associate with metics like Cephalus and his sons. Ferrari does not deny that Plato's brothers were politically ambitious; on the contrary, he cites Xenophon's account of Socrates' attempt to cure Glaucon of his political ambition, despite his political inexperience, in the *Memorabilia* 3.6.

In the remaining nine books of the *Republic* Socrates argues that it is necessary to banish the poets (but not the rhetoricians) in order to attain justice—for oneself or for the city.[103] As Adimantus points out at the beginning of book 2, the poets say that it is good to be just only for the rewards or to avoid the penalties of injustice. The poets even suggest that human beings can avoid possible penalties by deceiving others or bribing the gods with prayers and sacrifices. To comply with Glaucon and Adimantus' demand that he prove justice to be choiceworthy in itself, Socrates has to show that the poets' understanding of human existence is wrong.

A. Socrates' Descent into the House of Cephalus

The question of rewards and punishment is raised at the beginning of the dialogue when Socrates is brought somewhat unwillingly to the home of Cephalus, father of both Lysias and Polemarchus. Socrates had gone down to the Piraeus with Glaucon to see the processions in honor of the goddess. Spotting the philosopher at a distance, Polemarchus sends his slave to hold Socrates until he and his friends catch up with him. Socrates indicates a desire to go home, but Polemarchus reminds the philosopher that he and his friends are both more numerous and stronger. In this respect they resemble the "many" who rule in a democratic polis. Acting out the tenuous relation he later depicts between the philosopher and his fellow citizens, Socrates proposes to try persuading Polemarchus and his associates to let him go. Polemarchus points out the limits of the philosopher's power to persuade by observing that they cannot be forced to listen. Following the

103. In other words, book 10 is not the puzzling and unnecessary "excrescence" Julia Annas takes it to be in *An Introduction to Plato's "Republic"* (Oxford: Clarendon Press, 1981), 335, but is the culmination and conclusion of the entire argument. Nussbaum (*Fragility*, 122–35), on the other hand, presents Plato's dialogues as arguments with the tragic poets. Four other commentators argue that book 10 constitutes an appropriate conclusion to the whole argument, but on somewhat different grounds. In *Being and Logos*, John Sallis argues that book 10, especially the myth of Er, constitutes the appropriate conclusion to the meditation on the significance of human foreknowledge of our inevitable death. C. D. C. Reeve, *Philosopher-Kings* (Princeton: Princeton University Press, 1988), also argues against the "myth . . . that the *Republic* is neither a philosophically nor an artistically unified work" (xi). Both David Roochnik in *Beautiful City* and Kenneth Dorter, *The Transformation of Plato's "Republic"* (Lanham, MD: Rowman and Littlefield, 2006), emphasize the dialectical structure and ultimate unity of the dialogue. Dividing the dialogue into similar sections, Dorter sees the argument rising to the central images of the cave and divided line and then descending again to the cave. Like Benardete in *Second Sailing*, Roochnik argues that the dialogue explores three different conceptions of the city, soul, and philosophy in ascending order. Like this author, Roochnik emphasizes Socrates' need to distinguish philosophy from poetry at the end of the dialogue, but his account of both the need and the resolution of the question differs from that I am about to give.

lead of his young friend Glaucon, Socrates accedes to the will (or implicit vote) of the majority and accompanies them to Cephalus' house.

Attempting to wield a carrot as well as a stick, Polemarchus promises them dinner before they return to the harbor to see the torch race and meet many more young men for conversation. Testifying in deed to the superior attractions of an intellectual feast, the eleven men present never consume the promised dinner or return to view the race. In contrast to the easygoing, open-door dinner Agathon hosted at which guests discussed the benefits of love, the all-night meeting at the home of Cephalus at which they discuss the merits of a revolutionary new regime has the look of a conspiracy.[104] Arguments about who should rule are more dangerous than mere contests in speech. The former often take place behind closed doors in secret and at night, that is, in the dark.[105] As in the *Phaedrus*, so at the beginning of the *Republic*, we are reminded that human beings do not relate to one another solely on the basis of persuasion; threats of force and death lurk in the background.[106]

1. OLD AGE AS THE DEATH OF DESIRE (SOPHOCLES)

Cephalus greets Socrates by complaining about his not visiting more often. Now that the pleasures of the flesh have faded, the old man observes, he enjoys talking more. Cephalus claims, in effect, to have become philosophical in his old age. Socrates rather rudely responds by observing that most people would think Cephalus does not find old age burdensome because

---

104. Strauss, in his chapter "On Plato's Republic" (*City and Man*, 2–3), points out the parallel between the ten interlocutors here and the "Ten in the Piraeus" established by "men linked to Socrates and Plato by kinship or friendship [who] attempted a political restoration, putting down the democracy and restoring an aristocratic regime dedicated to virtue and justice" some years after the conversation depicted. The people involved in the "restoration" were not the same as those present at this conversation, however. As sympathizers with the democratic party, Polemarchus, Lysias, and Niceratus were victims of the Thirty. According to his *Seventh Letter*, it was his experience with "the eleven" in the city and "the ten" in the Piraeus, as well as Socrates' conviction by the democracy later, that convinced Plato himself no city would be just until philosophers became kings.

105. In terms of Socrates' later and arguably most famous image, this conversation thus takes place in the cave. Eva Brann argues that, as the place across the river, the Piraeus represents Hades: "Socrates 'descends' to the land beyond, is caught in conversation in the house of Pluto, and, like the phantom Heracles whom Odysseus meets on his own visit to the shades . . . he tells down there the story of his own descent (*Odyssey* 11.601)." Brann, "The Music of the Republic," *St. John's Review* 39, nos. 1 and 2 (1989–90): 11.

106. Sallis (*Being and Logos*, 312–455) picks up on Brann's suggestion and argues that the whole dialogue constitutes a meditation on the prospect of death. Because Socrates is forced by the number of Polemarchus' associates to defend philosophy as the only means of achieving justice, Bloom argues ("Interpretive Essay," 307–10), on the other hand, that the *Republic* constitutes the true and full "apology" of Socrates.

he is wealthy, and the old man concedes that wealth is advantageous—but only to a man of good character. Quoting Sophocles, Cephalus emphasizes the advantages of being free from sexual eros. No longer attached to physical pleasures, he can use his resources at the end of his life to pay his debts—particularly to the gods.

The investigation of the meaning of justice related in the *Republic* thus begins with Plato's reminding his readers of the two primary passions—sexual desire and fear of death—that have to be regulated if human life and community are to be preserved, the traditional means of imposing such restraint through fear of the gods, and the claim raised by the poets to produce and preserve such salutary beliefs. When he was young, Cephalus admits, he did not pay much attention to the stories about what happens to us after death, but in his old age he has come to believe that they might be true. He voluntarily retires, therefore, to make his sacrifices, leaving the argument to his son, Polemarchus.

2. Beginning Anew with the Young (Simonides)

The departure of the father represents the opportunity to innovate that arises with each new generation.[107] To take advantage of such an opportunity, however, would-be reformers like Socrates have to bring sons to question the opinions they have inherited. We thus see Socrates reformulate Cephalus' account of the advantages of wealth and good character into a definition of justice only in order to criticize it. "Telling the truth and giving back what you have taken from another" (*Republic* 331c) does not constitute an adequate definition, because there are occasions when it may be harmful to return someone's property (for example, to return a weapon to a man who has become mad) or to tell the truth.[108] The primary and central question for Socrates, we are reminded, is, what is good?

Polemarchus picks up the argument by quoting another poet, Simonides, who said that justice consists in giving each his due.[109] What the poet meant, Polemarchus explains, is that we should do good to friends and harm to enemies. Like "beauty" in the *Hippias Major*, justice so de-

---

107. Cf. Arendt, *Human Condition*, 9.

108. Quotations are based on the Bloom translation of *The Republic of Plato*, although slightly modified upon occasion on the basis of my own reading of the Greek text.

109. Supporting the general thesis of my treatment of the *Republic* as part of Socrates' contest with the poets, Blondell suggests that Socrates invites Polemarchus "to reject not just Simonides, but the whole poetic tradition" (*Play of Character*, 175).

fined consists in knowing what is fitting (*prepon*). As in the *Hippias Major*, however, the suggested definition is undermined by the problem of distinguishing apparent from real. Socrates asks what sort of knowledge enables someone to do good to friends and evil to enemies, and then shows that justice (or knowledge of good and evil) cannot consist in an art (*technē*). To do good a person needs to have knowledge of the specific goods in question: for example, horses, the power of various drugs to produce health or sickness, probable outcomes of various military strategies, and methods of making and keeping money. But, Socrates points out, the same kinds of "technical" knowledge can be used to deceive or harm: for example, potential buyers of horses, patients, and so forth. Knowing the properties or powers of the "goods" in question is not sufficient, moreover, to enable people to do good to friends; people also have to know who their friends are. If one does good to a person who only seems to be a friend, one actually does good for an enemy, a deceiver. Not knowing who one's friends are, one might also mistake a friend for an enemy and try to harm him. As in his previous conversation with Clitophon, Socrates ends by challenging Polemarchus' entire conception of justice by asking whether a just or virtuous person would ever harm another, that is, make him or her worse. Once again, we are reminded at the very beginning of the *Republic*, the decisive consideration for Socrates is what is good.

3. The Importance of Rhetoric (Thrasymachus)

At this point, Socrates reports, Thrasymachus jumped into the argument like a wild beast. Outraged by the political naiveté or, he suspects, duplicity of Socrates' apparently simplistic approach, Thrasymachus insists that Socrates answer rather than merely ask questions in order to feed his love of honor (by putting on an appearance of superior wisdom). And, the rhetorician warns, Socrates should not say that the just is the needful, helpful, profitable, gainful, or advantageous. Socrates protests that he may not have any other answer to offer, but the rhetorician announces that he does. He will give his answer, however, only if Socrates is willing to pay a penalty. As in his later trial, Socrates' friends promise to provide the necessary funds.[110]

---

110. This is one of the reasons Bloom suggests that the *Republic* is "the true apology of Socrates" ("Interpretive Essay," 307–11, 326).

Thrasymachus is not a citizen of Athens, but he nevertheless seems to speak for the city and its people when he identifies justice with the law.[111] Those who have the power to make the law (and thus prove that they are stronger) do so for their own advantage, the rhetorician insists. Socrates asks whether they do not need to know what is truly advantageous for them. A practitioner of an art himself, Thrasymachus rejects Clitophon's suggestion that they simply do what they believe is advantageous for them, even though such a move would have prevented Thrasymachus from seeming to contradict himself.[112] To be stronger—or better—one needs to know what one is doing. Like all other practitioners of arts, Socrates observes, rulers use their knowledge for the benefit of their clients or subjects. Like shepherds who tend flocks, Thrasymachus counters, rulers eventually fleece, if they do not kill and eat their charges. If rule were truly advantageous, Socrates objects, rulers would not demand compensation in the form of honor or money.

At each stage of the argument, Socrates notes, Thrasymachus agrees more and more reluctantly. Finally, when Socrates points out that those who know—music or medicine or any other art—do not claim to deserve more or take advantage of other knowers, but only claim to deserve more than those who do not know, the rhetorician blushes. A teacher of speech and argument himself, Thrasymachus realizes that he has been bested in front of an audience of potential students. Rather than get angry, however, the apparently aggressive speech-maker becomes docile. Although

---

111. The fact that the three men whose definitions of justice Socrates initially challenges are not Athenian citizens makes his inquiry safer than it might otherwise be. When Socrates turns to address young Athenians, he speaks in defense of justice (although not of Athenian democracy or law).

112. There has been much scholarly controversy about whether and, if so, why Thrasymachus contradicts himself. S. Everson, "The Incoherence of Thrasymachus," *Oxford Studies in Ancient Philosophy* 16 (1998): 99–131, thinks that he does. C. F. Hourani, "Thrasymachus' Definition of Justice in Plato's *Republic*," *Phronesis* 7 (1962): 110–20, argues that Thrasymachus does not put forward a definition of justice so much as an empirical observation, and that Thrasymachus is a conventionalist, that is, he identifies the just with the legal. G. B. Kerferd, "The Doctrine of Thrasymachus in Plato's *Republic*," *Durham University Journal* 40 (1947): 19–27, argues that Thrasymachus is shown not to be a defender of injustice (or "might makes right") or a conventionalist (justice is what the law says it is); he understands that justice is what is supposed to be for the good of the ruled, but perverted by rulers who make it or the laws to their own advantage. Dorter argues (*Transformation*, 32–50) that Thrasymachus' position is neither contradictory nor simply conventionalist. Socrates' elenctic examination of Thrasymachus leads him to state his true position, which Socrates does not, in fact, refute at the beginning of the dialogue, although he does so later. The undeniable fact is, however, that Thrasymachus admits that Socrates has defeated him in speech or argument, even though the rhetorician is not convinced of the truth of Socrates' claims.

he clearly has not been persuaded that justice is superior to injustice, Thrasymachus concedes Socrates' superior argumentative skill.

B. Justice: Natural or Necessary?

As Glaucon shows when Socrates asks him point-blank in the midst of his exchange with Thrasymachus whether it is better to be just or unjust, the young Athenian aristocrat knows that it is ignoble to appear to be openly or merely self-seeking.[113] Nevertheless, he admits at the beginning of book 2, he is no more persuaded than Thrasymachus that it is bad to satisfy one's own desires at the expense of others, if one can do so without acquiring a reputation for injustice or paying a penalty. Like Thrasymachus, Glaucon believes human beings naturally seek their own advantage. What is called "justice," that is, the law, comes into being when the many, who are individually weak, band together to protect themselves from depredations by the strong.[114] Justice, so understood, is based on convention and maintained by force; it is not natural, good, or choiceworthy in itself. Seeking a nobler understanding, Glaucon asks Socrates to prove to him that justice is good and choiceworthy. To do so, Adimantus points out, Socrates will have to controvert the claims of both traditional authorities and the poets.[115] By emphasizing the rewards of justice in terms of reputation and wealth, these authorities suggest that justice is not good or choiceworthy for its own sake.

As Adimantus presents it, the tradition is manifestly contradictory: it urges people to be just in order to gain the rewards or avoid the penalties

113. Socrates achieved his rhetorical victory over Thrasymachus partly by appealing to the sensibilities of the audience of young men concerning their reputations in opposition to Thrasymachus' intentionally shocking, unconventional, and de-bunking teaching about the self-interested, that is, unjust, sources of "justice" by asking Glaucon in front of his fellows whether he thought it was better to be just or unjust. At that point (347a–48a) Glaucon said he thought it was more profitable to be just. Now he recants.

114. Glaucon's claim that justice arises from a pact made by the weak to protect each other from tyranny at the hands of the strong has often been compared to modern social contract theory. There is a fundamental difference, however. According to modern social contract theory, the contract is based on and is an expression of the natural rights of the parties to it. For Glaucon the contract represents an agreement or convention that is contrary to (rather than in accord with or constituting a means of enforcing) what is right by nature. According to Glaucon, human beings are emphatically unequal by nature; according to modern natural rights thinkers like Hobbes, Locke, and Rousseau, we are equal—in our natural rights.

115. This reading of the *Republic* as Socrates' response to the poets is supported by the observation that, in stating the position to which they wish Socrates to respond, Adimantus quotes or cites Homer, Hesiod, Musaeus, and Orpheus (363a–64e) as sources, and Glaucon quotes Aeschylus *Seven against Thebes* 593–94.

of injustice, but it also suggests that people might receive the rewards without being just, if the gods so wish. However, as Plato showed in Socrates' earlier conversations, merely bringing out the contradictions in long-standing popular opinions does not suffice to dislodge such beliefs. As Glaucon states, most people believe that it is best to be able to satisfy one's own desires but worst to be subject to the arbitrary desires of others. Most people settle for laws and customs (*nomoi*) that prevent them from acting on all their own wishes but protect them from suffering at the hands of others.

To convince his interlocutors that the traditional views propagated, if not created, by the poets are wrong, Socrates could not merely bring out the contradictions or inadequacies. He had to propose an attractive alternative that was both more desirable and truer than the teachings of the poets. In response to this rhetorical necessity, we shall see, Socrates himself acts like a poet in two different respects. First, he constructs a novel image of a city in speech. Second, he uses his imaginary construction to show his auditors what is truly good in human existence. Unlike the rhetoricians and sophists, the poets did not claim merely to show their students how to obtain what is good. Like Homer, poets claimed to teach what is good and bad in human life. That was the reason Socrates equated poets with legislators in the *Symposium*. Both claimed to be teachers who formed the souls or character of their peoples. In the *Symposium* and *Phaedrus* Socrates did not criticize the form so much as the substance or teaching of the poets. In the *Republic*, however, Socrates does not content himself with suggesting that philosophy constitutes a higher, more beautiful and satisfying form of human existence than any depicted in an extant work of poetry—epic, tragic, or comic. He expands his argument with the poets to encompass questions of style as well as of content, because it is the form, even more than the substance, that makes poetry more attractive and hence more effective as a mode of popular teaching than philosophy. Socrates goes so far as to identify poetry with the form when he says, "I am not a poet; therefore, I will not speak in meter" (*Republic* 393d). It is the form that makes poetry so effective, because "rhythm and harmony most of all insinuate themselves into the inmost part of the soul and most vigorously lay hold of it" (401d).

1. Justice Writ Large

Expressing some doubt about his own ability to prove that justice is choiceworthy in itself, without regard to any extrinsic rewards, Socrates acknowledges that it would be "impious" not to try.[116] It is impossible, he reminds his interlocutors, to determine whether justice is good or choiceworthy in itself before they know what justice is. At the conclusion of his exchange with Thrasymachus Socrates admitted that his own argument was defective (*Republic* 354b); he had argued justice is more profitable than injustice without considering what justice is. To find out, he now suggests, they should first look for justice "writ big" in a city, where it would be easier to see than in an individual (where, in fact, as a virtue of the soul, it is literally invisible).[117]

2. THE TRUE CITY

Instead of the weak banding together against the strong, Socrates argues, the city comes into being when people discover they can satisfy their needs better if each does what he or she does best by nature and exchange products or services with others. What Socrates calls the "true city" (*Republic* 372e) thus comes into being to satisfy the needs of all equally, not merely the desires of the dominant part. It has a natural foundation; it does not exist merely by convention to serve the interests of the many as opposed to the more talented few.[118]

The desire to have more than is necessary and so to be distinguished from others is, however, what moves Glaucon.[119] He thus objects to the

116. Socrates thus claims to act on the basis of a virtue, piety, that he included in his list of the different kinds of virtues in the *Protagoras*, but that is not to be found in the city he is about to describe in speech. As in the *Alcibiades I, Charmides, Apology,* and *Phaedrus,* Socrates' piety is explicitly associated with a sense of the limits of his own powers.

117. As Strauss points out (*City and Man,* 92), in the *Republic* Socrates thus adopts a rather atypical mode of proceeding. He does not ask Glaucon and his brother Adimantus to try to identify the common element in different things said to be just—individuals, cities, laws, wars, etc.—or to find what is enduring. Socrates leads them to seek a definition of justice (which he lists in the *Parmenides, Phaedrus,* and *Phaedo* as one of the eternal ideas) by looking at the "coming-to-be" of a city. The account of the generation of the city he presents appears to represent a correction of that initially proposed by Glaucon. We should not be surprised that Socrates concludes later in the conversation that the definition of justice they come to on the basis of this image is defective.

118. In contrast to Aristotle in book 1 of the *Politics,* Rosen points out (*Plato's "Republic,"* 72–76), Socrates does not mention the erotic or procreative roots of the healthy city until the very end of his description. His emphasis on the more narrowly economic advantages of specialization and a division of labor for the preservation of individuals, as opposed to peoples, is related to the individual focus of the question whether a just life is better than an unjust one, to which the analysis of the city is merely a means.

119. Glaucon is thus both erotic, as Bloom ("Interpretive Essay") emphasizes, and spirited, as Nichols (*Socrates and the Political Community,* 59–66) and Benardete (*Second Sailing,* 35–43) argue. At *Republic* 548d–49b Socrates emphasizes that Glaucon is not simply a victory-loving timocrat; he is too fond of music and skilled at rhetoric. On the basis of this text, Roochnik (*Beautiful City*) points out that Glaucon could not live in the city they have founded, which is more regulated

absence of "relishes" in what he calls the "city of pigs." To satisfy his desire, Socrates observes, they will have to add warriors to the artisans currently composing the city. People who know how to use arms will be needed to seize land from neighbors to supply the luxuries Glaucon wants as well as to defend the city from attacks by others desiring more for themselves. In the "feverish" city we thus see the coming-to-be of both its justice (out of natural necessity) and its injustice (out of the desire for luxuries).

3. The Education of the Guardians

Once some people in the city have arms, the most pressing problem becomes how to prevent them from using those arms to oppress their fellow citizens. The first method Socrates proposes is to ban all images and stories of gods or heroes behaving in unjust, immoderate, or cowardly ways. The first reason Socrates expels poets from his city in speech is that they give expression to, and so encourage the development of, the kind of unjust desires that led Glaucon to object to the simple city. Poets are not banished simply because their works are fictional and hence false; their productions are censored because they reveal a powerful, if dangerous, truth about human motivation.

a. Music

Beginning with the stories (*mythoi*) they hear as children about the highest things—the first things in both senses—Socrates suggests that people who may become guardians should not be told about gods who fight with each other or commit incest (even though he will later admit that many people naturally imagine such in their dreams).[120] Gods must be believed only to cause good, not evil, and good gods would not change form or deceive human beings in any other way.[121] If, as Socrates suggested in both the *Symposium* and *Phaedrus*, there are eternally unchanging and hence intelligible objects of contemplation, these divine causes of good cannot be thought

---

and restrained, like his brother Adimantus. Dorter (*Transformation*, 55–57) argues that there is no good textual basis for distinguishing the brothers, whom Ferrari (*City and Soul*, 11–17) describes as "aristocratic quietists."

120. *Republic* 571c. As Aristotle points out (*Politics* 1264a10–40), it is not clear whether the education and institutions prescribed in the *Republic* apply only to the guardians or to the whole populace. If nurses are understood to be primary propagators of beliefs, it appears that the education must extend to all.

121. As Strauss points out (*City and Man*, 99), according to Socrates (*Republic* 389b), rulers may need to lie. If so, the gods he describes cannot rule. They may mete out justice, only if it, particularly punishment, is shown to be good. Would they care about human beings, however? That is not so clear, especially if, as Hesiod maintains in *Works and Days*, human existence is full of evils.

to be arbitrary or deceptive. Poetic images of the highest things should reflect the truth about the purely intelligible, not merely project human desires onto irresponsible, because immortal, deities.[122]

Because poetry has such a powerful formative effect, legislators should regulate not only the content but also the form and mode of presentation. In the just city they are constructing, poets must not be allowed to depict heroes bemoaning the terrors of death or their grief at the loss of loved ones; nor should poets be permitted to portray desires or acts of excess—with regard to food and sex or in expressions of grief and laughter. Those who watch or listen might be tempted to imitate the characters' lack of self-control. Because people learn so much through imitation, future guardians should not be allowed to play any role but that of a virtuous person. "Or haven't you observed that imitations, if they are practiced continually from youth onward, become established as habits and nature, in body and sounds and in thought?" Because guardians need to "know both mad and worthless men and women" (*Republic* 395d, 396a), they could be allowed to narrate stories about others. But dramatic poetry in which authors conceal their role by presenting only the speeches of others will not be tolerated. Citizens should not be taught to practice any form of deceit.

In banning dramatic poetry, Socrates admits, the legislators of the just city do not recognize or foster all kinds of human excellence. Thus

> if a man who is able by wisdom to become every sort of thing and to imitate all things should come to our city, wishing to display himself and his poems, we would fall on our knees before him as a man sacred, wonderful, and pleasing; but we would say that there is no such man among us in the city, nor is it lawful for such a man to be born there. We would send him to another city. (*Republic* 398a)

Socrates admits that poets have wisdom as well as power. He insists, however, that the power of poetry be subordinated to the requirements of civic education.

---

122. The Olympian gods Socrates describes in the *Phaedrus* do not engage in the activities to which he objects in the *Republic*. In both dialogues, the gods are "seen" by the mind or the soul. The gods there do not change form or deceive human beings. They lead "armies" of human souls up toward the eternal intelligibles, but there is no evidence that they care whether the human beings who follow them rise to the surface of the cosmos or fall to earth. Like Zeus they may be said to rule in the sense of providing a certain order or regular movements. Human souls are punished or rewarded for their behavior on earth once they become embodied, but not directly by the gods (in the *Phaedrus* or, as we see later in the myth of Er, in the *Republic*).

As in the *Phaedrus*, so Socrates concludes here, a good education should culminate in the right kind of love of the beautiful.[123] That love is intellectual rather than physical. Signs of affection such as kissing will be allowed among future guardians, but lovers will have to take care that they do not acquire a reputation for going any further.[124] As in both the *Phaedrus* and the *Symposium*, the purpose of education in the beautiful is the implanting, if not begetting, of immortal truths in the mind of the other.[125] In the *Republic* Socrates argues that as youths guardians should only be exposed to examples of virtuous behavior and speech, so that they will learn to love beauty (or nobility) before they encounter vice. He concludes that people will "never be musical—either ourselves or those whom we say we must educate to be guardians—before we recognize the forms of moderation, courage, liberality, magnificence, and all their kin, and, again, their opposites . . . both in themselves and in their images" (402b–c). Poetry can be instrumental in teaching people to recognize the forms of the virtues and the vices, but it remains merely instrumental. What is in truth is superior to mere images. Those who recognize the forms or images of the virtues in the dispositions of noble souls know no more beautiful sight, and they will love such human beings most of all.

In the *Phaedrus* the lover was said to perceive the image of the particular Olympian god his soul followed before it fell to earth and became embodied. In the *Republic* the images that arouse love are of the virtues, that is, of the eternal intelligible beings the gods in the *Phaedrus* easily rise to contemplate and human souls struggle to follow. In the *Republic* Socrates does not allow for differences—of individual inclination among human beings, characteristics among the gods, or between gods and the eternally intelligible beings. The reason Socrates abstracts from, if he does not deny, the existence of such differences in the *Republic* appears to be the political con-

<hr />

123. "Surely musical matters should end in love matters that concern the beautiful" (*Republic* 403c).

124. Socrates tells Glaucon that he will "set down a law in the city that's being founded; that a lover may kiss, be with, and touch his boy as though he were a son, for noble purposes, if he persuades him; but . . . his intercourse with the one for whom he cares will be such that their relationship will never be reputed to go further" (*Republic* 403b–c).

125. Cf. Socrates' later statement that "the nature of the real lover of learning [is] to strive for what is; he does not tarry by each of the many things opined to be but goes forward and does not lose the keenness of his passionate love nor cease from it before he grasps the nature itself of each thing which is with the part of the soul fit to grasp a thing of that sort. . . . and once near it and coupled with what really is, having begotten intelligence and truth, he knows and lives truly, is nourished and so ceases from his labor pains, but not before" (*Republic* 490a–b).

text. The guardians are guardians of the community; as such they should not have different characters or perceptions of the noble and good.[126]

b. Gymnastics

Having tried to arouse a desire for philosophy in his interlocutor by presenting him with a beautiful image of the human soul, in the *Phaedrus* Socrates proceeded directly to advocate the study of dialectics. In the *Republic* his account of the "musical" education of the guardians is immediately followed by the prescription of a certain kind of gymnastics. Only after he has argued the necessity of the rulers becoming philosophers does Socrates insist on the need for training in dialectics. In fabricating an image of the most beautiful city, it seems, Socrates finds it necessary to take account of the needs of the body in a way he had not in the private conversation about love he had with Phaedrus outside the walls of the city. One reason Phaedrus would never become a philosopher, we discovered there, was that he was too concerned about his physical well-being and not willing to engage in any activity requiring arduous effort. In the *Republic* Socrates gives a more complete account of the prerequisites for a philosophical education. At the same time, Plato reminds his readers of the difference between a philosophical friendship, which is purely voluntary, and a political association, which is not.

The physical training Socrates proposes in the *Republic* is explicitly related to the guardians' defensive functions. Warriors should not adopt the strict diets and schedules of professional athletes; to be effective soldiers, they need to learn not merely to moderate their desires for food, drink, and rest but to go without for long periods, if necessary. Socrates advocates a kind of physical training that allows intellectual development, however, more than a kind that simply produces stronger bodies, capable of enduring hardship. "Excessive care of the body," he concludes, "makes any kind of learning, thought, or meditation by oneself difficult" (*Republic* 407c).

Although the goal of the training of the body is ultimately the same as that of the musical formation of the soul, the two kinds of education impose somewhat different requirements. In order to judge both just and unjust behavior, Socrates argues, a person must first learn to be just. People who begin calculating how to satisfy their unjust desires at a young

126. Nichols (*Socrates and the Political Community*, 57–123) emphasizes the way Socrates abstracts from individuality or particularity in the proposals he makes in the *Republic*. She also traces this abstraction to the political context (as well as to Glaucon's "perfectionist" desires).

age do not believe it is possible to do anything else; they can never come to understand justice. The initial restrictions on the guardians' views of human action thus ultimately serve to broaden the scope of their knowledge. Only those who first learn to be just themselves can recognize both justice and injustice, when they encounter the latter in those they rule. In the case of medicine, it is otherwise. "Doctors . . . would prove cleverest if, beginning in childhood, . . . they became familiar with the greatest number of the worst bodies" (408d). Nevertheless, Socrates argues, in the city they are founding, doctors must not be allowed to extend their knowledge, because that attempt would distract them and their patients from the true goal of the education of the guardians. They are seeking the acquisition not of knowledge per se but of virtue. An unlimited concern with prolonging life undermines the development of courage in facing death.

By presenting unjust as well as just characters, the poets might argue, their works would provide future guardians and legislators with needed knowledge. If so, Socrates suggests, such knowledge should be made available only to those who had already formed just characters. It should not be available to youths or those who had not proved themselves. It certainly should not be presented in public performances of tragedies and comedies in front of crowds.

c. The Noble Lie

Having emphasized the power of poetry, Socrates brings out the limits of persuasion. To convince individual citizens to accept not merely their particular place or function in preserving the community, but the complete subordination of their individual desires to the requirements of that preservation, he concludes, it will be necessary to tell a noble lie. He does not know how anyone could persuade people of the desired beliefs—that citizens are born fully educated from their mother earth and that their functions are determined by the metallic character of their blood. The account of the autochthonous birth and education of all citizens or differences in the color of their blood would be disproved by simple observation of childbirth or bleeding.[127] It would not be easy to persuade people of claims that contradict the evidence of their senses, and even when they are per-

127. Attempting to soften the repugnance a reader may feel toward Socrates' insistence that rulers will need to lie, if nobly, Reeve (*Philosopher-Kings*, 210–11) argues that the lies are only "verbal" and not "real" because the lies benefit citizens by leading them as close to the good as they are capable of coming. Reeve does not pay enough attention to the goodness of the truth or philosophers' love thereof—or to the ease with which these lies could be shown to be such.

suaded (or claim to be), the opinions they acquire do not suffice to prevent them from acting on desires they feel. Such desires might be fostered by, but they are not simply products of, poetic depictions. To prevent guardians from acting on desires to have more than their fellows, Socrates thus tells his young companions, they will also have to deprive the guardians of all property and privacy (*Republic* 416c–17a). Effective legislation requires more than persuasive or poetic speech. To form the characters of citizens and control their behavior, rulers need to determine their economic condition and social relations. People do not acquire their opinions simply by hearing those of others; they also judge for themselves on the basis of experience. To shape their thoughts, one has to control that experience.

Why, Adimantus asks, would anyone want to be a guardian? They are no better than paid mercenaries, keeping constant watch for little pay and less honor. The purpose of their founding a city, Socrates reminds him, is not to discover the happiness of any one part but to find that of the city as a whole. In such a city, they may be able to find justice. He now urges them to look for it.

d. The Virtues as Opinions

As in his initial response to Glaucon, so when they turn to look for justice in the city, Socrates first tries to excuse himself and then proceeds in a way that is not only questionable but also uncharacteristic of him as a philosopher. If the city they have constructed is good, he suggests, it must contain all the virtues. If they can locate courage, wisdom, and moderation, they can then, by subtraction, find justice.[128] What they find—in all four cases—explicitly exists only in the form of opinion. And when they seek the analogue of the city with its three classes in three parts of the human soul, Socrates warns Glaucon "that in [his] opinion, we'll never get a precise grasp of it arguing the way we are now" (*Republic* 435c–d).[129]

---

128. As Annas points out (*Introduction*, 110–11), Socrates has not explicitly shown either that the city is good or that there are four and only four virtues.

129. As Strauss points out (*City and Man*, 109), the parallel between the city and the individual also breaks down at this point. Socrates explicitly compares the order of the three classes in the city to the order of the three parts of the soul. He gives no consideration to the needs of the body. Yet the city came into existence to satisfy the bodily needs of its members. The education of the guardians is not designed to make them the best human beings possible but to make them effective protectors of their (less educated) fellow citizens. Individuals whose reason directs and checks their desires by means of their spirit might be said to be well balanced, even happy, but we learn little about their relations to others or whether these relations are just. In the well-known analysis by Bernard Williams, "The Analogy of City and Soul in Plato's *Republic*," in *Exegesis and Argument*, ed. E. N. Lee, A. P. D. Mourelatos, and R. M. Rorty, 196–206 (Assen: Van Gorcum,

Although they not only reach a definition of justice in the city but also conclude that as the proper order of the parts of the soul, justice is manifestly desirable for every individual, the conversation continues.[130] It continues, however, not because the definition of justice is manifestly faulty—a matter of opinion rather than knowledge, applying in the case of the individual only to the soul without any account of its relation to the body—but because Socrates has aroused the interest of his interlocutors by referring in passing to the vast innovations in the organization of the household that would have to take place if such a city were to come into being.[131]

C. Socrates as Poet

Polemarchus asks his companions whether they should let it go, or whether they should protest Socrates' "robbing" them of part of the argument. All then "vote" to "arrest" Socrates and "compel" him to stay longer and complete his description of the regime. By means of the dramatic action, Plato subsequently shows us that Socrates not only understands and uses the power of poetry—epic and tragic—to shape the characters of its audience by presenting them with beautiful examples or images; he also comprehends and employs the appeal of novelty and hence the power of comic art.[132]

1973), Williams argues that the parallel breaks down, whether one equates a part of the soul with the dominant class in the city, in which case the souls of the dominant class, if not the souls of all the citizens are supposed to have only one of the three characteristic parts of a human soul, or whether all souls of all members of all classes are thought to have all three parts. Malcolm Schofield (*Plato*, 114–15) points out that although Williams acknowledges Socrates' observation that representatives of all forms of regime can be found in a democracy, Williams insists on drawing a strict parallel between the regime and the individual, which Socrates' description would make impossible in a democracy where all types reside. Roochnik (*Beautiful City*, 15–24) observes that the three-part description of the soul in book 4 is static, thus inadequate and incomplete, since we know from the *Phaedrus*, for example, that the soul is characterized by motion. Recognizing that this "arithmetical" description of the soul is not complete, Socrates in books 8 and 9 modifies and replaces it with a new image (of the hydra, the lion, and the little man) and narrative description of the conflicts among the interpenetrating parts. In other words, Socrates never thought there was a complete parallel between the order of individual souls and regimes.

130. Cf. Hans-Georg Gadamer, "Plato's Educational State," in *Dialogue and Dialectic*, 86–87.

131. "The possession of women, marriage, and procreation of children must as far as possible be arranged according to the proverb that friends have all things in common" (*Republic* 423e–24a).

132. Socrates himself thus provides an example of the poet he is said to have described at the end of the *Symposium* who understands and can "write" both tragedy and comedy. When Socrates says that he is not afraid of being laughed at but that he does worry that he will commit the worst crime by deceiving his friends about the noble, good, and just in legislation, Glaucon first excuses him and then laughs (*Republic* 451a–b).

In describing the innovations necessary to achieve justice—particularly the philosopher-king—Socrates leads (literally e-ducates) his companions to see human existence in a new light primarily by presenting them with a series of striking images—the legislator as the pilot of the ship of state, the sun as an image of the good, the divided line as an image of our knowledge, and the cave as an image of our nature in its education and want of education.[133] That is, Socrates acts as a poet. As in the *Phaedrus*, the purpose of his poetry (undertaken here in his own name and not in the guise of another) is to convince his young associates that philosophy is the best, most satisfying form of human existence. But at the same time that he uses poetry, Socrates also emphasizes its limits. The most he can do with the images he draws is to arouse the desires of his interlocutors; he cannot make them philosophers. To become philosophers, he states, they would have to undertake arduous studies in dialectics. Such studies could be imaged, if at all, only by mathematics; they are not and cannot be made poetic, even though they are beautiful and good.

I. THE BEAUTIFUL CITY

To unify the city as much as possible (and so to abolish the causes of war within and among cities), Socrates proposes (as Aristophanes does "later" in his *Ecclesiazusae*) to abolish not only all private property but also all exclusive family relations.[134] If everyone is to practice the art (a form of knowledge) for which he or she is best suited by nature, males and females must have the same education. To receive the same education and perform the same functions as men, women must be freed from their domestic duties and from confinement to a particular household and husband. As the comic poet shows dramatically at the conclusion of his play, and as Socrates suggests in requiring everyone to exercise in the nude and to mate on demand as the city requires, such provisions deny the character and force of human eros—for particular people.[135] By showing two old

---

133. To explain why cities will have no rest from evils before philosophers rule, Socrates says he needs to use an image "so you may see still more how greedy I am for images" (*Republic* 488a).

134. There is a dramatic anachronism here. In a conversation supposed to have taken place before his death in 399, Plato's Socrates quotes extensively from a play that was written and produced after his death. Strauss provides an extensive list of citations or quotations from Aristophanes in the *Republic*, especially to the *Ecclesiazusae* (*City and Man*, 61). Once more Plato reminds his readers of the imaginary, nonhistorical character of the conversations he relates.

135. At the conclusion of the *Ecclesiazusae* Aristophanes shows elderly crones exercising their legal right to demand sexual services from a young man before he pursues his own inclinations for a young and beautiful woman.

hags fighting over a reluctant young man, Aristophanes suggests that the communistic institutions proposed are unnatural. People will always be attached, first and foremost, to their private pleasures. There will therefore always be competition, frustration, conflict, and war. Socrates introduces another alternative. If, as he argued in the *Phaedrus*, human eros is intellectual more than physical, it can be redirected and thereby satisfied in a way that purely physical desire cannot. *The* innovation Plato's Socrates makes that goes beyond Aristophanes, and so implicitly corrects the comic poet, is the suggestion that philosophers should become kings.[136]

Glaucon's reluctant agreement at the end of the discussion of the communistic institutions to women serving in the military, primarily as reserves, shows that he has not fully accepted the proposition that, like dogs, male and female guardians should perform the same functions. Nor has he understood the implications of the proposed breeding when he accedes to Socrates' later suggestion that those who distinguish themselves in battle be rewarded with more frequent sexual liaisons as well as songs, food, and drink. (In that case the breeding would no longer be secret or anonymous.) In sum, Glaucon has not lost his desire for luxury or distinction. He perceives, however, that the greatest distinction or honor is to be achieved by bringing an entirely new kind of city into existence. He thus presses Socrates to show how they can become founders or legislators in fact.

2. PHILOSOPHER-KINGS

Socrates says that the least change in an existing city that would enable it to approximate the model they have outlined in speech—and the most extraordinary, original proposal he has to make—is the conjunction of philosophy with political power. It is admittedly unlikely, but not impossible, that a prince might develop a passion for learning.

As the need to educate the guardians had made clear, the justice of a city depends primarily on the character and knowledge of those in power. Philosophers have the requisite character, Socrates argues, by nature. As a result of their extraordinary love of truth, those with philosophical natures do not value other goods as highly. Not caring much about wealth or the pleasures it can buy, they are moderate in what they seek and liberal with what they have. Because they do not want much, they do not take from others; they are therefore also just. Seeking to discover what is eternally true, they do not greatly prize their own mortal life; not fearing

136. Strauss, *Socrates and Aristophanes*, 282.

death, they are therefore courageous. To succeed in their search for wisdom, philosophers also need to have quick wits and retentive memories. In describing their nature, however, Socrates emphasizes the effects of their dominant passion (erōs for the truth) on their character.

Adimantus objects that few people believe philosophers have such extraordinary virtues; rather than seeking them out as rulers, most people believe that philosophers are useless at best.[137] People hold such views about philosophers, Socrates responds, for three reasons. First, because it is against nature for those who know to beg the ignorant or rich to let them rule, philosophers do not claim a right to rule.[138] Second, since philosophers do not put forth their own just claims to rule based on knowledge, pretenders step in to take their place. Third and most important, most people have never seen a true philosopher. Those with the requisite nature are few, and most of them are corrupted before they mature. It is not the "pretenders" or "sophists" who turn youths with the natural bravery and moderation, quick intellects, and retentive memories of potential philosophers away from the search for wisdom, however. Parents, friends, and the whole citizen body with its laws and penalties do everything in their power to cajole or compel such youths to pursue wealth, fame, and empire instead of "useless" knowledge.[139] Only those whose circumstances or natures discourage them from engaging in political activity persist in the search for truth.[140] Having experienced the sweetness of the philosophical life and

137. Socrates explicitly says that it is necessary to respond to this popular misconception with an image. As he and Agathon agree in the *Symposium*, poetry is a more popular form of speech than philosophical argumentation. By following the example set by Aristophanes in his *Knights* of presenting the people as a large individual (Demos), physically strong, but shortsighted and hard of hearing, Socrates may be reminding his audience that the misperception was spread by poets as well. In his own image of the "ship of state," the sailors representing ambitious politicians compete for control of the ship by cajoling or compelling the owner (people) to give it to them. They deny that there is any other art of navigation beyond such persuasion or force that might qualify them as pilots. "They have no suspicion that the true pilot must attend to the time of year, seasons, sky, winds, stars, and all else that pertains to his art" (*Republic* 488d). Benardete (*Second Sailing*, 145–48) thus concludes that the philosophers Socrates is suggesting ought to rule are the "pre-Socratics" who studied the heavens and who were regarded, like Socrates himself in Aristophanes' *Clouds*, to be mere "idle babblers." He seems to take this part of Socrates' image literally. In the sequel, Socrates explicitly states that the "divine" knowledge the philosophers need in order to rule is of the purely intelligible forms of the virtues, not of the visible heavens.

138. One might understand Socrates to be referring here to a natural order of higher and lower. In the sequel it becomes clear, however, that the "nature" that prevents philosophers from contradicting the politicians is their overweening desire or erōs for truth. They do not put forward their claims to rule because they have no desire to do so.

139. Socrates' description of the potential philosopher here fits Alcibiades perfectly.

140. Socrates' mention of Theages as an example of a potential philosopher who remained out of politics because of his sickly physical constitution represents an anachronism, if, as Plato

"the madness of the many" as a result of which "no one who minds the business of cities . . . can go to the aid of justice and be preserved" (*Republic* 496a–d), these few withdraw from public life and mind their own business. According to the definition of justice they found in the city earlier, these philosophers are just. They do not have to rule.

At present, Socrates admits, youths with the requisite nature (like Alcibiades) represent the greatest danger to the maintenance of political order, precisely because they are corrupted—by the people themselves. However, if the people ever saw a true philosopher and heard speeches of the kind he had just given, they could be persuaded to accept philosophers as rulers.[141] Unlike the politicians now contending for control of the community, philosophers do not seek rule to benefit themselves at the expense of others. Seeking to understand the things that always *are*, philosophers have no leisure to concern themselves about human affairs; they are not, therefore, filled with envy, nor do they quarrel with others. Indifferent to human concerns, such philosophers would not appear to constitute caring or qualified rulers. Socrates thus adds that, contemplating things that exist always in a rational order, philosophers attempt to live in such an orderly fashion as far as that is possible for a human being. If some necessity arises for them to try to impress the order they see in the characters of others as well as in themselves, they will not "prove to be bad craftsmen of moderation, justice, and popular virtue" (500d). Socrates has thus included himself among the philosophers. As he demonstrates in action here, it is possible for a philosopher to act both as a poet and educator. Although he has not literally been "writing" on the blank slates or souls of others, he has been fabricating an image of justice—both in speech and in deed.

3. The Education of Philosophers

Although Socrates insisted earlier that the many could not philosophize, the difficulty of combining philosophy with political power does not appear to reside primarily in popular resistance. The problem appears, rather, to be finding people with the requisite natures and educating them to rule.

---

indicates at *Theages* 129d, the conversation in which Theages and his father Demodocus urged Socrates to take Theages as a student occurred in 409 during the expedition Thrasyllus undertook against Ephesus and Ionia. Socrates would not have known whether or not Theages had talent for philosophy at either of the two likely dramatic dates of the *Republic*, 422 or 412–411. For this reason some scholars have questioned the authenticity of the *Theages*.

141. At this point (*Republic* 498d) Socrates also observes that he and Thrasymachus have become friends; the philosopher and the rhetorician apparently agree not only on the desirability but also on the possibility of persuading the many to accept rule by the wise.

The question thus becomes, what studies and practices would make them fit to govern?

Neither the education in music and gymnastics nor the accompanying "psychology" they discussed earlier will suffice (*Republic* 504a–b). It thus becomes necessary to begin anew. Although Socrates had emphasized its passionate love of truth in his first description of a philosophical nature, he now stresses the need for potential rulers to combine intellectual virtues, quickness, and steadiness, which rarely coexist. As the warriors had to be tested to see whether they remembered the lessons they had been taught, so rulers have to be tested to see whether they are willing to engage in intellectual labor as well as physical. Only a few are able and worthy of undertaking the "greatest of all studies," the search for the "idea of the good."

This knowledge is not currently, or probably ever, available to human beings. But, Socrates points out, it is nevertheless what human beings want most of all, "what every soul pursues and for the sake of which it does everything. . . . Many men would choose to do, possess, and enjoy the reputation for things that are opined to be just and fair, even if they aren't, but when it comes to good things, no one is satisfied with what is opined to be so but each seeks the things that really *are*" (505d–e). No one is able to say with any precision, however, what the good is. Most people identify the good with the pleasant, yet they commonly speak of both "good" and "bad" pleasures. More "refined" people say the good is prudence, but when asked prudence about what, they answer in a circular fashion, the good.

a. The Good

Glaucon presses Socrates to say what the good is—or, if he does not know, at least what he supposes it to be—but Socrates demurs. Glaucon would not be able to follow an account of Socrates' opinion. Instead of a definition of the "idea of the good" (which Plato says in his *Seventh Letter* is impossible to articulate), Socrates presents Glaucon with a series of images he describes as the "children" or the "interest."[142] As Socrates indicates would be the case, the imagistic account he proceeds to give of "the greatest study" is

---

142. Derrida ("Plato's Pharmacy," 81–84) makes much of the fact that Socrates describes his doctrine as the *tokos*, the "token," which is left behind, the product or surplus, and that the Greek word for "being," *ousia*, originally referred to the property holdings of a household. As I argue more fully in the context of the *Phaedo*, the most Socrates can leave behind for his associates to inherit are opinions, images, and an example that will encourage them to continue seeking knowledge for themselves. He cannot directly pass such knowledge on to them.

not entirely clear or complete. The image suggests that the constitution of the whole is such that we can never entirely comprehend it.

Socrates introduces the analogy he proceeds to draw between the sun and the good by reminding Glaucon of the distinction he has often drawn between the many beautiful or good things and the beautiful or good in itself, which they call one idea, and that which really is. Rather than immediately draw a proportion between the visible and the intelligible realms as he subsequently does with the "divided line," Socrates points out that a third kind (*genos*) of thing is necessary for something to become visible. Not only must there be something with the power of sight and color in the object; there must also be light. Just as the god Helios (sun) is the cause (*aitia*) of the light that constitutes a necessary condition for things to become visible, so the good is the cause of the truth, in the light of which known things (*gignōskomena*) are known (*gignōskesthai*). The point of Socrates' excursus on the light seems to be to show that the good is not a god or cause in the sense of maker; it provides the necessary condition for knowledge and being, although it itself is neither.[143] There are three different factors that determine the knowability (or visibility) of something—the characteristics of the thing, the power of the "viewer," and the existence and/or amount of "light."

It makes sense, at least loosely, to say that it is both good in itself and good for us that there is being and knowledge.[144] As an "idea" the good is presumably one. But is it the whole or the ground, the cause—and in what sense—of the whole? Insofar as it is "beyond being" (*Republic* 509b), the idea of the good appears to be something different from the sum of its parts.[145] Socrates leaves the relation between the realm of the purely intelligible ideas ruled by the good and the sensible realm of generated things ruled by the sun—that is, the constitution and articulation of the order

143. The picture of the constitution of the whole given here is thus quite different from the "likely story" (*eikōs mythos*) Timaeus relates concerning the work of the *dēmiourgos*.

144. Martin Heidegger, *Nietzsche*, trans. David Farrell Krell (New York: Harper and Row, 1982), 4:167–72, argues in his explication of Plato, in his lectures on Nietzsche, that *agathos* (good) does not mean "moral." But it does seem to mean more than merely "useful," as Heidegger translates it (following Aristotle's notion of the "final" cause). In his later work Heidegger argues that the "Being" of the beings, that is, that which makes the disclosure of the beings in the light of truth (*a-letheia* or "un-concealment"), must itself remain concealed.

145. Inasmuch as Socrates suggests that the idea of the good is beyond being in dignity because it is older (*presbuteros*), it might appear to be the origin or *archē*. If the beings, or those things that truly are, are themselves eternal, however, their origin could not be in time or literally have age. The surpassing power (*dunamis*) that makes the idea of the good beyond being might be that of holding together being as a whole.

of the whole—as unclear as he had in his first articulation of his teaching about the ideas to Parmenides. There he had talked of "participation" (*metechein*) of the many sensible things in the purely intelligible ideas. Here he speaks primarily of "images" or, more precisely, similarities, relations of geometrical proportion. In both cases he denies that everything can be reduced to multiples of a single unit as in numbers (as the Pythagoreans had argued) or to one basic material (like the Milesians). Contrary to both the flux theorists and the Eleatics, Plato's Socrates insists from the beginning until the end of his public career as a philosopher that there are irreducibly different kinds of being. In his later images of the line and the cave, he suggests that we understand things insofar and only insofar as they are like the pure intelligibles. Only the intelligible can be intellected. But what, then, is responsible for some things becoming less than perfectly intelligible "images"? Is it a result of darkness, that is, the absence of light, and so presumably the limited power or range of the "lighting" of the good? Or are the sensible things in the realm of becoming products of a mixture of something like a formless matter with the intelligible forms? In either case, the good would appear to be the cause of being and knowledge, but not of the whole.

By calling the sun an "offspring" of the good "begot in proportion to itself" (508c) Socrates appears to conflate generation, the coming-into-being and passing away of sensible things in time, with purely intelligible relations of geometrical similarity. Insofar as he distinguishes sun and good, he suggests that only part of the world is intelligible. His account is explicitly incomplete. It is incomplete not merely as an image of the whole but also as a series of images of the subject(s) of potential study by human beings. Socrates says that he is "leaving out a throng of things" (509c).[146]

b. The Divided Line

One thing Socrates leaves out is the possibility of the intentional fabrication of "idols" or false opinions—in brief, poetry.[147] Turning from the

---

146. As Rosen points out, "Socrates is not precise in his use of technical terms, and in the present passage the idiom is metaphorical, not technical" (*Plato's "Republic,"* 263).

147. Observing that "in Book 10 Socrates says that a painter is like someone who carries a mirror and shows reflections of everything, and a poet does the same thing in words (596a–599a)," Dorter argues that "the poet's imitation of the visible world in words is also an example of *eikasia* [because] it cannot fit anywhere else on the line." Dorter admits that "Socrates could not give it as an example in the context of the metaphor of the Divided Line because words do not primarily belong to the visible world." Dorter ignores the problem of fabricated images like unicorns or gods (cf. Bloom, "Interpretive Essay," 428) as well as the fact that words may mark general types

source of our knowledge to what we can know, he asks Glaucon to draw a line in the sand, unevenly divided into two segments, each of which is then divided in the same proportion.[148] The lowest level represents the reflections or images of the sensible things on the upper part of the lower portion; sensible things are in turn said to be images of the definitions of the kinds of things human beings employ in trying to understand them (represented on the lower section of the upper part of the line), which definitions are then said to be composed, and so images, of the purely intelligible ideas on top. On this line there does not seem to be a place for metaphor, that is, the use of one kind of thing, for example, a lion, to represent an aspect rather than the whole of another kind of being, for example, a courageous man. Reflections or images may be more or less accurate, but none is simply false.[149] There is no place for the intentional lie—noble or otherwise. Socrates' image does not seem to allow either for his own political prescriptions (the noble lie) or his own use of images in educating Glaucon.

The line with its proportional segments is intended to show—or, more precisely, to image—a relation between sensible and intelligible forms of being that makes it possible for them to coexist in an intelligible, unified whole. (The line is divided into segments in equal proportions, and these proportions are, therefore, all equal to one.) Such relations of similarity— between reflections and things reflected, as well as between sensible examples of general categories of things and the intelligible categories—do exist in the world. But these intelligible relations of geometric similarity do not encompass all the particular beings and their distinctive character-

---

of things but do not reflect their shapes. (Cf. *Sophist* 239d–40a.) "Unless we take . . . *eikasia* to extend to verbal images as well as other kinds of reflections," Dorter sees, "one of the most common ways of looking at reality, one that focuses on what we hear about it rather than observing it in itself, would not be accounted for on the line at all" (*Transformation*, 191–92). Dorter does not want to admit that the image of the divided line is not complete, because he argues that the whole dialogue is organized on the basis of this image.

148. "Consider a line that is divided into two unequal segments and then cut each segment in two in accord with the same ratio. In other words, the line L is cut into two unequal parts A and B, and A is divided into parts C and D, whereas B is divided into E and F. A is to B as C is to D, and C is to D as E is to F" (Rosen, *Plato's "Republic,"* 263; cf. also illustrative chart in Bloom, *Republic*, 464). Tom Griffith, trans., *The Republic* (Cambridge: Cambridge University Press, 2000), points out: "From the description of the line, a mathematician would be able to prove that the two middle sections, corresponding to thought and belief, are invariably equal in length, regardless of the total length of the line and the location of its first cut" (note to 511d5).

149. As readers of Plato know, Socrates admits his own inability to account for the existence of false opinion in a subsequent conversation with the young geometer Theaetetus shortly before the philosopher's trial and death. Whether the Eleatic Stranger provides an adequate account of the possibility of false opinion in the *Sophist* remains to be seen.

istics—signified, for example, by proper names. And it is this multiplicity of kinds of beings as well as the diverse kinds of intelligible signifiers we use to distinguish and mark them that make the acquisition of knowledge so difficult.

c. The Cave

Socrates thus asks Glaucon to consider the cave as a third "image of our nature in its education and want of education" (*Republic* 514a). Human beings do not entirely lack knowledge, Socrates suggests with this third image, but we do not possess knowledge, properly speaking, of the whole. In contrast to the first two, Socrates' third image does seem to allow for the existence of poetry when he describes human beings carrying artifacts in front of a fire on a path leading out of the cave. These artisans shape the entire sensible experience of the prisoners chained to the floor. All the latter see are the shadows of the artificial objects on the wall in front of them, cast by a flickering, unsteady, artificially produced light.

Chained by their necks so that they cannot turn around and investigate the source(s) of the images they see and the sounds they hear behind them, Socrates notes, the prisoners would not "have seen anything of themselves." Bound to the floor of the cave, human beings do not understand their own condition. They do not understand that they are confined, by what, where, or with what results. Socrates suggests that the confinement is a result of their bodily needs and pleasures when he says that "if this part of such a nature were trimmed in earliest childhood and its ties of kinship with becoming were cut off—like leaden weights, which eating and such pleasures as well as their refinements naturally attach to the soul and turn its vision downward—and it were turned around toward the true things, it would see them most sharply" (519a–b).

Socrates does not say whether the "artifacts . . . and statues of men and other animals" of which the prisoners see only the shadows are simply copies of the real things in the world outside or include "imaginary" combinations fabricated by those who carry them. Nor does he say why some human beings, who were obviously freed from their chains and able to see something of the outside world, decided to make such a fire and to project images of artifacts into the cave. He does suggest that most human beings do not recognize sensible beings as images of intelligible kinds or principles of order as the image of the divided line indicates. (We know that none of the pre-Socratic philosophers, much less ordinary people, in fact, did.) Socrates' image suggests that most human beings understand things mediately rather than immediately, by means of man-made constructs—like words and the languages composed of them, or stories about the divine origins and causes of the generation of the things we encounter in the world around us. (Poets have been said to be the "makers" as well as the communicators of both.)[150] To understand what the things we perceive truly are and how they are related to each other as well as to us, human beings have to get beyond the human constructions, to see both the constructions and the things as they truly are.[151]

In his image of the cave Socrates thus suggests that human beings have to overcome two different kinds of impediments if they are to learn the true nature(s) of the beings. Not only do our own bodily needs and sensations direct our attention and efforts away from the intelligible toward the concrete and urgent. Human beings also lack direct or immediate access to the intelligible beings themselves. We have to use artificially devised languages, invent means of counting or measuring, and fabricate accounts of the origins, interconnections, and significance of our experiences, which distort both the experience and its purported causes, in order literally to dis-cover those causes—the intelligible beings and the man-made means of access to them.

To overcome both these impediments, Socrates further suggests, human beings need a "liberator"—someone who not only releases a prisoner from his chains but also forcefully turns him or her around and drags him or her up out of the cave, painfully, into the light. And the need for such a liberator changes the character of the education Socrates describes. What differentiates human beings from one another, according to Socrates here, is not intellectual ability—everyone is said to have the power—but the objects of their attention.[152] In contrast to what he said earlier about music and gymnastics, the education imaged by the emergence from the cave is no longer a matter of preventing young people from seeing bad examples of behavior. Nor is the goal simply the imitation or duplication of the

---

150. Socrates himself makes such a statement (*Cratylus* 391d–98c), as does Martin Heidegger, "The Origin of the Work of Art," in *Poetry, Language, Thought*, trans. Albert Hofstadter (New York: Harper, 1971), 73–78.

151. Rosen (*Plato's "Republic,"* 269–71) is thus correct in maintaining that the cave is not simply an image of the city, nor a full view of human nature. In contrast to Reeve, Rosen sees that there is not and cannot be a perfect parallel between the soul, much less its three parts, and the city, because in real human beings and their cities, souls are necessarily joined to bodies.

152. This description of a general human potential for learning, but directed to different objects, corresponds to the indications Socrates gave in his image of the human soul in the *Phaedrus* 249b–d.

ideas of the virtues in the soul of citizens. Socrates now states (518d–e) that all virtues but prudence are merely matters of habit. Philosophers are no longer described, therefore, as painters or sculptors who will copy the divine ideas of the virtues onto the blank slates of citizens. Now Socrates claims that their knowledge of what truly is enables them to distinguish the shadows better than the cave dwellers once the philosophers' eyes readjust to the dark.

It is no longer their knowledge that makes philosophers the only fit rulers, moreover. It is rather that, having experienced a better life, they do not desire the wealth or fame rule might bring. Only those who do not want to rule will rule for the sake of the community, not their own. Because such people do not desire to rule, they have to be compelled. They will be "compelled," it seems, by the force of argument. It would not be just to force these people to live a less satisfying life, Glaucon objects, by forcing them to sacrifice their own desires and happiness for the sake of others. Socrates responds that they would be reminded that they had received their education from the city, not for their own sake, but for the sake of the whole. In other words, they would be compelled to rule by their own understanding of what is just.[153]

Readers cannot help but ask whether philosophers who might actually arise in any city have actually been educated by their city (and so would be obliged, as they see it, to rule). Since the city (or the political authorities who rule it) determine what "shadows" or images their citizens are allowed to see, philosophers seeking to discover the true nature of things would have to question the laws of the city. In the last part of his image, Socrates thus emphasizes the antagonism with which a philosopher

---

153. Strauss (*City and Man*, 128) thus points out that self-compulsion is still compulsion. Cf. Howland, "The *Republic*'s Third Wave and the Paradox of Political Philosophy," *Review of Metaphysics* 51 (1993): 633–57; and Dorter, *Transformation*, 247. In arguing that philosophers rule for the sake of their own happiness (in order to avoid the rule of less able human beings), Reeve (*Philosopher-Kings*, 191–95) collapses the difference between the two reasons philosophers are said to be the best rulers: (1) their knowledge, and (2) the fact that they alone do not wish to rule, because they cannot achieve anything they particularly want by ruling. Reeve responds to this objection by arguing (*a*) that philosophers possess the knowledge all human beings want (whereas I have argued that Socrates contends only that philosophers know what they and all other human beings truly desire), and (*b*) that their rule is for the benefit of all, not merely their own. Insisting that both Socrates and Plato show philosophy to be essentially an erotic activity and that eros is a tyrant, Rosen, in his account of Plato's *Republic*, argues that, like Plato as he presents himself in the *Seventh Letter*, philosophers want to rule. In the *Republic* Plato shows them the need to restrain their own tyrannical urge by emphasizing the limits of their power and knowledge. Neither Reeve nor Rosen can make sense of Socrates' call for philosophers as rulers, if Socrates' insistence on human beings never acquiring complete knowledge is credited. Strauss can and does.

who had viewed the sunlight world would be greeted if he were forced to return to the cave and challenge the passionately held convictions of its prisoners. Popular opinion is not as malleable, nor will the many be as easily persuaded to accept the rule of philosophy, as Socrates initially suggested.

d. The Difference between Political and Philosophical Education

When Socrates asks what studies serve to turn souls from their attachment to sensible things toward the purely intelligible things that really are, we realize, the conversation related in the *Republic* has followed the image of education he has portrayed—up to this point. Socrates has acted as liberator. At the beginning of the dialogue, he tells us, he went *down* to the Piraeus. He was then compelled to stay and to discuss the character of justice with people who resided there. Glaucon and Adimantus admitted that the appearance of justice looked more advantageous to them than justice itself. Socrates has turned them around first by critically freeing them from the hold of accepted opinions about what is just, by showing them that these opinions are not merely contradictory but ignoble; next by drawing an image of a more beautiful city (*kallipolis*) in speech to arouse their interest and ambition; and finally by arguing that this city can be brought into existence only if a few people experience an even better form of life. In contrast to the brilliance of philosophy, the goals of actual political regimes and actors look much less attractive. Socrates has not made Glaucon or Adimantus a philosopher, however. He has merely persuaded them that the life of philosophy is more choiceworthy than that of an outstanding statesman and that their new aspiration to found a more beautiful city than any currently existing can be achieved only through the pursuit of wisdom. The education Socrates has provided them in the course of the conversation depicted in the *Republic* is thus an education in opinion, a *political* education, as he earlier defined it. Although he has educated his interlocutors about politics, we note, Socrates has not done so in a "political," that is, legal, manner. Rather than mandating certain beliefs or practices in public, he has gradually persuaded them to change their opinions in private, as individuals, without using the threat of punishment or force.[154] The conversation that Plato shows Socrates having with

---

154. He has, in other words, given them the sort of education or correction that Socrates urges in the *Apology* (26a) Meletus should have given Socrates instead of taking him to court.

his brothers constitutes an image, but only an image of a truly philosophical discourse.

Truly philosophical discourse begins, according to Socrates, with the study of mathematics. Neither gymnastics, dedicated as it is to the body, nor music, which transmits a certain harmoniousness and habits to the soul, but not knowledge, will suffice. The humble art of calculation—or simply counting—common to all arts provides the key. People begin to think when they are confronted by things that seem to combine contradictory characteristics. Such things are sensible, because sensations operate in terms of oppositions, for example, hard–soft, hot–cold, wet–dry. Since our senses cannot determine what a thing really is, as opposed to how it appears, we try to measure it. Calculations of number, surface, volume, motion, and harmony must be studied, however, not as they usually are, for their use in military or commercial affairs. They must be studied as means of teaching people the difference between the way things seem and the way they truly are. Studies of number in itself (as opposed to the mere use of such in calculations) will, in turn, introduce people to problems such as the conjunction of unity and an innumerable multitude in one, which the old Parmenides once drew out for the young Socrates.[155] Because the purpose of such studies is to teach people the difference between the sensible and the intelligible, Socrates warned, they must beware of mistaking astronomy, properly the study of the mathematics of the motion of solid bodies, for actual observations of the visible heavens, as previous cosmologists had.

The study of mathematics is merely preparatory, moreover, for dialectics, "when a man tries by discussion—by means of argument without the use of any of the senses—to attain to each thing itself that *is* and doesn't give up before he grasps by intellection itself that which is good itself" (*Republic* 532a–b). When Glaucon asks Socrates to instruct him by telling him what the power of dialectics is, the forms into which it is divided, and its modes, however, Socrates again tells Glaucon that he would not be able to follow, because he "would no longer be seeing an image of what we are saying, but rather the truth itself, at least as it looks to me" (533a).

In the *Republic*, we thus see, Socrates does not define or exemplify philosophy so much as he points toward it. In describing dialectics, Socrates explicitly does not say what it is; he does not fulfill Glaucon's request that

---

155. In the *Phaedo* (96e–97b) Socrates explains, he himself turned to the study of the *logoi* as a result of his meditations on the paradoxes involved in the relations of one and two.

he specify its powers, forms, and modes. Socrates uses the description of dialectics rather (1) to indicate the limits of poetry or images, in which the intelligible elements are always mixed with the sensible and (2) to distinguish philosophy as he understands it from two other kinds of intellectual activity with which it is often confused. As he indicates in his warning about the study of astronomy, cosmology is not philosophy, which consists in the search for knowledge of the things that *are* (and hence are not visible and do not move or change).[156] On the other hand, he insists, when he points out the evils that result from the practice of dialectics now, philosophy does not consist merely in knowing how to ask and answer questions. When arguments are not directed by a desire to discover what is truly good in itself, but serve only to discredit accepted opinions about the noble and good, Socrates reminds Glaucon, they produce lawlessness rather than order. That is one of the reasons philosophy has a bad name. Reflecting perhaps his own earlier experience, Socrates concludes, it is important to determine "that those with whom one shares arguments have orderly and stable natures, not, as now, sharing them with whomever chances by" (539d).

By summarizing the stages of the education of a future philosopher-guardian, Socrates reminds his interlocutors (and Plato's readers) that gymnastics and music are necessary, although not sufficient, parts. As Plato shows us in the case of Phaedrus, no one who pays undue attention to his bodily health or comfort will persist in the necessary intellectual labors; as Plato shows in the case of Alcibiades, no one who has failed to acquire the right disposition will aim at knowledge of the good (rather than wealth and reputation). To be sure, in describing the nature of a philosopher, Socrates argues that the love of truth is so intense that it produces all other virtues as by-products; Socrates also admits, however, such natures are usually corrupted by those closest to them. If the emergence of philosophers—and with them the only properly ordered souls and just cities—is to become anything but a matter of chance, the early education and hence the political circumstances of these extraordinary individuals

---

156. In the *Philebus* Socrates states that even if someone "believes he is inquiring into nature, you know he is seeking all his life for that which concerns this cosmos, how it has come to be, how it is a patient, and how an agent . . . not about the things that always are, but about the things that become, will become, and have become" (64b). Earlier in book 5 (*Republic* 476e–80a), Socrates contrasted the eternally unchanging objects of knowledge, which are, and the changeable objects of opinion, which participate in both being and not-being. Of not-being simply, Socrates agrees with Parmenides, there can be no cognizance at all.

must be regulated.[157] In the *Republic*, Plato shows, Socrates attempts to move in that direction by reforming the opinions of potential legislators. As in the *Phaedrus*, so in the *Republic*, Plato indicates that the influence of philosophy on human life is necessarily indirect. People cannot be literally re-formed by manipulation of their bodies, desires, or thoughts through any conceivable combination of coercion and persuasion.[158] The most educators can do is to induce people to undertake the necessary physical and intellectual labors by arousing a love of what is truly beautiful and good in human life, by presenting them with noble examples, by devising games that enable them to develop physical endurance and intellectual acumen, and by demonstrating the defects of other, more popular and seemingly pleasing ways of life, when students are prepared to understand the critique. If, as Socrates suggests in his most famous images, the whole is only intelligible in part, we can only seek knowledge; we can never simply possess it. We learn that the whole is only partly intelligible, however, only by seeking knowledge of the whole. What we learn in the process of seeking this knowledge is what is—or at least seems—to be good for us, the most satisfying, because not illusory (like the productions of the poets) form of human existence.

4. THE INFERIOR REGIMES

Having presented Plato's brothers images of the just life, both common and individual, Socrates seeks to demonstrate its superiority to injustice by examining inferior regimes and the souls of the citizens formed by them.[159] At the same time he continues his contest with the poets. Poets not only

---

157. The corrupting effects of the opinions of the people with whom a potential philosopher grows up are so great that Socrates concludes the discussion (*Republic* 540e–41a) by suggesting that everyone over the age of ten years must be banished.

158. As Socrates has shown in his sketch of the coming into being of the city, if necessity or force sufficed to control human action, education would not be necessary. On the other hand, if persuasion were sufficient to control human desire, we would not need institutions or laws.

159. Ferrari (*City and Soul*, 42–116) criticizes Williams ("Analogy") and Jonathan Lear, "Inside and Outside the *Republic*," *Phronesis* 37, no. 2 (1992): 184–215, who argue that there is a causal relation between the order of the regime and the character of citizens who internalize it, for misunderstanding the metaphorical character of the parallel. Ferrari is correct, I believe, in arguing that Socrates' analogy is between the order of the parts of the individual soul and the order of the classes in the various regimes. The Greek title of the *Republic*, *Politeia*, means "regime" or "order" (as can *dikē*, the subject of the discussion). The analysis of the relation between regimes and individuals brought up in them that Ferrari himself gives is, however, curiously static. He ignores the overall purpose of Socrates' account of the defective regimes in books 8 and 9, which is to explain the degeneration or change of regimes that occurs as a result of the disorder and division within individual souls. Like Lear, Roochnik (*Beautiful City*, 94–103) emphasizes the dynamic character of the account, which he argues can only be captured in a narrative.

undermine individual virtue by presenting examples of unrestrained passion, but, Socrates now charges, they also foster the development of inferior political regimes. "Tragedy . . . has the reputation of being wise," but "going around to the other cities, gathering crowds, and hiring fine, big and persuasive voices, [the producers of tragedies] draw the regimes toward tyrannies and democracies." Tragedians do not propagate their political message out of wisdom, so much as out of self-interest; "they get wages and are honored too, most of all by tyrants, . . . and, in the second place, by democracy" (*Republic* 568a, c). The tragedies thus appear to be the source of the understanding of "justice" that Glaucon initially articulated: the best life by nature is to have the power to do whatever one wants, that is, to become a tyrant. Those too weak to enforce their will on others band together to protect themselves from the depredations of the strong, that is, they found democracies.

In arguing that philosophers should rule, Socrates emphasized that rule is not in his or any other philosopher's own interest; they do not seek reputation or wealth. *The* difference between the best regime and all actually extant regimes is that, in the best regime, rule is for the sake of the whole community, rather than for the benefit of the rulers at the expense of the ruled.

a. Socrates versus Hesiod

Socrates presents these inferior, extant regimes as progressive stages of decay from the best community. Because he admits the best regime has not come into being anywhere as yet and may not ever, the account of the development of the inferior regimes he gives here cannot be taken literally as a historical development. It appears to be an adaptation of Hesiod's account of the ills of human existence in terms of a degeneration of the human race from the golden to the iron age.[160] As an indication of the importance of the institution of political rule and, with it, justice, Hesiod interrupted the decline from the golden to the silver, bronze, and finally iron age with the emergence of the heroes or demigods often said to be founders of later regimes. Since all these regimes are defective, Socrates' account contains no such exception to the general line of degeneration. His description of human life without justice is remarkably like that of the

---

160. Cf. Hesiod, *Works and Days*, 106–201. Socrates indicates the fictional, if not strictly poetic, character of his own account by somewhat playfully asking Glaucon if they should not "like Homer pray to the Muses" to tell them how faction first arose and then claim that the Muses speak to and through them "with high tragic talk" (*Republic* 545d–e).

epic poet. The difference is that Socrates suggests there is a rarely available, but possible alternative to the forceful, hence unpleasant imposition of "just" controls on unjust desires, whereas Hesiod, like the other "tragic" poets, does not envisage any such alternative.

The reason Socrates gives for the degeneration is important. By suggesting that the rulers of the best regime were not able to calculate the time at which future guardians should be born with sufficient accuracy, the philosopher reminds his interlocutors that the whole is not intelligibly ordered in a mathematical fashion. If it were, everything would stay exactly the same. Because everything that comes into being must eventually decay, generation cannot be so ordered. The guardians of *kallipolis* will not be able entirely to control the generation of future citizens, so the lines or signs of a natural division of talent and function will eventually become blurred. Failing to recognize that everyone contributes to the preservation of the community as a whole, those with arms will enslave the artisans and farmers. They will thus institute a "timocracy" rather like Sparta in which not the wise but the warlike rule. Because the "races" (or motives for seeking power) are now mixed, the "wise" are no longer trusted.[161]

b. Timocracy and Oligarchy

When Socrates gives an account of the development or formation of the soul of an individual who corresponds to the timocratic regime, he also shows how this development is linked to generation.[162] When members of the ruling class took land and servants as their own property, they also acquired their own families. The wife and servants of one such ruler then complained to the son that his father, who minded his own business according to the notion of justice that had prevailed earlier in the just regime, did not demand the honor and wealth he deserved (and in which they wanted to share). When the son went out, he heard people say that those who mind their own business are simpletons, whereas those who don't are honored and praised. Contrasting these statements with the

---

161. *Republic* 547e–48a. Socrates, in effect, collapses two of the "races" of Hesiod—the silver (stupid) and bronze (armed) into one regime, timocracy. He thus makes room for a regime Hesiod does not associate with a particular race or age, oligarchy. As he announces at the beginning of his poem, Hesiod thinks economic (as opposed to military and erotic) competition is good. He wants to encourage his brother to work and to control his desires so that he can hoard the results.

162. The change of regime and the developments within the souls of its typical citizens are presented as occurring simultaneously. Neither is said to be the cause of the other.

arguments and practices of his father, the youth found himself divided.[163] Whereas his father encouraged the development of the calculating part, his mother and her servants fed his spirit and desires.

Socrates had argued earlier that the souls of all human beings are divided into calculating, spirited, and desirous parts. They remain just only so long as reason (*logismos*) units with spirit to control the passions. When the spirited part becomes ascendant, people become harsh warriors who prize ability to fight above either wisdom or pleasure.

Those who seek honor eventually amass hoards of wealth.[164] Over time timocracies thus display a tendency to become oligarchies. The possession of wealth is taken increasingly as a sign of excellence, and human beings seek it above all else. As people accumulate the means of satisfying their physical desires, however, the desire to use those means also increases and the attachment to positions of preeminence fades. Wanting to free themselves from the restraints imposed by the calculations of their parents, the sons of oligarchs tend to become democrats.[165] To attain the freedom to do what they want, they unite with others to abolish the control of all superiors, including their own fathers.

c. Democracy and Tyranny

The order of the extant regimes Socrates describes is not determined by the merits of their respective goals or the relative "virtues" of their typical citizens. The search for honor (and hence the emphasis on war as the occasion for demonstrating military valor) does not obviously make a timocrat superior to a grasping oligarch (who is both calculating and self-controlled).[166] Nor is it clear that the repressive rapacity of the oligarch is superior to the easygoing freedom of the democrat. Indeed, Socrates observes, because every person is allowed to live as he or she wishes, democracies allow all sorts of human beings to develop. As the most varied and colorful regime, democracy appears to many to be the most beautiful. Because it allows all types to develop, it also appears to constitute the most favorable condition for inquiring, like Socrates, about the best way of life (*Republic* 557b–d). The

163. Dorter (*Transformation*, 253–81) argues not only that these divisions cause the decline, but also that there cannot, therefore, be a precise parallel between the soul of the individual and the regime.

164. In Greek, *timē* means "price" as well as "honor."

165. The oligarchs themselves fuel this tendency when, in order to increase their own holdings, they encourage the sons of others to spend their family's fortune.

166. Socrates observes that the timocrats secretly honor and hence hoard wealth (*Republic* 548a); oligarchs could thus be said to be more honest as well as more rationally calculating.

problem is that by inculcating a love of freedom above all other goods, democracy destroys all sense of order, hierarchy, and self-restraint in the souls of its citizens.

Seeking the means of satisfying their particular private desires, most citizens of a democracy tend to mind their own business. Externally viewed, democrats look like the artisan class of the city in speech. So long as its citizens do not band together to expropriate the goods of their wealthier brethren or their neighbors, democracy thus appears to embody the *political* definition of justice Socrates proposed earlier.[167] There is a crucial difference, however, between external behavior and the internal state of the individual souls. The absence of an internal order in the souls of democrats gradually tends to become manifest, Socrates suggests, in political disorder.

In a timocracy, the different functions of the different classes—ruling, military, craftsmen, and farmers—remain evident. Under an oligarchy, however, the same people rule, fight, and make money. As a result, Socrates observes, "this regime is the first to admit the greatest of all evils. . . . Allowing one man to sell everything that belongs to him, . . . and when he has sold it, allowing him to live in the city while belonging to none of its parts." When the competition of their compatriots for wealth results in the production of a sufficient number of such "drones," they unite in an attempt to seize the property of others, by theft or, if conditions are ripe, by mobilizing their fellow citizens against the evil oligarch (564d). Because they deny the superiority or consequent right to rule of any, the apparently just citizens of a democracy can be corrupted by leaders who promise them shares of the expropriation of the rich.[168] Fearing the censure of the decent, these leaders denounce, expropriate, exile, or murder anyone unwilling to serve their designs. The tyrannic nature of their ambition becomes apparent when they demand an armed guard to protect them from their fellow countrymen.[169]

The purpose of Socrates' review of the inferior regimes is to show Glaucon and Adimantus that the just life is superior to the unjust. The

---

167. Cf. Mara, *Discursive Democracy*, 141.

168. Although the democracy Socrates describes appears to be too tolerant to persecute anyone (such as a philosopher), he shows that the lack of order in the souls of its citizens allows it to be easily transformed into the harshest and most violent of all regimes. As Thucydides 5.69–85 observes in describing the effects of civil war in Corcyra, so Socrates argues that words change their meaning when citizens begin attacking their fellows. "Shame" becomes "simplicity," and "moderation" is called "cowardice."

169. Cf. Herodotus' description (1.59) of the feint Pisistratus used to persuade the Athenians to provide him with such a guard.

tyrant is an embodiment of injustice inasmuch as he is willing to sacrifice anyone and anything for the sake of satisfying his own immediate desires. In him, Socrates suggests, the desire to be free of all restraint, "to have intercourse . . . with a mother or anyone else—human beings, gods, and beasts, to attempt any foul murder, or to partake in any food" (571c) that many experience occasionally in dreams when the calculating part of their soul is asleep, becomes manifest. The power and hence freedom to do whatever one wants seem desirable. However, Socrates argues, contrary to Glaucon's initial suggestion, it is not possible to do whatever one wants without regard for the interests of others and acquire a reputation for justice, honor, or happiness. Everyone admits that the people living under a tyrant are miserable, prey as they are to his every passing whim. So is the tyrant himself, Socrates now urges. Knowing they will object to his designs, a tyrant cannot abide the company of the honest or virtuous. Nor can he trust his subordinates, who, in becoming such, have shown their willingness to sacrifice person and principle to further their own interests and ambitions. A tyrant thus lives without friends in constant fear of everyone with whom he comes into contact. He may be praised to his face by flatterers, but he is hated and blamed when he is not present to threaten those who speak.

Having read Socrates' characterizations of eros as the impulse toward philosophy in both the *Symposium* and *Phaedrus*, we may be surprised to see him characterize the soul of the tyrant in terms of its domination by eros.[170] In the *Republic* Socrates has shown, however, that the results of the passion that culminates most frequently in sexual generation (and hence in corruption) depend on the character of its object. A man who loves truth above all acquires all the other virtues as a result; a man who seeks power, wealth, and reputation without limit denies the legitimacy of any restraint. The "madness" of such overweening desire may not become immediately evident; as Socrates has observed, human beings can employ their ability to calculate to achieve low goals as well as high. Over time (and in the tragedies) it becomes clear that the person willing to sacrifice anyone or anything—to kill parents, commit incest, or betray the home-

---

170. The description of the development of a tyrannical soul in the son of a man of the people who was himself pulled between his desires and the law looks, however, very much like Alcibiades, who, Plutarch tells us (*Lives* 1.268), had Eros on his shield as his personal symbol and was the adopted son of Pericles. In his first speech in the *Phaedrus* (238a–b), Socrates thus opposed "moderation" to erotic excess, although he clarified the distinction in terms of the objects of law in his second speech.

land—lives, in the end, in constant uncertainty and fear, without friends, family, or people. Glaucon indicates that he sees Socrates' analysis of the inferior regimes as a dramatic, if not tragic production when, asked to declare which man and regime is happiest, he says: "I choose them, like choruses, in the very order in which they came on stage" (580b).

d. The City in Speech Finally as a Paradigm for an Individual

The parallel Socrates draws between regime and individual makes it easy to declare that the tyrant is the worst; his is clearly the worst regime. Socrates thus adds another proof of the happiness of the individual and his or her soul. Preparing readers for his analysis of the human good as a combination of knowledge and pleasure in the *Philebus*, he suggests that each of the three parts of the soul has its own peculiar pleasure. Only the person who has experienced all three is capable of judging; only the seeker of wisdom has experienced the pleasure of honor as well as of physical satisfaction, and he judges the pleasure of learning to be the greatest. Their objects fleeting, the other pleasures are necessarily mixed with pain. The pleasure the intellect takes in contemplating that which truly *is*, is pure.[171] Those who have felt it will therefore try to perpetuate the experience and thus to maximize both their knowledge (*phronēsis*) and pleasure; they will not seek to feed their transitory bodily desires by acquiring a great deal of money or a desire for honor by competing with others (and consequently suffering the pains associated with envy and anger, if not outright violence).[172] They certainly will not seek political power, except perhaps in the city in speech, which, Glaucon points out, does not exist anywhere on earth. That city serves, Socrates now explains, as "a paradigm laid up in heaven for the man who wants to see and found a city within himself" (*Republic* 592b). From the very beginning, the purpose of the description of the just city was not

---

171. Socrates thus somewhat playfully suggests (*Republic* 587d–e) that the philosopher lives 729 times as happily as the tyrant.

172. In his redescription of the life of "the many" (which seems to correspond to the cave) and the three parts of the soul, Socrates emphasizes that the only form of pleasure (and hence life, accompanied by sensation) that is distinctively human and not animal is intellectual. "Those who . . . don't . . . look upward toward what is truly above . . . but, after the fashion of cattle, always looking down with their heads bent to earth and table, feed, fattening themselves, and copulating; and, for the sake of getting more of these things, they kick and butt with horns and hoofs of iron, killing each other because they are insatiable; for they are not filling the part of themselves that is, or can contain anything, with things that are" (*Republic* 586a–b). The part of the soul Socrates now describes (586b–89b) as a little human being (as an image of reason) does not ally itself with the "lion" of *thymos* to control the many-headed hydra of the desires.

merely to show what justice is but also why it constitutes the best form of life for an individual.

D. Socrates versus Homer

In describing that city, Socrates concludes, they were especially right to exclude any form of imitative poetry. Imitative or, we would say, dramatic poetry that is publicly performed should be banned not simply because it has a deleterious effect on the formation of the character, disposition, or habits of potential guardians, but because the works of "the tragic poets and all the other imitators . . . maim the thought [*dianoia*] of those who hear them and do not have knowledge of what these things really are as a remedy [*pharmakon*]" (*Republic* 595b). In his concluding critique of imitation, we see that Socrates is concerned less with its power to shape opinions and attitudes than with its lack of truth and formative effect on the intellect.

The truth at stake, Socrates repeatedly reminds Glaucon in the concluding books of the *Republic*, is the good and bad of human existence. That is what Homer claimed to be able to teach, and in his concluding discussion of poetry Socrates testifies several times in different ways to the enduring appeal of the poet's work.[173] Indeed, at the very end of the *Republic*, in retelling his own "myth of Er," Socrates suggests that, as a practical matter, in the *Odyssey* Homer presented the effective or experiential truth about human life. Socrates' narrator reports that after ten years of labor and loss, Odysseus had learned that neither honor nor wealth was a satisfying goal,

---

173. Socrates begins his final critique of imitation by observing that "a certain friendship for Homer, and shame before him . . . since childhood, has prevented [Socrates] from speaking. For [Homer] seems to have been the first teacher and leader of all these fine tragic poets" (*Republic* 595b). At 598d–e Socrates again refers to "tragedy and its leader, Homer," who are said to "know all arts and all things human that have to do with virtue and vice, and the divine things too." At 601a–b Socrates emphasizes the charm of the meter, rhythm, and harmony with which the poets speak. And at 606e he tells Glaucon that "when you meet praisers of Homer who say that this poet educated Greece, and that in the management and education of human affairs it is worthwhile to take him up for study and for living by, by arranging one's whole life according to this poet, you must love and embrace them as being men who are the best they can be, and agree that Homer is the most poetic and first of the tragic poets, but you must know that only so much of poetry as hymns to gods and celebration of good men should be admitted into a city. And if you admit the sweetened muse in lyrics or epics, pleasure and pain will jointly be kings in your city instead of law and that argument which is best in the opinion of the community." Nevertheless, Socrates concedes, "if poetry, directed to pleasure, and imitation have any argument to give showing that they should be in a city with good laws, we should be delighted to receive them back from exile, since we are aware that we ourselves are charmed by them" (607c). In all cases, however, the claims of truth outweigh those of affection or pleasure.

and so Odysseus' soul, in choosing its next life in Hades, sought "for the life of a private man who minded his own business." That is exactly the choice Socrates has argued a just man would make.[174]

Socrates' much critiqued critique of imitative poetry should be understood in the context or "light" of both his apparent agreement and disagreement with Homer. Commentators have faulted Socrates, for example, for treating poetic images as if they were attempts merely to make carbon copies, that is, to duplicate the original things, which are in turn said to be imperfect copies of the ideas fabricated by the god and hence three times removed from the truth. Granted, poets do not merely describe things as they appear or have appeared in the past; such compositions would be prosaic. Socrates does not, however, simply criticize poets for making copies. He criticizes imitative poets more specifically, first, for claiming to represent and hence to know everything that is. By using sensible means of fabricating such representations, poets disprove their claim to know and represent the whole. As Socrates indicated with his image of the divided line, all kinds of being cannot be so represented or imagined. Second, he charges, because they do not recognize the existence of eternal, unchanging, and hence purely intelligible forms of being, poets cannot teach us how to direct or order our lives—individual or common.[175] They do not recognize and cannot imagine the goal or satisfactions of philosophical friendship.

1. On the Limits of the Poets' Knowledge

In considering what imitative poetry is, Socrates first asks Glaucon to consider a "handworker able to make not only all implements but also everything that grows naturally from the earth, [including] all animals—himself too . . . and in addition, earth and heaven and gods . . . and everything in Hades" (Republic 596c). When Glaucon observes that such would be a "wonderful sophist," Socrates suggests that Glaucon could do something similar merely by taking a mirror and carrying it around; "quickly [he] will make the sun and things in the heaven; the earth; himself and other animals and implements and plants and everything else that was just mentioned" (596d–e)—everything, that is, that is visible. Like a painter, a man with a

---

174. Sallis (Being and Logos), Brann ("Music"), and Jacob Howland, The "Republic": The Odyssey of Philosophy (New York: Twayne Publishers, 1993), all emphasize the parallels between the Republic and the Odyssey.

175. This charge, which Socrates made first in the Phaedrus, applies only to pre-Platonic poetry.

mirror makes images of the sensible things; the relation between images and things corresponds to that Socrates imaged on the lower portion of the divided line.[176] Socrates thus supposes that they would say that the intelligible ideas, of which these sensible things are said to be images, are made by a god. This passage is extremely puzzling. Nowhere else in the Platonic corpus does Socrates (or any other philosopher) suggest that the eternal, unchanging, hence purely intelligible ideas are made and so come into being, much less that the ideas are fabricated. We are led to suspect that the "god" here is said to be a maker only figuratively speaking—"we would say"—to suggest that divine or purely intelligible beings must have a divine origin or cause. The products of this "god" or *phytourgos* seem to include everything on the upper or intelligible part of the divided line, the ideas presupposed by the arts as well as the kinds of things to be found in nature—in sum, the models for the "artifacts, statues of men and other animals" Socrates said earlier cast the shadows human beings in the cave saw.[177] The central point appears to be that all the types or models of sensible things are not themselves sensible—and cannot, therefore, be fully or accurately reproduced in sensible form. All such sensible images are partial or perspectival, capturing one or another aspect of the intelligible being but not the whole.

Can an artist or poet who uses such sensible images present a picture of the whole? Socrates suggests that the medium of sensible imitation precludes it. Thus,

> when anyone reports to us about someone, saying that he has encountered a human being who knows all the crafts and everything else that single men severally know, . . . it would have to be replied to such a one that he is an innocent human being and that, as it seems, he has encountered some wizard and imitator and been deceived. Because he himself is unable to put knowledge and lack of knowledge and imitation to the test, that man seemed all-wise to him. (598c–d)

Socrates does not merely fault the poets' claim to know the whole; he also denies their claim to know and therefore teach the good and bad of human

---

176. Cf. Bloom, "Interpretive Essay," 428.

177. The *phytourgos* is not the same as Timaeus' *dēmiourgos*, who merely copies preexisting eternal models. Cf. *Timaeus* 28a–29a. Some of the ideas mentioned here (*Republic* 597b–e) are clearly derivative, for example, that of a couch from that of a human being and what such a being can use. According to Socrates' hypothetical logos in the *Phaedo* (101d–e), such ideas might, like the objects of the arts of legislation and justice in the *Gorgias*, be subsets of the more general idea of the good.

life. It has been said of "tragedy and its leader, Homer . . . that these men know all arts and all things human that have to do with virtue and vice and the divine things too" (598c–e). Socrates argues, however, that all these poets know is how to make pleasing images in speech that only persuade those who do not possess the knowledge of the things or activities in question. "Do you suppose that if a man were able to make both, the thing to be imitated and the imitation, he would permit himself to be serious about the crafting of the imitations and set this at the head of his own life as the best thing he has?" (599a). There is no evidence that Homer or any other poet actually knew an art like medicine or how to be a general and hence could teach another, Socrates charges.[178] No poet has actually drawn up laws for any city—or demonstrated his practical wisdom by inventing a useful tool or technique.[179]

Socrates' attack on the poets here does not appear to be entirely consistent with what he said in earlier dialogues. Socrates compares Homer and the poets unfavorably here to Lycurgus and Thales; he does not group poets like Homer and Hesiod together with legislators like Lycurgus and Solon, as Diotima had in the *Symposium* (209d). She characterized both legislators and poets as people who sought a deathless memory or renown for virtue by educating others through speeches about what makes human beings noble and good. Likewise, although Socrates faults the poets here for not even having a circle of students like the sophists who claim to be learning how to live from them, in his conversations with Hippias Socrates explicitly acknowledged that the sophists took the ideas of virtue

---

178. Socrates' suggestion that people would go to Homer or to any other poet for instruction might appear ridiculous. Who would believe he could learn to be a general or a doctor from Homer? Perhaps in response to that question, Plato in the *Ion* dramatizes a conversation between Socrates and a rhapsode who claims that someone can learn these arts by listening to or, even better, by memorizing and reciting Homer's epics. In that conversation Socrates quickly shows by interrogating Ion that (a) the rhapsode has no understanding of what an art or any other kind of knowledge really is, and that (b) unlike the practitioners of arts whom Socrates and Thrasymachus described in book 1, the rhapsode practices his "art"—or, more properly, trade—for the sake of making money by entertaining others. Unlike Hippias, the sophist who claimed to know and to be able to make everything a human being needs, Ion is satisfied merely with reciting, that is, copying Homer's imitation of human activities, arts, and virtues. His recitations are clearly copies of copies, three times—or more—removed from the truth. He gives them primarily to enrich himself, not to instruct, educate, or improve his auditors. In the *Ion* Plato shows that the worst effect poets have on their audience may not be to present them with bad examples or to tempt some to deceive others by acting a role. The worst effect poets have on their listeners is to make them believe that by merely hearing or repeating the words, they share the inspiration and wisdom of the poet, especially concerning the divine. Cf. Allan Bloom, "An Interpretation of Plato's *Ion*," in Pangle, *Roots*, 371–95.

179. In the *Timaeus* (21b–c) Critias reports that Solon was said not to have developed his talents as a poet precisely because he devoted himself to politics.

they claimed to teach primarily from Homer. At the end of the *Phaedrus* (277b–78b), however, Socrates explained his understanding of the limits of the intellectual children begotten by poets and legislators more clearly than he had in the *Symposium*: both poets and legislators mistakenly identify their writings with an actual education. In fact, education occurs only in the soul of another. Writings serve at most as reminders; they are not, nor do they produce, a "deathless memory." In the *Republic* Socrates further distinguishes those who present imitations of rulers from those who make laws on the basis of their knowledge of what is truly beautiful and good. Insofar as they present images of kings like Achilles and Odysseus who seek glory and wealth rather than knowledge, poets like Homer merely fabricate images of self-seeking, unjust rulers, which appeal to people who do not know. Socrates makes a similar claim, we should recall, in the *Phaedrus* (246c–d) with regard to the divine: it is not correct to speak or think of an immortal with both a soul and a body. When they speak of the Olympian gods, the poets show that they do not understand what is truly divine any more than they depict what is truly beautiful and good in human life. They cannot, because they do not recognize the necessary character or existence of that which is truly eternal or deathless.

The images the poets make merely appear to be that of which they are images. As Socrates emphasized earlier, images can distort, if not deceive us simply about what really is. In book 7 he pointed out that we use the arts of measurement to determine what truly is the case. These arts of measurement are not taught, nor can they be imaged by poetry. On the contrary, Socrates now urges, by sympathetically appealing to the passions and so arousing them, poetry strengthens the parts of the soul that calculation (*logismos*) should control. Poetry does not, therefore, provide the education necessary for the development of a well-ordered soul. It does not have the power of mathematics to redirect the mind from its attachment to sensible things to an investigation of the purely intelligible. Rather than help spectators bring order to their lives by directing their attention to that which is true and lasting, by giving expression to feelings of extreme joy and grief, which people learn to suppress (and then only in public) through long habituation and much practice, poetry tends to destroy the self-control or moderation of all but a few.

2. Socratic Poetry and the Good of Human Life

Because the charm of poetry is so great, Socrates nevertheless concedes, he would be delighted to readmit it, if poets could show that and how their works can contribute to the development of just human beings with well-ordered souls. He concludes his conversation with Glaucon and Adimantus by indicating what the nature of such poetry would be.

First, Socrates suggests that, like the speech he gave in the name of Stesichorus in the *Phaedrus*, poetry which promoted justice would have to inculcate belief in the immortality of the soul. Traditional Greek beliefs about the gods and the afterlife propagated by the poets did not. When Socrates asks Glaucon whether he has not perceived that our soul is immortal and indestructible, Glaucon responds, "No, by Zeus!" If he is not to do an injustice, Socrates states, he must maintain that the soul is immortal. Although Socrates assures Glaucon that it is not difficult to affirm that the soul is immortal, the reasons he gives for thinking so are not terribly persuasive.[180] Since souls are not destroyed by bodily disease (although they may be separated from the body when it is corrupted) or by their own vices or corruption, for example, injustice, he suggests that they are not destroyed at all. And in that case, he concludes, there would always be the same number of souls. Socrates admits that "it's not easy for a thing to be eternal that is both composed out of many things and whose composition is not the finest." Having argued that the soul has three parts, Socrates also concedes that we are not able "to see its true nature—whether it is many-formed or single-formed" so long as it is "maimed by community with body and other evils" (*Republic* 611b–12a). In other words, as Socrates acknowledged in the *Phaedrus*, we mortals will never be able to say or know definitively what the soul is.

Socrates' assertion of the indestructibility of the soul and the constant number of souls nevertheless allows him to relate a story, the myth of Er, to show that the rewards of justice and the punishments of injustice are even greater in the afterlife than they are while we are alive. This myth illustrates the kind of poetry that supports justice.[181] That poetry not merely asserts the immortality of the soul; it also makes individuals responsible

---

180. The fundamental problem is that Socrates never states in the *Republic* what he thinks the soul is. On the contrary, earlier, in drawing the parallel between the three parts of the city and the three parts of the soul, he explicitly said that "we'll never get a precise grasp of it this way; there is another longer road" (435c–d). In the *Phaedrus* 245c–46a he argued that the soul is immortal because it is self-moving, but he warned that it would take a discourse longer than any mortal could give to say what its idea is.

181. A computer search of the Platonic corpus on the Thesaurus Linguae Graecae for all the times Socrates explicitly says he is retelling "myths" or a combination of *mythos* and *logos* (*mythologia*) shows that the retellings concern the soul and the afterlife (in contrast to the "myths" about the origins of the city and not the soul or the afterlife told by Protagoras, the Eleatic Stranger, and the Athenian Stranger).

for the character and course of their own lives. They are not victims of impersonal fate or fates.

Socrates explicitly sets his myth of Er in contrast to the story Odysseus tells King Alkinoos about his own travels, including a trip to the underworld (*Odyssey* 11 entire). In Hades Odysseus talked to *psychai*, but these souls were able to speak only after they had drunk blood, that is, reacquired a connection with body. In their usual state, souls in Hades did not appear to be able to converse, think, or remember. Minos was said to judge, and some souls were shown to be suffering unending punishments. Only Heracles appeared to have been rewarded with an immortal life with the gods on Olympus. There was no suggestion of reincarnation or rebirth.

In Socrates' account of what Er saw in Hades, souls were first judged, rewarded, or punished and then brought to a field where they could contemplate the intelligible order and beauty of the cosmos in the orbits of the planets and the resultant harmony of the spheres both in color and music.[182] Although the three fates, said to be daughters of necessity, kept the spheres in motion, they merely sealed the choices the individual souls themselves made concerning their future lives. Neither the gods nor the intelligible order of nature determined the shape and outcome of human lives. On the contrary, individual souls chose the form of their future life on the basis of what they had learned or failed to learn, cherished or hated, in their previous existence. "Having lived in an orderly regime in his former life, participating in virtue by habit, without philosophy," Er reported, the first chose to be a tyrant without "noticing that eating his own children and other evils were fated to be a part of that life." When he saw what it actually entailed, he lamented his hasty choice, but too late. Er also described the selections of future lives made by individuals named in the *Odyssey*. Angry over the loss of Achilles' armor, Ajax decided to become a lion rather than a man; Agamemnon chose to become an eagle. Not wanting to be generated from a woman, Orpheus chose the life of a swan. Other musicians selected other birds; swans and musical animals decided to become human. "By chance Odysseus' soul had drawn the last lot and went to choose," Er concluded, "from memory of its former labors

---

182. Cornford (*Plato's Cosmology*, 75, 87–88) points out both the similarity and the difference between the depiction of the revolution of the spheres in the myth of Er and that to be found in the *Timaeus* 36c–d. In contrast to the description in the *Timaeus*, there is no allowance for the tilting of the earth in the description of the orbits in the *Republic*. The reason is that the vision described in the *Republic* is of intelligible motions presented directly to the soul; it is not embodied like the planets whose orbits become visible to the eye of the astronomical observer.

it had recovered from love of honor, so looked for a long time for the life of a private man who minds his own business, and with effort found one" (*Republic* 620c).

The emphasis of Socrates' story is not on the rewards and punishments people receive after death so much as the responsibility each has for the shape and direction of his or her own life. Even if our souls are not immortal, each of us is constrained and shaped by the particular place, family, and regime into which we are born as well as by our particular natural inclinations or talents and experience. Within these constraints, each of us still has the power to choose. Socrates' tale reflects a truth about human existence that does not depend simply on his problematic assertion concerning the immortality of the soul: "Each of us must . . . above all . . . seek to learn . . . to distinguish the good and the bad life" (618b–c). It is the philosopher who can teach us and not, as Homer claimed, the poet.

Didn't Er (and hence Socrates) acknowledge, however, that at least one of Homer's heroes learned how to choose? Shouldn't the *Odyssey*, if not the *Iliad*, be admitted, then, to provide the necessary education? To understand Socrates' expulsion of the poets, we have to investigate the agreement and disagreement between the philosopher and poet a bit further.

According to Er, "from memory of its former labors, . . . Odysseus' soul had recovered from love of honor . . . [and] so looked for the life of a private man who minds his own business" (*Republic* 620c). Minding one's own business was the definition of justice Socrates gave earlier (433a). As a result of his travels and homecoming, it appears that Odysseus became just. The question that first arises, however, is whether Er correctly stated the moral or teaching of Homer's epic. In the *Odyssey* we hear an account of the hero's trip to Hades, where he learns from a variety of shades—his mother as well as his fellow commanders—that the most important and satisfying aspects of human life are to be found in the mutual understanding and sympathy of those closest to us—parents, wives, and children. As members of a family, Homer suggested, we not only share the experience of birth and death; we consciously live in the face of it. In both his epics the poet shows that knowing we must die forces human beings to choose who and what is most important to them (the analogue to the choice that Er reports souls make before they are reborn). If our lives were unending, we would not have to choose or hence to know the good and the bad. Like the Homeric gods, immortal human beings would be childlike, irresponsible, and immoral; we would, as the sophists urged, willfully seek to maximize our own pleasure. When given an opportunity to live forever in apparent bliss with the nymph Calypso, Odysseus chose, as a result of what he learned in Hades, to return to Penelope. Love and friendship (as opposed to sexual union, pleasure, or ecstasy) are possible only on the basis of the mutual understanding and consequent trust that develop as a result of a shared experience of living in the face of death.[183] It is our foreknowledge of our inescapable demise and consequent separation that makes us cherish our love and loved ones while they last. Because everything that comes into being must also fade, however, Homer also indicated that Odysseus could not simply return home to stay. In Hades Tiresias told the hero that he would eventually have to leave Ithaca again and travel to a place where they know nothing of the sea. When he met a man who mistakes an oar for a winnowing fan, he should plant the oar as an offering to Poseidon, the god of the sea whose persecution forced Odysseus to undertake his ten years of travel and so acquire his education about the good and bad of human existence, especially the limits of fame. Then and only then could Odysseus return home and die in peace and prosperity (*Odyssey* 11.120–37).

Socrates agrees with Homer that what is truly good is to be found in private friendships. Socrates insists, however, that these friendships must not be based merely on shared experience of our mortality or—as in the case of both of Homer's heroes—dedicated to an accumulation of wealth and fame to bestow on one's heirs. In arguing that guardians should not be exposed to the description Homer gives of Hades and the lives of the shades because it would sap their courage, Socrates had objected first and foremost to Achilles' shade telling Odysseus that "I would rather work the soil, slave to a man with no alloted land whose means of life are not great than rule over all the dead who have perished" (*Odyssey* 11.489–91; *Republic* 386c). That very statement might be read to show that Achilles also had "recovered from love of honor" (as would his response to the ambassadors from Agamemnon, in *Iliad* 9.400–429, 595–619). Nevertheless, Homer also showed that, in light of the news of the glorious achievements of his son, Achilles walked away happy from his encounter with

183. When Odysseus returns to Ithaca and is greeted by Athena, we thus see him accept her claim that she has been with him the whole time, that they are two of a kind, and that she therefore loves and helps him without question. A prudent mortal does not challenge the truthfulness of an immortal—even concerning their differences. Cf. *Odyssey* 13.313–423. By way of contrast, at her urging we subsequently see him test the truthfulness and loyalty of all the members of his family and household.

Odysseus in Hades. Although Achilles denied that the honor and wealth Agamemnon promised were worth risking his life for, Achilles reentered the battle later, knowing that he would die, to avenge the death of his beloved friend. Homer did not show Odysseus returning to Ithaca merely to be reunited with his family, any more than he had Achilles return to Phthia as threatened. Odysseus returned to reclaim his kingdom. At the end of the poem Homer showed that Odysseus, to maintain his position, would have killed virtually all his fellow citizens, who attacked him to avenge the death of their sons among the suitors Odysseus had slain. As Plato reminded his readers in earlier Socratic conversations, most of those who heard the *Odyssey* recited did not conclude that the private life was best. On the contrary, Homeric heroes like Achilles and Odysseus were taken to embody heroic virtues, including dedication to the search for honor, political preeminence, and wealth.[184]

In his myth of Er, Socrates points both to a deeper reading of Homer and a deep disagreement with the epic poet. Socrates agrees with Homer that the desire animating the best human beings is not merely a desire to overcome death by winning fame. Even less is it a desire to avoid pain or to maximize pleasure. It is a desire to be both understood for what one is and is not—and yet to be loved. Human beings do not bond or stay together over time merely out of fear or greed. We do not simply try to avoid the bad. On the contrary, we positively admire the beautiful or noble and seek the good. Insofar as we possess self-knowledge, we recognize that as mortals we will never be perfect. We do not come to understand our imperfections merely in light of the inevitable end of our own existence and our yearning to negate, if not to overcome it. We positively long for a qualitatively better, more satisfying way of life and join with others in an attempt to achieve it. We love and are loved not so much for our achievements as for our aspirations. Because we are mortal creatures, the striving to improve our lives is necessarily ongoing and unending. It is, Socrates insisted, an effort to improve, not merely to preserve or defend. Improvement requires not only knowledge of our limitations; it also depends on our obtaining and regaining an intimation, if not a full-blown vision, of what is truly good and beautiful. In contrast to the dumb shades Odysseus encountered in Hades, the souls in Socrates' myth of Er

---

184. Such a reading of Homer is by no means limited to ancient authors. Cf. Arendt, *Human Condition*, 8–9, 19, 24–25; and Alasdair MacIntyre, *After Virtue*, 2nd ed. (Notre Dame: University of Notre Dame Press, 1984), 121–30.

were thus given a view of the beautiful, because intelligible, order of the whole before they chose the specific form of their future existence and were reborn.[185]

185. These reflections on the disagreement between Socrates and Homer concerning the good and bad of human life help explain two of the distinctive features of the dialogue in which Socrates explicitly takes up the question with which he concludes the *Republic*: what is the good life for us? First, in the *Philebus* the discussion of the question is shown to be ongoing. Socrates and Philebus are said to have been debating the issue before the dialogue begins, and the discussion between Socrates and Protarchus is said to continue after the dialogue ends. Jacob Klein, "About Plato's *Philebus*," *Interpretation* 2, no. 3 (1973): 157–82, emphasizes the lack of beginning or end to the conversation, as does Seth Benardete, *The Tragedy and Comedy of Life: Plato's "Philebus"*(Chicago: University of Chicago Press, 1993), 87–88. As we have seen in the *Symposium, Phaedrus, Clitophon,* and *Republic*, there are reasons to conclude that the investigation of what is truly good for human beings is necessarily unending. Our mortal nature prevents us from ever attaining, much less maintaining, a complete view of the purely intelligible beings or the order of the whole. We have constantly to strive to regain insights and truths we have learned but are continually in process of forgetting. That is why we need written reminders. The truth of the goodness of philosophy can be preserved, however, only through its transmission into the souls or lives of future generations. Second, the discussion of the question in the *Philebus* appears to be purely private. There is no mention of anything political. Cf. Joseph Cropsey, "On Pleasure and the Human Good: Plato's *Philebus*," *Interpretation* 16, no. 2 (Winter 1988–89): 167. As a result, the *Philebus* has no dramatic dating. According to Socrates, the good in human life can be known and achieved, if at all, only in private. That is the reason he states, both in his *Apology* (31c–32a) and in the *Republic* (496a–e), that he never actively engaged in politics. I thus disagree with Waller R. Newell, *Ruling Passion: The Erotics of Statecraft in Platonic Political Philosophy* (Lanham, MD: Rowman and Littlefield, 2000), 71, when he asserts that "Socrates 'practices politics' primarily by cultivating friendships." True, as Newell states, "although the *Republic* culminates in the lesson that one cannot impose the pattern of the good tout court on a city, one can begin to cultivate friends in one's actual city—friendships guided by the pattern of the good that one founds in the soul through philosophical investigations of politics." But I do not think that "beginning with these friendships . . . one can move outward gradually to effect larger reforms in the direction of the optimal *politeia*." At most, like Socrates in the *Republic*, one might convince ambitious political men that it would not be harmful and that it might even be useful to allow some of their fellow citizens to pursue not merely mathematical but philosophical inquiries. The "true city" as Socrates defines it provides people with the basic necessities of their existence. As he reminds Phaedrus with the story of the cicadas, we neglect those necessities at our peril. The city does not and cannot provide a philosophical education. As Socrates shows in his own life, such an education can be conducted only in private. What Socrates calls his *daimonion* or divine voice kept him from associating with young men who unambiguously and single-mindedly pursued political preeminence. It allowed him to pursue only those, like Alcibiades or Phaedrus, he had reason to believe might be persuaded to pursue a life of philosophy instead. Explicit mentions of the *daimonion* include *Alcibiades I* 103a, where Socrates said that it had kept him from approaching the young man until all his other lovers deserted him; *Phaedrus* 242c, where it prevents Socrates from leaving until he has given a second speech in praise of love, explicitly intended (257a–b) to persuade Phaedrus perhaps to persuade his lover Lysias to forsake rhetoric and pursue philosophy like Lysias' brother Polemarchus; and *Euthydemus* 272e–73a, when the *daimonion* keeps Socrates from leaving a gymnasium where he encounters Alcibiades' cousin Clinias, who seems open to being persuaded, as his cousin could not, that what he needs to pursue most is knowledge, not popularity. In both the *Apology* 31c–d and *Republic* 396c, Socrates says that his *daimonion* kept him out of politics. Particularly in democratic politics, Socrates charges, ambitious men promise the people wealth and glory rather than encouraging them to seek prudence and truth. In the *Theages* 128d–31a, Socrates claims that those who benefit from associating with

IV. The Human Good: *Philebus*

The *Republic* concludes with Socrates' admonition that, as we learn from the myth of Er, we must strive, above all, to learn "to distinguish what is the good and the bad life, and so everywhere and always to choose the better from among those that are possible" (618c). The *Philebus* begins with the question concerning the good life—is it the life of pleasure or the life of the mind? The conversation reported in the *Philebus* thus seems not merely to follow from but to complete that related in the *Republic*.

Indeed, in the *Philebus* Socrates appears to give the analysis of the good— the analysis he told Glaucon he could not give him because the young man could not follow. To be sure, in the famous images of sun, line, and cave that Socrates presented merely as "offspring" or interest, the "idea of the good" appeared to be the singular cause of all being and intelligibility, whereas in the *Philebus* Socrates and his interlocutor agree that the good for us humans is a mixture (although Socrates says he does not think this is true for the "divine *nous*" [22c]). Nevertheless, because Socrates appears to give a new account of the constitution and intelligibility of beings as mixtures of the limited and unlimited (or "definite" and "indefinite," *peras* and *apeiron*) in contrast to the imitations of the ideas in the *Republic*, several commentators have concluded that the *Philebus* constitutes a "late" dialogue in which Plato modified, if he did not entirely alter, his earlier teachings.[186] I contend, on the contrary, that in the *Philebus* Socrates expands and develops the argument he gave at the end of the *Republic* (585d–87e) concerning the superiority of the life of the mind, even on the grounds of pleasure, to any other.[187] In the *Philebus* he shows that both the common belief that pleasure is the good (to which we saw in the *Republic* even young aristocrats like Glaucon are tempted, despite their contempt for the many) and the more reflective modifications and extensions of this understanding in the works of the poets reflect an inadequate analysis of

---

him are those able to follow the advice of the *daimonion*. Socrates himself does not claim to be able to determine who will benefit from the beginning.

186. See, e.g., Sayre, *Late Ontology*, 78–86; Gisela Striker, *Peras und Apeiron: Das Problem der Formen in Platons Philebos* (Göttingen: Vandenhoeck & Ruprecht, 1970); and J. C. B. Gosling and C. C. W. Taylor, *The Greeks on Pleasure* (Oxford: Clarendon Press, 1982), 45–168. Dorothea Frede, "Disintegration and Restoration: Pleasure and Pain in Plato's *Philebus*," in *Cambridge Companion to Plato*, ed. Richard Kraut, 425–63 (Cambridge: Cambridge University Press, 1992), argues, on the contrary, that the "metaphysical" beginning lays a necessary foundation for the later analysis of pleasure.

187. By comparing the pleasures of the many, mixed with pain, to the phantom of Helen, which Stesichorus says the men at Troy fought over (586c), that is, a false or imagined rather than true beauty, Socrates also links this discussion in the *Republic* to his praise of love in the *Phaedrus*.

the phenomenon.[188] By showing that human beings do not take pleasure in the unconscious satisfaction of bodily wants and that human pleasure is not, therefore, necessarily associated with a continual process of becoming, Socrates seeks to combat the belief "that the sexual desires [erōtes] of beasts are more authoritative [kurioi] in determining how we humans can live well than the arguments and inspirations of the philosophical muse" (Philebus 67b).[189] As Socrates reminds his interlocutors (and readers) early in the dialogue (15a–c), however, the problems raised by his initial conversation with Parmenides remain.[190]

A. A Dialogue without Historical Setting, Characters, or Drama

Because the conversation about pleasure constitutes a ground-clearing operation rather than a positive enticement to philosophizing, the Philebus has an argumentative and rather abstract character. Socrates does not tell any stories (mythoi) or make any beautiful images. The dialogue is not set at any particular place or time in Athens. There is, indeed, no reference to politics whatsoever. Plato seems, moreover, to have named and created Socrates' two interlocutors particularly for their function in this argument.[191] Philebus, whose name means either lover of or beloved by the young, announces the doctrine that attracts them (and perhaps him to them)—namely, pleasure is the good that all living beings (zō[i]ois), not merely humans, seek. The way in which he might represent Socrates' chief opponent in a contest for the affections of young men is fairly obvious. Philebus is said to be beautiful or noble, that is, attractive (kalos) (11c). In the Symposium we learned that Socrates, despite his ugly appearance, was particularly able to attract young men like Alcibiades through his beautiful arguments; in that dialogue Socrates argued that the love of the beautiful was not beautiful or good itself. At the beginning of this dialogue (11b–d) we are told that in an earlier exchange with Philebus, Socrates had contended that the good is not pleasure but thought (phronein), mind (noein), memory (memnēsthai), and all things of that kind (suggenē), such as right

188. Donald Davidson, Plato's "Philebus" (New York: Garland, 1990), also argues that the examination of pleasure gives unity to this famously vexed, if not fragmented, discussion. He concentrates on "Plato's dialectical method," however, more than on the subject being examined.

189. Translations taken from Benardete (Philebus) are slightly modified.

190. Because of the apparent lack of integration of its arguments, Friedrich Schleiermacher suggested that the Philebus, like Phaedrus, was one of Plato's earlier, less expert compositions.

191. Unlike Gorgias, mentioned at Philebus 58a–c, they do not appear elsewhere in Greek history or literature.

opinion (*doxan orthēn*) and true calculations (*alētheis logismos*), for those who are able to participate in them (*dunata metalabein*). Because Philebus had indicated that he did not want to carry on the conversation, Socrates asked a young man named Protarchus (which means "the first principle") whether he would take up the argument.[192] Although neither the setting nor the characters have any political or historical significance, we are repeatedly reminded in the course of the conversation (16a, 19d–e, 23b, 28c, 50d–e, 67b) that there are many young men present who will force the philosopher to complete the argument. In other words, Socrates is compelled to present this argument because of the power (of the opinion) of the many. The threat to the philosopher is said to be "playful" because it is leveled by "boys" who do not yet have the force of the city or its fathers behind them.[193] The threat is, nevertheless, real. Socrates will not be able to attract youths to a life of philosophy so long as they believe that pleasure is the highest good and, consequently, follow Philebus' example in giving up argument when it appears to involve unnecessary painful effort. As we saw from Socrates' exchange with Alcibiades in the *Symposium*, not merely the perpetuity but the very truth of Socrates' claim that philosophy constitutes the best way of life depends on his ability to attract young people to it.

B. The Course of the Argument

Socrates indicates the course the conversation will take when he asks Protarchus to agree not only to take over Philebus' position but also to seek along with Socrates the disposition of soul in which pleasure and knowledge come to be. If they find a third state superior to either pleasure or

192. In saying that Philebus "withdrew" or "retired" (*apeireken*), Klein points out ("*Philebus*," 165), Plato puns on the association of Philebus' doctrine concerning not merely the supremacy but the infinite (or "unlimited," *apeiras*) character of pleasure. Cf. Benardete, *Philebus*, 87. Belonging to the class of the "more or less" but never entire or complete, Philebus' principle must always withdraw from sharp delineation in argument (*logos*). Protarchus thus indicates that he does not entirely agree with Philebus, although Protarchus does not yet realize it, when he states that he wishes them to take the argument out to its end (*peirōmetha perainein*) (*Philebus* 12b). When in withdrawing (12a–b) Philebus calls on his goddess, usually known as Aphrodite, but whose true name is Pleasure (Hēdonē), as a witness, he undermines his own suggestion that the goodness of pleasure is *alogos*, and hence evident to all living things, not merely humans with their distinctive faculty of *logos*. If things like pleasure have true or correct names, they and their names are and can be distinguished in speech (*logos*).

193. Benardete (*Philebus*, 97) points out that the word *polis* does not appear in the dialogue. Just as there is no reference to politics, so there is no mention of death. The only occurrence of *thanatos* is impersonal and with an alpha privative at 15d when *logos* is said to be *athanatos*.

mind, neither of the initial positions would be victorious. In that case, he and Protarchus will attempt to discover whether pleasure or mind is closer or more akin to the best.

Socrates then asks Protarchus if there are not different kinds of pleasure. If the young man agreed that there were, he would have reiterated the contradictory opinion of the many who believe that pleasure is the good but that there are both good and bad pleasures (cf. *Republic* 505c). Showing that he has a philosophical, if not sophistical education, Protarchus responds that different people may take pleasure in different things, but insofar as they are all pleasure, these pleasures are one and good.[194] Socrates objects that Protarchus is asking him to identify the most like and unlike things. The fact that the various sciences are all knowledge does not mean that there are not different kinds.[195] Impressed by Socrates' equal treatment of both pleasure and knowledge, Protarchus agrees to investigate the different kinds of both.[196]

C. The One and the Many

When Socrates asks Protarchus to agree to the further, all-encompassing "wonderful" (or "surprising," *thaumastos*) proposition (*logos*) that "gives all human beings trouble, whether they wish it or not" (*Philebus* 14c)—namely,

194. Socrates later identifies Protarchus as the "son of Callias" (*Philebus* 19b). According to Benardete (*Philebus*, 14n33), the name is too common to draw any definite connections or conclusions from it. Nevertheless, since Callias is regularly mentioned in the Platonic dialogues as a man who employs sophists to teach his sons (cf. *Protagoras* and *Apology*), it does not seem too much to suggest that the name points to Protarchus' having received such an education. Later in the conversation Socrates refers to the doctrines of pre-Socratic philosophers like Pythagoras and Anaxagoras, with which Protarchus seems somewhat familiar. Toward the end of the conversation (53a) Protarchus also brings up a claim he heard Gorgias make about the supremacy of persuasion as an art (*technē*).
195. Critics like Gosling and Taylor (*Pleasure*, 158ff.) and Klein ("*Philebus*," 166–68) regard Socrates' arguments in the *Philebus* as Plato's response to Eudoxus of Cnidus—an astronomer, mathematician, and geographer who firmly established the doctrine of ratios and proportions, including those of numerically incommensurable magnitudes, and tried to mix the *eidē*, as understood by Plato, with all sensible things—because, according to Aristotle *Nicomachean Ethics* 1172b9–15, 1172b35–73a5, Eudoxus argued that pleasure was the supreme good for both men and animals. The Gosling-Taylor argument rests, unfortunately, on speculative dating both of the time at which Plato wrote his dialogues and his competition with Eudoxus. Obviously Socrates could not credibly be imagined responding to Eudoxus.
196. As Cropsey points out ("Pleasure," 169), inasmuch as nothing is said about good and bad kinds of knowledge, the differences among the kinds of pleasure and knowledge are not exactly equivalent. The fact that Protarchus not only wants to see the argument taken to its completion (*peras*) but is also attracted by "fair play" indicates a certain nobility of character as well as thoroughness.

that the one is many and the many are one—the philosopher appears suddenly to elevate the conversation to the most general and abstract level. This *logos* appears surprising or "wonderful" inasmuch as it seems to constitute an outright contradiction. Are not the one (*hen*) and the many (*polla*) opposites? But why does Socrates say that this apparent contradiction gives *all* human beings trouble, whether they wish it (or we might say recognize it) or not?

The first reason the "surprising" *logos* gives at least some people trouble is that, although it may appear to be a contradiction, according to most if not all pre-Socratic philosophers, it is fundamentally true. If "being" is essentially one and the same, it can in principle be divided into an infinite number of parts or pieces and still remain essentially one and the same. Likewise, many parts or pieces of any particular quality remain one insofar as they all have that quality. In other words, essential differences are not established merely by plurality; the existence of true plurality requires essential differences. Mere division does not suffice. The manyness of the one and the oneness of the many could thus be said to have been the source of the *aporiai* at the heart of the antinomies in the "gymnastic" exercise in argumentation that the elder Parmenides once gave the young Socrates.[197] The old Eleatic gave the young Socrates such a demonstration, however, because Socrates was a young and aspiring philosopher. As Socrates and his interlocutors observed in the *Republic*, few people aspire to philosophy. Why does he say that this apparently contradictory *logos* about the one and the many gives trouble to all?

One reason everyone cares about this "amazing" proposition appears from the context in the *Philebus*. Like Protarchus, all human beings want, and therefore want to know, what is truly good. The dispute between Philebus and Socrates about the good can be restated as follows: is the good one and the same for all animals, including human beings, or is the good, as Socrates maintains, different for those who are able to participate in ratiocinative activities? To answer this question, one has to find out whether there are essential, unchanging differences, particularly among natural species.

197. The coexistence of the many and the one is not limited to Parmenidean philosophy, however. It would characterize all the forms of pre-Socratic philosophy that maintained there was one fundamental substratum or definition of "being." In emphasizing the importance of this "surprising" proposition, Socrates seems to recognize the reasons twentieth-century commentators like Karl Reinhardt and Martin Heidegger have maintained that in their apparently opposed theses concerning the character of being, Parmenides and Heraclitus said basically the same thing.

Most people do not understand the source of the difficulties involved in the conjunction of the one and the many, Socrates explains. It does not concern "the one . . . of the things that become and perish, for in that case, it has been conceded [that the one is many inasmuch as it changes from one thing to another]." Rather, he tells Protarchus:

> disputes arise whenever someone tries to set down human being as one and ox as one and the beautiful as one and the good as one . . . and unit[ie]s like them. . . . First, whether one should recognize that there are truly unit[ie]s of this kind; next, how, undergoing neither generation nor corruption, these unit[ie]s can remain the same; . . . and third, whether these unit[ie]s are to be posited as pulled apart and become many in the infinity of things which come into being or whether as a whole apart from itself, which would seem to be the most impossible of things, it comes to be one and the same simultaneously in one and many. (*Philebus* 15a–b)

The difficulties involve the existence of eternal beings of the kind Socrates called *eidē* in his youthful response to Zeno and the way in which sensible things "participate" in such ideas (the subject of much of Parmenides' critique of the young Socrates). Most people do not understand these difficulties—and have not, therefore, reached the threshold of Socratic philosophy—because they have not been shown, as Socrates himself was shown by Parmenides, that it is not sufficient to respond, as Protarchus does here (and Socrates had as a youth), that he himself could be considered a unity of many different qualities (*Parmenides* 129c–d). Like all other human beings, he and Protarchus are among the things that become. Most people have not asked whether there are permanently existing, unchanging unit(ie)s like species or the good (130b–c). They have been impressed, instead, with the way in which arguments that show the necessary coexistence of the one and the many can be used to refute any proposition.[198]

The conjunction of the one and the many is inherent in any speech (*logos*), Socrates observes. This is presumably the last and most fundamental reason why all human beings are troubled by the surprising *logos* about the conjunction of the one and the many, whether we wish to be or not; we are the *zō(i)on logon echon*. Speech is not possible until we move from particular signs or sounds for particular things to general words for kinds

---

198. Such arguments would include not only the paradoxes Zeno developed to defend his teacher from those who criticized Parmenides for failing to recognize the existence of motion or plurality; they would include all the "pre-Socratic" theories that reduced the apparent variety of the sensible world to one substratum.

of things, but the movement back to the particular things always remains. Once young people perceive the way in which the movement back and forth between the general and the particular or the one and the many can be used to refute the claims of others, they derive great pleasure from it. Enthusiastically refuting one argument after another, they perplex not merely themselves but whoever else is around, regardless of age, not even sparing their parents. Rather than lead to knowledge, the discovery of the conjunction of the one and the many in speech seems to result finally in complete *aporia*.

D. Socrates' Nobler or More Beautiful Way

Responding more to the critique of the young than to the substance of Socrates' claims, Protarchus asks Socrates whether he does not see their numbers. Isn't he afraid they will join with Philebus and attack him if he berates them? Merely criticizing the opinions and actions of others does not attract or persuade them. They will be willing to follow Socrates, however, if he has found a nobler or more beautiful (*kalliōn*) way of arguing.

Socrates claims to know such a way, which is easy to explain but difficult to use. It is the way of dialectic rather than eristic. Plato's Socrates is not primarily an elenctic philosopher, readers are reminded. He is not satisfied merely with showing that the opinions of his interlocutors are contradictory. His investigations are designed to help him discover whether there are eternal unit(ie)s, and if there are, what they are and how sensible things participate in them.

Socrates does not pursue that question or the matter fundamentally in dispute here, even though Protarchus invites him to do so. Instead, Socrates appeals to an ancient saying about the "things that are said to be," that is, the things in speech, "which have in themselves an innate limit and unlimitedness" (*Philebus* 16c). Neither the saying itself nor the examples of his mode of proceeding concern the eternal unit(ie)s. Socrates does not show here, as he admitted he did not know in his first encounter with Parmenides and continued to assert on the last day of his life in the *Phaedo*, whether there are eternal unit(ie)s like the human or the beautiful. Both in the general proposition and in the particular examples of letters and music that he uses to illustrate his point, Socrates deals explicitly with things that have come into being, exist in speech (*logos*), and hence have long been conceded to be a mixture of the one and the many. Through his procedure Socrates suggests that all pre-Socratic philosophy—including even Parmenides' famous "way" of truth—was based, fundamentally, on an analysis of things that come into being (or in the case of Parmenides, presumably, the negation of such) and was, therefore, inadequate. It did not account for the purely intelligible (which, in order to be intelligible, logical, and not fundamentally contradictory, required the existence of essential divisions that had to be plural and not merely negations).[199]

In demonstrating his nobler way of arguing, Socrates shows that the old Pythagorean-sounding saying is inadequate (although he does not say so explicitly). Understanding things as composed simply of the one and the many, or having the limited and the unlimited in themselves, is not sufficient to distinguish one from another or to define them; it leads, moreover, to eristic argumentation through the negation of one extreme by the other. To discover what the things are, Socrates urges, it is necessary to proceed "dialogically" by seeking first to identify the unit(y) within a thing or things and then to determine how many different kinds of this thing or unit(y) there are. Perceiving the unity in the many and the many in one is only the first step.

Protarchus admits that he does not completely understand, so Socrates gives two examples to illustrate his point. They indicate that nothing can be known or exist as what it is—a distinct or definite kind of being—before and unless it is differentiated not merely from other forms of being but within itself, into its varied aspects or "kinds." As in the case of letters, Socrates explains, so in the case of music, undifferentiated sound (*phōnē*) becomes something different if and only if it is articulated into its different elements. If tones and pitches are not separated into high and low, intervals and durations marked as long and short, and both then combined in various ways, there can be no melodies, scales, chords, harmonies, or rhythms. Undifferentiated sound, again, has to be divided into different kinds—vowels, labials, and consonants—to construct an alphabet of written letters. Apart from the articulation into its kinds or parts, neither music nor written speech exists. Nor do any of the "parts"—the notes, chords, or letters—exist except in conjunction with or in relation to the others. The one (*hen*), kind (*genos*), or idea (*eidos*) of music or of letters exists if and only if its constituent elements (*stoicheia*) are distinguished from one

199. Klein ("Concept of Number") points out that the Pythagorean discovery of the importance of number was important, but not sufficient, because the Pythagoreans did not distinguish the intelligibility of numbers from the sensible things numbers could be used to count, form, or organize, that is, the Pythagoreans did not distinguish sufficiently among the different kinds of being.

another. The undifferentiated, potentially fluctuating sound out of which both music and letters are constituted never becomes either without divisions or definitions (limits).[200] Socrates' two examples are by no means randomly chosen. Audible music and written letters are themselves two constituent parts of the art of poetry.[201] Socrates uses the constituent parts of the art of the poets to show that the poets' understanding of everything as fundamentally in flux cannot account for their own art or practice. Both the pleasure human beings take in poetry and its beauty depend on an underlying intelligible structure.

The fact that the articulation of the various aspects is necessary not merely to describe practices or forms of being, like music and letters in speech, but for their very existence or being does not show that such divisions necessarily exist or are eternal. We know that there are different kinds of music and letters (languages and alphabets) that have come into being and expired over time. The limits that define things that come into being do not appear to be the same as the eternal unities or ideas of which Socrates had spoken in previous dialogues.[202] Some of these limits might be eternal, but it does not look as if all of them are. The fact that the

200. Because Socrates first speaks of defining an idea as a unit(y) in terms of how many there are, and the divisions within sound that constitute music can be expressed in terms of mathematical relations, some commentators have suggested that Socrates is presenting a quasi-Pythagorean account of number as the exemplar, if not literally the component, of the constitution of all things. As Socrates' second example of letters shows, however, number is not the principle or exemplar. Not vowels, nasal diphthongs and consonants, nor the various kinds of each are distinguished from one another numerically or in terms of quantity. The result of this articulation of undifferentiated sound is, moreover, not music.

201. Cf. Benardete, *Philebus*, 120.

202. Because Socrates says that it is necessary to determine how many kinds, and not to characterize the many (*plēthos*—the same word used to describe "how many" young men are present) as infinite until they know how many kinds there are (*Philebus* 16d), some commentators have taken number to be the model of the kind of definition Socrates has in mind. The words "limit" (*peras*) and "unlimited" (*apeiron*) are Pythagorean terms. Not merely did the Pythagoreans argue that everything was composed of and defined by number; the sequence of numbers itself is infinite (because one can always add another "one"), but each number of units is definite (or limited). In ancient Greek thought, Klein explains, one is not a number because every number is a number of something. Such an understanding of number does not satisfy the demands of Socrates' dialogical method, however. According to Socrates, number(s) would also have to be defined according to the different kinds, for example, odd, even, prime, perfect. Cropsey ("Pleasure," 170–73), Sayre (*Late Ontology*, 155–61), and Klein ("*Philebus*," 167–68) all admit that Socrates does not call the unit(ie)s "kinds" or *eidē*. They argue, however, that the doctrine of the *Philebus* constitutes an advance on or refinement of the notion of the *eidē*. In doing so, Sayre and Klein both rely on Aristotle's statements in the *Metaphysics* (1073b17, 991a14, 1082a15, 8) concerning the two "elements" out of which everything, according to Plato, is constituted: the limitless composed of the "Great and the Small" and the sources of the "eidetic numbers" or kinds of kinds, the "indeterminate dyad" and the "one." I am arguing that this is Socrates' argument, which as such cannot simply be attributed to Plato. Neither Socrates nor Plato uses the Aristotelian terms.

nobler way of dialogically investigating what things are by finding a common factor or class and then identifying the different kinds or things that share in it resembles the hypothesis that Socrates said in the *Phaedo* he used to test the *logoi*, may tell us something about the reasons that on the last day of his life he presented his teaching concerning the ideas merely as a hypothesis and not the truth per se. Holding fast to that teaching, Socrates could show that things (or beings) are separated into different kinds (and kinds of kinds), but that finding did not in itself show that or which kinds are eternal and unchanging. This may be the reason Socrates says in the *Philebus* that the existence of such eternal unities and the way sensible things participate in them remains *the* subject of dispute.

Philebus asks, understandably, what the relevance of the discussion to the topic at hand is, and Socrates reminds him that they are inquiring what constitutes the good, pleasure or mind; they had agreed that each was one and were beginning to ask about the parts. Protarchus then announces that he understands the question—whether there are different species (*eidē*) of pleasure, and if so, how many and of what kinds? Protarchus sees what Socrates' way of investigating requires, but he also admits that neither he nor Philebus knows how to do it.[203] Socrates' way does appear to be easier to explain than to follow.

Protarchus thus demands that Socrates lead them. The young man has apparently heard Socrates converse before. He seems to be familiar with the philosopher's claim only to know that he does not know and his tendency, therefore, to question others rather than put forth his own views.[204] "Although it's noble for the moderate [or "wise," *tō(i) sōphroni*] to know everything," Protarchus observes, "it's thought to be a second sailing not to be unaware of oneself" (*Philebus* 19c). Recognizing his own ignorance, Socrates seeks knowledge.[205] It is not the young men but Socrates who initiates the conversation concerning the best of human possessions. To

203. By characterizing his own lack of knowledge as a "second sailing" (*Philebus* 19e) Protarchus indicates he may have heard something about Socrates' own famous stance or "turn." This is the second time the young man refers to himself or his own condition in a way reminiscent of Socrates. If so, Protarchus misuses the idiom. "Second sailing" refers to the use of one's own power or arms to man oars when the wind drops. Protarchus turns to Socrates to provide him with an argument he cannot formulate himself.

204. If Protarchus is son of the man named Callias at whose house Socrates met Protagoras, Protarchus has grown up among sophists and associates of Socrates. Callias' brother Hermogenes is Socrates' main interlocutor in the *Cratylus* and is said, in the *Phaedo* (59b), to be present at the philosopher's death.

205. There are, therefore, repeated references to the desirability of self-knowledge and the "saying" of Delphi in the *Philebus* (19c, 48c–d).

be sure, they playfully threaten not to allow him to leave until the question is settled. Nevertheless, he freely offers to talk with them. Protarchus concludes, therefore, that Socrates should stop perplexing them by asking them questions they are not able to answer and that he should deliberate on his own, by distinguishing the different kinds of pleasure and knowledge or showing in some other way whether pleasure or knowledge is best.[206]

E. The Good as a Mixture

Silently acting on Protarchus' suggestion that he take another route, Socrates claims to remember something he once heard to the effect that neither pleasure nor intelligence but some third thing is best. If that is the case, they will not have to distinguish the various kinds of pleasures to determine whether pleasure is the good. All that is necessary is, first, to ask whether the good sought by anyone with understanding is complete and hence adequate in itself to satisfy all their desires. If it is, Socrates quickly shows Protarchus, pleasure alone cannot constitute or be identical with the good. Without an admixture of mind, no one would know or remember that he enjoyed anything. To be good, pleasure must be mixed with mind. Protarchus is equally certain that no one would choose a life of the mind without any admixture of pleasure. Socrates is not so sure; he thinks this may be true only for us, that is, for those whose minds are embodied and hence mortal. A divine mind might not agree.[207]

Having convinced Protarchus that neither pleasure nor mind constitutes the human good, Socrates asserts that he would fight Philebus (in contrast to Protarchus) by insisting that mind is a more important element of, and therefore closer to, the human good than pleasure. But having achieved his initial goal, that is, having shown that pleasure is not the good, Socrates also says that he is willing to let the matter rest. Protarchus

---

206. The fundamentally asocial as well as *alogos* character of the thesis that pleasure is the good is reflected perhaps by the fact that in the two dialogues in which Socrates explicitly disputes the proposition that human beings should maximize their pleasure, he is forced by his interlocutor to deliberate on his own. Cf. *Gorgias* 505d. The *alogos* character of the thesis is reflected in the *Philebus* by Philebus' initial withdrawal from the conversation at the beginning of the dialogue and complete silence after 28b.

207. Once again, we see Protarchus (and Philebus) conclude that the two sides are equal when they are not. Is Plato suggesting that those who assert pleasure is the good do not calculate or reason with sufficient precision and clarity?

insists on continuing the argument by reminding Socrates that none of them will let him go until he completes it.

1. On the Constitution of Mixed Beings

If pleasure is not simply, immediately, and unquestionably good, the question again arises, what are the good or bad kinds? To answer that question, Socrates, proceeding in his dialogical way, has to specify what the different kinds are. And to do that, he states, he will need to use a new "contrivance" and "weapons."[208] In particular, he argues, it will be necessary to see that the beings said to be both one and many, and to have both the limited and the unlimited innately within them, are essentially different from either of their components, and that such mixtures must have a cause also distinct from the mixture. On the basis of such an analysis, Socrates shows that people like Philebus who conceive of pleasure as unlimited are mistaken, at least with regard to rational or human beings. It will not suffice to say, as they had of old, that "all things which are said to be are out of the one and the many have both a limit and unlimitedness innate within them," because even the unlimited and the limited themselves can be shown to be both one and many. These fundamental *eidē* do not appear to exist in themselves and apart from others. They are not the unit(ie)s, which are eternally unchanging.

Socrates first shows how the unlimited or indefinite is both one and many. The alpha privative (*a-peiron*) signaling that it literally has no external boundary, end, or limit suggests that the unlimited is, in a sense, many. That sense is not, however, of a plurality of units. The alpha privative signifies the absence of any definitive unity or parts. The term applies best to certain kinds of continua between two opposed states—hot and cold, dry and wet, great and small, quick and slow—on which things never reach the extremes or purity but always remain more or less. These continua are, nevertheless, more or less—something. In that sense, each of the continua is of one characteristic and not of something else. As Socrates' examples remind readers, there are different kinds of continua. What makes them unlimited or indefinite is not, moreover, simply their relational or comparative form. If it were, the comparatives of good and bad would also belong to the indefinite. The definitive characteristic of the unlimited or indefinite is the

---

208. Because the good is what human beings desire above all, they fight for and about it. Socrates himself has explicitly said that he is fighting—with Protarchus for the truth and against Philebus for second prize. To fight, one needs weapons.

impossibility of its ever reaching a state of completion, of purity, and hence an end to the more or less. For this reason, if pleasure belongs to the class of things of which there may always be more and hence are unlimited, as Philebus asserted (27e), pleasure cannot constitute the good. If, as Socrates and Protarchus previously agreed, the good per se is complete, things that share in it cannot be inherently better or worse without limit or end.

Socrates then turns to the opposite of the indefinite—the definite or limited. Just as the indefinite is both one and many insofar as all modes of being that are essentially relative and have no completion or purity in themselves are one, yet there are different kinds of indefiniteness, so, he suggests, all limits are one and the same (in fact or function) insofar as they give definition to various kinds of things. Qua limits or definitions, the double or the equal are what they are—never more or less. Anything that becomes differentiated from what was before by coming into being must be composed, therefore, of both the definite and the indefinite. The indefinite would never be completely distinguished from other being(s), whereas the completely and essentially limited would be complete in itself and would not therefore come into being. Whereas the indefinite cannot exist or be known simply by itself, that is, not in contrast or relation to the definite, it is not so clear that limits or definitions cannot exist in or by themselves, even though Socrates admits that there are many different kinds. Some might be lasting whereas others are not. Because his two examples of limits, the equal and double, both express quantitative relations, one is led to wonder whether they exist apart from the things they measure.

Failing to perceive the thrust of the argument (which Socrates has not made explicit), Protarchus admits that he has difficulty understanding why Socrates now maintains that there are three rather than two fundamental kinds of things. Protarchus does not yet see how the whole composite of the generated being is different from the sum of its parts. Socrates indicates the difference by pointing out that the goodness of the "offspring" generated through the mixture—whether it be health of the human body or the beauty of music (as opposed to raucous noise), the seasons (or order of the visible motions of the heavens and their results), and the human soul (or the invisible virtues that give it order)—depends on the combination being right (orthos) or having measure (metros). Not all generated beings are good, readers are led to see; the only mixtures that are good are "right" or have "measure."

Nothing comes into being, moreover, without a cause. To explain not merely the combination of definition and indefiniteness in generated things, but their very coming into being, Socrates states, it is necessary to posit yet another, fourth fundamental kind of being. By suggesting that "cause" and "maker" are merely different names for the same function, the bringing into being of something, Socrates ignores the distinction often drawn between nature and art. Socrates abstracts from these distinctions, it appears in the sequel, in order to draw a parallel between the constituent elements of animals and the cosmos as a whole.

2. MIND AS CAUSE

Having explained his "contrivance" or framework, Socrates suggests that they try to characterize both pleasure and mind in terms of his fourfold schema. All things that come into being, including the mixture of mind and pleasure they have identified with the human good, clearly belong to the mixed genus. Socrates asks Philebus whether pleasure and pain belong to those things that have no limit, and Philebus agrees that they do. If it were not possible always to have more, pleasure would not be completely good. But when Socrates asks where they would put knowledge, thought, or mind, Philebus objects to the philosopher's exalting his own god. Socrates accuses Philebus of exalting his goddess in the same fashion and insists that he answer the question. Rather than accept the discipline or limitation imposed by Socrates' method, Philebus reminds Protarchus of the young man's promise to speak for him. Feeling himself at a loss, Protarchus turns the entire argument over to Socrates. As a result, the issue at stake is not clearly stated, much less thoroughly canvassed.

Socrates claims that "all the wise exalt themselves" by agreeing "that the king of heaven and earth is mind [*nous*]" (*Philebus* 28c). If things are not organized in an intelligible manner, knowledge is impossible. The only "wisdom" human beings could have would be the knowledge that they cannot know. That is, however, exactly the kind of wisdom Socrates claims for himself in the *Apology*. According to his own statement in the *Phaedo*, he was prepared to believe that mind rules everything, but neither Anaxagoras nor anyone else had been able to show him how. The philosophers and poets before Parmenides who taught that everything is in flux also did not agree that mind is king.

Rather than simply take the testimony of the "wise" on authority, Socrates suggests, they could make further inquiries. Protarchus tells him to say whatever he wishes; he has already given over the argument as a whole to Socrates. So Socrates asks the young man whether they should say that everything is irrational and moves randomly, or whether something like mind directs and arranges everything that happens. When Pro-tarchus responds that it would not be holy (*hosion*) to deny that mind orders the movements of the heavenly bodies, Plato's readers see that the question here is the same one that the Athenian took up in book 10 of the *Laws*. The response Socrates gives to the question is not quite the same, however. He apparently does not have to convince the young man with whom he speaks to believe in the gods by observing the orderly movements of the stars. Socrates does, however, introduce an argument that agrees with what "those before us" said about mind arranging everything in opposition to the "terribly clever man [*deinos*] who says that everything is in disorder" (*Philebus* 29a). Like the Athenian, Socrates proposes to improve on Anaxagoras' argument, but the improvement he offers is different. Rather than showing that mind directs everything, the Athenian contented himself with showing that the regular movements of the heavenly bodies demonstrate that some motion or soul is not only orderly but also measurable and hence intelligible. He suggested, however, that the orderly forms of motion exist in constant and unending tension with the disorderly. If everything exists in opposition to everything else, Socrates sees, we cannot speak of a whole. And if there is no whole, nothing is, strictly speaking, knowable. Beginning with observations of the orderly motions of the heavenly bodies and their effects on the coming into being and passing away of things on earth through the seasons, Socrates suggests that the cosmos, having a beautiful order, is intelligible, and if it is intelligible, it must be a whole.[209] Just as we draw the relatively small portions of fire, earth, water, and air we find in our own bodies from a much greater quantity of such in the whole, so our souls must be drawn from and nourished or maintained by a greater soul. If the cosmos is a mixture of all these elements in a single body, it too must have a soul to hold all the different elements or parts together. The cause of this mixture of body and soul in all animals as well as in the cosmos is spoken of as mind or wisdom. But, Socrates quickly adds, mind or wisdom can never come to be without soul.

Socrates speaks explicitly of things which come to be (including mind and wisdom). All such things have limits or a de-finition. To be is to be something. The things that come to be (as opposed to those that always

209. In his poem, Parmenides had argued that being must have a form or limit (*peras*) if it is to be complete, not lacking anything. In the demonstration he has the philosopher give in his *Parmenides*, Plato suggests that the Eleatic philosopher's conception of being as homogenous does not allow him to maintain that being has a limit—or that being is a whole (and hence intelligible).

are) are mixtures—of the limited with the unlimited—caused or brought together by something like mind. (Mind itself appears to involve a mixture of motion with order.) Socrates thus fills in the gap he found in Anaxagoras' argument between the claim that mind rules everything and the description of things that come to be in the world as interactions or mixtures of preexisting elements by positing the existence of two essentially different kinds of things—definite and indefinite—which can mix with each other but are separate and distinct in themselves. There is no continuous, unregulated mixing or generation of all things indiscriminately, as Hesiod imagined and Heraclitus seems to have thought.

Socrates may thus give a more accurate description of what is and what comes to be than his predecessors; all things do not mix or fuse with all other things, and for there to be "things" or "beings" there must be essential distinctions or differences among them. But Socrates has not shown how these things come to be or why. Generation or mixing may not constitute adequate answers, but "mind" or intelligible distinctions and combinations do not provide an efficient cause. Protarchus may have been right in intuiting the need for a fifth (23d).

Socrates has, moreover, clearly made "animals," if not specifically human beings, the model of the cosmos—and animals, mixtures of soul and body, are mortal. As such, we are both incomplete and less than self-sustaining. Readers are led to ask, therefore, whether the animal is a satisfactory paradigm for the cosmos, which is supposed to encompass everything else— at least all other living beings—if it is a whole. The issue that underlies Philebus' assertion that pleasure can constitute the human good only if there is always more is human mortality. The pleasure we take in almost anything is colored more or less explicitly by our underlying sense that it will come to an end with death. In the *Philebus*, Socrates does not mention the foreknowledge human beings have of their inevitable death or the yearning somehow to overcome it. It is not clear, therefore, that he has fully confronted the issues, most immediately, of the human good, and more generally, of the extent to which the human (good or anything else) can serve as a model of the whole.

3. THE DIFFERENT KINDS OF PLEASURE

Socrates never claimed to be giving an account of the whole, however. He introduced both his "nobler" way of arguing dialectically (as opposed to the frustrating eristics of the sophists) and his fourfold framework concerning the aspects or kinds of beings to enable them to determine (*a*) whether there are different kinds of pleasure, and (b) if so, what they are. Having explained the framework, he proposes to use it to show what the different kinds of pleasure are.

Asked where pleasure would be found in the fourfold framework, Philebus asserts that it belongs to the unlimited, because it would not be good if there could not always be more. (In an aside, Socrates points out that if this were true, pleasure would also always be linked to its opposite, pain—even though Philebus does not want to admit it). Attempting to show that mind was closer to cause (and hence more like the good), Socrates had provisionally agreed with Philebus that pleasure belonged to the unlimited. If pleasure were truly unlimited or existed only on a continuum with pain, however, it would not be possible to say with any accuracy what pleasure is—or whether it is good. We would merely feel it. Having argued that mind is, or is at least like, the cause that brings limited and unlimited things into beautiful mixtures—in the cosmos or in human beings (through the harmony produced by the virtues)—Socrates proceeds to argue (a) that there are different kinds of pleasure and thus (b) that pleasure is not, therefore, unlimited. On the contrary, the purest kinds of pleasures prove to be quite restrained—or limited. These are the kinds of pleasures, moreover, that can be mixed with mind to produce the human good.

a. The Pleasure That Accompanies the Restoration of Bodily Order

Beginning, in effect, with Philebus' presumption that pleasure is a feeling, Socrates suggests that they try to determine in what feeling (*pathos*) each of the two alternative definitions of the good comes to be. Pleasure, he observes, is associated with the common (*koinon*) species. When Protarchus fails to understand what Socrates is talking about, the philosopher explains that by "common" he meant the "mixed" kind or third *eidos*. Using the popular (*dēmosia*) or common (*periphanē*, appearing on all sides) feelings of hunger and thirst as examples, he points out that pleasure accompanies the regaining of its natural order, unity, or wholeness by a composite being, just as pain accompanies the dissolution or corruption and eventual destruction of that order or unity. In discussing the need for a fourth *eidos* of cause in explaining how things come to be, Socrates and Protarchus had agreed that mind is the source of order or harmony in health and the beauty of the natural cosmos. In analyzing the first and most evident kind of pleasure, Socrates thus showed that it is tied to order (and ultimately the cause of that order in mind). Even the most basic and animal form of pleasure experienced primarily in and through body is not simply or purely a matter of feeling.

b. Anticipation

Socrates observes that there is a second kind of pleasure (or pain) to be found in the anticipation (*prosdokēma*) of a future state. Anticipation resides entirely in the soul, not in the body; also, Socrates predicts, the truth about pleasure will be found in these pure, unmixed kinds. Such anticipation could either contradict one's present condition or exaggerate it by "doubling." In either case, the anticipation is not the same as the feeling one presently has. If pleasure accompanies the restoration of order and pain accompanies the destruction of that order, things completely in order would feel neither. That is the condition of a life of wisdom or, presumably, the divine.[210] Socrates confines his analysis here to the things that come to be, because these and only these experience pleasure. There is, however, a higher state characterized by neither pleasure nor pain. That is presumably the condition of the divine mind he alluded to earlier (which did not want an admixture of pleasure to make something good).

Socrates' observations concerning the anticipatory kind of pleasure and pain lead him to a more general analysis of the relation between body and soul in the experience of pleasure. As Socrates has already reminded his listeners, human beings think of pleasure most commonly as associated with the satisfaction of desire. But, he points out, desire presupposes memory and hence a certain amount of intellect. Neither desire nor, presumably then, pleasure is or ought to be conceived of as purely or even fundamentally belonging to body. To desire something we lack, we have to remember what we want. There are vital bodily motions—breathing and digesting, for example—of which we are usually not aware and hence do not actively desire to engage in. Perception (*aisthēsis*) requires both body and soul. We remember only what we perceive. If memory is a function of the soul and not a property of body, then all inclination (*hormē*) and desire (*epithymia*), the ruling or directing principle (*archē*) of all living beings (*zō[i]a*), belongs to the soul. There is no such thing as simply or purely bodily desire.

Nor, Socrates concludes, does pleasure simply consist in a continuum with pain, like hot and cold, or dry and wet. He thus puts the soundness of their previous agreement with Philebus—that pleasure belongs to the

210. When Protarchus volunteers his opinion that the gods would not feel joy or its opposite, he shows that he associates divinity more with the cosmic "gods" than with the divinities said to dwell on Olympus. Such a pre-Socratic philosophical view is not compatible with the tragic view of human life, Socrates will show, even though most of the poets thought that it was.

unlimited—into question. Although it might seem that the pleasure that accompanies the restoration of order in a body results from the lessening of pain from the want, they had already observed that the person who is between pleasure and pain, that is, not feeling either, is not in the middle of the continuum. That person is not feeling either pain or pleasure because he or she has attained the order that was previously being acquired or disrupted, that is, at the end or limit of the continuum.

c. True and False Pleasures

Since desire depends on memory and memories can be distorted or false, Socrates asks Protarchus whether the pleasure or pain we anticipate feeling cannot also be true or false. At first Protarchus is willing to allow only that the opinion that accompanies or produces the pleasure may be false. Pleasure—still understood apparently to be pure feeling without any mental admixture—is only pleasure. Socrates accuses Protarchus of advocating the argument in favor of pleasure, but the youth responds that he is only saying what he had heard. Socrates reminds Protarchus of the way in which we are apt to misperceive things we see at a distance and also to misremember what we have experienced. Protarchus agrees that just as those who have false opinions are opining as much as those who opine truly, so those who take pleasure in anticipating pleasures they will not actually experience later, experience pleasure in the anticipation, but falsely, because they should truly be feeling the pain of anticipated disappointment. Socrates then points to the young man's fundamental concern by asking him to agree that they must also say the hopes of a just, pious, and good man are for the most part true, because such a man is beloved by the gods and so has reason to anticipate good things in the future, whereas bad people rejoice primarily in false pleasures, because (if the gods rule and care for human beings) such people should not expect a pleasant fate.[211] Protarchus seeks knowledge of the human good in order to show that there is a moral order. (Readers should remember that Protarchus thought it would be unholy to say that things occur randomly or by chance.) Socrates has already argued that the feeling of pleasure cannot be entirely separated from an intellectual, hence true or false, correct or incorrect, aspect. Although Socrates appears to have convinced Protarchus that there are

---

211. Socrates' suggestion would be more plausible if he said that those who have true or well-founded hopes tend to be just. He and Protarchus agree, we observe, only to what they should say (in public, perhaps, in contrast to what they may think privately).

different kinds of pleasures, Protarchus is not willing to agree that pleasures are bad simply because they are false. He thinks that bad or base pleasures are still pleasures. He does not understand the implications of Socrates' showing that all pleasure has an intellectual aspect, content, or presupposition.

Recognizing his failure to lead the young man away from the common perception of pleasure simply as a feeling, Socrates does not press Protarchus on the question of whether there are evil pleasures that are bad not simply because they are false. To show that there are really false pleasures, he simply says that he has to turn to another argument. In the course of this argument he identifies two additional kinds of pleasure—the pleasure heightened by its conjunction with pain in the most intense passions of the soul and pure pleasures, those without any admixture of pain. He then argues that we learn the nature of pleasure most from its pure and not its most intense forms.

To show not merely that there are two additional kinds of pleasure but that there are different kinds at all, Socrates explicitly has to modify their first agreement concerning pleasure—that it belongs to the indefinite. If pleasure were indefinite or unlimited, it would not be possible to discriminate one kind from another, for example, true from false. They had agreed, however, that pleasures are false when the pleasure is based on an incorrect opinion. Now Socrates points to another possible source of error: just as we often misperceive things we see at a distance, so pleasures and pain may not appear to be truly what they are when viewed from afar or too close.[212] There are also times when we feel neither pleasure nor pain. We do not perceive some of our own most vital motions—for example, when we are growing. It is an error, then, to identify pleasure and pain simply with changes in our constitution—filling or replenishing as opposed to emptying or decaying. The changes must have a certain magnitude and hence definition to be perceived as pleasant or painful.

d. Pleasure as the Absence of Pain

If pleasure and pain truly exist on an indefinite continuum of more and less, Socrates suggests, then those who deny that there truly is such a thing as pleasure other than the mere absence of pain would be correct. These are the true enemies of Philebus, because they show his good to be a mere

---

212. In the *Protagoras*, we may recall, Socrates led the sophists assembled at Callias' house to agree that they taught people how to measure or calculate their pleasures correctly.

negation, nothing positive. Socrates does not agree with such "epicure-ans." He asserts that there are at least five different kinds of pleasure that have no origin in or admixture of pain. He asks Protarchus to examine the claim that there is really no such "thing" as pleasure as a means of clarify-ing the nature and source of our understanding of it.

In order to learn the nature of a thing or quality, Socrates and Pro-tarchus agree, one should look at its most intense or extreme form. In the case of pleasure, the most intense forms appear to be associated with the body. Such extreme feelings are to be observed not so much in healthy people as in those recovering from illness. Nor are the most intense plea-sures often experienced by the morally upright. Foolish or hubristic peo-ple seek and enjoy extreme pleasures much more often than those who are self-restrained. On reflection it becomes clear that extreme pleasures are experienced as such, particularly by the sick or those with recurrent "itches," only in contrast to the extreme pain that precedes or accompanies them. That is the reason the haters of pleasure conclude that there is no such thing as pleasure, really; there is only the relief from or, even better, the absence of pain. They react as negatively as they do to pleasure seeking because they see it to be ignoble as well as stupid.

All three of the kinds of pleasure Socrates has identified involve a mix-ture of pain with pleasure: (1) the pleasure of recovering the order of the constituent parts of our body usually follows from the pain of a disrup-tion; (2) the anticipation of future pleasure creates pain in its absence; and (3) the pleasure we feel in the relief from the most intense pain obviously presupposes the latter. It is no accident, therefore, that most people under-stand pleasure and pain as existing on an indefinite continuum of more or less; what human beings most often and evidently experience as pleasure is mixed with pain. The fact that our most intense feelings involve such a mixture or constantly changing continuum is, moreover, the reason people have come to believe that not merely we but everything in the cosmos is constantly changing, or "as the wise assert, always flowing up and down" (*Philebus* 43a).[213]

In the *Symposium*, Plato attributed such a view to the poets Aristophanes and Agathon. Readers should not be surprised, therefore, to see Socrates present the works of poets—epic, tragic, and comic—as expressions of another kind of mixed pleasure. Analogous to the relief we feel recovering from an illness or scratching an itch, he observes, the painful psychic states

213. Socrates admits that not all the "wise" exalt themselves by declaring that mind rules all.

of anger, fear, longing, mourning, eros, emulation, and envy have certain pleasures associated with them. Neither the pain nor the pleasure involved is bodily, but these passions are our most intense. They are as deep and intense as they are because they result from a conjunction of pleasure with pain. Homer brought out the way in which pleasure and pain are combined in anger when the poet had Achilles talk about that "which sets even the very wise to anger, and is far sweeter than dripping honey" (*Philebus* 48a; *Iliad* 18.108). Like Achilles, people who become enraged are pained by the wrong they suffer but rejoice at the prospect of taking revenge. Likewise, the audiences of tragedies paradoxically take pleasure in weeping at the fate of the heroes. Members of the audience empathize with the pain, the terror, and the suffering of the characters, as if they too were experiencing what is happening on stage; they can pity the characters and their unjust fate, however, because as audience they know that the actors are not really undergoing it. Recognizing that it is only a play, audience members feel the abatement of their fear and rejoice in the fact that they are only the spectators.[214]

e. Laughter

Socrates admits that the combination of pleasure and pain in the reaction people have to comedies is more difficult to discern. Both the anger of Achilles and the fate of tragic heroes are explicitly associated with the pain we feel in contemplating our own inevitable death. Death is never conceived to be desirable, pleasant, or good—except, possibly, as the end of a miserable existence. That is why we can empathize with the fear tragic heroes feel in the face of death and yet pity them, because it is they and not we who are immediately in danger. What is puzzling about tragedy is our perception of beauty and hence our taking pleasure in what would appear to be awful events. What is puzzling about comedy is that it seems to be pure pleasure or entertainment, but is nevertheless intrinsically associated with pain.

Laughter could appear to be an expression of pure pleasure. It is a distinctively human, as opposed to more generally animal, phenomenon

---

214. Cf. Michael Davis, *Aristotle's "Poetics"* (Lanham, MD: Rowman and Littlefield, 1992), 39: "If the evil appearing before us is destructive or painful, we are forced to acknowledge the distinction between our perspective as spectators—*ta theatra*—and the perspective of the character undergoing what is destructive or painful— *autho kath' hauto* (1449a8–9). As spectators we pity; as participants we fear."

and has even been attributed to the immortal gods. Laughter has a claim, therefore, to be a part of, if not simply to constitute, the human good. Socrates argues, however, that laughter arises out of envy and in the face of perceived weakness.[215] It is not simply an expression of pleasure, much less of happiness or strength. Like anger, laughter is associated with immoderate behavior (exemplified by Aristophanes in the *Symposium* and condemned by Socrates in the *Republic*), because it constitutes a kind of relief from pain. It is not good or desirable in itself.

To show that laughter is not pure pleasure, Socrates first reminds Protarchus of the pain envious people feel when their friends prosper. If people were not envious, they would take pleasure in the advantages of their friends and be pained by their shortcomings. Taking pleasure in the revelation of the shortcomings of others presupposes envy or pain at one's own failure to do so well. Socrates and Protarchus agree, further, that ignorance of one's own limitations—whether with regard to wealth, beauty, virtue, or wisdom—is a shortcoming. But, Socrates points out, people laugh at the revelation of the ignorance of others only when they believe the others are too weak to take revenge. As in tragedy, the making public of the lack of self-knowledge, if not humiliation, of a strong man evokes fear, if not terror. Laughter presupposes a perception of weakness both in the brunt of the joke and in the person who rejoices. In the face of the perceived vulnerability of the other, those who laugh are relieved at least temporarily from their own sense of inferiority.[216] In both tragedies and comedies, Socrates suggests, members of the audience first identify with the protagonist, yet rejoice in the end that they are not she or he.

---

215. In the *Odyssey* 8.305–65, on the occasion when the Olympian gods are said to laugh most raucously, Homer explicitly connects laughter and ridicule to weakness and envy, as Socrates proceeds to argue here. When the lame Hephaestus takes revenge on his wife Aphrodite and Ares for their adultery by contriving to catch them in a net and then displays them embracing in public, Apollo tells Hermes that he would gladly suffer the ridicule if he could enjoy the embraces of the beautiful Aphrodite. Hermes agrees. All the gods but Poseidon laugh, because they envy the good fortune of Ares. The goddesses all hide in shame. They are weaker. Hephaestus lets the lovers depart after Poseidon, who strongly objects to the shaming of any divinity, demands that the weaker god let them go and promises him other compensation.

216. Hobbes defines glory as the "joy arising from imagination of a man's own power and ability" (*Leviathan*, pt. I, chap. 1, sec. 39), and then "sudden glory as the passion which maketh those grimaces called laughter, and is caused either by some sudden act of their own that pleaseth them, or by the apprehension of some deformed thing in another, by comparison whereof they suddenly applaud themselves. And it is incident most to them that are conscious of the fewest abilities in themselves, who are forced to keep themselves in their own favour by observing the imperfections of other men" (sec. 42).

f. The Conjunction of Intelligence and Pleasure in the Spectator and the Error in Dramatic Art

Socrates admits that he has concentrated on comedy in order to go through the kinds of pleasure as quickly as possible, so that they will let him go before midnight. Readers are thus led to suspect that his discussion of the intense, because mixed, pleasures and their presentation in dramatic art is sketchy, if not simply incomplete. On reflection, we see that this brief discussion does not recapitulate but it does complete Socrates' previous critique of the poets.

Socrates' inquiry about the disposition of our soul in comedies immediately after he has asked Protarchus to remember the combination of tears and rejoicing in the audience of a tragic spectacle makes it clear that he is concentrating on the reaction of the audience. In the *Symposium*, *Phaedrus*, and *Republic*, Socrates criticized the poets primarily for the inadequacy of what they represented on stage—for their presentation of beautiful illusions as truth, their presentation of immoderate behavior as heroic and thus exemplary, and their inability to represent the purely intelligible (and hence the true character of the whole). In the *Philebus* he focuses on dramatic art's evil effects on the understanding, especially the self-understanding, of its spectators. In his analysis of the mixed emotions both forms of drama depict and evoke, he indicates a bit more clearly than he had in the *Republic* why dramatic art is essentially a democratic form of art that not only appeals to a popular audience but also encourages its members to establish a democratic regime. Spectators of tragedies experience a mixture of pleasure and pain insofar as they empathize with the sufferings of the hero and yet rejoice in their own actual freedom from such suffering. They come to believe that they are better off than the great. Spectators of comedies rejoice in their superiority to the stupidity of the ridiculous protagonists. It is not the audience, however, but the artist who points out the foibles of his characters. By leading his audience to laugh at rather than to empathize with the failing of his characters, the comic artist tempts members of his audience to think they are wiser than they actually are. Rather than leading them to self-knowledge through a revelation of the limitations of the human situation, Socrates charges, both forms of dramatic art flatter the people (*dēmos*) by making them feel better and wiser than they actually are. Members of the audience thus feel justified in raising the claim not merely to rule themselves but to do what they want, that is, not to regulate their own desires.[217]

---

217. The Athenian levels a similar charge against the poets in *Laws* 700d–701c.

As Plato suggests in the speeches he attributes to Aristophanes and Agathon in the *Symposium*, so he shows Socrates explicitly arguing in *Philebus*: by presenting the strong emotions constituted by a mixture of pleasure and pain, dramatic art suggests that human desire can never be completely satisfied. Taking the most intense pleasures as exemplary, this art teaches that pleasure—the apparent object of human desire—is always mixed with pain. Because the pleasure we seek is never pure or complete, we are never satisfied. We can never achieve the good (which Protarchus and Socrates agreed earlier must be complete in itself). The belief that we can be happy, that happiness is or can be lasting, is an illusion.

The irony, Socrates indicates here, is that this "tragic" view of human possibilities not merely rests on a misunderstanding of human pleasure but on a misunderstanding of the kind of pleasure an audience takes in a dramatic production. As spectators, members of the audience do not experience the passions of the actors—much less the tragic or ridiculous effects of these passions—with the same intensity or seriousness as the characters. The audience knows that the characters are played by actors and that the emotions they express are not real. As spectators, members of the audience understand themselves to be seeing more and better than the characters. The pleasure the audience gets from a drama—like all human pleasure—has an intellectual, contemplative element. It is not merely a fleeting, essentially transitory sensation or illusion.

g. The Pure Pleasures

All the examples of pure pleasure that Socrates lists—the pleasures of viewing purely intelligible forms, seeing pure colors, hearing pure tones, smelling, or contemplating what we have learned (in abstraction from any longing or effort to learn)—have this passive, purely receptive, rather than desirous and hence actively seeking or striving character. These pleasures admittedly appear to be much milder and more measured than the extreme, intense variety associated primarily with sexuality (although Socrates never explicitly points out this association in the *Philebus*).[218]

---

218. Socrates lists eros as one of the strong passions that combine pleasure and pain (*Philebus* 47e, 50b–c). Explaining not only why such mixed emotions are most intense but also why they tend to characterize the disorderly and sick rather than the moderate and healthy, he uses the example of scratching an itch (46a, d–e), which can be taken, as in the *Gorgias* (494c–e), to refer to a base kind of sexual desire. Eros here is understood primarily as a desire to relieve a pain (and hence gives rise to the notion that pleasure consists merely in such a flight from pain) rather than as the desire for immortality (in other words, for a lasting good and not a fleeting temporary

Nevertheless, Socrates maintains, we should derive our understanding of the character of pleasure from its pure form (a) because it is pure rather than an admixture of something else, and (b) because as the contemplation of something complete in itself, such pleasure is associated with a state of being rather than a state of becoming like the more intense forms. Things come into being for the sake of being, not vice versa.

This concentration on the end rather than on the means of achieving it gives the conversation in the *Philebus* its abstract, relatively nondramatic character. As such, the good must be choiceworthy in itself, not necessary, and surely not that which is to be avoided. In determining what the good for us is, Socrates does not, therefore, deal with the necessity of facing our own inevitable demise or death. Nor does he take up the means of providing the necessities of our existence and defending them from others, that is, politics. He does not even consider the means by which human beings acquire the knowledge, intelligence, right opinion, and memory he argues are essential constituents of the human good. In contrast to the *Symposium*, *Phaedrus*, *Clitophon*, and *Republic*, in the *Philebus* Socrates does not consider either the content or the means of educating the young (although his leading of Protarchus to a correct view of the composite character of the human good might be considered an example of such). Unlike Protarchus, Socrates does not even refer to the need to seek self-knowledge. In the *Philebus* he limits himself to inquiring what the goal of our efforts is—and if that goal must include both knowledge and pleasure, how the two could be combined.

4. The Proper Mixture

If, as Socrates has shown by identifying no less than five kinds of pure pleasures, pleasure is not necessarily associated with becoming, is not unlimited, and hence is mixed with more or less pain, the good of human life cannot consist in seeking pleasure without end, as Philebus asserted. The question remains, however: what mixture of mind, intelligence, knowledge, right opinion, and memory with pleasure constitutes the human good?

To answer that question, Socrates has to distinguish the different kinds of knowledge just as he had sorted out the different kinds of pleasure. (He thus returns to the parallel between knowledge and pleasure that initially persuaded Protarchus to go on with the investigation.) Socrates first divides

---

pleasure) that Socrates argues it is in the *Symposium*. Toward the end of the dialogue, Protarchus observes that "sexual pleasures . . . are thought to be the greatest" (65c).

knowledge into the productive and the educative, then the productive into that which relies primarily on experience and that which employs the arts of number, measurement, and weighing. Even though music is often associated with mathematics in the Platonic dialogues (as it was earlier in the *Philebus*), Socrates uses flute playing as an example of a knack based on practice in contrast to a more precise art such as carpentry based on measurement. The distinction between pure and impure is not the same, he indicates, as that between noble and base, the beautiful and the ugly, or the freely chosen and the necessary. Dividing the more "precise" arts into two kinds as well, Socrates distinguishes the "arithmetic of the many," which measures unequal units such as armies or oxen, from the calculations and geometry practiced by philosophers, who employ purely intelligible concepts that are always the same. As noted earlier, Socrates does not take up or distinguish the different kinds of educative arts. He concentrates only on the products or cognitive results.

Protarchus does not have any difficulty agreeing that the arts of the philosophers are far superior to those of the many in both truth and accuracy, even when Socrates reminds him that those who are dreadfully clever in argumentation would object. Protarchus does not seem to remember that the existence of the eternally unchanging purely intelligible units philosophers were said to use is *the* greatest subject of dispute. Protarchus is troubled by what he used to hear from Gorgias about the art of persuasion being the best of all arts—and his perception of his own inability to maintain a position in opposition to either the great rhetorician or Socrates. Socrates lets Protarchus "off the hook" by saying that he is not looking for the greatest, the most beneficial, or even the most useful art; he is claiming merely that the philosophical arts, which might not be useful or grand, are simply the purest, truest, and most precise.[219] In this conversation, as

219. In a later conversation with Gorgias and his students, Plato shows Socrates arguing that rhetoric is not an art at all but only a knack; like sophistry, rhetoric appeals to the pleasure of the many and not to the good. Nevertheless, the evocation of the name of Gorgias serves to remind readers of the *Philebus* how "theoretical" the definition of the human good to which they come is. Socrates can respond to the threat posed by the "many" young men here with an argument, because the threat they pose is playful, neither serious nor mortal. As we are reminded by the *Gorgias* (521e), the Athenian demos, even though they act in some ways like children, would not be satisfied in a similar fashion. Because they were urgently aware of the needs as well as the desires of the body, the Athenian demos recognized the necessity not simply of declaring that the intense pleasures and pain that interfere with the operation of the mind are not good, but of restraining people under the sway of such passions with force. In other words, the demos saw the need for politics—from which this dialogue abstracts along with death. The Athenian demos threatened people like Socrates who did not accept their judgments of the good and bad in human life with

opposed to many others (for example, the *Phaedrus*, *Republic*, and *Gorgias*), Socrates is not competing with the sophists or rhetoricians as a potential educator.

In the *Philebus* Socrates concerns himself only with identifying the kinds of knowledge and pleasure human beings should seek, not the means of achieving them or of persuading others to do so.[220] He and Protarchus thus begin by mixing the purest knowledge with the purest pleasure. Socrates asks whether someone who knows geometrical concepts, axioms, and their corollaries, but has no idea how they can be applied to sensible materials and so tries to build a house on the basis of theory alone, can be said to possess adequate knowledge. Protarchus says such a character would be laughable. He lacks self-knowledge because he thinks he is wiser than he is. The good is supposed to be complete; theoretical knowledge is not full or adequate knowledge. If knowledge is a necessary part of the human good, Socrates and Protarchus agree, that good must include all kinds of knowledge: practices like flute playing as well as the more precise forms. The principle of inclusion is completeness, however—not regard for the necessary or the practical qua practical. Since they have also agreed that pleasure is a necessary part of the human good, the question arises whether they should likewise admit all forms of pleasure. The answer is no. All the various kinds of knowledge might not prove useful, but they are at least harmless. Some pleasures—the most intense and vicious kinds—positively hamper the acquisition of knowledge and the exercise of thought. Such pleasures could not, therefore, be mixed with intelligence in the constitution of the human good.[221]

---

capital punishment. Both in the *Gorgias* and the *Apology* (34c–35d) Socrates insists that he would not use the kind of forensic rhetoric necessary to defend himself effectively from such a charge. To do so would be to undermine the law and corrupt his fellow citizens.

220. He dismisses all concerns with things that come into being and pass away as matters of opinion rather than knowledge—even the cosmology he employed earlier. "Even if he believes he is inquiring into nature, you know he is seeking all his life for that which concerns this cosmos, how it has come to be, how it is a patient, and how an agent . . . not about the things that always are, but about the things that become, will become, and have become" (*Philebus* 59a). When Socrates turns, then, to show how the purest forms of knowledge are mixed with the purest pleasures in the constitution of the human good, the result is extremely theoretical. As Socrates states, "the present account appears to have been produced as if it were some bodiless cosmos destined to rule beautifully an ensouled body" (64b).

221. Why Socrates thinks it necessary to refer the question concerning the right mixture to personified "pleasures," then to "mind and thought," and to relay their answers in indirect discourse, is not immediately clear. He seems not to want to take responsibility for the exclusion of the strongest passions from the human good. Perhaps it is because of his eros, one of the passions he included earlier in those intense mixtures of pleasure and pain now said to be "thoughtless and vicious" (*aphronosynēs kai . . . kakias*) (*Philebus* 63e). As we have been indirectly reminded by the

For a mixture to be good, Socrates previously observed with regard to health and the seasons, the parts must be measured and in proportion. Because beauty and virtue always come with measure and proportion, he concludes, the human good has fled into the beautiful.[222] Because they have not been able to capture the good in one idea, Socrates suggests that to determine whether mind or pleasure is more akin to the good, they will have to see which is most similar to the three aspects of the good they have identified—the true, the measured, and the beautiful. First, they agree, mind is obviously closer to truth than pleasure. "Pleasure is the greatest of imposters; it is said that in the pleasures of love, which seem to be the greatest, perjury is pardoned by the gods, as if pleasures were like children devoid of mind" (Philebus 65c–d). Next, they agree that nothing seems to lack measure more than pleasure (which was initially said to be unlimited), whereas nothing seems more measured than mind and knowledge. Finally, with regard to beauty (or nobility), they observe that people often take pleasure in shameful activities, but neither mind nor thought ever appears to be shameful (or ugly).[223] If so, Socrates suggests, it is necessary to believe that it is not pleasure but measure that is by nature the first cause of a human being's possessing goodness. Beauty, proportion (symmetron), completeness, sufficiency, and qualities of that sort are second; mind and thought, third; the sciences, fourth; and the pure pleasures, fifth. Just as Socrates somewhat fancifully concluded in the Republic that the life of a tyrant is 729 times less pleasant than that of a philosophical king, so at the end of the Philebus (67a) he calculates that mind is 10,000 times more akin than pleasure to the good.[224]

Having shown that the lusts (erōtes) of beasts were not better guides in determining the good in human life than the divinations of the philosophic

---

Symposium and the Phaedrus, that was the way Hesiod had characterized (and therefore blamed) eros as irrational.

222. Gadamer (Dialectical Ethics, 208) points out that Socrates' saying that the power of the good has taken refuge in the nature of the beautiful is a way of saying that the power of the good becomes apparent in the beautiful. In the Phaedrus (250b–c) Socrates observed that the beautiful is the only eternal being that is sensibly evident to us as what it is. Here Socrates emphasizes that the beautiful is characterized by measure and proportion. Both characteristics suggest, as had Socrates in Hippias Major (301d–4a), that if the good becomes manifest in the beautiful, it becomes manifest, as he indicated earlier in the Philebus, as a complex order or ordered mixture.

223. The fact that calculations can appear to be base (aischros) may be the reason that Socrates dropped logismos from his list of the intellectual operations he thought belonged to the human good more than pleasure.

224. The point of Socrates' playfulness seems to be that number is not really an appropriate measure; good is not a question of quantity so much as of quality.

muse, Socrates reminds his auditors of the constraint under which he has been conducting the conversation by asking Protarchus whether he will now let the philosopher go. Protarchus responds that there is still a little bit left to be discussed. The philosopher is not finished, and it seems clear, he can never entirely finish. He is mortal, and there will be others, a great many others, who believe that pleasure is the good.[225] The most he can do, as he does in the *Philebus*, is to tell them what the goal of human life should be, that is, where to direct their attention and efforts. Arguing the abstract way he does in the *Philebus*, Socrates is not apt to persuade many of them. To convince people not merely to change their opinions but to change the direction and goals of their lives, Socrates tells Gorgias, when he meets the famous rhetorician in person, it is necessary to interrogate them as individuals. It is not possible to teach many people very much in a short time.

5. Why Socrates' Discussion of the Human Good is Incomplete

When, in the *Symposium* (175e), Socrates reminded Agathon how much more popular poetry is than philosophy, the poet did not take the comment as a compliment. He thought that the measure of the excellence of his art was the wisdom it contained, not merely its ability to please a crowd. The last piece of Socrates' debate with the poets thus concerns their wisdom—not merely concerning the good and bad of human life but more specifically about something poets appear to know much better than philosophers—namely, the character of the pleasure their works give to those who listen and watch. Socrates maintained that the poets' teaching concerning the tragedy of human life rests on an inadequate if common understanding of pleasure as essentially bodily and therefore inseparably connected to pain.

To show that human life has a good that is not merely transitory and hence essentially illusory and false, Socrates argued that (*a*) there is no pleasure for human beings separable from an awareness of it as pleasure and hence from mind or intelligence and (*b*) there are pleasures that do not entail corresponding pains. More specifically, he suggested, the pleasure audiences derive from dramatic poetry does not arise as much from the sensible beauty of the words or actions as from the audience members'

---

225. Cf. Socrates' statement in the *Republic* (519b) concerning the "leaden weights, which eating and such pleasures that follow along together with foolishness and the rest of vice attach to the soul" and hence, presumably, keep most tied to the floor of the cave looking at shadows.

perception of their own intellectual superiority to the characters. Because members of the audience do not, in fact, possess superior wisdom—at most they take over the views of the poets—the pleasure the poets give their audience is false.

Concluding his account of the human good by observing that it has "fled" into the beautiful (or noble) and that the good partakes more of intellect than of pleasure, because intelligence is more akin to truth, measure, and beauty than pleasure is, Socrates nevertheless seems to confront both his listeners and Plato's readers with a problem, if not a paradox. Because the human good is constituted of a variety of different qualities, which have to be in the correct proportion, Socrates argues that the human good is characterized, first and foremost, by measure, and second, by beauty and completeness. But Socrates' own argument about the human good appears to be much less beautiful or *kekosmēmenos* (dressed up) than the conversations that preceded it (related in the *Symposium*, *Phaedrus*, and *Republic*), embellished as they were with "poetic" devices like myths and images. In contrast to these explicitly more poetic conversations, moreover, the conversation related in the *Philebus* is explicitly incomplete. What are readers supposed to make of the apparent disjunction between the explicit teaching and the form or action of the dialogue?

Was Plato showing his readers that the famous stories about Diotima's education of Socrates and the images of "sun, line, and cave" are merely embellishments designed to make philosophy less threatening, if not positively attractive, to nonphilosophers? Did Socrates think the truth and beauty not merely of philosophy but of human life as a whole consist in the order and intelligibility of abstract arguments about the constitution of things that come to be out of mixtures of the limited and unlimited by mind? Did Plato, if not Socrates, think that the human good is attained primarily through the study of measure, and hence mathematics? This view of philosophy has led some commentators to concentrate on the first parts of the *Philebus* in abstraction from the discussion of pleasure for the sake of which the "metaphysical" discussion is introduced. It is a view fostered by Aristotle's report that Plato's lecture about the good surprised and confounded its auditors by its mathematical content. As we have seen, the conversation related in the *Philebus* might have struck some readers that way. In his *Seventh Letter* Plato famously said that the good itself is inexpressible (*alogos*). If so, it seems possible only to point to it indirectly through poetic images, not to explain it discursively or argumentatively. That is exactly what Plato showed Socrates doing in the *Republic*.

Unlike many modern philosophers, however, neither Socrates nor Plato thought that mathematics was the core of philosophy. At most, Socrates stated in the *Republic* and Plato indicated with the engraved warning at the entrance to the Academy, "Let no one ignorant of geometry enter here"; the study of mathematics constitutes a necessary preparation. By reading the *Philebus* in the context of the dialogues that precede it both dramatically and thematically, we see that Socrates' argument about the human good is directed primarily against the poets and the pre-Socratic philosophers who denied that there were any purely intelligible, unchanging forms of being. Socrates was combating the contention that everything is always in flux, moreover, not merely or primarily as a doctrine about the constitution of things but as an inference from and about human existence. Plato rarely depicts Socrates examining mathematicians; when he does (in the *Theaetetus*), he shows that Socrates tried to show the geometricians, like the politicians, poets, and artisans mentioned in the *Apology*, that they do not know what they think they do. Although both the Athenian Stranger and Socrates recommend the study of mathematics, especially as a way of raising questions about the accuracy of, and then correcting, our sense impressions, neither names any form of mathematics as the highest, most comprehensive, or most important form of knowledge. As we shall see, Socrates uses the "fact" of mathematical knowledge in conversing with geometers in the *Theaetetus* to show them that those who argue that everything is in flux are wrong. In the only mathematical proof to be found in the Platonic dialogues (*Meno* 82b–85c), Socrates leads a slave boy through the demonstration to illustrate another, more comprehensive kind of truth about the way in which we humans come to know and participate in the ideas through recollection.

At the beginning of the *Philebus* Socrates states that *the* question he and other philosophers face concerns (*a*) the existence of purely intelligible unit(ie)s; (*b*) the separation of these purely intelligible unit(ie)s from sensible things; and (*c*) the way in which sensible things participate in them. The kinds of "unit(ie)s" Socrates has in mind are not numbers or proportions; he refers explicitly to unities such as "human being," "ox," the "beautiful," and the "good," that is, to the different kinds of beings he often called "ideas." If a reader was convinced, like Aristotle, that the ideas could not exist separate from the sensible things to which they gave form, she might take Socrates' discussion of the constitution of things that come to be as mixtures as a discussion of the constitution of all things. Socrates, however, explicitly does not. He introduces the discussion of things that come to be as mixtures of the definite and indefinite caused by mind explicitly to show that there are different kinds of pleasure and that the poets are wrong about the possibilities and pleasures of human life. Even in its purest forms Socrates presents pleasure as something that occurs (comes to be) in sensible beings, even if the pleasure results from the contemplation of the purely intelligible.

At the end of the *Philebus*, Socrates and Protarchus agree that their discussion is incomplete. If, as they agreed earlier, purely theoretical knowledge (of building a house) is not sufficient, because complete knowledge would be practical as well as theoretical, the same principle would seem to apply to the human good. Knowledge of the human good also has to be practical as well as theoretical (or a matter of definition), and its truth has to demonstrated in deed rather than simply in speech. For this reason, I shall argue, Plato shows that Socrates proves himself to be both noble and good in deed at his trial and death. Practical knowledge of the human good would include not merely the end to be achieved but also knowledge of the means whereby one could achieve and sustain the good sought. There is no such discussion to be found in the *Philebus*, in which the conversation is explicitly said not to be complete. The definition of the human good Socrates articulates in this dialogue must therefore be filled out, if not completed, by his more "erotic" poetic and political accounts of the human search for the good in the other dialogues.

The only knowledge Socrates ever claimed to possess was knowledge of what human beings seek and desire. In the *Philebus* he defines the object of our desire or the "good" for human beings as a mixture of a mild form of pleasure with measure, beauty, intellect, and knowledge in order to show, in opposition to the poets, that the goal of human endeavor is not per se unattainable. Socrates does not even notice, much less explicitly account for, the major barrier to the achievement and preservation of that good—human awareness of our own mortality or inevitable death. Socrates does not, therefore, take account of the role or place of courage in the definition of human nobility. Plato shows that he demonstrated the meaning of human nobility at the end of his life, as much if not even more in deed than in speech.

As Socrates observed in the *Phaedrus*, the *kalon* is an especially important kind of purely intelligible, eternally unchanging being-in-itself or idea because it is the only one that manifests itself directly to human beings in sensible form. The question up for debate, according to Socrates, from the beginning to the end of his life as a philosopher, was whether there were any such eternal, unchanging intelligible ideas, and if there were, how sensible things participated in them. In the dialogues we have surveyed, Socrates has suggested that question can be answered, if at all, only in the realm of human existence, by showing not merely that but how ideas shape life. As Socrates indicated in his description of his dialogical method of arguing in the *Philebus*, he sought to discover what the various kinds of things are not merely by identifying their limits or de-finition by means of negation, but by identifying the different kinds within those limits. In the case of human life, we see in the Platonic dialogues, Socrates investigated the different kinds of human existence, especially in terms of their conception of the good and the noble (*kalos k'agathos*). He did not spend much time with representatives of the productive or defensive arts (although he often used them as examples), because arts such as farming, house building, warfare, and medicine are clearly means of achieving a greater good. He spent more time examining people who claimed to know how human beings could achieve virtue or happiness. In the case of the politicians and their imitators or servants—the sophists, rhetoricians, and poets—he showed that they did not know what they claimed to teach. The only form of human life that even promised to be able to achieve what all human beings sought was philosophy, understood as the search for knowledge of what is truly good.

The knowledge Socrates sought—and claimed only to seek, not to possess—was both limited and uncertain. It could not be achieved simply through argument; it had to be accomplished in deed or fact. Plato leads his readers to wonder, therefore, whether or at least why something more is not possible. How is the "vertical," so to speak, motion of human life and striving toward the good related to the calculable and hence intelligible circular motion of the heavenly bodies, which, the Athenian argued, testified to the existence of both the rule and the beneficence of mind or intellect in the cosmos as a whole? If we can acquire self-knowledge by looking at the reflection of our own soul in the soul of another human being, as Socrates told Alcibiades, why can't we acquire even more, better, and more certain, because more complete, knowledge by inquiring into the way in which the movements of our souls are reflected in, or are reflections of, the greater soul that unifies and directs the motions of the whole? In the *Phaedrus*, Socrates stated that it is impossible for a mortal to come to know and hence to describe the "idea" of soul as a whole, because it is too complex. No mortal has sufficient time. Couldn't a series of mortals put together such a description, however, on the basis of a series of arguments and studies conducted and passed down to succeeding generations over time?

In the *Timaeus*, Plato presents a statesman-philosopher from Locri giving a compilation of previous cosmological studies that appears to incorporate the Socratic ideas as well. Timaeus thus appears to solve the problem with which the *Laws* concluded. Even if it is only a "likely story" (*eikōs mythos*), his speech represents a philosophical tour de force. Unfortunately, we shall see, Timaeus' cosmology does not account for the erotic core of human existence, as Socrates describes it. There is a reason Socrates never suggests in the *Philebus* that the mixture of pleasure and mind that constitutes the human good also constitutes a paradigm of the mixture of sensible and intelligible forms of existence in the whole. Twice he observes that the good of the divine mind might not have or need an admixture of pleasure. The character of the divine or purely intelligible order and good is not the same as that which is in and possible for human beings. In contrast to Timaeus and the Athenian Stranger, Socrates never suggests that human beings can discover what is good for them by contemplating the intelligible order of the movements of the heavens. Not moved by the same wants or desires, the heavens cannot tell us what to do. But we cannot survive, much less live happily, if we do not make decisions, both singly and common, about what we need to do. We cannot just sit and watch. Nor, like other animals, can we simply follow our instincts (or "the erotic desires of the beasts"). We have to combine what our minds tell us about what is necessary and good with what gives us pleasure. We tend to call that combination in correct proportions (or measure) the "noble" or "beautiful." As the only purely intelligible "idea" that manifests itself to us directly in sensible form or forms, it is "difficult," as Socrates concluded in his conversations with Hippias. Inasmuch as it manifests itself both sensibly and intelligibly, it is complex; yet, precisely for that reason, it is the idea we discover, seek, and have to reflect on first. We have to ask not only what the beautiful is, but ultimately why it is also good.

6

Timaeus-Critias

COMPLETING OR CHALLENGING SOCRATIC POLITICAL PHILOSOPHY?

S ocrates concluded his discussion of the city in speech, which he proposed in the *Republic*, by observing that it did not matter whether this city ever actually came into being, because it would serve as "a paradigm laid up in heaven for the man who wants to see and found a city within himself" (592b). Nevertheless, in the *Timaeus* Plato has Socrates express a desire to see his city in motion at war with another, and two of his guests promise to satisfy his desire.[1] Critias volunteers to relate the story of how prehistoric Athens, with a regime remarkably like that described in the *Republic*, defeated the imperial ambitions of Atlantis when the latter set out to conquer the entire world. And Critias asks Timaeus to provide a cosmological prelude explaining not merely how the world, but more

---

1. Most scholars agree that the conversation related in the *Timaeus* is supposed to have taken place after that related in the *Republic*. Beginning with Proclus, some have thought the summary must refer to the *Republic* itself and that the conversation related in the *Timaeus* occurred a day after Socrates' narration of the *Republic*. See, e.g., Taylor, *Commentary on "Timaeus,"* 13, 45; Benjamin Jowett, trans., "The Republic," in *The Dialogues of Plato* (New York: Random House, 1937), 477–78; and Seth Benardete, "On Plato's *Timaeus* and Timaeus's Science Fiction," *Interpretation* 2, no. 2 (1971): 21–63. But other commentators—e.g., Brann, "Music," 29; Laurence Lampert and Christopher Planeaux, "Who's Who in Plato's *Timaeus-Critias* and Why," *Review of Metaphysics* 52 (September 1998): 90n10; and Diskin Clay, "The Plan of Plato's *Critias*," in *Interpreting the "Timaeus-Critias": Proceedings of the Fourth Symposium Platonicum*, ed. Tomas Calvo and Luc Brisson (Sankt Augustin: Academia Verlag, 1997), 52n6—point out that the specific dates on which the conversations are supposed to have occurred do not coincide. Socrates narrates the *Republic* the day after the first celebration of the festival of Bendis, which took place on the 19/20 Thargelion; *Timaeus-Critias* takes place during a festival devoted to Athena (21a), either the Panathenaea or a lesser one that took place two full months later. Plato also shows Socrates speaking to two entirely different groups of people. The summary presupposes the fuller statement in the *Republic* if only because Socrates emphasizes the novelty of his "three waves" of proposals in the *Republic*. This is one of the reasons I think that the dramatic date of the *Timaeus* should be set in 411 or later.

specifically how the people who were to become citizens of Socrates' city in speech, came into being.[2]

In his "prelude" Timaeus promises to present an account of the natural foundations of both politics and philosophy, which Socrates never provides.[3] Indeed, by suggesting that both the cosmos and the human constitution can be understood to be the products of a divine *dēmiourgos* (craftsman) who, intending the good, made imitations of the eternal forms in the shifting receptacle of becoming, Timaeus appears to give the explanation the young Socrates had hoped to receive from Anaxagoras (*Phaedo* 97b–99c) of why it is best for everything to be as it is.[4] Although Timaeus proceeds to argue that things are as they are as a result of an interaction between the good and the necessary—that is, it is not simply best that they are as they are—his speech provides ample support for Socrates' introductory praise of Timaeus as having attained the "peak of all philosophy" (*Timaeus* 20a).[5] In marked contrast to Socrates, Timaeus does not rest content with

2. Luc Brisson, "Le *Critias* de Platon," *Revue de Metaphysique et de Morale* 75, no. 4 (October–December 1970), writes: "Le *Critias* . . . s'insère dans une vision métaphysique unitaire proposant de régler l'action de la société actuelle sur celle de son passé qui s'inscrit dans le développement global de l'univers sensible, n'étant lui-même qu'une image en devenir de l'éternité du monde des formes intelligibles. C'est ainsi qu'on passe de la philosophie politique, fondée sur l'ontologie et la cosmologie, à l'epopée" (404). Christopher Gill, "The Genre of the Atlantis Story," *Classical Philology* 72, no. 4 (October 1977), argues: "There is a close parallel between the character of the Atlantis story and the character of Timaeus' creation. . . . both take as their starting point the political and ontological idealism of the *Republic*. . . . Both take as their subject not those ideals themselves but their relationship to the world of *genesis*. Both claim to have found, in some entity which has come into being in the past, a fitting image or embodiment of these ideals. Both set out to tell a story . . . which many of its readers have classed as a myth, but which is presented as an account of a past factual event" (302–3). R. Hackforth, "The Story of Atlantis," *Classical Review* 58 (1944): 7–9, also emphasizes the parallels between the story Timaeus tells about the construction of the cosmos and the story Critias tells about prehistoric Athens and Atlantis.

3. The closest Socrates ever comes to such a statement is in the *Philebus* 28d–30e, when he presents a relatively brief argument to show "that mind does belong to the genus of what is spoken of as the cause of all things" (30e). In the notes to the preceding chapter I pointed out that there has been considerable scholarly debate about whether the teaching about the limited, the unlimited, things as mixtures of the limited and the unlimited, and the cause of such, which Socrates presents immediately before this summary statement about mind as cause, is consistent with the teaching he presents about the ideas in the *Republic*. I argued that it does not—and that Socrates indicates his own understanding that it does not—solve the problems Parmenides first brought out in Socrates' teaching concerning the ideas. In contrast to Timaeus, Socrates never gives a specific account of the order of the movements of the heavenly bodies or the geometric construction of the four elements, which, in turn, constitute bodily things. At most in the *Philebus*, Socrates shows what is good for us. He never claims to know or to show what is good in itself.

4. Cf. Thomas Kjeller Johansen, *Plato's Natural Philosophy* (Cambridge: Cambridge University Press, 2004), 2.

5. In quoting the *Timaeus*, I have generally used the translation of Peter Kalkavage, *Plato's "Timaeus"* (Newburyport, MA: Focus Publishing, 2001), although I have checked it against the Greek text edited by John Burnet, *Platonis Opera*, vol. 4 (Oxford: Clarendon Press, 1903).

arguments showing that sensible things are intelligible to us only insofar as they participate in, or are imitations of, unchanging, purely intelligible ideas; Timaeus offers an explanation of how and why sensible things continually change their own shapes or forms. He also explains why most human beings fail to achieve the orderly, happy lives of which we are inherently, by nature, capable. In sum, whereas Socrates only seeks wisdom, Timaeus seems not merely to possess but to be able to share it with others.

By the time we finish reading Timaeus' account of the genesis of the cosmos and the human constitution, however, we are forced to conclude that his knowledge is neither complete nor entirely satisfactory as a basis for human life. Although he gives an impressive description of the way in which the cosmos might have come into being, his explanation of the way in which women and all other kinds of lower animals, as well as sexual generation among humans, resulted from the degeneration of the original males can be characterized, at best, as fanciful.[6] Moreover, Timaeus does not fulfill his promise to show how the people who are to become citizens of Socrates' city in speech come into being. If women arise only from cowardly men, the female guardians who were supposed to defend Socrates' city never existed.[7] On the basis of his cosmic paradigm, Timaeus is not able to give an adequate account of human desire and thus of the origins of political association. Rather than provide an explanation of the cosmological foundations of Socratic politics or philosophy, in the Timaeus Plato dramatizes the disjunction between the principles on the basis of which Timaeus claims that this is the best possible world and the only things Socrates ever claimed to know—ta erōtika.[8]

6. Joseph Cropsey, "The Whole as Setting for Man: On Plato's Timaeus," Interpretation 17, no. 2 (Winter 1989–90), concludes that Timaeus' myth is "'plausible' if the reader is amiably credulous" (190).

7. Jacob Howland, "Partisanship and the Work of Philosophy in Plato's Timaeus," Review of Politics 69, no. 1 (Winter 2007): 16n41, also notes that "Timaeus's emphasis on manly virtue seems to pick up on Socrates' remark that, in the regime described 'yesterday,' the natures of women 'were to be tuned to the men and so made similar to them' (18c), [but] . . . conflicts with [Socrates'] claim in the Republic that 'men and women have the same nature with respect to guarding a city, except insofar as the one is weaker and the other stronger'" (456a).

8. Admitting that the Timaeus is "a decidedly non-erotic dialogue," Jill Gordon nevertheless argues that the dialogue "provides surprising philosophical insight into the role and importance of eros in human life" ("Eros in Timaeus," 255). In opposition to the "traditional reading" (which actually follows the text, which says that the soul will acquire eros along with sensation after it is embodied), she claims that eros is said at 42a–b to be part of the immortal part of the human soul. More centrally, she points out, at 46d–e Timaeus says that the "lover of understanding and knowledge [ton de vou kai epistēmēs erastēn] must of necessity pursue as primary causes those that belong to intelligent nature [emphronos phuseōs] as first causes [aitias prōtas] and as secondary all those belonging to things that are moved by others and that set still others in motion by neces-

I. *Timaeus*

A. The Political Setting or Frame

1. The Initial Question: Who or What Is Missing?

Plato alerts readers to the possibility that someone, if not something, is missing in the *Timaeus* with Socrates' opening question: "One, two, three . . . but now where's our fourth, my dear Timaeus, of yesterday's feasters and hosts of today?" (17a).[9] When Timaeus responds that the fourth must be ill, because he would not willingly be absent, Plato's readers are reminded that human action is not entirely predictable, because we are subject to bodily disorders. When Socrates asks Timaeus whether he and his two companions will compensate for the absence of the fourth, and Timaeus responds that it would not be just if they did not attempt to repay Socrates in full measure for the feast of speech he had provided them the day before, we are also reminded that justice in human affairs does not occur

---

sity" (264). Although Timaeus also emphasizes the need to order and direct human eros, Gordon concludes, in opposition to Peter Kalkavage's translation of the *Timaeus* (10, 42), that philosophy, according to Timaeus, is fundamentally erotic, connected as it is to a divinely given ability to view something both beautiful and intelligible rather than something fundamentally thumotic. Neither she nor Howland ("Partisanship," 7–8, 22–27) takes sufficient account of the difference between the Timaean love of knowledge, which leads to contemplation of the intelligible movements of the heavenly bodies and imposes order on bodily passions and eros, in opposition to the eros characteristic of sensitive or perceptive beings, and Socratic eros, which is described as an extension, a form, or elevation and modification of the eros between human beings that expresses itself first in generation or procreation, then in the search for immortality, and finally in philosophical friendships.

9. Following Proclus, *The Commentaries of Proclus on the "Timaeus" of Plato, in Five Books*, trans. T. Taylor (London: Printed and Sold by the Author, 1820), 1:16, several commentators have suggested that the counting out of the numbers points forward both to the number of speeches that will be given and the numerical order of the cosmos described by Timaeus. See, e.g., Myles F. Burnyeat, "First Words: A Valedictory Lecture," *Proceedings of the Cambridge Philological Society* 43 (1997): 1–20; John Sallis, *Chorology: On Beginning in Plato's "Timaeus"* (Bloomington: Indiana University Press, 1999), 7–12; and Kenneth Dorter, "'One, Two, Three, but Where Is the Fourth?' Incomplete Mediation in the *Timaeus*," in *Politics, Philosophy, Writing*, ed. Zdravko Planinc (University of Missouri Press, 2001), 160–63. Although Socrates might be thought to substitute for the fourth guest, there are not four speeches. Socrates' speech was given the day before. He now gives a summary, followed by a preliminary summary of Critias' speech. Timaeus gives the only full speech, followed by the beginning of Critias' account, which breaks off in midsentence. Although in the *Critias* (108a) Socrates seems to expect Hermocrates to follow Critias, Hermocrates does not. What we have, therefore, is one past speech, two present summaries, one complete speech, and one beginning. Neither the number of participants nor their speeches parallel the numerical order of the cosmos, which is said to be one and unique, to have two component parts, body and soul, with the soul having three component elements and the "body" or receptacle, the traditional four. I suggest, therefore, that the first sentence points not to a parallel between the introductory human concerns and the cosmic order described by Timaeus but to a disjunction between them.

naturally or spontaneously. Human beings have to act intentionally to compensate for the absence of natural order or justice. At the very beginning of the dialogue, Plato thus indicates that the cosmological account of the foundations of Socrates' city in speech that is to follow will necessarily be incomplete.[10]

2. SOCRATES' REQUEST

Socrates himself was centrally concerned about the character and requirements of justice. In the speech he gave the day before, Socrates reminded his guests, he had described what he took to be the best regime and the men (*andrōn*; *Timaeus* 17c) of which it would be composed.[11] As summarized, that regime included most of the major provisions or features of the first two waves of the "city in speech" Socrates described in the *Republic*. Those who were to defend the regime from its enemies, both external and internal, were to be separated from the farmers and artisans. Functional assignments were to be based on natural capacity; each citizen was to perform the one task for which he or she was best suited. Those who were to serve as guardians had to be both spirited and philosophic by nature, so that they would treat enemies harshly but be gentle toward their fellow citizens; they were to be educated, correspondingly, in both gymnastics and music. They were not to own gold, silver, or, indeed, any private property. They were to live in common, continually exercising a care for virtue and free from all other tasks. Sex was not to be a determinant of function; females suited by nature to become guardians were to receive the same education and perform the same tasks as males, including fighting wars. "Marriages" and children were also to be common. Mating was to be secretly ordered so that the guardians would believe it occurred by lot and would not, therefore, resist or resent the arrangements. Because the results of generation could not be completely controlled, the rulers would have to keep a sharp lookout, educating the worthy offspring of the artisans and farmers to become guardians and replacing them with the progeny of the good who did not prove equal to their parents.[12]

---

10. As Kenneth Dorter argues in *Transformation* (351–68).

11. The use of "man" (the root of *andreia*, "manliness" or courage) is strange because Socrates proposes to give the same education to qualified women, but in the *Laws* (770c) the Athenian Stranger does the same thing in describing the purpose of the city and its laws.

12. At the end of his summary we see that Socrates' use of the term for the male (*anēr*) to describe citizens of both sexes serves to remind readers that when he describes the guardians going to war in the *Republic* (the place where his summary in the *Timaeus* breaks off, as Lampert and Planeaux ["Who's Who," 89] point out), he suggests that Greeks should not fight other Greeks

Although Timaeus says no when Socrates asks whether he has left any-thing out of his summary, many commentators have observed that Soc-rates fails to mention the philosopher-kings and their education.[13] Since Socrates introduced the philosopher-kings in the *Republic* as the only pos-sible means of bringing his city in speech into existence, he might not have considered them parts of the regime itself.[14] Timaeus and Critias will argue, in different ways, that the best regime comes into existence "naturally," not by the chance conjunction of philosophy with political power.

Socrates does not explicitly ask his interlocutors to show how the re-gime comes into existence or "to life," but rather to praise the city and its men "by giving a full account [*logos*] of how they struggled in con-tests [*athlous*] against other cities . . . and rendered appropriate payment for their education and upbringing . . . in deed and . . . in speech" (*Timaeus* 19c).[15] The speech he wants to hear sounds very much like an epic poem.[16] Socrates compares himself to someone who looks at beautiful animals, whether living or in pictures, and wants to see them in motion. Such a moving picture of his city in speech would have to be delivered in words to be seen with the "mind's eye." If Socrates believes that his city in speech

---

(because that is a form of civil war) and certainly should not take them as slaves (thus explaining why Critias later shows the "city in speech" at war with a foreign, non-Greek imperial power [*Republic* 469b–71b]). In adapting his speech to the prejudices of his young Athenian interlocu-tor Glaucon, Socrates also has to qualify both the arrangements for mating by lot (by granting superior soldiers rewards in the form of sexual favors [468 b–c]) and the equality of males and females. The latter are relegated to watching from the sidelines and serving as reserves (at 471d). By reasserting the original provisions, Socrates suggests that his interlocutors in the *Timaeus* may be more open to the strict requirements of justice.

13. See, e.g., Dorter, "Mediation"; Brann, "Music," 29–30; and Benardete, "On Plato's Ti-maeus," 378.

14. When Glaucon asks Socrates to show how it is possible for the regime they have been describing to come into being (*Republic* 472b), Socrates warns Glaucon not to expect him to show how the regime could come to exist in fact in every way they have described it in speech (473a). Then he states that the smallest change in the way things are done now in cities that would bring them closest to the regime they have described would be for philosophers to become kings or kings, philosophers (473c–d). Apparently following the example set by Socrates here in the *Ti-maeus*, Aristotle also fails to include the philosopher-kings in the description he gives in the *Politics* 1261a10–1264b25 of the regime proposed in the *Republic*.

15. Cf. Catherine Osborne, "Space, Time, Shape, and Direction: Creative Discourse in the *Timaeus*," in *Form and Argument in Late Plato*, ed. Christopher Gill and Mary Margaret McCabe (Oxford: Clarendon Press, 1996), 184.

16. Pierre Hadot, "Physique et poésie dans le *Timée* de Platon," *Revue de Théologie et de Philoso-phie* 115 (1983): 113, 118–19, thus emphasizes the epic, as well as mythological precedents for both Critias' and Timaeus' accounts. Hesiod, Xenophanes, and Parmenides had all written philosophi-cal poetry, Hadot reminds his readers.

could not come into existence without philosopher-kings, the speech he is requesting would have to be a work of fiction or poetry.[17]

Socrates says (19d) that he himself does not have the capacity (*dynamis*) to give the desired encomium (*egkōmiasai*). It is not clear, however, exactly what power he lacks. If he cannot give an adequate account of human beings—we might even say "things"—in motion, Socrates would be pointing to a major lacuna in his own philosophy. But in his famous image of the soul as a chariot in the *Phaedrus*, Socrates did describe the movements of souls. If there was a problem with his philosophical understanding of motion, it concerned the motion of bodies. Both Socrates' request and his acknowledgment of his own limitations can be read somewhat more narrowly. If we take him at his word in the *Republic* (378e, 393d), he is not a poet. In the *Symposium* (198d–e) he said that he understood praise to mean saying what is good and true, and not saying the bad. Socrates would not have been able to praise the citizens of his city in speech in war, because that would have required him to say something untrue about them. If, as he suggested in the *Republic* (372e–74d), the passions (especially love of one's own) that give rise to the need for such a defense and the ability to provide it are also the origin of both war and injustice, he cannot describe the guardians fighting to defend their city as simply just. According to Socrates, justice itself exists only as a purely intelligible being. Anything embodied is an imperfect copy.

Although poets and sophists could both be said to create images with words, Socrates does not think they are any more able to give the speech he desires than he is. Poets find it difficult to imitate anything with which they have not become familiar through their own upbringing, he observes, whereas sophists who travel from city to city cannot say how men who are both philosophers and statesmen act or speak. Since poets often depict imaginary regimes and sophists claim to teach their students how to become statesmen by speaking effectively in assemblies, Socrates' denial of their ability to depict statesmen in action seems strange.[18] On reflection, however, we realize that the knowledge Socrates thinks sophists lack is not simply experiential or affective. To present a credible imitation of just

17. Cf. Christopher Gill, "Plato's Atlantis Story and the Birth of Fiction," *Philosophy and Literature* 3 (1979): 65–77; Gill, "Genre," 300–304.

18. In his *Poetics* 1450b10, Aristotle observes: "Earlier writers made their characters speak like statesmen."

statesmen (who act in the common good rather than seeking to maximize their own fame and wealth), an author would have to know the sorts of things leaders do and say when they are attached to a particular people. The sophists lack such knowledge not merely because they travel from city to city, but because, as Socrates demonstrated in both the *Protagoras* and the *Symposium*, sophists teach that all human beings seek to maximize their own pleasure and minimize pain. Believing that everyone is essentially self-regarding, the sophists do not think any human beings act for the common good, or justly. To imitate what a philosopher would do or say, Socrates suggested in his critique of the poets at the end of the *Republic*, one has to be able to look beyond a particular time and place to see what is true in general. The guardians of his city in speech could not be shown speaking and acting merely on the basis of their love of their own—and remain perfectly just. Pre-Socratic poets had not failed to depict statesmen acting on the basis of general principles merely because their imitations were limited to their own time and place. On the basis of an analysis of their own experience, Socrates suggested in both the *Symposium* and the *Theaetetus*, pre-Socratic poets concluded that everything was in flux. They could not depict philosophic statesmen acting on the basis of general truths, because they denied that there were any such truths.

What prevents both the sophists and the poets from giving the desired praise is that they lack a certain kind of knowledge. But it is not clear from his introductory statement exactly what kind of knowledge Socrates lacks. Socrates says that he expects his present interlocutors to be able to give the desired account of his city in speech in motion, because they combine philosophical knowledge with practical political experience in particular cities. Socrates does not treat all of his interlocutors equally, however. He praises Timaeus most highly as one "being from Italian Locri, a city with most excellent laws, and inferior to no one there in wealth or birth, who has attained not only the highest offices and honors of his city but also, in my opinion, the peak of all philosophy" (20a). Of Critias Socrates says merely that he does not lack experience of these things.[19] We shall soon discover that Critias' understanding of truth is quite different from that held by Socrates and Timaeus. Of Hermocrates' nature and upbringing,

---

19. If Critias is the tyrant, we know from the *Charmides* that he was familiar not merely with philosophy in general but with Socrates' own teachings in particular.

Socrates admits he knows only by hearsay, and in Socrates' response to Critias' proposal, Plato reminds his readers that hearsay is not a reliable source of truth. It appears to be Timaeus, therefore, who has the kind of knowledge Socrates lacks. It is not clear at this point in the dialogue whether that knowledge is philosophical, the result of practical political experience, or both.

3. A POSSIBLE CONSPIRACY?

By having Socrates conclude his request by observing that he has come to the feast all dressed up (*kekosmēmenos*), Plato reminds his readers of the only other time in the dialogues Socrates is said to be (uncharacteristically) dressed up. That occasion, too, was for a "banquet of speeches."[20] But in the *Symposium* Socrates was a guest or speaker rather than a recipient or host, as in the *Timaeus*, and he came dressed up as a kind of defense for what he expected to be a contest, if not a battle with the poet(s). The participants in the symposium delivered their speeches in a contest to see who could praise Eros best. In his own speech, Socrates claimed that the only kind of knowledge he possessed was of *ta erōtika*.

In the *Timaeus* all the speakers appear to be friendly and cooperative rather than competitive or combative. At the beginning of the dialogue, Timaeus states that they are of one mind (*pasi kata noun*; 17c) about the goodness or desirability of Socrates' city in speech. After he proposes that they satisfy Socrates' request by identifying his city in speech with prehistoric Athens and showing her citizens in action in the war against Atlantis, Critias concludes: "All of us in common, each taking his part, will attempt to the best of our ability, to render what's fitting for what you've ordered us to do" (26d–e). That is, if Socrates agrees (*ei kata noun ho logos*). The agreement among the speakers in the *Timaeus-Critias* proves to be less than they initially suggested and the order of their speeches more problematic. At the beginning of the dialogue, nevertheless, it looks as if they are all committed to the fundamental principle of Socrates' city in speech—that each should do what he does best.

In the *Symposium* all the speakers were Athenians and thus citizens of the democracy. They had political as well as intellectual reasons (as sophists or poets) for appealing to the opinions and hence ultimately to the

20. Cf. Daniel J. Schoos, "'Timaeus' Banquet," *Ancient Philosophy* 19, supp. (1999): 103; Arieti, *Interpreting Plato*, 19.

pleasures or passions of the many. They were thus partisans of democracy, and democratic politics are competitive. Socrates won his contest with the poets in the *Symposium*, but, as all of Plato's readers know, the philosopher was subsequently killed by the Athenians for his lack of piety.

In the *Timaeus* all three of Socrates' interlocutors appear to be united in opposition to the Athenian democratic regime. There is no record outside the dialogue of a statesman or philosopher named Timaeus from Locri, but Locri was an enemy of Athens.[21] In contrast to the everchanging laws of a democracy (which Socrates characterized as both lax and gentle in the *Republic* 562c–63d), Locri was said to have possessed Europe's earliest written legal code, and that code was attributed to Zaleucus, who was known for his severity.[22] Hermocrates was responsible for the victory of Syracuse over Athens in Sicily that led to Athens' final defeat in the Peloponnesian War and the temporary replacement of the democracy by more oligarchic regimes.[23] Critias was the leader of the Thirty, who overthrew the democratic regime after the Athenians lost the war.[24] Like the all-night

21. Thucydides 3.86, 103, 115; 5.5. In 424 Locri was the only city in Sicily that would not make peace with Athens. In 422 Locri accepted assistance from Athens, but peaceful relations between the two cities did not last for long. Accepting the 424–422 date for the *Republic*, Lampert and Planeaux ("Who's Who," 94–95) argue that the dramatic date for the *Timaeus* is 421 (like the *Hippias*). It is, however, difficult to imagine Hermocrates leaving Sicily or being welcomed in Athens at that time. If the dramatic date of the dialogue is 409–408, it is also more likely that the Critias mentioned is the tyrant.

22. *Oxford Classical Dictionary*, 2nd ed., s.v. "Locri" and "Zaleucus."

23. Although Hermocrates has only one short speech in the *Timaeus* and another in the *Critias*, his presence helps more than anything else to establish the dramatic date of the dialogues. They must occur either before 427, when he began his attempt to unite Sicily against Athens, or after 411, when he set sail for Sparta to protest the policy Alcibiades suggested to Tissaphernes of delaying and underpaying the sailors in the Peloponnesian fleet. The later date seems more likely. Before the war Hermocrates was just making a name for himself; he had all he could do trying to prepare the Sicilians for the coming Athenian invasion. Having been exiled from Syracuse by the democratic party in absentia in 410 (Thucydides 8.29, 54, 85), Hermocrates was relieved of his duties as a general and told that he was free to go where he chose. According to Xenophon *Hellenica* 1.3.12, Hermocrates was nevertheless among the delegates from Sparta at the meeting Pharnabazus called with the Athenian ambassadors at Cyzicus in 408. No longer having any official position or country, Hermocrates might well be imagined to have visited Athens, and to have been welcomed into the home of a known opponent of the imperial Athenian democracy, on his way back to Syracuse in 408. Like Critias, Hermocrates had become an enemy of the democratic party in his own city; he might thus have wanted to confer with a leading citizen from Locri as well as two known critics of democratic rule in Athens about the possibilities of reform before he returned to his own city. In Syracuse the democratic party refused to rescind his banishment and finally killed him in 407.

24. Although Critias was taken to be the tyrant in antiquity (cf. Proclus *Commentaries on the "Timaeus"* 1.70), some twentieth-century scholars—e.g., Cornford, *Plato's Cosmology*, 1–2; Taylor, *Commentary on "Timaeus,"* 23; Sallis, *Chorology*, 26; and Warmen Welliver, *Character, Plot and Thought*

meeting of the eleven in the *Republic*, the gathering of known opponents of the Athenian democracy at Critias' house to discuss how Socrates' proposals could be put into practice has the look of a conspiracy. These visitors from Italy could well be imagined to have come to Athens to consult with Critias about ways of replacing the democratic regime in Athens with one they consider more just. They may even have heard rumors about the city Socrates had described to others earlier and asked him about it. Socrates appears willing to discuss changes that would make the government more just.

4. CRITIAS' SUMMARY SPEECH

Hermocrates informs Socrates that his three guests, on their walk back to Critias' home the day before, began considering how to repay him. Critias then mentions a story he would be willing to retell now to see whether it would serve, *if* Timaeus agrees. The fact that Timaeus had not agreed to this order previously suggests that there was a bit less agreement and coordination among the three visitors than we were initially led to believe.[25] Because Critias proceeds to give a summary of the speech he is proposing to present in fuller form if Socrates finds it acceptable, Critias' two partial accounts of the character and deeds of prehistoric Athens come to frame Timaeus' account of the origin and character of the cosmos. Read-

---

in Plato's "Timaeus-Critias" (Leiden: E. J. Brill, 1977), 50–57—have followed Burnet (*Early Greek Philosophy*, 338) in suggesting that the Critias in the dialogue is the tyrant's grandfather, because the tyrant (ca. 460–403) could not have had a grandfather who related a story Solon (ca. 630–558) told his father Dropides when Critias was ten years of age. Like A. Rivaud, trans. *Timée, Critias* (Paris: Société d'Édition "Les Belles Lettres," 1925), 17; W. K. C. Guthrie, *A History of Greek Philosophy* (Cambridge: Cambridge University Press, 1962–69), 5:298; Gill, "Genre," 302n33; and Clay, "Plan of *Critias*," 52n6, I think that Critias is supposed to be the tyrant, because the dramatic date of the *Republic* (which is presupposed by the summary) is more apt to be 411 than 422 or 424 BCE, for reasons stated in the previous note. I am inclined to agree with the suggestion made by J. K. Davies, *Athenian Propertied Families* (Oxford: Clarendon Press, 1971), 325–26, that Critias may have dropped a generation in tracing the story from his grandfather to his great grandfather rather than his great great grandfather. Like Pierre Vidal-Naquet, "Athens and Atlantis," in *The Black Hunter*, trans. Andrew Szegedy-Maszak (Baltimore: Johns Hopkins University Press, 1986), 283, I think Plato uses the confused chronology to remind his readers how unreliable stories related by word of mouth are.

25. Welliver (*Character*, 15–21) suggests that the change in the order of the speeches results from a conspiracy between Hermocrates and Critias to displace Timaeus as the leader of their small group. I think that the change in the order of the speeches serves to remind readers that Socrates and Timaeus are both philosophers, in contrast to the practical politicians, and that Timaeus' speech has a political purpose. Howland, in "Partisanship," follows Welliver in emphasizing the competition between Critias and Timaeus. He sees Timaeus engaging in a philosophical correction of Socratic erotic philosophy rather than posing an alternative to it.

ers are thus reminded of the political purpose of Timaeus' cosmology, but it becomes unclear, as a result of the change in the order of the speeches, whether Hermocrates is supposed to give one. What does become clear in Critias' preliminary summary is that his account of the victory of prehistoric Athens over Atlantis will not fulfill Socrates' desire to see his city in speech at war. The apparent agreement between Socrates and his interlocutors breaks down before Timaeus begins his long speech.

Critias proposes to retell a story he heard from his grandfather Critias, who heard it from his great grandfather Dropides, who heard it from Solon. Calling Solon both the wisest of the seven sages and Athens' great legislator, Critias suggests that his laws may be better than any Critias and his associates can derive from Socrates' speech. Critias appears to be more attached to his own—his city, its gods, and his family—than Socrates is. Critias' speech suggests, moreover, that the old is the good. Socrates described his city in speech in the *Republic* at a new celebration of a foreign goddess. Critias observes that his speech about the greatness of prehistoric Athens will serve not only as repayment to Socrates but also as a true and just praise of Athena on her festival day. Whereas Socrates' city in speech came into being as part of a philosophical attempt to determine what justice is, Critias' speech is explicitly a product of tradition or hearsay. Because that tradition emphasizes the prominence of his family in Athens, Plato leads his readers to suspect, Critias may have fabricated the story to elevate the status of his family and city.[26]

When Critias emphasizes the truth of his *logos* (*Timaeus* 20d) in contrast to Socrates' *mythos* (26c), we see that they have very different understandings of truth. According to Socrates (as well as Timaeus), nothing that comes into being and goes out of existence (such as prehistoric Athens)

---

26. Although Critias emphasizes the truth of his speech, Plato gives his readers reason to doubt its veracity. According to Critias, Dropides related the account of the battle between prehistoric Athens and Atlantis, which he first heard from Solon, to children during the Apaturia, a festival that celebrated an Athenian victory won by deceit. A legendary ancestor of Solon named Melanthos tricked a Boeotian named Xanthos by accusing him of violating the agreement to decide the battle in single combat by bringing a partner. When Xanthos turned around to see who had come with him, the Athenian attacked and killed him. As a result of his victory, Melanthos became king of Athens. Cf. Welliver, *Character*, 20–21. Not only do the origins of historical, as opposed to prehistorical, Athens appear to be less than just; readers are also reminded that Athenians past and present have not been unabashedly committed to the truth. Readers might wonder why none of Critias' contemporaries had heard about their noble ancestors. It looks as if Critias may have fabricated the story to glorify his own city and family. Cf. Johansen, *Natural Philosophy*, 37–38.

can be said truly to be. Critias disagrees. Like many others, he believes that what exists in fact or deed is truer than what exists only in speech.

Critias' description of the regime of prehistoric Athens departs in significant ways, moreover, from Socrates' city in speech. According to the priest from whom Solon first heard about the prehistoric city, old Athens was ruled by priests, not military or philosophical guardians, and the productive classes included shepherds as well as farmers and artisans. Although the priests had a certain kind of divine knowledge of cosmology or the heavens, they were not said to have known anything like the ideas of the virtues. The basis of their rule was different from that of the philosopher-kings in the *Republic*. Nor does the military function of the guardians appear to have been purely defensive. On the contrary, in order to enjoy the luxury of eating meat, the people of prehistoric Athens would have had to seize more land (from their neighbors) than was absolutely necessary to support themselves. But in the *Republic* Socrates pointed out that the desires for such luxuries are the source of war and injustice.

The kind of knowledge on which Critias bases his account of prehistoric Athens also differs greatly from that on which Socrates based his city in speech. In the *Republic* Socrates first examined the opinions of his interlocutors and then proposed his city in an attempt to find out what justice is; in his summary speech Critias relies on a combination of hearsay and natural history. Because the Egyptians in Sais worshiped the same god, Critias reports, they felt that they were related to the Athenians.[27] They thus received Solon with friendship rather than hostility and willingly shared their superior knowledge with him.[28] They were able to acquire and preserve information about what happened in past ages in a way no other people could, because of their unique topographical situation. Whereas Greeks like Solon knew only of the aftermath of the most recent flood, which swept away all people living on the plains, leaving only a few isolated and illiterate mountaineers, Egyptians knew that there had been

27. Critias points out that they had been ruled by the notorious Hellenophile King Amasis. According to Herodotus 2.172–81, Amasis had been a commoner who became king on the basis of his demonstrated virtue and deeds. His people are thus shown to have accepted the same principle of "equal opportunity" in selecting the best that the Athenians celebrated in their own city. Cf. Pericles' Funeral Oration, Thucydides 2.37–41, and Socrates/Aspasia in *Menexenus* 238b–e.

28. Solon's travels make him more like the Athenian Stranger and the select members of his Nocturnal Council who are sent abroad than like Socrates, who left Athens only to serve in its army.

many such disasters.[29] The city of Sais had existed for 8,000 years and had preserved records of events during the preceding millennium (including the battle between prehistoric Athens and Atlantis). Their location on the delta of the Nile enabled the Egyptians to do so because the combination of climate and location prevented them from suffering a disastrous flood (since there was no rain and excess water ran into the sea) or a fire or drought (which would be quenched by the flooding up of the Nile from below). Having had a great deal of time to investigate, the Egyptians had also been able to locate the causes of such natural disasters in the movements of the heavenly bodies, which regulate the weather. From its inception, the priest informed Solon, the law of their city had required them to study the cosmos as a whole in order to discover the effects of the divine beings (presumably the heavenly bodies) on humans, both by divination and through the study of medicine.

In relating the Egyptian's account of both the wisdom of his own city and the virtue of prehistoric Athens, Critias shifts the cause of the excellence of the city and its people from a division of labor based on the variety of inherent natural talents of individuals to piety and cosmology. He thus prepares his listeners for Timaeus' account of the cosmological origins as the cause of human nature and Plato's readers for the difference that gradually emerges between Timaeus' cosmology and Socratic philosophy. According to the priest, the goddess established Athens a thousand years before Sais. As in the traditional story about the founding of Athens with the autochthonous birth of Erechtheus, she took the "seed" from Ge (earth) and Hephaestus (fire)—the two "extremes" in Timaeus' later account of the four constituent elements of body—and "planted them" in a place where a good blending of the seasons (or climate, an effect in turn of the mix of Timaeus' two mediating elements, air and water) was apt to produce the wisest people.

Generated and educated by the gods, the Athenians surpassed all other humans in virtue and performed many great deeds. The greatest was the repulsing of the hubristic attack of Atlantis on all the peoples living around the Mediterranean. "At times leading the Greeks, at times standing alone, of necessity, when others defected, [Athens] was victorious. Having taken

---

29. These disasters included not only floods but also fires of the kind the Greeks describe in the story of Phaeton. When he tried to drive his father Helios' chariot across the heavens, Phaethon crashed it and scorched the earth where it was not submerged under water.

the most extreme risks and mastered the invaders, she prevented those who had not yet been enslaved from being enslaved and set free those living within the boundaries of the pillars of Heracles who had" (25c–d).

As many commentators have observed, the greatest deed of prehistoric Athens resembled the defeat of Persia by pre-Periclean Athens.[30] The problem with the victory of historical Athens, of which readers of the *Timaeus-Critias* are reminded by the presence of Hermocrates, was that the alliances and the navy she built up in defending the Greeks from the Persians not merely led other Greek cities to fear her; her allies and the tribute they paid also prompted the Athenians to attempt an unjust imperialistic conquest of Sicily. As in Socrates' account of the origins of the city in speech in the *Republic*, so in the history of Athens, the desires and abilities that enable a regime to defend itself from unjust aggression equip it to attack others. If a people does not come to possess the land on which they lived through autochthonous, divinely caused birth (as in Athenian tradition, the funeral oration Socrates attributes to Aspasia in the *Menexenus*, Socrates' own "noble lie" in the *Republic*, and Critias' account of prehistoric Athens), they will have seized land that might have been used equally well, if not better, by others.[31] The claim of all naturally or sexually generated peoples to the territory in which they live is never perfectly just. As Thucydides' history of the rise and fall of the Athenian empire shows, the land, wealth, forces, and dependents that a polity necessarily acquires in defending itself and others from conquest by a larger expansive imperial power just as necessarily makes the defending polity into an (unjust) empire. That empire not

---

30. See, e.g., Brisson, "*Critias* de Platon"; Vidal-Naquet, "Athens and Atlantis," 263–84; Gerard Naddaf, "The Atlantis Myth: An Introduction to Plato's Later Philosophy of History," *Phoenix* 48, no. 3 (Autumn, 1994): 189–209; and Gill, "Genre." Jean-François Pradeau, *Le monde de la politique: Sur le récit atlante de Platon, Timée (17–27) et Critias* (Sankt Augustin: Academia Verlag, 1997), 71–110, points out that the tradition of reading the Atlantis story as a political allegory containing a criticism of contemporary Athens goes back to Giovanni Bartoli, *Essai sur l'explication historique que Platon a donnée de sa République et de son Atlantide et qu'on n'a pas considerée jusqu'à maintenant* (Stockholm, 1779).

31. When Socrates/Aspasia explains in the *Menexenus* why it is just for Athens to be praised by all human beings, he emphasizes the autochthonous birth of its people (who did not, therefore, have to seize or take land from others by force but were born of and hence to it), the "aristocratic" regime in which the people chose to be ruled by their best citizens, and their role in preserving the freedom of Greece. He attributes the outbreak of the Peloponnesian War to the envy of others (242a) and describes the expedition to Sicily as an effort to preserve the freedom of the Leontinians and to help them keep their oaths. Like Thucydides, Socrates/Aspasia attributes the ultimate defeat of Athens to her own internal divisions. S/he never admits that Athens did anything but defend their own freedom and that of others. That is, at least, all that Athens deserves to be praised for.

only controls the fates of others; it also has to continue expanding, if it is not gradually to lose what it has gained or acquired.[32] To preserve the justice of his prehistoric city at war, Critias thus has to have prehistoric Athens and the empire it defeats destroyed by a natural calamity before Athens is forced to expand and become unjust.

Claiming only to have given the chief points of his speech (as, indeed, he had claimed earlier [23a] that the Egyptian priest gave Solon only a brief account of the laws and deeds of his ancestors and so raising for a second time a question about whether he had ever possessed a complete account of prehistoric Athens), Critias explains that he agreed to Socrates' request the previous day because he had been struck by the surprising degree of resemblance between the regime Socrates described and the city about which he had heard from his grandfather. Having given his associates a brief account on their way home, he spent the night attempting to recall the account as a whole. Believing that he had succeeded, ironically, because he had heard it first as a child, Critias related it to his companions at daybreak. By the end of this conversation, readers recognize, Critias will have repeated the outlines of his speech twice to Socrates and four times to his foreign visitors. Critias thus gives Timaeus both a context or background and some time to prepare the preliminary speech he now asks Timaeus, as the best student not merely of astronomy but of the cosmos as a whole, to give.[33] Neither the two versions of Critias' own speech nor his speech and Timaeus' prelude prove, however, to be entirely consistent with each other or with Socrates' summary description of his city in speech. Although human beings learn by repetition, they also tend to vary each repetition or sensible copy. Both in word (*logos*) and deed (*ergon*), Plato reminds his readers in this dialogue, hearsay is not a reliable or accurate source of knowledge.

5. SOCRATES' SILENCE

When Critias asks Socrates whether he will accept the account of prehistoric Athens as a response to his request to hear an account of his city in speech in action, Socrates responds that it would be appropriate as a

---

32. Cf. Cropsey, "Whole," 168.

33. It becomes unclear, therefore, whether Hermocrates is supposed to give a speech. Critias does not include a third speech in his preliminary plan here, although Socrates appears to expect such a speech in the *Critias* (108a) when he extends the indulgence he has granted Critias to Hermocrates as well.

celebration of the festival of the goddess. Socrates also emphasizes that Critias' speech had been *said* to be true. Socrates does not equate the story of prehistoric Athens with his own city in speech or agree that it is true. He says merely that he will remain silent.

As a whole, the dramatic preface to the *Timaeus* reminds us, there is no "place" or task in this regime—or cosmos—for Socrates.[34] To be sure, Socrates would not have been allowed to converse freely with anyone he chose in his own city in speech. In the *Republic* that regime was put forward not as a program for political action, however, so much as a way of convincing ambitious young Athenians that philosophy could be useful (and that it should, therefore, be tolerated, if not actively supported). Philosophy was defended in the end for enabling an individual to choose the best (private) way of life. In the *Timaeus* Socrates' interlocutors are all mature politicians who have already studied philosophy and thus do not have to be convinced of its utility or nobility. They agree with Socrates that human beings need to institute political order and laws and to study philosophy in order to learn how to subdue their unruly passions. Thinking that they know what to do, they propose to act on their knowledge. In the *Timaeus* philosophy is not presented as a quest for knowledge; we do not, therefore, see Socrates interrogating or examining the opinions of his interlocutors. He simply listens to their speeches as a "just" recompense for his own. Readers are led to wonder whether the speeches Timaeus and then Critias give do, in fact, fulfill Socrates' desire to see his city in speech in motion. Do their speeches fill out Socrates' vision? Do they point to the inadequacy of Socrates' own approach in contrast to a more complete form of wisdom? Or does Socrates' silence indicate a fault in Timaeus' cosmology?

B. Timaeus' Speech

The indications in his initial summary that Critias will not be able to show Socrates' city in speech in motion or at war are borne out in the subsequent dialogue when Critias' speech breaks off in midsentence before he gets to a description of the battle. Critias' inability to satisfy Socrates' request with his history does not prove, however, that Timaeus does not supply the necessary cosmological grounds for the coming into being of Socrates' city in speech.

---

34. Cf. Kalkavage, introduction to *Timaeus*, 37n57; Benardete, "On Plato's *Timaeus*," 382.

1. The Prologue: A "Likely Story"

Timaeus indicates some of his differences with Critias in the short introduction he gives to his "prelude." First, by giving a brief, general, and perfunctory evocation of the gods, in response to Socrates' reminder that such is customary, Timaeus shows that he is not conventionally pious.[35] He also displays both his modesty and superior rigor of thought when he insists, in striking contrast to Critias' assertion that his speech is a strange, but "true logos," that an account of the origin of the cosmos can be no more than a likely story (*eikōs mythos*).

Implicitly criticizing Critias' assumption that the cosmos, like everything else, comes into being, Timaeus insists (27d–28a) that we have to distinguish the beings that always are, unchanging, and understood by the mind (*nous*) with the help of reason (*logos*) from those that come to be and are perceived by unreasoning sensation (*alogos aisthēsis*). Not everything comes into being, but all things that do must have a cause. When the maker of any object that comes into existence uses that which never changes as the model, the copy will be beautiful. Since the heavens (which he equates with the cosmos) are visible, contain bodies, and are perceived by sensation, Timaeus reasons, the cosmos must have come into being. And, since the movements of the heavens are the most beautiful things we can imagine, the maker must have formed the cosmos on the basis of an eternal model. By fabricating the cosmos on the basis of such a model, the maker also shows that he is the best of all causes.

Like Socrates (and unlike the Athenian Stranger), Timaeus explicitly begins from the Parmenidean distinction between eternally existing, purely intelligible being and sensible becoming. Further like Socrates, Timaeus regards human beings as a locus and thus possible source of knowledge of the way in which intelligible and sensible can be joined. There proves to be a gap, however, between the timeless character of the intelligibility of the cosmos and the temporality of human intelligence; and this gap proves to be the fundamental reason Timaeus' account of the coming-into-being of the cosmos can only be a "likely story."

Because Timaeus first explains that his account explicitly concerns an image (*eikōn*), it looks as if the "likely" character of his account is a

---

35. That impression is reinforced by his acceptance (40d–41a) of the stories about the Olympian gods, even though they lack probability or necessary demonstration, because it is customary.

reflection of the subject matter.[36] At the end of the prologue (29c–d), however, Timaeus states that his arguments cannot be altogether consistent
and perfectly precise because both he and his judges are human beings.
Not only are human beings able to grasp the purely intelligible only by
means of its sensible manifestations, he later notes; there is also a fundamental difference between the eternity of that which is intelligible because it always is and the temporality of human discourse.[37] The content
of Timaeus' account can only be "likely" or "imagelike," therefore, not
only because it concerns a likeness but also because it takes the form of
a story or narrative that occurs as if it were in time, because it is told by
a human being to other human beings.[38] In fact, we learn from the narrative, "time" presupposes the creation of the orbits of the heavenly bodies;
the demiurge's initial fabrication of the world-soul cannot, therefore, occur in time. Nor can human beings, who are created later, have any direct
knowledge of the "god" or his work.[39] By the end of Timaeus' account,
if not the introduction, readers see that he could not have acquired his
understanding of the "likely" character of the intelligibility of the cosmos
the same way or in the same order he shows the demiurge constructing it.
Unlike the demiurge, but like other human beings, Timaeus does not have
direct access to or knowledge of the purely intelligible beings or model.
As Timaeus indicates in his introduction, he infers the existence of such a
good and intelligent maker from the character of his work.[40]

Human beings see a beautiful cosmos and with study discover the intelligible order implicit in it. What then must be the case, Timaeus asks, for

36. Giovanni Reale, "Plato's Doctrine of the Origin of the World," in Calvo and Brisson,
Interpreting the "Timaeus-Critias," 152, among others, makes this point.

37. Gretchen Reydams-Schils, "Plato's World Soul: Grasping Sensibles without Sense-
Perception," in Calvo and Brisson, *Interpreting the "Timaeus-Critias,"* 261–65, thus argues against
any simple parallel between the intelligibility of the cosmos and human intelligence or understanding.

38. Hans-Georg Gadamer, "Idea and Reality in Plato's *Timaeus,"* in *Dialogue and Dialectic,* trans.
Christopher Smith (New Haven: Yale University Press, 1980), 160–78, points out that Timaeus'
speech has a strangely dual character. When he speaks of the works of the "maker," "father," or
"god," his speech takes the form of a narrative, and he describes it as a *mythos*; when he describes
the numerical and geometrical forms of sensible things, however, his speech becomes more an
analysis or "account" he calls an *eikota logon* (*Timaeus* 53d).

39. "Narration de l'événement original, de la genèse du Dieu cosmique, c'est-à-dire d'un
événement qui, nous aurons encore à le redire, est caché et inaccessible à l'homme, le récit cos-
mologique du Timée ne peut être qu'une 'fable vraisemblable'" (Hadot, "Timée," 120). Although
Timaeus says that the souls later embodied in human beings do have a view of the divine order,
he also explains that their intellects (and thus this view) become entirely confused when they are
joined to bodies.

40. Cf. Johansen, *Natural Philosophy,* 75–76.

mortal, transient beings like ourselves to be able to acquire such knowledge? The cosmos must have an intelligible order, and the purely intelligible (which always is as it is) must therefore somehow get mixed with the sensible and transient, first in the cosmos and then in us. Timaeus' speech thus has three parts. First he explains the intelligible order of the cosmos, then he indicates how this order is related to sensible things in flux, and finally he describes the joining of the intelligible and the sensible or bodily in the constitution of human beings.

2. Cosmic Completion in Contrast to Human Neediness

Timaeus gives an account of the cosmos to show how it can be conceived as the product of a maker who intended the best. Timaeus does not identify the maker or show that he actually produced an intelligible order in and among all sensible things. On the contrary, Timaeus begins by affirming the incapacity of mere human beings to know the cause, maker, or god. At most we can become aware of the character of the work (*ergon*). In explicating the work of reason, Timaeus argues that the cosmos is good primarily because it provides the basis for a philosophical life.

Intending the best, Timaeus states, the god wanted everything to be as much like him, that is, as good as possible. He thus made the copy as much like the eternal paradigm as he could. Good and hence complete in himself, he did not envy anyone or anything. He is not a "jealous" god who wanted his inferiors to recognize his superiority or their dependence on his will. Doing only what is good (like Socrates' gods in the *Republic*), he is not responsible for the faults of the copy, which result from its nature as a copy and not from his intention.

The first result of goodness appears to be order. When the god "saw that everything visible was in a state of discordant and disorderly motion," Timaeus states, "he thus brought it into order" (30a).[41] Goodness, order, and beauty depend, further, on the presence of mind. Because neither good nor beauty exists apart from mind (*nous*), and intelligence cannot exist apart from soul, Timaeus explains, the god constructed the cosmos with mind within a soul within a body.

At the very beginning of Timaeus' account of the fabrication of the cosmos, we thus learn, the "soul" the god is about to construct is not the

---

41. Cornford (*Plato's Cosmology*, 34–35) is surely correct, therefore, when he objects to Taylor's characterization of the *dēmiourgos* in the *Timaeus* as a creator God. The god brings order to what already exists; he does not create de novo.

source of motion in the cosmos.[42] Inasmuch as it is fabricated by something else, the cosmic soul is not self-moving and therefore eternal, like the soul of which Socrates speaks in the *Phaedrus* or the Athenian argues in the *Laws* is the first and most fundamental kind of being. Timaeus' cosmic soul is the means of joining unchanging self-same being, which is intelligible to mind assisted by reason, to divisible bodily being, which is always becoming and hence sensible and changeable, so that the whole can be (made or become) orderly, beautiful, and intelligible. Motion inheres, we shall see, in the receptacle of becoming. The god and the soul he constructed bring order to that originally, in itself disorderly motion.

Because the cosmos has a soul, Timaeus says that it is a living being (*zō[i]on*). And if being as good as possible means being as complete as possible, he reasons, the intelligible paradigm of all living beings should contain all kinds. The cosmos and its paradigm should also be one. If either cosmos or paradigm thereof were more than one, the cosmos and its paradigm would not be all inclusive or complete.

Since the cosmos is both visible and tangible, Timaeus reasons, it also has a body. And since nothing can be visible without fire or tangible without solidity, the body of the cosmos must be composed of fire and earth. For two things to be conjoined, moreover, there must be a third. The most beautiful form of mediation is proportion. Since the body of the cosmos is not a plane but a solid figure, it must have two means. Timaeus identifies these "middle terms" with the other two of the four elements mentioned by pre-Socratic cosmologists such as Empedocles, air and water. In the subsequent section of his speech devoted to what necessarily exists, Timaeus explicitly combines this cosmological teaching about the four ele-

---

42. As Andrea Wilson Nightingale, *Spectacles of Truth in Classical Greek Philosophy* (Cambridge: Cambridge University Press, 2004), 58–59n169, points out, there is a long-standing scholarly argument about the way in which one should approach the *Timaeus* in general and this passage in particular. Like Cornford (*Plato's Cosmology*), Skemp (*Theory of Motion*), and Cherniss (*Aristotle's Criticism of Plato*), Nightingale maintains that the soul is the source of motion in order to make the *Timaeus* consistent with the *Phaedrus* and *Laws*. In doing so, like Gregory Vlastos, "Disorderly Motion in the *Timaeus*," *Classical Quarterly* 33 (1939): 71–83; H. Herter, "Bewegung der Materie bei Platon," *Rheinisches Museum für Philologie* 100 (1957): 327–47; and Richard D. Mohr, *The Platonic Cosmology* (Leiden: E. J. Brill, 1985), she has to concede that the *Timaeus* itself is inconsistent, that is, she does not base her reading on the *Timaeus* itself but on a combination of the dialogues (and arguments of different Platonic philosophers). Beginning with Proclus (if not earlier), commentators (again like Cornford) used the notion of a self-moving soul to attribute independent motion to the planets, which helped explain their "wandering."

ments with Pythagorean arguments showing how plane and solid figures can be constructed on the basis of numbers to create a mathematical basis for the "proportion."

Expanding on the shape and organs (or lack thereof) of the body of the cosmos, Timaeus concludes his summary description of the constitution of the cosmos by reminding his auditors of the disparity between the living whole and its human parts. In an argument reminiscent of Parmenides' account of the characteristics of being, Timaeus contends that the cosmos is unitary, indissoluble, and consequently everlasting (unless the god decides to destroy it), because there is nothing outside it. It includes everything else, and being complete in itself, it has no needs. It has mind, but no senses or locomotion, because there is nothing outside it to perceive and no place outside it to go. The god made it a sphere, the most perfect and self-similar of all shapes, and gave it the uniform circular motion that belongs to mind (*nous*) and intelligence (*phronēsis*). It always revolves in one place around its own axis (33b–34a). It is centered on itself and does not look beyond itself to the purely intelligible things that always are.

Because it is complete in itself, even though it does not bring itself into being, Timaeus calls the cosmos a blessed or happy god. It is beyond, above, and better than we imperfect, ever-needy, and desirous mortals. Because the cosmos is defined in terms of the negation of human limitations, however, the knowledge human beings have—or can attain—of it is not and cannot be simply the understanding like has of like.

3. The Tension between the Temporality of Human *Logos* and the Eternity of Intelligible Being

Having brought out the differences between human neediness and cosmic self-sufficiency in his description of the construction of the cosmos, Timaeus points out the gap between the temporality of human *logos* and the eternal, unchanging character of the intelligible beings. Because the soul rules and is intended to give order to body, it must come first. Yet in saying that the god brought order to the disorderly motions of the visible heavens, Timaeus had suggested that body or sensible becoming was first. The god "would never have let an elder be ruled by a younger—but we who somehow partake largely of the accidental and random do so when we speak" (*Timaeus* 34c). To be intelligible, the order of the cosmos has to be eternal. Since that order becomes manifest in the movement of visible objects, it is not, strictly speaking or completely, intelligible or eternal; it comes into being as a result of the demiurge's work, although it lasts forever (if he wills it). We humans cannot speak about the intelligible order of the cosmos without introducing the sensible and temporal.

Timaeus cannot entirely adhere to the priority of the divine soul over the body in his account of the coming into being of the cosmos, because what is first in itself or for the intelligibility of the cosmos is not first for us. Timaeus begins his description of the construction of the soul of the cosmos with an account of the intelligibility of the orbits of the heavenly bodies, because their order and intelligibility make human learning possible. If the movements of the heavens could not be mathematically calculated, human beings would not be able to learn the science of number or the kind of philosophy that enables them to bring order to their own thoughts by contemplating the orderly movements of the heavens (47a–c). In concluding his account of the works of necessity (69a), he admits that human beings are not able to discern or pursue anything that is not sensible. Because we learn about the purely intelligible only by means of the sensible, the sensible is first for us, even though the intelligible order inherent in the movements of sensible things is a prior requirement of our ability to learn from them.

a. The Cosmic Basis of Human Intelligence

According to Timaeus, the god constituted the soul of the cosmos out of being, which is always indivisible and the same, and that which is changing and divisible in bodies, the same and the other.[43] The Greek is simply not clear as to whether he forced together the three constituent elements (*eidē*), or whether he first divided being, the same, and the other into indivisible and divisible parts and then melded the six resulting parts together into one *idea*, forcing together the same and the different, which naturally resist mixing. If, however, the cosmic soul is to perform its function as the middle term between that which is eternally intelligible and that which continually becomes and is perceived by the senses, same and different would have to be both divided and joined, if there are going to be (and human beings are consequently going to be able to distinguish) different

---

43. Timaeus' treatment of the component parts of the soul—all of which are supposed to be purely intelligible—as substances or material that can be mixed reminds us powerfully of the reasons he describes the cosmos as an "image" and his own account of its construction a "likely story."

kinds of things in the cosmos that are the same as themselves but different from others.[44]

In the *Sophist*, the Eleatic Stranger also divides and defines things, according to whether they are the same or different. As a result, some commentators have thought this part of the *Timaeus* has to be understood in light of the *Sophist*.[45] One of the Eleatic Stranger's fundamental divisions of the *eidē* is, however, between rest and motion. In Timaeus' cosmos, everything is in motion; nothing is at rest. The intelligibility of things depends on the order imparted to the motions by the soul. Timaeus says that after constituting the soul out of being, sameness, and difference, the demiurge divided it, according to the powers of two and three, so that there are two "means," arithmetic and harmonic or geometrical, in each and every interval. As a result of these divisions, the motions of soul can be marked and measured in mathematical terms of number and proportion. It might seem that the soul had been constructed so that its parts would parallel, and therefore presumably fit, the four parts or elements of body, which were also said to be related to each other by two means. Instead of fitting soul to body, however, Timaeus says that the god split the proportionately divided soul in two, crossed the two parts, and then joined the ends of each half so that they formed two circles. One revolving always in the same place (and so named the motion of the same) holds the whole together. Placing the circle of the "other" at a diagonal to the same, he then divided it in six places into seven pieces, which revolve at different speeds in different directions, yet in proportion or ratio to each other. (These "pieces" correspond to the apparently irregular orbits of the planets.)

The function of the cosmic soul, as Timaeus describes it, is not to explain the kinds, the coming into being, or life of the various sorts of things to be found in the cosmos.[46] It is to make intelligible (or at least provide a speculative foundation for) the mathematically calculable order of the movements of the heavenly bodies, which in turn constitutes the basis for a kind of contemplative philosophy.

44. I think that Cornford (*Plato's Cosmology*, 59–61) is correct, therefore, when he argues that the god made three "intermediate" mixtures of indivisible and divisible being, indivisible and divisible sameness, and indivisible and divisible difference, and then melded the three intermediate mixtures to constitute soul.

45. See, e.g., ibid., 61–64, 96.

46. The tension, if not incompatibility, between Timaeus' account of the cosmos as a product of intentional fabrication and genesis or generative becoming becomes more evident at the end of his speech.

Rather than elaborate on the effects of the movements of the heavenly bodies on life (what comes to be) on earth, Timaeus emphasizes the ways in which the movements of the cosmos make knowledge possible. After the god constructed body within soul and made the two coextensive, the motions of the heavens became visible. As Timaeus later emphasizes, human beings learn about purely intelligible things only through their sensible manifestations. What human beings learn from observing the motions of the heavenly bodies, however, are the invisible, purely intelligible logical distinctions between same and other, the numerical measurements and geometrical relations of their movements.

Because the heavenly bodies move in different directions at different speeds, the intelligible order of their motion is not apparent to the naked eye. It has to be deduced and calculated from observed regularities of movement.[47] It can be calculated and deduced, however, only if there is an order inherent in the movements. That order, Timaeus explains, is of two kinds, corresponding to the two kinds of revolutions or circular movements. The movements that are always the same, intelligible, and therefore calculable become the source of true knowledge. Those that differ from themselves and from others, the movements that characterize sensible and divisible bodies, become the basis of true opinions (but not knowledge, because these opinions are about changeable things and hence change themselves). Timaeus describes this differentiated order of the movement of the cosmic soul as a *logos* without sound or noise (*aneu phthoggou kai ēchēs*). Like speech, the movements of the heavenly bodies constitute and communicate an intelligible order of differentiated visible, though not audible, parts. Like speech, the content of the heavenly *logos* is both sensible and intelligible; it thus provides a basis for and communicates both opinions and truth. Since the elements of this *logos* are not audible, composed of letters or words, it is not speech or discourse as we human beings understand it.[48] Although the order is communicated to humans who learn not only to observe but also to duplicate it in their own

47. As Kalkavage indicates in an appendix to his translation of the *Timaeus*, the calculations were complicated. There are apparent anomalies in the movements of the sun, moon, and planets in that the bodies appear to speed up, slow down, or even temporarily change directions in the course of a year. Later astronomers like Ptolemy responded to "the astronomical problem laid down by Plato according to Simplicius: 'What circular motions, uniform and perfectly regular, are to be admitted as hypotheses so that it might be possible to save the appearances presented by the planets?'" (153).

48. For this reason, it seems, Cicero translated *logos* by *ratio*. Cf. Peter Lautner, "Can Self-Reflection Be a Generative Principle? Atticus and Porphyry on *Timaeus* 37b3–6," *Ancient World* 32, no. 1 (2001): 71.

souls, communication to anything outside itself is not necessarily entailed by the orderly movements of the cosmic soul in itself. On the contrary, the order or logic of the motion of the cosmic soul is inherent in that soul and permeates the cosmos as a whole. It is the basis of human knowledge, that is, it makes human knowledge possible, but it does not necessarily produce such knowledge.

Just as Timaeus' account of the definition and character of the cosmic soul differs from the accounts of the immortal soul presented by both Socrates and the Athenian Stranger, so does his account of the knowledge that souls possess differ from Socrates' account of the knowledge that souls seek. Timaeus does not characterize the two parts of the dichotomy he initially draws between that which always is and that which continually becomes as *eidē* or *ideai* (although he will do so in his account of what comes into being by necessity as opposed to what comes into being because it is good or mind). Nor does he describe the eternal, completely intelligible animal that is the cosmos as an idea or "form." He does so characterize the three constituent elements of the cosmic soul, because being, same, and different appear to be the basic categories of thought, necessary for understanding or intelligibility. His purely intelligible *eidē* are not the same as those posited by either Socrates or the Eleatic Stranger. They do not include ideas of the virtues or mathematical concepts such as equality, of which Socrates speaks in the *Parmenides*, *Republic*, and *Phaedo*; nor are they the beings that are always, which, according to Socrates in the *Phaedrus*, souls strive to contemplate from the edge of the cosmos as it rotates. On the contrary, Timaeus' *eidē* are constituent parts of the soul of the cosmos itself. When he includes *eidē* of the inferior kinds of beings, defined by their location (heavens, sky, earth, or water) or their basic elements (which are, in turn, separated from each other and so defined by the geometric shapes of their component parts), it becomes clear that Timaeus' *eidē* are the purely intellectual divisions by which the sensible cosmos is organized and made intelligible.[49] Timaeus' *eidē* exist side by side, marking the different kinds or locations of things, unless, as in the construction of the cosmic soul, they are forced together contrary to their nature. They do not

49. Unlike the Eleatic Stranger, Timaeus does not include rest and motion along with being, sameness, and difference as fundamental or constitutive *eidē*. Insofar as the cosmos is visible and hence perceived by the senses, according to Timaeus, there is nothing at rest in it. Motion inheres in that which eternally becomes, which soul makes somewhat intelligible or calculable (*logistikos*) by "persuading" it to take the shapes of intelligible ideas. The Eleatic Stranger would object to Timaeus' account, therefore, as one of the "myths" that fail to make clear whether being is one, two, or many and why.

coexist in a "community" like the *eidē* of being, same and different, rest and motion, that the Eleatic Stranger describes. On the contrary, Timaeus suggests, like being and becoming, the heavens, air, water, and earth (or the four elements) have to remain distinct, if human beings are to perceive an order in their world.[50]

b. Being and Time

As in Timaeus' initial description of the god's construction of the body and soul of the cosmos, so in his description of the movements of the soul and its cognitive results, a contradiction arises between the temporality associated with intentional making (in which someone does something in order to do or achieve something else) and the constancy of intelligible order. Timaeus says (36e) that the soul, having been woven throughout the body of the cosmos, began a life unceasing and thoughtful through all time (*theian archēn ērxato apaustou kai emphronos biou pros ton sumpanta chronon*). Shortly thereafter (37b) he nevertheless refers to the soul as "self-moving" (*en tō[i] kinoumenō[i] huph' hautou pheromenos*), even though he has just described how it came into being when the god forced together being, same, and other, contrary to their natures.[51] In the *Phaedrus* (245c–e), Socrates argued that the soul has no beginning or end and is therefore eternal precisely because it is self-moved (and so never moved initially by something else).[52]

It is not possible for something that comes into being to be eternal, Timaeus insists, and the visible cosmos has come into being. The cosmic soul does not exist apart from its body; it is not in itself or strictly speaking eternal. The cosmos exists and continues to exist not in itself, because it is composite, but only on the basis of the will of the god, because it is good. Not being eternal in itself, the cosmos constitutes an image of eternity. That image in the circular movements of the heavenly bodies, measurable by numbers, is called time. Like the soul of the cosmos, time itself is invisible and intelligible; it does not exist, however, apart from visible things.

50. Erik Ostenfeld, "The Role and Status of the Forms in the *Timaeus*: Paradigmatism Revised?" in Calvo and Brisson, *Interpreting the "Timaeus-Critias,"* 170–76, also notices these differences between the forms described by Timaeus and those to be found elsewhere in the dialogues, but he tries to account for the difference in terms of the "development" of Plato's thought.

51. Since antiquity, commentators on the *Timaeus* have thus disagreed about whether the cosmic soul has a beginning in time or not. Cf. Plutarch, "On the Generation of the Soul in the *Timaeus*," in *Plutarch's Moralia*, trans. Harold Cherniss, vol. 1, pt. 1 (Cambridge: Harvard University Press, 1976).

52. Cf. Kalkavage, *Timaeus*, 66n37.

There is no such thing as time—days and nights, months or years—before the heavens come into existence. Time only exists or coexists with the cosmos.

We thus speak improperly or incorrectly, Timaeus argues, when we speak of eternal time. Eternal being always is; only things that come into being exist within time. In time they have become, are becoming, or will become. It is a continuous process or motion. Because it circles back on itself, the intelligible motion of the heavenly bodies, which we calculate on the basis of numbers, has no clear beginning, middle, or end. It appears to us to have gone and to continue to go on forever. But, Timaeus reminds his listeners, because it is constituted by a combination of two parts—the motion of becoming, which is made intelligible by calculations of unchanging numbers—which do not always or necessarily cohere, neither time nor the cosmos *is* necessarily always.

4. The Genesis of the Inferior Kinds

In order to make this the best possible cosmos, Timaeus suggested earlier, the god not only had to construct an order that was intelligible and hence beautiful; he also had to give it a soul, which made it a living animal. To be the best living animal, it had to be complete, and to be complete, it had to encompass all others. For that reason, he now explains, it had to include all four basic kinds (which are described variously as *ideai*, *eidē*, and *genē*). It might seem strange to have the basic kinds of living beings identified by their place (heavens, air, earth, or water) or related bodily element, but the definitions are intelligible products of mind (as opposed to ever becoming and infinitely divisible body), which distinguishes same from different. Timaeus cannot and does not define kinds or species of living things by their ability to procreate, because he associates generation with degeneration.

The most important distinction among the kinds of beings is between the immortal heavenly beings, constituted by the god, and the other mortal beings, which all began as male human beings. Although the visible gods in the heavens are composites (which can, therefore, in principle be dissolved; cf. Socrates *Phaedo* 78c), the "god" explains that things he himself binds together will stay together so long as he wills it. In other words, they continue to exist not because it is necessary, but because it is good. With regard to the visible cosmos, the god thus appears to act like Socrates' idea of the good in the *Republic*, although Socrates' idea was said to be the source of all other ideas, which Timaeus' god is not. He merely uses these preexisting purely intelligible ideas in constructing the cosmos.

If the cosmos was to be complete, it had to contain mortal as well as immortal beings. But the mortal beings could not be constituted directly by the god. He thus shaped the divine part of what would become human beings by dividing the impure remainder of the "soul stuff" into as many pieces as there were stars. While on their way to being "sown" in their respective stars, the god showed these souls the nature of all. Like Socrates, Timaeus suggests that human beings must have an inherent capacity to recognize general categories of thought like being, the same, and the other in order to develop the *logos* we observably possess.

The god also explains why the divine parts of human souls had to be born all at once. He would not be a just and good god if he favored some over others. Nor would human beings "grow into the most god-fearing of animals" (although Timaeus does not state the god's reasoning) unless he endowed them with divine minds, which enable them to appreciate his goodness as well as their own inferiority. Since human beings are of two kinds (*genē*) by nature, the god explains (*Timaeus* 42a), the stronger (and hence, according to the conventional meaning of the word *kreitton*) superior part will be called (*keklēsoito*) man (*anēr*). He left it to the "younger" gods to mold their bodies and so to make the parts of human beings that physically distinguish us from the divine. Having given all human beings equal souls at the beginning, the god does not appear to be responsible for the later inferiority of women. At this point, Timaeus has explained the coming into being of humans, both male and female, with souls that would enable them to become guardians in Socrates' city in speech, because souls have no sex. (Socrates himself [17c] spoke of all the citizens of his city as *andres*; by stating that the superior part would be called "men," Timaeus' god might be taken to suggest that the distinction in name is somewhat conventional.) The inferiority of women appears to be a product of necessity, not the work of the good god, although he knows what will necessarily happen.

By having their souls constituted from the same "stuff" as the cosmos, Timaeus indicates that it is their bodies that distinguish and separate human beings from the cosmos as whole. The cosmos has a spherical shape, no senses or limbs, and moves only by revolving in one place. The human soul is placed primarily in a spherical bone, which resembles the shape of the cosmos, but that head bone is joined to limbs, which enable it to move six ways, not simply in a circular revolution, and has a face with eyes to give it direction. Humans need senses and limbs to acquire the nourishment we require in order to grow. Unlike the cosmos, we are not self-sufficient.

When our souls are joined "by necessity" to bodies, Timaeus explains, the rush of sensation and the flow of nutrients are so great that they overcome and derange the revolutions of the same and the other in our souls. If human beings acquire the ability to master the force of sensations, erotic pleasures, and pains, as well as the terrors and anger that set us at odds with one another, they will live in justice. At death their souls will return to their lawful star. Those not able with age, correct upbringing, and education to re-create the orderly movement of the spheres within their own souls will be reborn as women or with a bestial nature. The inferiority of the "second sex" arises with the body.

In the best of all possible worlds, we might object, would human beings not be immortal and share the knowledge the cosmic soul has of being, sameness, and difference? Human beings would not be or be human, Timaeus suggests, except as mortal composites of body and soul. Life is good. In order to live, each kind of animal must have some shape (*idea*). The best possible life and world (or cosmos) for us is that in which we can regain the regular order of the revolutions of the circles of the same and the other in ourselves by observing and studying the mathematically calculable revolutions of the heavens. This—and not the acquisition of nutrition or self-preservation—is the purpose of our vision, "that by observing the circuits of intellect in heaven, having thoroughly learned them and partaken of the natural correctness in their calculations, and so imitating the utterly endangering circuits of the god, we might stabilize the wander-stricken circuits of thinking in ourselves" (47b–c).[53]

5. The Necessity of an Intelligible Ordering of the Sensible

Having described, if not explained, the intelligible order that human beings not only can discover but also can learn to duplicate in themselves by observing the movements of the heavenly bodies, Timaeus looks at the order of the sensible. If human beings learn about the purely intelligible

53. This is also the purpose of our sense of hearing. Although the proportions of the mixture constituting the cosmic soul form a musical scale in Pythagorean tuning for four octaves and a major sixth, there is no music of the cosmic sphere, according to Timaeus, because the cosmos has no senses. Using their sense of hearing along with their ability to learn and calculate the motions of the stars, human beings can compose music based on the mathematical order of the cosmos to bring order to their own souls. We are constituted so that we can make music not for the sake of our own pleasure, but for our own good (*Timaeus* 47c–d).

forms only by looking at their sensible manifestations (*Timaeus* 69a), how is it that ever-changing sensible becoming can be made or re-formed so that it resembles the intelligible, even though it itself is not?

It is necessary to examine the way in which the four basic elements constantly interact with and change into one another (as water can evaporate into air or condense into a solid). But, Timaeus warns his listeners, it is important to view the continual transformations of the elements that characterize the flux of becoming in light of their rational purpose. They must not, in other words, fall short in the way that Socrates thought Anaxagoras had when he said that mind was the source of everything, but then explained the character of all particular beings solely in terms of the interactions of their components.

a. The Three Kinds of Beings

Strictly speaking, Timaeus points out, there are no distinct elements before the construction or intelligible organization of the cosmos. In the stream of becoming, nothing is distinguished from anything else. In order to show how sensible things acquire the properties that enable us to recognize them, not merely as distinct from one another but also as having at least partially intelligible forms or definitions, it is necessary to go back to the beginning and to distinguish three different kinds (described as both *eidē* and *genē*). First, there are the things that are always the same and cognized by the mind; second, there are the sensible copies of these things about which we have opinions; and third, there is the stuff (*ekmageion*) or space (*chōra*) in which the sensible copies are made. (Timaeus did not need to speak of the "third" kind so long as he was concerned only with the invisible but intelligible order of the sensible things. To speak about the constitution of bodies, however, he has to divide their intelligible forms, even though these are mere imitations of the purely intelligible, from the stuff from which and in which the copies are constituted.) This third kind is difficult to speak about, precisely because it has no distinct properties of its own and thus cannot be defined or cognized in itself. We know about it only by means of a sort of "bastard" reasoning, which tells us that if sensible things must have bodies and hence volume, they must exist somewhere or in some space.

Within the Platonic corpus, mention of the *chōra* occurs only in the *Timaeus*. The concept appears to be unique to the philosopher-statesman from Locri. There is nothing like it in the arguments Plato ascribes to the Athenian, Parmenides, Socrates, or the Eleatic—probably because no other

Platonic philosophical spokesman even tries to give an account of how things come to be what they are (as opposed to what and why they are what they are).

Chōra seems to be the underlying substance out of which all sensible things are formed, but it is not uniform; if it were, it could not be the locus of shifting motion, because motion requires differentiation for something to move something else (*Timaeus* 57e). Parts or places in it are of different degrees of density, Timaeus explains, and, lacking balance or equilibrium, continually shift. *Chōra* has often been translated as "space," but unlike the modern concept, it is not empty nor does it represent mere extension. If it did, like time (which is joined to space in modern thought precisely for this reason), it could be mathematically measured and would therefore be intelligible in itself. *Chōra* is not.[54] If it were empty, it could not be the locus of the constant motion or shifting of its uneven parts.[55] It is the necessary precondition, not like space and time in Kant of intelligible existence, but of bodies in motion and hence of mortal life. It is the aspect of reality that Socrates seems to ignore or negate.

b. The Order of Sensible Things Is Neither Self-Evident nor Necessary

Not everything in the cosmos is good or intelligible, Timaeus admits. That is why the account he has given of the work of the good god must be supplemented by an account of what comes into being from necessity. It is not clear, however, that the combination of the two accounts is complete or true. Timaeus begins by insisting that his account of the genesis of the cosmos would only be a likely story.

He admits that the description he gives of the realm of necessity is not at all self-evident and may not persuade others. From the point of view of things in flux it is not clear that there is anything that exists always or in itself or that there is only one cosmos. These are both conclusions that follow from the requirements of mind and the good, not from an observation of sensible things. Timaeus reminds both his auditors and Plato's readers of the inferential character of his analysis when he "votes" to

54. Jacques Derrida, *"Khora," On the Name*, trans. David Wood (Stanford: Stanford University Press, 1995), 93, 147n2, suggests that Martin Heidegger erred when he traced Descartes' reduction of being to extension to this passage in Plato's *Timaeus*, in Heidegger, *Introduction to Metaphysics*, trans. Ralph Manheim (Garden City, NY: Doubleday, 1961), 55.

55. In contrast to atomists like Democritus, Timaeus has to insist that there is no void in order to explain the constant shifting, interpenetration, and interaction or flux of the basic elements or "stuff" out of which sensible things are constituted. If there were a void, like would be attracted to like, the kinds would gradually separate out, and the interaction would cease.

agree that there are three fundamental kinds or ideas. We acquire knowledge of the things that truly are by learning, whereas we are persuaded to have opinions about sensible things that change. The distinction between the intelligible and the sensible does not appear to arise so much from the things themselves as from us, the human observers, the different ways in which we acquire information about the external world, and the different character (firm or changeable) of that information. Timaeus emphasizes the nonnecessary character of the order he is describing in the realm of necessity by admitting, after he states the reasons the contents of *chōra* could be "persuaded" to accept the shapes of the four regular solids, that some might conclude that there would be at least five cosmoses, each shaped according to one of the five regular solids. He argues that there is only one cosmos on the grounds of what is good, not what is necessary. Later (*Timaeus* 59c) he describes the account of the intelligibility of sensible things he has given (in contrast to an account of the things that always are, of which we can acquire knowledge) as a moderate and prudent form of play.

Like the three fundamental kinds or ideas, the specific geometrical shapes of the four basic elements are inferred from our experience. For example, Timaeus suggests, the god persuaded the lighter parts to accept the shape of a pyramid constructed out of tiny, invisible scalene triangles (and so become copies of purely intelligible forms), because the sharp point of the pyramid is compatible with the cutting, burning sensations we associate with fire. Likewise, he persuaded the heavier parts to accept the shape of a cube, because the "solidity" of the cube corresponds to our belief in the firmness of earth. In themselves, Timaeus insists, the contents and material of *chōra* have no definitive or intelligible form.[56] If we were to speak precisely about the four basic elements, we would say that they are firelike or earthlike, not fire and earth or water and air.[57]

---

56. Before the god persuades the various parts to accept intelligible, geometrical forms, there is only a shifting mass of uneven density contained within an undefined space. The spherical shape of the cosmos as well as the revolving motion that holds everything together are results of the god's goodness and mind. They are thus imposed upon, not inherent in, *chōra* itself.

57. Some commentators—e.g., Cornford, *Plato's Cosmology*, 51; and Kenneth Sayre, "The Multilayered Incoherence of Timaeus' Receptacle," in *Plato's "Timaeus" as Cultural Icon*, ed. Gretchen J. Reydams-Schils (Notre Dame, IN: University of Notre Dame Press, 2003), 75–79—have complained that the four elements, as described, would not exist in the proportion Timaeus first suggested because the sides of the triangles of the cube earth are not the same as those that compose the other figures. Like Sayre, Cropsey ("Whole," 180) point outs that the sides of the triangles are not whole integers but radicals, and not the same radicals (in three cases the square root of three, in one the square root of two). The non-integer sides may be taken as a trace or indication of the

The fact that the varying densities of the shifting mass can accept and be understood in terms of four regular geometric solids not merely makes it possible for human beings to identify and distinguish them in an ordered and hence more beautiful cosmos (as opposed to the original chaos or flux). Describing the varied tendencies and consistencies of the originally undifferentiated mass in terms of geometrical figures also enables us to see how the elements can penetrate each other and interact.[58] Each element has its own geometrical shape and associated characteristics, but the sides of each solid can be broken up into its constituent parts (triangles), which can then be recombined to form the side of another. By showing how the triangles that constitute the planes or sides of one regular solid can be separated and then recombined to form another, Timaeus can explain phenomena such as fermentation, growth, and decay that the young Socrates found so puzzling that he turned away entirely from such inquiries (*Phaedo* 96a–d).[59]

c. On the Character and Causes of Human Sensations

Analyses of the interactions among the component parts of the basic elements further help us understand the way in which various parts of the cosmos affect us and so make the cause of our sensations somewhat

---

not wholly rational or intelligible character of the materials in flux. As John A. Black, *The Four Elements in Plato's "Timaeus"* (Lewiston, NY: Edwin Mellen Press, 2000), has shown, however, the four solid figures said to compose the elements could have been put in the two mean proportion Timaeus initially suggests on the basis of Pythagorean mathematics.

58. Both Cornford (*Plato's Cosmology*, 51) and Cropsey ("Whole," 180) point out that the demiurge could have composed all four of the elements (or regular geometric solids) out of equilateral triangles that, divided into two right triangles, would have made all four elements capable of interpenetrating and transforming one into another. Cornford suggests that Timaeus does not show how all four regular solids could be constructed out of equilateral triangles because he needs more triangles to make up each side of the invisible solids if triangles of different sizes are to be broken up and reconstituted. I think, on the other hand, that if there were not one element, the most solid, whose square sides composed of two right isosceles triangles did not interpenetrate with the other three, composed as they are out of scalene triangles, there would be no core or center of the cosmos. The flux would not generate or accept the kind of order Timaeus describes here, especially in his analysis of the difference between "light" and "heavy," as opposed to "above" and "below." At 54b–c Timaeus thus corrects his own earlier statement: "Something earlier that was said unclearly must at present be more thoroughly determined: the four kinds all appeared to have birth through one another into one another, but they didn't show themselves correctly. For out of the triangles we've chosen, four kinds are born; three come from the one triangle that has unequal sides, while the fourth is the only one joined together from the isosceles triangle. They are therefore not all capable, on being dissolved into one another, of becoming a few large bodies out of many small ones, and the other way around; but it is possible for three."

59. As Sayre points out ("Multilayered Incoherence," 72), the treatment of fire in the *Timaeus* differs significantly from that Socrates gives in the *Phaedo*.

intelligible. After he has described the way in which fire, air, water, and earth can be understood to be constructed in the shapes of the four regular solids and their interactions, Timaeus thus turns to an analysis of our sensations—even though he admits that he has not yet shown how the sense organs were constructed.

Once again Timaeus points out the way in which the temporal character and requirements of human discourse in which we have to put one thing before another make it impossible for us to describe the world or its simultaneous order and intelligibility with complete accuracy. He cannot describe the organs with which we sense at the same time that he describes what is sensed and how, even though the organs have to be present for sensation to occur. He begins with the sensations, because he recognizes that human beings acquire knowledge of the world only by sensibly interacting with it. Just as he began his account of the coming into being of the world by asking what has to be the case for us to perceive a beautiful cosmos, now he asks how the world must be conceived as having been organized so that (a) our various sensations are possible and (b) we can acquire understanding of the intelligible order and purpose of the world from reflections on these sensations.

Beginning with our sensations of hot and cold, Timaeus explains that the sharp points of the pyramids cut and so burn us. We become cold when, having forced out the smaller, lighter ones, the larger particles of fire condense and congeal into air or water. Because the smaller particles resist their expulsion, a shaking or trembling accompanies the transition from hot to cold. At the level of the sensible, everything that is in flux could also be said to be at war.[60] Hard and soft are determined by what does or does not resist our flesh. Heavy and light refer to the resistance something gives when moved: if great, it is heavy; if it can be moved easily, light.[61] Smooth and rough (feelings) are products of degrees of resistance mixed with more or less uniformity. Pleasures and pains are the most important affections of the body as a whole, but different parts of our bodies are more or less subject to these sensations, depending on whether the part (like bone) is difficult to move and so resists impressions or is soft like flesh and so more subject to attack by external bodies. We feel pain

60. This is the thought that informs Heraclitus' famous fragments.
61. "Heavy" and "light" do not refer to upward or downward movements, Timaeus explains, because the cosmos is spherical; there is no region that is above or below. Things are either at the center or the periphery.

and then pleasure when a violent departure from the natural equilibrium (perceived as pain) is remedied (with pleasure).

Because Timaeus understands sensations and hence pleasures and pains in terms of the resistance human beings feel to things, he does not acknowledge the existence of purely intellectual pleasures. He suggests that the most intellectual of the senses, vision, occurs without either pleasure or pain, because there is no resistance to the entrance or exit of light or fire in the eyes. In the *Philebus* Socrates had argued that there are several different kinds of pleasure. Not all arise from the removal of pain; only the pleasures of the body arise from the removal or satisfaction of wants. We can experience the intellectual pleasure of contemplating what we know without previous pain (although there would have been pain associated with the labor of learning). Nor do all bodily pleasures presuppose pain, according to Socrates. We can take pleasure in a good smell without having experienced pain at its absence beforehand. We may not have perceived the preceding void, Timaeus observes, but we nevertheless feel pleasure when the repletion occurs rapidly, as from an intense, quick infusion of scent. Timaeus does not admit the existence of the variety of kinds of pleasures Socrates brought out in the *Philebus*, because Timaeus insists that a hard and fast line be drawn between the things that are always and known by the mind and those that are sensible and changeable.[62] Only the latter can be felt as pleasurable or painful. For him the best life for human beings consists in observing the orderly movements of the heavens and duplicating those movements or order within. Although he says the life of philosophy is happy (*Timaeus* 68e) and best (90d), he does not claim that it is positively pleasant. If Socrates and Protarchus are right about human beings not believing that a life without pleasure would be good, human beings would not be satisfied with the life of philosophy Timaeus praises.

Having described sound "as the blow transmitted through the ears by the action of air upon brain and blood . . . , the motion produced by this blow beginning in the head and ending around the seat of the liver" (for reasons that become clearer in his discussion of divination in the next

---

62. Remi Brague, "The Body of the Speech: A New Hypothesis on the Compositional Structure of Timaeus' Monologue," in *Platonic Investigations*, ed. Dominic J. O' Meara (Washington, DC: Catholic University of America Press, 1985), 66–67, points out that Timaeus takes up and discusses particular human senses in the reverse order of the senses he stated earlier that the cosmos lacked, because it didn't need them—touch, taste, odors, colors.

section) as the cause of hearing, and the mixtures that may produce our perceptions of a variety of colors, Timaeus concludes his discussion of our affections (*pathē*) by emphasizing their fundamental unknowability—at least by us. No one but a god could give a full account of all our sensations and their causes. (This statement should be contrasted with Socrates' claim in the *Phaedrus* 246a that it is beyond the power of any mortal to speak adequately about the idea of the immortal soul.) Timaeus and Socrates agree that what is purely sensible is not knowable by human beings. We recognize and talk about the sensible images of intelligible beings; we cannot analyze undifferentiated flux. In contrast to Timaeus, however, Socrates insists on the mediating, even formative role of human *logos* and opinion (*doxa*) in our perceptions of sensible things. That is the reason he insists on examining the opinions of his interlocutors rather than analyzing human sensations as Timaeus does.

6. The Construction of the Human Being

Having laid out the two essentially different kinds of causes—the good and the necessary—that have to come together in the genesis of both the cosmos and the human being, Timaeus finally turns to the construction of the human. Ignored by most commentators who concentrate on his "cosmology," Timaeus nevertheless reminds his auditors that the generation of human beings was supposed to be the point or purpose of his entire discourse. The constitution of the human being proves to be an image of the way in which the good is combined with the necessary.[63] As we have already seen, Timaeus' account of the intelligible construction of the cosmos is inferred from human sensory experience.

a. The Body in Relation to the Soul

The physical organization of the body reflected the hierarchy of its psychic contents. Because anything the god made became immortal, he had to hand the construction of the human being over to his "offspring," the immortal heavenly god(s). Taking the divine part of the human soul from him, they placed it in a spherical bone called the head on top, an indication of its superiority to everything lower. Spreading the mortal soul, which contained all the affections—pleasures, pains, thoughtless rashness and fear, anger which is difficult to assuage, and credulous hope—mixed with

63. Brague (ibid., 34–83) shows that the three parts of Timaeus' speech correspond to the three parts of the human body, as Timaeus describes it.

irrational sensation and all-venturing eros throughout the body they create as soul's chariot, they separated the head from the trunk by a narrow
neck to prevent the defilement of the divine by the mortal.[64] They then
divided the human torso into two parts, housing the part of the soul that
partakes of courage and spirit in the upper part, so that it might cooperate
with reason in forcibly keeping down the desires in the lower part. The
upper part of the soul was thus associated with the heart, which heats up
the blood when reason sends word that some unjust action has occurred,
and the lungs, which cool the blood when it becomes overheated and so
restore equilibrium. The part of the soul that desires food and drink was
housed lower in the navel, "building a sort of trough for the feeding of the
body, . . . as though it were a wild beast which tied to the rest, they had to
feed if the mortal kind were to be" (*Timaeus* 70e).

Since human desires do not understand reason, although they have
some perception of it, Timaeus suggests, the god put the liver alongside
the bodily seat of the desires. Receiving the blows of sounds heard, the
liver produces images and phantasms that frighten the unreasoning desires into obedience. Nowhere do we see more clearly how the human is
constructed as well as possible as in the use of this base part as the seat of
the divinations to control our incontinent desires. Arising when human beings are asleep, delirious, or in the thrall of some enthusiasm, the images
produced in and by the liver are not works of people in their right minds.[65]
The length of the coils of their intestines also helps prevent human beings
from giving way to incontinence. If our bellies were not designed to hold
superfluous food and drink, we might not merely become diseased as a
result of gluttony; the insatiable desire for food and drink that would arise
if nourishment passed through us too quickly would prevent any human
from pursuing philosophy or music. The placement and design of our digestive organs thus secure the possibility of our leading not merely orderly
but happy lives.

64. Timaeus' use of the term "chariot" has led some commentators erroneously to equate his
account of the relation between the soul and body here with the image of the soul (but not the
body) as a chariot, drawn by Socrates in the *Phaedrus*.

65. Nowhere do we see the difference between Timaeus and Socrates more clearly than in
their respective characterizations of the images or visions people experience when not in their
right minds. In the *Phaedrus* (244a–45b) Socrates traces prophetic utterances or visions to the gods
(not the liver), and he characterizes the madness that sometimes arises from extreme grief as
a comfort rather than as a source of frightful images that serve to control the desires. Socrates
describes poetry, arising from the inspiration of the Muses, as a third sort of beneficent and hence
divinely sent madness, and philosophy as the fourth.

b. Differences between the Accounts of the Tripartite Soul and
Its Relation to the City in the Timaeus and the Republic

Timaeus may have heard Socrates give a similar account of the order of the three parts of the soul the day before in his delineation of the best regime. There are, nevertheless, important differences between the two descriptions of the tripartite soul, despite the superficial similarity. In the *Republic* (435d), Socrates explicitly stated that the account of the soul and its three parts (*eidē*), which he gives there, is not adequate; to give a precise account, he said, they would have to take a longer way. As we are reminded by comparing his account in the *Republic* with the *Timaeus*, Socrates did not relate the parts of the soul or its order to parts of the body. He associated the parts of the soul and its order with the four cardinal virtues.

Although the city Socrates described in the *Republic* came into being to facilitate the preservation of both the individual and species, its regime was explicitly designed to make its citizens as virtuous as possible. Describing not the coming into being of the city, but simply of human beings who might populate it, Timaeus contends that human beings are constituted in the best possible fashion because the organization of our digestive system allows us to learn music and become philosophers. Even though his account of the coming into being of the cosmos and the humans who inhabit it is supposed to serve as a prelude to an account of the city in action in war, he does not appear concerned about the defensive function of the guardians or about courage, the virtue most needed to perform it (even though he later puts a great deal of emphasis on the importance of gymnastic training as a source of equilibrium or balance). Courage is mentioned only once, as part of the mortal soul that cooperates with reason in repressing the gluttonous desires. Timaeus does not even mention the possibility of this part of the soul rebelling against reason (even though he acknowledged in passing that anger [*thymos*] is difficult to appease).

In the *Republic* Socrates did not, like Timaeus, divide the soul into mortal and immortal parts. Even though he stated that the soul has three parts (and so, according to his own argument in the *Phaedo*, is liable to decompose), Socrates argued that the soul is immortal. In the myth of Er he suggested that individuals should acquire an education so that they can choose their next life well. According to Timaeus, individual souls do not have the power to choose their own way of life in the future. Whether they are reborn as women or beasts, or return to their native stars, depends on the character of their present life; that character is determined more by the constitution and health of their body, the laws of the regime into which they are born, the arguments they have heard both in public and in private, and their education or lack of it, than by their individual efforts.

These differences between Socrates and Timaeus with regard to the character of the human soul can all be traced to Timaeus' contention that soul (whether cosmic or individual) does not exist separate from body, in contrast to Socrates' insistence that it does. The differences in the two philosophers' understandings of the soul in relation to the body seem, moreover, to reflect the different requirements of the good understood primarily in terms of intelligibility and the good understood primarily in terms of the just. According to Timaeus, soul is what links sensible flux to intelligible order or mind (*nous*) so that they can coexist. As a result of the soul's mediation between mind and body, both the cosmos and the constitution of the human body become intelligible. The price of that intelligibility appears, however, to be a complete loss of human freedom and individual morality. People cannot really choose how they live—or be held responsible for such a choice—if everything is ordered by reason or necessity. They cannot determine the direction or character of their own lives if everything is predetermined, by nature, for them. The extent to which the shape and character of human life are indeterminate, however, is not completely intelligible or rational.

c. The Rational and Material Elements of the Body

Having explained why it is good for human beings to have the physical constitution we do, Timaeus shows how the necessary elements were arranged to make human existence possible. This arrangement began with the marrow, composed of the best triangles mixed together to constitute a *panspermium*, from which all the different kinds of soul or animals the human could become can grow. Some of the marrow was then fired and cooled until it formed hard brittle bones to shelter the soft remainder inside. The bones were joined by softer, more flexible sinews, so that the human being could move, and the whole was protected from heat and cold by a layer of flesh.

The necessary and the good were not simply or entirely conjoined, however. Because the parts of the body most covered by flesh lost their ability to sense sharply, the gods constructing human beings had to choose whether to make us longer lived by protecting the head with more flesh, or more intelligent by leaving the head less insulated and more exposed.

They chose the latter, because a more intelligent life is superior to a longer life. When there is a tension or difference between the good and the necessary, Timaeus emphasizes, the good is and should be the supreme cause. The gods did provide the head with a covering of skin and hair to give it some protection. They also provided the fingertips with hard nails, because they knew nails would be useful for the animal reborn as a woman or beast. The mouth represented the conjunction of the best with the necessary insofar as it both emits speech and takes in food.

Because mortal animals perish unless they replenish their essentially transitory constituent elements, the divine craftsmen also engendered a nature akin to the human (so that it or the triangles of its constituent elements could be decomposed, absorbed, and reconstituted) to provide nutrition, although its looks and sensations were those of a different kind of animal. Plants can justly be called "animals" because they are living; they partake of the third form of soul, which is seated between the midriff and navel in humans, which shares in no way at all in opinion and reasoning and intellect, but only in sensation. Once again, Timaeus reminds his auditors, he does not define soul in terms of self-motion; precisely because it lacks self-motion, he states (77c), this form of soul or "animal" remains fixed and rooted down.

d. The Importance of Maintaining a Balance

Having described the entry (mouth) and what is to be taken in, Timaeus details the complex system of channels whereby human beings breathe, digest, and circulate the elementary triangular particles through the blood. Like the interpenetration of the elements, air and blood circulate through our bodies because of the pressure that bodies entering exert on those already present, in the absence of a void. When people are young, the triangles constituting the elements in their constitution are fresh and strong, so that they break up and absorb those that enter. When people get older, however, their constituent triangles weaken and disintegrate when they are pressed and penetrated by more active elements from outside.

All the diseases of the body derive from an excess or deficiency of the four elements, which results in the transformation of the blood into bile or phlegm, crumbling of the bones, or inflammation. Unable to replace necessary elements or grow, the body begins to disintegrate and destroy itself. The diseases (nosēmata) of the soul also result from excess or deficiency, in the first instance of pleasure and pain, but these sensory phenomena have their source in bodily deficiencies. Ignorance or folly (anoia) is a disease of the soul that arises from either madness (*mania*, "loss of one's right mind") or stupidity (*amathia*, "lack of learning"), and both these psychic conditions are produced by excessive pleasure or pain. "When a human is overjoyed or suffers in a contrary way from pain, and hastens inopportunely to seize the one while fleeing the other, he can neither see nor hear anything correctly, goes crazy, and is least able to partake of reason" (*Timaeus* 86b–c). Those who are full of sexual desire, for example, experience a combination of intense pleasure and pain that tends to drive them mad. People who blame sexual incontinence on a lack of mastery of pleasure (or immoderation) are mistaken, however. Sexual incontinence is generally a result of overly porous bones, which allow the marrow or seed to flow too freely. Other psychic disorders like bad temper, melancholy, recklessness, cowardice, and forgetfulness and slow learning (the affections he associated earlier with the mortal soul) can be shown to be the effects of bodily pains or deprivations as well. Such disorders are not the result, as Socrates often suggested, of erroneous opinions about what is truly good, which can be corrected by means of his elenctic examinations of his interlocutors.

Like Socrates, Timaeus insists that no one is willingly bad. When human beings are bad (because the cause of our existence is good, we should recall), we should blame their defective bodies on the bad regimes that did not force them to engage in studies that, if undertaken from childhood, might have remedied their defects.

Timaeus had been assigned to show how the cosmos and the human beings who were to people Socrates' city in speech came into being; the education of the guardians and the description of the regime in action had been left, respectively, to Socrates and Critias. Timaeus thus contents himself with a brief account of the ways in which the diseases of both body and soul can be remedied and health preserved. It is just, he observes, that the good receive more attention than the bad. The good is the beautiful, and the beautiful is a matter of proportion. "With respect to health and diseases and virtue and vices, there isn't a single proportion or lack of proportion more important than that of the soul in relation to body" (87d). We recognize the importance of proportion among the body parts: if they are ill-fitted to each other, they not only look ugly but they also do not function well. The same principle applies to the soul in relation to the body. If it is too strong, it puts too much stress on the body, which becomes weak and sick. Likewise, if the body is too strong for the soul, the person will become stupid. The remedy in all cases is to exercise both the soul and the body by keeping them constantly in motion and so to maintain a balance. If one undertakes such exercises in music and philosophy for the soul and gymnastics for the body, there will be no need to employ purgative drugs. Because thought should guide a man's life, it is important to exercise this part of the soul most vigorously. Those who do not will suffer the results, not only in an unpleasant, incontinent, and hence unhappy life now, but also in future reincarnations.

e. The Generation of the Other Species from Degenerate Men

Timaeus does not describe the generation of women, birds, beasts, and fish that follows in terms of justice (*dikaiosynē*) or penalties (*dikai*). If bodily defects or bad regimes cause disorders of the soul, the individuals are not justly to blame for their own faults.

Since his account of the cosmos would be incomplete if he did not describe the generation of other kinds of animals, Timaeus explains briefly that men who had been cowardly and lived unjustly were reborn as women. Only after some men were reborn as women did the organs that make the sexual generation of human beings possible come into being. Sexual intercourse among human beings is certainly not good, according to Timaeus; it was not even clearly necessary. (Timaeus was asked merely to explain the genesis of *andres*, not their preservation or propagation.) The animals living in the other regions also came into being from defective men. Birds resulted from a remodeling of men "harmless but light-minded" (*Timaeus* 91d), who studied the heavenly bodies but mistakenly believed that the truth about them was gained by sight rather than mind; these men sprouted feathers rather than hair. Men who constantly looked down toward their navel and its desires, no longer making use of the circuits in their heads or looking up to the heavens, were reborn as four-legged beasts or even worse, the footless kind that crawl on the earth. The lowest and stupidest, which no longer deserved to breathe air, were relegated to water.

7. THE APOLITICAL IMPLICATIONS

By the end of his speech it becomes clear that Timaeus has not given an account of the genesis of the cosmos that explains how the human beings who were to populate Socrates' city in speech came to be. On the contrary, Timaeus' account makes it impossible for there to be females who could perform the function of the guardians and so should receive the same education.[66] According to his account, females are cowardly by nature. Second and even more important, according to Timaeus, there were no differences in the divine parts or minds of human beings at the beginning. To avoid responsibility for making some better than others, Timaeus' god made humans equal in the highest and most important respect.[67] His argument may be good for establishing the dignity, if not partial divinity, of human beings in general; if, however, there are no natural differences in intellectual talents, proclivities, or potentials, there is no just basis for the division of labor. The assignment of functions in the city becomes a result of random or, at most, necessary (as in the case of sex) bodily differences. The natural ground of the definition of justice in Socrates' city has been erased.

The account Timaeus gives of the coming into being of humans indicates the need for a kind of civic education. People are not willingly bad, he insists. The motions of our souls were disrupted at birth by the juxtaposition with the body and its senses. To regain psychic order, people have to grow up with a good regimen and thus in a good regime.

Timaeus' emphasis on the disorderly motions of human beings at birth and the importance of teaching them order through regular exercise or motion of body and soul has reminded some readers of the Athenian Stranger. But the Athenian proposed laws to train all the citizens of his regime to be courageous and moderate—and a few future guardians to be knowledgeable not only about mathematics but also about the ideas of the virtues, the noble and the good. Timaeus regards education primarily as a means of enabling human beings to study the heavens not merely to learn numbers (which, the Athenian pointed out, have a lot of political uses), but to duplicate the intelligible movements of the heavenly bodies within themselves in thought and so to live happily. Timaeus does not prescribe any sort of training in civic virtues or beliefs.

66. Cf. David Krell, "Female Parts in *Timaeus*," *Arion*, n.s., 2/3 (1975): 400–421.

67. Socrates also suggests (*Republic* 518c) that all human beings qua human beings have a certain common intellectual capacity when he says that the power that enables humans to acquire knowledge is in the soul of each, but that the instrument with which each learns must be turned around from that which is coming into being to that which always is. Differences in knowledge are partly a product of education and hence of the political association, but in the *Republic* (485a–87a) Socrates also acknowledges natural differences in intellectual ability and philosophical desire. Likewise in the *Phaedrus* (249e–50a) Socrates insists that every human soul has had some glimpse of the beings-in-themselves. His description of a variety of different types of human souls nevertheless stands in marked contrast to Timaeus' account of the generation of different types of animals from a single kind of human soul.

Although in his account of the construction of the human head, Timaeus admits a tension, if not disjunction, between the best or intelligent and that which is necessary for protection or survival, he does not appear to recognize such a tension in human communities. He deals with human beings solely as individuals. Although he acknowledges a need for training, both of the body to become healthy and of the soul in mathematics, he never concerns himself with the content of what was traditionally thought to constitute the "musical" part of an education—stories about the gods (which he briefly included in his account only because they were old and not because they had any reason in or behind them), the coming into being of the cosmos, and the opinions concerning the good and bad in human life to which these stories gave rise.

When Socrates praises Timaeus as a poet (*poiētēs*) in the *Critias* (108b), he suggests that Timaeus' explanation of the genesis of the cosmos is vastly superior to that given by any of the previous poets or philosophers in terms of the gods or flux. It is not too difficult to see the reasons why. In contrast to poets like Hesiod and pre-Socratic philosophers like Heraclitus or Empedocles, Timaeus had incorporated Parmenides' insight into the unchanging character of purely intelligible being(s) as opposed to becoming. Timaeus had also incorporated Pythagoras' understanding of the way and extent to which sensible things can be described in numerical and geometrical terms. In contrast to the poets, Timaeus had thus shown how the sensible world could be made intelligible. Since sensibility is not possible without matter in motion, Timaeus had joined matter or the "stuff" of flux to intelligence by making its motions intelligible—either in themselves, like the movements of the heavenly bodies, or in their effects, like the geometric shapes of the elements and their interpenetration of each other as a result of the centripetal pressure exerted on them by the circular revolutions of the cosmic soul. He had even given an account of the component parts and construction of the human soul and body on the basis of his analysis of the intelligible order and material of the cosmos as a whole.

Unlike the pre-Socratic poets, Timaeus shows that there is a cosmological and hence natural basis for philosophy. He argues that it is possible, therefore, for human beings, by nature, to live orderly, just, satisfying, and hence happy lives. Unlike both the pre-Socratic poets and Socrates, however, Timaeus is not able to give an account of the origins and character of human politics, precisely because he recognizes only bodily desires or the desire for knowledge. He does not recognize a desire for honor.

He reduces the kind of inspired madness from which Socrates suggested both poetry and philosophy are born to a function of the liver. The "fantastic" images the liver produces serve to frighten the bodily desires into submission or to repress them. Timaeus is absolutely silent about the human ability to imagine a better state of human affairs, a state that does not currently exist—or, even to imagine a city that exists only "in speech"—as a dream, much less as a goal of human endeavor. His philosophers perceive and contemplate the intelligibility of regularly repeated motions; they do not show others how to improve.

In the *Republic* Socrates also suggested that human beings could live happy, orderly lives in the "true" simple city, if they restricted their desires to what they needed to survive. It was Glaucon who objected to life in this "city of pigs" and so expressed the characteristically human desire to have more than what is necessary, which, in giving rise to injustice, also gives rise to the need for guardians and so for a political as opposed to a simply economic division of labor between rulers and ruled. Philosophy was introduced into Socrates' city in speech primarily as a means of controlling the unjust desires of the nonphilosophers, especially the guardians. Thus far he and Timaeus are in agreement. They both also recognize a great natural desire (*erōs*) on the part of some human beings to obtain true knowledge. Both also suggest that philosophers alone possess true virtue. According to Timaeus, that virtue consists in duplicating the intelligible order of the cosmos in the mind of the philosopher who contemplates it. According to Socrates, philosophers possess all the other virtues as a result of the strength of their desire for the truth, not because they entirely possess it.[68]

Although he recognizes an erotic desire for knowledge, Timaeus treats all other forms of eros as signs of bodily inadequacy and sources of disorder. Because he treats eros, or desire more generally, simply as a sign of bodily deficiency and not as a spur to action, he has to posit a deux ex machina as both the origin and sustaining force of nature—cosmic as well as human. Timaeus does not merely abstract from the difference between generation and fabrication the way Socrates does in the *Philebus*;

---

68. Socrates also argued that philosophers would become the only just rulers because they could not obtain what they particularly want by means of political power. They would rule, therefore, not in their own interest but only for the sake of others. Timaeus suggests that philosophers should rule, that is, establish and maintain political order, because they understand the order of the whole and have replicated it in themselves. They will be able to design a regime that will enable others to acquire such order and impose it on those who do understand the reasons for it.

he substitutes fabrication for generation. As a result, he is able to make the order of things or the cosmos more intelligible. But he is not able to explain why animals, especially human beings, strive to perpetuate their own existence. Bodily existence is not good or worth preserving in itself, according to Timaeus; it is good and necessary only insofar as it completes the whole. The best life for a human being is to recapture and duplicate the orderly motions of the cosmos in his soul, so that soul will return to its star and not undergo the trauma of rebirth in sensible form. Socrates suggests something similar in the *Phaedrus* (248e–49a), when he says that the souls of philosophers will not be reborn in bodily form for 10,000 years, and in the *Phaedo* (82b–84b), where he suggests that they will go to live with the gods and not be reincarnated at all.[69] According to Socrates in the *Phaedrus*, however, an embodied soul can achieve knowledge of the purely intelligible beings it strives to contemplate only by seeing them, indirectly or mediately, in the countenance of a beloved and seeking to help the beloved person realize the virtue of which he was initially only an image by striving to become virtuous himself. According to Socrates, human beings can acquire knowledge only with the assistance and in the company of other human beings. For Timaeus, regimen, regime, and conversations are all merely means, preparing or preventing human beings from acquiring the bodily self-control and intellectual ability needed to discover and then contemplate the intelligible order of the heavens. There is nothing virtuous (just, moderate, or brave) about this order or the cosmic soul to be found in it. Nor is the intelligible order of the heavens discovered in or by conversations with other human beings. According to Timaeus, the happiness of the philosopher does not consist in or require friendship; his life is not pleasant so much as painless. He selflessly forgets the limitations imposed by his own body by contemplating the eternal order of the whole.

Inferring the intentional fabrication of the cosmos from its observable, intelligible order, Timaeus posits a divine demiurge. He does not claim to prove the existence of the demiurge. He does show that human beings have to learn both to control their own bodily urges and to understand the mathematics necessary to perceive and replicate the cosmic circles of the same and the other in their own minds. But Timaeus does not provide a motive or reason, for those who experience the benefits of

---

69. On his deathbed in the *Phaedo* (82a–84b), Socrates again suggests that philosophers can escape the punishment of rebirth. In this case he argues for the importance of an ascetic life, which, free from the attachments of the body, would be both moderate and brave.

contemplating the order of the heavens, to be concerned about the education of their fellow citizens or the form of the political regime.[70] His contemplative philosophers do not appear to fear harm from other animals or humans any more than they seek to improve themselves by educating others.

Timaeus admits that human beings are not complete or self-sufficient the way the cosmos is, but he does not seem to think that human beings must live together in order to survive or to procreate in order to preserve the species. Treating human beings as individuals rather than as essentially or necessarily social animals, he describes both human beings and their necessary nourishment as plants. Placed in suitable circumstances (like those of the Egyptians on the Nile), people can acquire everything they need. Timaeus does not speak, like the Eleatic Stranger, of the need human beings have to develop arts to protect themselves from wild animals; such animals only arise, according to Timaeus, from degenerate human beings. Nor does Timaeus observe, as Critias soon will, that human beings can seek knowledge only after they have acquired enough wealth not merely to provide for their vital necessities but to allow some leisure. Timaeus traces human sexuality to corruption rather than corruption to sexual generation (like Socrates in the *Republic*). According to Timaeus, human beings do not have to come together to procreate or to seek immortality by means of their more intellectual endeavors. Those who learn to duplicate the cosmic order in their own minds by contemplating it will return to the stars, where their souls had originally been planted.

Timaeus does not take any account of the need for the knowledge or virtue that well-educated human beings must develop to defend themselves from others less well proportioned or ruled. He treats human degeneration as a necessary result of physical inadequacies magnified by lack of training. By relegating each kind of animal to a different space or element, he hides the conflict—erotic and thumotic (desirous and aggressive as well as defensive)—that results from "degeneration." As initially agreed, he leaves the education of the guardians to Socrates, but he erases the natural source of that education and the division of labor that supports it. Timaeus does not give an account of the emergence or need for political

70. In terms of the famous cave image in the *Republic*, Timaeus indicates the motive or power—love of knowledge—that leads a philosopher to ascend the steep, rocky path to view the things in themselves, but he does not provide any reason for the philosopher to descend again to the cave.

associations, because he does not admit that nature or its god fails to provide human beings with everything they need or should truly desire.

II. *Critias*

Plato makes the limitations of Timaeus' speech as a foundation for political order even more evident in the *Critias*. First, he reminds his readers that, in striking contrast to the Athenian Stranger, Timaeus does not see much need for piety.[71]

Expressing relief at coming to the end of his long speech, Timaeus prays to the god he has just brought into being in speech (although he acknowledges that god, the cosmos, has long existed in fact) that if he has misspoken, his error will be corrected, as such errors should be, with knowledge. (Indeed, he equates such remedial knowledge with a punishment [*dikē*].) For Timaeus, in contrast to the Athenian Stranger, it is not simply the intelligible order to be found in the movements of the heavenly bodies that testifies to the existence of gods (behind, in, or somehow moving the heavens); for Timaeus, the cosmos itself is a god, because it is a whole, complete, and therefore incorruptible and everlasting (although not eternal—it is visible and has therefore come into being). Although the cosmology of the *Timaeus* has often been associated with that sketched in book 10 of the *Laws*, there is no strife between orderly and disorderly souls, according to Timaeus; human beings do not need, therefore, to seek assistance by allying themselves with the gods, as the Athenian urged.[72] Timaeus' god manufactures an orderly cosmic soul and then "persuades" the disorderly part of the whole to accept his order.

Popular acceptance of Timaeus' likely story about his constructed "god" would thus prevent two, but not all three, of the kinds of impiety the Athenian Stranger sought to counteract with his observations concerning the orderly movements of the heavens. Timaeus' cosmic god evidently

71. Neither *hosia* (referring usually to that which belongs to the gods as opposed to humans and is therefore sacred) nor *aidōs* (shame or awe) appears in the *Timaeus*. Forms of *sebas* (reverence or awe) occur twice. At 41e–42a Timaeus explains that the god shows future human souls the order of the whole (*tēn tou pantos phusin edeixe*) to make them the most god-reverencing animals (*zō[i]ōn to theosebestaton*). According to Timaeus, human reverence is a product of contemplative knowledge, not of fear or a sense of human inadequacy. At 69d6 he speaks of the reverence the created or cosmic gods have for their maker that leads them to separate his work as much as possible from the mortal parts of the human body.

72. See, e.g., Taylor, *Commentary on "Timaeus"*; Skemp, *Theory of Motion*.

exists and has effects on, even if it does not completely control, human life. It would not accept sacrifices or bribes. But it would be difficult to show that the cosmos, its maker, or soul cares about human beings or sees that justice is done. The "justice" of Timaeus' god is confined to his having all human souls begin with the same view of the cosmic order before they are planted in stars or given bodies. If these souls fail to recapture their original knowledge and order, it is not the god's fault. But the degeneration of those souls who are reborn as women, land animals, or even worse, fish is not their fault either; they failed to recapture their original orderly movements as a result of a bad body produced by a bad regimen and regime. No longer having the capacity to be educated, they have no hope of rebirth as the human beings they once were and are doomed to live unhappy lives without intelligence. Timaeus' god constitutes a cosmic order that is intelligible, even good as a whole, but that god and the order he produces appear to be perfectly indifferent to the fate or happiness of the particular living beings within it. Its goodness seems to consist, in the end, simply in supplying a foundation for contemplative philosophy.

The harsh necessities of the cosmic order might be used as an argument for the importance of establishing a good regimen and regime. Only those fortunate enough to be born and grow up under such have a chance of learning what they need to live a truly happy life. Timaeus has not provided any motive or incentive, however, for those who do manage to learn enough to duplicate the orderly motions of the cosmos within themselves to establish and maintain a good regime for others. His contemplative philosophers would appear to be as indifferent to the fate of others as their cosmic model is.

When Critias takes over the discussion, he thus expresses some dissatisfaction with the position in which he finds himself. No one in his right mind (*emphrōn*) would deny that Timaeus has spoken well, he observes. As generation after generation of scholars have agreed, Timaeus' speech was a tour de force in which he synthesized the best pre-Socratic philosophy and cosmology—Parmenidean teachings about the relation of thought to being, Pythagorean astronomy and mathematics, and Empedoclean cosmology and medicine. Partly because he has to follow such an impressive performance, Critias asks that he be given the same indulgence he claims Timaeus had requested (although he had not) in light of the magnitude of his task. Critias does not seem to have understood the reasons why Timaeus insisted that he could only give a "likely" account of the origins of the cosmos. Critias does not, because he does not share the Parmenidean understanding of truth as belonging only to that which always exists, from which both Timaeus and Socrates begin. Critias associates truth with factual description of particular things and deeds. He claims that his task is even more difficult than Timaeus', because he will be describing things with which his audience is familiar, and they will therefore be able to identify any mistakes he makes.

Critias acknowledges that there is something grudging and ungracious in his request, but Socrates grants it without hesitation. He extends the indulgence, unasked, to Hermocrates so that he will not have to repeat the request. Socrates merely warns Critias that in the mind (*dianoian*) of those gathered in this theater, the preceding poet (*poiētēs*; *Critias* 108b) has already gained wonderful renown.[73] Socrates treats Timaeus' speech as a performance that would make him famous; he does not say that he is persuaded of its truth.

Not wanting to accept the secondary status to which Socrates seems to relegate his more practical and less philosophical interlocutors, and anxious perhaps to move quickly from the promised praise of old Athens to a condemnation of the present regime, Hermocrates advises Critias to stop complaining and get on with it. Urging Critias to invoke Apollo as the god of victory and the Muses as the daughters of Memory and the source of inspiration for poets—and to proceed courageously to describe the virtue of the citizens of his ancient city—the Syracusan points to the two additional ways in which Timaeus' speech falls short and the task, therefore, that remains for Critias (as well as, perhaps, for Hermocrates himself).

For all its brilliance, Timaeus' speech did not perform the function he was assigned, inasmuch as he did not show how the people who were to populate Socrates' city in speech came into being. Critias has to supply that defect. Returning to the ancient stories concerning the Olympian gods, which Timaeus had grudgingly and briefly incorporated into his account merely as old stories, Critias describes the autochthonous birth, first of the citizens of Athens and then of the kings of Atlantis. In both cases the divine source and autochthonous birth serve to establish the original justice of the two cities by showing that they did not acquire their lands

---

73. In contrast to the *Republic* and *Phaedrus*, Socrates does not identify poetry here with speaking in meter. He follows Timaeus, perhaps, who called the demiurge a maker (*poiētēs*) as well as a father (*patēr*) in identifying poetry with the making of images and not confining poetry to speech at all.

or wealth by force and that their rulers deserved to be rulers because of their superior, divinely generated natures.

By describing the extent and wealth of the two ancient cities, Critias also shows how their people were able not merely to meet their needs and so to survive, generation after generation, but to obtain the wealth necessary to provide them with the leisure to acquire knowledge. He thus gives an account of the material conditions of both political order and philosophical investigations and, consequently, of human excellence or virtue that Timaeus had not.

As promised, Critias' description of prehistoric Athens echoes Socrates' description of the best city in speech—at least in certain respects. In the *Republic* (377e–78e), Socrates had warned legislators that they should not allow poets to tell stories about the gods fighting with each other for rule or adulterous sexual gratification. Rather than repeat the traditional tale about the competition between Athena and Poseidon to become the patron god(dess) of Athens, to which Socrates himself refers in the *Menexenus* (237c–d), Critias divides the hegemony of his two cities between the gods from the very beginning. Because the gods knew what was right and suitable, he states (*Critias* 109b), they accepted their allotments of land without strife. With the assistance of her half brother and fellow lover of the arts, Hephaestus, Athena not only planted the seeds of future Athenian citizens but also gave them their regime. According to the traditional account, Hephaestus spilled his sperm on the ground in an attempt to rape Athena. According to Critias, the people of prehistoric Athens did not grow up as a result of desire and force. The two gods cooperated in founding the city not only because they had the same father but also because they shared the same sort of practical wisdom.

The regime Critias describes in prehistoric Athens also mandated some of the most notable institutions of Socrates' city in speech. The guardians lived together in a single dwelling close to other public buildings and temples on the top of the acropolis, separated from the craftsmen and farmers who had homes on the sides of the hill or in the fields. Having no private property of their own (110c), the guardians received what they needed to survive and practice their art from their fellow citizens. Prehistoric Athens could support a large host of soldiers not otherwise engaged in productive labor, Critias explains, because the land was more extensive and richer than it now is, much of the soil having been washed away in erosion.

Nevertheless, the regime Critias describes differs in significant respects from Socrates' city in speech. Although the guardians lived together in a common dwelling on the top of the acropolis during the winter, and all their public buildings were devoid of gold or silver (of which they made no use), Critias also says that "they aimed at the mean between luxurious display and meanness, and built themselves attractive [kosmias] houses to live in during the summer and passed them on unaltered to their children" (112c). Unlike Timaeus (but like Socrates), Critias explicitly includes women among those who, renowned for both their beauty and virtue, acted as guardians of their own citizens and leaders, by their own consent, of the other Greeks. Maintaining their number at 20,000, Critias also suggests, the guardians practiced some sort of birth control. Nevertheless, it is clear, they did not have women and children in common or entirely eschew private property. They knew who their heirs were and had houses to bequeath to their descendants.

The limitations of Critias' speech as well as the reasons his account of prehistoric Athens cannot satisfy Socrates' desire to see his city in speech in action become clearer when Critias describes the aggressor from which prehistoric Athens saved Greece, imperial Atlantis. As several commentators have pointed out, the two sides in the great war look very much like two stages of Athenian history.[74] In describing the two warring cities, Critias thus falls prey to the fault of the poets, as Socrates initially described it (Timaeus 19d). Critias is able only to describe (or rearrange elements of)

---

74. Cf. Vidal-Naquet, "Athens and Atlantis"; Brisson, "Critias de Platon," 402–38; Gill, "Genre," 294–98; and Clay, "Plan of Critias," 49–54. Friedländer, Plato, 1:203, argues, on the contrary, that Atlantis represents Persia. There are indubitably common elements. In Thucydides 6.75 Hermocrates accuses Athens of having become the new Persia. I cannot subscribe to Vidal-Naquet's further claim that the conflict between the landed power of prehistoric Athens and the maritime empire of Atlantis reflects the fluctuation between the elements of earth and water in Timaeus' cosmology. In the latter, earth and fire constitute the poles; air and water are in between. Robert Brumbaugh, "A Note on the Numbers in Plato's Critias," Classical Philology 43 (1948): 40–42, points out the contrast between Critias' mention of one number (20,000) in describing prehistoric Athens and his use of many multiples of five and six in describing not only the land but also the meetings of the kings and the enormous army of Atlantis. Once again the numbers do not parallel the multiples (squares and cubes) of two and three that Timaeus employs in constructing the world soul or the elements out of the regular solids. Nor does the emphatic use of number and measurement seem to support the characterization of Atlantis as "fluid." Cf. Thomas G. Rosenmeyer, "The Numbers in Plato's Critias: A Reply," Classical Philology 44 (1949): 117–20. (Like Brisson, I am not persuaded by Rosenmeyer's further contention that the Critias with its famous mythical city is merely playful.) The reason for the numbers in Critias' description of Atlantis seems to me to make it more concrete and realistic; he did not need to specify the size of parts of Athens, because his interlocutors had seen them.

cities with which he is familiar.[75] Although he is an experienced practical politician with some philosophical education, he proves as unable to describe an entirely new, entirely just city in action as Timaeus proved unable to show how the people of such a city could have come into being.[76]

Like the brave Acharnians at Marathon, the guardians of prehistoric Athens fended off an attack on Greece by an aggressively expanding empire from across the sea. Like the Spartans (who also banned gold and silver within their city and dedicated their lives to training themselves to be virtuous soldiers rather than productive laborers) at Thermopylae, the prehistoric Athenian guardians also perished as a result—in this case, in a flood caused by an earthquake. Further like Sparta, prehistoric Athens was, according to Critias, a landed power. It had no harbors, ships, or walls. Before Pericles had all his fellow citizens move inside the city at the beginning of the Peloponnesian War, most of the citizens of historical Athens lived in the country. A conservative oligarch like Critias would look back with pleasure on his city's earlier customs and days.

Founded by the god of the sea, Atlantis looks in many ways like a glorified version of imperial, maritime Athens. As in Athens, according to both the traditional stories and Critias' account, the rulers of Atlantis were born autochthonously from divine seed.[77] Both their claim to the land and their rule were therefore just. According to Critias, however, the divine seed was not planted in the ground. Poseidon mated with the daughter of a man born autochthonously on the island, which was this god's allotment, and produced five sets of twins.[78] They and their heirs ruled the vast territory (larger than Libya or Africa and Asia combined) west of Gibraltar as allied monarchs on terms much like those of the original alliance of the Dorian kings of Sparta, Argos, and Messina (cf. *Laws* 690e–93b). Each was to rule on the basis of consent of the people of the territory and to come to the

75. Critias draws from other writings, both poetic, for example, the description of the Phaiakians' Scheria in Homer's *Odyssey* 7, and historical, for example, Herodotus' descriptions of Ecbatana and Babylon (1.98) with which he was familiar as well as from actual cities and events.

76. Aristotle *Politics* 1266a35 observes that all proposals for new regimes other than those "Socrates" presents in the *Laws* and the *Republic* are closer to regimes that have already been established.

77. Beginning his description of Atlantis, Critias explains (113a–b) that there is a reason he gives Greek names to barbarians. In transcribing the Egyptian records, Solon translated the names into Greek. The Greek names would nevertheless make Atlantis remind both Critias' auditors and Plato's readers of more recent Greek people, cities, and events.

78. The story is reminiscent of Homer's account of the heritage of the rulers of the Phaiakians in *Odyssey* 7.47–77. Atlantis also resembles the island kingdom of Phaiakia in its wealth.

assistance of any other king threatened with a violent overthrow. Perhaps because Poseidon left laws requiring the kings to meet together every five or six years (alternating odd with even) to judge infractions of the law and prohibiting the execution of any king without the explicit consent of a majority of the others, the alliance of Atlantic monarchies lasted much longer than that of the Dorians.[79] Perhaps the alliance of Atlantic monarchies lasted as long as it did merely because the combination of vast territory and commerce enabled them to amass as much wealth as they were able to use or imagine, so that they did not feel impelled to attack or to try to overthrow anyone else. Since their abundant land produced everything they might want, much less need (including metals and horses), the trade in which they engaged resulted in superfluous luxury. Unlike the prehistoric Athenians, the kings of Atlantis erected gold- and silver-plated temples and palaces. They also overcame the natural isolation, defenses, and self-sufficiency of the central island by building canals, bridges, and harbors.

Although Critias demonstrates much greater awareness than Timaeus of the need to satisfy the material requirements of human existence, he shows much less understanding of the ways in which human desires need to be formed, directed, and controlled by a regime. Rather than explaining the gradual corruption of the rulers of Atlantis by the absence of laws that directed their energies to the acquisition of virtue rather than the accumulation of wealth, Critias attributes the growth of the unjust imperial desires that led them to try to conquer the entire world to the increasing diminution of the divine portion of their nature, resulting from generations of intermarriage with other humans. "So long as the inherited nature of the god remained strong in them, they were led by his law and like-minded. Truly and prudently . . . they scorned everything but virtue . . . so their wealth did not make them drunk with pride so that they lost control and went to ruin" (*Critias* 120e–21a). Ironically predicting the reaction of later readers of the dialogue (who have been much more interested in resurrecting the lost continent than in the quasi-Socratic regime of prehistoric Athens), Critias concludes that just at the point Atlantis appeared most beautiful in all its wealth and glory to external observers, the souls of its rulers had become ugliest in the eyes of the all-seeing gods. He breaks off his account by observing, in words reminiscent of the beginning of the

---

79. Critias does not explicitly say so. Nor does he speculate on the way in which multiple sets of twin kings could have constituted some of the checks and balances characteristic of the mixed regime that saved Sparta, according to the Athenian Stranger.

Odyssey, that Zeus called an assembly of his fellow deities to inflict punishment on the unjust.

III. Conclusion

It is no accident, I think, that Plato ends the dialogue with Critias' evocation, if not imitation, of Homer. What Critias needs in order to show his two cities in war is a depiction of the motive force; that force, Homer showed in both his epics, is the righteous anger and consequent desire for revenge that leads human beings to overcome their fear of death and risk their lives to avenge the loss of those they love. Critias has gone beyond Timaeus in acknowledging not only that human beings need resources to enable them to seek knowledge but also that, recognizing our weaknesses and vulnerabilities as mortals, humans tend to seek assistance from higher powers. But Critias has not pointed toward anything like a thirst for justice. It was, however, a desire to know what justice is, in order to determine whether, and if so, why, living justly is superior to living unjustly, that gave rise to Socrates' elaboration of the city in speech in the *Republic*. There is a reason, it appears in the end, that the speech Socrates said he wanted to hear about his city at war sounds very much like an epic poem.

Even though they combine practical political experience with philosophical erudition, neither Timaeus nor Critias has been able to describe Socrates' city in speech at war, because neither of these philosopher-statesmen has the understanding of human passions possessed by the poet Homer. Yet, we recall, at the end of the *Republic* Socrates congratulated himself and his interlocutors for banishing the poets, because they corrupted their auditors by arousing and thus strengthening their passions at the expense of their reason, and failed to depict the way in which human beings could achieve happiness in a life of philosophy. Socrates held out a hope that the poets might be readmitted, however. In the *Timaeus-Critias* we learn why such a readmission is not merely desirable but necessary. The emergence of political order, much less a just political order, cannot be explained without taking account of human desires. Human beings cannot achieve order, in their relations with others or within themselves, simply by repressing or controlling the passions with reason. If human actions are to be ordered and directed, human desires must be attached to appropriate goals. Not merely must legislators learn from the poets how to persuade people to obey the laws, as the Athenian Stranger suggested with his preludes. We now see that philosophers, like Socrates, have to surpass the poets in discovering what human beings really desire or want.

In explicitly describing his account of the coming into being of the cosmos as an *eikōs mythos*, Timaeus suggested that his "prelude" had something in common with poetry not only in content but also in form. Like Hesiod, Timaeus described the genesis not only of the gods but also of the elements and of the living things constituted from them—human beings, animals, and plants. Like poets more generally, he explicitly presented his account in terms of images and in a narrative. Indeed, he suggested that the necessity of presenting an account to human beings, in a narrative, of the cosmic order in which all the parts exist simultaneously, that is, presenting the fabrication of that order as if it occurred in time, was one of the reasons his description could not be entirely consistent. He described the intelligible order of the cosmos in terms of images because human beings come to understand purely intelligible ideas only in sensible form. He thus examined the way in which our sensations inform and are informed by our thoughts. He did not show the way in which human beings combine sensible things or their experience with thought to imagine new and better states of affairs, like Socrates' city in speech, which could come into being, although so far they have not.

In terms of the famous image of the divided line Socrates employed in the *Republic*, Timaeus showed how the cosmos can be understood to be ordered according to the eternal, purely intelligible ideas of the same and the other (represented by the topmost portion of the line), composed of sensible things (the top portion of the bottom part of the line), which are constructed out of elements that can be described in purely intelligible geometric terms (the bottom portion of the top part of the line). He mentioned reflections of sensible things (the bottom portion of the bottom part) only as the fantastic images produced by the liver in a deranged mind to frighten the senses into obeying the strictures of reason. He did not even mention, much less take account of, the kinds of artifacts or images intentionally manufactured by poets or legislators that Socrates suggested, in his other famous image of the cave, gave rise to the shadows or opinions human beings mistake for the truth. These images were not derived from mere sensation. Like statues of Nike or Dike, they constituted sensible representations of the abstract because generalized objects of human striving, that is, the things people believe to be good, noble, or just. As Socrates observes in the *Phaedo* (100a), those who seek to discover what truly is (*ta onta*) by examining speeches or arguments (*logoi*) are not dealing any more (or, we might say in this context, any less) with images (*eikones*) than those who study facts (*erga*).

Looking back from the *Timaeus-Critias* to Socrates' own description of his city in speech in the *Republic*, we see that Plato's philosophers talk about two different kinds of ideas and three different kinds of images. Timaeus gives his account of the intelligibility and order of the cosmos on the basis of purely intelligible beings or concepts like same and other or the geometrical definitions of proportion, line, figure, and solid. Socrates suggests that philosopher-kings have to seek knowledge particularly of the purely intelligible forms of the virtues, the beautiful, and the good. The first kind of ideas makes the shapes or forms, interactions, and other movements of sensible beings intelligible as images of these ideas. The second kind of ideas constitutes the eternal, unchanging goals of human striving, goals that we never simply, completely, or always attain. The images of these ideas may take sensible form, as in the statues of "victory" or just deeds (*erga*) such as the defeat of Atlantis by Athens, but these sensible images are intelligible only as bodily representations of the ideas or, more precisely, of the opinions human beings have about the best way of life—the good, the beautiful, and the just. These opinions may, moreover, be true or false. They may be reflections of the eternally existing, unchanging ideas or artificial constructions fabricated by legislators and poets.

By contrasting the kind of ideas Timaeus employs in his account of the goodness and intelligibility of the visible cosmos with the kind of ideas Socrates uses in his analysis of the origins and ends of political association, we see the reasons Plato does not, like Aristotle, say that human beings are political by nature or that form does not exist apart from matter. In the persona of Socrates (as well as those of the Athenian and the Eleatic Strangers), Plato shows that human beings form political associations because nature does not spontaneously (despite Timaeus' suggestions to the contrary) provide for all of our needs. Likewise, in the person of Socrates, Plato insists that the forms or ideas of the virtues—the good and the beautiful—are and only are, properly speaking, in themselves, separate from sensible becoming, because they are not and cannot ever be completely realized in sensible form.

Plato's Socrates represents the contention—as controversial in his time as it is now—that human life cannot be understood or accurately described without appealing to some notion of the good, the noble, and the just. As Socrates tells his auditors in the *Phaedo* (98d–100a), it is impossible to describe the trial and conviction of a criminal simply in terms of matter in motion; as we have seen in the *Critias*, one has to take account not only of the claims about what is just but also of the desire to see it done in order to describe the actions, deeds, or facts (*erga*) of war. It is impossible to claim knowledge of the whole, if one does not have knowledge of the distinctively human. Not only do human beings constitute a part of the whole, which has to be accounted for; as Timaeus reminds us, human sensations, experience, and thought are also our only immediate sources of knowledge of the combination of the sensible and intelligible that constitutes the whole. We cannot claim knowledge of the whole, therefore, without explaining how we are able to acquire such knowledge. That is the reason, Socrates insists from the *Protagoras* and the *Alcibiades I* onward, that we have to begin our quest for knowledge with a quest for self-knowledge. In seeking to know ourselves, we necessarily ask what it is that we want; in asking what we want, we are led to inquire, in the first instance, what is good for us. Human beings cannot acquire any knowledge of the whole as good or complete in itself which is not initially colored by our desires and hence our opinions about what is good for us. We must, therefore, investigate and correct those opinions as a propaedeutic at least to acquiring knowledge of the whole.

As a comparison of the *Timaeus* with the *Philebus* quickly reminds us, the good in itself is not the same as the good for us. According to Timaeus, the cosmos is good because it is orderly, beautiful, and complete. As Socrates admits in the *Philebus*, however, human beings would not recognize a good that did not also include pleasure. Because our desires are rooted in our bodily senses of pleasure and pain, yet those pleasures and pains are shaped by our memories, experiences, and intellectual analyses of those experiences, the objects of human desire are not images of purely intelligible forms in the same way that cubes or circular revolutions of spheres are. In order to discover whether there are purely intelligible objects of human desire or whether such objects are, as both pre-Socratic poets and more recent positivistic social scientists have claimed, merely the illusory, because essentially transitory products of irrational feelings, we have to investigate not only the roots of human desires in our fundamental needs and experiences of pleasure and pain but also the inferences we draw from them, that is, our opinions. Some of the opinions we have about the good, the beautiful, or the just may be false—products of human fabrication rather than reflections of the things in themselves. In order to find out whether there is anything good, beautiful, or just in itself, we cannot simply look at what human beings do or take their statements at face value. As Socrates learned from Diotima, we have to question people about their opinions, some of which will be shown not merely to reflect their irrational roots in human desires or feelings but also to be inconsistent or false. As becomes clear in his *Apology* as well as many other dialogues, Socratic political philosophy was, therefore, necessarily confrontational.

The contrast Plato invites readers of the *Timaeus-Critias* to make between the philosopher who gives one very long speech about the construction of the entire cosmos and the silently listening Socrates, who usually stops his interlocutors from making long speeches and asks them to answer his questions briefly, does not simply point to the differences in the ideas the two philosophers have of the things that truly are, the different kinds of sensible embodiments of those ideas, or the different ways in which they seek to uncover the true in the sensible. Most important of all, Plato indicates, the two kinds of philosophy generate two different but equally partial truths. His wonder aroused by the beauty of the starry skies above, Timaeus asks what makes this vision possible. To discover and map the regular movements of the heavenly bodies as well as to give an account of our ability to perceive and calculate those movements, he demonstrates, a philosopher has to explain how sensible things can be shaped by, and move according to, intelligible principles. He also has to show how human beings are constituted so that we can come to understand the intelligible construction of the whole with our minds and sensory organs. Commentators on the *Timaeus* have often concluded, therefore, that the summary effect of his "prelude" is to show that human beings are microcosms of the whole.[80] Like the cosmos, Timaeus argues, human beings are constituted by a mixture of the good or rational with the necessary and sensible. His analysis culminates, however, in showing that there is a fundamental difference between the cosmos, which as a whole is complete and self-sufficient, and the human being, who is always needy. The sensory organs, by whose means we acquire knowledge of the external world, are signs of our own incompleteness. And it is in the area of human wants or desires that the limitations of Timaeus' contemplative philosophy come to the fore. Looked at from the perspective of the whole, human wants appear to be mere defects. Beginning from the fact of human wants, however, a philosopher like Socrates who asks what human beings truly want, and what, if anything will satisfy them, sees that human beings expand their

---

80. Both Cornford (*Plato's Cosmology*, 6) and Naddaf ("Atlantis Myth," 196) argue that there is just such a relation of macrocosm to microcosm in the *Timaeus*.

desires by imagining new and greater goods. Rather than a falling away from perfection, this philosopher sees human desires as pointing to it, as something to be achieved, but not yet existing or fully known.

It may seem as if the philosophy that looks down at the parts in light of the perfection of the whole and the philosophy that looks up, so to speak, from human desires to their satisfaction and completion should finally come together in a contemplative vision of what truly and eternally is. Looking back at the *Timaeus* in contrast to the *Symposium*, however, we see that the perfection of the whole the Timaean philosopher not merely contemplates but duplicates in himself in the circling (or sorting) of the same and the different in his mind is not the same as the vision of the beautiful in itself, which the Socratic philosopher seeks to attain. The Socratic philosopher recognizes that his view of the beautiful in itself will pass and have to be regained, because the contents of his mind are as mortal and hence changing as the components of his body. His own characteristic motion, striving, is not shared by the beautiful in itself. By comparing Timaeus' *eikōs mythos* with Socrates' image of the soul in the *Phaedrus*, we see, in the end, that the two philosophers do not have exactly the same view of what truly is or of the relation human beings have to it.

In both the *Symposium* and the *Phaedrus* we also saw that the Socratic philosopher has to determine whether his vision is merely a dream, a projection of his own desire, or true by seeing whether he can lead others to share it and the attempt to recapture it by continuing to seek knowledge. Socratic philosophizing thus requires ongoing interaction with other human beings in a way that Timaean contemplation does not. By comparing Socrates with Timaeus, we see indeed that Socratic philosophy is more political in two different respects. First, beginning with human desires, Socrates can explain why human beings form political associations and the ends as well as the characteristics of those associations in a way that Timaeus cannot. Second, because the Socratic mode of philosophizing requires a kind of social interaction, it makes its own political preconditions an explicit theme in a way Timaean contemplation does not.

Following Aristotle, many later thinkers have conceived of philosophy primarily on the basis of the Timaean model.[81] We conceive of science preeminently as knowledge of the universe; we seek it primarily by means

---

81. There are exceptions, of course. Xenophon, Cicero, Machiavelli, and Rousseau come immediately to mind. These writers have often been ignored or dismissed, however, by professional philosophers as well as by social scientists.

of empirical observations and analyses of the characteristics of sensible things, particularly as these can be expressed or enumerated in mathematical terms. In his dialogues, Plato just as clearly "privileges" Socrates. He is present in all but two of the dialogues and the major philosophical speaker in most. The preeminence of Socrates in the Platonic dialogues seems to reflect Plato's judgment that human beings must explain themselves and seek to discover what is good for them as a precondition for knowing anything else. It is not clear from the dialogues that Plato thinks that the whole is simply or perfectly intelligible. In the *Timaeus* he suggests that it is not. It is clear that Plato does not think that Socrates represents the only or even, in all respects, the best form of human knowledge. In the *Timaeus*, as in the dialogues that are shown to have occurred before and after it, Plato brings out the limits not only of Socrates' knowledge but also of its effects. Nevertheless, Plato seems to insist, we have to begin where Socrates does. The kind of philosophizing he represents is necessary, even if it is not altogether sufficient. It is necessary not merely to achieve knowledge, moreover; it is a necessary precondition for living a full and satisfying human life.

7

Socratic Practice

Even though the cosmos and human beings are both combinations of purely intelligible and sensible elements, Plato indicates in the *Timaeus*, the combination or order of the elements is different. The difference, most simply stated, is that as an intelligible whole, the cosmos is complete and self-sufficient. It moves, but its movements are circular and self-encompassing.[1] Human beings, on the other hand, are obviously not self-sufficient or complete. We are needy and desirous—of other things and other people. Both our minds and our bodies are thus directed outward, beyond the limits of our own physical constitution. Despite—or perhaps even because of—our incompleteness, Plato suggests through his depiction of Socrates, we have to begin our search for knowledge by examining the reasons for that search in our own needs and desires. Because we are human beings, we cannot, as Timaeus (and to a certain extent the Athenian Stranger) urges, look primarily to the order of the heavens to find guidance in ordering our own lives. In the dialogues that follow the *Timaeus* in dramatic dating, Plato thus returns to Socrates.[2]

---

1. Most scientists now think that the universe is constantly expanding. There is still a difference between the cosmos and the human, but the difference now is that the human remains finite whereas the cosmos appears to be infinite.

2. Although I argue that the *Theages*, *Euthydemus*, *Lysis*, *Gorgias*, and *Meno* form a group, all set toward the end of the fifth century, I recognize that their dramatic dating is controversial. As Pangle (*Roots*, 144n) notes in his translation of the *Theages*, the dramatic date of that dialogue is usually established by the reference at 129d to the expedition of Thrasyllus against Ephesus and Ionia in 409. Nails (*People*, 329), acknowledges the reference, but she points out that there is also a reference to the end of Archelaus' rule in Macedonia at 124d and that his rule ended in 399. She chooses the latter date as the dramatic date of the *Theages*, even though she ignores a similar reference in the *Alcibiades II* (141d) and suggests that the conversation related in the *Alcibiades II* prob-

ably follows closely the one related in *Alcibiades I* (332). (I do as well, primarily on the basis of its theme—the need for human beings to acquire self-knowledge, in this case, particularly because they are not gods.) A date of 399 would make the statements about Theages in the *Republic* even more anachronistic. The inconsistent dates have been one reason some scholars have concluded that both the *Theages* and the *Alcibiades II* are inauthentic (although the authenticity of the *Alcibiades II* was questioned in antiquity, whereas the authenticity of the *Theages* was not). Grote (*Plato*, 1:430) finds the reasons Schleiermacher, Stallbaum, and Ast gave for not considering the dialogue to be a work of Plato's unpersuasive. He observes that Dionysius of Halicarnassus not merely considered the dialogue authentic but pointed out "the peculiar phraseology assigned to Demodokus by remarking that the latter is presented as a person of rural habits and occupations" (1:430–31). For reasons I specify in the discussion of the dialogue later in the chapter, I do not find the case made by Mark Joyal, *The Platonic "Theages"* (Stuttgart: Franz Steiner Verlag, 2000), against Plato's authorship, convincing. Pace Joyal, I argue that what Plato shows about Socrates' practice in the *Theages* is consistent with what he shows elsewhere. The dramatic date of the *Euthydemus* has been determined primarily by the reference to Alcibiades at 275a. Nails (*People*, 316–18) suggests 407, when Alcibiades returned to Athens for four months and Clinias' father Axiochus, who had been exiled with Alcibiades, probably returned with him. She points out, correctly, that W. R. M. Lamb, the editor of the Loeb edition, incorrectly identified the famous Alcibiades with his grandfather (identified as the Alcibiades "of old" [*palaiou*], father of Clinias' father Axiochus) and thus concluded, erroneously (391n), that the dialogue must have taken place after his death in 404. Although the Alcibiades who is said "to be now" (in contrast to the Alcibiades "of old"; 275b) might be another, younger Alcibiades (b. 417/416), also a cousin of Clinias, it seems more likely that the reference is to the general and Socrates' former companion. If so, the conversation related in the *Euthydemus* should be imagined to have occurred before 404, but probably not before 407 (when it would not have been prudent to emphasize the family relation to the exiles). Observing that there is no evidence of a dramatic date of the *Lysis*, except for the fact that two of the characters (Ctesippus and Menexenus) appear in other dialogues, Nails argues that the conversation depicted in the *Lysis* must have occurred before the *Euthydemus* because the young males are called "boys" (*paides*) more frequently in the former and "youths" (*neaniskoi*) more frequently in the latter. Apparently relying on Phillip V. Stanley, "The Family Connection of Alcibiades and Axiochus," *Greek, Roman, and Byzantine Studies* 27, no. 3 (Summer 1986): 177, she claims that Plato uses the terms *pais* and *neaniskos* interchangeably to refer to Lysis (*Lysis* 205b–c). Neither she nor he seems to notice that Socrates asks about a *neaniskos* at that point unknown to him, but that Ctesippus replies by describing Hippocrates' *pais*. She does not take account of the difference in age between Ctesippus and Hippocrates, called youths at the beginning of the *Lysis* (203a), and the boys inside the palaestra (e.g., 206e), who include Lysis and Menexenus. Ctesippus appears as a member of a group of young male lovers in both the *Euthydemus* and the *Lysis* and thus to be not only approximately the same age himself but also older than the young boys depicted in the *Lysis*, who show no interest in (and perhaps even a bit of distaste for) becoming the *paidika* of an older lover (*erastēs*). Since Menexenus is said in the *Lysis* (211c) to have learned how to refute others from Ctesippus, who is shown to have learned how to argue eristically in the *Euthydemus* (294c–300d), I conclude that Plato wanted his readers to imagine the conversation related in the *Lysis* occurring not before but after the *Euthydemus* (although not very long after). The indications of the dramatic date of the *Lysis* based on the presence and depiction of Ctesippus are supported by the depiction there of Menexenus as a youth of ten to twelve years (preadolescent), who would have become old enough to compete to give the annual funeral oration, for which he seeks assistance from Socrates in the *Menexenus* (impossibly dated dramatically in 387 by the reference to the peace of Antalcidas, twelve years after Socrates died). Nails (*People*, 319) dates the *Menexenus* in 401/400 by excising the section of the text with the anachronistic reference to the battle of Corinth as an addition by copyists in the Academy. I think the conversations depicted in the *Euthydemus* and *Lysis* should also be imagined to have occurred before that related in the *Gorgias*, because, unlike the *Gorgias*, those dialogues do not contain any reference to the trial of the generals in 406 (in which Clinias' father Axiochus played an important part). Observing that Gorgias is known to have visited Athens in 427 and that Pericles, who is said to have died recently at 503c, died in the plague in 429, but that there is also a reference to the trial of the generals in 406, Arlene Saxonhouse, "An Unspoken

All Socrates ever claimed to know were *ta erōtika*, but if he truly knew about the erotic things, Socrates knew what human beings really wanted. Even though Socrates explicitly admits in both the *Philebus* and the *Phaedo* that he was never able to answer the objections Parmenides raised to his argument, Socrates was able to show, both in speech and in deed, how human life could and should be organized on the basis of purely intelligible principles. Beginning with Parmenides, other philosophers had maintained that there were purely intelligible forms of being. Unlike these other philosophers, Plato shows, Socrates saw that the intelligible principles shaped (or could shape) human life less by giving it a regular, observable, and predictable order than by providing it with true and lasting goals. That effect was, moreover, mediated by *logos*. The division of being into intelligible kinds constitutes the precondition for language, conversation, and thus philosophy, which in turn makes it possible for human beings to discover what they truly want.

All human beings want what is truly good, Socrates frequently reminds his interlocutors. But, he also recognizes, human beings do not learn to be virtuous, noble, or good merely by being told to be so. In the dialogues that follow the *Republic*, Plato does not, therefore, show Socrates trying to tell others what Glaucon could not understand—namely, his opinion about the good-in-itself. Nor does Plato show Socrates attempting to persuade other interlocutors to concur in his and Protarchus' judgment about

Theme in Plato's *Gorgias*: War," *Interpretation* 11 (May 1983): 143–44; and Benardete (*Rhetoric*, 7) point out that possible dramatic dates of the *Gorgias* span the Peloponnesian War. Nicias might appear to be alive, because at 472a Socrates says that Polus could bring the son of Niceratus along with the whole house of Pericles as witnesses. But Socrates could also mean simply that Polus could cite them as well-known examples in a speech before a court. Whereas Saxonhouse concludes that the dialogue is, therefore, explicitly fictional, E. R. Dodds, *Plato "Gorgias"* (Oxford: Clarendon Press, 1959), 7, suggests that there is no date at which we are supposed to imagine the conversation having occurred. I have dated the dialogue on the basis of the last chronological reference to the trial of the generals after Arginusae in 406. It would be possible for interlocutors to look back to people or events in the preceding two decades and declare that they are recent (compared to other historical events or personages); the reference to Pericles, "who died recently," serves to distinguish him in a list otherwise composed of leaders of previous generations: Themistocles, Miltiades, and Cimon. But it would not be possible for participants in the conversation to refer to events that had not yet occurred. Gorgias is known to have visited Athens in 427, but there is no reason that he could not have been imagined to have visited again later. Rosamond Kent Sprague, ed., *The Older Sophists* (Indianapolis: Hackett, 2001), 30, suggests that he visited the city repeatedly and may even have settled there. As Nails observes, there is little controversy about the dramatic date of the *Meno*. In *Anabasis* 2.6.21–8 Xenophon reports that Meno joined the forces of Cyrus in Asia Minor in 401 and disappeared, if he did not die shortly thereafter. Commentators generally believe that the dialogue is supposed to have occurred shortly before he left Greece in 402/401.

the character and contents of the human good. On the contrary, Plato depicts Socrates showing politically ambitious young men how to speak or argue better, by refuting others or being refuted. In demonstrating the way in which a person should conduct a conversation, Socrates does not merely exhibit a method of inquiry. The purpose of an argument or exchange is not to defeat one's opponent, Socrates often reiterates; it is to uncover the truth, in which all participants and auditors can share. Implicit in what might appear to be a merely methodological maxim is a more general principle of human behavior. People benefit—themselves as well as others—more by cooperating than by competing. We need to cooperate, because, as Socrates points out in the *Republic*, every mortal is limited in what he or she can do as an individual.

Socrates' own powers were limited, Plato shows in the dialogues set from approximately 409 through 401. He was able to benefit some of the youths who sought his company, but he was not able to benefit all.

Because these dialogues are short and conclude with admissions of ignorance or the need for further investigation, many commentators have grouped them together with the dialogues set during the first part of the Peloponnesian War as "early" and "elenctic."[3] There is, however, a notable difference. By the end of the fifth century Socrates had become a well-known public figure in Athens. He no longer had to build his own reputation, as in the *Protagoras*, by relating the story of his defeat of the famous sophist. Nor did he have to chase young men in the guise of an older lover, as he had Alcibiades. On the contrary, we see in the *Theages*, young men and their fathers came to Socrates to ask him to instruct them.[4] They believed that he could teach them something useful for succeeding in politics.

Because students and their parents sought out Socrates, he did not have to use his erotic knowledge to attract them. On the contrary, by inviting them to examine the desirability of their own goals or ambitions, he tested their ability to learn and so to benefit from associating with him. He never tried explicitly to instruct or persuade his interlocutors of the truth of specific doctrines. In the *Euthydemus* and the *Lysis*, we shall see, Socrates did show some of his associates how to argue better, primarily by example. As

3. Most notably, Vlastos (*Socrates, Ironist and Moral Philosopher*, 46–47) groups these dialogues together. Dodds (*Gorgias*, 18–30) places it late in the early group; Irwin (*Plato's Ethics*, 12) puts all but the *Theages* in an early–middle group.
4. Cf. Bruell, *Socratic Education*, 63.

he emphasizes in all these dialogues, however, his influence was limited.[5] He could not help or affect young people like Callicles and Meno, whom he could not convince to seek truth and prudence instead of the wealth, reputation, honor, and safety associated with political office.[6] Ironically, we see in the *Gorgias* and the *Meno*, Socrates angered his interlocutors and their parents more when he stopped approaching young people in the guise of a lover and instead looked more like a father figure who wished to advise and benefit them. Representatives of the family and the city began to see him as a threat rather than merely as a ridiculous character.[7]

I. *Theages*: Now They Come to Socrates

The authenticity of the *Theages* has often been disputed, because at the end of the conversation Socrates attributes a new, more positive function to his *daimonion* not found in other dialogues. Socrates' attribution of this new function to his *daimonion* can be understood, however, in terms of the circumstances and resolution of this particular conversation.

In the *Theages* Demodocus approaches Socrates to consult with him in private (*idiologēsasthai*; 121a) about the education of his son. Having heard from others about certain conversations in the city, Demodocus worries that his son has developed a desire to go and study with a sophist. The wealthy farmer is not concerned about the cost so much as the potential result, that is, that his son will be corrupted.

Socrates does not attempt to dissuade Demodocus from sending his son to study with a sophist. He recognizes that the person who needs to be

---

5. In the *Memorabilia* 1.2.12–18, Xenophon reports that Critias and Alcibiades associated with Socrates only so long as they thought he could show them how to argue more effectively. When they believed they had learned all they could, they left.

6. These dialogues provide examples of the way in which Socrates claims in his *Apology* to have gone to his fellow citizens and others individually, seeking to persuade them not to prize wealth, reputation, or honor, nor to fear death, but to seek truth and prudence, and to make their souls as good as possible—and the limited effects of those attempts.

7. In the dialogues he set at the end of the fifth century, there are, therefore, clear references to elements of the indictment, although not to the trial itself. In the *Theages* Socrates explains the function of his *daimonion*, which he suggests in his *Apology* may have been responsible, in part, for the accusation that he did not believe in the gods of the city but was introducing new ones. In the *Euthydemus*, readers are reminded how and why the Athenians confused Socrates with the sophists, and in the *Lysis* Socrates defends himself from the charge of corrupting the young. In the *Gorgias* he admits that if he were dragged into court, he would not be able to defend himself, and in the *Meno* Plato shows how Socrates aroused the anger of his main accuser.

persuaded is the son. Agreeing that counsel is sacred (*hieron*) and that there is nothing more divine about which to consult than education (*paideia*), Socrates observes that he and Demodocus may not have the same sort of thing in mind. Nor may the boy. Socrates thus suggests that they ask the boy what he wants.

Socrates knows Demodocus (whose name associates him with the *demos*), because the father has held high public offices in Athens, but he has not met the son. To address the son, Socrates has to ask his name. Hearing "Theages," Socrates comments on its relation to the divine.[8] Aware that both names and lineage can be deceiving, Socrates begins his interrogation of the youth by asking him what he wants to become "wise" about.

In answering a series of characteristically Socratic questions about whether he wants to learn what pilots, charioteers, and doctors know, Theages admits that he wants to become *sophos* (which can also mean clever in the sense of "wise guy") about ruling all kinds of human beings. He does not want to learn how to rule choruses or those who are exercising, that is, the arts of music and gymnastics, the core of a traditional Greek education (which his father has already provided him [*Theages* 122e]), any more than he wants to learn how to rule the sick or farm laborers. Concluding that Theages is moved by political ambition, Socrates names five tyrants and asks whether this is not the kind of rule the young man seeks.[9]

Socrates' berating of Theages as a scoundrel who wants to tyrannize his fellow citizens might lead readers to forget that like the Athenian Stranger, in the *Republic* Socrates suggested that the best form of rule would consist of people who know what to do having the power to do it. The problem with tyranny (*Republic* 575e–76c) is that a tyrant can never trust any

8. Socrates' not knowing the name of the son might indicate the philosopher had not identified Theages as a particularly promising youth (although in the *Theaetetus* 144c, Plato's readers see that Socrates does not know the name of the brilliant young geometer, even though he knows who his father was). In the *Republic* 496a–e, Theages is said to have pursued philosophy rather than a career in politics because he was sickly. If so, Theages was not apt to have been very good looking, and his prospects for a political career would not have been good. The fact that Socrates knows Theages in 411 (if not earlier) in the *Republic*, but has not yet met him in the *Theages*, is one of the many anachronisms to be found in the dramatic dates of the dialogues, but no commentator believes that the *Republic* is supposed to have occurred after the *Theages*. Many scholars have argued, however, that the conversation related in the *Republic* could not actually have occurred, because the people said to be present were not and could not have been present in Athens at the same time. Theages appears to be yet another example.

9. The tyrants include Archelaus, whom Polus raises as an example of the most desirable way of life in the *Gorgias* (470d).

of his associates. There is something a bit underhanded, therefore, about Socrates quoting Euripides' saying, "Tyrants are wise through keeping company with the wise" (*Theages* 125b).[10] In the *Protagoras* Socrates criticized the "wise" poet Simonides for associating with tyrants, and in the *Republic* he criticized tragedians more generally for flattering the tyrants and democracies on whom they depended for support.

By mocking and joking (125e) with him, Socrates provokes Theages to demonstrate both his own good sense and a certain familiarity with Socrates' arguments. Like all other human beings, Theages admits, he would like to have complete power and so "to become a god." He recognizes, however, that this is not possible or desirable for a mere human being. Theages thus corrects Socrates' presumption by conceding that he wants to rule human beings, but, he now adds, not tyrannically or with force. Like rulers who have good reputations, he only wants to rule those who are willing to submit to his rule. Whereas Socrates seemed to be leading Theages with his questions to confess an unjust ambition, readers now see, Theages has been leading Socrates on by giving the philosopher answers the youth thinks Socrates expects to hear. Socrates asks Theages whether he wants to rule like Themistocles, Pericles, Cimon, and others who were "clever in the art of politics" (*ta politika deinoi*; 126a), and the youth admits that he wishes to follow in the steps of the Athenian statesmen Socrates will criticize in the *Gorgias*. But when Socrates suggests that the youth could become wise in the art of politics by associating with the people who practice it, Theages objects, as Socrates had to Protagoras, that the sons of great Athenian politicians are "no better than the sons of shoemakers" (126d).[11] If great Athenian politicians were able to teach their own art, they would surely have taught their sons. So when Socrates further berates Theages for blaming his own father for not knowing how to educate him, despite his willingness to have his son associate with any Athenian gentleman experienced in politics, Theages asks Socrates whether he is not an Athenian gentleman. "Because if *you* would be willing to associate with [*syneinai*, literally "be with"] me," the youth quickly adds, "that will suffice and I will seek no one else" (127a). Demodocus' quick seconding of

10. Socrates frequently faults the poets, for example, Simonides in the *Protagoras* 339b–47c, and tragedians, for example, *Republic* 568a–c, where he cites the same passage from Euripides, for urging their auditors to seek the company if not the power of tyrants.

11. In this case, Theages seems to be referring particularly to Anytus, himself the son of a tanner, who, according to Xenophon (*Apologia Socratis*, 29), refused to give his own son the education his father had given him but insisted instead that his son learn the family trade.

the request increases the reader's suspicion that he and his son had sought out Socrates with this result in mind.[12]

Socrates' attempts to dissuade Theages from studying or associating with him have convinced some commentators (contrary to what he says in the *Republic*) that Socrates did not think Theages had the capacity to philosophize.[13] In fact, however, Socrates emphasizes his own limitations, not those of a youth he hardly knows. He first points out that Demodocus has more experience and renown as a politician in Athens than he does. But, if Theages and Demodocus are convinced that a son cannot learn the art of politics from his father, Socrates then suggests, Theages can take lessons from foreigners like Prodicus, Gorgias, and Polus, who claim to be able to teach young people how to succeed in politics for a fee. As in other dialogues, Socrates says that he does not know any "of these blessed and noble subjects" (128b). All he knows are the erotic things.

Having observed the effect their association with Socrates has had on other boys his age and little older, Theages wants to become superior to those to whom he had previously been inferior by associating with Socrates. Socrates thus concludes his conversation with Theages by emphasizing that the effects he himself has on those who associated with him are not under his control. Socrates hears a divine voice, which always dissuades. Those who refuse to heed its warnings, including the Athenians who went on the Sicilian expedition, experience death and destruction.[14] Socrates cannot associate with those against whom the *daimonion* warns him. But many of those it does not prevent him from associating with do not benefit at all; still others benefit only so long as they are actually with Socrates. They forget what they have learned as soon as they leave him.

One of the main reasons some commentators have concluded the *Theages* is not authentic is that Socrates has the *daimonion* not merely warning him away from some action but indicating to him that others should not do something. Since Socrates is famous for having made ad hominem arguments, however, readers should be prepared to look for explanations of changes in what he says in the character of his interlocutors or circumstances. Socrates does not always give the reasons the *daimonion* dissuaded

12. Cf. Bruell, *Socratic Education*, 110.

13. See, e.g., Pangle, *Roots*, 163–67.

14. Since Socrates assures his auditors in both the *Apology* and the *Republic* 496a–e that he never tried to give counsel in the public assembly, we must assume that he warned Athenians against the Sicilian expedition in private. The person he was most apt to warn appears to be Alcibiades. In the *Symposium* 216a–b, one year before he left to lead the expedition, Alcibiades says that he closed his ears to Socrates. Instead he listened to the demos.

him from an action, but the fact that he sometimes explains why he did not take the action in question (for example, approaching Alcibiades or going into politics) suggests that he could give a reason, if and when he thought it was appropriate. When he accounts for an action simply by referring to his *daimonion*, readers may infer that he does not want to tell his interlocutor what he is thinking. The reason he does not explain often seems to be that his thoughts would reflect badly on his interlocutor. In this case he does not say that various young men who were known to have associated with him did not have the requisite intelligence or character to benefit. He covers over the failings that prevented them from continuing their association with Socrates or from following his advice by referring to his *daimonion* (although he reports that they suffered when they refused to follow its, or his, advice; he had obviously not been able to persuade them that it would not be good for them to do as they wished). In this case he knows that Theages wants to associate with him and cannot easily be dissuaded, but he does not know whether Theages has the intelligence or the persistence to pursue philosophical investigations for some time. He might become discouraged, if not impatient, if he does not immediately see results. Socrates thus warns him without blaming him in advance for possible failure.

By having Socrates name Aristides, the son of Lysimachus, and Thucydides, the son of Melesias, as persons who benefited from associating with him only temporarily, Plato reminds his readers of the change that had occurred in Socrates' status in the fifteen years between the conversations related in the *Laches* and the *Theages*.[15] In the *Laches* the Athenian generals had to introduce Socrates to the older generation (although their children were aware of him) as someone who was particularly qualified to participate in a discussion about education. Now Socrates has generally become known as someone with whom it is advantageous for an ambitious young man to associate. He no longer has to persuade young Athenians like Alcibiades that they can benefit from associating with him; instead he has to warn them that everyone will not benefit equally or at all. The expansion of the subjects of the *daimonion*'s warnings seems, therefore, to be linked to the change in Socrates' circumstances as well as to the character of his interlocutor. As in the earlier dialogues, so in the *Theages*, Socrates insists that he does not possess knowledge, especially of the good and the

15. Socrates gives a similar description of Aristides, son of Lysimachus, as one who benefited from associating with Socrates only so long as he actually stayed with him, and of the influence of the *daimonion* on Socrates' willingness to associate with young men or not (*Theaetetus* 150e–51a).

noble; he only seeks it. He continues to insist that he does not teach (or take money). Now that he is famous, he also finds it necessary to tell his interlocutors there is no guarantee that merely associating with him will make them better speakers, more successful, more virtuous, or happier.[16] They must have a desire to learn as well as the natural capacity to do so.[17] They can prove that they have the necessary passion and talent, only in the future, in action, not at present or merely in speech. Although Socrates denies that he can teach Theages anything about politics, he does not deny that Theages might benefit from associating with him. He simply insists that he does not know whether Theages will benefit and that he cannot determine or control the result of their association.

II. *Euthydemus*: The Difference between Socratic Elenchus and Eristic Refutation

In the *Euthydemus* Plato depicts the way in which Socrates benefited a young man who became one of his regular companions by having Socrates give an account of a conversation he had with two sophists.[18] His *daimonion* not merely allowed him to have this conversation but caused it, Socrates tells his old friend Crito, by telling him not to leave the Lyceum as planned.

In the *Euthydemus* readers see not merely that Socrates teaches Ctesippus how to argue more effectively by example more than by giving him explicit instructions or lessons. We also see that several of Socrates' other

16. Admitting the similarities other scholars have pointed out between what Socrates says in the *Theages* and the *Alcibiades I*, and conceding that Socrates' presentation of his relation to Theages and others is consistent with his presentation of himself as the only true *politikos* in the *Gorgias*, Joyal (*Theages*, 41, 72–103) nevertheless concludes that the attribution of a new function to Socrates' *daimonion*, having it give him advice to relate to others, rather than merely signal what he should not do, makes the *daimonion* more like an ordinary *daimōn*, and so indicates the author was someone other than Plato. (Xenophon, in *Memorabilia* 1.1.4–5, also says that Socrates counseled his companions on the basis of what the *daimonion* told him and uses that fact as evidence of Socrates' piety.) I have argued that Socrates' attribution of a new function to his *daimonion* can be explained by the new circumstances in which he finds himself. As in the other cases when Socrates refers to his *daimonion*, a thoughtful reader can discover the reasons why Socrates did what he did on the basis, purportedly, of a prompting by his *daimonion*. The *daimonion* does not point to an irrational aspect of Socratic philosophy so much as his sense that he should not always tell his interlocutor the reasons why he did what he did. I have more to say about the untraditional character of Socrates' piety at the end of this chapter and in the next.

17. Cf. the discussion in chapter 3 of the significance of Alcibiades as a failed student of Socrates.

18. Ctesippus is named as one of the associates present at Socrates' death in the *Phaedo*. Phaedo tells his interlocutor that they (this group) have been coming every day for a month to talk to Socrates.

close associates fail to pick up the lessons implicit in his demonstrations. In the *Euthydemus* Plato thus indicates not only why some of Socrates' young associates improved markedly, whereas others did not. He also brings out some of the reasons Socrates' fellow citizens continued to confuse him with the sophists, even though he did not claim to teach virtue or charge a fee for listening to him converse.

A. Why Socrates Talks to the Sophists

In the *Euthydemus* Plato once again depicts a father consulting with Socrates about the education of his son. As in the *Theages*, readers are reminded by the opening of the *Euthydemus*, Socrates had become rather well known in Athens, particularly for and by means of his associations with the young. The question in the *Euthydemus* is not, however, whether Socrates will allow Crito's son, Critobulus, to become an associate of his. At the end of the dialogue (306d), Crito indicates that he has been associating (*suggenōmai*) with Socrates for some time. So, it would seem, has his son.[19] But Crito has not been satisfied with the results. He has therefore been seeking other teachers. When he is with Socrates, Crito feels that he has been foolish to have put so much effort into gaining wealth and marrying well in order to have good sons but without being able to educate them. When he looks at those who claim to be able to educate others, however, he is not inclined to press his sons toward "philosophy" (307a). In contrast to the sophists, Socrates did not claim to teach anyone how to become virtuous. Socrates did often claim to be engaged in philosophical investigations, but his old friend Crito does not appear to be able to tell the difference. Nor does the association of father and son with Socrates appear to have benefited Critobulus as much as his father wants.

Knowing that Crito has been seeking a teacher for Critobulus, Socrates urges Crito to come with him to take lessons from the brothers, Euthydemus and Dionysodorus—and to bring his sons. Crito sensibly asks Socrates what the brothers teach. Having asked them to give a demonstration of their art the day before, Socrates relates the entire conversation he, Alcibiades' cousin Clinias, and his lovers had with the sophists. Because exchanges between him, his young Athenian friends, and the sophists prove to be comical, if not farcical, readers cannot but wonder at the end

---

19. In his *Apology* (33d) Socrates names Critobulus first of the youths whose relatives have not complained that their association with Socrates has corrupted them.

why Socrates urges Crito to join him in taking lessons from the sophists and to bring his sons. As Socrates demonstrates in the conversation he relates to Crito, he understands the sophists' tricks and can show his young friends how to overcome them. By the end of the dialogue it is clear that there is nothing Socrates can learn from them.

Socrates converses with the sophists for three other reasons. First, as readers learn from Socrates' account of the exchange he had with the brothers the previous day, youths need to learn how the sophists defeat their opponents in argument, if they are not, like Clinias, to be discouraged from pursuing philosophy, or, like Ctesippus, to get angry and attack the teachers.[20] Crito and his sons have obviously not picked up the argumentative tricks Socrates pointed out both in speech and in deed to his young Athenian interlocutors. If Crito and Critobulus had accompanied Socrates to hear more such exchanges, they might have come to recognize the difference between sophistry and Socratic philosophy. Socrates did not attempt simply to benefit his fellow Athenians by exposing the sophists' tricks, however. The second reason Socrates conversed with the sophists was to benefit them. As Ctesippus demonstrates, people refuted by the sophists often became angry and struck out at them in retaliation. Socrates would not always be there to mollify such angry disputants by showing them how to refute their sophistical opponents. In an attempt to prevent the sophists from arousing any more anger than necessary, Socrates urges them at the end of the conversation not to give any more public displays of their art. Having shown Ctesippus how to defeat them in one sitting, Socrates tells the brothers that they will deprive themselves of their source of income if they give any more free exhibitions, because their tricks are so easily learned. Unfortunately, Plato indicates, the brothers lack the practical wisdom to benefit from Socrates' prudent advice. At the end of the dialogue, Plato shows, Crito was not the only Athenian who had trouble distinguishing Socratic philosophy from eristic sophistry. Like the speechwriter

---

20. Commentators like Richard Robinson, "Ambiguity," *Mind* 50 (1941): 140–55; Robinson, "Plato's Consciousness of Fallacy," *Mind* 51 (1942): 94–114; Robinson, *Plato's Earlier Dialectic*; and M. A. Stewart, "Plato's Sophistry," *Proceedings of the Aristotelian Society*, supp. 51 (1977): 20–44, have suggested that Plato did not recognize or know how to expose the fallacies in the sophists' arguments (as Aristotle later did in his *Sophistical Refutations*). Yet Rosamund Kent Sprague, *Plato's Use of Fallacy* (New York: Barnes and Noble, 1962); Thomas Chance, *Plato's "Euthydemus": Analysis of What Is and Is Not Philosophy* (Berkeley: University of California Press, 1992); and R. S. W. Hawtrey, *Commentary on Plato's "Euthydemus"* (Philadelphia: American Philosophical Society, 1981), have all shown in more detail than I can here how Socrates not merely points out the fallacies in the brothers' arguments but shows young Athenians how to counter them.

who tells Crito his friend Socrates made himself look ridiculous by conversing with such silly fellows, many of the auditors failed to understand what Socrates was trying to accomplish. The third reason Socrates talked to the sophists was, therefore, to protect himself from the results of his being confused with them.

B. The Differences between Socrates and the Sophists

Plato brings out some of the differences between Socrates and the sophists at the very beginning of Socrates' narration. Crito does not notice them, because Socrates leaves many of the differences implicit in the exchange he relates instead of explicitly pointing them out.

1. THE SOPHISTS BRAG, SOCRATES IS MODEST

The first difference readers see is that the sophists brag, falsely, both about their argumentative abilities and the effects their arguments have on their interlocutors. Socrates understates both his victories in the argument and the beneficent effects he has on the listeners.

Socrates tells Crito that the brothers are all-wise (*passophoi*) and that he wants to become as clever (*deinos*) as they by taking lessons from them, but Socrates does not equate their ability to wield words as if they were weapons and to refute any argument, whether it be true or false, with the teaching of virtue as the brothers do when they describe what they teach to Clinias. Socrates expresses his skepticism about their ability not merely to teach virtue but to persuade those who do not believe that virtue can be taught by asking the sophists to give a demonstration of their art. The brothers say that is the reason they have come to Athens, to exhibit and teach their wisdom to anyone who wants to learn.

Quite a crowd had gathered around them, Socrates explains. What he does not say, but what becomes evident in the course of the conversation, is that a violent conflict might have erupted between the students of the brothers and the lovers of Clinias, if Socrates had not been there to mollify Ctesippus. Socrates merely tells Crito that, as he was about to leave the Lyceum, his *daimonion* indicated that he should not. In response to this divine warning (or premonition of possible trouble), Socrates sat down. Seeing Socrates sitting alone, Alcibiades' cousin Clinias joined him. Seeing Socrates sitting next to a potential student, the brothers sat themselves on either side of the pair. The foursome was quickly surrounded by the admiring students of the brothers and lovers of the handsome Clinias. Socrates does not point out his own ability to attract young, noble companions like Clinias (and his cousin) any more than he brags about the practical wisdom that induced him to stay.

2. The Sophists Don't Care about the Character of Their Interlocutor or the Truth

Assuring the brothers that everyone present would like to acquire the wisdom they claim to possess, Socrates urged them to demonstrate with Clinias how they persuade young men to philosophize and care about virtue. Socrates thus implied that Clinias was among those who did not believe that virtue could be taught. (In the *Protagoras* Socrates had pointed out that democratic Athenians generally did not believe that virtue was teachable.) In beginning the demonstration, Euthydemus immediately brought out one of the fundamental differences between the kind of refutations in which he engaged and those Socrates administered by stating that the characteristics of the interlocutor do not matter so long as he is willing to answer. The character of the interlocutor does not matter, because the brothers are not interested in anything but refuting the contentions of their victims. They want to show off their own cleverness in debate. They are not concerned about improving the character or life of their interlocutor or about the truth or falsity of the proposition in question. Clinias will be refuted whichever way he answers, Dionysodorus whispers to Socrates. The sophists do not require their interlocutors to say what they really think, as Socrates does (cf. *Gorgias* 487a–b).

3. The Sophists Discourage, Socrates Encourages

In the first exchange of speeches, the sophists show that they discourage rather than encourage young men like Clinias from trying to become virtuous by seeking wisdom. They pummel the young man with a quick set of either/or questions that he cannot answer without contradicting himself and so being refuted. Euthydemus begins by asking Clinias whether the wise (*sophoi*) or unlearned (*amatheis*) are the best students. When Clinias answers that it is the wise, Euthydemus gets the young man to admit that he and others go to teachers to learn what they do not know. But when Clinias responds that those who have no learning learn, Dionysodorus reminds him that people who do not know their letters cannot take dictation and so learn speeches by memory. Euthydemus quickly steps in and asks Clinias whether learners learn what they know or what they do not know. Clinias answers, the latter, and Euthydemus reminds him that people cannot learn by taking notes unless they already know their letters; Dionysodorus tells him, however, that learning is the reception of knowledge, which presupposes its previous absence. At each stage, students of the brothers laugh and applaud their teachers' cleverness.

Seeing that Clinias was becoming despondent, Socrates stepped in and showed how he, in contrast to the sophists, encouraged rather than discouraged his interlocutors. First, he explained to Clinias how the brothers played on the double meaning of the word "learning," which can refer both to the process and to the result or content. Then Socrates assured Clinias that such playing on the meaning of words was merely *play*. Even if Clinias were to learn such argumentative tricks from the brothers, he would not be any wiser. The brothers had not fulfilled their promise to demonstrate how they would convince him to care about wisdom and virtue. Socrates will give a demonstration of what he has in mind.

Rather than shame the youth by refuting him, the way the brothers had, Socrates began by taking the burden of potential shame on himself. Since he would be speaking impromptu, and thus perhaps laughably, he first asked the brothers and their students to restrain themselves and so protected himself and his young interlocutor from their ridicule. Then he asked Clinias whether all human beings want to do well. That question might seem ridiculous, Socrates admitted, because everyone obviously wishes to do well. But if everyone agrees, it would be absurd to deny his first premise. Socrates did not pose an either/or question like the brothers had. He characteristically inquired about what people really want, so that they could then investigate the means of acquiring it. In general, he and Clinias quickly agreed, people want good things. Among these goods are wealth, health, good looks, good birth, talents, and honors, but most of all, the virtues, especially wisdom. Then in a curious turn of the argument, Socrates first suggested that they had forgotten the most important thing, which is good fortune, only to argue that people who have the relevant knowledge do not need good luck. The sort of wisdom he described was so complete that it did not allow for any error or for any role for the gods in directing human affairs, but Clinias did not object. Like his famous cousin, the young man was apparently not very pious. As he had told Alcibiades as a youth, so Socrates now reminded Clinias, human beings cannot benefit from the possession of any good, including wisdom, unless they know (have the *phronēsis* and *sophia*) how to use it. Socrates concluded that human beings should therefore seek wisdom above all—as a legacy from their fathers or benefit from their friends and lovers, whether strangers or citizens. As he had told Alcibiades earlier, so Socrates again told Clinias, people should be willing to be slaves—or to perform any other honorable service—in order to become wise—*if* wisdom is teachable.

Clinias demonstrated how effective Socrates' protreptic speech was by immediately responding that he believed wisdom was teachable (although Socrates indicated earlier that Clinias had doubted it). Socrates challenged the brothers to give an equally effective display.

4. THE SOPHISTS PROVOKE, SOCRATES CHALLENGES

In the second set of speeches the sophists showed that they not merely discouraged youths from philosophy by refuting and thus making them look foolish in front of others. They also angered onlookers as well as participants. The sophists made themselves look ridiculous, moreover, by using arguments to refute others that denied the possibility of teaching or refuting anyone. Socrates merely tells Crito that he found their obviously inept, self-contradictory arguments "surprising" (*thaumasious*).

Dionysodorus tried to turn Socrates' critique of the brothers back onto Socrates himself by asking whether he was playing with them. Socrates insisted that he was serious, so Dionysodorus asked whether Clinias was now wise or whether they wished to make him what he was not now. On behalf not only of himself but also of the friends of Clinias surrounding them, Socrates said the latter, and Dionysodorus responded that they were "some" lovers who wished the young man dead!

Ctesippus got angry and accused Dionysodorus of lying when he asserted that Ctesippus wished Clinias dead. So Euthydemus asked the irate young Athenian whether he thought it was possible to talk about that which is not. Plato's readers are thus reminded that both the form and the philosophical basis of the sophists' arguments could be traced back to Parmenides, although Socrates does not say this explicitly.[21] His narration focuses on the frustration and potential conflict such seeming abstract arguments arouse. Although Ctesippus agreed that, speaking about what is, gentlemen say what is true, he protested that Dionysodorus had spoken about what is, but not as it is. Dionysodorus said that gentlemen would speak evil of evil things, and Ctesippus warned the sophist to beware of

21. Cf. Hermann Keulen, *Untersuchungen zu Platons "Euthydem"* (Wiesbaden: Otto Harrassowitz, 1971),77–92, on the Eleatic sources of eristics. Also Taylor, *Plato*, 89–102.

being included in the evil himself. The young man already knew that the sophists' way of arguing was "cold." They had shown that they did not care about the welfare of those they refuted.

In the first exchange Socrates had intervened to prevent the brothers from entirely discouraging Clinias from philosophy. In the second exchange he has to intervene to diffuse the antagonism. He does so, first in action, by challenging Clinias' young lovers to demonstrate their courage as well as their affection for him. He urges Ctesippus to accept what the visitors are willing to tell them. Pointing to the way the brothers had again played on the ambiguous meaning of words by equating not-being with death, he advises Ctesippus to let the brothers transform Clinias, if they actually know how to do away with people who are wicked and witless so as to make them useful and prudent. The arguments the sophists use in effecting the change may be irritating, but it would be worth enduring their aggravating contentions if the end result were good. Socrates then, in effect, dares Clinias' professed lovers to show that they were as brave as he "in the face of death" by adding that, if the young men are afraid to risk their own destruction, he, an old man, will volunteer to let Dionysodorus demonstrate his ability to transform a human being by destroying him in order to make him good.

Just as Socrates showed the brothers in the first exchange that they should not be trying to shame those they were seeking to persuade to take lessons from them, so in the second exchange of speeches he shows the assembled youths the kind of courage a person needs in order to learn. A student must be able to endure looking ridiculous in order to be shown that he does not know what he thinks he does.

5. SOCRATES REFUTES THE SOPHISTS BUT COVERS OVER HIS VICTORY

Ctesippus wanted to show that he was courageous, even though he doubted that courage could be demonstrated in a mere contest of words. Not wanting to look less willing than Socrates to risk his life for the benefit of his beloved, Ctesippus offered himself to be skinned by the strangers—so long as he was not made into a wineskin like Marsyas but into the shape of virtue.[22] Attempting to put a good face on the confrontation,

22. In the *Symposium* 215a–16a, Alcibiades compares Socrates to Marsyas with regard to his ability to entrance listeners but points out that Socrates does not need an instrument. Alcibiades does not refer to the fate of the satyr, however, or suggest that something similar might happen to the philosopher. Ctesippus here provides an example of the way in which love can make a lover courageously sacrifice himself in an attempt to get the attention of his beloved. In the *Symposium*

he observed that Dionysodorus believed that Ctesippus was vexed with him, but that he had merely contradicted (*antilegein*) a remark the youth thought was inappropriately aimed at him. But Dionysodorus denied that there was any such thing as a contradiction. If it is impossible to say what is not, the sophist argued, people speaking about the same thing must either agree or be talking about different things.

Not knowing how to respond to someone who claimed that it was impossible to contradict him or anyone else, Ctesippus fell silent. Socrates had to step in and explain why he found Dionysodorus' arguments "surprising." Followers of Protagoras often used this argument, but the proposition that it is not possible to speak or opine falsely seems in the end to turn against itself. If it is not possible to say or think anything false, there is no such thing as ignorance nor is anyone able to err. But if no one can err or contradict another, it would appear to be impossible to refute anyone. And if it is impossible to refute another, what *do* the brothers teach?

Rather than answer his question, Dionysodorus responded to Socrates' reference to their initial claim to be able to communicate virtue to anyone willing to learn their art of refutation with an insult: Socrates had shown himself to be an old "Cronus" by "recollecting" (*anamimnē[i]skē[i]*) what the brothers had said in the past, instead of responding to what the sophist was now saying. Socrates asked Dionysodorus what he meant (*bouletai*), and the sophist asked Socrates whether he thought that phrases could have intentions (*bouletai*). Socrates protested the high-handed, arbitrary, if not tyrannical way in which Dionysodorus insisted on others answering him, even though he refused to answer them. And having pointed out a second way in which the sophists tripped up their opponents, Socrates returned to the fundamental contradiction in the sophists' position: if it is impossible to speak falsely or err, it is impossible to contradict (*antilegein*) or refute (*exelegchein*). By pointing out the contradiction between the sophists' claim to teach anyone how to refute others in speech and their contention that it is impossible to contradict or refute anyone, Socrates had refuted the sophists.

Unlike the sophists, however, Socrates understood that refuting one's interlocutors is not the point of an argumentative exchange. People who seek merely to win arguments in order to demonstrate their own superiority

---

Phaedrus uses this phenomenon as an example of the way in which eros promotes virtue. In the *Euthydemus* Plato seems to be showing the way in which eros arouses competition as much, if not more, than eristics. Ctesippus' desire to look good in the eyes of his beloved appears to stand in the way of his willingness to look ridiculous in the process of learning.

are apt to provoke their interlocutors to respond to their defeats in speech with contests in deed, that is, with force. Rather than announce, much less glory in, his refutation of the eristic sophists, Socrates sought to remind his young associates of the reasons they needed to seek knowledge (and not merely to win arguments).

Socrates' refutation of Dionysodorus' contention that it is impossible to refute anyone elicited the same kind of response from Ctesippus that Socrates' faulting of the brothers' first display had elicited from Dionysodorus—an insult. The youth not merely accused the sophists of speaking nonsense.[23] By pointing out that they had no home, he appeared to be threatening them with the possibility of prosecution and expulsion from Athens. Fearing that the young man would become even more abusive, Socrates tried, for a second time, to soothe him. As he told Clinias before, so he now assured Ctesippus, the brothers had merely been playing with them. As Ctesippus suspected, people should not take winning or losing purely verbal exchanges seriously. Having demonstrated that it is not possible to persuade human beings to seek to become virtuous merely by winning arguments with them, Socrates urged the brothers to get serious and show how they could teach young people to become virtuous. For a second time Socrates offered to give a demonstration himself as a challenge to the brothers to do the same.

Socrates' second demonstration appears, however, to be much less successful than the first. In their first discussion Socrates had convinced Clinias to seek wisdom, but in the second he and Clinias prove unable to identify the kind of knowledge they want. Socrates and Clinias agree that neither wealth nor immortality nor any other good benefits someone who does not know how to use it. Since people need to have the goods in order to use them, Socrates and Clinias also agree that the knowledge they seek would include both how to make or acquire the goods and how to use them. Although Socrates admitted that he thought the knowledge they were seeking would be something like the art of speech making (*tēn logopoiikēn technēn*), which exerts a kind of charm on juries, assemblies,

23. In response to Crito's initial question about where the sophists came from, Socrates explains that they were born in Chios but had gone as colonists to Thurii, where, Hawtrey points out (*Commentary*, 14), they may have encountered Protagoras. Francisco J. Gonzalez, *Dialectic and Dialogue: Plato's Practice of Philosophical Inquiry* (Evanston, IL: Northwestern University Press, 1998), 95, suggests that Socrates' report that they had been exiled from Thurii and had been wandering around Greece ever since put them in a bad light, but Nails observes, "they were probably subject to the general expulsion of Athenians and their sympathizers from Thurii in 412, at the end of the Athenian army's defeat in Sicily" (*People*, 318).

and other kinds of crowds, he and Clinias agree that it is possible for some people (like the critic of Socrates at the end of the dialogue) to know how to write speeches without also being able to deliver them effectively in an assembly. On similar grounds, Clinias then argued that generals do not have the knowledge that they are seeking, because generals turn their captives over to politicians to use.

In both his demonstrations, readers should observe, Socrates concludes by pointing out what he and his interlocutor do not know. In obvious contrast to the sophists, Socrates does not boast about his own wisdom or glory in his ability to refute others.

C. Crito's Failure to Understand the Point of Socrates' Narration

Crito breaks into the narration at this point to express doubt that either Clinias or Ctesippus could have formulated such good arguments. In contrast to the brothers, readers see that in relating this conversation Socrates has demonstrated that he can show young men how to argue more critically and effectively. Crito does not believe Socrates, perhaps because Socrates' account of Clinias and Ctesippus makes Critobulus look bad by comparison. He too should have learned to argue well merely by associating with Socrates. Insinuating that it was Socrates (and not Clinias or Ctesippus who could make such superior arguments), Crito is nevertheless anxious to learn whether they discovered the art they sought. For Crito, readers see, neither the arguments nor the character and intentions of the people who make them are as important as the outcome. Precisely because he is concerned primarily, if not solely, about the "bottom line," Crito does not see how Socrates produces the results he does.

Socrates indicates that he understands why Crito finds it difficult to believe him. By telling Crito that he and Clinias did not find the kind of knowledge they were seeking but made themselves ridiculous running around after it, Socrates reminds Crito (and Plato's readers) of what he had shown Ctesippus and the other young men listening in action: a person needs to be willing to risk making himself look ridiculous by admitting that he does not know something, if he is to learn. Crito's unwillingness to make himself look ridiculous by going with Socrates to take lessons with the brothers indicates the reason he and many other older men find it difficult to learn. It is not their failing memory so much as their unwillingness to lose their sense of their own dignity, particularly in front of their own children, that makes it hard for fathers to admit that they do not know.

Such an admission is a necessary prerequisite for learning, however. Like his fellow Athenian democrats, Plato shows, Crito tries to decide things for himself. Rather than simply believe the speechwriter who told him that his friend Socrates had made himself look ridiculous conversing with such foolish fellows, Crito asks Socrates to give his own account of the conversation. Having heard it, Crito admits that he would rather be refuted than to refute others with such silly arguments. He will not go with Socrates to take lessons from the brothers.

D. Why Socrates Claims To Have Failed

Socrates explains that he and Clinias initially believed they had found the knowledge they were seeking in the kingly art. Because generals and all the other craftsmen give their products to the king to be used, he and Clinias asked what effect (*ergon*) kings had, but they were unable to find a satisfactory answer. Since the art they sought was supposed to include knowledge not only of how to use but also of how to make some good, the effect of kingship had to be the production of some good. Because nothing is good for human beings who don't know how to use it, however, the good that kingship produces also had to include knowledge or wisdom. But Socrates and Clinias could not discover an art capable of making all human beings good and wise in all respects.

Readers might object that the kingly art need not make everyone good or wise in all respects.[24] In the *Republic* Socrates argues that guardians need to be taught a certain kind of gymnastics and music to make them good, effective, and just defenders of the city. But they have to learn much more, for example, mathematics and dialectics, to become just rulers. In the *Statesman* the Eleatic Stranger argues that the kingly art consists in knowing how to use all the other arts to make the people of the city moderate and courageous enough to defend and preserve it. It is one thing to know how to teach people to become virtuous, if it is possible. (Socrates is famous for denying that it is possible to teach virtue, even though he maintains that virtue is knowledge. Showing or demonstrating and teaching are not, moreover, exactly the same.) It is another thing to know whom to teach what. Both Socrates and the Eleatic agree that a ruler needs to test

24. Except for this last requirement, that the art be equally effective on all, the art Socrates and Clinias seek corresponds to the "royal art" the Eleatic Stranger defines in the *Statesman*. The last requirement thus reveals the way in which the argument is particularly aimed at the brothers.

his citizens to find out which are capable of learning and what they are capable of doing.

By identifying the problems with Socrates' argument, readers can see why he made it. The sophists claimed that they could persuade anyone to learn to be virtuous; the character of the interlocutor did not matter. Socrates has shown not only that the sophists dissuade rather than persuade young people to learn what is necessary to become virtuous with their refutations. He has also shown that the way to encourage young people to learn is first to show them what they truly need to know in order to be virtuous (as Socrates had shown Clinias in their first exchange), and then to show them that they do not possess the requisite knowledge (as Socrates showed Clinias in their second exchange), so that they will seek it.

Because Socrates emphasizes his and Clinias' failure to find the specific kind of knowledge they were seeking, most commentators have concluded that Socrates' second demonstration is a failure.[25] Whether we think that Socrates succeeds or fails depends, however, on what we think Socrates was attempting to demonstrate. In contrast to the sophists, Socrates has reminded the audience, he does not claim to be all-wise, nor does he (or they) know anyone who is all-wise, in fact. He has shown not only that he can refute (and so best) the sophists at their own game, but also that the ability to play this game, that is, to refute others, is not the knowledge that makes someone virtuous and qualified to rule. Even more important, he has shown that he knows not only how to mollify but also how to moderate both the speech and action of the youths who associate with him by challenging them to demonstrate their own courage by admitting that they do not know.

E. Socrates Shows Ctesippus How to Refute the Sophists

Having shown how he encouraged young people to pursue knowledge in his first exchange of speeches with the sophists and how he was able to moderate his young companions in the second, Socrates challenged the brothers for a third time to demonstrate their knowledge. His emphasis on his own inability to identify the kind of knowledge they are seeking in contrast to the brothers' obviously exaggerated claims about their own wisdom adds to the ironical, if not buffoonish, humor of the dialogue.

25. See, e.g., David Roochnik, "The Sensuous Play of Plato's *Euthydemus,*" *Interpretation* 18 (1991): 211–32.

Socrates nevertheless has a useful, if not serious, purpose in initiating this third exchange. By repeatedly giving the brothers answers they will not allow, Socrates points out the way in which the sophists artificially constrain arguments so they can refute their interlocutors, but he does not explicitly say that is what he is doing. Plato shows that Ctesippus nevertheless got the message. Following Socrates' lead, the youth first asked the brothers to answer empirical questions they deny are relevant. Then, perceiving the pattern Socrates had indicated, Ctesippus defeated the sophists using their own characteristic moves or tricks. Having learned how to play their game, he no longer took it or them seriously. Instead of getting angry, or even glorying in his victory, he and Clinias joined the students of the brothers in laughter at the end.

In response to Socrates' third request that they exhibit their wisdom, Dionysodorus asks Socrates whether he would prefer to be instructed or to be shown that he already knows. At his age, Socrates responds, it would be a relief to be shown that one does not have to make an effort to learn new things. Unfortunately for the sophists, if everyone knows everything from birth, as they proceed to argue, no one needs to learn anything from them. As in the second exchange, so in the third, the sophists put forward arguments that deny the possibility of their own art. This is what happens, he suggests, to people who care only about winning the argument and not about its truth. But, as in their second exchange, so in the third, Socrates does not point out the effective meaning of this argument to the sophists and their potential students until the end of their conversation. He uses the opportunity to show Ctesippus how the sophists refute their opponents by inducing them to repeat some of their characteristic moves several times in a row.

Dionysodorus asks Socrates whether he knows anything, and Socrates concedes that he knows some things. Dionysodorus concludes that Socrates knows everything, because if Socrates knows (something), he cannot not know (something). By turning the question back on the brothers and asking them whether, if they know one thing, they know all, and then whether the "things" they know include carpentry and cobbling, Socrates shows Ctesippus how the sophists abstract from all particular qualifications of the propositions they treat strictly in terms of the opposition between affirmation and negation, all or nothing. Quickly grasping the point, the young man breaks in to ask, first, whether Dionysodorus knows how many teeth Euthydemus has and can prove it by counting them. The sophists do not regard such requests for specific knowledge, much less empirical proof, as serious, because they do not fall within the rules of the sophists' game. Socrates incredulously asks the elderly Dionysodorus whether he knows how to dance. Dionysodorus responds not only that he knows how to dance but also that he and his brother and everyone else, including Socrates, know everything—not merely at present but from birth.[26] Even though it has reminded other commentators of the "theory of recollection" that Socrates presents in the *Meno* and the *Phaedo*, according to which the soul has seen and thus knows everything before it is reunited with a body and reborn, Socrates expresses doubt that he has such wisdom. (According to his own theory, he would have to work hard to "recollect" it.) Euthydemus offers to prove it. He asks Socrates whether he has knowledge by means of something or not. Socrates asks him whether he is referring to the soul. Euthydemus reprimands Socrates for responding with a question rather than answering. Protesting that he cannot respond accurately, if he does not know what Euthydemus means, Socrates again points out the way in which the sophists not only refuse to allow their propositions or questions to be qualified in any way but also use the ambiguous meaning of words to refute their interlocutors. Like Clinias in the first exchange, they invite their respondent to answer on the basis of one possible meaning of a word, and then object to his response on the basis of another.

Socrates tells Crito that he ceased objecting so that the sophist would not refuse to give him lessons. Agreeing that he would always know all things, if that is what Euthydemus wishes ("means" or "intends," *bouletai*), Socrates nevertheless catches the brothers up by asking whether Dionysodorus thinks Socrates knows that good men are unjust (although he implies that he does not think or, therefore, "know" any such thing), and then, after Dionysodorus affirms that he knows, inquiring where he learned it. People cannot learn anything, according to the brothers, because learning entails people not knowing something at one time that they come to know later (and thus, abstracting from the difference in time, that they both know and do not know). Dionysodorus thus answers Socrates' query with "nowhere." But, Socrates points out, on the basis of the same reasoning, he does not know that good men are unjust (because he could not have learned it). Euthydemus criticizes his brother for spoiling the

---

26. The Parmenidean form of their arguments made it necessary for the brothers to claim that they always had the wisdom they now possess. If they did not always have all of it, there would have been some time when they had both known (something) and not known (something) which they proceeded to learn.

argument, and Dionysodorus blushes. Socrates again proves that he knows how to refute the brothers, using their own techniques or arguments, but he does not emphasize his victory. He wants to let Ctesippus publicly win the argument, glory in his victory, and so overcome his antagonism to the sophists.

Rather than exult in his own demonstrated superiority in argument, Socrates let Dionysodorus quickly recover by asking the philosopher what he meant by saying he was Euthydemus' brother. He veils his own cleverness by complaining that the brothers had not only refused to answer his questions but had also ganged up on him, two against a single interlocutor, that is, by criticizing their injustice rather than their ineptitude.

Euthydemus first proves that Socrates has no father, because his father is not father to his (half) brother and therefore is no father. Having observed the pattern of the previous exchange, in which agreements were applied first to the interlocutor and then to the questioner (as well as having heard the implicit appeal in Socrates' reference to Iolaus, the young helper of Heracles), Ctesippus asked Euthydemus if he too does not have a father. Euthydemus proves that his father, being a father, is father to all (since a father cannot be no father)—to animals as well as to humans. Dionysodorus then suggested that Ctesippus' dog, which had fathered a litter, is his father too. But instead of getting angry, Ctesippus laughed when Dionysodorus pointed out that the young man thus beat his father. Ctesippus' spirits rose even higher when he proved able to silence Euthydemus in the next two exchanges about how much of a good thing is good and whether silent things can speak. Ctesippus was particularly delighted, Socrates observes, because his beloved Clinias now laughed (instead of being laughed at). But remembering that Crito has already shown himself unwilling to admit that either young Athenian had learned to argue so cleverly merely from listening to Socrates, Socrates suggests that Ctesippus must have overheard the brothers talking (even though Socrates had shown, in relating the conversation, how he pointed out their characteristic moves and tricks).

F. Why Socrates Let the Sophists Appear to Refute Him

Seemingly to prove that he was not the source of Ctesippus' newfound cleverness, Socrates concludes his account of the conversation by showing how Dionysodorus refuted him. Like the sophist's showing that Socrates' young associate beat his father, both the final arguments contain, if in humorous form, serious objections that others have made to Socrates' arguments.[27]

Raising the question of "participation" that Parmenides first posed about Socrates' argument concerning the ideas, Dionysodorus inquires whether Socrates thought that beautiful things were the same as the beautiful. Socrates answers, admittedly in perplexity (aporia), that beautiful things are different from the beautiful, although the beautiful is present in them. But Dionysodorus points out that he (or an ox) would then be Socrates, because he (or an ox) was present with Socrates. How can something be different by having something different present in it and so be different from itself? Like the Eleatic Stranger in the Sophist, as we shall see, Socrates effectively replies to this particular question by pointing out that the different cannot be the same (that is, that difference is not opposition or negation).[28] But Socrates again covers over his own showing of the inadequacy of the sophist's refutation by praising the "wisdom" in Dionysodorus' second quick recovery.

Picking up on Socrates' mention of craftsmen, the sophist argues that the proper use of an artisan's own craft (such as cooking or sculpting) is to apply the art to the artisan himself. The application of an argument to the person who makes it is a characteristically Socratic move. The sophists had failed to make it in both the second and third demonstrations of their "wisdom," when they put forward arguments that denied the possibility of their own art. Rather than pointing out what they learned from him, however, Socrates expresses desire that such wisdom could be his.

Dionysodorus points to the most obvious difference between the philosopher (who only seeks wisdom) and the sophists (who claim to possess and to sell it) by getting Socrates to agree that we can do what we want

27. As Chance points out (Plato's "Euthydemus," 160–61), scholarly comment on the arguments in the last section of the dialogue has been restricted to characterizations of the arguments as "zany" or "absurd." Although Hawtrey directs his readers to the references to Aristophanes at 276d, 283e, and 285c (Commentary, 34–35, 64, 99, 105)—first collected by Winckelmann—and included in Dorothy Tarrant, "Colloquialisms, Semi-Proverbs and Word-Play in Plato," Classical Quarterly 40 (1946): 109–17; and "More Colloquialisms, Semi-Proverbs, and Word-Play in Plato," Classical Quarterly, n.s., 8 (1958): 158–60—neither he nor any other critic has pointed out the connection between the subjects of the last, most "absurd" disputations and the accusations made against Socrates by Aristophanes in his Clouds, of encouraging father beating and of denying the existence of the "ancestral" Zeus. Socrates is called a sophist in the Clouds (line 359) and accused or criticized as such. In the Apology (18d) Socrates says that a certain comic poet was one of his first accusers.
28. It is extremely important to observe that Plato's Socrates did not fail to give the argument Plato attributes to the Eleatic Stranger because he had not thought of it.

with what we own. The sophist also indicated the way in which Socrates got himself into trouble by engaging in such disputations. If people can sell, give, or sacrifice what they own, Dionysodorus argued, people like Socrates (and his fellow Athenians) who claim to have ancestral gods can sell, give away, or sacrifice them. Like the arguments about father beating that denied the differences between human beings and animals, the exchange the sophists have with Socrates about his ability to dispose of his ancestral gods should remind readers of the charges against the philosopher that were first comically leveled in Aristophanes' *Clouds* and later repeated, more seriously, in court.

Although Socrates reports that everyone present—both the students of the sophists and Clinias' lovers—joined in laughter and applause at the end of their disputation, readers are reminded by Crito's account of the speechwriter's critique that not everyone in Athens took a positive view of such verbal sparring. The speechwriter, for example, thought such "philosophy" was base and inconsequential. If he had been told that his efforts to help his beloved city or son were in fact destroying them, the speechwriter might, like Ctesippus here or Lycon and Anytus later, have become angry and tried to strike back not merely with arguments but with force. Although Socrates was clearly not a sophist who traveled from city to city selling arguments, the apparent similarity between his refutations of his interlocutors and theirs, along with his willingness to associate and converse with them, contributed to popular suspicion of the effects and character of his philosophy. The content of their exchanges would have given angry accusers grounds to charge him with impiety and corrupting the young. By keeping both his own interrogations and displays by the sophists private, Socrates attempted to minimize the negative effect. As we see in the *Euthydemus*, however, Socrates could not entirely control what passed by word of mouth, even when he narrated the conversation. Like the audience of Aristophanes' *Clouds*, as Socrates suggests in his *Apology* (18b–c), many Athenians came to believe that his disputations were not merely ridiculous but positively dangerous—especially when the arguments, as they almost always did, concerned the education of the young and, sometimes, the gods.

The *Clouds* was not merely a play but a comedy. But that comedy had serious effects. As Socrates reminds his interlocutors and auditors in the *Euthydemus*, different people have different ideas about what is play and what is serious. It is easy to confuse the two. Socrates enjoyed playing with the sophists, but the sophists did not regard their disputes merely as "play."

Nor did those who were refuted and made to look ridiculous by them—unless like Ctesippus they learned how to refute the sophists in turn. Socrates tried to expose the argumentative tricks the sophists used in refuting their interlocutors so that the young would not become discouraged from further study of philosophy or strike out in anger against the sophists (with whom Socrates was associated). He also tried to moderate the views older Athenians like Crito tended to take of the sophists, by showing that their arguments were amusing, that they were playing a kind of game, and that exchanges with them were not really serious. Although he demonstrated both in practice and in precept that he knew how to refute the sophists, Socrates let himself appear to be defeated by them in speech, and so look ridiculous, to show in deed, as he had insisted in speech, that it is not important to win such arguments.

Because they did not pay sufficient attention to the arguments and took account only of the apparent conclusion, people like Crito and the speechmaker failed to perceive the lessons Socrates gave Ctesippus and the superiority of Socrates to the foolish brothers. In response to Aristophanes' critique of his teacher in the *Clouds*, Plato showed in the *Euthydemus* that Socrates enjoyed sparring with the sophists precisely because he understood the limits of speech better than the sophists, who thought that winning arguments was the most important thing in life, or the Athenians, who were concerned about what others would say. Socrates could not prevent all of those refuted by sophistical arguments from becoming indignant. Nor could he prevent them from confusing him with the ridiculous fellows with whom he sometimes conversed. To distinguish Socrates from the sophists, they would have had to pay more attention to the form and intention of the arguments than they were willing or able. The most Socrates could do was repeatedly to demonstrate the difference—both in form and intention—in speech and in deed.

III. *Lysis*: Socrates as Friend Rather Than Lover of the Young

In the *Euthydemus* Ctesippus experienced the kind of help Socrates could provide a young lover of a handsome youth. In the *Lysis* we see Ctesippus solicit Socrates' assistance on behalf of another. As a result, we are presented not only with an investigation of the meaning of friendship but also with a demonstration of the cooperative kind of association Socrates sought to establish with the young, in contrast to the competitive debates of the eristic sophists. Just as Ctesippus appears to have become a regular companion of Socrates after the conversation related in the *Euthydemus*, so Ctesippus' younger cousin Menexenus seems to have become a regular companion of Socrates after the conversation related in the *Lysis*. (Both are named in the *Phaedo* among the close companions of Socrates present at his death.)

Socrates had more success attracting young men able and interested in arguing than he did with handsome youths such as Clinias, Lysis, and Meno. As Socrates observes in the *Meno*, these "pretty boys" were apt to be spoiled by the flattery of their lovers and did not, therefore, strive to improve themselves. Socrates' greatest failure to improve a handsome young man was Clinias' cousin, Alcibiades. Socrates had publicly pursued Alcibiades as a lover, but he had not been able to persuade the handsome young man to give up his political ambitions and join him in a search for self-knowledge. Alcibiades had not merely entered Athenian politics "with a vengeance"; threatened with prosecution for impiety, he had become a traitor by fleeing first to Sparta and then to Persia. Socrates' purported love for Alcibiades hangs as a kind of backdrop for these dialogues, even when Alcibiades' name is not explicitly mentioned, because these dialogues are dramatically set during the years (409–405) when Socrates' former companion was trying to return to Athens. Was Alcibiades the example par excellence of the pernicious effect Socrates had on the young?

Socrates had explicitly approached Alcibiades as a lover. Although he is purportedly showing Hippothales how to attract a beloved boy, Socrates in the *Lysis* just as explicitly approaches the boys as friends. Because their discussion appears to be inconclusive, commentators have generally regarded the *Lysis* as an early aporetic statement on "love" that Plato later completed in the *Symposium* and *Phaedrus*.[29] The dramatic dates indicate,

---

29. See, e.g., Terry Penner and Christopher Rowe, *Plato's "Lysis"* (Cambridge: Cambridge University Press, 2005); David Bolotin, *Plato's Dialogue on Friendship* (Ithaca: Cornell University Press, 1979); Michael Davis, *The Autobiography of Philosophy* (Lanham, MD: Rowman and Littlefield, 1999), 67–82; Friedländer, *Plato*, vol. 2; Guthrie, *History of Greek Philosophy*, vol. 4; Grote, *Plato*; and Donald Norman Levin, "Some Observations concerning Plato's *Lysis*," in *Essays in Ancient Greek Philosophy*, ed. John Peter Anton and George L. Kustas (Albany: SUNY Press, 1971), 236–58. Commentators who emphasize Plato's development—e.g., Max Pohlenz, *Aus Platos Werdezeit* (Berlin: Weidmann, 1913)—and those who insist on the unity of Plato's thought—e.g., von Arnim, *Platos Jugenddialoge*; and Shorey, *Unity of Plato's Thought*—argue that the investigation of the meaning of love and friendship that Socrates begins in the *Lysis* is filled out, if not completed, in the *Symposium* and *Phaedrus*. Laszlo Versenyi, "Plato's *Lysis*," *Phronesis* 20, no. 3 (1975): 85–98, represents a partial exception. Like this author, he argues that the friendship Socrates describes

however, that Plato intended his readers to imagine the conversation related in the *Lysis* as having occurred well after both the *Symposium* and
the *Phaedrus*.[30] Moreover, the apparently aporetic conversation in the *Lysis*
contains a critique of both the definitions of love presented in the two
earlier dialogues. In the *Symposium* Socrates (in the guise of Diotima) suggested that human eros begins with the desire for a particular beautiful
young person but that it culminates in the love of the beautiful in itself. In
the *Lysis* he argues that the erotic desire to possess what we now lack, even
if that is what is held to be most dear, the *prōton philon* (or "first friend,"
which has reminded so many commentators of the good-in-itself), does
not constitute an adequate definition of friendship. In the first place, the
relation is not mutual. He who holds the good—or knowledge—most dear
is not himself held to be dear (or a friend). Nor does the "friendship" last, if
the desire is satisfied and the good possessed. In the *Phaedrus* Socrates had
thus suggested that a lover perceives the image of the god he would become, if he could, in the face of his beloved. The lover's attempts to enable
his beloved to realize the potential indicated by his imaging of the divine
arouse a reciprocal affection and corresponding desire to improve him on
the part of the beloved. As lover and beloved change roles, they become
more like and their desire mutually felt. In the *Lysis*, however, Socrates
points out not only that all "loves" are not mutual, but also that people
who do the same things tend to compete with each other. The friendships
he seeks to establish with his young associates are not relations among
people who are or ever become completely alike. As Socrates reminds his
audience and Plato reminds his readers with the philosopher's demonstration of his "erotic speech," Socrates obviously knows more than the young
people with whom he associates. But Socrates and his associates are not entirely unlike either. Neither he nor they possess the good, the wisdom, they
come together to seek. He cannot simply give it to them; he does not claim
to possess it or even to represent a beautiful image of it. On the basis of a
shared desire for wisdom, which he both communicates to and awakens

---

is fundamentally educational, but he emphasizes the utilitarian aspect of Socrates' discussion of
friendship and downplays the identification of the "first friend" with the good too much.

30. As noted earlier, the dramatic date of the conversation Socrates narrates in the *Lysis* is
indicated primarily by the age of two of the participants in relation to their depiction in the
Euthydemus and the *Menexenus*. Even if the conversation narrated in the *Euthydemus* (275b) is supposed to have taken place in 407, as Nails argues, the conversation Socrates narrates in the *Lysis*
would definitely have occurred after the *Symposium*, set dramatically in 416, and the *Phaedrus*,
usually thought to be set in 412–411, if not earlier.

in his companions, they form an association or "family" of those who are related (*oikeiou*) by nature because they seek to obtain and share in the same good. The "aporetic," uncertain, and incomplete conclusion of the dialogue images the character of philosophy as a never-ending, essentially uncertain search.

A. Socrates' Attempt to Change His Public Image

As in the *Euthydemus*, so in the *Lysis*, Socrates narrates the dialogue. As in the *Euthydemus*, so in the *Lysis*, Socrates not merely describes but enacts, in front of an audience, the kind of conversation he has with young Athenians. Instead of addressing the concerns of a specific individual like Crito, however, in the *Lysis* Socrates relates the conversation to an anonymous audience. Later, by relating the conversation to another anonymous audience, Socrates goes out of his way to make the contents and results known to others, as he had in the *Protagoras*, when he was seeking to establish his reputation, but not in the *Symposium* or *Phaedrus*, where Plato shows him speaking in private.

In earlier dialogues such as *Protagoras*, *Alcibiades I*, *Charmides*, *Symposium*, and *Phaedrus*, Socrates had allowed himself and his desire to associate with noble youths to be characterized, somewhat playfully, in terms of the conventional pursuit of beautiful boys by older males (*erastai*). Even though the only things he claimed to know were *ta erōtika*, he never sought to have sexual intercourse with his young companions; all he wanted was to converse with them. Nevertheless, after he became famous, Socrates apparently realized that this conventional misrepresentation of the character of his association with the young was dysfunctional, if not dangerous. He was ten years older, so his pursuit of young men as a lover was apt to make him took even more foolish, if not degenerate, than it had when he was younger. (He was later convicted of corrupting the young.) Just as Socrates dramatized the difference between his refutations of his interlocutors and those of the eristic sophists in his narration of the *Euthydemus*, so in the *Lysis* he brought out the difference between the beneficent friendship he sought to establish with young boys and the sexual desires of an older male lover like Hippothales.[31] Socrates recognized that if he

---

31. Drew A. Hyland, "*Erōs, Epithumia,* and *Philia* in Plato," *Phronesis* 13, no. 1 (1968): 32–46, argues that *philia* is more associated with reason than either *epithymia* (desire) or *erōs* (love) in the Platonic dialogues.

continued to present his relations with young men in terms of eros, their fathers might restrict his contact with their sons. Unfortunately, Plato indicates, the more Socrates depicted himself as something like a father figure instead of a lover, the more he appeared to compete with parents for the affection and respect of their progeny. Rather than merely appearing to be a ridiculous old man, the philosopher began to look like a threat to the traditional order of the family. As Aristophanes suggests in his *Clouds*, so Plato shows in the dialogues he set in the last decade of Socrates' life, it was not the alleged atheism of the philosopher so much as the alienation of their sons' affection that angered the Athenians.

B. The Suspicious Look of Socrates' Associations with the Young

In the opening scene of the *Lysis*, Socrates appears in the guise of the expert in erotic affairs he claimed to be in both the *Symposium* (177e) and *Phaedrus* (257a). Walking outside the city walls from the Academy to the Lyceum (where the conversation related in the *Euthydemus* took place), he was accosted by Hippothales and Ctesippus, who urged him to join them in discussions with other young people in a nearby palaestra. Socrates did not accept their invitation immediately, however. He suspected, correctly, that they wished to obtain his assistance in pursuing their own erotic endeavors. He seemed to recognize that in entering the palaestra he might be contravening Athenian customs or law. According to Aeschines (*Contra Timarchum* 10), during the Hermaea (the festival the boys are celebrating) the rules governing palaestra were relaxed to allow youths to talk to the boys and their slave guardians to get drunk, but adults like Socrates were not permitted to join them.[32] Instead of seizing the opportunity to converse with noble young Athenians, as we might have expected on the basis of his behavior in earlier dialogues, Socrates made a series of preliminary inquiries. First, he asked who was in charge of the school. Hearing that the teacher was a sophist named Miccus, with whom Socrates was not merely

---

32. In the *Symposium* 182a–85b, Pausanias reports that Athenian law was ambiguous. Although it allowed lovers to act openly in ways that were not otherwise thought to be seemly, the law also had fathers hire tutors to guard their sons from such lovers. Pausanias interprets this ambiguity as constituting a test to make lovers go to great efforts to show that not merely do they desire the bodies of their beloved but they wish to improve their souls as well. The fact that Pausanias proposes a new law that would outlaw love of boys whose minds had not yet developed (as a waste), but allow those lovers who did not approach the very young to pursue adolescents and allow adolescents to gratify them, suggests that Athenian law did not allow older men to pursue young boys, even though the law was not strictly or effectively enforced or followed.

acquainted but who had even commended the philosopher, Socrates seemed to have felt assured that his transgression would not be reported to the civil authorities. He then asked on what terms he would be entering the palaestra and who the beautiful one was. He thus forced Hippothales to admit that he was seeking Socrates' assistance in wooing a boy.

Although Hippothales responded to Socrates' question by observing that different people have different notions of beauty, Socrates declared that his god-given ability to recognize lovers and beloveds let him see that Hippothales was in love with a particular youth. Since Hippothales was too embarrassed to tell Socrates the name of his beloved, Ctesippus had to inform the philosopher not only that his young friend was in love with Democrates' son Lysis but also that Hippothales had proved himself to be an inept lover. Rather than saying anything specially about his beloved, Hippothales had praised Lysis' family, their wealth, and their history. Socrates commented that Hippothales had been celebrating his triumph before he had achieved it. Although Hippothales would not admit it, he had been lauding his prey to make his conquest appear all the more glorious. Hippothales obviously did not know much about love. Not only was his success uncertain; he had been making it more difficult by giving the object of his desire more reason to be proud and less apt to grant favors. Hippothales admitted he would be grateful for any assistance Socrates could offer him. Socrates said that could not tell Hippothales how to approach a beloved but that he would show him.

At the beginning of the *Lysis*, Plato thus depicts Socrates acting in a highly questionable, if not improper, manner—both legally and morally. The philosopher may have been violating Athenian social norms. (The young men's easy invitation to Socrates to join them in the palaestra suggests that the regulations were not strictly or regularly enforced.) Socrates also and more shockingly appears to be actively and willingly engaged in procuring the favors of a young boy for an older male. To put it bluntly, as Seth Benardete states, Socrates looks like a pimp.[33] If Socrates' claim to fame as a philosopher consisted in his knowledge of *ta erōtika*, the begin-

---

33. Cf. Seth Benardete, "On Plato's *Lysis*," in *The Argument of the Action: Essays on Greek Poetry and Philosophy* (Chicago: University of Chicago Press, 2000), 198–202. James Haden, "Friendship in Plato's *Lysis*," *Review of Metaphysics* 37 (December 1983): 344–52, points out the way in which the setting of Socrates' initial encounter with the young men at the gate of Panops (the all-seeing Hermes), as well as the festival the boys are celebrating in the palaestra, evokes the sexual associations of the god (and thus exaggerates the impression that Socrates' meeting with the boys is illicit).

ning of the *Lysis* makes it look as if the Athenians had fairly good reasons for prosecuting Socrates as a corrupter of the young.

C. Socrates' Demonstration of His Erotic Knowledge

When readers see that the "erotic" speech Socrates gives to show Hippothales how to approach a beloved constitutes an argument for the need to acquire knowledge in order to become useful to and thus loved by one's family or strangers, it does not look quite so sleazy. We observe, moreover, that Socrates chooses to discuss the nature of love in his own name (as opposed to that of Diotima or Stesichorus), in the context of an obviously asexual and apparently reciprocal relation between two young boys. He does not use the desire of a lover for gratification as his beginning point or model, the way he did in the *Symposium* and *Phaedrus*. He does suggest that young people will have to question the character and grounds of the control parents customarily exercise over their children in order to form a new association with those who are "akin" or belong to each other by nature, because they seek knowledge of the good (and not merely because they are blood related). Socrates thus appears to admit that the philosophical friendships he seeks to form with young people constitute a challenge to the authority parents were accustomed to exercise over their progeny. That is presumably the reason, Plato indicates in the opening of the dialogue, that Socrates had to cross conventional boundaries in order to show his young associates what friendship or love involves.

Hippothales did not know how to arouse Lysis' interest or affections, but he could tell Socrates how to approach him. If Socrates were to enter the palaestra with Ctesippus and begin talking, Hippothales predicted, Menexenus would join his relative, and Lysis would follow Menexenus, whom he has made his special companion (*hetairos*). Having watched his beloved closely, Hippothales knew that Lysis loved to listen to arguments. (Readers might infer that Hippothales was not able to engage in such arguments and so attract Lysis to him, whereas Socrates is able to do so.)

On entering the palaestra, Socrates sees Lysis standing alone with a garland around his head and comments that the youth looks not merely beautiful but both beautiful and good (*kalos k'agathos*), that is, the image of an Athenian gentleman. By remaining aloof from the others, Lysis indicates he is proud of his looks as well as of his wealthy, aristocratic family. Unsure of his ability to speak, he is also shy. Although he looks eager to join the conversation Socrates begins with Ctesippus, Lysis comes over, as Hippothales predicted, only after Menexenus does.

Having observed Lysis' reticence, Socrates addresses his questions initially to Menexenus. Although his queries bring out the free and easy relations between the two boys, they also point to possible grounds of dissension. Socrates begins by asking who is older and hence better born. The boys say they argue about their age and birth (and thus suggest that they are close), but they laugh at the question of who is most beautiful. Lysis obviously is. Does that mean he is (or thinks that he is) superior—better and more beautiful (or noble)? Socrates tells the boys that he will not ask them about their relative wealth, because, according to an old saying, friends share everything in common.[34] Socrates reports that he did not have an opportunity to ask who is wiser or more just, because Menexenus was called away. Those listening to Socrates' account of the conversation might have remembered, however, that Menexenus was said to know more about arguing than Lysis. Socrates later reminds Lysis that Menexenus, having been tutored by his cousin Ctesippus, is a keen disputant (*eristikos*). Might Menexenus have appeared to be wiser and thus more deserving of honor than his good-looking friend? Although they appear to be close, relations between the two young comrades could easily become competitive.[35] Without Socrates' intervention, they might have not remained friends for long.

Socrates takes the opportunity created by Menexenus' absence to ask Lysis about his relation to his parents.[36] Does he think they love (*philein*) him? He does. In contrast to the friendship between the two boys, the relation between parents and child is obviously very unequal. Lysis' parents not merely do not allow him to do as he wishes; they do not give him the same access to or control over their property they give to slaves. They even put a slave in charge of his movements. Lysis justifies the control by ob-

---

34. In the *Laws* 739c–e, the Athenian observed that this was impossible for human beings (at least in a regime), and in the *Republic* 457b–66d, Socrates first argued that it would be necessary for the guardians to hold all property, including children and wives, in common, but then suggested that the city he had described was not likely to come into existence. Members of households, especially husbands and wives, do share, however, which is one reason the *oikos* becomes the model association in the *Lysis*.

35. Cf. Penner and Rowe, *Lysis*, 12.

36. Even though in the *Symposium* Diotima teaches Socrates that erotic relations are properly understood to be educational (210a–12a), Socrates begins his "speech" in "praise" of Eros (199c–d) by explicitly excluding relations between parents and children or between siblings from his discussion of eros. Such relations would obviously be incestuous, although he does not say so. They are, however, as Socrates shows here, properly seen to be loving (*philia*) and educational.

serving that he is not yet of age. Like the friendship between the two boys, the friendship between Lysis and his parents also appears to be temporary, lasting only until the boy matures. Making explicit the principle implicit in the control exercised over the young, Socrates asks whether Lysis' parents allow him to read and write letters for them. Told that he is trusted to do this (as a slave probably would not have been), Socrates generalizes: a person is allowed to do what he knows. Not merely Lysis' parents, but his neighbors, the Athenians, and even the Great King entrust their lives and most precious possessions to those who show they know what to do with them. Those who demonstrate their practical intelligence (*phronimoi genōmetha*) not merely are free themselves but have control of others, because they in effect own and derive the advantages from the things they know how to use. Those who do not possess such practical wisdom are not allowed to do as they wish but are constrained by others.

The message is clear. Lysis should not think well of himself until he has acquired practical wisdom. Once he has acquired it, however, everyone will be his friend. Since he does not possess practical wisdom yet, he needs someone to help him acquire it. As the person who has just told him what he needs to do, Socrates appears to be volunteering. Lysis should look to him, rather than to his parents, to learn what he needs to know in order to become free himself and command others. Ruling on the basis of knowledge instead of force, he will be loved rather than feared. The model of the kind of love Socrates describes is familial affection rather than sexual desire. Just as parents do everything they can to help their children become as good as possible, because they love their children, so Socrates will instruct Lysis, and Lysis will benefit others with the knowledge he acquires. Just as children love their parents for the benefits received or expected, so Lysis will love Socrates, and those he rules will love Lysis.

Socrates' demonstration of the way in which one ought to approach a beloved youth is thus similar to the first conversation he had with Alcibiades (to whom the philosopher had presented himself as his last and best lover [*erastēs*], because he loved the young man's soul and not his body [*Alcibiades I* 103a])—with two important exceptions. Alcibiades' father was dead, and his guardian Pericles was not apt to become jealous of Socrates, as Lysis' father might. There is, moreover, an audience whose members will probably relate Socrates' conversation with Lysis to others, as there had not been for Socrates' first encounter with Alcibiades. Like Alcibiades, Socrates shows Lysis that the youth's looks, family, wealth, and native intelligence will not suffice to enable him to realize the great ambitions he had not been aware he had. From their first conversation the youth learns that he has to look to Socrates to find out what he wants to do, as well as how to do it.

Socrates underlines the character and thrust of the demonstration of his "erotic" speech by reporting that he almost made an error by telling Hippothales that this is the way to endear oneself to another—not by puffing him up but by showing him how you can help him become better. When Socrates turned to look at Hippothales, however, he saw that the young lover was in an agony of embarrassment. His embarrassment points to the difference between the Socratic and his more ordinary kind of love. Socrates shows youths what they really want and promises to help them achieve it; Hippothales knows only what he wants. Having nothing to offer his beloved but his own desire, he has to hide himself and his desire. Socrates can openly proclaim his own desire for wisdom and the knowledge he has acquired of love matters, because both are associated with a promise to benefit others, as much, if not more than oneself. The problem, to which he is responding in the *Lysis*, is that his kind of love of the young was often mistaken for the other. By showing that the love he felt for the young was more like that of a parent than that of a lover, however, Socrates made the potential competition between him and the boys' parents for their loyalty and affection more evident.

D. Who or What Is a Friend (*Philos*)?

1. The Question Raised in Action

Hippothales was probably even more discomfited when he saw Socrates and Lysis whispering together in private. Had Socrates not supplanted the young would-be lover by persuading the boy of the need to seek wisdom with him? Ctesippus indicates that Socrates and Lysis were acting like exclusive lovers, when he complains about their not sharing their speeches with the others present. (As in the *Euthydemus*, so in the *Lysis*, Socrates is thus shown to be conversing with a beautiful youth surrounded by a group of other young lovers.)

Having attracted Lysis by indicating the benefits the youth might attain by conversing further with him, readers see that Socrates did not immediately engage Lysis in a search for what is truly good and beautiful, as we might have expected from the *Alcibiades I, Symposium*, or *Phaedrus*. Instead, Socrates turned, at Lysis' request, to examine Menexenus on the character of friendship. As a result, the dialogue seems to focus on the relation between the two boys rather than on the relation Socrates is forming with them, even though Socrates says at the end of the dialogue that he counts himself in with them.

Younger and less self-confident than Alcibiades, Lysis does not privately beseech Socrates to teach him how to make friends and influence people. Instead he asks Socrates to tell Menexenus what Socrates has just told him. Still a boy, Lysis is willing to have Socrates show him that he does not yet know everything he needs to. Nevertheless, he also wants Socrates to show that his comrade does not know any more or better. Lysis feels, even if he does not say, that his relation with his comrade is competitive. Socrates asks Lysis, in effect, to demonstrate what he has just learned by repeating what he has heard, but Lysis demurs. Socrates had reminded Lysis that Menexenus is skilled in eristic debates, and Lysis may not have believed that he could show his friend that he needed to learn the way Socrates had shown him. Lysis assures Socrates that he will repeat what he had heard later; now he wants Socrates to give another speech so he can listen (and not himself be interrogated further).

Although Socrates' initial exchanges with the boys indicate that their relations are more competitive than cooperative, they understand themselves to be drawn together as friends primarily by what they have in common. In responding to Ctesippus' complaint that they are not sharing their speeches with the others, Socrates states his question to Menexenus so that all can hear; Socrates also acts, as the ancient saying he had quoted said a friend would act, by sharing the conversation that follows not only with the others present but also with his anonymous auditors. Socrates asks Menexenus, in effect, whether the understanding of friendship as sharing things in common is adequate.

According to Socrates, Lysis had not understood something Socrates said but thought that Menexenus might. Socrates does not tell Menexenus that Lysis asked him not merely to question but to correct his friend. Nor did Socrates tell Lysis that he was talking to him in order to show Hippothales how to seduce a young man. Socrates' failure to be completely open or honest with his young interlocutors might lead readers to ask whether he is a good friend of the boys. The question of who or what a friend is, is thus raised in the action as well as explicitly in the argument of the dialogue.

Socrates apparently recognized that there was something not entirely friendly about Lysis' request. By asking Menexenus what a friend (*philos*) is, Socrates suggests that this is what Lysis did not understand. If Lysis had recognized the way Socrates had benefited him by showing him that he needed to acquire practical wisdom in order to achieve his ambitions, Lysis might have wanted his friend Menexenus to enjoy the same benefits. But if that was what he wanted, Lysis would have asked Socrates to examine and correct Menexenus in public rather than whispering his request in private.

The "erotic" attraction Socrates appears to have exercised on Lysis seems, moreover, to consist, as it had in the case of Alcibiades, in the promise of providing the youth with the means of besting all his rivals. As soon as Lysis has learned everything he can from Socrates, he will presumably cast the old man aside. What Plato has indicated about Lysis' pride and competitiveness makes us wonder whether he would have accepted the same disclosing of his own lack of freedom and knowledge from Hippothales, a young man closer to him in age and position. If not, Socrates has not provided Hippothales with an example of an approach he can actually use to get what he wants. The opening exchanges of the dialogue should lead readers to ask more broadly what Socrates thinks he is demonstrating to whom.

2. Why Friends Cannot Be Merely Like or Unlike

Socrates may not have simply been dissimulating when he told Menexenus (*Lysis* 211e) that he had passionately longed (*erōtikōs*) to possess friends (*philōn*) and thus congratulated Lysis and Menexenus for having become friends at such a young age. Socrates explained that he did not know how to acquire a friend (*philos*), because he did not know how one becomes dear (*philos*) to another (despite his knowledge of *ta erōtika*). "When someone loves [*philē(i)*] someone," he asks Menexenus, "which one becomes friend (or dear) to the other, he who loves [*philōn*] the beloved [*philomenou*] or the beloved [*philomenos*] of the lover [*philountos*]? Or is there no difference?" (212a). It might seem incredible that the expert in *erōs* has never had a friend, but Socrates' question points to a difference between *erōs* and *philos* and the difficulty therein. Whereas *erōs* is a passionate desire for an object or person, it is not clear whether the *philos* is the one who holds something dear or what is held dear (and thus what it would mean to have a friend, someone who holds you dear or whom you hold dear).

The difficulty would disappear if there were no difference between friend and befriended, that is, if friends share everything in common. Believing that they do, Menexenus responded to Socrates' question by saying that there is no difference. Socrates reminded him that young people often resent and are angered by the attentions of older lovers (*erastai*) or parents. (Lovers and parents can arouse the same negative reaction, even though their motives and the kind of love they have for the young person are quite different.) People are also said to love animals or things, like wine or wisdom, that cannot love them back. The holding of something dear does not appear to be a reciprocal relation. But if children sometimes hate parents who love them, and those who hate are enemies, Socrates pointed out, then friends (or the beloved) can be enemies of their friends (lovers), and lovers (or friends) can be enemies of their beloved. But friends and enemies are thought to be opposites.

By reducing the "eristic" Menexenus to a state of *aporia* (*ou pany euporō*), Socrates induced Lysis to reenter the conversation and actively engage in their attempt to discover who a friend is. Aware of Lysis' reluctance to be interrogated further and again found wanting, Socrates suggested they might not have been proceeding correctly. Not having enjoyed having his own lack of understanding exposed, Lysis emphatically agreed. In fact, by asking whether friends are simply "like" or, soon, "unlike" without any qualification concerning the respects in which they are like or unlike, Socrates had proceeded the way he showed, in the *Euthydemus*, that eristic sophists did in refuting their interlocutors. The difference here, as it was in the *Euthydemus*, was that Socrates was not seeking merely to demonstrate that the young boys contradicted themselves or, in the case of Menexenus, that they had not quite mastered the techniques of eristic debate. Socrates was trying to benefit his young interlocutors. He was bringing out the problems with their current opinions so that they could acquire a new and better understanding of their own condition. As the initial action indicated, Menexenus and Lysis were not apt to remain friends if they did not acquire a new understanding of friendship. Although he readily admitted that Lysis was handsomer than he, Menexenus believed that friends are friends because they are like. He did not seem to realize that Lysis believed he was beloved because of his beauty and that he associated with Menexenus because Menexenus was clever at arguments and thus useful, at least temporarily, to the more reticent Lysis. If and when Lysis learned how to argue, from Socrates, for example, he would no longer need Menexenus. He would be free, and perhaps even feel entitled as his superior, to command his former "friend." In any case, Lysis did not understand Menexenus to be "like" or "equal" to him.

To prevent the boys from feeling discouraged the way Clinias was when he was refuted by the sophists, Socrates deflected the criticism away from his young interlocutors by attributing to Homer Menexenus' belief that friendship consists in the attraction of like to like. Having shown the problems with that definition, he then attributed the more instrumental view of friendship Lysis accepted in his first exchange with Socrates to the cosmologists and showed the difficulty with their view.

As Socrates indicates by quoting a line from Homer's *Odyssey* (17.218) in which the poet says that god draws like to like, the poets were the source of the understanding of friendship Menexenus articulated.[37] In this statement, we should note, the god already constitutes a third factor or cause of the friendship between others. Socrates plays this role in the dialogue, we shall see, although Socrates does not point out the connection or his role explicitly. This is the aspect of friendship people generally do not understand, that friendship does not exist simply between two people or a person and a thing, but that two or more are united for the sake of something else.

Leading the young people through the argument one step at a time, Socrates first showed them why friendship cannot be understood to be merely the attraction of like to like. Although they are like, he pointed out, the wicked and unjust do not become friends. Friends must be like in sharing certain qualities and not sharing others.[38] It might seem, therefore, that those who are like because they are good will be friends. But, Socrates reminds them, in their first exchange he and Lysis agreed that friends are useful. If the good is self-sufficient, then a good person will not need anyone or anything else or find anyone or anything useful, and so "dear." Socrates and Lysis had agreed, however, that friends must somehow be both good and useful to others.

Taking the argument one step further, Socrates referred to authors he said were even wiser than the poets because they discussed nature as a whole. These authors maintained that friends are unlike. Socrates showed without explicitly stating that the poets disagree with one another by quot-

37. As Davis (*Autobiography*, 81), Benardete ("On Plato's *Lysis*," 215), and Bolotin (*Plato's Dialogue*, 125–27) point out, Socrates wrenches the line from its context. It is said disparagingly of Eumaios, the swineherd, and Odysseus, disguised as a beggar, by the goatherd who is serving the suitors. To a certain extent, however, the layers of deceit parallel the many steps of Socrates' argument in the *Lysis*, an argument that appears to go back and forth between opposites. Not only is Odysseus a disguised king; the swineherd who serves him was also once a prince, who was enslaved as a result of defeat in war. There is, therefore, a question concerning nature and convention here as well as one of appearance and reality. The "like" are both like and unlike each other and themselves. The god suggests that similar people may be drawn together more by circumstances or chance than by choice.

38. If Lysis and Menexenus had observed Socrates argue with the sophists and learned from his demonstrations the way Ctesippus had, Socrates would not have been able to convince them that friends are simply not like, the way he does here.

ing another poet, Hesiod, who observed that people who engage in the same activities tend to compete rather than to cooperate with each other, and thus challenged Homer's claim that the god draws like to like. The poets themselves thus seemed to support the cosmologists' claim that those who are alike compete and thus oppose each other not only in word but also in deed. More generally, both the poets and the cosmologists suggested, as the poor in need must be friendly to the rich, and the sick man is friend to the doctor, so opposed elements in the cosmos such as hot and cold, dry and wet, sweet and bitter, empty and full, seem to be attracted to each other by what one party to the "friendship" lacks and another provides.

But just as Socrates had objected to the definition of friendship as the attraction of like to like in his previous exchange with Menexenus, because the unjust cannot be friends with each other, so, he now told both Lysis and Menexenus, those who are experts in refuting others (*antilogikoi*) would gleefully point out that as hatred is the opposite of love, so friends are the opposite of enemies, and the just are the opposite of the unjust. Those who are unlike cannot be said to be friends any more than those who are like. Socrates has made it clear that friendship cannot be defined in terms of these mutually exclusive categories. Because Socrates has not explicitly or directly refuted or shamed them, the way an eristic sophist would, both boys are willing to follow his lead in articulating a new, more complex understanding of friendship.

3. Friendship Is Not Merely a Desire for a Good That One Lacks

Having shown that it is impossible to define friendship in terms of a reciprocal relation between likes or unlikes, and that both the poets and the cosmological philosophers who refined and broadened the poets' understanding of nature were wrong, Socrates recalled another old saying and thus opened up a third avenue of inquiry. According to this (unattributed) saying, the beautiful (*kalos*) is friend (*philos*). This definition of *philos* makes it sound very much like *erōs*, as Socrates described it in the *Symposium*, especially when he goes on to ask Menexenus whether the beautiful is not also the good. In the *Symposium* Socrates defined *erōs* primarily in terms of the absence or want of, and consequent desire to possess, not merely the beautiful but the good—forever. But in the *Lysis* Socrates argues that those who desire the good do not hold it to be dear (*philos*) merely on account of its absence. The desire for a good that one lacks may be considered to be a special case of the attraction of opposites (empty and full).

Socrates pointed out that those who completely lack the good would exist in the opposite state, that is, be bad. Those who love the beautiful because it is good can be neither good, in which case they would not want the good, nor bad, in which case their badness would exclude the presence of its opposite. (They are like the in-between of opinion, which Diotima taught the young Socrates is neither of the mutually exclusive poles of knowledge or ignorance, and which is the locus of philosophical inquiry.) Those who want to acquire and possess the beautiful and good must be changeable, although the object they wish to possess need not be. If they have no hope of possessing and retaining the object of their love, their love of it would be based on an illusion. (Such is the tragic understanding of eros that Agathon articulates in the *Symposium*.)

In the *Lysis* Socrates explains to both of the boys (217a) how it is possible for something or someone to be neither good nor bad by describing two different ways in which something can be present (*parousia*) to something else. If something is externally juxtaposed to something else, as, for example, when hair is painted white, the first thing may affect the external appearance, but it will not affect or express the character of the thing, the way the white hair of an aged man reveals his actual condition.[39] As Socrates' example reminds us, things or opinions are apt to be external when they are newly appended to something or someone young; over time, with age, they tend to become internalized. As in the *Symposium*, so in the *Lysis*, Socrates uses philosophy as an example of this in-between condition. Philosophers who love knowledge are not knowers, but they are also not completely ignorant or stupid. They know that they don't know and seek knowledge because it is good. Lacking what is good, but seeking it, they cannot be said to be simply bad, although they are not simply good either. Socrates does not say that philosophers are the only true friends or that wisdom is the only thing that is truly good and beautiful

Socrates merely concludes that all absences or deprivations of goods cannot and should not be regarded simply as bad. Desires like hunger can be instrumental to goods, like remaining alive. Neither friendship nor philosophy (if it is, indeed, a form of friendship) can be adequately defined in terms simply of a desire and its satisfaction in the possession of the object or the remedy of the want. If human beings become friends, like an invalid

---

39. He also shows how he could have responded to Dionysodorus' objection to his argument about participation in the *Euthydemus*, if he had wished.

and a doctor, for the sake of some good (in this case, health), because of some remediable bad (in this case, illness), the "friend" will cease to be a friend when the bad is removed and the good is acquired.[40] The "friend" appears to be merely instrumental and transitory; if "friends" are means of acquiring some other good, there must be a first or final good (or "friend," *to prōton philon*), for which all others are means and on account of which we call the others friends (*hou heneka kai ta alla phamen panta phila einai*; 219c). What is good and is therefore held to be a friend (or dear) cannot be adequately defined merely in terms of the absence of its opposite or the bad.

4. SOCRATES' MORE COMPLEX BUT INCOMPLETE DEFINITION OF FRIENDSHIP

If desire is a cause of friendship, that which desires is a friend of what it desires, and it desires what it lacks, Socrates concluded: *erōs*, *philos*, and *epithymia* (desire) must be for that which belongs to one (*oikeiou*). By saying that if Lysis and Menexenus are friends they belong to each other by nature, Socrates not only raises the question of whether the boys actually are friends (which he had implicitly raised earlier). He also suggests that the inadequacies human beings perceive in themselves that cause them to seek friends are natural.

As Socrates indicated by describing the different reactions the boys and Lysis' young lover have to his arguments, it is not the perception of inadequacy and consequent need in individuals that cause the problem or make it difficult to say what a friend is. Human beings desire and thus hold a large number of things to be "dear." Problems arise with regard to private or exclusive possession as opposed to common ownership, particularly with regard to the person or thing held to be dear. Do persons or things belong to others, by nature, simply because they desire but are deprived of them? Because individuals want many of the same things, there would be much conflict about who owns what (as Hobbes points out in *Leviathan* 1.13) unless things (and persons—wives and children) are owned in common (as Socrates suggested they should be in the *Republic*). That may be the reason Socrates restricted *erōs*, *philos*, and *epithymia* to relations among humans, when in the very next sentence (222a) he stated that no

---

40. Cf. Bolotin (*Plato's Dialogue*, 60) and Gadamer ("*Logos* and *Ergon* in Plato's *Lysis*," in *Dialogue and Dialectic*, 16) on the meaning and difference between *heneka*, "for the sake of," and *dia ti*, "because of," something.

one will love, befriend, or desire another unless that person belongs (or is akin) to him in soul or in some character (*ēthos*), ways (*tropous*), or form (*eidos*) of soul.[41]

Why should a psychic similarity give one person a right to claim another as his property? Plato dramatizes the difficulty by having Socrates report that Menexenus, the boy who believed from the beginning that friendship is a reciprocal relation between like persons, emphatically agreed with him, whereas Lysis, the boy who acknowledged the right of his parents to control him and his property until the age of maturity, when he hoped to be free to command others, remained silent (and so indicated his dissent). Ignoring the difference in the reactions of his two interlocutors, Socrates concludes that it is necessary for human beings to love what belongs to them by nature. He brings out the way in which he has identified *philos* with *erōs* in this last definition, and yet at the same time points to the difference, when he adds that it is necessary, therefore, for the genuine rather than pretended lover (*erastēs*) to be loved (*phileisthai*) by his favorite (*paidikon*), that is, that true love among human beings is mutual. Socrates indicates that this conclusion is by no means necessary or uncontroversial by reporting that both boys signified their assent, but with difficulty, by silently nodding, whereas Hippothales radiated with pleasure.

In his first conversation with Menexenus, Socrates reminded the boy that children often greet the attentions of older lovers, as they do the admonitions of their parents, with distaste, if not anger. These boys obviously do not share the desire of their lovers or feel that they belong by nature to them. Socrates might have responded that these older lovers are not genuine lovers, if they do not seek the good of the boy's soul rather than bodily pleasure for themselves, using him as a means. (Hippothales would therefore have to change not only his way of approaching Lysis but also his aim in doing so in order to become a genuine lover.) In the *Symposium* and the *Phaedrus* Socrates acknowledged that human beings perceive their erotic longings initially as physical urges, whether to procreate or to attain pleasure. In both these dialogues he had argued that true love is, nevertheless, love of the soul. That love is, moreover, ultimately a desire to obtain a higher or more beautiful good or god. The "friend" as Socrates describes him or it in the *Lysis* appears to be something lesser.

41. Socrates appears here to be close to Aristophanes' suggestion in the *Symposium* that eros consists in the desire to become whole again by reuniting with one's other half, but for Aristophanes such a temporary reunion is bodily.

The "friend" appears in Socrates' initial exchange with Lysis to be useful; he knows and can tell others how to get what they want. The "friend" cannot simply be good in himself, Socrates then tells Menexenus, because those who are completely good do not need anyone else. Even though people say that the beautiful, and hence the good, is what we hold dear (and so a friend), and that all the things we hold dear, because they are means of achieving something else we desire, point to this final or first "friend," neither the good in itself nor the bad that results from its absence can be said to cause us to seek friends. Our desires are the cause of our seeking friends. These desires are not necessarily bad, but they are signs of our deficiencies. As desirous, humans are neither entirely good nor entirely bad. Socrates claims that those things or persons that remedy our deficiencies and so satisfy our desires belong to us by nature. Although Socrates casts this description of the friend in terms of eros as well, his auditors do not all accept the equation. They do not because they do not understand themselves to share the same need, deficiency, or desire as their "lovers."

Socrates' description of friends as those who belong to each other by nature describes relations among the citizens of the simple or "true" city in the *Republic*, in which each contributes what he or she does best by nature in order most efficiently to satisfy the needs of all, better than a pair of lovers. Each member of the "true city" is needy as an individual, but together they produce everything they need or, apparently, desire. The relations of these citizens are friendly, but they don't seem to be very erotic.[42] As Glaucon's protest indicates, these political friends cooperate in satisfying the needs of their bodies. They do not feel deprived of the truly beautiful, because their souls do not yearn passionately for it. (All human beings or souls may not. As Socrates points out in the famous "ladder of love" in the *Symposium*, the desire to possess what is truly beautiful has to be awakened and cultivated.) The kind of possession Socrates has associated with friendship is not like the erotic madness he describes in the *Phaedrus*. On the contrary, from the beginning of the discussion (*Lysis* 211d) in which Socrates speaks of his erotic desire to possess (*ktasthai*) a friend until the end, when he speaks of friends belonging to each other by nature as parts of a household (221e), he treats friends as kinds of property.

Political communities might be described in terms of friendship as Socrates has just defined it. But can philosophy? Socrates objected to

---

42. Socrates indicates (*Republic* 372b) that they will have to exercise some means of birth control to limit the number of citizens to those the city can support.

Menexenus' initial definition of friendship as reciprocal on the basis of examples like philosophy, that is, of human loves of things (or people) that could not (or did not) love them back. If philosophy is understood, as Socrates often seems to understand it, as the search for knowledge of what will make us happy, then philosophy would be an activity that arises out of human needs and desires. Even if those needs and desires could be satisfied by the achievement of practical wisdom (*phronēsis*) about the best way for a human being to live (cf. *Apology* 38a), such practical wisdom would not constitute the possession of the truly beautiful or the good in itself. It would still be a means of remedying a human deficiency. Since this best way of life consists in conversing with others and examining others about what is truly virtuous, it requires the participation of others who share the same interests. Philosophical conversations cannot take place among those who are alike in all respects, however, any more than economic or political exchanges can. In order to give a full definition of friendship, who or what belongs to whom or what by nature, Socrates would have to specify what character or form of soul friends must have in order to be "akin," and in what respects they must differ in order to be able to remedy each other's deficiencies.

5. WHY THE DEFINITION OF FRIENDSHIP REMAINS INCOMPLETE

Observing that his interlocutors had not entirely agreed with his argument and surmising that they may have had difficulty following all its twists and turns, Socrates asks them, although they are "drunk [and thus presumably confused], as it were, from the argument" (*Lysis* 222b), simply to agree that the akin is something other than the like. He then tests the boys by asking them whether the good is akin to everyone and the bad alien, as it would have to be if what is akin to people by nature is what satisfies their desires by remedying their deprivations, or whether the good is akin to the good, the bad to the bad, and the neither good nor bad to its like. The boys erroneously opt for the latter, and Socrates is forced to conclude that they have fallen back on the account of friendship in terms of the attraction of like to like they had dismissed earlier. So he counts up the possible definitions they have considered of the "friend" as "the wise in law courts do" (222e) (even though he rejects such a procedure in both the *Gorgias* and the *Theaetetus* as a means of arriving at the truth). He lists the beloved, the loving, the like, the unlike, the good, and the akin, and then claims not to remember all the things they have gone through. If none of these was a friend, he concludes, he no longer knows what to say.

Socrates has not shown that his last definition of "friend" as one who is akin or belongs to someone is faulty. He has shown that his interlocutors did not see the difference between that which is said to be akin and the like or the good. But he has not explained what he means by the friendship of those who are akin by nature very clearly. He has not suggested that people might become friends because they share the same desire but are able to compensate for each other's inability to achieve it alone by contributing different talents to a common enterprise. When he engages these young boys in a conversation, for example, Socrates contributes most of the knowledge or wisdom. The boys contribute their youth, a characteristic Socrates no longer possesses but one that he needs in others if his philosophy is to be perpetuated in the future. Nor has Socrates explained how his definition of friendship can be applied to the household, the polity, or philosophy—or to the differences among these kinds of "friendly" associations.

E. Why Socrates Could Not Entirely Overcome the Suspicions of the Fathers

Although Socrates says that he no longer has anything to say, *if* a friend was none of the things he and the boys had mentioned, he clearly did not think their conversation about the meaning of friendship was finished. On the contrary, he reports that he "had in mind [intended] to set one of the older fellows in motion" (*Lysis* 223b). He was prevented from doing so (and thus from completing his investigation of the meaning of friendship or the education of the boys and the young men grouped around them listening) by the return of the slave tutors, who told the boys that it was time for them to go home. Socrates and his companions tried to drive the tutors away, but they appeared to be drunk and were unwilling to listen. The conversation was thus broken up by the threat of physical force on the part of the tutors, legitimated by law.

At the very end of the conversation, Socrates, his auditors, and Plato's readers are thus reminded that his ability to hold philosophical conversations with the young depended on the toleration of such conversations by their parents and the law. Although the law prohibiting such conversations was not strictly enforced, it could be. Socrates' ability to approach and to converse with the very young, who were apt to be most impressionable and hence most educable, would have been much less precarious if he had been able to persuade their fathers and the Athenian people more generally that he was not a lover who wanted take advantage of inexperienced boys to satisfy his own sexual desires. Unfortunately for Socrates, in making the character of his own affection for and attraction to the young clearer, he also made the way in which his philosophy challenged both the wisdom of their own fathers and the law about what was truly good in human existence more evident.

Socrates' parting words indicate the change he had effected by means of the conversation, as well as its limits. "Now, Lysis and Menexenus, we have become ridiculous—I, an old man, and you. For these fellows will say, as they go away, that we suppose we're one another's friends—for I also put myself among you—but what a friend is we have not yet been able to discover" (223b). At the beginning of the conversation, Socrates complained that he had never acquired a friend and congratulated Lysis and Menexenus for having done so; at the end, however, Socrates put himself among them as a friend. He made himself their friend by showing them that they did not know what a friend is, that they needed to learn, and that he could help them learn in future conversations. He had become a friend of the two young boys by persuading them to engage in a philosophical investigation of the character of their relations with one another and their true desires under his guidance. That investigation was admittedly not complete. It could not be complete, if philosophy means the search for wisdom rather than the possession of it. Nor could Socrates know after a single conversation that their friendship would endure. With Menexenus, it did; with Lysis, not.

What becomes clearer in Socrates' conversation with the two boys is the character of the philosophical friendship he tried to form with younger men. Socrates was not seeking pleasure or any other good simply for himself. He was not, therefore, so much a lover as a friend. He was attempting to help other young people acquire the kind of self-knowledge he himself was seeking. All human beings desire what is truly good, Socrates repeatedly insisted. Human beings thus form different kinds of associations, beginning with the family but extending to the polis and philosophy, in order to find out what is truly good and then to acquire it. Like the family, Socrates' relations to his younger associates involved a certain amount of inequality. He knew more and better than they. In order to prove that his opinions were correct and that philosophy constitutes the best form of human existence, Socrates nevertheless had to engage such youths in a similar search. Although they had less knowledge, Socrates' younger friends also had something essential to contribute—their future potential to become philosophers. As in a family, the attraction and affection of Socrates' associates for the philosopher were reciprocated. In contrast both to the family and to the city whose laws supported and secured the authority of the fathers, however, the association of the philosopher and the youths he sought to educate was completely voluntary.

IV. *Gorgias*: Socrates as Sole Practitioner of the True Political Art

The tension between the philosophical friendships Socrates attempted to form with the young and the political friendships among citizens that emerges at the end of the *Lysis* becomes thematic in the *Gorgias*, particularly in the concluding exchange between Socrates and a young Athenian named Callicles. Claiming to be his friend (*Gorgias* 499a), Callicles urges Socrates to give up philosophy and enter the political arena. Philosophy is an appropriate activity only for the young, Callicles asserts. Once he has learned how to speak and argue, a real man (*anēr*) will turn his attention to public affairs, because that is the only way a human being can protect himself and those he loves from the injustice of others. Admitting that he will be unable to defend himself if he is unjustly indicted and dragged into court, Socrates nevertheless tries to show the Athenian youths listening to the conversation that they will not be able to achieve what they want through political action as it is ordinarily understood. He goes so far as to claim (521d), paradoxically, that he is the only one in Athens at his time even trying to practice the true political art!

As Socrates defines it, the true political art is dedicated to achieving the good of the souls of the citizens. It has two branches: formative or legislative and remedial or judicial. Insofar as Socrates "corrects" the opinions of his interlocutors by refuting them, he claims to be exercising the remedial branch of the art. The effectiveness of Socrates' art is, however, necessarily limited. Not only is it impossible for him to interrogate each and every one of his fellow citizens individually. Like Callicles, some of the individuals he examines refuse to have their opinions refuted and so corrected. They do not see the utility of Socrates' "art" and are exasperated by his questions. They believe that it is much more worthwhile to learn from rhetoricians like Gorgias how to persuade their fellow citizens in assemblies to adopt the legislation they wish or to speak in court in their own defense.

Just as Plato dramatized the differences between Socrates and the eristic sophists in the *Euthydemus* and showed that Socrates was not the ordinary kind of elderly lover of the young in the *Lysis*, so he brings out the differences between the kind of argumentative speech in which the philosopher engages and political rhetoric in the *Gorgias*. In all the dialogues set in the decade leading up to his trial and conviction, Plato depicts Socrates' attempts to show his fellow Athenians what his philosophical investigations really involved, what they could achieve, and what they could not.

A. The Limits of the Power of Persuasion

Young Athenians took lessons from foreign teachers of rhetoric like Gorgias and Polus (to whom, we might recall, Socrates referred Theages) in order to acquire political power. But in the *Gorgias* Socrates shows his interlocutors and audience that the power of persuasion is much more limited than the famous rhetorician or his students recognize.

At the beginning of the dialogue, Gorgias' Athenian host Callicles expresses surprise that Socrates has come to hear the rhetorician declaim. In fact, we see, Socrates is not interested in witnessing a demonstration of Gorgias' prowess as a speaker. Socrates blames their failure to arrive on time to hear Gorgias' exhibition on Chaerephon's keeping him in the marketplace. When Callicles and Chaerephon offer to press their friend to give another display, however, Socrates says that can wait. He has some questions he wants to ask Gorgias: what the power of his art is and what he teaches. Since Gorgias had offered to answer any questions after his speech, he agrees to respond to Socrates' queries.

Why was Socrates so interested in the power of rhetoric or what Gorgias teaches? Some commentators have suggested that Socrates might have been interested in enlisting the famous rhetorician's assistance, as he presumably had enlisted the assistance of Thrasymachus in the *Republic*, in persuading people of the beneficial character of philosophy.[43] If not to make philosophers kings, Gorgias might at least convince people not to prosecute philosophers by providing them with a defense, as he had Helen. If so, Socrates' hopes are dashed in the course of the dialogue when Gorgias proves unable to persuade his host Callicles to continue conversing with Socrates, much less to agree to the beneficial character of his philosophy. Rather than a hope of enlisting the cooperation of the famous rhetorician, Socrates' relatively courteous treatment of Gorgias expresses his convic-

---

43. Benardete, *Rhetoric*, 5; James H. Nichols, Jr., trans., *Plato: "Gorgias"* (Ithaca: Cornell University Press, 1998), 131, 148–49, 173; Devin Stauffer, *The Unity of Plato's "Gorgias"* (Cambridge: Cambridge University Press, 2005), 38.

tion, first stated to Polemarchus in the *Republic* and then reiterated to Crito in prison, that not only should one attempt to benefit friends but that one should also not harm or be unjust to anyone, be they competitors or enemies. Socrates tries to benefit Gorgias by showing him that he endangers himself by making the great claims he does for the power of his art. But in the *Meno* Plato shows that all Gorgias learned from his conversation with Socrates was to make his claims consistent. He no longer claimed to teach virtue—or justice—as he does in the *Gorgias*, and he ridiculed the sophists who did. The fact that Socrates does not seek to interrogate Gorgias in private indicates, moreover, that the philosopher was not trying to benefit the rhetorician himself so much as the audience of young Athenians.[44] More than helping Gorgias, Socrates wanted to show their young listeners that rhetoric could not achieve what its teachers claimed it could by refuting its most famous exponent.

In order for them to converse, Socrates emphasizes, Gorgias has to keep his responses short. Although Gorgias sensibly observes that all questions cannot be answered adequately with brief replies, his first responses to Socrates' questions are short. Since Gorgias claims to be a knower and practitioner of an art, Socrates asks what he does and makes others capable of doing too. Gorgias replies, speeches; Socrates then asks what the speeches are about. "The greatest of human affairs, and the best" (451d), Gorgias vaguely and evasively responds. Pressed to be more specific, he finally declares that his art provides "the greatest good and cause both of freedom for human beings themselves and rule over others in each man's own city" by enabling them to make speeches that "persuade judges in the law court, councilors in the council, assemblymen in the assembly, and in every other . . . political gathering" (452d–e).[45]

1. THE GROUNDS OF GORGIAS' CLAIMS

If Gorgias had not been restricted to brief replies by his agreement with Socrates, he might have explained the reasons for his vast claims with

---

44. In the *Gorgias* it is unclear exactly where the conversation takes place or who is listening. Socrates has apparently gone to Callicles' home, where Gorgias is said to be staying (447b). Since Callicles refers to Gorgias' asking of "those inside" to pose any question to him, and Socrates refers later (455c) to "those inside" as possible students, it sounds as if Socrates and Chaerephon have met Callicles, Gorgias, and Polus outside the house. But when Gorgias worries about those before whom he made a display earlier getting tired, and Chaerephon says that Gorgias will hear an "uproar from these men, wishing to hear what you'll say" (458b), it sounds as if there are more listeners present.

45. Nichols, *Plato: "Gorgias,"* 33 (slightly altered).

arguments like those found in two of his remaining fragments. In his "Encomium to Helen" he demonstrates the overwhelming power of speech, and in "On the Non-Existent" he explains the basis of this power by arguing that there is no form of being that exists independent of our sensations.

Gorgias begins his "Encomium" by suggesting that there is a certain kind of proportion and order to all things: "What is becoming to a city is manpower, to a body beauty, to a soul wisdom, to an action virtue, to a speech truth." That proportion seems to create a duty: Because "man and woman and speech and deed and city and object should be honored with praise if praiseworthy and incur blame if unworthy . . . , it is the duty of [a] man both to speak the needful rightly and to refute the unrightfully spoken."[46] Gorgias concludes that it is right for him to refute those who have rebuked Helen for having caused so much suffering as a result of her lack of fidelity to her husband. He claims to be doing what is right, but the arguments he gives on behalf of Helen undermine any legal conception of justice.

Helen is not responsible for the suffering she is said to have caused, Gorgias argues, because she did not choose to do so. Her beauty, a result of her divine parentage, caused men to desire her love and thus brought many men together in order to achieve their ambitions for wealth and glory by displays of personal vigor or knowledge in victorious conquest. Helen was moved to act as she did by divine command or necessity, by force, by speech, or by passion. In the first two cases it is fairly easy to see why Helen was not able to resist. The gods are more powerful than mortals, and it is impossible for a weak woman to resist the superior physical force of a man. Gorgias explains that speech and passion are equally irresistible, however. Because human beings are mortal, we do not know the past, present, or future. We are reduced in all cases to acting on the basis of opinions (or beliefs). But these opinions are easily changed. Astronomers have persuaded human beings to believe things about the heavens contrary to their own observations. Philosophers, too, are able to undermine the beliefs of others by refuting them. Most importantly, speakers who know how to arouse the passions of their audience can change their opinions. Fear is stronger than thought. So is desire or love. The power of speech on the soul is analogous to the power of drugs on the body. Speakers who know how to produce and use speeches to arouse specific passions change what other people think.

With a bit of reflection it becomes clear that the four factors Gorgias says must have determined Helen's actions, so that she is not responsible,

46. Sprague, *Older Sophists*, 50.

would apply to any "criminal." We see, therefore, what kind of speech Gorgias claimed would be the cause of freedom for human beings and why it would enable them to rule over others. Ability to make arguments like those Gorgias gave on behalf of Helen would not only free a potential felon from the threat of punishment in court by persuading a jury of his innocence. Someone able to arouse the passions of others by means of speech could also persuade an assembly to adopt the measures he proposed as law.

In "On the Non-Existent," Gorgias set Parmenides' famous argument showing that being is one, homogeneous, unchanging, eternal, immobile, intelligible but not sensible on its head by arguing on the basis of the same kinds of mutually exclusive alternatives that nothing exists.[47] If it did exist, it would not be intelligible, because things in our minds do not necessarily correspond to things that are. And "even if it should be apprehended, it would be incapable of being conveyed to another. For if existent things are visible and audible and generally perceptible, which means that they are external substances [and perceived by the respective senses of sight and hearing], how can these things [in the mind] be revealed to another person?"[48] Human beings communicate by means of *logos*, a separate faculty from sight or hearing. *Logos* is not a substance or existing thing, however; it arises from things impinging on us. In opposition to Parmenides' claim that being is one, intelligible, and unchanging, Gorgias asserts that all existence is perceptible, hence ever changing and malleable. Because our perceptions are products of interactions between external things and those who perceive them, they change and can be changed. There is no independently existing "being" or "reason" (*logos*) by which to test or measure the truth of our changing perceptions. These perceptions can, moreover, be intentionally manipulated by a rhetorician who knows how to affect the passions and therewith the perceptions and beliefs of his audience.

2. SOCRATES' REFUTATION OF GORGIAS

In his conversation with Gorgias, Socrates does not explore the philosophical basis of the rhetorician's claims. That fact alone suggests that Socrates

47. Edward Schiappa, "Interpreting Gorgias's 'Being' in *On Not-Being* or *On Nature*," *Philosophy and Rhetoric* 30, no. 1 (1997): 15–27, shows the parallels between Gorgias' text and Parmenides' poem. He and the other interpreters he mentions are wrong, however, to think that readers are forced to choose between a serious "philosophical" reading of Gorgias' argument and one in which it is seen to be a clever parody. It is both.

48. Sprague, *Older Sophists*, 46.

is not as concerned about examining the rhetorician as he is about persuading those who are listening.[49]

Socrates simply gets Gorgias to agree, first, that a rhetorician does not need to know the subject about which he speaks in order to persuade an ignorant audience, and second, that the rhetorician's speeches concern the just and unjust, noble and base, good and bad. Because the rhetorician does not claim to have much substantive knowledge, Socrates concentrates on the potentially corrupting, destructive effects of the claims Gorgias makes about the power of his art. According to Gorgias' understanding of the character of human access to the world, we do not have knowledge of the things in themselves, only of the way in which we can affect the perceptions other people have of them. In refuting Gorgias, Socrates proceeds on the basis of the rhetorician's own presuppositions, not the philosophical claims and arguments he mocked. Socrates insists on beginning his examinations of the opinions of others with propositions to which they agree, because, we see in his later abortive exchange with Callicles, if Socrates does not, his interlocutor can follow his reasoning to the end and then simply object to the first premise. In that case, the interlocutor is not led to reconsider his initial commitments as a result of having been refuted or corrected.

There is an implicit problem in a foreign teacher seeking students in Athens who is making such claims—and Socrates knows it. If Gorgias is able to do what he says he can, he is offering to teach all who are willing to pay him how they can manipulate, if not overthrow, the democratic regime. Gorgias recognizes the problem. After Socrates reminds him that there may be "someone inside who wishes to become a student of yours" (*Gorgias* 455c), Gorgias thus adds an otherwise inexplicable qualification to his exultation in the "power of his art." Having bragged that a rhetorician can "go into any city" and persuade any gathering to accept his advice rather than that of an expert, he cautions: "one should use rhetoric just as every other competitive skill," not against family, friends or fellow citizens, but "against enemies and doers of injustice" (456c–e). If someone learns the art of rhetoric and uses it unjustly, "the man who taught him should not be hated and expelled from the cities" (457b).

---

49. Socrates' treatment of the famous rhetorician is like his treatment of the famous sophist in the *Protagoras*. Socrates does not examine the theoretical basis of the sophist's views until much later, in the *Theaetetus*, after the sophist is dead and his views have to be explained and defended by someone else.

SOCRATIC PRACTICE / 537

Socrates highlights the refutation he is about to inflict on Gorgias by asking his interlocutor if he is a man like Socrates, who would rather learn the truth by having his own false opinion refuted than enjoy a victory in speech by refuting another. Not to lose face, Gorgias claims that he too would rather get to the truth of the matter than win the argument. He nevertheless tries to escape the refutation Socrates has threatened by expressing concern that those who have been listening to him for a long time may be tired. Chaerephon and Callicles assure him, however, that nothing could give them greater pleasure than for the conversation to continue.[50] So Socrates asks Gorgias if he would teach a student of rhetoric what is just, if the student does not know. Gorgias says that he would, and Socrates observes that someone who knows what is just would necessarily be just.[51] If Gorgias teaches his students to be just, there is no reason for him to worry about their misusing the skill he has taught them. But, Socrates concedes, they would have to talk further in order to settle the issue.

Socrates' exchange with Gorgias is inconclusive. If Gorgias knows and teaches his students what is truly just, there is no problem with his teaching them how to persuade others. He would be acting in the public interest of any decent city. If, however, Gorgias does not know or does not teach his students what is just, he is selling potentially unjust people the means of overturning the laws of a democratic polity like Athens. And if the latter is an accurate description of Gorgias' practice, Socrates indirectly

---

50. As in the *Protagoras*, so in the *Gorgias*, Socrates traps the famous speaker by appealing to the pleasure of the audience in listening to the debate or debunking of another, the pleasure to which sophists and rhetoricians themselves usually appealed. Socrates understands the basis of their business and practices, it seems, better than they do. Both dialogues constitute examples of what Nietzsche describes as Socrates' attracting the attention, admiration, and emulation of young Athenian aristocrats by presenting them with a new form of *agōn*, even though Socrates explicitly denies that was what he was doing. Nietzsche, "Das Problem des Sokrates," *Götzen-Dämmerung*, in *Sämtliche Werke*, vol. 6; translated by Richard Polt as "The Problem of Socrates," in *Twilight of the Idols* (Indianapolis: Hackett, 1997).

51. The argument is highly abbreviated and hence problematic. It depends on an equation of the kind of knowledge a just man has of justice with the kind of knowledge of medicine that makes a doctor a doctor. (Socrates gets Gorgias to agree that someone who knows what is just would be a just person, and a just person would do just things.) Socrates indicates some of the differences between the kind of knowledge a ruler—or even a practitioner of the general art of moneymaking—should have and that possessed by various kinds of artisans, in his discussion with another rhetorician, Thrasymachus, in the *Republic* (345b–47e). As Aristotle makes clear in his discussion of *akrasia* in book 7 of the *Nicomachean Ethics*, it is by no means clear that someone who knows what is just will necessarily do it. In defense of Socrates, however, one might respond that such an "incontinent" person would not really know what is just. The question would then again become, What, if any, kind of knowledge of justice would make the knower just?

reminds the famous rhetorician, he endangers himself by making the extensive claims he does about the power of his art. In fact, Socrates indicates, rhetoric is not as powerful as Gorgias thinks. Insofar as it consists in an ability to persuade people in assemblies what is just and unjust, rhetoric has the power Gorgias claims for it only in democratic regimes, where the people make the law. The power of persuasion is thus limited by the regime. It is also limited by law and by a force that underlies the law, trust. Although he claims to be a rhetor and to be able to make others rhetors, as a foreign teacher of rhetoric Gorgias promulgates an art he cannot practice in Athens, where, as a foreigner, he is not allowed by law to speak in a public assembly. Nor does it seem likely that, as a foreigner, he would have been able to persuade the Athenians to pass laws he thinks best, if he had been allowed to speak. The Athenians would not have trusted him and his advice the way they would trust one of their fellow citizens to say what is best for the city, because, unlike them, he would not have to suffer the consequences of a bad policy. As a foreigner, Gorgias would not even have been able to defend himself in court from the charge that he had shown an unjust man how to seize power in Athens by persuading the ignorant demos. By relating Gorgias' claims about the power of his art to the rhetorician's own situation, Socrates shows that the power of persuasion is limited not only by law (which might be changed through persuasion in a democracy) but also by familiar association, trust, or friendship.

B. The Limits of Coercion: Polus

Gorgias' follower Polus is not convinced. Like many commentators who have taken his objection as Plato's last word on the subject, Polus observes that Gorgias was forced to contradict himself merely because he was ashamed to admit that he did not teach justice. Unlike Gorgias, Polus does not understand or heed Socrates' implicit warning.

In contrast to Gorgias, who argued that speech has the power to shape and reshape everything, Polus understands rhetoric to be merely a means. He sees that young people take lessons from teachers of rhetoric to learn to speak persuasively in order to acquire political power so that they can do what they want. The personal liberty and ability to command others that Gorgias boasted a rhetorician could acquire by persuading a public assembly rest ultimately on the threat of enforcement. A foreign teacher of rhetoric himself, Polus also sees that all leaders are not native born. Instead of Themistocles and Pericles, he names a foreign tyrant, Archelaus, as an example of the power he thinks everyone wants.[52]

Attached to his own freedom and aware that members of the Athenian audience also prize individual liberty, Polus protests the restriction on his freedom of speech when Socrates agrees to examine him—on the condition that the young rhetorician restrain his tendency to give long speeches. Socrates admits that it would be terrible to deprive anyone of that freedom in Athens, the city in Greece where there was most freedom to speak. But, Socrates points out, he has a corresponding freedom to leave, if he does not want to listen. Readers see that Polus has not only failed to understand the reason Socrates was able to refute Gorgias (because he has not recognized his own vulnerability to prosecution). He has also failed to understand another point implicit in Socrates' exchange with Gorgias: people are not able to persuade others to obey them, if others are not willing to listen (cf. *Republic* 327c). Persuasion, and thus the power of rhetoric, is not simply a product of the skill of the speaker; it also depends on the relation the speaker has to the audience and thus on the character of the audience.

I. What Is Rhetoric?

Having written a book on the subject, Polus believes that persuasion is a matter of technique. So, having observed that Socrates gained an advantage over Gorgias by interrogating him, Polus volunteers to ask rather than answer questions. But Socrates quickly shows that Polus does not know how to conduct a dialectical investigation. Polus does not understand the difference between asking what something is and asking what sort of thing it is, Socrates suggests, because he has studied the writings of pre-Socratic philosophers such as Anaxagoras, who affirm that things are all mixed up together in the same place (*Gorgias* 465d).[53] As a result of his study of pre-Socratic philosophy, Polus does not recognize the existence of things-in-themselves, independent of human perception or evaluation. He is therefore only concerned about what people think about things, not what the things in themselves are. In the central exchange in this dialogue,

52. Cf. Rutherford: "Polus' main contribution to the dialogue is his emphasis on the power which rhetoric . . . can bring to its user" (*Art*, 151).

53. Plato reminds his readers that Socrates' own characteristic "what is . . .?" question also presupposes a certain understanding of the character of beings—that they exist distinct from others, in themselves. Although Socrates does not mention the ideas in the *Gorgias*, Socrates' characteristic way of investigating and refuting the opinions of others presupposes such an argument.

Plato thus reminds his readers that there is a philosophical basis for the claims made by the rhetoricians. But, as we have seen in his treatment of Gorgias, Socrates concentrates on the effects of these errors, not their philosophical foundation.

In order to say what something is, Socrates argued in the *Philebus*, it is necessary not only to say what it is or is not, but also to specify the kinds. When Polus asks Socrates what he thinks rhetoric is, Socrates thus says that it is a kind of experience or practice (*empeiria*) that produces a certain pleasure, but Polus does not press the question of what kind of practice until Socrates prompts him.[54] Since Polus does not see any need for a rhetorician to know or teach justice, Socrates informs him that a rhetorician who teaches anyone how to persuade people in an assembly to do what he wants, without knowledge of what is just or unjust, engages in a kind of flattery (*kolakeia*) that constitutes an image (*eidōlon*) of a part of the art of politics (*politikē*).

Polus does not understand, so Socrates expands his definition. Having ascertained that Polus distinguishes soul from body (that is, that he is not simply a materialist),[55] Socrates explains: just as there are two arts, gymnastics and medicine, which train or return bodies to a good condition, so there are two arts of legislation and justice, jointly called politics (*politikē*), which shape or remedy defects in souls. There are also four corresponding types of flattery: cosmetics and cookery, which imitate gymnastics and medicine; and sophistry and rhetoric, which imitate legislation and justice. Socrates calls these pursuits imitations because they seek what appears to be good, the pleasant, rather than what is truly good. These pursuits are forms of flattery because they suggest that what pleases their recipients is good (and so flatter their customers by acting as if they know what is good). Although these pursuits require a certain kind of facility on the part

---

54. Socrates was not willing to proceed, however, until he was assured that Gorgias would not be insulted by his negative definition of rhetoric. Since Gorgias had claimed that he taught his students justice, he did not have to feel insulted and thus urged Socrates to continue. Socrates' delicacy in treating Gorgias and Gorgias' interest in the conversation have made some readers think that Socrates may be trying to see if he can persuade Gorgias to use his rhetorical skills to convince people to undergo the kind of correction Socrates administers. In the Callicles section, we see that this attempt fails. Gorgias is no more able to convince Callicles to continue than Socrates himself is. In the *Meno* we then see that Socrates has persuaded Gorgias simply not to claim that he taught virtue.

55. Following Aristotle (*Metaphysics* 987b1–8), modern commentators such as Vlastos and Irwin have included the *Gorgias* among the "early" dialogues in which Socrates seeks to define the moral virtues but does not, like "Plato," put forward a broader philosophical teaching about the "ideas." It is important to observe, therefore, that in this section of the *Gorgias* Socrates indicates his own recognition that his moral teachings have a philosophical foundation.

of practitioners, they do not constitute arts, because their practitioners do not know what is truly good. Not knowing the goal, these practitioners cannot give a reasoned account of how they achieve their effects, that is, relate means to ends; like cooks, they rely on their experience of what gives people pleasure.

"Are good rhetoricians merely thought to be flatterers?" Polus incredulously asks. Polus cannot understand or agree with Socrates' definition of rhetoric, because he does not recognize a difference between what people think is good and what really is. Tyrants are well regarded (*nomizesthai*), Polus tells Socrates (*Gorgias* 466b), because they have the greatest power in their cities (*megiston dynantai en tais polesin*); they are able to kill, imprison, or confiscate the goods of anyone they wish. Socrates has to remind Polus that people do not envy the tyrant's ability to kill, imprison, or confiscate goods per se; they envy his ability to get other people to do what he wants by threatening them with such penalties if they do not obey his commands. The teacher of rhetoric does not seem to understand the way in which the threat of force functions as a kind of persuasion. If a ruler has to kill a man who defies his orders, the ruler cannot get much more out of him.

Nor, Socrates points out, is the power of a tyrant worth much if it does not enable him to obtain what he wishes. If everyone wishes what is truly good or advantageous for himself, it is then necessary to determine what that is. Believing he already knows what everyone wants, Polus does not try to refute Socrates when Socrates invites him to do so by showing that rhetoric does not merely depend on experience but involves intelligence (*nous*).[56] Instead, Polus agrees to answer Socrates' questions in order to find out what Socrates means (because Polus cannot believe Socrates really means what he seems to be saying).

2. SOCRATES' REFUTATION OF POLUS

Socrates begins his refutation of Polus by observing (somewhat like Hobbes) that everyone has the power to kill another if he goes into the marketplace with a concealed dagger. Objecting that such a person would be punished, Polus states his own position more precisely. What he and others envy is the ability to do whatever one wishes—without having to pay a penalty. In other words, everyone wants to be free. They understand

---

56. In other words, Polus does not accept Socrates' invitation to explain how appeals based on bodily pleasures and pains are governed or directed by mind, as Anaxagoras claimed the interactions of the material elements of the cosmos were.

freedom negatively, as the absence of restraint. They do not, like Socrates, seek to know and do what is positively good. Like Polus, they believe that doing whatever one wishes is the highest good for human beings.

Just as Socrates told Gorgias that he would prefer to be refuted and so learn the truth rather than win the argument, so he now tells Polus that it would be best not to need correction, but if one does, it is better to be corrected and so make one's life or soul more orderly than to escape punishment. Even more incredulous, Polus says even a child could refute this claim. He mentions Archelaus as a man who did everything people generally consider unjust and impious and yet became ruler of Macedonia. Socrates points out that Polus is arguing rhetorically, the way lawyers do in court, by calling witnesses to support his claims. But, Socrates objects, the number of people who share an opinion does not make that opinion true. Nor will Socrates be frightened into agreeing with something he does not think is true by a large number of people threatening him with terrible punishments (or ridicule). He seeks the agreement only of his interlocutor. Readers have to ask why, because Polus does not.

Like most people, Polus thinks it is worse to suffer injustice than to do it, because suffering injustice is painful. Socrates shows by asking him, however, that like most people, Polus also believes it is nobler to suffer injustice than to do it. Since suffering is obviously painful, Socrates points out, suffering injustice must be considered nobler than doing injustice because it is useful or beneficial and thus good in some other way. The good and the pleasant are not identical. That is the reason Socrates denies rhetoric is an art; it appeals only to the pleasant and is not based on knowledge of what is truly good.[57]

By asking Polus to submit himself to the argument as to a doctor, Socrates reminds him (and us) of the parallel not only between justice and medicine but also between Socrates' refutations of his interlocutors and these remedial or corrective arts. If people think it is worse to do injustice than to suffer it, because it is more ignoble, Socrates points out, they must not think that it is the greatest of evils for a criminal to pay a just penalty. They must think it is better for people to suffer the penalty and so to be corrected, made just, and thus better. If people have done something wrong, he concludes, they should go to court and accuse themselves first,

---

57. To consider the question fully, Socrates would have had to lead Polus (and Plato's readers) through an examination of the complex relation between the noble and the good. Because Polus does not believe in the existence of goodness or nobility apart from what people think or believe, Socrates is able to confine his argument with Polus to the level of popular opinion.

then their family and friends. They should not accuse enemies or those who have wronged them. On the contrary, people should seek to prevent their enemies from being corrected and so benefited![58]

Although he agrees that Socrates' argument seems to lead to this conclusion, Polus is not persuaded: "To me, Socrates, these things seem strange; but perhaps you make them agree with the things said before" (480e). Punishment is admittedly painful and unpleasant, and Socrates has not explained how inflicting pain on the body can remedy faults of the soul. In his refutation of Polus, Socrates appears, indeed, to abstract from the distinction between body and soul he had insisted on in his own earlier definition of the political art. As Socrates' auditors and Plato's readers see, however, Socrates' interlocutors suffer a kind of psychological pain when they are refuted (and so corrected)—shame. Socrates does not point out the kind of pain involved in the corrections of the soul he attempts to administer, and his shameless young interlocutor seems to understand the embarrassment simply as a matter of public face or presence.[59] Polus does not see the way in which the embarrassment might lead a thoughtful person to correct himself (or "internalize" the argument). He sees only that Socrates has shown that two common opinions he holds about suffering injustice are contradictory, and that in trying to make them consistent, Socrates has come to the extraordinary conclusion that, rather than using his rhetorical skill to evade punishment himself or to help others do so, Polus should use it to accuse himself, his family, and his friends.

Socrates refutes (elegchein) Polus, but he does not succeed in correcting (kolazein) him. There is no evidence in the dialogue that Socrates convinces Polus to change his opinions about what is good and so to bring order to his life (or soul) by making his thoughts consistent with each other as well as with his own deeds and desires. It does not look as if he tries. Rather than persuade Polus, the second half of Socrates' argument seems designed to provoke one of the young Athenian listeners to protest—as Callicles eventually does.

If Socrates had wanted to persuade Polus to change the arguments he made on behalf of his own art, Socrates would have reminded the young

---

58. In the *Republic* 334c–36a, Socrates questions the common Greek belief that one should benefit one's friends and harm one's enemies. Socrates' urging of Polus and others not to seek to punish their enemies does, however, have shock value for them.

59. On the role of shame in Socrates' arguments in the *Gorgias*, see Richard McKim, "Shame and Truth in Plato's *Gorgias*," in *Platonic Writings, Platonic Readings*, ed. Charles L. Griswold, 34–48 (New York: Routledge, 1988).

teacher that ambitious young Athenians (like Theages) do not say that they want to be tyrants. They take lessons from foreign teachers of rhetoric like Polus to learn how to persuade their fellow citizens to do what they recommended to the assembly and so to accept their rule willingly.[60] Tyrants might be feared, even secretly envied, but they were not well thought of. If Polus had been brought to recognize and reflect on this well-known fact, he would have understood why Gorgias felt impelled to say that he would teach a student of rhetoric what is just, if he did not already know. But, Plato shows, Polus was not a very thoughtful or self-reflective young man. By following in the footsteps of his mentor Gorgias, Polus has shown in deed (*ergon*) that he does not envy or desire to acquire the power of a tyrant in his own city so much as he wants to become world renowned by traveling from city to city exhibiting and teaching his rhetorical skills. He truly believes, both in speech and in deed, that public opinion determines the value of things. He thus accepts and follows it uncritically.[61] He does not reflect on the tension between what he says and teaches others, and what he really wants and thus does.

Perhaps with tongue in cheek (although virtually all other commentators have taken him seriously and literally), Socrates has shown the young rhetorician how he can acquire the power Polus initially claimed everyone wants: to kill, imprison, or confiscate the goods of anyone he wishes, respectably and with the protection of law. Polus does not exhibit any inclination to become a public prosecutor, however. In response to Socrates' questions, he admits that no one really wants to kill, imprison, or confiscate goods per se; people wish to have such powers only in order to get what they want from others—without fear of punishment. What Socrates shows Polus directly is that people cannot get what they want by means of force alone. What he merely indicates to his auditors (and Plato's readers) is that one cannot benefit others merely by the use of force. If the goal of punishment is the reform of the soul of the criminal, punishment should not be aimed at the body. It should not take the form, therefore, of killing or inflicting physical pain. Insofar as it is aimed at the soul, corrective punishment may employ shame, as a form of psychic pain, but shame too

---

60. See, e.g., Young Socrates in the *Statesman* 276d–77a, 293e, who sees that there is an important difference between ruling on the basis of law and consent and ruling tyrannically on the basis of force, and Theages in the dialogue that bears his name.

61. Cf. Kahn, *Plato and the Socratic Dialogue*, 135: "Polus is refuted because he cannot reconcile his admiration for power and wealth, no matter how obtained, with his recognition that unjust or criminal acts are generally regarded as dishonorable and 'shameful.'"

is only a means that may not be effective in achieving the end. The desired correction of the soul occurs only if the subject recognizes the contradictions in his or her own opinions or actions *and* wishes to correct them. If the subject merely tries to escape further embarrassment in front of others by hiding his or her true opinions from them, there will be no real improvement. That is the reason Socrates says he cares only about obtaining the agreement of his interlocutors. He does not want to subject them, any more than he himself wants to be subjected, merely to the opinions of others.

C. The Limits of Protective Politics: Callicles

The understanding of politics and punishment Socrates put forth in his exchange with Polus was very different from that of his contemporaries—as well as from that of most people today—as Callicles indicates when he objects that if what Socrates says is true, the world as we know it would be turned upside down.[62] Like Gorgias, Polus, and Callicles, we understand political action primarily as a means of getting what we want. Like Gorgias, Polus, and Callicles, we understand persuasion and force to be the primary means of attaining and exercising political power. As Socrates points out to Polus, however, means are not truly means if they cannot help us achieve our ends. If our end is to live a good life, which requires associating with other good people, neither persuasion nor force will suffice to get us what we seek. As Socrates tries to show Callicles, political power cannot even enable people to band together to protect themselves from the injustice of others (a lesser goal than living the good life, but the reason that political associations are first formed, according to Socrates in the *Republic*), unless the people become moderate and just.

---

62. Danielle S. Allen, *The World of Prometheus: The Politics of Punishing in Democratic Athens* (Princeton: Princeton University Press, 2000), 30–50, 246–50, shows how different Socrates' understanding of punishment as a form of "correction" was from that of his contemporaries, who understood the justice of punishment basically in terms of revenge. In 574 Solon had made it possible for individuals to accuse others of crimes against the public, not just against themselves or their kin. Yet, Allen reports, "the surviving oratorical corpus yields only four cases in which a prosecutor claims to act as a purely disinterested public actor" (39–40). Without the anger (*thymos* or *orgē*; neither word appears in the *Gorgias*) aroused by a sense of personal injury or injustice, people did not feel moved to bring accusations in court against others (although they were willing to testify falsely, as sycophants for a fee). The inquisitorial politics to which Socrates' exchange with Polus seems to point, and which we moderns have seen realized in later history, might unfortunately have their origins in Plato.

1. CALLICLES' "FRIENDSHIP" FOR SOCRATES

Although he has been castigated as a criminal and a brute because he argues for the natural right of the stronger and refuses to submit to the discipline of reason, Callicles puts forth a more decent view of politics than does Gorgias or Polus.[63] The latter two urge their students to learn rhetoric in order to acquire political power that would enable them to do what they want and to command others. Callicles tells Socrates that he should give up philosophizing and learn how to speak effectively in public in order to care for his own soul, to contribute to public councils, and to protect himself, his family, and friends from the injustice of others (*Gorgias* 485e–86c).

As a fellow Athenian, Callicles claims to be Socrates' friend. Because he is a fellow Athenian, Socrates predicts, Callicles will be less restrained by shame (or a sense of his precarious position) than his foreign friends (*philoi*) Gorgias and Polus are.[64] If he says what he thinks, Callicles will be the best possible test of the truth of Socrates' opinions. Not only will Callicles be honest; he also has knowledge—or at least "an education as many Athenians would say" (487b) (although not necessarily Socrates). Callicles has demonstrated his goodwill toward Socrates by urging the philosopher to follow the same course of action he and his friends have adopted for themselves.

Socrates begins his conversation with Callicles by pointing out what they have in common. Not only are they both Athenians and thus political friends. Both also share a passion (*pathos*, not, we should observe, a conviction, a belief, or a way of life); both are lovers. Nevertheless, Socrates

---

63. There has been a great deal of scholarly debate about Callicles' character. Scholars of the last generation tended to see Callicles as an "immoralist," if not "amoralist." See, e.g., Friedländer, *Plato*, 2:244–72; Grote, *Plato*, 2:90–151; Paul Shorey, *What Plato Said* (Chicago: University of Chicago Press, 1968), 54; and Eric Voegelin, *Plato* (Baton Rouge: Louisiana State University Press, 1981), 24–25. Recently, scholars have given a more complex view. Like Euben (*Corrupting Youth*, 227), Benardete (*Rhetoric*, 61–102), Newell (*Ruling Passion*, 9–41), Saxonhouse ("Unspoken Theme," 162–69), and Devin Stauffer, "Socrates and Callicles: A Reading of Plato's *Gorgias*," *Review of Politics* 64 (Fall 2002): 627–58, I argue that Callicles is not simply immoral or amoral. Like Benardete and Saxonhouse, I think his character mimics and so reflects the regime under which he has grown up, Athenian democracy during the Peloponnesian War. I cannot agree with Arieti, who maintains that "Socrates, spurning every opportunity to reconciliation and agreement with Callicles, has transformed the patriotic, well-meaning man into a tyrant-loving, antiphilosophical man" (*Interpreting Plato*, 90). Callicles reproves Socrates for persisting in his pursuit of philosophy, that is, shows himself to be antiphilosophical, at the beginning of their exchange.

64. By calling the foreigners friendly (*philoi*), Socrates nevertheless suggests that they are no less close or well intentioned toward him than Callicles and thus silently questions the proposition that fellow citizens have more in common than those who devote their lives to speeches delivered in private.

suggests, they cannot become true friends so long as the objects of their affection are different or changing. The character of the "first friend," or that for the sake of which people become friends, is decisive. Shared natural desire, eros, or need does not constitute a sufficient basis for a true friendship, which we now learn must be philosophical rather than merely political. As in the *Phaedrus*, so in his exchange with Callicles, Socrates observes that lovers try to please their beloved by doing what the beloved wants and so becoming more like him. Because most people hold contradictory opinions and change them frequently, Callicles has been forced to change his own opinions frequently and thus to contradict himself in attempting to please his beloved Demus and the Athenian people (*dēmos*). Although Socrates loves Alcibiades (who, like Callicles, was a lover of the *dēmos* and who did not, therefore, remain a friend of Socrates), Socrates loves philosophy more. Driven by his political passions, Alcibiades changed not merely his opinions but the city or nation to which he gave service.[65] Rather than following the twists and turns of his beloved in deed or in speech, Socrates has remained in and loyal to Athens. He thus accepts as a compliment Callicles' complaint that he always says the same things. As a philosopher, Socrates prizes what is true and unchanging more than the whims of a changeable youth. He tries to become like what he loves as much as possible by seeing that his opinions remain the same and consistent.

Callicles will never agree with himself, the philosopher warns, if he does not refute Socrates' contention that it is better to pay the penalty than to escape and remain unjust. Trying to please the public that makes and enforces the laws in democratic Athens, Callicles has not merely appealed to but has absorbed one of the three major justifications for punishment: correction. (The other two are retribution and deterrence.) By not only accusing Socrates of wronging himself and his fellow Athenians but also suggesting that the old man needs a beating (485d), Callicles has been acting as if he agreed that a just man should accuse his friends and seek to have them punished for their own good.[66]

65. If the dramatic date of the dialogue is 405, Socrates' mention of his love for Alcibiades may be taken as a warning to Callicles. Alcibiades had not only changed his political opinions and allies; they too had changed. Although the Athenians had been willing to let him return in 407, they changed their minds after he lost several naval battles.

66. Because Callicles accuses Socrates of making himself ridiculous by continuing to engage in private philosophical arguments as an old man rather than taking part in serious public deliberations and was himself a young man who recommended beating his elder as a beneficial and deserved punishment, commentators have often compared his accusation to that leveled earlier by Aristophanes in his *Clouds*. Although Aristophanes also depicts Socrates as a laughable figure, the accusation the comic poet levels at the philosopher is different from that leveled by the young

2. Callicles' Understanding of Natural
Right and Socrates' Refutation of It

Callicles certainly does not think that he agrees with Socrates. On the contrary, thinking that almost everyone else agrees with him and disagrees with Socrates, Callicles, like Polus, believes that Socrates will be easy to refute. Just as Polus objected that Socrates had shamed Gorgias into contradicting himself, so, Callicles charges, Socrates tricked Polus into refuting himself by silently shifting between nature and convention in the questions he put to the young rhetorician. By nature, the stronger have a right to take what they want and so to rule. The belief that it is nobler to suffer than to commit injustice is merely conventional. To protect themselves, the weak join together in attempting to convince those who are stronger not to act according to nature but according to law and what is publicly, that is, generally, praised. Like Glaucon in the *Republic*, Callicles thinks any man who can, will break through these conventions and do what he wants. The behavior of animals and foreign rulers shows that by nature the stronger rule the weak. Like Darius and Xerxes, those who believe they are powerful enough to expand their empire by conquering others are not restrained by any laws.[67]

Socrates quickly proves that Callicles' understanding of natural right is neither tenable nor coherent.[68] If better (*beltion* or *ameinon*) means stronger (*kreitton*), the many have a right to rule the few, by nature and not merely by convention, because the many are stronger. He did not mean

---

Athenian in several important respects. In the *Clouds* Aristophanes suggests that Socrates did not understand the effects his teachings about the nonexistence of the gods had on other human beings. Because he himself was so ascetic, he did not see the way in which his teaching freed others to pursue their own unjust desires. His teachings relieved them from fear of punishment not only in the afterlife but also in this, because in Aristophanes' play Socrates is able to show anyone how to talk his way out of any lawsuit. Believing that he cannot sue Socrates successfully in court, the unjust father, at the end of the play, tries to destroy Socrates and his school with fire for alienating the affections of his son. Both Aristophanes and Callicles warn Socrates that his political naiveté will be dangerous to him. Unlike the comic poet and Socrates' later Athenian accusers, Callicles does not charge Socrates with impiety or corrupting the young. Indeed, Callicles shows no concern about piety and recommends that people become unjust themselves, if necessary, by serving an unjust tyrant. According to Callicles, Socrates is ridiculous because he and his philosophy are completely ineffective. Callicles says he is castigating Socrates for his own good, as a friend, and not like Aristophanes as a competitor in wisdom on behalf of the city. Cf. *Clouds* 517–62; *Frogs* 1480–1510.

67. As Saxonhouse points out ("Unspoken Theme," 157), Callicles does not seem to notice that both these emperors failed.

68. Cf. George Klosko, "The Insufficiency of Reason in Plato's *Gorgias*," *Western Political Quarterly* 36 (1983): 590.

just physically stronger, Callicles retorts; he meant "better" in the sense of more courageous (literally, more manly) and prudent. Not challenging the proposition that the courageous and intelligent have a right to rule, Socrates asks what they get and deserve more of. Callicles does not think that they would receive more food or clothes; he seems to believe that rulers would receive more of the honor and wealth usually associated with political power. If ruling others is a sign of superiority, Socrates objects, its advantage cannot consist primarily in external rewards. Is it not better to be able to rule oneself as well as others? Moderate or self-controlled people are no better than dead stones, Callicles responds. If living is feeling, the best life is one of the most extreme passions or desires with the ability to satisfy them.[69] Pressed to say whether he truly thinks it better to be always desirous, hungry or "itching," like a catamite, Callicles objects to the disgusting, shameful examples Socrates is introducing. Callicles finally admits that, like everyone else, he distinguishes between better and worse pleasures.

Callicles proves to be neither so frank nor friendly as he initially claimed. Realizing that he is about to contradict himself as a result of Socrates' interrogation, he answers so "that the speech should not contradict me" (*Gorgias* 495a) and does not say what he really thinks. "Claiming at one time that things are this way, and at another time that the same things are otherwise," Socrates complains, "you deceive me! And yet I did not think at the beginning that you would willingly deceive me, because you were my friend" (499c).

Having proved that Callicles' stated views are contradictory, Socrates attempts to show that Callicles actually agrees with him. But even though Callicles has admitted that there are better and worse pleasures, he is not willing to endorse the distinction Socrates restates between the arts that seek the good and the corresponding kinds of flattery that seek only to please. Trying to please Gorgias (and so flattering rather than trying to benefit his friend), Callicles merely grants what Socrates says (501c) so that he can finish the argument. Callicles agrees that speaking in a public assembly of Athenians or free men in other cities is a kind of "popular speaking" that differs from tragic poetry addressed to an audience of women, children, and slaves only by the absence of tune, rhythm, and meter. Rhetoric

69. Because of Callicles' praise of natural masters and his equation of human excellence with strength of passion, some commentators have equated his position with that of Nietzsche. See, e.g., Euben (*Corrupting Youth*, 227–28) and Newell (*Ruling Passion*, 17).

is not, in other words, defined primarily by its audience or setting. He agrees, further, that rhetoric can be said not to be merely pleasing, only if its content makes its audience better. He does not think there are any rhetoricians who improve their fellow citizens in Athens at present, but he believes that there were some in the past: Themistocles, Cimon, Miltiades, and Pericles. He also agrees that craftsmen aim at achieving some order or form in what they produce, and that we call this form produced in the human body health and strength. But he refuses to say that the order to be achieved in the soul through law is called justice and moderation.

Callicles does not think all pleasures are equally good or noble, but he even more emphatically does not think that self-restraint or moderation is good or desirable. When Socrates reintroduces the parallel he drew between medicine and justice to argue that, just as a doctor would not prescribe drugs merely because they tasted good to a sick man, so a legislator would not attempt to please an intemperate public but would restrain it by not letting it do what it wants, Callicles rebels. He refuses to answer any further questions—even to gratify Gorgias. Socrates concludes, "This man will not allow himself to be benefited by suffering what the argument is about, being corrected" (*kolazomenos*; 505c).

Plato thus confronts his readers with two questions. First, what is it about Callicles that makes him unwilling to answer Socrates and risk being refuted like Gorgias and Polus? Not all of Socrates' interlocutors are convinced by his arguments. Like Polus, they may conclude that what he says is strange (and so indicate that they themselves are not persuaded), but they do not usually rebel angrily against any further interrogation. Second, why does Socrates insist on obtaining the agreement of an interlocutor and examining their opinions in common? As he demonstrates after Gorgias begs him to complete the argument, Socrates is perfectly capable of presenting it on his own.

3. CALLICLES' REAL POSITION

Callicles' reaction to Socrates' refutation shows that the friendship he claims to feel for Socrates masks a kind of contempt. Callicles is willing to offer Socrates some free advice about the superiority of his own mode of life. If Callicles thought Socrates represented any kind of danger, however, he would have used force against him without compunction. Callicles believes that the strong have a right to rule and that this ridiculous old man not only is entirely defenseless but also deserves a beating (which Callicles would presumably have administered, if he really cared about Socrates and was

not restrained by his fear of the law). Callicles admires men like Themistocles, Miltiades, Cimon, and Pericles, who were able to persuade the people
to pass the laws they thought best and were honored because they showed
the people not only how to protect themselves from foreign aggression but
also how to acquire an empire for themselves. He contemns Athenian leaders at the end of the Peloponnesian War for the same reasons; they were
not able to defend Athens or to preserve her empire. As his name indicates,
Callicles would like to be renowned for his nobility.[70] He would like to be
recognized not merely as an equal but as a superior man. He seeks to please
the Athenian demos so they will elect him to a prominent position. If he
fails to gain the recognition he desires, however, he wants at least to protect
himself and his family from unjust prosecution in court.

As his disdain for moderation indicates, Callicles believes that the best
thing for human beings is to be able to do what they want. He resists all
forms of constraint, internal or external. He does not see any reason for
anyone to restrain or discipline himself. As Callicles understands it, self-
restraint is merely a product of weakness and hence ultimately of fear.
If he cannot rule others by himself, he will join with them in trying to
preserve himself, his family, and his friends from external control.[71] He will
not discipline himself any more than he will accept the dictates of "philosophy" coming from Socrates. Callicles thus embodies the forces or desires
that make the rule of reason impossible to achieve for and in most human
beings.

Completing the argument on his own, Socrates first shows why someone like Callicles, who refuses to exercise any self-restraint, cannot be a
friend to others or a good citizen. Then Socrates proves that no one can
attain happiness, freedom, or security by seeking political power, as Callicles urges.

Socrates first indicates why people who do not subscribe to these principles cannot be friends. If political associations are defined in terms of

70. There is no evidence that such a person existed outside this dialogue. His name appears
to be a compound of the word for "most noble," *kallistos*, and "glory" or "acclaim," *kleos*. Cf.
Benardete, *Rhetoric*, 63.

71. Although Callicles praises those who are masters by nature, Newell points out that he
speaks of the conventions established by the many as ways in which "we" persuade those who
are stronger to obey. "He does not really seek unlimited and indiscriminate pleasure, but pleasure
mediated by honor. A life of pure hedonism . . . might more easily be achieved by a man of means
who lives in private luxury and avoids the toils and danger of a political career. Callicles wants
Demos and the demos to honor him. . . . At bottom, freedom is more important to Callicles than
hedonism. 'How can a man be happy,' he asks Socrates, 'if he's a slave to anything?' (491e5–6)"
(*Ruling Passion*, 17, 25, 27).

friends and enemies, as Socrates and his interlocutors often assert (cf. *Clitophon* 410b; *Republic* 332a–b), agreement on these principles constitutes the foundation of a true political association, and the argument (*logos*) Socrates puts forward here constitutes the basis of his claim to be the only one in Athens now attempting to practice the true art of politics.

Socrates begins by reemphasizing the difference between the good and the pleasant. The pleasant is for the sake of, and hence subordinate to, the good. People become good insofar as good is present in them, and like other things, humans become good or excellent (virtuous) by means of an appropriate arrangement, correctness, and art (*taxis, orthotēs*, and *technē*). In human beings, that order (*kosmos*) is an order of the soul, or moderation. Because the moderate soul is good, it does what is fitting to other human beings and to the gods. It is therefore just (toward others), pious (toward the gods), courageous (presumably not fearing death), and, possessing all these virtues, blessedly happy. It would be best not to need punishment in order to learn moderation, but it is better to learn by being corrected than to live in perpetual misery. Those who do not cannot be friends of others. Like Callicles' natural masters or robbers, those who do not learn to be self-restrained become competitors of, and hence hostile to, others precisely because they are always seeking more. Callicles has not learned this lesson, Socrates suggests, because he has not studied enough geometry to know about proportional equality. Rather than greedily taking more and more from others, the orderly, moderate, and just attempt to give each his due. Only those who can control themselves are trustworthy or responsible. Fellow Athenians who not merely announce but attempt to act on the principles articulated by Callicles are even less trustworthy than foreign teachers of rhetoric or "sophists" like Gorgias. By making such arguments, Socrates indicates, Callicles is not furthering his own political ambitions.

Responding to Callicles' reproach that Socrates will not be able to protect himself, his family, or his friends from injustice so long as he persists in philosophizing, Socrates argues that the only way people can protect themselves from injustice is to make those with whom they associate more just. He begins critiquing Callicles' political alternative to philosophy by asking whether one needs some power (*dynamis*) or art to protect himself from injustice. Callicles agrees that some power (but not art) is needed. Socrates reminds him that, in earlier speeches, Socrates and Polus had agreed that no one commits injustice willingly; people are unjust only because they do not know any better or are compelled. To avoid compulsion, one needs power, but to avoid ignorance, one needs knowledge or an "art." Callicles refuses to admit that people need knowledge to avoid doing injustice and becoming unjust themselves.

When Socrates suggests that the power and art needed to avoid suffering injustice might include ruling a city, however, Callicles not only emphatically agrees but praises Socrates for speaking nobly. If a person cannot rule alone but has to associate with others, and those others are tyrannical and unjust, Socrates points out, that person will necessarily suffer injustice by becoming unjust himself. A savage, uneducated tyrant could not trust people who were better than he and apt to contemn him as he himself contemns the base. To be a friend of a tyrant (or of a tyrannical people like the Athenian demos), a young person would have to become like the tyrant (cf. *Republic* 580a).

Callicles protests that those who do not imitate and so become like the tyrant will be killed. A tyrant may kill, imprison, or confiscate the goods of a man who refuses to become unjust like the ruler, Socrates admits, but it will be a base man killing a noble and good one. Those who consider Callicles to be completely immoral must be surprised by hearing him respond, "Isn't this the irritating thing?" (*Gorgias* 511b). Callicles' understanding of politics is by no means completely immoral or even amoral, even though it is patently self-contradictory. At the beginning of their conversation he had insisted that it is not baser to do injustice than to suffer it. Sensible people know that they have to die, Socrates reminds Callicles. Although they acquire and use various means of preserving their lives under a variety of circumstances, neither they nor Callicles greatly esteems arts like swimming or navigation, which enable them to save their own lives or those of others but do not improve their bodies or souls. Callicles does not esteem the practitioners of such arts highly enough to allow his children to intermarry with them. He does not really believe that saving lives—one's own or those of others—is the highest good.

Callicles admits that what Socrates has just said seems good to him, but he "suffers the experience of the many and is not entirely persuaded" (513c). Callicles is torn between the nobler but not uncommon belief that trying to save one's own life at any cost is base, and the desire he shares with most human beings and animals to preserve his own life or that of his family. That is the reason he urges Socrates to stop philosophizing and to enter politics; it is also the reason Callicles "loves," that is, flatters, the demos. Socrates attempts to show Callicles that it is impossible to protect himself or anyone else by trying to please the people. They have turned against those who have served them, as much if not more than against those who opposed them.

Callicles accuses Socrates of seeking a cheap victory by asking Callicles if he can name an Athenian he has made better. Just beginning his political career, Callicles is too young and untried to have had much effect. If he were choosing to learn an art or to employ an artisan, Socrates replies, wouldn't he first look at the students or works of the artisan? If he were prudent, he would not choose a teacher or craftsman who could not point out examples of the beneficent results of his art. Applying this test to the famous rhetoricians of the past whom Callicles admires, Socrates argues that Pericles, Themistocles, Miltiades, and Cimon cannot be said to have improved the Athenians by making them more just. Although all four of these general-statesmen served the Athenian demos by protecting them from foreign aggression, the people had unjustly "rewarded" them with punishments—fines (Pericles), exile (Themistocles), near execution (Miltiades), or ostracism (Cimon). Instead of improving the Athenian people, these leaders allowed the souls of the people to become increasingly disorderly by feeding their desire for glory, conquest, power, and wealth.[72] They had no better reason to complain about their "unjust" treatment by the people they corrupted than do the sophists, who make themselves ridiculous by claiming to teach their students to become more virtuous and then complain about their students not paying the promised fees. No just man would deny just recompense to someone who truly taught him how to become better. Indeed, Socrates adds, no just man would ask any further compensation for making his fellows better; he would reap the benefits of associating with better men. Callicles errs in contemning the sophists while admiring the "rhetoricians." By claiming to teach virtue, the sophists show that they at least recognize the only true and effective means of achieving human happiness, even if they do not, in fact, successfully teach it and undercut their own claims by demanding fees.[73]

72. In criticizing Socrates or Plato for giving an unfair picture of these Athenian statesmen, James L. Kastely, "In Defense of Plato's *Gorgias*," *PMLA* 106, no. 1 (January 1991): 102, points out that E. R. Dodds, Brian Vickers, and Terence Irwin all fail to note that Socrates admits that these statesmen were exceptionally able servants, even though they failed to improve the character of their people. Dodds, *Gorgias*, 359; Brian Vickers, *In Defense of Rhetoric* (Oxford: Clarendon Press, 1988), 89–90; and Terence Irwin, trans., *Gorgias* (Oxford: Clarendon Press, 1979), 119, 237.

73. Although Callicles speaks contemptuously of the sophists, Gorgias is his guest. There has been much scholarly debate about whether Gorgias should be considered a sophist. See, e.g., E. L. Harrison, "Was Gorgias a Sophist?" *Phoenix* 18 (1964): 183–92; Henry Sidgwick, "The Sophists," in *Lectures on the Philosophy of Kant and Other Philosophical Lectures and Essays*, 323–71 (London: Macmillan, 1905); G. B. Kerferd, *The Sophistic Movement* (New York: Cambridge University Press,

4. CALLICLES' RESISTANCE TO SOCRATES' POLITICAL ART

Although he does not claim to teach virtue, Socrates does claim to be the only person in Athens currently attempting to practice the true art of politics. As he emphasizes in both the *Republic* and the *Apology*, however, he does not attempt to legislate. Like the art of justice, as he defines it in the *Gorgias*, Socrates' political art is remedial. He seeks to improve his fellow citizens by refuting and so correcting them. By leading them to subordinate their contradictory, self-regarding desires to the discipline of reason, he tries to make them more moderate (self-ruling) and just (having regard for others). Socrates is well aware of the limited power and effects of his art. If he were unjustly accused of crime and dragged into court, he admits, he would not be able to save himself. He would be like a doctor defending himself before a jury of children from a charge leveled by a pastry chef that, rather than gratifying them with sweet cakes, he has forced them to swallow bitter, pain-causing drugs.

Socrates' description of his own plight makes it sound as if the force that prevents people from being just—or accepting correction—is their natural attachment to pleasure and aversion to pain. In this dialogue, Socrates draws a hard and fast line between the pleasant and the good (along with the just and noble), to which he does not always adhere.[74] Nevertheless, Plato shows in the *Gorgias*, Callicles does not refuse to be corrected simply because he wishes to maximize his pleasure. On the contrary, Callicles admits that like most other people, he distinguishes good from bad pleasures. What he adamantly maintains from the beginning to the end of the conversation is that it is ignoble not to be able to defend oneself from the injustice of others. Acting on that belief, Callicles makes himself as much like the Athenian demos as possible. The passionate conviction that leads him not merely to resist but to contemn Socrates animates many others.

1981), 29–94; H. D. Rankin, *Sophists, Socratics, and Cynics* (Totowa, NJ: Barnes and Noble, 1983), 37; and Jacqueline de Romilly, *The Great Sophists in Periclean Athens*, trans. Janet Lloyd (New York: Oxford University Press, 1992), 6–7, 63, 170. In the *Gorgias* 465c, Socrates says that sophists and rhetoricians are often confused, although he insists on a distinction. Like Gorgias, sophists such as Protagoras promised to teach their students how to speak effectively in public assemblies. Gorgias was a student of Empedocles, and in refuting Parmenides he displays his knowledge of pre-Socratic philosophy and logic. Cf. Sprague, *Older Sophists*, 43–46. Perhaps in response to Socrates' criticism here, in the *Meno* we hear that Gorgias did not claim to teach virtue; he only claimed to teach rhetoric. In the *Apology* 19e, Socrates includes Gorgias along with Hippias and Prodicus among those who travel from city to city and claim to teach virtue to young people, for a fee.

74. In the *Philebus* he admits that purely intellectual pleasures are part of the human good.

The source of the resistance to reason embodied by Callicles is not simply the attraction to pleasure and the aversion to pain that human beings share with all other animals. It is our fear of death. Unlike other animals, human beings recognize that we have to die. What we fear or object to is not death per se, however, so much as an early, unnecessary, especially painful, or prolonged demise as a result of the violence and injustice of others. As Socrates points out in the *Republic*, human beings band together to form political associations to protect themselves and their families from the depredations of others, at home and abroad. When the leaders who help found and maintain these associations fail to provide the protection and accustom the people to demanding ever more wealth and glory, the people strike out angrily at the leaders they are easily led to believe have betrayed them. Callicles and his like see that they need to cooperate with others to protect themselves and those dearest to them. What they do not and apparently cannot be made to see is that they will not achieve the protection they seek unless they themselves and their fellow citizens become moderate and just. They are too attached to their liberty, the negative ability to do what they wish, to submit willingly to restraint, whether imposed by others or themselves. Ancient democracies were not ruled by law, therefore, so much as by the will of the majority and thus ultimately by force.

In depicting Callicles' refusal to submit to correction by Socrates, Plato not only points out the forces that make most people and most polities resist the rule of reason or philosophy. He also shows why Socrates insists on obtaining the agreement of his interlocutors to each point as the argument progresses. Sitting back and letting Socrates state his case, Callicles remains entirely unmoved by the long speech. He grants the points with which he does not agree to let Socrates finish the argument and approves when Socrates says something with which he agrees. As a result, Callicles is not confronted by the contradictions in his own opinions or forced to reconsider them. Human beings can be forced to do and say things they do not believe are true or right, but in this dialogue Plato shows that no one can be persuaded if he is not willing to listen, or be reformed if he is not willing to be corrected.

D. Socrates' "Mythical" Explanation of His Own Practice

After Callicles has refused to be corrected, Socrates shifts at the end of the dialogue to another kind of speech. He says that he regards the story he tells about the reform and character of the judicial process in the afterlife as an argument (*logos*), even though he thinks Callicles will view it as a myth. Since Callicles told Socrates earlier (*Gorgias* 493d) that he would not be persuaded by myths any more than he was by arguments, the purpose of Socrates' final speech does not seem to be to persuade Callicles.[75]

Socrates' account of justice after death reminds his auditors (and Plato's readers) why it is difficult, if not impossible, for human beings to avoid suffering injustice in this life; it also reminds us why an art of rhetoric, as Socrates defined it in the *Phaedrus*, does not exist. So long as the human beings and the gods who judged them had bodies, and the human beings were able to prepare for the day of judgment, the decisions were inaccurate and bad. "For those on trial . . . [were] tried clothed; . . . many . . . who had base souls were clothed in fine bodies, ancestry, and wealth. When the trial took place, many went with them to bear witness that they had lived justly" (*Gorgias* 523c–d). Having bodies themselves, the divine judges were deceived by their own senses as well as by the men. Zeus reformed the judgment of the gods by postponing it until the humans had died and insisting that the judges be dead also, so that soul would confront soul without any bodily inference. It is not hard to see that the conditions that prevented the gods from making just decisions before still exist among human beings.[76]

Callicles had urged Socrates and others to go into politics specifically to avoid being dragged into court and unjustly condemned. Citing Homer's description of the famous punishments of former tyrants in the *Odyssey*, Socrates reminds Callicles that people who acquire political power are most likely to do the greatest injustices and so to be punished in Hades. The most effective means of protecting oneself from unjust prosecution by others in this life is to avoid their notice by living a retired, private life. The Athenian statesmen who corrupted the people by feeding their desires may have deserved their punishments, but, Socrates now acknowledges, those few politicians, like Aristides, who were able to remain just had also been treated badly by their fellow citizens.

75. Gorgias could only get Callicles to go through the motions so that Socrates could finish his argument. Gorgias was not able to provide an example of the true use of rhetoric by persuading Callicles to accept his verbal punishment. Nor does the student of philosophy appear to be moved by Socrates' recourse to the gods.

76. Cf. Alessandra Fussi, "The Myth of the Last Judgment in the *Gorgias*," *Review of Metaphysics* 54 (March 2001): 529–52; and James Boyd White, *When Words Lose Their Meaning* (Chicago: University of Chicago Press, 1984), 101, both of whom also argue that the "myth" describes life on earth.

E. Why Socrates Converses Only in Private

In the *Gorgias* Socrates thus indicates more clearly than in any other dialogue why he did not engage in political action as ordinarily understood but insisted on examining his interlocutors individually in private. Human beings do not have and, while living, cannot acquire the knowledge needed to institute and administer justice.[77] By examining the opinions of his interlocutors, Socrates was at least attempting to acquire the knowledge of individual souls, both his own and those of others, that would be required. By refuting them or being refuted himself, he was trying to correct and so order their souls as well as his own. Such corrections were the necessary prerequisites for anyone learning to rule himself, much less to rule others. It was not possible for Socrates to persuade or correct anyone who was not willing to be persuaded or corrected, however. Like Gorgias, Polus, and Callicles, most people do not like to be shown up or made ashamed in public. People will be corrected, therefore, if at all, most effectively in private. Because human beings are combinations of body and soul, the correction cannot consist merely in showing that a person has logically inconsistent opinions; it has to relate the general arguments to that person's particular situation and character, if it is going to be accurate or effective.

Socrates concludes the *Gorgias* by pointing out that none of his interlocutors has been able to refute his contentions that people should beware of doing injustice more than suffering it; that if people become unjust, they should accept their punishment; and that rhetoric should always aim at what is just. His arguments do not depend on fear of punishment in the afterlife, although they are compatible with such beliefs. Not claiming he has acquired the knowledge needed to judge, Socrates urges Callicles to join him in practicing justice and the rest of virtue. Only after they have practiced bringing order to their own souls as individuals, in private, should they turn their attention to political affairs.

A glance back at the preceding conversation should lead readers to interpret Socrates' parting suggestion cautiously. The practice (*askēsantes*) Socrates recommends could not be easily or quickly completed. Callicles has studied philosophy in preparation for a career in politics. But in his

---

77. As in the *Apology* 40c–e and *Phaedo* 61d, Socrates admits that we do not know what happens after death. He believes (*Gorgias* 524b) that death is nothing, that death is the separation of the body from the soul, and that like corpses individual souls continue to bear the marks of their experiences and character (even longer) after death. (If souls did not, there would be no basis for the judgment and punishment of the base.)

conversation with Socrates, Callicles has shown that he has not studied long or hard enough; he has not learned to argue cogently, nor has he learned to be moderate, pious, or just. As represented by Socrates, philosophy is a life-long endeavor. Socrates told Callicles (*Gorgias* 487e) that if they could come to an agreement, they would have reached the truth and would not need to test it further. By the end of the dialogue it is clear, however, that such an agreement would have consisted in Callicles' admission that Socrates is right, that human beings should strive above all to become moderate and just. That is exactly what Callicles refused and apparently could not be persuaded to admit. And Callicles expresses the opinions and desires of most people, who resist philosophical instruction as well.

In the *Republic* (498c–d) Socrates suggests that the people could be persuaded to accept the rule of a philosopher by a rhetorician like Thrasymachus. In the *Gorgias* he shows, however, why philosophic rule will not come about through persuasion alone. In order to mold or reform the souls of their fellow citizens, Socrates says in the *Republic*, philosophers would have to begin by taking "the city and the dispositions of human beings, as though they were a tablet, which they would first have to wipe clean" (501a). That would hardly be easy, he admits; such a "clean slate" is achieved in the *Republic* (540e–41a) by sending away everyone more than ten years of age.[78] Only the souls of the young can be shaped. Yet Socrates also insists in both the *Republic* (497d–98c) and the *Gorgias* that philosophy is not an occupation for the young. They need to be trained by good institutions and laws to be able to study more intensely later. It would be better if people did not need punishment or correction. Legislation thus appears to be a higher, more positive branch of the art of politics than is justice in Socrates' definition of the art of politics. In the *Republic* (518d), Socrates admits, however, that the virtues inculcated by law are like bodily habits. To obtain the knowledge necessary to rule justly, philosophers require further education in dialectics. The opinions and habits young people acquire as a result of a good upbringing have to be subjected to critical examination before they are taken to be true. In the *Gorgias* (as in the *Charmides* and *Alcibiades*), Plato shows his readers that such critical examinations are conducted most effectively on an individual basis in private.

---

78. Such a purge is suggested, if not mandated, for similar reasons by both the Athenian Stranger (*Laws* 735d–36a) and the Eleatic Stranger (*Statesman* 308e–9a), whereas in the *Timaeus* it appears to be impossible to reverse the original corruption that results in human procreation. The most one can achieve is a regime in which some are able to become philosophers themselves.

Socrates never expected more than a few exceptionally talented young people to be able and willing to pursue philosophical investigations with him. Even if he were to succeed in persuading a few to become philosophers and they were to acquire the power to legislate, as legislators they could achieve nothing more than molding the opinions and habits of their fellow citizens. Without critical examination and correction of their opinions, these citizens would not become truly moderate or just. If citizens whose opinions had not been criticized and corrected acquired the power or freedom to do so, they were apt to mistreat their rulers the way the Athenians had mistreated the just Aristides.[79] Young people who joined Socrates in trying to make themselves more just before they took up public affairs were apt to be more like Aristides than the political leaders who corrupted the Athenian people further by feeding their unjust desires. And these just leaders might be able to keep the unjust desires of their compatriots in check by enforcing the law.

Socrates confined himself to private life not simply because he realized that his interrogations tended to anger others and that he would be defenseless in court because most of his fellow citizens could not understand why he persisted in activities that irritated others. He did not engage in public activity merely because neither he nor any other rhetorician was able to establish the necessary conditions for the rule of philosophy by convincing an entire people to hand their children completely over to the care of others and peacefully depart. (Socrates has shown that rhetoric does not have the power that Gorgias claimed for it: to enable one to be free and rule others in one's own city.)[80] Socrates persisted in conducting his philosophical investigations in private—and yet paradoxically claimed to be the only one at his time in Athens even attempting to practice the true political art—because he saw that his private interrogations of individuals were the only means of achieving the goals and purposes of political associations. People like Polus and Callicles thought that honor, wealth, and power would make them happy, but Socrates reminded his auditors that it is necessary to know

---

79. In the *Laws* the Athenian Stranger emphasizes the need to supervise citizens in all their associations and activities, from birth until death, even though the citizens of his regime are trained from birth to be courageous and moderate. He proposes the establishment of a Nocturnal Council in the end, because, like Socrates and unlike his Dorian interlocutors, the Athenian recognizes that people truly learn the most important things only in private conversations. Because people cannot be made virtuous by means of laws, in the *Statesman* (291c) the Eleatic Stranger will declare that all actual rulers are sophists. By passing laws or issuing decrees, rulers claim to know, in effect, what is good for their citizens.

80. Cf. Strauss, *City and Man*, 127.

what is truly good for us in order to achieve what we want. The only way people can be happy is to become virtuous and to associate with other virtuous people. If the people with whom one associates cannot be trusted (and neither the immoderate nor the unjust can be trusted), members of a political association cannot even succeed in protecting themselves from the injustice and violence of others, at home or abroad.

Socrates recognized that he could benefit only a limited number of people by conversing with individuals and that these conversations would have to be repeated if they were to have much effect. He admitted that he was not able to benefit everyone and that some of those who improved while they associated with him and listened to him conversing with others degenerated as soon as they left his side. He modestly claimed only to be attempting to practice the true art of politics, not to be a successful practitioner. In interrogating and refuting the opinions of others, Socrates did not present a positive teaching. Although he described a city in speech in the *Republic*, he presented it ultimately as a paradigm that individuals could use to order their own souls; unlike the Athenian Stranger, Socrates did not present his city in speech as a set of laws that could be used by actual statesmen in founding a new colony. Nor like the Eleatic Stranger did he ever outline a royal science or art of politics that consisted in knowing what to order or command. Socrates did not think that people could be made virtuous by command any more than they could be forced to be free. He admitted that he benefited from the conversations in which he tested the opinions of others, but, he insisted, he was not the only one who benefited. If justice consists in doing what is both in one's own interest and in the interest of others, that is, the common good, Socrates was just. Although the claims Socrates made on behalf of his philosophy were much more modest than the promises politicians regularly made about the benefits they would bring their fellow citizens, Plato shows that the benefits of Socratic philosophy were much more real.

V. *Meno*: Socrates as "Teacher"

In the *Meno* Plato shows that Socrates' refutation of Gorgias had not persuaded the rhetorician that he should teach his students to be just. Gorgias had learned merely that he should not claim to teach virtue, so that he would not be forced to contradict himself again in public. Meno reports (95c) that one of the things he admires most about Gorgias is that Gorgias never promises to teach virtue and laughs at those who do, even though he thinks there is a need to make men speak skillfully. In the *Meno* Plato thus reminds his readers of the limits of Socrates' ability to benefit those with whom he conversed. Socrates was not able to persuade Gorgias to teach his students to be just, and, we shall see, Gorgias did not teach his student Meno to be just. But Socrates does not prove to be any more able than Gorgias to arouse a desire to become just in Meno. As in the *Gorgias*, so in the *Meno*, Plato shows his readers how limited the power of argument is. Recognition of the limits of his power to influence others did not keep Socrates from trying, however. If he could not convince young people to join him in a philosophical investigation of what is truly virtuous, good, noble, and just, he would try, as he does with Meno, to provide them with a better, more salutary set of opinions.

As the understanding of friendship he proposed in the *Lysis* indicates, Socrates could only befriend and so benefit people who were willing to admit their own deficiencies and consequent needs—particularly with regard to knowledge. One of the main reasons he sought to associate with the young was that they find it easier to acknowledge their ignorance than adults do; ignorance is less shameful in the young. Not all young people are willing to concede their lack of learning, however. In the *Meno* Plato shows that Socrates fails to persuade a young Thessalian he cannot learn how to be virtuous unless he asks what virtue is. Meno believes that he already knows. After Socrates refutes the three definitions he offers, Meno does not seek to inquire further. He gets angry and threatens to prosecute Socrates, as does Meno's Athenian host, Anytus, even though Socrates criticizes him only in private.[81] Because people will not blame themselves or others for things beyond human control, Socrates concludes the dialogue by telling Meno that he would benefit the Athenians if he were to persuade Anytus that the fate of human beings lies in the hands of the gods.

A. If Not a Method, What?

It is ironic, in light of Socrates' failure to persuade Meno to inquire what virtue is, that the dialogue has often been taken to epitomize the "Socratic method" of investigation, because in the famous scene with the slave boy,

---

81. Bruell (*Socratic Education*, 165–66) also emphasizes the importance of the presence of Socrates' later accuser, Anytus, in the *Meno*.

Socrates claims to demonstrate how a human being can be led to "recollect" the truth solely by means of questioning.[82] But at the conclusion of the demonstration Socrates says that he is not entirely confident of the truth of what he has reported about the immortality of the soul or its ability to "recollect" (*Meno* 86b–c). The only thing he will assert with confidence is his conviction that it is better for human beings to persist in their efforts to acquire knowledge than to give up in the face of the difficulties involved.[83] Explicitly based on things he has heard from others, the truth of which he is not willing to affirm in the end, the demonstration does not appear to constitute an illustration of the way Socrates usually approaches questions. (In fact, it represents an unusual, if not singular, incident in the Platonic corpus. Socrates is not shown giving any other such geometrical proof.) Nor, in light of Socrates' explicit disavowal, does what he says about recollection appear to constitute his own (or Plato's) theory (about the possibility or grounds of knowledge or anything else). To be sure, in the *Phaedo* (72e) Cebes reports that Socrates was wont to say that learning is nothing but recollection. Cebes also says (73a) that the best argument for Socrates' accustomed saying consists in showing that when people are questioned correctly, they answer correctly. They could not do this if they did not, in some sense, have knowledge (*epistēmē*) and right reason (*orthos logos*) within them, and this can be proved (*katēgorein*) most clearly with a mathematical diagram. But in the *Phaedo* (73b–76a) Socrates gives a different account of the character and basis of recollection through an association of images. He presents this account, moreover, only after Cebes' friend Simmias says that he does not "recollect" the argument very well; in other words, it does not look as if Socrates repeated it in their presence all that frequently. In the *Phaedo* Socrates is trying to comfort his friends at the prospect of his death by convincing them of the immortality of the soul. In the *Meno* he asserts the immortality of the soul, largely on the basis of the authority of others, as part of an attempt to show Meno that

82. See, e.g., Malcolm Brown, "Plato Disapproves of the Slave Boy's Answer," *Review of Metaphysics* 20 (1967): 57–93; and Kenneth Seeskin, *Dialogue and Discovery: A Study in Socratic Method* (Albany: SUNY Press, 1987).

83. Roslyn Weiss, *Virtue in the Cave* (New York: Oxford University Press, 2001), emphasizes the importance of Socrates' disavowal. Jerome Eckstein, *The Platonic Method: An Interpretation of the Dramatic-Philosophic Aspects of the "Meno"* (New York: Greenwood Publishing, 1968), also argues that the "demonstration" does not constitute an example of Socratic inquiry or produce a tenable "theory" and is not intended to do so—but on somewhat different grounds—as does Robert C. Bartlett, "Socratic Political Philosophy and the Problem of Virtue," *American Political Science Review* 96, no. 3 (September 2002): 529–30.

a critical examination and disproof of his current opinions will not necessarily result in *aporia*. The fact that Meno refuses to take up Socrates' question about virtue afterward, even though the young man praises Socrates' speech, ought to make readers wary of taking the demonstration as the example par excellence of Socrates' mode of teaching.[84]

If the exchange with the slave boy does not represent the example par excellence of the way in which Socrates led his interlocutors by questioning them to see the truth, however, what does? What did Socrates do? In the *Meno*, as in many other dialogues, we see Socrates transform his interlocutor's initial question, for example, in the *Republic*, whether it is better for a human being to live justly or unjustly, into a "what is . . . ?" question. And in the *Meno*, as in many other dialogues, the result of Socrates posing that "what is . . . ?" question is to show his interlocutors that they do not know what they are talking about. As Plato shows in the *Euthydemus*, Socrates knew that merely refuting his interlocutors might discourage them from engaging in further philosophical inquiries. If he wanted to persuade others to join him in making such inquiries, Socrates not only had to persuade them that they did not know what they thought they did; he also had to hold out the promise of their learning. That was the purpose of his demonstration with the slave boy.[85] When Meno still refused to pursue the question of what is virtue, after Socrates demonstrated the possibility of recollection, Socrates thus proposed that they seek to learn whether virtue is teachable by means of a hypothesis: if virtue is knowledge, it must be teachable. He could at least show Meno that it was possible to acquire knowledge and so virtue. Socrates was not in, nor did he lead his interlocutor into, a complete and irremediable state of *aporia*. So when they failed to identify any teachers of virtue, Socrates pointed out that right opinion

---

84. Following Robert S. Brumbaugh, "Plato's *Meno* as Form and Content of Secondary School Courses in Philosophy," *Teaching Philosophy* 1–2 (1975): 107–15, Seeskin (*Dialogue and Discovery*, 118, 125) claims that the demonstration has a positive effect on Meno, because he enters the discussion more wholeheartedly from that point onward. These scholars fail to take account of Socrates' observation that he must be ruled by Meno and therefore will take up the question with which Meno began—whether virtue is teachable—because Meno will not be ruled by Socrates or take up the question of what is virtue, which Socrates insisted they had to answer before they could determine whether it is teachable. In other words, Meno has not budged—or learned anything from the conversation in the meantime.

85. Gail Fine, "Inquiry in the *Meno*," in Kraut, *Cambridge Companion to Plato*, 209, 221, argues, contra Gregory Vlastos, "Elenchus and Mathematics: A Turning Point in Plato's Philosophical Development," *American Journal of Philology* 109 (1988): 375, that the demonstration with the slave boy constitutes an example of Socratic elenchus, which results in the slave boy's coming to true opinions about that which he does not know, not knowledge.

could be as good as knowledge for the sake of action. The problem was that opinions are easily changed. They concluded, therefore, that virtue must be a product of divine dispensation, that is, that human power alone is not sufficient to produce or secure it. Although Socrates took care not to discourage Meno completely the way Euthydemus and Dionysodorus threatened to discourage Clinias, Socrates would not allow Meno to leave thinking that he was virtuous as he was by nature and did not need any further instruction or support.

In the *Meno* readers thus see Socrates "at work," first trying to persuade his interlocutor to join him in philosophizing, and failing that, then attempting to improve his interlocutor's opinions. The demonstration with the slave boy represents only a partial example of the way Socrates usually proceeded. In the Platonic dialogues Socrates consistently insists that he does not know the most important things and that he cannot therefore teach others what is virtuous, noble, or good. By questioning the opinions of others, however, he can show them that they hold contradictory views that will prevent them from achieving the goods they seek. By asking his interlocutors to think about what is virtuous, noble, or good, he asks them to inquire, in general, what human beings should do. In leading his interlocutors to ask that question with particular regard to their own desires and circumstances, he gives them a lesson in acquiring what might be called practical wisdom (*phronēsis*). Not only here in the *Meno* (88c–89b) but also in the *Republic* (518e), Socrates identifies this wisdom as what makes people virtuous. The ability not merely to formulate general principles but to apply them in specific circumstances cannot be taught by precept. But what cannot be taught may nevertheless be learned.[86] Since the acquisition of practical wisdom requires a certain amount of experience, it cannot be said to be simply "by nature" (*Meno* 89b). It seems to be acquired by means of a certain practice (*askēsis*)—the option Meno drops when he restates his question concerning the ways in which human beings might become virtuous after Socrates' demonstration (86c–d).[87] But the "practice" does not appear to consist in a kind of training or mere repetition any more than it consists in engaging in practical affairs, as usually understood. It consists in the kind of dialectical questioning of others along with oneself in which

---

86. Meno misses the distinction. When Socrates suggests at 89c that the soul must become good by learning (*mathēsei*), Meno replies that they must then conclude that, according to their hypothesis, virtue is knowledge (*epistēmē*) and can be taught.

87. Cf. Gilbert Ryle, "The *Meno*: Many Things Are Odd about Our *Meno*," *Paideia* 5 (1976): 1.

Socrates engages and Meno refuses.[88] It is not the same as knowledge or a kind of science (*epistēmē*). If we take seriously what Socrates says in the *Gorgias* about his attempting to practice *hōs alethōs politikē technē*, it might be considered to be part of "the true political art."

B. The Man Who Refused to Ask What Virtue Is

From Xenophon's *Anabasis* Plato's readers would have known that Meno proved to be a traitor who betrayed his fellow Greeks to agents of the Great King. But Plato's dialogue is set before the Greek mercenaries set sail for Asia Minor in 401. When Meno opens the conversation by asking Socrates if he can say whether virtue is acquired by teaching, through practice, by nature, or in some other way, it looks as if the young Thessalian wants to become virtuous.

As the dialogue proceeds, however, Meno's initial question begins to look more like a challenge than a genuine inquiry. Socrates indicates how abrupt and ill-mannered the young man's query is when he comments that Thessalians must have acquired the habit of answering any question put to them, both fearlessly and magnificently, from Gorgias. (As we know from the *Gorgias*, the famous rhetorician began his exhibitions of his skill by offering to answer any question put to him. Ordinarily people would not pose such a question without explanation or introduction.) Later in the dialogue Meno suggests that Gorgias was the source of his question when he says (*Meno* 95c) that one of the things he most admires about Gorgias is that he does not promise to teach virtue and laughs at those who do. An admitted admirer and follower of Gorgias, Meno also seems to doubt that virtue is teachable. He asks Socrates, in effect, whether he agrees—and if not, to prove that Meno and Gorgias are wrong. When Socrates tells Meno that he cannot say whether virtue is teachable, because he does not know what virtue is and has never met anyone who does, Meno asks Socrates whether he met Gorgias when the rhetorician was in Athens.[89] If he had, Gorgias could have told him. Meno thinks that Gorgias knows what virtue is, because, we soon learn, Meno thinks that virtue consists of the ability

---

88. Martin Andic, "Inquiry and Virtue in the *Meno*," in Plato's "*Meno*," ed. Malcolm Brown (Indianapolis: Bobbs-Merrill, 1971), 264, comes to the same conclusion, if by quite a different path.

89. Meno's question suggests that Gorgias had been in Athens within Meno's memory. Because the *Meno* is usually thought to have taken place in 402–401, just before Meno went to Asia Minor, his question should lead readers to believe that the conversation related in the *Gorgias* should be imagined to have taken place closer to 405 than to 427.

to rule. In the *Gorgias* the rhetorician claimed that he taught people the means of becoming free themselves and commanding others in their own cities.

Socrates' initial response to Meno's question points to the role that not merely foreign teachers, but political regimes more generally, might be thought to have in determining whether people are virtuous or not (and so to a possible answer to Meno's question). The Thessalians may have learned to expect anyone to be able to answer any question like Gorgias, but people in Athens do not claim to be so all knowing. Like Socrates, they would tell the "stranger" (*Meno* 71a) that they could not say whether virtue is teachable because they do not know what virtue is. In fact, we see later in the dialogue, Socrates' fellow citizens do not say what he claims they will. On the contrary, Meno's Athenian host and Socrates' later accuser, Anytus, asserts (92e–93a) that any young Athenian can learn to be virtuous from any Athenian gentleman (*kalos k'agathos*) of the previous generation. Socrates exaggerates the unanimity of opinion among members of different regimes at the beginning of the dialogue, it seems, to highlight the actual differences among individuals growing up in various regimes and so to indicate the limited effects the regime has on the formation of belief and character. Socrates knows that the regimes in Thessaly and Athens do not even attempt to give their citizens the same opinions or "wisdom." In the *Crito*, Socrates observes, as he does not here for reasons of courtesy, that the Thessalians are renowned not only for their wealth and their horses but also for their lawlessness. A generation earlier, in discussing with Protagoras the question of whether virtue could be taught, Socrates had stated that the Athenians did not think it possible. In other words, most of Socrates' fellow citizens agreed with Meno and Gorgias. In asking whether virtue could be taught, both Meno and Socrates are calling one of the fundamental presuppositions of their respective regimes into question.

Socrates does not, therefore, treat Meno simply as a representative of his regime for long. On the contrary, he asks the young Thessalian to tell him what he thinks virtue is. Socrates characteristically addresses his interlocutor as an individual and points out the problems with his current opinions in order to show him that he does not know what he thinks he does and that he should join Socrates in seeking wisdom.

Thinking there are many virtues, Meno believes he can easily say a great deal about them. Whereas the virtue of a man is to be able "to carry on the affairs of the city, . . . to do well by his friends and harm to his enemies, and not to suffer himself," the virtue of a woman is "to manage the household well, conserving what is inside and being obedient to her man." Likewise, the virtue of a child is different from that of an elderly man, a freeman, or a slave. In sum, Meno thinks, "there is a virtue, according to each activity and each time of life relative to each task for each of us" (*Meno* 71e–72a).

Meno has described a great many virtues without saying what they all have in common that makes them virtues, Socrates objects. Meno's statement resembles what Aristotle says in the first book of his *Politics* about the varied virtues of men, women, children, and slaves. But unlike Aristotle, Meno is not able to respond to Socrates' question about what makes all the different kinds of virtues, virtues, by observing that they result in what is best under the circumstances for everyone involved—or that the truly virtuous person knows what to do to achieve the best possible result. Although he says that what is virtuous is different not only for every person, but even for every task, Meno is not a relativist like Protagoras. Pressed by Socrates to say what the virtues have in common, Protagoras responded with a long speech suggesting that what is good varies according to the circumstances. Having agreed that health, size, and strength are the same for men and women, Meno declares, when pressed by Socrates to say how the virtue of men and women is the same, that virtue consists in the ability "to rule over human beings" (73c–d). Socrates immediately points out that this definition would not apply to slaves or children.

Although he claims that there are many different kinds of virtues, Meno shows that he actually holds a single, rather conventional ancient Greek view of human excellence. When Socrates asks him whether rule must not also be just and moderate in order to be virtuous, Meno easily agrees, because this too is the publicly accepted view. When Socrates asks him whether justice is a virtue or virtue itself, however, Meno is nonplussed. People commonly speak about a variety of different virtues—courage, moderation, wisdom, and magnificence. Meno cannot say, therefore, what virtue itself is.[90]

Socrates' questioning of Meno's understanding of virtue shows, first, that Meno has not thought much about it. Meno merely repeats what he has heard not only from Gorgias but also from others. Socrates tries to improve Meno's intellectual habits by asking him to practice finding the common element in different things he calls by the same name in simpler

---

90. Cf. Jacob Klein, *A Commentary on Plato's "Meno"* (Chapel Hill: University of North Carolina Press, 1965), 72.

cases, such as shape or color, so that he will be able to answer the question about virtue, but Meno refuses. He asks Socrates to tell him instead. Socrates agrees to gratify him by defining shape, if Meno promises then to try once more to define virtue. But after Socrates defines shape as that which follows color, Meno not merely dismisses the definition as simpleminded. He insists on Socrates defining color in addition to shape before he abides by his promise to attempt another definition of virtue. Meno shows that he is not merely unreflective; he is lazy and unjust. He has been spoiled by his lawless upbringing in Thessaly, his wealth, and his having become accustomed to being gratified by teachers like Gorgias. Socrates comments, "Even someone who is blindfolded could know from conversing with you, Meno, that you are handsome and still have lovers. Because you do nothing but impose commands in your speeches, the very thing that spoiled people do, so as to tyrannize as long as they are in their prime" (*Meno* 76b).

In marked contrast to Callicles, who refused to answer any more questions from Socrates much more emphatically than Meno did, Meno never tries to instruct or benefit Socrates by telling him what is truly virtuous. Unlike Callicles, Meno is not moved by a desire to protect himself, his family, and his friends from the injustice of others. Meno is only concerned about prospering himself. It is no accident that he finally defines virtue (77b) as the desire for fine things (*kala*) and the ability to get them. Observing that Meno is an ancestral friend of the Great King (and so linking the portrait in the dialogue to that drawn by Xenophon), Socrates concludes that virtue, according to Meno, is the ability to provide oneself with gold and silver. Yet when Socrates asks Meno whether he would agree that such acquisitions are virtuous, if they are not justly or piously acquired, Meno asserts that he would not. Meno is not a simple or pure hedonist. He does not determine what he thinks is good on the basis of a calculation of what will maximize his pleasure and minimize his pain in the long term, like a sophist. Meno wants public recognition, the offices, and the honors as well as the wealth and the power that come with political rule.[91]

Socrates' initial exchange with Meno thus leads readers to ask: could Socrates have persuaded Meno to be more just by appealing to his desire for recognition? In other words, did Socrates have an opportunity to reform

91. Alexander Nehamas, "Meno's Paradox and Socrates as a Teacher," *Oxford Studies in Ancient Philosophy* 3 (1985): 4, points out that the "virtue" Meno inquired about, whether it could be taught, had been understood from earliest times in Greece to be almost the equivalent of fame.

Meno before he went to Asia Minor and proved himself a traitor? The answer given not merely by Meno's subsequent history but in the dialogue itself is that Socrates did not. Even if Socrates had persuaded Meno to change his opinion about the teachability of virtue, the philosopher concludes the dialogue by pointing out that mere opinion does not constitute an adequate foundation for virtuous human action in the future, because opinion is too easily changed. To change Meno's disposition, Socrates would have had to converse with him more than once. In their first encounter Meno indicates (77a), however, that he will remain with Socrates only if Socrates gives Gorgias-like answers that gratify him. Meno would not have accepted the sort of correction Socrates offered.

C. The Failure of Socrates' Demonstration

Meno gets angry when Socrates points out that he has fallen back again into saying that there are many virtues without specifying what virtue is. Meno realizes that he has nothing left to say and is ashamed to be left speechless. Meno has heard from Gorgias that learning to speak well will help him attain power. Regarding Gorgias as an exemplar of good speech, Meno believes that speaking well means (as in his first "definition" of virtue) having a lot to say.

Refusing to admit any failing—intellectual or moral—on his own part, Meno blames Socrates for his inability to answer. He has heard that Socrates is always perplexed and brings others into the same sorry condition. Now Socrates is bewitching and perplexing him. Claiming that he is jesting, Meno compares the philosopher to a torpedo fish that numbs its victims. Nevertheless, he warns, Socrates will be "well-advised not to sail away or emigrate from [Athens]: for, if [he] were to do this sort of thing in a foreign city, [he] would probably be arrested as a sorcerer" (Meno 80b).

Responding to the joke rather than to the threat, Socrates says that Meno almost tricked him. The handsome young man has made a likeness of Socrates in order to provoke Socrates into drawing a gratifying image of him in return. Socrates will not play Meno's game, however. Socrates admits that he does not know what virtue is and observes that Meno, who claimed to know, now appears not to know. Although Socrates is not willing to adopt the mode of speaking characteristic of Gorgias to gratify Meno, he is willing to search for knowledge with Meno.

Unwilling to engage in any further investigations of this kind with Socrates, Meno poses his famous paradox: How can Socrates seek for something, if he does not know anything about it? And if he happens upon it, how will he know it is what he seeks, if he does not know what he seeks? Socrates objects to this eristic argument, formulated to best or silence Socrates rather than to get to the truth. As reformulated by Socrates, Meno's argument cuts off any further inquiry: one cannot seek what one knows, because one already knows it, but one cannot seek what one does not know, because one does not know it. The paradox does not take account of Socrates' usual mode of proceeding (as in his initial exchanges with Meno), beginning with an opinion (but not knowledge) and subjecting that opinion to examination.[92]

Perceiving that Meno will not answer any more questions, Socrates takes a new tack, designed to appeal to the tastes Meno displayed in their initial encounter. In responding to Socrates' definitions of shape and color, Meno indicated that he preferred more technical or esoteric explanations to those based on ordinary observation. The latter were available to anyone who thinks, whereas the former required wealth (to pay for lessons) and could be given only by a few. Although Meno preferred Socrates' formal geometric definition of shape as the limit of a solid to the definition based on reflections on immediate sense perception, he had liked the definition of color Socrates attributed to Empedocles even better. Empedocles was one of the pre-Socratic philosophers who wrote as a poet and claimed or seemed to claim that he was divinely inspired, and in putting forth his third definition of virtue Meno himself had referred to the words of a poet. Socrates thus begins by telling the young Thessalian that something he had heard from "men and women wise about things divine" (81a) convinced him that Meno's eristic objection to the search for wisdom was not well taken.

Meno begs Socrates to tell him who these wise people were and what they said. Socrates says that they included priests and priestesses as well as

92. There has been a great deal of scholarly controversy about whether Meno's paradox merely constitutes an eristic objection or whether it poses a genuine problem. Cf. Weiss, *Virtue in the Cave*, 52–76; Shorey, *What Plato Said*, 157; Taylor, *Plato*, 135; Bernard Phillips, "The Significance of Meno's Paradox," in *Plato's "Meno": Text and Criticism*, ed. Alexander Sesonske and Noel Fleming (Belmont, CA: Wadsworth, 1965), 78; and Nehamas, "Paradox," 8–30. I agree with Francis M. Cornford, "Anamnesis," in Brown, *Plato's Meno*, 124–35; Julius Moravcsik, "Learning as Recollection," in *Plato*, ed. Gregory Vlastos (Garden City, NY: Doubleday, 1971), 1:57; Brian Calvert, "Meno's Paradox Reconsidered," *Journal of the History of Philosophy* 12 (1974): 147; Samuel Scolnicov, "Three Aspects of Plato's Philosophy of Learning and Instruction," *Paideia* 5 (1976): 52–53; and John F. Thomas, *Musings on the "Meno"* (The Hague: Martinus Nijhoff, 1980), 123, 128–29, that the all-or-nothing character of Meno's objection makes it eristic and invalid. It resembles the argument the brothers use to refute Clinias at the beginning of the conversation in the *Euthydemus* (276c–d) by asking him whether one learns things one already knows or things one does not. Either way he answers, he is shown to be wrong.

Pindar and other divine poets, that is, a few people who claimed to have divine knowledge not available to other human beings. They declared "the human soul to be immortal, that at one time it comes to an end called dying, and at another time it comes into being, but that it is never destroyed" (81b). They urged people, therefore, to live as piously as possible. Socrates quoted lines that have been attributed to Pindar, stating that those souls whose penance is accepted by Persephone will be sent back into the sun and become glorious kings and heroes.

The priests and poets who presented the immortality of the soul as a reason for human beings to live piously, so that they may be rewarded in the hereafter with fame in the future, may have appealed to Meno's own desire for public recognition. Socrates, however, drew a different lesson, not about the way in which human beings should live or future rewards but about how and what they can learn now.[93] Because the soul is immortal and has been born many times, it has seen everything here and in Hades. There is nothing surprising, therefore, about its ability to recollect things it knew before, including virtue. (In contrast to the poet he quotes, Socrates speaks about "soul" only in the singular.) Since everything in nature is related (suggenēs), he then suggested, there is nothing to prevent someone who has recollected (or, as we usually say, learned) one thing from discovering everything else, so long as he is brave and does not tire of searching.[94] Rather than telling Meno that he should live piously, Socrates concluded that he "should not be persuaded by the eristic argument, because it would make us lazy and please only the weak" (81d–e).

Socrates does not persuade Meno to reopen the investigation of what virtue is with this speech, however. Instead Meno asks Socrates to teach (didaxai) him what he means by calling all learning (mathēsis), recollection (anamnēsis). For a second time, Socrates calls Meno a rogue (panourgos).[95]

93. Cf. Stewart Umphrey, Zetetic Skepticism (Wakefield, NH: Longwood Academic, 1990), 14–15.
94. It is difficult to make Socrates' gloss on what he has heard into a consistent argument or doctrine. Combining what Socrates says about "recollection" in the Meno with what he says in the Phaedo, scholars such as Nicholas White, Plato on Knowledge and Reality (Indianapolis: Hackett, 1976), have explicated the notion in terms of the "ideas." Although Socrates asks Meno what the eidos of virtue is (Meno 72c), in the version of the "doctrine" of recollection he presents in the Meno he does not say that what the soul recollects are the ideas. On the contrary, his claim that everything is (literally) co-generated (81d) suggests that, like soul itself, everything is continually coming into being and "dying," that is, that there are no eternally unchanging things like the ideas. What those who are "wise" about "divine" things told Socrates is, in other words, more like the teaching attributed to Empedocles (as well as other pre-Socratic philosophers and poets; cf. Theaetetus 152e) than the argument enunciated elsewhere in various versions by Socrates.
95. The first was when Meno compared the philosopher to a torpedo fish at Meno 80b.

Socrates had just denied that there is such a thing as teaching (*didachēn*) and insisted that there is only recollection. Meno apologizes that he was speaking only from habit, and Socrates agrees to show him what he meant by learning as recollection.

By choosing to demonstrate what he meant by recollection by leading a slave boy through the steps of a geometric proof, Socrates once again adapts his speech to Meno's taste. As the questions Socrates addresses to Meno, as he and the boy go through the proof, indicate, Socrates' demonstration is not intended to establish the truth of the result. Meno already knew the answer to the question Socrates puts to the boy, that is, how to form a square double the area of another. The demonstration is designed to persuade Meno that it is necessary to show someone that he does not know what he thinks he knows to make him eager to seek knowledge.

In order to use the boy to show Meno what he meant by saying that all learning is recollection, Socrates has to make sure that the slave speaks Greek. If he does not, the boy will not understand Socrates' questions. Socrates does not point out this aspect of his demonstration to Meno, because it is not immediately relevant to his attempt to persuade Meno that *aporia* is a necessary precondition for learning. But if learning by recollection occurs, as Socrates emphasizes, by means of questioning (as opposed to instruction), it requires not only that another person pose the questions but also that the questioner and respondent speak a common language. Learning so understood is a social rather than a solitary activity with a conventionally established prerequisite. But neither the interpersonal character nor the conventional prerequisite can be inferred simply from the immortality of the soul. Socrates' own account of the significance and character of his own demonstration is thus incomplete.

Having learned that the slave speaks Greek, Socrates also makes sure that he understands what a square is and how to count. With his initial questions Socrates indicates that a human being will not only have to speak the same language as the questioner; he will also have to be familiar with some concepts and possess certain intellectual skills in order to learn by recollecting. (In order to learn virtue, it thus seems by analogy, Meno needs to know, first, what virtue is. He might have to generalize or abstract the common intelligible element in various specific examples of virtue in the way Socrates suggests human beings learn what is equal in the *Phaedo* [74d–75b].)

After Socrates and the boy agree that a square area is bounded by four equal lines and that this area can be divided into four smaller squares by two intersecting lines drawn from the midpoints of the sides, Socrates asks the boy (*a*) whether a square double the area of the original would have eight of the smaller squares and (*b*) what the length of the line on its side would be. Would it be two times as large as the original? When, following Socrates' suggestion, the boy says that it would, Socrates asks Meno: "Do you see that I am not teaching him anything, but all that I do is ask questions?" Meno agrees that the boy thinks he knows what sort of line it is from which the eight-foot area would come to be but that he does not. The boy has to be shown, first, that the area of the square with sides double the length of the sides of the first is not twice but four times as great. Nor is the area of a square with sides one and one-half times as great as the first double the area. It contains nine smaller squares rather than the desired eight. In other words, the boy not merely has to be shown that his first responses or opinions are wrong; he apparently has to be reduced to a condition of *aporia*, not knowing what else to say, in order to be ready to learn the correct answer. Socrates points out the relevance of what he has just shown to Meno's recent experience by asking him whether, "by making [the boy] perplexed [*aporein*] and numbing him, just like the torpedo-fish, they have harmed him" (84b). Meno concedes that the boy does not appear to have been harmed, and Socrates concludes that they have "done something useful for the work at hand. . . . For now he, not knowing, can carry on the search gladly, whereas then he could easily think that he could speak well about the double area before many people and many times" (84b–c). Not merely has the boy not been harmed, but, Socrates gets Meno to agree, the boy has positively benefited from his "numbing." So, Meno should reflect, has he benefited from Socrates' showing him that he does not know what virtue is, although he thought he knew. Meno is now—or ought to have been—ready to inquire and learn. A mere slave, much Meno's social inferior, has proved able to do so. By demonstrating what he means by "recollection" with a slave, Socrates indicates that the capacity to recollect belongs to human beings per se, by nature (and not exclusively to a wealthy, pampered few).

In showing the slave boy what the line is upon which a square double the area of the first can be constructed, readers should also observe, Socrates literally shows rather than tells him. Socrates points to "the line that the sophists call the diagonal" and shows the boy that a square composed of four halves of the four smaller squares into which the original has first been divided, bisected on the diagonal, has double the area of the original.[96] Socrates cannot tell the boy the answer or solve the problem simply in speech, through argument, or by means of calculation (counting), because the line is not commensurable with (and hence not describable in terms of) the sides. The name "diagonal" does not reveal the relation between it and the sides, nor can that relation be expressed in terms of whole numbers; it can be depicted or described only as a relation between the squares.

Socrates' showing, by means of the particular geometric proof he chose to demonstrate, that all the intelligible relations of things cannot be expressed in words or numbers indicates that human beings need to use their senses in acquiring knowledge. We learn different things by seeing, hearing, smelling, and thinking about what we have experienced. Our sensory impressions are, to be sure, often inaccurate, so the opinions we form on the basis of these impressions have to be corrected (often by measuring), like the slave's first guesses about the length of the desired line. Nevertheless, Socrates' proof reminds us, there are things that cannot be known simply by means of calculation or reduction to a common element.[97] The best, perhaps only, way to discover what things are—in themselves and in relation to others—is to reflect on our sensible experiences, trying to identify the common elements in the variety of particular examples we encounter, the way Socrates first identified shape as that which we perceive following color. Meno thought that Socrates' first definition was simpleminded and objected that it contained another unknown. If, as Socrates' argument about the ideas suggests, being exists only in differentiated form or as beings, then any attempt to define any particular form of being will necessarily contain a reference to an unknown.

96. I cannot, therefore, agree with Norman Gulley (*Plato's Theory of Knowledge*, 11–12) in his claim, reaffirmed by Gregory Vlastos, in his widely reprinted article "*Anamnēsis* in the *Meno*," *Dialogue* 4 (1965–66): 144, that "no mention at all is made of sense-experience either in the dialogue with the slave or in the subsequent discussion of its significance." However, I do not agree with W. D. Ross, *Plato's Theory of Ideas* (Oxford: Clarendon Press, 1951), 18, in his assertion that the method Socrates uses in instructing the boy is "purely empirical."

97. Brown ("Plato Disapproves," 199–242) thus argues that for Plato, geometry represents a lesser form of knowledge than arithmetic. To say, as did the German scholar quoted by Brown (O. Toeplitz, "Das Verhältnis von Mathematik und Ideenlehre bei Plato," in *Quellen und Studien zur Geschichte der Mathematik* [Berlin: Springer, 1931], 4), that Plato took the distinction between the two kinds of mathematics seriously, does not mean Plato thought one a superior form of knowledge. In book 7 of the *Republic*, Plato (or Socrates) distinguishes calculation from knowledge of numbers (525a–c) but makes both (along with all other forms of mathematics) inferior to knowledge of the ideas or dialectics, in an education that requires a philosopher to proceed both "up" the line from sensations and back down again from the ideas to their sensible images.

Reflecting on what they had seen in the demonstration, Socrates and Meno agree that the boy only "recollected" opinions; he does not have knowledge. The questioning (or what Socrates called "refutation" and "correction" in the *Gorgias*) would have to be repeated many times, the questions asked in different ways, before the slave would understand the reasons the opinions he had just come to were true. Nevertheless, Socrates has Meno affirm, the boy had never been taught geometry. So if he came to articulate those opinions in response to Socrates' questioning, the slave must somehow have drawn the opinions out of himself. And if he did not articulate them or realize that he had them before he was questioned, he must have drawn them out of that part of himself that was not always part of him as a human being, that is, his immortal soul. (What the immortal soul now appears to have, we might note, is true opinion and not knowledge [of the ideas or anything else].) Since this soul is said to exist both before and after it comes to life as a human being, it would not appear to be individual. It seems to constitute a certain kind of knowledge or capacity to acquire it which human beings share.

Socrates concludes his demonstration by urging Meno to be bold and try to recollect what he does not now remember. But although he thought Socrates spoke well, Meno is no more inclined to take up the question of what is virtue after the geometric demonstration than he was before. Unmoved by the conversation, he states that he would get most pleasure from inquiring about that which he first asked, whether virtue is teachable or by nature or comes to human beings in another way. As Socrates had charged earlier, Meno does not want to learn so much as he wants to be gratified.

D. If Virtue Is Prudence, No One Can Teach It

Although Socrates continued to insist that it would not be possible to answer Meno's question without determining what virtue is, he was forced to acknowledge Meno's unwillingness to investigate that question. Meno had not merely refused to be ruled by Socrates; believing (like Callicles) that it is the way to remain free, Meno would not even try to rule himself but had attempted, successfully, to rule Socrates. Socrates thus asked Meno to relax his rule a bit and allow the philosopher to formulate a hypothesis on the basis of which they might answer Meno's query. Socrates again proposed a mode of proceeding used by geometricians. He made it clear, however, that this is not the way he would proceed if he were free to do what he thinks will lead to the truth. Why, readers might ask, did

Socrates try to carry the argument further? Why didn't he just give up on Meno, who had already proved to be difficult to persuade, if not impossible to teach? The answer Socrates gives to this question at the end of the dialogue is that the Athenians would benefit if Meno persuades Anytus of what Socrates tries to persuade Meno.

1. Virtue Is Prudence, as a Whole or in Part

Although Socrates suggested that they would be arguing on the basis of a hypothesis—that if virtue is teachable, it must be some kind of knowledge—he actually gives an argument to show that virtue must be some kind of knowledge. By getting Meno to agree that virtue is good, that what is good must be beneficial, and that all the things we call good—both the goods of the body and the virtues of the soul (courage, justice, moderation, aptitude for learning, memory, and great-souledness)—are beneficial only if they are combined with mind (*nous*) and directed prudently (*hēgoumenēs phronēseōs*), Socrates answers the question he put to Meno about what makes the various kinds of virtue virtuous, that is, what virtue is.

If virtue is practical wisdom, either as a whole or in part, Socrates points out, virtue cannot be by nature. If people were born virtuous, the only way to keep them in their virtuous condition would be to protect them from any outside influence. People cannot learn or acquire wisdom, however, if they are kept in isolation from each other or the world. People are not good by nature, therefore, but must become good by learning (*mathēsei*). But it is Meno (and not Socrates) who concludes that if virtue is knowledge (*epistēmē*), as they hypothesized, it can be taught.

Socrates suggests that they might not have agreed to this correctly. Meno does not see the problem. He does not seem to remember what Socrates just demonstrated with the slave boy, that learning occurs through recollection and not by teaching. Although it does not seem to have impressed Meno, Socrates has pointed out, several times, that teaching and learning are not the same. But having failed to convince Meno through argument or demonstration, Socrates is reduced to appealing to his prejudices. Socrates now says that he doubts virtue can be taught, because he has not been able to find anyone who teaches it.

2. Socrates' Attempt to Tame Anytus

At that moment Meno's Athenian host and Socrates' later accuser, Anytus, arrives. Socrates greets him by observing that Anytus is especially well suited to participate in their search for teachers of virtue for three reasons:

(1) Anytus' father demonstrated his own practical wisdom not only by acquiring considerable wealth through his own efforts, instead of by chance or as a gift, but also by not allowing his wealth to make him arrogant or disorderly; (2) Anytus' father made sure his son was well brought up and educated; and (3) a majority of the Athenians have shown that they believe Anytus was well brought up and educated by electing him to high office.

Just as Socrates had pointed to one possible answer to the question of whether virtue is acquired by teaching, at the beginning of the dialogue, by commenting on the differences between the Thessalians and the Athenians without explicitly discussing the role of the regime in forming the character of its citizens, so in introducing Anytus Socrates points to another: children are taught to be virtuous by their parents. Rather than taking up this traditional notion immediately, however, Socrates begins their quest for teachers of virtue by looking at the professionals. If a man wants to learn an art, Socrates points out, he goes not merely to a practitioner but to one who also claims to be able to teach it and thus charges a fee. The people who claim to teach virtue are called sophists.

The suggestion that young people be sent to study with the "sophists" arouses Anytus' anger. "These men are the debasement and corruption of those who associate with them" (*Meno* 91c), he objects. If cobblers or tailors returned goods in worse condition than they received them, Socrates responds, they would not stay in business for a month. Yet Protagoras was famous for his wisdom and acquired a great deal of wealth from the fees he charged students in the forty years he practiced his art (*Protagoras* 314e–15a). Were he and his students mad? No, Anytus retorts; the families who continue to send their children to study with sophists and "the cities that allow them to come in and do not drive them out, whether it's some foreigner . . . or a fellow citizen" (92b) are.

By means of this exchange, Plato shows that conditions in Athens had changed significantly in a generation. When Socrates went to Callias' house to ask the famous sophist whether virtue was teachable, he observed Pericles' two sons among Protagoras' followers.[98] Thirty years later a popularly elected leader of the Athenians declares that they ought to ban all such "teachers," not merely foreigners but fellow citizens. Seeking to discover the source of Anytus' animosity, Socrates asks whether a sophist had wronged him. Anytus admits that he has never associated with a sophist nor allowed anyone in his family to do so. Having absolutely no

98. Cf. Aristotle *Athenian Constitution* 27, 34; Xenophon *Hellenica* 2.3.42; Nails, *People*, 37–38.

experience with sophists himself, Anytus is nevertheless convinced that the sophists corrupt others and wants to take action against them.

What happened between the time of Socrates' earlier conversation with Protagoras about the teachability of virtue and his present encounter with Anytus was not only that Athens had fought and lost the Peloponnesian War, but also that the democratic regime had been overthrown by the Thirty. Anytus had been prosecuted for failing to recapture Pylos from the Spartans in 409, although he escaped the fine by bribing the jury. Perhaps because he was angry at the demos for blaming him for bad luck (bad weather), he had supported Theramenes' faction of the Thirty in 404 but was later banished by them. He was then made *stratēgos* (general) by the democrats at Phyle and returned with Thrasybulus to the Piraeus to become one of the leaders of the newly restored democracy.[99] In a speech in 402, Isocrates (18.23–24) praised Anytus for abiding by the amnesty and not seeking vengeance on anyone. But in the *Meno*, Plato indicates, Anytus has not forgiven or forgotten. Rather than blame himself, the Athenian people, or past leaders for their misfortunes, Anytus attributes the corruption of his people to the influence of "sophists" domestic as well as foreign.[100] But he does not seem to have identified the guilty party or parties by name—yet.[101]

Having brought out Anytus' animosity toward the sophists, Socrates does not even attempt to defend them. Instead, he tries to show the leader of his people that the transmission of virtue is more difficult than he seems to believe. "We are not seeking those whose company would make Meno worthless," Socrates reminds Anytus; you can call them sophists if you wish. Tell Meno "to whom he can go in this great city to become worthy of mention in virtue" (*Meno* 92c–d). The democratic politician

99. In the *Republic* Socrates observed, "many believe that certain young men are corrupted by sophists, . . . but it is the very men who say this who are the biggest sophists. . . . Gathered together in assemblies, courts, theaters, army camps, or any other common meeting of a multitude, they blame some of the things said and done, and praise others, with a great deal of uproar, . . . and so completely educate . . . young and old . . . just the way they want" (492a–b).

100. In the *Apology* 23d–3, Socrates claims that his accusers charged him with investigating the things in the heavens and under the earth and corrupting the young by doing so, that is, with the usual charges against philosophers, because they do not know, in fact, what Socrates does or teaches. It may appear from the *Meno* that Anytus had some idea of what Socrates did and talked about, but as Plato shows in the *Meno*, Anytus had already made up his mind about sophists—not merely foreign but domestic (like Socrates)—before he talked to him.

101. As noted earlier, Xenophon (*Memorabilia* 1.212–18) makes the same point about Critias and Alcibiades. Under the terms of the amnesty, Anytus could not accuse Socrates of having corrupted Critias, in particular, although he no doubt had these two notorious examples of Socrates' purported influence in mind when he referred to domestic sophists.

refuses, however, to name anyone in particular. A true democrat believes that everyone is equally able to serve in high office and so, perhaps, equally virtuous. Seeming to ignore the pains his own father took to educate him and thus displaying a characteristically democratic lack of filial piety, Anytus claims that contact with any Athenian gentleman (*kalos k'agathos*) will make a young man better if he is willing to listen. Socrates asks whether these men have not only become virtuous but also able to teach others through their own efforts, and Anytus maintains that they too learned from those who came before them. Beginning with Themistocles, Socrates then names a series of renowned Athenian leaders—Aristides, Pericles, and Thucydides—who had demonstrated a desire to educate their sons by providing them with lessons of various sorts, but nevertheless failed to pass on their own virtue. If such virtuous fathers could not teach their own sons, Socrates concludes, virtue might not be teachable.

Anytus responds to this characteristically Socratic, but also fundamentally democratic, observation that virtue is not passed on through the generations by heredity or the formal instruction money can buy, with a threat slightly veiled as advice. Socrates appears to be carelessly willing to say bad things about people, but Anytus warns, "it is perhaps easier to harm human beings than to benefit them in other cities; in Athens it is certainly so" (94e–95a).

In the concluding exchange between Socrates and Meno, Plato suggests that Anytus was correct. Plato shows that Socrates attempted to benefit the Athenians by persuading Meno that human beings become virtuous by means of divine dispensation, in the hope that Meno would persuade Anytus and make him gentler. We know, however, that Meno soon left Athens and that Anytus subsequently accused Socrates of impiety and corrupting the young.

Nevertheless, we should ask: why would such a belief have made Anytus gentler? If we think back on Anytus' own history and Socrates' first example of a truly outstanding Athenian statesman unable to pass on his own virtue, we see a possible reason. Just as Themistocles was able to save Athens not only because he persuaded the people to abandon their homes and man the ships but also because a storm destroyed the Persian fleet, so Anytus had been blamed for his failure to lead an attack by the Athenian navy on Pylos, when the attack had been frustrated by a storm. If people were convinced that both great victories and defeats are results of factors over which human beings have no control, they would not blame or glorify their leaders quite so much. They would not treat their leaders unjustly, as the Athenians had treated both Themistocles and Anytus, and thus incline, if not force the most outstanding to leave and become traitors. Nor would their leaders be as apt to become angry in response to their own unjust treatment or to seek other scapegoats to blame for public disasters.

The outcomes of battles are not the only thing human beings cannot control. As Socrates told Theages, he could not control the effects associating with him had on others. By having Socrates use both Aristides and Thucydides as other examples of outstanding political fathers who were not able to pass on their virtue to their sons, Plato reminds his readers not only that in the *Laches* Socrates volunteered to help both their sons and their grandsons discover what virtue is and how to acquire it, but also that in the *Theages* Socrates admitted that their grandsons, Aristides and Thucydides, appeared to benefit from associating with him for a time but that the benefits did not last.[102] Nor did other teachers appear to have any more predictably lasting results. Although in the *Phaedrus* (269e–70a) Socrates says that Pericles was able to become the great rhetorician he was because he had studied nature as a whole and the place of mind in it with Anaxagoras, in the *Protagoras* and the *Meno* Socrates reminds his auditors that Pericles was not able to produce the same result in his sons, even though he, unlike Aristides and Thucydides, paid attention to the education of his heirs and sent them to study with teachers he respected. Plato may or may not have known what the historian Thucydides said about Themistocles:

> By his own native capacity, which was neither shaped by education nor developed by later training, he was at once the best judge in those sudden crises which admit of little or of no deliberation, and the best prophet of the future, even to its most distant possibilities. An able expositor of all that came within the sphere of his practice, he was not without the power of passing an adequate judgment in matters in which he had no experience. He could also excellently divine the good and evil which lay hidden in the unseen future. To sum up, whether we consider the extent of his natural powers, or the slightness of his application, this extraordinary man must be

---

102. Pericles asked Protagoras to draft a constitution for the colony of Thurii, where Pericles then sent Cephalus and his sons Polemarchus and Lysias. Perhaps exemplifying the same problem in the relations of one generation to another, Thurii later revolted from its "mother" Athens. For that reason Cephalus and his family returned to Athens (and were able to take part in the discussion related in the *Republic*).

allowed to have surpassed all others in the faculty of intuitively meeting an emergency. (1.138.3)[103]

But, as Socrates pointed out earlier, Themistocles' natural ability would not have been exercised or evident if, as a youth with an exceptionally good nature, he had been closeted away to protect him from all other possibly "corrupting" influences. In sum, Socrates' discussion with Meno and Anytus indicates that the virtue displayed by certain individuals, particularly in the form of practical wisdom, cannot be acquired merely by practice; nor does it arise spontaneously by nature. It seems to require all these factors—a good nature or capacity, some education, suitable associates, experience and practice, as well as the proper occasion or circumstances— and more. Themistocles might not have been able to save Athens, if not all of Greece, without the storm, but the storm alone was not sufficient. The leader of Athens also had to know what was best to do under the dire circumstances and be able to persuade his people to follow his advice.

3. Opinion and Divine Dispensation

Socrates concludes his conversation with Meno, therefore, by pointing out an option they have not considered. To prepare Meno to accept it, Socrates asks him whether there are gentlemen in Thessaly and, if there are, whether they teach or think that virtue can be taught. Like him, Meno says, Thessalian gentlemen vacillate between thinking that virtue can be taught and that it cannot. Perhaps because he doubts that virtue can be taught, he admires Gorgias for laughing at people who claim they can teach it; Meno, however, does not display the same animus against the sophists that Anytus does. His people had not just lost a war or had their government overthrown, and he had not lost his own fortune as a result.

Socrates points out that the poet Theognis also seems to vacillate between thinking that human beings can be taught to be good and that they cannot. The poet advises young people to associate with the rich and powerful, because "from good men you will be taught good things," but, the poet also warns, "if you mingle with the bad, you will lose even the mind you have" (*Meno* 95d). No one can make thoughts and put them into the mind of another. If they could, a bad son would never be born from a good father. "But by teaching you will never make the bad man [*anēr*] good" (96a). If readers put the lines together, they see that, like Socrates, the poet understands that the effect of teaching or association depends on the character of the learner as well as the would-be instructor. Bad associations ruin the mind, even if it is good by nature, and once a person or his mind is ruined, he cannot be made good by instruction. Goodness is not hereditary, partly because it depends on associations or circumstances and instruction.

There is no other subject (*pragma*), Socrates points out, that those who claim to teach are not thought to know, and that those who seem to possess have so much doubt about whether it can be conveyed to others. Since neither the professional instructors nor virtuous gentlemen appear able to teach it, there do not seem to be teachers or learners. But, in line with his quotation from Theognis, Socrates observes that he and Meno may have had their minds made bad by their instruction by Prodicus and Gorgias. They have not seen that there is another way in which human beings can learn to do what is right (*orthos*). For the purpose of directing action, right opinion is just as good as knowledge.

Why, then, do people think knowledge is superior to opinion, Meno asks. Human beings easily lose their right opinions, if they are not "tied down" by calculations of cause, Socrates explains. Such calculations are what he earlier called "recollection" (*anamnēsis*). But he immediately adds a reservation: he does not speak as one who knows. He claims only to know that there is a difference between right opinion and knowledge.

Appearing to summarize their conversation, Socrates concludes: if human beings can be good and benefit their cities only on the basis of knowledge or right opinion, people are not good by nature. Because people are not good by nature, he and Meno have inquired whether virtue can be taught. If virtue is prudence, virtue appears to be teachable. They have not been able to find any teachers, however, so they have agreed that virtue is not teachable and that it is not prudence. Reversing the terms of his initial hypothesis, Socrates observes that if virtue is not teachable, it must not be a product of knowledge. But he and Meno still agree that virtue is good and beneficial. Since human beings are directed to right action only by right opinion or knowledge, but people cannot be taught to know what is right, it cannot have been by wisdom but only by good opinion (*eudoxia*) that men like Themistocles led their cities. They were not able to teach their virtue to others because their virtue was a product of opinion and not of knowledge. Because such men could not explain why or how they were able to settle great affairs, they should be said to be divinely inspired like poets and soothsayers.

Meno thinks that Socrates speaks correctly, although he suspects that Anytus may be vexed (presumably by the suggestion that political leaders do not know what they are doing). Predicting that he will converse with Anytus again, Socrates insists that they must conclude that human beings act correctly in politics not by nature or as a result of education, but only by divine dispensation, so long as they cannot teach another to act in the same way. Meno concludes that Socrates speaks beautifully, but Socrates disowns the result of their conversation by insisting, as he had from the beginning, that it is impossible to know whether virtue can be taught until they determine what virtue is.

E. What We Learn about Virtue

In fact, readers learn a great deal about what virtue is, particularly the kind of virtue exemplified by famous statesmen, from Socrates' conversation with Meno. As in the *Protagoras*, so a generation later in the *Meno*, Socrates argues that virtue is not teachable, even though he insists that it is something like knowledge. But Socrates indicates the reason he comes to such a paradoxical conclusion more clearly in the *Meno* than he had in the *Protagoras*. The problem is not simply that neither the sophists nor the gentlemen can say what virtue as a whole is. Even if they were able, like Socrates, to identify the common element as prudence, the preconditions for acquiring this human excellence are so complex that it seems to exceed human communication and control.

In the *Protagoras*, Plato showed, Socrates had begun to establish his own reputation as a clever speaker by besting the famous sophist. Confident of his own rhetorical abilities, Protagoras accepted his defeat gracefully. He graciously displayed his own wisdom by praising Socrates. The sophist was certain that his own reputation would not (as it was not) be destroyed in a day. A generation later, Plato showed in the *Meno*, Socrates aroused the ire of both a young foreigner and a mature Athenian politician, when the philosopher demonstrated that the young man did not know what virtue is and his host could not show that it was passed down from generation to generation the way he claimed. Socrates made these interlocutors angry, even though there was no audience before whom they might have been embarrassed. Unable themselves to counter Socrates' arguments, they both threatened Socrates with prosecution in the courts (where they could employ other more effective speakers or speechwriters).

Socrates did not emphasize the limits of human knowledge and power—his own and those of others—merely as an apology for his own ineffectiveness. As we see in the *Meno*, he tried to show others their limits, as he had Anytus, both directly and indirectly, in an attempt to make them less angry and thus less unjust.[104] People who were convinced that human beings cannot completely control the course of events would not be as apt to blame others for the disastrous effects of their own greed. They would not form unreasonable expectations or believe the exaggerated claims political leaders often make about their own powers, especially in democracies. Because Socrates recognized that people could not simply be talked out of their strongest desires and deepest fears, he knew that his own efforts would have limited effects. He simply tried to do the good that he could.

Like his evocation of his own *daimonion*, Socrates' emphasis on the limitations of human knowledge and power indicates that he had a kind of piety. That piety was, however, untraditional. In the Platonic dialogues we often see Socrates conclude that the outcome of associating with him, for example, depends on the god. But we never see him pray to the god or the gods to produce desired results.[105] He did not seem to believe in the existence of deities who would respond to specific sacrifices or requests. The obviously untraditional character of Socrates' understanding of the divine along with his proclivity for associating with the young made it possible for an unscrupulous angry man like Anytus to accuse him of not believing in the gods of the city and corrupting the young.

104. Sallis (*Being and Logos*, 64) also emphasizes the depiction of Socrates revealing the ignorance of others and the way in which this serves the city in the *Meno*, although Sallis comes to these conclusions by a different route.

105. Xenophon (*Memorabilia* 1.2–9) says that Socrates often made sacrifices at public temples and used divination. Plato reports Socrates' references to his *daimonion* but not the public sacrifices. Like the Athenian Stranger (*Laws* 687c–d), Socrates warned Alcibiades (*Alcibiades II* 138b–c) that he should be careful what he prays for, because his prayers for what he believes is good, but is not, might be granted. As we shall see more emphatically in the *Euthyphro*, Socrates' arguments for piety take the form of emphasizing the limits on human knowledge and power and the need, therefore, for human beings to seek knowledge (including knowledge of their limits).

CONCLUSION TO PART II

What the Contrast with Timaeus
Tells Us about Socrates

At the acme of Socrates' philosophical career, we have seen, Plato
sets up a contrast between him and Timaeus. This contrast shows
what a strange (*atopos*) kind of philosopher Socrates was. Perhaps
because of the influence of Plato's student Aristotle, Timaeus represents a
more familiar understanding of philosophy than the more famous Socrates.
Timaeus has achieved order in his own soul by learning and then contemplating the intelligible order of the movements of the heavenly bodies. On
the basis of his understanding of the order of the heavens, he is also able to
perceive the geometric ordering of the elements and the reason informing
the construction of the human body. Timaeus is not simply a theoretical
philosopher, however. As a philosopher-statesman, he has also been able to
legislate a regime in Locri that presumably makes it possible for some of
its citizens to achieve and maintain this order in themselves and for their
descendants.

As we have seen, the problem with the kind of philosophical understanding represented by Timaeus consists in his inability to give a persuasive account of generation (as opposed to intentional fabrication) in general
and human eros in particular. He has to posit the intentional construction
of the cosmos by an unknown and unknowable "god"; he cannot explain
how the cosmos came to be or acquired an intelligible order on its own. Timaeus acknowledges his own erotic desire for learning, but there appears
to be an almost complete disjunction between this desire and all the other
disorderly "erotic" human desires that have to be strictly regulated if human beings are to live orderly, much less reflective or knowledgeable lives.

Socrates claims to know nothing but *ta erōtika*. Nowhere in the Platonic dialogues does he articulate a view of the cosmos.[1] Nowhere in the Platonic dialogues does he give an explication of the character of being or the whole. The closest he comes to such a statement is in the *Republic* in his famous images of the sun, divided line, and the cave. As emphasized in chapter 5, these are explicitly "images," not arguments or explications. Although Socrates claims that "the idea of the good" is source, ground, or principle of all knowledge and being, he also says that it is "beyond being." Socrates cannot even tell Glaucon his own opinion concerning it.

In his *Metaphysics* (987b1–10) Aristotle concludes that Socrates engaged solely in the study of ethical questions. It is "Plato" who posits the existence of the "forms" that exist separately from their sensible manifestations. As we have seen in chapter 3 of part I, however, Aristotle's account of the relation between "Socrates" and "Plato" does not accord with Plato's presentation of Socrates' description of his own philosophical development in the *Phaedo*. Aristotle apparently did not credit the way Plato shows that Socrates' search for definitions of justice or virtue in itself led him to emphasize the way in which human desire and thought prompt us to look beyond our immediate circumstances to what is purely intelligible, for direction in living our lives. Plato's Socrates calls that more or less articulate "looking," *erōs*, and he states several times that *ta erōtika* are the only things he knows.

Socrates explains what he understands by *erōs* first in the *Symposium* and then in the *Phaedrus*. Socrates does not speak in his own name in either of these dialogues. In the *Lysis*, however, he gives a demonstration in deed as well as in speech of his knowledge. He shows a young man how to become a true friend (*philos*) of the boy he loves by conversing with him in a way that lets the young boy see that he does not know what he needs to know in order to achieve his own ambitions and desires. Reading the three dialogues in conjunction with one another makes it clear that Socratic philosophy constitutes the culmination and purest expression of human *erōs* and *philia*. That "philosophy" does not consist in a set of doctrines or arguments so much as a continuing conversation about what is truly noble and good.

1. Cf. Aristotle *Metaphysics* 987b1–5. As we shall see, the explicitly "mythical" description Socrates gives of the "true" earth at the end of the *Phaedo* is much less detailed and scientific than Timaeus' "likely story."

As explained in the *Symposium*, Socrates' knowledge of *erōs* consists, first, in understanding that it is the power of communication between the divine and the human rather than the power of generation (as the pre-Socratic philosophers and poets thought). Eros is one of the *daimones* or the "daimonic" power (*to daimonion* [*Symposium* 202e], in which, Socrates says in other dialogues, he shares) that binds together the whole. It is not limited to the ethical, as Aristotle claims Socrates' philosophical investigations were. Indeed, the word "ethical" (*ēthikē*) does not appear in the Platonic corpus. Plato's Socrates emphasizes that his knowledge is limited, but the limits are defined in a different way. As the similarity between Diotima's description of the *daimōn* Eros and Socrates indicates, Socrates' knowledge of *ta erōtika* consists in the self-knowledge or kind of "human wisdom" he says, in the *Apology*, lets him see that he knows only that he does not know the most important things. Socrates knows, in other words, what is most important. He knows what he and other human beings most want to know.

As the "love" of something, Diotima explains in the *Symposium*, eros constitutes a relation between that which lacks something and, considered simply as that which is lacking, the opposite of that which it lacks, that is, that which is desired. What is unlike, in other words, wants to become like what it desires. Insofar as it is desirous, the unlike thus wants to change, to be moved, if not to move or cause motion elsewhere. In the case of human beings, Socrates consistently claims, that which we want is what is truly good. What is good will not remain good for us, however, if it is gained and then lost. What we want is to possess the good forever. But because we are mortal, we can never really attain or completely become what we want, that is, to become immortal. We cannot become one in the knowledge of the only things that truly can be known, that is, the eternally unchanging, purely intelligible beings, because we forget what we have learned and have to strive to relearn and remember. We can, however, approach, "imitate," or "share" in the eternal purely intelligible beings by coming to understand that they exist and that sensible beings "participate" in them.

In the *Symposium* Socrates has Diotima present the promise of such learning as an "initiation" into the highest mysteries in the famous "ladder of love." In opposition to the poets, she argues, eros does not consist in love of one's other half or of the beautiful. It is not the beautiful but the good that human beings want to possess—forever—in order to be happy. We desire the beautiful, because it appears good to us. As Socrates points out in the *Republic*, human beings can be satisfied with the apparently beautiful or just in a way that they will never be content with the only apparently good. We are, nevertheless, observably attracted by the beautiful. We are so attracted, she suggests, because as mortals we cannot achieve the immortality we desire. We wish, therefore, more or less knowingly, to "beget in the beautiful," that is, to perpetuate ourselves or the best aspects of ourselves. Sexual generation is the bodily form of such perpetuation. The psychological or intellectual expression of such a desire is to be seen in the works of poets like Homer and Hesiod as well as in legislators like Lycurgus and Solon. These individuals sought immortality in the form of fame or glory by educating noble youths and so begetting virtue in their souls. Both the virtues they generated and the fame they achieved were, however, essentially matters of opinion. Diotima thus describes a new kind of "begetting in the beautiful" that comes as close as a mortal can to possessing the good forever. Her account of the ladder of love is described explicitly as an initiation and takes the form of a promise, because, before Socrates, there was no one who sought to ascend to the truth in this manner.

As Socrates subsequently demonstrates in the *Lysis*, such a "lover" begins by seeking to attract an individual youth by begetting "speeches." These "speeches" do not consist in declamations so much as conversations that show the youth that he does not know what he thinks he knows and thus that he needs to seek knowledge in the company of the philosopher. Neither the lover nor the beloved possesses the knowledge the lover seeks in all kinds of pursuits and studies. She describes the object of that search as a glimpse of "the beautiful in itself" and not the good, because, as Socrates observes in the *Phaedrus* (250d), the beautiful in itself is the only kind of being in itself that makes itself manifest directly to the senses. The search or ascent to knowledge culminates only in a temporary "glimpse," because philosophers are changeable mortals who cannot remain simply the same in mind any more than in body. This glimpse of the beautiful in itself nevertheless gives each of them an incentive to continue to seek to recapture it as well as knowledge of other kinds of beings in themselves, especially of what lies beyond it, the good in itself. Even if they never acquire more than this glimpse, she promises, philosophers will nevertheless beget true virtue in themselves. Like the natural philosopher Socrates describes in the *Republic*, whose desire for truth overwhelms all other desires, philosophical lovers will become courageous, moderate, just, and wise as a result of the power of their love of truth. Having seen an image of that truth in the face of their beloved, philosophers try to communicate their own desire for true beauty and good to their beloved and so to enable their beloved to beget similar virtues in themselves.

If human beings become virtuous only by engaging in a philosophical search for knowledge of what is beautiful and good in itself, human beings can be educated only on an individual basis and in private. In the *Gorgias* Socrates thus emphasizes that the conversations in which he refutes and so corrects his interlocutor, or is himself refuted and so corrected, have to occur on an individual basis and so in private. Because such private examinations of human opinions and the institutions based on them constitute the only means of acquiring true virtue, Socrates claims to be the only person in Athens at this time even trying to practice the true political art. The corrections or psychic punishments he administers belong to the lower, remedial part of the political art called justice. But, Socrates repeatedly shows, human beings need to undergo such corrections in order to become good, just, moderate, and hence trustworthy citizens.[2] We are not born knowing exactly what we want or how to obtain it. Our unexamined desires and opinions point us in contradictory directions. So long as these opinions and desires remain unexamined and uncorrected, we tend to work against ourselves by seeking to achieve contradictory goals.

Like Theages, young men who observed the effect Socrates had on his associates saw that it improved them in a politically relevant fashion, even if they did not understand exactly in what respects or how. Socrates did not, and could not, tell them directly. Not claiming to know anything but *ta erōtika*, and questioning rather than directly trying to persuade anyone of anything, Socrates did not claim to teach anything to anyone. Because learning requires both desire and effort on the part of the learner, Socrates attributed his ability to affect his associates to his *daimonion*. He was not entirely able to determine whether he would be able to communicate his own desire to them.

Plato shows that Socrates produced a great many beautiful speeches in his attempts to arouse the love of truth in his young interlocutors. The famous images at the center of the *Republic*, the myth of Er, and his "palinode" in the *Phaedrus* can all be understood to constitute visions or glimpses of the beautiful in itself, designed to arouse the intense love of truth that

---

2. At the beginning of the *Seventh Letter* (325d), Plato (or his imitator) says he gave up his political ambitions and turned to philosophy, because in the corrupt regimes that existed it was impossible to find good and virtuous friends or associates.

would in turn beget all the virtues in Socrates' young interlocutors. In contrast to the "myths" related by Protagoras, Timaeus, the Athenian, and the Eleatic Stranger, which concern the origins of the cosmos or political order, all the "myths" Socrates tells concern the immortality of the soul. They contain the promise of a view of the purely intelligible undistorted by the senses, unattainable, but conceivable by a mortal.

Impressed not only by the beauty of his speeches but also by the superiority of argument he demonstrated in his exchanges with others, politically ambitious young Athenians like Alcibiades were attracted to Socrates, especially when he initially appeared to honor them by seeking their company. Like Plato's brothers Glaucon and Adimantus, Socrates was able to persuade some of these young Athenians that philosophy constituted their only hope of achieving justice, in themselves if not in their city, even if he did not succeed in making them philosophers. Like Alcibiades, other handsome Athenian youths were attracted by Socrates' seeming ability to teach them politically relevant skills. Neither Clinias nor Lysis became a regular associate of Socrates, however. They appeared to think that their own good looks and aristocratic heritage would secure them a preeminent place in the polis. Only their less handsome friends, Ctesippus and Menexenus, who learned how to argue by listening to Socrates, remained with him.

Socrates did not convince most of his young associates to become philosophers. But Plato shows in the dialogues set during the last decade of the fifth century that, as the apparently inexplicable attraction Socrates had for young ambitious Athenians became better and more widely known, Socrates' situation in Athens became more dangerous. Older democratic politicians like Anytus became suspicious of the influence Socrates apparently had on the young, especially young aristocrats like Alcibiades, who might be scheming to overthrow the regime. Their suspicions were aroused not only by the inexplicable fact of Socrates' attraction for the young, but also by his apparent unwillingness to say what, or even to admit that, he taught them. Because he not only seemed able to defeat his interlocutors in argument but also had the temerity to defend the foreign teachers, neither his older friends like Crito nor his enemies like Anytus were able to tell the difference between him and the sophists. As we all know, Callicles had reason to warn Socrates that he might be dragged into court and unjustly convicted.

Socrates' critiques of the poets in the *Symposium, Republic,* and *Philebus* clearly show that he did not believe in the traditional stories about the "gods of the city." He did not merely think that these stories were intellectually incoherent (cf. *Phaedrus* 246d). He thought the conceptions of the divine to be found in the works of the poets undermined all possibility of human happiness, individual or communal, by hinting that there was nothing eternal. Like the Athenian Stranger, Socrates saw that legislators would never be able to achieve the goal of political life by making each and every citizen as virtuous as possible, if they did not know what virtue is. Like the Athenian Stranger, Socrates saw that meant knowing what is noble and good in itself. By arguing that there were essentially different kinds of purely intelligible beings, the ideas, Socrates was able to provide the basis for an ongoing investigation of what these kinds were "in themselves" as well as of their relation to the sensible forms of being that "participated" in them. In contrast to both the Athenian Stranger and Timaeus, Socrates did not join his argument concerning the ideas to observations about the mathematically calculable, hence intelligible motions of the heavenly bodies, which obviously affect growth and so life on earth. He did not, because, as he indicates at the beginning of the myth of Er, he recognized that no sensible mortal would ever be able to recognize the purely intelligible ideas in the motions of sensible bodies. As Timaeus also indicates, all human sensation and cognition is affected, that is, distorted, by time and space. Rather than look to the heavens for a model of the order human beings seek to achieve in their own lives, Socrates analyzed the structure and consequences of his own deepest and most distinguishing desire. The love of the beautiful, which he saw characterized all human beings to a greater or lesser extent, was actually a desire to possess the good forever. As such, it pointed us toward that which is and must be unchanging and hence purely intelligible, even though we ourselves are not and can never be. In human eros Socrates found the way in which the sensible is directed toward and thus shaped by the intelligible. He had thus found a way of responding to the objections Parmenides raised to his argument concerning the ideas.

But was Socrates' response to the political-philosophical problems bequeathed to him by his predecessors satisfactory? Wasn't the effect of his philosophical practice limited to individuals? Didn't Socrates' illumination of the inadequacies of the opinions on which all existing institutions and laws rest undermine political order? Did his insight into the beneficent effects of the desire for, but necessarily limited and uncertain character of, human knowledge constitute an adequate basis for philosophy? In the eight dialogues explicitly linked to his trial and conviction, Plato thus has another philosophical challenger raise these and other fundamental questions about the adequacy and effects of Socratic philosophy.

PART III

The Trial
and Death
of Socrates

8

The Limits of Human Intelligence

After his initial exchange with Parmenides, in the dialogues set at the beginning and end of the first part of the Peloponnesian War, Plato showed Socrates talking to people—ambitious youths, sophists, poets, rhetoricians, politicians—who were primarily concerned about human affairs. In these dialogues Socrates could, therefore, have been understood to be concerned solely with ethical questions, as Aristotle later maintained (*Metaphysics* 987a1–5). Socrates was attempting to improve his fellow citizens by revealing the inadequacies and inconsistencies of their conceptions of the noble and good. So long as people sought contradictory or false goals, he recognized, they would never achieve satisfaction or happiness. Socrates proved, moreover, that the sophists who claimed to be able to teach young Athenians how to become virtuous could not do so in fact because the sophists held the same inadequate conceptions of the noble and good.

In dialogues set during the second part of the war, Plato then depicted Socrates presenting something like a positive teaching when, in the *Symposium*, *Phaedrus*, and *Republic*, he challenged the traditional understanding of the noble and good that had been put forth by the poets. But, Plato emphasized in the dialogues he set in the last decade of the fifth century, Socrates did not try to propagate that positive teaching by persuading others. He tried to correct his interlocutors by revealing the inadequacies of their current opinions and by urging them to reorganize their lives in light of what they had learned about what they and others really and truly want. Emphasizing the limits of his own knowledge and power, Socrates conveyed what he thought was truly good for human beings as much by his own example as by the arguments he gave.

In the first five dialogues explicitly leading up to Socrates' trial and death, however, Plato shows his teacher conversing with interlocutors who claim to know higher things. If these interlocutors proved, on examination, to have the knowledge they claim, Socrates' boast that no one was wiser than he would be shown to be hubristic and false.

Socrates looks better than his interlocutors in the first three of these eight dialogues—all of which are supposed to have occurred on a single day—because he at least knows what he does not know. Although Theaetetus, Euthyphro, and Cratylus all claim to know something eternal, none of them can explain how. Explicitly recognizing his own limitations, Socrates understands why it is difficult for human beings to acquire knowledge. In the *Theaetetus* he observes that he and the mathematicians both find themselves between those who argue, on the basis of an analysis of human sensation, that everything is in motion, and those who argue, on the basis of logic, that everything is one and motionless. He and the mathematicians both claim that there is an essential plurality, but neither he nor they can say what all the different parts, kinds, or numbers of things are, much less how they fit together to constitute a whole. Although he suggests in the *Theaetetus* that human beings should become as much like the god as they can by becoming as just and pious as they can, he does not, like Euthyphro, think that mortals should try to act like immortals. Nor does Socrates imagine, like Cratylus, that human beings can learn what the beings truly are merely from their names.

When the Eleatic Stranger shows the next day in the *Sophist* how motion and rest coexist with and within being as fundamental kinds (*eidē*), it looks as if he has come not merely to refute but to supersede Socrates. According to the Eleatic, it is possible to have more knowledge and so to be wiser than Socrates thinks. In the *Statesman* it appears, however, that the kind of knowledge the Eleatic argues anyone must have in order truly to be a statesman (*politikos*) is not possible for a human to attain. Plato thus prepares his readers to ask whether the combination of speech (*logos*) and deed (*ergon*), sensation (*aisthēsis*) and intelligence (*phronēsis* or *nous*), motion (*kinēsis* or *metabolē*) and rest (*stasis*), represented by the dying Socrates does not give a better, because a nobler, more beautiful, and hence more attractive answer to the fundamental problems all of Plato's philosophers seek to address.

In this chapter I examine the reasons Plato shows it is difficult for human beings to acquire knowledge and the grounds therein for Socrates' claim to be the wisest of all, because he knows that he does not know. In the next chapter I investigate the challenge the Eleatic Stranger poses to Socrates, both philosophically and politically. Finally, I look at Plato's presentation of Socrates' trial and death as a response to that challenge.

I. *Theaetetus*: What the Geometers Don't Know or Understand

A. Prologue: The Question of Socrates' Legacy and Plato's Role in Defining It

The story of Socrates' trial and death raises the question of his legacy and thus points to the importance and basis of Plato's own work. Plato reminds his readers of both of those issues in the prologue with which he begins the first of the dialogues explicitly leading up to Socrates' trial and death.[1]

From the prologue readers learn that most of the dialogue we know as the *Theaetetus* is supposed to consist of a transcript that Euclides, the founder of the Megarian school of philosophy, made of the conversation Socrates had with the geometers Theodorus and Theaetetus. Socrates narrated the conversation to Euclides when he visited Socrates in jail. Returning home, Euclides wrote down what he could remember of Socrates' narration, cutting out comments such as "then I said" or "he agreed." The next time he visited Socrates, Euclides inquired about what he had not remembered.

Euclides' account stands in marked contrast to Plato's own work. Although Plato himself wrote both nine narrated and twenty-six dramatic dialogues, he never tells his readers that he consulted with Socrates about them. He notes that he was present at Socrates' trial, but he never claims, like Euclides, to have heard about the conversations, many of which are supposed to have occurred before he was born, from Socrates himself. Does Plato mean to suggest that he did not? That the conversations he

---

1. Ronald M. Polansky, *Philosophy and Knowledge: A Commentary on Plato's "Theaetetus"* (Lewisburg, PA: Bucknell University Press, 1992), points out, "Only the *Phaedo* and *Theaetetus* have introductory conversations set outside Athens, appropriately enough, because these are just the two dialogues which enclose the series of dialogues surrounding Socrates' trial and death. . . . It might be coincidence . . . , but there is good reason for thinking not. Locating the listeners to Socrates' discourses at places and times removed from the original occurrence bestows special prominence on the conversations. They remain so profoundly interesting that many years later his circle wishes to be reminded of Socrates by listening to preserved dialogues" (35).

reports are fictions or mere likenesses of conversations that might have occurred? Plato does have Socrates relate conversations he had to others in six of his dialogues, but in none of those dialogues does Socrates suggest that anyone recorded his narrative. On the contrary, in the *Phaedrus* Socrates argues that the most any writing can do, like the reminders Euclides wrote down for himself right after he returned home, is to enable people to recall what they have thought. In the writing itself, Euclides' account reminds us, the connectives between the marks, words, and sentences, on the one hand, and the things to which they refer as well as to the one who is contemplating them, on the other, are severed. Readers have to reconstitute the subject matter, what the writing is about, for themselves in their own minds in order to understand it. They cannot merely say orally what is written, or merely repeat the words, like the slave who reads Euclides' manuscript to his tired masters.

Does Socrates' willingness to supplement Euclides' memory indicate that he changed his mind about the value of writing when he saw himself nearing death? We know about Socrates' narrative as well as his additions only from Euclides' report, and Euclides admits that his report is not entirely literal or complete. If one of the main ways people learn about what happened before they were born is by means of a written record, Plato reminds his readers in the prologue to the *Theaetetus*, our knowledge of the past is always going to be partial. No mortal can possibly see or experience everything, so we have to rely on the reports of others if we are to know anything beyond our own immediate experience. But like Euclides' transcript, the reports of others can never be entirely literal or complete. Our knowledge of ourselves as well as of the world in which we find ourselves is necessarily and unavoidably mediated—by language as well as by written reports and our own faulty memories. Like Socrates' interlocutors in the *Theaetetus*, *Euthyphro*, and *Cratylus*, however, people tend to identify understanding with "seeing" the "light." We misconstrue what we have learned as an immediate impression rather than as the product of analyses and syntheses that occur in time. By eliminating the narrative connections, Euclides reinforces this kind of misunderstanding by presenting the conversation between Socrates and the geometers as if it were happening as they listen.[2] In fact, readers learn from the prologue, the conversation

2. Cf. Seth Benardete, *Theaetetus* (Chicago: University of Chicago Press, 1986), 1:88; Howland, *Paradox*, 43.

occurred in 399, shortly before Socrates' trial. A slave is reading the manuscript to the two Megarians years later, after a battle at Corinth (in either 391/390 or 369) in which Theaetetus was wounded.[3] If Euclides had not seen Theaetetus on his way to the harbor, he might not have been reminded of the conversation and had the transcript read. What is preserved by means of writing is not merely partial; whether the writing is preserved or read depends on external circumstances.[4]

In the prologue to the *Theaetetus* Plato reminds his readers that what we know about Socrates depends on what others, primarily Plato, wrote down about him, and that what they wrote is necessarily incomplete and therefore not entirely accurate. No writing about the life and thought of another human being can provide a literal copy of that person. The written "reminder" has to be filled in on the basis of the experience and thoughts of the reader. Not only in recalling, but also in understanding what we see and hear around us, we have to organize things into types, which we mark by names. We never perceive all the details at the time; we have to fill in specifics from our experience to flesh out the written reminders. The problem of writing thus points to the fundamental philosophical problem that runs through Plato's entire corpus, that is, the problem of relating the ever-changing character of sensible existence to stable, hence intelligible, types of being. That problem is explicitly taken up later in the *Theaetetus* in the discussion of Heraclitus and Parmenides.

---

3. Commentators disagree about which battle at Corinth, depending on the age at which they think Theaetetus died. Some believe he must have died relatively young (in which case they see the exchange between Euclides and Terpsion as occurring in 390), because he would not have been actively fighting if he had been more than forty years old; e.g., H. Thesleff, "Platonic Chronology," *Phronesis* 34 (1989): 18n47. Others think he would have had to have lived longer in order to make the mathematical discoveries attributed to him, in which case they (like Benardete, *Theaetetus*, 1:184) date the prologue in 369. Although most ancient writers took the report of Theaetetus' discovery to be historical, Myles Burnyeat, "The Philosophical Sense of Theaetetus' Mathematics," *ISIS* 69, no. 249 (1978), concludes that the "story is a fiction, devised by Plato for his own purposes in the dialogue" (489), because it is difficult to imagine a sixteen-year-old making such an important mathematical discovery. There is little if any evidence that a mathematician named Theaetetus made the discovery about the roots he reports in Plato's dialogue beyond the dialogue itself. On the other hand, one might object, students of mathematics often make their most important discoveries when they are very young.

4. Benardete points out: "The publication of the logos is due to Plato; Euclides was content to render an illusion of the original conversation, in conformity with Socrates' recommendation in the *Phaedrus*, as his own private reminder, though one might suppose that he would not have gone to so much trouble had he not intended to publish it at some time or other. Had not Plato intervened, and Euclides got around to bringing it into the light, we might have had a non-Platonic Socratic dialogue, which would have had a purely accidental link with Plato's *Sophist* and *Statesman*" ("Plato's *Theaetetus*: On the Way of the Logos," in *Argument of the Action*, 298).

Plato presents an image of the problem of relating things in motion to those at rest at the very beginning of the dialogue in the prologue. Terpsion had difficulty finding Euclides, because his fellow Megarian was not in the marketplace as Terpsion expected. Euclides was a student of Parmenides, who denied that being had or was in motion, but Plato shows that, contrary to his mentor's teaching, Parmenides' student moved. Euclides was going down to the harbor when he encountered Theaetetus being carried to Athens from the camp at Corinth. Dying of dysentery, Theaetetus should have reminded Euclides of the transitory character of human life. Instead, their meeting reminded Euclides of Socrates' surprising ability to prophesy (*hōs mantikōs . . . eipe*) that Theaetetus, a mere boy when the philosopher met him, would become much talked of if he lived to be a man. Having denied, contrary to Aristotle, that there is such a thing as "potential," Euclides found it amazing that Socrates could see the potential in a young man's nature.[5] Plato thus raises questions about the adequacy of his narrator's understanding through both the deeds and the speeches he reports in the prologue.

In reporting Euclides' surprise, Plato also reminds his readers that Socrates had more than one legacy. His students and their students took away different understandings. Said to be present at Socrates' death in the *Phaedo* (59c), Euclides and Terpsion were close associates of his. Their memories nevertheless appear to be as partial and selective as their writings. Euclides did not write down an account of the conversations Socrates and his interlocutors in the *Theaetetus* had the next day with the Eleatic Stranger. As a follower of Parmenides, Euclides appears to have been more interested in the critique Socrates gave of the "streamers" than he was in the critique the Eleatic gave of his "father" Parmenides and the "friends of the forms." Perhaps Socrates did not tell him about the extension of his conversation with Theaetetus in the *Sophist* and *Statesman*. Perhaps Euclides did not remember to ask Socrates to refresh his memory. Plato does not tell us how he learned about this further conversation.

In the scene he paints in the prologue to the *Theaetetus*, Plato does remind his readers that there are different kinds of motion and rest—intellectual and physical. Tired by their travels, the Megarians ask a slave boy to read the transcript of Socrates' conversation to them while they are resting. Having read the *Republic*, we are led to wonder whether their minds will be able to work energetically enough to comprehend the arguments if

5. Cf. *Metaphysics* 1047a15–17; Howland, *Paradox*, 41.

their bodies are fatigued. Motion and rest are not any more easily or completely separated in human existence than body and mind. To understand ourselves, we need to know how motion and rest are related in us. This is the "self-knowledge" that pre-Socratic philosophy, divided between those who maintained that everything is always in motion and Parmenides, who argued that being is always the same and motionless, could not provide.

B. Why Socrates Interrogates the Geometers

Socrates initiates the conversation by telling Theodorus that, if he cared more about Cyrene and its affairs than he did about Athens, he would ask the geometer about his hometown and the people there. Since he cares more about Athens, Socrates wants to know if Theodorus has found any of his young Athenian students to be particularly worthy of note. Theodorus has found one of his Athenian students to be extremely promising—so much so that Theodorus says he would be ashamed to say how highly he thinks of the student if the student were handsome (*kalos*); people might think Theodorus is a lover. Because this young man has a snub nose and protruding eyes like Socrates, Theodorus does not think that he has to worry. Combining an ability to learn quickly with exceptional gentleness and bravery, Theodorus says, this student has the best nature he has ever encountered.

If Socrates cared so much about Athens, why did he go to a foreign teacher of geometry to ask about promising youths? In previous dialogues Plato showed Socrates interrogating foreign sophists and rhetoricians, largely at the behest or for the sake of young, politically ambitious Athenians, when he was not examining the young Athenians themselves. Theodorus' commenting on how rare it is to see someone with a quick mind and good memory who is not irascible, but gentle, should remind Plato's readers that the rare combination of qualities Theaetetus possesses is very much like the combination of apparently opposed qualities Socrates said would be necessary in the guardians of his city in speech.[6] Those guardians had to be trained in mathematics, moreover, if they were to become rulers and not merely soldiers. Whereas the politically ambitious young men to whom Socrates had been speaking would seem, like Alcibiades, to have already been corrupted by their fellow citizens, family, and friends and so

---

6. Cf. Benardete, *Theaetetus*, 1:90: "Theaetetus has all the qualities except gracefulness that Socrates lists as prerequisites for potential philosophers."

unlikely to pursue philosophy, the students of the geometrician appear to be moving in the right direction. Might Socrates have been looking for potential philosophers among them?[7]

The day the dialogue occurs, the seventy-year-old man knows that he is about to be indicted for a capital crime. It would not make sense for him to look for new associates; he would not have time to affect them. (As he later tells Theaetetus, some of his associates lost what progress they had made by leaving Socrates too soon.) From the prologue, we have learned that Theaetetus subsequently became a very good soldier or guardian but not a philosopher.[8] By bringing out the difference between the way in which Socrates understands mathematics as part of a philosopher's education and the way mathematicians understand their own art, in the *Theaetetus* Plato indicates the reasons why the young geometer did not become a philosopher and Socrates did not seek to associate primarily with young mathematicians (although we learn in the *Phaedo* that there were several Pythagoreans among his close companions).

I. INITIAL DIFFERENCES OF INTEREST AND APPROACH

One difference between the philosopher and the older geometrician emerges at the very beginning of the dialogue. As we saw in the *Protagoras* and *Alcibiades I*, Socrates is willing to appear in the guise of a lover of young men; Theodorus emphatically is not. Theodorus does not merely want to avoid the charge of corrupting the young. His desire to avoid the appearance of a lover reflects the character of his teaching. Unlike Socrates, the geometrician does not promise to help young people get what they desire. He does not even claim that the knowledge he conveys is useful (although we know from the *Republic* that he could have made that claim). From the very beginning of the dialogue, the art Theodorus teaches appears to be completely theoretical or, we might say, objective. It is not a product of, or affected by, human passions. In modern, but perhaps not only modern, terms, it appears to be more scientific, if not more philosophical, than Socrates' own inquiries. It encourages its practitioners to look away from rather than at themselves.

---

7. Rachel Rue, "The Philosopher in Flight," in *Oxford Studies in Ancient Philosophy* 11 (1993): 93, points out that Socrates asks Theodorus, "which youths show an active interest in 'geometry or any other philosophy' (143d3)."

8. In emphasizing the similarities between Socrates and Theaetetus in *Play of Character* (251–313), Blondell neglects this fundamental difference.

Because they pursue different kinds of knowledge, Socrates and Theodorus notice different characteristics of the young people who associate with them. As a foreign teacher in Athens, Theodorus obviously does
not think that the national origin or civic loyalties of his students are
important. Their political associations do not affect their ability to learn
geometry. Socrates is concerned about the political identities and family
backgrounds of his young companions, because they affect, if not shape,
what the young people want. Theodorus forgot the name of Theaetetus'
father, but Socrates recognizes him on sight as the son of Euphronius (literally good or well minded), who, he adds, was very much like Theaetetus,
as Theodorus has described him. Heredity makes a difference with regard
to the distinctive natures of individuals as well as to their wealth. Understanding inheritance primarily in terms of wealth, Theodorus reports that
even though his guardians have squandered much of his estate, Theaetetus
continues to be remarkably generous. Like his art, Theodorus is concerned
about what is present (and not where it comes from). Geometric figures
do not change over time, and foreign teachers need to be paid. Socrates
agrees that Theaetetus is well born (*gennikon*), but he appears to be more
anxious to discover whether the son has inherited the intelligence of his
father than to hear about his estate.

Socrates good-humoredly dismisses the unflattering comparison Theodorus had drawn between Socrates and Theaetetus with regard to their
physical appearance, on the grounds that the geometrician is not a painter
(and so not an expert in visible appearances or images, although his knowledge of proportion might qualify him as a judge of the truly beautiful). Instead of dwelling on their physical resemblance, Socrates asks Theaetetus
whether they should not eagerly seek to find out if he has the virtue and
wisdom of soul for which Theodorus has praised him. Theaetetus modestly says that Theodorus may have been joking, but Socrates asserts, "That
is not Theodorus' way" (*Theaetetus* 145c). Readers are thus confronted with
two more differences between the philosopher and the mathematician.
Socrates is willing to appear in the guise of an elderly lover because he is
willing to appear laughable or ridiculous. Theodorus is not.

Socrates' knowledge and investigations concern human characteristics and qualities—political and natural (or inherited). He has to ask not
only about what is the case at present, but also about what people have
been and can become in the future. His inquiries thus combine what is
unchanging and therefore intelligible with what becomes. The serious,

straightforward geometer seeks to prove what is true (now and in the past and in the future without changing). Unable to countenance a significant difference between appearance (his visible constructions) and reality (the intelligibility of the proofs), he does not joke. So when Socrates suggests that in seeking to determine what is knowledge, they ought to play a game in which those who fail to answer the question adequately sit down and declare themselves asses whereas he who remains is to be declared king, Theodorus excuses himself. Unaccustomed to answering questions of the sort Socrates asks, he does not want to be shown up. He is not willing to admit or expose the limitations of his own knowledge the way the explicitly erotic Socrates does.

2. THEAETETUS' FIRST ATTEMPT AT A DEFINITION AND THE INSIGHT IT GIVES INTO HIS NATURE

Following Theodorus' injunction to address his questions to Theaetetus rather than to the group as a whole or, in particular, to Theodorus, Socrates asks Theaetetus what he thinks knowledge is. Socrates had treated knowledge and wisdom as if they were the same (*Theaetetus* 145e), but then admitted that he did not know what knowledge is. That was the reason he proposed the game—to solicit answers from others. Socrates did not wish to restrict his inquiry to Theaetetus, but Theodorus gave him no choice. From his first exchange with Theaetetus, Socrates learns that the youth follows his teacher without questioning or resisting him in any way. Just as in the *Charmides*, where Socrates had to interrogate Critias to get to the source of Charmides' opinions, so he now has to interrogate Theodorus to get to the source of Theaetetus' views. But just as Critias urged Socrates to question his favorite until Charmides proved unable and unwilling to defend the views he had acquired from his friend, so Theodorus now forces Socrates to show that the opinions Theaetetus has acquired from his mentor are not tenable before he is willing to risk possible embarrassment by engaging in a dialogue with Socrates.

Theaetetus says that knowledge is what he is learning from Theodorus—geometry, astronomy, harmony, and arithmetic (145c–d). But the young geometer indicates that he is also familiar with what Socrates says by adding cobbling and the arts (*technai*) of the other craftsmen to the list of subjects that Theodorus teaches in his definition. Playing on the terms of Theodorus' earlier praise of his pupil, Socrates comments that his answer shows that the young man is both noble and generous; asked for one thing, he has responded with many. But Socrates then asks Theaetetus, as he had asked Meno with regard to virtue, what do all these forms of knowledge have in common that makes them all knowledge?[9]

The apparently faulty examples of definitions of something ordinary (*phaulos*), such as mud, that Socrates gives Theaetetus should remind readers of the criticism Parmenides made of the young Socrates' own argument concerning the ideas (130d–e): that he did not include such lowly things because he was too concerned about what other people thought. These faulty definitions also point toward a possible characterization of knowledge, of its parts in relation to a whole. Theaetetus agrees that it would be ridiculous, in saying what mud is, to distinguish the clay used by potters from that used by oven makers or bricklayers. Yet we later readers of Aristotle recognize that the use to which something is put might constitute the most important, "final" element of its definition. (Socrates himself makes this point in his critique of the poets in book 10 of the *Republic*.)[10] Theaetetus might have objected to Socrates' demand that he define "mud" or knowledge in terms of an element common to all specific examples by observing that the constitutive kinds of knowledge could both be distinguished and finally united on the basis of their use, for the sake of improving human existence. If Theaetetus had thus suggested that things can be understood, finally, only in relation to the good, Socrates might have agreed. But as a student of geometry, Theaetetus is not used to defining things in terms of their purpose. Socrates and Theaetetus thus agree merely that a thing cannot be defined simply by naming it. It is necessary to know the thing to which the name refers. As Socrates had argued in the *Charmides*, so he suggests here that knowledge has an object, although here the object seems to be knowledge itself.[11] Because knowledge has an object (or subject matter that exists independent of the knowledge or knower), knowledge cannot be defined merely by the person said to possess it—in this case, the artisan. (Socrates does not suggest, as Critias had, that knowledge of knowledge constitutes self-knowledge.) Having denied that knowledge can be defined simply in terms of its use or its maker (Aristotle's final and efficient causes), Socrates observes that things are often

9. According to Dorter (*Form and Good*, 71): "The *Theaetetus*, in fact, recalls the *Meno* at almost every turn." If virtue is knowledge, as Socrates often says, then the questions raised in the two dialogues should be closely related. It does not appear to be an accident that Plato shows the conversation related in the *Theaetetus* following that related in the *Meno* closely in terms of the dramatic dating as well as the content of the two dialogues.

10. Those who judge arts by the utility of their products tend, moreover, to be common people. Cf. Aristotle *Politics* 1282a1–23.

11. Cf. Grote, *Plato*, 1:497.

defined in terms of their constituent materials—in the case of mud, earth mixed with water. The different kinds of mud represent different proportions of the constituent elements, according to the intended use.

Theaetetus thinks that he knows the kind of answer Socrates is looking for. It would be equivalent to a discovery he and the young Socrates made when they were talking about Theodorus' proof that the sides of squares containing 3, 5, 7, 10, 11, 12, 13, 14, 15, and 17 square feet were not evenly divisible into units of one foot. Theodorus stopped at 17, but it occurred to his students that the number of squares with incommensurable sides would be infinite. They thus tried to find a way of gathering all the incommensurables under one name, that is, of describing what the incommensurable sides had in common, as opposed to the commensurable sides of squares. Treating the sides (or lines) in terms of numbers (which, as ancient Greeks, they understood to be multiples of one),[12] they represented the sides whose length could be constructed by multiplying equal factors with squares, and the sides whose length could not be produced by the multiplication of equal factors by oblongs. They then named the first group of sides "lines" (*mēkē*) and the second "powers" (*dynameis*). Modern commentators have asked whether the groupings of lines or "sides," whose length corresponds to what we call an "irrational" (not whole) number, which Theaetetus and young Socrates suggested, represents a mathematical improvement or step beyond Theodorus' proofs of the particular examples, and whether Theaetetus can really be imagined to have made this discovery as a youth of sixteen (which he is said to be in the dialogue).[13] They have not seen the way in which the two kinds of numbers parallel the division Socrates will point out in Theaetetus' own understanding between the things that can be counted (and so characterized as indivisible units) and the sensible things we perceive only as a result of an interaction with (and thus in relation to) our sense organs. Theaetetus is not perplexed by the results of his own division the way he is by Socrates' account of the dice, because Theaetetus' division seems to show that lines that cannot be divided into units nevertheless become commensurable with others in terms of squares when they are made into plane figures. There are, then, two reasons that

12. Cf. Klein, "Concept of Number."

13. Cf. Burnyeat, "Philosophical Sense," 489–513; Knorr, *Evolution of Euclidean Elements*; Arpad Szabo, "Theaitetos und das Problem der Irrationalität in der griechischen Mathematikgeschichte," *Acta Antiqua Academiae Scientia Hungaricae* 14 (1966): 303–58; Thomas L. Heath, *A History of Greek Mathematics* (Oxford: Clarendon Press, 1921), 1:202ff.; and David Fowler, *The Mathematics of Plato's Academy* (Oxford: Clarendon Press, 1999), 371–81.

Theaetetus does not respond to Socrates' query by suggesting that all forms of knowledge concern things that can be counted. First, Theaetetus suspects, Socrates would reply by asking him about arts such as shoemaking, agriculture, or medicine, which do not involve the counting of things (or reducing them to countable units) as obviously as do the sciences Theodorus teaches.[14] Second, Theaetetus has seen that the length of all lines cannot be counted, that is, calculated in terms of units, but that the length of the line can nevertheless be made intelligible in relation to others.[15]

By giving a general answer rather than a series of examples, Theaetetus had improved on his mentor. But the young man was not able to explain how or why he made the improvement he did. Like many mathematicians, he had an immediate intuition as to how a problem could be solved. But he could not generalize the process, which is to say, he could not describe the logic that had enabled him to come to the solution he proposed. Theodorus would say that Theaetetus' inability to generalize was a sign of his youth and inexperience; he had "seen" a way to solve the problem but could not yet give the proof (as Euclid, *Elements* 10, later did). More critical observers might object that mathematicians often peak at a very young age precisely because their discoveries are based on this kind of immediate insight that qua mathematician they cannot explain.

Rather than explore the reasoning that underlay Theaetetus' "solution" and so appear to be criticizing rather than praising him and his teacher, Socrates appeals to (and perhaps seeks to test) the other side of Theaetetus' remarkable nature, as described by Theodorus—his courage. Urging Theaetetus to be bold (*tharrei*) and believe what Theodorus has said about him, Socrates asks him to imitate his answer about the *dynameis* by trying to encompass all the different kinds of knowledge in one definition (or literally "argument," *logos*). Indicating that he does not like to risk embarrassing himself by showing what he does not know any more than his mentor does, Theaetetus admits that he has heard about the questions Socrates poses and has tried to answer them, but has not been able to do so himself or find anyone else who can. Readers know from the preface that Theaetetus later showed himself to be brave, physically and politically, in the face of death. Early in the dialogue, however, we learn that as a youth

---

14. Cf. Benardete, "Logos," 302; and Polansky, *Philosophy and Knowledge*, 54–57. Even though he is and obviously should be familiar with proportions, the sums of which can equal 1, readers have no reason to believe that Theaetetus would know about the other kind of measure, that of the "mean" or "fitting," upon which the Eleatic Stranger will tell young Socrates, the arts depend.

15. Cf. Cropsey, *Plato's World*, 27.

Theaetetus was not intellectually courageous or daring. His unwillingness to confront questions he did not feel able to answer indicates that, despite his apparent modesty and willingness to be corrected by his elders, he has perceived Theodorus' high opinion of him and does not want the limits of his talents to be exposed. In the course of the dialogue, Socrates will try to moderate Theaetetus' intellectual pride. As a result, Socrates suggests at the end of the dialogue, Theaetetus may be able to conceive truer thoughts in the future. But even if he remains barren, Theaetetus will become a better citizen, as we see in the prologue he did, because he will no longer believe himself to know what he does not know and so feel superior to his fellows.

3. Why Socrates Presents Himself as a Midwife Rather Than as a Lover

In response to Theaetetus' admission of his own incapacity, Socrates gives his famous description of his own "art of midwifery." As Richard Robinson observes, the image of Socrates as a midwife has appeared so appropriate to later readers that they have taken it "as a feature of all the Socratic literature and of the real Socrates."[16] The image occurs only once, however, in the *Theaetetus*. Readers should ask, therefore, why Socrates describes himself and his "art" this way here and nowhere else. The fact that the *Theaetetus* is the only dialogue in which Socrates presents himself as an intellectual midwife indicates that this particular description of his art is related to the character of his interlocutor.

In the *Gorgias* Socrates also claimed to be attempting to practice an art, the true political art. And the art of midwifery Socrates claims to practice, secretly, in the *Theaetetus* sounds very much like his attempts to discover the truth by refuting or being refuted by his interlocutors, as described in the *Gorgias*, with the addition of the operation of his *daimonion*, as described in the *Theages*. There was nothing particularly feminine, however, about Socrates' descriptions of his art and divine guidance to the politically ambitious Callicles and Theages. Socrates did not claim to be the only one in Athens trying to practice the true political art until late in his conversation with Callicles, but he did not ask that young Athenian to keep

16. Richard Robinson, "Forms and Error in Plato's *Theaetetus*," *Philosophical Review* 59 (1950): 4. Cf. A. R. Lacey, "Our Knowledge of Socrates," in *The Philosophy of Socrates*, ed. Gregory Vlastos (Garden City, NY: Doubleday, 1971), 42, cited in Myles Burnyeat, "Socratic Midwifery, Platonic Inspiration," *Bulletin of Classical Studies* 24 (1977): 14.

the nature of his activity secret. Why, then, does Socrates characterize his art in feminine terms and urge his interlocutors to keep it secret in the *Theaetetus*?

By comparing his art to that of his mother, Phaenarete (whose name literally means "apparent virtue" or, perhaps, "bringing virtue into the open"), Socrates seems to be contrasting the feminine character of his own activity and knowledge with Theaetetus' manly character and knowledge. Rather than impressing form onto matter, as Aristotle says the male does in generating, or announcing and purveying a teaching for others to receive, like the serious Theodorus, Socrates claims merely to help others develop, give birth to, and articulate their own thoughts. But although his art appears to be merely auxiliary and hence subsidiary to the activity of others, Socrates asks Theaetetus not to tell anyone else that he has it. Not knowing that he practices an art, Socrates explains, people think he is extremely odd (*atopōtatos*) because he perplexes people (literally by "leaving them without means," *aporein*). Since his interrogations not merely perplexed but angered others, as Socrates points out in both the *Meno* and his *Apology*, it would seem to be in his interest to tell people that he has an art. Why keep it secret? Might Socrates be trying to entice Theaetetus to associate with him rather than continue his studies with Theodorus by suggesting that he has a secret teaching, which he shares only with a select few? Although Theaetetus may be proud of his intellect, he does not appear to be attracted to the mysterious or covert any more than his mentor is.[17] Socrates' desire to keep his art secret seems to be connected to the way in which his intellectual art of midwifery differs from the bodily art of his mother. Ordinary midwives help women to give birth; they do not have to be able to judge, as Socrates does, whether the progeny are true or false. It is his demonstration of the inadequacy of their opinions (or intellectual progeny), in particular, that angers others. Nevertheless, Socrates suggests, if people understood the power of his art, they would all want to associate with him (presumably because all people want to know what is truly good). Fortunately, his divine voice indicates which individuals will benefit from associating with him and which will not. As Socrates states explicitly in the *Gorgias*, no one can teach (as opposed to persuade) large groups of people all at once. If anyone is to benefit from Socrates' art, Socrates has to be able

17. Socrates later introduces Theaetetus to the "mysteries" of the "myth" of Protagoras. But since Theaetetus was previously unaware of any such mystery, it is hard to believe that was what attracted him to Protagoras.

to converse with individuals, one by one, in private. To remain able to seek wisdom by conversing with others, Socrates has to prevent most people from understanding how much they could gain from philosophizing with him, lest they mob and press him. That might be one reason Socrates repeatedly states he does not mind looking ridiculous; most other people do. They seek to avoid company that will make them appear laughable.

In the *Symposium* Socrates also presented philosophy as a mode of intellectual pregnancy and begetting. Diotima had taught him that all human beings—male and female—are pregnant and desire, therefore, to beget in the beautiful. In the *Symposium* the beautiful thus appeared to be the necessary matrix or condition for such begetting. If Socrates had presented his art of midwifery in terms of the knowledge of the erotic things he claimed he had acquired from Diotima, in claiming to know how to help others give birth he would have been claiming to have a beautiful soul himself. At first glance, his presentation of his art in the *Theaetetus* appears to be more modest. Just as midwives are drawn from women who have given birth but are no longer able to do so, Socrates says, he is barren of thoughts or insights. He can merely help others conceive—and then determine whether their conceptions are true or false. Claiming that all human beings desire to beget, whether physically or intellectually, for the sake of attaining immortality, Diotima had not distinguished bodily and intellectual forms on the basis of sex; instead she ranked the various expressions of the desire for immortality—procreation, founding a new regime, and philosophy—according to the virtue they produced. Strictly dividing bodily from intellectual progeny, in the *Theaetetus* Socrates not merely separates female from male forms of begetting; he also claims that only some males are pregnant. It is part of his art to determine which. Socrates' claim to be able not only to determine who is pregnant but also whether what they conceive is true makes his presentation of his art look a bit less modest than it initially appears. If Socrates is able to help others give birth, like the female midwives, not only because he himself is no longer able to conceive but also because he has conceived in the past, it looks as if he has had ideas in the past that he has subjected to examination and can now use in testing the conceptions of others. He is forty years older in the *Theaetetus* than he was when he talked to Diotima, and he now admits he has an art.[18] He knows how to

18. Just as Socrates cum Diotima presented Eros as a *daimōn*, a mixture of the divine and the human, in the *Symposium*, so Socrates presents the midwife as like the goddess Artemis in being barren but having had the human experience of pregnancy and conception.

question, refute, correct, and so improve others. He can say that he does not have and has not conceived any wisdom (*Theaetetus* 150c–d) because he knows only that and what he does not know.

Just as midwives know what combinations of male and female will produce the best children, so Socrates claims to be able to predict (with the assistance of his *daimonion*) what associations of teacher and student will have the best results. Midwives do not usually admit that their art includes matchmaking, he explains, because they do not want to be taken for pimps. Lacking knowledge of the good, the unjust pimps seek to line their own pockets by catering to the pleasure of their clients without regard for the long-term results. Like the midwives, Socrates claims to be able to match teachers with students in order to obtain the best results. He never claims to be able to teach or even persuade anyone else of anything. He knows only how to elicit the opinions of others and test them. Nevertheless, he admits, some people improve markedly and rapidly as a result of associating with him. Observing this improvement, we saw in the *Theages*, other young people wish to associate with him. Socrates does not always accede to their wishes, however. Seeking the good and the true, as opposed to the pleasant, he lets his *daimonion* or "the god" decide. Socrates does not want to hurt the feelings of those he does not deem to be promising. Nor does he simply throw them back on their own inadequate resources. Unlike pimps, who merely seek pleasure—their own and that of others—Socrates tries to be just. He thus suggests other teachers who may be able to help those he cannot. He mentions Prodicus, in particular.[19]

Theaetetus already has a teacher with whom he is pleased and whom he pleases. He does not feel deprived of what he desires or believes is rightfully his, even by the guardians who have squandered his estate. Because the youth does not feel himself wanting, Socrates does not tell Theaetetus, as he had once told Alcibiades, that he knows what the young man wants or suggest that he can help Theaetetus attain it. Nor does Socrates respond to Theodorus' insulting characterization of his own appearance by saying that even though the youth has an ugly body like his own, Theaetetus has a beautiful soul and Socrates loves it.[20] Because Theaetetus does not feel

---

19. It is not clear in this or other dialogues whether Socrates thinks that the precise use of words that Prodicus emphasized was positively beneficial. Socrates does not appear to think that Prodicus' emphasis on verbal distinctions harmed the souls of his students the way the promises the other sophists made to make their pupils virtuous could.

20. Later in the conversation (*Theaetetus* 185e) Socrates declares that Theaetetus has a beautiful soul. Socrates never suggests that he sees his own soul reflected in that of the young

himself full of unfulfilled desire, Socrates does not approach Theaetetus as a lover. Nor does he suggest that the young man has been corrupted and needs to be corrected, as he had in the case of both Alcibiades and Callicles. Theaetetus has admitted that he has not only heard about, but has also been perplexed by, Socrates' questions and his own inability to answer them. This perplexity has left Theaetetus ill at ease with himself and, potentially, with others. He is willing to learn from others, but he does not want to be shown up or refuted. By presenting himself as an intellectual midwife, Socrates tries literally to en-courage Theaetetus to submit to the questions he fears he cannot answer by promising to help him through a painful process that will relieve him in the end of his perplexity.

By eliciting Theaetetus' opinions about what knowledge is and examining them, Socrates will show the brilliant young geometer that he does not know what he thinks he does. Theaetetus thinks that he is acquiring knowledge from Theodorus; by examining what Theaetetus believes knowledge to be, Socrates shows him (and Plato's readers) that neither the young geometer nor his mentor understands the status, foundations, or limitations of his own art. They do not, in a word, recognize the difference between mathematics and philosophy. Socrates emphasizes the negative results of his own art of refutation, and not its positive corrective potential, because he has already learned that Theaetetus does not have a philosophical nature. Theaetetus may display the combination of docility and spiritedness Socrates argued is necessary for a guardian, but he does not have the overwhelming love for the truth characteristic of a truly philosophical nature. If Theaetetus desired to know the truth of things above and beyond everything else, he would not have stayed away from Socrates because he did not feel able to answer the questions he had heard that Socrates posed. He would have gone to hear others examined, if not to be examined himself. Even more than Theodorus, Theaetetus has shown at the very beginning of the conversation that neither he nor his search for knowledge is erotic.

C. Socrates' Explication of Theaetetus' Protagorean Thesis

Buoyed by Socrates' promise to help him deliver, Theaetetus ventures another definition. Because "whoever knows something perceives that which

---

mathematician. Like philosophers and mathematicians more generally, Socrates and Theaetetus resemble each other externally, not internally.

he knows," the young man reasons, "it appears that knowledge is nothing else but perception" (*Theaetetus* 151e).

Theaetetus proves, however, not to understand the definition he admits he has taken over from Protagoras. Socrates has to explain it before they can investigate whether it is true or false. Socrates' explanation of Protagoras' saying has seemed so plausible to some contemporary readers that they have attributed the view defended to Plato himself.[21] Because modern readers tend, like Protagoras, to believe that everything is in motion, Socrates' critique of this thesis has enduring relevance.

1. Theaetetus' Failure to Reflect on His Own Opinions and Experience

Socrates begins to draw out what Theaetetus thinks by showing that the young man has acquired this understanding of knowledge by reading the writings of others, not by reflecting on his own experience of learning.[22] Observing that Protagoras said something similar when he proclaimed that "human being is the measure of all things, that (or how) they are and that (or how) they are not," Socrates asks Theaetetus whether he has read it. "Yes," the youth admits, "and often." By describing the probable basis and reasons for Protagoras' saying, Socrates then shows Theaetetus that this understanding of knowledge is not consistent with some of the fundamental principles of the mathematics he practices. It denies that anything has existence or unity in itself and can therefore be counted (or said to be equal or unequal to itself or to anything else). Theaetetus begins to understand why it is difficult to say what knowledge is only after Socrates has shown him that the opinions he has acquired from experts are incompatible.

2. The Atheistic Character of the Protagorean Thesis

Socrates reminds Theaetetus of the apparent and most immediate basis for the Protagorean claim by observing that individuals experience what appear to be the same things differently; for example, wind that feels cold to some does not feel cold to all. It is not so clear, however, why Socrates

---

21. Burnyeat, "Socratic Midwifery"; John McDowell, *Plato: "Theaetetus"* (New York: Oxford University Press, 1973); and Rosemary Desjardins, *The Rational Enterprise: Logos in Plato's "Theaetetus"* (Albany: SUNY, 1990).

22. Theaetetus thus manifests some of the problems with reading to which Plato alerted his readers in the prologue.

suggests that Protagoras' statement is intended to be enigmatic to most people but that it conveys a secret teaching to his students.[23]

That secret teaching is, as all other previous philosophers and poets except Parmenides have more or less covertly taught, that everything is always in motion, and that nothing is or has any being in itself. In drawing out the reasons so many intelligent authors thought that everything was in flux (or always becoming), Socrates indicates why some of them (the poets who Protagoras had claimed in his first conversation with Socrates were sophists but unwilling to admit it) tried to keep it secret. If everything is always in motion and thus changing, there is nothing unchanging or immortal. There are no gods. And if there are no gods, as the Athenian Stranger points out (*Laws* 889e–90a), there is no basis for human laws, order, and justice except convention and force.

Although Protagoras openly advertised his ability to teach others how to persuade their fellows to enact laws that would favor the speaker's own interests, Socrates showed in the *Protagoras* that the sophist did not so openly admit that he defined the "good" of the speaker by calculating what would give him most pleasure in the long run, that is, on the basis ultimately of sensation. Nor, Socrates now points out in his conversation with Theaetetus, was Protagoras willing to declare openly that this notion of the human good depends on an understanding of the world that is inherently atheistic. On the contrary, in his writings Protagoras explicitly denied that he knew whether the gods existed or not (even though his claim that "man is the measure" implies that they do not). The mathematicians to whom Socrates is speaking are not interested, however, in the status of poetic myths or conceptions (even though Socrates later calls Protagoras' saying or position a "myth") or their political results.

3. How and Why Socrates Generates Perplexity in Theaetetus

Because Theaetetus merely repeated something he has read, Socrates has to explicate the basis and implications of the thesis that everything that exists is in motion, before they test its truth. One of the reasons people believe that everything is in motion, Socrates points out, is that life seems to consist in a kind of motion. Both bodies and minds develop and remain healthy only so long as they are active; ceasing to move, they atrophy. The

---

23. As McDowell (*Theaetetus*, 129–30) and David Bostock, *Plato's "Theaetetus"* (Oxford: Clarendon Press, 1988), 50, both point out, it is not immediately evident why Socrates should equate Protagoras' saying with the thesis attributed to Heraclitus (or, on the basis of the surviving fragments, why he attributed this position to the philosopher).

generation and growth of all living things on the earth depends, further-more, on the motions of the heavenly bodies, especially the sun. If every-thing is in motion, perception (or "sensation," *aisthēsis*) results from the interaction of the organs of perception (for example, eyes) with the things seen. Nothing has sensible qualities in itself. The characteristics of things are not merely products of the interaction, but they vary according, and are thus relative, to the things with which they interact.

By giving Theaetetus the famous example of the dice, in which six are greater than four by half, but also less than twelve by half, Socrates lets the young geometer see that the results of his understanding of knowledge are not consistent with fundamental principles of his mathematical art. The point of Socrates' maieutic art is not merely to refute Theaetetus by showing that he holds contradictory opinions, however. Rather than hav-ing the youth agree to the results of the current argument, contrary to his cherished and deeply held convictions, Socrates reminds him that they are talking to each other in private in order to examine their thoughts to see whether they are consistent. He then spells out the problem by stating three principles on which they agree: nothing becomes greater or less, in bulk or number, so long as it remains equal to itself; nothing increases or decreases unless something is added to or subtracted from it; and nothing can become something else later if it has not come into being earlier. The problem represented by six in comparison to four and twelve is not simply that six is not large or small in itself, but only in relation to something else. The problem is that six cannot acquire these contradictory characteristics in relation to other things if six has not come into being (and thus will change later). Six may be "generated" by adding one to five or subtracting one from seven, but as numbers were then understood in Greece, six is and always will remain the sum of six units, which becomes something dif-ferent if anything is added to or subtracted from it. As a geometer would surely be aware, numbers can exist in different proportions (and thus re-lations) to others without changing the original numbers or their char-acteristics, for example, from odd to even, even though the addition or subtraction of two numbers to constitute a third can.[24]

Perceiving the incompatibility of the position to which he has just agreed, because it seemed sensible, and his considered, mathematically derived first principles, Theaetetus declares that he is perplexed. Having

---

24. That is the puzzle with which Socrates confronted Hippias when he pointed out that 1 is odd but that the sum of two 1's, or 2, is even.

admitted earlier that he and his questions perplex others, Socrates assures Theaetetus that this perplexity is the beginning of philosophy. Lest Theaetetus shrink back, as he had in the past, from pursuing the question, Socrates promises to help him ferret out the truth in the thought of the renowned author.

4. The True Basis and Character of the Protagorean Thesis

The "truth" in Protagoras' statement does not, as it first appeared, consist in a generalized extrapolation from our experience of sensation, that is, that our awareness and hence knowledge of the external world arise only as a result of our contact with something else, and that sensations differ from person to person because persons do not have a stable identity or being any more than the things they perceive. The "truth" of Protagoras' saying lies in the "secret teaching" about the relative existence of all "things" as a result of an unending process of interactions. Socrates and Theaetetus thus dismiss the "uninitiated" view of "those who believe that nothing is except whatever they are capable of getting a tight grip on with their hands" (*Theaetetus* 155e), and who therefore deny the existence of the "actions, becomings, and everything invisible," which, Socrates, Theaetetus, and Protagoras have suggested, actually cause sensations. Socrates then initiates Theaetetus into the "mysteries" of those who are cleverer than those "without Muses," by explaining that those who claim, like Protagoras, that nothing is, but that everything becomes, maintain that there are two kinds of motion or "powers" (*dynameis*), the power to affect something else and the power of being affected. Just as nothing appears or "is" red where there are no eyes to see it, so our eyes do not perceive red or anything else unless it strikes them.

Theaetetus protests that he does not know whether Socrates believes the argument he is giving, so Socrates reminds the young man that he has no thoughts of his own; he merely brings out and examines the conceptions of others. He begins both to distance Theaetetus from his Protagorean thesis and to show what it entails more fully by asking the youth whether, if we know what we perceive, it is then possible to say that what people dream is any less true for them so long as they are dreaming, than what they experience while they are awake.

Theaetetus admits that he is perplexed, for a third time, by his inability to say whether or how there could be a difference, so Socrates points out that the changes in our perceptions are not caused simply by changes in the things; we also are affected and changed by each perception. We think that we are the same, whereas the things that make an impact on us are not. But if we feel an effect, we are changed. So are the things we perceive. We do not know them "in themselves," separate from our perceptions; our perceptions change, because we change. All there is (or, more strictly speaking, becomes) is an infinite number and series of interactions. There is nothing that simply and always affects or is itself affected. A dream is as true for the dreamer as the "real world" is when he wakes up (although we might ask how people know they have been dreaming).

D. How Socrates Draws Theodorus into the Conversation

Having drawn out the full meaning and implications of Theaetetus' Protagorean thesis, Socrates proposes to examine it to see whether it is sound. Theodorus breaks into the conversation at this point to urge Socrates "by the gods" to show what is wrong with this view, and readers learn not only that Protagoras was a comrade of the old geometer's but also that Socrates knew it. His explication of the understanding of knowledge Theaetetus acquired from reading Protagoras was designed to show Theodorus as well as his student that such an understanding is incompatible with mathematics. If Theaetetus is as docile a student as Theodorus has said, he is not apt to disavow Protagoras unless his teacher does. Theodorus' urging Socrates to prove that Protagoras is wrong suggests, however, that the old geometer cannot show where the sophist is wrong; he needs and wants Socrates' assistance.

Socrates' first critique and subsequent exchange with "Protagoras" are designed not only to force Theodorus to answer Socrates directly rather than simply listen to the examination of his student, but also to show why Theodorus thinks his art is compatible with that of Protagoras and why the geometer is wrong. Combined with their discussion of the relation between theoretical and political speech (or argument) in the "digression" and the objections to Heraclitean philosophy that follow, the critique of Protagoras brings out the limitations of Theodorus' understanding not only of mathematics but also of its relation to other kinds of knowledge and thus of knowledge itself.

1. SOCRATES' INITIAL CRITIQUE OF PROTAGORAS

All three of Socrates' first set of objections to Protagoras' saying bring out the opposition between the apparently egalitarian, democratic character of Protagoras' teachings and his aristocratic claim to possess a rare and valuable form of knowledge.[25] First, Socrates says that he doesn't under-stand why Protagoras did not say a pig or a baboon was the "measure." If knowledge is perception, and these animals have senses, they should be as able as humans are to determine what is for them. Second, Socrates ob-jects, if every human is as much a measure of truth as any other, he does not understand how Protagoras can claim to be wiser than others. But third, if Protagoras does not have knowledge others lack, there is no basis for his demanding a fee—and a high one at that—for teaching them.

2. Why the Geometers Don't See the Conflict between Protagoras and Mathematics

Although Theodorus emphatically expressed his desire to hear Socrates show how and why Protagoras' "relativistic" claim that everything is a product of an interaction and thus always changing is wrong, the old ge-ometer refuses to join in refuting his friend (*philos*). Nor is he willing to defend Protagoras by arguing, contrary to his own opinion, that no one is wiser than anyone else. Socrates has to demonstrate Theaetetus' lack of comprehension of Protagoras' doctrine and the objections to it in order to force Theodorus to answer.

Unlike his teacher, the modest student admits that he is surprised to hear that he is the equal of all other human beings, perhaps even the gods, in wisdom. And readers see that Socrates' first three objections require a speaker to apply his own doctrine, first and foremost, to his own activity. If a teacher's doctrine does not account for his own activity, the basis as well as the truth of his doctrine are brought into question.[26]

Socrates points to the difference between the kind of arguments he characteristically employs and those the geometers use by suggesting that Protagoras or someone on his behalf would object to their faulting his doctrine on the basis of mere probability rather than a logical demonstra-

25. Speaking to an audience of politically ambitious young Athenians, in the *Protagoras* Socrates had faulted the sophist for claiming to teach virtue in opposition to the democratic belief that virtue cannot be taught. Speaking to mathematicians, who believe that they have knowledge others lack, Socrates criticizes Protagoras in effect for having too democratic a teaching. Like the truth, according to his own saying, the character of Protagoras' teaching changes according to his audience.

26. Theodorus had not been impressed or persuaded the way Protarchus had been in the *Philebus* by Socrates' treating his own thesis in the same way he treated the thesis of his opponent. Socrates had pointed out that if Protagoras' saying were true, it would be as impossible for him to show that anyone else was wrong in a conversation as it was for Protagoras to claim that he had a greater truth or wisdom. Theodorus is not as interested in seeing justice done as Protarchus and Theaetetus are.

tion or proof. Regarding his own art as exemplary, Theaetetus agrees that they will not have treated the sophist justly unless they offer necessary proofs (even though Protagoras had not given anything resembling a logical proof for his own claim).

Socrates then raises three other possible objections to Protagoras' equation of "perceiving" or, literally, seeing with knowledge, objections that do not involve the applicability of the saying to the sophist himself. But Theaetetus' answers show that he does not understand the difficulties involved.

By asking Theaetetus whether we know a foreign ("barbarian") language when we hear or see it, Socrates first points to the difference between sensing and understanding. By responding that we would perceive the language by hearing it or seeing it written but that we would not have the knowledge of an expert, Theaetetus shows that he does not recognize the difference between perceiving and comprehending. He and his teacher were attracted to Protagoras' definition of knowledge because they too understand knowledge to be a kind of *aisthēsis*, that is, immediate perception, of the way things are. They do not recognize the temporal implications of having to prove the truth of propositions or "corollaries" in steps or stages.

It is no accident, then, that Socrates' next question concerns the temporal character of knowledge: If knowledge is perception, do we know what we remember? Theaetetus again shows that he does not understand the question—or what it involves—by asserting that it would be monstrous if we did not. Certain that human beings know what they remember, because it is present in and to their minds, Theaetetus does not consider the difficulties associated with the source of memory in past perception or the apparent differences between what one perceives at present and what one recalls.[27]

Because it appears to be so literal, Socrates' third question seems almost playful. If we cover one eye, do we see and thus know at the same time that we do not see and thus do not know (and so contradict ourselves)? Rather than explore the questions of the necessity of simultaneity or presence as opposed to sequential ordering and completeness as requirements of knowledge implicit in the apparent contradiction between seeing with one eye and not seeing with the other, Socrates dismisses the question as eristic almost as soon as he raises it.[28]

27. Socrates reintroduces these difficulties in the second half of the dialogue, in his famous images of the block of wax and the dovecote, when he conclusively demonstrates that Theaetetus does not know what knowledge is.

28. Martin Heidegger emphasizes both in his historical explication of the meaning of Protagoras' famous saying, in his lectures in *Nietzsche* (4:91–95).

3. Socrates' Defense of Protagoras

Implicitly commenting on Theaetetus' inability to explain or defend the thesis he took over from Protagoras, Socrates politely suggests that the "father of the myth" would be able to defend it, if he were still living. (Socrates thus reminds readers of his own critique of writing in the *Phaedrus.*) Theodorus still refuses to act as the "guardian" of the "orphan" left by his friend, so Socrates volunteers to help. He explicitly addresses comments he imagines Protagoras would make in his own defense to both geometers. These comments are nevertheless designed to draw Theodorus into the conversation; they are, moreover, inadequate to defend Protagoras' position—and Socrates knows it. (He thus apologizes at the end for having done what little he could on the basis of his own ability. Not perceiving the problems, Theodorus thinks he is joking.)

By having Protagoras object first to him frightening a mere child, Socrates begins his defense by laying the grounds for his later insistence that Theodorus come to the assistance of his friend. Responding to the surface, and not to the deeper issues implicit in Socrates' exchange with Theaetetus, Protagoras affirms that he would have no difficulty admitting that our memory of what we perceive is different from the perception, that someone can know and not know at the same time, and that the perceiver himself changes. If everything changes, all three of these propositions have to be true. With regard to the conflict between his teaching and his own activity, he accuses Socrates of speaking demagogically (as Socrates had earlier accused himself, when he suggested that Theaetetus was too easily persuaded by such demagogic speeches), that is, of flattering the "masses" by suggesting that everyone is equally wise. Recognizing that everyone has his or her own private perceptions that are true for that person does not prevent Protagoras from claiming to be wiser than others. All perceptions are equally true, but the way in which any person perceives things is a reflection of that person's condition. Just as doctors know how to change the way sick people perceive things by administering drugs that restore their health, so sophists know how to change the way people in cities perceive what is noble, just, and holy, by giving speeches that persuade and so alter the souls of their audience. This knowledge justifies Protagoras' claim to be wiser than others, and the utility of this knowledge justifies his charging a fee for teaching what he knows.

Picking up on Theaetetus' concern that Protagoras be treated justly, the sophist admonishes Socrates that arguing unjustly will undermine his claim to care about virtue. If Socrates wishes to dispute the sophist's claims, he should present a contrary position. Or, if he prefers to proceed by question and answer, he should not try merely to refute his opponent. On the contrary, if and when his opponent is knocked down, Socrates should pick him up and put him back on his feet, explaining exactly where and how he went wrong. If Socrates proceeds in this manner, Protagoras promises, his interlocutors will blame themselves, not him, for their perplexity. And hating themselves, they will flee to philosophy. If, however, Socrates continues merely to refute, they will blame him for their perplexity and come to hate philosophy.

Earlier, Socrates had suggested that he had not treated Protagoras fairly, because he had not disproved the sophist's proposition with a geometric proof. Now, however, having just set the sophist on his feet, in effect, by revising the statement of his position and then defending it, Socrates has made his own way of arguing the model of a just response. Socrates also reminds his interlocutors that Protagoras did not give geometric-like proofs. Protagoras was famous for his wisdom and acquired a great deal of money, not so much because people thought what he said was true or just but because people thought his knowledge was useful in politics.

E. Separating the Geometer from the Sophist

Having not only critiqued but also defended the sophist, Socrates can now insist that Protagoras' self-declared friend Theodorus do the same. Socrates reminds the geometer that Protagoras had objected to his attributing his position to a "mere child," that is, Theaetetus. To be just to Protagoras, Theodorus must join the conversation.

Accusing Socrates of an immoderate love of argumentative contests, Theodorus reluctantly agrees with the expressed expectation that he will be refuted (*Theaetetus* 169d). (Like Theaetetus, Theodorus is familiar with Socrates' usual mode of proceeding.) But, Theodorus warns, he will not participate any longer than necessary to examine Protagoras' saying.

1. Why Most People Disagree with Protagoras' Saying but Nevertheless Find His Claims Plausible

Theodorus must have been pleasantly surprised. Rather than obviously or directly refuting the geometer, Socrates quickly and easily gets him to agree that most people do not think they are as wise as everyone else. On the contrary, when they face a crisis and need assistance, for example, when they are sick or threatened with a shipwreck, most people consult experts, such as doctors or pilots. Nor do most people believe that all opinions are equally true. In fact, Socrates points out, if the opinions of all human beings are equally true, Protagoras has to agree that their opinions are as true as his own saying. He is therefore forced to contradict himself.

Believing that this critique is devastating, Theodorus protests that they are running down his comrade too much. Apparently from respect for Theodorus' concern for his friend, Socrates suggests that they leave Protagoras behind and consider their own opinions. Socrates had introduced Protagoras and his saying, after all, as a means of bringing out and examining the opinions of the geometricians. Since Protagoras is older than they, Socrates rather conventionally observes, he is probably wiser. Socrates seems to be complimenting Protagoras, but he concludes his examination of the sophist with a devastating comment. They will never be able to determine how wise Protagoras or his saying is because, according to this saying, the (presumably rigid, because dead) sophist might pop his head (intellect, but not body) up (out of the earth) for a moment, but he would run off, and they would not be able to catch or force him to answer. Stated in general terms, Socrates' point is that if everything is always in motion, no one, no person, no saying, no thing has an identity or meaning that persists over time.

Theodorus clearly does not agree with Protagoras in thinking that everything is always in motion, but he continues to feel a somewhat diminished connection to his "comrade" (hetairos; Theaetetus 171c). To show the geometers the incompatibility between their art and the sophist's teaching, Socrates has to explain why they, like many others, find Protagoras' saying plausible.

Although most people do not think all opinions are equally true, Socrates points out, they nevertheless observe that certain kinds of opinions, the opinions people hold about the noble and base, just and unjust, holy and unholy, differ from city to city. On the basis of this observation, they conclude that opinions about such things are merely matters of convention; there is no truth about such matters. And these are the subjects about which Protagoras teaches his students to speak persuasively.

Like most people, Socrates implies, the geometers also think that the noble, the just, and the holy are merely matters of convention. (Like many contemporary students of natural science and mathematics, they regard the subjects of mousikē and politikē as matters of taste or opinion, that is, value judgments based on emotional reactions, not knowledge.) Socrates does not state the reasons the geometers think the sophist's teaching is compatible with their own. He merely points out that people do not think what they believe to be advantageous is necessarily so. Rather than observe more generally, as he had in the *Republic*, that many people are willing to settle for what is only apparently noble or apparently just, but that no one wants what is only apparently good, he simply says that they are approaching a huge question.

2. Creating an Alliance between Mathematics and Philosophy

Theodorus seems eager to pursue the question. Echoing the contrast Socrates had drawn earlier between a sophistic contest in which speakers seek to win by refuting the other and the kind of examination of their own opinions he and Theaetetus were conducting in private, "very much at our leisure" (*Theaetetus* 155a), Theodorus asks, "aren't we at leisure?" (172c). Socrates knows that he is not at leisure; he has to go to the porch of the king to be indicted. Socrates does not tell Theodorus this, however. Instead he agrees that they are "apparently" at leisure. Theodorus' expression of interest in investigating the question has provided Socrates with an opportunity to create a kind of alliance with the geometer. In contrast to those who seek preeminence and power, both the geometer and the philosopher are dedicated to finding the truth.

Provoked by Theodorus' question to remember his own impending trial, Socrates says that he has been reminded of how ridiculous philosophers look when they try to give public speeches in court. Most people believe that the politicians who actively prosecute and defend others in court are the freest, if not the most powerful, individuals in cities. But, Socrates reflects, these politicians look like domestic servants when they are compared to philosophers. Philosophers speak at their leisure on any topic they wish, for as long as they wish, so long as they eventually get to what truly is. Those who speak in court have a set time in which to make their arguments, the topics or questions determined by the prosecution or case. Instead of seeking the truth of things for themselves, moreover, these speakers have to defend a particular person by pleasing and so persuading another set of judges. Although they believe that they are terribly clever, because they know how to manipulate the system, that is, the laws and the people who make them, such politicians tend to develop a narrow and crooked view of human life. But, Socrates implicitly reminds Theodorus, these clever speakers possess the kind of wisdom Protagoras was proud to teach.

At Theodorus' behest Socrates then gives a description of their own "chorus" of philosophers, who freely exchange speeches at their leisure. They "don't know the way to the marketplace, or where a court is." They are not familiar with the laws, spoken or written, nor do they join clubs or participate in banquets and revelries with flute girls. They do not ask whether someone is well born or not, because they don't think such things are worth knowing about. Their bodies are situated in the city, but their "thought . . . flies 'deep down under the earth' and measures the planes with geometry, 'and above the heaven' star-gazing, everywhere exploring the nature of each thing as a whole" (173e).

As many commentators have noted, this description of the philosopher does not fit Plato's Socrates so much as the figure Aristophanes satirized in the *Clouds*.[29] As Socrates demonstrated at the beginning of the *Theaetetus*, he pays attention to family background. In the *Apology, Gorgias, Symposium*, and *Republic* Socrates also shows that he knows the way to the marketplace, participates in banquets, and associates with politically ambitious people, even if he does not seek office, conspire to overturn the regime, or speak in the assembly. Socrates indicates that he is describing a popular view of philosophers (shared, ironically, as we have seen, by the geometer) by relating the famous tale of the Thracian girl who laughed at Thales when, looking at the stars, he fell down a well. Philosophers do not pay attention to any of the particular people around them, Socrates explains, because they seek to know the nature of each kind of being (including human being) as a whole, how it acts or is acted on differently from all others. As a result, philosophers look ridiculous when they are dragged into court and compelled to speak. They do not know anything "peculiar to revile anyone with." Nor are they able to praise or hear other people praised without laughing themselves. When a tyrant or king is praised, a philosopher reflects, "it's a shepherd, or some cowherd . . . milking a more peevish and conspiratorial animal than most, [who necessarily] becomes boorish from lack of leisure" (*Theaetetus* 174c–d). If a philosopher hears someone lauded for owning 10,000 acres of land, he wonders how anyone could credit such a pittance, compared to the whole surface of the earth.

29. See, e.g., Rue, "Philosopher in Flight," 87–89; Howland, *Paradox*, 59–60; Paul Stern, "The Philosophic Importance of Political Life: On the 'Digression' in Plato's *Theaetetus*," *American Political Science Review* 96, no. 2 (June 2002): 275–89. The parallel is limited. The philosophers described by Socrates here are like the foolish fellow in the *Clouds* only in their impracticality and contempt for the "ephemerals" below. Neither Theodorus nor Socrates' philosophers in the digression teach rhetoric the way Aristophanes' Socrates does.

And when people take pride in their ancestry, he concludes that they suffer from an incapacity to calculate and foolish vanity; they do not seem to recognize that all human beings are related and can all be traced back to much more ancient common progenitors. On such occasions, people laugh at the arrogance as well as the ignorance and perplexity of the philosophers.

Although this common view of philosophers does not fit Socrates, Theodorus emphatically and enthusiastically accepts it as a description of his own activity and "kind." By contrasting the freedom and broad, cosmic perspective of the apparently ridiculous and ineffective philosophers with the servility of public speakers (and the sophists who teach them), Socrates thus wins an enormous rhetorical victory. Before Socrates contrasted philosophers with public speakers, Theodorus associated himself with his "friend" Protagoras, who like Theodorus was a foreigner in Athens, claiming not only to possess but also to teach an art for a fee. As a result of the contrast Socrates draws in the "digression," Theodorus begins to associate himself with Socrates in opposition to "public speakers" such as Protagoras. Theodorus thus becomes willing to criticize and dismiss Protagoras after the digression as he had not before.

F. The Enduring Difference between Socrates and Theodorus

Indicating the shift in Theodorus' sense of allegiance by addressing him as a friend (*Theaetetus* 176b), Socrates gives a further description of the philosopher's possible relation to nonphilosophers that does correspond to his own activity.[30] Echoing his famous description of the freeing and educating of a soul in the cave in the *Republic*, Socrates says that the people who would drag philosophers into court by accusing them of particular crimes and laugh at the philosophers' inability to defend themselves prove to be equally perplexed and thus ridiculous, at least in the eyes of the educated, if and when a philosopher is able to drag them (or their minds) up by turning their attention from personal responsibility for particular acts by asking them more generally: What is just in itself? Or, what really and truly makes human beings happy?

Theodorus shows that he does not understand the necessity of the conflict between philosophers and those who would please the many when he observes that if Socrates were to persuade everyone of what he has just

---

30. Cf. Scott R. Hemmenway, "Philosophical Apology in the *Theaetetus*," *Interpretation* 17, no. 3 (1990): 323–46.

said, "peace would be more widespread and evils less among human be-ings" (176a). But Socrates informs him that it is not possible to rid the lives of mortals of all bad things any more than it is necessary for the immortal gods to suffer evil. The evils of human life appear to be rooted in our mor-tality, but, Socrates insists, death is not the evil. That is what the "clever speakers" think. Like Callicles they engage in politics in order to secure their own safety by appearing to be just rather than prudently attempting to become as much like the gods as possible by becoming as just and pi-ous as possible.[31] They do not recognize that there are two paradigms of human life, one modeled on the eternal order of the immortals and the other modeled on the lives of unjust people. Nor do they recognize the true penalty, which (as Socrates told Callicles) is to live an unjust and so disorderly existence among other unjust, disorderly people.

Most emphatically showing that he is now talking about the kind of philosophy he practices, Socrates tells his now merely "comrade" The-odorus (177b), such people will not change unless "they have to give and receive an account [logos] of the things they blame in private, and they are willing to put up with it for a long time and not take flight" (177b). In that case, they end up not being satisfied with themselves and their rhetoric.

1. Socrates' Examination of the Geometer's Opinions

Instead of allowing Theodorus to continue listening to him speak persua-sively, Socrates ceases to reflect on his own situation and returns to an ex-amination of the geometer's opinions. As in the Gorgias, Socrates suggests, the only way a person will be corrected is through such an examination. Although Theodorus has become more willing to criticize Protagoras, we see in the following exchange that he is not willing to undergo a thorough examination of his own opinions or to be corrected.

Socrates begins by reiterating the point at which they had digressed. Al-though Theodorus and others might grant that things are for each as each perceives them, and that the just in each city is what its citizens believe is just, they are not so willing to agree that what people think is good for

31. In the Gorgias Socrates observed that Callicles' erroneous opinions showed that the young Athenian had not studied enough geometry. In other words, Socrates suggested that study of geometry might help human beings overcome their irrational fear of death by teaching them to deal proportionately with humans and gods. Drawing such proportions would be impossible, of course, for persons who followed Protagoras in making "man" the measure. As Socrates demon-strated in the Gorgias, however, neither Socrates nor anyone else would be able to persuade such people to change their ways, so long as they believed that death and pain were the worst penalties or ills that human beings can suffer.

them or will benefit them in the future necessarily is or will be advantageous for them. In his restatement, Socrates not only stresses the difference between what people believe and what will really benefit them; he also points out that in contrast to changeable opinion, knowledge is manifested and retained over time. People consult experts, he now explains, because they believe that those who know what worked in the past are best able to judge what will work in the future. Because only some people know what has been in the past and thus what will probably be in the future, as opposed to what merely appears to be the case at present, Theodorus agrees that Protagoras was wrong in declaring that all human beings are the measure of what is. Only those who know what has been, is, and will continue to be the case are.

Theodorus concludes that Protagoras' speech seems to have been overtaken, first, by the fact that everyone is not a knower, and second, by the observation that the sophist's speech makes the opinions of others equally authoritative, even though the others do not agree with his saying. Like his student Theaetetus, Theodorus does not recognize the importance of truth remaining the same over time. He does not, therefore, recognize the fundamental difference between the status and basis of the proofs he teaches and the propositions of the sophist.

2. THE CRITIQUE OF HERACLITUS AND THE EXPANSION OF THE QUESTION

They have not touched what Socrates (as opposed to Theodorus) considers to be the core of Protagoras' position: the claim that everything is in motion. When Socrates attributes the argument to Heraclitus rather than to Protagoras, however, Theodorus does not evince any reluctance to participate in refuting the claim. On the contrary, Theodorus declares that it is impossible to converse with the Ionian proponents of this thesis, because, in accord with their own principle, they never say or mean the same thing.

Unlike his naive young student, Theodorus understands the conflict between the contention that everything is in flux and the presuppositions of his own art. (Before Socrates explicated Protagoras' saying, Theodorus seems not have understood the way in which Protagoras agreed fundamentally with Heraclitus. Theodorus understood Protagoras to be talking only about the "human" things.) Theodorus clearly prefers Protagoras to the Ionians, but Socrates thinks there is more to be said on behalf of the Heracliteans. Observing that Theodorus has only seen the Heracliteans fighting, and that they would say something different to their pupils, Socrates suggests that the philosopher and his followers recognize the tension between the enduring truth of their central contention, that everything always becomes, and the change they observe in all (sensible) things. (Having indicated here that he has a higher opinion of flux philosophy than the geometer does, Socrates gives his own, quite different criticism of flux philosophy in the *Cratylus* [412c–13d].)

Theodorus objects that such people cannot have students or teachers (because there is nothing that remains the same to pass on), and Socrates admits that the geometer speaks "with measure" (*metriōs*). He then enlarges the problem he and Theodorus confront by reminding the geometrician that there are also philosophers like Parmenides and Melissus who argue that everything is one and stable.

Socrates does not explain why he says that he and Theodorus find themselves in the middle of the two opposing philosophical camps. On reflection, readers realize that both Socrates and the mathematician find themselves in the middle because they both maintain there are a plurality of things that remain the same in themselves (whether these be "ideas" or numbers). Both Socrates and the geometricians thus appear to be closer to the Eleatics. Their recognition not only of plurality but also of the existence of the two opposed claims about the character of all being nevertheless suggests that the Heracliteans, who say that everything is at war, may be correct.

When the geometer responds that it would be unendurable for them not to examine both of these philosophical positions (*Theaetetus* 181c), it looks as if Socrates has dragged Theodorus up out of his conventionalism (or dependence on agreements) and turned his attention to an examination of first principles. Beginning with those who maintain that everything is in motion, Socrates points out that motion includes alteration (*alloiōsis*) as well as locomotion (*phora*). And if it does, the result of the interaction of affect with affected, which constitutes the momentary perception, must itself be changing so that perception occurs along with nonperception. But if perception is knowledge, and perception cannot be separated from nonperception, knowledge cannot be distinguished from not-knowledge any more than being can be separated from nonbeing.

3. Theodorus' Retreat from Truth to Agreement

Protagoras has been proved wrong. That being the case, Theodorus announces, his obligation to answer Socrates' questions, on the basis of their previous agreement, has come to an end. Theaetetus expresses his desire to have them examine the arguments of those who maintain that everything is at rest as well, but Theodorus objects: would the younger teach the older to be unjust? Theodorus understands himself to be a "philosopher" concerned about measuring and so defining everything under the ground as well as on it and in the heavens. He agrees with Socrates that common people find such philosophers ridiculous because they do not pay attention to those who are nearest, if not dearest, to them. He does not agree with Socrates that there is a paradigm (or form) of justice in itself or that human beings should try to approximate the divine by becoming as just and pious as they can. Like Protagoras, Theodorus thinks that what is just in every city is what the people believe and so agree is just. His own art begins with agreements or "axioms," the truth of which cannot be proved, but which nevertheless appear to be true immediately or intuitively to those who hear them. He does not question these first principles any more than he challenges the laws of the regime in which he finds himself. In terms of the "divided line," he does not seek to ascend to the "ideas" by means of dialectic. He considers such philosophical investigations to be empty, "bare" speeches (*psiloi logoi*), in contrast to the fuller, visible proofs that can be given of geometrical propositions. Theodorus would not have accepted Socrates' characterization of geometry (*Gorgias* 450d) as an art that is conducted solely through speech (*logos*).

G. Socrates' Midwifing and Thus Moderating of Theaetetus

In the same way that Theaetetus seemed to proceed more dialectically and thus philosophically than his mentor, when he and the young Socrates divided the sides of squares and cubes into "lines" or "powers" instead of trying to give a separate proof in each case like Theodorus, so he seems to express more philosophical passion than Theodorus when he urges Socrates to examine Parmenides' argument. But to Theodorus' surprise, Socrates refuses. He is not a "bag" of speeches, as Theodorus imagines. Indeed, Socrates has shown, it is the mathematicians who are full of the speeches of others, speeches they have merely accepted rather than examined, even to see whether they are compatible with their own art. As his exchange with Theodorus has just demonstrated, moreover, merely refuting the position taken by another, particularly by showing that it is not compatible with the interlocutor's deepest convictions and claims to knowledge, will not necessarily lead Socrates' interlocutor to examine those convictions or claims. Neither geometer will be willing or able to investigate the question concerning knowledge until he is led to question the adequacy of his own understanding and art. Theodorus has proved unwilling to do so. Theaetetus is younger and more docile, however. His soul can perhaps be turned not only from the visible to the intelligible, but also to an examination of the first principles and assumptions of arts like geometry.

Socrates refuses to take up Parmenides' argument until he has examined the viability of Theaetetus' understanding of knowledge, because he realizes that a critical examination of the adequacy of the geometers' understanding of knowledge is a necessary prerequisite for the broader inquiry. As he points out in quickly demonstrating the inadequacy of the equation of knowledge with perception, it is impossible "to hit upon truth if one does not hit upon being," and "if one does not hit upon truth, one will never be a knower" (*Theaetetus* 186c). As Socrates understands it, knowledge is not possible, if being is (or really, if the beings are) not intelligible. Theaetetus would not be able to answer Socrates' question without engaging Parmenides' argument. He will not be able to engage that argument, however, until he has brought out, critiqued, and thus freed himself (with Socrates' assistance) from his own preconceptions. (Socrates' "midwifing" of Theaetetus is therefore a necessary condition, at least as Socrates understands it, for the Eleatic Stranger's subsequent instruction of Theaetetus.) In presenting himself as a midwife, Socrates had indicated early in the conversation that his exchange with Theaetetus could have only negative results.

1. KNOWLEDGE IS SOMETHING OTHER THAN PERCEPTION

In refuting Theaetetus' first two attempts at a definition of knowledge, Socrates fills out the critique of Protagoras he left implicit in the earlier discussion. By asking Theaetetus whether human beings do not have different kinds of sense perceptions by means of various bodily organs, for example, sight by means of eyes, hearing by means of ears, Socrates indicates both how Protagoras could have distinguished human beings from baboons and why he did not. Human beings share such senses and organs with beasts, but, Theaetetus points out, human beings recognize these nonsensible aspects of things by means of their souls, not their bodies. They have to undergo a long and arduous education, moreover, to learn to recognize nonsensible characteristics of things—that they have being, are similar or dissimilar, same or different, even or odd, noble or base, good or bad. If Protagoras had acknowledged the peculiar ability human beings display to recognize and mark types of things with words, he could have explained why they (and not baboons) are the "measure." But in that case the sophist would have had to admit not only that some people know more truth than others, but also that persistent, intelligible types or kinds of things exist independent of human perception.

2. FALSE OPINION AND THE INADEQUACY OF MEMORY AS AN UNDERSTANDING OF KNOWLEDGE

Having concluded that knowledge cannot be defined as "nothing other than perception" (*Theaetetus* 151e), Socrates asks Theaetetus to begin anew, as if they had wiped the slate clean.[32] Realizing that human awareness of things cannot be traced merely to the impressions things make on our senses but involves coordinating and sorting our various sense perceptions and thus our minds, Theaetetus suggests that knowledge consists in a kind of opinion. Since there are false as well as true opinions, knowledge must consist in true opinion.

In refuting the claim that knowledge consists (merely) of true opinion, Socrates fills out the implications of two other questions he had asked earlier about Protagoras' saying. These questions concerned the role of memory in the acquisition and possession of knowledge and the apparently contradictory claims involved in the assertion that everything is always changing, which result in people simultaneously knowing and not knowing.[33]

Socrates reintroduces these questions by asking about what he claims has long perplexed him—how false opinion is possible. Socrates might well be perplexed about the difference between true and false opinions. On the basis of the divided line, all opinions would be images of things, which are in turn images of the mental constructs arts or artisans employ. The images could be more or less accurate, but qua opinions, they would all seem to be less than completely true and hence, of necessity, somewhat false. In the *Republic* (478c–d) Socrates defined opinion, as Diotima had taught him in the *Symposium*, as belonging to the realm of becoming, that which was between knowledge of the things that always are and ignorance

---

32. By asking Theaetetus to begin anew, Socrates thus indicates, in passing, that his refutations in the *Republic* serve the purpose of expelling everyone over ten years of age, without the use of force, by, as it were, "wiping the slate clean."

33. Dorter (*Form and Good*, 101) also points out the identification of knowledge with memory in this section.

of nothing. And in the *Philebus* he explained how it is possible to define things that come into being as mixtures of the unlimited (usually sensory characteristics) and the limited (intelligible divisions like numbers), which are caused (perhaps ultimately by the good). What he claimed neither he nor anyone else knows is whether there are eternally existing, unchanging unities, and if there are, what they are, and how they can be broken apart and spread through an infinity of things or united into a whole.

Socrates does not take up the question of opinion, true or false, in terms of his own argument in the *Theaetetus*, however. Instead, he takes up the problem of false opinion as it arises from the refutation of Protagoras. If Protagoras' saying were correct, there would be no such thing as false opinion. Protagoras has been shown not to be correct, however, and Theaetetus shares the opinion of most—that some people have false opinions. If false opinion does not arise from perception, it must have its source in mistakes in the mental coordinating and sorting operations Theaetetus saw had to be added to perception in order to generate knowledge.

At first the problem appears to be a more serious version of the puzzle Socrates introduced earlier about a man who covered one eye and thus could simultaneously see and not see. Socrates and Theaetetus agree that it is not possible for a person to have an opinion about something of which he knows nothing or, more simply, to have an opinion about nothing. People who have false opinions must therefore mix up things that they know (in some sense). People do not usually mistake abstract or general concepts like the noble or the even for their opposites, the base or the odd. The mistakes seem to arise when an immediate perception is erroneously identified with a remembered impression of something similar, for example, when someone sees Socrates in the distance and mistakes him for Theaetetus. Human beings are able to acquire knowledge, Socrates suggests, if they are able to receive accurate impressions, retain them, and match their current perceptions with these past impressions. In that case, human beings (like Theaetetus) learn more or less basically by nature, depending on whether they have better or worse memories or "wax blocks." If the block is too hard, it will not receive accurate or detailed impressions; if it is too soft, it will not be able to retain old impressions. In both these cases, it will mismatch impressions and form false opinions.

Socrates recognizes that the wax block represents far too simple an account of the way in which human beings actually learn things. It does not indicate the importance of the synthesizing and sorting functions Theaetetus has attributed to the human soul. Socrates presents the image of the wax block and then points out the limitations of the understanding of knowledge as immediate perception plus memory it represents, because both geometers have shown that they understand the basis of their art to consist in immediate perceptions of the truth of the "axioms" from which they reason and the persuasiveness of the proofs they derive from these axioms to result from their visible expression as well as their logic. Neither geometer has shown an appreciation for the temporal character of human reasoning or the problems associated with it.[34]

Apologizing for his garrulity (perhaps because he is making a point he made earlier, although in a somewhat different context), Socrates points out that the explanation of error (or false opinion) in terms of a mismatch of perception with memory does not account for errors about purely intelligible concepts like numbers. (Even when memory is added to perception, Socrates shows, the geometers have not reflected on the character of their own art in the understanding of knowledge they hold and voice.) A person who concludes that the sum of 5 and 7 is 11 has not mismatched a perception with a memory.

Relating the inquiry into false opinion to their own endeavors, Socrates points out (*Theaetetus* 196d–e) that they have shamelessly (*anaides*) been talking about recognizing (*gignōskomen*) and knowing (*epistametha*), while admitting that they are ignorant (*agnooumen*).[35] When Theaetetus protests, Socrates admits that it is not possible to converse otherwise. One has to begin with the views or opinions about things indicated by the words we use to describe them, as Socrates does here, and then test them to see whether they are true or false. Socrates admits that he and Theaetetus become liable to the eristic objection that they are contradicting themselves in speaking about something they claim not to know. They avoid Meno's paradox by admitting that they have initial views about the matter in question that may not be true *and* by testing the validity of those initial views in a cooperative search for the truth rather than merely trying, like an eristic sophist, to show up their opponent in an argumentative contest.

34. Theodorus agreed that Protagoras was mistaken in identifying knowledge with immediate perception, because those who have arts are better able to predict what will happen in the future. They are able to predict because of what they know about what happened in the past, that is, their marking and remembering of regularities. And Theaetetus had declared that it would be monstrous if people were not said to know what they remembered.

35. Myles Burnyeat, The *"Theaetetus" of Plato* (Indianapolis: Hackett, 1990), 65–66, points out, in examining Theaetetus' second definition of "knowledge" as true judgment, that they are investigating an example of false judgment. A dramatic artist such as Plato was not apt to be unaware of the self-referential character of the discussion.

Socrates attempts to avoid the difficulty they have encountered in defining knowledge merely as a correspondence between memory and perception by distinguishing between knowledge they passively hold or possess and the knowledge they bring to mind and actively use. Comparing the mind to a dovecote in which specific pieces of knowledge fly around like birds until the "owner" catches and uses them, Socrates suggests that the person who concluded that 5 and 7 were 11 seized something he knew (the number 11, as well as the numbers 5 and 7). But, Socrates points out, they are still attributing his false opinion, error, and hence ignorance to his knowledge and so contradicting themselves. And if, as Theaetetus suggests, some of the "birds" or opinions held were taken to represent non-knowledge, they would still be contradicting themselves by asserting that the person with false opinions simultaneously knows and does not know.

What is so remarkable about Socrates' arithmetic example is that the answer contained within is so close at hand. Yet he and Theaetetus miss it, even though Socrates suggests, in turning from their examination of the source of false opinion back to the question of knowledge (201a), that the answer might be lying right at their feet. Someone who mistakenly concludes that 5 and 7 equal 11 has not counted or calculated correctly.[36] Someone who merely memorizes sums without understanding the basis or reasons for the result does not know them. We have here an example of the difference between true opinion and knowledge. As Socrates observes at the end of the Meno, true opinions are changeable, but knowledge, pinned down by reasoning, is not. Ancient Greek mathematicians distinguished arithmetic as the knowledge of numbers from both calculation and geometry (Republic 522c–29a). One would nevertheless expect a geometer to recognize the difference not only between the slave boy's initial error in thinking that a square could be doubled in area by doubling its sides, but also between the true opinion, to which the boy came as a result of Socrates' corrections, and the knowledge he would acquire if he were able to give the proof on his own, or that a boy, learning his sums, would gain by counting rather than by memorizing.

Theaetetus admitted at the beginning of the dialogue that he was not able to answer Socrates' question about knowledge by generalizing from his own mathematical experience. Rather than investigate the adequacy of Theaetetus' second definition of knowledge as true opinion by applying it

36. Cf. Burnyeat, Theaetetus, 109; Dorter, Form and Good, 106. Neither commentator points out the way in which this fact reflects on Theaetetus and his lack of self-reflection.

to mathematical propositions, Socrates thus concludes their examination of his second definition by reminding Theaetetus of the public speakers with whom Theodorus contrasted his own studies. If true opinion were knowledge, public speakers would not be able to convince juries to come to a true opinion about events they have not seen and could not, therefore, remember. Perhaps because the objection incorporates his own faulty equation of knowledge with perception and memory, the docile Theaetetus agrees that his second definition has been refuted.

3. Knowledge Is Not Simply Analytic or Synthetic

Socrates' example of the mistaken addition of 5 and 7 should have prepared Plato's readers, if not Theaetetus, for his third definition of knowledge as true opinion with reasoning (*logos*). A person who broke the numbers down into their component units and then added them up would not have made a mistake.

Theaetetus says that he does not remember who said that knowledge consists in true opinion supported by reason. Commentators have argued about whether the source is Antisthenes (as Aristotle claims), Socrates (who says similar things in the *Meno* and *Phaedo*), or Plato himself.[37] It is not as important to identify the source of the definition, however, as to see that Theaetetus does not understand what it (or *logos*) entails. He characteristically repeats a definition he has heard or read elsewhere, rather than reflecting on his own experience.

Offering to exchange a "dream" for a "dream," Socrates suggests that dreams are, like Theaetetus' third definition, composed of faded memories.[38] In his dream Socrates "heard some people say that the first things, just like the elements [*stoicheia*], out of which we and everything else are

37. Cf. McDowell, *Theaetetus*, 229–31; Polansky, *Philosophy and Knowledge*, 101, 209; Burnyeat, *Theaetetus*, 128–87.

38. Several other explanations of Socrates' reference to a "dream" here have been given. Taylor, *Plato*, 346; Francis M. Cornford, *Plato's Theory of Knowledge* (London: Routledge and Kegan Paul, 1939), 144; and Bostock (*Theaetetus*, 202) all think Plato indicated that this theory had in fact been announced only after Socrates' death by having Socrates call it a dream. According to Myles Burnyeat, "The Material and Sources of Plato's Dream," *Phronesis* 15 (1970), "'telling someone his own dream' was a proverbial expression for telling him something he already knows only too well from his own experience" (105–6). This would apply to the passage as I read it. Amelie Rorty, "A Speculative Note on Some Dramatic Elements in the *Theaetetus*," *Phronesis* 17 (1972), thinks that "his dream is that a certain theory about recollection is true" (230), whereas Stanley Rosen, "Socrates' Dream," *Theoria* 42 (1976), argues that "dreaming produces the unity of the whole" (183). Dorter suggests "that the theory . . . is one that we should be able to recognize as true, but only indistinctly" (*Form and Good*, 108).

composed, have no logos" (*Theaetetus* 201e). Because these first elements are absolutely simple, they cannot be described; they can only be named. Just as all things are constituted by a plaiting of the elements, so, Socrates points out, speech (*logos*) is constituted by a weaving together of the names.

The description of things (and their names) that Socrates gives here would describe a world in which things could be accounted for by numbers (as the Pythagoreans, themselves students of geometry, claimed).[39] As Parmenides points out in the first argument to Aristotle, "one" cannot even be said to be, because if being is added to "one," it becomes more than one. One is the simple element out of which all other numbers are composed. But the analogy Socrates draws between the composition of things out of elements (which are perceptible, even though they cannot be known or explained by an argument) and the composition of syllables (which can be spoken and understood, out of letters, which can only be seen or heard) obscures the possible recourse to a Pythagorean account of the intelligibility of things in terms of numbers. If Theaetetus had been thinking in terms of numbers rather than in terms of letters, syllables, and words, he would not have agreed that the whole is different from the sum of its parts, as Socrates shows when he introduces six as an example.

Socrates' use of the first syllable in his own name, *S-O*, to inquire whether something intelligible can really be constituted by combining unintelligible elements, points to the differences between letters or, more generally, language and numbers, or still more generally, mathematics as means by which human beings acquire knowledge of things. One is not a number or intelligible as such, but all numbers are composed of units and intelligible as such. Because all units are the same as all other units, they can be combined in any order. There is no difference between a whole number and the sum of its parts.

Unlike the units out of which numbers are composed, letters differ from one another in appearance as well as sound. They cannot all be indiscriminately combined to make syllables, much less words. The order in which they are combined makes a difference: *O-S* is not and does not sound like *S-O*.[40] Not merely do the letters or sounds merge together to

39. Glenn R. Morrow, "Plato and the Mathematicians: An Interpretation of Socrates' Dream in the *Theaetetus* (201e–206c)," *Philosophical Review* 79 (July 1970), points out that "the term *stoicheia* had long been used to designate the basic premises of arithmetic and geometry" (326).

40. Cf. Burnyeat, *Theaetetus*, 210n94. If we can know a number without knowing all of the operations (additions, subtractions, etc.) that might produce it, Dorter argues (*Form and Good*,

form something different from the components taken singly; the words formed out of the syllables acquire their meaning and intelligibility only in reference to other words and things. It may be true, in a limited sense, as Socrates and Theaetetus agree, that the number of an army is the same as the army; it is obviously not true that the letters A, R, M, Y or their combination in a single word is the same as a collection of people organized to fight.

Precisely because words, sentences, and languages are composed of different elements, which can be recognized and distinguished from one another, and do not all combine, language seems to provide a more accurate reflection of the complex character of the world than mere numbers. But, as Socrates reminded Theaetetus earlier, different peoples speak different languages in different times and places. There is no necessary correspondence between names and things. Language is at most a distorted (and thus distorting) image of things, impressed, as it were, in defective wax blocks. Language (*glōtta*) is not the same as *logos*.

Inquiring what *logos* is such that, added to right opinion, it constitutes knowledge, Socrates and Theaetetus quickly conclude that it is not merely "making one's thought evident through sound with words and phrases, imaging the opinion in the stream that flows through one's mouth, as if in a mirror or water" (*Theaetetus* 206d). Having been challenged and shown to be wrong earlier when he suggested that the whole is not the sum of its parts, Theaetetus is now willing to accept a definition of *logos* as an analysis and specification of all the parts. But returning to the various components of words, letters, and syllables, Socrates reminds him that the same elements can be parts of different things. To know whether a component has been left out of a specification and analysis, one needs to know the whole or—at the very least—its distinguishing characteristics, whether these are to be found in the order of the elements (as in a word or name), the particular identity of a person like Theaetetus, or the purpose or function of a thing like a wagon. But having suggested that a right opinion about something might become knowledge if one could specify the way in which it differed from everything else, Socrates points out that the acquisition of knowledge would then depend, in a circular fashion, on knowledge (in this case of everything else).

103n39), a number is more than the sum of its parts. Considering the "parts" to be units, and talking solely about the ancient Greek conception of number as a number of units, I disagree.

Socrates and Theaetetus conclude that the young geometer has now been emptied of all the conceptions he had of knowledge. Indeed, Theaetetus comments, Socrates has brought out much more than Theaetetus ever imagined he had. If Theaetetus were to become pregnant again, Socrates promises, he will conceive on a better basis. Even if he remains barren, Theaetetus will have become more moderate, less hard on his associates, and tamer as a result of his encounter with Socrates, because he no longer believes that he knows what he does not. Socrates has to go to meet the indictment Meletus has drawn up against him, but, he urges Theodorus, they should meet again tomorrow morning at the same place.

H. Conclusion: On the Geometers' Lack of Self-Knowledge

Just as it is remarkable that Socrates and Theaetetus do not mention the way in which a false opinion about the sum of 5 and 7 could be corrected by counting, so it is equally remarkable that in asking what *logos* (speech or reason) could be added to right opinion to make it knowledge, they do not consider the example of a geometrical proof. Such a proof would appear to constitute an example par excellence of the way in which a proposition, hypothesis, or opinion can be transformed into knowledge by reason. But, as Plato showed most dramatically in Theaetetus' first definition, the young geometer does not consider his own experience in formulating his understanding of knowledge. He merely repeats what he has heard. Theaetetus' failure to reflect on what he himself does as a mathematician is not accidental. It results from the understanding of knowledge he has absorbed, even though he himself does not articulate it, from his practice of geometry. Theaetetus agreed when Socrates suggested that they might not be treating Protagoras justly, that knowledge requires a necessary proof of the kind geometers give. Socrates admitted that reflections on the way in which human beings learn do not constitute necessary proofs. Through his examination of Theaetetus and Theodorus, Socrates has nevertheless shown that human beings will not be able to say what knowledge is unless they engage in such reflections.

Plato has Socrates demonstrate the need for human beings to seek self-knowledge, if they are to acquire any knowledge at all, with mathematicians, because, as the root of the ancient Greek word *mathēmata* indicates, mathematics provides the clearest example of human learning. That learning begins with counting, measuring, and calculating. In the form of geometry it extends to plane surfaces and solids, whose motions (as in astronomy) can then also be studied. Because geometers study plane and solid figures, we see in the *Theaetetus*, they tend to conflate intellection with sensation in "perception." Both Theodorus and Theaetetus thus adopted Protagoras' understanding of knowledge. Recognizing that all lengths are not commensurable, these geometers were nevertheless tempted to believe that everything could be made commensurable by transforming lines into figures (as in Theaetetus' sorting of the two kinds of lines or shapes). As Socrates shows in the *Theaetetus*, such mathematicians do not recognize the essential difference between the intelligible and the sensible; they are not, therefore, able to show how sensible things, which are always in motion, are related to the purely intelligible, unchanging principles of thought they employ in their own art, even though they (like many contemporary scientists) believe they do. To show how the purely intelligible concepts used in geometry do and can explain things in the sensible world, geometers would have to explain the character and relevance of their art. They would have to begin by explaining what a geometrical proof is and what kind of knowledge it produces. Such an explanation could not be given as a geometrical proof, however. It would require a philosophical investigation of the kind in which Socrates engages.

II. *Euthyphro*: The Importance of Recognizing the Difference between the Human and the Divine

The conversation depicted in the *Euthyphro* occurs right after the conversation related in the *Theaetetus*. At the end of the *Theaetetus* (210c), Socrates says he has to go to the porch of the king to receive the indictment Meletus has drawn up against him. At the beginning of the *Euthyphro* (2a), the diviner asks Socrates what he is doing at the porch of the king. The sequence and thus connection between the two dialogues appear to be merely coincidental.[41] Only when we discover that piety (and hence the crime of impiety of which Socrates was accused) involves a claim on Euthyphro's part to possess knowledge do we see that Socrates continues to pursue the same questions he raised with Theaetetus in the conversation

41. Leo Strauss, "On the *Euthyphron*," in *The Rebirth of Classical Political Rationalism: An Introduction to the Thought of Leo Strauss*, ed. and with an introduction by Thomas L. Pangle (Chicago: University of Chicago Press, 1989), 193.

he has with Euthyphro—namely, what is knowledge, and how do human beings acquire it?

A. The Charges against Socrates

Euthyphro's surprise at meeting Socrates at the porch of the king not merely reminds readers that Socrates and his ways were well known; it also shows that Socrates' ways were such that people would not expect him to prosecute someone in court. We are led to ask, why not? In the *Gorgias* Socrates told Polus that people should accuse first themselves, then their family and friends, so that they would be corrected. But Socrates also insisted that people would be corrected only if their judges were just. Socrates did not think that either he or his fellow Athenians really knew what is just. He thus went around testing his own opinions, and those of others in private conversations, by trying to refute them or be refuted himself. As he tells Euthyphro at the end of this conversation, he would not prosecute anyone, certainly not his father, in opposition to custom or convention, unless he knew for sure that the prosecution would be pious and just. Socrates' awareness of his own ignorance prevented him from attempting to impose his own views on others by means of law—or, ultimately, by force.

Although Socrates was well known, his accuser was not. Euthyphro does not recognize Meletus by name, deme, or physical description. Readers are led to suspect that the unknown young poet may have been attempting to make himself better known by prosecuting Socrates. Socrates, nevertheless, gives a remarkably positive account of his accuser: Meletus must be very wise if he knows how the young are corrupted and who corrupts them. Meletus is the only politician (statesman) who begins correctly by taking care of the young first. By clearing out the older corruptors of the young, Meletus will "become the cause of the greatest good things for the city" (*Euthyphro* 3a). Like the philosopher mocked by Aristophanes in the *Clouds*, Plato's Socrates believes that young people who possess the requisite wisdom have a right, if not an obligation, to correct their elders. As the proposals he makes in the *Republic* also make clear, Plato's Socrates is not pious in the sense of believing that the old is the good or that the elderly should always take precedence over the young.

By attempting to do Socrates an injustice, Euthyphro thinks, Socrates' accuser will be harming rather than benefiting the city. Euthyphro asks how Meletus claims that Socrates corrupts the young, and the philosopher explains: "He asserts that I am a maker of gods," or, more precisely, "that I make novel gods and don't believe in the ancient ones" (*Euthyphro* 3b). This version of the indictment differs in significant ways from that found in the *Apology*, in which Socrates is said to do "injustice by corrupting the young, and by not believing in the gods in whom the city believes, but in other *daimonia* that are novel" (24b–c).[42] By stating the charge in terms of "making," Socrates reminds us not only that he often pointed out that he was not a poet (literally, "maker"), but also that the Greek gods could, in a sense, have been said to have been made by the poets. If, as many commentators believe, Socrates considers the divinities to be something like his "ideas," Socrates believes in more ancient (eternal and unchanging) gods than those described by Homer or Hesiod that neither he nor anyone else made or created. Socrates is, in other words, not guilty as charged in the *Euthyphro* (3b).

B. Euthyphro's Defense of Socrates

Euthyphro immediately traces the charges to Socrates' claim that a *daimonion* sometimes speaks to him and dismisses the accusation as a reflection of the envy many people feel for those who have special knowledge of the divine. In the assembly, Euthyphro reports, people often laugh at his predictions for the same reason, even though he has never said anything untrue. Readers are led to wonder whether Euthyphro's advice was true or prudent, however, when Euthyphro counsels Socrates not to give any thought to the charges but to confront his accusers. That is what Socrates did—and he was convicted and killed as a result.

Euthyphro emphasizes the ways in which he and Socrates are similar— both are religious innovators—but Socrates immediately distances himself. He characteristically states that he does not mind being laughed at. Unlike Euthyphro, moreover, Socrates does not think the Athenians care whether someone is clever; he supposes that their *thymos* is aroused only by someone they believe able to make others like him. As we have learned from the *Symposium*, however, that is exactly what Socrates has been trying to do. He has been attempting to persuade others, especially the young, to join him in philosophical investigations, as the only way of showing that

---

42. Socrates' restatement of the charges in the *Euthyphro* also differs from the account found in Xenophon's *Defense of Socrates before the Jury* 1–10, which is usually considered to be the closest to the actual indictment in fact.

the philosophical life is not only the best—the happiest and most self-suf-ficient—but also the truest. Socrates is not sure that the antagonism others feel toward such teachers is merely a matter of envy, as Euthyphro claims. Like the poet Aristophanes, whom he calls his old accuser in the *Apology*, Plato's Socrates recognizes that fathers resent not merely the challenge to their authority but the alienation of the affection of their progeny that results from a philosophical education (cf. *Apology* 23c–e). He politely sug-gests that Euthyphro may have avoided arousing anger and been assailed only with laughter, because the diviner has made himself available only infrequently and has not been willing to teach his own wisdom. Because of his own "philanthropy," many people believe that Socrates tells everything he knows to anyone willing to listen, for the sheer pleasure of it, without being paid.[43]

C. Socrates' Admission of Guilt

Socrates is amazed when he hears that Euthyphro is prosecuting his own father for murder. Euthyphro must have precise knowledge about the di-vine to be certain that he is not acting impiously! Socrates wants, therefore, to become Euthyphro's student. Appearing to be anything but courageous and something of an opportunist, Socrates begs Euthyphro to teach him about the divine things. If Meletus persists in accusing Socrates of making innovations concerning the divine things, Socrates can then tell him to charge his teacher instead, "on the ground that he is corrupting the old, me and his own father, by teaching me and by admonishing and punishing him" (*Euthyphro* 5b). Meletus has charged Socrates with the crime of "mak-ing new gods," but, Socrates suggests, it is Euthyphro who is innovating.

In prosecuting his own father, Euthyphro certainly appears to be acting not merely unconventionally but impiously. Yet, Euthyphro claims, he is acting according to the law. "People believe that Zeus is the best and most just of the gods, even though they agree that he bound his own father, because he gulped down his sons without justice, and that the latter, in

---

43. As Leo Strauss points out, Socrates does not admit that he does, in fact, say everything he knows to everyone who wants to listen. Nor does Plato show him doing so. On the contrary, Plato's Socrates is famous for arguing ad hominem. In the dialogues, he is never shown conversing with others in the marketplace, as he claims he often does in the *Apology*. On the contrary, he is shown speaking to particular individuals in private, sometimes as a result of his own choice, but sometimes as a result of their specifically seeking him out. In this case, the conversation is forced on Socrates, who tries to help Euthyphro by convincing him not to sue his father. Strauss, "On the *Euthyphron*," 204–6.

turn, castrated his own father because of other such things" (5e–6a). The Athenians contradict themselves, the diviner charges, when they get angry at him for proceeding against his father. Since his father has done him an injustice, his father should be punished. Like Zeus, Euthyphro is seeking to see that his father receives his due. Like Socrates, it seems, the diviner is trying to make the opinions of the Athenians, if not the Greeks as a whole, consistent. The philosopher and the diviner appear to be more similar than Socrates would like to admit.

In response to Euthyphro's "proof," Socrates distances himself from the seer again by observing that he always gets annoyed when people say things like this about the gods. As he explains later (7c–d), the stories about the gods' quarreling suggest that the gods do not agree about what is just and unjust, noble and base, good and bad, and thus that the gods do not know any more or better than the humans who also disagree about these things. If gods are no better than human beings, they do not deserve to be worshiped. Yet, Socrates points out (6b–d), the stories about the war among the gods are depicted on public monuments and literally woven into the robe carried in the procession in the most important Athenian civic celebration, the Great Panathenaea. Although he explicitly claims not to know anything about the gods (6b), in objecting to these stories Socrates admits that he does not believe in the gods of the city.

In the *Euthyphro* Socrates appears to be guilty as charged in the *Apology*, at least with regard to his lack of belief in the gods of the city. It is not clear that he has introduced a new god by referring to his *daimonion* or that he corrupts the young. On the contrary, Euthyphro's accusation of his father suggests that the young have been led to turn against their elders and thus perhaps corrupted more by the old beliefs and stories than by Socratic philosophy.

D. Euthyphro's Purported Knowledge

Euthyphro's account of the facts of the case he is prosecuting makes the justice of his cause and thus the knowledge on which it is purportedly based look highly questionable. The man he has accused his father of murdering was a laborer hired by Euthyphro. In a drunken fit, this laborer got angry with one of the family servants and cut his throat. Euthyphro's father bound the murderer's hands and feet together, threw him into a ditch, and sent a messenger to an exegete to find out what they should do next; the hired man, however, died as a result of hunger, the cold, and his bonds before the messenger returned. At most, Euthyphro's father appears to be guilty of manslaughter. As Socrates reminds Euthyphro, moreover, under Athenian law, members of the victim's family were expected to bring changes against a murderer, not relatives of the person accused of the crime.[44]

"It's laughable that you suppose that it makes any difference whether the dead man is an outsider or of the family," Euthyphro responds. "One should keep watch only to determine whether the killer killed with justice or not." Euthyphro is trying to make Athenian law more impersonal and thus more logical and consistent. Switching from criminal to religious law, he points out that "the pollution is equal if you knowingly associate with such a man and do not purify yourself, as well as him, by proceeding against him in a lawsuit" (4b). Euthyphro begins from the old stories, but he tries to apply them and their lessons uniformly. In response to Socrates' questioning, he insists, however much gods and human beings may disagree about what is good, just, or noble, they all agree that it is just to punish a wrongdoer. Euthyphro understands the law and justice to consist in rules of behavior to which everyone agrees and to which everyone is, therefore, subject. In this respect he is more like a rationalist philosopher than an advocate of piety, traditionally understood.

E. Socrates' Examination of Euthyphro's Piety

By pointing out the problematic character and results of the poetic stories about the gods on which Euthyphro relies, Socrates reveals the problematic character not merely of the diviner's admittedly idiosyncratic understanding of justice and piety, but of the understanding of the gods and the way in which human beings are related to them that was characteristic of ancient Greece as a whole. Because his views are derived, rationally and logically, from the traditional stories, Euthyphro's inability to give a satisfactory definition of piety shows that the traditional understanding of the gods in ancient Greece was not and could not be made to be logically

---

44. On the relevant Athenian laws (which were carried over into Magnesia and made more consistent by the Athenian Stranger in the *Laws*, book 9), see Arlene Saxonhouse, "The Philosophy of the Particular and the Universality of the City: Socrates' Education of Euthyphro," *Political Theory* 16 (May 1988): 287. The fact that Socrates has to explain the difference between a *graphē* and a *dikē* to Euthyphro at the beginning of the dialogue suggests that Euthyphro did not know Athenian law very well.

consistent. The contradictions in the traditional views did not lie, however, where Euthyphro thinks.

Although Euthyphro offers to tell him many other wonderful things about the divine, Socrates presses him on a single question: what is pious? Socrates wants to learn what the *eidos* (*Euthyphro* 6d) or *idea* (6e) of the pious is, that is, what makes pious things pious, so that he can use the *idea* as a pattern (*paradeigma*) to determine whether what Euthyphro or anyone else is doing is like it, and thus pious or not. Euthyphro's first and most revealing response to Socrates' request had been that "the pious is just what I am doing now: proceeding against whoever does injustice regarding murders or thefts of sacred things, or is doing wrong in any other such thing, whether he happens to be a father or mother or anyone else at all; and not to proceed against him is impious" (5d–e). Pressed by Socrates to give a definition rather than an example, Euthyphro could have said simply that it is impious not to prosecute anyone who has committed a serious crime. Not seeing or at least not willing to admit that he conflates piety and justice, Euthyphro says, instead, that the pious is what is dear to the gods. Socrates objects that if the gods quarrel, they are not apt to hold the same things dear, and Euthyphro responds that the gods do not disagree on the proposition that anyone who acts unjustly should be punished. Neither do human beings who bring cases to court, Socrates counters; what they disagree about is what is just or unjust. He thus challenges Euthyphro to prove that the gods believe that his own case is just.

Although Euthyphro would have to give the argument Socrates requests in court in order to prosecute his father, he declines to do so, not because he is unable to give such a proof but because it would be "no small work." Wryly commenting that Euthyphro thinks him less able or quick at learning than most other potential Athenian jurors, Socrates admits that Euthyphro's demonstration that his own case is just would not tell Socrates what is pious. When Socrates reiterates his question, and Euthyphro repeats his answer that the pious is what is dear to the gods, Socrates points out an ambiguity. According to this definition, things may be pious because they are dear to the gods, or they may be dear to the gods because they are pious. Euthyphro does not perceive the problem, so Socrates contrasts a series of things acted upon (carried, led, or loved) with those that act upon them (by carrying, leading, or loving). If things are said to be pious because they are dear to the gods, we see, there cannot be anything that is pious in itself (or an "idea" of piety), not merely because various gods may hold different things dear but more fundamentally because the pious character of things would be a product of an affect (*pathos*) produced by something else. Piety would not be an inherent quality of things in themselves.

If things dear to the gods are pious, Socrates concludes, these things must then be dear to the gods because they are pious. He thus asks Euthyphro once more what the pious is. Euthyphro balks. He is not able to tell Socrates what he means because Socrates seems to make whatever he says go around in circles. Denying that he does so intentionally, Socrates offers a suggestion: doesn't Euthyphro think that the pious is the just? Although we have seen there is a great deal of evidence that Euthyphro does believe that the pious is the just, he doesn't understand the question. He does not understand, we see in the exchange that follows, because, like other ancient Greeks who accepted the traditional stories, Euthyphro holds two contradictory views about the gods without seeing the contradiction between them.

On the one hand, Euthyphro believes that the gods think that criminals should be punished. If piety consists in doing what is dear or pleasing to the gods, piety then consists in doing justice. On the other hand, when Socrates asks Euthyphro whether the just is the pious, or whether the pious is only a part of the just, Euthyphro affirms the latter. He says that piety consists in knowing how to tend the gods, that is, "how to say and do things gratifying to the gods by praying and sacrificing" (14b). In that case, Socrates comments, piety consists in a kind of exchange. Human beings try to give the gods what is pleasing to them, so that the gods will grant us what we need or want. Since the gods do not need and cannot be benefited by anything from us, but we desperately need their protection and assistance, the exchange would not appear to be just.

F. Socrates' Attempt to Moderate and So Benefit Euthyphro

The contradiction between the belief that the gods support the enforcement of justice and the belief that the gods can be bribed or cajoled into favoring particular human beings or communities was not peculiar to Euthyphro. On the contrary, Euthyphro reminds Socrates, the ancient Greeks generally regarded Zeus as the best and most just of the gods; he was thought to use his powerful thunderbolts to punish the guilty. In the *Clouds* Aristophanes had criticized Socrates for denying that Zeus is a god and trying to introduce worship of the clouds instead, precisely because Zeus was believed to care about the enforcement of justice, whereas the goddesses of the poets and sophists cared only about images. As Socrates reminded us with his reference to the Great Panathenaea, like most other ancient Greeks, his fellow Athenians held public festivals not merely as expressions of gratitude to the gods for establishing and preserving the city and its laws, but to beseech the gods, especially their particular civic patrons, to favor them.

As Socrates indicates when he says that he disagrees with the poet who said "where dread is, there too is awe" (*Euthyphro* 12b), gods who saw that justice was done would not merely be feared; they would be revered. If the gods reliably and obviously ensured the existence of a just order among human beings, justice and piety would be the same. Human beings would not merely dread the gods' disapproval and punishment, if they acted unjustly; humans would also have reason to thank such divinities for establishing and preserving a just order on earth. Human beings might express their gratitude in public ceremonies, sacrifices, and hymns of praise.[45] They might recognize their dependence on the gods by praying to them, but human beings could not rationally or piously ask such just or avenging gods for special favors, even mercy, because they would be asking the just gods to be unjust.

As Socrates hints when he observes that human beings dread poverty, disease, and many other bad things without being in awe of them, human beings do not only fear punishment. We are afraid of many kinds of disasters, for example, famine or defeat in war, the causes of which we do not know and the effects of which are beyond our control. We thus pray to intelligent beings with superhuman powers, to the gods, to protect and preserve us. Precisely because we believe that they are better and more powerful than we, we do not believe that we can benefit them with our gifts or praise. At most we may honor them by recognizing our own dependency and inferiority.

If Euthyphro recognized the necessarily limited and hence uncertain character of his own mortal knowledge, Socrates suggests, he would not persist in his prosecution of his father. Admitting his own lack of knowledge like Socrates, Euthyphro would seek to discover what is just and pious so that he could have become as much like a god as a human being can by becoming as just and pious as possible (cf. *Theaetetus* 176b). But

---

45. In the *Republic* 607a, the only kind of poetry Socrates says would be allowed in their city consists of hymns to the gods or celebrations of good men.

when Socrates urges Euthyphro to reopen the question at the end of their conversation, Euthyphro refuses. Although he was waiting to bring his case at the beginning of the conversation, he now says that he is in a hurry to go somewhere else. It is not clear whether he will return to the porch of the king to press charges against his father or not.

Because Euthyphro's claims to know the divine things appear to be so ridiculous by the end of the dialogue, it looks as if the main point of the *Euthyphro* is to show how Socrates tried to dissuade the young diviner from bringing the case against his father by showing Euthyphro what he does not know and so to moderate and benefit him.[46] The parallel between the action and the lesson of the *Theaetetus* and the *Euthyphro* is clear. Although Socrates emphasizes his own lack of wisdom in both of these dialogues, he is able (or at least tries) to benefit his young interlocutors by demonstrating that they do not know what they think they do.

G. The Broader Problem of Piety

The practical "lesson" of both the *Theaetetus* and the *Euthyphro* is the same: people who recognize their own lack of knowledge will be more virtuous, moderate, and courageous than people who believe they know what they do not. It would be a mistake, however, to emphasize the common lesson and ignore the larger issue that emerges in the exchange between Socrates and Euthyphro.

In bringing out the contradictions in Euthyphro's opinion about the pious, Socrates points to the ways in which the stories about the gods accepted by most of the ancient Greeks gave rise to two of the three kinds of impiety the Athenian Stranger warned against in the *Laws*. Zeus was said to punish wrongdoers. If he did not punish them directly, he was supposed to have established and supported governments that did. When people saw injustice go unpunished, they began to wonder, therefore, whether the gods existed. Or, if the gods existed, people began to wonder whether the gods cared about human beings, particularly whether humans were

---

46. Cf. Strauss, "On the *Euthyphron*," 190, 196; and Bruell, *Socratic Education*, 117–33. Both authors conclude that Euthyphro was too stupid to benefit from his conversation with Socrates. Saxonhouse ("Philosophy of the Particular," 285–91) leaves the question open as to whether Euthyphro learned from the conversation. Jan Blits, "The Holy and the Human: An Interpretation of Plato's *Euthyphro*," *Apeiron* 14 (1980), observes: "Since we are never told whether Euthyphro has already seen the king or, like Socrates, is waiting to do so, the extent of Socrates' success in dissuading him must remain conjectural" (36).

justly treated or not. The traditional practice of sacrificing and praying to gods to favor particular people augmented the suspicion that the gods did not really care about seeing justice done. These practices suggested that the gods were not just, because they could, in effect, be bribed.

Neither Socrates nor Euthyphro mentions the third source of impiety with which the Athenian Stranger was most concerned—the cosmological philosophy that maintains that everything is fundamentally a product of chance, and that justice and the gods are therefore merely matters of convention. In his *Apology*, Socrates will suggest that he was accused of impiety because most of his fellow citizens could not distinguish him from earlier cosmological philosophers. But in the conversation that precedes Socrates' trial as related in the *Euthyphro*, Plato indicates that natural philosophy is neither so common nor so powerful a source of impiety as the desire for justice. The Socrates who talks to Euthyphro is not a natural philosopher. Neither he nor Euthyphro questions the existence, the beneficence, or even the intelligibility of the gods. On the contrary, Euthyphro insists that in seeking to do justice, he is doing what is dear to the gods. Insofar as he wants to act as the gods do, Euthyphro impiously ignores the essential difference between immortal and mortal beings. Claiming that he does not know what is just or pious, Socrates appears to be much more pious than Euthyphro when he asserts that the gods are the source of all good things. But the question that arises with regard to the "theology" Socrates proposes to Adimantus in the *Republic* arises in the *Euthyphro* as well. Could gods who are completely beneficent and intelligible also care for human beings or see that justice is done? Such gods could punish human beings because punishment can be beneficial, even if the recipients do not admit that or want it. Purely beneficent, intelligible gods could inflict pain and use force.[47] But would the transitory affairs of mortals be worthy of the attention of immortals? Plato raises the same question in an exchange between the Athenian and Megillus in the *Laws* (803c–4b). In the absence of direct divine action on behalf of justice, good and intelligible gods might provide a basis on which human beings could erect a just regime, if humans were able to know what is good and purely intelligible. Socrates repeatedly emphasizes the desire human beings share to obtain

47. Some commentators on the *Republic* have suggested that such gods could not rule, because Socrates later admits that (human) rulers have to lie. It is not clear to this reader that completely intelligible immortal forces or beings would have to deceive human beings in order to control human action—certainly in the long run. Mortal beings and actions could not negate or escape immortal, unchanging rules or laws.

such knowledge, but he also repeatedly suggests that it is impossible for mortal beings to acquire and retain it. If so, human beings will continue to desire justice—as one of the good things—but will not be able to achieve it. One of the strongest human desires, a desire that gives rise both to piety and to impiety, will remain unsatisfied.

III. *Cratylus*: What Words Cannot Tell Us

A. The Importance of the Dramatic Date

In contrast to the explicit link between the end of the *Theaetetus* and the beginning of the *Euthyphro*, the dramatic connection between the *Euthyphro* and *Cratylus* is not made clear at the end of the former or the beginning of the latter. Only after Socrates has begun "to utter oracles like an inspired prophet" in explaining the giving of names by poets does he say that Euthyphro is the cause, "for he had been with and listened to [the diviner] for a long time early that morning" (*Cratylus* 396d).

Although Socrates refers to the inspiration he has taken from Euthyphro three more times in the *Cratylus* (399a, 400a, 409d), many commentators dismiss the apparent dramatic connection.[48] Some argue that it would be impossible for Socrates to have had the conversations related in the *Theaetetus*, *Euthyphro*, and *Cratylus* in a single morning.[49] Others insist that Euthyphro had not said enough to have inspired Socrates, even ironically,

48. John Sallis is a notable exception. In *Being and Logos* he observes: "We are, of course, not told explicitly that this conversation is the same as the one present in the dialogue *Euthyphro*. . . . But if we attend to the *Euthyphro* and to the basic connection of its problematic to that of the *Cratylus*, there can be no question. . . . The connection becomes still more evident and more significant if the portrait of Euthyphro provided by the discussion itself is recalled. . . . Earlier on the same day as the conversation presented in the *Cratylus*, there occurs the conversation with Euthyphro presented in the dialogue so named; . . . and the dialogue concludes by ironically linking that knowledge of divine things which Euthyphro claims with the charge being brought against Socrates regarding his relation to the gods (15e–16a). The conversation presented in the *Sophist* occurs on the following day. In turn, the conversation in the Sophist is designated as a continuation of the conversation of the day before—presented in the *Theaetetus*—which Socrates had with Theaetetus 'shortly before his own death' (*Theaet.* 142c) and which concludes with Socrates' going off to the magistrate's for the hearing regarding the writ filed against him by Meletus while, at the same time, promising Theodorus that they will continue the conversation on the following day (210d). Thus, the conversation presented in the *Theaetetus* occurs still earlier on the same day as that reported in the *Euthyphro*. Therefore, the conversations presented in the *Theaetetus*, the *Euthyphro*, and the *Cratylus* all have as their dramatic date the day of Socrates' hearing before the magistrate" (228–30).

49. J. V. Luce, "The Date of the *Cratylus*," *American Journal of Philology* 85 (1964): 138–39; and G. E. L. Owen, manuscript, cited in Timothy M. S. Baxter, *The "Cratylus": Plato's Critique of Naming* (Leiden: E. J. Brill, 1992), 28.

in the *Euthyphro*.[50] Still others point out that Hipponicus II (d. 420) must still be alive, because his son Hermogenes is said not to have control of his patrimony (although Hermogenes' brother Callias is said to have plenty of money to spend on sophists and so appears to have control of the family fortune).[51] Most commonly, however, commentators suggest that the conversation related in the *Cratylus* had to have taken place before 399, if Plato learned about Heraclitus from Cratylus before he became a student of Socrates, as Aristotle states (*Metaphysics* 987a32–b1).[52]

It may not have been possible for Socrates actually to have had these three conversations in a single morning, but, as I argued earlier, Plato gives his readers plenty of reasons to see that the dialogues are not literal reports of actual historical events. He uses dramatic dates to indicate connections, particularly the sequence in which the dialogues should be imagined to have taken place. Socrates' claim to have been "inspired" by Euthyphro should warn readers not to take the "etymologies" altogether seriously. Plato could have juxtaposed Cratylus and Socrates simply to show why he thought the latter articulated a superior understanding.

Many commentators not merely refuse to credit the dramatic connection between the *Cratylus* and the *Euthyphro*. They also fail to notice that Socrates disowns the fanciful etymologies he gives in the *Cratylus* by describing them as an inspiration from Euthyphro. These commentators inquire about the theory of naming that "Plato" may be putting forward, without taking account of the fact that Plato attributes the arguments to Socrates or, even more saliently, that Socrates explicitly describes the etymologies he gives as the "inspiration" of a foolish, hubristic diviner, from which he says he will

50. Nails, *People*, 153.

51. Ibid., 163. Admitting that Xenophon depicts Hermogenes as impoverished, Nails argues that a man who talks about the way slaves are named (*Cratylus* 384d) does not sound poor. But having grown up in a wealthy household, Hermogenes would know how slaves are treated, even if he did not inherit.

52. John Burnet gives the dramatic date of the *Cratylus* as 399 BCE, but Taylor (*Plato*, 76) concludes, on the basis of a reference to "curfew regulations" in Aegina at 433c, that the dramatic date was not long after the Athenian military occupation of the island and that Socrates was thus in his forties. Nails (*People*, 106) finds Taylor's dating plausible because Plato could then have encountered Cratylus before he became an associate of Socrates. Having said that Plato learned about flux theory insofar as it concerned sensibles in his *Metaphysics* at 987a–b, Aristotle reports at 1010a7–15 that Cratylus later declared, radicalizing Heraclitus' famous statement, that it is not possible to step into the same river even once, and that he came to believe on Heraclitean grounds that it is not possible to speak at all. D. J. Allan, "The Problem of *Cratylus*," *American Journal of Philology* 75 (1954): 271–87, argues, however, that Plato could have depicted Cratylus as a young man in 399, whose thought later developed into the radical skepticism Aristotle also notes. Allan also points out that Aristotle did not say that Plato was a pupil of Cratylus; at 987a he merely said that Plato was *synēthēs* (familiar with) Cratylus.

need to be purged the next day.[53] Such commentators not merely miss the humor. They fail to see the way in which the *Cratylus* is linked, thematically as well as dramatically, to the *Theaetetus* and *Sophist*.[54] Nor do they see the way the three distinct sections of the *Cratylus* form one sustained line of argument.[55] That argument does not consist in a "theory of naming" so much as a showing that names are merely tools to be used in discovering the different kinds of beings. Names or words (*onomata*) do not directly reveal or image the character of specific beings or their interrelations any more than numbers do. In the *Cratylus* Plato thus completes the defense he began in the *Theaetetus* of Socrates' claim to be the wisest human being, because he knows that he does not know, by showing the problematic character of the access human beings have to the intelligible character and order of things.

B. The Dramatic Introduction and Statement of the Problem

Hermogenes begins the dialogue by asking Cratylus' permission to invite Socrates to join their discussion. For Hermogenes, it seems, the agree-

---

53. Sedley (*Cratylus*) argues against a dramatic reading of the dialogues in terms of characters (much less plots or settings) on the grounds that the dialogue form merely represents Plato's thinking, the kind of internal thinking as conversing that he describes in "late" dialogues such as the *Theaetetus* and *Sophist*. Sedley does not take account of the fact that "Plato" presents thinking in these dialogues as an internal conversation; he does not present an interpersonal conversation as a representation of internal thinking. Nor does he pay attention to the one dialogue (*Hippias Major*) in which Socrates in effect converses with himself as a character. Plato could have written a dialogue of a philosopher with himself if he had wanted. Instead he showed specific philosophers in conversation with specific others. Rachel Barney, *Names and Nature in Plato's "Cratylus"* (New York: Routledge, 2001), observes that the attributions of the etymological speeches to Euthyphro "suggest that the real function of the genre of inspiration is . . . to distance the contents presented from the figure of Socrates" (58). But she does not think the dialogue form should prevent us from talking about "Plato's" argument. Other scholars who treat the *Cratylus* as presenting "Plato's" theory include Charles H. Kahn, "Language and Ontology in the *Cratylus*," in Lee, Mourelatos, and Rorty, *Exegesis and Argument*; and Julia Annas, "Knowledge and Language: The *Theaetetus* and the *Cratylus*," in *Language and Logos*, ed. Malcolm Schofield and Martha Craven Nussbaum, 95–114 (Cambridge: Cambridge University Press, 1982). Malcolm Schofield, in "Denouement of the *Cratylus*," on the other hand, writes about Socrates' argument and "Plato's authorial strategy" (65), as does Bernard Williams in his account titled "Cratylus' Theory of Names and Its Refutation." Both are found in Schofield and Nussbaum, *Language and Logos*, 61–81 and 83–93, respectively.

54. Allan, in "Problem of *Cratylus*," does.

55. For example, even though Mary Margaret Mackenzie, "Putting the *Cratylus* in Its Place," *Classical Quarterly* 36, no. 1 (1986): 124–50, brings out the thematic connections between Socrates' argument with Hermogenes in the first part of the dialogue and the *Theaetetus* as well as between Socrates' critique of Cratylus in the third part and the argument of the *Sophist*, she entirely neglects the long central etymological section. So, to a considerable extent, do Georgios Anagnostopoulos, "The Significance of Plato's *Cratylus*," *Review of Metaphysics* 27 (1973): 318–45; and Rudolph Weingartner, "Making Sense of the *Cratylus*," *Phronesis* 15 (1970): 5–25, even though both argue that the dialogue is united by a single argument concerning the correctness of names.

ment of others constitutes a necessary if not the highest form of authority. We are not surprised to learn, therefore, that Hermogenes believes that "the correctness of names is determined by convention" (*Cratylus* 384c). Cratylus, however, is indifferent to the participants or results of the discussion. He tells Hermogenes to do as he pleases. Cratylus not merely thinks "that there is a correctness of name for each thing, one that belongs to it by nature, . . . which is the same for everyone, Greek or foreigner" (383a–b). He also claims to know what the correct names of things are. In response to questions from Hermogenes, Cratylus affirms that he himself and Socrates are both truly named. But Cratylus does not think that his knowledge of correct names requires conversations with, much less the agreement of, others. Hermogenes complains that Cratylus treats him ironically. Cratylus claims to possess some private knowledge that would force Hermogenes to agree with him, if Cratylus were to state it clearly, but Cratylus refuses to tell Hermogenes how he knows that things have correct names by nature. Cratylus is not even willing to explain why he says that Hermogenes is not his interlocutor's true name, even if that is what people call him. Hermogenes thus asks Socrates to "interpret Cratylus' oracular utterances," or, even better, to say what he himself thinks about the correctness of names.

Characteristically denying that he knows, Socrates agrees to investigate the correctness of names with Hermogenes, whom he identifies as the "son of Hipponicus."[56] As we saw in the *Theaetetus*, Socrates thinks a person's parents or origins have as much if not more to do with who or what he is than his name. By saying that Hermogenes could have learned about the correctness of names directly, if he had taken Prodicus' fifty-drachma course, Socrates reminds us that the correctness of names was a question of concern particularly to this sophist.[57] Socrates thus gives us two reasons to suspect at the very beginning of the conversation that he does not think that there are correct names for things by nature or that this is a profitable subject of inquiry. We should not be surprised to discover in the course of the conversation that Socrates does not agree with either Hermogenes or Cratylus. Names are not simply conventional, Socrates first points out in a critique of Hermogenes' thesis, if names refer to distinct things that really

---

56. Toward the end of the dialogue, he thus distinguishes Cratylus from Hermogenes as a "son of Smicrion." We are also reminded that Socrates knew who Theaetetus' father was, even though he did not know the youth's name.

57. In the *Protagoras* (339a–42a) Socrates gently mocked Prodicus' emphasis on the precise definition and use of words.

and always are. But, Socrates then shows in a long series of etymologies as well as in his final exchange with Cratylus, names do not disclose the character of things.

Why, then, does Socrates agree to join an inquiry into the correctness of names with Hermogenes and Cratylus? There appear to be two reasons, corresponding to the two characters. First, although Hermogenes shows himself to be a collector of opinions and speeches like Meno, Hermogenes is not a pretty boy who expects to be flattered. On the contrary, he wants to hear the argument that opposes his own beliefs. He is, in other words, a potential if not yet a true philosopher. And his lack of wealth has prevented him from coming under the influence of the sophists, as his brother Callias has.[58] Nor does Hermogenes, like many of Socrates' other interlocutors, appear to desire political power and preeminence. As we first encounter him, Hermogenes wants but does not know how to seek wisdom. His complaint against Cratylus shows that Hermogenes perceives the connection between justice and the sharing of wisdom. But at the beginning of the dialogue, Hermogenes shows himself to be too concerned about what other people say—their opinions as well as their arguments.[59] Socrates has to show him that it does not suffice merely to collect all relevant arguments; it is necessary to examine the reasons given for different claims and to develop the best possible case for the alternative to one's own, before one critiques it. There is evidence that Hermogenes absorbed at least part of the lesson. Although he accompanies Cratylus part of the way on his trip into the country at the end of this dialogue, we know from the *Phaedo* that Hermogenes (unlike Theaetetus or Euthyphro) returns and becomes a close companion of Socrates.[60] He seems to have learned the value of Socratic philosophy.

Whereas Hermogenes shows himself to be a potential seeker of knowledge, Cratylus demonstrates that the problematic character of claims to

58. As Socrates observes later (391b–c), Hermogenes' brother Callias paid a great deal of money to the sophists for lessons. His patronage of the sophists was indeed notorious. Cf. *Protagoras* 314c–15e; *Apology* 20a. Like Theages' sickness, Hippocrates' poverty appears to have saved him for philosophy. Socrates does not try to "marry" him to Prodicus, even for the one-drachma course, as he says in the *Theaetetus* he did youths whom he did not think would benefit from associating with him.

59. Parmenides faulted the young Socrates, however, for the very same trait.

60. By presenting Hermogenes as one who accompanies (and so plays the role of Hermes), Barney (*Names*, 160), Sedley (*Cratylus*, 156), and C. D. C. Reeve in his translation of *Cratylus*, in Cooper, *Plato: Complete Works*, 156n65, point out that Socrates suggests, at the very end of the dialogue, contrary to Cratylus' initial claim, that Hermogenes may have been correctly named after all.

wisdom is not explicated and supported by arguments. Like Euthyphro's "divinations," Cratylus' wisdom is less original and unconventional than he thinks; like Euthyphro's divinations, Socrates indicates in his "etymologies," the wisdom Cratylus claims to possess is based on the inspired works of the poets. Further, like Euthyphro's divinations, Socrates shows in the end, Cratylus' position is contradictory. Cratylus does not recognize the problematic character of his own claim to know the true names of things (and hence the things themselves), ironically, because he is not willing to communicate and consequently to subject his "wisdom" to the questions of others. The refusal of the knower of words to use words is a major part of the obvious humor of the dialogue. In depicting the refutation of Cratylus, Plato nevertheless presents an important justification for Socratic investigations: there is no such thing as unexamined wisdom.

C. Socrates' Critique of Hermogenes' Conventionalism

Cratylus was probably making fun of him, Socrates suggests, when he said that Hermogenes was incorrectly named. Unable to make money, Hermogenes has shown that he is not kin to the patron deity of traders and bankers. Humorous or not, the question of the correctness of Hermogenes' name points to a difference in the use of names that Hermogenes ignores when he maintains that all names exist merely by convention. As a proper name, "Hermogenes" refers to an individual. Just as masters have the power to call their slaves whatever they please, Hermogenes claims, so people generally can call anything whatever they want, so long as they abide by the same habits and customs.[61] If "Hermogenes" is taken to refer to a relative of the god Hermes, however, the name refers to a certain type of person. Socrates shows that he recognizes the difference between names understood to be arbitrary marks assigned to things by their private owners and publicly recognized signs denoting types of things, as well as the fact that the power of individuals to name things in their own households is supported, if not granted by law, by asking Hermogenes if it makes any difference whether the name is given by a private person or public authority. Hermogenes says that it does not, and Socrates observes that different

---

61. In arguing that Hermogenes represents a very unconventional "conventionalist" insofar as he insists that individuals can have their own private names for things, Weingartner ("Making Sense") ignores the fact both that slaves become slaves and that masters acquire the right to name them by convention.

people call the same thing by different names. To name it correctly, even if they use different words to do so, they still have to perceive the same thing. It does not make a difference what we call something, that is, the specific sound, sign, or name; it does, however, make a difference what "something" we are referring to with the name, that is, whether we are perceiving and denoting the same type or particular thing.

Speeches and words can be true or false only if they correspond (or fail to correspond) to things that are (or are not). That is why Socrates next asks Hermogenes whether he thinks that speeches, and then the words of which speeches are composed, can be true or false.[62] Emphasizing the fact that different individuals, like different peoples using different languages, call the same thing by a variety of names, Hermogenes reiterates his conviction that names are entirely conventional and not at all natural. Since Hermogenes also observes that names or the meaning of words tend to change over time, Socrates asks Hermogenes whether he agrees with Protagoras' contention that things are for each as they appear to each (and thus can presumably be named by each to reflect what he or she sees at that moment). Hermogenes says that he does not, even though he admits he has at times been tempted to agree with Protagoras, and Socrates has grounds to believe that he will be able to free Hermogenes from his conventionalism. He thus asks Hermogenes whether he also disagrees with Euthydemus' suggestion that if anything shares in a characteristic (for example, knowing), everything has to share it (because it is impossible simultaneously to claim that something is known and not known without contradicting oneself; cf. *Euthydemus* 293b–96d).[63] If Hermogenes thinks, in opposition to both sophists, that things (or literally "beings," *onta*) have distinct forms that persist over time, independent of the perceiver (or namer), he will see the necessity of knowing what the enduring kinds of things are in order to name them correctly—in Greek or any other, "barbarian" language. If the function of language is to indicate things, as the conventionalist thesis suggests, language cannot be entirely conventional. On the contrary, if there are distinctive kinds of things, various words serve more or less well to distinguish and mark them.

62. Like Mackenzie ("Place," 127n7), I do not agree with Malcolm Schofield, "A Displacement in the Text of the *Cratylus*," *Classical Quarterly* 22 (1972): 246–53, who argues that this section of the text is misplaced. Socrates commits what is often called a fallacy of composition in affirming that the parts must all share in a characteristic of the whole.

63. On the basis of a similar argument, Euthydemus' brother Dionysodorus had argued earlier that there is no such thing as false speech, because "no one speaks what is not" (*Euthydemus* 285d–86b).

If "things" have distinct natures, Socrates argues, the best names are those that best indicate these distinctive natures and so enable people to see and distinguish them.[64] And if things are distinct by nature, the actions or practices (*praxeis*) of these things must also be naturally distinct. Some practices require tools as well as materials on which to work; for these practices, the best tools, like the best materials, will be those most suited to the nature of the practice. Speaking is a kind of practice, of which naming is a part. Names are tools that enable teachers to separate things according to their distinctive natures and to teach others, but all names do not do this equally well. Contrary to Hermogenes' initial claim, everyone does not have the ability to name anything as he or she pleases in private. If names are to be used to teach others the distinctive natures of things, the name-maker must act as a kind of legislator in public. This legislating name-maker will perform his task well, moreover, only if he knows how to put what each of the beings is by nature into syllables and sounds, so that it will be easily recognized by others. Speaking different languages, legislating name-makers will use somewhat different syllables or sounds. Which are the best, true, and correct names can only be determined by a person who knows how to ask and answer questions in order to determine the distinctive natures of things by sorting them, that is, by a dialectician (*dialektikos*).

Because Socrates' reference to a name-making legislator is followed by an attempt to get back to the original form and meaning of words in the etymological section, some commentators conclude that the *Cratylus* represents a Platonic investigation of the origin of language.[65] Socrates' statement that a dialectician should judge whether names are correct shows, however, that this cannot be the case. Presupposing recognition of the enduring existence of essentially different kinds of things, dialectical philosophy was a relatively recent development. Plato shows that it began with Socrates' articulation of his argument about the ideas as a young man, in

---

64. Socrates speaks both of the *pragmata*, "things" particularly of concern to us, and the beings, *onta*, themselves. As Seth Benardete points out in "Physics and Tragedy: On Plato's *Cratylus*" (in *Argument of the Action*, 146–66), human beings are most apt to name the *pragmata* with which they are concerned, that is, not to name the whole range of beings per se. If so, names are less extensive than being or nature as a whole, even though proper names for individuals appear to be more numerous.

65. H. N. Fowler, trans., *Cratylus*, Loeb ed. (Cambridge: Harvard University Press, 1953), 4; Taylor, *Plato*, 78; Shorey, *What Plato Said*, 259; W. Lutoslawski, *The Origin and Growth of Plato's Logic* (London: Longmans, 1897), 228; U. Wilamowitz-Möllendorff, *Platon*, 1:220–29; and G. S. Kirk, "The Problem of *Cratylus*," *American Journal of Philology* 72 (1951): 22.

the *Parmenides* in approximately 450.[66] In the *Theaetetus* Socrates pointed out that all previous poets and philosophers except Parmenides had shown things in the world to be fundamentally in flux, and that even Parmenides had maintained that everything is one.[67] If everything is fundamentally the same, Socrates demonstrates in much greater detail in the "etymological" section of the *Cratylus*, distinctions among things in name must be basically arbitrary, conventional, and false. The fact that most if not all human beings speak languages in which they distinguish various kinds of things as well as people by name suggests, however, that they perceive enduring differences among things, even if they do not agree about what these differences are, much less on the names. To determine what the correct names of things are—or should be—Socrates argues here and reiterates at the end of the dialogue, it is necessary to determine what kinds of things there are, that is, to engage in dialectical investigations.

In his initial critique of Hermogenes' conventionalism, Socrates has merely shown, first, that the names used to signify various things cannot be simply private, if names are to be used to teach others. Second, the fact that various peoples use different names to signify different things, which Hermogenes emphasized, indicates that language is not purely or entirely conventional. On the contrary, it shows that different peoples in different places perceive enduring differences among things. The specific words they use to mark those differences may be more or less correct. But insofar as the use of different names indicates recognition of different kinds of things, Socrates concludes (*Cratylus* 391a), names have a certain (or some) correctness.

D. Socrates' Inquiry into the Correctness of Greek Names

In arguing that names or naming cannot be entirely conventional, Socrates had not shown that there are correct names for things, much less that names disclose the nature of things by means of their syllables and sounds.[68] Her-

66. Citing references elsewhere in the dialogues to the name-makers of old and thus taking Socrates to believe in the existence of such intentional wordsmiths or legislators, Sedley (*Cratylus*, 69) points out that the word "dialectics" does not appear before Plato. It does not appear because the phenomenon it names was not known.

67. Euthydemus' contention that if anything has a given characteristic, then everything must have it, represented an extension of Parmenides' argument.

68. For this reason commentators such as Baxter and Barney have concluded that the "theory of naming" that Socrates—or Plato—puts forward in the *Cratylus* is prescriptive rather than descriptive. I argue, on the contrary, that by the end of the dialogue, chiefly by means of the etymo-

mogenes admits that he cannot respond to Socrates' argument. But he is not entirely persuaded by it, so he asks Socrates to show him how names can be correct by nature. Socrates insists he has not said that he knows there are correct names for things by nature. He merely agrees, again, to inquire with Hermogenes whether there are correct names for things by nature.

1. The Poetic or "Inspired" Sources

Seeking someone who claims to know, Socrates again suggests that they consult the sophists.[69] But having stated his disagreement with Protagoras earlier, Hermogenes is emphatically not willing to beg his brother to tell him what Callias had learned from the lessons that he, unlike Hermogenes, was able to pay for. So Socrates suggests they consult the other professional wordsmiths, the poets. The first thing they learn from Homer is that he distinguishes between the names by which the gods and human beings call the same things. If the names the gods use are correct by nature, as Socrates and Hermogenes immediately agree (*Cratylus* 391e), the names humans use are wrong.

The three examples of differences between divine and human names in Homer that Socrates mentions all concern things human beings think are merely natural phenomena—a river, a bird, and a hill—which, we learn by checking the specific references to the *Iliad*, the gods know to be signs for something else—a god, sleep, and a tomb.[70] If the names of things the gods use are correct, the correct names of things point to kinds of beings that are not immediately or naturally observable, and so not nameable, by human beings (who are not, like the poets, inspired by the gods).

---

logical section, Socrates has shown, contrary to Cratylus, that there are not and cannot be simply correct names that tell us what the beings are, as well as having shown already that names are not entirely conventional.

69. Socrates' references to the sophists in general, and Prodicus in particular, as experts in the correct use of words are not altogether facetious. In the *Euthydemus* 277e, Socrates tells Clinias that he could have defended himself from refutation by the eristic sophists, who had played on the double meaning of words, if the young man had learned about the correct use of words (*peri onomatōn orthotētos mathein*) from Prodicus.

70. At *Cratylus* 391e Socrates observes that, according to Homer (*Iliad* 21.332–80), the Trojan river that had single combat with Hephaestus is "called 'Xanthos' by the gods and 'Skamandros' by men." Then at 392a Socrates quotes Homer's statement (*Iliad* 14.291) that "the gods call it 'chalcis' but men call it 'cymindis.'" (Benardete ["Physics," 153] points out that the "bird" the gods call *chalkis* and men call *kumindis* [*Iliad* 14.289–91] is actually "Sleep," which Hera uses to deceive Zeus.) Finally, referring to *Iliad* 2.813ff., Socrates asks Hermogenes whether it is more correct to call a certain hill Bateia (the Hill of the Thicket), as men do, or the burial mound of dancing Myrina (Murine), as the gods do.

Socrates' demonstration to Hermogenes (and Plato's readers) that if there are correct names for things by nature then we do not yet have them, proceeds in stages. Admittedly lacking the kind of insight the gods have into the true nature of things, Socrates suggests they begin by examining the basis (natural or not) of the names human beings choose to call each other. Human beings may have more insight into the purely human things. Socrates' examination of the two names used to refer to Hector's son shows, however, not merely that human beings often refer to the same individual by different names. The proper names of individuals reflect the hopes their parents had for their progeny at birth (but could not know would be realized) or the social rank and function of the parents the child is expected to inherit. These names do not reflect the character of the individual so named. For example, Hector's son may have been named Astyanax in the expectation that he would become lord of the city, but as all readers of the *Iliad* know, he did not. Nor are the moral characteristics of the parents any more reliably inherited than their social stations. Pious parents may name their babe Theophilus, but neither the name nor their wishes suffice to make the man loving or beloved of the gods. Because different names like Archepolis (ruler of the city), Agis (leader), Polemarchus (warlord), and Eupolemus (good warrior) can refer to similar if not the same civic functions, Socrates points out, various names for individuals could be correct, even if those names were entirely different, certainly if the words are altered by a letter or so. The names of mythical heroes such as Orestes (mountain man) and their ancestors—Agamemnon (admirable for remaining), Atreus (ruinous), Pelops (he who sees only what is near), Tantalus (most wretched), even Zeus (a combination of *zēna* and *dia*, which means "through whom we receive life")—often do signify the character of the person named, because they are given afterward by those who live to tell the tale.

By commenting that he would have continued his examination of the correctness of the names of even earlier gods if he had remembered the genealogy of Hesiod, Socrates indicates not only that the poets were the source of the names and corresponding characteristics of the gods in ancient Greece, but also that the account of the names of the gods he is about to give is based on a different understanding than that contained in the *Theogony*.[71] By relating the names of gods to specific natural charac-

---

71. Sallis (*Being and Logos*, 221–22) points out not only the difference between Socrates' account of the origins and Hesiod's but also the difficulty with Socrates' account of the genealogy

teristics or forces, Socrates also suggests that the poets were the source of the notion that there are correct names by nature for individual people (like Hermogenes), if not for things. Like the poets, Socrates claims to be speaking on the basis of wisdom, which has suddenly come upon him, he knows not whence. Hermogenes' concurrence that Socrates appears to be artlessly uttering oracles leads the philosopher to attribute this "wisdom" to the "inspiration" of Euthyphro, whose words "possessed" his soul earlier that morning. Like Euthyphro's generalizations about the stories of the gods as they apply to his own life, Socrates' comments represent a kind of rationalization of the names and associated stories related by the poets. Because the poets shaped both the language and opinions of his contemporaries, Socrates suggests that they ought to persist in their investigation of his newly acquired, "inspired wisdom." But recognizing that claims to "inspiration" constitute a problematic basis for knowledge, Socrates also says they ought to find someone who can purify or cleanse them of this seeming wisdom the next day. (As Plato's readers know, the next day Socrates meets an Eleatic Stranger, and they commence an investigation of whether they have the same "thing" [ergon] in mind when they use the word or name "sophist." The Eleatic suggests, moreover, that the noblest form of "sophistry" consists in purifying another person of the greatest form of ignorance by showing him that he does not know what he thinks he does.) Socrates thus indicates at the beginning of his investigation of the meaning of names that the etymologies he is about to offer do not represent his own considered opinions. Although he claims to have been "possessed," Socrates does not, like the poets, claim that his "inspired" speech has a divine source.

2. The Names of the Things That Always Are

Having learned from their brief examination of Homer that the proper names of individual human beings reflect their ancestors' social position or their parents' hopes more than their own character or nature, Socrates proposes that they look instead at the names of things that always are. Not subject to the same kind of unpredictable changes as human individuals, eternal beings could have been named more accurately, perhaps

---

of the gods here. If Socrates had followed Hesiod, he would have found that the next god(dess) is "earth" (much below sky). Rather than looking up beyond himself—the meaning Socrates attributes to the name Uranus, which is then associated with pure mind—Hesiod's god not merely looked but pressed hard downward (to prevent anything else from coming into being).

even by a superhuman power. Socrates begins with the gods (*theoi*). "The earliest men in Greece believed only in those gods in whom many barbarians believe now—sun, moon, earth, stars, and sky. They saw that these were always moving in their courses and running, so they called them gods (*theous*) from this running (*thein*) by nature" (*Cratylus* 397c–d). Suggesting that the divine part of human beings might be equally eternal or undying, Socrates then reports that, according to Hesiod, the *daimones* are the "spirits" of good, wise (*phronimoi*), and knowing (*daēmones*) men.[72] But when Hermogenes takes Socrates further back into the poetic realm of the legendary by asking him to explain "hero" (*hērōs*), Socrates gives not simply one but two derivations of the word: from the love (*erōs*) between gods and mortals that generated the heroes, or because the heroes were wise and clever speakers able to ask questions (*erōtan*). If, as the name of the gods in general suggested, everything is in flux, the meaning of specific words must also fluctuate. That is the reason "hero" can have two derivations. Shifting back from the subjects of poetry to naturally observable phenomena, Socrates then suggests that human beings in general are called *anthrōpoi* because the word represents a combination of *anathrei*, which means "looking up" and "what he has seen" (*opōpe*), and human beings are the only animals that look up and think (*logizetai*) about what they have seen. He thus returns to his original thesis. The names human beings use to indicate things reflect their observations of nature: first and most immediately, the tendency of progeny to inherit the characteristics of their progenitors, but second and more fundamentally, the nature and movements of the heavenly bodies, which determine what grows on earth.

Unfortunately, Socrates reminds Hermogenes, human beings disagree about the meaning and derivation of the names of natural phenomena as well as about the proper names of individual persons. Socrates uses the names of the two constituent parts of human beings as examples of the kinds of disagreement one finds. Socrates "think[s] the people who gave the soul its name thought that when it was present in the body, it was the cause of its living by giving it the power to breathe and so revive it" (*ana-*

---

72. In the *Apology* and *Symposium*, Socrates uses a more conventional understanding of *daimones* as the offspring of gods who mate with humans, rather than the understanding of the word he attributes here to Hesiod. But, Sallis points out (*Being and Logos*, 241), Socrates' claim here that *daimones* are the spirits of good and wise men would make the association of Socrates the philosopher with the *daimōn* Eros who communicates between humans and gods even closer. Socrates then gives an etymology of "hero," moreover, that not only brings out its association with *erōs* but also results in the claim that, because of the relation to *erōtan*, the hero is a dialectician, able to ask questions.

psychon; 399d–e). People like Euthyphro would contemn such a simple, naturalistic explanation, however. Preferring something more noble or intellectual, along the lines of Anaxagoras, who thought that mind orders everything by nature, they would call the soul "that power which carries and holds nature [*physechēn*]" (400b). Having believed that all names are conventional, Hermogenes thinks that the second explanation is more "artful" (*technikōteron*). Socrates agrees but adds that it seems ridiculous (*geloion*) to think that things were truly named in this way, that is, on the basis of the words of others rather than on the basis of observations of natural phenomena. In the case of the body, he then observes, people disagree about whether the name *sōma* is derived from *sēma*, because the body is the tomb (*sēmainei*) of the soul, or because the soul uses the body to give signs (*sēma*). Both these derivations point to the way in which the invisible soul is encased into the body. By stating that he believes the word for "body" can be traced back to the Orphic poets, who thought the soul was undergoing punishment so long as it was imprisoned or entombed in the body, Socrates suggests not merely that the poets were the source of many of the names people continue to use. He also indicates his belief that, if words are tools human beings use to separate and mark the kinds of things (*pragmata*) with which they are particularly concerned, poetic names will also contain indications of the "use" or reasons why human beings are concerned with the "thing" in question.

3. The Names of the Olympian Gods

More attracted by Socrates' explication of the constitution and derivation of the names customarily used for the highest things than with the implicit order and importance of the natural phenomena named, Hermogenes asks Socrates to go back and fill out the account of the names of the gods he had begun with Zeus. Hermogenes obviously does not believe that Socrates' failure to remember Hesiod prevented him from proceeding further with the names of the gods. Socrates had, after all, referred to Hesiod's other poem in explicating the meaning of *daimones*. If he is speaking, as claimed, from inspiration, Hermogenes may have reflected, Socrates doesn't need to remember the inspired words of others. Even if Socrates is not truly inspired himself, his memory of the words of the poets does not appear to be as bad as he claims. Hermogenes later (*Cratylus* 413d) bluntly admits that he thinks Socrates has been making everything up—with the important exception of his account of the conversations he had with others about justice.

In a significant variation of Protagoras' famous statement that, of the gods, we know not whether they are or are not (for if man is the measure, his knowledge cannot extend beyond the human), Socrates tells Hermogenes that if we are intelligent (*noun echoimen*), we recognize that we do not know anything about the gods or their true names, that is, what they call themselves. Nevertheless, Socrates admits, there is a secondary kind of correctness with regard to the names of the gods, what it is customary to call them in prayers. But in investigating these names, he insists, we should recognize that we are inquiring about the thoughts human beings had in giving them names and not about the gods themselves. If names express the opinions people have about things rather than the things themselves, however, it is already clear that we cannot learn the nature of things from the names, as Cratylus had asserted.

One might have thought that Socrates would return to the poets Homer and Hesiod in particular to find the origin of the gods' names customarily used in prayers. Reiterating his general thesis about the basic meaning of all Greek words, Socrates contends, instead, that the first people who gave the gods names were observers of the heavens (*meteōrologoi*) as well as big talkers (*adoleschai*). Like the people who called the gods *theoi*, because they saw that the heavenly bodies were always in motion, the people who named the Olympian gods "agreed with Heraclitus that all things move and nothing remains still" (401d). Socrates points out that variants of "Hestia" refer to being (*ousia* or *essia*) or flow (*ōsia*).[73] Homer traces everything to divinities named after streams: Oceanus, Rhea, and Cronus. And with prompting from Hermogenes, Socrates explains a variety of ways in which the names of other particular Olympian deities could have been derived from words referring to motion and/or intelligence.

As in the case of the human soul and body, Socrates' suggestion of a variety of derivations for the names of the Olympians indicates that no one of the etymologies he suggests is certain. Even more than the word for "body," Socrates indicates, the names of the gods have implications for the kinds of relations human beings can have with the gods. After having given multiple possible derivations of the name of Zeus's brother Poseidon, Socrates thus challenges the traditional derivation of the name of

73. The association Socrates suggests here between "Hestia" and "flow" stands in marked contrast, however, to his suggestion in the *Phaedrus* that Hestia is the one god who remains (stationary) at the center of things, as opposed to the other Olympians, whose souls rise to the edge of the cosmos to be nourished by contemplation of the good, beautiful, justice, and knowledge in themselves. Cf. Sallis, *Being and Logos*, 246.

Zeus's other brother, Hades, from "invisible" (*aeidēs*)—to which Socrates himself refers in the *Phaedo*. Human beings call Hades by the name Pluto (wealth), Socrates observes here, not only because wealth is often buried but also because they erroneously fear him (or death) and so do not want to refer to him or it directly. Rather than being taken to refer to an "invisible" and hence unknown region, Socrates contends, the name "Hades" is (or should be) derived from knowing (*eidenai*) all noble things. Refusing to consort with humans so long as they have bodies, Hades associates only with pure souls, free from the evils and desires of the body. Hades thus shows himself to be a philosopher who knows how to bind souls to himself permanently, not by necessity but with the stronger bonds of desire or love (for knowledge). Hades certainly should not be feared.[74]

Because Socrates has not yet succeeded in freeing Hermogenes from the conventional stories about the gods of the city, he accedes to his interlocutor's request for explanations of the names of Demeter, Hera, Apollo, Athena, Hephaestus, Ares, and the others. Not surprisingly, Socrates proceeds to show that the names of all these gods—as well as those of the Muses, Leto, Artemis (whom Socrates adds to Hermogenes' list), Dionysus, and Aphrodite (added as a kind of second thought by Hermogenes to the civic gods of Athens)—can be taken to refer to the beauty of things in motion or the intellectual ability to perceive them. Perhaps remembering that he has just been indicted for impiety after he gives an interpretation of the meaning of the name of the patron goddess of his city, however, Socrates tells Hermogenes that he is afraid to talk any more about the gods.

Having shown particular sensitivity about the meaning of his own name, Hermogenes asks Socrates to explain, before he quits, the meaning of the name of his patron deity. And by linking "Hermes" to *hermēneus* (interpreter), *eirein* (to use words), and *emēsato* (contrive), Socrates not merely convinces Hermogenes that he has been incorrectly named, because (in implicit contrast to Socrates) he is not "good at devising speeches." By observing that speech signifies all things (*to pan*) and keeps them always going round, Socrates suggests that all speech is inherently and necessarily deceptive. It thus has two forms—true and false.[75] Like Hermes' son Pan,

---

74. Socrates' account of the meaning of the name Hades here is thus compatible with the arguments he presents in the *Phaedo* concerning the reasons philosophers do not fear but actually seek death. The fact that Socrates draws the same lesson from two different definitions of Hades indicates that the meaning of the words or names is not decisive for Socrates himself.

75. Cf. Sallis, *Being and Logos*, 251.

who has a "true part that is smooth and dwells among the gods above, while the false part dwells below among the human masses and is rough and goatish [*tragikon*]" (408b–d), speech (*logos*) has a high, divine, because purely intelligible part. Unfortunately, however, among humans its pure intelligibility is distorted and so disfigured by its "rough" animal origin in our tumultuous passions and disordered perceptions.

Socrates brings out the "rough" animal origin of the words the Greeks used, however, in the etymological explanations he suggests for the names not only of the gods but also of human virtues and vices. Understanding Socrates' reluctance to discuss the names of the gods any further to apply specifically to the gods of the city, Hermogenes asks him to see how far "the horses of Euthyphro," that is, his inspired wisdom, will go, by explaining the names of particular cosmic gods such as the sun. Having argued earlier that the gods in general acquired their name from the movements of the heavenly bodies, Socrates quickly shows that the names of the sun and moon, as well as the measures of time associated with the movements of the heavens, the seasons, and months, are all associated with motion and light.

Noting that the inspiration of Euthyphro seems have to failed him, Socrates admits that the names of two of the four basic elements cannot be derived in this manner in Greek; he is thus forced to speculate that the words for fire (*pyr*) and water (*hydōr*) must be foreign imports. The need to posit such "borrowings" in order to explain the names of half (or more) of the constituent elements of all things nevertheless indicates the severe limitations of such "etymologies" as explanations of the intelligibility of things.

4. THE MISUNDERSTANDING UNDERLYING THE NAMES OF THE VIRTUES AND VICES

Turning at Hermogenes' request to explicate the names of the intellectual virtues that presumably enable us to understand the world, Socrates explains why the names they have inherited from their ancestors do not describe things correctly. Claiming to have a new "inspiration" (which does not presumably come from Euthyphro), Socrates observes:

> Most of the wise now get so dizzy going around and around in seeking the
> nature of the things that are, that the things themselves appear to them to
> be turning around and moving every which way. Well, I think that the hu-
> man beings who gave things their names of old were exactly like the wise

now. They don't see the cause in their own feeling, but think that it is the nature of the things themselves, which are never stable or steadfast, but flowing and moving, always full of every sort of motion and constant coming into being. (*Cratylus* 411b–d)

The words or names the Greeks use to indicate can be taken to express a certain understanding of things, as Socrates has been demonstrating. It is the "Heraclitean" understanding of things that Socrates attributed to all previous poets and philosophers, with the exception of Parmenides, in the *Theaetetus*. But if this understanding basically constitutes a projection of the observer's inner turmoil and confusion onto the world, as Socrates suggests here, this understanding of things is obviously wrong. If the motion people have observed in things is merely a reflection or product of their own inner turmoil, people have not described things accurately in naming them on account of their seeming motion. As Socrates argued much more fully in his explication of Protagoras' saying in the *Theaetetus*, our perceptions of the world are initially and fundamentally sensations, based on an interaction with external things. But the fact that we move and are moved in perceiving things in the world does not mean that everything in the world moves in the same way—or at all. In order to discover what the characteristics of the nonhuman things are, we have to become aware of our own characteristics and limitations (so that we will not continue to read our own characteristics or perceptions into the things we perceive). That is the reason Socrates regularly urges his interlocutors to seek self-knowledge. Because the knowledge sought is of the human and not merely of the individual, it cannot be gained merely by introspection. It can be gained only by comparing "notes" or perceptions and opinions with others. To be sure, we cannot communicate or compare our perceptions and opinions without using words. But, Socrates is showing Hermogenes, we have to be alive to the possibility that the words we have inherited reflect an inadequate, if not simply incorrect, understanding of things. We can use words as tools, to mark and so separate out the different kinds of things we think we perceive. We should be wary, however, of believing that the words themselves directly communicate or reflect the character of the things (as opposed to some human perceptions of them).

For example, Socrates explains, the names people gave the intellectual virtues—*phronēsis, gnōmē, noēsis, sōphrosynē,* and *epistēmē*—all point to an understanding of things as always coming to be and thus as always in motion. On this basis, it is easy to conjecture that justice (*dikaiosynē*) refers to the understanding (*synesis*) of the just. But is difficult to determine what the just (*dikaion*) itself means. People disagree. "Those who think everything is in motion believe that the greater part of it is such as to be a mere receptacle [*chōrein*], and that there is something which passes through it all by means of which things are generated." What passes through must be very subtle as well as swift, Socrates observes, in order to pass through all things. Because "it superintends and passes through [*diaïon*] all things, it is correctly called *dikaion*, the sound of the kappa being added merely for the sake of euphony" (412d–e). When Socrates asked the people who believe everything is in motion what it is that passes through or causes generation, they told him, in secret (indicating they knew that they were reinterpreting the meaning of the name of the chief god of the city, who had traditionally been said to secure justice with his lightning bolts), that it is correctly called Zeus because it causes generation. But when he asked further, what is just, he was given a variety of answers and mocked. One told him that "the sun is justice, for the sun alone superintends all things, passing through and burning [*diaïonta kai kaonta*] them." But another, laughing, asked Socrates whether he thought "there is not justice among humans when the sun has set" (413b). He said that justice is "fire," not fire literally but the heat that is in fire. Yet a third laughed at all this and asserted that justice is what Anaxagoras said, mind. For mind rules itself, is mixed with nothing else, but orders (*kosmein*) and runs through (*ionta*) everything. As Socrates explains more fully in his "autobiography" in the *Phaedo*, his studies of the cosmologists and Anaxagoras left him perplexed (in a state of *aporia*), because their theories could not tell him what is truly good or just. Here (413d) he simply concludes that the word "justice" was based on the (mis)understanding that everything is in motion.

If the names the ancient Greeks gave things constituted projections of their own inner motion onto the world, we are not surprised to discover, the names they gave to the virtues and vices express the same sensations. Socrates thus shows how the words *andreia* (courage), *technē* (art), *aretē* (virtue), *kalon* (noble), *deon* (obligation), *agathon* (good), *sympheronta* (advantageous), *lysitelounta* (profitable), *ōphelima* (useful), *kerdalea* (gainful), and their opposites can all be shown to express different stances, fostering or hindering, toward motion. The names of human passions and desires are shown even more easily to refer to different kinds of e-motion than the names for virtues and vices.

5. WHY WORDS CANNOT BE TRUSTED TO REVEAL THE TRUE NATURE OF THE BEINGS

When Hermogenes emphasizes the difference between Socrates' account of his conversations with other philosophers about justice and the etymologies by saying that he believes Socrates really heard the varied accounts of justice, Socrates tells Hermogenes to listen carefully.[76] Socrates may be able to deceive Hermogenes into thinking that he has also made up everything he is about to say. Socrates continues to argue that Greek words can be shown to reflect a basically Heraclitean understanding of things—an understanding Socrates is known not to accept. But Socrates now explicitly admits that the extent to which Greek names reflect even this understanding is problematic, because "the original words have before now been completely buried by those who wished to dress them up. They have added and subtracted letters for the sake of euphony and have distorted the words in every way for ornamentation or merely with the lapse of time." But "if we are permitted to insert and remove any letters we please in words," he acknowledges, "it will be perfectly easy to fit any name to anything" (*Cratylus* 414d).

Having warned Hermogenes not to expect too much precision from an analysis of words (414e), Socrates seems to return to the understanding of words he sketched in his initial critique of Hermogenes' conventionalism when he suggests that "*onoma* seems to be a word composed from a sentence signifying 'this is a being about which our search is'" (421a).[77] Socrates does not follow up his own suggestion at this point in the conversation, however. Instead, he reiterates his general thesis about the original meaning of all Greek names by arguing that *alētheia* (truth) refers to the divine motion and *pseudos* (false) to its opposite. His skepticism about the validity of Socrates' arguments becoming ever more explicit, Hermogenes comments that Socrates has bravely knocked all these words into pieces to show that they refer to motion. But, he asks, how would Socrates explain or defend the meanings he has attributed to the component syllables or parts of these words—*ion* (going), *rheon* (flowing), and *doun* (shackling)?

---

76. Sedley (*Cratylus*, 108) indicates the importance of this exchange, near the center of the dialogue, when he observes that the tone of the conversation changes at this point.

77. As in the case of "Zeus," understood to be the composite name of that through which or on account of which (*dia*) things come into existence or life (*zēna*), Socrates suggests here, a word that actually represents the contraction of a sentence may disclose more of the truth than a word that is supposed simply to reflect the being (becoming) of the thing named.

In response, Socrates states the demands of correctness in names more explicitly and precisely than he had in the preceding etymologies. If we did not have words, he points out, we would use gestures. But he observes, gestures work best to communicate the thing we have in mind if they imitate it. If words are to indicate the nature of the things named, they must imitate not merely the sound, like music, or the shape, like painting, but the very being of the things. Words have to "imitate the being of each thing by means of letters and syllables" to "show what each thing is" (423e). In order to discover whether there are correct names of things, they would have to break words down into their smallest parts, letters. They would have to sort the letters into different kinds—vowels, consonants, and mutes—and determine what each of the letters refers to. Like grammarians, they would have to determine which letters can be combined and which cannot. They would have to sort the possible syllables and determine what they mean, both in themselves and when combined to make words. Finally, they have to see how the words themselves, nouns and verbs, could be combined into sentences in order to see whether they were true.

Socrates does not claim to be able to show how words are correct by dividing them into their component elements and then reconstituting them. On the contrary, he twice states that the whole project seems laughable (425d, 426b). Having agreed with Hermogenes to do the best he can, Socrates nevertheless points out meanings associated with certain letters—movement with *rho* because *r*'s are rolled, swift and easy penetration with *iota* because of its light sound, stickiness and sweetness with *gamma*, smoothness with *lambda*, inwardness with *nu*, *alpha* as a big letter, and *o* with roundness—as a beginning. Although he admits the project seems ridiculous, Socrates can think of no better argument for the proposition that names are correct by nature. Those who trace the origins of names to foreign words, gods (poetic inspiration), or a time too long ago to know—all of which Socrates himself did in parts of the etymologies—make the basis and meaning of words fundamentally unknowable.

Contrary to Hermogenes' initial assertion, Socrates' etymological investigations have shown that human beings do not name things entirely on the basis of convention in a completely arbitrary manner. As Socrates pointed out in their initial discussion of Homer, like Archepolis or Hermogenes, the proper names by which human beings call others are often composed out of other words and have meaning. Proper names are not reliable indicators of the true character of individuals, however, because these names often reflect either the hopes or the status of the parents more than the nature or accomplishments of the person so named. Next, Socrates showed, the names by which human beings call the gods—both cosmic and Olympian—can be seen to refer to an understanding of things as always in motion. So can the words used to describe human virtues and vices. But, Socrates also suggested, this Heraclitean understanding of things represents a projection of the inner state of the human observer onto the phenomena, that is, it does not represent an accurate view of things as they are. Nor does it provide a definition of justice on the basis of which human beings can order their lives. Since the parts of words have been shown to have meaning, Socrates not only told Hermogenes that it would be necessary to break each word down into its smallest elements and then reconstitute each and every word in sentences to determine whether words constitute correct imitations of things that reveal what they truly are. He also reminded Hermogenes that there are meanings regularly associated with certain sounds or letters. However, Socrates' comments on his own etymologies—that he has had to posit foreign origins for some words, that the original meanings of words get covered over with time, both intentionally and unintentionally, and that anyone can make any word refer to anything by adding and subtracting letters—have given both his interlocutor and Plato's readers reasons to doubt that human beings can learn the true nature of things from the words used to indicate, if not to imitate and so describe them. In his concluding exchange with Cratylus, Socrates brings out more directly and explicitly the reasons human beings cannot learn the nature of things directly from the names human beings have given them.

E. Socrates' Refutation of Cratylus

Hermogenes may not have taken Socrates' attempt to disclose the original meaning of the Greek words used to describe the highest things—the gods and the virtues—seriously enough. The etymologies Socrates suggests in the *Cratylus* provide some support for his contention in the *Theaetetus* that all previous poets and philosophers subscribed to a Heraclitean view of things. Believing that Socrates has made up everything except his account of the conversations he had with students of cosmology about justice, Hermogenes nevertheless thinks that Socrates has given an extraordinary performance. He thus challenges Cratylus to present a better argument for the correctness of names, to instruct them, or to learn from Socrates.

Cratylus tries to put Hermogenes off, as he had in their initial exchange, by asking him whether he believes such important things are learned so easily and quickly.

Characteristically assuming a cooperative rather than a competitive stance, Socrates flatters Cratylus to induce him to state his own position. Once again indicating that he does not fully accept or endorse the etymologies, Socrates observes that "nothing [he has] said is set in stone. [He has] merely said what has appeared from [his] investigations with Hermogenes" (*Cratylus* 428a). Since Cratylus has not only pondered these things himself but has also had instruction, he is apt to have a better argument. Cratylus again seeks to cut off further inquiry by saying simply that he agrees with Socrates.

Socrates will not let him escape so easily. In the etymologies Socrates presented to Hermogenes as an explanation of what correct names by nature might be, he did not put forward an unambiguous position with which another could simply agree or disagree. To get Cratylus to say what he thinks, Socrates observes that self-deception is the most difficult kind of deception to escape, because we cannot simply avoid the deceiver (as Cratylus is trying to avoid Hermogenes' questions and Socrates' request). To avoid deceiving themselves, people need to reexamine their own opinions in the company of others.

Socrates conceals the extent to which he is directly challenging Cratylus by asking him about propositions on which they presumably agree. He begins by asking Cratylus whether he thinks names are correct if they show what things (*pragmata*) are. He then gets Cratylus to agree, as Hermogenes had, that names are given for the sake of instruction and that those who instruct have an art (*technē*). Although Cratylus also agrees that some artisans produce better and worse works than others, he is not willing to admit, as Hermogenes had, that some legislators make better laws than others or that some set down names that are more correct than others. On the contrary, Cratylus asserts, a name that is not correct is not a name. Like Hermogenes, the person named should have the nature indicated by the words, that is, in this case he should be kin to Hermes (as the person indicated has already admitted he is not). If not, the people who call him by that name are not simply using an incorrect name (and so still pointing to, signifying, or meaning him). They are making unintelligible noise.

By asking Cratylus whether he thinks that those who name things incorrectly are speaking falsely, Socrates not merely shows that he and Cratylus do not, in fact, agree. Socrates had insisted that words and speeches can be both true and false at the very beginning of his exchange with Hermogenes. By getting Cratylus to state that he does not think it is possible to say something false, because that would be to say nothing at all, Socrates also shows that Cratylus' position rests on a sophistical argument like the one Dionysodorus makes in the *Euthydemus*. In the *Euthydemus* Socrates had shown that the sophists who argued that it is impossible to speak falsely contradicted themselves; in the *Theaetetus* he explained why it is difficult to give an account of false opinion—on the basis of an understanding of knowledge as immediate or stored perceptions. Here Socrates merely observes that many have denied the possibility of false speech the way Cratylus does and thereby suggests that Cratylus' "wisdom" is not quite so rare or esoteric as the young man seems to believe. Instead of disputing the proposition directly, and so challenging if not insulting Cratylus, Socrates simply says that the argument is too sophisticated (*kompsoteros*) for an old man like himself. By commenting on his age, he nevertheless reminds us, if not his interlocutors, of the serious context in which this apparently frivolous debate occurs, that is, his trial.

In the etymologies of the Greek names for the gods, Socrates had suggested not only that these words referred in general to a Heraclitean understanding of all things as in flux but also that this view of things did not generate a conception of justice on which human beings could agree. Such disagreements about the meaning of justice could not be an indifferent fact to an old man about to be tried for his injustice or to a young man who thinks he has been deprived of his inheritance by his older brother and of wisdom by Cratylus' irony. According to Heraclitus, human beings call things just and unjust, but for Zeus, everything is equally just or unjust.[78] If such an understanding of things was implicit in the names the ancient Greeks had given the gods, which had then been disseminated by the poets, people in general were not merely apt to absorb such an understanding without realizing it. The more reflective they became, the more they were apt to conclude that nothing is really just and to act merely on the basis of their irrational fears and hopes.

By asking Cratylus whether someone who addressed him as "my friend from Athens, Hermogenes, son of Smicrion" would have named him (from Athens and son of Smicrion) incorrectly, Socrates reminds Cratylus that, as he had pointed out earlier in Homer, names are often compounds, each part having a distinct meaning. Not merely can some of the parts

78. Fragment 102, in Freeman, *Ancilla to the Pre-Socratic Philosophers*, 31.

be true, but incorrectly or impossibly combined; the names themselves often reflect the ancestry of the person more than his nature or character. Socrates' compound examples also point to the probable source of Cratylus' initial claim that names are correct by nature and that if a name does not express the nature of the thing named, it is not a name. Having observed that names like Hermogenes or Archepolis have meanings that suggest descriptions of the character or deeds of the person, Cratylus had concluded that "proper" or real names do just that. Any name that does not is, therefore, not a name.

By asking Cratylus whether he agrees that there is a difference between the name and the thing named, Socrates shows that Cratylus' initial understanding of names is not tenable. If there is a difference, names must be imitations (*mimēmata*) or likenesses (*eikones*) of things. And if there is a difference between copy and original, as there must be, if the copy is not to be the same as the original, copies can be more or less accurate. Cratylus objects, stating that grammarians would not say a word that has been misspelled by adding or subtracting a letter from it has been written incorrectly; they would say that the incorrect version does not represent the word. But Socrates responds that, if Cratylus admits a difference between the name and thing (which does not exist in the example of the misspelling of a word), he must admit that the name can be more or less correct. It will be a name so long as it expresses the inner being of the thing—more or less clearly.

At this point, Cratylus "bravely" switches from his initial understanding of names as direct expressions of the beings to names as imitations of the beings without explicitly admitting that he is doing so. He initially resists the conclusions that seem to follow from the observation that just as imitations can be more or less full and accurate, so names can be names even if they are not entirely or in all respects correct. He does not want to admit that names can indicate the character of things, even if all the syllables or letters do not exactly correspond to the being of the thing. Nor does he want to concede that names can be given more or less well. But if Cratylus does not admit that names are imitations, which may be more or less correct, Socrates points out, Cratylus will be driven to agree with Hermogenes that all names are conventional. Admittedly given to things by human beings, names are different from the things that exist by nature.

Socrates then uses the Greek word for "hardness" to show that different peoples can represent the same thing equally well by using two slightly different forms of the word *sklērotēs* in Attic Greek, which the Eritreans call *sklērotēs*. Not only can *r* (*rho*) and *s* (*sigma*) be used interchangeably without fundamentally altering the meaning of the word. Letters that have contradictory meanings or associations, like *r*, which they have agreed indicates motion, and *l* (*lambda*), which signifies the opposite of hardness, can also be found in a word without preventing not just one but several peoples from understanding what the word signifies. Cratylus expostulates, "That is by custom, my friend!" (*Cratylus* 434e), and Socrates points out that Cratylus agrees then "that both convention and custom must contribute something to the meaning of words" (435b).

Socrates does not conclude that the meaning of words is wholly conventional.[79] On the contrary, he says that he would prefer names to have the power to be as much like the things as possible. We are compelled, however, to recognize the role of convention in naming (which is not to say that names are entirely or completely conventional). Socrates' own position thus differs from both of the opposed contentions of his two interlocutors. Because words are not simply or entirely expressions of the things that are, he argues, we cannot learn what the beings really are merely by studying their names, as Cratylus initially suggested. But the fact that various peoples use a variety of words to distinguish different kinds of things in the world should also make us hesitant to conclude, as the ancient makers of Greek names seem to have thought, that everything is always in flux.

Hermogenes, Socrates, and Cratylus have all agreed that names are and should be used to instruct. But, Socrates now explicitly points out, if the names people give things represent their understanding of things, the names people gave things of old will not be correct unless their understanding of things was correct. Apparently returning to his initial position, Cratylus responds that the first names must have been accurate, otherwise they would not be names at all. Socrates must agree that the first names were correct. Hasn't he shown that the original name-givers all had the same thing in mind? Had he not argued that the original names were given on the basis of the same observation of the fundamental movement or flux of all things? The fact that later names have been consistently derived from earlier conceptions does not show that the earlier conceptions were correct, Socrates counters. The consistency merely perpetuates the original error. But Socrates does not think that names are consistent.

79. Pace Anagnostopoulos, "Significance of *Cratylus*," 327–28.

They should reexamine what they said. They had agreed previously that the names that indicated all things were in motion disclosed their nature. But, Socrates now points out, words like *epistēmē* (knowledge) suggest that it makes our souls stand still. *Historia* (inquiry) refers to that which stops the flow, as does *piston* (trust), and *mnēmē* (memory) connotes rest. There are also negative terms like *hamartia* (error) and *symphora* (misfortune), which refer to the flow. In fine, all words do not express an understanding of everything always in motion. Even if most do, as Cratylus contends, such an issue cannot be settled by majority rule. The fact that words reflect a view of things both in motion and at rest means that we cannot determine the true nature or being of things simply by learning their names. Nor can we simply posit a higher power, a god, to be the ultimate source and guarantee of the correctness of names, as Cratylus suggests, because such a power would not have contradicted himself in the names he gave things. We have no recourse but to investigate the things themselves.

Socrates explicitly admits (439b) that the way to learn and make discoveries about the beings may be too great a thing for either of them to know. The observation he makes here about the superiority of studying the thing itself, as opposed to its image, raises intriguing questions about his decision (related in the *Phaedo* 99d–100a) to study the arguments (*logoi*) human beings give about things, because these arguments are no less images of the things than sensible facts. Why can't we get to the things themselves? How and why are "speeches," arguments, or mere propositions more revealing of the true nature of things than the words of which these speeches are composed? Is the advantage (indicated by Socrates' explication of "Zeus" and *onoma*) that speeches are obviously and explicitly composites of smaller units and thus more clearly indicate the essentially differentiated and hence complex nature of things? In his conversation with Hermogenes and Cratylus, Socrates claims only to have shown that the true natures of things cannot be learned simply from the names that have been given to them. He does not claim to have shown that everything is not in flux, as most of the names suggest. He concludes merely by pointing out that there cannot be knowledge of anything, if everything is always changing. By saying that he "dreams" of things like the beautiful or the good in itself, Socrates points toward his own argument about the ideas as indicating what must be posited if human beings are to believe they can achieve knowledge. But he does not make that argument here. He simply urges Cratylus to investigate the matter thoroughly and courageously, observing that Cratylus is young and in his prime and so implying that he may still be able to learn something new.

Cratylus agrees to do so, but adds that he has already investigated the matter thoroughly and "things seem to [him] to be as Heraclitus says" (440d–e). Cratylus seems, indeed, to have acquired this view from Socrates' etymologies. Cratylus' first "oracular" claims about the correctness of names did not evince such an understanding. On the contrary, in contending that "Cratylus" and "Socrates" are correct names but that "Hermogenes" is not, Cratylus suggested that names have different meanings that may or may not disclose the nature of the particular thing to which they are attached. If they do not, they are not truly names. Socrates has persuaded Cratylus that the true nature of things is not immediately disclosed in this manner by particular or proper names, but that most Greek names for the highest things refer to a general and unending flux. Cratylus does not explicitly acknowledge that he has changed his stance. He begins to advocate Socrates' Heraclitean argument only toward the end in order to save his own original contention—for which he himself had offered no argument—that names are correct by nature. If we can trust Aristotle, Cratylus later came to realize the logical consequences of the Heraclitean understanding of things he had adopted and jettisoned his belief that names are correct by nature. Turning from word back to gesture, he declared that all one could do is to point (to something that would be changing as one spoke).

IV. The Problems Raised by Socrates' Assertion of His Own Ignorance

In the three dialogues introducing the account of his trial and death, Socrates shows that none of his interlocutors has the immediate or direct knowledge of things he claims to possess. All the forms of knowledge they claim to possess are, in fact, the results of different forms of mediation—of mathematical reasoning, numbers, and calculations in the case of the geometricians, of reasoning on the basis of the purported inspiration of the poets in the case of the diviner, and of the naming of things in the past by poets and philosophers in the case of Cratylus. In showing that the knowledge claimed by Socrates' interlocutors was not and could not be immediate or direct, Plato reminds his readers that all three forms of mediation between things and knowers have both temporal and bodily aspects. Geometric proofs involve potentially audible sentences or arguments as well as visible constructions. Yet both the definitions on which these proofs depend and the results of the reasoning are purely intelligible and unchanging. The poets who originally related the stories on which the diviner Euthyphro depends claimed to be inspired by the Muses, who were, in turn, said to be the daughters of Memory. Their stories and the knowledge of the gods said to be contained in them last only so long as they are remembered and retold. But, as Socrates reminds Theaetetus with the image of the wax block, human memory is often defective. Even when human beings recall the images of things they have stored in their memory correctly, moreover, they may incorrectly apply these images to other similar things they currently perceive and so mistake them. In the *Cratylus* Socrates suggested that many of the Greek words people of old used to name and describe things expressed their own feelings and confusion more than the nature of the things observed. Yet, Socrates also shows, people cannot learn or reason about the different kinds of things without naming or counting them. He also observes, both in the *Theaetetus* and in the *Cratylus*, that the assumptions and results of naming or describing things in words and arguments are different from the assumptions and results of counting them. The nature of a whole number does not differ from the sum of its parts. The nature or meaning of a word does.

In disputing the claims of his interlocutors to possess knowledge, Socrates raises serious questions about the basis and character of his own endeavor as well. Asserting his own ignorance, he seeks knowledge by examining the arguments other people make about them. But what is the character of argument or *logos*? How and why is *logos* or the *logoi* it produces able to reveal the character of things in a way that sensation, memory, or words do not? How is the human ability not merely to name but to describe the characteristics of things in sentences and to link those propositions about things logically in arguments related to our ability to enumerate and calculate? What is the significance of the enduring difference between the two fundamental ways in which human beings acquire knowledge about and bring order to the world in which we live?

Socrates does not explicitly raise these questions, much less offer answers to them. When Theodorus and his students come, as promised, to rejoin Socrates the next day, however, they bring an Eleatic Stranger with them. And he, in contrast to Socrates, explicitly claims to give an explanation of the basis of *logos*. We shall have to see, of course, whether that explanation is adequate.

Socrates does not merely raise questions about the means and foundations of all human hopes of acquiring knowledge in the *Theaetetus, Euthyphro,* and *Cratylus,* moreover. He also explicitly links the problems we have acquiring knowledge to the quest for justice. In the *Theaetetus* he not only reminds the geometer of the disdain he and other more theoretical "philosophers" feel for the more "practical" politicians who concern themselves with transitory matters like laws and punishments. He also shows that the geometers do not understand the character and basis of their own art precisely because they have not taken proper account of their own mortality and vulnerability as human beings. Likewise, in the *Euthyphro* Socrates does not simply show that the diviner does not have the knowledge of the gods he claims to possess. Not merely is Euthyphro's purportedly singular knowledge of what the gods desire derivative, in fact, from the works of others, that is, from the stories told by poets. Euthyphro's prosecution of his father shows that he does not understand the connection between civic piety and family attachments. Lacking self-knowledge, Euthyphro does not recognize the love of one's own that has prompted him, as it does many other human beings, to strike out at those they believe have wronged them. He does not understand the desire for justice that leads human beings both to hope and believe that there are gods, who will be able to see justice done when and where human beings cannot, and to rebel against those gods, if not to deny their existence entirely, when justice is not achieved. In the *Cratylus* Socrates then shows that Euthyphro is by no means alone in his failure to understand the power and significance of the desire for justice in human affairs. The poets and philosophers who projected their own inner confusion and lack of order onto the world by teaching that everything is in flux also ignored or denied this powerful human impulse.

Does Socrates' admission of his own lack of knowledge and inner turmoil (cf. *Phaedrus* 230a) provide a better basis for determining what is just and thus guiding human life, both individual and communal, than all previous poetry and philosophy have done? That is the question to which Plato turns finally, and most famously, in his depiction of Socrates' trial and death.

9

The Eleatic Challenge

In the first three of the eight dialogues culminating with his trial and death, Socrates shows that those who believe they can acquire knowledge by means of their mathematical skill (*technē*), divination, or names are mistaken. Socrates appears to be wiser than Euthyphro, Cratylus, and the geometers with whom he converses in the *Theaetetus*, because he at least recognizes that he does not know. Socrates' refutations of his interlocutors' various claims to knowledge nevertheless leave Plato's readers with a serious problem. If we cannot acquire knowledge of the world through numbers or words, and the gods do not clearly tell us what to do, how are we to learn? The only possible way for human beings to gain knowledge seems to be to use our *logos* to sort beings into kinds or classes. As Socrates emphasizes at the end of the *Cratylus*, such a sorting constitutes a necessary precondition for counting or naming things. But when Theodorus and his students return the next day to recommence their dialogue with Socrates, the anonymous Eleatic stranger they bring with them suggests that Socrates cannot explain the character or basis of *logos*.[1] Socrates ad-

---

1. I have followed Seth Benardete (*Being of the Beautiful*) in translating *xenos* as "stranger" or "foreigner" rather than "visitor," like C. J. Rowe (in Cooper, *Plato: Complete Works*, 294–358), and Robin Waterfield, *Plato: Statesman* (Cambridge: Cambridge University Press, 1995), to emphasize the difference between Socrates, who stayed in Athens except when called on to defend the city's interests militarily, and who explicitly said in the *Theaetetus* that he cared more about his fellow citizens, especially the young, than about others, and the philosophers who traveled around in search of knowledge. This "political" difference is obviously related to, if not a direct reflection of, the "methodological" difference the Eleatic points out between sorting things "equally" into same and other, in contrast to Socrates' evaluation of things in terms of their participation in the good or noble. As Henri Joly points out in *La question des étrangers* (Paris: Vrin, 1992), *xenos* is

mits that he does not know, but, the Eleatic intimates, Socrates' mode of philosophizing does not offer any hope of alleviating his ignorance.

Some commentators have called the two dialogues that occur the day after the *Theaetetus, Euthyphro,* and *Cratylus* Socrates' "philosophical trial," because the charges the Eleatic implicitly levels against Socrates in the *Sophist* and the *Statesman* are so serious.[2] First, the Eleatic suggests, Socrates is a sophist. According to the Eleatic, sophists are not distinguished primarily by their attempt to attract wealthy young students by promising to teach them virtue for a fee. Sophists are defined (*Sophist* 268b–d) by their ability to appear wise to others by refuting their interlocutors in private conversations, even when they themselves know, ironically, that they are not wise. In the *Apology* (23a) Socrates admits that the people who heard him interrogate others concluded that he knew the subjects about which he refuted his interlocutors. But Socrates insists, as he had in his first conversation with Theaetetus, that he does not have any wisdom of his own. In his conversation with Theaetetus he could not even show how false opinion is possible. In the *Sophist* the Eleatic does. In modifying the argument of his "father" Parmenides to show how false opinion, and therefore sophistry, is possible, the Eleatic also indicates the reason Socrates has not acquired the wisdom he has been seeking. He has not divided up the beings into the right kinds of classes (*eidē*). Socrates has sought to divide things hierarchically into better and worse kinds (according to their closeness or distance from the good) rather than sorting them horizontally, the way the Eleatic himself does, into same and other. "Friends of the forms" like Socrates, who draw a hard and fast distinction between the eternally unchanging beings which are intelligible and the sensible, changing things which are not, are not able to give an account of their own thought or soul, because thought and soul both involve motion. As a result, these "friends" have not been able to acquire the self-knowledge Socrates says he has been seeking any more than they are able to acquire knowledge of things. As Socrates also seemed to demonstrate at the end of the *Theaetetus,* they are not even able to explain how different kinds of letters can be combined to make words

---

contrasted with "citizen"—whether as mere foreigner, enemy, or barbarian—elsewhere in Plato's works.

2. According to Miller (*Philosopher in "Statesman,"* 2–3), the Eleatic offers the philosophical defense of Socrates that Socrates himself cannot give to a popular audience in his political trial. Both Rosen (*Web of Politics,* 6–7) and Howland (*Paradox,* vii, 3–8) see that the Eleatic is implicitly accusing Socrates of philosophical and political failings. Both nevertheless conclude that the Eleatic's position is compatible with Socratic philosophy. I argue that Plato's two philosophical spokesmen represent fundamentally different understandings of the basis and conduct of philosophy.

and then sentences that disclose the truth about things in *logos*. In sum, the Eleatic charges in the *Sophist*, Socrates is a sophist who appears to be wise by refuting others, but who, according to his own admission, knows nothing. He cannot explain the basis or character of the *logoi*, which, he says in the *Phaedo*, he investigated instead of the beings themselves. Nor does Socrates' proclaimed knowledge of "the erotic things" enable him to guide human action. On the contrary, the Eleatic charges in the *Statesman*, Socrates' attempt to discover the true political art by questioning his contemporaries' opinions about the *kalos k'agathos* reveals his failure to understand the limits of consent-based politics and the requirements of the rule of law. Socrates has brought his indictment and probable conviction for a capital crime by his fellow Athenians on himself.[3] He knows even less about politics than he does about being and *logos*. According to the Eleatic, Socrates is not a paradigm of either philosophical or political practice.[4]

I. The Initial Contrast between Socrates and the Stranger

Theodorus indicates his belief that the Eleatic represents a better form of philosophy than does Socrates when, in the very first sentence of the *Sophist*, he tells Socrates that he and his students have returned as they agreed yesterday morning (at the conclusion of the *Theaetetus* [210d]), and that they have brought with them a stranger from Elea who is a "real" or, literally, manly philosopher (*anēr philosophos*; 216a). The implicit contrast to Socrates' feminizing description of himself as a midwife seems clear.

Reminding readers of his appreciation for if not complete agreement with Homer (which we shall see also distinguishes him from the Eleatic),

---

3. Christopher Rowe ("Killing Socrates," 63–76) attempts to forestall such a reading of the *Statesman* by offering a new translation of 300a1–7. As Rowe himself admits, however, the Greek text does not settle the issue in and by itself.

4. Emphasizing the fact that the Eleatic never names Socrates specifically as a sophist or lawbreaker, Blondell argues that "there is no ad hominem attack. The combination of clear allusions to the elenctic Sokrates with elements detaching those allusions from his specific representations in Plato generates an indeterminacy that enables the visitor's critique (and appreciation) of elenctic methods to incorporate Sokrates without being confined to him" (*Play of Character*, 385). She agrees with the many commentators who, relying on the chronology of composition, suggest that Plato marked his increasing independence from Socrates by using other philosophical spokesmen in his "late" dialogues. She suggests that the Eleatic's anonymity, in contrast with Socrates' marked individuality—readers know not only his name, parents, city, and social standing but also his physical appearance, characteristic haunts, and dress—makes "the visitor" a better, because more impersonal, paradigm of philosophy.

Socrates paraphrases parts of the *Odyssey* (9.271, 17.485–87) in wondering whether the anonymous stranger is not a god in disguise who has come to refute those who are poor in arguments (*logoi*). (Socrates' interlocutors would not know, as Plato's readers do, that Socrates had told Hermogenes the previous day that they would need to seek a sophist or priest to cleanse themselves of the "inspirations" Socrates had imbibed from Euthyphro by refuting them. In that case, what might appear to be a punishing or avenging god would prove to be a benefactor.) Theodorus assures the group, however, that the Eleatic does not engage in refutation. He is more measured (*metrioteros*) than those (again implicitly like Socrates; *Theaetetus* 169b–d) who are zealous in contention. Theodorus does not believe the Eleatic Stranger is a god, but the geometer thinks that, like all philosophers, the Stranger is divine. Indirectly questioning Theodorus' ability to judge what is divine as he had explicitly questioned the geometer's ability to judge beauty the previous day in the *Theaetetus*, Socrates observes that philosophers are not much easier to discern than gods. Philosophers also appear in many guises, traveling from city to city (like the Eleatic), looking down from on high on the life of those below.[5] Perhaps because they have to look up—and hence into the sun—the nonphilosophers below do not agree on the character of the philosophers' activity. Some think philosophers are worthless; others, that they are worth everything. Sometimes philosophers appear to be sophists; at other times, they appear to be statesmen; and at yet other times, they even appear to be mad. In any case, Socrates reminds his interlocutors, there is by no means universal agreement about who is a philosopher or whether philosophy is a worthwhile activity.

Attempting to find out just what kind of philosopher the Eleatic Stranger is, Socrates asks him whether people from Elea believe that the sophist, statesman, and philosopher are one, two, or, like their names, three. When the Stranger responds three, although it is no small work to distinguish them clearly, Socrates knows that the Eleatic is not simply a follower of Parmenides; if the Stranger were, he would have said that these activities are erroneously thought to be three by mere mortals, but that like all being, these three are truly one. Admitting it would take a lot

---

5. At the beginning of his poem, Parmenides describes the knower as one who looks down on many cities. See Kirk, Raven, and Schofield, *Presocratic Philosophers*, 243. Nightingale (*Spectacles*, 63–70) gives an account of the development of the practice in ancient Greece of traveling in search of knowledge into a philosophical practice or motif.

of effort to distinguish the three, Socrates urges the Eleatic to do so. By asking the Eleatic whether he would prefer to go through the argument by himself in a long speech or to proceed by means of question and answer, the way he had once heard Parmenides, Socrates lets the Stranger know that he is familiar with Eleatic teachings.

Socrates' recalling of the conversation he had with Parmenides when he was young also serves to remind Plato's readers that Socrates too is a follower of Parmenides, insofar as he agrees, in opposition to all other previous philosophers and poets, that everything is not becoming or in flux. Like Parmenides, Socrates argues that the only things that truly are, are the things that do not come into being or fade but remain always the same, and that these eternally unchanging, purely intelligible things are the only things that can be known. Unlike Parmenides, however, Socrates thinks that there is an irreducible plurality of such eternally unchanging, purely intelligible *eidē*. To the very last day of his life, Socrates could not say exactly how many or what "ideas" there are, but he regularly suggested that there are ideas of the good, the beautiful, and the just. Although particular, sensible beings can be said to "participate" in several different "ideas," Socrates, even if he also fails to explain clearly what he means by "participation," insists that the ideas themselves are completely separate entities that do not intermingle or coexist with one another.

Later in the *Sophist*, when the Eleatic Stranger is led to violate Parmenides' stricture concerning the impossibility of thinking or saying "what is not" in order to explain how a sophist can present a false appearance of knowledge, he also argues that there is a plurality of fundamental *eidē* in contrast to his mentor's one. Indeed, the Eleatic suggests that things could not be described and thus made intelligible in *logos*, if being itself were not differentiated into the same (*t'auton*) and other (*thateron*). In his conversation with Socrates, Parmenides had suggested that philosophy would be impossible without something like Socrates' argument concerning the ideas, even though the elder Eleatic did not find Socrates' version to be entirely satisfactory (*Parmenides* 135b–d). In contrast to Socrates, who clearly and emphatically distinguishes the eternally unchanging, purely intelligible ideas from the sensible, changing things that somehow participate in them, the Eleatic Stranger speaks of *genē* and *eidē* interchangeably. He indicates that not all *eidē*, as he understands them, are eternal, when he identifies two kinds (*genē*) of persuasive speaking, public and private, as *eidē* (*Sophist* 222d). In contrast to "friends of the forms" like Socrates, the Eleatic argues that the *eidē* do not exist purely and independently of each other. On the contrary, he shows that the "greatest and first principle" (*megistou te kai archēgou protou*) of being (*to on*) not merely coexists but mingles with mutually exclusive conceptions or classes (*genē, ideai,* and *eidē*) such as motion and rest, same and other, that are said to be among the greatest.

At the beginning of the *Sophist* Plato merely indicates that both Socrates and the Eleatic Stranger are similar insofar as they are both philosophical followers of Parmenides, who break with their teacher by positing the existence of essentially different kinds of being. When the Stranger begins by asking what is a sophist, he seems to be asking the same kind of "what is . . . ?" question for which Socrates became famous. Given the choice of giving one long speech or proceeding through question and answer the way Parmenides had done in the conversation he had had with Socrates long ago, the Stranger observes that it is easier to proceed by question and answer with a tractable interlocutor and that he is embarrassed by the prospect of seeming to lecture Socrates. It thus looks as if the Eleatic is not only asking the same kind of question that Socrates usually does, but that he will also use a similar method of investigation. Plato quickly shows his readers, however, that the questions the Eleatic Stranger asks are not the same questions Socrates asks, even though the wording is the same. (Plato thus gives his readers an example in action of the problem with which the Eleatic begins—that people can use the same word or words to indicate different conceptions.) Likewise, when the Eleatic demonstrates his distinctive method of defining things by means of diairesis with the simple example of the angler, readers also see that the Eleatic's mode of questioning is very different from that of Socrates.

Although the Eleatic appears to be asking a Socrates-like question when he inquires what a sophist is, he describes the problem in terms quite different from those Socrates usually employs. Rather than inquire what sophists claim to teach (as Socrates does in the *Protagoras*) or whether sophistry is an art (*technē*), as Socrates explicitly asks in the *Gorgias*, the Eleatic comments (*Sophist* 218c) that he and Theaetetus may have only the name (*onoma*) of the sophist in common. In private (*idia[i]*) they may have different notions of the fact, work, or deed (*ergon*) they signify by that name. The aim of the argument is to come to an agreement about the matter with which they are concerned (*pragma*), that is, what is referred to by the name "sophist." The kind of answer the Eleatic seeks to his "what is . . . ?" question is thus very different from the kind of answer Socrates seeks. The reason for the difference, we discover later, is that the Eleatic does not think that anything is or can be known in itself; on the contrary, he argues, all things are and are known only in relation to others. He thus asks what we mean by "sophist" rather that what a sophist in itself is. Because sophistry constitutes a certain kind of imitation, the Eleatic shows in the end, it cannot be accurately described in itself. The term "sophist" does not constitute merely a conventional mark or evaluative label, however; it denotes a determinate or definable form of human activity and power (*pragma* and *dynamis*), which he, in dramatic contrast to Socrates, describes from beginning to end as a kind of knowledge or art (*technē*).

Just as the Eleatic's question differs from those of Socrates, although it resembles Socrates' typical question in form or "name," so his method of seeking an answer to such a question differs from Socrates' typical mode of proceeding, even though there is a certain degree of external resemblance here as well.[6] The Eleatic agrees to proceed by means of question and answer, rather than give a long speech, largely for the sake of his own ease and as a courtesy to Socrates. He thus indicates that the definitions of the sophist and statesman to which he comes do not depend on whether he proceeds by question and answer or presents one long argument; nor does the character of his interlocutor make any difference—except that he be tractable. Unlike Socrates, the Eleatic does not try to draw out Theaetetus' opinions or to force the young man to reexamine them. Nor does he, like Socrates in the *Crito*, subject his own opinions to reexamination. The Eleatic later admits to having come to a state of great perplexity (*aporia*) about being as well as not-being, but in explicit contrast to Socrates in his conversation with Theaetetus, the Eleatic proceeds to show how he resolved his perplexity with arguments he tells Theodorus he remembers from having heard them before (*Sophist* 217b).

Like Socrates (and all other philosophers, according to the Eleatic's own characterization of the "science of the free" or "dialectics" [253c–d]), the Eleatic attempts to sort things into different kinds, according to which ideas they share or do not share in. Also like Socrates, the Eleatic begins with a rather lowly, everyday example—an angler rather than a cobbler. The Eleatic's method of "sorting" is nevertheless clearly different from that of Socrates. Socrates tends to characterize "arts" such as shoe making

6. In the *Phaedrus* (265c–66c), Socrates also describes the division of things into kinds as diairesis and part of the science of dialectics, which involves collection as well as division. But Socrates never engages in the kind of dichotomizing the Eleatic does; Socrates speaks rather, like the Eleatic when he sorts out the parts of a political order late in the *Statesman* (287c), of separating things like a butchered animal at the joints.

and medicine in terms of the goods their practitioners claim to produce (the ends or purposes); the Eleatic begins by asking Theaetetus to agree that angling and sophistry are kinds of arts. The Eleatic then determines what kind of art angling is by sorting the different kinds according to the method or mode of externally observable action—making (*poiēsis*) as opposed to acquisition (*ktētikē*), acquiring by means of exchange or coercion, openly or secretly, of living as opposed to lifeless things, in the water rather than on land, by snaring rather than by speaking. He never characterizes angling—or sophistry—in terms of its purpose, motive, or any other sort of "good." He describes what the angler (or later sophist) does, where, with what, and to what or whom, but not why.

Although all the steps or specific dichotomies in the diairesis may not appear to be absolutely necessary, the Eleatic's divisions succeed in isolating the distinctive characteristics of angling as an activity. As becomes clearer in their much longer investigation of the sophist, the Eleatic does not ask his interlocutor to state his own opinion and then examine it the way Socrates does. The Eleatic proposes a statement or alternatives and asks his interlocutor whether he agrees or disagrees. His method of interrogation is thus much less confrontational than Socrates'. As a result it has a different effect. Culminating in an agreement on the definition of a term, it does not produce the kind of perplexity (*aporia*) that Theaetetus experienced the day before and that angered Socratic interlocutors such as Callicles and Meno.[7]

Because of the apparent, if superficial, similarity between Socrates and the Eleatic Stranger in the questions they pose as well as their method of answering and the eidetic conceptual basis of both the questions and the answers generated, many commentators have concluded that Plato's two philosophical spokesmen represent basically the same philosophical orientation.[8] If commentators note differences, they tend to conclude that the Eleatic represents a better, more mature version of insights and methods Plato may have learned from Socrates but developed much further on his own.[9] I argue that by having Socrates listen quietly as the Eleatic questions

7. Michael Frede, "Plato's Arguments and the Dialogue Form," in *Methods of Interpreting Plato and His Dialogues*, ed. James C. Klagge and Nicholas D. Smith (Oxford: Clarendon Press, 1992), 203–4, distinguishes "didactic dialogue," that is, leading an interlocutor by means of questions to the conclusion preordained by the speaker, as the Eleatic does, from the Socratic elenchus, which forces an interlocutor to confront and compare his own, often contradictory opinions.

8. Shorey (*Unity of Plato's Thought*) is the most famous advocate of the unitarian approach.

9. E.g., Sayre, *Late Ontology*; Friedländer, *Plato*, vol. 3; G. M. A. Grube, *Plato's Thought* (Indianapolis: Hackett, 1980); and J. B. Skemp, *Plato's "Statesman"* (New Haven: Yale University Press,

first Theaetetus and then Young Socrates, Plato, in the *Sophist* and *States-man*, sets two fundamentally different philosophical orientations in confrontation with each other in order to dramatize the advantages and deficiencies of both for his readers. The differences between the Eleatic and Socrates become clearer when the Eleatic develops a definition of the sophist that seems to fit Socrates better than anyone else.

II. Who or What Is a Sophist?

From the introductory exchange readers learn that both Socrates and the Eleatic are modified or pluralistic Parmenideans. As such they both recognize a difference between appearance and reality. They both thus speak about human beings who claim or appear to know what they do not and, perhaps, cannot know, whom they both call sophists. As the Eleatic observes at the beginning of his analysis of the sophist, however, people can use the same name but have very different ideas about it. And if we compare what the Eleatic says about the sophist with what Socrates says in other dialogues, we find that their conceptions of the "beast" are different because the knowledge sophists are said to claim, but do not in fact possess, is different.

Plato shows Socrates conversing with men who explicitly call themselves or are called sophists in the *Protagoras*, *Hippias Major*, *Hippias Minor*, and *Euthydemus*.[10] Although Protagoras, Hippias, Euthydemus, and Dionysodorus teach somewhat different subjects and skills—persuasive speech in the case of Protagoras, a comprehensive set of arts and sciences that includes speech in the case of Hippias, or methods to defeat their opponents in argumentative contests in the case of the brothers—they all claim to teach their students how to become virtuous or, somewhat conventionally put, *kalos k'agathos*, and thus to live the best possible form of human existence.[11] By asking them what virtue is and why they teach what they do,

---

1952). Dorter argues (*Form and Good*, 216, 235–43), however, that the Eleatic's arguments have to be supplemented by the concern for the good characteristic of Socrates. Mara ("Constitutions," 377–80) also finds Socrates to be superior.

10. I exclude Gorgias and Thrasymachus, often included among the "sophists," because they claimed and were known particularly for their teaching of "rhetoric" as opposed to sophistry, especially as defined and exemplified in these other dialogues.

11. We do not see Socrates questioning Prodicus, with whom Aristophanes particularly associates Socrates as a sophist in *Clouds* (360). Socrates refers to Prodicus' emphasis on the precise definition and use of words in several dialogues, and in the *Protagoras* he is said to have a circle of

Socrates shows that all these sophists understand themselves to be teaching their students the means of acquiring status and wealth. Pressed about the reasons anyone would want to attain political preeminence and position, these sophists concede that they teach their students how to maximize their pleasure—especially the pleasure human beings experience in feeling superior to others—with a minimum of pain (especially the pain involved in learning many difficult things).[12]

In the *Gorgias* (464b–65e) Socrates thus defines sophistry as a false imitation of one of the two branches of the art of politics, legislation. Forensic rhetoric is the false imitation of the other branch, corrective or punitive justice. This definition of sophistry was plausible to Socrates' audience, because the sophists all taught various forms of speech and argument, and laws were made, especially in democratic Athens, by persuading people in assemblies. The true art of politics, as Socrates defines it, aims at the formation or reformation of the human soul. The art of politics, as Socrates defines it, thus requires knowledge of the good—at least, knowledge of what is truly good for human beings, if not of the good in itself.[13] Sophistry is not an art, but only an imitation of an art, because it does not represent or rest on the requisite knowledge. It is a mode of flattery, because in appealing to what the people want, it falsely suggests that they know what is good. For this reason Socrates argues in the *Republic* (492a–b) that "the multitude seated together in assemblies or court-rooms or theaters or camps or any other public gathering" are the greatest sophists; in making policy decisions about what is noble, just, or advantageous, whether formal or informal, the multitude claim, in effect, to know what is good. Sophistry

---

students around him the way Protagoras and Hippias do. By referring to his fifty-drachma exhibition in the *Cratylus* (384b), Socrates shows that Prodicus also charged a fee.

12. In the *Protagoras* (358a) all the assembled sophists agree that they teach such calculations. In the *Hippias Major* Hippias insists from beginning to end that he himself seeks to please his audience by describing models of human virtue or preeminence as conventionally understood for them to emulate. In the *Hippias Minor* Socrates shows that Hippias' own vaunting of his own comprehensive knowledge contradicts the conventional belief, to which Hippias also claims to subscribe, that Achilles is superior to Odysseus because the former is simple and honest, whereas the latter is crafty and knowledgeable but devious. In the *Euthydemus* Socrates not only reports the brothers' insistence that they teach the only art necessary to make human beings virtuous and superior; he also shows how the students of the brothers take pleasure in—they laugh and applaud—their teachers' ability to best others in argument.

13. Cf. Gregory Vlastos, "The Historical Socrates and Athenian Democracy," *Political Theory* 11, no. 4 (November 1983): "Plato's Socrates most certainly has *a* doctrine of the 'royal art,' but it is not the same doctrine; . . . the knowledge Socrates has . . . has nothing to do with knowledge of the instrumentalities of the good life; it is knowledge of ends or, more precisely, knowledge of *the* end of the good life . . . the perfection of the soul . . . on which . . . the whole of human happiness depends" (506).

and rhetoric are not truly arts but are merely "knacks" (empeiria), Socrates thus states in the Gorgias (465a), because if they were arts, practitioners and teachers would be able to give an account (logos) of what they do and why. Neither sophists nor rhetoricians can give an account of what they do, because they do not know the purported end (the good) for which the ability to speak they purvey is purportedly the means of attainment.[14]

The Eleatic indicates that his understanding of sophistry is different from Socrates' when he asks Theaetetus at the beginning of their examination to agree that sophistry has the power of art (technē; Sophist 219a, 221c–d). By using another, simpler technē, angling, to demonstrate the diairetic method he thinks they will need to use to pinpoint the distinctive features and character of sophistry, he continues to treat sophistikē as a form of art. In both the cases of the angler and the sophist, he begins the diairesis by dividing the productive from the acquisitive arts.

When the Eleatic applies this method to the sophist, however, he begins with an understanding of sophistry that seems close to Socrates' understanding of sophistry and obscures the difference between them. Like the angler, the Eleatic observes, the sophist appears to be a kind of hunter. He tries to lure and then capture wealthy, leisured young men by promising to educate them in virtue by means of persuasive speeches delivered to them in private, as individuals, rather than in public. Unlike older lovers, however, sophists ask a fee for their speeches rather than giving them as gifts. If the sophist sells not only the speeches of others but also those he has composed himself, the Eleatic admits in his next several definitions and diaireses, sophistry appears on both sides of the dichotomy he drew between productive and acquisitive arts at the beginning of their definition of the angler. Both his interlocutor and Plato's readers might begin to wonder whether the Eleatic's bifurcating method will enable him to isolate or define the sophist.

The Eleatic seems willing to raise questions about the power and accuracy of his method in order to show that the sophist resembles Socrates more than that self-proclaimed philosopher is willing to admit. By presenting a series of descriptions of the sophist as a seller of speeches—his own, those of others, or a combination—who travels from city to city or

---

14. Both Harvey Scodel, Diaeresis and Myth in Plato's "Statesman" (Göttingen: Vandenhoeck and Ruprecht, 1987), 40–43; and R. S. H. Bluck, Plato's "Sophist" (Oxford: Clarendon Press, 1971), 40–46, point out the contrast between Socrates' definition of sophistry and the Eleatic's definitions in the Sophist, but neither identifies the centrality of knowledge of the good for Socrates, as opposed to the Eleatic.

remains entirely at home, the Eleatic shows that the sophist cannot be defined simply by the acquisitive aspect of his art.[15] The sophist must also be defined in terms of what he makes. Sophists not merely prove to be unable to make their students virtuous, even though they (falsely) claim to know how to do so and thus charge a fee for their lessons, as Socrates points out in the *Apology* (19e–20c); the Eleatic suggests that sophists appear and thus lead others to believe that they are wise, even when they themselves know—and perhaps even, like Socrates, openly and emphatically admit—they are not.

To show how the sophist produces (*poiein*) the false appearance of wisdom, the Eleatic next observes (without explaining why he does so) that the sophist not merely hunts young men by producing and exchanging speeches for a profit. Bringing back together kinds of activity they had separated out in their definition of the angler (and so indicating further how poorly that art serves as a paradigm of sophistry), he observes that the sophist also engages in a kind of fighting or competition—in speech rather than by means of force, with individuals rather than groups, by question and answer rather than long speeches, artfully about any subject, but particularly with regard to the just and unjust. The Stranger contrasts the sophists who compete with those who idly converse with others without giving the audience pleasure.

Having proved unable to pinpoint the defining characteristics of the sophistic art by comparing it to various aspects of angling or, more generally, by defining it as a branch of the acquisitive art, the Eleatic suggests that they try to understand sophistry in terms of another kind of menial task—sorting, sifting, or winnowing. Grouping these all together as arts of discrimination (*diakritikē*), he then identifies two basic kinds: the sorting of like from like as opposed to the sorting of better and worse. The first does not have a name, but it includes his own diairetic method of argument (*logos*). His mode of sorting things does not, like Socrates' definition of an art, take account of whether the activity benefits the recipients or whether it looks ridiculous or dignified. In considering kinds of hunting, for example, it makes no distinction between a general and a lice catcher. The Eleatic's method seeks only to determine which things in the arts are related, not

---

15. *Sophist* 259e–60a. The complexity of the descriptions of the sophist as a seller as well as a producer have led commentators (as well as Theaetetus and the Eleatic) to disagree about how many definitions of the sophist the Eleatic actually offers, as well as what exactly those individual definitions are. The diagram in Howland (*Paradox*, 195) is particularly helpful in showing the causes or places in which the confusion occurs.

what enables one to acquire intellectual understanding (*tou ktēsasthai gar heneka noun . . . katanoein*). The Eleatic does not, like Socrates, claim that the acquisition of intellectual understanding is itself useful or beneficial.

The second kind of discriminating, sorting better from worse, is generally called purification (*katharsis*). In the case of the body, it includes washing the outside as well as cleansing the interior by means of gymnastic training or medicine. There are also two different kinds (*eidē*) of evils (*kakia*) from which the soul needs to be freed. By distinguishing wickedness, which is cured primarily by "justice" or punishment, from ignorance, which is cured by instruction, the Eleatic shows that he differs from Socrates not only in argumentative method but also in substantive understanding of both the source and cure for human evil. According to Socrates, no one does evil willingly. Since everyone wants what is good (especially for himself), people do bad things because they don't know what is really good. By leading individuals to admit that they hold contradictory opinions, particularly about what is noble and good (*kalos k'agathos*), and so refuting them, Socrates says in the *Gorgias*, he corrects or punishes (*kolazein*) them. For that reason he claims to be the only person in Athens at his time even attempting to practice (one of the two branches of) the true art of politics. The Eleatic, too, maintains not only that refutation is an art but also that it cures the greatest form of ignorance and so benefits its subjects. Like Socrates, the Eleatic declares that believing that one knows what one does not know constitutes the greatest kind of ignorance. Further like Socrates, the Eleatic thinks most people have to be freed from this sort of ignorance before they will be willing to learn. Unlike Socrates, however, the Eleatic does not appear to think that virtue is knowledge. If it were, the cure for ignorance and vice would be the same (as it is, according to Socrates). The differences between the Eleatic and Socrates with regard to the character and source of human vice thus appear to be rooted in their different understandings of the character, extent, and possible content of human knowledge. So, more obviously, are their different views of pretended knowledge or sophistry.

Like Socrates, the Eleatic emphasizes (233a) that human beings cannot know everything. According to the Eleatic, the distinguishing feature of a sophist thus proves to be his ability to give others the false impression of knowing all things (as opposed to Socrates' understanding of sophistry as the claim to know "simply" what is good for human beings). The sophist creates this impression by refuting others. As Socrates observes in the *Apology* (23a), people believed that he knew when he refuted others, even though he insisted that he knew only that he did not know. The Eleatic does not agree with Theaetetus that the sophist is defined simply by his art (knowledge) of how to refute the opinions of others, however. As the Eleatic describes it, the art of refutation constitutes an important part or stage in the art of education. As readers see in the way in which he examines first one and then another aspect of the popular understanding of sophistry in order to show that it is inadequate and inaccurate, the Eleatic's own method of sorting like from like constitutes another way of cleansing human souls of false opinions, so that they can improve their intellectual understanding. Unlike the Socratic elenchus, however, the Eleatic's mode of sorting is neither confrontational nor productive of *aporia* (and thus anger). On the contrary, we see in the *Sophist*, the Eleatic gradually challenges and corrects widespread opinions, particularly the belief that the sophists are defined by their demand to be paid for lessons in virtue, which his interlocutor shares. The Eleatic does not ask Theaetetus to state his own views and then criticize them the way Socrates did. He merely inquires whether Theaetetus agrees with a widely held view and then examines that view.

According to the Eleatic Stranger, the sophist is not distinguished by his practice of the art of refutation, whether he asks a fee or not. *Sophistikē*, as the Eleatic finally defines it, consists in knowing how to make other people believe you know everything, even if the sophist himself recognizes that he does not, in fact, possess such comprehensive knowledge. A sophist knows how to make himself into an image or imitation of someone who knows what his interlocutors do not by refuting them in short speeches in private. As knowledge of how to create an image, it belongs to the productive rather than to the acquisitive arts.

Although Theaetetus points out that people study with the sophists primarily because of the political knowledge they claim to have and purvey (232d), the Eleatic insists that it is the all-encompassing rather than the specifically political character of the pretended knowledge that is crucial. Because it is impossible for a human being to know everything in truth, the sophist's apparent knowledge must be false.

In order to show how it is possible for a human being to appear to know everything, the Eleatic has to explain (*a*) how, contrary to the apparent teaching of his mentor Parmenides, something that is not (the case) can nevertheless appear to be (the case), and (*b*) how it is possible to create completely verbal as opposed to visible images. The Eleatic explains how it is possible to distinguish a copy from the original and thus appearance from reality by showing how we can differentiate one thing from another without contradicting ourselves by simultaneously maintaining that it is (exists) and is not (does not exist). He explicitly says that he presents his famous teaching about the *koinōnia* of the greatest *eidē* in order to show how *logos* is possible.[16] He does not explicitly say how the sophist's ability to create images entirely in words is related to or different from that of the poets, even though in book 10 of the *Republic* Socrates criticizes poets for seeming to make images of everything and so claiming to have a kind of comprehensive knowledge they do not possess. Although Socrates groups sophists and poets together with rhetoricians as people able to make persuasive speeches that use images, the Eleatic does not even mention poetry (although it would surely be included among the "poetic" arts).[17] The reason he does not may be that, in ancient Greece, the poets did not claim to be speaking out of their own knowledge; they claimed to be inspired by the gods and so to speak for them. The images the poets created were, moreover, of the speeches and deeds of others. As the Eleatic points out in his culminating definition, the sophist imitates using his own body. He does not pretend to be someone else, however, as an actor does. The sophist makes himself appear to be all knowing and wise by refuting others. No one ever mistook Socrates for a poet, but many of his fellow citizens were unable to distinguish him from the sophists.

The Eleatic's definition of a sophist seems to fit Socrates much better than it fits the foreign teachers Socrates and others called sophists. Protagoras propounded the notion that "man is the measure," which Socrates disputes at length in the *Theaetetus*, and Hippias paraded himself as a polymath; both tended to give long persuasive speeches; neither was content merely to refute his interlocutors. Euthydemus and Dionysodorus did teach the art of refutation, but they did not content themselves merely with refuting their interlocutors; they too claimed to teach virtue. Nor did they ironically admit that they themselves did not know.

16. The gist of his brief and perforce incomplete, if not inadequate, argument is this: just as being is broken up into and yet constituted by different kinds, some of which combine with one another, whereas others do not, and words can be broken up into letters and yet are composed of them, some able to combine and some not, so *logos* is constituted by combinations of different kinds of words, names and verbs, some of which can be combined and produce true statements whereas others cannot. If the latter are nevertheless put together, they produce false, if not nonsensical propositions.

17. In this dialogue, the only poem from which the Eleatic quotes is that by the philosopher Parmenides. It is Socrates who paraphrases Homer at the beginning. In completely ignoring poetry, the Eleatic goes even further than his teacher Parmenides, who quoted a single line from Ibycus (*Parmenides* 137a) to express his own feelings.

Why does the Eleatic Stranger suggest that Socrates is the sophist par excellence, in contrast to the statesman and the philosopher? Like the public, political indictment, the Stranger's accusation appears to have two parts. First, the Stranger charges, Socrates does not speak truly when he says that he knows only that he does not know the most important things. In the conversation he had with Theaetetus the previous day, Socrates claimed to possess an art of intellectual midwifery that looked very much like the art of refutation Socrates suggested in the *Gorgias* was at least part of the true art of politics. In claiming to be the only person at his time even attempting to practice the true art of politics, Socrates was claiming, in effect, to be not only a philosopher but also a statesman. All philosophers do not have to be kings or statesmen, according to Socrates, but all just rulers have to be philosophers. When Socrates says that he does not possess knowledge but merely seeks it, the Eleatic implicitly charges, Socrates does not merely "ironically" dissimulate about the character and extent of his knowledge. He makes himself look better and wiser than he is. The deception does not lie simply in the fact that the people who listen to Socrates conversing tend to conclude that he knows that about which he refutes the opinions of others. The problem, more fundamentally, is that Socrates presents a false image of philosophy. Because human beings cannot know everything or the whole, Socrates concludes, philosophy can only consist in a search for wisdom. Socrates claims to know, in other words, that human beings cannot attain knowledge properly speaking. Although the Eleatic agrees that a human being cannot know everything, in both the *Sophist* and the *Statesman* he maintains that human beings can acquire particular kinds of knowledge. Likewise, because Socrates argues that evils will not end in cities until philosophers become kings, the Eleatic will suggest in the *Statesman*, Socrates also presents a false understanding of statesmanship. According to the Stranger, statesmanship constitutes a particular kind of knowledge; it is not the same thing as philosophy, nor does the acquisition of statesmanship require a philosophical education. The second and more fundamental charge the Stranger levels against Socrates is, therefore, that Socrates does not understand the character and kind of knowledge human beings can attain.

III. Who or What Is a Philosopher?

From antiquity onward, commentators have speculated about the reasons Plato did not write a dialogue titled "The Philosopher." At the beginning of the *Sophist* the Stranger says he will be able to show that the sophist, states-man, and philosopher are three, even though it is difficult to distinguish them. But we have only two dialogues on the sophist and the statesman. Shouldn't there be a third?

It is important to note that in the course of their seeking the sophist, the Stranger remarks at a certain point (*Sophist* 253c), they seem to have found the philosopher. The philosopher as the Stranger defines him has a science (*epistēmē*)—perhaps the greatest—called *dialektikē*. This science consists in the "art" (suggested by the *-ike* suffix) of dividing things accord-ing to their class (*eidos*). Someone who has this ability (or "power," *dyna-mis*) can perceive the one *idea* that extends through many things separately situated, the many such ideas that differ from one another and yet are included in one, the one that arises from the combination of many such wholes, and the many ideas that exist completely apart and separate from one another.[18]

So described, the Stranger's understanding of dialectics and thus of phi-losophy bears the same name and initially looks very much like the peak of the education of the philosopher Socrates describes in the *Republic* (531d–34c). Whatever differences there may be in Socrates' and the Eleatic's understanding of sophistry, it appears that they have basically the same understanding of philosophy. That might even be a reason the discussion of philosophy per se is so short.

On examination, however, it becomes clear that Socrates and the Eleatic have different understandings of dialectics, corresponding to their different conceptions of the *eidē* and the two different kinds of "sorting" they prac-tice. According to Socrates, a person learns how to philosophize by gradu-ally moving up the "divided line" from looking at reflections or images of sensible things to the things themselves, and then from these "things," which are always changing and becoming, to the arts or "sciences," which enable us to recognize and understand sensible things as embodiments of intelligible types and principles, finally to examine the purely intelligible concepts and assumptions on which these "sciences" (which are not prop-erly so called) are based. But, Socrates insists, such a person or movement

18. To be sure, the Eleatic later says that "they may go on to consider him (the philosopher) with greater clarity, *if it's still our wish*" (*Sophist* 254b). At the end of their second conversation in the *Statesman*, no one expresses a desire to go on—not even the Eleatic, who steps in at various points in the conversation to challenge what Theaetetus or young Socrates thinks is an adequate understanding (e.g., *Statesman* 277a). They seem to agree that they have discovered what the phi-losopher is in defining his look-alikes, the sophist and the statesman.

should not be called dialectical "unless he [or it] is able to separate out the *idea* of the good from all other things" (534b). Neither naming nor apparently recognizing a supreme "idea of the good" among the "greatest *eidē*," the Eleatic does not identify *dialektikē* with the ability to isolate and give an account of the "idea of the good." As a result, he does not sort and define things, as Socrates does, according to whether they are better or worse. He separates like from like by determining whether and the extent to which they are same and different. Rather than posit, like Socrates, the "idea of the good" as the highest and most fundamental source (*archē*) of both being and intelligibility, the Eleatic treats being as the most comprehensive kind (*eidos*) that can be defined and so understood only as differentiated into same and other. He does not speak of the "being of the beings" or of a source.

In explaining why his "father" Parmenides' argument about the oneness of being has to be modified to allow for the coexistence of the greatest kinds (*eidē*) within being, the Eleatic presents a trenchant critique of all previous philosophy—pre-Socratic as well as Socratic. No previous philosopher has given an adequate account of being, he argues, because they have all limited themselves to inquiring about what kinds of things are, how many, and what sort. None has asked which kinds mix with one another and which do not—the finding the young Socrates had told Parmenides and Zeno would be truly "wonderful," because he argued that each of the kinds of being or forms is discrete. This argument is the one the Eleatic proceeds to challenge.

Those who have attempted to specify the character of being have conversed with us too nonchalantly, the Eleatic Stranger tells Theaetetus. In telling stories (*mythoi*) in which some claim that being is one, and others that it is two or even three, at war with itself or alternating between strife and marriage, previous philosophers have not cared enough about whether others followed their arguments. Swearing "by the gods" in an unusual display of emotion and so giving his statement emphasis, the Eleatic says that he thought he understood these "stories" when he was young; now, however, he sees that he is as perplexed about the character of being as he is about unsayable and unthinkable not-being. In explaining his own perplexity, he criticizes the theories of Empedocles and Heraclitus as well as Parmenides. Those like Empedocles who say that being consists in a kind of opposition of two elements cannot explain how the two different elements are related to being. If being consists in the relation of two other elements, would being not then be some third (thing) beyond the opposed pair? But if both of the elements in the opposition partake equally in being, as Heraclitus suggests, is being not some more fundamental one?

Those, like Parmenides, who speak of the all as one, face two other problems. First, in claiming that being is one, they are not able to account for the existence or being of the name as something separate from the thing or being itself. They do not, therefore, allow for the existence or intelligibility of *logos*. Second, the Eleatic observes that, according to Parmenides' poem, being is a sphere with parts. But if being is one, it cannot have parts (any more than it can have a name); it cannot, therefore, be a whole (or be counted).

Those who speak in a less "diacritical" way, not about the number of elements or principles in being but about its nature or character, also face insuperable problems. First, there are the thinkers who identify being with body. Second, there are those who dispute with the materialists by insisting that being is constituted by some purely intelligible, bodiless forms (*eidē*); these thinkers break bodies up into little pieces and describe them as always becoming.

Theaetetus comments that he has met many of the dreadful materialists, so the Eleatic Stranger asks Theaetetus to respond on their behalf to his questions. By having them engage in an argument, the Eleatic claims, he and Theaetetus are improving the materialists, if not in fact, at least in speech. The question arises, however, whether the "improved" version of their argument that the Stranger and Theaetetus critique actually represents the materialists' position; they, after all, deny the existence of anything immaterial, including presumably *logos*, as something other than sound and thought (*noēsis*). The Eleatic asks the "improved" (more rational and hence "tamer") materialists whether they would admit the being of soul, and Theaetetus suggests that they would declare soul to be a kind of body. Concerning intelligence (*phronēsis*), justice, and the other virtues the Eleatic asked about, the materialists would be ashamed either to deny that they have being or to insist that they are bodily.

In their original "autochthonous" condition, the Eleatic observes, the materialists would shamelessly deny the existence of anything nonbodily. But if they were to admit the being of anything bodiless, they might agree to the following restatement of their thesis: anything with the power to affect or be affected by anything else has being. In this refined version, the materialist thesis proves to be no other than the secret teaching Socrates attributed to Protagoras, Heraclitus, the poets, and all the other "flux" theorists, excluding only Parmenides, in his conversation the previous morning. Both Socrates and the Eleatic suggest that the thesis that being consists in a kind of opposition arises from reflections on the character of sensation (*aisthēsis*), how and what sorts of things are perceived. The problem the Eleatic pointed out with this thesis earlier was that it did not give an independent characterization of being (separate from the opposed forces or pair constituting it). Here he suggests such a unitary characterization—power (*dynamis*). Because the Eleatic does not take up this characterization or criticize it directly, some commentators have concluded that this is his own understanding as well.[19] The difference between the position the Eleatic attributes to the "improved" giants and his own nevertheless emerges in the course of the conversation. Although the Eleatic suggests that everything exists in relation to everything else, he does not agree that everything is constantly in motion. On the contrary, he argues, there are *eidē* of both rest and motion, which are mutually exclusive with each other, although both are compatible with being. There are some kinds or aspects of being which are at rest and not in motion.

In the *Theaetetus* (182a–b) Socrates and Theodorus agreed that a characterization of being in terms of the power to affect or be affected meant that nothing is in itself; everything exists only in relation to other things. And if everything is constantly both affecting and being affected by other things, both things and their relations are always changing. Everything is always in motion or flux. There are no purely intelligible units or enduring definitions of things. Neither *logismos* nor *logos* has any foundation in being.

Socrates and Theodorus initially agreed to examine Parmenides' thesis as well as that of Heraclitus, but when Theodorus withdrew, much to Theaetetus' disappointment, Socrates refused to proceed. It is not Socrates, but the Eleatic, who brings out a similar problem with his mentor's doctrine—in criticizing the "friends of the forms" who dispute the materialist thesis.

Socrates is clearly one of these "friends" who argue that being consists in some kinds of intelligible and bodiless forms, whereas bodies are characterized by becoming. The problem with this thesis, the Eleatic points out, is that it fails to explain cognition. Isn't that which is known affected by

---

19. See, e.g., Stanley Rosen, *Plato's "Sophist": The Drama of Original and Image* (New Haven: Yale University Press, 1983), 93, 101. The Eleatic does not say that everything or all attributes are "power," however. In his subsequent discussion of being, he can simply remind Theaetetus that the claim that everything is in motion deprives everything of intelligibility, because he probably knows from their account of the conversation Socrates had with Theaetetus the previous day (and, in any case, Plato's readers know) that Socrates has already shown the difficulties with the "improved" or "sophisticated" form of this thesis.

becoming known? And isn't the soul that knows it also affected? Moreover, isn't "the being that is cognized, to the extent that it is being cognized, to just that extent in motion" (*Sophist* 248e)? In other words, both thought and calculation (*logismos*) involve motion. According to the "friends of the forms," however, the pure intelligibles that have being are unchanging and hence at rest. If mind and soul both involve motion, there has to be some kind of interaction to overcome the fundamental difference between the mind and the being(s) it is supposed to apprehend. The Eleatic's critique of the friends of the forms thus resembles the last critique Parmenides made of Socrates' argument concerning the forms in their early conversation (*Parmenides* 134d–35b): the unchanging intelligibles could not be known by changing mortals. The Eleatic indicates that the same objection could be raised against Parmenides' own argument.

Theaetetus and the Eleatic agree that they would not want to deny motion, life, soul, and intelligence (*phronēsis*; *Sophist* 248e) to that which perfectly is. As a result, they face the following dilemma: "if the things which are, are motionless [as Parmenides maintained in his poem], there never is mind [*nous* from 249a] in anything about anything [contrary to Parmenides' saying that 'to be' (*einai*) and 'to think' (*noein*) are the same]." However, if they "concede that all things are sweeping along and moving [as Heraclitus and his ilk argued, they also] remove [mind] by this speech from the things that are" (249b). The intelligibility of being seems to require that it somehow be both in motion and at rest.

Reviewing his previous critique of the thinkers who maintained that being was characterized by a fundamental opposition, for example, between rest and motion, the Eleatic suggests that they might solve the problem if they agreed that being is something other than rest and motion, in which both rest and motion share, even though they themselves are mutually exclusive. He and Theaetetus might appear to be providing a "feast" for the young and the late learners who would object that they are contradicting themselves by saying that being is simultaneously both one and many. However, to those who are interested in discovering what being is (that is, potential philosophers), rather than merely in showing up or defeating others in argument (that is, eristic sophists), they would respond by pointing out that opposed qualities such as rest and motion cannot be said to be one, yet people who maintain that each and every form of being is entirely separate from all others make themselves ridiculous by saying that each "is" separate (and so in effect claiming that it has something, "being," in common with others). The only "solution" is to show that some of the things that are (like being) mix with others (like rest and motion), whereas others (like rest and motion) do not.

Just as there are certain letters (vowels) that mix with others (consonants), and others (consonants) that do not mix, so that one must possess a certain kind of knowledge (*grammatikē*) to distinguish and hence be able to combine them correctly, the Eleatic suggests, we need to have a science that can determine which of the kinds of being go through all so as to make them capable of mixing and which are unmixable and hence causes of the divisions among them. That "science of the free" would appear to be philosophy, that is, the dialectical science of dividing (things or beings) into kinds (genera or *genē*) according to their ideas (*ideai*). In seeking the sophist, the Eleatic exclaims, they seem to have found the philosopher. So long as they do not possess the requisite knowledge of the kinds of beings, however, both philosopher and sophist remain opaque—for different reasons. Whereas the philosopher is difficult to see because he lives in such a brilliant place, the sophist hides in the darkness of "that which is not." To discern either philosopher or sophist clearly, they have to identify the principle of differentiation more clearly. That is what the Eleatic proceeds to do.

He suggests that they review not all the *eidē* (which would include such specific or specialized *erga* as the angler) but only the greatest to see which combine and which do not. Both rest and motion combine with being, he reiterates, although not with each other. These *eidē* are thus three: "each of them is other than the two others, and itself the same as itself" (254d). Since sameness and difference are such crucial elements or aspects in the definition of any idea, the Eleatic inquires further about the character of this pair. "Are they themselves a kind of pair of two genera, different from these three [being, motion, and rest], but always of necessity joining them in a mixture?" (254e). Being and same cannot be one, the Eleatic points out, because if they were, nothing would be different. But he and Theaetetus have already agreed that rest and motion differ. He and Theaetetus thus agree that "same" (*t'auton*) constitutes a fourth of the largest and most basic *eidē* and that "other" (*thateron*) constitutes a fifth, because things are the same as themselves but differ relative to others. "And we'll assert besides that it has gone through all of them, for it's not on account of its own nature that each one is different from all the rest, but on account of its participation in the *idea* of the other" (255e). In other words, everything that has being is different from everything else; being is, exists, and is intelligible only as differentiated. It is differentiated, however, not only because it participates in the idea of the other but also because it remains the same as itself. If it did not, it and everything else would be reduced to ever-changing differentiation or flux and thus all be essentially the same.

The Eleatic's explication of the interrelations among the five biggest *eidē* lets us see that when the Eleatic states (253d) that a philosopher possesses the dialectical science of dividing (*diaireisthai*) things according to their class (*genos*), not supposing that the same and the other belong to the same kind (*eidos*), he is describing his own understanding and practice. His own distinctive method of identifying a class of things (in these dialogues, arts) and then dividing them (*diairesis*), that is, showing how they are the same and yet different, is based on his understanding that everything that is, is both the same and different and can be known only as such. He shows how the flatness of his own method of sorting things according to whether they are like or unlike, as opposed to Socrates' attempt to determine which is better or worse, is based on the same understanding of the fundamentally differentiated character of being when he asks Theaetetus about the opposites of the beautiful and the just. According to the argument they have just gone through about the mixing of the basic kinds of being, they agree that the beautiful does not have more being than the not-beautiful (as Socrates' understanding of the ideas suggests). On the contrary, they agree, that which is not beautiful is simply other than the beautiful. It participates in being as much as the beautiful. So the not-just participates equally in being with the just.

By reconceiving that which is not as that which is other, the Eleatic admits, he and Theaetetus have disobeyed Parmenides' injunction not to force "whatever is not to be" and to "keep your thought away from this way of searching." They have not, however, asserted the being of not-being and thereby contradicted themselves. They have not gone down the forbidden "way" of not-being. On the contrary, they have solved the two fundamental problems the Eleatic pointed out in his teacher's argument. They have shown how it is possible to have a name for being that is different from being itself. Also, by showing how being can be one and a whole, yet be differentiated and partly in motion, they have explained how being can be known by mere mortals.

Indeed, the Eleatic declares, the purpose of his argument about the intermixture of the basic kinds of being was to show how *logos* could be, "for if we were deprived of this, we would be deprived of philosophy" (260a). If they had not been able to show how *logos* can be, they would not have been able to say another word. Having used the way in which some kinds of letters (vowels) can be combined with others (consonants), which cannot themselves be combined, to make words as a paradigm of the mixing and nonmixing of the different basic kinds of being, the Eleatic points out that speech (*logos*) is also composed of two different kinds of words, nouns (*onomata*) and verbs (*rhēmata*), that is, the names of things (which remain accurate only so long as the things themselves remain the same in the relevant respect) and actions (which involve motion). Because all things cannot perform all actions, all names or nouns cannot truly be combined with all verbs. Human beings can, for example, truly be said to learn, but Theaetetus cannot truly be said to fly. The words "Theaetetus" and "flies" can be spoken in combination without obvious lack of sense, because they refer to something and not nothing, and there is nothing in their respective forms as a noun and a verb that prevents their being put together. The possibility of false speech (or in its silent form within the mind of the speaker, thought or opinion) thus arises from combinations of words that are formally correct but substantively not. Likewise, a person who mistook Theaetetus at a distance for Socrates would have not perceived "nothing." He would have perceived something as other than it really is and so have been deceived by a false appearance.

Theaetetus is amazed to see the perplexities with which he and Socrates had struggled the previous day so easily resolved. Plato's readers, however, should not be so quick to accept the superiority of the Eleatic's account of philosophy and *logos* as is the uncritical and somewhat impatient youth. In the *Theaetetus* Socrates had used arguments in questioning the possibility of false opinion that we know from the *Euthydemus* Socrates considered to be sophistic. Socrates was explicitly trying merely to act as "midwife" to Theaetetus; that is, he was trying to show the proud young man that he did not really know nearly so much as he thought. Socrates was not presenting his own view of things the way the Eleatic does in the *Sophist*. In the *Republic* Socrates treated images and opinions as mixtures of being and becoming, sensible and intelligible. In the *Theaetetus* Socrates showed the young mathematician (as well as Plato's readers) not only that perception is not an adequate basis or definition of knowledge, because it cannot account for mathematics; he also showed Theaetetus that there is a difference between true opinion and knowledge by reminding him that rhetoricians can persuade a jury of a true account of things without the jury thereby acquiring knowledge of what really happened. To be sure, in asking whether true opinion would become knowledge if it were explained by an argument (*logos*), Socrates was not able to give a definition of *logos* such that its addition would or could transform true opinion into knowledge. (The qualification is important.) Socrates took up three possibilities. The first was that speech consisted merely in making one's thought evident in sound. In that case, the addition of *logos* (sound) could not make a thought or opinion true or false, much less knowledge, because *logos* would be merely an image, as it were, of thought in sound (*Theaetetus* 208c). Nor could *logos*, understood to be the specification of the component parts of a thing, generate knowledge as opposed to an opinion about what the thing is. As they had seen earlier that a word could not be defined merely by specifying the letters or even the syllables that compose it, so they saw that no one could understand what a wagon is merely from a list of its component parts. In other words, it was necessary to pay attention to the order of the elements. In the case of words, as opposed to numbers, the whole was something more than merely a sum of its parts. In the case of a wagon, it was necessary to consider its use or purpose. But, Socrates finally observed, if they considered a *logos* to consist in a specification of what anything is by showing how it is distinctive, that is, how it differs from all other things, knowledge of any one thing would presuppose knowledge of everything else. This last difficulty appears, however, to be relevant to the Eleatic's way of defining things by sorting them into the same and different. If nothing is what it is in itself, because the kinds of being (*eidē*) are intermixed in themselves as well as in the particular sensible things that participate in them, nothing can be completely known until it is shown how it is not only the same as itself but different from everything else. Complete knowledge of anything would thus appear to require knowledge of everything.

In his definition of the sophist, we have seen that the Eleatic agrees with Socrates that no mortal can know everything. The Eleatic comes to that conclusion for a different reason, however. Socrates thinks human beings can never achieve full knowledge (*epistēmē*), because the cosmos consists not only of eternally unchanging, hence purely intelligible, entities but also of sensible, changing, and hence not fully intelligible things. And if the whole is not perfectly intelligible, it is difficult to say that or how it is perfectly good or to know what is good in itself. If the order or kinds of being are not hierarchically organized, the Eleatic suggests, on the contrary, a dialectician can sort out many different kinds of things and activities. The reason no human being can know everything is that there are so many different kinds (*eidē*). Human beings can, however, sort out and come to know some specific kinds of things. Whereas Socrates denies that anything short of knowledge of the good should be called science (*epistēmē*) and suggests that studies like geometry should not, therefore, strictly speaking, be called arts, the Eleatic observes that "science is one, but when the area covered by part of that knowledge becomes distinct, that part gets a name of its own. So the arts and sciences are spoken of as many" (*Sophist* 257d). He thus speaks of sophistry as one branch of the art of imitation, statesmanship as another kind of art or science that is paradoxically more cognitive than practical or productive, and philosophy as dialectical science. He indicates both the difference he sees between statesmanship and philosophy and their relative value in the *Statesman* when he tells young Socrates that they have not been seeking to find the statesman "as a problem set for its own sake but rather for the sake of their becoming more skilled in dialectics about everything" (285d).

Because Socrates and the Eleatic Stranger agree that no human being can attain complete knowledge, they both understand philosophy to consist in a search that has, at best, partial results. But each of these two Platonic philosophical spokesmen emphasizes one of the two aspects of the activity more than the other. The Eleatic is primarily concerned about the knowledge that results, whereas Socrates stresses the love that fuels the search. When Socrates questions his interlocutors, he is not as concerned about their learning what virtue, courage, justice, or beauty is as in showing them that they do not know what they think they do. Only when they come to question their own beliefs about the good, the noble, and the just will they join him in seeking knowledge of what is truly good and try to achieve it. Demonstrating little if any interest in human motivation or striving, the Eleatic does not seek to show his interlocutors that they hold contradictory opinions.[20] He tries to give them practice in sorting things dialectically so that they will be able to distinguish different kinds of knowledge. He claims to know something about what human beings do and can learn, whereas Socrates claims to know only about what human beings want.

Although he presents a comprehensive argument about the character of being as a whole in his digression in the *Sophist*, Plato shows the Eleatic speaking primarily about kinds of human knowledge. Like Socrates, the Eleatic Stranger may therefore be said to concentrate on the human things—in contrast to both the Athenian Stranger and Timaeus, who try to find guidance and support for human life and organization in the intelligible

---

20. The Eleatic mentions eros in the *Sophist* only in connection with one of his proposed definitions of the sophist as a person who pursues young boys, but asks wages rather than giving them gifts like a lover. He never talks about a desire for wisdom. Nor does he mention *thymos* in his discussion of the *Statesman*.

order of the movements of the cosmos. Like Socrates, the Eleatic concentrates on the human things, because, again like Socrates, the Eleatic finds *logos*, the distinctively human capacity, to be the key to the intelligibility of the whole. As we have seen, the Eleatic sees an analogy, if not parallel, between the intelligible structure of being and the structure of *logos*. As we have also had occasion to remark, in the *Theaetetus* Socrates raises questions about the intelligibility of the component elements as well as of the composite structure of words and hence about the parallel between *logos* and "being" the Eleatic would draw. Words are better keys to the character and organization of the whole than numbers, Socrates suggests, because words contain and allow for differences other than in quantity. In contrast to the Eleatic, however, Socrates concludes that the elements must be intelligible in themselves and not just in relation to one another, if they and things composed of them are to be intelligible as well. With the example of the wagon, Socrates suggests that combinations of different component parts can only be understood in terms of their purpose or function. In the *Phaedo* Socrates indicates that *logoi* are images of the beings as much as sensible facts or *erga*. Like sensible things, it appears, Socrates thinks that the arguments and opinions (*logoi* and *doxai*) he examines are distorted reflections of the things that are truly intelligible. Things sensible and intelligible can ultimately be understood only in terms of what they are good for—and hence the good in itself. Socrates does not claim to know the good in itself. Nor does he claim to understand the intelligible structure of being as a whole the way the Eleatic Stranger does.

If the Eleatic is an exemplar of the dialectical science and thus of philosophy, as he suggests, then in his judgment Socrates cannot be a philosopher, even though the Eleatic is too urbane to say so explicitly. He contents himself with intimating that Socrates is a sophist who imitates a knower by refuting his interlocutors in private conversations, even though he himself is perfectly and ironically aware that he does not know.

IV. Who or What Is a Statesman?

When the Eleatic answered Socrates' question of whether he thought the sophist, statesman, and philosopher were one, two, or three by saying that they were three, Socrates learned not only that the Eleatic was not simply a follower of Parmenides; he also learned that the Eleatic was not a Socratic, because a Socratic would have answered two. In the *Republic*, Socrates proclaimed that evils would not cease in cities until philosophers became kings or kings learned to philosophize. He argued that the knowledge required to be a philosopher and a just ruler were the same. Because they claimed to be able to teach virtue (and thus to know what it is), Socrates treated sophists as false imitators of both philosophers and statesmen. Although the Eleatic also describes those who rule without possessing the knowledge required to do so as "the greatest enchanters of all the sophists" (*Statesman* 303c), and the "science of the rule of human beings [as] pretty nearly the hardest and greatest to acquire" (292d), he does not agree that philosophers and statesmen have the same kind of knowledge. On the contrary, having defined a philosopher in the *Sophist* (253e) as one who possesses the dialectical science, he tells young Socrates in the *Statesman* (285d) that they have not been investigating the statesman for its own sake (and surely not in order to become one), but only for the sake of becoming more skilled in dialectics (and thus better philosophers). In explicit contrast to Socrates in the *Republic*, the Eleatic does not include dialectics in the many arts a statesman must know. Nor, according to the Eleatic, does the knowledge a person requires to rule justly and well consist in the ability to refute others that Socrates not merely possessed but, in the *Gorgias*, suggested was a part of the true art of politics, or in knowledge of the ideas, especially the idea of the good, which Socrates argued in the *Republic*, philosopher-kings must have. If, as the Eleatic concludes (*Sophist* 305d–e), the royal art of the king (*basilikē*) or politics (*politikē*) does not itself consist in a kind of practice (*prattein*), but in knowing how to weave together all the arts that do have practical effects (*tōn dynamenōn prattein*) to produce and maintain a population sufficiently moderate and courageous to preserve the polity, it is different from both philosophy and sophistry (as the Eleatic has defined them). According to the Eleatic's definition, neither Socrates nor his philosopher king is a statesman.

A. The New Interlocutor: Socrates

In the *Statesman* the differences between the Eleatic Stranger and Socrates become clearer than they were in the *Sophist*. Plato marks the heightened sense of confrontation by introducing a new interlocutor—named Socrates!

The Eleatic suggests that since Theaetetus had been questioned by Socrates the previous day and then by him, the young geometer may be tired. Theaetetus' companion agrees to take his place. Much has been made of the kinship the elder Socrates points outs out between himself and the two young Athenians: whereas Theaetetus looks like Socrates, the young Socrates shares his name. Socrates and the Eleatic agree, however, that neither the look (the literal meaning of *eidos*) nor the name of a thing necessarily reveals what it is. Readers see the truth of this point in action when neither Theaetetus nor young Socrates proves to have the philosophical interests or abilities of the older and more famous Socrates.

How, then, can we discover what something is—in this case, a statesman—if we cannot rely on the way things look or on names? According to the Eleatic, we need to look at its effect (*ergon*) or concern (*pragma*). Just as Socrates demonstrates his understanding of the art of politics in the *Gorgias* by attempting to correct Callicles, so, we shall see, the Eleatic demonstrates his understanding of statesmanship (*politikē*) as knowing how to mold the opinions of others to make them both courageous and moderate in the effect he has on his two young Athenian interlocutors. Whereas Socrates succeeded in moderating the hidden but nevertheless great pride the young geometer took in his intellect in the *Theaetetus*, in the *Sophist* the Eleatic explicitly encourages the modest, docile, and thus apparently moderate Theaetetus.[21] In the *Statesman* the Eleatic then seeks to moderate his explicitly "manly" companion, the young Socrates.[22]

The fact that Theaetetus' companion has the same name as the older philosopher has another, even more important dramatic effect. When the Stranger speaks to his interlocutor by name, he addresses "Socrates." He can be and, Plato reminds his readers, is addressing the elder as well as the younger.

B. The Eleatic's Indirect Critique of Traditional Views of Statesmanship

As in the *Sophist*, so in the *Statesman*, the Eleatic comes to his final definition by means of a circuitous series of bifurcating diaireses, broken up by several digressions. As in the *Sophist*, so in the *Statesman*, the Eleatic appar-

---

21. Cf. *Charmides* 157d–61b, where the title character is said to be moderate because he is (apparently although not really) modest.

22. Just as in the *Sophist* (265d), the Stranger claims to know Theaetetus' nature and thus to know what the young man will be inclined to think in the future, as well as at present, so in the *Statesman* (262c) the Stranger comments on the goodwill he has for young Socrates' nature and addresses him as "manliest of all" (263d). Rosen is not correct, therefore, when he claims (*Plato's "Sophist,"* 21) that the Stranger has no interest in identifying the specific characteristics of his interlocutors in order to persuade them.

ently needs to free his young interlocutor from some popular misconceptions that he also holds before they can come to a truer, more accurate view.[23] As with Theaetetus, and in explicit contrast to the elder Socrates, however, the Eleatic does not say that he is criticizing other views or ask his interlocutor to state these opinions as his own in order to refute them.

The Eleatic first takes up and corrects the widespread view of the statesman as a commander. Virtually all political leaders in ancient Greece were generals. The Eleatic points out, however, that rulers govern more by means of their intelligence than by force. Next, the Eleatic suggests that the statesman serves as a kind of shepherd. That was the mythological view of kings like Agamemnon, who were formulaically called shepherds of their people by Homer.[24] Perhaps for that reason the Eleatic corrects this view by reinterpreting three old myths about the foundings of cities. Unlike a shepherd, the Eleatic points out, a statesman does not belong to a different, higher species. Because he is a human being ruling other human beings, people will not agree to his rule unless it is based on laws to which they have consented. In discussing the relation between statesmanship (*politikē*) and legislation, the Eleatic concedes that a statesman would have to rule by means of law, because he could not be everywhere at all times. But, he points out, decisions based on generalizations like laws will always be inferior to those a statesman would make himself on the basis of his understanding of what is necessary or opportune in specific circumstances. Precisely because most people lack that understanding, however, they will regard anyone who claims the right to go beyond or to question the law as a potential tyrant and prosecute him. This is what, the Eleatic suggests (299b–d), the elder Socrates has failed to understand.

1. THE COGNITIVE COMMANDER

In seeking the sophist, the Eleatic first (*Sophist* 219b–c) divided those who had an art (*technē*) from those who did not, and then divided the arts between the acquisitive (*ktētikē*) and productive (*poiētikē*). Now, the Eleatic suggests, they must seek the statesman among those who possess a

23. Cf. Christopher Gill, "Rethinking Constitutionalism in *Statesman*," in *Reading the "Statesman": Proceedings of the Third Symposium Platonicum*, ed. C. Rowe, 291–303 (Sankt Augustin: Academia Verlag, 1995), 292.

24. Cf. Miller, *Philosopher in "Statesman*," 40–41.

science (*epistēmē*). Both arts and sciences are kinds of knowledge. The Eleatic does not explicitly draw a distinction between these kinds of knowledge, perhaps because he will identify the science a ruler ought to possess with the royal art (*basilikē*). But the initial division among the sciences he proposes is different from the initial division of the arts he used to define the sophist. The first distinction he draws, using arithmetic (more precisely, number theory) as an example, between arts (*technai*) that simply produce knowledge (*gnōnai*) and those like carpentry which have practical effects (*praxeis*), suggests that the sciences are more purely cognitive, if not theoretical, than the arts.

Readers may be surprised to learn that the kingly art is one of the former, "because a king can do much less by means of his hands and his body to maintain his rule than with the strength and intelligence of his soul" (259c). And if a statesman is defined by the knowledge he possesses rather than the effects of his actions, it does not matter whether he has a position of power. Since the knowledge required to rule a slave, household, small city, or vast empire is the same—the difference being merely one of size or number in the ruled—master, householder, statesman (*politikos*), and king are merely different names for people who have basically the same art.[25] The Eleatic's emphasis on the purely cognitive character of the statesman's knowledge appears to be a bit less strange, when he goes on to observe that instead of merely knowing how to distinguish one kind of thing from another, like a student of numbers, a statesman knows what orders to give others to bring something into being. He does not simply communicate the commands of others, as a priest or seer does the command of a god. The statesman knows what and how to command.

At the end of the first set of diairetic disjunctions between the purely cognitive and practical, injunctive or merely critical, self-originating as opposed to merely communicative arts, the statesman looks more like an architect than a carpenter. The question then arises concerning what kind of thing—living (*empsycha*) or not—the statesman brings into being with his commands. This question would be difficult to answer for those who understand statesmen primarily to be founders of regimes. Regimes order the lives of human beings but are not in themselves, strictly speaking,

25. The Stranger obviously disagrees with Aristotle, who begins his *Politics* (1252a7–23) by maintaining that kings, statesmen, household managers, and slave masters do not differ merely in the number of people they rule. According to Aristotle, these four kinds of rule constitute different kinds of relations, "partnerships," or associations (*koinōniai*).

living. Thinking in terms of a leader giving commands to his subordinates, and not distinguishing a statesman from a head of household, the Eleatic and young Socrates agree that the statesman gives orders concerning the becoming of the ensouled. As a result, they prove unable to distinguish statesman from other forms of nurturers and caretakers. If the Eleatic and Young Socrates had distinguished between the component parts and the whole or purpose of a political association, as the elder Socrates would have insisted they must, the course of the conversation and the definition of the statesman reached would have been very different.

2. THE SHEPHERD OF TWO-LEGGED PIGS OR FEATHERLESS BIPEDS

In contrast to the Eleatic's emphasis on the primarily cognitive character of the statesman's knowledge, his contention that statesmen deal with groups rather than with individuals in private seems commonsensical; it accords with the experience people have of politics. The humorous results of their attempt to determine the characteristics of the living beings the statesman herds are far from commonsensical, however. And the reasons why the Eleatic pushes young Socrates to describe human beings as featherless bipeds or two-legged pigs rather than as rational animals are far from clear.

The Eleatic asks how the art of tending might be divided, and Socrates answers, again quite sensibly, that the art of nurturing human beings could be separated off from the nurture of other kinds of animals. At first, the Eleatic's objections to this division appear to be principled, if not technical: Socrates had not distinguished between a part and a species; all species are parts, but not all parts are species. The distinction Socrates drew between humans and other animals is analogous to that Greeks commonly draw between themselves and "barbarians." The Eleatic seems to be suggesting that the difference between humans and animals is merely conventional, not natural. He also complains that the division between humans and other animals is lopsided and arbitrary, like a distinction drawn between the numbers between one and ten thousand, on the one hand, and all the other numbers, on the other. He says that distinctions, according to species, should be drawn down the middle, like that between male and female or odd and even. They are not made simply by separating one part off from all the rest (the not-x).

When the Eleatic tells the "manliest of all" young Socrates that other reputedly intelligent creatures such as cranes might divide themselves off the same way, however, the Eleatic's objection begins to appear to be more moral or pedagogical than technical. Human beings should not base their understanding of politics on the pride they take in their intelligence (especially when they are brilliant mathematicians like Theaetetus and young Socrates). As the Eleatic will make clear at the end of his "myth," human beings have to form political societies in order to preserve and protect themselves, not because we are particularly well endowed by nature with reason, but because we are much less well equipped than other animals with means of defense.

In their second attempt to find the distinguishing characteristics of the herd the statesman tends, the Eleatic thus begins with the distinction he first drew in the *Sophist* between tame animals, which can be domesticated, and wild animals, which cannot. He then divides those that can be domesticated according to whether they live in the water or on land, fly or walk, on two feet or four, with or without cloven hooves, have horns or don't, and interbreed or not. All but the last of these characteristics are directly related to the animals' ability to fight or flee from those who might attack.

"It is now more evident than in their search for the sophist," the Eleatic states, "that by this method of argument what is august is not cared for more than what is not or the great honored more than the small" (*Statesman* 266d). The Eleatic is not propounding a logical technique of definition, however, so much as he is gradually moving toward an understanding of politics as arising not from human nobility but from human need. As in his definition of the sophist, where the distinctions between the ability to sell retail or wholesale, whether in his own city or traveling from city to city, made the number and the order of the bifurcations unclear, so the Eleatic now admits that there are two different ways, one longer and one shorter, that produce somewhat different definitions of a human being. There are two ways, because the bifurcations do not follow neatly one from another in the case of numbers of legs, hooves, and interbreeding. The Eleatic acknowledges (266c), moreover, that the definitions to which they come are comical.

At first glance it looks as if the definitions of the sophist and statesman to which the Eleatic leads his young interlocutors are products of a technical process of bifurcation. As we examine the way in which he leads them to the final definition, however, it becomes increasingly clear that he is trying to get them to jettison common partial or contradictory notions they share without challenging them or the adequacy of their opinions directly, the way the elder Socrates would.

C. The Mythical Correction

The problem the Eleatic explicitly points out in the definition of the states-man to which they have come is that there are many different kinds of artisans who claim to know what to do (or command) to nourish and nur-ture the human herd. He does not explain why he needs to use a "large part of a myth" that he calls "childish" (*Statesman* 268d–e) to distinguish the statesman from these other artisans. Only after he has retold and rein-terpreted three old stories do we realize that his initial definitions of the statesman as a wise commander (or legislator) and caring shepherd reflect, if obliquely, traditional views. The Eleatic recognizes that mathematically educated young Athenians like Socrates and Theaetetus are not apt to be-lieve such old stories. He thus acknowledges that there is something play-ful about his use of the myth. He sees that he will not be able to free the young from the misconceptions they have inherited by confronting and trying to refute these views of the statesman directly, the way the elder Socrates might have done; if he tried, the young men would simply tell him that they don't believe such old wives' tales. Having shown that young Socrates retains something of the traditional view of a statesman as an all-wise commander and caring shepherd by arguing very untraditionally that the statesman's knowledge is more cognitive than practical and that the human herd he tends is a bunch of comically defenseless two-legged ani-mals, the Eleatic reinterprets three old stories to show that the traditional view is childish. In defining the statesman as a wise and caring shepherd, they have been looking up to him the way young children look up to their parents. In adopting the image of the shepherd, the Eleatic points out at the end of his myth, they have even implied that the statesman belongs to a higher species—that he is, in a word, a god.

As originally told, all three of the old stories the Eleatic reinterprets— Zeus's changing the direction of the movement of the heavens to signal his preference for Atreus over Thyestes, the rule of Cronus in the golden age, and the autochthonous birth of the original inhabitants of cities such as Athens and Thebes—represent accounts of the origins of political re-gimes. According to the Eleatic, however, all three of these stories refer to one cosmic event. In explicating the reasons for, and the effects of, the re-verse in the motion of the cosmos, which all three of these ancient stories reflect in different ways, the Eleatic also gives an account of the origins of political rule. But the account he gives differs significantly from the tradi-tion. Whereas the old stories suggest that political rule arises from the concern gods have for human beings, the Eleatic reinterprets the stories to show that human beings have to develop arts, particularly the political art, in order to protect themselves from hostile natural forces. The gods may have cared for human beings in the past, but, the Eleatic concludes his myth by pointing out, the gods no longer rule us directly. Human beings have to take care of themselves.

The Eleatic begins his account of the reverse in the motion of the cosmos by reminding his interlocutors that only the divine is eternal and unchanging. Because the heavens or cosmos is visible, it is obviously bodily, and neither it nor its motion can be maintained without change. For something like the motion of the cosmos to begin, a divine (preexisting, because eternal) cause must therefore be posited. Because nothing bodily remains entirely the same, the motion of the cosmos once begun could not persist without change; because the gods do not change, a god cannot be thought to be responsible for the reverse in the motion of the cosmos. Nor, because that which is eternally unchanging is intelligible as such, can the gods be thought to work in opposed or contradictory directions. The traditional story about Zeus's changing the direction of the movement of the heavens is not true. The motion of the cosmos first changed when the god ceased directing it. The god had to stop directing it because the cosmos is not, like a god, eternal and cannot move or be directed forever in the same way. When the god let it go, the cosmos tried to retain as much of its original motion as possible, rotating in the same place in the same way, although not in the same direction, by twisting back like a spinning top toward the direction from which it had initially been propelled. But when it had finally exhausted its initial momentum, a god had to take control and reverse the motion lest the cosmos, having used up its own resources, dissolve into an "infinite sea of dissimilarity." Rather than direct its motion himself, he gave the cosmos an order of its own (thus making it truly a cosmos), deathless and ageless.

Although the picture of the cosmos the Eleatic presents has some things in common with the cosmic views presented by other Platonic philosophers, it differs from them in significant respects. Like Socrates and Timaeus, the Eleatic begins by emphasizing that only the divine is eternal and unchanging. Because the heavens and the cosmos are visible and thus bodily, they are neither eternal nor perfectly intelligible. No human being could be present or know their origin. Like Socrates (or Er) in the *Republic* and Timaeus, the Eleatic presents his account of the cosmos and its motion explicitly as a myth. Socrates and Timaeus also observe that heavenly bodies move in opposite directions, but they depict these contrary movements occurring simultaneously as part of a beautiful, intelligible order they call good. Like the Athenian Stranger, the Eleatic Stranger suggests that the two kinds of motion remain in opposition. But in dramatic contrast to the Athenian, who associates the orderly intelligible motion of the heavens with the gods and urges human beings to ally themselves with them in opposing the disorderly motion of the bad soul, the Eleatic sketches a two- or three-part development that culminates in a godforsaken universe.[26]

The Eleatic associates the first era when the god directly guided the motion of the cosmos with the traditional stories about the rule of Cronus. During that era, the Eleatic says, Cronus appointed lesser divinities (*daimones*) to rule different parts of the cosmos and kinds of animals. Like shepherds, these divinities saw that all the needs of their respective flocks were met. As a result, there was no conflict or savagery. Among human beings "there were no regimes or possession of women and children either, for everyone came alive from the earth without any memory of those before" (*Statesman* 271e–72a). According to the Eleatic, the age of the rule of Cronus thus coincided with the age of autochthonous births. Because food was ready at hand, people did not need to farm. Nor did they need to find shelter or clothe themselves.

In the *Laws* (713b–14a) the Athenian urges people to imitate the way of life instituted by Cronus to the greatest extent possible. The Eleatic says, however, that this age was happier than ours only if people used the opportunity to philosophize provided by their leisure as well as their ability at that time to converse with other animals, "inquiring from every nature, whether with its kind of particular capacity it was aware of something different from all the rest, to gather intelligence" (*phronēsis*; *Statesman* 272c). But it does not seem likely that these peaceful, prosperous people philosophized, since the Eleatic later states that human beings developed the arts (and thus their practical intelligence) only when forced to do so by necessity.[27] And if people in this earlier age did not philosophize, life at that time was neither happier nor better than it is now.[28]

---

26. There has been much debate about whether there are two or three periods. Cf. Mary Margaret McCabe, "Chaos and Control: Reading Plato's *Politicus*," *Phronesis* 42, no. 1 (1997): 94–117.

27. As Scodel points out (*Diaeresis*, 81n9), because they were continually growing younger, people at that time were continually forgetting rather than acquiring knowledge. McCabe ("Chaos and Control" 107), and Rosen ("Plato's Myth of the Reversed Cosmos," in *Quarrel*, 71) also emphasize the importance of the lack of memory.

28. The implicit question here is why human beings develop their theoretical intelligence. Timaeus and the Athenian Stranger suggest that human beings are drawn to philosophy by

Because nothing bodily can remain entirely the same, the god and his subordinates had to stop guiding the movement of the cosmos and caring for the animals living in it. Bereft of divine direction, during this second era, the cosmos stopped turning as it had and swung back, revolving on its own momentum in the opposite direction. Great climatic changes and other natural disasters like floods resulted from the change in the motions of the heavens. Most human beings and animals died as a result. Because the generation of plants and animals is observably associated with the movement of the heavens (in the timing of menstrual cycles or mating seasons), the order of generation changed with the movements of the heavens. People and animals were still spontaneously born from the earth, but now they emerged old, with gray hair, and gradually became younger and younger until they faded back into the earth to become the seeds of another rebirth. With the passage of time, however, both the reverse movement of the cosmos in reaction to the cessation of its original impulsion and the generations of living beings living on the earth became weaker and weaker. Having used up its own resources and thus existing in a state of *aporia*, the cosmos was in danger of dissolving into a "sea" of infinite dissimilarities.

To prevent the degeneration of the cosmos into complete disorder and unintelligibility, the god again took charge and reversed the motion of the cosmos. Rather than perpetuate a cycle of divine rule followed by threatened chaos when the gods had to depart, the god made the motions of the cosmos self-regulating.[29] Because the god had made the cosmos self-regulating, the animals also now had to generate, nurse, and grow by themselves—rather than simply receiving what they needed from the earth or the gods. As a result, human beings find themselves living in an era of conflict. The cosmos they inhabit is a mixture of the previous two eras. Because it still contains some beautiful elements left by its divine maker (*dēmiourgos*) and father, it is not entirely unintelligible; it is not entirely in-

---

reflecting on the beauty and order of the movements of the heavenly bodies. Although Socrates says that philosophy begins with wonder in the *Theaetetus*, he is speaking there of the surprise that results from the perception of one's perplexity about something a person believed he knew. In general, Socrates traces the philosophical impulse to a love (*erōs*) of truth or the desire all humans share to know, so they can acquire, what is truly good. The Eleatic gives no reason or impulse for the development of his dialectical science.

29. The Eleatic describes the cosmos as a "living animal" (*zō[i]on*) presumably because it is self-moving and thus appears to have a soul. Perhaps because the god applies his divine mind to the ordering of the sensible world, the Eleatic also says that the cosmos has *phronēsis*.

telligible either, since everything is in flux. Because of the cosmos' bodily nature, many aspects of the existing order are harsh. Animals have to struggle to get and keep what they need to survive. Weak and unguarded by nature, human beings have to develop arts to protect and provide for themselves, lest they be torn apart by wild beasts.

According to the older, more traditional tales to which the Athenian Stranger recurred, the gods cared for human beings by ruling them or appointing other, suitable rulers and giving human beings the knowledge they needed in order to survive. Like Timaeus, the Athenian thus urged human beings to seek to understand and imitate the divine order. According to the Eleatic Stranger's reinterpretation and revision of these tales, human beings now and perhaps always live in a godforsaken universe in which they have to rule and provide for themselves.[30] Although he observes in passing that other old stories attribute the arts to gifts from gods like Hephaestus or Athena, the Eleatic maintains that the kinds of knowledge or arts human beings need to protect and preserve themselves are developed and acquired by the humans themselves without divine assistance or support.

Although the Eleatic had initially said that he would need to use "a large part of a big myth" (268d) to distinguish the statesman from other human caretakers, at the conclusion of his tale he blames himself and young Socrates for having "raised up an amazing bulk of the myth" and having been "compelled to use a greater part than they should have" (277b). It is easy to see why the Eleatic emphasizes how big his myth is: it concerns the origins, development, and final character of the cosmos. He had to use such a big, cosmic myth to show young Socrates (and the assembled auditors) that human beings do not acquire political knowledge as a result of their god-given or natural advantages. Human beings do not form political associations in order to develop their natural potential for self-rule or to become excellent by acquiring virtue.[31] They have to learn how to form political associations and to develop other defensive arts, because of their natural weakness and vulnerability.[32]

---

30. In both his account of the "Myth of the Reversed Cosmos," in *Quarrel* (68–77), and *Web of Politics* (40–63), Rosen persuasively argues that the previous eras represent different aspects of our current existence. The Stranger says that the cosmos now contains beautiful things from its divine origin, but he also emphasizes that it is not entirely beautiful or friendly to human beings.

31. The contrast with Aristotle is evident.

32. Readers thus see, retrospectively, why the Eleatic had insisted on characterizing the human herd not in terms of its intelligence but in terms of the means it has—or lacks—of defending itself (with horns or hooves) or fleeing from danger (with wings or numbers of legs).

As the Eleatic's use of the myth indicates, our understanding of the function or work (*ergon*) of the statesman depends on our understanding of nature as a whole. The first reason the Stranger criticizes himself for using a myth is thus that his account of the cosmos is and remains essentially mythical. Unlike the explicitly mythical descriptions of the motions of the heavenly bodies given by Socrates, Timaeus, and the Athenian Stranger, the Eleatic's account of the effects of the reversed motion of the cosmos is not based on observations of the mathematically calculable orbits of the heavenly bodies. His reinterpretation and rationalization of the three old tales does not appear to be very scientific. The cosmological basis of his argument about the kind of political knowledge human beings need to develop thus seems weak.

If the Eleatic had begun not with old stories but with astronomical observations of the mathematically calculable orbits of the heavenly bodies, he would have been led, like Socrates, Timaeus, and the Athenian Stranger, to emphasize the intelligible and thus beneficent order of the world. All three of these philosophers suggest that studying the intelligible motions of the heavenly bodies will help human beings learn not merely how the cosmos is ordered but, even more important, how to order their own souls. Political societies are established and maintained, according to all three of these philosophers, to enable human beings not merely to preserve themselves but to live the best life possible by acquiring as much virtue as possible.[33] Political societies should encourage some of their members to study the orderly movements of the heavens, because such studies help people learn how to become more virtuous by bringing order to their own souls.

Both in practice and in precept, the Eleatic objects that beginning with the first, the highest, and most beautiful things does not result in a true view of politics.[34] As he emphasizes by giving an explicitly myth-based account,

33. Cf. Charles L. Griswold, *"Politikē Epistēmē* in Plato's *Statesman,"* in *Essays in Ancient Greek Philosophy,* ed. John Anton and Anthony Preus (Albany: SUNY Press, 1989), 3:150, who notes "a fundamental difference between the ES's cosmology and that of Socrates . . . as well as a striking difference between their respective notions of political science and dialectic." Andrea Wilson Nightingale, "Plato on the Origins of Evil: The *Statesman* Myth Reconsidered," *Ancient Philosophy* 16 (1996): 65–83, also draws out the many differences, indeed incompatibilities, between the cosmological myth in the *Statesman* and those to be found in the *Timaeus* and the *Laws*. Convinced that "Plato" must somehow be made consistent (and that he apparently was unable to imagine different characters putting forth different understandings), she nevertheless tries in the end to merge them.

34. Skemp points out that "the *Timaeus* tries to give us a fully consistent cosmology in which astronomical facts have a supreme significance, whereas the *Politicus* uses for didactic purposes the notion of a periodic cosmic reversal which no astronomer could accept and which would be inconsistent even with the earlier half-mythical astronomy of the myth of Er in *Republic* X. Yet once

human beings do not observe and cannot know their origins. Rather than relying on high-minded speculations or inferences, he suggests, we should begin from what we do know—our own immediate, present experience. He acknowledges that the existence of some beautiful intelligible things indicates that the cosmos has a divine origin. (The Eleatic never suggests that the world is completely unintelligible, that everything exists in conflict with everything else, or that everything is in flux.) But, he insists, we do not know the origins. And when we reflect on our own experience, without the mythological or cosmological dressing up we have inherited, we are confronted with our own natural weakness. Whatever may have been the case in the past, we have no direct experience of divine care or rule.

The Eleatic says that they were compelled to use too large a part of the myth, because his retelling of the old stories appears to represent a sketch of the view of nature as a whole on which his view of politics is based. In fact, he has merely reinterpreted three old stories in order to free young Socrates (and their audience) from the remnants of the old, mythologically based views of statesmen or kings as godlike shepherds and all-knowing commanders. The Eleatic knows that he has not presented an empirically based, scientific account of the character of the cosmos.[35] That is not, as he sees it, the place to begin trying to understand politics or the art of the statesman. We should instead acknowledge our lack of natural equipment and then investigate the means, the arts human beings have gradually developed to protect and preserve themselves, beginning with the smallest and most menial. If the art of the statesman is a discrete form of knowledge, distinguishable from both sophistry and philosophy, it does not require knowledge of nature as a whole to determine what that art is.

By having the Eleatic complain about the necessity of using such a large myth—larger and more than he thought appropriate—Plato indicates that our understanding of human nature cannot be entirely severed from a broader understanding of nature as a whole. Yet if, as the Eleatic emphasizes, human beings cannot know the origins or first principles, human knowledge will always be incomplete. And if human knowledge is incomplete, human

---

the impossible 'reversal of rotation' is tolerated, the *Politicus* account seems to do less violence to observed facts than the *Timaeus* does—for the basic principle that reason causes circular physical movement leads in the *Timaeus* to extraordinary psychological and physiological conclusions" (*Plato's "Statesman,"* 89).

35. I thus agree in part, but only in part, with Christopher Rowe's warning against taking the myth as "serious history or cosmology"; Rowe, "The *Politicus*: Structure and Form," in Gill and McCabe, *Form and Argument*, 160n17.

beings will disagree not only about the character of the natural order but also, and more stridently, about the ends of politics. At the end of his myth, the Eleatic points out that they had erred not only in treating the statesman as a shepherd and thus implicitly as a member of a higher species; by neglecting to differentiate between caring (*therapeuein*) and nourishing (*trophē* or *agelaiotrophikē*), they had also failed to distinguish care for the entire community from concern for a part. Finally and perhaps most importantly, they had not paid attention to the difference between rule based on force and rule based on consent. If human knowledge is both rare and tenuous, the few who actually learn what is needed to establish and maintain a polity will have difficulty persuading the many who lack such knowledge. That is the reason, we shall see, that the rule of law becomes a problem—perhaps the central problem—when the Stranger begins to define the art of politics, as it really exists, rather than as it has been traditionally and more nobly portrayed, using the menial, even feminine art of weaving as a paradigm.

D. Weaving as a Paradigm of Statesmanship

Young Socrates thinks they have come to an adequate definition of the statesman as a human ruler who knowledgeably cares for the entire community on the basis of consent rather than force. Because this definition hides a fundamental problem, the Eleatic insists, they have just begun. Having brought out the defects of the old model or paradigm of divine rule, they need a new example—or, really, two.

Like Socrates in the *Theaetetus* and himself in the *Sophist*, the Eleatic uses the learning of letters as a model of learning more generally. Just as children who are able to recognize different letters in simple combinations make mistakes when they confront more complicated words and sentences, so "we should not be surprised if our soul is naturally affected the same way with regard to the elements of all things, that sometimes it is consistent and gets to the truth, but that sometimes it becomes distracted, opining correctly about some mixtures, but failing to recognize the same elements when they are rearranged and placed in the long and difficult syllables of the things of concern particularly to human beings [*pragmata*]" (*Statesman* 278d). To avoid making mistakes, human beings need to divide things into their basic elements and look at those elements in smaller, simpler combinations so as to learn how to decipher larger, more complex mixtures.

They are not concerned with the character of learning or knowledge generally, however. They are seeking to identify the kind of knowledge human beings need to defend themselves from the attacks of wild beasts. The Eleatic does not raise questions, therefore, about the character (intelligible or not) of the elements or their combination, as Socrates had in the *Theaetetus*, or about whether the combinations of letters and words reflect the character of the things to which they refer, as he had in the *Sophist*. On the contrary, having indicated earlier that the political art involves the co-ordination of other lesser arts when he compared the statesman to an architect (259e), the Eleatic proposes another paradigm of a simpler kind of coordination of arts (which, as opposed to elements, are intelligible) that enables human beings to protect themselves from natural afflictions.[36] Because defense is not a good in itself, the Eleatic does not talk about the end (*telos*) of politics; he describes its function (*ergon*) or concerns (*pragmata*).[37] By choosing an art practiced primarily by women in ancient Greece as a paradigm of politics, the Eleatic emphasizes the source of its defensive character and thrust in physical weakness.[38] According to the Eleatic, politics is not essentially acquisitive or aggressive.[39]

The Eleatic quickly defines the character of the product of weaving (279c–d) by contrasting it in a series of bifurcations to arts that positively achieve some effect (*poiein*), as opposed to repelling or preventing (*mē paschein amuntēria*). Then he points out that weavers need to employ two other kinds of artisans—those who know how to make the instruments they use and those who produce the materials they weave together with those instruments—in order to exercise their own art. To define the art of weaving, it will not suffice to determine what no other artisan but a weaver does (plaiting the warp and the woof); one also has to show how the weaver uses the products of other arts.

---

36. As forms of knowledge, the arts are intelligible. Their intelligibility may be a product simply of the intelligence of the human artisan. The materials with which the artisans work—or the "elements"—may not be intelligible in themselves.

37. Pace Rosen, who declares that "weaving is . . . also defective as a paradigm . . . because it is a peaceful, feminine art of the household" (*Web of Politics*, 153). Melissa Lane, *Method and Politics in Plato's "Statesman"* (Cambridge: Cambridge University Press, 1998), 164–71, notes that Aristophanes had used weaving as a metaphor for politics in his *Lysistrata*.

38. This statement is in contrast, for example, to that of the Cretan elder Clinias at the beginning of the *Laws* (625e–26b).

39. This statement is in contrast, for example, to that of the Cretan elder Clinias at the beginning of the *Laws* (625e–26b).

Having indicated more fully than he had in his first diairesis how the statesman, like an architect or a weaver, has to bring together the work of a variety of different artisans in order to bring something into being, the Eleatic now clarifies the difference between the kind of knowledge involved in this kind of coordination and that represented by other primarily cognitive arts like mathematics. Readers see that the Eleatic has not entirely abandoned his initial definitions of the statesman as a commander and caretaker.[40] He used the myth to show that the knowledge involved is human, that is, of things that come into being and are therefore not eternal, and that human beings seek and develop such knowledge not because of their extraordinary natural intelligence so much as their natural defenselessness. But, having demoted the status of statesmanship from the divine to the human and compared it to the relatively menial art of weaving, the Eleatic has to prevent the brilliant young mathematician from contemning the knowledge of the statesman or, even worse, denying that the statesman has any knowledge whatsoever.

E. The Necessity of Recognizing Two Kinds of Measure

The Eleatic points out that, like other clever men who want to appear wise, the young geometer may later observe that everything that becomes can be measured mathematically and thus recognize one and only one kind of measurement. If he does, he will deny that the "arts" that bring beautiful and good things into existence are, strictly speaking, forms of knowledge. He will reduce them, as Socrates reduced cookery and rhetoric, to mere knacks for which some clever people display a natural talent.[41]

There are two ways of determining whether something is excessive or deficient, the Stranger explains. The first way is that characteristic of mathematical arts—such as calculation, geometry, and astronomy—which measure things relative to each other in terms of a common standard, for example, units, inches, pounds, motion. The arts that produce good and beautiful things or people—like architecture, weaving, and politics—also

40. Cf. Christopher Rowe, introduction to *Reading the "Statesman,"* 14.

41. Contemporary social scientists tend to regard outstanding individual leaders this way, if they pay attention to leadership or leaders at all. Leadership (or, in more old-fashioned terms, statesmanship) is not the sort of thing that can be counted (or, therefore, known, according to these quantitative social scientists), although leadership can in a sense be quantified. Some people display more; others demonstrate less.

use this kind of measure. As Rosen points out, one has to know how big a man is to make an effective cloak; this kind of measurement, however, does not enable a cloak maker to know how soft the woof should be to provide the requisite amount of warmth to repel the cold under the particular climatic conditions, or how tough the warp should be to make the cloak fit to repel rain.[42] Arts that involve a bringing together of a variety of different materials and skills must employ a different kind of measure. Because the component parts of these arts are not commensurable, expert practitioners of these arts cannot determine how much of any given part is fitting, opportune, or needful by using a single external standard to measure them all relative to each other. Such artisans have to look to a place in the midst of things, where all the requisite parts come together in the proper proportion to produce the desired outcome. They must look, in other words, to the mean (*metrion*).

Because the softness or toughness of the fiber used to make a cloak seems to depend on its purpose, protecting people from the natural elements, commentators such as Rosen have identified the mean with the purpose of the art in question. As we have already seen, however, the Stranger does not define arts in terms of their ends (*telē*); he speaks instead about their work or function (*ergon*). He does not, therefore, talk about purposes or ends in this passage. Although ends and functions may appear to be similar so long as we are talking about things, human purposes have to be intentional whereas functions do not. It is possible to determine how something functions simply by observing it, but to determine what someone's purpose is, you must ask him. Most of the Eleatic's arguments thus rest on externally observable characteristics and acts of human beings. He does not have to interrogate his interlocutors the way Socrates does in an attempt to discover their motives and intentions.

The Eleatic's description of the mean as the measure of what is fitting, opportune, or needful sounds a great deal like Aristotle's definition of the moral virtues in terms of the mean. Indeed, because the Eleatic's definition of the mean as the fitting, opportune, and needful sounds particularly like Aristotle's definition of practical wisdom, as knowing the right thing to do, in the right way, at the right time, by the right person, commentators such as Rosen have taken the Eleatic's description of the mean to refer

---

42. Rosen's discussion of the two kinds of measure in *Web of Politics* (123–25) is extremely useful.

to the prudence a statesman must possess.[43] As Rosen admits, however, the Eleatic does not mention *phronēsis* in this passage any more than he does *telos*. Although the Eleatic says that good and bad people differ primarily in exceeding or falling short of the mean (*Statesman* 283e), he does not propose the mean as a measure of virtue. He introduces it as the kind of measure that has to be used in the productive arts more generally, those that fabricate things as well as those that form human beings.

If the Eleatic had defined arts, as Socrates does, in terms of the good they produce, arts could be evaluated, that is, praised or blamed, in terms of how much or little of that good they actually produce. Because he evaluates everything in terms of a single standard, the good, Socrates does not need to introduce a teaching about two kinds of measure in order to explicate the character of political knowledge. On the contrary, in the *Republic* he points out the way in which studies of mathematics prepare young people for philosophy and thus for rule. As the Eleatic emphasizes in the *Sophist*, he sorts like from like. He does not evaluate things by sorting them hierarchically into better and worse. Nor does he define things in terms of their end. He defines things in relation to each other, how they are same and different; he does not use a common unit or standard to measure them. As he proceeds, readers see that the Eleatic describes the two kinds of measure to show both his own audience and Plato's readers that neither his method of diairesis nor his understanding of philosophy as *dialektikē* is fundamentally mathematical. Despite his earlier emphasis on the importance of dividing things down the middle (from which he is about to depart), the distinctions or divisions the Eleatic makes are not quantitative. They are qualitative. Insofar as the Eleatic was trying, like his teacher Parmenides, to separate the "is" from the "is not," the divisions were supposed to be down the center. We now know, however, that his sorting of things was in terms of the ways they were the same and the ways they differed from others.

The Eleatic does not introduce the two different arts of measurement (*metrētikē*) simply or perhaps even primarily in order to describe the art of the statesman. He uses this methodological digression to defend his

---

43. Cf. ibid., 125–26. As Griswold points out, the Stranger's use of *phronēsis* (including his attribution of it to the cosmos at *Statesman* 269d) is "rather far from Aristotle's notion of *phronēsis* (which is not an *epistēmē* or *technē* for him); in particular, the ES's political science does not seem guided by 'moral virtue,' at least not in any sense of 'virtue' more edified than that useful to a city and its citizens for their survival" ("*Politikē Epistēmē*," 152–53).

own apparently circuitous way of defining the statesman's art. Just as they had "compelled 'that which is not' to be" in the *Sophist*, in order to show how it was possible for someone to make false images in speech, so, the Stranger tells Socrates, "they must compel the more and less to become measurable relative not only to one another but also to the becoming of the mean, if anyone is to become a scientific knower of matters of action [like a statesman]" (*Statesman* 284b–c). But observing that an explanation of "the precise itself," which includes both arts of measurement, would require an even more extensive argument than the one he had presented about the being of that "which is not," the Eleatic concludes that it is sufficient at present for them to believe that there are these two forms of measurement, because such a belief prevents them from grouping all arts of measurement together without investigating the differences among them.[44]

They have been investigating not merely the art of weaving but even the kingly art of the statesman, the Eleatic announces, not so much for its own sake as to practice dialectics. People who fail to distinguish between the two kinds of measure (whom commentators frequently identify as geometricians, especially Pythagoreans) show that they are not in the habit of dividing things into classes (*eidē*).[45] Such people group similar things together as the same without inquiring about the differences among them. Just as children learning letters spell out words not merely for the sake of mastering that particular word but in order to read and write more generally, so, the Eleatic tells Socrates, they have had to practice by using simpler, more immediately perceptible paradigms like weaving in order to learn how to sort things dialectically. It is necessary to use examples that are "naturally there for easy understanding . . . which are not difficult to

---

44. As Seth Benardete, *Plato's "Statesman"* (Chicago: University of Chicago Press, 1984), 3:116, points out, the "precise itself" looks like the "good in itself." Jacob Klein, *Plato's Trilogy* (Chicago: University of Chicago Press, 1977), identifies them (175) and thus argues that the Eleatic's statesman must be a philosopher (177). The Stranger does not explain "the precise itself" any more than Socrates explained the "good in itself." The precise obviously does not have the moral connotations of the good, however. Nor are the reasons the two philosophers give for their failure to explain the primary and most important "thing" the same. Whereas Socrates tells Glaucon that he cannot even state his opinion about the good in a way the young man could understand, the Stranger tells young Socrates that it would take too long to explain the precise itself. He postpones the explanation; he does not indicate that such an explanation cannot be given or that he himself could not give it. Contrary to Klein's inference, the Eleatic never says that a statesman needs to know the precise in itself. He thinks they can specify what a statesman knows without giving the lengthy argument necessary to explain the precise itself.

45. Benardete, *Statesman*, 117; Miller, *Philosopher in "Statesman,"* 68.

make plain . . . apart from speech" because "no image has been devised as plain as day for human beings in the case of the biggest and most honorable things" (285e–86a). The Eleatic does not say whether the science of the statesman (*epistēmē politikē*) or the kingly art (*basilikē*) is one of the biggest and most honorable things. It seems to be somewhere in between the easily perceptible and the entirely bodiless. Although it is easy to see leaders and cities, both the intelligence it requires to maintain a city and the regime or order the statesman establishes in it are invisible, difficult to discern, and extremely important.

Anyone who complains about the disagreeable length or circular orbitings of the arguments he has given "about the art of weaving, about the unwinding of the all, and, in the case of the sophist, about the being of 'that which is not,'" the Eleatic concludes, needs to show that it would be possible to make them "more capable of dialectic and making the way things are plain in speech" (286b, 287a) with briefer, more direct remarks. The proper length of speeches is not measured by the pleasure they give. Like Socrates, the Eleatic concedes that others may not see the point of his mode of arguing and find it disagreeable. It is important to note that the Eleatic admits here that he has been trying to teach his young associates how to argue dialectically and that the way he has chosen to do so is indirect (*kuklō[i]*).[46]

F. The Statesman and His Art

Using weaving as an example, the Eleatic now admits that it is difficult to separate the art of the statesman from the products and services other artisans contribute to the final product by cutting down the middle. They will proceed, therefore, as Socrates does in the *Phaedrus* by dividing it as if it were a "sacrificial animal," limb from limb. It is tempting to conclude that the Eleatic's insistence on cutting things down the middle in his diaireses earlier had been a rhetorical ploy, designed particularly to appeal to two young geometers. We should resist that temptation, however, by remembering that the Eleatic's method of division arises from his contention that beings can be sorted into classes not only according to the

46. Cf. John M. Cooper, "Plato's *Statesman* and Politics," in *Proceedings of the Boston Area Colloquium in Ancient Philosophy*, ed. John J. Cleary and Gary M. Gurtler (Lanham, MD: Rowman and Littlefield, 1997): "The Visitor From Elea['s] . . . main . . . purpose is to teach Young Socrates . . . and the others present how to be better dialecticians" (71).

respects in which they are the same but also according to the several ways in which they may differ. Politics has been shown to require a different kind of knowledge than mathematics. The Eleatic thus has to use a different method of sorting, proceeding in stages or parts, rather than simply bifurcating, to separate it not only from the arts that contribute to it but also from its competitors and imitators.

The Eleatic first cuts off all the arts that provide useful tools and services. The tools include instruments, vessels, supports, defenses, ornaments, raw materials, and all forms or sources of nourishment. The services begin with the labor of slaves, who obviously do not claim to be kings, and include merchants as well as free laborers, heralds, scribes, and priests. The most important public servants from which the statesman must be distinguished are, however, those who pretend to be statesmen by actually governing. These are "the greatest enchanter[s] of all the sophists" (*Statesman* 291c).

These "enchanters" do not look like imitators of the wise, that is, sophists as the Eleatic had finally defined them in the *Sophist*. They do not give others the false impression that they know everything by refuting interlocutors in private conversations. Like the sophists, as Socrates defined them in the *Gorgias*, they pretend to be legislators and kings. We see the connection between the Eleatic's earlier definition and his present identification of the "greatest" examples, however, if we think of the elder Socrates silently listening to the conversation. By refuting and so correcting his interlocutors in the *Gorgias*, Socrates had claimed to be the only person in Athens even trying to practice the true art of politics. But, as the Eleatic indicated in the *Sophist* and argues more explicitly in the *Statesman*, Socrates cannot practice the true political art because he does not possess it. If he did, he would know that people who want to preserve the rule of law will not allow individuals to go around questioning the wisdom of their laws in private any more than they will tolerate them in public assemblies. Socrates is not the example of a sophist par excellence simply because he gives his interlocutors the impression that he knows everything by refuting everyone else; like the politicians, Socrates appears to be an even greater "enchanter" and sophist when he claims that his refutations constitute the true political art.[47]

---

47. The Eleatic actually uses the singular, *megiston goēta*. In the *Symposium* (203d), *erōs*, and thus by implication Socrates, is also described as a *goēs*.

I. The Tension between Knowledge and Law

Governments are usually characterized by the number of people in power, the Eleatic observes. They are also differentiated by whether the rule is voluntary or compulsory, whether rulers are rich or poor, and whether their rule is by law or lawless. If the statesman is distinguished from all others by his knowledge, however, none of these characteristics suffices to define him. But it is clear, if the only true and best form of government requires knowledge, that democracy never represents the best form of government because few people are able to possess even lesser forms of knowledge, much less the complex kind of knowledge called statesmanship. That one person—or perhaps a few—who employs science justly to improve the city as much as he can while still keeping it safe rules correctly, whether he uses force or persuades others.[48] Because no one or small number of rulers can supervise each and every citizen individually at all times, scientific rulers must lay down laws to guide people in general. But these laws never represent more than general rules of thumb—stating what is best most of the time, in most places, for most people. Because "the dissimilarities of human beings and their actions are so great, and the human beings themselves are constantly changing" (Statesman 294b), no scientific or true ruler will feel unalterably bound by these general rules.

Those who would acquire and practice the art of politics face an obstacle, however, of a kind no other artisans or scientists confront. People recognize that expert physicians or pilots may not merely have to contravene the rules and go against accepted practice, they may even have to force their patients or passengers without their consent to do what is good for them. The "proof" is in the proverbial pudding—whether the people who claim to have knowledge can save lives or, in cases when they

48. Because the Eleatic speaks about just rule and improving the city, commentators such as Dorter have argued that, in the end, the Eleatic's understanding of politics is no different from that which Socrates presents in the *Republic*. It is important, therefore, to stress the Eleatic's explicit qualifications on rulers "employing science and the just and, *in keeping it safe*, make it better from worse, *to the best of their ability*" (*Statesman* 9293e) and later his distributing "to those in the city that which with mind and art is most just, and *can keep them safe* and make them better from worse *as far as possible*" (297b). Although Socrates introduces guardians as needed for defense, in legislating for *kallipolis* later, he does not pay much if any attention to the requirements of defense. His concern becomes, first, the justice, and then the preservation or decay, of the regime. In the *Laws* the Athenian Stranger more explicitly disagrees with the Eleatic when he insists that nothing—not even the preservation of the regime or the city itself—should take precedence over the attempt to enable "every member of the community, male or female, young or old, . . . to acquire the virtue of soul that befits a human being" (770d–e).

fail, show that they had to do what they did in attempting to do so. Things are quite different in politics. Not only does a statesman have to see that a variety of activities are undertaken by others to produce a variety of incommensurable goods in order to preserve the life of the city. Those he must rule have also learned from bitter experience with lawless rulers who used their power to enrich themselves at the expense of their people that they must insist on their rulers also obeying the law—to the letter—unless they can persuade the people beforehand to change the law or can justify their lawless actions after the fact in a public audit. In either case the expert and his knowledge are subordinated to the opinions of those who do not have that knowledge. It is, indeed, their lack of knowledge that makes the ignorant, but not entirely inexperienced multitude insist that everyone be equally subordinated to received opinion or tradition.

Not merely would someone who understands politics refuse to serve under such conditions. It becomes extremely dangerous for someone to try to acquire real knowledge of politics.

> If it's evident that someone is seeking, contrary to the writings, an art of piloting . . . or . . . medicine, and . . . sophistically devising anything whatsoever about things of this sort, first he will be called not a skilled physician or captain, but a talker about highfalutin things, a kind of garrulous sophist. Then, second, on the grounds that he's corrupting people younger than himself by convincing them to engage in piloting and medicine not in conformity with laws, but to rule ships or the sick on the basis of their own authority, anyone who wants . . . will be permitted to draw up an indictment and haul him into court where, if it's decided that he persuades either young or old contrary to the laws and what is written, he will be punished with extreme penalties, because no one is allowed to be wiser than the laws, and anyone who wants can learn what has been written as well as the established ancestral customs. (299 b–d)

As several commentators have observed, the Eleatic's description of the plight of a person who seeks to acquire political knowledge that goes beyond the law seems to fit the elder Socrates.[49] He had been called a sophist by his old accuser Aristophanes, and as the Eleatic had probably learned from his companions on their way to meet Socrates, he had been indicted the day before for corrupting the young. The fact that he has been indicted shows, the Eleatic intimates, that Socrates did not understand the

---

49. Miller, *Philosopher in "Statesman,"* 98–99; Howland, *Paradox,* 275–76.

CHAPTER NINE / 730

obstacles imposed by popular ignorance and experience on the attainment of knowledge about politics (*politikē*). The interrogations of individuals, which Socrates characterized as part of the practice of the true political art in the *Gorgias* and which he describes as service to the god in the *Apology*, appeared to his fellow citizens to amount to a claim that he is wiser than the laws.

In the *Gorgias* Socrates explicitly acknowledged that he—or anyone else—could be unjustly indicted in Athens. He was not oblivious of the risk he ran. The Eleatic's accusation is, however, more precise. Socrates questioned his interlocutors about their understanding of what is truly good and noble because he believed that the goal of politics was to achieve the human good and that good could not be achieved by anyone who did not know what it was. In the description of the knowledge a statesman needs in order to rule justly and well that the Eleatic proceeds to give, he shows that the requisite knowledge can and must be defined more specifically. By asking his questions, Socrates could not learn the arts of the general, rhetorician, and judge that every statesman needs to employ, much less how to coordinate all the lesser, more practical and productive arts, in order to preserve a city. Nor would he learn to mix courage and virtue in the citizen body. Socrates has unnecessarily brought himself into danger in seeking the true political art, the Eleatic suggests, because he has not understood the distinctive characteristics and problems of politics.

Young Socrates underlines the Eleatic's point by observing that if the practitioners of other arts were subjected to the kinds of restraints placed on the statesman, all the arts would perish. Having been reminded by the myth that human beings need to develop arts in order to survive, he adds that life, which is hard enough now, would become unbearable in the absence of art.

The Eleatic assures the young Socrates that all is not lost. If rulers were allowed to do whatever they think is best for the sake of profit or any other whim, without knowledge of the law or past practice, things would be worse because "the laws have been laid down on the basis of much experience" (*Statesman* 300b). Certain advisors have examined these experiences in detail and persuaded the multitude to set down the laws that embody them. Someone who went against the law would therefore be going against accumulated wisdom. The rule of law is admittedly a second best or "second sailing." It is nevertheless better than lawlessness. Regimes in which rulers are forced to obey the law are more like the true regime than the lawless ones, and thus better "imitations" of it, because the rule of law is based on a kind of knowledge, not merely on the desires, pleasure, or superior force of the rulers.

If someone able to rule with virtue and knowledge were to arise, the Eleatic claims, he would be welcomed warmly and, in piloting with precision, would steer the right regime in happiness. Unfortunately, it is never evident to others who has the requisite ability, because "a king does not come to be in cities as a king-bee is born in a hive, one individual clearly superior in body and mind" (301e). Unable to recognize true virtue and wisdom, people have no choice but to rely on the "second-best" laws.

If the best possible regimes are those based on law, which itself represents, at best, partial knowledge, the Eleatic observes, we should not be surprised that bad things occur in them; we should be surprised that cities survive despite the sorry state of their captain and crews. We see that "a city is something strong by nature" (302a). It can be improved by art, but it does not require much art on the part of its leaders to survive awhile. The three regimes ruled by one, a few, or many on the basis of law are better than the three lawless varieties. Although the lawful rule of many is the least good imitation, because a great many people do not and cannot possess a great deal of wisdom, democracy is the least bad of the lawless regimes because power in it is so diffused. For that reason, some commentators have concluded, the Eleatic recommends democracy as the best possible practical option.[50] It is, as the elder Socrates' life seems to prove, the least dangerous to philosophy. The Eleatic says, however, that "monarchy, if it's confined by good . . . laws, is the best of all the six" (302e).[51] It bears the same name and looks the most like the rule of the one virtuous and knowledgeable statesman, whose right regime should be separated from the others "as a god from human beings" (303b). Because it is a question of knowledge, the differences between the regime based on law and rule based on knowledge and the differences between lawful and lawless rule are much more important, according to the Eleatic, than the differences in the number of lawful or lawless rulers.

Because other people do not possess the virtue or knowledge of the true statesman, they will not recognize him or allow him to rule. It does not look as if he can even serve as a founder or legislator for subsequent

50. See, e.g., Griswold, "Politikē Epistēmē"; David Roochnik, "Residual Ambiguity in Plato's *Statesman,*" *Plato: The Internet Journal of the International Plato Society* 5 (2005): 4–10. Mara observes that "the best inferior regime according to the criterion of freedom is the lawful democracy" ("Constitutions," 377).

51. Cf. Mara, "Constitutions," 377.

generations. There is no incentive for anyone to acquire the requisite knowledge, nor does the Eleatic suggest that there is. People can learn from experience; on the basis of that experience, clever advisors can persuade them to incorporate and preserve it in laws. Laws can, therefore, be improved over time. Since the rule of law never can or will equal the rule of knowledge, however, the Eleatic does not consider lawgivers, be they founders or reformers, to be statesmen, properly speaking. They, like all actual rulers, are mere imitators and hence sophists.

The Eleatic does not explicitly state the most remarkable conclusion that flows from his argument: the reason it is so difficult to find the true statesman is that no true statesman will ever actually be found in office or exercising political power. The statesman is defined by his knowledge. As the Eleatic pointed out at the beginning of the dialogue, that means his art is not practical or productive so much as it is cognitive. He certainly does not need to hold a powerful position in the city in order to possess it. On the contrary, the Eleatic has shown, no one who truly understands politics would accept a position of responsibility under the conditions those who lack the knowledge themselves would impose. He would not even try to benefit his fellow citizens in private, like Socrates, by showing them what they do not know, because he recognizes that, not knowing, they will prosecute and condemn him. He would travel around from city to city like the Eleatic, talking to those who wish to learn, sharing his wisdom with those willing to listen, and perhaps gathering some wisdom of his own.

2. The Statesman's Knowledge

The fact that a true statesman will never seek or accept office does not mean that it is impossible to isolate and define the particular kind of knowledge he has. Having successfully distinguished the statesman, who would necessarily lay down laws as part of his rule but not feel himself bound by them, from the law-abiding regimes that resemble his, precisely because they rule according to laws based on a certain kind and degree of knowledge, the Eleatic is finally able to isolate and describe the distinctive kind of knowledge a statesman would possess. He would use the three kinds of knowledge that are closest to his in ruling—the arts of the rhetorician, the general, and the judge—but his art is not the same as any of theirs. There is a difference between knowing how to persuade (though not instruct) a large crowd and knowing when to use persuasion and when to use force. The first kind of knowledge belongs to the art of rhetoric; the second is part of the royal art (*basilikē*) or statesmanship (*politikē*). Likewise, it requires one kind of knowledge to fight wars and another kind to determine when they should be fought. Rulers also need to know how to apply their own laws and uphold contracts between particular people under specific circumstances; such judgments are, however, obviously subordinate to the laws rulers make. The true king or statesman knows how to care for everything in the city by weaving together these arts with the laws. On the basis of his comprehensive knowledge, the statesman, like an architect, commands and supervises other artisans to produce and preserve political order.

Above all, the Eleatic explains, a statesman needs to know how to weave together two different kinds of people—the moderate and the courageous—in order to preserve the city. Like the elder Socrates, the Eleatic observes, most people think that courage and moderation are two kinds of virtue. But he boldly suggests that, instead of being friendly, these two kinds of virtue are actually opposed. Whereas moderate people are gentle, slow, and orderly, courageous people tend to be quick, speedy, and intense; these opposed virtues or natural inclinations in people create a problem for the statesman. Because moderate people tend to be "exceptionally well-ordered," they live a "quiet life, minding their own business" (Socrates' definition of political justice in the *Republic*). As a result, they are unprepared for war and become the prey of aggressors. The courageous are always tensing up for wars, which they wage until they are defeated and enslaved by their enemies. If a city is to remain free and well ordered but able to defend itself, its population has to combine both these virtues. Since like is naturally attracted to like, however, it requires art to produce the necessary composite. Like a weaver, a knowledgeable statesman must get others to test and purify the materials with which he will work by purging—punishing, exiling, killing, or enslaving—people who prove themselves "incapable of sharing in a manly and moderate character and everything else that pertains to virtue, but are prone to godlessness, insolence and injustice by a bad nature" (*Statesman* 308e). Then he must bind together the moderate and courageous, both with divine ties, by seeing that they acquire true opinions about the beautiful, just, and good things in the part of their soul that is eternal, and with human ties, by arranging suitable marriages and exchanging children, with other cities as well as within the city itself. He holds the community together by making sure that in allocating offices and honors, they go to individuals who are both moderate and courageous themselves or to groups that have members with each of the contrary tendencies to balance each other.

G. The Limitations of the Eleatic's Definition of the Statesman

The Eleatic never indicates how a statesman acquires the knowledge he needs to coordinate all the other arts and to bind the courageous and moderate together. Nor does he suggest any means for the statesman's passing of his knowledge on to his successors. Like the guardians in Socrates' city, the Eleatic's statesman will first test his citizens as children in play, and after purging those without any capacity to become virtuous, he will turn them over to educators, although he will prescribe what and how they teach. Further like Socrates' guardians, before the introduction of philosopher-kings, the Eleatic's statesman merely shapes the opinions of his people. He is never said to teach, write down, or otherwise communicate his wisdom to others. The Eleatic does not suggest that his statesman will institute anything like the Nocturnal Council, much less the philosophical curriculum that Socrates mandates in the *Republic*. In contrast to both Socrates and the Athenian, the Eleatic does not manifest any concern about the education of future rulers. He does not, because, as he has already indicated, he does not expect a true statesman ever actually to rule or, therefore, to have successors. No people will ever consent to his rule; most will never be able to recognize the kind of knowledge necessary to guide a polity, much less understand its necessity or desirability. The Eleatic's description of the knowledge a statesman must possess thus takes place without any consideration of consent, as if the people once purged will be perfectly malleable.

Practicing the dialectical science he said characterized a philosopher, the Eleatic helps young Socrates to sort the statesman from his closest imitators, the governors of actual regimes, as well as from philosophers and sophists. As the Eleatic announced early in the dialogue, if the statesman is defined by his knowledge, it does not matter whether he actually holds a position of power. By encouraging Theaetetus and moderating young Socrates, the Eleatic indicates in his own practice that he possesses some of the knowledge he attributes to the statesman. It is not clear, however, that he possesses the arts of the general, the rhetorician, and the judge, to say nothing of the ability to coordinate all the other arts needed and practiced in a city. According to his own understanding, the Eleatic would not have to possess knowledge of those arts in order to sort the kind of knowledge the statesman possesses from those of his closest competitors and imitators. He understands himself to be a philosopher, not a statesman or a sophist. He is not interested in ruling, nor are his young, mathematically inclined interlocutors.

The question the dialogue raises by having the elder Socrates sit and listen to the Eleatic's discourse is whether such a completely external, dispassionate, or as we would say, "objective" description of the knowledge needed to rule is sufficient. Isn't it necessary to understand the desires or drives that lead some people to want to rule others? Isn't it necessary to examine the different claims they raise in order to determine why knowledge alone gives some human beings a right to rule others? Doesn't the Eleatic need to say more about the reasons a person who knows how to coordinate all the arts and mix moderate with courageous individuals would use that knowledge justly in order to make the people as good as possible? Peoples have not wanted their rulers to be restrained by law primarily because they were worried about their lack of knowledge; they have insisted on placing legal restraints on rulers after experiencing the extortions and cruelty of an unjust tyrant. Nor is either justice or knowledge in rulers an absolute requirement of communal self-preservation. As the Eleatic observes, cities have been known to survive without just or knowledgeable rulers.

Plato presents Socrates' response, as it were, to the challenges raised by the Eleatic in the dialogues that follow, the dialogues that depict Socrates' trial and death. In the *Apology* Socrates responds to the Eleatic's insinuation that he does not understand the way in which his interrogations of his fellow citizens undermine the rule of law by pointing out that his interrogations were not contrary to the laws or "writings" of Athens.[52] He may have impoverished himself and his family, but he had been allowed to philosophize in Athens until he was seventy years old. The risk involved in his mode of philosophizing was not as great as the Eleatic suggested. Instead of claiming to be wiser than the laws, Socrates set an example of extraordinary law-abidingness—both during his life and in his death. On the day of his death he explained, in contrast to the Eleatic, what he found unsatisfactory about previous philosophy.

By presenting Socrates' response in an evidently dramatic form in this last "trilogy" of dialogues, Plato suggests that the practice and defense of philosophy cannot be simply a matter of dialectical sorting. As an activity of an embodied individual who must interact with others in order to survive, philosophy must make itself and its effects evident in deed as well as in speech.

52. Cf. Lane, *Method and Politics*, 154.

10

The Trial and Death of Socrates

In the *Apology of Socrates*, *Crito*, and *Phaedo*, Plato presents a Socratic response to the charges—both political and philosophical—made by the Eleatic Stranger. In the *Apology* and the *Crito*, Plato depicts Socrates' answer to the charge that he did not understand politics—particularly the grounds, necessity, and limits of the rule of law. In the *Phaedo* Plato then sketches a Socratic response to the Eleatic's philosophical criticism of his argument about the ideas by having Socrates tell his young friends why he turned to examine speeches (*logoi*) rather than facts (*erga*), and why he clung to the argument (*logos*) he found safest, his argument about the ideas, even though he could only posit, not prove it.

To answer the Eleatic's political charges, Socrates needed to show that the questions he posed to private individuals concerning their opinions about what is good and noble did not threaten to undermine the laws or corrupt the young. In doing so, Socrates emphasized, he faced a great rhetorical challenge. Because the fear of death is naturally so strong in human beings, none of his interlocutors—his fellow Athenian citizens, nonphilosophical friends like Crito, or younger philosophical associates—was apt to be persuaded by his arguments that he ought to obey the law and accept the death penalty. He could only convince them after the fact, in deed, by calmly letting the city kill him. As a seventy-year-old man, Socrates emphasized, he would have to die soon in any case. Never conceding that he was guilty as charged, Socrates chose to die the way he did to convince his contemporaries and their successors that the kind of philosophy he practiced did not undermine the rule of law.[1] On the contrary, it benefited both the city and the individual philosophers. It not merely helped human beings, like Socrates, to overcome their fear of death. It showed people how to live with the irremediable ignorance associated with mortality that gives rise to both resentment of, and resistance to, the rule of reason because of its inescapable limitations.

I. The Argument: Socrates' Response to the Eleatic Stranger's Political Charges

If Socrates had understood why the best form of rule generally possible is by law, and that the rule of law depends on the wisdom of the law not being questioned, the Eleatic intimated in the *Statesman* (299b–c), Socrates would not have sought knowledge of the true political art by questioning his contemporaries "contrary to the writings." He would have known that such a person would not be recognized as the sole practitioner of the "true political art" that Socrates claimed to be in the *Gorgias*. He would be called "a talker about highfalutin things, a kind of garrulous sophist" and hauled into court by anyone who wanted to accuse him of corrupting the young by convincing them to act not in conformity to the laws but autocratically.

A. Socrates' Interrogations Were Not Contrary to Athenian Law

In the *Apology* Socrates indirectly reminds Plato's readers that the Eleatic Stranger was a foreigner who did not know what the law actually was in Athens. Until the time of his trial, Socrates had not disobeyed Athenian law. Athens was famous for the freedom of speech her citizens enjoyed (*Gorgias* 461e; Thucydides 2.37–41). If Socrates raised questions about the wisdom of current Athenian laws or policies, he would not have been acting contrary to Athenian law. Socrates does not defend his practice of philosophy as a result or expression of Athenian freedom of speech, however.[2] Nor does he admit that he challenged the wisdom or authority of

---

1. On the importance of Socrates' age, see Leo Strauss, "On Plato's *Apology of Socrates* and *Crito*," in *Studies in Platonic Political Philosophy* (Chicago: University of Chicago Press, 1983), 51–54.

2. This fact has not prevented later commentators from viewing Socrates' trial in terms of the freedom of speech and its (lawful) extent in Athens. I. F. Stone, *The Trial of Socrates* (New York: Anchor Books, 1989), points out, with wonder, that Socrates did not rest his case on freedom of

Athenian law. On the contrary, Socrates brags, he obeyed the law more regularly and rigorously than his contemporaries did. He was the only person to protest when the Athenians failed to follow their own legal procedures and tried the generals from the battle of Arginusae as a group rather than as individuals. On trial for a capital crime himself, Socrates refuses to beg the jury for mercy; instead he insists that they should do their duty, which is to decide what is just (and legal), and not allow their judgment to be swayed by compassion. There is only one law Socrates admits that he would disobey, *if* it were to become law: that law would tell him that he must "no longer spend time in this investigation or philosophize" (*Apology* 29c).[3] Until Socrates' trial, there had been no such law in Athens. Socrates had been questioning the opinions of his contemporaries, Athenians and foreigners, as individuals in private, for at least thirty-five years. Some of his interlocutors became angry and threatened him, but no one suggested that he was guilty of a crime against the city. As Callicles admitted in the *Gorgias*, anyone could unjustly indict and drag anyone else into court in Athens; this fate was not one reserved particularly for philosophers. The problem was that a philosopher could not defend himself and his activity successfully to a popular audience.

B. The Athenians Did Not Understand the Difference between Socrates and Other Philosophers

Socrates suggests in the *Apology* that because he questioned people in private and did not go into the assembly, where he admits he would have endangered his life by criticizing the injustice of the demos, most of his fellow Athenians did not understand what sort of a philosopher he actually was. When the wealthy young men who enjoyed listening to him interrogate others imitated him by interrogating their elders, and their elders could not answer the questions they posed, they blamed Socrates. When the elders were asked what Socrates taught or did, they did not know. So they repeated the old charges against natural philosophers, that

speech; Arlene Saxonhouse, *Free Speech and Democracy in Ancient Athens* (New York: Cambridge University Press, 2006), takes Socrates' condemnation to reveal the limits of that freedom.

3. Cf. Gerasimos Xenophon Santas, *Socrates: Philosophy in Plato's Early Dialogues* (London: Routledge and Kegan Paul, 1979), 50; Gary Young, "Socrates and Obedience," *Phronesis* 19 (1974): 29. In arguing that Socrates' philosophizing meant that his questioning could not be limited to one law, Roslyn Weiss, *Socrates Dissatisfied* (New York: Oxford University Press, 1998), 13n9, fails to distinguish between Socrates' questioning of the opinions of others in private and public disobedience of a law.

by investigating "the things aloft and under the earth" and "not believing in gods" and "making the weaker speech the stronger," Socrates corrupted the young. Despite Aristophanes' caricature of him in the *Clouds*, Socrates insisted, he was not a natural philosopher who talked about highfalutin things, nor did he take money like the sophists did for teaching young people how to become virtuous or effective public speakers. Those in the audience who had heard him speak could serve as witnesses.

Precisely because Socrates conducted his investigations in private, however, most of the jurors had no immediate experience of what kind of philosophy he practiced. And in the *Apology* we see that when Socrates tries to show the jury what he does, he provokes outrage, if not outright disbelief. He begins by relating the (in)famous story about his reaction to the oracle at Delphi's answer to his associate Chaerephon's question, Is there anyone wiser than Socrates? Even though it was Chaerephon, not Socrates, who went and posed the question, and even though Socrates emphasizes how difficult it was for him to understand the oracle's answer, because he knew that he knew nothing important, Socrates' relating of the story had to appear to be an only slightly veiled form of boasting. He has to ask the jurors not to make disturbances at this point in his speech. Oracular sayings were notoriously difficult to understand correctly, so Socrates' attempt to discover what the oracle could possibly have meant may not have appeared to be as impious to his Athenian judges as it has to some modern commentators.[4] The questions Socrates posed to the politicians, poets, and artisans may have angered them, but his interrogations vindicated the truth of the oracle. Socrates modestly concluded, moreover, that his superior wisdom consisted in his knowing, as the others apparently did not, that he did not know anything important. Human wisdom is worth little compared to the divine. But, as Socrates observes in his second speech after the jurors have voted to convict him (37e–38a), when he claims to be investigating the oracle, they do not believe him; they think he is being ironic.

C. Socrates' Arguments Looked Sophistic

Socrates tells the jurors that he has been indicted as a result of the anger his interrogations of politicians, poets, and artisans produced by demonstrating that they did not know what they claimed to know. His three

---

4. Herodotus gives several examples of the disastrous consequences of individual misunderstandings of the apparently evident meaning of the oracles they received.

new accusers—Anytus, Meletus, and Lycon—represent the three groups Socrates had questioned. Socrates admits that the people who have heard him interrogate others suppose that he knows the things about which he refutes others. But Socrates takes the opportunity offered by the one and only speech he delivers to a large public audience to insist that he does not know these things. He is not a sophist of the kind the Eleatic Stranger described.

When Socrates attempts to show his jurors what his interrogations of individuals are like by examining Meletus, however, his demonstration once again provokes audible protests or "disturbances" from the jurors. In proving that Meletus does not know who improves the young or what Socrates actually says about divine things, Socrates appears to be cleverly leading his accuser to contradict himself and so to be proving his own superiority. The philosopher does not seem to be defending himself from the charges that he corrupts the young by convincing them not to believe in the gods of the city and introducing new divinities. Socrates' speech appears to be contentious and evasive rather than truthful or to the point. Socrates cannot show the jury what he does any more than he can simply describe his interrogations without appearing to be vaunting his argumentative superiority.[5] If he is convicted, Socrates concludes, it will not be a result of the charges leveled by Anytus or Meletus, but by the slander and envy of the many (28a).

D. Why Socrates Could Serve the Public Only by Speaking in Private

Far from admitting that he is impious or that he corrupts anyone, Socrates insists that he has piously been serving the god of Delphi by questioning others to show them that they do not know what they believe that they do. He should be regarded as the gift of the god to the city and will be difficult to replace. He has not only risked his life by arousing the anger of others in the service of the deity, but he has also impoverished himself and his family by devoting all his time to reforming his fellow citizens. Like a gadfly, he has irritated them by persistently asking why they, citizens of such a great city, continue to fear death and try to amass ever more wealth and fame rather than seek truth, prudence, and the good of their soul.

---

5. Both Brann ("Offense of Socrates," 1–21) and West (*Apology of Socrates*, 76) emphasize the way in which Socrates provoked the Athenian jurors with his boasting. Neither commentator admits that Socrates could not tell the whole truth about his activity without seeming to brag.

Although he claims to have selflessly served others, Socrates admits that he could not have spoken or acted in public. It would have been too dangerous for him to offer advice to the demos gathered together in a legislative assembly: "For there is no human being who will preserve his life if he genuinely opposes . . . any multitude and prevents many unjust and unlawful things from happening in the city. If someone who fights for the just is going to preserve himself even a short time, he has to lead a private rather than a public life" (31e–32a). The distinction Socrates draws here between acting in public and in private constitutes his most direct answer to the Eleatic's charge that he undermined the law by asking how political practice could be improved. Socrates did not question the wisdom of the laws directly or in public; on the contrary, he obeyed the laws and urged others to do so as well. Socrates questioned the integrity and wisdom of individuals, some (but only some) of whom participated in making Athenian laws. The distinction Socrates makes between public and private questioning points, however, to a fundamental difference between Socrates and the Eleatic Stranger concerning both the extent and the way in which philosophical knowledge can affect politics.

E. The Fundamental Difference: How Philosophy Can Affect Politics

Socrates and the Eleatic agree that most human beings will never be able to acquire the knowledge required to become a statesman.[6] They also agree that a statesman with the requisite knowledge would have to rule by means of laws, even though both see that laws involve generalizations that do not take sufficient account of particular circumstances.[7] Neither Socrates nor the Eleatic thinks, however, that individuals with the requisite knowledge will seek to rule. Socrates says so explicitly in the *Republic*. The Eleatic denies that it is necessary to use or practice the royal art in order to acquire or possess it. He does not raise the question in the *Statesman* of why anyone would want to acquire or exercise such an art; nor does he indicate how an individual who possessed the requisite art might pass it on

---

6. Statesmen are indeed rare. We can still name distinguished examples—Solon, Pericles (although Socrates would object), Julius Caesar, Charlemagne, Henry V, Elizabeth I, Frederick the Great, George Washington, Abraham Lincoln, and Winston Churchill—partly because there are so few of them to remember.

7. In the *Republic* Socrates argues that evils in cities will not cease unless philosophers become kings, but he also suggests that such philosophers will be properly educated and that they will supervise others on the basis of laws he and his young interlocutors have laid down.

to his or her successors. Socrates and the Eleatic also agree that other human beings are not able to recognize the rare individuals who actually possess the knowledge required to rule and thus to compel them to use it.

Socrates and the Eleatic Stranger disagree about the way in which people acquire political knowledge and how it can be made effective. According to the Eleatic, people learn from experience not to trust individuals or groups who ask to rule without limitation or constraint. Although such people claim to be acting for the good of the community, they often, if not always, subordinate it to their own interests by executing their opponents and enriching their own coffers at the expense of others by means of heavy taxes, if not outright extortion. After they overthrow the criminal ruler, prudent leaders gather the multitudes together and persuade them not merely to forbid unfettered rule in the future but to collect and write down some common opinions and to preserve other unwritten customs that mandate not only periodic selection of rulers by election or by lot but also subject those rulers to audits and possible indictments afterward. People who have the knowledge required to rule a city would not allow their deeds and judgments to be subordinated to the opinions, passions, and possible resentments of an ignorant popular body, however. The best possible outcome, which the Eleatic dubs a "second sailing," is thus for the multitude to be persuaded by certain advisors to write down as law what they have learned from past experience, particularly concerning the dangers of unlimited rule, and to prohibit any individual or group from doing anything contrary to the law. Laws can be changed and thus presumably be improved, but they will always be subject to the experience and consent of the multitude, who can never attain precise knowledge of what is necessary or just under particular circumstances. Laws will therefore always represent mere opinion backed by force. They will never allow for the rule of knowledge per se, which would, in turn, never allow itself to be constrained by past experience or general regulations, if circumstances demanded something different.

The rule of law makes the ruler subject to the consent of the ignorant people, but, the Eleatic points out, democracy is the weakest form of government, unable to do anything very, very good or very, very bad, because power is dispersed into so many offices held by so many different individuals. Of all the law-abiding regimes, it is thus the worst, although it is the best (because the weakest) of the lawless. It is better to live in a democracy than in any other immoderate regime, but, he concludes, "it is by far best to live in the first regime [a law-abiding monarchy, which can presumably most effectively enforce or execute the law because it has a single leader], except for the seventh [the rule of the knower], which must be separated from all the rest of the regimes as a god from human beings" (*Statesman* 303b).[8] Like Socrates in the *Republic*, the Eleatic appears both to criticize democracy and yet to praise it, in a partial, backhanded fashion. The Eleatic does not go so far as Socrates did in the *Republic*, however, by pointing out the advantages for a seeker of knowledge of living in a regime in which representatives of all regimes are allowed to rise and flourish. As has already been noted, the Eleatic never expresses any concern about the ways in which individuals acquire political knowledge. Instead, he emphasizes how amazing it is that cities continue to exist for any time. They must be something "strong by nature," since "they know almost nothing about politics, but suffer from the greatest kind of ignorance in thinking that they do" (302b). The most someone who possesses political knowledge could do, according to the Eleatic, would be to use the art of rhetoric and the force of law to shape opinions and control intermarriages so that the city maintains the balance of courage and moderation (but not justice and wisdom) in its citizen body and among its officers needed to preserve the city.

In the *Gorgias* Socrates suggested that the most laws can do is shape opinions and inculcate desired habitual behaviors in the people subject to them. For these people to come to understand what they truly want, that is, what is truly good, they must be subjected to the kind of individual interrogation in private he alone provides. People do not subject themselves to the rule of law merely because they have experienced the evil results of lawless rule by others. People also know that they themselves, at least occasionally, share the unjust desire to profit at the expense of others and so pass laws to check and regulate themselves. There is, in other words, an enduring difference between what people genuinely believe is in the common interest and what they privately want for themselves, both as individuals and en masse. Because democratic assemblies are easily persuaded to act on the basis of widely shared desires or fears, they are easily persuaded by ambitious politicians and "clever rhetoricians" to adopt unjust policies, and it is dangerous for an individual like Socrates to oppose them, especially when their passions are aroused.

---

8. This conclusion raises serious problems for the contention made by both Griswold ("*Politikē Epistēmē*") and Roochnik ("Residual Ambiguity") that the Eleatic Stranger favors democracy because the rule of a true statesman or knower is so unlikely.

Like government itself, Socrates argues in opposition to the Eleatic, the rule of law does not arise simply because most people do not know what is best to do under a staggering variety of possible circumstances and have experienced the evils of unconstrained rule. Socrates consistently maintains that not merely laws, but an ongoing education in the form of a reexamination of our own motives and opinions is necessary to bring order to the lives of human beings, characterized as we are by souls divided by desires, anger, and the capacity to calculate alternative means to our various ends. Laws do not make or administer themselves, moreover. When Socrates asks Meletus who makes young Athenians better, and the poet answers, the laws, Socrates thus insists that Meletus tell him not what or how, but who, that is, which persons educate and improve the youth. The Eleatic recognizes that political offices must be occupied by individuals with the requisite opinions and character, but he does not acknowledge the need for ongoing education by means of individual examinations in private.

Socrates responds to the Eleatic's slightly veiled criticism of him in the *Statesman* by pointing out that the rule of law is not compromised primarily by people who question the wisdom of the laws or seek to acquire better knowledge about politics. The rule of law is more ordinarily and regularly challenged by the unjust desires of the people who originally make and administer laws in an attempt to control those very desires in themselves as well as others. These people need to reminded of the reasons they initially formulated, established, and need to enforce their conceptions of justice by means of law. Asked what he does, if he does not corrupt the young, Socrates says that he serves "the god" of Delphi over whose shrine is inscribed the command "Know thyself." Rather than trying to persuade his fellow Athenians to change public policy in the assembly, he goes to them individually and in private to ask them why they continue to feed their unjust desires for wealth and to fear death. He does not address them together and in public, because he recognizes that public speakers often, if not always, must appeal to, and thus arouse, the very passions laws seek to control. Whereas the Eleatic includes rhetoric in the arts a statesman must know how to use, Socrates denies that rhetoric is an art. Refusing to corrupt the jurors further by using the kind of speeches he knows would persuade them, Socrates insists on telling the truth about what he does—even though he recognizes it will outrage his fellow citizens and result in his conviction and death.

The stakes are high, and Socrates knows it. By addressing his fellow Athenians as citizens of a great city, Socrates reminds them (as well as

Plato's readers) that the Athenian democratic regime was not as weak as either the Eleatic or he in the *Republic* had suggested democracies would be. Athens had been an imperial city tyrannically ruling others in the not distant past. Nor was the dangerous exercise of Athenian power limited to foreign relations. The question posed by Socrates' trial was not merely whether he would be allowed to continue to live peacefully in Athens; the more general and greater question was whether one of the few cities that had allowed philosophers to seek knowledge, freely and in public, would outlaw philosophy—particularly Socratic philosophy—in the future. If Socrates were convicted, foreign teachers like the Eleatic might not find it safe to come to Athens and converse with the young, even in private.

II. The Action: Socrates' Defense of His Philosophy to His Fellow Citizens

In the *Apology*, Plato shows Socrates, in the only speeches he ever delivered to a public assembly, attempting to convince his fellow citizens that the kind of philosophy he practices does not undermine the rule of law. In the *Crito* Socrates then urges one of his oldest and closest friends, in a private conversation Socrates has reason to believe will be related to others, that they should both obey the law. Socrates does not tell his friends in private something different from what he proclaimed in public, particularly concerning the reasons he did not seek exile and decided instead to accept the death penalty.

A. Socrates' Public Defense

According to Crito (*Crito* 45e), it would have been possible to prevent the introduction of the lawsuit against Socrates in court. The philosopher did not, in other words, have to go on trial. He chose to do so. He had something he wanted to prove—in deed, if not in speech.

I. SOCRATES' SPEECH

In his defense Socrates maintains that, if he is convicted, it will be on the basis of an old prejudice. Because they investigate things under the earth and in the heavens, philosophers are thought to be atheists. Some years earlier in Aristophanes' *Clouds*, Socrates had been shown to be such a philosopher as well as a teacher of rhetoric. In line with that picture, his current accusers have claimed that he is a clever speaker. They have warned the jurors that he will be able to talk his way out of court.

Socrates begins his defense, therefore, by reminding the jurors of what they can see with their own eyes: he is an old man. This is, moreover, the first time he has appeared in court. Proceeding as he usually does, he will show them that, far from a teacher of rhetoric, he is artless (*atechnōs*) and foreign (*xenōs*) to the manner of speech usual in court. Asking them not to pay attention to the way he speaks so much as to the content, he urges them to demonstrate the virtue of a judge, which is to determine whether what he says is just or not. He promises to display the virtue of an orator, which is to speak the truth. It will be difficult in a short time to overcome the prejudices the jurors have acquired from those who have slandered him, but, he emphasizes, "the law must be obeyed and a defense speech must be made" (19a). Rather than teaching or showing others how to evade punishment with clever arguments, Socrates is a model of a law-abiding citizen. He does not merely obey the law. He also exhorts others, the jurors in this case, to perform their civic duty as well.

Socrates denies not only that he is a clever speaker but also that he is a natural philosopher and atheist. Not contemning such knowledge, Socrates insists that he is not a "wise man," who investigates things in the heavens and under the earth, and who does not, as a result, believe in the gods. In the *Euthyphro* Socrates had observed that the Athenians do not care what someone believes or does not believe, "unless he happens to be a skillful teacher of his own wisdom. But their spiritedness is aroused against anyone they suppose makes others like himself" (3c). Socrates thus also reminds his jurors that he is also not a sophist who claims to teach virtue or even, merely, the ability to speak effectively to public assemblies. He suggests that some of his fellow citizens have been aroused against him because he appears able to make others like him, when he explains that the source of the slander and prejudice against him are interrogations that young men, imitating Socrates, have made of their elders.

Rather than allaying the suspicions of his audience, however, Socrates outrages the jurors by speaking in his usual manner; they protest audibly when he first describes and then demonstrates the kind of speeches in which he usually engages. He explicitly has to ask the jurors not to make disturbances after he tells the story about the oracle (20e), accuses Meletus of being careless and hubristic (26e–27b), and seems to defy the city by announcing that he does not care whether they "obey Anytus or not, or let him go or not; [he] will not [cease his philosophizing], even if [he] were going to die many times" (30b).

Socrates cannot describe or demonstrate what he does to his fellow citizens without appearing to boast. It is, indeed, his apparent hubris combined with his unwavering determination not to do anything unjust out of a fear of death that make Socrates look so much like a tragic hero in his last three dialogues. Socrates' hubris may only be apparent inasmuch as he insists that the oracle declared that no one was wiser, because Socrates alone appears to know that he does not know anything important. It is this recognition of his own ignorance, moreover, that makes Socrates so brave in the face of death. "To fear death is nothing other than to seem to be wise, but not to be so," he informs the jurors. "No one knows whether death does not even happen to be the greatest of all goods for human beings; but people fear it as though they knew well that it is the greatest of evils" (29a).

Recognizing that they will not believe his mere protestations, Socrates offers his fellow citizens proofs of a kind they value and find more persuasive than speeches—deeds. The first proof he gives of his unwillingness to do anything unjust because of fear of death is his protesting the trial of the generals en masse, even though the orators threatened to indict and punish him with prison or death. The second is his refusal to follow the command of the Thirty to go with four others to arrest Leon of Salamis and bring him to die.[9] He then concludes his speech by pointing out the externally observable evidence of arguments he made earlier. He has never claimed to be anyone's teacher or charged a fee to those who wished to listen to him converse. On the contrary, he has freely shared his wisdom with anyone who wants to listen. Although his accusers have charged him with corrupting the young, they have not named any particular individuals he corrupted. The relatives of young people known to have associated with Socrates regularly are, however, present in court to testify on his behalf. Skeptical readers might wonder whether the youths or their relatives would want to admit publicly that they had been corrupted. In the *Gorgias* Socrates had urged individuals who felt that they were corrupt to accuse themselves as well as their relatives in order to cure them; if they followed his advice and thought that they were corrupt or unjust, they should have

---

9. Commentators err, however, when they take Socrates' refusal to obey the Thirty as an example of his disobeying the law. Tyrants were characterized by their failure to rule by law, ruling instead through arbitrary decrees backed by force.

done so. And in the *Euthyphro* he had praised Meletus for doing what a politician should by caring for the young. Most of Socrates' audience would not know about the content of either of these conversations. But they would have seen that the families of the individuals who had associated most frequently with Socrates were not accusing him, whereas the man who had accused him of corrupting the young, Meletus, had been shown not to know what Socrates actually said when he examined the young poet before their eyes in court.

Finally, Socrates suggests, some of the jurors might feel indignant when they see that Socrates refuses to bring his family to plead for mercy they way they themselves had in the past. Again providing an example in court of the way in which he has attempted to reform his fellow citizens by accusing them, Socrates observes that "it is shameful for anyone reputed to be distinguished, whether in wisdom or courage or any other virtue to act this way" (35a). If he were to beg them to acquit him, contrary to the oath they took to give a judgment according to the laws, he would prove in deed that he was not pious and sought to corrupt his fellow citizens.

In concluding his defense, Socrates reiterates his insistence earlier (30d) that he is not giving this speech for his own sake. He is going to die in any case. He will not be able to enjoy the benefits of his philosophizing for long. It is they and their successors who will lose the benefits of his interrogations and find him difficult to replace, if they convict him. Anticipating many later, critical readings of his apology, Socrates insists that he is not speaking as he is because he is stubborn (*authadizomenos*) and unwilling to change his behavior, because he dishonors (*atimazōn*) or contemns them, or because he is daring (*tharraleōs*) in the face of death. Again, he emphasizes, he is old. He will not act like the people who "suppose that they will suffer something terrible if they die—as though they would be immortal if you did not kill them" (35a). Whether it is true or false, Socrates now admits, he has a reputation that he wants to preserve after his death. He urges his Athenian auditors to be concerned about their reputation for acting nobly and not basely as well.

Socrates' concluding statement is carefully ambiguous. Because he says that he believes in the gods as none of his accusers does, some commentators have argued that in the *Apology*, which they consider to be a historical report more than a Platonic invention, Socrates is acting on the basis of his religious belief or "inspiration."[10] Socrates' statement is,

10. Kahn, *Plato and the Socratic Dialogue*, 96; Thomas C. Brickhouse and Nicholas D. Smith, "The Origin of Socrates' Mission," *Journal of the History of Ideas* 44, no. 4 (1983): 657–66; Brick-

however, fully in line with his admission in the *Euthyphro* (6a) that he becomes annoyed when people retell the poet's stories about the gods fighting each other, even though he knows that these stories are sculpted and woven into the sacred things of Athens (6b–c). As in the *Euthyphro*, Plato shows that Socrates often posited the existence of the eternal, unchanging, fully intelligible entities like the "ideas." In the *Apology* he declares that he has been ordered to engage in his philosophical investigations and conversations "by the god, from divinations and dreams and every way any divine allotment ever ordered a human being to do anything" (33c). He was not an atheist of the kind Meletus accused him of being; he literally did believe as none of his accusers and few other Athenians did.[11] He was guilty of not believing in the gods of the city and introducing new divine things (although not literally "making" them, as Socrates restates Meletus' accusation in the *Euthyphro* [3a]), but he would not admit that the propagation of such opinions and arguments corrupted the young.

2. Socrates' Reaction To His Conviction

Socrates had more success persuading the jurors that they should not condemn him than he expected. If thirty votes had changed sides, he observes, Meletus would have had to pay the fine for bringing a frivolous lawsuit. Socrates certainly did better than he suggested in the *Gorgias* when he told Callicles that, if the philosopher were hauled into court, his position would be similar to that of a doctor defending himself in front of a jury of children from the charge, leveled by a pastry cook, that he had given them painful drugs instead of gratifying their desire for sweets. Socrates was not angered by the jurors' decision because he expected to be convicted. Surprised perhaps by his own success in persuading the assembled jurors, however, for the first time in his life he proposed a change in Athenian

---

house and Smith, "The Paradox of Socratic Ignorance in Plato's *Apology*," *History of Philosophy Quarterly* 1, no. 2 (1984): 125–31; and Brickhouse and Smith, *Plato and the Trial of Socrates* (London: Routledge, 2004).

11. Mark L. McPherran, *The Religion of Socrates* (University Park: Pennsylvania State University Press, 1999), 139–67, reminds his readers both of Socrates' declared convictions concerning gods and the divine as well as the ways in which his declarations did not fit Athenian "cult" practices. David Corey, "Socratic Piety," *Review of Politics* 67, no. 2 (2005): 201–28, faults secular critics like Dana Villa, *Socratic Citizenship* (Princeton: Princeton University Press, 2001); George Kateb, "Socratic Integrity," in *Nomos XL: Integrity and Conscience*, ed. Ian Shapiro and Robert Adams (New York: New York University Press, 1989); Arendt, "Philosophy and Politics"; and Arendt, "Thinking and Moral Considerations," *Social Research* 38 (1971): 417–46, for ignoring or denying the relevance of Socrates' piety, even though Corey also admits that Socrates' piety was not traditional.

law before a public assembly.[12] (The change would have made Athenian law more like Spartan law, although Socrates prudently did not say so.) Socrates no longer had to worry about unscrupulous orators hauling him into court, and thus the risk to his life, by making such a proposal.

If Athens had a law that prohibited jurors from deciding a capital case in one day but instead required them to take many days, Socrates asserted (*Apology* 37a–b), he could have persuaded them to acquit him. It takes time, he suggested, for a popular audience to understand the benefits of having a philosopher among them. Socrates had practiced his philosophy in Athens for thirty-five years, but few of his fellow citizens had witnessed or heard one of his conversations. Many more of them had heard that Alcibiades and Critias had been close associates of Socrates for a time, however, even though neither of these known traitors could be named, because of the declaration of amnesty that accompanied the reinstitution of a democratic regime in Athens in 403.[13] Socrates could remind the jurors that a known partisan of the democracy, Chaerephon, had also been a close associate of his for even longer than Alcibiades or Critias, but he could not prove merely by assertion or even one demonstration that his interrogations did not generally have a corrupting effect. His accusers asserted that he did corrupt; he asserted that he did not. The jurors did not know what Socrates said or what effect he had in his private conversations.

Socrates had to try to show them the effect his philosophy had in a visible, external, and generally observable fashion. At his trial he did so by demonstrating that he would accept the death penalty rather than perform an illegal or unjust act. Socrates recognized, however, that the meaning of deeds is no more evident than the meaning of speeches. Just as speakers can misunderstand what they describe or lie, so deeds may be inaccurately observed and their significance misunderstood. To persuade his auditors (and later readers) that his philosophy did not harm but in fact benefited the city, Socrates had to explain what he was doing and why.

Asked to state what he deserves instead of the death penalty proposed by Meletus, Socrates insisted, "something good" (36d). From the beginning of his defense, he had claimed that he would tell the jury the truth. He had

12. West and West, *Four Texts*, 91n68.

13. Stone (*Trial*, 177) argues that we know from a speech of Lysias, titled "Against the Corn-Dealers" and delivered in 386, that far from being disgraced or accused of having acted unjustly, Socrates' chief accuser Anytus was elected to high office after the trial.

refused to remain quiet, to care about moneymaking or holding office or having political influence in the city, because that would not benefit them or him. Instead, he had gone to each of them privately in an attempt to confer what he believes is the greatest benefit by trying to persuade them (as, Plato shows, he had tried to persuade Alcibiades, Critias, and Callicles) to care for themselves by becoming as good and as prudent as possible, before they tried to care for the city. He thus proposed that the city of Athens honor him the way they do Olympian victors by giving him his meals in the Prytaneum. In the *Apology*, Socrates claims to have embodied all the virtues—wisdom, courage, justice, and piety—except moderation (which is not mentioned). Socrates could not tell his fellow Athenians what he deserves according to his worth in truth (36d) without appearing to be completely hubristic, that is, lacking self-restraint.

Socrates' refusal to propose an alternate penalty—a substantial fine, prison, or exile—that he knows to be bad, instead of death, which he does not know to be bad or good, clearly outraged the jury. More of them voted to kill him than had voted to convict him after his first speech. Not convinced that he has been unjust to anyone else, Socrates tells them, he will not be unjust to himself. Surmising that the jury would have accepted an alternate proposal of exile, Socrates explains that it would be neither reasonable nor noble for him to suggest it. Once again, he emphasizes that he is an old man. At a younger age, it might have made sense for him to leave and begin again in a new city. As an old man, he has no chance of persuading strangers that his philosophizing benefits them, if he cannot persuade his fellow Athenians. The problem is not restricted to Athens. On the contrary, "wherever [he] goes, the young will listen. . . . If [he] drive[s] them away, they persuade their elders to drive [him] out. But if [he] does not drive them away, their fathers and families will drive [him] out" (37d–e).

Socrates aroused the anger of Athenian fathers by raising questions about the noble and good, that is, about the best way for a human being to live, that they could not answer. Because he raised—and by his example led their sons to raise—questions about traditional answers to this question, Athenian fathers accused Socrates of impiety. He cannot convince them otherwise with speeches or explain why he cannot remain silent. If he says "this is to disobey the god," they won't believe him, thinking he is being ironic. But if he says "this happens to be a very great good for a human being—to make speeches every day about virtue and the other things about which [they] hear me conversing and examining both myself and others—

and that the unexamined life is not worth living for a human being, [they] will be persuaded even less" (37e–38a). The benefits of Socratic philosophy cannot be appreciated by people who have not experienced them. Because he cannot tell them, Socrates has to show them by provoking them to kill him, an old man, and then fearlessly dying rather than cease questioning the opinions of others. As a penalty, he finally proposes that the jury fine him the thirty minae that Plato, Crito, Critobulus, and Apollodorus have offered to pay on his behalf—which is as much as to say that Socrates proposes that he pay no penalty at all.

3. SOCRATES' INTERPRETATION OF THE SIGNIFICANCE OF HIS DEATH

Socrates shows, in the two speeches he gives to the jurors after they have voted to convict him, that he wants to determine the meaning of his trial and death. Again he reminds the jurors who voted to convict that he is old and would have died soon in any case. They will not have succeeded in freeing themselves of Socrates' annoying interrogations so much as acquiring blame for killing a wise man, "for those wishing to reproach you will assert that [he was] wise, even if [he was] not" (38c). Despite his claim at the beginning of his defense that he lacks experience speaking the way they do in court, Socrates assures them that he has not been convicted because he did know the kind of speeches that would have persuaded them. Emphasizing the intentional character of his speech and action, Socrates reiterates that he would not have acted as shamefully as many of them have by begging for his life. He much prefers "to die having made [his] defense speech as he did than to live that way" (38e).

Once the question concerning the best way for a human being to live has been raised, Socrates warns those who voted to condemn him, it cannot be repressed or silenced by killing human beings. They will not escape the need to give an account of their lives. There will, on the contrary, be more people to refute them. Socrates admits that he has had some influence on the young (although he does not concede that he has corrupted them). And, he warns, they will be harsher in criticizing their elders than he has been, because they are younger. Indeed, Socrates claims that he has been holding them back. It is not clear whom exactly Socrates has in mind, but Plato comes immediately to mind as a younger man, obviously influenced by Socrates, who blamed the Athenians for his death.[14] Nor is

---

14. As Bruell notes (*Socratic Education*, 136), Plato specifically says that he was present at Socrates' defense.

it clear how exactly Socrates had been holding them back. This much is evident from the *Apology* itself. In his defense speech Socrates claimed that the prejudice against him had arisen as a result of the questions young people, imitating him, had put to their elders. Angered by their inability to answer, the elders blamed Socrates. But after he is dead, the elders will no longer be able to blame him. Nor, after his public defense, will they be able to claim that the "corruption" they complain about can be attributed to Socrates' engagement in natural philosophy. They will have little recourse but to try to defend themselves and their way of life with reasons. They will not want to kill their own children, if they persist in asking questions, nor will the city allow them to do so.

Both the threats Socrates makes to the jurors who voted to convict and the comfort he offers those who would have acquitted him seem to presuppose the continuation of his kind of philosophizing. Socrates seeks to perpetuate his kind of philosophy, but he cannot know that he will succeed. He thus calls his predictions about the probable future "oracles," uttered by a man about to die. He says that he takes comfort in the fact that his divine voice, the *daimonion* Meletus had misconstrued in his accusation, had not indicated that Socrates should not come to court or say what he did in his defense. Since in the past that voice had warned him away from dangerous actions, Socrates concludes that his trial and death will be something good. Death is nothing to be feared, he tells the jurors he considers to have decided justly in his favor and so to be true judges, but not merely because such fear presupposes that we know what we do not. Having declared that the unexamined life is not worth living, he points out that death may be merely the loss of all sensation. If so, it would be like a long dreamless sleep, a relief from the frustrations and pains of usual human striving. If death results not in the loss of perception but in our souls' change of place by journeying to Hades, it would be a wondrous gain. In Hades, we would not only confront "those who are judges in truth"; we would be able to associate and converse with the greatest heroes and wisest human beings. Socrates would continue to philosophize as he had in Athens, and others would be able to imitate him. Seeking to perpetuate his kind of philosophy as the only form of human life worth living, he concludes by urging his friendly auditors to treat his sons as he has treated his fellow Athenians, by admonishing them not to care for money or reputation more than virtue. He cannot say whether it will be better for him to die and converse with great men or for them to live, carrying on his practice.

B. Socrates' Defense of His Actions in Private to Crito

In the *Crito* Socrates seeks to persuade his old friend that the philosopher will make a mockery of his own public statements in the *Apology* if he seeks to escape punishment.[15] Since Crito heard Socrates proclaim at his trial that he would choose death, which he did not know to be good or bad, rather than exile, which he knows to be bad for an old man, readers might wonder why Crito presses Socrates to accept his assistance and flee the night before he has to die. One possible reason is the close proximity of the philosopher's death. Crito may have believed that Socrates could bravely accept death when it was merely a future prospect; we all know that we have to die—sometime. After the ship from Delos had been sighted at Sunium, however, it was clear that it would arrive in Athens that day and Socrates would have to die the next. Nor is Crito dissuaded by the dream Socrates reports in which a woman told him, echoing a statement of Achilles in the *Iliad*, that he would arrive in Phthia the third day.[16] As in the *Euthydemus*, Crito appears to take Socrates' claims to divine inspiration with the proverbial grain of salt.[17]

Crito's sense of urgency led him to bribe the jailor to let him into Socrates' cell before daybreak.[18] Unable to sleep himself, Crito is amazed

15. Cf. Gregory Vlastos, "Socrates on Political Obligation," *Yale Review* (Summer 1974): 517–34. On ways in which the arguments are specifically addressed to Crito, see Drew A. Hyland, "Why Plato Wrote Dialogues," *Philosophy and Rhetoric* 1 (1968): 38–50; Young, "Socrates and Obedience," 1–29; Frederick Rosen, "Obligation and Friendship in Plato's *Crito*," *Political Theory* 1, no. 3 (August 1973): 307–16; and Ann Congleton, "Two Kinds of Lawlessness," *Political Theory* 2, no. 4 (November 1974): 432–46. Attempts to find a general theory of legal obligation in *Crito* do not take sufficient account of the fact that the arguments are explicitly addressed to Crito and concern Socrates' own singular life and condition at the end. See, e.g., R. E. Allen, *Socrates and Legal Obligation* (Minneapolis: University of Minnesota Press, 1980); Richard Kraut, *Socrates and the State* (Princeton: Princeton University Press, 1984); and A. D. Woozley, *Law and Obedience: The Arguments of Plato's "Crito"* (London: Duckworth, 1979). Indicating his failure to take account of the dialogue form, Allen describes the *Crito* as "an early essay" (66).

16. For a careful analysis of the dream and its significance, see Thomas Payne, "The *Crito* as a Mythological Mime," *Interpretation* 11 (1983): 1–23. As in the *Apology* (28c–d), so in his report of his dream at the beginning of the *Crito*, Socrates compares his own situation with that of the hero. Acknowledging the comparison, both Strauss ("*Apology*," 44) and Richard Holway, "Achilles, Socrates, and Democracy," *Political Theory* 22, no. 4 (November 1994): 561–90, suggest that it is not altogether flattering to Socrates. Strauss notes a "slight incongruity" in Socrates' comparison of himself to a young beautiful warrior. Holway argues that both Achilles and Socrates are engaged in something rather like adolescent rebellion. N. A. Greenberg, "Socrates' Choice in the *Crito*," *Harvard Studies in Classical Philology* 70 (1965): 73–75, argues, on the other hand, that Socrates' choice is far more daring and meaningful than that of the Homeric hero.

17. Cf. Strauss, "*Apology*," 57.

18. The image of a man shackled (as we know from the beginning of the *Phaedo*) in a confined space in the dark with another there ready to free him has reminded some readers of Socrates'

by Socrates' ability to rest so peacefully. Crito obviously does not share Socrates' stated conviction that it would be untoward for a man of his age to be vexed at the prospect of his death.[19] Crito does not appear to be as concerned about the loss Socrates is about to suffer, however, as he is about the consequences of Socrates' death for himself. Addressing Socrates as "daimonic," Crito suggests that the philosopher has a strange if not superhuman indifference to his own demise. But, Crito objects, "if you die, it is not just one calamity for me; apart from my being deprived of such a companion as I will never discover again, I will also seem to many to have been able to save you if I had been willing to spend money. . . . And yet what reputation would be more shameful than to seem to regard money as more important than friends? For the many will not be persuaded that you were not willing to go away from here although we were eager for it" (*Crito* 44b–d).

Socrates reminds Crito that he has frequently and consistently argued that they should not pay attention to the opinions of the many, because most people are ignorant. Socrates' current predicament has convinced Crito, however, "that it is necessary to care about the opinion of the many, [because] the many can produce not the smallest of evils, but almost the greatest, if someone is slandered among them" (44d). In the *Crito* Plato thus shows how little power Socrates' arguments had in shaping the opinions of one of his oldest associates. When faced with the prospect of significant loss—of life, wealth, or reputation—Crito ceases to adhere to the Socratic position and succumbs instead to the opinion of the many.

To persuade Crito, which Socrates says he thinks is important to do before he acts (48e), Socrates has to address the opinions and concern of the many, which Crito seems to share. At the very least Socrates needs to provide Crito with reasons that many will believe as to why Socrates was not willing to escape, even though Crito urged him to do so. Crito will be able to repeat Socrates' speeches in defending himself from the slanderous charge that he cared more about money than about saving his friend.[20]

---

famous image of our nature with regard to education, in the *Republic*. If so, the *Crito* constitutes an admirable transition to the *Phaedo*, where Socrates famously argues that the only way a philosopher can free himself from the body and the errors into which it brings us is to die.

19. Cf. Kraut, *State*, 4n1.

20. Like J. Peter Euben, "Philosophy and Politics in Plato's *Crito*," *Political Theory* 6, no. 2 (May 1978): 157–59, I am arguing that Socrates is not indifferent to the opinion of the many, even though he denies that their opinion determines what is just. Also like Euben, I am arguing that the arguments are directed at Crito, in the first place, but not only at Crito. Unlike Euben, however, I am arguing that the focus of the arguments is on the philosopher's relation to the rule of law.

Because Socrates dismisses the relevance of the concerns he shares with the many, Crito seeks to persuade Socrates to accept his assistance and escape by appealing to concerns Crito believes Socrates shares. So Crito assures Socrates that if he is concerned about the danger or cost to his companions, he need not worry. Foreign associates of Socrates like Simmias and Cebes of Thebes have offered to put up the money; they are not subject to Athenian law or the accusations of informers the way Crito is.[21] At his trial, Crito recalls, Socrates said that he would not propose exile, because there was nowhere to go. Crito has friends in Thessaly, however, who will welcome Socrates. Most important of all from Socrates' point of view, Crito argues, the philosopher's unwillingness to escape is neither just nor virtuous. In his central speech at the trial Socrates had asserted that he would not be unjust to himself. But, Crito now asks, isn't Socrates being unjust to himself by enabling his enemies to harm him? Furthermore, isn't Socrates abandoning his sons and foisting the responsibility for their nurture and education onto others? Finally, can Socrates credibly claim to be courageous or to foster manliness in his companions if they act in a way that allows others to kill him?

Perceiving the difference between Crito's two sets of arguments, Socrates reminds his old friend that he is "not only now, but always such as to obey nothing . . . but the argument that appears best" (46b). Socrates will not dismiss his previous arguments in reaction to recent events; he will only yield to a better argument. He thus invites Crito to reconsider the arguments to which they have agreed in the past. It looks as if Socrates will be giving the reasons for his own actions. But in restating these arguments, Socrates consistently asks Crito whether he agrees. Socrates does not say whether he agrees, particularly with the arguments Socrates attributes to "the laws." At the end he simply says that the "echo of these speeches booming within makes [him] unable to hear others" (54d). The fact, pointed out by many commentators, that in the *Crito* Socrates does not mention the two concerns he argued in the *Apology* were most important both for himself and for others—namely, his philosophy and the good of the soul—leads us to suspect that the arguments Socrates presents to Crito are designed to persuade Crito and the many, who do not believe that Socrates would have willingly stayed if Crito had urged him not to.[22]

21. Cf. J. Adam, ed., *Plato: Crito* (Cambridge: Cambridge University Press, 1888), 34.
22. Strauss, "*Apology*," 62; Bruell, *Socratic Education*, 217; West and West, *Four Texts*, 25.

Socrates begins by reminding Crito of an argument Socrates had made many times in the past, for example, in his refutation of Meletus. People should not heed the opinions of the many, because the many do not know; if a person turns the care of anything, for example, his own body, a horse, or a child, over to someone who does not know how to care for it, that "thing" will be corrupted. The problem with this argument in the context is that in the *Apology* Socrates had admitted that he did not know the most important things. In prison with a day remaining before his death, he and Crito are unlikely to find the "expert" they have presumably been seeking for some time. Lacking knowledge themselves, Socrates and Crito do not seem to be any better equipped than "the many" to decide what Socrates should do.

Because merely living appears to be a necessary, if not sufficient condition for living well, Socrates suggests, "someone" might object that the many are able to kill us. Crito emphatically agrees. Socrates responds by asking his friend, have they not agreed in the past that living well is more important than merely living, and that living well is the same as living justly and nobly? If the good, the noble, and the just in human life are the same, Socrates concludes (explicitly dismissing Crito's first set of concerns as those of the "mindless many"), "we should not consider anything but whether we will do just things by paying money and gratitude to those who will lead me out of here, or whether in truth we will do injustice—those of us who lead out as well as those who are led" (48c–d). Socrates will not let Crito escape responsibility. Since it is certainly illegal for Socrates to escape and for others to assist him, the question becomes, in effect, whether it is just for them to break the law in this particular instance.

Socrates narrows the question further by reminding Crito of another argument he frequently made, to which Crito had agreed: no one harms himself by doing what is bad or unjust voluntarily. If so, Socrates argues as he had in the *Republic* speaking to Polemarchus: "even someone who has been done injustice, should not do injustice in return, as many suppose" (49c). In making this argument, Socrates also reminds Crito that, old men as they are, they look foolish if, like children, they jettison the results of many serious, lengthy conversations in reaction to a few recent events. In other words, acting as Crito urges will be bad for both of their reputations. At the same time, Socrates makes the premise of the argument that follows an agreement that the conviction and sentencing of Socrates were unjust.

Even if he has been unjustly convicted, Socrates proceeds to argue, it is not just for Socrates and Crito to disobey the law by escaping from prison.

The question, of course, is why not? The first reason Socrates has given is that it is not just to retaliate for one injustice by doing another.[23] The unjust harm being done Socrates is evident; not only has he been publicly condemned and shamed, but he is also about to be killed. But what exactly is the injustice Socrates and his friends would commit by arranging his escape? Is it unjust to refuse to obey an unjust decree or law? Socrates did not appear to think so in the *Apology*, when he reminded the jurors that not only had he been the only one to protest the illegal trial of the ten generals but also that he had refused to obey the tyrannical decree of the Thirty.

Socrates seems to base the reasons he is about to give, in the name of "the laws," concerning why it would be unjust for him to escape on a third "argument" to which he reminds Crito they had also agreed in the past— namely, that one ought to do what he has agreed to, if just, and not to try by deception to get out of doing what he promised to do. This "argument" appears to be little more than an assertion, even if it is widely agreed to. (In the *Republic* Socrates showed Cephalus why it would not always be just to do as one had previously agreed.) The qualification "if just" seems, moreover, to beg the question—what is just?

To answer the question in his own case, Socrates explains, they have to determine whether he would be harming those he least should harm and not abiding by his agreements—again, if they are just—by going away without persuading the city. There are thus two questions: first, is Socrates harming anyone by escaping, and if so, whom? And, second, would Socrates be deceptively evading a just deed he had agreed to perform if he left without persuading the city that it was just for him to do so? We should not fail to note that the condition Socrates lays down here, persuading the city, is exactly the condition the Eleatic Stranger had argued no wise man would accept. Socrates has not claimed the knowledge of a statesman, however. On the contrary, he has emphasized his ignorance. He has, moreover, presented his problem defending himself as a problem of persuasion inasmuch as his fellow citizens will not believe him when he declares that it is a great good for human beings to talk about virtue and the other things about which he converses daily and that the unexamined life is not worth living.

---

23. Socrates could, although he does not, refer to Aeschylus' *Oresteia*, in which the tragedian shows that justice understood as revenge leads to an interminable chain of injuries, which can only be ended by a public agreement to transform injuries to individuals, to be privately punished in turn by other individuals, into crimes against the city, which then determines what should be done in response for the sake of the common good through public deliberations.

Since Crito cannot answer Socrates' questions, Socrates asks him to imagine "the laws" and "the community of the city" standing before them and asking whether Socrates is not doing what he can to destroy them. "Is it possible," they inquire, "for a city to continue to exist, in which judicial decisions are rendered ineffective by private individuals?" (*Crito* 50b). Socrates' escape would surely not overturn the laws of Athens or destroy the city in and of itself. The only way to make sense of the laws' claim is to generalize it. Socrates' escape would threaten the continued existence of a legal order in Athens to the extent to which his escape set an example for others. *The* question for both Socrates and the laws is what kind of precedent he is setting and for whom.

Instead of asking whether he has an obligation to obey an unjust law, as many contemporary legal theorists have, Socrates asks Crito whether they should object that the city has treated Socrates unjustly by not judging him correctly.[24] By stating the question as he does, Socrates suggests that he would be doing the city an injustice by escaping in return for its injustice to him, and that he would, therefore, be acting contrary to his own previous arguments.

In response to the two questions Socrates put to Crito, "the laws" claim not only that Socrates would be harming them and the city but also that he would be failing to abide by his former agreements. They point to three such agreements, each of which applies more and more specifically to Socrates. The first "agreement" the laws attribute to Socrates is an agreement to honor and obey them, more even than a child is obliged to honor his father or a slave to obey his master, because the laws required his parents not only to marry (and so make his birth legitimate) but also to nurture and educate him. This is a claim virtually all fatherlands make, especially when they order their citizens to sacrifice their lives in defense of the city. It is not a claim peculiar to Athens or particularly applicable to Socrates, insofar as he believes his philosophy constitutes the most important form of education a human being can receive. At most the laws of Athens had allowed Socrates to educate himself by talking to others. Apparently referring to Socrates' vaunt at his trial that just as he had risked dying when ordered by the elected rulers to defend Athenian interests at Potidaea and Delium, so he risked dying by remaining at his station when ordered by the god, "the laws" argue that he must do what his city and

---

24. See, e.g., Allen, *Socrates and Legal Obligation*; Kraut, *State*; and Woozley, *Law and Obedience*.

fatherland bid in war and court—or persuade them of what is just by nature. In mentioning the just by nature as an alternative, "the laws" may be admitting that they were not literally or directly responsible for Socrates' birth. That was a natural result of the conjunction of male and female humans. Parents do not necessarily or naturally stay together and provide their progeny with an education, however, unless they are required to do so by law. In return for nurturing him, preserving his life, and, if not fully and completely, educating him, "the laws" thus demand that Socrates obey them unless he can convince his fellow citizens to adopt a higher (divine) or more general (natural) standard of justice in his case. Is there a reason Socrates should escape the punishment meted out to other individuals convicted of a capital crime by a jury of their fellow citizens? Is Socrates an exception, or should he be treated as one? At his trial, Socrates had argued that he was an exceptional citizen and should be treated as such, but he had not persuaded the jury.

Silently acknowledging that individual human beings do not have an opportunity to choose the families or cities into which they are born and so agree to obey the laws under which they were raised, the laws of Athens point to a second kind of agreement Socrates would be breaking if he tried to escape. Treating their citizens as free adults, able to choose the community and way of life they think best, the laws of Athens allow individuals, once mature, to take their property and go wherever they choose.[25] Those individuals who have chosen to stay in Athens have, as we would say, "tacitly" agreed in deed (as opposed to "expressly" consenting in speech) to obey the laws or persuade their fellow citizens to change their ignoble commands.[26] The emphasis on the option of changing the laws through persuasion is democratic and so more specific to Athens than the previous "agreement." Socrates had been exceptional, they point out, in the extent to which he stayed in Athens, not traveling the way other human beings do, for example, to see how other cities conduct their affairs. And the fact

25. The laws of Athens are thus more generous than John Locke is in his account of tacit consent. Cf. *Second Treatise* sec. 119: A person tacitly consents to obey the laws so long as he enjoys any privilege or owns property. So long as he has not explicitly consented to the laws of a nation, he has a right to leave, but he must leave his property behind.

26. The laws' elocution, persuade or obey, has puzzled commentators, e.g., Terry Penner, "Two Notes on the *Crito*: The Impotence of the Many, and 'Persuade or Obey,'" *Classical Quarterly* 47, no. 1 (1997): 153–66, because one does not literally "persuade" laws. The alternative "the laws" put forward must, therefore, mean that in Athens the laws allow a citizen like Socrates either to persuade jurors that their actions should not be seen to have been illegal or, having like Socrates failed to persuade, to obey.

that Socrates not only has lived himself but also has had children in Athens suggests that he has found the laws satisfactory—not merely for himself or his philosophy, but for others as well.

The problem with the second argument "the laws" make is that Socrates' tacit "agreement" to obey the laws lasts only so long as he remains in Athens. He would signal the end of his agreement by leaving, as Crito is urging. "The laws" thus point to a third and last "agreement." By agreeing to stand trial, rather than running away beforehand, Socrates had agreed to abide by the verdict of the court.

This third "agreement" applies most specifically to Socrates, "the laws" emphasize. Although Socrates had stated on occasion that Sparta and Crete had good laws, he had never proposed moving to either city. On the contrary, Socrates had stayed in Athens for seventy years. His choice must have been based on long deliberation and was not a mere reaction to current events.

"The laws" do not describe the third "agreement" in terms of justice. Instead, they ask Socrates what good he would be doing himself or his friends by escaping that could compensate for the harm he would be doing himself as well as his companions. They would be in danger of being exiled themselves or losing their property, whereas he would irrevocably damage his own reputation. Because he is an old man, he cannot travel far. The citizens of any city to which he could travel would have heard about his trial, conviction, and escape. Citizens of a nearby city with good laws, like Thebes or Megara, would suspect him of corrupting their young people the way he had been accused of corrupting them in Athens; if he escapes, he will have become an exemplary lawbreaker. (As we know from the *Laws* and *Hippias Major*, neither of the farther-away cities that Socrates said had good laws [Sparta and Crete] would have allowed him to philosophize in front of their young people, even if he had been able to travel so far and arrive as an anonymous "stranger.")[27] But if he goes to a disorderly place like Thessaly, as Crito urges, Socrates will appear not merely to have

27. In the *Laws*, which Pangle (*Laws*, 378–79) suggests may depict just this alternative, the Athenian Stranger has to obey the "Dorian law of laws," which forbids anyone from raising questions about the goodness or wisdom of the laws in front of young people. But in the *Apology* (37d–e) Socrates declares that he knows that wherever he goes, the young will listen to him when he speaks, just as they do in Athens. If he tries to drive them away, they will drive him out by persuading their elders; if he does not drive them away, their elders will. Because Crete was a law-abiding regime far away, Strauss argues (*Argument and Action*, 2), the location in Crete does not suffice to explain why Socrates is not the philosophical spokesman in the *Laws*. The reason is that Socrates did not directly engage in political activity because it was too dangerous.

escaped by using a disguise or deceit. "An old man with only a little time left in his life" (53d), he will make himself look ridiculous and his previous speeches about justice and virtue into laughing matters by acting as if he prizes the few remaining moments of his life more than he fears breaking the law. And if Socrates were to reply that he seeks to live not for his own sake but for the sake of his children, he would be casting doubt on the devotion of his friends, who would have to take charge of the education of his sons, in any case, if he escaped.

In sum, "the laws" conclude, Socrates can do himself little good by escaping, but his escape would not merely damage his own reputation; it would also harm his family and friends. Admitting that Socrates has been treated unjustly, if only by "human beings" and not "the laws" (54b–c), "the laws" urge the old man to concern himself about what will happen after his death, about his reputation on earth and the defense he will have to make to their "brothers," the true laws or judges in Hades. "The laws" can no longer promise to supply Socrates with life, education, or protection during his life in exchange for his obedience. They can, however, still harm his friends and family, as they threaten they will, if he makes them angry.

With the echo of the laws' speeches booming so loudly in his ears, Socrates tells Crito, he cannot hear anything else. But if Crito has something else to say, Socrates invites him to try. Crito, however, has nothing to say. "Let us act in this way," Socrates concludes, "since in this way the god is leading" (54e). Socrates does not say that he agrees or has been convinced by the arguments he attributes to "the laws." He suggests, on the contrary, that like Apollo on the pediment of the temple at Olympia, he can only indicate or point, he cannot say, why he is doing what he is doing. As he pointed out in the *Apology*, his fellow Athenians will not believe him when he tries.

Socrates has not interrogated "the laws," we should note, as he has interrogated other individuals in private. He does not raise questions about what the laws declare to be just. They interrogate him and raise questions about the justice of the action his friend would have him undertake. In other words, Plato does not present Socrates as an exemplar of what we have come to call "civil disobedience," that is, a man who accepts the punishment while challenging the justice of the law by which he is punished.[28]

---

28. Although I agree with Kraut (*State*, 75) that it is anachronistic to describe Socrates' decision in the *Crito* in terms of civil disobedience, I argue that Socrates is trying to persuade later generations that philosophy is not dangerous to the law by publicly going to his death.

Why did Socrates attribute the arguments intended to persuade Crito that the philosopher should not try to escape to "the laws" instead of putting them forth in his own name? The first reason is that Crito has admitted that he is no longer, if he had ever been, convinced by the arguments he has heard Socrates make in the past, to which Socrates adheres until he comes across better arguments. It doesn't look as if Crito can be convinced merely by Socrates speaking in his own name, therefore. Socrates needs something stronger. "The laws" have force as well as persuasion behind them, as Socrates reminds Crito, when "the laws" threaten to act against his friends at the conclusion of their speech. "The laws" act in character by not allowing Socrates to question them. Laws constitute commands for which individuals are punished if they do not obey.

Socrates does not want Crito merely to be silenced by the threat of coercion, however. Socrates wants to persuade his old friend (as well as Crito's critics and friends to whom Socrates can be fairly sure Crito will repeat his arguments). Socrates thus confronts Crito, who says that he agrees with the opinion of the many, with another set of opinions, also held by many, with which, as a citizen of Athens, Crito may be presumed to agree. What do "the laws" represent, especially in democratic Athens, but the opinions of the many concerning what they publicly declare to be just? Socrates had dismissed the concerns Crito initially voiced about money, reputation, and the nurture of his children as the opinions of the "mindless" many. But, as Crito recognized in the second set of concerns he voiced, Socrates shares his desire to act virtuously—courageously and justly. The question—the only question—before them, according to Socrates, thus becomes whether it would be just for him to escape. According to the law, it clearly and obviously is not. Once Socrates defers to the authority of "the laws" by letting them cross-examine him, the question is settled.

Socrates brings "the laws" forward to speak on their own behalf only after Crito has agreed that one should not respond to one injustice by committing another. Although Socrates points out that this understanding of justice is not shared by many, as Aeschylus shows in the *Oresteia*, the rule of law depends on individuals giving up the notion that they must revenge injustices committed against them and allow the community as a whole to decide what constitutes an injustice and how that injustice should be punished. If most people, unlike Socrates' friend Crito, believe that persons unjustly convicted, like Socrates, have a right to escape and thus break the law, because they have been treated unjustly, most people do not understand the basis of the rule of law. By clearly enunciating this principle,

Socrates not only gets Crito and those who hear Crito's recitation of the conversation later to agree that Socrates has been treated unjustly and thus, in effect, that philosophizing should not be declared to be illegal. By reminding Crito and those who listen to him of the true but frequently forgotten basis of the rule of law, Socrates demonstrates in action as well as in speech how the kind of philosophy he practiced helps preserve the rule of law.

By having "the laws" come forward and examine Socrates as he examined others, Socrates makes "the laws" appear to be much more reasonable than they do when they appear simply to be commands backed by force. As Socrates indicates in the arguments he attributes to "the laws," most people obey the law most of the time because they find it advantageous to do so. They acquire a debt for the benefits they enjoyed as a result of the rule of law when they were children, and they tacitly consent to obey the laws if they remain in the city as adults. As the laws of Athens emphasize, they also give citizens an opportunity to persuade them to change. This provision becomes especially important in the third argument "the laws" make with regard to Socrates' case. Socrates could have decided that the benefits he had enjoyed from living in Athens would not continue, and hence compensate for his death, if he were convicted of a capital crime. He could have fled before the trial rather than taking a chance. By deciding to stay and stand trial, Socrates appeared to have agreed to accept the judgment of the court. He had been given an opportunity to persuade the jury that he and others should not be prohibited from philosophizing, because it led to a denial of the gods of the city and corruption of the young.

As Crito states early in the dialogue, the critical decision Socrates made was to stand trial rather than to flee.[29] As we know from the *Apology*, Socrates did not expect to persuade the jury that he was not guilty and thus to be exonerated. He predicted that they would convict him on the basis of an old prejudice and that he would not be able to undermine, counteract, or change that prejudice in a single day. An old man, Socrates reminded the jury in public as he now reminds Crito in private, he would die soon in any case. The question was what reputation he and they would acquire as a result of the court's decision. By having "the laws" admit that he had not been treated justly by "human beings," Socrates suggests that

---

29. Cf. Greenberg, "Choice," 68. I do not, however, agree with Greenberg's further argument that Socrates becomes a hero because he gambles with his life.

the "men of Athens" who voted to convict him were already acquiring a reputation for unjustly killing a wise man.[30] If so, public opinion and thus the law of Athens were already shifting from an ignorant suspicion to a more knowing toleration, if not acceptance, of philosophy. As Plato depicts them, both Socrates' speeches and deeds were designed to produce precisely that result. If Socrates had tried to evade suffering the death penalty, he would have made a mockery of his speeches concerning the irrationality of fearing death and the worthlessness of an unexamined life. He would have appeared to have valued his own life, that is, merely living, more than his philosophy, that is, living well. By allowing the jury to convict him and then staying to accept the death penalty, when he was old and about to die in any case, Socrates used the opportunity to demonstrate both in speech and in deed that the kind of philosophy he practiced did not threaten to undermine the rule of law or corrupt his fellow citizens. Socrates did not claim to know what is just. On the contrary, he continued to investigate that question up to the day of his death. In the absence of knowledge or an expert, however, Socrates steadfastly maintained, both in public and in private, that it was better for human beings to do what they believed to be just, that is, for the common good, especially when they were willing to declare such an opinion in public, support it with reasons, and subject those reasons to cross-examination, than it was to act on the basis of private, clearly unjust selfish desires.

III. The Denouement: The Death of Socrates and the Perpetuation of Philosophy

In the *Crito* Socrates failed to take any notice of one of his friend's chief complaints—that if Socrates died, Crito would lose an irreplaceable friend (44b). Socrates had concentrated on showing why he and Crito should obey the law. But in the *Phaedo* other close friends of Socrates reiterate Crito's complaint. In the *Phaedo* (63b) Socrates thus recognizes that he must give another defense (63b), as if he were in court, against the charge that, by committing suicide, he is unjustly abandoning his friends as well as impiously and imprudently rebelling against the rule of the gods. Socrates' close associates were not all citizens of Athens, so they could not be sat-

---

30. Stone (*Trial*) denies that this was the case, in fact. It was Plato who convinced later generations that Socrates had not been treated justly.

isfied by an argument showing what Socrates owed Athens or even that escaping would not do Socrates any good. What about the good of his companions, especially those who had come to Athens to converse with him and who would, therefore, have been apt to follow him to another city? To satisfy his foreign associates, Socrates needed to show his friends how they could continue philosophizing in his absence and so perpetuate the activity he and they both held most dear.

The defense Socrates presents of himself and his philosophy in the *Phaedo* has two parts.[31] In the first part he argues that a philosophical life is best not merely because it relieves philosophers from the fear of death but also because it results in their possessing the true forms of all the virtues. Socrates' initial arguments seem to depend on the immortality of the soul, however, and he admits that these arguments are open to doubt. So in the second part of his defense Socrates makes himself, his experience, and his central teaching concerning the ideas into the example of the way in which human beings can live with the inescapable ignorance associated with their mortality and the uncertainty to which it gives rise.[32] In making his own way of life and teaching exemplary, Socrates not merely responds to the difficulty dramatized in the first three dialogues in the eight-dialogue series depicting his trial and death—namely, how and why should human beings continue to seek wisdom, if we cannot acquire reliable knowledge of ourselves or of the world from sensation, numbers, or words. In describing not only the way in which he came to his argument about the ideas but also how it applies to questions of life and death, Socrates responds to the critique the Eleatic made of the arguments of "friends of the forms." In the *Phaedo* Plato thus describes the way in which Socrates attempted on the last day of his life to show his close companions, both in word and deed, how and why they could perpetuate the peculiar kind of philosophical practice he had initiated.

31. As Seth Benardete, "On Plato's *Phaedo*," in *Argument of the Action*, 277–96; and Eva Brann, Peter Kalkavage, and Eric Salem, *Plato's "Phaedo"* (Newburyport, MA: R. Pullins, 1998), 5–23, have pointed out, the organization of the *Phaedo* is exceptionally symmetrical. At the very middle of the dialogue (88a, between 58a and 118a), the narrator Phaedo and his auditor Echecrates break into the narration to express their sympathy with the distress Socrates' auditors felt when the soundness of his arguments about the immortality of the soul was questioned. At this point (89c–d), Socrates states they should not be worried so much about the fear of death as about the onset of misology. The latter would be fatal to the perpetuation of philosophy.

32. In fact, as Benardete points out ("*Phaedo*," 281–82), Socrates makes his own experience the subject of conversation on his last day from the very beginning, when he reflects on the experience he has just had of the combination of pleasure with pain. The fact that the entire dialogue is an account of his experience does not become clear, however, except in retrospect.

A. The Problem of Socrates' Philosophical Legacy Revisited

The narration of Socrates' life and death raises the question, What will live on beyond him? That question was also raised at the beginning of the series of eight dialogues explicitly associated with his trial and death. Like the *Theaetetus*, the *Phaedo* begins with a prologue explaining the way in which Socrates' words have been recorded or related. The prologues to the *Theaetetus* and *Phaedo* thus constitute a frame for the series as a whole in which Plato points more or less explicitly to the question, How will Socratic philosophy be passed on and perpetuated?

1. THE FOUNDING OF SCHOOLS

As in the *Theaetetus*, so in the *Phaedo*, the person responsible for relating Socrates' speeches became the founder of a philosophical school. Indeed, in the *Phaedo*, Plato reminds his readers even more emphatically than he had at the beginning of the *Theaetetus* that Socrates' philosophical legacy was varied. Not merely did the narrator himself found a school of philosophy at Elis; he relates the account of what Socrates said on the last day of his life to Echecrates at the school he founded in Phlia. And, Phaedo tells Echecrates, not only Euclides and Terpsion, founders of the Megarian school, but also Aeschines and Antisthenes, founders of two other philosophical schools in Athens, were among the close associates present at Socrates' death. We readers are aware that Plato also founded a school as well.

By reminding his readers, at the beginning of the *Phaedo*, that so many of Socrates' former associates not only founded schools but also wrote dialogues, Plato might appear to be emphasizing the differences between Socrates and his followers. In fact, however, Plato indicates that both in establishing schools and in writing, Socrates' companions were following the example Socrates set at the very end of his life.

As Phaedo tells Echecrates, he and Socrates' other regular associates waited outside the prison before they were allowed in. And readers see that the conversations they had been having with Socrates each day in his cell could have constituted the model for a certain kind of school. Whether the philosopher and his companions met in a single place regularly depended on the location and resources of the philosopher. Not having a home or building capable of housing such a group, Socrates had previously met with his regular companions (like Chaerephon) in the market or at the houses of others. But after Socrates was imprisoned, his most dedicated companions came to talk to him there. There was a certain convenience in having a set time and place. Conversing in private, they may also have experienced a certain degree of freedom from public scrutiny.

Although Socrates' associates founded different philosophical schools, Plato, by noting the absence of Aristippus, reminds his readers that the Socratics had one feature in common. They were not hedonists, that is, they did not think pleasure was the highest good. At the beginning of the *Phaedo*, Plato reports, both Socrates and the narrator observed the conjunction of pleasure and pain. Rubbing his legs after they had been freed from the irons, Socrates commented on the way in which human beings feel pleasure in the absence or withdrawal of pain. Although Socrates had argued in the *Philebus* that the conjunction of pleasure and pain he notes here is particularly characteristic of bodily sensations and is not true of all pleasures, he reminded his auditors here that human existence cannot be entirely pleasant so long as we inhabit bodies. Nor are our own bodies the only sources of pain. Phaedo tells Echecrates that he did not feel the pleasure he usually experienced in philosophizing, because he was pained by the prospect of Socrates' imminent death. He did not feel pity for Socrates, "for the man appeared to me to be happy, both in his manner and his words, so fearlessly and nobly did he meet his end" (*Phaedo* 58e).

Consisting in the search for wisdom rather than the possession of knowledge, Socratic philosophy could not constitute pure pleasure. It involved effort and entailed disappointment, at least temporarily. As Socrates had reminded his auditors in the *Symposium*, mortals cannot gain or retain anything—intellectual or physical—permanently. *The* question posed by Socrates' example as well as by his speeches was why human beings should keep trying to acquire wisdom.

By naming the associates of Socrates who became founders of philosophical schools, Plato reminds his readers not only that Socrates had a varied philosophical legacy, at least with regard to doctrine, but also that Socrates had convinced a number of younger people not merely to devote their own lives to philosophy but to teach and so attempt to attract others to the pursuit of wisdom. At the beginning of the *Phaedo* Plato thus leads his readers to ask not only how Socrates persuaded so many others to adopt a life of philosophy but also how Plato understood his own writings and founding of the Academy in relation to the life and thought of his mentor.

2. THE CHARACTER AND INTENTION OF "SOCRATIC POETRY"

In the prologue to the *Theaetetus*, Plato tells his readers, Euclides wrote down a conversation Socrates had related to him. Euclides had not been present at the conversation, but Socrates obviously had, and Euclides checked the accuracy of his account with Socrates. In the prologue to the *Phaedo*, Plato lets his readers observe that he has written down the account of a person present at Socrates' last conversation who related it to someone who had not been there. In both cases we are reminded of the advantages of writing; it not only preserves but also makes possible the communication of words to persons who were not and usually could not have been present, whether for reasons of time or space.[33] Unlike Socrates, but like Plato, we are reminded at the beginning of the *Phaedo*, many of Socrates' close associates not only founded schools but also wrote dialogues as a means of perpetuating the life of philosophy.[34] Socrates did not write—at least until the very end of his life.

Reflecting on the close conjunction of pleasure and pain when he was freed from his chains, Socrates told his companions that Aesop would have composed a story about the way pleasure and pain were yoked at the head, if he had observed the phenomenon. And Socrates' mention of Aesop reminded Cebes, one of the Thebans who had offered to furnish funds to bribe Socrates' jailors and was present at his last conversation (apparently by chance, but really, of course, as a result of Plato's art), that he and others had been wondering why Socrates had been spending his last days putting a hymn to Apollo as well some of Aesop's sayings (*logous*) into verse.

Socrates explained that he had a dream many times during his life that commanded him "to make music and work at it" (*mousikēn poiei kai ergazou* [60e]). Believing that philosophy was the greatest kind of music, he had thought the dream was simply encouraging him to keep doing what he was doing. After his trial, however, while the festival of the god prevented him from dying, Socrates began to wonder whether the dream had been commanding him to make a more popular (*dēmōdike*) form of music. Having been convicted of impiety by the city of Athens, he decided that it would be safer to acquit himself of any possible impiety by composing a

33. Both the conversations in the *Theaetetus* and *Phaedo* were read or related some time after the fact. Echecrates reminds Plato's readers of the obstacle that distance (as well as political differences—Phlia had been an ally of the Spartans during the Peloponnesian War) put on communication when he observes that "none of our fellow citizens from Phlia even visits Athens at all nowadays, nor has any stranger arrived from there in a long time" (*Phaedo* 57a). All they had heard was that Socrates "drank the potion and died." They had not learned why so much time had elapsed between the trial and his death, what the man said before his death, or how he met his end.

34. Diogenes Laertius (*Lives* 2.64) reports that both Aeschines and Phaedo were reputed to have written dialogues, although only fragments remain from Aeschines' writings and nothing of Phaedo's.

hymn to the god whose festival it was than to continue assuming he knew what the dream meant.

As in the case of the oracle, so in the case of his dream, Plato shows, Socrates understood the meaning of such phenomena to be neither self-evident nor certain. In both cases, he thus tried to determine the meaning of communications that may have had divine origin, but are nevertheless unclear, by testing them in deed. Thinking that a poet, qua poet, would use stories and not arguments, and not being a maker of stories himself, Socrates began to put stories (*mythous*) of Aesop he happened to have at hand (*procheirous*) into verse in an attempt to produce a more popular form of "music."[35]

Because Socrates had not put stories into verse before but had explicitly argued against the goodness of both poetry and writing, critics such as Friedrich Nietzsche have suggested that Socrates' turn to composing verses in the face of death represented an admission of the inadequacy of the philosophy in which he had previously engaged, if not a kind of recanting.[36] If we look back at Socrates' critiques of writing in the *Phaedrus* and of poetry in the *Republic*, however, we see that his belated attempts to produce a more popular form of music do not fall prey to most of them. In the *Phaedrus* Socrates argued that writing does not constitute a substitute for either knowledge or memory; he admits, however, that written signs can serve as aids in calling back to mind things learned in the past. The stories Socrates is writing down in verse do not purport to convey knowledge, but they could serve to remind their readers of moral lessons they might have wanted to forget. In book 10 of the *Republic* Socrates explicitly allowed hymns to the gods to be composed and sung in his city of speech, even when he sadly had to forbid most other kinds of poetry. He stated, however, that he would be anxious to readmit poetry that did not have the deceptive, corrupting effects of most earlier Greek verse. The first criticism of poetry he made was that its images were imitations of imitations and so three degrees removed from the truth. Full of animals that speak, Aesop's stories would not be understood to imitate things that really exist. Nor do these stories present false images of leadership. Socrates does not tell us exactly which tales he had put into verse, but Aesop's "fables" do not usually feature gods, heroes, or even statesmen who claim to know

---

35. As Stern points out (*Socratic Rationalism*, 25), Socrates corrects Cebes' characterization of Aesop's stories as *logoi*.

36. Nietzsche, *Birth of Tragedy*, sec. 14.

how a regime should be ordered. Most important, the tales Socrates was putting into verse would not be apt to arouse passions that tend to make their auditors less moderate and just in the way Socrates charged epic, tragic, and comic poetry does. Aesop's tales have morals; they often depict the bad results of ambition, greed, laziness, and excessive desire as well as the way such passions lead "animals" foolishly to put themselves under the control of those with the ability to harm them and, often, with an interest in doing so.[37] Aesop's fables are thus rationalistic and explicitly foster a kind of moderation, but they are also definitely popular and prosaic in form as well as content. By putting them into verse, Socrates would beautify these stories and thus perhaps make them nobler as well as more attractive.[38] Neither Socrates' sense that there might be something lacking in his philosophy, particularly with regard to exhibiting his piety, nor his choice of subject matter to put into verse and thus make the practical implications of his philosophy more intelligible to a popular audience, contradicts his previous arguments. His recent experience of the trial and the delay in his execution would have made him more aware, however, of the need to do so.

Insofar as the *Phaedo* shows how happy Socrates was in nobly and courageously meeting his death, the dialogue provides the popularly accessible picture of the goodness of the philosophical life Socrates had begun to think at the end of his life might be necessary. In writing the *Phaedo*, Plato thus appears to have been carrying out Socrates' intention in composing verses.

3. Is The *Phaedo* a Tragedy?

Tragedy was the most popular form of Greek art (cf. *Laws* 658d). The fact that the sequence of the three dialogues or "plays" in which Plato depicts Socrates' trial, conviction, and death looks very much like a tragic "trilogy" thus leads us to ask: Did Plato present his teacher as the hero of a prose drama in an attempt to make his nobility more evident to a popular audience?

---

37. Like "The Grasshopper and the Ant," Aesop's stories dramatize the advantages of calculation (*logismos*), foresight (*phronēsis*), and hard work over passion, easy pleasure, and instant gratification. Unlike epic or tragic poetry, stories such as "The Lion and the Mouse" depict ways in which the apparently weaker can help the strong. Aesop's fables do not glorify worldly greatness, wealth, or fame, even though, like "The Lion and the Ass," they illustrate the ugliness of envy and resentment.

38. As a cursory look at Homer and the tragedies shows, Greek epic and tragic poets often, if not always, used existing stories, although they tended to modify them.

No less a commentator than G. W. F. Hegel has declared the trial and death of Socrates to be a tragedy. It was a tragedy in the sense Hegel defined tragedy, that is, the result of an irreconcilable conflict between two principles, both of which should be affirmed in its own right. According to Hegel, the conflict in the case of Socrates was between the freedom of subjective consciousness and the requirements of the state instituted to protect and preserve individual freedom. As a philosopher, Socrates had to demand complete freedom of thought; as a state, Athens had to punish those who would undermine the efficacy of its laws. As we have seen, however, in the *Apology* and *Crito* Plato suggests that neither the trial nor the death of Socrates at the hands of the city was necessary. Socrates did not have to stand trial, according to Crito; if he had proposed exile, Socrates surmises, the Athenians would have let him go.

Plato's account of the trial and death of Socrates could, however, be construed as "tragic" in another, less technical, more poetic sense. Not only do the three dialogues constitute a tragedy-like trilogy; there are also explicitly "tragic" aspects of Plato's depiction of Socrates' death in the *Phaedo*. Although it is written as a narrative rather than as a performed dialogue (and therefore in accord with some of Socrates' prescriptions in the *Republic* [396c–e]), the *Phaedo* has often been read as history rather than the product of a literary imagination, although Plato states that he was not present and thus could not verify Phaedo's account of what was said, if Plato ever heard it.

"Can we remain unaware of the fact that the dialogue does not give a so-called 'historical' account of Socrates' death," Jacob Klein asks, "but gives a mythical presentation of that crucial event, which however is truer than the tale about Theseus and the Minotaur, accepted as true by the average Athenian?"[39] As Aristotle reminds readers of the *Poetics*, tragedians re-presented old stories or myths. And what Nietzsche later dubbed "the myth of the dying Socrates" definitely has elements of tragedy. Phaedo's explanation of the reasons for the delay of Socrates' execution makes the story of Theseus' saving of the fourteen young Athenians from the Minotaur a backdrop for his own account of Socrates' death. By listing fourteen companions, divided into groups of nine and five, Klein observes, Plato seems to draw an analogy between Theseus' saving of his fellow citizens

---

39. Jacob Klein, "Plato's *Phaedo*," in Willamson and Zuckerman, *Lectures and Essays*, 377–78.

from death and Socrates' saving of his companions from the fear of such.[40] He thus makes Socrates look like a hero.

According to Plato's student Aristotle, tragedies also purified their audiences of fear and pity. And there is an element of catharsis in the reason for the delay of Socrates' execution. Even though it seems to be a result of chance rather than intention or art, Socrates' trial happened to occur right after the ritual ship, which sailed to Delos and back every year in commemoration of Theseus' deed, had departed; the city of Athens purified itself by banning all public executions for the duration of its voyage.[41]

Despite the tragic elements in Plato's depiction of the death of Socrates, however, both Plato and his protagonist make it clear that Socrates' death was not a tragedy. First, as Ronna Burger points out, the *Phaedo* is a narrated dialogue; it is not drama or performed.[42] The narration serves to distance readers from the action and thus enables them to be more reflective. Second, as Klein points out, the parallel between Theseus and Socrates is not complete. The fourteen named individuals said to be present at the philosopher's death do not include the narrator, Phaedo, who was also explicitly said to have been present. He is made Socrates' helpmate in the second part of the dialogue when they battle the misology to which their doubts about the soundness of the arguments for the immortality of the soul threaten to give rise rather than the fear of death per se. With his long hair and past experience of sexual exploitation, Phaedo could appear to be a substitute for Ariadne (who showed Theseus how to escape from the labyrinth after he killed the Minotaur). Like Ariadne, Phaedo may have been left, perhaps even pregnant (with thought), deserted by Socrates, but living on to give birth to their common progeny.[43] Theseus saved the Athenian youths by killing a monstrous combination of the human with the bestial that would tyrannize over if not destroy them.[44] If Socrates were

---

40. Ibid., 375–78; Burger, *Platonic Labyrinth*, 17–20. For example, Theseus was supposed to take seven males and seven females, but reputedly dressed up two smooth-faced young men as women to improve the fighting force of his contingent (Plutarch, "Theseus," in *Lives* 23.2). Of the fourteen individuals named as present at Socrates' death, nine are Athenians and five from other cities.

41. Rather than purifying itself by executing Socrates, as Derrida contends ("Plato's Pharmacy," 63–171), Plato indicates that Athens purified itself by delaying his execution. This delay made it possible for Socrates to explain to his friends the reasons he was accepting the death penalty.

42. Burger, *Platonic Labyrinth*, 7.

43. Klein, "Phaedo," 377.

44. As Klein reports ("Phaedo," 375), King Minos' wife Pasiphae fell in love with a white bull; the famous craftsman Daedalus (who is said to have been an ancestor of Socrates; *Euthyphro* 11b–c;

shown to be doing something similar by destroying the fear of death in his listeners by teaching them that philosophy consists in the search for death, Plato would be suggesting that the combination of soul and body in human life on earth is equally unnatural and undesirable. That seems to be the meaning of the story Socrates first tells, to which Simmias and Cebes object, and which Socrates therefore modifies. According to the old story, moreover, Theseus was so happy on his return from Crete that, after stopping to sacrifice in gratitude to the gods at Delos, he forgot to change the color of his sail from black to white to signal his waiting father that he was returning with the hostages alive. Theseus thus saved future generations of Athenians, but at the cost of his father's death. Did Plato wish to suggest that, just as Theseus' father Aegeus killed himself when he saw the ship returning with a black sail and so did not live to celebrate his son's victory or his subsequent reordering of the regime, so Socrates killed himself when the ritual ship returned and did not live to see the victory his intellectual son won in his name over the popular prejudice against philosophy and the political improvements that victory made possible?

In fact, Plato emphasizes, Socrates did everything he could to prevent his companions from viewing his death as a tragedy or mourning him as Theseus and the city of Athens did Aegeus. Instead of trying to arouse and then purify them of their fear and pity, Socrates sent away his wife, so that his companions would not follow her example, by feeling pity for him or themselves, or by giving voice to their grief. He reminded his companions of other stories they had heard, especially those related by the Pythagoreans, which suggested death is not something to be feared. Most of all, however, Socrates presented them with the example of a man facing his own death fearlessly and nobly.

Like the catharsis of pity and fear that tragedies work in the audience, according to Aristotle, the delay of Socrates' execution and hence the purification of Athens were only temporary. If Athens were to be purified or freed of its guilt for unjustly killing Socrates, Plato indicates, people generally would have to acquire a new understanding of philosophy. To give them such a new understanding, however, Socrates would have to speak in a more popularly accessible way than he had in the past. As Socrates

---

Alcibiades I 121; *Meno* 97b) designed a way for her to satisfy her desires. But, as Plutarch reports, and Plato's readers would know from the *Minos*, there were alternate versions of the story. According to some, the youths were not sacrificed to or devoured by the monster but were enslaved and became servants of King Minos.

stated in his *Apology*, that meant showing them the benefits of philosophy in deed rather than simply in speech. In the interpretation of his dream, he reports in the *Phaedo*, he seems to recognize a need to speak in a more popular manner, telling stories as well as giving arguments. In the *Phaedo*, Plato thus shows, Socrates combined *mythoi* and *logoi*. By reporting what Socrates did and said on the last day of his life, through the eyes and words of another admirer, Plato presents the popularly intelligible picture of the goodness of a philosophical life for which Socrates appeared to be striving. Although Plato innovated by writing dialogues in prose whereas his teacher had turned, late in life, to putting prosaic stories into verse, Plato's writing was in accord with Socrates' intention. Not only did Plato dramatize the good effects of a philosophical life by showing how it enabled Socrates to confront his death so fearlessly and nobly. He also showed what Socrates was trying to achieve: the perpetuation of the life of questioning and reason, instead of the relapse into irrationality that the fear of death and the pity it arouses often provoke.[45] By stating that he was not present, Plato lets his readers know that he is not giving them a literal report of what occurred on the last day of Socrates' life. That the report be based on fact was nevertheless important for the persuasiveness of Plato's depiction of the goodness of philosophy in the death of Socrates as well as for Socrates' attempt to convince his companions to follow his example and thus to perpetuate his philosophical activity. The hero of Plato's prose drama was not a mythical character from the distant past. On the contrary, Socrates was known to have lived and died in Athens. Plato may have embellished it, but the story of Socrates' death was not entirely a fabrication of Plato's imagination and art.

4. SOCRATES AND THE PYTHAGOREANS

Phaedo reports that fifteen of Socrates' close companions joined him in his prison cell the last day of his life, but we hear the philosopher speaking primarily to Simmias and Cebes, two Thebans Socrates explicitly identifies as students of Philolaus. The question thus arises as to why Plato shows

45. Nietzsche (*Birth of Tragedy*, sec. 14,) suggests that by writing dialogues in prose rather than verse, Plato created a new form of art, the novel (the only genre of literature later critics have observed the Greeks did not recognize along with lyric, epic, tragic, and comic poetry). If so, Plato's distinctive form of writing reflected the distinctive character of Socratic education insofar as novels depict the private lives of individuals (as opposed to the public acts of kings) and are designed to be read by individuals in private, not performed in public in front of a group. Cf. Ian Watt, *The Rise of the Novel* (London: Chatto and Windus, 1957).

Socrates speaking at the very end of his life primarily to Pythagoreans (among whom Phaedo and Echecrates might also be included). The answer appears to be that Pythagoras was the most important example, before Socrates, of a philosopher who insisted that philosophy involved a certain way of life, not merely a set of doctrines or arguments.[46]

Concerned about the perpetuation of Socratic philosophy in the *Phaedo*, Plato wanted to bring out both the similarities and the differences between Socrates and the Pythagoreans. The list of the companions present points to one of the most important similarities as well as the most obvious difference. Like Socrates, Pythagoras left no writings, but unlike Socrates (although like Plato) Pythagoras founded a school. In this school (or later schools) students were not only taught that everything in the world is constituted by number; they were also supposed to follow certain rituals and regulations concerning what they ate and wore.

In the *Theaetetus* Socrates pointed out that he had something important in common with students of mathematics. His argument about the ideas, which he reiterates in the second half of the *Phaedo*, put him, like the students of numbers, in the middle, between Parmenides, who argued that being is one, and Heraclitus, who maintained that everything is always in flux. Arguing that everything is composed of numbers, the Pythagoreans shared Socrates' understanding that there is more than one kind of being, even though being itself is purely intelligible.[47] This underlying similarity in the basic understanding of the character of being—or to speak more properly, beings—as well as a corresponding tendency to devalue the evidence and pleasures of the bodily senses, might have been the reason these students of Philolaus had come to Athens to converse with Socrates. Like the fellow citizens and admirers of Anaxagoras who came to hear about the conversation Socrates was reputed to have once had with Parmenides, these visitors wanted to find out where exactly and why the Athenian disagreed with their mentor, in order to determine who was right.

After they were expelled from Croton, the Pythagoreans appear to have given up their political aspirations and organization (which, I have argued,

---

46. In the introduction to her translation, Brann points out that the first word of the dialogue, *autos* or "self," was the way in which Pythagoras referred and had his students refer to him. Following Benardete ("*Phaedo*") to a certain extent, Michael Davis ("Socrates' Pre-Socratism") suggests that the first word of the dialogue indicates that the question of the *Phaedo* is how body and soul can be combined to make a "self."

47. According to Aristotle *Metaphysics* 987b10–14, 29–32, the Pythagoreans thus differed from Plato only in denying any separation between the first principles—which they identified with numbers rather than "ideas"—and the things said to be their imitations.

constituted a precedent for the Athenian's attempt to found a school as part of a new colony on Crete in the *Laws*). They nevertheless retained certain ritualistic teachings about how people should live (associated with a belief in the reincarnation of the soul) as well as a mathematical understanding of the order and organization of the beings. Like the later Pythagoreans, if not Pythagoras himself, Socrates urged his associates to devote themselves to philosophy in private, rather than to seek political power or influence. As Plato makes clear in the introductory sections of the *Phaedo*, however, Socrates did not establish anything like a sect.

Trying to assuage the grief, if not fear his companions express at the prospect of his demise, Socrates in the first part of their conversation tries to persuade them that death is not terrible by relating stories and arguments he says they must have heard from Philolaus, even though Cebes indicates at the beginning that he has some doubts about the truth of such tales.[48] Adapting these stories to make them consistent with his own view of the character and requirements of knowledge—that it can only be of what is always and unchanging, accessible, therefore, only to the mind and not the senses—Socrates initially emphasizes what he shares with the Pythagoreans.

Having led his Pythagorean interlocutors to recognize the difficulties in arguments and stories they have heard from Philolaus, in the second half of the dialogue Socrates explains why he found Pythagorean as well as other previous philosophical arguments wanting and developed his argument about the ideas. Unlike the Pythagoreans, Socrates argues not only that there are different kinds of beings but also that the different kinds cannot be distinguished from each other merely by number (because differences in numbers of units do not constitute essential differences in kind). Although Socrates agrees with both Parmenides and the Pythagoreans that to be means to be intelligible, he does not think that intelligibility can be,

---

48. Christoph Riedweg, *Pythagoras: His Life, Teaching, and Influence*, trans. Steven Rendall (Ithaca: Cornell University Press, 2005), 42–97, shows that by the time of Philolaus (who is explicitly said to have been the teacher of Simmias and Cebes in Thebes, at *Phaedo* 61d), there were different kinds of Pythagoreans, some adhering to the ascetic rules for living that had been passed down on the basis of the oral tradition (*akousmata*), whereas others like Philolaus emphasized the cosmological and mathematical arguments. Although Riedweg disputes the validity of the grounds on which Walter Burkert denies that Pythagoras himself had or taught any mathematical knowledge, in *Lore and Science in Ancient Pythagoreanism*, trans. Edwin L. Minar, Jr. (Cambridge: Harvard University Press, 1972), he points out (62–63) that all the different kinds of Pythagoreans agreed that some (aristocrats) might live in such a way (ascetically) so that they could acquire immortality (but that neither they nor other ancient Greeks believed that all individual souls were immortal) and that others would be reborn. In other words, Riedweg shows that the specific things Socrates says merely that he has heard (*Phaedo* 61d) were Pythagorean teachings.

or always is, entirely separate from, or completely identical with, sensible existence. On the contrary, he argues, sensible things acquire their specific characteristics by participating in the purely intelligible ideas or forms.

By presenting his own experience as exemplary, Socrates shows that he does not consider philosophy to be "the practice of dying" by restricting bodily pleasure to an absolute minimum. As we are reminded at both the beginning and end of the dialogue, Socrates had a wife and young children. He did not try to abstain from bodily pleasure or ignore the requirements of bodily preservation. He maintained that human beings can never have perfect or certain knowledge, because we are combinations of body and soul. He called his own argument about the ideas merely a "hypothesis," that is, something that he posited, and urged his companions to subject this hypothesis to constant reexamination the way he has. The only "rule" or requirement of a philosophical life he laid down consisted in the need for such constant reexamination of one's convictions in conversations with others, especially concerning the good of the soul. He never proposed dietary rules like those attributed to Pythagoras; nor did he voice any concern, when explicitly asked by Crito, about how his body would be clothed for burial.[49]

In the *Phaedo* Plato reminds his readers, both in the description of the circumstances of the philosopher's death and in the narration of what he said, that Socrates founded a philosophical tradition, if not literally a school. He left his associates no writings or specific doctrine. Instead he urged them, both in word and in deed, to continue philosophizing, testing every argument they thought was sound in ongoing "dialectical" conversations with others. He showed, both in his own arguments and by means of his own example, that such conversations had to take place in private among friends. Nevertheless, he also indicated at the end of his life, such efforts could be pursued and perpetuated in writing as well as by means of direct personal exchanges. Plato was, to a certain extent, following Socrates' example both in writing dialogues and in founding a school. In his dialogues Plato not only related conversations Socrates had with specific individuals; he also dramatized the example Socrates set for others, the example of a man who understood philosophy to be a way of life, not a matter of secret rituals or a means of acquiring covert political influence.[50]

49. The Pythagoreans had a taboo on burying the dead in woolen garments. See Riedweg, *Pythagoras*, 63–64.

50. As Stern suggests when he observes, "In the *Phaedo*, unlike the *Clouds*, we are permitted to hear Socrates' indoor teaching" (*Socratic Rationalism* 190n45), this making public of his teaching is part of the defense of Socrates by Plato.

B. Socrates' Second Apology: Philosophy Is Concerned
with Nothing but Dying and Death

Having explained that he had not begun composing poetry in order to compete with sophists like Evenus, Socrates told Cebes to bid Evenus farewell and to urge him, if he is of sound mind (*sōphronein*), to follow (*diōkein*) Socrates as quickly as he can. The meaning of Socrates' admonition is actually unclear inasmuch as *diōkein* could mean "banish" (and so perhaps erase from his memory the fact that Socrates was being punished) or "prosecute" (and so distinguish himself and his activity from the philosopher). But however the verb is translated, it is clear that in the *Phaedo* Socrates is urging his auditors, just as Plato in effect is urging his readers, to follow Socrates' example, that is, to continue philosophizing in his manner.

Cebes understands Socrates to be referring to his imminent death and so a trip to Hades; Socrates adopts that understanding when he asks Simmias, who has expressed surprise if not shock at the message, whether Evenus is not a philosopher (although Socrates did not appear to regard him as such in the *Apology* [20b], where Evenus is explicitly mentioned as someone who claims to possess the kind of knowledge Socrates has found no human to possess). Simmias responds that Evenus seems to him to be a philosopher, and Socrates states that, in that case, Evenus will take his advice, even though he may not do violence to himself, "for they say it is not right [*themiton*]" (61c). Cebes then asks Socrates to explain what he means by saying that it isn't right to kill oneself but that a philosopher should follow one who is dying.

By having Socrates ask with some surprise whether Cebes has not heard similar things from Philolaus, Plato lets his reader know that the account of philosophy as a search for death that Socrates is about to give is not Socratic so much as Pythagorean in origin, even though in responding to Socrates' question, Cebes says he has heard "nothing clear and distinct [*saphes*]." As we shall see in the course of the conversation, this student of Philolaus is more convinced of the truth of geometrical proofs than of the stories and rites associated with Pythagorean sects. Socrates explicitly states that he knows such things only from hearsay (*akoēs*) but observes that it is fitting for someone about to emigrate to that place to investigate (*diaskopein*) and tell stories (*mythologein*) about the emigration (61e). It is ironic that so many later readers and commentators have taken these investigations and stories, explicitly attributed to others and characterized as hearsay, to epitomize Platonic if not Socratic doctrines.[51]

Certain that Evenus will not follow Socrates' advice about following him, Cebes nevertheless asks the philosopher to explain why he and Philolaus say that it is not right for human beings to take their own lives. Socrates explains that it would be impious of us to end our own lives before the gods decree it because we are their property. Simmias then asks why a wise man would leave good masters or unjustly desert his friends the way Socrates appears to be doing. Socrates recognizes that he is again being charged with impiety, imprudence, and injustice, this time not by the law or the Athenians but by his close associates, and that he must therefore give a new defense.

Socrates responded to the charges at his trial with arguments and accounts of his deeds, but his apology to his philosophical companions is, paradoxically, explicitly mythological. He emphasizes both the limits of human knowledge and the wisdom to be found in old stories.[52] In his *Apology* he had stated that to fear death is to claim to know what no human does or can know. But, as at the end of the *Apology*, so in the *Phaedo*, Socrates shows himself to be willing to explore, with his true "judges" and friends, stories about what may happen to human beings after they die.[53] Stressing the connection between his second and first apologies, Socrates later observes, "not even a comic poet would say that I am chattering and making arguments about things that do not concern me" (70c). Socrates' repeated reminders to his interlocutors that he has an immediate interest in establishing the truth of the stories and arguments they are considering and that they should therefore be wary of simply accepting what he says without question have not always prevented Plato's readers from doing so.

Cebes and Simmias show themselves not to be interested in stories about the afterlife, however, so much as in the reasons Socrates is acting as he is. Cebes asks Socrates to explain why he and Philolaus say people are for

---

51. See, e.g., Dorter, *Phaedo*, ix.

52. Although Socrates had told Phaedrus that he did not have time to investigate or "decode" the meaning of old stories even as he showed that he was able to do so, because he had such an urgent need of acquiring self-knowledge, the stories here would concern what kind of being he and other humans are and so be relevant to his search.

53. As West and West observe (*Four Texts*, 94n78), in the *Apology* Socrates does not call the jurors "judges" (*dikastai*), as was conventional; he addresses them as "men of Athens" and calls only those who voted for his acquittal "judges." In the *Phaedo* (63b) he expresses the hope that he will defend himself more persuasively to his friends than he had to his judges (*dikastas*) and then (63e) calls his associates his judges.

bidden to take their own lives. Cebes has apparently been persuaded that, as Socrates stated in his first *Apology*, the unexamined life is not worth living. In light of Socrates' own fate, Cebes may have begun to wonder whether the examined life is worth living either.[54] He laughs when Socrates asks him to consider whether it might not be better for some humans to be dead than alive, even though it is not pious for them to take their own lives.

Defending himself from the renewed charge of impiety, Socrates explains that it is not pious for human beings to take their own lives, even though proponents of the mysteries claim that the human body constitutes a kind of prison for the soul because the gods care for us and we are their possessions. Like our own slaves or property, human beings do not have a right to take their own lives without the permission of their benevolent masters. We are permitted to die only by some divinely sent necessity of the kind that has come upon him.[55] It is not altogether clear, however, that Socrates' death by order of the Athenians was necessary, much less divinely decreed. According to Crito, Socrates could have evaded the trial and thus his conviction. The necessity seems to have inhered more, as Socrates emphasized in both the *Apology* and the *Crito*, in his age.

Perhaps for that reason, Socrates praises Cebes when he objects by stating that a prudent person would not willingly leave the service of good masters (or choose to die before his allotted time). Socrates admits that it would have been unjust (although not imprudent) for him not to have been vexed at his death (which he has consistently maintained he did not deserve as a punishment for wrongdoing), if he did not believe that he would be among better masters and human beings after he dies. He insists that he does not know what death will bring, but he has high hopes that it will bring "something good." Although he complained earlier about Socrates' desertion of them, Simmias acknowledges that if Socrates shares the thought (*dianoian*) that leads him to have such hopes and so to meet his death with such equanimity with his companions, he will have demonstrated his justice by letting them share in a good that should be held in

54. See David Bolotin, "The Life of Philosophy and the Immortality of the Soul: An Introduction to Plato's *Phaedo*," *Ancient Philosophy* 7 (1987): 39–55; Peter J. Ahrensdorf, *The Death of Socrates and the Life of Philosophy* (Albany: SUNY Press, 1995), 30; Stern, *Socratic Rationalism*, 20.

55. It is not clear what exactly the necessity is or how it is divinely ordained. Does Socrates equate the decision of the Athenians with a divine necessity? The attribution of necessity to the official punishment does not square with Crito's report that Socrates could have evaded the trial entirely, but it would accord with Socrates' emphasis on the necessity of his dying soon, in any case, as a result of old age, by nature.

common. The question remains whether Socrates' passive acceptance of death at the hands of others is prudent.

Socrates makes his famous suggestion that philosophy is nothing but the search and preparation for death, in response to the question of whether it is prudent (as opposed to just) for Socrates to accept his death so calmly. Simmias laughs, observing that many people see philosophers just that way, as little better than dead while still alive. Like Callicles, Socrates comments, such people associate living with feeling, especially the pleasures of the body. Philosophers recognize that bodily pleasures and pains not merely do not enable them to acquire the good they seek; the demands of the body positively get in the way of acquiring the knowledge philosophers seek. Human beings cannot gain knowledge of the purely intelligible things-in-themselves by means of their senses; "things" like the good, the noble, the just, the healthy, the big, or the strong in themselves are accessible only to the mind (*dianoia*) by means of reason (*logismos*). Not only do our bodily senses distort what we perceive; human beings also find it difficult to find the leisure necessary to seek wisdom, because our bodily necessities and desires require us to seek food and shelter and even to fight wars with others in order to attain and preserve such necessary goods.[56] If death consists in the separation of body and soul, philosophers can be understood to be seeking death, insofar as they try to purify themselves of their bodily desires and sensations in order to acquire knowledge of the things that truly are.

In his first, explicitly mythological explanation of the reasons a philosopher will not become upset by the prospect of his death but might even be tempted to seek it, Socrates not only points out that separation of the soul from all bodily influences appears to constitute a necessary condition for the acquisition of true knowledge. He also suggests that freedom from bodily concerns is a necessary condition of human excellence. Socrates says that he hopes to find better companions among those who have successfully learned how to die, because true virtue also requires freeing the soul from the influence of bodily pleasures and pains. Because most people fear death, Socrates reminds his interlocutors, most people understand

---

56. I am puzzled, therefore, by David Bostock's claim (*Phaedo*, 26) that Socrates does not give any reasons or examples of the way in which sense perception makes it difficult for human beings to acquire knowledge, even though I recognize that Socrates will claim, in the account of recollection he later gives, that our senses are the way in which we are reminded of what we knew before birth and so enable us to acquire knowledge. Bostock apparently thinks that all the arguments Socrates (or Plato) gives are or ought to be consistent with one another. I not only observe that the arguments are not consistent with one another but also argue that Plato intends us to observe the inconsistency and to recognize the difficulties posed by the inconsistencies.

courage to consist in overcoming this fear. The way it is usually overcome, however, is by another fear—of dishonor or losing a loved one, for example. Likewise, what most people call moderation consists in exchanging the satisfaction of one kind of desire (usually short term or immediate) for the satisfaction of another (longer lasting or greater). Because such an exchange of one fear for another, or one desire for another, retains both a fear or desire, Socrates suggests that true virtue may not consist in, or result from, such an exchange; it may exist only where there is a certain kind of wisdom (*phronēsis*) that frees a person from all such fears and desires.[57]

Socrates does not explain exactly what kind of purification he has in mind. But he identifies this purification with philosophizing correctly and states that he has done everything in his power to achieve it. In the *Apology*, we are reminded, Socrates suggested that he exemplified the virtues of piety, courage, and justice (although not moderation), because he possessed a certain kind of human wisdom. Knowing that he did not know, Socrates did not fear death or seek wealth and reputation as his fellow Athenians did. Because he did not try to get the better of others but attempted to convince them to seek the good of their souls, truth, and prudence by showing them they did not know what was truly good and noble, he was not merely law-abiding but just. As the Eleatic Stranger reminded us, Socratic refutations constituted a kind of purification. They freed—or were at least intended to free—his interlocutors from the greatest kind of ignorance, the ignorance involved in thinking one knows what one does not. What most people think they know, but do not, Plato reminds his readers in the dialogues depicting Socrates' trial and death, is that death is bad.

Socrates concludes his second defense by suggesting that the people who instituted the ancient rites spoke with a hidden meaning when they said that "whoever arrives in Hades ignorant of the mysteries and uninitiated will lie in muck, but he who arrives purified and initiated will dwell with gods" (*Phaedo* 69c). On the basis of his own experience, Socrates has identified and brought out the truth, not literal but implicit, in the stories and rites passed on from the Orphic mysteries within Pythagorean sects. As in the *Apology*, so in the *Phaedo*, Socrates' defense consists primarily in an account of his own life.

As Aristophanes showed in his caricature of Socrates in the *Clouds*, but Plato also depicted more nobly, Socratic philosophy involved a kind of

---

57. "Moderation and justice and courage and prudence itself may be nothing but a kind of purification" (*Phaedo* 69c).

asceticism.[58] In his *Apology* Socrates reminded the jurors that he lived in great poverty. He explicitly urged both his companions and his fellow citizens not to seek wealth, fame, or pleasure until they had acquired knowledge of what is truly good. Socrates' refutations thus constituted the noblest, truest, and most important forms of purification. By showing his interlocutors that they did not know what they thought they did, Socrates hoped to cure them of their fear of death. He did not cure them, completely, effectively, or truly, by telling stories, although he did tell or retell stories such as the myth of Er at the end of the *Republic* and the stories he claimed to have heard about the immortality of the soul from wise men and women, on which he based his account of learning as recollection in the *Meno*. Socrates tried to cure his interlocutors of their fear of something they irrationally believed to be bad by showing them, in practice even more than in principle, what is truly good for human beings. Although the unexamined life of pleasure seeking is not worth living, he insisted, the examined life of philosophy is. Such a life does not require belief in the immortality of the soul, separated from the body. Nor is it completely ascetic or without pleasure. On the contrary, Socrates affirmed in his *Apology*, the conversations in which he and his associates engaged were not unpleasant. As Plato tells his readers by means of Crito's interjection at the beginning of Socrates' mythologizing, philosophical conversations tend to heat up—or, we might say, further enliven human beings. Socratic philosophizing did not prepare him to die merely by reducing his sensations to a minimum. Both in the *Apology* and in the *Phaedo*, Socrates maintains that a life of philosophy is good and satisfying so long as it lasts, and that the philosopher has nothing to fear when it comes to an end.

C. Socrates' Three Faulty Proofs of the Immortality of the Soul

Failing to notice Socrates' mention of a hidden meaning in the old stories, Cebes observes that the reasons Socrates says a philosopher will not fear death all depend on the immortality of the soul. But, Cebes objects, many people (including Cebes, we surmise) believe that when the body dies, the soul also dies or is dispersed. He asks Socrates, therefore, to prove that the soul is immortal.

---

58. In the *Clouds*, Aristophanes comically depicts the necessity for Socrates' followers to put mind over matter by having the philosopher force Strepsiades to think about how he can solve his problems while bitten by fleas. In the *Symposium* Plato describes Socrates' own apparent indifference to physical pain and pleasure, rising above them because he is so absorbed in his own thought, in Alcibiades' speech and at the conclusion of the dialogue.

Readers of Plato seem to agree on very little, but commentators on the *Phaedo* are virtually unanimous in finding the "proofs" Socrates gives inadequate.[59] Plato shows that Socrates' interlocutors were not persuaded by them. Both Simmias and Cebes continue to have doubts about the adequacy of Socrates' arguments after he has stated them. And at the end of his last and presumably best argument, Socrates not merely praises the Thebans for raising objections but urges them to go on questioning. As Hans-Georg Gadamer observes, the purpose of Socrates' arguments does not appear to be proving the immortality of the soul and thus providing grounds for the hopes he has expressed concerning the afterlife so much as to enable his companions to overcome their fears and so to be able and willing to continue philosophizing after he has gone.[60]

One indication that the primary purpose of Socrates' speech is not to prove that the soul is immortal is that Socrates never asks what soul is. At the end of the first book of the *Republic*, Socrates pointed out how foolish it was for him to have tried to prove that justice was good without first having determined what justice is. Yet in the *Phaedo* we see the philosopher who was famous for asking "what is . . . ?" questions attempt to prove that the soul is immortal without first trying to define soul. We can find a reason for his failure to raise the question in the *Phaedrus*, where Socrates argues that the self-moving soul must be immortal because nothing else causes and so begins (or ends) its motion, but he concedes that it would take more time than any mortal has at his disposal to describe the soul's form (*eidos*), that is, to say what it is. On the last day of his life, Socrates would have been acutely aware of the limitations his own mortality put on his time as well as his knowledge. He thus contents and constrains himself to *mythologein*.[61]

---

59. See, e.g., Dorter, *Phaedo*, ix; Stern, *Socratic Rationalism*, 49.

60. Cf. Hans-Georg Gadamer, "The Proofs of Immortality in Plato's *Phaedo*," in *Dialogue and Dialectic*, 36.

61. The connection between Socrates' arguments in the *Phaedrus* and the *Phaedo* can be seen by observing in the *Phaedrus* how Socrates presents philosophy as the form of eros that enables human beings to escape repeated reincarnations; in the *Phaedo* he also presents philosophy as the means of escaping future reincarnations (although not as a form of love). To free his companions of their fear of death, particularly the consequences of his death, Socrates has to try to free them from their attachment to, and dependence on, him as an individual with his erotic knowledge of how to arouse a desire for wisdom in others. Rather than entice others to investigate with him, in the *Phaedo* Socrates has to persuade them to continue seeking wisdom with each other without him. It is perhaps no accident that in beginning his famous palinode in the *Phaedrus* (242b), Plato has Socrates comment that only Simmias the Theban is fonder of hearing arguments than Phaedrus is.

1. THE GENERATION OF EVERYTHING FROM ITS OPPOSITE

Instead of referring directly to the cosmological understanding of soul as self-moving, which would not have provided any comfort for his friends in a teaching about the immortality of individual human souls, Socrates begins his first "proof" by referring to the ancient tale that says that souls *are* (always), that after death they go to Hades, and that they then come back to earth reborn.[62] This ancient tale was associated with the Pythagorean belief in reincarnation (as well as judgment after death), to which he returns explicitly in his third "proof."

Simmias and Cebes have already indicated their skepticism about such tales, so Socrates suggests that, to see the truth of these stories, they should think about everything that becomes. (He also reminds us, Plato's readers, of the reasons he associated the poets with the philosophers of flux.) He then asks his interlocutors whether it is possible for anything to come to be something else or different from what it has been except from what it is or has not been, that is, its opposite. Socrates combines several different kinds of opposition in the examples he gives. Whereas some of the opposites, like life and death, seem to be mutually exclusive, others, like big and little, increasing and decreasing, are comparative, existing along a spectrum.[63] Other kinds of oppositions he mentions, like the noble and base or just and unjust, allow things to be neither. Still others, like strong and weak, or hot and cold, could be understood to be more or less, even the negation of a single quality (or existence). All these "opposites" appear, moreover, to be characteristics of a third "something"—soul or substance or being—which fluctuates or "becomes" between them. But if this is the case, Socrates is

---

62. As in Homer *Odyssey* 11, such stories treat *psychai* as very thin, perhaps diaphanous, bodies insofar as they occupy spaces.

63. As Dorter points out (*Phaedo*, 35–40), Socrates treats life and death as if they were mutually exclusive opposites, like odd and even (which he does not mention here), although things can be neither living nor dead, the same way they can be neither just nor unjust, neither pleasant or painful. In the *Philebus* Socrates provides a critique of this thesis by arguing that there are pure pleasures without any admixture of, or connection to, pain. At the beginning of the *Phaedo*, he observes that pleasure and pain appear to be "yoked" together at the head when he observes that what people call pleasure always follows pain. The difference between the analysis of pleasure he gives in the *Philebus* and the connection between pleasure and pain he emphasizes at the beginning of the *Phaedo* is but one of the many reminders to Plato's readers that Socrates is not giving his own arguments in this part of the *Phaedo* so much as he is examining the stories and arguments given by others. As Dorter also points out, it would have ruined Socrates' argument here to admit that there are things that do not share in either pole of the oppositions he names. But to be fair to Socrates, we should note that thinkers like Heraclitus had also declared that everything existed in opposition and there were no middle points.

either assuming the existence of the soul that he is supposed to be proving, which moves between life (on this earth) and Hades, or he is identifying the soul with the process of becoming as a whole, which persists in and through all the fluctuations. Socrates points to one of the grounds of the plausibility of the thesis he is taking from flux philosophers such as Heraclitus (as well as from poets and sophists) when he observes that in the world of becoming, everything has to move back and forth between opposed poles or states, because if things did not move back and forth, everything would end up at one pole or in one condition (dead), and becoming would cease.

2. IF KNOWLEDGE IS RECOLLECTION

Cebes points to the irony—or problem—when he easily agrees to Socrates' conclusion that the soul is deathless—on the basis of another argument. No more attracted to reflections on the character of sensible experience or becoming as a whole than he is to the poetry and tales out of which such reflections partly arose, Cebes says that he has already been persuaded of the immortality of the soul by the arguments and demonstrations Socrates had given in the past to show that learning is recollection.

If human beings learn by recollecting, their souls must have come to know the purely intelligible things they recollect before they were joined to bodies. Cebes seems to be referring to the kind of demonstration Socrates gave with the slave boy in the *Meno*, when he reminds Simmias, who admits he has forgotten: "If the questions are put well, when people are questioned, they themselves are able to speak about everything. Yet if they did not happen to have knowledge [*epistēmē*] and right reason [*orthos logos*] within them, they would not be able to do so. This is shown most clearly if you charge them with mathematical diagrams or something of that sort" (*Phaedo* 73a–b). Neither Cebes nor many of the commentators on this passage seem to remember that in the *Meno*, Socrates premised the demonstration and the lessons he extracted from it on stories he has heard from priests and priestesses who say that the soul is immortal. Like the tale with which Socrates began his first "proof," the argument about recollection appears to assume what it is supposed to prove.

The restatement of his argument about recollection that Socrates gives to Simmias here is very different, moreover, from the argument he makes about the significance of the demonstration in the *Meno*.[64] Here he does

---

64. Cf. Norman Gulley, "Plato's Theory of Recollection," *Classical Quarterly* 54 (1954): 194; and J. L. Ackrill, "*Anamnesis* in the *Phaedo*: Remarks on 73c–75c," *Phronesis*, supp. 1 (1973): 175.

not demonstrate the capacity of an untutored boy to follow the logical steps in a geometrical proof by questioning him "correctly," demonstrating visibly that the boy's first responses are not correct and then showing him how to give the correct answer. Nor does Socrates emphasize the need to repeat the steps of the proof many times in order to change correct opinion into knowledge.[65] Instead, he asks Simmias to reflect on the ability human beings have to recall one thing or person when they see another, often very unlike—especially where there is a love interest. Rather than "recollection," we would ordinarily call this an example of the power of association, based on a perception of the frequent coincidence of the two things, if not a perceived similarity of some kind between them.

Socrates' use of the examples of a person's recalling the boy who plays a lyre when he sees a lyre, as well as our ability not merely to recognize a person from his painted image but to connect him or his image with a beloved friend, has puzzled some commentators, because it does not lead neatly or logically to the "theory of forms," with which Socrates here, although not in the *Meno*, associates our ability to "recollect," that is, recognize, them in sensible things.[66] The implicit difficulty, on which Socrates does not explicitly comment here, does, however, appear to be of the same kind that Socrates later says led him to develop his own distinctive argument and method of investigation. He was puzzled by the fact that the same outcome (here "recollection"; later, that units become two) results from two different, apparently opposed processes (here perception of likeness or unlikeness; later, both addition and division). Like the difficulties in Socrates' first proof, the difficulties in the second point to the reasons which Socrates explains later in the conversation led him to develop a novel kind of philosophical practice.[67]

Socrates appears to reduce the range of recollection to the perception of similarity when he asks Simmias if people do not necessarily note whether the thing they perceive falls short of what it leads them to rec-

65. Such a demonstration would have highlighted the role of the questioner and so contributed to the fear both Simmias and Cebes confess at the end of this discussion that they will not be able to find another such "singer" as Socrates to assuage their fears by engaging them in further, repeated philosophical conversations in the future.

66. See, e.g., David Gallop, trans., *Plato's "Phaedo"* (Oxford: Clarendon Press, 1975), 88–90.

67. This suspicion is further supported by the observation that both of the apparently anomalous characteristics of the first examples of recollection that Socrates puts forth here, that they are prompted by love and that they can arise from either similarities or dissimilarities, are said in other dialogues to be the source of our attempts to learn more by questioning: eros in the *Symposium*, and the observation that a finger can be both longer and shorter than others in the *Republic*. Cf. Stern, *Socratic Rationalism*, on the significance of the love factor.

ollect. However, the difference between the thing perceived and what is recollected in or through it could be stated just as well in terms of likeness and unlikeness, sameness and difference. It is impossible, indeed, to distinguish image or imitation from original without specifying the differences as well as the similarities. As in the cases of the lyre and the boy or the picture and the man, the differences can be in kind as well as in amount of similarity.

The example Socrates chooses of equality brings out the reasons Cebes finds Socrates' explanation of learning as recollection persuasive, as well as the problems involved. Equality appears to be a purely intelligible concept. It might be inferred from a series of comparisons between sensible objects, which are the same in a respect that can be measured by an external standard, but it cannot be acquired by means of sensation alone, nor does it inhere in sensible objects like sticks perceived to be equal to each other. Both Cebes and Simmias have been said to be students of Philolaus, a Pythagorean who emphasized the study of geometry; and as students of geometry they would have been aware of the difference between the sensible constructions used to illustrate geometrical proofs and the logic of the proof itself. As students of geometry they would also have understood the necessity of beginning proofs with axioms that cannot be proved in the same way. One of those axioms is that equals of equals are equal. But how do people come to acquire and understand the concept of equality if it is not deduced from something else? They infer or generalize it from a series of examples of sensible things said to be equal by others. Neither the examples nor the saying prove that the things are equal, however, nor do they communicate the concept per se. Most people seem to recognize, to intuit, or, Socrates might say, to "recollect" it—somehow. They don't go through all the reasoning necessary to define the concept precisely, yet what it means for things to be equal is commonly, if loosely understood.

The unstated problem that comes to the fore when Socrates emphasizes the difference between the equal itself and the equal sensible things is that equality is a relation. Things cannot be perceived or understood to be equal if they are not understood to be separate from each other and thus different in some respect as well. As a relation, equality would appear to be a bad example of a quality that is always and unchanging in itself, even though it is a good example of a concept that is purely intelligible. The equal, the greater, and the lesser are not, as Socrates asserts, just like the beautiful, the good, the just, and the holy in themselves. All these concepts are like insofar as they are not and do not refer to things or aspects of things perceptible by the senses; they are all purely intelligible. The two kinds of purely intelligible concepts differ, however, inasmuch as the first three "mathematical" concepts are relative measures, whereas the last four qualities can be in, or possessed by, sensible things to a greater or lesser extent, but the quality itself is the measure, not measured or established in terms of another standard of measure, for example, size or number. In the account of the purely intelligible ideas or forms Socrates gives here as well as in his later description of his own hypothesis, Socrates abstracts from the difference between the kinds of intelligible measures (units and proportions) the Pythagoreans thought gave order to things and the distinctive, nonquantifiable, but nevertheless purely intelligible, qualities he himself regularly emphasized—the good, the noble, and the just.

By emphasizing that we acquire such purely intelligible concepts only by means of sensible experience (*Phaedo* 75a), Socrates shows (although he does not say so explicitly) that philosophy cannot consist in the ascetic attempt to minimize sensation he suggested it was in his first, somewhat playful account of philosophy as a search for death. Socrates had concluded that account by suggesting that those who insisted on the importance of purifying one's soul before arriving in Hades had a "hidden teaching," which was that philosophizing correctly was the best if not only means of achieving such a purification in this life. But Simmias and Cebes had concluded, more literally, that everything depended on a showing that the human soul is in fact immortal.

Although Socrates appears to have persuaded his interlocutors that, if learning is recollection, the soul must have existed independent of the body before it was joined to it in birth, Socrates' second proof does not show that the soul is immortal any more than his first did. The fact that human beings observably have a capacity to discern things as similar to and different from each other, and to generalize or abstract the characteristic differences as intelligible concepts, does not prove that either our soul or this capacity exists before we are born, or that it does not die with us. Insofar as the concepts themselves are purely intelligible, they may be in principle, if not in practice or fact, eternal and unchanging. But must the intelligence that recognizes the intellibility of these principles also be eternal and unchanging?

3. The Soul Is Not the Sort of Thing That Disintegrates

Simmias is convinced, as Cebes affirmed that he had been earlier, that Socrates' argument about learning as recollection proves that the soul pre-exists the body. But neither thinks that Socrates has shown that the soul does not dissolve and become dispersed the way the body decomposes at death. Socrates first tries to persuade the Thebans that they will find a proof that the soul exists after as well as before death by merely combining the two arguments he has already given: "Every living thing comes to be from what's dead. For if the soul *is* beforehand, and if it's necessary for it, when it enters into life and is born, to come to be from nowhere else than death and being dead, how is it not necessary for it to *be*, even after it's died, since it must be born again?" (*Phaedo* 77c–d). He thus points clearly to the connection between belief in the immortality of the soul and reincarnation, which he makes explicit in the elaboration of his argument that follows. As Pythagoreans, the Thebans should and would be familiar with both doctrines. The belief that souls not only were immortal but that they would be reincarnated, often as animals, was the basis of the restrictions on eating, drinking, and wearing animal products characteristic of Pythagorean sects.

As Plato makes clear at this point in the dialogue, their Pythagorean beliefs and ritual practices do not prevent Simmias and Cebes from feeling apprehensive at the prospect of Socrates' death. Nor has Socrates been able to purge them of their fears with the stories and arguments he has given thus far. On the contrary, the Thebans' inability to show the inadequacy of his statements has added to their conviction that they will never find another "singer" of "incantations" able to relieve them of such apprehensions. The fear of death they are suffering is not, we should note, fear of their own demise. They are pained by the prospect of the loss not only of the company but also of the speeches of the man whose activity makes their lives worth living. Socrates thus urges them to seek another such singer not only energetically and broadly, abroad as well as at home, but also together and in themselves. Socrates had stated earlier that he regarded philosophy as the highest and best form of music. In the *Symposium*, we might recall, he had also compared himself (and Eros) to a magician (*goēs*) who produced incantations. Simmias and Cebes will find comfort and relief in his absence, Socrates suggests, only by persisting in the kind of philosophical conversations they have had with him with each other and anyone else they can find. Socrates' third proof of the immortality of the soul thus culminates in praise of the philosophic life. As in his initial, somewhat playful description of philosophy as the search for death and in both of the preceding proofs of the immortality of the soul, which seemed to be assumed in the initial description, in his third proof

Socrates appeals to a combination of practices and teachings characteristic of the Pythagoreans with arguments and practices that were distinctively Socratic. Only after he has brought the two young Pythagoreans to admit openly, both to themselves and to the assembled company, that they do not find these arguments satisfactory does Socrates openly and explicitly present his own practice and distinctive argument as exemplary.

In response to the Thebans' expressed fear that the soul dissipates along with the body, Socrates does not ask what the soul itself is, but whether it is the sort of thing that is apt to dissipate. The characteristics of the soul he identifies, in contrast to those of the body, are characteristics Parmenides had argued inhered in being itself—noncomposite (or unitary), unchanging, and hence nonsensible. Socrates does not ask whether, and therefore does not deny that, soul, like Parmenides' being, moves. That question would have brought to the fore *the* question about soul and its relation to being the Eleatic Stranger had posed in objecting to the arguments of "the friends of the forms." Both soul (understood as living) and thought (*dianoia*) involve motion; motion, however, appears to involve change. According to Socrates and students of geometry, such as the Thebans to whom he is speaking, that which changes cannot, strictly speaking, be known.

Unlike Parmenides, Socrates reminds his interlocutors, they agree that there are different kinds of being—the equal in itself and the beautiful or noble in itself, for example—but these kinds do not change. He thus returns to his initial description of philosophy as the attempt to free the soul from the confusion and corruption caused by its incorporation. He seems to forget that in the second proof of the immortality of the soul, which he gave on the basis of his own argument about learning as recollection, he had not merely conceded but had emphasized that the embodied soul begins to learn through sensation. We would never learn if we tried, as he now apparently urges his interlocutors to try, to keep the soul entirely free of the effects of sensation and thus of body. He asserts that when the soul investigates, in itself by itself, it is carried (*oichetai*) to "what's pure and *is* always and is deathless and keeps to the same condition." He goes so far as to declare that "since the soul is akin [*syggenes*] to this [deathless, unchanging being], it continually comes to be [*gignetai*] with what is always in itself" (79d). This state of the soul is called intelligence (*phronēsis*). And if the soul is divine, deathless, intelligible, uniform, self-same, and indissoluble, whereas the body is mortal, having many forms, unintelligent, dissoluble, and never the same, they agree, the soul must be indissoluble—or nearly so. By qualifying the conclusion in this way, Socrates admits that he has not actually responded to their concern before he has even finished the argument.

Although Socrates and Cebes agree that "nature ordains the body to be a slave and ruled by soul" (80a), the suspicion arises that the soul does not exist any longer than the body, because most souls are in fact ruled by their bodily sensations and desires. Those who do not purify their souls of such sensations and desires by seeking to know the truly intelligible, unchanging beings do not merely lack the leisure and peace to seek wisdom and fail to acquire true virtue, because of the conflict among and aroused by their bodily desires, as Socrates emphasized in his first account of philosophy as the search for death. Those who do not purify their souls of their attachment to bodily pleasures suffer the greatest and most extreme evil of all—thinking that the sensible things that give them the most intense pleasures and pains are the most evident and true. Having been shaped by their bodily desires and fears while alive, such souls remain close to earth after they die and quickly become entangled in the bodies of animals that instinctively act according to their strongest passions—donkeys in the case of gluttons, falcons or wolves in the case of tyrants, and so on. Having made themselves as much like the purely intelligible, unchanging beings they seek to contemplate while alive, the souls of philosophers are not at all terrified of becoming separated from their bodies. They alone do not fear death.

The emphasis in Socrates' account of the state of a philosopher's soul after death has nevertheless changed slightly. He no longer talks about philosophers associating with better gods or human companions. Having become like the eternal unchanging beings they sought to contemplate while alive, these souls do not talk, reason, think, or suffer; they are no longer affected by anything and so do not feel any pain or fear. They are no longer divided or composite, changeable or visible, but we would not be apt to describe them as living individuals either.

Socrates has not proved that individual souls like his are immortal, nor do his Theban companions think he has done so. So when Socrates falls silent, having apparently finished his argument, they continue to whisper. Asked what they are murmuring about, the Thebans admit they have not found Socrates' arguments entirely persuasive. Although Socrates' *mythologia* has not convinced his companions that the soul is immortal, it does succeed in bringing out the reasons for their apprehensions and doubts so that the philosopher can address them more directly. Even though Simmias said that Socrates' argument that learning is recollection had convinced him that the soul exists before it is united with body, he now shows that he clings to the Pythagorean notion that the soul merely constitutes a harmony of the bodily elements, which dissipates along with those elements in death. More attached to Socrates' argument about learning as recollection, Cebes agrees, perhaps on the basis of his familiarity with the Pythagorean notion of reincarnation, not only that souls exist before the bodies with which they are joined but also that the same souls can be incorporated into several different bodies. But, he objects, the fact that a soul outlasts several bodies does not mean that it lasts forever.

In responding to these objections or settled questions, if not beliefs, Socrates does not try to prove that the soul, whether individual or cosmic, is immortal so much as he attempts to show the Pythagoreans that they do not know that there are no eternally unchanging, purely intelligible beings. If human beings prematurely conclude that there is nothing eternally unchanging and hence knowable, Socrates worries, they will deprive themselves of all possibility of acquiring knowledge.

D. The Battle against Misology

Although Socrates reassured the Thebans that he would not be discomfited by their objections, Phaedo reports that he and Socrates' other companions were shaken, because they, unlike Simmias and Cebes, had been persuaded by Socrates' arguments. But perceiving that his disappointed companions might be tempted to jettison the attempt to discover the truth by examining various, apparently conflicting arguments, Socrates rallied them. He urged them not to conclude that no argument is true merely because many arguments can be disputed, if not shown to be invalid. They should blame themselves or their own lack of art for their failure to find a valid argument, and they should continue striving, lest they be robbed of the truth about the things that truly are by their own failure to persevere.

This dramatic interlude constitutes the climax of the dialogue. Phaedo reports that he "never admired [Socrates] more, . . . first, how pleasantly and kindly and admiringly he received the young men's argument, second, how keenly he perceived how we'd suffered under their arguments, and, third, how well he healed us and, as if we were men who'd fled and been laid low, rallied us and turned us about to follow him and consider the argument with him" (*Phaedo* 88e–89a). Socrates rallied his companions, we should observe, by redefining the issue. The question is no longer so much if the soul—whether that be personal or general had not been made clear in the previous arguments—is immortal as it is how to discover an argument that will preserve the possibility of discovering the truth about the things that are always.

Simmias and Cebes had been urging each other to state their objections to Socrates' argument. Both wanted to hear Socrates' response. They had been afraid, however, "that it might be unpleasant for [Socrates] in his present misfortune" (84d). Like swans who sing most beautifully as they are about to die, Socrates assured them, he is not afraid of death.[68] In presenting his last set of arguments for the immortality of the soul, Socrates had been said to be "singing incantations" to assuage their fears, not his own.

After being reassured that it would not be giving Socrates further pain, Simmias first gave a general statement of his own stance that appears quite Socratic. Recognizing how difficult it is for mortals to know about these matters, Simmias insisted that only a "soft man" will "not test what's said about them in every way or cease investigating in every way possible." He who perseveres will either learn what the case is or, if that proves to be impossible, "sail through life in the midst of danger, seizing on the best and the least refutable of human arguments, . . . as if on a raft, unless he can find a more stable carrier, some divine account" (85c). Socrates had just claimed to possess a prophetic art. Simmias, therefore, did not rule out the possibility of a man's acquiring wisdom through divine inspiration.

Socrates had urged them to state their objections to his previous argument, so Simmias then asked: why, on the grounds Socrates has maintained that the soul is undying—that it is noncomposite, unchanging, invisible, and divinely beautiful—could one not say equally well that the soul is a harmony that perishes with the body? Just as the strings of a lute, if it is well tuned and played, produce a sound that not only is unified but also can be expressed in the purely intelligible terms of a geometrical relation, so the soul can be regarded as that which orders the constituent parts of the body but dissolves along with those parts.

Plato highlights the Pythagorean source of Simmias' objection by having Echecrates, who was also a Pythagorean, break into the narrative (88c) to say that he too has been persuaded that the soul is a kind of harmony.

---

68. Although Socrates claims to be a servant of Apollo, like the swans, and endowed with a prophetic art no less than theirs, he does not claim to have the "foreknowledge of the good things in Hades," which the swans do. He states simply that he is "not being freed from life any more sad of heart than they" (*Phaedo* 85b). As the Thebans are about to learn, Socrates' equanimity in the face of death does not arise from a firm belief on his part in the immortality of the soul.

Echecrates was particularly anxious, therefore, to hear Socrates' response to Simmias' objection.

What Plato's readers learn from the action or exchange is, first, that Simmias is only partly a follower of Socrates. Like Socrates, he thinks that opinions need to be tested; he wishes, therefore, to hear Socrates' response to his objections. Unlike Socrates, however, Simmias does not do the testing himself. He looks to others, like Socrates or his friend Cebes. When there is no clear resolution of the issue, he falls back on the most plausible opinion he has heard in the past. He does not actively pursue the issue or, arguably, learn much from the exchange.

Second and more important, however, Plato confronts his readers with the debilitating effects of such easy-going skepticism by depicting the reaction of the assembled group. Socrates had assured Simmias and Cebes that stating their objections to his arguments would not cause him pain, but Socrates' other associates were discouraged by the cogency of the objections once stated. Like people who become haters of all human beings because they have trusted some too unconditionally and have been disappointed by them, Socrates worried, his companions might become haters of arguments. Like most human beings who are neither entirely good nor completely bad, he observes, most arguments contain some but not the entire truth. Rather than blame their own lack of art for their failure to discern the partial truth or problems in specific arguments, his companions might be tempted to conclude, like those who engage in eristic debates, that nothing is sound or stable but that everything simply tosses to and fro. By too easily and quickly jumping to such a general conclusion from specific failures, they would deprive themselves of any chance of discovering the truth about things that are (and do not simply become).

Socrates' companions had been discouraged by the objections to his arguments because they had accepted his arguments too easily and uncritically. Socrates thus warned them about trusting him and the arguments he put forth too much. About to die himself, he might appear to be like the eristic debaters who desire victory more than truth. The difference, he pointed out to his companions, is that he wants to make the case particularly to and for himself, whereas the eristics are concerned primarily about winning in the eyes of others. Socrates will benefit, if what he argues is true; his companions will benefit from his not paining them with laments for his demise, even if it is not true. His mindlessness will not last long, if they follow his advice and "give little thought to Socrates and much more to the truth. They should agree with him, if he seems to be speaking truth, but strain against him with every argument they've got, if he does not" (91c). They should, like Simmias, greet all arguments with a degree of critical skepticism, but they should not let this skepticism serve as a substitute for energetic effort to find the truth or as an excuse for merely falling back on familiar old opinions. What Socrates clearly wanted was for his companions to persist in their philosophical investigations after he was gone. So and only so would the force that had ruled his existence persist in theirs.

1. SOCRATES' RESPONSE TO SIMMIAS

Socrates first responded to Simmias' objection by pointing out that the notion that the soul is a harmony of the parts of the body is not compatible with the notion that the soul must exist before the body, if learning is recollection. Socrates thus reminded the assembled group that Simmias had contradicted his own earlier agreement. So when Cebes reaffirmed his belief that learning is recollection and that this argument showed that the soul exists before and independent of the body, Simmias quickly conceded that the notion that the soul is a harmony is based simply on a plausible likeness and hence probability rather than a demonstration. As we have already seen in his response to the restatement of Socrates' argument about learning as recollection, Simmias tended not only to be less contentious than Cebes but also to follow his lead. Although he seemed to insist on the desirability of testing all arguments in his earlier statement, Simmias relied on his friend to do the testing.

Socrates did not, therefore, merely accept Simmias' speedy concession. If he had, Simmias might have continued to hold onto his belief that the soul is a kind of harmony, not because he thought that it was true but because he believed that it was the most plausible account he could find. Socrates pointed out that the notion that the soul is merely an order of the various parts of the body also conflicts with the notion they earlier agreed to, that the soul rules the body. But this response was not good or persuasive. An order of the parts may presuppose the existence of those parts, but so does rule of a city presuppose the existence of the city. (The difference here is between something earlier in time and something superior.) So Socrates quickly added two other arguments to show that the understanding of soul as a harmony is inconsistent with the understanding of soul as that which gives order (more or less) to a living person. Neither of these arguments was much better, however. If a harmonious soul is one, as it would have to be to incorporate all the aspects he had earlier said made the soul something closer to the immortal than the mortal, Socrates pointed out, it could not be said to be more or less harmonious, better or worse, virtuous or vicious. All souls would be the same. Socrates' contention that souls are noncomposite had attributed all their bad and disorderly characteristics to the effects of body. So Socrates added a second objection: the notion of the soul as a harmony would not allow for the seemingly forcible repression, on occasion, of some base desires by higher psychic aspects or elements. Socrates' contention in the *Phaedo* (as opposed to the *Republic*) that the soul is noncomposite makes it difficult to maintain that soul simply, automatically, always, or even frequently rules body. If what determines the character and direction of a living thing rules the thing, it looks as if most human souls are ruled by their bodies' needs and desires. It is easier and more plausible to argue that the body is ruled by the soul, if the human soul is understood to be characterized by conflict, as in the *Republic*, between reason and the desires, and that the reason needs to be dominant.

Despite the difficulties, if not inadequacy, of Socrates' response to Simmias, both he and Cebes said they were completely convinced. They believed that soul definitely rules body so long as soul and body are conjoined, because bodies live only so long as they are ensouled. When separated from soul, the body dies. What is decisive or "ruling" even in nonintelligent forms of life is therefore "soul." Whereas Simmias feared that the order or "harmony" soul gives to body would also disappear with death, Cebes was willing to concede, if only because of the recollection argument, that soul can survive, separated from one body, and be reincarnated in another. But, he objected, the capacity of soul to be reborn does not show that soul is imperishable. Like a weaver who makes and wears a series of cloaks, a soul may occupy several bodies but gradually be worn down and perish.

Although the Pythagoreans believed that the sensible world was mathematically ordered and constituted, the objections Simmias and Cebes raised to Socrates' arguments show us that, like the geometers to whom Socrates spoke in the *Theaetetus*, the Pythagoreans did not think the purely intelligible numbers or relations existed separate from their material embodiments. Although they did not think being was simply unitary, uniform, or homogeneous, they were not able to recognize, much less explain, the existence of essentially different kinds of being. To do so, they needed something like Socrates' hypothesis and argument concerning the ideas.

2. SOCRATES' AUTOBIOGRAPHICAL RESPONSE TO CEBES

Socrates appears to have found it more difficult to respond to Cebes' objection than to Simmias', even though we are reminded by Echecrates' interjection that Simmias' suggestion that soul is a harmony was embraced by later, more geometrically inclined Pythagoreans, whereas the belief in reincarnation was not. Phaedo reports that Socrates paused for a long time, searching within himself. Socrates indicates the character, if not the source of the difficulty when he observes that in order to respond to Cebes' objection they must consider the cause (*aitia*) of generation and decay as a whole.

Thinking back to the account Socrates gives of his own intellectual development (which we considered in chap. 3), we see that it is impossible to prove that anything is indestructible on the basis of the understanding of life and death with which he began, in terms of the conjunction and separation of soul and body. Such an understanding had been implicit, if not explicit, in the traditional stories passed down by Greek poets and made more systematic by later pre-Socratic philosophers. As Socrates pointed out in his first proof of the immortality of the soul, things could become different, but only from what they were not, that is, their opposites. But as Cebes' objection indicates, this fact or observation did not show that either the opposites or the oscillation between them would go on forever.

In seeking the cause or origin (*archē*) of the coming to be, existence, and perishing of the beings, Socrates discovered that it could not be found in the addition or subtraction of the component parts, whether these be considered material or numerical. Addition did not always result in increase in size, any more than division always resulted in a diminution of number. Although Socrates did not say so, the conundrum he describes—that two units can be transformed from odd to even by means of addition, but that one can also be made two and thus even by means of division—constitutes a critique of the Pythagorean contention that everything is constituted by number. Such an explanation does not show why changes in number, whether by addition or subtraction, result in changes of quality (like living and dead). Socrates initially thought that he had found a more satisfactory account of the reason (*aitia*) all things are as they are, come to be, and perish, in Anaxagoras' declaration that mind rules all. According to Socrates, that would have meant that everything is as it is, because it is best. But Socrates discovered that Anaxagoras explained everything in terms of its component parts, not purpose. Although Socrates came to see that human actions (*erga*) could not be adequately explained without taking account of what the people involved thought was good (hence sought and intended), he could not explain everything that happened in the world as a result of one overriding purpose, nor could he find anyone else who could.

Having discovered that the people who tried to explain things as products of their components, like Anaxagoras, mixed everything up together,[69] and that he would destroy his mind by seeking to contemplate the beings themselves, the way people who look at the eclipse of the sun directly rather than in its reflections in mirrors or water blind their eyes, Socrates took his famous "second sailing" by seeking the truth of the beings in the speeches (*logoi*) given about them rather than in the beings themselves.[70] Although these speeches are no less reflections of the beings than their sensible effects (*ergois*), Socrates warned, these speeches are not simply images.[71] Socrates concluded with such a warning not only because he knew that theorists such as Cratylus thought they could discover the truth of the beings directly from a study of their names; Socrates also knew that Pythagoreans like his interlocutors tended to understand the sensible things (*erga*) they encountered in the world as images of the truly intelligible beings, that is, numbers.

Socrates presents both the content of the hypothesis and his use of it to test other *logoi* in a way designed to show Simmias that Socrates' argument concerning the ideas constitutes the "safe" raft the Theban had stated he sought when he could not find the truth. Socrates has indicated, if he has not shown conclusively, that no one has been able to demonstrate why things come to be, are, and then perish. He has therefore given up that investigation as fruitless, if not positively harmful. He admits that those who follow his example will remain in an inescapable condition of uncertainty, but he holds out a potentially saving branch or hope, designed to appeal to these particular interlocutors.[72] Socrates posits, and urges them also to

69. As we have seen in the *Theaetetus* this is true even more emphatically of the "hidden" or more sophisticated version of the thesis put forward by Protagoras. If everything is the product of an interaction, nothing is or remains clearly (in) itself.

70. Cf. chapter 3 for a fuller statement.

71. This statement casts doubt on the parallel Dorter (*Phaedo*, 116) draws between the divided line Socrates describes in the *Republic*, on which objects represented by each segment are images of those represented by the higher segment(s), and Socrates' autobiographical account of the way he decided to seek knowledge.

72. Simmias and Cebes have already declared in the discussion of recollection that they think such ideas exist and that human beings know them. As Plato reminds his readers in the *Meno*, moreover, geometers (such as these Pythagoreans) regularly used the kind of hypothetical argument Socrates recommends here.

posit, the existence of "things" like beauty, good, and big that are in themselves. The safe argument he develops on the basis of that hypothesis is
that all the things with which we human beings are particularly concerned
(*pragmata*) come to be and are as they are only because they share in some
of these essential beings in themselves, not because of their composition,
their order, or constitution.[73]

Echecrates' interjection at the conclusion of Socrates' description of
the hypothetical argument by which he tests all others indicates how persuasive it was to Pythagoreans. Echecrates had been particularly sympa-
thetic to Simmias' objection to Socrates' proof of the immortality of the
soul, because he shared the understanding of the soul as harmony.

Socrates had not explicitly responded to Cebes' objection, however. To
show that the soul is not merely reborn but imperishable, Socrates had
to add another argument. None of his first three proofs would suffice. If
everything were always coming to be from its opposite, as Socrates argued
in his first proof of the immortality of the soul, the only thing indestructible would be the process of becoming itself. To identify this unending
process of becoming with (perhaps a "world" or cosmic) soul would be
to deny not only the significance of any difference between human and
nonhuman or good and bad, but also the immortality of individuals. In
his second proof, Socrates had suggested that there were some purely intelligible beings in themselves—like equality, beauty, and good—that the
soul cognizes before birth but then forgets and has to recollect. Precisely
because the soul forgets and has to learn, however, it does not appear to be
one of these eternally unchanging ideas. Although in the *Phaedo* Socrates
has not explicitly distinguished human souls from others by their ability
to recognize the intelligible forms of sensible things, the way he did in
the *Phaedrus*, he has maintained—both in his account of the philosophers'
escape from reincarnation and in his response to Simmias' thesis that the
soul is a kind of harmony—that there are different kinds of souls.

Socrates' response to Cebes is complex. First, he distinguishes the things
(*pragmata*) that share in certain unchangeable ideas (such as big or small)
from the ideas, even though the things are often named after the ideas

---

73. Like Robert Bolton, "Plato's Discovery of Metaphysics," in *Method in Ancient Philosophy*,
ed. Jyl Gentzler (Oxford: Clarendon Press, 1998), 91–95, I do not think Socrates is talking about
efficient causation or "physics" in our, or Aristotle's, sense. Socrates has explicitly given up investigations of nature. I hesitate, however, to use the term "metaphysics" with regard to Socrates or
Plato, since that term and study first arise in the context of Aristotle's investigations of nature and
being, which, we have just seen, proceed in a different way and in different terms.

in which they participate. Then he observes that a thing, like Simmias, can participate in two contradictory ideas, even if the ideas themselves are contradictory, and neither of the ideas can share in its opposite. There seem, as a result, to be two possible sources of confusion—between the name and the thing, which bears the name because it participates in the idea, and between the name and the idea (as opposed to the thing). When an unnamed "someone" asks whether Socrates has not contradicted his earlier contention that opposites are generated out of opposites, Socrates uses the distinction he has just drawn between the ideas and the things that participate in them to distinguish between the opposed ideas, which never partake in their contraries, and the things that can and do participate in opposite qualities. But Socrates then complicates the relation between things and ideas by pointing out that there are things such as fire that do not bear the name of the quality they embody, in this case heat, but that will not admit or participate in the opposite of that quality, in this case, cold, or a thing like snow that embodies it. The phenomenon of things sharing in ideas from which they do not take their names and which do not admit the opposite idea is extended to numbers—three, five, and ten—which, as odd or even, do not ever admit or participate in the opposite and yet, because they are more specifically defined, are not identical with either the odd or the even per se. In the case of ten, the number may even be composed of parts that have an opposite quality not possessed by the whole.

This complex set of distinctions allows Socrates to draw an analogy between fire and soul. Just as fire, which is not the same as heat, will not admit cold or the snow that participates in cold, but goes away if something with the opposite quality approaches, so soul, which is not the same as the *eidos* of life (*Phaedo* 106d) but carries or contains life, will not admit the opposite of life, death. Socrates can affirm, moreover, that soul, being deathless (*athanatos*), is also imperishable (*anōlethros*), without having to say whether the soul is sensible (like fire) or denying, even if it is purely intelligible and yet can mix with sensible body, that it can have more specific, particular definitions, like the numbers three and ten, as opposed to the more general ideas of odd and even in which these numbers participate.

Socrates' fourth attempt to show that the soul is immortal without saying what the soul itself is does not succeed, however, any better than his first three. Fire may not admit cold or snow, but fires are not observed to burn forever. Likewise, although the purely intelligible conception of the number three may survive the addition or subtraction of a unit to any particular number and the transformation of that number into something different, the particular number three does not survive, nor does its "oddness." Cebes indicates that he sees problems in Socrates' fourth "proof" by agreeing only that the soul "apparently" departs and goes to Hades when death approaches. As in his previous three proofs of its immortality, so in his fourth and final attempt to show that the soul is not only deathless but also indestructible, Socrates seems to assume that the soul is a discrete kind of being that not only participates in a variety of different, even opposed specific ideas or characteristics but also can move from place to place. Soul thus appears to be somewhat bodily, and if it is bodily, it would be subject to decay or dissolution in the long run.

Cebes chooses not to press the issue, however. On the contrary, he says that he has no further objections but that Simmias may. Cebes' observation that there would be no better occasion to continue the discussion leads us to suspect that his compliance has to do with the circumstances and his continuing desire not to distress Socrates. They are all aware that the hour of Socrates' death approaches. Simmias also has nothing specific to say at this point, but he admits that both the magnitude of the subject and the weakness of the human intellect leave him with a lingering distrust. It is Socrates, therefore, who not only praises Simmias again for his generally skeptical stance but who also insists that "our very first hypotheses—even if to all of you they're trustworthy—must nevertheless be looked into." And, he concludes, "if you sort them out, you will be following up the argument as much as it's possible for a human being to follow it" (107b).

E. Socrates' Emphasis on the Limitations of His Own Arguments

Several commentators have pointed out defects in Socrates' last argument, but few have emphasized the way in which Socrates himself steps back from it.[74] Yet we have seen that at the conclusion of his argument for the immortality of the soul, Socrates emphasizes the need for his companions to inquire further, especially about the soundness of the hypotheses he has suggested and to which they have agreed. Socrates has offered his argument about the ideas to his companions in the way one extends a branch from the shore to a man drowning in a rapid current (of uncertainty). His

74. David Keyt, "The Fallacies in *Phaedo* 102a–107b," *Phronesis* 8 (1963): 167–72; David O'Brien, "The Last Argument of Plato's *Phaedo*," *Classical Quarterly* 17 (1976): 198–231, and 18 (1968): 95–106; Dorter, *Phaedo*, 151–54.

hypothesis provides them with a place or position from which to begin; it does not guarantee them knowledge or safety.

Socrates knows very well that his argument is liable to powerful objections. As we know from the *Parmenides*, Socrates used his argument about the ideas to respond to Zeno's paradoxes and then heard his argument critiqued by Zeno's teacher. Responding to that critique on the basis of what he learned from Diotima about opinion and eros, Socrates attempted to show how purely intelligible beings could shape sensible existence by enticing other young men to live a life of philosophy. That is, we have seen, what he has continued to do up to and through the last day of his life.

In presenting his companions his hypothesis concerning the ideas on the basis of his own intellectual autobiography, Socrates has been urging them to begin where he began and thus to follow his example. Since they will truly be engaged in a Socratic philosophical investigation only if they question their own presuppositions, opinions, or hypotheses, he does not tell them what the results will be. On the contrary, he emphasizes, they cannot know what the results of their inquiries will be and probably will not ever reach a condition of complete certainty. Signaling his own recognition of the defective character of the arguments he has given to prove the immortality of the soul, Socrates concludes by stating that "*if* the soul is immortal, we must care for it, not merely for the time we call life, but for all time" (*Phaedo* 108a).

F. The Implications of Socrates' Admittedly Inconclusive Arguments

Was Plato indicating his own judgment that Socrates had failed as a philosopher, even though he was a good and noble human being, by showing that on the last day of his life Socrates returned to the problem with which he began his philosophical investigations, admitted his own continuing uncertainty, and explicitly focused on *stories* told about the afterlife? The answer to that question, I believe, must be no.

Plato has consistently depicted Socrates as a seeker of wisdom, not as the proponent of a specific doctrine or argument. On the last day of his life, Plato shows, Socrates was still trying, if possible, even more emphatically, to encourage his young associates to continue philosophizing the way he has. To do so, they would need to begin where Socrates did. He thus attempted to lead them to that point—and no further. To expose his young associates to the difficulties and criticism he had encountered when he began employing his argument about the ideas would be to discourage them at the outset.

Although Plato has Socrates present only the beginning of his investigations, he also shows Socrates reaffirming his attachment to the hypothesis and his use of it to test others on the very last day of his life. Socrates' Pythagorean interlocutors may not have been aware of Parmenides' criticisms of Socrates' argument—or those raised more recently by a visiting member of his school. But, as Plato has shown his readers in previous dialogues, partly in response to Parmenides' critique (and his purported instruction by Diotima), Socrates turned to an investigation of human opinions, especially about the beautiful, as the realm where the sensible and intelligible most evidently meet. By leading noble youths to examine and correct their own opinions, Socrates hoped to show how ideas could reform bodily creatures. As he and we were reminded by Alcibiades, Socrates could never be sure that he would succeed. On the last day of his life in the *Phaedo*, Plato not only shows that Socrates persisted in his attempt to persuade his young companions to adopt and persevere in a life of philosophy until the very last moment. Plato also reminds his readers that Socrates succeeded in persuading a number of young men to establish a variety of schools in which to educate others to continue the search for wisdom—with Plato, first and foremost.

The critique the visitor from Elea made of the arguments of the "friends of the forms" was somewhat different from that Parmenides made of the young Socrates. And the fact that Plato shows this critique leveled the day after Socrates was indicted, as well as Socrates' failure to respond to the Eleatic's implied accusations in either the *Sophist* or the *Statesman*, has led many commentators to conclude that Plato thought Socrates was unable to respond. In the *Apology* and *Crito* we saw, however, that Socrates responded to the Eleatic's accusation that he was a sophist whose questioning of others undermined the rule of law (as well as to the implied judgment that Socrates' fellow citizens were, therefore, justified in accusing and convicting him), even though Socrates did not explicitly address his philosophical accuser. So, on reflection, we see that Socrates' presentation of his hypothesis, concerning the ideas, as the "strongest" and "safest" *logos* he knows, in the *Phaedo* constitutes an answer to the objections the Eleatic raised to the position taken by "friends of the forms," even though Socrates does not say that is what he is doing.

In the *Sophist* (218c–d) the Eleatic Stranger objected that, by separating the realm of being completely from the realm of becoming, "friends of the forms" were not able to recognize that beings that were or became known were affected (and thus changed), as was the mind that came to know them. Like Parmenides, the Eleatic suggested, a strict separation between the sensible and the intelligible makes human knowledge impossible. The response we see Socrates making in the *Phaedo* begins with his contention that the beings-in-themselves (or the ideas) do not change and are not affected in themselves. The whole (*holos*) or the "all" (*pan*), as the Eleatic dubbed it (*Sophist* 244b), is composed of both sensible and intelligible kinds of beings. Like Simmias, Socrates observes, sensible beings can and do usually participate (*metechein*) in many different, even contrary, kinds of intelligible beings, but pace the Eleatic Stranger, the purely intelligible beings or ideas do not mix or share in each other. If they did, they would not be intelligible in themselves (as, indeed, nothing is, according to the Eleatic).

Socrates admits that he cannot give an account of how or why everything we sense or understand constitutes a beneficently ordered whole, as opposed to a mere sum of the constituent parts. (We should recall the distinction between the whole and the all, of which Socrates reminded Theaetetus in their discussion of *logos*.) But, Socrates reminds us, no one else has been able to present such an account either. Insofar as both sensible and more particular kinds of intelligible being (for example, specific numbers such as three, five, and ten) are like and thus participate in broader, more fundamental, and therefore higher kinds of being or ideas, Socrates suggested in his famous image of the divided line in the *Republic*, sensible things and the hypotheses on which the various arts and sciences such as geometry are based can be understood to be imitations. In his autobiography in the *Phaedo*, Socrates has pointed out that speeches (*logoi*) are no less images than deeds (*erga*), but he also emphasized that speeches are not simply imitations or images of being. In opposition to the Eleatic Stranger (as well as to his "father" Parmenides, who famously declared that thinking [*noein*] and being [*einai*] are the same), Socrates contends that being is not organized the same way as *logos* or *nous*. *Logos* is composite, as the Eleatic emphasized, whereas, Socrates argues, the purely intelligible beings are not, if they are eternally unchanging. Socrates has not merely admitted but has stressed that our minds and souls are affected, purified, made orderly, and so moved if and when we perceive the truly intelligible beings. But, he has insisted, the purely intelligible beings are not, do not exist and are not defined merely in relation to others, as "other." They exist in themselves, separate and thus different from everything else. Both intelligible and sensible kinds of being can be "like" and "unlike" others in specific respects, but, according to Socrates, kinds of being are never the same as themselves (which implies some kind of internal division) any more than they are different in themselves. Human beings sort beings, both intelligible and sensible, into kinds, according to how they are like and unlike or same and different, but the kinds, the ideas properly speaking, are only in themselves. This is true, even according to the "more beautiful method" Socrates sketches in the *Philebus* (which many commentators have taken to be a criticism of the "theory of the ideas" Plato supposedly put forward in his "middle" dialogues). According to that method, it is necessary to identify all the different variations included in any particular kind or form in order to define or know it. As in the *Parmenides*, so in the *Philebus*, Socrates continues to insist that the limited (that which participates in a form or idea) and the unlimited (the potentially sensible, but in itself undefined) must be mixed together in any kind of generated kind of being, but that the ideas do not mix. As in his account of his disappointment in Anaxagoras in the *Phaedo*, so in the *Philebus*, Socrates also argued that each kind of generated mixture must also have a cause. That cause would presumably be the good, but Socrates never claims to know what the good in itself is.

G. The Moral of Socrates' *Mythologia*

Having done everything in his power to convince his companions, in deed as well as in speech, that a philosopher who is good, moderate, and just has no reason to fear death, Phaedo reports, Socrates concluded his reflections on the stories told about what may happen to us after we die by attempting to deprive evil, unjust human beings of the comfort they might take in the thought Socrates had suggested at his defense, that death may merely signify the end of all our striving and suffering. The place of Socrates' final account of what is said about the true idea of the earth (*idean tēs gēs*; 108d) in the *Phaedo* thus appears to be parallel to the place of the myth of Er in the *Republic*. Just as at the end of the *Republic* Socrates requested permission from his interlocutors to reintroduce considerations of the rewards and punishments after he had attempted to prove that the just life is choiceworthy, so, having attempted to show that there is no reason for just and prudent philosophers to fear death, at the end of the *Phaedo* he asked permission to talk about the fates said to await the unjust in the bowels of the earth as well as the beautiful sights and experiences awaiting those with well-ordered souls who ascend to the surface.

There are, however, significant differences between the picture of human life after death that Socrates gives in the myth of Er at the end of the

Republic and that he presents at the end of the *Phaedo*. These differences not merely point out the way in which Socrates shapes his speech to the occasion, his particular interlocutors, and their specific concerns. They also highlight significant divergences between Socrates' view of the place human beings have in the cosmos and those of Plato's other philosophical spokesmen, Timaeus and the Eleatic Stranger.

The first difference concerns the path or paths souls take to the place of judgment. In the *Republic*, Er says that his soul went in the company of others. Er does not say that theirs was the only path, but he does not indicate the existence of another. In the *Phaedo* Socrates emphasizes differences among the paths on which their individual *daimones* take various kinds of soul. The well ordered know where they are going and proceed directly to their destination; the unjust and those who have been attached to bodily pleasures linger and must be taken by more difficult, tortuous routes. The souls Er describes all move in groups in preset directions, whether up to see beautiful sights or below to be punished; in the *Phaedo* Socrates says that the worst souls will be shunned by all others. Whereas Er is purportedly sent back to earth to warn all living people about their future fate and so emphasizes the common aspects, Socrates emphasizes the different fates of various kinds of souls. Er thus describes the upper and lower regions of the afterlife very generally and rather briefly. Socrates describes in much greater detail life on the surface of the earth and the effects of the rivers of water, fire, and mud that circulate within the earth on the criminal souls thrust into them.

The cosmological geography of the two explicitly mythical descriptions of the afterlife differs even more significantly. According to Er, souls proceed after judgment to and from two openings upward to the heavens, where they are said to view beautiful sights, or they enter and, in most cases, exit from two openings to a lower world, where they are punished for their crimes. In Er's afterworld, the souls reassemble after they have traversed their respective paths and tell each other about their experiences before they proceed to a plain where they see a column of light, which holds the revolutions of the heavens together. Having not only observed but also having heard the harmony of the heavens, each soul is then asked to choose its next life. A required drink from the river Lethe finally makes them forget all they have experienced before they are reborn.

Socrates' vision of the afterlife is almost entirely terrestrial. He does not claim to know whether the picture of the earth he gives is true, but he says that he is persuaded that "if it is round and in the middle of the heaven, it doesn't need either the air or any other such compulsion not to fall. The self-similarity of the heaven in every direction and the equilibrium of the earth are sufficient to hold it. For a thing that is in equilibrium and placed in the middle of something self-similar will be in no condition to incline more or less to either side" (*Phaedo* 109a). As in the picture of the revolution of the spheres in the myth of Er, so in Socrates' description of the place of earth there is no adjustment for the way the circuits of the heavenly bodies actually appear to humans who observe them, as there is in the *Timaeus*. Socrates explains why when he goes on to suggest that human beings live in hollows on the surface of the earth where a vapor (air) gathers that prevents them from seeing the heavens clearly or precisely, the way water prevents those underneath from seeing things on or above its surface clearly and distinctly. Only souls that rise to live on the true surface of the earth, where air has the same status as water does on what we take to be the surface, can see "the sun and moon and stars as they really are" (111c). Since pious and well-ordered souls can see the heavens as they are only after they die, they cannot become well ordered while they are embodied, as Timaeus suggests, by contemplating the orderly movement of the heavens. In the *Phaedo* Socrates has proposed that human beings seek knowledge of the purely intelligible beings-in-themselves or ideas in a very different way, by examining the *logoi*. Only the souls of philosophers who have devoted their lives to seeking such knowledge will live on forever, without bodies, on the surface of the earth where they are able not only to observe the heavens without distorted vision but also to communicate directly with gods. As in the *Phaedrus* so in the concluding myth of the *Phaedo*, only the souls of philosophers escape the ongoing cycle of reincarnation. According to the myth of the *Phaedo*, however, these purified souls do not return to their homes in the stars, as Timaeus had suggested. They remain on the surface of the earth, where they are able not only to perceive the beauty but also to converse with other human beings and gods.

Socrates' description of the apparently static equilibrium of the earth in the midst of the self-same heaven also stands in marked contrast to the mythical description of the cosmos the Eleatic Stranger gave in the *Statesman*. There the cosmos was said to undergo the least possible change that must accompany bodily existence by periodically reversing the direction of its movement. But by changing the order of life and death on earth, the least possible change in the movement of the cosmos produced great havoc and destruction among animals and humans. According to Socrates, the churning motion of the rivers, which moves things to and fro, is within the earth; such motion does not characterize the cosmos or the heavens, whose beauty suggests order, even if human souls cannot correctly perceive that order so long as they are embodied.

The last and most striking difference between the account of the afterlife Socrates attributes to Er in the *Republic* and that which he gives in his own name, without assurance of knowledge, in the *Phaedo* appears to be the absence of individual choice in the determination of a soul's next reincarnation in the latter. According to Er, after it has been judged, punished, and reassembled with all the other souls, each has an opportunity to choose its form and way of life during its next reincarnation. Socrates thus concludes that "each of us must, to the neglect of other studies, see to it that he is a seeker and student of that study by which he might be able to learn and find out who will give him the capacity and the knowledge to distinguish the good and the bad life, and so everywhere and always to choose the better from among those that are possible" (618b–c).

In the mythical account of the earth he gives in the *Phaedo*, Socrates does not describe a choice on the part of souls. Insofar as souls make a choice concerning their way of life, they make it in this life. In the afterlife souls are rewarded, punished, and reincarnated (or not) as a result of the way they chose to live when embodied. (Indeed, in his third proof of the immortality of the soul, Socrates had suggested that the souls of recently departed human beings who had been driven by bodily desires would hover close to the earth and often enter the bodies of animals with similar traits—without passing through judgment and punishment before reincarnation.) Since each of the souls Er describes chooses its fate on the basis of its dominant passion or experiences in its previous life—and not as a result of the punishment or reward it received in the afterlife or the view it had of the harmonic order and beauty of the cosmos—the effective choice in both myths is made or determined by the way a soul chose to live when embodied. In both myths, human beings are shown to be responsible for their own fate—here and now. The most important difference in the myths appears to be a reflection of the character of Socrates' interlocutors. In the *Republic* Socrates was talking to young men who were tempted to seek political power but whom he was trying to persuade to engage in philosophy. In that dialogue he thus emphasized the importance of learning to make the right choice—here and now. In the *Phaedo* he is talking to young men who have already chosen philosophy. He does not emphasize the necessity of learning how to make the best choice of a way of life, therefore, so much as the results of that choice in the hereafter.

From the very beginning of the conversation in which Socrates suggested that it would be particularly appropriate for them to examine speeches and tales about the afterlife he has been striving to show his associates that philosophers have nothing to fear in death—for themselves, for friends like Socrates, or from the loss of such friends. Philosophers can hope not merely that they will acquire the knowledge they have been seeking when their souls are separated from their bodies. They can also hope to associate with better, more virtuous companions. Because Socrates shares such hopes, his associates should not grieve for him. Nor should they worry about their inability to persist in a philosophical life without him. He has shown them how they can persist, both in speech and in deed, through his own example. Now at the end of the dialogue, he has even promised them a reward. He does not insist that everything is just as he has said. These stories and arguments constitute "incantations" he urges them to sing to themselves repeatedly to help them persevere in philosophy.

H. Socrates' Last Dramatic Act

Socrates knew that he would persuade his associates (as well as Plato's later readers) that his kind of philosophy enables human beings to face their inevitable death calmly and nobly more by means of his own deeds than merely by giving speeches. He indicates his own awareness of the dramatic character of his own last act by declaring as he ends his speech that "as a man in a tragedy might declaim, 'Destiny calls'" (*Phaedo* 115a).

Everything Socrates does from this point on is intended to demonstrate his lack of fear and his concern for others. He proposes first to take a bath so that the women will not have to struggle to clean a heavy corpse after he is dead. Crito asks if he has any last requests, and Socrates says simply that he wishes his companions to continue to take care of themselves the way he has been urging them (as he urged Alcibiades in their very first conversation). The perpetuation of the search for wisdom, which has given shape to Socrates' life, depends on his associates continuing to philosophize in his fashion. By doing so, Socrates thus states, they will do the most they can for him as well as for his children (by providing them with virtuous associates) and themselves, whether or not they explicitly agreed to do so now. Their words now will not be as important as their later speeches and deeds.

The significance of Socrates' life and death depends on his philosophical legacy. He does not care how he will be buried, he tells Crito with a laugh. Socrates cannot persuade his old friend, as he has attempted to persuade both his own associates and Plato's readers, that he will not be contained in the body they will have to dispose of on the morrow. Recognizing that what they say now will not determine their action in the distant future, he asks them to swear now that after he dies, Socrates will not remain in his body, so that Crito (who cannot be so convinced) will bear his death more lightly and will not do or say anything false or harmful, to himself or others, in the process of burying him. Socrates again demonstrates his lack of concern about his own fate and his care about the good of those who survive him.

Because Crito continues to understand Socrates' legacy primarily in bodily terms, carried through his family or progeny, Socrates takes his old friend with him when he goes away to bathe and to have his final conversation with his sons and wife. Neither Phaedo nor Plato tells us what Socrates said. Although he spends some time with his immediate family, Socrates returns to spend his final moments with his assembled associates. They are or represent his true heirs.

Socrates does not express anger at the unjust reasons or men that have caused him to be condemned to death any more than he allows himself or his fellows to express grief. When the servant of the eleven comes to see whether Socrates is ready to take the potion, he states his conviction that Socrates will not rage at him the way others have, because Socrates understands that the executioner is only the instrument. Declaring that Socrates is the noblest, gentlest, and best man he has ever encountered in the prison, the executioner bursts into tears. Although Socrates praises the executioner as a man of the city (*asteios*), he will not allow his associates similar expressions of grief. Crito wants Socrates to delay imbibing the potion until the very last moment, but Socrates says that such a delay would make him appear unreasonable and ridiculous. He would seem to be admitting in practice what he has denied in argument—namely, that death is something terrible and to be avoided at all costs. After Socrates readily drinks the potion, and his associates uncontrollably burst into tears, he sternly tells them to control themselves. Implying that they are demonstrating a lack of courage, he says that he sent the women away precisely in order to avoid such wailing. Socrates' associates can express their respect for him only by acting as if they believe what he has been telling them.

Instead of anger or grief, Socrates expresses a kind of piety at the end of his existence. Having asked if he could pour a libation of the "medicine" to the gods, as if it were wine, and being told that the authorities prepared only enough to serve its function, Socrates simply prays to the gods that his trip "from here to there will be fortunate" (*Phaedo* 117c). He walks around until his legs began to feel heavy and his body numb. Then he lies down.[75] His last words, after he uncovers his face, are "Crito, we owe a cock to Asclepius. So pay the debt and don't be careless" (118a).

Because Asclepius was the god of medicine, Nietzsche takes these parting words to constitute an admission on Socrates' part that his life has been a long illness from which he is finally being healed.[76] As David Gallop observes, however, there is little support in the dialogue for such a conclusion.[77] Socrates has insisted that he has nothing to fear in death. He has not sought death—indeed, he has argued that the gods forbid human beings from seeking to end their lives prematurely—even though he has sought the knowledge he has suggested human beings would actually be able to

75. There has been some controversy about whether Socrates could have died as peacefully as Plato claims. Having consulted later medical sources, ancient and modern, some scholars argue that he did not: Christopher Gill, "The Death of Socrates," *Classical Quarterly*, n.s., 23, no. 1 (May 1973): 25–28; Bonita M. Graves, G. M. Graves, A. K. Tsakopoulos, and J. P. Anton, "Hemlock Poisoning: Twentieth-Century Scientific Light Shed on the Death of Socrates," in *The Philosophy of Socrates*, ed. K. J. Boudouris, 156–68 (Athens: Center for Greek Philosophy, 1991); and William Ober, "Did Socrates Die of Hemlock Poisoning?" *New York State Journal of Medicine* 77 (1977): 254–58. Hemlock poisoning would have resulted in his suffering violent seizures. Having reviewed the sources, Enid Block, "Hemlock Poisoning and the Death of Socrates," in *The Trial and Execution of Socrates: Sources and Controversies*, ed. Thomas C. Brickhouse and Nicholas D. Smith, 255–78 (New York: Oxford University Press, 2002), persuasively argues that there is more than one kind of hemlock and that Socrates could have died peacefully as described. Gill's conclusion that Plato created a literary fiction would not be incompatible with the argument of this book—that Plato's dialogues are works of art and not historical reports. Plato states he was not present at Socrates' death and so reminds us that the *Phaedo* in particular is not an eyewitness report. It would be better, however, to believe that his teacher did not die painfully in fact.

76 Nietzsche, "Problem of Socrates," 17. Although this has become the most common modern interpretation, Glenn W. Most, "A Cock for Asclepius," *Classical Quarterly* 43 (1993): 96–111, points out that among ancient authors, this interpretation is attested only once, in a scholium to this passage by the Neoplatonist Damascius. It became popular again in the Italian Renaissance and in the Romantic period of the nineteenth century.

77 Gallop, *Phaedo*, 225. Agreeing with Gallop, Most ("Cock") follows Pamela M. Clark, "A Cock to Asclepius," *Classical Review*, n.s., 2, no. 3–4 (1952): 146, and Burger (*Platonic Labyrinth*, 216) in arguing that since the cock is to be from Crito, who is still living, as well as from Socrates, it cannot be offered in gratitude for Socrates' death. It must rather and more conventionally be a sacrifice to request that Asclepius bring someone back to health. From the dialogue, the person whom we know is ill is Plato, so it must be a prayer for his recovery. Unfortunately, Socrates does not state such a wish. J. Peter Euben, *Platonic Noise* (Princeton: Princeton University Press, 2003), argues that Socrates' parting words can be taken in four different senses: (1) that he is giving thanks for his release from the sickness of life; (2) that he is making a joke to deflate the pretentiousness of the first reading; (3) that by saying "we" owe the debt to the god (which Nietzsche changed to "I"), Socrates is emphasizing the collective nature of sacrifice; and (4) that by recognizing his joint obligation with Crito, Socrates also is recognizing in the end that he is "a man with a body, attached to family, friends, and the city he has always refused to leave" (159).

acquire, if they are able to acquire it at all, only if and when their souls are separated from their bodies. He has not argued unambiguously or without "myth" that individual souls exist apart from bodies. He accepts his death at the hands of the city (although he never admits that it is just), and ultimately, as a natural necessity, it is unreasonable for anyone to try to escape or delay in old age. He has repeatedly maintained, as he had in earlier dialogues, that the only way of life that is truly worth living—in this life or the next—is the life of philosophy. He thus affirms the goodness of his own existence and his desire that his associates persevere in the search for wisdom to which he has dedicated himself. He recognizes that the ability of any individual to do so is not entirely under his own control; it depends on the circumstances of one's birth and life, and hence on "chance" or "the gods." Socrates thus concludes his life by expressing his gratitude to the gods for having allowed him to live as he has—and by showing that neither his piety nor his philosophy is associated primarily with ritual, as it had been for and among the Pythagoreans. In telling Crito that they owe Asclepius a cock, Socrates does not specify the color. Just as he has stated his indifference to the way in which he is buried, including the fabric of the shroud, which had been specified for the Pythagoreans, so he fails to warn his friend away from sacrificing a "white" cock, which was regarded as a sacrilege and thus forbidden by the same sect. For Socrates, philosophy constitutes a way of life, but not an external "discipline" of the kind Michel Foucault has described among later groups or that the Pythagoreans imposed on their initiates. Like Socrates' own dying acts, his philosophical way of life was not merely dictated by, but was an externally observable expression of, his speeches and arguments.

CONCLUSION

Why Plato Made Socrates His Hero

R eading the Platonic dialogues in the order of their dramatic dates, we see that Plato concluded his story with the presentation of Socrates, in the words of Phaedo, as "the best, most prudent, and most just" (*Phaedo* 117c) man he ever met. Present in all but two of the dialogues, and the leading philosophical spokesman in most, Socrates is obviously the most prominent character in Plato's prose dramas. At the conclusion of the series in the *Phaedo* we have seen that Plato presents Socrates as an exemplary figure not only in speech but also in deed. The question nevertheless remains: exemplary in what respect? Was Socrates as good a philosopher or as good a citizen as he was a good human being? Phaedo says that Socrates was the most prudent or intelligent man (*andros . . . phronimōtatou*) he ever met, but intelligent (*phronimos*) is not necessarily the same as wise (*sophos*). As we have seen in his use of other philosophical spokesmen, Plato dramatizes the limitations, if not defects, of Socrates' speeches and deeds. But if Plato understood the limitations of Socrates both as a philosopher and statesman, why did he make Socrates the star, so to speak, of his dialogues?

I. Socrates' Second, Political Legacy: *Menexenus*

Socrates distinguished himself most visibly from other ancient Greek philosophers by remaining always in his native city rather than traveling to other cities in search of students or knowledge. Socrates was an exceptionally good citizen of Athens, Plato shows in the last view he gives of the philosopher, not merely during his lifetime but even after his death.

Both in the *Apology* and the *Republic* Plato had Socrates state that he could not have gone into the public assembly to protest the injustice of current policies without endangering his life. Socrates had to content himself with interrogating and so, he hoped, correcting individuals privately. If he had an effect on public opinion, that effect would be produced only gradually and indirectly.

In the *Menexenus* Plato suggests that there was another way Socrates (and later philosophers who followed his example) could have a beneficial effect on the opinions of their fellow citizens. Rather than directly challenge the adequacy of their political convictions—in public assemblies or private conversations—a philosopher might shape public opinion by offering his fellow citizens a just account of their own history. Like Socrates' attempts to practice "the true art of politics" by refuting and so correcting individuals in private, Plato indicates in the *Menexenus*, such a remolding of a city or its citizens' self-understanding could be achieved only indirectly and with the passage of time. Plato emphasizes both the indirectness and the temporal distance involved in the *Menexenus* not only by having Socrates present his version of Athenian history in a speech he gives to his young associate to use in the annual contest, but also by showing Socrates, incredibly, delivering this speech twelve or more years after his death.

Scholars have been puzzled by the *Menexenus*, first, because Plato has Socrates refer (245e–46a) to battles and a peace that occurred more than a decade after his death in 399.[1] This anachronism, along with the other peculiar features of the dialogue, led the famous nineteenth-century German philologist Eduard Zeller to declare that the dialogue was spurious, even though Aristotle refers twice to the dialogue in his *Rhetoric* (at 1367b and 1415b) and so testifies to its authenticity.[2] If we needed further proof that Plato was not merely writing down conversations he had heard or heard about, the *Menexenus* constitutes decisive evidence.[3]

A second feature of the *Menexenus* that has puzzled scholars is the introduction of a funeral oration, presumably a sober speech given on a somber occasion, with a lighthearted exchange between Socrates and his

1. See Dodds, *Gorgias*, 24; Louis Meridier, *"Ménexène,"* in *Platon "Oeuvres complètes"* (Paris: Belles Lettres, 1920), 5:82; Friedländer, *Plato*, 2:216; Charles Kahn, "Plato's Funeral Oration: The Motive of the *Menexenus*," *Classical Philology* 58 (October 1963): 220; and Susan Collins and Devin Stauffer, introduction to *Empire and the Ends of Politics* (Newburyport, MA: Focus Publishing, 1999), 2n.

2. Eduard Zeller, *Platonische Studien* (Tübingen: C. F. Osiander, 1839), 146.

3. Strauss, *Argument and Action*, 2.

young associate. Can we take the dialogue or the long speech it contains seriously?[4]

Both the anachronism and the lighthearted character of the exchange become more intelligible if we read the *Menexenus* as following the *Phaedo* on the basis of the indications of its dramatic date. Menexenus was one of the close associates of Socrates, present at his death, whom Socrates urged to follow his example by continuing to philosophize. This was the only way, Socrates insisted, that he wanted to be remembered and honored after he died. Meeting Menexenus on his way back from the council chamber, Socrates begins the dialogue by asking the young man whether he believes that he has "come to the end of education and philosophy" and thinks that he is adequately prepared to rule his elders (234a–b). Socrates sees that instead of following his own example and dedicating his entire life to philosophy, Menexenus has political ambitions. Like Socrates' most notorious earlier companions, Pericles' nephew Alcibiades and Plato's cousin Critias, Menexenus appears to have associated with Socrates in order to learn how to speak and argue effectively so that he could use the skill later to acquire political power.[5] Although Menexenus assures Socrates that he will not seek to rule unless Socrates advises him to do so, we readers are aware that, in fact, Socrates is no longer there to restrain Menexenus and his ambitions. Nor does Socrates expect to be able to do so. Menexenus represents an example of an associate who no longer feels the attraction of philosophy when Socrates himself is not present, in contrast to Plato, who became disillusioned with politics when he saw how the Athenians treated Socrates and saw that his fellow citizens no longer obeyed their own laws and customs (*Seventh Letter* 324c–26b). Not believing that he can prevent Menexenus from giving up philosophy and entering politics, Socrates presents his young associate with an interpretation of Athenian history that would lead him to advocate adherence to the old laws and not to undertake revolutionary projects the way Alcibiades and Critias had.

The *Menexenus* thus represents the second part of Socrates' legacy. In the *Phaedo* Socrates presented himself as a model for those who would

---

4. Robert Clavaud, *Le "Ménexène" de Platon et la rhétorique de son temps* (Paris: Belles Lettres, 1980), 15–77, presents a survey of the controversy. Stephen G. Salkever, "Socrates' Aspasian Oration: The Play of Philosophy and Politics in Plato's *Menexenus*," *American Political Science Review* 87, no. 1 (March 1993): 141n., explains that ancient commentators like Cicero thought the dialogue contained a serious funeral oration but that commentators since the eighteenth century have emphasized the comic aspects.

5. Cf. Xenophon *Memorabilia* 1.12–16.

follow him in a life of philosophy. In the *Menexenus*, we then see, Socrates tries to disseminate an understanding of Athenian history that, if accepted and absorbed by his fellow citizens, would make them more just and perhaps happier, even if they did not become philosophers. Whereas the *Phaedo* depicts Socrates' "private" gift and encouragement to philosophically inclined individuals, the *Menexenus* contains his public, political teaching, particularly with regard to his own city. Athens, as depicted in the *Menexenus*, is a better city than the democracy Socrates describes in the *Republic*, in which the philosopher can find and study the products of all kinds of regimes.

A third aspect of the *Menexenus* that commentators have found puzzling can also be explained if the dialogue is read as a sequel to the *Phaedo*. In earlier dialogues such as the *Gorgias*, Socrates had criticized rhetoricians; in the *Menexenus*, however, Socrates presents himself as an accomplished rhetorician. He gives his young associate a speech that the young man can presumably repeat and use to win the annual contest to deliver the funeral oration honoring the soldiers who died that year defending Athens. Socrates prefaces the long speech he delivers in the *Menexenus*, however, with a critique of rhetoricians who praise the dead as well as their survivors and ancestors for more virtues than they actually possessed, and who thus mislead their listeners into believing that they were better than they really were. As in the *Gorgias*, so in the *Menexenus*, Socrates describes rhetoric, unflatteringly, as a form of flattery. He distances himself from the speech (1) by attributing it to his "teacher," Aspasia, (2) by having her attribute sections of the speech to others, particularly the dead soldiers, and (3) by stating his willingness to repeat the speech to Menexenus only because they are speaking in private and the youth promises not to let anyone else know of its authorship. (The effective result of this promise is that Menexenus can claim the speech as his own, if he should choose to repeat it.) In the *Menexenus* Socrates thus maintains the same critical stance he took toward rhetoric in earlier dialogues like the *Apology*, *Republic*, and *Gorgias*, where he emphasized that he never addressed the assembly but only conversed with other individuals in private.

By attributing the authorship not only of his own speech but also of Pericles' famous funeral oration to Aspasia, Socrates not merely casts aspersion on the originality, rhetorical skill, and manliness of the famous Athenian leader. By suggesting that his own speech has the same questionable origin and truth value, Socrates also contrasts his account of fifth-century

Athenian history with that of his famous predecessor.[6] Pericles had not only made the Athenian regime more radically democratic than it had previously been by paying people to serve on juries. He had also promoted its imperial policy, with results Socrates had decried in the *Gorgias* and that were known to his contemporaries in a way that they could not have been known to Pericles himself.

As related by Thucydides, Pericles' speech is designed to encourage his fellow Athenians to persist in the war against Sparta and its allies in order to expand their empire even farther and so attain even greater glory and grandeur. As related by Plato, Socrates' speech is designed to inculcate beliefs he had argued in the *Republic* were a necessary foundation for a just city. In the same way that Socrates argued in the *Republic* that a just city will engage in wars only to defend itself and its allies, so in the speech he attributes to Aspasia Socrates presents Athens as having waged war only to defend her own freedom and that of the other Greeks. As in the *Republic* (469b–71b), so in the *Menexenus*, Socrates suggests that Greeks ought to regard each other as kin and treat each other better than they treat the barbarians. Even more fundamental and problematic, in the *Republic* Socrates explained that the citizens of a just city would need to be persuaded of a noble lie. Convincing them that they were all born from the ground, where they had been nurtured and educated by the god before their birth, would reduce faction, because they would regard each other as brothers and sisters who had been born from the same mother earth. They would also avoid the problems involved in justifying the taking and holding of any particular piece of land by force by any particular people to the exclusion of others. So in the speech Socrates attributes to Aspasia in the *Menexenus*, he repeats the old stories about the autochthonous birth of the Athenians and the blessings the gods had bestowed on them, including their old regime, customs, and laws.

The character and future actions of the regime depend very much on the opinions the people have about the excellence of their polity. By contrasting the speeches of Pericles and Socrates, Plato reminds his readers

---

6. On the contrast between Socrates and Pericles (or "Plato" and "Thucydides"), see Salkever, "Oration," 133–40; R. E. Allen, "Plato's *Menexenus*, Translation and Commentary," in *The Dialogues of Plato* (New Haven: Yale University Press, 1985), 1:319–43; Saxonhouse, *Fear*, 117ff.; Kahn, "Funeral Oration," 220–34; Bruce Rosenstock, "Socrates as Revenant: A Reading of the *Menexenus*," *Phoenix* 43 (1994): 331–47; S. Sara Monoson, "Remembering Pericles: The Political and Theoretical Import of Plato's *Menexenus*," *Political Theory* 26, no. 4 (August 1998): 489–513; Susan Collins and Devin Stauffer, "The Challenge of Plato's *Menexenus*," *Review of Politics* 61 (Winter 1999): 85–115.

that these opinions are variable and hence subject to change. By having Socrates attribute both Pericles' funeral oration and his own to Aspasia, Plato indicates that neither of the understandings of Athens put forward may be entirely true or factually accurate. Pericles understood the greatness of Athens to consist in the free institutions that made the Athenians clever and daring enough to seize an empire. But is the speech Thucydides attributed to Pericles any truer or more accurate than the speech Plato attributes to Socrates and that Socrates attributes to Aspasia? Thucydides did not claim to have recorded the speeches word for word; he wrote that he presented speakers saying what he thought they should have said under such circumstances (Thucydides 1.22). By quoting from parts of Pericles' funeral oration, Plato shows the way in which the words of past orators acquire new meaning when incorporated into the speeches of others. From the contrast drawn between Pericles' and Socrates' speeches, readers learn that the meaning of events depends on the intentions of the actors. The "facts" of the history are basically the same. But, according to Pericles, the Athenians waged war because they loved glory. According to Socrates, the Athenians were seeking to defend themselves and the other Greeks. Readers are also reminded that our understanding of the intentions, motives, or reasons polities act as they do, especially in war, depends on what their leaders say about them. Unfortunately, these leaders can and do lie. The value of their public speeches thus appears to consist primarily in their effects. Did Pericles' adulation of empire and honor lead his nephew Alcibiades to seek both without restraint? Socrates had not been able to restrain Alcibiades by speaking to him in private; according to his own testimony in the *Symposium*, Alcibiades covered his ears and ran away so that he could listen to the acclaim of the demos instead. What if Socrates been able to shape the opinions of the demos? Would later politically ambitious young Athenians have been more restrained?

Plato reminds his readers that Socrates did not actually give such a speech, that is, that the *Menexenus* is a fiction, by prefacing the recitation with an exchange in which Socrates assures Menexenus that he remembers what Aspasia said. He is reluctant to repeat the speech, however, because she (also dead by the dramatic date of the dialogue) might be angry. Socrates fears, moreover, that the youth will laugh at him if he seems to be playing. Socrates nevertheless agrees to gratify his young associate, partly because no one else is there to hear or report what he says. No one will ever be able to prove that he did. The anachronistic dramatic date of the dialogue provides fairly good evidence that he did not. What Plato does in the *Menexenus*

is present a description of Athenian history and politics on the basis of Socratic principles, in contrast to the account his fellow citizens had acquired
from Thucydides. According to Thucydides, Pericles emphasized Athenian
freedom and the acquisition of empire. According to Plato, Socrates would
have stressed the importance of obeying the law, recognizing the role of the
gods, and acting justly.

The speech Socrates attributes to Aspasia has the same form as other
funeral orations that survive from the period. It begins with a statement
of the requirement by Athenian law (*nomos*) that such speeches be given; it
centers on praise of the dead heroes and Athens; and it ends with a conso-
latory exhortation to the living.[7] The content and proportion of the speech
dedicated to each of these parts differ markedly, however. Pericles presents
the legal obligation to speak at the funeral as something far subordinate to
the deeds of those who had died serving their city; Socrates begins by emphasizing the importance of giving such a speech. According to Socrates,
such a speech not only should lead its auditors to remember and honor
those who have acted well but also should counsel younger survivors to
imitate the virtues of those who have died and console their parents.

Socrates begins the counsel to be conveyed to the young by observing
that the dead deserve praise insofar as they were good. Athenian soldiers
are considered good for three reasons: (1) their birth, (2) their nurture and
education, and (3) their deeds. In contrast to Pericles, Socrates emphasizes
the inheritance the young soldiers received from their ancestors, their
birth and upbringing, more than their deeds. The Athenian soldiers' birth
is good because their ancestors did not migrate from another land and
seize the ground they now possess with force. As in the city in speech in
the *Republic*, Athenians have reason to treat each other as brothers and
sisters, born from the same mother earth. Their origins and relations with
one another have been peaceful and just.

Like Critias in his description of the autochthonous origins of ancient
Athens, and again in contrast to Pericles, Socrates also emphasizes the
love of Athens that led the gods to contend for possession. Thucydides
explained both the relative peace of Athens and the growth of her population by the fact that the soil of Attica was barren and so did not invite
invasion, but attracted refugees from invasions elsewhere. Socrates uses

7. Here I am relying on Nicole Loraux, *The Invention of Athens: The Funeral Oration in the Classical City*, trans. Alan Sheridan (Cambridge: Harvard University Press, 1986); Salkever, "Oration,"
134.

the fertility of the ground, which he claims first produced not only human beings but also the food crops necessary to support them, as evidence of the gods' favor. These gods (and not the human beings themselves, much less Pericles) ruled and educated the early Athenians, so that they were able to defend the country and establish a regime that would produce later generations of good and noble citizens.

Pericles praises the novel regime of Athens, which, by treating all its citizens as free and equal, encouraged its soldiers to become clever and daring beyond all others and so enabled them to acquire an empire. Socrates describes the Athenian regime as an aristocracy, which has been in place almost since the founding. Recognizing that others call Athens a democracy, Socrates observes not only that Athens still has kings (even if the office had been reduced to ritual functions) but also, and more importantly, that "although the multitude has control over most of the city's affairs, they give the ruling offices and authority to those who are deemed to be best" (*Menexenus* 238c). Like Pericles, Socrates emphasizes, no one is left out because of obscurity (low birth) or poverty. Because all citizens are thus equal (in opportunity, as we would say), Socrates points out, Athens cannot be accurately characterized as an oligarchy or tyranny, in which one man or a few use force to rule all the rest for the sake of their own interest.[8] Believing that all citizens are equally children of the same mother earth, Athenians seek to be ruled, equally, under law, yielding only to those reputed to be virtuous and prudent.

According to Socrates, the ancestors of the dead soldiers benefited them not only by preserving the regime initially given to Athens by the gods, but also by providing later generations with examples of Athenians giving their lives to defend the safety and freedom of their own and of all Greek cities. The fighters at Marathon who blocked Darius' invasion are first; the sailors at the naval battles of Salamis and Artemisium are second; and the joint action of the Spartans and the Athenians in securing Greece from the Persians at Plataea is third.

8. Both Kahn ("Funeral Oration," 225ff.) and M. M. Henderson, "Plato's *Menexenus* and the Distortion of History," *Acta Classica* 18 (1975): 38, treat Socrates' description of Athens as an "aristocracy" as an error. Thucydides 2.65 observes, however, that "what was nominally a democracy was becoming in [Pericles'] hands government by the first citizen." To be sure, Thucydides also says that it was different after Pericles. Nevertheless, Athenian leaders continued to be elected, and elections, according to Aristotle, are aristocratic means of selecting officials, in contrast to the lot characteristic of democracy.

Athens acquired her empire, according to Thucydides, after the Spartans abandoned leadership of the alliance of Greek cities against Persia, and the allies asked Athens to take their place. Athens did not force member cities to pay tribute instead of providing ships and so finance the Athenian fleet, and she helped additional Greek cities to free themselves from Persia.

Was Athens unjustly attempting to acquire an empire that would have eventually included all of Greece, as Thucydides intimates, both in the speeches he attributes to Pericles and in his judgment that the cause of the war was Spartan fear of Athenian expansion? Or was Athens simply doing what was necessary to defend Greece from renewed Persian assaults? Did the Spartans declare war on Athens out of fear, as Thucydides states, or were they moved by envy and jealousy, as Socrates maintains, when they saw Athens threatening to supplant them as the leading Greek power?[9] Pericles may have done his best to provoke the war with his Megarian decree (ironically, according to Aristophanes [*Acharnians* 525–35], at the behest of Aspasia), but it is nevertheless the case that Sparta attacked Athens, her former ally, and that a peace was negotiated only after Sparta lost the battle and left some of her men as hostages at Sphacteria. Athens did not initiate or perpetuate the war. Socrates' depiction of Athenian military action as primarily defensive is not and need not be read as simply comic or erroneous (as so many recent commentators have).

Socrates describes the continuation of what was, according to Thucydides, the second part of the war between Athens and Sparta as a separate, third war, "unexpected and terrible." Plato thus shows Socrates rewriting history. But it is not clear that his version is less accurate or true than Thucydides' description of "the greatest motion" that seemed to proceed to its denouement with the same inevitability as a Greek tragedy.[10] There are reasons to think that the continuation of the war was not necessary, and that its second outbreak could, therefore, be said to have been unexpected. Could the machinations of the ambitious young Alcibiades, which led to violations of the treaty on both sides, be said to be necessary? Was Laches' defeat, a result of his inability to stand up to his troops, at Mantineia inevitable? Could not the Athenians' defeat on Sicily, which resulted, according to Thucydides, from a combination of bad luck, lack of cavalry, and bad

---

9. Lysias also made envy and jealousy the motives for Athens' enemies in his funeral oration.

10. For a contemporary challenge to Thucydides' account of the war, see Donald Kagan, *The Outbreak of the Peloponnesian War* (Ithaca: Cornell University Press, 1969).

judgment on the part of Nicias, have been avoided? Thucydides emphasizes both the enormity of the Athenian invading force and the pathos of their ultimate defeat in Sicily. Socrates takes the official justification for the expedition, the freeing of the Leontinians, seriously. Like Thucydides, Socrates points out that Athens was able to continue waging war in her own defense for many years afterward. Socrates also concurs with Thucydides' judgment that the Athenians were "vanquished not by others but by [their] own discord" (243d). Unlike Thucydides, however, Socrates points out that the civil strife in Athens that produced several regime changes was milder than it had been elsewhere in Greece. And he emphasizes that the Athenians have become reconciled not only to each other but also to the other Greeks.

Critics have pointed out several ellipses and inaccuracies in Socrates' brief account of Athenian history during the fifth and early fourth centuries. He does not mention the Spartan contribution to the sea battle at Artemisium, and he downplays the violence associated with Athenian civil strife. (He does not, for example, mention the fact that several of his close associates, such as Chaerephon and Polemarchus, were killed, or that he was condemned to death after the official amnesty—not for war crimes, to be sure, but for corrupting unnamed young people, who might well have included some individuals with whom the democrats had supposedly become reconciled. In remaining silent, he is seeking to preserve the reconciliation rather than dwell on past injuries.) Socrates also seems to misdescribe some of Athens' most recent battles with the Spartans and Persians over Ionian Greek cities in the so-called Corinthian War.[11] Plato might be using these inaccuracies to remind his readers, who would know what had happened during their own lifetime best, that Socrates could not actually know what happened after his death. But the brief history of Athens that "Aspasia" gives is generally in accord with the understanding of praise that Socrates articulates in the *Symposium*: to say what is good and true, and to remain silent about what is not. Socrates remains silent about the Athenian striving for empire, because that striving on the part of leaders like Pericles and Alcibiades was unjust. He has Aspasia rewrite Athenian history to show his fellow citizens a better, more just way of understanding their experience. And he does so without distorting the record much, if any, more than his most famous predecessor had.

11. Athens was never "completely at peace" at the end of the fifth century (as Socrates claims; *Menexenus* 244b), nor was there a known war on behalf of the Parians (245b). See Collins and Stauffer, introduction to *Empire*, 48; and C. E. Graves, *The "Euthyphro" and "Menexenus" of Plato* (London: Macmillan, 1935), 111.

Having given a brief and generally plausible account of the Athenian regime and its history that is most in accord with principles of justice Socrates had argued for earlier, "Aspasia" concludes with the exhortation to the survivors not merely to imitate but to exceed those who have died in the virtues indicated by their history. She sounds most like Socrates when she tells her auditors that she "will exhort the children of these men, just as in war, not to leave the post of their ancestors," and that she will "now exhort you, and whenever I meet one of you in the future . . . to strive eagerly to be as good as possible" (246b). Recognizing that she (like Socrates) has less status with the children of the dead heroes than their fathers, she puts the admonition not to soil the reputation of their ancestors by acting ignobly into the mouths of the dead heroes. Likewise she delivers the advice from the heroes, to their parents, not to add to their own grief with lamentations and to remember that they had "prayed not that their children become immortal, but that they become good and well-reputed [*eukleeis*]" (247d) in indirect discourse. Parents would honor the dead better "by nurturing and caring for their children and wives" than by grieving for their loss. "Not only would [their] parents be able to forget their misfortune, but they would live more nobly and correctly" (248c–d).

Both the length and content of this part of the speech distinguish it from other extant funeral orations.[12] And the exhortation that the heroes finally extend to the city as well as their families, to take care of their parents and sons, sounds a great deal like the parting admonition Socrates gave his close associates. The funeral oration is, as Menexenus recognizes in his parting comments about both Aspasia and Socrates, a Socratic work. It is, however, a Socratic public or political work, and so not delivered in his persona as philosopher.

The difference between Socrates' own admonition to his friends and that delivered to the families and cities becomes clear when the author of the speech restates the message on her own and not merely in words she claims to have heard from the fathers. The heirs of the dead soldiers are to obey the laws and defend the city, not only militarily but also by preserving the customary rites along with the gymnastic, equestrian, and musical contests that serve to educate the young. Like "the laws" in the *Crito*, Aspasia suggests at the end of her speech that the city is the parent of its citizens. It both nurtures and educates them. The city does not edu-

---

12. Cf. Henderson, "Distortion," 28–33; Salkever, "Oration"; Collins and Stauffer, introduction to *Empire*.

cate or care for others by questioning and exhorting them individually, the way both Socrates and the author of this speech do. As the author of this speech observes, "the multitude has control over most of the city's affairs" (238d), and the multitude do not philosophize (cf. *Republic* 494a).

Another, related difference between the individual philosopher named Socrates and the author of this speech becomes clear when we observe that Plato does not record Socrates' parting words to his wife and children, but he does show that Socrates had a relatively long final conversation with them. He spoke in private with his private family. At the conclusion of the speech Socrates says was composed of leftovers from the funeral oration she composed for Pericles, Aspasia has even fewer words of comfort for the wives than Pericles does, who curtly admonishes them to suffer in silence. This may have been a reason Socrates attributed the authorship of both speeches to Aspasia. A courtesan would not be apt to show sympathy for wives. She would know all too well that it was contrary to Athenian customs and laws for a woman to speak in public; her words would have to be delivered by a man, and it would not be appropriate in a public rite celebrating the sacrifice soldiers had made of their own, private lives and fortunes on behalf of the city to dramatize the private losses their spouses had to endure.[13] Socrates, the philosopher who spoke only in private to individuals, was and could be more humane.

II. Socrates in Light of Plato's Other Philosophers

In his dramatic presentation of the rise, the advantages, and the limitations of Socratic philosophy, we have seen that Plato contrasts his teacher with four other philosophers. Each of these other philosophers is able to do or

---

13. The attribution of the speech to Aspasia is, of course, as fictional as the supposed delivery of the speech to Menexenus by Socrates. No one knows exactly when she was born or died; having been a friend of Pericles, however, she too was probably dead by the dramatic date of the dialogue. And she had as good if not better reasons than Socrates not simply to praise Athens. The son she had with Pericles had finally been made a citizen, but he was one of the generals illegally condemned and killed as a result of the simultaneous trial of all ten of the generals at the battle of Arginusae (cited in her speech as a preeminent example of Athens' continuing determination to defend its own freedom). Since Socrates alone protested the illegality of the trial, she had reason to be friends with him. Yet in the face of this history, "Socrates" has her declare, at the end of the account she gives in this speech, that if one wishes to accuse Athens justly, "the only thing one can truly say is that she was too compassionate" (*Menexenus* 244e). And this in light of the (in)famous Melian dialogue! Apparently Plato blamed the Melian oligarchs, who would not let the people hear the Athenian offer for the fate of the city.

explain something that Socrates is not. The contrasts Plato draws work both ways, however; for Socrates is able to address problems and take account of phenomena—especially in the human realm—that none of the other philosophers can. By reviewing the differences in the questions they ask, the methods they use to answer these questions, and the results of the arguments they put forward, we learn not only why Plato thought that human intellectual endeavor would always consist in a search for wisdom, but also why he made Socrates his chief philosophical protagonist.

A. The Athenian: Politics and Piety

Socrates' indirect political action in the *Menexenus* leads us back to the contrast between Socrates and the Athenian Stranger with which this book began. At first glance, the anonymous Athenian appears to be superior to Socrates, at least with regard to political effectiveness, in two related respects. First, the Athenian is able to affect the deeds of public men directly in a way Socrates never did. Second, by showing the elderly Dorians why it was necessary for city elders to be able to prove to the young that the gods exist and that they care about human beings, the Athenian defends himself, in advance as it were, from the accusations of impiety and corrupting the young which brought about Socrates' death.

1. Politics and Education

The Athenian was able to convince the two elderly Dorians to accept his legislative proposals only by articulating and accepting the "Dorian law of laws" at the beginning of their conversation. He assured his elderly interlocutors that no young people would be present when they questioned the wisdom and justice of the current laws of their respective cities. By defending a distinctive institution of his own regime, the Athenian then showed the old Dorians that they did not know or fully understand all political possibilities. By describing the failures and limitations of their own polities, he gradually convinced them that he could propose a better way of doing things.

Socrates did not think he could assert or enforce anything like the Dorian law of laws. Explaining why he did not propose exile as an alternative to the death penalty at his trial, Socrates not only insisted that he did not deserve something bad and that he would not propose an unjust penalty. He also predicted that wherever he went, young people would want to listen to him converse. If he did not allow them to do so, they would complain to their fathers, who would drive him away. But if he allowed young people to listen to him converse, their fathers would prosecute him for the same reasons the Athenians had.

Could the young be excluded from discussions of how to institute the best possible regime, as the Athenian suggests? Or would they demand to be included in such discussions, as Socrates claims? What did Plato think would happen or was best? By having the Athenian argue at the end of the *Laws* that it would be necessary to establish a school to which older guardians would bring their younger potential successors, Plato seems to recognize the impossibility of establishing the best possible regime without incorporating a discussion of the reasons for the laws. Legislators cannot proclaim the best possible laws in the best possible way if they do not understand why they are best. They cannot pass on that knowledge to their successors, and so maintain the best possible regime, if they do not give their potential successors both the time and opportunity to acquire the necessary intellectual skills to pursue the difficult questions involved. To legislate well, the Athenian reminded the old Dorians, legislators would have to understand the goal of the regime, which is to make its citizens as virtuous as possible. To make people virtuous, it is obviously necessary to know what virtue is, and thus to understand in what way virtue is one and how it is differentiated. Potential legislators would have to ask the same questions, how it is one and how many, of the noble and the good. They would, in other words, have to raise the questions for which Socrates became famous.

To be sure, the discussions of the Nocturnal Council were not completely public or open to everyone. But neither were Socrates' conversations. Although in his defense Socrates emphasized that he never barred anyone from listening to him converse or asked a fee, he also observed that sons of wealthy fathers had the leisure to listen to him. Although Socrates did not say so explicitly, tradesmen and their sons did not. The selection of the members of the Nocturnal Council might appear to be more intentional and potentially more just because it was based on the merits of the individuals rather than the moneymaking capacities of their parents. Since the youths would have to be citizens and would be chosen by individual officeholders, however, they and the officeholders would also be chosen partly on the basis of their parents and partly on the basis of the somewhat arbitrary choices of the guardians or the groups that elected them. The most significant differences between the discussions that would take place in the Nocturnal Council and the conversations Socrates held with a variety of private individuals were, first, that the discussants in the Nocturnal Council included public officials, who were elected to perform specific public functions, and, second, that the discussions of the council were therefore necessarily limited in time to a few hours before dawn. Would young people or busy men and women, responsible for conducting public business during the day, be able to answer questions Socrates could not answer entirely to his own satisfaction, even though he devoted all of his adult life to pursuing the answers to them?

In the dialogues Socrates suggests that no embodied mortal will ever be able completely to attain or retain knowledge of the noble or the good in itself. It would appear, therefore, to be impossible for human beings to attain the knowledge the Athenian argues is necessary to institute and maintain the best regime. According to Socrates, philosophers can be virtuous—not because they possess knowledge of what virtue is, but as a result of their overwhelming love and consequent search for the truth. If so, philosophers achieve the goal of political association not by schooling themselves or others to rule or by engaging in political activity but by seeking wisdom.

In the *Republic* (518d) Socrates admits that the "virtues" inculcated in his city in speech are like bodily habits. Laws succeed at most in enforcing external obeisance to authoritative public opinions. They cannot produce knowledge or true virtue in any individual or people. Although Socrates says that legislation is the highest part of the political art in the *Gorgias*, he claims to be the only person in Athens at his time even trying to practice the true political art—and his art was clearly corrective. He did not accuse himself, members of his family, or his fellow citizens of doing wrong in a public assembly or in court, as he suggested that Polus should. As Socrates states in his *Apology*, he examined each of his interlocutors individually, in private, urging them to care for truth, prudence, and the good of their souls. He did not interrogate only Athenians, but he spoke mostly to Athenians. He did not simply seek to convince them that they were seeking impossible goals when, out of fear, they tried to escape death or to amass as much wealth and reputation as possible. Nor did he content himself with showing them that they held contradictory opinions and that if they acted on the basis of these contradictory opinions, they would necessarily be acting against themselves. He attempted to show them, in deed as much as in speech, the sorts of virtues a philosopher comes to possess through seeking the truth. He realized that he would only persuade a few to join him in a life of philosophy, but he recognized this as the only path to true virtue.

Plato's depiction of Socrates' "legacy," both philosophical and political, makes the Athenian's political superiority appear to be less than it initially seems. Like the Athenian, we saw in the *Phaedo*, Socrates persuaded many of his close associates—Plato first and foremost—to establish schools. Unlike the Nocturnal Council, however, these schools were devoted more to the study of philosophy than to maintaining any specific laws or regimes. The Socratics established schools in many different cities, and these schools were less subject than the secretive Nocturnal Council might have been to accusations that they served a certain political party and constituted a kind of sect, if not conspiracy (like its Pythagorean precedent). *The* difference between the kind of influence the Athenian wanted to exercise on future Dorian legislators and that Socrates had on his associates is the difference between the ability to use the force of the laws to establish certain institutions and to prohibit people from voicing certain views, and the need to persuade individuals to adopt a set of practices and opinions freely.

The same difference shows up with regard to the use of writings. Late in his life Socrates appears to have recognized the need for a more popular, widespread means of conveying the goodness of the philosophical life, and many of his associates subsequently wrote accounts of "Socratic" conversations. People were not required to read these records by law, however, in the way the Athenian suggests the written record of his conversation with the old Dorians should be. The effects of the indirect dissemination of opinions through schools and writings that are publicly available, but not mandated or required, are less immediate and harder to see than the effects of direct legislation. But the indirect effects of teaching (as opposed to commanding) that the Athenian presents in his image of the free doctor as opposed to the slave doctor are more lasting and real. The Athenian and Socrates agree that the goal of the city (or political action) is to make citizens virtuous so that they can live together happily, and that no one is or can be truly virtuous without choosing to be so. They agree, in other words, that virtue cannot be required or forced.

2. Two Untraditional Forms of Philosophical Piety

According to the Athenian, guardians of the laws need to know not only what the goal of the city is, that is, what is truly noble, good, and virtuous. They also need to learn the proof of the existence of the gods that the Athenian urged the elderly Dorians to use in responding to rebellious youths who asked why they should follow ancestral tradition. If no one can answer the youths, the Athenian warned, their questions will arouse the anger of the elders, who will then be tempted to impose their rules by force rather than try to persuade the younger generation that their ways are best.

In the *Apology* Socrates observed that young people enjoyed listening to his interrogations of others, and they imitated him when they went home by questioning their fathers. Unable to answer the questions their sons asked, the fathers became angry and blamed Socrates. Not knowing what he did, the fathers repeated the old accusations against natural philosophers, that they were atheists who corrupted the young.

Both the anonymous Athenian and Socrates recognize that ancestral authority cannot be maintained simply on the basis of age. Unless the implicit claim to possess wisdom on the basis of experience can be defended to young people who chafe under the rule of others, rule will come to depend solely and unjustly on superior force, which the elders may or may not possess. Armies are usually composed and often led by irreverent young men like Achilles and Alcibiades. When the Athenian tells his Dorian interlocutors that the guardians of the laws will need to be able to prove the existence of the gods to young rebellious atheists, he admits that the Dorian law of laws, which mandates praise and forbids any questioning of the laws in front of the young, will not be sufficient to ensure their obedience. The rule of law requires a reasoned defense, which the elders qua elders cannot provide.

In contrast to Socrates, the Athenian does not worry about the stories of the gods that show them acting in immoral ways, although he does not praise such stories. These stories are a part of the tradition he is teaching the elders to defend. According to these stories, the gods not only exist but also care about human beings. The gods are, indeed, usually said to be the source of the laws of well-ordered polities like Crete and Sparta. As readers are shown in the course of the dialogue, however, the Dorians never took poetry as seriously as the Athenians did. They were more impressed by the fact of war and the role of force.

According to the Athenian, the old Dorians had not yet experienced the most serious threat to the rule of law. That threat is posed by a "new" kind of philosophy, which teaches that everything is a product of nature, chance, or art. Gods are products of human convention or art; there are no divine beings, in fact. There is, in other words, no divine source of justice. Laws merely represent the agreements and interests of the strongest.

According to this new philosophical understanding of things, there is no reason the elders should not try to impose their will on the young, if they can, any more than there a reason is for the young not to rebel, if they can. There is a reason, however, for the elders to try to repress not only the rebellious youth but also the teaching of the argument that justifies their rebellion.

The Athenian recognizes that repression is not going to succeed against ever new generations of young skeptics. He thus urges the old Dorians to fight fire with fire— or philosophy with philosophy. They should respond to the contention that everything is matter in motion by pointing out that motion is primary, and if motion is primary, there must be something self-moving, that is, soul. The locus of mind thus becomes the source and foundation of everything. There are admittedly different kinds of motion. Those that are orderly, like the motions of the heavenly bodies, are good and divine. These motions or powers support us and should be supported by us in a war against the bad, disorderly forms of motion or "soul." According to the Athenian, the natural investigations of the pre-Socratic philosophers are the source both of the most serious threat to political order and the basis of a response to it.

In his *Apology* Socrates predicts that he will be convicted on the basis of an old prejudice, the prejudice against natural philosophers. Although he denies that he is a natural philosopher or has the knowledge they seek, Socrates does not contemn it. Nor does he think natural philosophy is the greatest threat to the rule of law or source of corruption in the young. On the contrary, Socrates maintains that fathers angered by their own inability to answer the questions their sons ask blame Socrates for their own lack of knowledge. Not knowing what Socrates does, they repeat the old charges against natural philosophers. But, as Socrates tells Euthyphro, it is not the claim to possess greater knowledge or wisdom that gets other people upset. It is the demonstrated ability of a speaker to make others like him and thus to forsake the ways of their fathers.

Like the Athenian, Socrates recognizes that human beings need to be regulated by laws, because their unordered passions lead them into conflict. It is their passions—especially their fear of death and their desires to amass wealth, power, and honor—that make them resist the rule of law. Unlike the Athenian, Socrates thus objects to the stories told by the poets that show gods acting on the basis of a desire for pleasure or to avoid pain, because they set bad examples. Like the fathers who object to their sons' questions, Socrates knows that imitation constitutes a powerful form of teaching. Like Euthyphro, Socrates knows that some young people will be tempted to do as the gods do, rather than as they say. Socrates does not object merely to the bad effects the traditional depictions of gods may have on human beings, however. He thinks the poets' depictions of the gods are untrue. The poets' characterizations of the gods may portray what human beings would like to do, if they had the power to do what they want and did not have to fear death; Socrates insists, however, that good and intelligent beings would not act this way. In the *Phaedrus* (246c) Socrates observes that we have no reason to think an immortal being could have a body or the passions associated with it. Nothing eternal can change or be embodied.

Neither Socrates nor the Athenian (who explicitly recognizes only the intelligent force [*nous*] in or behind the intelligible movements of the heavenly bodies to be divine) believes in the "gods of the city," if those are the gods the poets described. But the two philosophers represent different responses to the problematic basis and effects of traditional Greek beliefs. The Athenian attempts to replace the stories about the divine sources of Cretan and Spartan legislation with a "rational" theology, based in part on cosmological observations. Because this theology serves as the public justification of the laws, the Athenian cannot rely merely on the persuasiveness of reason. He also tells the old Dorian legislators that they will have to incarcerate or kill anyone who publicly doubts the existence of the gods, their care for human beings, or their justice.

Socrates does not propose the enforcement of any such public teaching. Although he suggests in the *Republic* that a just city would have to be founded on a "noble lie" about the origins and education of the populace, he also says that he does not know how any legislator could persuade anyone to believe it. Socrates regularly posits the existence of divine beings—eternally unchanging, intelligible, if not intelligent, and good—but he does not propose that his hypothesis about the ideas become a public teaching in any actual city or that people should not question the truth of his argument. On the contrary, he urges his close associates to do just that. Nor does Socrates try to moderate the ambitions of rebellious youths like Alcibiades and Critias by presenting them with a rational theology.[14]

14. Just as the Athenian seeks to teach the elderly Dorians to appreciate the necessity for moderation as well as for courage by having them join him in the founding of a new "city in speech," so Socrates seeks to show Plato's brothers the political utility of philosophy by having them join him in describing a "city in speech." In dramatic contrast to the Athenian and his Dorian interlocutors, however, Socrates, Glaucon, and Adimantus conclude that their city in speech will serve as a paradigm for individuals. They do not state their intention to found it in fact.

Instead, he attempts to show them how great their ambitions are and how slight their own resources to achieve those ambitions. Then he seeks to persuade them that they will need the assistance of others to attain their goals, and that to obtain that assistance, they will have to learn to be just. For Socrates, there is a close connection between justice and piety. Because the laws of actual cities are not always wisely formulated or justly administered, Socrates recognizes, "the laws" often claim to have divine support. They promise that individuals, who are not treated justly in this life, will be rewarded or punished rightly by the gods in the next (*Crito* 54b–c). The problem with this claim, Socrates suggests in the *Euthyphro*, is that it can produce the sort of atheistic rebellion the Athenian fears. Observing that justice is not done, and that the gods have apparently allowed it, people begin to doubt that the gods care about human beings, if the gods exist.

Although Socrates objected to the stories traditionally told about the gods in ancient Greece, he appears to have believed in the existence of divine beings or forces. Several times in the dialogues he claims to be ruled by the god or gods. In contrast to the Athenian (and Timaeus), however, Socrates does not base his belief in the existence of gods on observations of the regular, hence intelligible, movements of the heavens. On the contrary, in the *Phaedo* we hear him remind his close associates that human beings cannot directly, accurately, or completely observe the intelligible order of the heavens, so long as their minds are dulled and confused by their senses. Socrates' piety is based not on observed intelligibility or contemplation, but on a reasoned awareness of the limitations of human reason and knowledge. Mortals can never entirely know the truth about the immortal or divine, he acknowledged. All we can know is that there are some immortal and completely intelligible things in themselves, which are not merely beyond but superior to us. As mortal and not entirely intelligible beings ourselves, we do not and may never be able to know how the purely intelligible is related to the not entirely unintelligible aspects of being. If we examine our own experience carefully, we do know that we have access to some entirely intelligible beings or concepts. We could not learn to speak or to count if we did not have some perception of purely intelligible forms of being. From our own experience we also learn that the irrational and unintelligible are harmful and bad. We thus know that the intelligible is good, even if we are never able to achieve knowledge of the good or intelligible in itself.

Socrates tried to propagate his own peculiar brand of piety by urging individuals to examine their own opinions critically so that they would see that they did not know what they thought they knew and that, lacking such knowledge, they could not do everything they desired. Socratic piety could not be propagated by means of legislation or the requiring of a specified set of beliefs. To acquire the knowledge of their own ignorance that Socrates associated with the Delphic oracle (and hence with a kind of piety as well as moderation), young people would have to be encouraged to question the truth and wisdom not only of the stories told by the poets but also of the opinions held by most of their elders. They should be encouraged to ask whether avoiding death and maximizing their wealth, honor, and pleasure would really enable them to live happily, as most of their elders thought (*Apology* 29d–30b; *Republic* 492a–94b). As Socrates indicates in the *Menexenus*, the opinions that led the Athenians to seek empire over others were impious. Young people should be taught to respect their ancestors, but only insofar as their ancestors were good. Neither the elderly nor the young would continue to obey laws they do not believe are rational or just.

As both the dialogues and the external historical record show, Socrates did not succeed in all of his attempts to persuade individual Athenians to seek truth, prudence, and the good of their souls instead of wealth and honor. It is not clear, however, that Socrates' arguments about the limits of human knowledge and the consequent limitations of our ability to control our fates were any less valid or persuasive than the Athenian's attempt to legislate piety on the basis of a rational cosmology.

B. Parmenides: The Problematic Relation of the Intelligible to the Sensible

In the *Parmenides* the elderly Eleatic raises three objections to Socrates' argument about the ideas: (1) Socrates could not say exactly what there are ideas of; (2) Socrates could not explain how sensible things participate in the purely intelligible ideas; and (3) Socrates could not show how such unchanging, purely intelligible ideas could be known by changeable mortals.

In the *Symposium* Socrates suggests that he learned how to overcome Parmenides' third objection as a result of a kind of divine inspiration. The oppositions Parmenides drew between the "is" and the "is not," and thus between knowledge and ignorance, were too sharp and absolute. They did not encompass becoming, which exists somewhere between the "is" and the "is not," or opinion, which exists somewhere between knowledge and ignorance. By examining their opinions, discovering where their opinions contradicted each other or their own experience and desires, and then modifying their views accordingly, Socrates found that mortal human beings could move closer to something like knowledge. Socrates never claimed that human beings could acquire knowledge, simply and unambiguously. On the contrary, Socrates explicitly recognized that their mortal nature not merely prevented human beings from retaining whatever knowledge they acquired, but required them constantly to reconsider their opinions in light of new experiences. But by demonstrating in deed as well as in speech how the pursuit of truth could make a philosopher virtuous— courageous, moderate, and just as well as wise—Socrates showed how purely intelligible concepts could form sensible human existence, even if the human being concerned did not possess complete knowledge of them.

Parmenides criticized the young Socrates for caring too much about what other human beings thought. But Plato shows that Socrates was not concerned about what others thought of him so much as what they thought was truly noble and good. Human beings are the only animals who voice opinions, because humans are the only animals with the power of speech. That power, in turns, depends on a perception of types or kinds. As *the* place in the cosmos where the intelligible and the sensible come together, human beings and their opinions became the focus of Socrates' investigations. Socrates admitted on the last day of his life that he had never been able to explain how sensible things generally participated in the perfectly intelligible forms or exactly what there are ideas of, that is, he never could entirely answer Parmenides' objection.

In the *Phaedo* Plato suggests that these admitted defects with regard to the possession of knowledge may nevertheless have proved advantageous in Socrates' attempt to perpetuate his kind of philosophizing. Socrates could show his young associates where to begin and how to progress. Precisely because he recognized that mortals can never attain or retain perfect knowledge, he could not present them with "the" answer or even a "table"—a list, hierarchy, or chart—of all the possible types of being, and their relations to one another or to sensible things. As he shows most clearly in the *Euthydemus*, Socrates was able to encourage youths to join him in ongoing philosophical investigations, because he could show them how to improve their understanding, especially of what is truly noble and good. He did not claim to possess such knowledge himself or present a set method of attaining it. Even though he began by refuting or correcting his interlocutors, Socrates did not discourage them from undertaking further inquiry the way the eristic followers of Parmenides did, by arguing for or against one proposition and then turning around and proving the contrary. As Socrates demonstrated in his exchanges with Euthydemus and Dionysodorus, the sophists used the opposition Parmenides had posited between the "is" and the "is not" to refute any proposition. They could play this game because the addition of any specific quality to a claim of "is" entails a claim that the specific thing "is not" something else. But, as the Eleatic Stranger argues in partial opposition to his "father" Parmenides, differentiation does not entail negation. Indeed, Plato's Parmenides concedes in talking to Socrates (although the author of the poem does not) that something like Socrates' argument concerning the ideas, that is, the possibility of sorting things into intelligible types, is a necessary condition for the possibility of philosophy. Like Socrates in the *Phaedrus*, the Eleatic Stranger also points out, *logos*—speech and reason—presupposes the capacity to perceive such types.

As Plato shows in the dramatic prologue to the *Parmenides*, Parmenides and Zeno had not been able to maintain much of a following in Athens. The individuals who had once listened to the exchange between Socrates and the Eleatic philosophers no longer had any interest in the argument. Plato indicates, although he does not state, the reason. Parmenides and his followers were not able to say why they or anyone else should seek knowledge. Parmenides' demonstration of the philosophical gymnastics Socrates should practice appeared to be an exercise in pure logic. His reasoning about "one" did not seem to have any application to the lives of the participants or listeners. And, Plato shows, the youths who once listened to Parmenides and Zeno argue turned to more practical pursuits when they got older. The eristic sophists who used Parmenidean logic to refute their interlocutors did not seek merely to impress or to entertain their students, although initially they did both. They claimed to be teaching virtue, because they believed that the ability to best someone else in argument would give a man the ability to obtain power, wealth, and honor. But, as Plato shows in the *Euthydemus*, *Gorgias*, and *Meno*, these sophists eventually frustrated and bored or angered their audiences. Neither pure Eleatic philosophy nor its sophistical application had a wide or enduring following.

Socrates did attract a following. That was the reason he was the first philosopher to be dragged into court and convicted of a capital crime. Politically ambitious young men like Alcibiades, Critias, Theages, and Clinias saw that Socrates could show them how to argue as well as, if not better than, the sophists. As Xenophon reports (*Memorabilia* 1.2.12–16), so Plato shows, these youths associated with Socrates for a time, but they did not remain close to him. They were not interested in seeking truth or wisdom; they wanted the wealth and honor they could acquire in politics. Plato does not suggest that Socrates represented a more promising philosophical path than Parmenides merely because Socrates' often-stated desire to discover what is truly noble and good had more popular, practical appeal. As Socrates often observed, few people are willing to make themselves look ridiculous the way he did—especially if they wish to attain high political office. Socrates nevertheless continued to insist that it was necessary to admit that one does not know, and so to look ridiculous in the eyes of those who think they know what they do not, if one is to learn,

Plato suggests that Socrates was superior to Parmenides as a philosopher. Both Parmenides and Socrates confronted the same basic problem: how can ever-changing sensible existence be shaped by what is unchanging and purely intelligible? At the end of his life, Plato's Socrates explicitly admitted that he had not entirely solved the problem. But, Plato indicates, Socratic philosophy represented an improvement on that of Parmenides in two fundamental respects. First, by positing a variety of purely intelligible forms of being, Socrates could at least begin to give an account of the different kinds of beings we observe and experience—sensible and intelligible. The first and most fundamental difference in the kinds of beings may be just that—some are purely intelligible, whereas others exist only in their sensible embodiments or other manifestations. The second, almost equally fundamental difference is between intelligent (human) and not-intelligent, although possibly intelligible, forms of being. Parmenides' arguments concerning whether one is or is not could not come to a resolution, because homogeneous being cannot be defined except, as in the poem, through its opposition to not-being. But according to Parmenides, not-being cannot be said or thought. If that is the case, there can be no intelligible limit or, literally, definition to being. Second, neither Parmenides nor his followers could explain why human beings should want to acquire knowledge or how they could acquire it, if they desired. Socrates repeatedly shows his interlocutors that they will not be able to live happily unless they come to know what is truly good. He thus explains, if he does not supply, a motive and justification for philosophy. Even more important, Socrates suggests that human beings and their opinions are *the* place where the fundamental question about the participation of the sensible in the intelligible can begin to be answered, if it can be answered. In other words, Parmenides lacked the self-knowledge that Socrates explicitly seeks. Socrates understands that knowledge of "the human things" is not knowledge of the whole or knowledge properly speaking. But, he insists, we will never be able to attain knowledge if we do not know why we seek it and cannot explain how we are able, as changeable mortals, to achieve something like it.

C. Timaeus—The Whole and Its Parts

By asking whether or not one is, Parmenides was at least attempting to speak about the whole, even if he could not explain the existence of sensible things or human cognition. In seeking knowledge of the good-in-itself and the beautiful or noble-in-itself, Socrates clearly did not restrict his inquiries to the human per se. But although Socrates says in the *Republic* that the idea of the good is the source and basis of all other beings and knowledge, and that it is beyond being itself, he does not even give his opinion about the intelligible structure and composition of the whole. He presents his most comprehensive "account" merely as an image. He never claims to know exactly what ideas there are, much less show how they are related to each other or how they can be said to arise out of, or exist on the basis of, the idea of the good.

In the *Timaeus* the statesman-philosopher from Locri initially appears able to give a much more comprehensive account of the whole and its parts, particularly the way in which purely intelligible and sensible forms of being can be combined, than either Parmenides or Socrates does. Socrates even praises Timaeus for having achieved the "peak of all philosophy" (20a).

To be sure, Timaeus characterizes his account of the intelligible organization of the cosmos as a "likely story." Such an account can only be likely, Timaeus explains, because only the purely intelligible is truly knowable. He is describing the visible, hence sensible, cosmos. He is, moreover, delivering this account to human beings, who cannot cognize everything simultaneously but have to hear things spelled out in a linear, temporal order. Like Parmenides and Socrates, Timaeus begins by recognizing the difference between eternally unchanging, purely intelligible being and ever-changing, sensible becoming. Unlike Parmenides and Socrates, who begin with purely intelligible being or beings, and ask how sensible things share in this intelligibility or not, Timaeus begins with the visible cosmos. Because it is visible and thus sensible, he reasons, the cosmos has to have come into being; because it is beautiful, its origin had to be good. From this beauty, which inheres in and arises from its intelligible order, Timaeus infers that the cosmos had an intelligent and good cause—or maker. Timaeus never claims to know that there was a divine craftsman; he infers the existence of such from the intelligibility of the organization and movements of the sensible things we perceive.

Timaeus describes first the intelligibility of the orbits of the heavenly bodies, which are the bases, among other things, of human perceptions of time, of the seasons, and hence of the growth of all living things on earth. He then shows how the bodily things that come into being and perish can be understood to be composed of four basic elements—fire, air, water, and earth—and that these elements can also be understood to be organized into different kinds of geometrical solids. Because these solids can all be broken up into triangles, Timaeus can explain how they disintegrate and are recombined into other things in the process of becoming.

Because he is describing the intelligible organization of sensible things, Timaeus admits, the intelligibility of the cosmos is not complete. In constituting the world soul (the locus of intelligence combined with motion), he states, the god had to force the same and the different, which would otherwise have remained opposed, together with being. The god then divided this mixture into pieces that constitute a series of geometrical and harmonic mean proportions, so that they could serve as the two means necessary to bind the four elements of body together. In contrast to the numbers the Pythagoreans suggested formed the intelligible constitution of all things, Timaeus recognizes that bodily things cannot be reduced to any homogeneous material or definition and remain intelligible. Being must, therefore, be mixed with the same and the other, that is, be differentiated, as both Socrates and the Eleatic Stranger argue. Timaeus does not claim that the various densities of the shifting matter of becoming, within what he calls chōra, actually have the geometric shapes he attributes to them, moreover; he maintains merely that they will "accept" such shapes or descriptions.

Having shown how both the orbits of the heavenly bodies and the components of sensible things can be described and related to each other in geometrical, hence intelligible, terms, Timaeus finally shows how the kind of intelligibility to be found in the heavens is combined with the essential disorder of sensible bodies in the construction of the human being. We can perceive the order in the movements of the heavens because our souls are composed of the same intelligible "stuff." The order of our souls is overcome by the disorder of body when the two are combined. But the construction of our bodies—with the encasing of the soulish material in the head, almost entirely separated from and placed on top of the rest of the body—makes it possible for us to recapture the intelligible order our souls share with the heavens and impose that order on ourselves. By looking up and contemplating the order there, human beings can regain the original order in their souls. Their heads can then rule their disorderly bodily desires and movements.

Having initially praised Timaeus as a philosopher and statesman, Socrates warns Critias, at the beginning of the dialogue that follows Timaeus' exposition, that the other poet (*poiētēs*) has become wonderfully well reputed in the mind of the observer (*tēn tou theatrou dianoian*; *Critias* 108b). It is not difficult to see why Socrates characterizes Timaeus as a "poet" as well as a philosopher. Timaeus had described the cosmos as something made. He had, moreover, characterized his description as a "likely story" or image presented as a narrative. Greek poets like Hesiod had also described the way in which the cosmos came to be, as the result of divine forces, if not intentional action. But in contrast to these poets and all previous philosophers with the exception of Parmenides, Timaeus had not presented becoming as an unending process in which everything is always being transformed into something else. Like Parmenides and Socrates, Timaeus recognized the existence of purely intelligible, eternally unchanging beings—categories or divisions—in addition to the ever-changing sensible. He had not only recognized the distinction, moreover; he had shown how the sensible can be understood to have intelligible organization and form (shapes—the basic meaning of *eidē*). Most important of all, in contrast to the pre-Socratic poets, Timaeus had shown not only that philosophy is the best way of life, but also how and why it is possible.

The problems with Timaeus' "likely story" come to the surface only when we look at it, as Socrates (and Aristotle) surely would, in terms of its end or purpose. Timaeus defines the end (*telos*) of the cosmos as its perfection or completeness. Critias had asked Timaeus merely to explain how the human beings who were to populate Socrates' city in speech came into being. As I argued in chapter 6, Timaeus' speech fails to fulfill this more limited purpose, because he does not—and, in fact, cannot—explain how there could be female guardians. According to Timaeus, all females are re-born from cowardly males. The failure of his speech to perform the function assigned points, moreover, to a much broader and more fundamental problem. Timaeus' suggestion that the intelligible organization of the cosmos, both in the heavens and in the sensible things on earth, can be described in geometrical terms as a result of its intentional fabrication, makes it impossible for him to describe anything as the spontaneous, unpredictable result of a chance mixing or mating of essentially different elements, such as the male and female. His top-down explanation of the intelligibility of the cosmos as a whole, containing within it all other possible forms of sensible being, not only culminates in a ridiculous account of the coming into being of all inferior kinds of animals from the degeneration of the initial male humans. It also leads him to treat every human being as having the same kind of organization and, therefore, essentially the same nature. All have the potential to regain the order of their soul that corresponds to the orderly movements of the heavenly bodies; all human souls are disordered by the conjunction with body and its conflicting desires. Differences among human beings result from defective education, nurture, or regime. If differences among individual human beings are products of bodily differences or the failure of other human beings to provide the necessary remedial education, however, there are no natural differences that justify the assignment of different tasks in the city to different individuals. (Timaeus does not propose anything like Socrates' "myth of the metals.")

Like Socrates, Timaeus recognizes that there is a fundamental difference between the human part of the whole and the whole. The cosmos would not be good or beautiful, Timaeus argues, if it were not complete. Because they are only parts, human beings are defective and have needs. In contrast to both Socrates and the Eleatic Stranger, however, Timaeus argues that the cosmos would not be complete if it did not provide means of satisfying those needs. Unlike Socrates, Timaeus claims that human beings can attain knowledge of the whole. Conflict among human beings can be avoided by means of good government. The essentially disorderly desires and motions of the body could result in conflict among human beings, but Timaeus suggests that these conflicts can be regulated by human statesmen who have learned how to replicate the orderly motion of the heavens in their own souls. For Timaeus there is the order impressed on bodies by the mind, on the one hand, and essentially disorderly bodily motion, on the other. The first is good; the second is a product of necessity. Understanding human beings in these cosmic terms, Timaeus regards the desire for knowledge as good. He does not admit that there is anything like intellectual pleasure, however. On the contrary, he suggests that all desires for pleasure are bodily and should be regulated, if not entirely repressed. He does not see the attraction human beings have for anything or anyone as beautiful to be anything but an appreciation of intelligible, mathematically described order or harmony. Failing to see a necessity for procreation in an intentionally fabricated cosmos, except as a result of the defective education and training of the first human beings, Timaeus does not recognize the desire "to beget in the beautiful" that Diotima taught Socrates is expressed most generally in sexual desire, but more intellectually and rarely in the work of poets and legislators, and even more rarely in philosophy. Because he traces all the differences among particular kinds of beings basically to bodily differences or location, Timaeus also does not recognize, much less explain, the feeling of injustice that leads some human beings to imagine a better life than the one they now have and thus to rebel against the established order. He does not recognize and cannot give an explanation for the passions that lead human beings like Glaucon to demand more than they need. But, as Socrates maintains in opposition to both Timaeus and the Eleatic Stranger, these passions are *the* source of conflict and injustice in human life—not mere need.

As Plato reminds his readers by having Socrates sit silently while Timaeus gives his extraordinary account of the fabrication and order of the cosmos, Socrates never presents anything like Timaeus' explanation of the way in which ever-changing sensible becoming can be understood to be geometrically and thus intelligibly ordered. No other philosopher in the Platonic dialogues does. At most, in the *Philebus* Socrates asks Protarchus to agree that the cosmos cannot be a product of mere chance. They agree that the order perceptible in the cosmos indicates that it had an intelligent author, but Socrates does not explain or describe the work of such an author. He argues that everything is a combination of the "limited" and the "unlimited," rather like Timaeus' understanding of the imitation of the eternal ideas by the good god in the fabrication of the cosmic soul and imposition of limited forms on the undefined material of becoming. (The similarity is not entirely accidental, insofar as both arguments have Pythagorean roots.) Socrates also argues that every such mixture must have a cause. That cause would appear finally to be the good in itself. But Socrates never explains how that cause operates except in the actions of human beings who desire to get what they want. Human beings have intentions, because they have desires. It is not at all clear that the divine, eternally unchanging, and purely

intelligible ideas do or could. It is not clear, in fact, that it is best for everything to be as it is, or if it is best, why. Socrates had hoped to learn that it
was so from Anaxagoras, who claimed that mind is the cause of everything.
He did not. Nor does Socrates think he has learned why it is best for everything to be as it is from Timaeus. He silently listens to Timaeus' speech
and then declares that he is a wonderfully well-reputed (*thaumastōs* . . .
ēudokimēken; *Critias* 108b) poet.

Timaeus had shown how the study of the orderly movements of the
heavenly bodies would make the souls of the philosophers themselves orderly and thus make them capable of impressing order on other human
beings by means of laws, education, and training. But he had not shown
why these philosophers would care about imposing such order, except as
the condition for their own existence. Timaean philosophers would need
other human beings to teach them the mathematics necessary to appreciate the intelligibility of the motions of the heavens as well as to provide
them with the necessary means of survival—food, clothes, shelter, and
defense. But Timaean philosophers would not need to converse with others in order to contemplate the orderly movement of the heavens or to be
happy. Timaeus does not, in a word, recognize the existence or necessity
of human love. He does not recognize the sort of attraction the presence
of beauty in other people, as opposed to the heavens, arouses in human
beings. He does not recognize the nobility involved in striving for a better
way of life. The city from which he comes and in which he served as a
statesman was famous for having very old, that is, unchanging, laws. As
the Athenian Stranger points out, it is not good for the laws to change or
appear to change frequently. Because the laws have to be applied in changing circumstances, however, they need to be modified in application if they
are to remain just and effective. Timaeus' account of the cosmic basis of
human order does not allow for any change but degeneration. Nor does he
recognize the need mortals have to seek and retain knowledge by means
of conversations (or more broadly, communication) with others. He does
not, in sum, possess Socrates' knowledge of *ta erōtika*. He does not recognize the full implications of the fact that mortals desire to be what they are
not and cannot, as mortals, ever be, that is, to be immortal. We can participate in the immortal insofar as we understand or contemplate it. But if we
have self-knowledge, we have to recognize that we are something lesser
and that we would like to be something more.

In opposition to Timaeus, Socrates observes (implicitly in the myth of
Er at the end of the *Republic* and explicitly at the end of the *Phaedo*) that

our embodied natures make it impossible for human beings to acquire clear and accurate knowledge of the movements of the heavenly bodies. Our vision—both bodily and intellectual—is clouded by our senses. Nature may provide for what human beings need, but human beings are not satisfied with what they need. We act and have to act intentionally, in concert with others, not merely to secure what we need to survive and procreate, but also to increase the beauty of, and the pleasure we take in, our own lives. It is certainly not clear to most human beings that it is best for things to be as they are.

The gap between the cosmic whole and the human parts is not merely the disjunction between the complete and the partial, or the perfect and the defective. The causes of cosmic motion—orderly or disorderly—are different from the causes of human action. Neither the spheres nor other animals nor other nonliving forms of being are moved by the kinds of intense passions that human beings are. Contrary to his own suggestion at a certain point in the *Republic*, Socrates recognizes that the lives of human beings cannot be brought to order by compelling philosophers to impose such an order on them. The unruly desires of the nonphilosophers might be repressed for awhile, but they would eventually break out. As Socrates effectively acknowledges in his account of the mistakes rulers would eventually make in calculating and administering the "nuptial number," human procreation cannot be managed the way Socrates and his interlocutors imagine. Human beings do not mate on command, instinctively, or indifferently. If the rule of philosophers were ever to be established, they would not be able to maintain their rule in the face of the opposition of the desires of others, covert or open. In apparent contrast to Timaeus, however, Socrates does not think that philosophers have ever ruled or that they will rule in the future. It is not possible for human beings to acquire the kind of comprehensive knowledge Timaeus suggests they can, because the world is not as orderly as Timaeus claims. Generation is a fact. Timaeus' feeble attempt at the conclusion of his speech to explain the need for procreation by the degeneration of some of the original *andres* indicates Plato's own recognition of the limitations of this "comprehensive" view.

D. The Eleatic Stranger: On Human Knowledge— Philosophical and Political

Socrates admitted that he could not give an account of the whole. He also admitted that he could not go into the public assembly of Athens to speak on behalf of justice and survive. In the dialogues leading up to his trial and death, Plato thus shows that Socrates faced his most serious challenge from an Eleatic Stranger who questioned the adequacy of both Socrates' philosophy and his understanding of politics.

1. Is the Whole Completely Intelligible?

In the *Sophist* the Eleatic Stranger finally proposes a definition of the "beast" that fits Socrates much better than other known "sophists" such as Protagoras, Prodicus, Hippias, Euthydemus, and Dionysodorus: a sophist knows how to persuade those who listen to him refute others in private conversations that he knows what the others do not, even though he may ironically recognize that he does not actually possess such knowledge. Socrates did not claim to teach virtue, nor did he demand a fee for doing so like other "sophists," but in his defense speech Socrates admitted that those who listened to him refute others in private concluded that he knew that about which he refuted the others—even if he, ironically, knew that he did not.

In the *Apology* Socrates replied to the Eleatic's implicit charge by publicly declaring that he does not know the most important things, particularly what is truly noble and good, about which he queried others. That is why he continued to seek knowledge by examining the opinions of others and urged his fellow Athenians to do the same. To declare that he is a sophist because he knows that those who listened to him refute others often drew a false conclusion is to maintain that neither his intentions nor his public statements of them are relevant to the character of his speeches and deeds.

The Eleatic does not insinuate (and he never impolitely declares) that Socrates is a sophist merely because listeners think he knows that about which he refutes the opinions of others, however. The Eleatic's implicit accusation that Socrates is a sophist, not a philosopher, rests on deeper and firmer grounds.

According to both Socrates and the Eleatic Stranger, philosophers dialectically sort and so come to know what kinds of beings there are, by showing how many things share in one trait, and how one thing can share in many traits, that is, how it differs from itself and other things in a variety of respects. But, the Eleatic intimates, Socrates does not practice the philosophical art of dialectics correctly. He sorts things hierarchically, according to whether they are good or bad, just or unjust, useful or useless; the Eleatic sorts things according to whether they are similar or different. By showing the individuals he refutes that they do not know what they think

they know, the Eleatic suggests, Socrates practices a noble form of sophis-
tics. Although Socrates is able to rid his interlocutors of the worst sort of
ignorance, his refutations remain a form of sophistry, because Socrates
cannot lead his interlocutors to knowledge. He cannot, because he does
not understand the way the basic *eidē*—being, rest, motion, sameness, and
difference—coexist.

Like other "friends of the forms" who draw a sharp line between the
unchanging intelligible ideas of things-in-themselves and sensible, changing things that are supposed to be mixtures, the Eleatic charges, Socrates
cannot show either how the sensible things participate in the intelligible
or how it is possible for the changeable minds of mortals to comprehend
the unchanging, perfectly intelligible beings. Because he sorts things according to whether they are the same or different, the Eleatic both shows
how motion and rest can coexist with being and how sensible things share
in the intelligible.

After his trial and conviction (as well as his two conversations with the
Eleatic), on the last day of his life Socrates admits that he cannot explain
how ever-changing sensible things share in the purely intelligible. By enabling him to explain how any particular sensible thing can share in several
different, even contradictory intelligible ideas, his hypothesis allows him to
say what things are, but not how sensible things come to share in the ideas
that make them intelligible to us. Socrates admits that his hypothesis is not
final or complete. He suggests that it may need to be explained by some
higher and better hypothesis (*Phaedo* 101d–e), but he does not indicate what
that hypothesis would be, for example, whether it would involve the idea
of the good as the cause of all. Nor does he provide a list of potential
ideas or suggest how they might be related to each other. It clear, however,
that he does not think that the *eidē* can coexist with or contain others, the
way Eleatic argues that the idea of being contains the ideas of both rest
and motion, even though rest and motion are mutually exclusive. Socrates
maintains that each idea exists "in itself."

Socrates does not object to the Eleatic's argument about the coexistence of the greatest *eidē* when he hears it. The criticism Socrates makes
of Anaxagoras in the *Phaedo* shows, however, that Socrates would not have
found the Eleatic's account of the intelligibility of the whole acceptable.
To show how mind is the cause of everything (and so that everything is
fundamentally intelligible), Socrates says, Anaxagoras would have had to
show why it is best for everything to be as it is. Anaxagoras did not, and

Socrates could not find anyone else who could provide such an explanation. Socrates does not explain why he thought it was necessary to show why it was best for everything to be as it is in order to demonstrate the intelligibility of the whole. But his reasons were probably as follows: if it cannot be shown that it is best for things to be as they are, they perhaps can and should be ordered in a different way. If things can be ordered in a different way, the present order is essentially accidental. Things might necessarily be as they are, but, as Timaeus shows, the necessary is not the same as the good or entirely orderly (and hence intelligible) in itself. But if things could be ordered better, they lack order in some essential sense as they are (because order itself is good). But if things lack order, they are not completely intelligible.

2. The Character and Limits of Human Knowledge

The Eleatic does not claim to have sorted, defined, and thus made intelligible everything. On the contrary, he expresses doubt (*Sophist* 233a) that any human being can know everything. It would seem that everything could, in principle, be defined by showing all the respects in which it is the same and different from all other forms of being, but that no mortal has enough time to do this for each and every thing. The Eleatic confines himself to showing how the greatest ideas coexist. It might still be possible for a series of mortals to define specific kinds of beings and areas of activity, and so for human beings to acquire more knowledge about more things over time. The Eleatic thinks he can show that it is possible for human beings to learn how to produce certain kinds of effects in certain areas of endeavor, that is, how to appear to be wise by refuting others (*sophistikē*), how to coordinate all the arts, breed, and inculcate the opinions necessary to preserve people in cities (*politikē*), and how to sort things into their kinds (*dialektikē*). According to the Eleatic, human beings can acquire particular kinds of knowledge, even if they do not possess knowledge of the whole. According to Socrates, human beings can only seek wisdom. Knowledge, properly speaking, can only be of the whole; to acquire such knowledge, one would have to be able to show why it is best for everything to be as it is.

Socrates would not find the Eleatic's arguments satisfying for two basic reasons. First, the Eleatic does not show, any more than Anaxagoras had, why it is best for everything to be as it is. He has not, therefore, shown how everything is in principle intelligible. Second, the kind of intelligible order the Eleatic finds in things does not respond to the concerns of human beings. What we want to know, above all, is what is truly good—first and foremost for us. Human beings are, admittedly, only a part of the whole. But, with regard to the search for knowledge, human beings are arguably the most important part of the whole, because humans are the only kinds of beings that seek and can even potentially possess it. And in the *Phaedo*, Socrates points out, human actions cannot be understood without regard to the intentions of the actors. Human actions cannot be understood, therefore, merely in terms of their externally observable effects. The Eleatic abstracts from both intention and passionate motivation in his accounts of sophistry, statesmanship, and philosophy. But if the Eleatic cannot explain human action, he cannot explain the whole or its intelligibility—partial or complete. Timaeus at least tried to show how the cosmos was constructed to be as good as possible, even if he had to admit that it was not entirely good or, therefore, entirely intelligible. Timaeus had not been able to account for the intense desire human beings have for what they believe is good, however. The Eleatic is even less able to do so. That is, the Eleatic has even less of the only kind of knowledge Socrates claimed to possess.[15] The Eleatic may be able to say what a philosopher is, but he cannot explain why anyone would want to engage in philosophical investigations. According to the Eleatic, a philosopher is an expert in dialectics; he is not necessarily virtuous or happy.

3. *Logos*

Because he could not find anyone who could explain why it was best for things to be as they are, Socrates tells his associates in the *Phaedo*, he took a different tack. Rather than investigate the beings themselves, he began looking at the *logoi*. But, the Eleatic intimates in the *Sophist*, Socrates was not able to give an account of *logos*, what it is or how it enables human beings to acquire knowledge.[16] If, as Socrates maintains, every idea exists

---

15. Socrates claims in the *Gorgias* to be the only person of his time in Athens even trying to practice the true political art (and so presumably at least to possess that art). In the *Theaetetus* he also claims to practice the art of intellectual midwifery. These claims might appear to qualify, if not simply to contradict, his earlier claims in the *Symposium* and *Phaedrus* that the only kind of knowledge he possesses is that of *ta erōtika*. In the *Symposium*, however, we have seen that Socrates learns about the need to examine his own opinions as well as the opinions of others from Diotima. He also learns that opinion constitutes the realm between knowledge and ignorance, and the place where the connection between the intelligible and sensible may be found. And Diotima convinces him, finally, that eros constitutes a desire for the beautiful and good, rather than something beautiful and good in itself. Socrates' "arts" are thus a part of his "erotic" knowledge.

16. From talking to Theodorus and his students on their way to meet Socrates, the Eleatic probably learned that Socrates had been unable to give an adequate account of *logos* the day before.

separately "in itself," the Eleatic suggests (*Sophist* 259e–60a) that all *logoi* would disappear. Our ability to decipher a variety of different kinds of things in the world and show how they are related to one another presupposes the kinds of intelligible distinctions among and the coexistence of the kinds of being that the Eleatic sketched in his argument about the coexistence of the greatest *eidē*. In other words, we are able to understand and describe the world because of the similarity between the structure or organization of our speech (*logos*) and the intelligible structure and organization of the beings.

Socrates had not maintained that "there is no mixing of anything with anything" (*Sophist* 260b), however. Both in his early reply to Zeno and in his final presentation of his hypothesis about the ideas in the *Phaedo*, Socrates observed that sensible things participate in a number of different, even contradictory, ideas. Like the Eleatic and unlike Parmenides, Socrates argues that being is differentiated. Socrates goes further than the Eleatic, indeed, by suggesting that there is no single idea of undifferentiated being that underlies and encompasses all others. If to be is to be intelligible, as Parmenides argued, there is no such thing as undifferentiated being, because undifferentiated being is unintelligible. The "unlimited" of which Socrates speaks in the *Philebus* corresponds to the essentially undefined flux of becoming, which becomes defined and thus intelligible only when it is combined with the "limited" forms. This combination must, moreover, have a cause. Socrates does not claim to know the cause, which would appear ultimately to be the idea of the good. Like Timaeus and the Eleatic he thus attributes the apparent intelligibility of the things in the cosmos to the work of a "god."

Socrates' characteristic "what is . . . ?" question indicates that he thinks it is possible for human beings to speak and reason without subscribing to the Eleatic's argument about the coexistence of the greatest *eidē*. On the contrary, Socrates argues in his third abortive attempt to say what *logos* might mean at the end of the *Theaetetus*, if knowledge requires showing how something differs from everything else, as the Eleatic suggests, knowledge is impossible. There are too many possible differences to take into account.

At first glance, Socrates and the Eleatic appear to have very similar, if not identical understandings of *logos*. Both describe *logos* as the "weaving together of names" (*Theaetetus* 202b; *Sophist* 262c). Both observe that names are composed of syllables, which are combinations of letters (*Theaetetus* 202d–5e; *Statesman* 278a–c). Both use children's learning of letters as a paradigm of human learning simply. Both suggest that human error arises from mistaken combinations of discrete elements, be they letters or numbers. Both also agree that the combination of letters or numbers may be correct in itself, but incorrectly applied to things. Because there is always a difference between the name used to signify a thing and the thing itself, people may use the wrong name to signify a thing. They may also not have a correct understanding of the characteristics of the thing named. To remedy such errors, both suggest, people need to analyze complex things down into their basic elements or *eidē* and then recombine them to give a correct account of the whole. Both philosophers thus point out the connection between the human ability to speak and reason, that is, between *logos* and *dianoia*.

The apparently slight differences in the two philosophers' descriptions of *logos* nevertheless point to much more significant differences about the basis and limits of human reason. In the *Theaetetus* Socrates begins by observing that the elements (*stoicheia*) of *logos* (which seem to include the units of which numbers are composed as well as letters) are themselves *aloga*. As constituent parts of the words used to describe the names that constitute a *logos*, these elements cannot themselves have a *logos*. They can only be named, that is, marked, and so distinguished from others. The Eleatic does not say anything about the apparently somewhat arbitrary isolation of certain sounds from others, which is a necessary precondition of speech. Nor does the Eleatic observe, as Socrates does in the *Philebus*, that these distinctions mark off and define certain parts of otherwise undifferentiated audible sound. The Eleatic apparently thinks that the distinction between the same and different he applies in sorting things will suffice to distinguish letters as well as words. More important, the Eleatic does not observe, as Socrates does, that the formation of syllables does not depend solely on the constituent letters or which letters will combine with others and which will not. The order of the component letters is also decisive. The syllable *OS* is not the same as the syllable *SO*. Socrates generalizes this observation to show that the whole is not merely the sum of its parts. To explain what a wagon is, he shows, it does not suffice merely to analyze it into its component parts and list them. To know how these parts go together and perform their function, one has to know the purpose, that is, what the combined product is good for. Socrates consistently maintains that all knowledge must be related finally to what is good.

As we have seen, the Eleatic does not take account of purposes, although he does speak of functions. In the case of words, as with the elements and the *eidē*, he simply observes that some elements or words can be put together to constitute compound wholes, whereas others, such as consonants with consonants or nouns with nouns, cannot. Even if the kinds of words can be put together, he further observes, the sentence will still be false if it makes an untrue claim about the character or powers of the subject. (His famous example is the perfectly good sentence in terms of its form, but nevertheless false: Theaetetus flies.) To explain the existence of false opinion, and thus sophistry, the Eleatic insists, pace his teacher Parmenides, that there is always a difference between the name and thing named. He thus recognizes two sources of error—mistakes in the constitution of the names or combinations of names in sentences, and ignorance of the powers of the things named. He does not distinguish between unintended errors and intentional lies; he does not take account of intention at all. He explains the existence of sophistry or false opinion on the basis of a fourfold categorization of things and their images, which resembles the lower part of the divided line Socrates draws in the *Republic*: Just as the god makes things in the world and reflections or images of them, in water, for example, so human beings fabricate artifacts and images of them, verbal as well as visual. These images or opinions are true or false depending on whether the image maker possesses knowledge of what he is depicting or talking about.

As we see in the *Republic* when Socrates says that the rulers of a just city will need to persuade their people of the truth of a "noble lie," Socrates does distinguish error and ignorance from intentional deception. As he clearly states in the *Phaedo*, he does not think that human actions can be accurately described or explained without taking account of the intentions of the people involved. People err unintentionally, but they deceive others intentionally. Even though Socrates recognizes that human beings do not always say what they truly think, he nevertheless turned from study of the beings (*ta onta*) to the *logoi* because he discovered that human beings cannot attain knowledge of the purely intelligible things directly by means of their reason (*nous*) or their senses (*aisthēseis*). Like the Eleatic, Socrates sees that the perception of types of things along with the consequent ability to name them, that is, *logos*, makes it possible for human beings to acquire some knowledge of the intelligible organization of the whole. Unlike the Eleatic, however, Socrates does not think that sorting things merely according to the ways in which they are similar and different will produce knowledge. Because things differ from each other in so many ways, the definitions so derived would be multiple and changing. That appears to be the reason the Eleatic tells young Socrates, once they have separated the statesman from everything else, they will have to stamp a single look on it (*dei gar autēn aneurein, kai chōris aphelontas apo tōn allōn idean autē[i] mian episphragisasthai; Statesman* 258c). The Eleatic tries to contain all the possible differences by demanding that things be divided down the middle, not merely in terms of what they are or are not, but according to how they are the same as well as different from others. But in the *Sophist* and *Statesman* Plato shows that the Eleatic is not able to maintain his method of bifurcation in all instances. The need to stamp a single idea onto the statesman is telling. All the *eidē* or intelligible divisions and definitions of things are not eternally unchanging, that is, always the same, according to this Eleatic. On the contrary, human beings impress the types or divisions they find onto things.

Although Socrates recognizes that *logos* enables human beings to acquire some knowledge of the purely intelligible beings by sorting things dialectically, he does not think that the structure of *logos* parallels the intelligible order of the whole. Nor would sorting things according to their sameness and difference be sufficient to produce knowledge. Perceiving that there is something between being and nothing (becoming), just as there is between knowledge and ignorance (opinion), Socrates does not merely examine the arguments (*logoi*) of others to see whether they are consistent with his hypothesis about the ideas. Some parts of the whole are perfectly intelligible and so eternally unchanging, but other parts are not. Because the whole is not completely intelligible, we cannot have complete knowledge of it. At most our *logos* enables us to acquire some knowledge of the perfectly intelligible ideas. As human beings, what we most want to know for the sake of living the best possible lives is what is truly beautiful and good. Socrates thus interrogates other people specifically about their opinions concerning the noble and good. Human beings will never be able to possess knowledge about everything; we can try, however, to learn as much as possible about the things that are most important to us. Following Parmenides in equating being with intelligibility, Socrates does not think that all forms of being participate equally in it. According to the Eleatic, the unjust has as much being as the just. According to Socrates, the ugly does not have as much being as the beautiful. Both the just and the beautiful are more intelligible, because they are more orderly than the unjust and ugly. As the Eleatic charges, Socrates understands things hierarchically, not only in terms of which kinds of intelligible being they participate in but also in terms of how orderly, intelligible, and thus good they are.

4. Knowledge and Politics

In the *Gorgias* Socrates claims to be the only person at his time in Athens even trying to practice the true political art. But in the *Statesman*, the Eleatic implicitly charges, Socrates does not understand what kinds of knowledge a statesman needs to order and preserve a city. A statesman does not need to learn dialectics or the "idea of the good" from which Socrates suggests all knowledge and being arise. A statesman needs to know how to coordinate all the arts necessary to establish and preserve a political association, especially the arts of the rhetorician, general, and judge. Above all, he needs to know how to blend courage and moderation in citizens by means of interbreeding, the inculcation of proper opinions, and the allocation of offices. It is not likely that someone with the requisite knowledge will ever come to power. Lacking such knowledge themselves, most people will not recognize it in another. They will, moreover, have learned the risks involved in giving someone unchecked power, from bitter experience with lawless rulers who used their power to enrich themselves. The people will thus listen to prudent rhetoricians who tell them to write down the customs and opinions that worked best in the past and to insist that anyone who comes to power follow these written instructions. Someone who knows what is best to do under specific circumstances will not agree to have his judgment subject to the opinions or laws of the ignorant, however. The rule of law is the best possible political result we can expect. By publicly questioning the opinions of the politicians, poets, and artisans, Socrates showed that he did not understand the limited power of knowledge in politics. As a result of this lack of understanding, he brought about his own trial and conviction. He did not understand that the rule of law is the best possible practical outcome, and that the rule of law cannot be maintained if private individuals openly question it.

In the *Apology*, I argued in chapter 10, Socrates responds to the Eleatic's veiled accusation that he undermines the rule of law by questioning the opinions of his contemporaries by pointing out that he is one of the most law-abiding citizens of Athens. In the *Crito* Socrates then suggests that the rule of law cannot be maintained merely by forbidding anyone to question its wisdom. If citizens are to obey the laws willingly, not merely from fear of punishment or death, the justice of the law needs to be demonstrated. The philosopher serves his city primarily by providing such a demonstration.

Socrates recognizes the limited role knowledge can play in politics just as well as the Eleatic. Socrates agrees with the Eleatic that most human beings will never be able to acquire the knowledge required to become a great or true statesman.[17] He does not agree, however, about what that knowledge is.

Like the Athenian Stranger, Socrates argues that the goal of politics is to make citizens as virtuous as possible. And to do this, he further agrees with the Athenian, it is necessary for rulers to know what virtue is. Cities are among the mortal things that cannot last forever. Like the Athenian, Socrates thus argues that making citizens virtuous is a more important goal than mere preservation. It is not rational for a human being to want to live forever or to expect something made by mortals to last. In the *Republic* Socrates initially suggests that philosophers will be able to impress the ideas of the virtues onto the souls of citizens by means of breeding, habituation, and legislation. But he also argues that philosophical natures possess all the virtues as a result of the strength of their desire for truth. The "virtues" inculcated in citizens are opinions and like bodily habits. True virtue consists in *phronēsis* (*Republic* 518d–e). By *phronēsis* Socrates does not mean the ability to know what to do to save the city under specific circumstances to which the Eleatic refers; Socrates refers to the kind of practical knowledge underlying and encompassing all the virtues that enables a person both to know and to do what is best and most just under all circumstances.[18] Socrates does not conclude that philosophers should rule, therefore, simply because they know the ideas. (In other dialogues such as the *Symposium*, Socrates explicitly admits that mortal philosophers cannot retain what knowledge they attain and must continue to strive to regain it; as in the *Republic* he argues that philosophers act virtuously as a result of their search for truth.)[19] According to Socrates, philosophers should rule because they know what virtue is, and they know what virtue is because they have self-knowledge. In the *Republic* Socrates finally argues that philosophers will make the only just rulers because they are the only human beings who cannot satisfy their own particular desires by means of

17. As I pointed out in chapter 10, n. 6, statesmen are rare.

18. By making *phronēsis* the ground and sum of all true virtue, Socrates comes close to Aristotle in *Nicomachean Ethics* 6.13.1144b1–1145a10. Unlike Aristotle, however, Socrates suggests that *phronēsis* includes, because it is grounded on, knowledge of the beings-in-themselves or "theoretical" wisdom. As I argued in chapter 9, the understanding of nature suggested by the Eleatic in his myth concerning the reversed motion of the cosmos would make it impossible for a philosopher to achieve the kind of knowledge Socrates suggests, in his famous image, that a person freed, turned around, and dragged up out of the cave to see things in the light of the sun would acquire.

19. Cf. Nightingale, *Spectacles*, 99.

rule. They may not know what is good in itself, but, like Socrates himself, they know what the best form of human life is. Because they cannot get what they really want by means of political power, they will rule not for their own sake but only for the common good. They will not seek rule, however, and they can justly be compelled to rule only by a community that provided them with the education they needed to become philosophers. But, Socrates agrees with the Eleatic, it is unlikely that the citizens of any actual city will compel a philosopher to rule. They will think that philosophers are useless "stargazers," if not sophists, who corrupt the young.

Socrates and the Eleatic agree that a ruler qua ruler cannot make his or her people truly virtuous. The most a ruler can do by means of laws and institutions is to inculcate virtuous opinions. Socrates and the Eleatic also agree that no people is apt to put a philosopher into power to shape, if not simply to control, what they think.

Socrates distinguishes himself most visibly from the other philosophers Plato depicts by remaining in Athens rather than traveling to other cities. He thus indicates in deed as well as in speech that he has a different understanding of the relation that should exist between a philosopher and the political community.

As "the laws" in the *Crito* point out, Socrates often suggested that the regimes of Crete or Sparta were better ordered than the democracy of Athens, but he stayed in Athens. The reason, we infer from the *Apology* and *Crito*, is that the laws of Athens allowed him to philosophize, whereas the laws of these "better-ordered" regimes would not.[20] Socrates did not think that Athenian democracy represented the best possible regime, because he thought the purpose of a political community was to make its citizens as virtuous as possible. No one wants the people with whom he associates to be corrupt, Socrates reminded Meletus. Everyone wants to be able to trust the people among whom they live and work, but people can only trust those they believe to be just. Insofar as democratic Athenian laws allowed everyone to do as they pleased, these laws made no attempt to improve the character of the citizens. The laws of better-ordered regimes constituted better, because closer, images of the best possible regime. But, Socrates also clearly indicates, even the laws of the best possible regime would not

20. In the *Republic* (557c–58c), Socrates goes so far as to argue that the freedom characteristic of a democracy allows all sorts of human beings to develop there. Democracies thus provide a kind of laboratory of types of regimes for a philosopher to observe. He does not need to travel.

make citizens truly virtuous. In the myth of Er at the end of the *Republic*, he suggests that a man raised in a good regime would choose to be a tyrant in his next life. Holding (or voicing) good opinions will not have made him want to be truly virtuous. Only later, in light of the horrible consequences, will he regret his choice.

Like the Athenian, Timaeus, and the Eleatic, Socrates recognizes that human beings do not have rational well-ordered souls by nature. Those who are not educated come into conflict. The question then becomes what sort of education enables human beings to rule themselves by means of their reason, rather than continue to act and fight on the basis of their desires and irrational anger. As the Athenian observes in the *Laws* (666e), traditional forms of ancient Greek education treated young people in "herds" by giving them the same instruction in music and gymnastics. The laws of Crete and Sparta mandated certain practices and institutions that required potential leaders to learn how to master their fear of death and sensual desires and so to become courageous and moderate, but these laws did not and could not make future rulers either wise or just.

Because human beings are not blank slates upon which rulers or educators can draw whatever shapes they desire, Socrates suggests in the *Gorgias*, human education must be remedial rather than simply formative.[21] Before Callicles seeks to determine the course of public affairs, he needs to learn how to control himself. Self-control can only be acquired, however, in private on an individual level. To learn what to attain as well as how to attain what a person really wants, Socrates tells politically ambitious young Athenians like Alcibiades, Lysis, Clinias, and Callicles, it is necessary to examine one's own opinions and desires in conversation with another. It is possible to force people to act against their desires and to shame them into saying what they do not truly think or wish, but it is possible to change their desires only by changing what they believe is truly good. Because he

---

21. Like Socrates in the *Republic*, the Athenian and the Eleatic both recognize that all human beings cannot be made to act in virtuous ways, much less themselves to be virtuous, when they argue that the first act a legislator or statesman must undertake is a purge of the population. As the Athenian explicitly observes, such purges are extremely difficult to execute with the consent of the population. The most convenient and possible form would be to send a colony of potentially disruptive people abroad. Socrates' suggestion that the rulers expel everyone over ten years of age is one of the major reasons he admits that his city in speech is unlikely to be actualized. According to Timaeus, all human souls become disorderly when they are joined to bodies, that is, all human beings are disorderly by nature, and have to be educated or ruled by people who have reacquired order in their own souls by learning how to contemplate the intelligible movements of the heavenly bodies.

is the only person in Athens who conducts such examinations, Socrates claims to be the only person even trying to practice the true political art.

III. Plato's Presentation of Socrates

By showing the way in which Socrates examined the opinions of other individuals, especially about the noble and good, in private in Athens, Plato self-consciously and intentionally presented a new form of education—political as well as philosophical. Socrates did not attempt to reform his associates by means of legislation. On the contrary, he showed why such attempts would never truly work. Plato admitted that Socrates did not convince, much less reform, most of the individuals to whom he spoke. Socrates nevertheless demonstrated, both in deed and in speech, how a human being could become truly virtuous.[22]

As he emphasizes in the *Apology*, Socrates devoted his life first and foremost to his philosophical investigations. But unlike the philosopher by the same name in Aristophanes' comedy, Plato's Socrates did not forget that he was a human being or mortal. On the contrary, he recognized that he was a man as well as a citizen by having a family (and generating future citizens). He also served in the military and participated in public debates when required by law to do so. He clearly subordinated these more general obligations to his higher calling, but he did not deny their importance or refuse to fulfill these lesser duties.[23] As he explains in both the *Republic* and the *Apology*, he did not go into the assembly and try to change the laws or government of Athens, because he did not think he could do so and survive. Recognizing that he would soon die in any case, he did attempt at the end of his life to effect two and only two changes in the laws of Athens (as well as those of other cities). The first and narrowest change he proposed was that his city not make decisions in capital cases in a single day. Serious decisions should be made as dispassionately as possible. The

22. At the end of the *Phaedo* (116c, 118a), Plato thus has not only Socrates' regular associate, Phaedo, but also the jailor, an ordinary citizen charged with retaining and administering punishment to the prisoner, testify that Socrates is the best man he has ever met. Whereas Phaedo states that Socrates was wisest and most just as well as best, the jailor characterizes him as most noble and gentle.

23. Cf. Euben, *Platonic Noise*, 159–60: "In this, the final moment of his life, Socrates becomes again a citizen among citizens, a man with a body, attached to family, friends, and the city he has always refused to leave. In these terms, he heals the rift between philosophy as he had practiced it and as he had described it in the *Apology*. But healing does not mean that the tension between philosophy and politics is erased. How could it be, given the circumstances?"

laws should thus seek to give judges time to deliberate, to reconsider their first impressions, and to allow their passions to cool.[24] Second, and much more broadly, Socrates sought to convince Athens (as Plato sought to convince other cities, more generally, by means of his writing) not to outlaw philosophy.

As presented by Plato, Socratic philosophy did not challenge or undermine the rule of law. On the contrary, Plato shows that Socratic examinations were designed to lead politically ambitious young men to see why they needed to take account of the necessities and desires of others, that is, to be just. Socratic examinations demonstrably did not always have the beneficent effects desired. The conversations Socrates held about virtue were not a substitute for legal regulation. Most people would need to have their passions regulated by the law most of the time. In order for just laws to be established and maintained, however, some people would need to understand the reasons for them. Insofar as Socrates' conversations led his interlocutors to understand why their own passions needed to be restrained or redirected, these conversations represented a necessary support for and supplement to the rule of law. Socrates himself emphasized that examinations of the opinions of his interlocutors, which he conducted, would have to be repeated many times in order to work. Because individuals must be willing to cooperate in their own "correction" and education, Socratic conversations could not be forced or enforced. Unlike the Nocturnal Council, the Athenian suggests, the ongoing conversations that Plato shows Socrates conducting, and that Plato himself later institutionalized in his Academy, did not have public support or sponsorship. They would not have worked as desired, if they did. People can be forced to say what they do not believe or act as they do not desire by fear of death, shame, or hope for reward, but they cannot be forced to think or desire what they do not. They can be swayed by effective public speakers, at least for a time, but they cannot be convinced to change their minds or the objects of their desire unless they are led to reflect on their opinions and desires. They have to be brought to see that they will be working against themselves so long as they hold contradictory opinions and that some of the goals they now seek are impossible to attain. Both the controversial character and the urgency of making some decision make it almost impossible to engage

24. The Athenian also makes such a recommendation. Suggested improvements in existing laws presuppose knowledge of the ways in which things are done elsewhere—a knowledge available to citizens (or visitors) of a commercial regime such as Athens but not available to legislators of other regimes, unless they traveled, as Timaeus and the Eleatic did.

in such reflections in public. Individuals have to be freed from pressures to conform to the opinions of others, if they are to determine what they truly think. As Socrates recognized, such reflections can take place only in private in the company of another person, who will ask the questions his interlocutor might be tempted to avoid if he were entirely alone.

As Plato suggests in the *Menexenus*, a philosopher might also try to affect the opinions of his fellow citizens by offering a reinterpretation of their common history. He could retell the story of the founding and progressive development of the polity in terms of the requirements of justice, rather than merely as the way they attained peace, prosperity, and power. As the humorous cast of the dialogue indicates, however, Plato did not think that philosophers should expect much success by adopting this mode of public education. Socratic examinations of the opinions individuals hold about the noble and good are admittedly limited in power, both in their scope and their effect. In the dialogues, Plato nevertheless shows, they are the only truly effective means of education—public or private.

As Hannah Arendt emphasizes, Socratic examinations always remained within the realm of opinion. Attempting to draw a hard and fast line between Socrates and Plato, however, Arendt does not acknowledge that Socrates saw the realm of opinion as between and thus bounded by knowledge of the purely intelligible beings, of which we have at least a glimmer, and that which is not known at all.[25] It is important, in other words, to see Plato's Socrates as a philosopher who had a particular, defined way of understanding and thus approaching things as well as people. In the *Apology* Socrates presents himself as an exemplary citizen, but he never presents himself simply as such.[26] It is a mistake, therefore, to see him or to regard his interrogations of others as serving a primarily negative or critical function.[27] Socrates interrogated individuals about their opinions concerning

25. Arendt, "Philosophy and Politics," 81. Like her mentor Heidegger, Arendt thinks Plato initiated the attempt to impose a rational order on the world.

26. See, e.g., Villa, *Socratic Citizenship*. In advocating a return to a Socratic understanding of philosophy as a way of life, Pierre Hadot goes to the other extreme, however, by suggesting that Socrates' relation to the public was largely hostile because the goals of the philosopher were radically opposed to those most people seek. See Hadot, *Philosophy as a Way of Life*, trans. Michael Chase (Oxford: Blackwell, 1995), 104.

27. Søren Kierkegaard gives the most powerful statement of this essentially negative view of Socrates in his dissertation, published as *The Concept of Irony*, trans. Howard V. Hong and Edna H. Hong (Princeton: Princeton University Press, 1989). In his *Philosophical Fragments*, Kierkegaard (or his pseudonymous Johannes Climacus) modifies his view of Socrates to emphasize the way in which his lack of knowledge led him to seek the company of others in his search for wisdom. Kierkegaard contrasts the love or desire represented by this seeker with the overflowing of wisdom

the noble and good in order to convince them, as well as those sometimes listening, that they ought to join him in an ongoing investigation of what is truly noble and good. He did not expect to persuade all or even most other people of his own opinions. He did not even hope to persuade most of those he refuted or the young people who listened to him to join him in further inquiry. He did claim that the conversations in which he engaged were not unpleasant, and that those individuals with the requisite intellectual ability who joined him in seeking the truth above all else would acquire all the virtues, if they engaged wholeheartedly in the search. Socrates recognized that there was an irreducible element of chance in human affairs (*Euthydemus* 279c–d), but, "the gods willing," he promised that those who joined him in a life of philosophy would be happy.

By making Socrates his chief philosophical protagonist, Plato not merely dramatized the best form of human existence as he understood it. By contrasting Socrates with other philosophers, Plato also indicated why philosophy will always remain a search for wisdom rather than the possession of knowledge. Human beings cannot claim knowledge, properly speaking, unless they can give an account of the whole. To explain the order of the whole, they would have to give an account of the relation between the purely intelligible kinds of being and their sensible manifestations that does not negate the distinctions. They would have to explain the difference and the relation between human intentional action and the repetitive, if not random, motions to be found in the cosmos. And as part of that explanation, they would have to show how the distinctively human faculty of *logos* enables us to perceive and describe the relation between purely intelligible and sensible forms of being. Plato did not think that mortals could give such a comprehensive account of the intelligibility of the universe, although he was also convinced that they should not cease trying. Beginning with Plato's own student Aristotle, later philosophers thought that they could. Their comprehensive accounts have not proved satisfactory to their successors, however. As a result, thoughtful individuals in the twenty-first century face many of the same, if not the very same problems Socrates did.

In his presentation of Socrates in contrast to the other philosophers, Plato not only brings out these fundamental problems. He also indicates the direction in which human beings need to move. We may never be

---

and love of "the god." In his depiction of Zarathustra, Friedrich Nietzsche contrasts with previous philosophers this vision of a "knower" who overflows.

able to obtain knowledge, properly speaking, but we can learn something about the limitations of our power and, consequently, how we should restrict our ambitions to command others—much less to conquer the world, or to remake it entirely—by seeking knowledge. We may never be able to understand, much less give order to the universe, but we can learn what we mortals most want and seek knowledge of that. The Socratic demand that human beings seek self-knowledge, first and foremost, remains, ironically, as radical in the twenty-first century as it was when he made it.

Bibliography

Ackrill, J. L. "*Anamnesis* in the *Phaedo*: Remarks on 73c–75c." *Phronesis*, supp. 1 (1973): 177–95.

Adam, J., ed. *Plato: Crito*. Cambridge: Cambridge University Press, 1888.

Ahrensdorf, Peter J. *The Death of Socrates and the Life of Philosophy*. Albany: SUNY Press, 1995.

Alfarabi's "Philosophy of Plato and Aristotle." Trans. Muhsin Mahdi. Glencoe, IL: Free Press, 1962.

Allan, D. J. "The Problem of *Cratylus*." *American Journal of Philology* 75 (1954): 271–87.

Allen, Danielle S. *The World of Prometheus: The Politics of Punishing in Democratic Athens*. Princeton: Princeton University Press, 2000.

Allen, R. E., trans. and with commentary. *Plato: "Ion," "Hippias Minor," "Laches," "Protagoras."* In *The Dialogues of Plato*, vol. 3. New Haven: Yale University Press, 1996.

———, trans. and with commentary. "Plato's *Menexenus*." In *The Dialogues of Plato*, vol. 1. New Haven: Yale University Press, 1985.

———, trans. and with commentary. *Plato's "Parmenides."* In *The Dialogues of Plato*, vol. 4. New Haven: Yale University Press, 1997.

———. *Socrates and Legal Obligation*. Minneapolis: University of Minnesota Press, 1980.

———, ed. *Studies in Plato's Metaphysics*. New York: Humanities Press, 1965.

Anagnostopoulos, Georgios. "The Significance of Plato's *Cratylus*." *Review of Metaphysics* 27 (December 1973): 318–45.

Andic, Martin. "Inquiry and Virtue in the *Meno*." In *Plato's "Meno,"* ed. Malcolm Brown, 262–314. Indianapolis: Bobbs-Merrill, 1971.

Annas, Julia. *An Introduction to Plato's "Republic."* Oxford: Clarendon Press, 1981.

———. "Knowledge and Language: The *Theaetetus* and the *Cratylus*." In *Language and Logos*, ed. Malcolm Schofield and Martha Craven Nussbaum, 95–114. Cambridge: Cambridge University Press, 1982.

———. "Self-Knowledge in Early Plato." In *Platonic Investigations*, ed. Dominic J. O'Meara, 111–38. Washington, DC: Catholic University of America Press, 1985.

Annas, Julia, and Christopher Rowe, eds. *New Perspectives on Plato, Modern and Ancient*. Cambridge: Harvard University Press, 2002.

Arendt, Hannah. *The Human Condition*. Chicago: University of Chicago Press, 1958.

———. "Philosophy and Politics." *Social Research* 57, no. 1 (Spring 1990): 73–103.

———. "Thinking and Moral Considerations." *Social Research* 38 (1971): 417–46.

Arieti, James. *Interpreting Plato: The Dialogues as Drama*. Savage, MD: Rowman and Littlefield, 1991.

Arnim, Hans von. *Platos Jugenddialoge und die Entstehungzeit des Phaidros*. Leipzig: G. B. Teubner, 1914; repr., Amsterdam: A. M. Hakkert, 1967.

Ausland, Hayden. "La 'seconde navigation' dans la philosophie politique de Platon." *Revue Française d'Histoire des Idées Politiques* 16 (2002): 275–93.

———. "Who Speaks for Whom in the *Timaeus-Critias*?" In *Who Speaks for Plato*? ed. Gerald A. Press, 183–98. Lanham, MD: Rowman and Littlefield, 2000.

Bacon, Helen. "Socrates Crowned." *Virginia Quarterly Review* 35 (1959): 418–20.

Barker, Ernest. *Greek Political Theory: Plato and His Predecessors.* London: Methuen, 1918.

Barnes, Jonathan, trans. and ed. "Parmenides." In *Early Greek Philosophy.* Harmondsworth, UK: Penguin Books, 1987.

Barney, Rachel. *Names and Nature in Plato's "Cratylus."* New York: Routledge, 2001.

Bartlett, Robert. "Political Philosophy and Sophistry: An Introduction to Plato's *Protagoras.*" *American Journal of Political Science* 47, no. 4 (October 2003): 612–24.

———. "Socratic Political Philosophy and the Problem of Virtue." *American Political Science Review* 96, no. 3 (September 2002): 525–33.

Bartoli, Giovanni. *Essai sur l'explication historique que Platon a donnée de sa République et de son Atlantide et qu'on n'a pas considerée jusqu'à maintenant.* Stockholm, 1779.

Baxter, Timothy M. S. *The "Cratylus": Plato's Critique of Naming.* Leiden: E. J. Brill, 1992.

Belfiore, Elizabeth. "Wine and Catharsis of the Emotions in Plato's *Laws.*" *Classical Quarterly* 36, no. 2 (1986): 421–37.

Benardete, Seth. *The Argument of the Action: Essays on Greek Poetry and Philosophy.* Chicago: University of Chicago Press, 2000.

———. *The Being of the Beautiful: Plato's "Theaetetus," "Sophist," and "Statesman."* Translation and commentary. Chicago: University of Chicago Press, 1984.

———. "On Interpreting Plato's *Charmides.*" *Graduate Faculty Philosophy Journal* 11, no. 2 (1986): 9–36.

———. "On Plato's *Lysis.*" In *The Argument of the Action: Essays on Greek Poetry and Philosophy*, 198–229. Chicago: University of Chicago Press, 2000.

———. "On Plato's *Phaedo.*" In *Argument of the Action: Essays on Greek Poetry and Philosophy*, 277–96. Chicago: University of Chicago Press, 2000.

———. *On Plato's "Symposium."* Munich: Carl Friedrich von Siemens Stiftung, 1993.

———. "On Plato's *Timaeus* and Timaeus's Science Fiction." *Interpretation* 2, no. 2 (1971): 21–63.

———. "Physics and Tragedy: On Plato's *Cratylus.*" In *Argument of the Action: Essays on Greek Poetry and Philosophy*, 146–66. Chicago: University of Chicago Press, 2000.

———. *Plato's "Laws": The Discovery of Being.* Chicago: University of Chicago Press, 2000.

———. *Plato's "Statesman."* Chicago: University of Chicago Press, 1984.

———. "Plato's *Theaetetus*: On the Way of the Logos." In *The Argument of the Action: Essays on Greek Poetry and Philosophy*, 297–321. Chicago: University of Chicago Press, 2000.

———. *The Rhetoric of Morality and Philosophy: Plato's "Gorgias" and "Phaedrus."* Chicago: University of Chicago Press, 1991.

———. *Socrates' Second Sailing.* Chicago: University of Chicago Press, 1989.

———. *Theaetetus.* Chicago: University of Chicago Press, 1986.

———. *The Tragedy and Comedy of Life: Plato's "Philebus."* Chicago: University of Chicago Press, 1993.

Benson, Hugh H. "A Note on Socrates' Self-Knowledge in the *Charmides.*" *Ancient Philosophy* 23 (2003): 31–48.

Billings, Grace Hadley. *The Art of Transition in Plato.* Menasha, WI: George Banta, 1920.

Black, John A. *The Four Elements in Plato's "Timaeus."* Lewiston, NY: Edwin Mellen Press, 2000.

Blits, Jan. "The Holy and the Human: An Interpretation of Plato's *Euthyphro.*" *Apeiron* 14 (1980): 19–40.

Blitz, Mark. "An Introduction to the Reading of Plato's *Laches.*" *Interpretation* 5, no. 2 (Winter 1975): 185–225.

———. "Plato's *Alcibiades I.*" *Interpretation* 22, no. 3 (Spring 1995): 339–58.

Block, Enid. "Hemlock Poisoning and the Death of Socrates." In *The Trial and Execution of Socrates: Sources and Controversies*, ed. Thomas C. Brickhouse and Nicholas D. Smith, 255–78. New York: Oxford University Press, 2002.

Blondell, Ruby. *The Play of Character in Plato's Dialogues*. Cambridge: Cambridge University Press, 2002.

Bloom, Allan. "An Interpretation of Plato's *Ion*." In *The Roots of Political Philosophy*, ed. Thomas L. Pangle, 371–95. Ithaca: Cornell University Press, 1987.

———. "Interpretive Essay." In *The "Republic" of Plato*. New York: Basic Books, 1968.

———. *Love and Friendship*. New York: Simon and Schuster, 1993.

———. *The "Republic" of Plato*. New York: Basic Books, 1968.

Bluck, R. S. H. *Plato's "Sophist."* Oxford: Clarendon Press, 1971.

Blundell, Mary Whitlock. "Character and Meaning in Plato's *Lesser Hippias*." Oxford Studies in Ancient Philosophy supp. Oxford: Clarendon Press, 1992.

Bobonich, Christopher. *Plato's Utopia Recast: His Later Ethics and Politics*. Oxford: Clarendon Press, 2002.

Bolotin, David. "The Life of Philosophy and the Immortality of the Soul: An Introduction to Plato's *Phaedo*." *Ancient Philosophy* 7 (1987): 39–55.

———. *Plato's Dialogue on Friendship*. Ithaca: Cornell University Press, 1979.

Bolton, Robert. "Plato's Discovery of Metaphysics: The New *Methodos* of the *Phaedo*." In *Method in Ancient Philosophy*, ed. Jyl Gentzler, 91–111. Oxford: Clarendon Press, 1998.

Bonitz, Hermann. "Zur Erklärung Platonischer Dialoge." *Hermes* 5 (1871): 413–42.

Bostock, David. *Plato's "Phaedo."* Oxford: Clarendon Press, 1986.

———. *Plato's "Theaetetus."* Oxford: Clarendon Press, 1988.

Brague, Remi. "The Body of the Speech: A New Hypothesis on the Compositional Structure of Timaeus' Monologue." In *Platonic Investigations*, ed. Dominic J. O'Meara, 53–83. Washington, DC: Catholic University of America Press, 1985.

Brandwood, Leonard. *The Chronology of Plato's Dialogues*. Cambridge: Cambridge University Press, 1990.

Brann, Eva. "The Music of the Republic." *St. John's Review* 39, nos. 1 and 2 (1989–90): 1–103.

———. "The Offense of Socrates: A Re-Reading of Plato's *Apology*." *Interpretation* 7 (May 1978): 1–21.

Brann, Eva, Peter Kalkavage, and Eric Salem, trans. with commentary. *Plato's "Phaedo."* Newburyport, MA: R. Pullins, 1998.

Brickhouse, Thomas C., and Nicholas D. Smith. "The Origin of Socrates' Mission." *Journal of the History of Ideas* 44, no. 4 (1983): 657–66.

———. "The Paradox of Socratic Ignorance in Plato's *Apology*." *History of Philosophy Quarterly* 1, no. 2 (1984): 125–31.

———. *Plato and the Trial of Socrates*. London: Routledge, 2004.

———. *Socrates on Trial*. Princeton: Princeton University Press, 1989.

Brisson, Luc. "De la philosophie politique l'épopée: Le *Critias* de Platon." *Revue de Metaphysique et de Morale* 75, no. 4 (October–December 1970): 402–38.

Brown, Malcolm. "Plato Disapproves of the Slave Boy's Answer." *Review of Metaphysics* 20 (1967): 57–93.

———, ed. *Plato's "Meno."* Indianapolis: Bobbs-Merrill, 1971.

Bruell, Christopher. *On the Socratic Education*. Lanham, MD: Rowman and Littlefield, 1999.

———. "Socratic Politics and Self-Knowledge: An Interpretation of Plato's *Charmides*." *Interpretation* 6, no. 3 (1977): 141–203.

Brumbaugh, Robert. "A Note on the Numbers in Plato's *Critias*." *Classical Philology* 43 (1948): 40–42.

———. *Plato on the One: The Hypotheses in the "Parmenides."* New Haven: Yale University Press, 1961.

———. "Plato's *Meno* as Form and Content of Secondary School Courses in Philosophy." *Teaching Philosophy* 1–2 (1975): 107–15.

Brunt, P. A. "The Model City in Plato's Laws." In *Studies in Greek History and Thought*, 245–81. Oxford: Clarendon Press, 1993.

Burger, Ronna. *The "Phaedo": A Platonic Labyrinth*. New Haven: Yale University Press, 1984.

———. *Plato's "Phaedrus": A Defense of a Philosophic Art of Writing*. University: University of Alabama Press, 1980.

Burkert, Walter. *Lore and Science in Ancient Pythagoreanism*. Trans. Edwin L. Minar, Jr. Cambridge: Harvard University Press, 1972.

———. *Weisheit und Wissenschaft: Studien zu Pythagoras, Philolaus, und Platon*. Nuremberg: Hans Tarl, 1962.

Burnet, John. *Early Greek Philosophy*. London: Adam and Charles Black, 1892.

———, ed. *Platonis Opera*. Vols. 1–5. Oxford: Clarendon Press, 1901–3.

———. *Plato's "Euthyphro," "Apology of Socrates," and "Crito."* Oxford: Oxford University Press, 1924.

Burnyeat, Myles F. "First Words: A Valedictory Lecture." *Proceedings of the Cambridge Philological Society* 43 (1997): 1–20.

———. "The Material and Sources of Plato's Dream." *Phronesis* 15 (1970): 101–22.

———. "The Philosophical Sense of Theaetetus' Mathematics." *ISIS* 69, no. 249 (1978): 489–513.

———. "Socratic Midwifery, Platonic Inspiration." *Bulletin of Classical Studies* 24 (1977): 7–16.

———. *The "Theaetetus" of Plato*. Indianapolis: Hackett, 1990.

Bury, J. B. *A History of Greece*. New York: Modern Library, 1913.

Bury, R. G., trans. *Laws*. Loeb ed. Cambridge: Harvard University Press, 1926.

———. "Plato and History." *Classical Quarterly* 45 (1951): 86–93.

———. *The "Symposium" of Plato*. Cambridge: Cambridge University Press, 1966.

Callahan, J. H. "Dialectic, Myth and History in the Philosophy of Plato." Special issue, "Interpretations of Plato," ed. Helen North. *Mnemosyne* (1977): 64–85.

Calvert, Brian. "Meno's Paradox Reconsidered." *Journal of the History of Philosophy* 12 (1974): 99–104.

Calvo, Tomas, and Luc Brisson, eds. *Interpreting the "Timaeus-Critias": Proceedings of the Fourth Symposium Platonicum*. Sankt Augustin: Academia Verlag, 1997.

Chance, Thomas. *Plato's "Euthydemus": Analysis of What Is and Is Not Philosophy*. Berkeley: University of California Press, 1992.

Cherniss, Harold. *Aristotle's Criticism of Plato and the Academy*. Vol. 1. Baltimore: Johns Hopkins University Press, 1944.

———. *The Riddle of the Early Academy*. Berkeley: University of California Press, 1945.

Clark, Pamela M. "A Cock to Asclepius." *Classical Review*, n.s., 2, no. 3–4 (1952): 146–48.

Clavaud, Robert. *Le "Ménexène" de Platon et la rhétorique de son temps*. Paris: Belles Lettres, 1980.

Clay, Diskin. "The Plan of Plato's *Critias*." In *Interpreting the "Timaeus-Critias": Proceedings of the Fourth Symposium Platonicum*, ed. Tomas Calvo and Luc Brisson, 49–54. Sankt Augustin: Academia Verlag, 1997.

———. *Platonic Questions: Dialogues with the Silent Philosopher*. University Park: Pennsylvania State University Press, 2000.

Coby, Patrick. *Socrates and the Sophistic Enlightenment: A Commentary on Plato's "Protagoras."* Lewisburg, PA: Bucknell University Press, 1987.

Cohen, David. "Law, Autonomy, and Political Community in Plato's *Laws*." *Classical Philology* 88 (1993): 301–17.

Collins, Susan, and Devin Stauffer. "The Challenge of Plato's *Menexenus*." *Review of Politics* 61 (Winter 1999): 85–115.

———. *Empire and the Ends of Politics*. Newburyport, MA: Focus Publishing, 1999.

Congleton, Ann. "Two Kinds of Lawlessness." *Political Theory* 2, no. 4 (November 1974): 432–46.

Cooper, John M., ed. *Plato: The Complete Works*. Indianapolis: Hackett, 1997.

———. "Plato's *Statesman* and Politics." In *Proceedings of the Boston Area Colloquium in Ancient Philosophy*, ed. John J. Cleary and Gary M. Gurtler, 71–103. Lanham, MD: Rowman and Littlefield, 1997.

Corey, David. "Socratic Piety." *Review of Politics* 67, no. 2 (2005): 201–28.

Cornford, Francis M. "Anamnesis." In *Plato's "Meno,"* ed. Malcolm Brown, 124–35. Indianapolis: Bobbs-Merrill, 1971.

———. *Plato and Parmenides*. London: Routledge and Kegan Paul, 1939.

————. *Plato's Cosmology: The "Timaeus" of Plato*. London: Routledge and Kegan, 1937.

————. *Plato's Theory of Knowledge*. London: Routledge and Kegan Paul, 1939.

Craig, Leon. *The War-Lover: A Study of Plato's "Republic."* Toronto: University of Toronto Press, 1994.

Cropsey, Joseph. "On Pleasure and the Human Good: Plato's *Philebus*." *Interpretation* 16, no. 2 (Winter 1988–89): 167–92.

————. "Plato's *Phaedrus* and Plato's Socrates." In *Political Philosophy and the Issues of Politics*, 231–51. Chicago: University of Chicago Press, 1977.

————. *Plato's World*. Chicago: University of Chicago Press, 1995.

————. "The Whole as Setting for Man: On Plato's *Timaeus*." *Interpretation* 17, no. 2 (Winter 1989–90): 165–91.

Davidson, Donald. *Plato's "Philebus."* New York: Garland, 1990.

Davis, Michael. *Aristotle's "Poetics."* Lanham, MD: Rowman and Littlefield, 1992.

————. *The Autobiography of Philosophy*. Lanham, MD: Rowman and Littlefield, 1999.

————. "Philosophy and the Perfect Tense: On the Beginning of Plato's *Lovers*." *Graduate Faculty Philosophy Journal* 10, no. 2 (1980): 75–97.

————. "Socrates' Pre-Socratism: Some Remarks on the Structure of Plato's *Phaedo*." *Review of Metaphysics* 33 (March 1980): 559–77.

Denyer, Nicholas. *Plato: Alcibiades I*. Cambridge: Cambridge University Press, 2001.

Derrida, Jacques. *The Ear of the Other*. Ed. Christie V. McDonald. New York: Schocken Books, 1985.

————. *Edmund Husserl's "Origins of Geometry."* Trans. John Leavey, Jr. Stony Brook, NY: Nicolas Hays, Ltd., 1978.

————. *"Khora," On the Name*. Trans. David Wood. Stanford: Stanford University Press, 1995.

————. *Of Grammatology*. Trans. Gayatri Spivak. Baltimore: Johns Hopkins University Press, 1976.

————. *Otobiographies: L'enseignement de Nietzsche et la politique du nom propre*. Paris: Galilée, 1984.

————. "La pharmacie de Platon." In *La dissemination*. Paris: Seuil, 1972. Translated by Barbara Johnson as "Plato's Pharmacy," in *Dissemination*. Chicago: University of Chicago Press, 1981.

————. *The Postcard*. Trans. Alan Bass. Chicago: University of Chicago Press, 1987.

Desjardins, Rosemary. *The Rational Enterprise: Logos in Plato's "Theaetetus."* Albany: SUNY, 1990.

Des Places, Edouard. *Études platoniciennes*. Leiden: E. J. Brill, 1981.

Devereux, Daniel. "Courage and Wisdom in Plato's *Laches*." *Journal of the History of Philosophy* 15 (1977): 129–41.

Diogenes Laertius. *Lives of Eminent Philosophers*. Trans. R. D. Hicks. Cambridge: Harvard University Press, 1925.

Dobbs, Darrell. "For Lack of Wisdom: Courage and Inquiry in Plato's *Laches*." *Journal of Politics* 48 (1986): 825–40.

Dodds, E. R. *Plato "Gorgias."* Oxford: Clarendon Press, 1959.

Dönt, E. "Bemerkungen zu Phaidros 249 und Nomoi 897." *Hermes* 96 (1968): 369–71.

Dorter, Kenneth. *Form and Good in Plato's Eleatic Dialogues*. Berkeley: University of California Press, 1994.

————. "Imagery and Philosophy in Plato's *Phaedrus*." *Journal of the History of Philosophy* 9 (1971): 279–88.

————. "'One, Two, Three, but Where Is the Fourth?' Incomplete Mediation in the *Timaeus*." In *Politics, Philosophy, Writing: Plato's Art of Caring for the Souls*, ed. Zdravko Planinc. Columbia: University of Missouri Press, 2001.

————. *Plato's "Phaedo": An Interpretation*. Toronto: University of Toronto Press, 1982.

————. *The Transformation of Plato's "Republic."* Lanham, MD: Rowman and Littlefield, 2006.

Dover, Kenneth. *Lysias and the Corpus Lysiacum*. Berkeley: University of California Press, 1968.

Dusanic, Slobodan. "The Laws and the Foreign Policy of Eubulus' Athens." In *Plato's "Laws" and Its Historical Significance*, ed. Francisco L. Lisi, 227–39. Sankt Augustin: Academia Verlag, 2001.

Eckstein, Jerome. *The Platonic Method: An Interpretation of the Dramatic-Philosophic Aspects of the "Meno."* New York: Greenwood Publishing, 1968.

England, E. B. *The "Laws" of Plato*. Manchester: Manchester University Press, 1921.

Euben, J. Peter. *Corrupting Youth: Political Education, Democratic Culture, and Political Theory*. Princeton: Princeton University Press, 1997.

———. "Philosophy and Politics in Plato's *Crito*." *Political Theory* 6, no. 2 (May 1978): 149–72.

———. *Platonic Noise*. Princeton: Princeton University Press, 2003.

Everson, S. "The Incoherence of Thrasymachus." *Oxford Studies in Ancient Philosophy* 16 (1998): 99–131.

Ferrari, G. R. F. *City and Soul in Plato's "Republic."* Chicago: University of Chicago Press, 2005.

———. *Listening to the Cicadas: A Study of Plato's "Phaedrus."* Cambridge: Cambridge University Press, 1987.

Fine, Gail. "Inquiry in the *Meno*." In *Cambridge Companion to Plato*, ed. Richard Kraut, 220–26. Cambridge: Cambridge University Press, 1992.

Forde, Steven. "On the *Alcibiades I*." In *The Roots of Political Philosophy*, ed. Thomas L. Pangle, 222–39. Ithaca: Cornell University Press, 1987.

Fowler, David. *The Mathematics of Plato's Academy*. Oxford: Clarendon Press, 1999.

Fowler, H. N., trans. *Cratylus*. Loeb ed. Cambridge: Harvard University Press, 1953.

Frank, Erich. *Plato und die Sogenannten Pythagoreer*. Halle: Niemeyer, 1923.

Frede, Dorothea. "Disintegration and Restoration: Pleasure and Pain in Plato's *Philebus*." In *Cambridge Companion to Plato*, ed. Richard Kraut, 425–63. Cambridge: Cambridge University Press, 1992.

Frede, Michael. "Plato's Arguments and the Dialogue Form." In *Methods of Interpreting Plato and His Dialogues*, ed. James C. Klagge and Nicholas D. Smith, 201–20. Oxford: Clarendon Press, 1992.

Freeman, Kathleen, trans. *Ancilla to the Pre-Socratic Philosophers: A Complete Translation of the Fragments in Diels, "Fragmente der Vorsokratiker."* Cambridge: Harvard University Press, 1948.

Freud, Sigmund. *Beyond the Pleasure Principle*. Trans. James Strachey. New York: Bantam, 1959.

Friedländer, Paul. *Plato*. Trans. Hans Meyerhoff. 2nd ed. 3 vols. Princeton: Princeton University Press, 1969.

Fussi, Alessandra. "The Myth of the Last Judgment in the *Gorgias*." *Review of Metaphysics* 54 (March 2001): 529–52.

Gadamer, Hans-Georg. "Idea and Reality in Plato's *Timaeus*." In *Dialogue and Dialectic*, trans. Christopher Smith, 156–93. New Haven: Yale University Press, 1980.

———. *The Idea of the Good in Platonic-Aristotelian Philosophy*. Trans. Christopher Smith. New Haven: Yale University Press, 1986.

———. "*Logos* and *Ergon* in Plato's *Lysis*." In *Dialogue and Dialectic*, trans. Christopher Smith, 1–20. New Haven: Yale University Press, 1980.

———. "Plato and the Poets." In *Dialogue and Dialectic*, trans. Christopher Smith, 39–72. New Haven: Yale University Press, 1980.

———. *Plato's Dialectical Ethics: Phenomenological Interpretations Relating to the "Philebus."* Trans. Robert M. Wallace. New Haven: Yale University Press, 1991.

———. "Plato's Educational State." In *Dialogue and Dialectic*, trans. Christopher Smith, 73–92. New Haven: Yale University Press, 1980.

———. "The Proofs of Immortality in Plato's *Phaedo*." In *Dialogue and Dialectic*, trans. Christopher Smith, 21–38. New Haven: Yale University Press, 1980.

Gaiser, Konrad. *Platon und die Geschichte*. Stuttgart: Fromman, 1961.

Gallop, David, trans. and ed. *Parmenides of Elea: Fragments*. Toronto: University of Toronto Press, 1984.

———. trans. *Plato's "Phaedo."* Oxford: Clarendon Press, 1975.

Geach, P. T. "The Third Man Again." *Philosophical Review* 65, no. 1 (January 1956): 72–82.

Gill, Christopher. "The Death of Socrates." *Classical Quarterly*, n.s., 23, no. 1 (May 1973): 25–28.

———. "The Genre of the Atlantis Story." *Classical Philology* 72, no. 4 (October 1977): 287–304.

———. "Plato's Atlantis Story and the Birth of Fiction." *Philosophy and Literature* 3 (1979): 65–77.

———. "Rethinking Constitutionalism in *Statesman*." In *Reading the "Statesman": Proceedings of the Third Symposium Platonicum*, ed. C. Rowe, 291–303. Sankt Augustin: Academia Verlag, 1995.

Gill, Christopher, and Mary Margaret McCabe, eds. *Form and Argument in Late Plato*. Oxford: Clarendon Press, 1996.

Gill, Mary Louis. Introduction to *Plato: "Parmenides."* Indianapolis: Hackett, 1996.

Gonzalez, Francisco J. *Dialectic and Dialogue: Plato's Practice of Philosophical Inquiry*. Evanston, IL: Northwestern University Press, 1998.

Gordon, Jill. "Eros and Philosophical Seduction in *Alcibiades I*." *Ancient Philosophy* 23 (2003): 11–29.

———. "Eros in Plato's *Timaeus*." *Epoche* 9, no. 2 (Spring 2005): 255–77.

Görgemanns, Herwig. *Beiträge zur interpretation von Platons Nomoi*. Munich: Beck, 1960.

Gosling, J. C. B., and C. C. W. Taylor. *The Greeks on Pleasure*. Oxford: Clarendon Press, 1982.

Graves, Bonita M., G. M. Graves, A. K. Tsakopoulos, and J. P. Anton. "Hemlock Poisoning: Twentieth-Century Scientific Light Shed on the Death of Socrates." In *The Philosophy of Socrates*, ed. K. J. Boudouris, 156–68. Athens: Center for Greek Philosophy, 1991.

Graves, C. E. *The "Euthyphro" and "Menexenus" of Plato*. London: Macmillan, 1935.

Greenberg, N. A. "Socrates' Choice in the *Crito*." *Harvard Studies in Classical Philology* 70 (1965): 45–82.

Griffith, Tom, trans. *The Republic*. Cambridge: Cambridge University Press, 2000.

Griswold, Charles L., Jr. "Philosophy, Education, and Courage in Plato's *Laches*." *Interpretation* 14, nos. 2–3 (May and September 1986): 177–93.

———. "*Politikē Epistēmē* in Plato's *Statesman*." In *Essays in Ancient Greek Philosophy III: Plato*, ed. John Anton and Anthony Preus, 141–67. Albany: SUNY Press, 1989.

———. *Self-Knowledge in Plato's "Phaedrus."* New Haven: Yale University Press, 1986.

Grote, George. *Plato, and the Other Companions of Sokrates*. 3 vols. London: J. Murray, 1865.

Grube, G. M. A. *Plato's Thought*. Indianapolis: Hackett, 1980.

Gulley, Norman. *Plato's Theory of Knowledge*. London: Methuen, 1962.

———. "Plato's Theory of Recollection." *Classical Quarterly* 54 (1954).

Guthrie, W. K. C. *A History of Greek Philosophy*. 6 vols. Cambridge: Cambridge University Press, 1962–81.

Hackforth, R. *Plato's "Phaedrus."* Cambridge: Cambridge University Press, 1952.

———. "The Story of Atlantis: Its Purpose and Its Moral." *Classical Review* 58 (1944): 7–9.

Hadot, Pierre. *Philosophy as a Way of Life*. Trans. Michael Chase. Oxford: Blackwell, 1995.

———. "Physique et poésie dans le *Timée* de Platon." *Revue de Théologie et de Philosophie* 115 (1983).

Hamilton, Walter, trans. *Phaedrus and Letters VII and VIII*. London: Penguin, 1973.

Harrison, E. L. "Was Gorgias a Sophist?" *Phoenix* 18 (1964): 183–92.

Havelock, Eric. *The Liberal Temper in Greek Politics*. New Haven: Yale University Press, 1957.

Hawtrey, R. S. W. *Commentary on Plato's "Euthydemus."* Philadelphia: American Philosophical Society, 1981.

Heath, Thomas L. *A History of Greek Mathematics*. 2 vols. Oxford: Clarendon Press, 1921.

Heidegger, Martin. *Early Greek Thinking*. Trans. David Farrell Krell and Frank A. Capuzzi. New York: Harper and Row, 1975.

———. *Introduction to Metaphysics*. Trans. Ralph Manheim. Garden City, NY: Doubleday, 1961.

———. *Nietzsche*. Vol. 4. Trans. David Farrell Krell. New York: Harper and Row, 1982.

———. "The Origin of the Work of Art." In *Poetry, Language, Thought*, 73–78. Trans. Albert Hofstadter. New York: Harper, 1971.

———. *Platon "Sophistes."* In *Gesamtausgabe*, vol. 19. Frankfurt-am-Main: Vittorio Klostermann, 1992. Translated by Richard Rojcewicz and André Schuwer as *Plato's "Sophist."* Bloomington: Indiana University Press, 1997.

———. *Question concerning Technology*. Trans. William Lovitt. New York: Harper, 1977.

———. *What Is Called Thinking?* Trans. Fred Wieck and J. Glenn Gray. New York: Harper and Row, 1968.

———. *What Is Philosophy?* Trans. William Kluback and Jean T. Wilde. New Haven: Yale University Press, 1956.

Hemmenway, Scott R. "Philosophical Apology in the *Theaetetus.*" *Interpretation* 17, no. 3 (1990): 323–46.

Henderson, M. M. "Plato's *Menexenus* and the Distortion of History." *Acta Classica* 18 (1975): 25–46.

Herodotus. *The History.* Trans. David Grene. Chicago: University of Chicago Press, 1987.

Herter, H. "Bewegung der Materie bei Platon." *Rheinisches Museum für Philologie* 100: 327–47.

Hesiod. *Theogony.* Trans. Norman O. Brown. Indianapolis: Bobbs-Merrill, 1953.

Holway, Richard. "Achilles, Socrates, and Democracy." *Political Theory* 22, no. 4 (November 1994): 561–90.

Hourani, C. F. "Thrasymachus' Definition of Justice in Plato's *Republic.*" *Phronesis* 7 (1962): 110–20.

Howland, Jacob. *The Paradox of Political Philosophy: Socrates' Philosophical Trial.* Lanham, MD: Rowman and Littlefield, 1998.

———. "Partisanship and the Work of Philosophy in Plato's *Timaeus.*" *Review of Politics* 69, no. 1 (Winter 2007): 1–27.

———. *The "Republic": The Odyssey of Philosophy.* New York: Twayne Publishers, 1993.

———. "The *Republic*'s Third Wave and the Paradox of Political Philosophy." *Review of Metaphysics* 51, no. 3 (1998): 633–57.

———. "Re-Reading Plato: The Problem of Platonic Chronology." *Phoenix* 45 (1991): 189–214.

———. "Socrates and Alcibiades: Eros, Piety, and Politics." *Interpretation* 18, no. 1 (Fall 1990): 63–90.

Hyland, Drew A. "*Erōs, Epithumia,* and *Philia* in Plato." *Phronesis* 13, no. 1 (1968): 32–46.

———. *The Virtue of Philosophy.* Athens: Ohio State University Press, 1981.

———. "Why Plato Wrote Dialogues." *Philosophy and Rhetoric* 1 (1968): 38–50.

Iamblichus. *Life of Pythagoras.* Trans. Thomas Taylor. London: John M. Watkins, 1965.

Irigaray, Luce. "Sorcerer Love: A Reading of Plato's *Symposium,* Diotima's Speech." Trans. Eleanor H. Kykendall. *Hypatia* 3, no. 3 (Winter 1989): 32–44.

Irwin, Terence, trans. *Gorgias.* Oxford: Clarendon Press, 1979.

———. *Plato's Ethics.* New York: Oxford University Press, 1995.

———. *Plato's Moral Theory.* Oxford: Clarendon Press, 1977.

Johansen, Thomas Kjeller. *Plato's Natural Philosophy: A Study of the "Timaeus-Critias."* Cambridge: Cambridge University Press, 2004.

Joly, Henri. *La question des étrangers.* Paris: Vrin, 1992.

Jowett, Benjamin, trans. "The *Republic.*" In *The Dialogues of Plato.* New York: Random House, 1937.

Joyal, Mark. *The Platonic "Theages."* Stuttgart: Franz Steiner Verlag, 2000.

Kagan, Donald. *The Outbreak of the Peloponnesian War.* Ithaca: Cornell University Press, 1969.

Kahn, Charles H. "Language and Ontology in the *Cratylus.*" In *Exegesis and Argument,* ed. E. N. Lee, A. P. D. Mourelatos, and R. M. Rorty, 152–76. Assen: Van Gorcum, 1973.

———. "A New Look at Heraclitus." *American Philosophical Quarterly* 1, no. 3 (July 1964): 189–203.

———. "On Platonic Chronology." In *New Perspectives on Plato, Modern and Ancient,* ed. Julia Annas and Christopher Rowe, 93–127. Cambridge: Harvard University Press, 2002.

———. *Plato and the Socratic Dialogue: The Philosophical Use of a Literary Form.* Cambridge: Cambridge University Press, 1996.

———. "Plato's Funeral Oration: The Motive of the *Menexenus.*" *Classical Philology* 58 (October 1963): 220–34.

———. *Pythagoras and the Pythagoreans: A Brief History.* Indianapolis: Hackett Publishing, 2001.

Kalkavage, Peter, trans. *Plato's "Timaeus."* Newburyport, MA: Focus Publishing, 2001.

Kastely, James L. "In Defense of Plato's *Gorgias.*" *PMLA* 106, no. 1 (January 1991): 96–109.

Kateb, George. "Socratic Integrity." In *Nomos XL: Integrity and Conscience,* ed. Ian Shapiro and Robert Adams, 77–112. New York: New York University Press, 1989.

Kerferd, G. B. "The Doctrine of Thrasymachus in Plato's *Republic.*" *Durham University Journal* 40 (1947): 19–27.

———. *The Sophistic Movement.* New York: Cambridge University Press, 1981.

Keulen, Hermann. *Untersuchungen zu Platons "Euthydem."* Wiesbaden: Otto Harrassowitz, 1971.

Keyt, David. "The Fallacies in *Phaedo* 102a–107b." *Phronesis* 8 (1963): 167–72.

Kierkegaard, Søren. *The Concept of Irony.* Trans. Howard V. Hong and Edna H. Hong. Princeton: Princeton University Press, 1989.

———. *Philosophical Fragments.* Trans. Howard V. Hong. Princeton: Princeton University Press, 1962.

Kirk, G. S. "The Problem of *Cratylus.*" *American Journal of Philology* 72 (1951): 225–53.

Kirk, G. S., J. E. Raven, and M. Schofield. *The Presocratic Philosophers.* 2nd ed. Cambridge: Cambridge University Press, 1983.

Klein, Jacob. "About Plato's *Philebus.*" *Interpretation* 2, no. 3: 157–82.

———. *A Commentary on Plato's "Meno."* Chapel Hill: University of North Carolina Press, 1965.

———. "The Concept of Number in Greek Mathematics and Philosophy." In *Jacob Klein: Lectures and Essays*, ed. Robert B. Williamson and Elliot Zuckerman, 43–52. Annapolis: St. John's College Press, 1985.

———. "Plato's *Phaedo.*" In *Jacob Klein: Lectures and Essays*, ed. Robert B. Williamson and Elliot Zuckerman, 43–52. Annapolis: St. John's College Press, 1985.

———. *Plato's Trilogy.* Chicago: University of Chicago Press, 1977.

Klosko, George. *The Development of Plato's Political Theory.* New York: Methuen, 1986.

———. "The Insufficiency of Reason in Plato's *Gorgias.*" *Western Political Quarterly* 36 (1983): 579–95.

———. "The Nocturnal Council in Plato's *Laws.*" *Political Studies* 36 (1988): 74–88.

Knorr, Wilbur Richard. *The Evolution of the Euclidean Elements.* Dordrecht: D. Reidel, 1975.

Kochin, Michael S. *Gender and Rhetoric in Plato's Political Thought.* Cambridge: Cambridge University Press, 2002.

———. "Plato's Eleatic and Athenian Sciences of Politics." *Review of Politics* 61 (Winter 1999): 1–28.

———. "The Unity of Virtue and the Limitations of Magnesia." *History of Political Thought* 19, no. 2 (1998): 125–41.

Krämer, Hans Joachim. *Plato and the Foundations of Metaphysics.* Trans. John R. Catan. Albany: SUNY Press, 1990.

Kraut, Richard, ed. *Cambridge Companion to Plato.* Cambridge: Cambridge University Press, 1992.

———. *Socrates and the State.* Princeton: Princeton University Press, 1984.

Krell, David. "Female Parts in *Timaeus.*" *Arion*, n.s., 2/3 (1975): 400–421.

Lacey, A. R. "Our Knowledge of Socrates." In *The Philosophy of Socrates*, ed. Gregory Vlastos, 22–49. Garden City, NY: Doubleday, 1971.

Lamb, W. R. M., ed. and trans. *Lysis, Symposium, Gorgias.* Loeb ed. Cambridge: Harvard University Press, 1925.

Lampert, Laurence. "Socrates' Defense of Polytropic Odysseus: Lying and Wrong-doing in Plato's *Lesser Hippias.*" *Review of Politics* 64, no. 2 (Spring 2002): 87–125.

Lampert, Laurence, and Christopher Planeaux. "Who's Who in Plato's *Timaeus-Critias* and Why." *Review of Metaphysics* 52 (September 1998): 87–125.

Lane, Melissa. *Method and Politics in Plato's "Statesman."* Cambridge: Cambridge University Press, 1998.

Lautner, Peter. "Can Self-Reflection Be a Generative Principle? Atticus and Porphyry on *Timaeus* 37b3–6." *Ancient World* 32, no. 1 (2001): 257–69.

Leake, James. "Introduction to the *Lesser Hippias.*" In *The Roots of Political Philosophy*, ed. Thomas L. Pangle, 300–306. Ithaca: Cornell University Press, 1987.

———. "*Lesser Hippias.*" In *The Roots of Political Philosophy*, ed. Thomas L. Pangle, 281–99. Ithaca: Cornell University Press, 1987.

———. "*Lovers.*" In *The Roots of Political Philosophy*, ed. Thomas L. Pangle, 80–89. Ithaca: Cornell University Press, 1987.

Lear, Jonathan. "Inside and Outside the *Republic.*" *Phronesis* 37, no. 2 (1992): 184–215.

Ledger, Gerard R. *Re-Counting Plato.* Oxford: Oxford University Press, 1989.

Levin, Donald Norman. "Some Observations concerning Plato's *Lysis*." In *Essays in Ancient Greek Philosophy*, ed. John Peter Anton and George L. Kustas, 236–58. Albany: SUNY Press, 1971.

Lewis, W. Bradley. "The Nocturnal Council and Platonic Political Philosophy." *History of Political Thought* 19, no. 1 (1998): 1–20.

Loraux, Nicole. *The Invention of Athens: The Funeral Oration in the Classical City*. Trans. Alan Sheridan. Cambridge: Harvard University Press, 1986.

Luce, J. V. "The Date of the *Cratylus*." *American Journal of Philology* 85 (1964): 138–39.

Ludlam, Ivor. *"Hippias Major": An Interpretation*. Stuttgart: Franz Steiner, 1991.

Ludwig, Paul. *Eros and Polis*. Cambridge: Cambridge University Press, 2002.

———. "Portrait of the Artist in Politics: Justice and Self-Interest in Aristophanes *Acharnians*." *American Political Science Review* 101, no. 3 (2007): 479–92.

Lutoslawski, W. *The Origin and Growth of Plato's Logic*. London: Longmans, 1897.

Lutz, Mark J. *Socrates' Education to Virtue: Learning the Love of the Noble*. Albany: SUNY Press, 1998.

MacIntyre, Alasdair. *After Virtue*. 2nd ed. Notre Dame: University of Notre Dame Press, 1984.

Mackenzie, Mary Margaret. "Putting the *Cratylus* in Its Place." *Classical Quarterly* 36, no. 1 (1986): 124–50.

Mara, Gerald. "Constitutions, Virtues, and Philosophy in Plato's *Statesman* and *Republic*." *Polity* 13 (Spring 1981): 355–82.

———. *Socrates' Discursive Democracy: Logos and Ergon in Political Philosophy*. Albany: SUNY Press, 1997.

McCabe, Mary Margaret. "Chaos and Control: Reading Plato's *Politicus*." *Phronesis* 42, no. 1 (1997): 94–117.

McDowell, John. *Plato: "Theaetetus."* New York: Oxford University Press, 1973.

McKim, Richard. "Shame and Truth in Plato's *Gorgias*." In *Platonic Writings, Platonic Readings*, ed. Charles L. Griswold, 34–48. New York: Routledge, 1988.

McPherran, Mark L. *The Religion of Socrates*. University Park: Pennsylvania State University Press, 1999.

Meridier, Louis. *"Ménexène."* In *Platon "Oeuvres complètes,"* vol. 5. Paris: Belles Lettres, 1920.

Miller, Mitchell H., Jr. "Parmenides and the Disclosure of Being." *Apeiron* 13, no. 1 (1978): 12–35.

———. *The Philosopher in Plato's "Statesman."* The Hague: Martinus Nijhoff Publishers, 1980.

———. *Plato's "Parmenides": The Conversion of the Soul*. Princeton: Princeton University Press, 1986.

Mitchell, Robert Lloyd. *The Hymn to Eros: A Study of Plato's "Symposium."* Lanham, MD: University Press of America, 1993.

Mohr, Richard D. *The Platonic Cosmology*. Leiden: E. J. Brill, 1985.

Monoson, S. Sara. "Remembering Pericles: The Political and Theoretical Import of Plato's *Menexenus*." *Political Theory* 26, no. 4 (August 1998): 489–513.

Moore, John D. "The Dating of Plato's *Ion*." *Greek, Roman, and Byzantine Studies* 15 (Winter 1974): 425–39.

Moravcsik, Julius. "Learning as Recollection." In *Plato*, ed. Gregory Vlastos, 1:53–69. Garden City, NY: Doubleday, 1971.

Morrison, Donald. "On the Alleged Historical Reliability of Plato's *Apology*." *Archiv f. Gesch. D. Philosophie* 82 (2000): 235–65.

Morrow, Glenn R. "Plato and the Mathematicians: An Interpretation of Socrates' Dream in the *Theaetetus* (201e–206c)." *Philosophical Review* 79 (July 1970): 304–33.

———. *Plato's Cretan City*. Princeton: Princeton University Press, 1960.

Most, Glenn W. "A Cock for Asclepius." *Classical Quarterly* 43 (1993): 96–111.

Mourelatos, Alexander D., ed. *The Pre-Socratics*. Princeton: Princeton University Press, 1974.

———. *The Route of Parmenides*. New Haven: Yale University Press, 1970.

Müller, Gerhard. *Studien zu den Platonischen Nomoi*. Munich: C. H. Beck Verlag, 1951.

Munk, Eduard. *Die Natürliche Ordnung der Platonischen Schriften*. Berlin: Dümmler, 1857.

Munn, Mark D. *The School of History: Athens in the Age of Socrates*. Berkeley: University of California Press, 2000.

Naddaf, Gerard. "The Atlantis Myth: An Introduction to Plato's Later Philosophy of History." *Phoenix* 48, no. 3 (Autumn, 1994): 189–209.

Nails, Debra. *Agora, Academy, and the Conduct of Philosophy*. Dordrecht: Kluwer Academic Publishers, 1995.

———. *The People of Plato: A Prosopography of Plato and Other Socratics*. Indianapolis: Hackett, 2002.

Neel, Jasper. *Plato, Derrida, and Writing*. Carbondale: Southern Illinois University Press, 1988.

Nehamas, Alexander. "Confusing Universals and Particulars in Plato's Early Dialogues." *Review of Metaphysics* 29 (1975): 288–306.

———. "Meno's Paradox and Socrates as a Teacher." *Oxford Studies in Ancient Philosophy* 3 (1985): 1–30.

———. "Socratic Intellectualism." In *Proceedings of the Boston Area Colloquium in Ancient Philosophy*, ed. J. Cleary, 2:275–316. Lanham, MD: Rowman and Littlefield, 1986.

Nehamas, Alexander, and Paul Woodruff, trans. *Phaedrus*. Indianapolis: Hackett, 1995.

Newell, Waller R. *Ruling Passion: The Erotics of Statecraft in Platonic Political Philosophy*. Lanham, MD: Rowman and Littlefield, 2000.

Nicgorski, Walter. "Cicero's Socrates." In *Law and Philosophy*, ed. John A. Murley, Robert L. Stone, and William T. Braithwaite, 1:213–33. Athens: Ohio University Press, 1992.

Nichols, James H., Jr., trans. *Plato: "Gorgias."* Ithaca: Cornell University Press, 1998.

Nichols, Mary P. *Socrates and the Political Community: An Ancient Debate*. Albany: SUNY Press, 1987.

———. "Socrates' Contest with the Poets in Plato's *Symposium*." *Political Theory* 32, no. 2 (April 2004): 186–206.

Nietzsche, Friedrich. "Das Problem des Sokrates." In *Götzen-Dämmerung. Sämtliche Werke*, vol. 6.3, ed. Giorgio Colli and Mazzino Montinari. Berlin: De Gruyter, 1980. Translated by Richard Polt as "The Problem of Socrates." In *Twilight of the Idols*. Indianapolis: Hackett, 1997.

———. *Die Geburt der Tragödie*. In *Sämtliche Werke*, vol. 1, ed. Giorgio Colli and Mazzino Montinari. Berlin: De Gruyter, 1980. Translated by Walter Kaufman as *The Birth of Tragedy*. In *Basic Writings*. New York: Modern Library, 1968.

———. *Jenseits von Gut und Böse*. In *Sämtliche Werke*, vol. 5, ed. Giorgio Colli and Mazzino Montinari. Berlin: De Gruyter, 1980. Translated by Walter Kaufman as *Beyond Good and Evil*. In *Basic Writings*. New York: Modern Library, 1968.

Nightingale, Andrea. "Historiography and Cosmology in Plato's *Laws*." *Ancient Philosophy* 19, no. 2 (Fall 1999): 299–326.

———. "Plato on the Origins of Evil: The *Statesman* Myth Reconsidered." *Ancient Philosophy* 16 (1996): 65–83.

———. *Spectacles of Truth in Classical Greek Philosophy*. Cambridge: Cambridge University Press, 2004.

———. "Writing/Reading a Sacred Text: A Literary Interpretation of Plato's *Laws*." *Classical Philology* 88, no. 4 (October 1993): 279–300.

Nussbaum, Martha. *The Fragility of Goodness*. Cambridge: Cambridge University Press, 1986.

———. " 'This Story Isn't True': Poetry, Goodness, and Understanding in Plato's *Phaedrus*." In *Plato on Beauty, Wisdom, and the Arts*, ed. J. M. E. Moravcsik and Philip Tenko, 79–124. Totowa, NJ: Rowman and Littlefield, 1982.

Nye, Andrea. "Irigaray and Diotima at Plato's *Symposium*." *Hypatia: A Journal of Feminist Philosophy* 3, no. 3 (Winter 1989): 46–61.

Ober, William. "Did Socrates Die of Hemlock Poisoning?" *New York State Journal of Medicine* 77 (1977): 254–58.

O'Brien, David. "The Last Argument of Plato's *Phaedo*." *Classical Quarterly* 17 (1967): 198–231; 18 (1968): 95–106.

O'Brien, Michael. "The Unity of the *Laches*." In *Essays in Ancient Greek Philosophy*, ed. John Anton and George Kustas, 1:303–25. Albany: SUNY Press, 1971.

Orwin, Clifford. "On the *Cleitophon*." In *The Roots of Political Philosophy*, ed. Thomas L. Pangle, 117–31. Ithaca: Cornell University Press, 1987.

Osborne, Catherine. "Space, Time, Shape, and Direction: Creative Discourse in the *Timaeus*." In *Form and Argument in Late Plato*, ed. Christopher Gill and Mary Margaret McCabe, 179–212. Oxford: Clarendon Press, 1996.

Ostenfeld, Erik. "The Role and Status of the Forms in the *Timaeus*: Paradigmatism Revised?" In *Interpreting the "Timaeus-Critias": Proceedings of the Fourth Symposium Platonicum*, ed. Tomas Calvo and Luc Brisson, 165–77. Sankt Augustin: Academia Verlag, 1997.

Owen, G. E. L. "The Place of the *Timaeus* in Plato's Dialogues." *Classical Quarterly*, n.s., 3 (1953): 79–95.

Pangle, Thomas L., trans. *Plato's "Laws."* New York: Basic Books, 1980.

———. "The Political Psychology of Religion in Plato's *Laws*." *American Political Science Review* 70, no. 4 (December 1976): 1059–77.

———, ed. *The Roots of Political Philosophy*. Ithaca: Cornell University Press, 1987.

Pappus. *Commentary on Book X of Euclid's "Elements."* Ed. Gustav Junge and William Thomson. Cambridge: Harvard University Press, 1930.

Parke, H. W., and D. E. W. Wormell. *The Delphic Oracle*. New York: Oxford University Press, 1956.

Parmenides of Elea. *Fragments*. Ed. and trans. David Gallop. Toronto: University of Toronto Press, 1984.

Pemberton, Harrison J. *Plato's "Parmenides": The Critical Moment for Socrates*. Darby, PA: Norwood Editions, 1984.

Penner, Terry. "Two Notes on the *Crito*: The Impotence of the Many, and 'Persuade or Obey.'" *Classical Quarterly* 47, no. 1 (1997): 153–66.

Penner, Terry, and Christopher Rowe. *Plato's "Lysis."* Cambridge: Cambridge University Press, 2005.

Phillips, Bernard. "The Significance of Meno's Paradox." In *Plato's "Meno": Text and Criticism*, ed. Alexander Sesonske and Noel Fleming. Belmont, CA: Wadsworth, 1965.

Planinc, Zdravko. *Plato's Political Philosophy: Prudence in the "Republic" and the "Laws."* Columbia: University of Missouri Press, 1991.

Platonis Opera. Vol. 1. Ed. E. A. Duke, W. J. Hicker, W. S. M. Nicoll, D. B. Robinson, and J. C. G. Strachan. Oxford: Oxford University Press, 1995.

———. Vols. 2–5. Ed. John Burnet. Oxford: Clarendon Press, 1901–7.

Plochmann, George Kimball. "Socrates, the Stranger from Elea, and Some Others." *Classical Philology* 49, no. 4 (October 1954): 223–31.

Plutarch. *Lives of Noble Grecians and Romans*. Ed. Arthur Hugh Clough. New York: Modern Library, 1932.

———. "On the Generation of the Soul in the *Timaeus*." In *Plutarch's Moralia*, 133–345. Trans. Harold Cherniss. Cambridge: Harvard University Press, 1976.

Pohlenz, Max. *Aus Platos Werdezeit*. Berlin: Weidmann, 1913.

Polansky, Ronald M. *Philosophy and Knowledge: A Commentary on Plato's "Theaetetus."* Lewisburg, PA: Bucknell University Press, 1992.

Pottenger, John R. "The Sage and the Sophist." *Interpretation* 23, no. 1 (February 1995): 41–60.

Pradeau, Jean-François. *Le monde de la politique: Sur le récit atlante de Platon, Timée (17–27) et Critias*. Sankt Augustin: Academia Verlag, 1997.

Proclus. *Alcibiades I*. Trans. William O'Neill. The Hague: Martinus Nijhoff, 1965.

———. *The Commentaries of Proclus on the "Timaeus" of Plato, in Five Books*. Trans. T. Taylor. London: Printed and Sold by the Author, 1820.

———. *A Commentary on the First Book of Euclid's "Elements."* Trans. Glenn Morrow. Princeton: Princeton University Press, 1970.

———. *Proclus' Commentary on Plato's "Parmenides."* Trans. Glen R. Morrow and John M. Dillon. Princeton: Princeton University Press, 1987.

Rankin, H. D. *Sophists, Socratics, and Cynics*. Totowa, NJ: Barnes and Noble, 1983.

Reale, Giovanni. "Plato's Doctrine of the Origin of the World." In *Interpreting the "Timaeus-Critias": Proceedings of the Fourth Symposium Platonicum*, ed. Tomas Calvo and Luc Brisson, 149–64. Sankt Augustin: Academia Verlag, 1997.

Reeve, C. D. C., trans. *Cratylus*. In *Plato: The Complete Works*, ed. John M. Cooper, 101–56. Indianapolis: Hackett, 1997.

———. *Philosopher-Kings*. Princeton: Princeton University Press, 1988.

Reinhardt, Karl. *Parmenides und die Geschichte der griechischen Philosophie*. Frankfurt-am-Main: Vittorio Klostermann, 1959.

Reydams-Schils, Gretchen. "Plato's World Soul: Grasping Sensibles without Sense-Perception." In *Interpreting the "Timaeus-Critias": Proceedings of the Fourth Symposium Platonicum*, ed. Tomas Calvo and Luc Brisson, 261–65. Sankt Augustin: Academia Verlag, 1997.

Riedweg, Christoph. *Pythagoras: His Life, Teaching, and Influence*. Trans. Steven Rendall. Ithaca: Cornell University Press, 2005.

Roberts, W. Rhys, ed. *On Literary Composition*. London: Macmillan, 1910.

Robinson, Richard. "Ambiguity." *Mind* 50 (1941): 140–55.

———. "Forms and Error in Plato's *Theaetetus*." *Philosophical Review* 59 (1950): 3–30.

———. "Plato's Consciousness of Fallacy." *Mind* 51 (1942): 94–114.

———. *Plato's Earlier Dialectic*. Ithaca: Cornell University Press, 1941.

Romilly, Jacqueline de. *The Great Sophists in Periclean Athens*. Trans. Janet Lloyd. New York: Oxford University Press, 1992.

Roochnik, David. *Beautiful City: The Dialectical Character of Plato's "Republic."* Ithaca: Cornell University Press, 2003.

———. "Residual Ambiguity in Plato's *Statesman*." *Plato: The Internet Journal of the International Plato Society* 5 (2005): 4–10.

———. "The Riddle of the *Cleitophon*." *Ancient Philosophy* 4, no. 2 (Fall 1984): 132–45.

———. "The Sensuous Play of Plato's *Euthydemus*." *Interpretation* 18 (1991): 211–32.

Rorty, Amelie. "A Speculative Note on Some Dramatic Elements in the *Theaetetus*." *Phronesis* 17 (1972): 227–38.

Rosen, Frederick. "Obligation and Friendship in Plato's *Crito*." *Political Theory* 1, no. 3 (August 1973): 307–16.

Rosen, Stanley. *Plato's "Republic."* New Haven: Yale University Press, 2005.

———. *Plato's "Sophist": The Drama of Original and Image*. New Haven: Yale University Press, 1983.

———. *Plato's "Statesman": The Web of Politics*. New Haven: Yale University Press, 1995.

———. *Plato's "Symposium."* New Haven: Yale University Press, 1968.

———. *The Quarrel between Philosophy and Poetry*. New York: Routledge, 1988.

———. *The Question of Being*. New Haven: Yale University Press, 1993.

———. "Socrates as Concealed Lover." In *The Quarrel between Philosophy and Poetry*, 91–101. New York: Routledge, 1988.

———. "*Sōphrosynē* and *Selbstbewusstsein*." *Review of Metaphysics* 26, no. 4 (1973): 617–42.

Rosenmeyer, Thomas G. "The Numbers in Plato's *Critias*: A Reply." *Classical Philology* 44 (1949): 117–20.

Rosenstock, Bruce. "Socrates as Revenant: A Reading of the *Menexenus*." *Phoenix* 43 (1994): 331–47.

Ross, W. D. *Plato's Theory of Ideas*. Oxford: Clarendon Press, 1951.

Rowe, C. J. "The Argument and Structure of Plato's *Phaedrus*." *Proceedings of the Cambridge Philological Society* 32 (1986): 106–25.

Rowe, Christopher. "Killing Socrates." *Journal of Hellenic Studies* 121 (2001): 63–76.

———. "The *Politicus*: Structure and Form." In *Form and Argument in Late Plato*, ed. Christopher Gill and Mary Margaret McCabe, 153–78. Oxford: Clarendon Press, 1996.

———, ed. *Reading the "Statesman": Proceedings of the Third Symposium Platonicum*. Sankt Augustin: Academia Verlag, 1995.

Rue, Rachel. "The Philosopher in Flight: The Digression (172c–177c) in Plato's *Theaetetus*." In *Oxford Studies in Ancient Philosophy*, 11 (1993): 71–100.

Runciman, W. G. "Plato's *Parmenides*" (1959). In *Studies in Plato's Metaphysics*, ed. R. E. Allen. New York: Humanities Press, 1965.

Rutherford, R. B. *The Art of Plato*. Cambridge: Harvard University Press, 1995.

Ryle, Gilbert. "The *Meno*: Many Things Are Odd about Our *Meno*." *Paideia* 5 (1976): 1–9.

Sabine, George H. *A History of Political Theory*. Rev. ed. New York: Henry Holt, 1950.

Salkever, Stephen G. "Socrates' Aspasian Oration: The Play of Philosophy and Politics in Plato's *Menexenus*." *American Political Science Review* 87, no. 1 (March 1993): 133–43.

Sallis, John. *Being and Logos*. 2nd ed. Atlantic Highlands, NJ: Humanities Press International, 1986.

——. *Chorology: On Beginning in Plato's "Timaeus."* Bloomington: Indiana University Press, 1999.

Santas, Gerasimos. *Socrates: Philosophy in Plato's Early Dialogues*. London: Routledge and Kegan Paul, 1979.

——. "Socrates at Work on Virtue and Knowledge in Plato's *Laches*." In *The Philosophy of Socrates*, ed. Gregory Vlastos, 177–208. Garden City, NJ: Doubleday, 1971.

Saunders, Trevor J. "Penology and Eschatology in Plato's *Timaeus* and *Laws*." *Classical Quarterly* 23 (1973): 232–44.

——. "Plato on Women in the *Laws*." In *The Greek World*, ed. A. Powell. London: Routledge and Kegan Paul, 1995.

——. "Plato's Later Political Thought." In *Cambridge Companion to Plato*, ed. Richard Kraut, 464–92. Cambridge: Cambridge University Press, 1992.

Saxonhouse, Arlene. *Fear of Diversity*. Chicago: University of Chicago Press, 1992.

——. *Free Speech and Democracy in Ancient Athens*. New York: Cambridge University Press, 2006.

——. "The Philosopher and the Female in the Political Thought of Plato." *Political Theory* 4, no. 2 (May 1976): 195–212.

——. "The Philosophy of the Particular and the Universality of the City: Socrates' Education of Euthyphro." *Political Theory* 16 (May 1988): 281–99.

——. "An Unspoken Theme in Plato's *Gorgias*: War." *Interpretation* 11 (May 1983): 139–69.

Sayre, Kenneth. "The Multilayered Incoherence of Timaeus' Receptacle." In *Plato's "Timaeus" as Cultural Icon*, ed. Gretchen J. Reydams-Schils, 60–79. Notre Dame, IN: University of Notre Dame Press, 2003.

——. *Parmenides' Lesson*. Notre Dame, IN: University of Notre Dame Press, 1996.

——. *Plato's Late Ontology: A Riddle Resolved*. Princeton: Princeton University Press, 1983.

——. *Plato's Literary Garden*. Notre Dame, IN: University of Notre Dame Press, 1995.

Schiappa, Edward. "Interpreting Gorgias's 'Being' in *On Not-Being* or *On Nature*." *Philosophy and Rhetoric* 30, no. 1 (1997): 15–27.

Schleiermacher, Friedrich Daniel Ernst. *Über die Philosophie Platons*, including *Geschichte der Philosophie: Vorlesungen über Sokrates und Platon* (1819–23) and *Die Einleitungen zur Übersetzung des Platon* (1804–28). Ed. Peter M. Steiner. Hamburg: Felix Meiner, 1996.

Schmid, W. T. *On Manly Courage: A Study of Plato's "Laches."* Carbondale: Southern Illinois University Press, 1992.

——. *Plato's "Charmides" and the Socratic Ideal of Rationality*. Albany: SUNY Press, 1998.

Schofield, Malcolm. "Denouement of the *Cratylus*." In *Language and Logos*, ed. Malcolm Schofield and Martha Craven Nussbaum, 61–81. Cambridge: Cambridge University Press, 1982.

——. "A Displacement in the Text of the *Cratylus*." *Classical Quarterly* 22 (1972): 246–53.

——. *Plato*. New York: Oxford University Press, 2006.

Schofield, Malcolm, and Martha Craven Nussbaum, eds. *Language and Logos*. Cambridge: Cambridge University Press, 1982.

Schoos, Daniel J. "Timaeus' Banquet." *Ancient Philosophy* 19, supp. (1999): 97–108.

Scodel, Harvey. *Diaeresis and Myth in Plato's "Statesman."* Göttingen: Vandenhoeck and Ruprecht, 1987.

Scolnicov, Samuel. "Three Aspects of Plato's Philosophy of Learning and Instruction." *Paideia* 5 (1976): 50–62.

Scott, Gary Alan. *Plato's Socrates as Educator*. Albany: SUNY Press, 2000.

Scott, Gary Alan, and William A. Welton. "Eros as Messenger in Diotima's Teaching." In *Who Speaks for Plato?* ed. Gerald A. Press, 147–59. Lanham, MD: Rowman and Littlefield, 2000.

Sedley, David. *Plato's "Cratylus."* Cambridge: Cambridge University Press, 2003.

Seeskin, Kenneth. *Dialogue and Discovery: A Study in Socratic Method.* Albany: SUNY Press, 1987.

Sellars, W. "Vlastos and 'The Third Man.'" *Philosophical Review* 64, no. 3 (July 1955): 405–37.

Sesonske, Alexander. "Hedonism in the *Protagoras." Journal of the History of Philosophy* 1 (1963): 73–79.

Shorey, Paul. *The Unity of Plato's Thought.* Chicago: University of Chicago Press, 1903.

———. *What Plato Said.* Chicago: University of Chicago Press, 1933.

Sidgwick, Henry. "The Sophists." In *Lectures on the Philosophy of Kant and Other Philosophical Lectures and Essays,* 323–71. London: Macmillan, 1905.

Skemp, J. B. *Plato's "Statesman."* New Haven: Yale University Press, 1952.

———. *The Theory of Motion in Plato's Later Dialogues.* Cambridge: Cambridge University Press, 1942.

Sprague, Rosamond Kent, ed. *The Older Sophists.* Indianapolis: Hackett, 2001.

———. *Plato's Use of Fallacy.* New York: Barnes and Noble, 1962.

Stalley, R. F. *An Introduction to Plato's "Laws."* Oxford: Basil Blackwell, 1983.

Stanley, Phillip V. "The Family Connection of Alcibiades and Axiochus." *Greek, Roman, and Byzantine Studies* 27, no. 3 (Summer 1986): 173–81.

Stauffer, Devin. "Socrates and Callicles: A Reading of Plato's *Gorgias." Review of Politics* 64 (Fall 2002): 627–58.

———. *The Unity of Plato's "Gorgias."* Cambridge: Cambridge University Press, 2005.

Stern, Paul. "The Philosophic Importance of Political Life: On the 'Digression' in Plato's *Theaetetus." American Political Science Review* 96, no. 2 (June 2002): 275–89.

———. *Socratic Rationalism and Political Philosophy: An Interpretation of Plato's "Phaedo."* Albany: SUNY Press, 1993.

———. "Tyranny and Self-Knowledge: Critias and Socrates in Plato's *Charmides." American Political Science Review* 93, no. 2 (June 1999): 399–412.

Stewart, M. A. "Plato's Sophistry." *Proceedings of the Aristotelian Society,* supp. 51 (1977): 20–44.

Stone, I. F. *The Trial of Socrates.* New York: Anchor Books, 1989.

Strang, Colin. "Plato and the Third Man." *Proceedings of the Aristotelian Society,* supp. 37 (1963): 147–64.

Strauss, Leo. *The Argument and the Action of Plato's "Laws."* Chicago: University of Chicago Press, 1975.

———. *The City and Man.* Chicago: Rand McNally, 1964.

———. "How Farabi Read Plato's *Laws.*" In *What Is Political Philosophy? and Other Studies.* Glencoe, IL: Free Press, 1959.

———. *Natural Right and History.* Chicago: University of Chicago Press, 1953.

———. "On Plato's *Apology of Socrates* and *Crito.*" In *Studies in Platonic Political Philosophy.* Chicago: University of Chicago Press, 1983.

———. *On Plato's "Symposium."* Ed. and with a foreword by Seth Benardete. Chicago: University of Chicago Press, 2001.

———. "On the *Euthyphron.*" In *The Rebirth of Classical Political Rationalism: An Introduction to the Thought of Leo Strauss,* ed. and with an introduction by Thomas L. Pangle. Chicago: University of Chicago Press, 1989.

———. "On the *Minos.*" In *Liberalism Ancient and Modern.* New York: Basic Books, 1968.

———. *Socrates and Aristophanes.* New York: Basic Books, 1966.

———. *Xenophon's Socrates.* Ithaca: Cornell University Press, 1972.

———. *Xenophon's Socratic Discourse.* Ithaca: Cornell University Press, 1970.

Striker, Gisela. *Peras und Apeiron: Das Problem der Formen in Platons Philebos.* Göttingen: Vandenhoeck & Ruprecht, 1970.

Sweet, David. "Introduction to the *Greater Hippias.*" In *The Roots of Political Philosophy,* ed. Thomas L. Pangle, 340–55. Ithaca: Cornell University Press, 1987.

Szabo, Arpad. "Theaitetos und das Problem der Irrationalität in der griechischen Mathematikge-
schichte." *Acta Antiqua Academiae Scientia Hungaricae* 14 (1966): 303–58.
Szlezak, Thomas A. *Reading Plato.* Trans. Graham Zanker. New York: Routledge, 1999.
Tarrant, Dorothy. "Colloquialisms, Semi-Proverbs and Word-Play in Plato." *Classical Quarterly* 40
(1946): 109–17.
———. *The "Hippias Major" Attributed to Plato; With Introductory Essays and Commentary.* Cam-
bridge: Cambridge University Press, 1928; repr., New York: Arno Press, 1973.
———. "More Colloquialisms, Semi-Proverbs, and Word-Play in Plato." *Classical Quarterly,* n.s.,
8 (1958): 158–60.
Taylor, A. E. *A Commentary on Plato's "Timaeus."* Oxford: Clarendon Press, 1928.
———. "On the Date of the Trial of Anaxagoras." *Classical Quarterly* 11 (1917): 81–87.
———. *Plato: The Man and His Work.* Cleveland: World Publishing, 1956.
Taylor, C. C. W. "The Origins of Our Present Paradigms." In *New Perspectives on Plato, Modern
and Ancient,* ed. Julia Annas and Christopher Rowe, 73–84. Cambridge: Harvard University
Press, 2002.
Tejera, V. *Plato's Dialogues One by One: A Structural Interpretation.* New York: Irvington Publishers,
1984.
Tennku, J. *The Evaluation of Pleasure in Plato's Ethics.* Helsinki: Societas Philosophica, 1956.
Thesleff, Holger. "Platonic Chronology." *Phronesis* 34 (1989): 1–26.
———. *Studies in Platonic Chronology.* Helsinki: Societas Scientiarum Fennica, 1982.
Thomas, John F. *Musings on the "Meno."* The Hague: Martinus Nijhoff, 1980.
Thucydides. *The Landmark Thucydides.* Ed. Robert B. Strassler. Trans. Richard Crawley. New York:
Free Press, 1996.
Tigerstedt, E. N. *Interpreting Plato.* Stockholm: Almqvist & Wiksell, 1977.
Umphrey, Stewart. *Zetetic Skepticism.* Wakefield, NH: Longwood Academic, 1990.
Vernant, J. *L'individu, la mort, l'amour, soi-même et l'autre en Grèce ancienne.* Paris: Gallimard, 1989.
Versenyi, Laszlo. "The Cretan Plato." *Review of Metaphysics* 15, no. 1 (September 1961): 64–80.
———. "Plato's Lysis." *Phronesis* 20, no. 3 (1975): 85–98.
Vickers, Brian. *In Defense of Rhetoric.* Oxford: Clarendon Press, 1988.
Vidal-Naquet, Pierre. "Athens and Atlantis." In *The Black Hunter,* trans. Andrew Szegedy-Maszak.
Baltimore: Johns Hopkins University Press, 1986.
———. "Platon: L'histoire et les historiens." In *Histoire et structure,* ed. J. Brunschwig, C. Imbert,
and A. Roger, 147–60. Paris: Vrin, 1985.
Villa, Dana. *Socratic Citizenship.* Princeton: Princeton University Press, 2001.
Vlastos, Gregory. "Anamnēsis in the Meno." *Dialogue* 4 (1965–66): 143–67.
———. "Disorderly Motion in the Timaeus." *Classical Quarterly* 33 (1939): 71–83.
———. "Elenchus and Mathematics: A Turning Point in Plato's Philosophical Development."
American Journal of Philology 109 (1988): 362–96.
———. "The Historical Socrates and Athenian Democracy." *Political Theory* 11, no. 4 (November
1983): 495–516.
———. "The Individual as an Object of Love in Plato." In *Platonic Studies,* 221–65. Princeton: Prince-
ton University Press, 1973.
———. *Socrates, Ironist and Moral Philosopher.* Ithaca: Cornell University Press, 1991.
———. "Socrates on Political Obligation." *Yale Review* (Summer 1974): 517–34.
———. *Socratic Studies.* Cambridge: Cambridge University Press, 1994.
———. "The Third Man Argument in the Parmenides." *Philosophical Review* 63, no. 3 (July 1954):
319–49.
———. "The Unity of the Virtues in the Protagoras." In *Platonic Studies.* Princeton: Princeton Uni-
versity Press, 1973.
Voegelin, Eric. *Plato.* Baton Rouge: Louisiana State University Press, 1981.
Wallach, John R. *The Platonic Political Art.* University Park: Pennsylvania State University Press,
2001.

Waterfield, Robin, trans. *Plato: Statesman*. Cambridge: Cambridge University Press, 1995.

Watt, Ian. *The Rise of the Novel*. London: Chatto and Windus, 1957.

Weingartner, Rudolph. "Making Sense of the *Cratylus*." *Phronesis* 15 (1970): 5–25.

———. *The Unity of the Platonic Dialogue*. Indianapolis: Bobbs-Merrill, 1973.

Weiss, Roslyn. *Socrates Dissatisfied*. New York: Oxford University Press, 1998.

———. *The Socratic Paradox and Its Enemies*. Chicago: University of Chicago Press, 2006.

———. *Virtue in the Cave*. New York: Oxford University Press, 2001.

Welliver, Warman. *Character, Plot and Thought in Plato's "Timaeus-Critias."* Leiden: E. J. Brill, 1977.

West, Thomas G. *Plato's "Apology of Socrates": An Interpretation, with a New Translation*. Ithaca: Cornell University Press, 1979.

West, T. G., and Grace Starry West, trans. *Charmides*. With an introduction by Thomas G. West. Indianapolis: Hackett, 1986.

———. *Four Texts on Socrates*. Ithaca: Cornell University Press, 1984.

White, David A. *Rhetoric and Reality in Plato's "Phaedrus."* Albany: SUNY, 1993.

White, James Boyd. *When Words Lose Their Meaning*. Chicago: University of Chicago Press, 1984.

White, Nicholas. *Plato on Knowledge and Reality*. Indianapolis: Hackett, 1976.

Wilamowitz-Möllendorff, Ulrich von. *Platon*. 2 vols. Berlin: Weidman, 1920.

Williams, Bernard. "The Analogy of City and Soul in Plato's *Republic*." In *Exegesis and Argument*, ed. E. N. Lee, A. P. D. Mourelatos, and R. M. Rorty, 196–206. Assen: Van Gorcum, 1973.

———. "Cratylus' Theory of Names and Its Refutation." In *Language and Logos*, ed. Malcolm Schofield and Martha Craven Nussbaum, 83–93. Cambridge: Cambridge University Press, 1982.

Williamson, Robert B., and Elliot Zuckerman, eds. *Jacob Klein: Lectures and Essays*. Annapolis: St. John's College Press, 1985.

Wolfsdorf, David. "Interpreting Plato's Early Dialogues." *Oxford Studies in Ancient Philosophy* 27 (Winter 2004): 16–40.

Woodruff, Paul, trans. *Plato: "Hippias Major."* With commentary and essay. Indianapolis: Hackett, 1982.

Woozley, A. D. *Law and Obedience: The Arguments of Plato's "Crito."* London: Duckworth, 1979.

Young, Gary. "Socrates and Obedience." *Phronesis* 19 (1974): 1–29.

Zeller, Eduard. *Die Philosophie der Griechen in ihrer geschichtlichen Entwicklung*. 5th ed. Leipzig: O. R. Reisland, 1922.

———. *Plato and the Older Academy*. Trans. F. Alleyn and A. Goodwin. London: Longmans, Green, 1888.

———. *Platonische Studien*. Tübingen: C. F. Osiander, 1839.

Zuckert, Catherine H. "On the Rationality of Rational Choice." *Political Psychology* 16, no. 1 (1995): 179–98.

———. "Plato's *Laws*: Postlude or Prelude to Socratic Political Philosophy?" *Journal of Politics* 66 (May 2004): 374–95.

———. *Postmodern Platos*. Chicago: University of Chicago Press, 1996.

———. "The Socratic Turn." *History of Political Thought* 25 (Summer 2004): 189–219.

Index

gymnastics: analogue of legislative art, 540; as component of traditional education, 28, 70n37, 73n44, 333; and education of guardians in *Republic*, 349–50, 461–62; and political history in *Laws*, 73

Hegel, G. W. F., 2–3, 35, 772

Heidegger, Martin, 40n53, 153n13, 158n21, 170nn45–46, 173, 175n53, 184n8, 186n12, 214, 312n70, 358n144, 362n150, 389n197, 451n54, 619n28, 860n25

Heracles, 264, 286, 289, 339n105, 380

Heraclitus, 262, 290, 400, 614n23, 776; and Cratylus, 651–77 passim; his doctrine as same as that of Parmenides, 173, 389n197; Eleatic Stranger on, 697–700; in *Theaetetus*, 627–28

Hermocrates, 37, 427, 430–31, 470, 472n74; and dramatic date of *Timaeus-Critias*, 429n21, 429n23; and order of speeches in *Timaeus-Critias*, 423n9, 430n25, 435n33; and Sicilian war with Athens, 429, 434

Hermogenes, 394n204, 651–77

Herodotus, 59n24, 259n76, 371n169, 432n27, 473n75, 582n103, 739n4

Hesiod, 196, 286, 287, 295, 312, 319, 400, 464, 476, 589, 641, 660, 849; Athenian Stranger's use of, 75n49, 86n78; Socrates' critique of, 368–70

Hesiod, works of: *Theogony*, 192, 287n14, 291n93, 300, 307n57; *Works and Days*, 346n121, 368n160

Hipparchus, 27, 29

Hippias, 257–73, 297n34, 377, 688, 689n12, 694; in *Protagoras*, 219, 224, 282n1

Homer, 196, 311, 312, 319, 406, 475, 557, 589, 641, 709; Athenian Stranger's use of, 74–75, 86n78, 116, 126; and names (*Cratylus*), 659, 661, 664; origin of traditional conceptions of virtue, 215, 247, 256, 268–71, 275–77, 279, 344; Socrates' critique of, 374–84

Homer, works of: *Iliad*, 269n94, 270, 276, 285n8, 381, 382, 406, 659, 659n70, 660, 754; *Odyssey*, 60n26, 74, 240, 256, 256n72, 276, 281, 339n105, 374, 375n174, 380–83, 407n215, 473n75, 473n78, 475, 522, 557, 683, 786n62

ideas, forms, kinds (*eidē, ideai*), 12, 24, 30n46, 148, 157–58, 313n72, 390; Eleatic Stranger on, 30n46, 36, 38, 40, 178–79, 443, 445–46, 696–706, 846–47; extent of, 34, 197n38; of the good, 149, 178, 186n13, 357–59,

385, 447, 587, 696–97, 839, 850; as hypothesis, 35, 186n13, 188–89, 197, 394, 778, 798, 800–801, 803–4, 805, 847; in *Laws*, 137, 147; Parmenides' critique of, 34, 158–62; in *Philebus*, 393n202, 416; Timaeus on, 36–38, 442–43, 445–46, 447, 450, 841. *See also* being; dialectic; images; *logos*

images: in cave, 361; in divided line, 360, 575n97, 631, 696; heavenly motion as image of intelligent cause, 125, 127n129; and the ideas, 359; *logoi, erga* as images of being, 185, 186n13, 676, 706, 800, 806; and poetry, 346–47, 366, 375–78, 470n73, 476; Socrates' use of, 318, 352–53, 359–67, 587; and the sophist, 693–94, 852; three kinds of, 477; Timaeus' *mythos* as, 437–38

Irwin, T. H., 8n18, 148, 227n20, 485n3, 540n55, 554n72

kinds. *See* ideas, forms, kinds (*eidē, ideai*)

Klein, Jacob, 168n40, 187n14, 384n185, 387n192, 388n195, 392n199, 393n202, 568n90, 606n12, 725n44, 772–73

Krämer, Hans Joachim, 29n45

Laches, 247–57, 273, 823

Locri, 427, 429

logos (argument, explanation, speech), 69, 171, 308, 313, 395n192, 388–89, 484, 678; and combination of one and many, 388–91; and conjunction of sensible and intelligible, 212, 444, 666; and deed or fact (*ergon*), 164, 185n12, 200, 211, 435, 476–77, 596, 706, 806; Eleatic Stranger on, 40, 678, 682, 806, 850; Eleatic Stranger vs. Socrates on, 849–53; Gorgias on, 534–35; and ideas, 40, 187, 188n17, 189, 837; and limits of knowledge, 202, 312–13, 328–29, 861; and *mythos*, 185n9, 129n33, 221, 309, 379n181, 431, 437, 438n38, 557, 775; and opinion, 192n30, 200, 202, 317, 456, 635–38; as requiring motion, 166; Socrates' investigation of, 8, 13, 24, 185–87, 186n13, 192n30, 196–97, 206, 306, 326, 365n155, 394, 676, 682, 706, 736, 800, 809; as temporal, 441–46

Lycon, 204, 508, 740

Lysias, 307–10, 311n68, 322–32; and dramatic dates of *Phaedrus, Clitophon, Republic*, 301n43; political activity of, 339n104, 581n102

Lysis, 22, 483n, 510–31, 591, 857